Managerial Accounting

INTERNATIONAL ADAPTATION

Managerial Accounting

Tools for Business Decision Making

Ninth Edition

INTERNATIONAL ADAPTATION

Jerry J. Weygandt PhD, CPA
University of Wisconsin—Madison, USA

Paul D. Kimmel PhD, CPA
University of Wisconsin—Madison, USA

Jill E. Mitchell MS, MEd, CIA
Northern Virginia Community College, USA

WILEY

Managerial Accounting
Tools for Business Decision Making
Ninth Edition

INTERNATIONAL ADAPTATION

Copyright © 2024 The content provided in this textbook is based on Managerial Accounting: Tools for Business Decision Making, by Jerry J. Weygandt, Paul D. Kimmel, and Jill E. Mitchell, 9th edition [2021]. John Wiley & Sons Singapore Pte. Ltd

John Wiley & Sons, Inc., Hoboken, New Jersey

Cover image: © Adobe Stock

Contributing Subject Matter Expert: Dr M. Venkateshwarlu, Professor of Accounting and Finance, Indian Institute of Management Mumbai, India

Founded in 1807, John Wiley & Sons, Inc. has been a valued source of knowledge and understanding for more than 200 years, helping people around the world meet their needs and fulfill their aspirations. Our company is built on a foundation of principles that include responsibility to the communities we serve and where we live and work. In 2008, we launched a Corporate Citizenship Initiative, a global effort to address the environmental, social, economic, and ethical challenges we face in our business. Among the issues we are addressing are carbon impact, paper specifications and procurement, ethical conduct within our business and among our vendors, and community and charitable support. For more information, please visit our website: www.wiley.com/go/citizenship.

All rights reserved. This book and series is authorized for sale in Europe, Middle East, Africa, Asia, Australia and New Zealand only and may not be exported. Exportation from or importation of this book to another region without the Publisher's authorization is illegal and is a violation of the Publisher's rights. The Publisher may take legal action to enforce its rights. The Publisher may recover damages and costs, including but not limited to lost profits and attorney's fees, in the event legal action is required.

No part of this publication may be reproduced, stored in a retrieval system, or transmitted in any form or by any means, electronic, mechanical, photocopying, recording, scanning, or otherwise, except as permitted under Section 107 or 108 of the 1976 United States Copyright Act, without either the prior written permission of the Publisher or authorization through payment of the appropriate per-copy fee to the Copyright Clearance Center, Inc., 222 Rosewood Drive, Danvers, MA 01923, website www.copyright.com. Requests to the Publisher for permission should be addressed to the Permissions Department, John Wiley & Sons, Inc., 111 River Street, Hoboken, NJ 07030, (201) 748-6011, fax (201) 748-6008, website http://www.wiley.com/go/permissions.

ISBN: 978-1-394-22532-3

ISBN: 978-1-394-22533-0 (ePub)

ISBN: 978-1-394-22534-7 (ePdf)

Printed and bound by CPI Group (UK) Ltd, Croydon, CR0 4YY

C9781394225323_261023

About the Authors

JERRY J. WEYGANDT, PhD, CPA, is Arthur Andersen Alumni Emeritus Professor of Accounting at the University of Wisconsin–Madison. He holds a Ph.D. in accounting from the University of Illinois. Articles by Professor Weygandt have appeared in *The Accounting Review*, *Journal of Accounting Research*, *Accounting Horizons*, *Journal of Accountancy*, and other academic and professional journals. These articles have examined such financial reporting issues as accounting for price-level adjustments, pensions, convertible securities, stock option contracts, and interim reports. Professor Weygandt is author of other accounting and financial reporting texts and is a member of the American Accounting Association, the American Institute of Certified Public Accountants, and the Wisconsin Society of Certified Public Accountants. He has served on numerous committees of the American Accounting Association and as a member of the editorial board of the Accounting Review; he also has served as President and Secretary-Treasurer of the American Accounting Association. In addition, he has been actively involved with the American Institute of Certified Public Accountants and has been a member of the Accounting Standards Executive Committee (AcSEC) of that organization. He has served on the FASB task force that examined the reporting issues related to accounting for income taxes and served as a trustee of the Financial Accounting Foundation. Professor Weygandt has received the Chancellor's Award for Excellence in Teaching and the Beta Gamma Sigma Dean's Teaching Award. He is on the board of directors of M & I Bank of Southern Wisconsin. He is the recipient of the Wisconsin Institute of CPA's Outstanding Educator's Award and the Lifetime Achievement Award. In 2001 he received the American Accounting Association's Outstanding Educator Award.

PAUL D. KIMMEL, PhD, CPA, received his bachelor's degree from the University of Minnesota and his doctorate in accounting from the University of Wisconsin. He was an Associate Professor at the University of Wisconsin–Milwaukee for more than 25 years and is now a Senior Lecturer at the University of Wisconsin–Madison. He has public accounting experience with Deloitte & Touche (Minneapolis). He was the recipient of the UWM School of Business Advisory Council Teaching Award and the Reggie Taite Excellence in Teaching Award, and a three-time winner of the Outstanding Teaching Assistant Award at the University of Wisconsin. He is also a recipient of the Elijah Watts Sells Award for Honorary Distinction for his results on the CPA exam. He is a member of the American Accounting Association and the Institute of Management Accountants and has published articles in *Accounting Review*, *Accounting Horizons*, *Advances in Management Accounting*, *Managerial Finance*, *Issues in Accounting Education*, and *Journal of Accounting Education*, as well as other journals. His research interests include accounting for financial instruments and innovation in accounting education.

JILL E. MITCHELL, MS, MEd, CIA, is a Professor of Accounting at Northern Virginia Community College (NOVA), where she has taught face-to-face, hybrid, and online courses since 2008. Since 2009, she has been an adjunct instructor at George Mason University (GMU). She is a past president of the Washington, D.C. Chapter of the Accounting and Financial Women's Alliance (AFWA), and she served on the board of directors of the Virginia Society of CPAs (VSCPA). She is a member of the American Accounting Association (AAA) and the Institute of Internal Auditors. Jill serves on the AAA Education Committee and is the co-chair for the Conference on Teaching and Learning in Accounting (CTLA). Prior to joining the faculty at NOVA, Jill was a senior auditor with Ernst & Young's Business Risk Services practice in Miami, Florida. She is a certified internal auditor and earned an MS in Accountancy from the University of Virginia and a BBA in Management Information Systems from the University of Georgia honors program. Recently, she earned an MEd in Instructional Design Technology from GMU. Jill is a recipient of the Outstanding Faculty Award, the Commonwealth's highest honor for faculty of Virginia's universities and colleges presented by the State Council of Higher Education for Virginia; the Virginia Community College System Chancellor's Award for Teaching Excellence; the AFWA's Women Who Count Award; the AAA Two-Year College Educator of the Year Award; and the AAA/J. Michael and Mary Anne Cook/Deloitte Foundation Prize, the foremost recognition of an individual who consistently demonstrates the attributes of a superior teacher in the discipline of accounting.

From the Authors

Dear Student,

Why This Course? Remember your biology course in high school? Did you have one of those "invisible man" models (or maybe something more high-tech than that) that gave you the opportunity to look "inside" the human body? This accounting course offers something similar. To understand a business, you have to understand the financial insides of a business organization. A managerial accounting course will help you understand the essential financial components of businesses. Whether you are looking at a large multinational company like **Samsung** or **Starbucks** or a single-owner software consulting business or coffee shop, knowing the fundamentals of managerial accounting will help you understand what is happening. As an employee, a manager, an investor, a business owner, or a director of your own personal finances—any of which roles you will have at some point in your life—you will make better decisions for having taken this course.

> "Whether you are looking at a large multinational company like **Samsung** or **Starbucks** or a single-owner software consulting business or coffee shop, knowing the fundamentals of managerial accounting will help you understand what is happening."

Why This Text? Your instructor has chosen this text for you because of the authors' trusted reputation. The authors have worked hard to provide instructional material that is engaging, timely, and accurate.

How to Succeed? We've asked many students and many instructors whether there is a secret for success in this course. The nearly unanimous answer turns out to be not much of a secret: "Do the homework." This is one course where doing is learning. The more time you spend on the homework assignments—using the various tools that this text provides—the more likely you are to learn the essential concepts, techniques, and methods of accounting.

Good luck in this course. We hope you enjoy the experience and that you put to good use throughout a lifetime of success the knowledge you obtain in this course. We are sure you will not be disappointed.

Jerry J. Weygandt
Paul D. Kimmel
Jill E. Mitchell

DEDICATED TO

Our spouses, Enid, Merlynn, and Sean,
for their love, support, and encouragement.

New to the International Adaptation

DATA ANALYTICS

The authors carefully considered how to thoughtfully and meaningfully integrate data analytics into the managerial accounting course, and are pleased to provide the following data analytics resources.

Data Analytics in the Real World

Real-world examples that illustrate engaging situations in companies are provided throughout the text.

> **DATA ANALYTICS INSIGHT**   **The Walt Disney Company**
>
> ### Using Data in Its Own World
>
>
>
> Paulbr/Getty Images
>
> **The Walt Disney Company** (USA) makes fun seem effortless at its theme parks, but there is a magic mountain of data collection going on behind the scenes. For example, Disney employs behavioral analytics, which uses data to both predict and influence customer behavior, in countless ways. Disney collects the data through its "MagicBands" worn by visitors to the parks. While the MagicBands provide visitors with many benefits (e.g., delivering customized itineraries, reducing wait lines, and providing customer recognition by Disney characters), these bands are also delivering continual information to the company about the locations, activities, eating habits, and purchases of Disney visitors.
>
> Disney uses the MagicBand information to support daily adjustments of operations as well as long-term planning. For example, the company can use this information to monitor park usage and subsequently encourage visitors to change their itineraries to different activities that will require a shorter wait time. If customers are waiting in line, they aren't happy—and they also aren't spending money. Long-term planning uses of MagicBand information include designing new attractions and updating menu options in response to supply and demand.
>
> **Source:** Randerson112358, "How Disney World Uses Big Data," *medium.com* (May 18, 2019).
>
> **What is behavioral analytics, and how does Disney use it to minimize lines at its theme parks? (Answer is available in the book's product page on www.wiley.com)**

Data Analytics and Decision-Making

The text also provides numerous discussions on how managers are increasingly relying on data analytics to make decisions using accounting information.

> Companies have never had so much available data. In many companies, virtually every aspect of operations—the employees, the customers, even the manufacturing equipment—leaves a data trail. However, while "big data" can be impressive, it can also be overwhelming.
>
> - Having all the data in the world will not necessarily lead to better results.
> - The trick is having the skills and know-how to use the data in ways that result in more productive (and happier) employees, more satisfied customers, and more profitable operations.
>
> It is therefore not surprising that one of the most rapidly growing areas of business today is data analytics. **Data analytics** is the use of techniques, which often combine software and statistics, to analyze data to make informed decisions.
>
> Throughout this text, we offer many examples of how successful companies are using data analytics. We also provide examples of one analytical tool, data visualizations. **Data visualizations** often help managers acquire a more intuitive understanding of (1) the relationships between variables and (2) business trends. *The end-of-chapter homework material provides opportunities to perform basic data analytics and data visualizations in selected chapters.*

Data Analytics in Action

Most chapters offer *Data Analytics in Action* problems, to offer students the opportunity to see how they might use data analytics to solve realistic business problems. Excel templates for each of the *Data Analytics in Action* problems provide students a framework for solving the problem.

Using Data Visualization to Analyze Costs

DA5.1 Data visualization can be used to compare options.

Example: Consider the *Management Insight* box "Are Robotic Workers More Humane?" presented in the chapter. Data analytics can help **Kroger** (USA) determine if using robots in its warehouse would be a cost-effective decision. Consider the following chart, which compares income effects in both a manual and a robotic system. When using human labor in a manual system, we see that labor costs are substantial. When a robotic system is utilized, we see that depreciation is a larger cost item, and labor is much less.

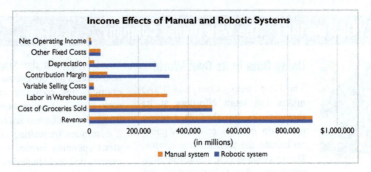

If we assume that revenues will increase 40% due to an increased sales volume, what effect will we see on net operating income? As shown in the following chart, the increase in net operating income is larger in an automated system. This is because the labor increase was a smaller dollar amount than the respective increase in a manual system, coupled with no increase in total fixed costs. This effect is often referred to as **operating leverage**, which is discussed further in Chapter 6.

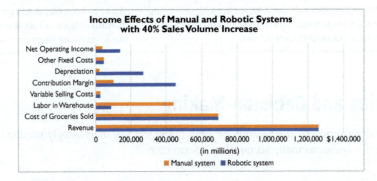

For this case, you will use an approach similar to that used in the example just presented. You will help a fast food restaurant evaluate the benefits of installing a kiosk in the lobby to automate customer orders, thus reducing the need for cashiers. This case requires you to compare income statement data for traditional and digital ordering for the restaurant, and then create and analyze a bar chart.

CHAPTER-BY-CHAPTER CHANGES

Chapter 1: Managerial Accounting

- NEW section on the value of data analytics in helping managers understand the relationship between CVP variables and business trends.
- NEW Data Analytics Insight box on how **Disney** uses its MagicBands as a source of data to analyze the behavior of its customers.
- Expanded discussion within "Manufacturing Costs" section to ensure student understanding of raw materials versus direct materials as well as what is considered to be manufacturing

overhead. Also updated Illustration 1.4 (assignment of costs to cost categories) to include an explanation for each cost classification, again to ensure student understanding.
- Moved up discussion of balance sheet (before income statement) in "Manufacturing Costs in Financial Statements" section for more logical presentation of topics.
- Updated each "Managerial Accounting Trends" section subtopic for the latest information on service industries, lean manufacturing, balanced scorecard, ethics, and social responsibility.
- Expanded focus on "Code of Ethical Standards" by including the EU Audit Regulation and Directive (EU Directive 2014/56/EU) which was adopted in 2014.
- NEW Data Analytics in Action problems allow students to perform basic data analytics and data visualization.

Chapter 2: Job Order Costing

- NEW Data Analytics Insight box on how **Autodesk** uses data analytics to improve its software and profitability.
- More discussion on assigning raw materials costs and assigning factory labor costs, to improve student understanding.
- Updated time ticket discussion for more recent process involving scanning of employee identification codes.
- NEW Data Analytics in Action problems allow students to perform basic data analytics and data visualization.

Chapter 3: Process Costing

- Production cost report now has the "Cost Reconciliation Schedule" section to include costs to be accounted for, not just costs accounted for.
- Carefully scrutinized discussion to ensure complete student understanding. For example, in the "Transfer to Next Department" section, have added explanation of what department transfers entail.

Chapter 4: Activity-Based Costing

- NEW data analytics discussion added to section of identifying cost drivers.
- NEW Data Analytics Insight box on how companies such as **GE** and **UPS** use data analytics to help reduce non–value-added activities.
- NEW section ("Assigning Nonmanufacturing Overhead Costs") and income statement presentations, to help highlight differences between traditional costing and activity-based costing.

Chapter 5: Cost-Volume-Profit

- NEW discussion on CVP and the use of data analytics, using **DHL Express** as an example.
- NEW expanded highlighted equations, to show more detailed calculations for improved understanding.
- NEW expanded explanation of what CVP analysis is.
- NEW illustration and discussion on how a traditional income statement differs from a CVP income statement.
- NEW discussion on the variable cost ratio.
- Enhanced end-of-chapter assignments by offering students more opportunities to prepare CVP income statements, as well as a new problem on regression analysis.

- NEW Data Analytics in Action problems allow students to perform basic data analytics and data visualization.

Chapter 6: Cost-Volume-Profit Analysis: Additional Issues

- NEW Data Analytics Insight box on how **Caesars Entertainment** uses data analytics to determine how to maximize profits from its customers.
- NEW Data Analytics in Action problems allow students to perform basic data analytics and data visualization.

Chapter 7: Incremental Analysis

- Highlighted the decision rules, as well as additional factors to consider, for incremental analysis decisions.

Chapter 8: Pricing

- NEW Data Analytics Insight box on how **Big Data Pricing** helps customers use data analytics to improve dynamic pricing practices.
- NEW Data Analytics in Action problems allow students to perform basic data analytics and data visualization.

Chapter 9: Budgetary Planning

- NEW Data Analytics Insight box on how **Dickey's Barbecue Pit** uses data analytics to improve restaurant sales performance.
- NEW Data Analytics in Action problem allows students to perform basic data analytics and data visualization.
- New Service Company Insight on the financial challenges for Tokyo Olympics 2020.

Chapter 10: Budgetary Control and Responsibility Accounting

- NEW Data Analytics Insight boxes on rolling forecasts and zero-based budgeting.
- Updated section on "Judgmental Factors in ROI" with "Alternative Measures of ROI Inputs" for more precise discussion and improved student understanding.
- NEW Data Analytics in Action problems allow students to perform basic data analytics and data visualization.

Chapter 11: Standard Costs and Balanced Scorecard

- NEW Data Analytics Insight box on how manufacturing companies are using technology such as 5G cellular to improve the amount and speed of data collection to improve operations.
- NEW highlighted applications of determining standard costs in "A Case Study" section, for improved student understanding.
- NEW Data Analytics in Action problem allows students to perform basic data analytics and data visualization.

Chapter 12: Planning for Capital Investments

- NEW Data Analytics Insight box on how **Electronic Arts** uses data from its current online video games to help it develop future products.
- Improved illustration showing computation of cash payback period by including detailed steps and computations.

- NEW Management Insight box on 5G and how it presents a risky investment to telecom companies.
- NEW Data Analytics in Action problems allow students to perform basic data analytics and data visualization.

Chapter 13: Statement of Cash Flows

- Added more T-accounts and journal entries to increase understandability of preparing the statement of cash flows using the indirect method.
- Used 2019 **Apple** financial statements for example of how to analyze the statement of cash flows using free cash flow calculation, for increased student engagement.
- Updated "Accounting Across the Organization: Net What?" to include the recent annual reports of FMCG companies operating out of Europe, including that of **Nestle A.G.**
- Updated "Anatomy of Fraud" to include a case on **Allianz Australia Insurance Limited** and **AWP Australia**.

Chapter 14: Financial Analysis: The Big Picture

- NEW section on how data analytics can assist in improving valuation models.
- NEW presentation of discontinued operations on the income statement (previously on the statement of comprehensive income) as well as discussion and format of the statement of comprehensive income.
- Updated "Anatomy of Fraud" to include a case on **Freeman FinTech Corporation Limited**.

Hallmark Features

Our text opens with a story about **Current Designs** kayaks, and each chapter contains a case that illustrates how managerial accounting can help in the kayak production process. The kayaks thus represent areas of active learning, of learning that's best accomplished through full engagement, commitment, and practice.

In this International Adaptation of the ninth edition of *Managerial Accounting*, all content has been carefully reviewed and revised to ensure maximum student understanding. At the same time, the time-tested features that have proven to be of most help to students have been retained, such as the following:

Infographic Learning

Over half of the text is visual, providing students alternative ways of learning about accounting.

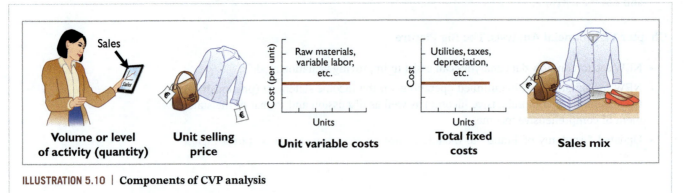

ILLUSTRATION 5.10 | Components of CVP analysis

Real-World Decision-Making

Real-world examples, which illustrate engaging situations in companies, are provided throughout the text. Answers to the critical thinking questions are available in the book's product page on www.wiley.com.

PEOPLE, PLANET, AND PROFIT INSIGHT | **Synergy**

Between a Rock and a Hard Place

Alessandro2802/Getty Images

Households in Western Australia that install solar panels sometimes generate several times the amount of energy that they use. For these surplus kilowatts generated that can be fed back into the grid, their electric company **Synergy** (AUS) pays them a rebate (referred to as a feedback tariff). However, the amount recently paid by Synergy has been cut to a third of what imported electricity costs, so household users (and electricity producers) have to export a lot to break even. This rebate or feed-in tariff was reduced considerably because the surplus uptake due to renewables has been so great.

What this means is that when the initial customers that installed solar panels signed up for a 10-year contract under "The Premium Feed-In Tariff Scheme," Synergy agreed to pay customers 40 cents per unit of power they fed back into the grid. The tariff was then reduced to 20 cents, and now new customers are paid just 7.135 cents per unit under the Renewable Energy Buyback plan and have to buy electricity back at night for 26 cents per unit.

Customers, who wanted the greatest return on their investment, installed the maximum-size solar system (five-kilowatt equipment). These customers are now investigating the use of batteries to reduce the amount of power they purchase—their overnight costs—while looking to pay off their equipment investment.

Source: K. Diss, "Solar Panel Owners Caught Between a Rock and a Hard Place," *ABC News* (October 22, 2016).

If a five-kilowatt solar system costs A$24,000 to install, how many units of power were required to break even under the original Premium Feed-In Tariff Scheme? How many units are currently required? (Answer is available in the book's product page on www.wiley.com)

DO IT! Exercises

DO IT! Exercises in the body of the text prompt students to stop and review key concepts. They outline the Action Plan necessary to complete the exercise as well as show a detailed solution.

DO IT! 4 ▶ Break-Even Analysis

Lombardi NV has a unit selling price of €400, unit variable costs of €240, and fixed costs of €180,000. Compute the break-even point in sales units using (a) a mathematical equation and (b) unit contribution margin.

Solution

a. The equation is €400Q − €240Q − €180,000 = €0; (€400Q − €240Q) = €180,000. The break-even point in sales units is 1,125.

b. The unit contribution margin is €160 (€400 − €240). The calculation therefore is €180,000 ÷ €160, and the break-even point in sales units is 1,125.

Related exercise material: **BE5.8, BE5.9, DO IT! 5.4, E5.8, E5.9, E5.10, E5.11, E5.12, and E5.13.**

ACTION PLAN
- Apply the profit equation: Sales − Variable costs − Fixed costs = Net income.
- Apply the break-even equation: Fixed costs ÷ Unit contribution margin = Break-even point in sales units.

Decision Tools

Accounting concepts that are useful for management decision-making are highlighted throughout the text. A summary of Decision Tools is included in each chapter as well as a practice exercise and solution called Using the Decision Tools.

USING THE DECISION TOOLS | Amazon.com

Amazon.com (USA) faces many situations where it needs to apply the decision tools presented in this chapter, such as calculating the break-even point to determine a product's profitability. Amazon's dominance of the online retail space, selling other company's products, is well known. But not everyone may realize that Amazon also sells its own private-label electronics, including USB cables, mice, keyboards, and audio cables, under the brand name AmazonBasics. Assume that Amazon's management was provided with the following information regarding the production and sales of Bluetooth keyboards for tablet computers for 2023.

Cost Schedules

Variable costs		
Direct labor per keyboard	$ 8.00	
Direct materials per keyboard	4.00	
Variable overhead per keyboard	3.00	
Variable cost per keyboard		$15.00
Fixed costs (per year)		
Manufacturing	$ 25,000	
Selling	40,000	
Administrative	70,000	
Total fixed costs		$135,000
Selling price per keyboard		$25.00
Sales, 2023 (20,000 keyboards)		$500,000

Instructions

(Ignore any income tax considerations.)

a. What is the operating income for 2023?
b. What is the unit contribution margin for 2023?
c. What is the break-even point in sales units for 2023?
d. Assume that management set the sales target for the year 2024 at a level of $550,000 (22,000 keyboards at the same unit selling price). Amazon's management believes that to attain the sales target in 2024, the company must incur an additional selling expense of $10,000 for advertising in 2024, with all other unit variable costs and fixed costs remaining constant. What will be the break-even point in sales dollars for 2024 if the company spends the additional $10,000?
e. If the company spends the additional $10,000 for advertising in 2024 and unit variable costs, unit selling price, and all other fixed costs remain at 2023 levels, what is the sales level in dollars required to equal 2023 operating income?

Solution

a. Sales $500,000
Less:
Variable costs (20,000 keyboards × $15) 300,000
Fixed costs 135,000
Operating income $ 65,000

b. Selling price per keyboard $25
Variable cost per keyboard 15
Unit contribution margin $10

c. Fixed costs ÷ Unit contribution margin = Break-even point in sales units: $135,000 ÷ $10 = 13,500 units

d. Fixed costs ÷ Contribution margin ratio = Break-even point in sales dollars: $145,000* ÷ 40%** = $362,500

*Current fixed costs $135,000
Additional advertising expense 10,000
Revised fixed costs $145,000

**Unit contribution margin remains $10, as unit variable cost and unit selling price did not change. Contribution margin ratio = Unit contribution margin ÷ Unit selling price: 40% = $10 ÷ $25

e. Sales = (Fixed costs + Target net income) ÷ Contribution margin ratio
$525,000 = ($145,000 + $65,000) ÷ 40%

REVIEW AND PRACTICE

Practice Exercises

Analyze a job cost sheet and prepare entries for manufacturing costs.

1. **(LO 1, 2, 3, 4)** A job cost sheet for Whitstable plc is shown below.

Job No. 92				For 2,000 Units
Date		Direct Materials	Direct Labor	Manufacturing Overhead
Beg. bal. Jan.	1	3,925	6,000	4,200
	8	6,000		
	12		8,500	6,375
	25	2,000		
	27		4,000	3,000
		11,925	18,500	13,575

Cost of completed job:	
Direct materials	£11,925
Direct labor	18,500
Manufacturing overhead	13,575
Total cost	£44,000
Unit cost (£44,000 ÷ 2,000)	£ 22.00

Instructions

a. Answer the following questions:
　1. What was the balance in Work in Process Inventory on January 1 if this was the only unfinished job?
　2. If manufacturing overhead is applied on the basis of direct labor cost, what overhead rate was used in each year?

b. Prepare summary entries at January 31 to record the current year's transactions pertaining to Job No. 92.

Solution

1. a. 1. £14,125, or (£3,925 + £6,000 + £4,200).
　　2. Last year 70%, or (£4,200 ÷ £6,000); this year 75% (either £6,375 ÷ £8,500 or £3,000 ÷ £4,000).

b. Jan. 31	Work in Process Inventory	8,000	
	Raw Materials Inventory		8,000
	(£6,000 + £2,000)		
	31	Work in Process Inventory	12,500	
	Factory Labor		12,500
	(£8,500 + £4,000)		
	31	Work in Process Inventory	9,375	
	Manufacturing Overhead		9,375
	(£6,375 + £3,000)		
	31	Finished Goods Inventory	44,000	
	Work in Process Inventory		44,000

Online Supplements

This edition provides a multitude of online resources which are available via the related resources link found in the product page on www.wiley.com.

Instructor's Manual The Instructor's Manual offers helpful teaching ideas. This manual contains chapter learning objectives, lesson outlines, chapter key concepts, and suggested activities.

Solutions Manual includes detailed solutions to the Questions, Brief Exercises, Do It! Exercises, Exercises, and Problems given at the end of each chapter.

PowerPoint Presentations contain a combination of chapter's key concepts, figures and tables, problems and examples, and illustrations.

Test Bank With over 2,000 questions, the test bank allows instructors to tailor examinations according to study objectives and difficulty. Multiple-choice, true/false, and short answer essay questions are included.

Excel Templates for selected end-of-chapter problems, including those on data analytics, provide students a model of best practices for setting up problems in Excel and applying Excel functions to solve problems.

Excel Working Papers provide working paper templates for select exercises and problems in the book.

Brief Contents

Cost Concepts for Decision-Makers

1. Managerial Accounting 1-1
2. Job Order Costing 2-1
3. Process Costing 3-1
4. Activity-Based Costing 4-1

Decision-Making Concepts

5. Cost-Volume-Profit 5-1
6. Cost-Volume-Profit Analysis: Additional Issues 6-1
7. Incremental Analysis 7-1
8. Pricing 8-1

Planning and Control Concepts

9. Budgetary Planning 9-1
10. Budgetary Control and Responsibility Accounting 10-1
11. Standard Costs and Balanced Scorecard 11-1
12. Planning for Capital Investments 12-1

Performance Evaluation Concepts

13. Statement of Cash Flows 13-1
14. Financial Analysis: The Big Picture 14-1

APPENDIX A Time Value of Money A-1

COMPANY INDEX I-1

SUBJECT INDEX I-3

RAPID REVIEW: CHAPTER CONTENT

Contents

1 Managerial Accounting 1-1

Just Add Water ... and Paddle: Current Designs 1-1
Managerial Accounting Basics 1-3
Comparing Managerial and Financial Accounting 1-3
Management Functions 1-3
Organizational Structure 1-5
Managerial Cost Concepts 1-7
Manufacturing Costs 1-7
Product versus Period Costs 1-9
Illustration of Cost Concepts 1-9
Manufacturing Costs in Financial Statements 1-12
Balance Sheet 1-12
Income Statement 1-12
Cost of Goods Manufactured 1-14
Cost of Goods Manufactured Schedule 1-15
Managerial Accounting Trends 1-16
Service Industries 1-16
Focus on the Value Chain 1-17
Balanced Scorecard 1-18
Business Ethics 1-19
Corporate Social Responsibility 1-20
The Value of Data Analytics 1-21
Data Analytics Insight: Using Data in Its Own World 1-21
Data Analytics in Action 1-43

2 Job Order Costing 2-1

Profiting from the Silver Screen: Disney 2-1
Cost Accounting Systems 2-3
Process Cost System 2-3
Job Order Cost System 2-3
Data Analytics Insight: Providing Service Through the Cloud 2-4
Job Order Cost Flow 2-5
Accumulating Manufacturing Costs 2-5
Assigning Manufacturing Costs 2-7
Raw Materials Costs 2-8
Factory Labor Costs 2-10
Predetermined Overhead Rates 2-13
Entries for Jobs Completed and Sold 2-16
Assigning Costs to Finished Goods 2-16
Assigning Costs to Cost of Goods Sold 2-17
Summary of Job Order Cost Flows 2-18
Job Order Costing for Service Companies 2-19
Advantages and Disadvantages of Job Order Costing 2-20
Applied Manufacturing Overhead 2-22
Under- or Overapplied Manufacturing Overhead 2-22
Data Analytics in Action 2-41

3 Process Costing 3-1

Famed Soft Drink in the Outback: Back o' Bourke Cordials 3-1
Overview of Process Cost Systems 3-3
Uses of Process Cost Systems 3-3
Process Costing for Service Companies 3-3
Similarities and Differences Between Job Order Cost and Process Cost Systems 3-4
Recording Costs 3-6
Process Cost Flow 3-6
Assigning Manufacturing Costs—Journal Entries 3-6
Equivalent Units 3-9
Weighted-Average Method 3-10
Refinements on the Weighted-Average Method 3-10
The Production Cost Report 3-12
Compute the Physical Unit Flow (Step 1) 3-13
Compute the Equivalent Units of Production (Step 2) 3-14
Compute Unit Production Costs (Step 3) 3-14
Prepare a Cost Reconciliation Schedule (Step 4) 3-15
Preparing the Production Cost Report 3-16
Costing Systems—Final Comments 3-17
Appendix 3A: FIFO Method for Equivalent Units 3-20
Equivalent Units Under FIFO 3-20
Comprehensive Example 3-21
FIFO and Weighted-Average 3-25

4 Activity-Based Costing 4-1

Wellness for Customers and the Company: Technogym SpA 4-1
Traditional vs. Activity-Based Costing 4-3
Traditional Costing Systems 4-3
Illustration of a Traditional Costing System 4-3
The Need for a New Approach 4-4
Activity-Based Costing 4-5
ABC and Manufacturers 4-7
Identify and Classify Activities and Allocate Overhead to Cost Pools (Step 1) 4-8
Identify Cost Drivers (Step 2) 4-8
Compute Activity-Based Overhead Rates (Step 3) 4-9
Assign Overhead Costs to Products (Step 4) 4-9
Comparing Unit Costs 4-10
ABC Benefits and Limitations 4-13
The Advantage of Multiple Cost Pools 4-13

xvii

xviii CONTENTS

The Advantage of Enhanced Cost Control 4-15
The Advantage of Better Management Decisions 4-18
Some Limitations and Knowing When to Use ABC 4-18
Data Analytics Insight: Delivering People and Packages 4-19
ABC and Service Industries 4-20
Traditional Costing Example 4-20
Activity-Based Costing Example 4-21
Appendix 4A: Just-in-Time Processing 4-24
Objective of JIT Processing 4-25
Elements of JIT Processing 4-25
Benefits of JIT Processing 4-26

5 Cost-Volume-Profit 5-1

Don't Worry—Just Get Big: Amazon.com 5-1
Cost Behavior Analysis 5-3
Variable Costs 5-3
Fixed Costs 5-4
Relevant Range 5-5
Mixed Costs 5-7
Mixed Costs Analysis 5-8
High-Low Method 5-8
Importance of Identifying Variable and Fixed Costs 5-10
CVP Analysis 5-11
Basic Components 5-11
CVP Income Statement 5-12
Break-Even Analysis 5-16
Mathematical Equation 5-16
Contribution Margin Techniques 5-17
Graphic Presentation 5-19
Target Net Income and Margin of Safety 5-20
Target Net Income 5-20
Margin of Safety 5-22
CVP and Data Analytics 5-23
Appendix 5A: Regression Analysis 5-25
Data Analytics in Action 5-45

6 Cost-Volume-Profit Analysis: Additional Issues 6-1

The Secret to Supermarket Profitability: Aldi 6-1
Basic CVP Concepts 6-2
Basic Concepts 6-2
CVP and Changes in the Business Environment 6-4
Sales Mix and Break-Even Sales 6-7
Break-Even Sales in Units 6-7
Data Analytics Insight: Taking No Chances with Its Profits 6-9
Break-Even Sales in Euros 6-9
Sales Mix with Limited Resources 6-12
Operating Leverage and Profitability 6-14
Effect on Contribution Margin Ratio 6-15
Effect on Break-Even Point 6-16
Effect on Margin of Safety Ratio 6-16
Operating Leverage 6-16
Appendix 6A: Absorption Costing versus Variable Costing 6-19
Example Comparing Absorption Costing with Variable Costing 6-20
Net Income Effects 6-22
Decision-Making Concerns 6-26
Potential Advantages of Variable Costing 6-28
Data Analytics in Action 6-47

7 Incremental Analysis 7-1

Keeping It Clean: Method Products 7-1
Decision-Making and Incremental Analysis 7-3
Incremental Analysis Approach 7-3
How Incremental Analysis Works 7-4
Qualitative Factors 7-5
Relationship of Incremental Analysis and Activity-Based Costing 7-5
Types of Incremental Analysis 7-6
Special Orders 7-6
Make or Buy 7-8
Opportunity Cost 7-9
Sell or Process Further 7-11
Single-Product Case 7-11
Multiple-Product Case 7-12
Repair, Retain, or Replace Equipment 7-14
Eliminate Unprofitable Segment or Product 7-16

8 Pricing 8-1

They've Got Your Size—and Color: Zappos.com 8-1
Target Costing 8-3
Establishing a Target Cost 8-4
Cost-Plus and Variable-Cost Pricing 8-5
Cost-Plus Pricing 8-5
Limitations of Cost-Plus Pricing 8-7
Variable-Cost Pricing 8-8
Time-and-Material Pricing 8-9
Transfer Prices 8-13
Negotiated Transfer Prices 8-14
Cost-Based Transfer Prices 8-17
Market-Based Transfer Prices 8-19
Effect of Outsourcing on Transfer Pricing 8-19
Transfers Between Divisions in Different Countries 8-19
Data Analytics Insight: Setting the Optimal Price 8-20
Appendix 8A: Absorption-Cost and Variable-Cost Pricing 8-22
Absorption-Cost Pricing 8-22
Variable-Cost Pricing 8-24
Appendix 8B: Transfers Between Divisions in Different Countries 8-25
Data Analytics in Action 8-43

9 Budgetary Planning 9-1

What's in Your Cupcake?: Erin McKenna's Bakery NYC 9-1
Effective Budgeting and the Master Budget 9-3
Budgeting and Accounting 9-3
The Benefits of Budgeting 9-3
Essentials of Effective Budgeting 9-4
The Master Budget 9-7
Sales, Production, and Direct Materials Budgets 9-8
Sales Budget 9-8
Production Budget 9-10
Direct Materials Budget 9-11
Direct Labor, Manufacturing Overhead, and S&A Expense Budgets 9-14
Direct Labor Budget 9-14
Manufacturing Overhead Budget 9-15
Selling and Administrative Expense Budget 9-16
Budgeted Income Statement 9-17
Data Analytics Insight: That's Some Tasty Data! 9-18
Cash Budget and Budgeted Balance Sheet 9-19
Cash Budget 9-19
Budgeted Balance Sheet 9-22
Budgeting in Nonmanufacturing Companies 9-24
Merchandisers 9-24
Service Companies 9-25
Not-for-Profit Organizations 9-26
Data Analytics in Action 9-47

10 Budgetary Control and Responsibility Accounting 10-1

Pumpkin Madeleines and a Movie: The Roxy Hotel Tribeca 10-1
Budgetary Control and Static Budget Reports 10-3
Budgetary Control 10-3
Static Budget Reports 10-4
Flexible Budget Reports 10-7
Why Flexible Budgets? 10-7
Developing the Flexible Budget 10-9
Flexible Budget—A Case Study 10-10
Flexible Budget Reports 10-12
Data Analytics Insight: These Forecasts Move with the Times! 10-13
Responsibility Accounting and Responsibility Centers 10-14
Controllable versus Noncontrollable Revenues and Costs 10-16
Principles of Performance Evaluation 10-16
Data Analytics Insight: Hitting the Road with Zero-Based Budgeting 10-18
Responsibility Reporting System 10-18
Types of Responsibility Centers 10-19
Investment Centers 10-24
Return on Investment (ROI) 10-24
Responsibility Report 10-25
Alternative Measures of ROI Inputs 10-26
Improving ROI 10-26
Appendix 10A: ROI versus Residual Income 10-30
Residual Income Compared to ROI 10-30
Residual Income Weakness 10-31
Data Analytics in Action 10-50

11 Standard Costs and Balanced Scorecard 11-1

80,000 Different Caffeinated Combinations: Starbucks 11-2
Standard Costs 11-3
Distinguishing Between Standards and Budgets 11-4
Setting Standard Costs 11-4
Direct Materials Variances 11-8
Analyzing and Reporting Variances 11-8
Calculating Direct Materials Variances 11-10
Direct Labor and Manufacturing Overhead Variances 11-13
Direct Labor Variances 11-13
Data Analytics Insight: Speedy Data to the Rescue! 11-16
Manufacturing Overhead Variances 11-16
Variance Reports and Balanced Scorecards 11-18
Reporting Variances 11-18
Income Statement Presentation of Variances 11-19
Balanced Scorecard 11-20
Appendix 11A: Standard Cost Accounting System 11-24
Journal Entries 11-24
Ledger Accounts 11-26
Appendix 11B: Overhead Controllable and Volume Variances 11-26
Overhead Controllable Variance 11-26
Overhead Volume Variance 11-28
Data Analytics in Action 11-46

12 Planning for Capital Investments 12-1

Floating Hotels: Holland America Line 12-2
Capital Budgeting and Cash Payback 12-3
Cash Flow Information 12-3
Illustrative Data 12-4
Cash Payback 12-4
Net Present Value Method 12-6
Equal Annual Cash Flows 12-7
Unequal Annual Cash Flows 12-8
Choosing a Discount Rate 12-9
Simplifying Assumptions 12-10
Comprehensive Example 12-10

xx CONTENTS

Capital Budgeting Challenges and Refinements 12-12
Intangible Benefits 12-12
Profitability Index for Mutually Exclusive Projects 12-14
Risk Analysis 12-15
Post-Audit of Investment Projects 12-16
Internal Rate of Return 12-17
Comparing Discounted Cash Flow Methods 12-18
Annual Rate of Return 12-19
Data Analytics Insight: Increasing the Chances of Gaming Wins 12-21
Data Analytics in Action 12-35

13 Statement of Cash Flows 13-1

Got Cash?: Microsoft 13-1
Statement of Cash Flows: Usefulness and Format 13-3
Usefulness of the Statement of Cash Flows 13-3
Classification of Cash Flows 13-3
Significant Noncash Activities 13-4
Format of the Statement of Cash Flows 13-5
Preparing the Statement of Cash Flows—Indirect Method 13-6
Indirect and Direct Methods 13-7
Indirect Method—Computer Services International 13-7
Step 1: Operating Activities 13-9
Summary of Conversion to Net Cash Provided by Operating Activities—Indirect Method 13-12
Step 2: Investing and Financing Activities 13-14
Step 3: Net Change in Cash 13-15
Analyzing the Statement of Cash Flows 13-17
Free Cash Flow 13-17
Appendix 13A: Statement of Cash Flows—Direct Method 13-20
Step 1: Operating Activities 13-20
Step 2: Investing and Financing Activities 13-26
Step 3: Net Change in Cash 13-27
Appendix 13B: Statement of Cash Flows—T-Account Approach 13-27

14 Financial Analysis: The Big Picture 14-1

Making Money the Old-Fashioned Way 14-2
Sustainable Income 14-3
Discontinued Operations 14-3
Comprehensive Income 14-4
Changes in Accounting Principle 14-6
Horizontal Analysis and Vertical Analysis 14-8
Horizontal Analysis 14-8
Vertical Analysis 14-11
Ratio Analysis 14-14
Liquidity Ratios 14-15
Solvency Ratios 14-16
Profitability Ratios 14-16
Financial Analysis and Data Analytics 14-17
Comprehensive Example of Ratio Analysis 14-17

Appendix A Time Value of Money A-1

Interest and Future Values A-2
Nature of Interest A-2
Future Value of a Single Amount A-3
Future Value of an Annuity A-5
Present Values A-8
Present Value Variables A-8
Present Value of a Single Amount A-8
Present Value of an Annuity A-11
Time Periods and Discounting A-13
Present Value of a Long-Term Note or Bond A-13
Capital Budgeting Situations A-15
Using Financial Calculators A-17
Present Value of a Single Sum A-18
Present Value of an Annuity A-19
Future Value of a Single Sum A-19
Future Value of an Annuity A-20
Internal Rate of Return A-20
Useful Applications of the Financial Calculator A-21

COMPANY INDEX I-1

SUBJECT INDEX I-3

RAPID REVIEW: CHAPTER CONTENT

Acknowledgments

Managerial Accounting has benefited greatly from the input of users, focus group participants, manuscript reviewers, ancillary authors, and proofers. We greatly appreciate the constructive suggestions and innovative ideas of users and reviewers from this and previous editions as well as the creativity and accuracy of the ancillary authors and checkers.

Users and Reviewers

Dawn Addington, *Central New Mexico Community College*
Joe Atallah, *Coastline Community College*
Melody Barta, *Evergreen Valley College*
Bruce Bradford, *Fairfield University*
Ann K. Brooks, *University of New Mexico*
Robert Brown, *Evergreen Valley College*
Leroy Bugger, *Edison State College*
Melodi Bunting, *Edgewood College*
Lisa Capozzoli, *College of DuPage*
Renee Castrigano, *Cleveland State University*
Wanda Causseaux, *Siena College*
Sandy Cereola, *James Madison University*
Gayle Chaky, *Dutchess Community College*
Julie Chenier, *Louisiana State University—Baton Rouge*
James Chiafery, *University of Massachusetts—Boston*
Bea Chiang, *The College of New Jersey*
Cheryl Clark, *Point Park University*
Toni Clegg, *Delta College*
Maxine Cohen, *Bergen Community College*
Stephen Collins, *University of Massachusetts—Lowell*
Solveg Cooper, *Cuesta College*
William Cooper, *North Carolina A&T State University*
Cheryl Copeland, *California State University, Fresno*
Alan E. Davis, *Community College of Philadelphia*
Larry DeGaetano, *Montclair State University*
Michael Deschamps, *MiraCosta College*
Bettye Desselle, *Texas Southern University*
Judy Dewitt, *Central Michigan University*
Cyril Dibie, *Tarrant County College—Arlington*
Jean Dunn, *Rady School of Management at University of California—San Diego*
Ron Dustin, *Fresno City College*
Barbara Eide, *University of Wisconsin—La Crosse*
Dennis Elam, *Texas A&M University—San Antonio*
James Emig, *Villanova University*
Janet Farler, *Pima Community College*
Anthony Fortini, *Camden County College*
Jeanne Franco, *Paradise Valley Community College*
Chad Frawley, *Rutgers University—Northeast Normal*
Patrick Geer, *Hawkeye Community College*
John Hogan, *Fisher College*
Bambi Hora, *University of Central Oklahoma*
M.A. Houston, *Wright State University*
Jeff Hsu, *St. Louis Community College—Meramec*
Janet Jamieson, *University of Dubuque*
Kevin Jones, *Drexel University*
Don Kovacic, *California State University—San Marcos*

Lynn Krausse, *Bakersfield College*
Craig Krenek, *Elmhurst College*
Steven LaFave, *Augsburg College*
Eric Lee, *University of Northern Iowa*
Jason Lee, *SUNY Plattsburgh*
Harold Little, *Western Kentucky University*
Dennis Lopez, *University of Texas—San Antonio*
Suneel Maheshwari, *Marshall University*
Lois Mahoney, *Eastern Michigan University*
Diane Marker, *University of Toledo*
Tom Marsh, *Northern Virginia Community College*
Christian Mastilak, *Xavier University*
Josephine Mathias, *Mercer County Community College*
Edward McGinnis, *American River College*
Florence McGovern, *Bergen Community College*
Pamela Meyer, *University of Louisiana—Lafayette*
Mary Michel, *Manhattan College*
Joan Miller, *William Paterson University*
Jill Misuraca, *University of Tampa*
Earl Mitchell, *Santa Ana College*
Syed Moiz, *University of Wisconsin—Platteville*
Linda Mullins, *Georgia State University Perimeter College*
Johnna Murray, *University of Missouri—St. Louis*
Michael Newman, *University of Houston*
Lee Nicholas, *University of Northern Iowa*
Cindy Nye, *Bellevue University*
Obeua Parsons, *Rider University*
Glenn Pate, *Palm Beach State College*
Nori Pearson, *Washington State University*
Joe Pecore, *Rady School of Management at University of California—San Diego*
Dawn Peters, *Southwestern Illinois College*
DeAnne Peterson, *University of Wisconsin—Eau Claire*
Judy Peterson, *Monmouth College*
Timothy Peterson, *Gustavus Adolphus College*
Robert Rambo, *Roger Williams University*
Jim Resnik, *Bergen Community College*
Jorge Romero, *Towson University*
Luther Ross, *Central Piedmont Community College*
Maria Roxas, *Central Connecticut State University*
Christina Ryan, *College of New Jersey*
Susan Sadowski, *Shippensburg University*
Richard Sarkisian, *Camden County College*
Karl Schindl, *University of Wisconsin—Manitowoc*
Debbie Seifert, *Illinois State University*
Valerie Simmons, *University of Southern Mississippi*
Mike Skaff, *College of the Sequoias*
Charles Skender, *University of North Carolina—Chapel Hill*
Karyn Smith, *Georgia Perimeter College*
Patrick Stegman, *College of Lake County*
Richard Steingart, *San Jose State University*
Gracelyn Stuart-Tuggle, *Palm Beach State University*
Karen Tabak, *Maryville University*
Diane Tanner, *University of North Florida*
Tom Thompson, *Savannah Technical College*
Mike Tyler, *Barry University*

Jin Ulmer, *Angelina College*
Linda Vaello, *University of Texas—San Antonio*
Manuel Valle, *City College of San Francisco*
Huey L. Van Dine, *Bergen Community College*
Joan Van Hise, *Fairfield University*
Claire Veal, *University of Texas—San Antonio*
Sheila Viel, *University of Wisconsin—Milwaukee*
Suzanne Ward, *University of Louisiana—Lafayette*
Dan Way, *Central Piedmont Community College*

Online Course Developers and Reviewers

Carole Brandt-Fink
Heidi Hansel
Laura McNally
Melanie Yon

Ancillary Authors, Contributors, Proofers, and Accuracy Checkers

Ellen Bartley, *St. Joseph's College*
LuAnn Bean, *Florida Institute of Technology*
Debby Bloom, *Queens University*
Jack Borke, *University of Wisconsin—Platteville*
Ann K. Brooks, *University of New Mexico*
Melodi Bunting, *Edgewood College*
Bea Chiang, *The College of New Jersey*
Lawrence Chui, *University of St. Thomas*
Carleton Donchess, *Bridgewater State University*
Dina El Mahdy, *Morgan State University*
James Emig, *Villanova University*
Mary Ewanechko, *Monroe Community College*
Larry Falcetto, *Emporia State University*
Vicki Greshik, *University of Jamestown*
Michael Griffin, *University of Massachusetts—Dartmouth*
Heidi Hansel, *Kirkwood Community College*
Coby Harmon, *University of California—Santa Barbara*
William Heninger, *Brigham Young University*
Lisa Hewes, *Northern Arizona University*
Derek Jackson, *St. Mary's University of Minnesota*
Craig Krenek, *Elmhurst College*
Y. Robert Lin, *California State University—East Bay*
Lisa Ludlum, *Western Illinois University*
Kirk Lynch, *Sandhills Community College*
Donald R. Majors II, *Elmhurst College and Utica College*
Susanna Matson, *Southern New Hampshire University*
Jill Misuraca, *University of Tampa*
Barbara Muller, *Arizona State University*
Linda Mullins, *Georgia State University—Perimeter College*
Yvonne Phang, *Borough of Manhattan Community College*
David Polster, *Oakton Community College*
Laura Prosser, *Black Hills State University*

Angela Sandberg, *Shorter University*
Vincent Shea, *St. John's University*
Margaret Shackell, *Forsyth Technical Community College*
Alice Sineath, *University of Maryland University College*
Teresa Speck, *St. Mary's University of Minnesota*
Lynn Stallworth, *Appalachian State University*
Diane Tanner, *University of North Florida*
Sheila Viel, *University of Wisconsin—Milwaukee*
Dick Wasson, *Southwestern College*
Lori Grady Zaher, *Bucks County Community College*

Advisory Board

Jimmy Carmenate, *Florida International University*
Sandra Cereola, *James Madison University*
Norma Holter, *Towson University*
Frank Ilett, *Boise State University*
Christine Kloezeman, *Glendale Community College*
Johnna Murray, *University of Missouri—St. Louis*
Nori Pearson, *Washington State University*
Karen Russom, *Lone Star College—Greenspoint*
Joel Sneed, *University of Oregon*

We thank Benjamin Huegel and Teresa Speck of St. Mary's University for their extensive efforts in the preparation of the homework materials related to Current Designs. We also appreciate the considerable support provided to us by the following people at Current Designs: Mike Cichanowski, Jim Brown, Diane Buswell, and Jake Greseth. We also benefited from the assistance and suggestions provided to us by Joan Van Hise in the preparation of materials related to sustainability.

We appreciate the exemplary support and commitment given to us by editor Veronica Schram, marketing manager Christina Koop, course content developer Jenny Welter, instructional designer Matt Origoni, senior course production operations specialist Nicole Repasky, editorial supervisor Terry Ann Tatro, designer Jon Boylan, program assistant Natalie Munoz, senior production editor Rachel Conrad, and Julie Perry, Cindy Durand, Amy Kopperude, Jennifer Collins, Gladys Soto, and Richard Bretan at Lumina. All of these professionals provided innumerable services that helped the text take shape.

We will appreciate suggestions and comments from users—instructors and students alike. You can send your thoughts and ideas about the text to us via email at: AccountingAuthors@yahoo.com.

Paul D. Kimmel
Madison, Wisconsin

Jerry J. Weygandt
Madison, Wisconsin

Jill E. Mitchell
Annandale, Virginia

CHAPTER 1

Managerial Accounting

CHAPTER PREVIEW

This chapter focuses on issues illustrated in the following Feature Story about **Current Designs** (USA) and its parent company **Wenonah Canoe** (USA). To succeed, the company needs to determine and control the costs of material, labor, and overhead, and understand the relationship between costs and profits. Managers often make decisions that determine their company's fate—and their own. Managers are evaluated on the results of their decisions. Managerial accounting provides tools to assist management in making decisions and evaluating the effectiveness of those decisions.

FEATURE STORY

Just Add Water ... and Paddle

Mike Cichanowski grew up on the Mississippi River in Winona, Minnesota. At a young age, he learned to paddle a canoe so he could explore the river. Before long, Mike began crafting his own canoes from bent wood and fiberglass in his dad's garage. Then, when his canoe-making shop outgrew the garage, he moved it into an old warehouse. When that was going to be torn down, Mike came to a critical juncture in his life. He took out a bank loan and built his own small shop, giving birth to the company **Wenonah Canoe** (USA).

Wenonah Canoe soon became known as a pioneer in developing techniques to get the most out of new materials such as plastics, composites, and carbon fibers—maximizing strength while minimizing weight.

In the 1990s, as kayaking became popular, Mike made another critical decision when he acquired **Current Designs** (USA), a premier Canadian kayak manufacturer. This venture allowed Wenonah to branch out with new product lines while providing Current Designs with much-needed capacity expansion and manufacturing expertise. Mike moved Current Designs' headquarters to Minnesota and made a big (and potentially risky) investment in a new production facility. Today, the company's 90 employees produce about 12,000 canoes and kayaks per year. These are sold across the country and around the world.

Mike will tell you that business success is "a three-legged stool." The first leg is the knowledge and commitment to make a great product. Wenonah's canoes and Current Designs' kayaks are widely regarded as among the very best. The second leg is the ability to sell your product. Mike's company started off making great canoes, but it took a little longer to figure out how to sell them. The third leg is not something that most of you would immediately associate with entrepreneurial success. It is what goes on behind the scenes—accounting. Good accounting information is absolutely critical to the countless decisions, big and small, that ensure the survival and growth of the company.

Bottom line: No matter how good your product is, and no matter how many units you sell, if you don't have a firm grip on your numbers, you are up a creek without a paddle.

Source: www.wenonah.com.

 Watch the *What Is Managerial Accounting?* video at https://wileyaccountingupdates.com/video/?p=76 for an introduction to managerial accounting and the topics presented in this course.

CHAPTER OUTLINE

Learning Objectives	Review	Practice
LO 1 Identify the features of managerial accounting and the functions of management.	• Comparing managerial and financial accounting • Management functions • Organizational structure	**DO IT! 1** Managerial Accounting Overview
LO 2 Describe the classes of manufacturing costs and the differences between product and period costs.	• Manufacturing costs • Product versus period costs • Illustration of cost concepts	**DO IT! 2** Managerial Cost Concepts
LO 3 Demonstrate how to compute cost of goods manufactured and prepare financial statements for a manufacturer.	• Balance sheet • Income statement • Cost of goods manufactured • Cost of goods manufactured schedule	**DO IT! 3** Cost of Goods Manufactured
LO 4 Discuss trends in managerial accounting.	• Service industries • Focus on the value chain • Balanced scorecard • Business ethics • Corporate social responsibility • The value of data analytics	**DO IT! 4** Trends in Managerial Accounting

Go to the Review and Practice section at the end of the chapter for a targeted summary and practice applications with solutions.

MANAGERIAL ACCOUNTING BASICS

Managerial accounting provides economic and financial information for managers and other internal users. The skills that you learn in this course will be vital to your future success in business. You don't believe us? Let's look at examples of some of the crucial activities of employees at **Current Designs** (USA) and where those activities are addressed in this text.

> **LEARNING OBJECTIVE 1**
> Identify the features of managerial accounting and the functions of management.

- In order to know whether it is making a profit, Current Designs needs accurate information about the cost of each kayak (Chapters 2, 3, and 4). To be profitable, Current Designs adjusts the number of kayaks it produces in response to changes in economic conditions and consumer tastes. It needs to understand how changes in the number of kayaks it produces impact its production costs and profitability (Chapters 5 and 6).
- Further, Current Designs' managers often consider alternative courses of action. For example, should the company accept a special order from a customer, produce a particular kayak component internally or outsource it, or continue or discontinue a particular product line (Chapter 7)? Related to this decision is determining what price to charge for the kayaks (Chapter 8).
- In order to plan for the future, Current Designs prepares budgets (Chapter 9), and then compares its budgeted numbers with its actual results to evaluate performance and identify areas that need to change (Chapters 10 and 11).
- Finally, Current Designs sometimes needs to make substantial investment decisions, such as the building of a new factory or the purchase of new equipment (Chapter 12).

Someday, you are going to face decisions just like these. You may end up in sales, marketing, management, production, or finance. You may work for a company that provides medical care, produces software, or serves up mouth-watering meals. No matter what your job position or product, the skills you acquire in this class will increase your chances of business success. Put another way, in business you can either guess or you can make an informed decision. As former **Microsoft** (USA) CEO Steve Ballmer said, "If you're supposed to be making money in business and supposed to be satisfying customers and building market share, there are numbers that characterize those things. And if somebody can't speak to me quantitatively about it, then I'm nervous." This course gives you the skills you need to quantify information so you can make informed business decisions.

Comparing Managerial and Financial Accounting

There are both similarities and differences between managerial and financial accounting.

- Each field of accounting deals with the economic events of a business. For example, *determining* the unit cost of manufacturing a product is part of managerial accounting. *Reporting* the total cost of goods manufactured and sold is part of financial accounting.
- Both managerial and financial accounting require that a company's economic events be quantified and communicated to interested parties.

Illustration 1.1 summarizes the principal differences between financial accounting and managerial accounting.

Management Functions

Managers' activities and responsibilities can be classified into three broad functions:

1. Planning.
2. Directing.
3. Controlling.

Feature	Financial Accounting	Managerial Accounting
Primary Users of Reports	External users: stockholders, creditors, and regulators.	Internal users: officers and managers.
Types and Frequency of Reports	External financial statements. Quarterly and annually.	Internal reports. As frequently as needed.
Purpose of Reports	General-purpose.	Special-purpose for specific decisions.
Content of Reports	Pertains to business as a whole. Highly aggregated (condensed). Limited to accrual accounting and cost data. Accounting standards.	Pertains to subunits of the business. Very detailed. Extends beyond accrual accounting to any relevant data. Evaluated based on relevance to decisions.
Verification Process	Audited by accountants.	No independent audits.

ILLUSTRATION 1.1 | **Differences between financial and managerial accounting**

In performing these functions, managers make decisions that have a significant impact on the organization.

Planning requires managers to look ahead and to establish objectives.

- These objectives are often diverse: maximizing short-term profits and market share, maintaining a commitment to environmental protection, and contributing to social programs.
- A key objective of management is to **add value** to the business under its control. Value is usually measured by the price of the company's stock and by the potential selling price of the company.

For example, **Hewlett-Packard** (USA), in an attempt to gain a stronger foothold in the computer industry, greatly reduced its prices to compete with **Dell** (USA).

Directing involves coordinating a company's diverse activities and human resources to produce a smooth-running operation.

- This function relates to implementing planned objectives and providing necessary incentives to motivate employees.
- Directing also involves selecting executives, appointing managers and supervisors, and hiring and training employees.

For example, manufacturers such as **Samsung Electronics Company** (KOR), **Volkswagen** (DEU), and **Dell** (USA) need to coordinate purchasing, manufacturing, warehousing, and selling. Service corporations such as **Emirates Airlines** (ARE), **Federal Express** (USA), and **British Telecommunications** (GBR) coordinate scheduling, sales, service, and acquisitions of equipment and supplies.

The third management function, **controlling**, is the process of keeping the company's activities on track.

- In controlling operations, managers determine whether planned goals are met.
- When there are deviations from targeted objectives, managers decide what changes are needed to get back on track.

Scandals at companies like **Theranos** (USA) and **Danske Bank** (DNK) attest to the fact that companies need adequate controls to ensure that the company develops and distributes accurate information.

How do managers achieve control? A smart manager in a very small operation can make personal observations, ask good questions, and know how to evaluate the answers. But using this approach in a larger organization would result in chaos. Imagine the president of **Apple** (USA) attempting to determine whether the company is meeting its planned objectives without some record of what has happened and what is expected to occur. Thus, large businesses typically use a formal system of evaluation. These systems include such features as budgets, responsibility centers, and performance evaluation reports—all of which are features of managerial accounting.

Decision-making is not a separate management function. Rather, it is the outcome of the exercise of good judgment in planning, directing, and controlling.

Organizational Structure

Most companies prepare **organization charts** to show the interrelationships of activities and the delegation of authority and responsibility within the company. **Illustration 1.2** shows a typical organization chart.

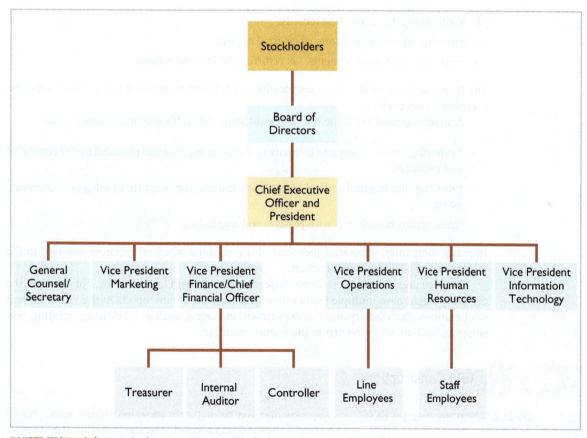

ILLUSTRATION 1.2 | **A typical corporate organization chart**

Stockholders own the corporation. They provide oversight indirectly through a **board of directors** they elect.

- The board formulates the operating policies for the company or organization.
- The board selects officers, such as a president and one or more vice presidents, to execute policy and to perform daily management functions.

The **chief executive officer (CEO)** has overall responsibility for managing the business. As the organization chart shows, the CEO delegates responsibilities to other officers.

Responsibilities within the company are frequently classified as either line or staff positions.

- Employees with **line positions** are directly involved in the company's primary revenue-generating operating activities. Examples of line positions include the vice president of operations, vice president of marketing, factory managers, supervisors, and production personnel.
- Employees with **staff positions** are involved in activities that support the efforts of the line employees. In a company like **Unilever** (GBR) or **Facebook** (USA), employees in finance, legal, and human resources have staff positions.
- While activities of staff employees are vital to the company, these employees are nonetheless there to support the line employees who engage in the company's primary operations.

The **chief financial officer (CFO)** is responsible for all of the accounting and finance issues the company faces. The CFO is supported by the **controller** and the **treasurer**. The controller's responsibilities include:

1. Maintaining the accounting records.
2. Ensuring an adequate system of internal control.
3. Preparing financial statements, tax returns, and internal reports.

The treasurer has custody of the corporation's funds and is responsible for maintaining the company's cash position.

Also serving the CFO is the internal audit staff. The staff's responsibilities include:

- Reviewing the reliability and integrity of financial information provided by the controller and treasurer.
- Ensuring that internal control systems are functioning properly to safeguard corporate assets.
- Investigating compliance with policies and regulations.

In many companies, these staff members also determine whether resources are used in the most economical and efficient fashion.

The vice president of operations oversees employees with line positions. For example, the company might have multiple factory managers, each of whom reports to the vice president of operations. Each factory also has department managers, such as fabricating, painting, and shipping, each of whom reports to the factory manager.

MANAGEMENT INSIGHT — DPR Construction

Sam Edwards/Caiaimage/Getty Images

Does a Company Need a CEO?

Can a company function without a person at the top? Nearly all companies have a CEO although some U.S. companies, such as **Oracle**, **Chipotle**, and **Whole Foods**, have operated with two people in the CEO position. **Samsung** (KOR) even had three CEOs at the same time. On the other hand, **Abercrombie & Fitch** (USA) operated for more than two years without a CEO because its CEO unexpectedly quit and a suitable replacement was hard to find. In fact, some companies replace the CEO position with a management committee. These companies feel this structure improves decision-making and increases collaboration. For example, the 4,000 employees of **DPR Construction** (USA) are overseen by an eight-person committee. Committee members are rotated off gradually but then continue to advise current members. The company notes that this approach provides more continuity over time than the sometimes sudden and harsh changes that occur when CEOs are replaced.

Source: Rachel Feintzeig, "Companies Manage with No CEO," *Wall Street Journal* (December 13, 2016).

What are some of the advantages cited by companies that choose a structure that lacks a CEO? (Answer is available in the book's product page on www.wiley.com)

> **DO IT! 1** ▶ **Managerial Accounting Overview**
>
> Indicate whether the following statements are true or false. If false, explain why.
>
> 1. Managerial accountants have a single role within an organization: collecting and reporting costs to management.
> 2. Financial accounting reports are general-purpose and intended for external users.
> 3. Managerial accounting reports are special-purpose and issued as frequently as needed.
> 4. Managers' activities and responsibilities can be classified into three broad functions: cost accounting, budgeting, and internal control.
> 5. Managerial accounting reports must comply with accounting standards.
>
> **Solution**
>
> 1. False. Managerial accountants do determine product costs, but they are also responsible for evaluating how well the company employs its resources. As a result, when the company makes critical strategic decisions, managerial accountants serve as team members alongside personnel from production, marketing, and engineering.
> 2. True.
> 3. True.
> 4. False. Managers' activities are classified into three broad functions: planning, directing, and controlling. Planning requires managers to look ahead to establish objectives. Directing involves coordinating a company's diverse activities and human resources to produce a smooth-running operation. Controlling keeps the company's activities on track.
> 5. False. Managerial accounting reports are for internal use and thus do not have to comply with accounting standards.
>
> Related exercise material: **BE1.1**, **BE1.2**, **DO IT! 1.1**, and **E1.1**.

ACTION PLAN

- Understand that managerial accounting is a field of accounting that provides economic and financial information for managers and other internal users.
- Understand that financial accounting provides information for external users.
- Analyze which users require which different types of information.

MANAGERIAL COST CONCEPTS

In order for managers at **Current Designs** (USA) to plan, direct, and control operations effectively, they need good information. One very important type of information relates to costs. Managers should ask questions such as the following:

1. What costs are involved in making a product or performing a service?
2. If we decrease production volume, will costs change?
3. What impact will automation have on total costs?
4. How can we best control costs?

LEARNING OBJECTIVE 2
Describe the classes of manufacturing costs and the differences between product and period costs.

To answer these questions, managers obtain and analyze reliable and relevant cost information. The first step is to understand the various cost categories that companies use.

Manufacturing Costs

Manufacturing consists of activities and processes that convert raw materials into finished goods. Contrast this type of operation with merchandising, which sells products in the form in which they are purchased.

- Manufacturing costs incurred to produce a product are classified as direct materials, direct labor, and manufacturing overhead.
- Typically, manufacturing costs are incurred at the production facility (the factory). The terms *manufacturing cost* and *product cost* are used interchangeably.

Direct Materials

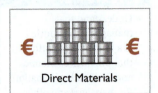

To obtain the materials that will be converted into the finished product, the manufacturer purchases raw materials. **Raw materials** are the basic materials and parts used in the manufacturing process.

Raw materials that can be physically and directly associated with the finished product during the manufacturing process are **direct materials**. Examples include flour in the baking of bread, syrup in the bottling of soft drinks, and steel in the making of automobiles. A primary direct material of many Current Designs' kayaks is polyethylene powder. Some of its high-performance kayaks use Kevlar®.

Some raw materials cannot be easily associated with the finished product. These are called indirect materials. **Indirect materials** have one of two characteristics:

1. They do not physically become part of the finished product (such as polishing compounds used by Current Designs for the finishing touches on kayaks).
2. They are impractical to trace to the finished product because their physical association with the finished product is too small in terms of cost (such as cotter pins and lock washers used in kayak rudder assembly).

Companies account for indirect materials as part of **manufacturing overhead**. So, all direct materials are raw materials, but not all raw materials are direct materials.

Direct Labor

The work of factory employees that can be physically and directly associated with converting raw materials into finished goods is **direct labor**. Bottlers at **Coca-Cola** (USA), bakers at **Aryzta** (CHE), and equipment operators at **Current Designs** (USA) are employees whose activities are usually classified as direct labor. **Indirect labor** refers to the work of manufacturing-related employees that has no physical association with the making of the finished product or for which it is impractical to trace costs to the goods produced. Examples include salaries and wages of factory maintenance people, factory security, product quality inspectors, and factory supervisors. While these employees work in the production facility, they are not directly involved in converting raw materials into the finished product. Like indirect materials, companies classify indirect labor as **manufacturing overhead**.

Manufacturing Overhead

Manufacturing overhead consists of manufacturing costs that are indirectly associated with the manufacture of the finished product.

- Manufacturing overhead includes indirect materials, indirect labor, depreciation on factory buildings and machines, insurance, taxes, and maintenance on factory facilities.
- If the cost is manufacturing-related but cannot be classified as direct materials or direct labor, it should be considered manufacturing overhead.

One study of manufactured goods found the following magnitudes of the three different product costs as a percentage of the total product cost: direct materials 54%, direct labor 13%, and manufacturing overhead 33% (see **Alternative Terminology**). Note that the direct labor component is the smallest. This component of product cost is dropping substantially because of automation. Companies are working hard to increase productivity by decreasing labor. In some companies, direct labor has become as little as 5% of the total cost.

Tracing direct materials and direct labor costs to specific products is fairly straightforward. Good recordkeeping can tell a company how much plastic it used in making each type of gear, or how many hours of factory labor it took to assemble a part. But tracing overhead costs to specific products presents problems. How much of the purchasing agent's salary is attributable to the hundreds of different products made in the same factory? What about the grease that keeps the machines running smoothly, or the electricity costs of the factory? Boiled down to its simplest form, the question becomes: Which products cause the incurrence of which costs? In subsequent chapters, we show various methods of aggregating and allocating overhead to products as these costs cannot be directly traced.

ALTERNATIVE TERMINOLOGY
Some companies use terms such as *factory overhead*, *indirect manufacturing costs*, and *burden* instead of manufacturing overhead.

MANAGEMENT INSIGHT Whirlpool

bikeriderlondon/Shutterstock

Why Manufacturing Matters for U.S. Workers

Prior to 2010, U.S. manufacturing employment fell at an average rate of 0.1% per year for 60 years. At the same time, U.S. factory output increased by an average rate of 3.4%. As manufacturers relied more heavily on automation, the number of people they needed declined. However, factory jobs are important because the average hourly wage of a factory worker is $22, twice the average wage of employees in the service sector. Fortunately, manufacturing jobs in the United States increased by 1.2% in 2010, and they were forecast to continue to increase through at least 2015. Why? Because U.S. companies like Whirlpool, Caterpillar, and Dow are building huge new plants to replace old, inefficient facilities. For many products that are ultimately sold in the United States, it makes more sense to produce them domestically and save on the shipping costs. In addition, these efficient new plants, combined with an experienced workforce, will make it possible to compete with manufacturers in other countries, thereby increasing export potential.

Sources: Bob Tita, "Whirlpool to Invest in Tennessee Plant," *Wall Street Journal Online* (September 1, 2010); and James R. Hagerty, "U.S. Factories Buck Decline," *Wall Street Journal Online* (January 19, 2011).

In what ways does the shift to automated factories change the amount and composition of product costs? (Answer is available in the book's product page on www.wiley.com)

Product versus Period Costs

Each of the manufacturing cost components—direct materials, direct labor, and manufacturing overhead—are product costs. As the term suggests, **product costs** are costs that are a necessary and integral part of producing the finished product (see **Alternative Terminology**).

- All manufacturing costs are classified as product costs.
- Companies record product costs, when incurred, as an asset called inventory.
- These costs do not become expenses until the company sells the finished goods inventory.
- At that point, the company records the expense as cost of goods sold.

Period costs are costs that are matched with the revenue of a specific time period rather than included in inventory as part of the cost to produce a salable product.

- These are nonmanufacturing costs.
- Period costs include selling and administrative expenses.
- In order to determine net income, companies deduct these period costs from revenues in the period in which they are incurred.

ALTERNATIVE TERMINOLOGY

All manufacturing costs are product costs, which are also called *inventoriable* costs.

Illustration 1.3 summarizes these relationships and cost terms. Our main concern in this chapter is with product costs.

Illustration of Cost Concepts

To improve your understanding of cost concepts, we illustrate them here through an extended example. Suppose you started your own snowboard factory, Lapland Boards. Think that's impossible? Burton Snowboards (USA) was started by Jake Burton Carpenter, when he was only 23 years old. Jake initially experimented with 100 different prototype designs before settling on a final design. Then Jake, along with two relatives and a friend, started making 50 boards per day in Londonderry, Vermont. Unfortunately, while they made a lot of boards in their first year, they were only able to sell 300 of them. To get by during those early years, Jake taught tennis and tended bar to pay the bills.

Illustration 1.4 shows some of the costs that your snowboard factory, Lapland Boards, would incur. We have classified each cost as a product cost or a period cost, as well as provided an explanation for the classification. We have also specified whether product costs are direct materials, direct labor, or manufacturing overhead.

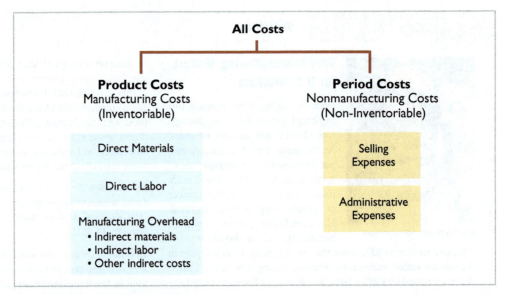

ILLUSTRATION 1.3 | Product versus period costs

Cost	Product Cost (direct materials, direct labor, or manufacturing overhead)	Period Cost (non-manufacturing)	Explanation
1. Wood cores, fiberglass, and resin (€30 per board)	Direct materials		Essential elements of finished product
2. Labor to trim and shape boards (€40 per board)	Direct labor		Physically and directly associated with converting raw materials into finished goods
3. Factory equipment depreciation (€25,000)	Manufacturing overhead		Factory cost that is not direct materials or direct labor
4. Property taxes on factory building (€6,000 per year)	Manufacturing overhead		Factory cost that is not direct materials or direct labor
5. Advertising costs (€60,000 per year)		X	Not a cost associated with producing product
6. Sales commissions (€20 per board)		X	Not a cost associated with producing product
7. Factory maintenance salaries (€25,000 per year)	Manufacturing overhead		A factory cost, but employees are not physically and directly involved with converting raw materials into finished goods
8. Salary of factory manager (€70,000 per year)	Manufacturing overhead		A factory cost, but employees are not physically and directly involved with converting raw materials into finished goods
9. Cost of shipping boards to customers (€8 per board)		X	Not a cost associated with producing product
10. Salary of product quality inspector (€20,000 per year)	Manufacturing overhead		A factory cost, but employees are not physically and directly involved with converting raw materials into finished goods

ILLUSTRATION 1.4 | Assignment of costs to cost categories

Total manufacturing costs are the sum of the **product costs**—direct materials, direct labor, and manufacturing overhead—incurred in the current period. If Lapland Boards produces 10,000 snowboards the first year, the total manufacturing costs would be €846,000, as shown in **Illustration 1.5**.

Once it knows the total manufacturing costs, Lapland Boards can compute the average manufacturing cost per unit. Assuming 10,000 units, the cost to produce one snowboard is €84.60 (€846,000 ÷ 10,000 units).

The cost concepts discussed in this chapter are used extensively in subsequent chapters. So study Illustration 1.4 carefully. If you do not understand any of these classifications, go back and reread the appropriate section.

Cost Item	Manufacturing Cost
1. Material cost (€30 × 10,000)	€300,000
2. Labor cost (€40 × 10,000)	400,000
3. Depreciation on factory equipment	25,000
4. Property taxes on factory building	6,000
7. Factory maintenance salaries	25,000
8. Salary of factory manager	70,000
10. Salary of product quality inspector	20,000
Total manufacturing product costs	**€846,000**

ILLUSTRATION 1.5 | Computation of total manufacturing product costs

---

DO IT! 2 ▶ Managerial Cost Concepts

A bicycle company has these costs: tires, wages of employees who put tires on the wheels, factory building depreciation, advertising expenditures, factory machine lubricants, spokes, salary of factory manager, salary of accountant, handlebars, salaries of factory maintenance employees, and salary of product quality inspector. Classify each of these costs as a product cost or a period cost. Specify direct materials, direct labor, or manufacturing overhead for product costs.

Solution

Cost	Product Cost	Period Cost
Tires	Direct materials	
Wages of employees who put tires on the wheels	Direct labor	
Factory building depreciation	Manufacturing overhead	
Advertising expenditures		X
Factory machine lubricants	Manufacturing overhead	
Spokes	Direct materials	
Salary of factory manager	Manufacturing overhead	
Salary of accountant		X
Handlebars	Direct materials	
Salaries of factory maintenance employees	Manufacturing overhead	
Salary of product quality inspector	Manufacturing overhead	

Related exercise material: **BE1.3, BE1.4, BE1.5, BE1.6, DO IT! 1.2, E1.2, E1.3, E1.4, E1.5, E1.6,** and **E1.7.**

ACTION PLAN
- Direct materials: any raw materials physically and directly associated with the finished product.
- Direct labor: the work of factory employees directly associated with the finished product.
- Manufacturing overhead: any costs indirectly associated with the finished product.
- Costs that are not product costs are period costs.

MANUFACTURING COSTS IN FINANCIAL STATEMENTS

LEARNING OBJECTIVE 3
Demonstrate how to compute cost of goods manufactured and prepare financial statements for a manufacturer.

The financial statements of a manufacturer are very similar to those of a merchandiser. For example, you will find many of the same sections and same accounts in the financial statements of **Procter & Gamble** (USA) that you find in the financial statements of **Dick's Sporting Goods** (USA). The principal differences between their financial statements occur in two places:

1. The current assets section in the balance sheet.
2. The cost of goods sold section in the income statement.

Each step in the accounting cycle for a merchandiser also applies to a manufacturer.

- For example, prior to preparing financial statements, manufacturers make adjustments.
- The adjustments are essentially the same as those of a merchandiser.

DECISION TOOLS
The balance sheet helps managers determine whether sufficient inventory exists to meet forecasted demand.

Balance Sheet

The balance sheet for a merchandising company shows just one category of inventory. In contrast, the balance sheet for a manufacturer may have three inventory accounts, raw materials, work in process, and finished goods, as shown in **Illustration 1.6** for Current Designs' kayak inventory (see **Decision Tools**).

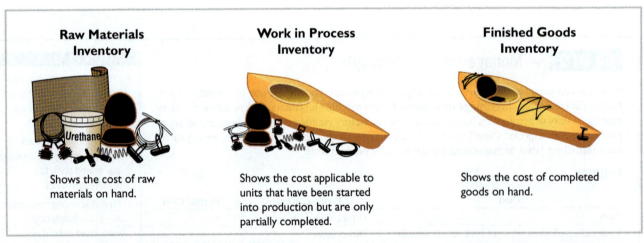

ILLUSTRATION 1.6 | Inventory accounts for a manufacturer

Finished Goods Inventory is to a manufacturer what Inventory is to a merchandiser. In both cases, these represent the goods that the company has available for sale. The current assets sections presented in **Illustration 1.7** contrast the presentations of inventories for merchandising and manufacturing companies. The remainder of the balance sheet is similar for the two types of companies.

Income Statement

Under a periodic inventory system, the income statements of a merchandiser and a manufacturer differ in the cost of goods sold section.

Merchandising Company Balance Sheet December 31, 2023		Manufacturing Company Balance Sheet December 31, 2023		
Current assets		Current assets		
Cash	€100,000	Cash		€180,000
Accounts receivable (net)	210,000	Accounts receivable (net)		210,000
Inventory	400,000	Inventory		
Prepaid expenses	22,000	Finished goods	€80,000	
Total current assets	€732,000	Work in process	25,200	
		Raw materials	22,800	128,000
		Prepaid expenses		18,000
		Total current assets		€536,000

ILLUSTRATION 1.7 | Current assets sections of merchandising and manufacturing balance sheets

- Merchandisers compute cost of goods sold by adding the beginning inventory to the **cost of goods purchased** and subtracting the ending inventory.
- Manufacturers compute cost of goods sold by adding the beginning finished goods inventory to the **cost of goods manufactured** and subtracting the ending finished goods inventory.

Illustration 1.8, which assumes a periodic inventory system, shows these different methods.

ILLUSTRATION 1.8 | Merchandiser versus manufacturer cost of goods sold calculations

A number of accounts are involved in determining the cost of goods manufactured. To eliminate excessive detail, income statements typically show only the total cost of goods manufactured. A separate statement, called a Cost of Goods Manufactured Schedule, presents the details (see Illustration 1.11).

Illustration 1.9 shows the different presentations of the cost of goods sold sections for merchandising and manufacturing companies. The other sections of an income statement are similar for merchandisers and manufacturers.

Merchandising Company
Income Statement (partial)
For the Year Ended December 31, 2023

Cost of goods sold	
Inventory, Jan. 1	€ 70,000
Cost of goods purchased	650,000
Cost of goods available for sale	720,000
Less: Inventory, Dec. 31	400,000
Cost of goods sold	€320,000

Manufacturing Company
Income Statement (partial)
For the Year Ended December 31, 2023

Cost of goods sold	
Finished goods inventory, Jan. 1	€ 90,000
Cost of goods manufactured (see Illustration 1.11)	370,000
Cost of goods available for sale	460,000
Less: Finished goods inventory, Dec. 31	80,000
Cost of goods sold	€380,000

ILLUSTRATION 1.9 | Cost of goods sold sections of merchandising and manufacturing income statements

Cost of Goods Manufactured

An example may help show how companies determine the cost of goods manufactured. Assume that on January 1, **Current Designs** (USA) has a number of kayaks in various stages of production. In total, these partially completed manufactured units are called beginning **work in process inventory**. These are kayaks that were worked on during the prior year but were not completed. As a result, these kayaks will be completed during the current year. The cost of beginning work in process inventory is based on the **manufacturing costs incurred in the prior period**.

Current Designs first incurs manufacturing costs in the current year to complete the kayaks that were in process on January 1. It then incurs manufacturing costs for production of new orders. The sum of the direct materials costs, direct labor costs, and manufacturing overhead incurred in the current year is the **total manufacturing costs** for the current period.

We now have two cost amounts:

1. The cost of the beginning work in process.
2. The total manufacturing costs for the current period.

The sum of these costs is the **total cost of work in process** for the year.

At the end of the year, Current Designs may have some kayaks that are only partially completed. The costs of these unfinished units represent the cost of the **ending work in process inventory**. To find the **cost of goods manufactured**, we subtract the ending work in process inventory from the total cost of work in process. **Illustration 1.10** shows the calculation for determining the cost of goods manufactured.

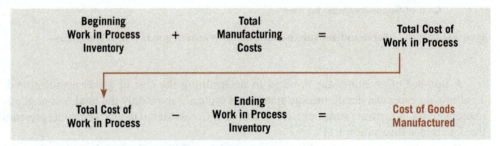

ILLUSTRATION 1.10 | Cost of goods manufactured calculation

Cost of Goods Manufactured Schedule

The **cost of goods manufactured schedule** reports cost elements used in calculating cost of goods manufactured. **Illustration 1.11** shows the schedule for Current Designs (using assumed data). The schedule presents detailed data for direct materials and for manufacturing overhead (see **Decision Tools**).

You should be able to distinguish between "Total manufacturing costs" and "Cost of goods manufactured."

DECISION TOOLS

The cost of goods manufactured schedule helps managers determine if the company is maintaining control over the costs of production.

- As Illustration 1.11 shows, total manufacturing costs is the sum of all manufacturing costs (direct materials, direct labor, and manufacturing overhead) **incurred during the period**.
- Cost of goods manufactured is the cost of those goods that were **completed during the period** and are no longer work in process; these costs relate to finished goods.
- If we add beginning work in process inventory to the total manufacturing costs incurred during the period and then subtract the ending work in process inventory (the calculation given in Illustration 1.10), we arrive at the cost of goods manufactured during the period.
- Cost of goods manufactured represents the costs related to items that were completed during the period and are therefore included in finished goods.

Current Designs
Cost of Goods Manufactured Schedule
for the Year Ended December 31, 2023

Work in process, January 1		$ 18,400
Direct materials		
Raw materials inventory, January 1	$ 16,700	
Raw materials purchases	152,500	
Total raw materials available for use	169,200	
Less: Raw materials inventory, December 31	22,800	
Direct materials used		$146,400*
Direct labor		175,600
Manufacturing overhead		
Indirect labor	14,300	
Factory repairs	12,600	
Factory utilities	10,100	
Factory depreciation	9,440	
Factory insurance	8,360	
Total manufacturing overhead		54,800
Total manufacturing costs		376,800
Total cost of work in process		395,200
Less: Work in process, December 31		25,200
Cost of goods manufactured		$370,000

*To simplify the presentation, assumes that all raw materials used were direct materials.

ILLUSTRATION 1.11 | **Cost of goods manufactured schedule**

DO IT! 3 ▶ Cost of Goods Manufactured

The following information is available for Gonzalez SpA.

	March 1	March 31
Raw materials inventory	€12,000	€10,000
Work in process inventory	2,500	4,000
Raw materials purchased in March	€ 90,000	
Direct labor in March	75,000	
Manufacturing overhead in March	220,000	

Prepare the cost of goods manufactured schedule for the month of March 2023. (Assume that all raw materials used were direct materials.)

Solution

Gonzalez SpA
Cost of Goods Manufactured Schedule
For the Month Ended March 31, 2023

Work in process, March 1		€ 2,500
Direct materials		
Raw materials, March 1	€ 12,000	
Raw materials purchases	90,000	
Total raw materials available for use	102,000	
Less: Raw materials, March 31	10,000	
Direct materials used	€ 92,000	
Direct labor	75,000	
Manufacturing overhead	220,000	
Total manufacturing costs		387,000
Total cost of work in process		389,500
Less: Work in process, March 31		4,000
Cost of goods manufactured		€385,500

Related exercise material: **BE1.7, BE1.8, BE1.9, BE1.10, DO IT! 1.3, E1.8, E1.9, E1.10, E1.11, E1.12, E1.13, E1.14, E1.15, E1.16,** and **E1.17.**

ACTION PLAN
- Start with beginning work in process as the first item in the cost of goods manufactured schedule.
- Sum direct materials used, direct labor, and manufacturing overhead to determine total manufacturing costs.
- Sum beginning work in process and total manufacturing costs to determine total cost of work in process.
- Cost of goods manufactured is the total cost of work in process less ending work in process.

MANAGERIAL ACCOUNTING TRENDS

LEARNING OBJECTIVE 4
Discuss trends in managerial accounting.

In this rapidly changing world, managerial accounting needs to continue to innovate in order to provide managers with the information they need.

Service Industries

Much of the global economy has shifted toward an emphasis on services.

- Today, approximately 80% of U.S. workers are employed by service companies.
- Airlines, marketing agencies, cable companies, and governmental agencies are just a few examples of service companies.
- Service companies differ from manufacturing companies in that services are consumed immediately by customers.

For example, an airline uses special equipment to provide its product, but the output of that equipment is consumed immediately by the customer in the form of a flight. A marketing agency performs services for its clients that are immediately consumed by the customer in the form of a marketing plan. In contrast, a manufacturing company like **Boeing** (USA) records the airplanes that it manufactures as inventory until they are sold.

This chapter's examples feature manufacturing companies because accounting for the manufacturing environment requires the use of the broadest range of accounts. That is, the accounts used by service companies represent a subset of those used by manufacturers because service companies are not producing inventory. Neither an airline nor a marketing agency produces an inventoriable product. However, just like a manufacturer, each needs to keep track of the costs of its services in order to know whether it is generating a profit (see Ethics Note). An airline needs to know the cost of flight service to each destination, and a marketing agency needs to know the cost to develop a marketing plan. The techniques shown in this chapter to accumulate manufacturing costs to determine manufacturing inventory are equally useful for determining the costs of performing services.

Many of the examples we present in subsequent chapters, as well as some end-of-chapter materials, will be based on service companies.

ETHICS NOTE

Do telecommunications companies have an obligation to provide service to remote or low-user areas for a fee that may be less than the cost of the service?

SERVICE COMPANY INSIGHT   Allegiant Airlines

Stephen Strathdee\iStock.com

Low Fares but Decent Profits

When other airlines were cutting flight service due to recession, **Allegiant Airlines** (USA) increased capacity by 21%. Sounds crazy, doesn't it? But it must have known something because while the other airlines were losing money, it was generating profits. In fact, it often has the industry's highest profit margins. Consider also that its average one-way fare is only $83. So how does it make money? As a low-budget airline, it focuses on controlling costs.

Allegiant purchases used planes for $3 million each rather than new planes for $40 million. It flies out of small towns, so wages are low and competition is nonexistent. It minimizes hotel costs by having its flight crews finish their day in their home cities. The company also only flies a route if its 150-passenger planes are nearly full (it averages about 90% of capacity). The bottom line is that Allegiant knows its costs to the penny. Knowing what your costs are might not be glamorous, but it sure beats losing money.

Sources: Susan Carey, "For Allegiant, Getaways Mean Profits," *Wall Street Journal Online* (February 18, 2009); and Scott Mayerowitz, "Tiny Allegiant Air Thrives on Low Costs, High Fees," http://bigstory.ap.org (June 28, 2013).

What are some of the line items that would appear in the cost of services performed schedule of an airline? (Answer is available in the book's product page on www.wiley.com)

Focus on the Value Chain

The **value chain** refers to all business processes associated with providing a product or performing a service. **Illustration 1.12** depicts the value chain for a manufacturer.

- Note that the value chain includes both manufacturing and nonmanufacturing costs.
- Many of the most significant business innovations in recent years have resulted either directly, or indirectly, from a focus on the value chain.

For example, **lean manufacturing** was originally pioneered by Japanese automobile manufacturer **Toyota** (JPN) but is now widely employed. Lean manufacturing requires a review of all business processes in an effort to increase productivity and eliminate waste, all while continually trying to improve quality.

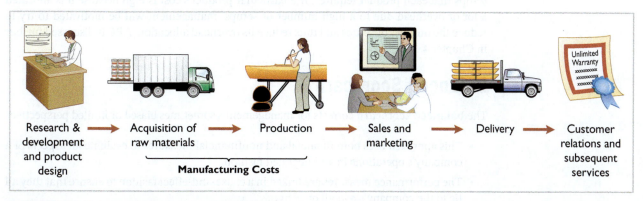

ILLUSTRATION 1.12 | A manufacturer's value chain

Just-in-time (JIT) inventory methods, which have significantly lowered inventory levels and costs for many companies, are one innovation that resulted from the focus on the value chain.

- Under the JIT inventory method, goods are manufactured or purchased just in time for sale.
- However, JIT also necessitates increased emphasis on product quality. Because JIT companies do not have excess inventory on hand, they cannot afford to stop production because of defects or machine breakdowns. If they stop production, deliveries will be delayed and customers will be unhappy.

Partially as a consequence of JIT, many companies now focus on **total quality management (TQM)** to reduce defects in finished products, with the goal of zero defects. **Toyota** (JPN) was one of the pioneers of TQM processes as early as the 1940s. Some of the largest companies in the world, including **Ford** (USA) and **ExxonMobil** (USA), have benefitted from these practices.

Another innovation is the **theory of constraints**.

- This involves identification of "bottlenecks"—constraints within the value chain that limit a company's profitability.
- Once a major constraint has been identified and eliminated, the company moves on to fix the next most significant constraint.

General Motors (USA) found that by applying the theory of constraints to its distribution system, it could more effectively meet the demands of its dealers and minimize the amount of excess inventory in its distribution system. This also reduced its need for overtime labor.

Technology has played a big role in the focus on the value chain and the implementation of lean manufacturing. For example, **enterprise resource planning (ERP) systems**, such as those provided by **SAP** (DEU), provide a comprehensive, centralized, integrated source of information to manage all major business processes—from purchasing, to manufacturing, to sales, to human resources.

- ERP systems have, in some large companies, replaced as many as 200 individual software packages.
- In addition, the focus on improving efficiency in the value chain has resulted in adoption of automated manufacturing processes.

As overhead costs have increased because of factory automation, the accuracy of overhead cost allocation to specific products has become more important. In response, managerial accountants devised an allocation approach called **activity-based costing (ABC)**.

- ABC allocates overhead based on each product's use of particular activities in making the product.
- In addition to providing more accurate product costing, ABC can contribute to increased efficiency in the value chain.

For example, suppose one of a company's overhead pools is allocated based on the number of setups that each product requires. If a particular product's cost is high because it is allocated a lot of overhead due to a high number of setups, management will be motivated to try to reduce the number of setups and thus reduce its overhead allocation. ABC is discussed further in Chapter 4.

Balanced Scorecard

The **balanced scorecard** corrects for management's sometimes biased or limited perspective.

- This approach uses both financial and nonfinancial measures to evaluate all aspects of a company's operations in an integrated fashion.
- The performance measures are linked in a cause-and-effect fashion to ensure that they all tie to the company's overall objectives.

> **MANAGEMENT INSIGHT** — **Inditex SA**
>
>
> Pixel-shot / Alamy Stock Photo
>
> **Supplying Today's (Not Yesterday's) Fashions**
>
> In terms of total sales, **Inditex SA** (ESP) is the planet's largest fashion retailer. What does it do differently than its competitors? How did it double its sales over a recent seven-year period while competitors such as **Gap Inc.** (USA) stumbled badly? Inditex distinguishes itself in its value chain's ability to react quickly to constantly changing customer tastes. First, designers and commercial staff sit side by side in a massive, open workspace facility, taking direct input from sales staff around the world regarding new product ideas. Manufacturing facilities are located relatively near company headquarters, allowing more direct input and oversight into production. Also, all goods (other than online sales) are shipped straight from the production facility to stores, rather than warehouses. As a result of its unique approach to how it designs, manufactures, and distributes its goods, Inditex can actually sometimes get a new product from initial idea to the store shelf in two weeks rather than the industry norm of two to eight months. And because Inditex provides customers with designs that competitors don't have yet, it can charge higher prices while also continuing to look for ways to increase efficiency and thus cut costs.
>
> **Source:** Patricia Kowsmann, "Fast Fashion: How a Zara Coat Went from Design to Fifth Avenue in 25 Days," *Wall Street Journal* (December 6, 2016).
>
> **What steps has Inditex taken that make its value chain unique?** (Answer is available in the book's product page on www.wiley.com)

For example, to increase return on assets, the company could try to increase sales. To increase sales, the company could try to increase customer satisfaction. To increase customer satisfaction, the company could try to reduce product defects. Finally, to reduce product defects, the company could increase employee training. The balanced scorecard, which is discussed further in Chapter 11, is now used by many U.S. companies, including **Hilton Hotels**, **Walmart**, and **HP**.

Business Ethics

All employees within an organization are expected to act ethically in their business activities. Given the importance of ethical behavior to corporations and their owners (stockholders), an increasing number of organizations provide codes of business ethics for their employees.

Creating Proper Incentives

Companies like **Siemens** (DEU), **Novartis** (CHE), **Nestle** (CHE), and **Unilever** (GBR) use complex systems to monitor, control, and evaluate the actions of managers. Unfortunately, these systems and controls sometimes unwittingly create incentives for managers to take unethical actions.

- Because budgets are also used as an evaluation tool, some managers try to "game" the budgeting process by underestimating their division's predicted performance so that it will be easier to meet their performance targets.
- But, if budgets are set at unattainable levels, managers sometimes take unethical actions to meet the targets in order to receive higher compensation or, in some cases, to keep their jobs.

In a recent example, **Carlsberg A.S.**, a Danish multinational brewer, mentioned that "Carlsberg is investigating its Indian unit for financial irregularities, including incorrect payments, embezzlement, and kickbacks from customers." The company said the probe followed accusations made by its local partner, with which it is "engaged in a very difficult commercial conflict."

Code of Ethical Standards

In response to company scandals, many countries throughout the world have begun to establish ethical rules and practices. For example, the U.S. Congress enacted the **Sarbanes-Oxley Act (SOX)** to help prevent lapses in internal control.

- CEOs and CFOs are now required to certify that financial statements give a fair presentation of the company's operating results and its financial condition.
- Top managers must certify that the company maintains an adequate system of internal controls to ensure accurate financial reports.
- Companies now pay more attention to the composition of the board of directors. In particular, the audit committee of the board of directors must be comprised entirely of independent members (that is, non-employees) and must contain at least one financial expert.
- The law substantially increases the penalties for misconduct.

The EU equivalent of the Sarbanes-Oxley Act (SOX) for internal controls is the EU Audit Regulation and Directive **(EU Directive 2014/56/EU)** which was adopted in 2014.

- The purpose of the EU Directive 2014 is to enhance the quality and transparency of the audits in the European Union.
- These regulations establish requirements for statutory audits of financial statements and impose certain obligations on auditors and audit firms.
- While the EU Audit Regulation and Directive does not mirror all the provisions of the Sarbanes-Oxley Act, it addresses similar objectives of strengthening internal controls, improving corporate governance, and enhancing the independence and reliability of auditors.
- In EU, auditors are expected to adhere to a statement of ethical professional practice that sets the principles and standards governing their behavior and conduct.
- The essential reference for auditors' ethical responsibilities is the International Ethics Standards Board for Accountants (IESBA) Code of Ethics, which provides a global framework for ethical conduct in accounting. European auditors typically align with these international standards.

To provide guidance for managerial accountants, the Institute of Management Accountants (IMA) has developed a code of ethical standards, entitled *IMA Statement of Ethical Professional Practice.* Management accountants should not commit acts in violation of these standards. Nor should they condone such acts by others within their organizations. Throughout the text, we address various ethical issues managers face.

Corporate Social Responsibility

The balanced scorecard attempts to take a broader, more inclusive view of corporate profitability measures. Many companies, however, have begun to evaluate not just corporate profitability but also **corporate social responsibility**.

- Corporate social responsibility considers a company's efforts to employ sustainable business practices with regard to its employees, society, and the environment.
- This is sometimes referred to as the **triple bottom line** because it evaluates a company's performance with regard to **people, planet, and profit**.
- Recent reports indicate that nearly 80% of the 500 largest U.S. companies provide sustainability reports.

Make no mistake, these companies are still striving to maximize profits—in a competitive world, they won't survive long if they don't. In fact, you might recognize a few of the names on a recent list (published by Corporate Knights) of the 100 most sustainable companies in the world. Are you surprised that **General Electric** (USA), **adidas** (DEU), **BMW** (DEU), **Coca-Cola** (USA), or **Apple** (USA) made the list? These companies have learned that with a long-term, sustainable approach, they can maximize profits while also acting in the best interest of their employees, their communities, and the environment. In fact, a monetary bonus was provided by 87% of the companies on the list to managers that met sustainability goals. At various points within this text, we discuss situations where real companies use the very skills that you are learning to evaluate decisions from a sustainable perspective, such as in the following Insight box.

PEOPLE, PLANET, AND PROFIT INSIGHT | Phantom Tac

aabeele/Shutterstock.com

People Matter

Many clothing factories in developing countries are known for unsafe buildings, poor working conditions, and wage and labor violations. One of the owners of Phantom Tac (BGD), a clothing manufacturer in Bangladesh, did make efforts to develop sustainable business practices. This owner, David Mayor, provided funding for a training program for female workers. He also developed a website to educate customers about the workers' conditions. But Phantom Tac also had to make a profit. Things got tight when one of its customers canceled orders because Phantom Tac failed a social compliance audit. The company had to quit funding the training program and the website.

Recently, Bangladesh's textile industry has seen some significant improvements in working conditions and safety standards. As Brad Adams, Asia director of Human Rights Watch, notes, "The (Dhaka) government has belatedly begun to register unions, which is an important first step, but it now needs to ensure that factory owners stop persecuting their leaders and actually allow them to function."

Sources: Jim Yardley, "Clothing Brands Sidestep Blame for Safety Lapses," *The New York Times Online* (December 30, 2013); and Palash Ghosh, "Despite Low Pay, Poor Work Conditions, Garment Factories Empowering Millions of Bangladeshi Women," *International Business Times* (March 25, 2014).

What are some of the common problems for many clothing factories in developing countries? (Answer is available in the book's product page on www.wiley.com)

The Value of Data Analytics

Companies have never had so much available data. In many companies, virtually every aspect of operations—the employees, the customers, even the manufacturing equipment—leaves a data trail. However, while "big data" can be impressive, it can also be overwhelming.

- Having all the data in the world will not necessarily lead to better results.
- The trick is having the skills and know-how to use the data in ways that result in more productive (and happier) employees, more satisfied customers, and more profitable operations.

It is therefore not surprising that one of the most rapidly growing areas of business today is data analytics. **Data analytics** is the use of techniques, which often combine software and statistics, to analyze data to make informed decisions.

Throughout this text, we offer many examples of how successful companies are using data analytics. We also provide examples of one analytical tool, data visualizations. **Data visualizations** often help managers acquire a more intuitive understanding of (1) the relationships between variables and (2) business trends. *The end-of-chapter homework material provides opportunities to perform basic data analytics and data visualizations in selected chapters.*

DATA ANALYTICS INSIGHT | The Walt Disney Company

Paulbr/Getty Images

Using Data in Its Own World

The Walt Disney Company (USA) makes fun seem effortless at its theme parks, but there is a magic mountain of data collection going on behind the scenes. For example, Disney employs behavioral analytics, which uses data to both predict and influence customer behavior, in countless ways. Disney collects the data through its "MagicBands" worn by visitors to the parks. While the MagicBands provide visitors with many benefits (e.g., delivering customized itineraries, reducing wait lines, and providing customer recognition by Disney characters), these bands are also delivering continual information to the company about the locations, activities, eating habits, and purchases of Disney visitors.

Disney uses the MagicBand information to support daily adjustments of operations as well as long-term planning. For example, the company can use this information to monitor park usage and subsequently encourage visitors to change their itineraries to different activities that will require a shorter wait time. If customers are waiting in line, they aren't happy—and they also aren't spending money. Long-term planning uses of MagicBand information include designing new attractions and updating menu options in response to supply and demand.

Source: Randerson112358, "How Disney World Uses Big Data," *medium.com* (May 18, 2019).

What is behavioral analytics, and how does Disney use it to minimize lines at its theme parks? (Answer is available in the book's product page on www.wiley.com)

DO IT! 4 ▶ Trends in Managerial Accounting

Match the descriptions that follow with the corresponding terms.

Descriptions:

1. _____ All activities associated with providing a product or performing a service.
2. _____ A method of allocating overhead based on each product's use of activities in making the product.
3. _____ Systems implemented to reduce defects in finished products with the goal of achieving zero defects.
4. _____ A performance-measurement approach that uses both financial and nonfinancial measures, tied to company objectives, to evaluate a company's operations in an integrated fashion.
5. _____ Inventory system in which goods are manufactured or purchased just as they are needed for use or sale.
6. _____ A company's efforts to employ sustainable business practices with regard to its employees, society, and the environment.
7. _____ A code of ethical standards developed by the Institute of Management Accountants.

Terms:

a. Activity-based costing.
b. Balanced scorecard.
c. Corporate social responsibility.
d. Just-in-time (JIT) inventory.
e. Total quality management (TQM).
f. Statement of Ethical Professional Practice.
g. Value chain.

ACTION PLAN
- Develop a forward-looking view, in order to advise and provide information to various members of the organization.
- Understand current business trends and issues.

Solution

1. g 2. a 3. e 4. b 5. d 6. c 7. f

Related exercise material: **BE1.11, DO IT! 1.4, and E1.18.**

USING THE DECISION TOOLS | Current Designs

Current Designs (USA) faces many situations where it needs to apply the decision tools in this chapter, such as analyzing the balance sheet for optimal inventory levels. For example, assume that the market has responded enthusiastically to a new Current Designs' model, the Otter. As a result, the company has established a separate manufacturing facility to produce these kayaks. Now assume that the company produces 1,000 of these kayaks per month. Current Designs' monthly manufacturing costs and other data for the Otter are as follows:

#	Item	Cost
1.	Rent on manufacturing equipment (lease cost)	$2,000/month
2.	Insurance on manufacturing building	$750/month
3.	Raw materials (plastic, fiberglass, etc.)	$180/kayak
4.	Utility costs for manufacturing facility	$1,000/month
5.	Utility costs for administrative office	$800/month
6.	Wages for assembly-line workers in manufacturing facility	$130/kayak
7.	Depreciation on administrative office equipment	$650/month
8.	Miscellaneous manufacturing materials used (lubricants, solders, etc.)	$12/kayak
9.	Property taxes on manufacturing building	$24,000/year
10.	Manufacturing supervisor's salary	$5,000/month
11.	Advertising for the Otter	$30,000/year
12.	Sales commissions	$30/kayak
13.	Depreciation on manufacturing building	$4,000/month

Instructions

a. Prepare an answer sheet with the following column headings:

	Product Costs			
Cost Item	Direct Materials	Direct Labor	Manufacturing Overhead	Period Costs

Enter each cost item on your answer sheet, placing an "X" under the appropriate headings.

b. Compute total manufacturing costs for the month.

Solution

a.

	Product Costs			
Cost Item	Direct Materials	Direct Labor	Manufacturing Overhead	Period Costs
1. Rent on manufacturing equipment ($2,000/month)			X	
2. Insurance on manufacturing building ($750/month)			X	
3. Raw materials ($180/kayak)	X			
4. Manufacturing utility costs ($1,000/month)			X	
5. Office utility costs ($800/month)				X
6. Wages for assembly workers ($130/kayak)		X		
7. Depreciation on administrative office equipment ($650/month)				X
8. Miscellaneous manufacturing materials used ($12/kayak)			X	
9. Property taxes on manufacturing building ($24,000/year)			X	
10. Manufacturing supervisor's salary ($5,000/month)			X	
11. Advertising cost ($30,000/year)				X
12. Sales commissions ($30/kayak)				X
13. Depreciation on manufacturing building ($4,000/month)			X	

b.

Cost Item	Manufacturing Cost
Rent on manufacturing equipment	$ 2,000
Insurance on manufacturing building	750
Raw materials ($180 × 1,000)	180,000
Manufacturing utilities	1,000
Labor ($130 × 1,000)	130,000
Miscellaneous materials ($12 × 1,000)	12,000
Property taxes on manufacturing building ($24,000 ÷ 12)	2,000
Manufacturing supervisor's salary	5,000
Depreciation on manufacturing building	4,000
Total manufacturing costs	$336,750

Current Designs' monthly manufacturing cost to produce 1,000 Otters is $336,750.

REVIEW AND PRACTICE

Learning Objectives Review

LO 1 Identify the features of managerial accounting and the functions of management.

The *primary users* of managerial accounting reports, issued as frequently as needed, are internal users, who are officers, department heads, managers, and supervisors in the company. The purpose of these reports is to provide special-purpose information for a particular user for a specific decision. The content of managerial accounting reports pertains to subunits of the business. It may be very detailed, and may extend beyond the accrual accounting system. The reporting standard is relevance to the decision being made. No independent audits are required in managerial accounting.

The functions of management are planning, directing, and controlling. Planning requires management to look ahead and to establish objectives. Directing involves coordinating the diverse activities and human resources of a company to produce a smooth-running operation. Controlling is the process of keeping the activities on track.

LO 2 Describe the classes of manufacturing costs and the differences between product and period costs.

Manufacturing costs are typically classified as either (1) direct materials, (2) direct labor, or (3) manufacturing overhead. Raw materials that can be physically and directly associated with the finished product during the manufacturing process are called direct materials. The work of factory employees that can be physically and directly associated with converting raw materials into finished goods is considered direct labor. Manufacturing overhead consists of costs that are indirectly associated with the manufacture of the finished product. Manufacturing costs are typically incurred at the manufacturing facility.

Product costs are costs that are a necessary and integral part of producing the finished product (manufacturing costs). Product costs are also called inventoriable costs. These costs do not become expenses until the company sells the finished goods inventory.

Period costs are costs that are identified with a specific time period rather than with a salable product. These costs relate to non-manufacturing costs and therefore are not inventoriable costs. They are expensed as incurred.

LO 3 Demonstrate how to compute cost of goods manufactured and prepare financial statements for a manufacturer.

Companies add the cost of the beginning work in process to the total manufacturing costs for the current year to arrive at the total cost of work in process for the year. They then subtract the ending work in process from the total cost of work in process to arrive at the cost of goods manufactured.

The difference between a merchandising and a manufacturing balance sheet is in the current assets section. The current assets section of a manufacturing company's balance sheet presents three inventory accounts: finished goods inventory, work in process inventory, and raw materials inventory.

The difference between a merchandising and a manufacturing income statement is in the cost of goods sold section. A manufacturing cost of goods sold section shows beginning and ending finished goods inventories and the cost of goods manufactured.

LO 4 Discuss trends in managerial accounting.

Managerial accounting has experienced many changes in recent years, including a shift toward service companies as well as an emphasis on ethical behavior. Improved practices include a focus on managing the value chain through techniques such as just-in-time inventory, total quality management, activity-based costing, and theory of constraints. The balanced scorecard is now used by many companies in order to attain a more comprehensive view of the company's operations, and companies are now evaluating their performance with regard to their corporate social responsibility. Finally, data analytics and data visualizations are important tools that help businesses identify problems and opportunities, and then make informed decisions.

Decision Tools Review

Decision Checkpoints	Info Needed for Decision	Tool to Use for Decision	How to Evaluate Results
What is the composition of a manufacturing company's inventory?	Amount of raw materials, work in process, and finished goods inventories	Balance sheet	Determine whether there are sufficient finished goods, raw materials, and work in process inventories to meet forecasted demand.
Is the company maintaining control over the costs of production?	Cost of material, labor, and overhead	Cost of goods manufactured schedule	Compare the cost of goods manufactured to revenue expected from product sales.

Glossary Review

Activity-based costing (ABC) A method of allocating overhead based on each product's use of activities in making the product. (p. 1-18).

Balanced scorecard A performance-measurement approach that uses both financial and nonfinancial measures, tied to company objectives, to evaluate a company's operations in an integrated fashion. (p. 1-18).

Board of directors The group of officials elected by the stockholders of a corporation to formulate operating policies and select officers who will manage the company. (p. 1-5).

Chief executive officer (CEO) Corporate officer who has overall responsibility for managing the business and delegates responsibilities to other corporate officers. (p. 1-6).

Chief financial officer (CFO) Corporate officer who is responsible for all of the accounting and finance issues of the company. (p. 1-6).

Controller Financial officer responsible for a company's accounting records, system of internal control, and preparation of financial statements, tax returns, and internal reports. (p. 1-6).

Corporate social responsibility The efforts of a company to employ sustainable business practices with regard to its employees, society, and the environment. (p. 1-20).

Cost of goods manufactured Total cost of work in process less the cost of the ending work in process inventory. Cost of all the items completed during the period. (p. 1-14).

Data analytics The use of techniques, which often combine software and statistics, to analyze data to make informed decisions. (p. 1-21).

Direct labor The work of factory employees that can be physically and directly associated with converting raw materials into finished goods. (p. 1-8).

Direct materials Raw materials that can be physically and directly associated with manufacturing the finished product. (p. 1-8).

Enterprise resource planning (ERP) system Software that provides a comprehensive, centralized, integrated source of information used to manage all major business processes. (p. 1-18).

EU Directive 2014/56/EU Directive of the European Parliament which lays down the conditions for the approval and registration of persons that carry out statutory audits, the rules on independence, objectivity and professional ethics applying to those persons, and the framework for their public oversight. (p. 1-20).

Indirect labor Work of factory employees that has no physical association with the finished product or for which it is impractical to trace the costs to the goods produced. (p. 1-8).

Indirect materials Raw materials that do not physically become part of the finished product or that are impractical to trace to the finished product because their physical association with the finished product is too small. (p. 1-8).

Just-in-time (JIT) inventory Inventory system in which goods are manufactured or purchased just in time for sale. (p. 1-18).

Line positions Jobs that are directly involved in a company's primary revenue-generating operating activities. (p. 1-6).

Managerial accounting A field of accounting that provides economic and financial information for managers and other internal users. (p. 1-3).

Manufacturing overhead Manufacturing costs that are indirectly associated with the manufacture of the finished product. (p. 1-8).

Period costs Costs that are matched with the revenue of a specific time period and charged to expense as incurred. (p. 1-9).

Product costs Costs that are a necessary and integral part of producing the finished product. All manufacturing costs are classified as product costs and are included in inventory. (p. 1-9).

Sarbanes-Oxley Act (SOX) Law passed by the U.S. Congress intended to reduce unethical corporate behavior. (p. 1-19).

Staff positions Jobs that support the efforts of line employees. (p. 1-6).

Theory of constraints A specific approach used to identify and manage constraints in order to achieve the company's goals. (p. 1-18).

Total cost of work in process Cost of the beginning work in process plus total manufacturing costs for the current period. (p. 1-14).

Total manufacturing costs The sum of direct materials, direct labor, and manufacturing overhead incurred in the current period. (p. 1-11).

Total quality management (TQM) Systems implemented to reduce defects in finished products with the goal of achieving zero defects. (p. 1-18).

Treasurer Financial officer responsible for custody of a company's funds and for maintaining its cash position. (p. 1-6).

Triple bottom line The evaluation of a company's social responsibility performance with regard to people, planet, and profit. (p. 1-20).

Value chain All business processes associated with providing a product or performing a service. (p. 1-17).

Work in process inventory Partially completed manufactured units. (p. 1-14).

Practice Multiple-Choice Questions

1. **(LO 1)** Managerial accounting:
   a. is governed by accounting standards.
   b. places emphasis on special-purpose information.
   c. pertains to the entity as a whole and is highly aggregated.
   d. is limited to cost data.

2. **(LO 1)** The management of an organization performs several broad functions. They are:
   a. planning, directing, and selling.
   b. planning, directing, and controlling.
   c. planning, manufacturing, and controlling.
   d. directing, manufacturing, and controlling.

3. **(LO 2)** Direct materials are a:

	Product Cost	Manufacturing Overhead Cost	Period Cost
a.	Yes	Yes	No
b.	Yes	No	No
c.	Yes	Yes	Yes
d.	No	No	No

4. **(LO 2)** Which of the following costs would a computer manufacturer include in manufacturing overhead?
   a. The cost of the disk drives.
   b. The wages earned by computer assemblers.
   c. The cost of the memory chips.
   d. Depreciation on testing equipment.

5. **(LO 2)** Which of the following is **not** an element of manufacturing overhead?
   a. Sales manager's salary.
   b. Factory manager's salary.
   c. Factory repairman's wages.
   d. Product inspector's salary.

6. **(LO 2)** Indirect labor is a:
   a. nonmanufacturing cost.
   b. raw material cost.
   c. product cost.
   d. period cost.

7. **(LO 2)** Which of the following costs are classified as a period cost?
   a. Wages paid to a factory custodian.
   b. Wages paid to a production department supervisor.
   c. Wages paid to the CEO.
   d. Wages paid to an assembly worker.

8. **(LO 3)** For the year, Klein SpA has cost of goods manufactured of €600,000, beginning finished goods inventory of €200,000, and ending finished goods inventory of €250,000. The cost of goods sold is:
   a. €450,000.
   b. €500,000.
   c. €550,000.
   d. €600,000.

9. **(LO 3)** Cost of goods available for sale is a step in the calculation of cost of goods sold of:
   a. a merchandising company but not a manufacturing company.
   b. a manufacturing company but not a merchandising company.
   c. a merchandising company and a manufacturing company.
   d. neither a manufacturing company nor a merchandising company.

10. **(LO 3)** A cost of goods manufactured schedule shows beginning and ending inventories for:
    a. raw materials and work in process only.
    b. work in process only.
    c. raw materials only.
    d. raw materials, work in process, and finished goods.

11. **(LO 3)** The calculation to determine the cost of goods manufactured is:
    a. Beginning raw materials inventory + Total manufacturing costs − Ending work in process inventory.
    b. Beginning work in process inventory + Total manufacturing costs − Ending finished goods inventory.
    c. Beginning finished goods inventory + Total manufacturing costs − Ending finished goods inventory.
    d. Beginning work in process inventory + Total manufacturing costs − Ending work in process inventory.

12. **(LO 4)** After passage of the Sarbanes-Oxley Act:
    a. reports prepared by managerial accountants must be independently audited.
    b. CEOs and CFOs must certify that financial statements provide a fair presentation of the company's operating results.
    c. the audit committee, rather than top management, is responsible for the company's financial statements.
    d. reports prepared by managerial accountants must comply with accounting standards.

13. **(LO 4)** Which of the following managerial accounting techniques attempts to allocate manufacturing overhead in a more meaningful fashion?
    a. Just-in-time inventory.
    b. Total quality management.
    c. Balanced scorecard.
    d. Activity-based costing.

14. **(LO 4)** Corporate social responsibility refers to:
    a. the practice by management of reviewing all business processes in an effort to increase productivity and eliminate waste.
    b. an approach used to allocate overhead based on each product's use of activities.
    c. the attempt by management to identify and eliminate constraints within the value chain.
    d. efforts by companies to employ sustainable business practices with regard to employees and the environment.

Solutions

1. b. Managerial accounting emphasizes special-purpose information. The other choices are incorrect because (a) financial accounting is governed by accounting standards, (c) financial accounting pertains to the entity as a whole and is highly aggregated, and (d) cost accounting and cost data are a subset of management accounting.

2. b. Planning, directing, and controlling are the broad functions performed by the management of an organization. The other choices are incorrect because (a) selling is performed by the sales group in the organization, not by management; (c) manufacturing is performed by the manufacturing group in the organization, not by management; and (d) manufacturing is performed by the manufacturing group in the organization, not by management.

3. b. Direct materials are a product cost only. Therefore, choices (a), (c), and (d) are incorrect as direct materials are not manufacturing overhead or a period cost.

4. d. Depreciation on testing equipment would be included in manufacturing overhead because it is indirectly associated with the finished product. The other choices are incorrect because (a) disk drives would be direct materials, (b) computer assembler wages would be direct labor, and (c) memory chips would be direct materials.

5. a. The sales manager's salary is not directly or indirectly associated with the manufacture of the finished product. The other choices are incorrect because (b) the factory manager's salary, (c) the factory repairman's wages, and (d) the product inspector's salary are all elements of manufacturing overhead.

6. c. Indirect labor is a product cost because it is part of the effort required to produce a product. The other choices are incorrect because (a) indirect labor is a manufacturing cost because it is part of the effort required to produce a product, (b) indirect labor is not a raw material cost because raw material costs only include direct materials and indirect materials, and (d) indirect labor is not a period cost because it is part of the effort required to produce a product.

7. c. Wages paid to the CEO would be included in administrative expenses and classified as a period cost. The other choices are incorrect because (a) factory custodian wages are indirect labor, which is manufacturing overhead and a product cost; (b) production department supervisor wages are indirect labor, which is manufacturing overhead and a product cost; and (d) assembly worker wages is direct labor and is a product cost.

8. c. Cost of goods sold is computed as Beginning finished goods inventory (€200,000) + Cost of goods manufactured (€600,000) − Ending finished goods inventory (€250,000), or €200,000 + €600,000 − €250,000 = €550,000. Therefore, choices (a) €450,000, (b) €500,000, and (d) €600,000 are incorrect.

9. c. Both a merchandising company (periodic inventory system) and a manufacturing company use cost of goods available for sale to calculate cost of goods sold. Therefore, choices (a) only a merchandising company, (b) only a manufacturing company, and (d) neither a manufacturing company or a merchandising company are incorrect.

10. a. A cost of goods manufactured schedule shows beginning and ending inventories for raw materials and work in process only. Therefore, choices (b) work in process only and (c) raw materials only are incorrect. Choice (d) is incorrect because the schedule does not include finished goods.

11. d. The calculation to determine the cost of goods manufactured is Beginning work in process inventory + Total manufacturing costs − Ending work in process inventory. The other choices are incorrect because (a) raw materials inventory, (b) ending finished goods inventory, and (c) beginning finished goods inventory and ending finished goods inventory are not part of the computation.

12. b. CEOs and CFOs must certify that financial statements provide a fair presentation of the company's operating results. The other choices are incorrect because (a) reports prepared by financial (not managerial) accountants must be independently audited; (c) SOX clarifies that top management, not the audit committee, is responsible for the company's financial statements; and (d) reports by financial (not managerial) accountants must comply with accounting standards.

13. d. Activity-based costing attempts to allocate manufacturing overhead in a more meaningful fashion. Therefore, choices (a) just-in-time inventory, (b) total quality management, and (c) balanced scorecard are incorrect.

14. d. Corporate social responsibility refers to efforts by companies to employ sustainable business practices with regard to employees and the environment. The other choices are incorrect because (a) defines lean manufacturing, (b) refers to activity-based costing, and (c) describes the theory of constraints.

Practice Exercises

1. (LO 2) Favre AG reports the following costs and expenses in May.

Factory utilities	CHF 15,600	Direct labor	CHF 89,100
Depreciation on factory equipment	12,650	Sales salaries	46,400
Depreciation on delivery trucks	8,800	Property taxes on factory building	2,500
Indirect factory labor	48,900	Repairs to office equipment	2,300
Indirect materials	80,800	Factory repairs	2,000
Direct materials used	137,600	Advertising	18,000
Factory manager's salary	13,000	Office supplies used	5,640

Determine the total amount of various types of costs.

Instructions

From the information, determine the total amount of:

a. Manufacturing overhead.

b. Product costs.

c. Period costs.

Solution

1. a.

Factory utilities	CHF 15,600
Depreciation on factory equipment	12,650
Indirect factory labor	48,900
Indirect materials	80,800
Factory manager's salary	13,000
Property taxes on factory building	2,500
Factory repairs	2,000
Manufacturing overhead	CHF175,450

b.

Direct materials used	CHF137,600
Direct labor	89,100
Manufacturing overhead	175,450
Product costs	CHF402,150

c.

Depreciation on delivery trucks	CHF 8,800
Sales salaries	46,400
Repairs to office equipment	2,300
Advertising	18,000
Office supplies used	5,640
Period costs	CHF 81,140

Compute cost of goods manufactured and sold.

2. (LO 3) Shi Ltd. incurred the following costs during the year.

Direct materials used in production	NT$1,200,000		Advertising expense	NT$450,000
Depreciation on factory	600,000		Property taxes on factory	190,000
Property taxes on store	75,000		Delivery expense	210,000
Labor costs of assembly-line workers	1,100,000		Sales commissions	350,000
Factory supplies used	250,000		Salaries paid to sales clerks	500,000

Work in process inventory was NT$100,000 on January 1 and NT$140,000 on December 31. Finished goods inventory was NT$605,000 on January 1 and NT$506,000 on December 31. (Assume that all raw materials used were direct materials.)

Instructions

a. Compute cost of goods manufactured.

b. Compute cost of goods sold.

Solution

2. a.

Work in process, January 1			NT$ 100,000
Direct materials used		NT$1,200,000	
Direct labor		1,100,000	
Manufacturing overhead			
Depreciation on factory	NT$600,000		
Factory supplies used	250,000		
Property taxes on factory	190,000		
Total manufacturing overhead		1,040,000	
Total manufacturing costs			3,340,000
Total cost of work in process			3,440,000
Less: Ending work in process			140,000
Cost of goods manufactured			NT$3,300,000

b.

Finished goods inventory, January 1	NT$ 605,000
Cost of goods manufactured	3,300,000
Cost of goods available for sale	3,905,000
Less: Finished goods inventory, December 31	506,000
Cost of goods sold	NT$3,399,000

Practice Problem

(LO 3) Wang Industries has the following cost and expense data for the year ended December 31, 2023.

Raw materials, 1/1/23	¥ 300,000	Property taxes, factory building	¥	60,000
Raw materials, 12/31/23	200,000	Sales revenue		15,000,000
Raw materials purchases	2,050,000	Delivery expenses (to customers)		1,000,000
Work in process, 1/1/23	800,000	Sales commissions		1,500,000
Work in process, 12/31/23	500,000	Indirect labor		1,050,000
Finished goods, 1/1/23	1,100,000	Factory machinery rent		400,000
Finished goods, 12/31/23	1,200,000	Factory utilities		650,000
Direct labor	3,500,000	Depreciation, factory building		240,000
Factory manager's salary	350,000	Administrative expenses		3,000,000
Insurance, factory	140,000			

Prepare a cost of goods manufactured schedule, an income statement, and a partial balance sheet.

Instructions

a. Prepare a cost of goods manufactured schedule for Wang Industries for 2023. (Assume that all raw materials used were direct materials.)

b. Prepare an income statement for Wang Industries for 2023.

c. Assume that Wang Industries' accounting records show the balances of the following current asset accounts: Cash ¥170,000, Accounts Receivable (net) ¥1,200,000, Prepaid Expenses ¥130,000, and Short-Term Investments ¥260,000. Prepare the current assets section of the balance sheet for Wang Industries as of December 31, 2023.

Solution

a.

Wang Industries
Cost of Goods Manufactured Schedule
For the Year Ended December 31, 2023

Work in process, January 1			¥ 800,000
Direct materials			
Raw materials inventory, January 1	¥ 300,000		
Raw materials purchases	2,050,000		
Total raw materials available for use	2,350,000		
Less: Raw materials inventory, December 31	200,000		
Direct materials used		¥2,150,000	
Direct labor		3,500,000	
Manufacturing overhead			
Indirect labor	¥1,050,000		
Factory utilities	650,000		
Factory machinery rent	400,000		
Factory manager's salary	350,000		
Depreciation, factory building	240,000		
Insurance, factory	140,000		
Property taxes, factory building	60,000		
Total manufacturing overhead		2,890,000	
Total manufacturing costs			8,540,000
Total cost of work in process			9,340,000
Less: Work in process, December 31			500,000
Cost of goods manufactured			¥8,840,000

b.

Wang Industries
Income Statement
For the Year Ended December 31, 2023

Sales revenue		¥15,000,000
Cost of goods sold		
Finished goods inventory, January 1	¥1,100,000	
Cost of goods manufactured	8,840,000	
Cost of goods available for sale	9,940,000	
Less: Finished goods inventory, December 31	1,200,000	
Cost of goods sold		8,740,000
Gross profit		6,260,000
Operating expenses		
Administrative expenses	3,000,000	
Sales commissions	1,500,000	
Delivery expenses	1,000,000	
Total operating expenses		5,500,000
Net income		¥ 760,000

c.

Wang Industries
Balance Sheet (partial)
December 31, 2023

Current assets		
Cash		¥ 170,000
Short-term investments		260,000
Accounts receivable (net)		1,200,000
Inventory		
Finished goods	¥1,200,000	
Work in process	500,000	
Raw materials	200,000	1,900,000
Prepaid expenses		130,000
Total current assets		¥3,660,000

Questions

1. a. "Managerial accounting is a field of accounting that provides economic information for all interested parties." Is this true? Explain why or why not.

   b. Julien Baptiste believes that managerial accounting serves only manufacturing firms. Is Julien correct? Explain.

2. Distinguish between managerial and financial accounting as to (a) primary users of reports, (b) types and frequency of reports, and (c) purpose of reports.

3. How do the content of reports and the verification of reports differ between managerial and financial accounting?

4. Ying Li is studying for the next accounting mid-term examination. Summarize for Ying what she should know about management functions.

5. "Decision-making is management's most important function." Is this true? Explain why or why not.

6. Explain the primary difference between line positions and staff positions, and give examples of each.

7. Daehyun Kim is unclear as to the difference between the balance sheets of a merchandising company and a manufacturing company. Explain the difference to Daehyun.

8. How are manufacturing costs classified?

9. Vinay Jha claims that the distinction between direct and indirect materials is based entirely on physical association with the product. Is Vinay correct? Why?

10. Shinji Takahashi is confused about the differences between a product cost and a period cost. Explain the differences to Shinji.

11. Identify the differences in the cost of goods sold section of an income statement between a merchandising company and a manufacturing company.

12. The determination of the cost of goods manufactured involves the following factors: (A) beginning work in process inventory, (B) total manufacturing costs, and (C) ending work in process inventory. Identify the meaning of X in the following equations:

    a. $A + B = X$ b. $A + B - C = X$

13. Yavuz A.S. has beginning raw materials inventory ₺120,000, ending raw materials inventory ₺150,000, and raw materials purchases ₺1,700,000. What is the cost of direct materials used?

14. Cheung Ltd. has beginning work in process HK$260,000, direct materials used HK$2,400,000, direct labor HK$2,200,000, total manufacturing overhead HK$1,800,000, and ending work in process HK$320,000. What are the total manufacturing costs?

15. Using the data in Question 14, determine (a) the total cost of work in process and (b) the cost of goods manufactured.

16. In what order should manufacturing inventories be reported in a balance sheet?

17. How does the output of manufacturing operations differ from that of service operations?

18. Discuss whether the product costing techniques discussed in this chapter apply equally well to manufacturers and service companies.

19. What is the value chain? Describe, in sequence, the main components of a manufacturer's value chain.

20. What is an enterprise resource planning (ERP) system? What are its primary benefits?

21. Why is product quality important for companies that implement a just-in-time inventory system?

22. Explain what is meant by "balanced" in the balanced scorecard approach.

23. In what ways can the budgeting process create incentives for unethical behavior?

24. What rules were enacted under the Directive 2014/56/EU to address unethical accounting practices?

25. What is activity-based costing, and what are its potential benefits?

Brief Exercises

BE1.1 (LO 1), C Complete the following comparison table between managerial and financial accounting.

Distinguish between managerial and financial accounting.

	Financial Accounting	Managerial Accounting
Primary users of reports		
Types of reports		
Frequency of reports		
Purpose of reports		
Content of reports		
Verification process		

BE1.2 (LO 1), C Listed below are the three functions of the management of an organization.

1. Planning.   2. Directing.   3. Controlling.

Identify which of the following statements best describes each of the above functions.

Identify the three management functions.

a. _____ requires management to look ahead and to establish objectives. A key objective of management is to add value to the business.

b. _____ involves coordinating the diverse activities and human resources of a company to produce a smooth-running operation. This function relates to the implementation of planned objectives.

c. _____ is the process of keeping the activities on track. Management determines whether goals are being met and what changes are necessary when there are deviations.

BE1.3 (LO 2), C Determine whether each of the following costs should be classified as direct materials (DM), direct labor (DL), or manufacturing overhead (MO).

Classify manufacturing costs.

a. _____ Frames and tires used in manufacturing bicycles.
b. _____ Wages paid to production workers.
c. _____ Insurance on factory equipment and machinery.
d. _____ Depreciation on factory equipment.

BE1.4 (LO 2), C Indicate whether each of the following costs of an automobile manufacturer would be classified as direct materials, direct labor, or manufacturing overhead.

Classify manufacturing costs.

a. _____ Windshield.
b. _____ Engine.
c. _____ Wages of assembly-line worker.
d. _____ Depreciation of factory machinery.
e. _____ Factory machinery lubricants.
f. _____ Tires.
g. _____ Steering wheel.
h. _____ Salary of painting supervisor.

BE1.5 (LO 2), C Identify whether each of the following costs should be classified as product costs or period costs.

Identify product and period costs.

a. _____ Manufacturing overhead.
b. _____ Selling expenses.
c. _____ Administrative expenses.
d. _____ Advertising expenses.
e. _____ Direct labor.
f. _____ Direct materials.

Classify manufacturing costs.

BE1.6 (LO 2), C Presented here are Brooks AG's monthly manufacturing cost data related to its tablet computer product.

a. Utilities for manufacturing equipment	€116,000
b. Raw materials (CPU, chips, etc.)	85,000
c. Depreciation on manufacturing building	880,000
d. Wages for production workers	191,000

Enter each cost item in the following table, placing an "X" under the appropriate classification.

	Product Costs		
	Direct Materials	Direct Labor	Manufacturing Overhead
a.			
b.			
c.			
d.			

Compute total manufacturing costs and total cost of work in process.

BE1.7 (LO 3), AP Francis plc has the following data: direct labor £209,000, direct materials used £180,000, total manufacturing overhead £208,000, and beginning work in process £25,000. Compute (a) total manufacturing costs and (b) total cost of work in process.

Prepare current assets section of balance sheet.

BE1.8 (LO 3), AP In alphabetical order, here are current asset items for Roland Company's balance sheet on December 31, 2023. Prepare the current assets section (including a complete heading).

Accounts receivable	$200,000
Cash	62,000
Finished goods	91,000
Prepaid expenses	38,000
Raw materials	83,000
Work in process	87,000

Determine missing amounts in computing total manufacturing costs.

BE1.9 (LO 3), AP The following are incomplete manufacturing cost data. Determine the missing amounts for these three independent situations.

	Direct Materials Used	Direct Labor	Manufacturing Overhead	Total Manufacturing Costs
1.	A$40,000	A$61,000	A$ 50,000	?
2.	?	A$75,000	A$140,000	A$296,000
3.	A$55,000	?	A$111,000	A$310,000

Determine missing amounts in computing cost of goods manufactured.

BE1.10 (LO 3), AP Use the data from BE1.9 and the data that follow. Determine the missing amounts.

	Total Manufacturing Costs	Work in Process (Jan. 1)	Work in Process (Dec. 31)	Cost of Goods Manufactured
1.	?	A$120,000	A$82,000	?
2.	A$296,000	?	A$98,000	A$331,000
3.	A$310,000	A$463,000	?	A$715,000

Identify important regulatory changes.

BE1.11 (LO 4), C The Sarbanes-Oxley Act (SOX) has important implications for the financial community. Explain two implications of SOX.

DO IT! Exercises

Identify managerial accounting concepts.

DO IT! 1.1 (LO 1), C Indicate whether the following statements are true or false. If false, indicate how to correct the statement.

1. The board of directors has primary responsibility for daily management functions.
2. Financial accounting reports pertain to subunits of the business and are very detailed.
3. Managerial accounting reports must follow accounting standards and are independently audited.
4. Managers' activities and responsibilities can be classified into three broad functions: planning, directing, and controlling.

DO IT! 1.2 (LO 2), C A music company has these costs:

Advertising	Paper inserts for DVD cases
Blank DVDs	DVD plastic cases
Depreciation of DVD image burner	Salaries of sales representatives
Salary of factory manager	Salaries of factory maintenance employees
Factory supplies used	Salaries of employees who burn music onto DVDs

Identify managerial cost classifications.

Classify each cost as a period or a product cost. Within the product cost category, indicate whether the cost is part of direct materials (DM), direct labor (DL), or manufacturing overhead (MO).

DO IT! 1.3 (LO 3), AP The following information is available for Petrov SA.

Prepare cost of goods manufactured schedule.

	April 1	April 30
Raw materials inventory	R$100,000	R$140,000
Work in process inventory	50,000	35,000

Materials purchased in April	R$ 980,000
Direct labor in April	800,000
Manufacturing overhead in April	1,600,000

Prepare the cost of goods manufactured schedule for the month of April 2023. (Assume that all raw materials used were direct materials.)

DO IT! 1.4 (LO 4), C Match the descriptions that follow with the corresponding terms.

Identify trends in managerial accounting.

Descriptions:
1. _____ Inventory system in which goods are manufactured or purchased just as they are needed for sale.
2. _____ A method of allocating overhead based on each product's use of activities in making the product.
3. _____ Systems that are especially important to firms adopting just-in-time inventory methods.
4. _____ Part of the value chain for a manufacturing company.
5. _____ The U.K. economy is trending toward this.
6. _____ A performance-measurement approach that uses both financial and nonfinancial measures, tied to company objectives, to evaluate a company's operations in an integrated fashion.
7. _____ Requires that top managers certify that the company maintains an adequate system of internal controls over financial reporting.

Terms:
a. Activity-based costing.
b. Balanced scorecard.
c. Total quality management (TQM).
d. Research and development, and product design.
e. Service industries.
f. Just-in-time (JIT) inventory.
g. Directive 2014/56/EU.

Exercises

E1.1 (LO 1), C Mukta Joshi has prepared the following list of statements about managerial accounting, financial accounting, and the functions of management.

Identify distinguishing features of managerial accounting.

1. Financial accounting focuses on providing information to internal users.
2. Staff positions are directly involved in the company's primary revenue-generating activities.
3. Preparation of budgets is part of financial accounting.
4. Managerial accounting applies only to merchandising and manufacturing companies.
5. Both managerial accounting and financial accounting deal with many of the same economic events.
6. Managerial accounting reports are prepared only quarterly and annually.
7. Financial accounting reports are general-purpose reports.
8. Managerial accounting reports pertain to subunits of the business.
9. Managerial accounting reports must comply with accounting standards.
10. The company treasurer reports directly to the vice president of operations.

1-34 CHAPTER 1 Managerial Accounting

Classify costs into three classes of manufacturing costs.

Instructions

Identify each statement as true or false. If false, indicate how to correct the statement.

E1.2 (LO 2), C The following is a list of costs and expenses usually incurred by Souza Furniture in its factory.

1. Salaries for product inspectors.
2. Insurance on factory machines.
3. Property taxes on the factory building.
4. Factory repairs.
5. Upholstery used in manufacturing furniture.
6. Wages paid to assembly-line workers.
7. Factory machinery depreciation.
8. Glue, nails, paint, and other small parts used in production.
9. Factory supervisors' salaries.
10. Wood used in manufacturing furniture.

Instructions

Classify these items into the following categories: (a) direct materials, (b) direct labor, and (c) manufacturing overhead.

Identify types of costs and explain their accounting.

E1.3 (LO 2), C Wulin Cycles incurred the following costs while manufacturing its bicycles.

Bicycle components	NT$1,000,000	Advertising expense	NT$450,000
Depreciation on factory	600,000	Property taxes on factory	140,000
Property taxes on retail store	75,000	Customer delivery expense	210,000
Labor costs of assembly-line workers	1,100,000	Sales commissions	350,000
Factory supplies used	130,000	Salaries paid to sales clerks	500,000

Instructions

a. Identify each of the above costs as direct materials, direct labor, manufacturing overhead, or period costs.

b. Explain the basic difference in accounting for product costs and period costs.

Determine the total amount of various types of costs.

E1.4 (LO 2), AP Jin Ltd. reports the following costs and expenses in May.

Factory utilities	₩15,500,000	Direct labor	₩69,100,000
Depreciation on factory equipment	12,650,000	Sales salaries	46,400,000
Depreciation on delivery trucks	3,800,000	Property taxes on factory building	2,500,000
Indirect factory labor	48,900,000	Repairs to office equipment	1,300,000
Indirect materials	80,800,000	Factory repairs	2,000,000
Direct materials used	137,600,000	Advertising	15,000,000
Factory manager's salary	8,000,000	Office supplies used	2,640,000

Instructions

From the information, determine the total amount of:

a. Manufacturing overhead.
b. Product costs.
c. Period costs.

Classify various costs into different cost categories.

E1.5 (LO 2), C Jang Electronics is a manufacturer of laptop computers. Various costs and expenses associated with its operations are as follows:

1. Property taxes on the factory building.
2. Production superintendents' salaries.
3. Memory boards and chips used in assembling computers.
4. Depreciation on the factory equipment.
5. Salaries for quality control inspectors.
6. Sales commissions paid to sell laptop computers.
7. Electrical components used in assembling computers.

8. Wages of workers assembling laptop computers.
9. Soldering materials used on factory assembly lines.
10. Salaries for the night security guards for the factory building.

The company intends to classify these costs and expenses into the following categories: (a) direct materials, (b) direct labor, (c) manufacturing overhead, and (d) period costs.

Instructions

List the items (1) through (10). For each item, indicate the cost category to which it belongs.

E1.6 (LO 2), C Service The administrators of Chesterfield County's Memorial Hospital are interested in identifying the various costs and expenses that are incurred in producing a patient's X-ray. A list of such costs and expenses is presented here:

1. Salaries for the X-ray machine technicians.
2. Wages for the hospital janitorial personnel.
3. Film costs for the X-ray machines.
4. Property taxes on the hospital building.
5. Salary of the X-ray technicians' supervisor.
6. Electricity costs for the X-ray department.
7. Maintenance and repairs on the X-ray machines.
8. X-ray department supplies.
9. Depreciation on the X-ray department equipment.
10. Depreciation on the hospital building.

The administrators want these costs and expenses classified as (a) direct materials, (b) direct labor, or (c) service overhead.

Classify various costs into different cost categories.

Instructions

List the items (1) through (10). For each item, indicate the cost category to which the item belongs.

E1.7 (LO 2), AP Service National Express reports the following costs and expenses in June 2023 for its delivery service.

Classify various costs into different cost categories.

Indirect materials used	A$ 6,400	Drivers' salaries	A$16,000
Depreciation on delivery equipment	11,200	Advertising	4,600
Dispatcher's salary	5,000	Delivery equipment repairs	300
Property taxes on office building	870	Office supplies	650
CEO's salary	12,000	Office utilities	990
Gas and oil for delivery trucks	2,200	Repairs on office equipment	180

Instructions

Determine the total amount of (a) delivery service (product) costs and (b) period costs.

E1.8 (LO 2), AP Evilene Company makes industrial-grade brooms. It incurs the following costs:

1. Salaries for broom inspectors.
2. Copy machine maintenance at corporate headquarters.
3. Hourly wages for assembly workers.
4. Research and development for new broom types.
5. Salary for factory manager.
6. Depreciation on broom-assembly equipment.
7. Salary for the CEO administrative assistant.
8. Wood for handles.
9. Factory cleaning supplies.
10. Lubricants for broom-assembly factory equipment.
11. Salaries for customer service representatives.
12. Salaries for factory maintenance crew.
13. Sales team golf outings with customers.
14. Salaries for the raw materials receiving department employees.
15. Advertising expenses.
16. Depreciation on the CFO company car.
17. Straw for brooms.
18. Salaries for sales personnel.
19. Shipping costs to customers.

Classify various costs into different cost categories.

Compute cost of goods manufactured and sold, and discuss classification of various costs.

Instructions

a. Indicate whether each cost is direct materials, direct labor, manufacturing overhead, or nonmanufacturing.

b. Indicate whether each cost is a product cost or a period cost.

E1.9 (LO 3), AP Lopez Corporation incurred the following costs during 2023.

Direct materials used in product	$120,000	Advertising expense	$45,000
Depreciation on factory	60,000	Property taxes on factory	14,000
Property taxes on store	7,500	Delivery expense	21,000
Labor costs of assembly-line workers	110,000	Sales commissions	35,000
Factory supplies used	23,000	Salaries paid to sales clerks	50,000

Work in process inventory was $12,000 on January 1 and $15,500 on December 31. Finished goods inventory was $60,000 on January 1 and $45,600 on December 31.

Instructions

a. Compute cost of goods manufactured.

b. Compute cost of goods sold.

c. For those costs not included in the calculations in part (a) or part (b), explain how they would be classified and reported in the financial statements.

Determine missing amounts in cost of goods manufactured schedule.

E1.10 (LO 3), AP An incomplete cost of goods manufactured schedule is presented here:

Hinata Group
Cost of Goods Manufactured Schedule
For the Year Ended December 31, 2023

Work in process, January 1			¥21,000,000
Direct materials			
Raw materials inventory, January 1	¥ ?		
Raw materials purchases	15,800,000		
Total raw materials available for use	?		
Less: Raw materials inventory, December 31	2,250,000		
Direct materials used		¥18,000,000	
Direct labor		?	
Manufacturing overhead			
Indirect labor	1,800,000		
Factory depreciation	3,600,000		
Factory utilities	6,800,000		
Total manufacturing overhead		12,200,000	
Total manufacturing costs			?
Total cost of work in process			?
Less: Work in process, December 31			8,100,000
Cost of goods manufactured			¥54,000,000

Instructions

Complete the cost of goods manufactured schedule for Hinata Group. (Assume that all raw materials used were direct materials.)

Determine the missing amount of different cost items.

E1.11 (LO 3), AN Manufacturing cost data for Reis A.S. are presented as follows:

	Case A	Case B	Case C
Direct materials used	₤ (a)	₤684,000	₤1,300,000
Direct labor	570,000	860,000	(g)
Manufacturing overhead	465,000	816,000	1,020,000
Total manufacturing costs	1,956,500	(d)	2,537,000
Work in process 1/1/23	(b)	165,000	(h)
Total cost of work in process	2,215,000	(e)	3,370,000
Work in process 12/31/23	(c)	110,000	700,000
Cost of goods manufactured	1,852,750	(f)	(i)

Instructions

Determine the missing amount for each letter (a) through (i).

E1.12 (LO 3), AN Incomplete manufacturing cost data for Horizonte SpA for 2023 are presented as follows for these four independent situations.

Determine the missing amount of different cost items, and prepare a condensed cost of goods manufactured schedule.

	Direct Materials Used	Direct Labor	Manufacturing Overhead	Total Manufacturing Costs	Work in Process Jan. 1	Work in Process Dec. 31	Cost of Goods Manufactured
1.	€117,000	€140,000	€ 87,000	€ (a)	€33,000	€ (b)	€360,000
2.	(c)	200,000	132,000	450,000	(d)	40,000	470,000
3.	80,000	100,000	(e)	265,000	60,000	80,000	(f)
4.	70,000	(g)	75,000	288,000	45,000	(h)	270,000

Instructions

a. Determine the missing amount for each letter.

b. Prepare a condensed cost of goods manufactured schedule for situation (1) for the year ended December 31, 2023.

E1.13 (LO 3), AP Lindgren Corporation has the following cost records for June 2023.

Prepare a cost of goods manufactured schedule and a partial income statement.

Indirect factory labor	CHF 4,500	Factory utilities	CHF 400
Direct materials used	20,000	Depreciation, factory equipment	1,400
Work in process, 6/1/23	3,000	Direct labor	40,000
Work in process, 6/30/23	3,800	Maintenance, factory equipment	1,800
Finished goods, 6/1/23	5,000	Indirect materials used	2,200
Finished goods, 6/30/23	7,500	Factory manager's salary	3,000

Instructions

a. Prepare a cost of goods manufactured schedule for June 2023.

b. Prepare an income statement through gross profit for June 2023 assuming sales revenue is CHF92,100.

E1.14 (LO 2, 3), AP **Service** Marilla Cuthbert, the bookkeeper for Winston Consulting, a political consulting firm, has recently completed a managerial accounting course at her local college. One of the topics covered in the course was the cost of goods manufactured schedule. Marilla wondered if such a schedule could be prepared for her firm. She realized that, as a service-oriented company, it would have no work in process inventory to consider.

Classify various costs into different categories and prepare cost of services performed schedule.

Listed here are the costs her firm incurred for the month ended August 31, 2023.

Supplies used on consulting contracts	£ 1,700
Supplies used in the administrative offices	1,500
Depreciation on equipment used for contract work	900
Depreciation on administrative office equipment	1,050
Salaries of professionals working on contracts	15,600
Salaries of administrative office personnel	7,700
Janitorial services for professional offices	700
Janitorial services for administrative offices	500
Insurance on contract operations	800
Insurance on administrative operations	900
Utilities for contract operations	1,400
Utilities for administrative offices	1,300

Instructions

a. Prepare a schedule of cost of contract services performed (similar to a cost of goods manufactured schedule) for the month.

b. List the costs not included in (a), and then explain how they would be classified and reported in the financial statements.

Determine cost of goods manufactured and prepare a partial income statement.

E1.15 (LO 3), AP The following information is available for Abelman Company.

	January 1, 2023	2023	December 31, 2023
Raw materials inventory	$21,000		$30,000
Work in process inventory	13,500		17,200
Finished goods inventory	27,000		21,000
Materials purchased		$150,000	
Direct labor		220,000	
Manufacturing overhead		180,000	
Sales revenue		910,000	

Instructions

a. Compute cost of goods manufactured. (Assume that all raw materials used were direct materials.)

b. Prepare an income statement through gross profit.

c. Show the presentation of the ending inventories on the December 31, 2023, balance sheet.

d. How would the income statement and balance sheet of a merchandising company be different from Abelman's financial statements?

Indicate in which schedule or financial statement(s) different cost items would appear.

E1.16 (LO 3), C University Company produces collegiate apparel. From its accounting records, it prepares the following schedule and financial statements on a yearly basis.

a. Cost of goods manufactured schedule.

b. Income statement.

c. Balance sheet.

The following items are found in the company's accounting records and accompanying data.

1. Direct labor.
2. Raw materials inventory, January 1.
3. Work in process inventory, December 31.
4. Finished goods inventory, January 1.
5. Indirect labor.
6. Depreciation expense of factory machinery.
7. Work in process, January 1.
8. Finished goods inventory, December 31.
9. Factory maintenance salaries.
10. Cost of goods manufactured.
11. Depreciation expense of delivery equipment.
12. Cost of goods available for sale.
13. Direct materials used.
14. Heat and electricity for factory.
15. Repairs to roof of factory building.
16. Cost of raw materials purchases.

Instructions

List the items (1)–(16). For each item, indicate by using the appropriate letter or letters, the schedule and/or financial statement(s) in which the item would appear.

Prepare a cost of goods manufactured schedule, and present the ending inventories on the balance sheet.

E1.17 (LO 3), AP An analysis of the accounts of Lau Ltd. reveals the following manufacturing cost data for the month ended June 30, 2023.

Inventory	Beginning	Ending
Raw materials	HK$90,000	HK$131,000
Work in process	50,000	70,000
Finished goods	90,000	80,000

Costs incurred: raw materials purchases HK$540,000, direct labor HK$470,000, manufacturing overhead HK$199,000. The specific overhead costs were: indirect labor HK$55,000, factory insurance HK$40,000, machinery depreciation HK$40,000, machinery repairs HK$18,000, factory utilities HK$31,000, and miscellaneous factory costs HK$15,000. (Assume that all raw materials used were direct materials.)

Instructions

a. Prepare the cost of goods manufactured schedule for the month ended June 30, 2023.

b. Show the presentation of the ending inventories on the June 30, 2023, balance sheet.

E1.18 (LO 3), AP *Writing* McQueen Motor Company manufactures automobiles. During September 2023, the company purchased 5,000 head lamps at a cost of A$15 per lamp. Fifty of these lamps were used to replace the head lamps in autos used by traveling sales staff, and 4,600 lamps were put in autos manufactured during the month.

Of the autos put into production during September 2023, 90% were completed and transferred to the company's storage lot. Of the cars completed during the month, 70% were sold by September 30.

Determine the amount of cost to appear in various accounts, and indicate in which financial statements these accounts would appear.

Instructions

a. Determine the cost of head lamps that would appear in each of the following accounts on September 30, 2023: Raw Materials, Work in Process, Finished Goods, Cost of Goods Sold, and Selling Expenses.

b. Write a short memo to the chief accountant, indicating whether and where each of the accounts in (a) would appear on the income statement or on the balance sheet on September 30, 2023.

E1.19 (LO 4), C The following is a list of terms related to managerial accounting practices.

1. Activity-based costing.
2. Just-in-time inventory.
3. Balanced scorecard.
4. Value chain.

Identify various managerial accounting practices.

Instructions

Match each of the terms with the statement below that best describes the term.

a. _____ A performance-measurement technique that attempts to consider and evaluate all aspects of performance using financial and nonfinancial measures in an integrated fashion.

b. _____ The group of activities associated with providing a product or performing a service.

c. _____ An approach used to reduce the cost associated with handling and holding inventory by reducing the amount of inventory on hand.

d. _____ A method used to allocate overhead to products based on each product's use of the activities that cause the incurrence of the overhead cost.

Problems

P1.1 (LO 2), AP Wong Company specializes in manufacturing a unique model of bicycle helmet. The model is well accepted by consumers, and the company has enough orders to keep the factory production at 10,000 helmets per month (80% of its full capacity). Wong's monthly manufacturing costs and other expense data are as follows:

Classify manufacturing costs into different categories and compute the unit cost.

Rent on factory equipment	S$11,000
Insurance on factory building	1,500
Raw materials used (plastics, polystyrene, etc.)	75,000
Utility costs for factory	900
Supplies used for general office	300
Wages for assembly-line workers	58,000
Depreciation on office equipment	800
Miscellaneous materials used (glue, thread, etc.)	1,100
Factory manager's salary	5,700
Property taxes on factory building	400
Advertising for helmets	14,000
Sales commissions	10,000
Depreciation on factory building	1,500

Instructions

a. Prepare an answer sheet with the following column headings:

Cost Item	Product Costs			Period Costs
	Direct Materials	Direct Labor	Manufacturing Overhead	

Enter each cost item on your answer sheet, placing the amount under the appropriate heading. Total the amounts in each of the columns.

b. Compute the cost to produce one helmet.

P1.2 (LO 2), AP Bulan Music Company has been a retailer of audio systems for the past three years. However, after a thorough survey of audio system markets, Bulan decided to turn its retail store into an audio equipment factory. Production began October 1, 2023.

Direct materials costs for an audio system total Rp740,000 per unit. Workers on the production lines are paid Rp120,000 per hour. An audio system takes 5 labor hours to complete. In addition, the rent on the equipment used to assemble audio systems amounts to Rp49,000,000 per month. Indirect materials cost Rp50,000 per system. A supervisor was hired to oversee production; her monthly salary is Rp30,000,000.

Factory janitorial costs are Rp13,000,000 monthly. Advertising costs for the audio system will be Rp95,000,000 per month. The factory building depreciation is Rp78,000,000 per year. Property taxes on the factory building will be Rp90,000,000 per year.

Instructions

a. Prepare an answer sheet with the following column headings for October 2023.

Cost Item	Product Costs			Period Costs
	Direct Materials	Direct Labor	Manufacturing Overhead	

Assuming that Bulan manufactures, on average, 1,500 audio systems per month, enter each cost item on your answer sheet, placing the amount per month under the appropriate heading. Total the amounts in each of the columns.

b. Compute the cost to produce one audio system.

P1.3 (LO 3), AN Incomplete manufacturing costs, expenses, and selling data for two different cases for the year ended December 31, 2023, are as follows:

	Case 1	Case 2
Direct materials used	€ 9,600	€ (g)
Direct labor	5,000	8,000
Manufacturing overhead	8,000	4,000
Total manufacturing costs	(a)	16,000
Beginning work in process inventory	1,000	(h)
Ending work in process inventory	(b)	3,000
Sales revenue	24,500	(i)
Sales discounts	2,500	1,400
Cost of goods manufactured	17,000	24,000
Beginning finished goods inventory	(c)	3,300
Cost of goods available for sale	22,000	(j)
Cost of goods sold	(d)	(k)
Ending finished goods inventory	3,400	2,500
Gross profit	(e)	7,000
Operating expenses	2,500	(l)
Net income	(f)	5,000

Instructions

a. Determine the missing amount for each letter.

b. Prepare a condensed cost of goods manufactured schedule for Case 1.

c. Prepare an income statement and the current assets section of the balance sheet for Case 1. Assume that in Case 1 the other items in the current assets section are as follows: Cash €3,000, Accounts Receivable (net) €15,000, Raw Materials €600, and Prepaid Expenses €400.

---

a. DM S$75,000
DL S$58,000
MO S$22,100
PC S$25,100

Classify manufacturing costs into different categories and compute the unit cost.

a. DM Rp1,110,000,000
DL Rp900,000,000
MO Rp181,000,000
PC Rp95,000,000

Determine the missing amount of different cost items, and prepare a condensed cost of goods manufactured schedule, an income statement, and a partial balance sheet.

b. Ending WIP € 6,600
c. Current assets €29,000

P1.4 (LO 3), AP The following data were taken from the records of Wagner Ltd. for the fiscal year ended June 30, 2023.

Raw Materials Inventory 7/1/22	£ 48,000	Accounts Receivable	£ 27,000
Raw Materials Inventory 6/30/23	39,600	Factory Insurance	4,600
Finished Goods Inventory 7/1/22	96,000	Factory Machinery Depreciation	16,000
Finished Goods Inventory 6/30/23	75,900	Factory Utilities	27,600
Work in Process Inventory 7/1/22	19,800	Office Utilities Expense	8,650
Work in Process Inventory 6/30/23	18,600	Sales Revenue	534,000
Direct Labor	139,250	Sales Discounts	4,200
Indirect Labor	24,460	Factory Manager's Salary	58,000
		Factory Property Taxes	9,600
		Factory Repairs	1,400
		Raw Materials Purchases	96,400
		Cash	32,000

Prepare a cost of goods manufactured schedule, a partial income statement, and a partial balance sheet.

Instructions

a. Prepare a cost of goods manufactured schedule. (Assume that all raw materials used were direct materials.)

b. Prepare an income statement through gross profit.

c. Prepare the current assets section of the balance sheet on June 30, 2023.

a. CGM £386,910
b. Gross profit £122,790
c. Current assets £193,100

P1.5 (LO 3), AN Empire Company is a manufacturer of smartphones. Its controller resigned in October 2023. An inexperienced assistant accountant has prepared the following income statement for the month of October 2023.

Prepare a cost of goods manufactured schedule and a correct income statement.

Empire Company
Income Statement
For the Month Ended October 31, 2023

Sales revenue		$780,000
Less: Operating expenses		
Raw materials purchases	$264,000	
Direct labor cost	190,000	
Advertising expense	90,000	
Selling and administrative salaries	75,000	
Rent on factory facilities	60,000	
Depreciation on sales equipment	45,000	
Depreciation on factory equipment	31,000	
Indirect labor cost	28,000	
Utilities expense	12,000	
Insurance expense	8,000	803,000
Net loss		$ (23,000)

Prior to October 2023, the company had been profitable every month. The company's president is concerned about the accuracy of the income statement. As her friend, you have been asked to review the income statement and make necessary corrections. After examining other manufacturing cost data, you have acquired additional information as follows:

1. Inventory balances at the beginning and end of October were:

	October 1	October 31
Raw materials	$18,000	$29,000
Work in process	20,000	14,000
Finished goods	30,000	50,000

2. Only 75% of the utilities expense and 60% of the insurance expense apply to factory operations. The remaining amounts should be charged to selling and administrative activities.

Instructions

a. Prepare a schedule of cost of goods manufactured for October 2023. (Assume that all raw materials used were direct materials.)

b. Prepare a correct income statement for October 2023.

a. CGM $581,800
b. NI $2,000

Continuing Case

Current Designs

CD1 Mike Cichanowski founded **Wenonah Canoe** (USA) and later purchased **Current Designs** (USA), a company that designs and manufactures kayaks. The kayak-manufacturing facility is located just a few minutes from the canoe company's headquarters in Winona, Minnesota.

Current Designs makes kayaks using two different processes. The rotational molding process uses high temperature to melt polyethylene powder in a closed rotating metal mold to produce a complete kayak hull and deck in a single piece. These kayaks are less labor-intensive and less expensive for the company to produce and sell.

Its other kayaks use the vacuum-bagged composite lamination process (which we will refer to as the composite process). Layers of fiberglass or Kevlar® are carefully placed by hand in a mold and are bonded with resin. Then, a high-pressure vacuum is used to eliminate any excess resin that would otherwise add weight and reduce the strength of the finished kayak. These kayaks require a great deal of skilled labor as each boat is individually finished. The exquisite finish of the vacuum-bagged composite kayaks gave rise to Current Designs' tag line, "A work of art, made for life."

Current Designs has the following managers:

Mike Cichanowski, CEO
Diane Buswell, Controller
Deb Welch, Purchasing Manager
Bill Johnson, Sales Manager
Dave Thill, Kayak Factory Manager
Rick Thrune, Production Manager for Composite Kayaks

The company's accounting data for the most recent period is as follows:

			Product Costs			
	Payee	Purpose	Direct Materials	Direct Labor	Manufacturing Overhead	Period Costs	Amount
4	Winona Agency	Property insurance for factory					3,200
5	Bill Johnson (sales manager)	Payroll check—payment to sales manager					1,700
6	Xcel Energy	Electricity for factory					450
7	Winona Printing	Price lists for salespeople					85
8	Jim Kaiser (sales representative)	Sales commissions					1,250
9	Dave Thill (factory manager)	Payroll check—payment to factory manager					1,450
10	Dana Schultz (kayak assembler)	Payroll check—payment to kayak assembler					760
11	Composite One	Bagging film used when kayaks are assembled; it is discarded after use					260
12	Fastenal	Shop supplies—brooms, paper towels, etc.					890
13	Ravago	Polyethylene powder which is the main ingredient for the rotational molded kayaks					3,170
14	Winona County	Property taxes on factory					5,480
15	North American Composites	Kevlar® fabric for composite kayaks					4,930
16	Waste Management	Trash disposal for the company office building					660
17	None	Record depreciation of manufacturing equipment					4,540

Instructions

a. What are the primary information needs of each manager?

b. Name one special-purpose management accounting report that could be designed for each manager. Include the name of the report, the information it would contain, and how frequently it should be issued.

c. When Diane Buswell, controller for Current Designs, reviewed the accounting records for a recent period, she noted the cost items and amounts shown above (amounts are assumed). Enter the amount for each item in the appropriate cost category. Then sum the amounts in each cost category column.

Data Analytics in Action

Using Data Visualization to Determine Performance

DA1.1 Data visualization can be used to review company results.

Example: Recall the *Management Insight* "Supplying Today's (Not Yesterday's) Fashion" presented in the chapter. Data analytics can help **Inditex** (ESP) determine how it is performing over time. For retailers, the gross margin percentage is a good measure of how the company is doing, as it indicates what percentage of sales is available to cover selling and administration costs and generate profit. From publicly available data, we can calculate Inditex's gross margin percentage [(Sales − Cost of goods sold) ÷ Sales] and track it over time. What do you observe when you look at the following chart?

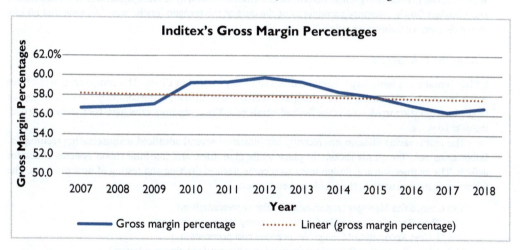

Hopefully, you immediately noticed that Inditex is able to maintain a high and stable gross margin over the time period shown. Management should be quite pleased with this. But another measure of success, revenue per employee, can provide management with even more insight concerning its sales. This case will require you calculate and graph this data for Inditex, and then analyze the results.

Go to the book's product page on www.wiley.com for complete case details and instructions.

Data Analytics at Inditex Corporation

DA1.2 You are excited about your upcoming job interview at **Inditex** (ESP). You realize that you need to have a better understanding of the company so that you can have several thoughtful questions prepared to ask during the interview. For this case, you will use Inditex's performance information to create several visualizations that will help increase your knowledge of the company's operations.

Go to the book's product page on www.wiley.com for complete case details and instructions.

Expand Your Critical Thinking

Decision-Making Across the Organization

CT1.1 Wendall Company specializes in producing fashion outfits. On July 31, 2023, a tornado touched down at its factory and general office. The inventories in the warehouse and the factory were completely destroyed, as was the general office nearby. However, after a careful search of the disaster site the next morning, Bill Francis, the company's controller, and Elizabeth Walton, the cost accountant, were able to recover a small part of the manufacturing cost data for the current month.

"What a horrible experience," sighed Bill. "And the worst part is that we may not have enough records to use in filing an insurance claim."

"It was terrible," replied Elizabeth. "However, I managed to recover some of the manufacturing cost data that I was working on yesterday afternoon. The data indicate that our direct labor cost in July totaled $250,000 and that we had purchased $365,000 of raw materials. Also, I recall that the amount of raw materials used for July was $350,000. But I'm not sure this information will help. The rest of our records are blown away."

"Well, not exactly," said Bill. "I was working on the year-to-date income statement when the tornado warning was announced. My recollection is that our sales in July were $1,240,000 and our gross profit ratio has been 40% of sales. Also, I can remember that our cost of goods available for sale was $770,000 for July."

"Maybe we can work something out from this information!" exclaimed Elizabeth. "My experience tells me that our manufacturing overhead is usually 60% of direct labor."

"Hey, look what I just found," cried Elizabeth. "It's a copy of this June's balance sheet, and it shows that our inventories as of June 30 are Finished goods $38,000, Work in process $25,000, and Raw materials $19,000."

"Super," yelled Bill. "Let's go work something out."

In order to file an insurance claim, Wendall Company needs to determine the amount of its inventories as of July 31, 2023, the date of the tornado touchdown.

Instructions

With the class divided into groups, determine the amount of cost in the Raw Materials, Work in Process, and Finished Goods inventory accounts as of the date of the tornado touchdown. (Assume that all raw materials used were direct materials.)

Managerial Analysis

CT1.2 Tenrack is a fairly large manufacturing company located in China. The company manufactures tennis rackets, tennis balls, tennis clothing, and tennis shoes, all bearing the company's distinctive logo, a large green question mark on a white flocked tennis ball. The company's sales have been increasing over the past 10 years.

The tennis racket division has recently implemented several advanced manufacturing techniques. Robot arms hold the tennis rackets in place while glue dries, and machine vision systems check for defects. The engineering and design team uses computerized drafting and testing of new products. The following managers work in the tennis racket division:

> Yan Chen, Sales Manager (supervises all sales representatives)
> Tian Zhao, Technical Specialist (supervises computer programmers)
> Jun Li, Cost Accounting Manager (supervises cost accountants)
> Lixia Chen, Production Supervisor (supervises all manufacturing employees)
> Xinxin Wang, Engineer (supervises all new-product design teams)

Instructions

a. What are the primary information needs of each manager?
b. Which, if any, financial accounting report(s) is each likely to use?
c. Name one special-purpose management accounting report that could be designed for each manager. Include the name of the report, the information it would contain, and how frequently it should be issued.

Real-World Focus

CT1.3 The **Institute of Management Accountants** (IMA) is a global organization dedicated to excellence in the practice of management accounting and financial management.

Instructions

Go to the IMA's website to locate the answers to the following questions:

a. How many members does the IMA have, and what are their job titles?
b. What are some of the benefits of joining the IMA as a student?
c. Use the chapter locator function to locate the IMA chapter nearest you, and find the name of the chapter president.

Communication Activity

CT1.4 Refer to P1.5 and add the following requirement:

Prepare a letter to the president of the company, Shelly Phillips, describing the changes you made. Explain clearly why net income is different after the changes. Keep the following points in mind as you compose your letter.

1. This is a letter to the president of a company, who is your friend. The style should be generally formal, but you may relax some requirements. For example, you may call the president by her first name.
2. Executives are very busy. Your letter should tell the president your main results first (for example, the amount of net income).
3. You should include brief explanations so that the president can understand the changes you made in the calculations.

Ethics Case

CT1.5 Steve Morgan, controller for Newton Industries, was reviewing production cost reports for the year. One amount in these reports continued to bother him—advertising. During the year, the company had instituted an expensive advertising campaign to sell some of its slower-moving products. It was still too early to tell whether the advertising campaign was successful.

There had been much internal debate as how to report advertising cost. The vice president of finance argued that advertising cost should be reported as a cost of production, just like direct materials and direct labor. He therefore recommended that this cost be identified as manufacturing overhead and reported as part of inventory costs until sold. Others disagreed. Morgan believed that this cost should be reported as an expense of the current period, so as not to overstate net income. Others argued that it should be reported as prepaid advertising and reported as a current asset.

The president finally had to decide the issue. He argued that advertising cost should be reported as inventory. His arguments were practical ones. He noted that the company was experiencing financial difficulty and that expensing this amount in the current period might jeopardize a planned bond offering. Also, by reporting the advertising cost as inventory rather than as prepaid advertising, less attention would be directed to it by the financial community.

Instructions

a. Who are the stakeholders in this situation?
b. What are the ethical issues involved in this situation?
c. What would you do if you were Steve Morgan?

All About You

CT1.6 The primary purpose of managerial accounting is to provide information useful for management decisions. Many of the managerial accounting techniques that you learn in this course will be useful for decisions you make in your everyday life.

Instructions

For each of the following managerial accounting techniques, read the definition provided and then provide an example of a personal situation that would benefit from use of this technique.

a. Break-even point (Chapter 5).
b. Budget (Chapter 9).
c. Balanced scorecard (Chapter 11).
d. Capital budgeting (Chapter 12).

Considering Your Costs and Benefits

CT1.7 Because of global competition, companies have become increasingly focused on reducing costs. To reduce costs and remain competitive, many companies are turning to outsourcing. Outsourcing means hiring an outside supplier to provide elements of a product or service rather than producing them internally.

Suppose you are the managing partner in an accounting firm with 30 full-time staff members. Larger firms in your community have begun to outsource basic tax-return preparation work to India. Should you outsource your basic tax-return work to India as well? You estimate that you would have to lay off six staff members if you outsource the work. The basic arguments for and against are as follows:

YES: The wages paid to Indian accountants are very low relative to U.S. wages. You will not be able to compete unless you outsource.

NO: Tax-return data are highly sensitive. Many customers will be upset to learn that their data are being emailed around the world.

Instructions

Write a response indicating your position regarding this situation. Provide support for your view.

CHAPTER 2

Job Order Costing

CHAPTER PREVIEW

The following Feature Story about **Disney** (USA) describes how important accurate costing is to movie studios. In order to submit accurate bids on new film projects and to know whether it profited from past films, the company needs a good costing system. This chapter illustrates how costs are assigned to specific jobs, such as the production of the most recent *Avengers* movie. We begin the discussion in this chapter with an overview of the flow of costs in a job order cost accounting system. We then use a case study to explain and illustrate the documents, entries, and accounts in this type of cost accounting system.

FEATURE STORY

Profiting from the Silver Screen

Have you ever had the chance to tour a movie studio? There's a lot going on! Lots of equipment and lots of people with a variety of talents. Running a film studio, whether as an independent company or part of a major corporation, is a complex and risky business. Consider **Disney** (USA), which has produced such classics as Snow *White and the Seven Dwarfs* and such colossal successes as *Frozen*. The movie studio has, however, also seen its share of losses. Disney's *Lone Ranger* movie brought in revenues of $260 million, but its production and marketing costs were a combined $375 million—a loss of $115 million.

Every time Disney or another movie studio makes a new movie, it is creating a unique product. Ideally, each new movie should be able to stand on its own, that is, the film should generate revenues that exceed its costs. In order to know whether a particular movie is profitable, the studio must keep track of all of the costs incurred to make and market the film. These costs include such items as salaries of the writers, actors, director, producer, and production team (e.g., film crew); licensing costs; depreciation on equipment; music; studio rental; and marketing and distribution costs. If you've ever watched the credits at the end of a movie, you know the list goes on and on.

The movie studio isn't the only one with an interest in knowing a particular project's profitability. Many of the people involved in making the movie, such as the screenwriters, actors, and producers, have at least part of their compensation tied to its profitability. As such, complaints about inaccurate accounting are common in the movie industry.

In particular, a few well-known and widely attended movies reported low profits, or even losses, once the accountants got done with them. How can this be? The issue is that a large portion of a movie's costs are overhead costs that can't be directly traced to a film, such as depreciation of film equipment and sets, facility maintenance costs, and executives' salaries. Actors and others often complain that these overhead costs are overallocated to their movie and therefore negatively affect their compensation.

To reduce the risk of financial flops, many of the big studios now focus on making sequels of previous hits. This might explain why, shortly after losing money on the *Lone Ranger*, Disney decided to make more *Avengers* movies—much safer bets.

CHAPTER OUTLINE

Learning Objectives	Review	Practice
LO 1 Describe cost systems and the flow of costs in a job order system.	• Process cost system • Job order cost system • Job order cost flow • Accumulating manufacturing costs	**DO IT! 1** Accumulating Manufacturing Costs
LO 2 Use a job cost sheet to assign costs to work in process.	• Raw materials costs • Factory labor costs	**DO IT! 2** Work in Process
LO 3 Demonstrate how to determine and use the predetermined overhead rate.	• Predetermined overhead rate • Applying manufacturing overhead	**DO IT! 3** Predetermined Overhead Rate
LO 4 Prepare entries for manufacturing and service jobs completed and sold.	• Finished goods • Cost of goods sold • Summary of job order cost flows • Job order for service companies • Advantages and disadvantages of job order costing	**DO IT! 4** Completion and Sale of Jobs
LO 5 Distinguish between under- and overapplied manufacturing overhead.	• Under- or overapplied manufacturing overhead	**DO IT! 5** Applied Manufacturing Overhead

Go to the Review and Practice section at the end of the chapter for a targeted summary and exercises with solutions.

COST ACCOUNTING SYSTEMS

Cost accounting focuses on measuring, recording, and reporting product costs for manufacturers and service costs for service organizations. Companies determine both the total cost and the unit cost of each product.

- The accuracy of the product cost information is critical to the success of the company.
- Companies use this information to determine which products to produce, what prices to charge, and how many units to produce.
- Accurate product cost information is also vital for effective evaluation of employee performance.

LEARNING OBJECTIVE 1
Describe cost systems and the flow of costs in a job order system.

A **cost accounting system** consists of accounts for the various manufacturing and service costs. These accounts are fully integrated into the general ledger of a company. An important feature of a cost accounting system is the use of **a perpetual inventory system**. Such a system **provides immediate, up-to-date information on the cost of a product**.

There are two basic types of cost accounting systems:

1. A process cost system.
2. A job order cost system.

Although cost accounting systems differ widely from company to company, most involve one of these two traditional product costing systems.

Process Cost System

A company uses a **process cost system** when it manufactures a large volume of similar products. Production is continuous. Examples of a process cost system are the manufacture of cereal by **Kellogg** (USA), the refining of petroleum by **ExxonMobil** (USA), and the production of chocolate by **Lindt & Sprüngli** (CHE).

- Process costing accumulates product-related costs **for a period of time** (such as a week or a month) instead of assigning costs to specific products or job orders.
- In process costing, companies assign the costs to departments or processes for the specified period of time.

Illustration 2.1 shows examples of the use of a process cost system. We will discuss the process cost system further in Chapter 3.

Job Order Cost System

Under a **job order cost system**, the company assigns product costs to each **job** or to each **batch** of goods. An example of a job is the manufacture of a jet by **Airbus** (FRA), the

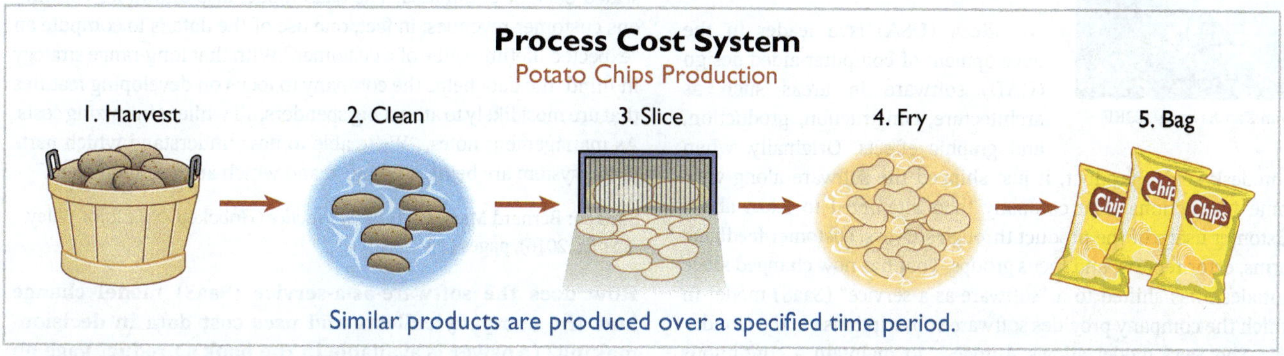

Process Cost System
Potato Chips Production

1. Harvest → 2. Clean → 3. Slice → 4. Fry → 5. Bag

Similar products are produced over a specified time period.

ILLUSTRATION 2.1 | **Process cost system**

production of a movie by **Disney** (USA), or the making of a fire truck by **Pierce Manufacturing** (USA). An example of a batch is the printing of 225 wedding invitations by a local print shop, or the printing of a weekly issue of *Fortune* magazine by a high-tech printer such as **Quad Graphics** (USA).

- An important feature of job order costing is that each job or batch has its own distinguishing characteristics. For example, each house is custom built, each consulting engagement by an accounting firm is unique, and each printing job is different.
- **The objective is to compute the cost per job.** At each point in manufacturing a product or performing a service, the company can identify the job and its associated costs.
- A job order cost system measures product costs for each job, rather than for set time periods.

Illustration 2.2 shows the recording of product costs in a job order cost system for Disney as it produced two different films at the same time: an animated film and an action thriller.

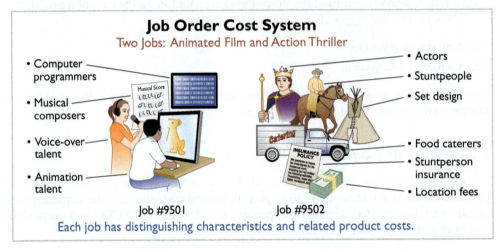

ILLUSTRATION 2.2 | Job order cost system for Disney

Can a company use both job order and process cost systems? Yes. For example, **General Motors** (USA) uses process cost accounting for its standard model cars, such as Malibu and Corvettes, and job order cost accounting for a custom-made limousine for the president of the United States.

The objective of both cost accounting systems is to provide unit cost information for product pricing, cost control, inventory valuation, and financial statement presentation.

DATA ANALYTICS INSIGHT   Autodesk

Providing Service Through the Cloud

Kran Kanthawong/123RF

Autodesk (USA) is a leader in the development of computer-aided design (CAD) software in areas such as architecture, construction, production, and graphic effects. Originally, when Autodesk sold a product, it just shipped the software along with some instructions. The company then attempted to learn about customer usage of the product through surveys, customer feedback forms, error reports, and focus groups. That has now changed since Autodesk has shifted to a "software-as-a-service" (SaaS) model in which the company provides software subscriptions via the cloud.

The SaaS model allows Autodesk to maintain a continuous customer relationship as well as provides immediate access to tremendous amounts of data. The company knows which aspects of its software are being used, what needs fixing, and what features can be scaled back or eliminated. The SaaS model also allows for continuous customer revenues; in fact, one use of the data is to compute an "expected lifetime value of a customer." With that long-range strategy in mind, the data helps the company to focus on developing features that are most likely to attract big spenders, all while minimizing costs. As management notes, "We're able to now understand which parts of the system are being used most, and which are cost inefficient."

Source: Bernard Marr, *Big Data in Practice* (Hoboken, N.J.: John Wiley & Sons, 2016), pages 205–210.

How does the software-as-a-service (SaaS) model change how the company collects and uses cost data in decision-making? (Answer is available in the book's product page on www.wiley.com)

Job Order Cost Flow

We first address the flow of costs for a manufacturer (service company costs are addressed in a later section). The flow of product costs (direct materials, direct labor, and manufacturing overhead) in job order cost accounting parallels the physical flow of the materials as they are converted into finished goods and then sold (see **Illustration 2.3**).

1. Companies first **accumulate** manufacturing costs in the form of raw materials, factory labor, or manufacturing overhead.
2. They then **assign** manufacturing costs to the Work in Process Inventory account.
3. When a job is completed, the company transfers the cost of the job to Finished Goods Inventory.
4. Later, when the goods are sold, the company transfers their cost to Cost of Goods Sold, reported on the income statement.

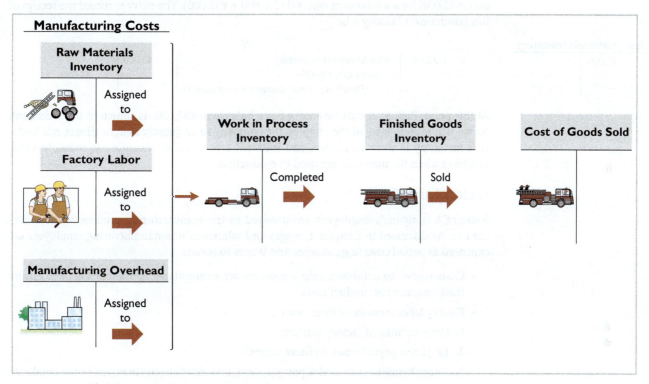

ILLUSTRATION 2.3 | Flow of costs in job order costing

Illustration 2.3 provides a basic overview of the flow of costs in a manufacturing setting for production of a fire truck. (A more detailed presentation of the flow of costs is provided near the end of this chapter in Illustration 2.15.) There are two major steps in the flow of costs:

1. *Accumulating* the manufacturing costs incurred.
2. *Assigning* the accumulated costs to the work done.

The following discussion shows that the company accumulates manufacturing costs incurred by debits to Raw Materials Inventory, Factory Labor, and Manufacturing Overhead. The company does not attempt to associate these costs with specific jobs when it initially incurs the costs. Instead, the company makes subsequent entries to assign manufacturing costs incurred to specific jobs as they are consumed. In the remainder of this chapter, we will use a case study to explain how a job order cost system operates.

Accumulating Manufacturing Costs

To illustrate a job order cost system, we will use the January transactions of Martinez Electronics, which makes custom electronic sensors for corporate safety applications (such as fire and carbon monoxide) and security applications (such as theft and corporate espionage).

Raw Materials Costs

When Martinez receives raw materials (both direct and indirect) it has purchased from a supplier, **it debits the cost of the materials to Raw Materials Inventory**.

- The company debits Raw Materials Inventory for the invoice cost of the raw materials and freight costs chargeable to the purchaser.
- It credits Raw Materials Inventory for purchase discounts taken and purchase returns and allowances if applicable.
- Martinez makes **no effort at this point to associate the cost of these materials with specific jobs or orders**.

To illustrate, assume that Martinez purchases, on account, 2,000 lithium batteries (Stock No. AA2746) at €5 per unit (€10,000) and 800 electronic modules (Stock No. AA2850) at €40 per unit (€32,000) for a total cost of €42,000 (€10,000 + €32,000). The entry to record the receipt of this purchase on January 4 is:

Raw Materials Inventory

42,000	

(1)[1]

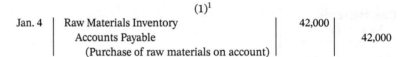

Jan. 4	Raw Materials Inventory	42,000	
	Accounts Payable		42,000
	(Purchase of raw materials on account)		

At this point, Raw Materials Inventory has a balance of €42,000, as shown in the T-account. As we will explain later in the chapter, the company subsequently assigns **direct** raw materials inventory to work in process and **indirect** raw materials inventory to manufacturing overhead when the materials are used in production.

Factory Labor Costs

Some of a company's employees are involved in the manufacturing process, while others are not. As discussed in Chapter 1, wages and salaries of nonmanufacturing employees are expensed as period costs (e.g., Salaries and Wages Expense).

- Costs related to manufacturing employees are accumulated in Factory Labor to ensure their treatment as product costs.
- Factory labor consists of three costs:
    1. Gross earning of factory workers.
    2. Employer payroll taxes on these wages.
    3. Fringe benefits (such as sick pay, pensions, and vacation pay) incurred by the employer.
- **Companies debit labor costs to Factory Labor as they incur those costs.**

To illustrate, assume that Martinez incurs €32,000 of factory labor costs. The entry to record factory labor (both direct and indirect) for the month is:

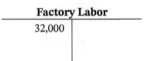

(2)

Jan. 31	Factory Labor	32,000	
	Payroll Liabilities		32,000
	(To record factory labor costs)		

At this point, Factory Labor has a balance of €32,000, as shown in the T-account. The Factory Labor account accumulates all manufacturing labor costs, that is, both direct labor and indirect labor. The company subsequently assigns direct factory labor to work in process and indirect factory labor to manufacturing overhead.

Manufacturing Overhead Costs

A company has many types of overhead costs.

- If these overhead costs, such as property taxes, depreciation, insurance, and repairs, relate to overhead costs of a nonmanufacturing facility, such as an office building, then these

---

[1] The numbers placed above the journal entries for Martinez Electronics are used for reference purposes in the summary provided in Illustration 2.15.

costs are expensed as period costs (e.g., Property Tax Expense, Depreciation Expense, Insurance Expense, and Maintenance and Repairs Expense).

- If the costs relate to the manufacturing process, they are accumulated in Manufacturing Overhead to ensure their treatment as product costs.

Using assumed data, the summary entry for manufacturing overhead (other than indirect materials and indirect labor) for Martinez Electronics is:

		(3)		
Jan. 31	Manufacturing Overhead		13,800	
	Utilities Payable			4,800
	Prepaid Insurance			2,000
	Accounts Payable (for repairs)			2,600
	Accumulated Depreciation			3,000
	Property Taxes Payable			1,400
	(To record manufacturing overhead costs)			

Manufacturing Overhead

13,800	

At this point, Manufacturing Overhead has a balance of €13,800, as shown in the T-account. The company subsequently assigns manufacturing overhead to work in process.

DO IT! 1 ▶ Accumulating Manufacturing Costs

During the current month, Tamara Constructions incurs the following manufacturing costs.

a. Raw material purchases of €4,200 on account.
b. Factory labor of €18,000.
c. Factory utilities of €2,200 are payable, prepaid factory insurance of €1,800 has expired, and depreciation on the factory building is €3,500.

Prepare journal entries for each type of manufacturing cost.

Solution

a. Raw Materials Inventory		4,200	
Accounts Payable			4,200
(Purchases of raw materials on account)			
b. Factory Labor		18,000	
Payroll Liabilities			18,000
(To record factory labor costs)			
c. Manufacturing Overhead		7,500	
Utilities Payable			2,200
Prepaid Insurance			1,800
Accumulated Depreciation			3,500
(To record manufacturing overhead costs)			

Related exercise material: **BE2.1, BE2.2, DO IT! 2.1, E2.1, E2.7, E2.8, and E2.11.**

ACTION PLAN
- In accumulating manufacturing costs, debit at least one of three accounts: Raw Materials Inventory, Factory Labor, and Manufacturing Overhead.
- Manufacturing overhead costs may be recognized daily. Or, manufacturing overhead may be recorded periodically through a summary entry.

ASSIGNING MANUFACTURING COSTS

Assigning manufacturing costs to work in process results in the following entries:

1. **Debits** made to Work in Process Inventory.
2. **Credits** made to Raw Materials Inventory, Factory Labor, and Manufacturing Overhead.

LEARNING OBJECTIVE 2
Use a job cost sheet to assign costs to work in process.

> **DECISION TOOLS**
>
> A completed job cost sheet helps managers to compare costs with those of previous periods to ensure that costs are in line.

An essential accounting record in assigning costs to jobs is a **job cost sheet**, as shown in **Illustration 2.4**. A **job cost sheet** is a form used to track the costs chargeable to a specific job and to determine the total and unit costs of the completed job (see **Decision Tools**).

Job Cost Sheet

Job No. _____   Quantity _____
Item _____   Date Requested _____
For _____   Date Completed _____

Date	Direct Materials	Direct Labor	Manufacturing Overhead

Cost of completed job
   Direct materials   €_____
   Direct labor   _____
   Manufacturing overhead   _____
Total cost   €_____
Unit cost (total cost ÷ quantity)   €_____

ILLUSTRATION 2.4 | Job cost sheet

Companies keep a separate job cost sheet for each job, typically as a computer file.

- The job cost sheets constitute the subsidiary ledger for the Work in Process Inventory control account in the general ledger. A **subsidiary ledger** consists of individual records for each individual item—in this case, each job.
- The Work in Process Inventory account is referred to as a **control account** because it summarizes the detailed data regarding specific jobs contained in the job cost sheets.
- **Each debit entry to Work in Process Inventory must be accompanied by a corresponding posting to one or more job cost sheets**—the assignment of direct materials, direct labor, or manufacturing overhead.

Raw Materials Costs

Assignment of raw materials costs involves two steps:

1. Posting detailed information to individual job cost sheets.
2. Journalizing summary data in the general journal.

Companies assign raw materials costs to jobs when their materials storeroom issues the materials in response to requests. Requests for issuing raw materials are made by production department personnel on a prenumbered **materials requisition slip**. The materials issued may be used directly on a job, or they may be considered indirect materials.

- As **Illustration 2.5** shows, the requisition should indicate the quantity and type of materials withdrawn and the job to be charged (see **Ethics Note**).
- Note in Illustration 2.5 the specific job to be charged (Job No. 101). The materials requisition slip is also an example of the internal control of documentation (in this case, prenumbering as R247).
- The company will charge direct materials to Work in Process Inventory, and indirect materials to Manufacturing Overhead.

> **ETHICS NOTE**
>
> Approvals are an important internal control feature of a requisition slip because they establish individual accountability over inventory.

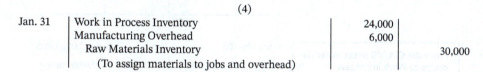

ILLUSTRATION 2.5 | Materials requisition slip

The company may use any of the inventory costing methods (FIFO, LIFO, or average-cost) in costing the requisitions **to the individual job cost sheets**. In an automated system, the requisition is entered electronically. Once approved and delivered to production, the direct materials are charged automatically to an electronic job cost record.

Periodically, the company journalizes the aggregated requisitions. For example, if Martinez uses €24,000 of direct materials and €6,000 of indirect materials in January, the entry on January 31 is:

		(4)		
Jan. 31	Work in Process Inventory		24,000	
	Manufacturing Overhead		6,000	
	Raw Materials Inventory			30,000
	(To assign materials to jobs and overhead)			

This entry reduces Raw Materials Inventory by €30,000, increases Work in Process Inventory by €24,000 as the direct costs are assigned to jobs, and increases Manufacturing Overhead by €6,000, as the following shows:

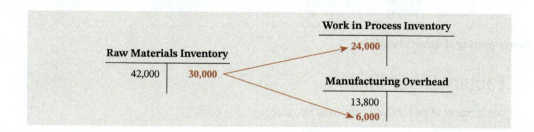

Illustration 2.6 shows the posting of requisition slip R247 to Job No. 101 for €1,000 and other assumed postings to the job cost sheets for materials requested on other materials requisition slips. The requisition slips provide the basis for total direct materials costs of €12,000 for Job No. 101, €7,000 for Job No. 102, and €5,000 for Job No. 103. After the company has completed all postings, the sum of the direct materials columns of the job cost sheets (the **subsidiary** account amounts of €12,000, €7,000, and €5,000) should equal the direct materials debited to Work in Process Inventory (the **control** account amount of €24,000).

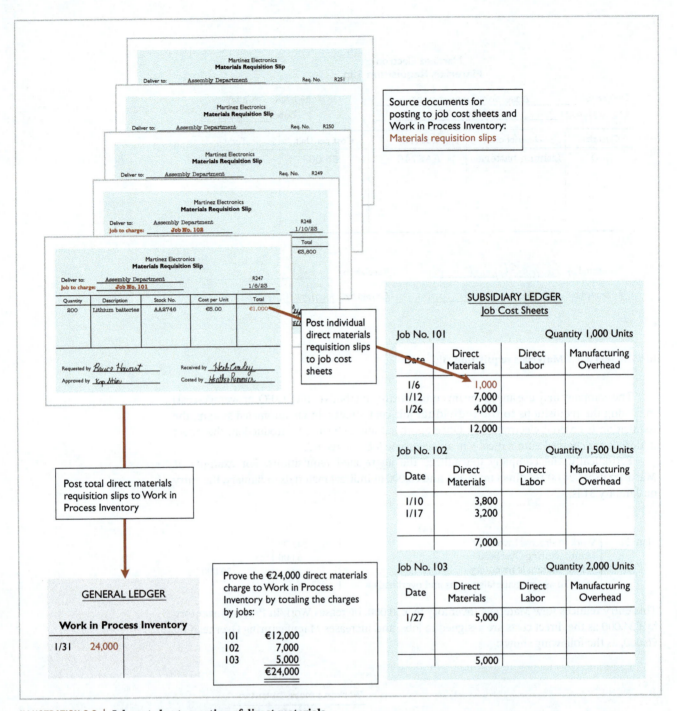

ILLUSTRATION 2.6 | Job cost sheets–posting of direct materials

Factory Labor Costs

Assignment of factory labor involves two steps:

1. Posting detailed information to individual job cost sheets (subsidiary ledger).
2. Journalizing summarized data in the general journal.

Companies assign factory labor costs to specific jobs (direct labor) or to manufacturing overhead (indirect labor) on the basis of time tickets prepared when the work is performed.

- The *time ticket* indicates the employee name, the hours worked, the account and job to be charged, and the total labor cost.

- When direct labor is involved, the time ticket must indicate the job number, as shown in **Illustration 2.7**. The employee's supervisor should approve all time tickets.
- Many companies accumulate this information through the use of bar coding and scanning devices instead of physical time tickets. When they start and end work, employees scan bar codes on their identification badges and bar codes associated with each job they work on.

Martinez Electronics
Time Ticket

Date: 1/6/23
Employee: John Nash
Employee No.: 124
Charge to: Work in Process
Job No.: 101

Time			Hourly Rate	Total Cost
Start	Stop	Total Hours		
0800	1200	4	10.00	40.00

Approved by *Bob Kadler* Costed by *M Cher*

ILLUSTRATION 2.7 | Time ticket

The time tickets are subsequently sent to the payroll department.

- The payroll department combines the employee's hourly gross wages from the time tickets with any applicable payroll taxes and associated fringe benefits. This total direct labor cost is posted to the job cost sheets.
- In an automated system, after factory employees scan their identification codes, labor costs are automatically calculated and posted to electronic job cost sheets.
- After posting to individual job cost sheets, the company completes the assignment process with a journal entry for total labor cost. It debits Work in Process Inventory for direct labor and debits Manufacturing Overhead for indirect labor.

For example, if the €32,000 total factory labor cost consists of €28,000 of direct labor and €4,000 of indirect labor, the entry is:

(5)

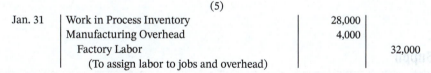

Jan. 31	Work in Process Inventory	28,000	
	Manufacturing Overhead	4,000	
	Factory Labor		32,000
	(To assign labor to jobs and overhead)		

As a result of this entry, Factory Labor is reduced by €32,000 so it has a zero balance, and labor costs are assigned to the appropriate manufacturing accounts. The entry increases Work in Process Inventory by €28,000 and increases Manufacturing Overhead by €4,000, as the following shows:

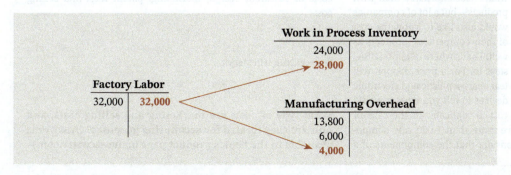

Let's assume that the labor costs chargeable to Martinez's three jobs are €15,000, €9,000, and €4,000. **Illustration 2.8** shows the Work in Process Inventory and job cost sheets after posting. As in the case of direct materials, the sum of the postings to the direct labor columns of the job cost sheets (subsidiary accounts Job 101 €15,000, Job 102 €9,000, and Job 103 €4,000) should equal the posting of direct labor to the Work in Process Inventory control account (€28,000).

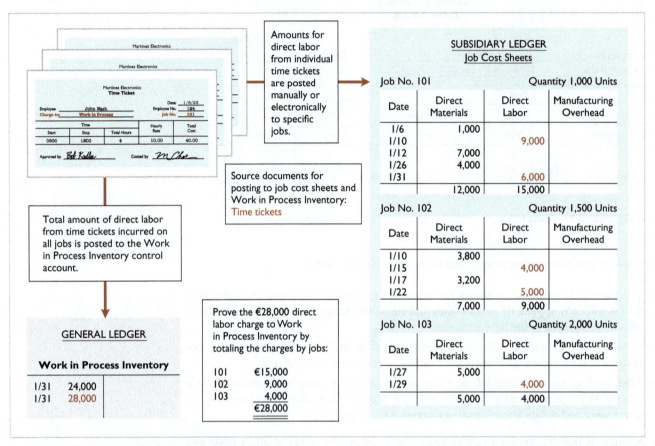

ILLUSTRATION 2.8 | **Job cost sheets–direct labor**

MANAGEMENT INSIGHT — iSuppli

© TommL/iStockphoto

The Cost of an iPhone? Just Tear One Apart

All companies need to know what it costs to make their own products—but a lot of companies would also like to know the cost of their competitors' products as well. That's where **iSuppli** (USA) steps in. For a price, iSuppli will tear apart sophisticated electronic devices to tell you what it would cost to replicate. In the case of smartphones, which often have more than 1,000 tiny components, that is no small feat. Consider that the components of a recent iPhone model cost about $221. Assembly adds only about another $5. However, the difference between what you pay (about triple the total component cost) and the "cost" is not all profit. You also have to consider the additional non-production costs of research, design, marketing, patent fees, and selling costs.

Source: 2016 IHS Markit.

What type of costs are marketing and selling costs, and how are they treated for accounting purposes? (Answer is available in the book's product page on www.wiley.com)

DO IT! 2 — Work in Process

Heinz NV is working on two job orders. The job cost sheets show the following:

 Direct materials—Job 120 €6,000; Job 121 €3,600

 Direct labor—Job 120 €4,000; Job 121 €2,000

Prepare the two summary entries to record the assignment of costs to Work in Process from the data on the job cost sheets.

Solution

The two summary entries are.

Work in Process Inventory (€6,000 + €3,600)	9,600	
Raw Materials Inventory		9,600
(To assign materials to jobs)		
Work in Process Inventory (€4,000 + €2,000)	6,000	
Factory Labor		6,000
(To assign labor to jobs)		

Related exercise material: **BE2.3, BE2.4, BE2.5, DO IT! 2.2, E2.2, E2.7, and E2.8.**

ACTION PLAN
- Recognize that Work in Process Inventory is the control account for all unfinished job cost sheets.
- Debit Work in Process Inventory for the materials and labor charged to the job cost sheets.
- Credit the accounts that were debited when the manufacturing costs were accumulated.

PREDETERMINED OVERHEAD RATES

Companies charge the **actual** costs of direct materials and direct labor to specific jobs because these costs can be directly traced to specific jobs. In contrast, manufacturing **overhead** relates to production operations **as a whole**.

- As a result, overhead costs cannot be assigned to specific jobs on the basis of actual costs incurred because these costs cannot be traced to (identified with) specific jobs.
- Instead, companies assign (or "apply") manufacturing overhead to work in process and to specific jobs **on an estimated basis through the use of a predetermined overhead rate** (see **Alternative Terminology**).
- The **predetermined overhead rate** is based on the relationship between estimated annual overhead costs and estimated annual operating activity, expressed in terms of a common **activity base**.
- The company may state the activity in terms of direct labor costs, direct labor hours, machine hours, or any other measure that will provide an equitable basis for applying overhead costs to jobs.

LEARNING OBJECTIVE 3
Demonstrate how to determine and use the predetermined overhead rate.

ALTERNATIVE TERMINOLOGY
Assigning manufacturing overhead is also referred to as applying manufacturing overhead.

Companies establish the predetermined overhead rate at the beginning of the year. Small companies often use a single, company-wide predetermined overhead rate. Large companies often use rates that vary from department to department. The equation for calculating a predetermined overhead rate is shown in **Illustration 2.9**.

$$\text{Estimated Annual Overhead Costs} \div \text{Estimated Annual Operating Activity} = \text{Predetermined Overhead Rate}$$

ILLUSTRATION 2.9 | Equation for predetermined overhead rate

Overhead consists only of indirect costs and relates to production operations as a whole. To know what "the whole" is, it might seem logical to wait until the end of the year's operations. At that time, the company knows all of its actual costs for the period. As a practical matter, though, managers cannot wait until the end of the year.

- To cost products effectively as they are completed, managers need information about product costs of specific jobs completed during the year.

- Using an estimated predetermined overhead rate enables costs to be determined for the job immediately and identifies when these costs may be different from those planned.

Illustration 2.10 indicates how manufacturing overhead is assigned to work in process.

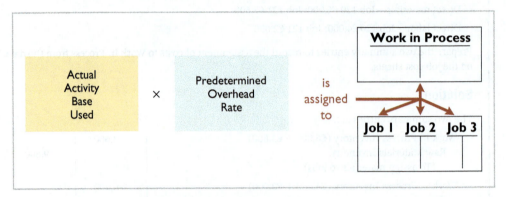

ILLUSTRATION 2.10 | **Using predetermined overhead rates**

Martinez Electronics uses direct labor cost as the activity base. Assuming that the company estimates annual overhead costs to be €280,000 and direct labor costs for the year to be €350,000, the overhead rate is 80%, computed as shown in **Illustration 2.11**.

Estimated Annual Overhead Costs	÷	Estimated Direct Labor Cost	=	Predetermined Overhead Rate
€280,000	÷	€350,000	=	80%

ILLUSTRATION 2.11 | **Calculation of predetermined overhead rate**

This means that for every euro of direct labor, Martinez will assign 80 cents of manufacturing overhead to a job. The use of a predetermined overhead rate enables the company to determine the approximate total cost of each job **when it completes the job**.

Historically, companies have used direct labor costs or direct labor hours as the activity base. The reason was the relatively high correlation between direct labor and manufacturing overhead.

- Today, more companies are using **machine hours as the activity base, due to increased reliance on automation in manufacturing operations**.
- Or, as mentioned in Chapter 1 (and discussed more fully in Chapter 4), many companies now use activity-based costing to more accurately assign overhead costs based on the activities that give rise to the costs.
- A company may use more than one activity base.

For example, if a job is manufactured in more than one factory department, each department may have its own overhead rate. A company might also use two bases in assigning overhead to jobs: direct materials euros for indirect materials, and direct labor hours for such costs as insurance and supervisor salaries.

Martinez uses a single predetermined overhead rate and applies manufacturing overhead to work in process after it assigns direct labor costs. It also applies manufacturing overhead to specific jobs at that time. For January, Martinez applied overhead of €22,400 in response to its assignment of €28,000 of direct labor costs (direct labor cost of €28,000 × 80%). The following entry records this application.

	(6)		
Jan. 31	Work in Process Inventory	22,400	
	Manufacturing Overhead		22,400
	(To assign overhead to jobs)		

This entry reduces the balance in Manufacturing Overhead and increases Work in Process Inventory by €22,400, as shown below.

Manufacturing Overhead		Work in Process Inventory	
13,800	22,400	24,000	
6,000		28,000	
4,000		22,400	
1,400			

The overhead that Martinez applies to each job will be 80% of the direct labor cost of the job for the month. **Illustration 2.12** shows the Work in Process Inventory account and the job cost sheets after posting. Note that the debit of €22,400 to Work in Process Inventory equals the sum of the overhead applied to jobs: Job No. 101 €12,000 + Job No. 102 €7,200 + Job No. 103 €3,200.

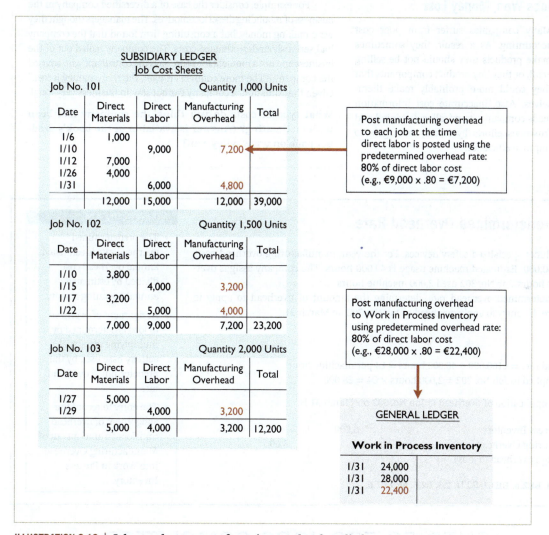

ILLUSTRATION 2.12 | Job cost sheets–manufacturing overhead applied

After posting the credit of €22,400 to manufacturing overhead, a debit balance remains.
- This means that the overhead applied to jobs using the predetermined rate was less than the actual amount of overhead incurred during the period.
- This situation is referred to as underapplied overhead.

We address the treatment of under- and overapplied overhead in a later section.

At the end of each month, the **balance in Work in Process Inventory should equal the sum of the costs shown on the job cost sheets of unfinished jobs.**

Illustration 2.13 presents proof of the agreement of the control and subsidiary accounts for Martinez. (It assumes that all jobs are still in process.)

Work in Process Inventory		Job Cost Sheets	
Jan. 31	24,000	No. 101	€ 39,000
31	28,000	102	23,200
31	22,400	103	12,200
	74,400 ◄ ──────────		€74,400

ILLUSTRATION 2.13 | Proof of job cost sheets to Work in Process Inventory

MANAGEMENT INSIGHT

© Tony Tremblay/iStockphoto

Jobs Won, Money Lost

Many companies suffer from poor cost accounting. As a result, they sometimes make products they should not be selling at all, or they buy product components that they could more profitably make themselves. Also, inaccurate cost information leads companies to misallocate capital and frustrates efforts by factory managers to improve efficiency.

For example, consider the case of a diversified company in the business of rebuilding diesel locomotives. The managers thought they were making money, but a consulting firm found that the company had seriously underestimated costs. The company bailed out of the business and not a moment too soon. Says the consultant who advised the company, "The more contracts it won, the more money it lost." Given that situation, a company cannot stay in business very long!

What type of costs do you think the company had been underestimating? (Answer is available in the book's product page on www.wiley.com)

DO IT! 3 ▶ Predetermined Overhead Rate

Hudson Company produces specialized safety devices. For the year, manufacturing overhead costs are estimated to be €160,000. Estimated machine usage is 40,000 hours. The company assigns overhead based on machine hours. Job No. 302 used 2,000 machine hours.

Compute the predetermined overhead rate, determine the amount of overhead to apply to Job No. 302, and prepare the entry to apply overhead to Job No. 302 on March 31.

Solution

Predetermined overhead rate = €160,000 ÷ 40,000 hours = €4 per machine hour
Amount of overhead applied to Job No. 302 = 2,000 hours × €4 = €8,000

The entry to record the application of overhead to Job No. 302 on March 31 is:

Work in Process Inventory	8,000	
Manufacturing Overhead		8,000
(To assign overhead to jobs)		

Related exercise material: **BE2.6, BE2.7, DO IT! 2.3, E2.5, and E2.6.**

ACTION PLAN
- The predetermined overhead rate is estimated annual overhead cost divided by estimated annual operating activity.
- Assignment of overhead to jobs is determined by multiplying the actual activity base used by the predetermined overhead rate.
- The entry to record the assignment of overhead transfers an amount out of Manufacturing Overhead into Work in Process Inventory.

ENTRIES FOR JOBS COMPLETED AND SOLD

Assigning Costs to Finished Goods

LEARNING OBJECTIVE 4
Prepare entries for manufacturing and service jobs completed and sold.

When a job is completed, Martinez Electronics summarizes the costs and completes the lower portion of the applicable job cost sheet. For example, if we assume that Martinez completes Job No. 101, a batch of electronic sensors, on January 31, the job cost sheet appears as shown in **Illustration 2.14**.

Job Cost Sheet

Job No.	101		Quantity	1,000
Item	Electronic Sensors		Date Requested	January 5
For	Tanner Company		Date Completed	January 31

Date	Direct Materials	Direct Labor	Manufacturing Overhead
1/6	€ 1,000		
1/10		€ 9,000	€ 7,200
1/12	7,000		
1/26	4,000		
1/31		6,000	4,800
	€12,000	€15,000	€12,000

Cost of completed job
  Direct materials   € 12,000
  Direct labor   15,000
  Manufacturing overhead   12,000
  Total cost   € 39,000
  Unit cost (€39,000 ÷ 1,000)   € 39.00

ILLUSTRATION 2.14 | **Completed job cost sheet**

When a job is finished, Martinez makes an entry to transfer its total cost to Finished Goods Inventory. The entry is as follows:

(7)

Jan. 31	Finished Goods Inventory	39,000	
	Work in Process Inventory		39,000
	(To record completion of Job No. 101)		

This entry increases Finished Goods Inventory and reduces Work in Process Inventory by €39,000, as shown in the following T-accounts:

Work in Process Inventory		Finished Goods Inventory
24,000 39,000	⟶	39,000
28,000		
22,400		

Finished Goods Inventory is a control account. It controls individual finished goods records in a finished goods subsidiary ledger, which includes all the job cost sheets for completed jobs that have not yet been sold.

Assigning Costs to Cost of Goods Sold

Companies using a perpetual inventory system recognize cost of goods sold when each sale occurs. To illustrate the entries a company makes when it sells a completed job, assume that on January 31 Martinez Electronics sells on account Job No. 101. The job cost €39,000, and it sold for €50,000. The entries to record the sale and recognize cost of goods sold are:

(8)

Jan. 31	Accounts Receivable	50,000	
	Sales Revenue		50,000
	(To record sale of Job No. 101)		
31	Cost of Goods Sold	39,000	
	Finished Goods Inventory		39,000
	(To record cost of Job No. 101)		

This entry increases Cost of Goods Sold and reduces Finished Goods Inventory by €39,000, as shown in the T-accounts below.

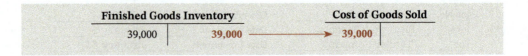

Summary of Job Order Cost Flows

Illustration 2.15 shows a completed flowchart for a job order cost accounting system. All postings are keyed to entries 1–8 in the example presented in the previous pages for Martinez Electronics.

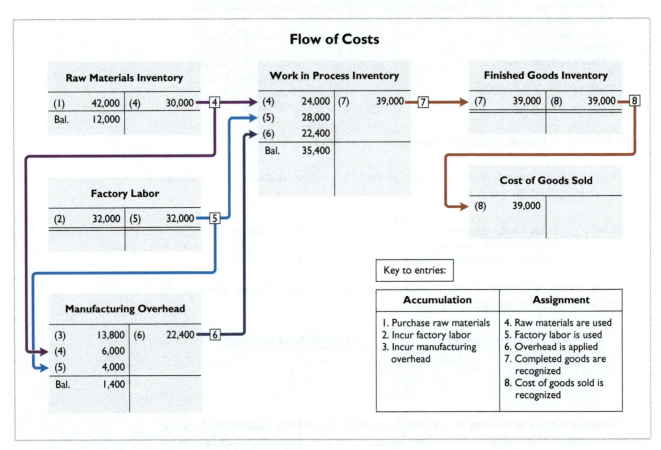

ILLUSTRATION 2.15 | **Flow of costs in a job order cost system**

The cost flows in the diagram can be categorized as one of four types:

- **Accumulation.** The company first accumulates costs by (1) purchasing raw materials, (2) incurring labor costs, and (3) incurring manufacturing overhead costs.
- **Assignment to jobs.** Once the company has incurred manufacturing costs, it must assign them to specific jobs. For example, as it uses raw materials on specific jobs (4), the company assigns them to work in process or treats them as manufacturing overhead if the raw materials cannot be associated with a specific job. Similarly, the company either assigns factory labor (5) to work in process or treats it as manufacturing overhead if the factory labor cannot be associated with a specific job. Finally, the company assigns manufacturing overhead (6) to work in process using a *predetermined overhead rate*. This deserves emphasis: **Do not assign overhead using actual overhead costs but instead apply overhead using a predetermined overhead rate.**

- **Completed jobs.** As jobs are completed (7), the company transfers the cost of the completed job out of Work in Process Inventory into Finished Goods Inventory.
- **When goods are sold.** As specific items are sold (8), the company transfers their cost out of Finished Goods Inventory into Cost of Goods Sold.

Illustration 2.16 summarizes the flow of documents in a job order cost system.

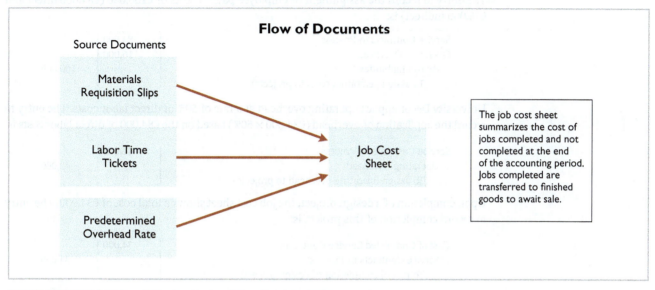

ILLUSTRATION 2.16 | Flow of documents in a job order cost system

Job Order Costing for Service Companies

Our extended job order costing example focuses on a manufacturer so that you see the flow of costs through the inventory accounts.

- Job order costing is also commonly used by service companies.
- While service companies do not have inventory, the techniques of job order costing are still quite useful in many service-industry environments.

Consider, for example, the U.S. companies of **Mayo Clinic** (healthcare), **Pricewaterhouse-Coopers** (accounting), and **Goldman Sachs** (investment banking). These companies need to keep track of the cost of jobs performed for specific customers to evaluate the profitability of medical treatments, audits, or investment banking engagements.

Many service organizations bill their customers using cost-plus contracts (discussed more fully in Chapter 8).

- Cost-plus contracts mean that the customer's bill is the sum of the costs incurred on the job, plus a profit amount that is calculated as a percentage of the costs incurred.
- In order to minimize conflict with customers and reduce potential contract disputes, service companies that use cost-plus contracts must maintain accurate and up-to-date costing records.

Up-to-date cost records enable a service company to immediately notify a customer of cost overruns due to customer requests for changes to the original plan or unexpected complications. Timely recordkeeping allows the contractor and customer to consider alternatives before it is too late.

A service company that uses a job order cost system does not have inventory accounts. It does, however, use an account similar to Work in Process Inventory, referred to here as Service Contracts in Process, to record job costs prior to completion. It also uses an account called Operating Overhead, which is similar to Manufacturing Overhead. To illustrate the journal entries for a service company under a job order cost system, consider the following transactions for University Decor, an interior design company. The entry to record the assignment of €9,000 of supplies to projects (€7,000 direct and €2,000 indirect) is:

Service Contracts in Process	7,000	
Operating Overhead	2,000	
Supplies		9,000
(To assign supplies to projects)		

The entry to record the assignment of employee payroll costs of €100,000 (€84,000 direct and €16,000 indirect) is:

Service Contracts in Process	84,000	
Operating Overhead	16,000	
Payroll Liabilities		100,000
(To assign personnel costs to projects)		

University Decor applies operating overhead at a rate of 50% of direct labor costs. The entry to record the application of overhead (€84,000 × 50%) based on the €84,000 of direct labor costs is:

Service Contracts in Process	42,000	
Operating Overhead		42,000
(To assign operating overhead to projects)		

Upon completion of a design project, the job cost sheet shows a total cost of €34,000. The entry to record completion of this project is:

Cost of Completed Service Contracts	34,000	
Service Contracts in Process		34,000
(To record completion of design project)		

Job cost sheets for a service company keep track of materials, labor, and overhead used on a particular job, similar to a manufacturer. Several exercises at the end of this chapter apply job order costing to service companies.

SERVICE COMPANY INSIGHT   General Electric

Lagereek/Getty Images

Sales Are Nice, but Service Revenue Pays the Bills

Jet engines are one of the many products made by the industrial operations division of **General Electric (GE)** (USA). At prices as high as $30 million per engine, you can bet that GE does its best to keep track of costs. It might surprise you that GE doesn't make much profit on the sale of each engine. So why does it bother making them? For the service revenue. During one recent year, about 75% of the division's revenues came from servicing its own products. One estimate is that the $13 billion in aircraft engines sold during a recent three-year period will generate about $90 billion in service revenue over the 30-year life of the engines. GE hopes to have 44,000 engines in service in the near future.

Because of the high product costs, both the engines themselves and the subsequent service are most likely accounted for using job order costing. Accurate service cost records are important because GE needs to generate high profit margins (estimated to be 30%) on its service jobs to make up for the low margins on the original sale. It also needs good cost records for its service jobs in order to control its costs. Otherwise, a competitor, such as **Pratt & Whitney** (USA), might submit lower bids for service contracts and take lucrative service jobs away from GE.

Sources: Paul Glader, "GE's Focus on Services Faces Test," *Wall Street Journal Online* (March 3, 2009); and Steve Heller, "General Electric's Untapped Opportunity in Aviation," *The Motley Fool* (August 27, 2016).

Why would GE use job order costing to keep track of the cost of repairing a malfunctioning engine for a major airline? (Answer is available in the book's product page on www.wiley.com)

Advantages and Disadvantages of Job Order Costing

Job order costing is more precise in the assignment of costs to projects than process costing (discussed in Chapter 3). For example, assume that a construction company, Malone Construction, builds 10 custom homes a year at a total cost of €2,000,000. One way to determine the cost of each home is to divide the total construction cost incurred during the year by the number of homes produced during the year. For Malone Construction, an average cost of €200,000 (€2,000,000 ÷ 10) is computed. If the homes are nearly identical, then this approach is adequate for purposes of determining profit per home.

- But if the homes vary in terms of size, style, and material types, using the average cost of €200,000 to determine profit per home is inappropriate.
- Instead, Malone Construction should use a job order cost system to determine the specific cost incurred to build each home and the amount of profit made on each.
- Thus, job order costing provides more useful information for determining the profitability of particular projects and for estimating costs when preparing bids on future jobs.

However, job order costing requires a significant amount of data entry. For Malone Construction, it would be much easier to simply keep track of total costs incurred during the year than it is to keep track of the costs incurred on each job (each home built). Recording this information is time-consuming, and if the data is not entered accurately, the product costs are incorrect.

- In recent years, technological advances, such as bar-coding devices for both labor costs and materials, have increased the accuracy and reduced the effort needed to record costs on specific jobs.
- These innovations expand the opportunities to apply job order costing in a wider variety of business settings, thus improving management's ability to control costs and make better-informed decisions.

A common problem of all costing systems is how to assign overhead to the finished product. Overhead often represents more than 50% of a product's cost, and this cost is often difficult to assign meaningfully to the product. How, for example, is the salary of a project manager at Malone Construction assigned to the various homes, which may differ in size, style, and cost of materials used?

- The accuracy of the job order cost system is largely dependent on the accuracy of the overhead allocation process.
- Even if the company does a good job of keeping track of the specific amounts of materials and labor used on each job, if the overhead costs are not assigned to individual jobs in a meaningful way, the product costing information is not useful. We address this issue in more detail in Chapter 4.

DO IT! 4 ▶ Completion and Sale of Jobs

During the current month, Crysta Corporation completed Job 109 and Job 112. Job 109 cost €19,000 and Job 112 cost €27,000. Job 112 was sold on account for €42,000. Journalize the entries for the completion of the two jobs and the sale of Job 112.

Solution

Finished Goods Inventory	46,000	
Work in Process Inventory		46,000
(To record completion of Job 109, costing €19,000 and Job 112, costing €27,000)		
Accounts Receivable	42,000	
Sales Revenue		42,000
(To record sale of Job 112)		
Cost of Goods Sold	27,000	
Finished Goods Inventory		27,000
(To record cost of goods sold for Job 112)		

Related exercise material: **BE2.8, BE2.9, DO IT! 2.4, E2.2, E2.3, E2.6, E2.7, and E2.10.**

ACTION PLAN
- Debit Finished Goods Inventory for the cost of completed jobs.
- Debit Cost of Goods Sold for the cost of jobs sold.

APPLIED MANUFACTURING OVERHEAD

LEARNING OBJECTIVE 5
Distinguish between under- and overapplied manufacturing overhead.

At the end of a period, companies prepare financial statements that present aggregated data for all jobs manufactured and sold.

- The cost of goods manufactured schedule in job order costing is the same as presented in Chapter 1 with one exception: **The schedule shows manufacturing overhead applied, rather than actual overhead costs.**
- **The company adds this amount to direct materials used and direct labor assigned to determine total manufacturing costs.**
- Companies prepare the cost of goods manufactured schedule directly from the Work in Process Inventory account (see **Helpful Hint**).

HELPFUL HINT
Companies usually prepare monthly financial statements for management use only.

Illustration 2.17 shows a **condensed** schedule for Martinez Electronics for January.

Martinez Electronics
Cost of Goods Manufactured Schedule
For the Month Ended January 31, 2023

Work in process, January 1		€ –0–
Direct materials used	€24,000	
Direct labor	28,000	
Manufacturing overhead applied	22,400	
Total manufacturing costs		74,400
Total cost of work in process		74,400
Less: Work in process, January 31		35,400
Cost of goods manufactured		€39,000

ILLUSTRATION 2.17 | Cost of goods manufactured schedule

Note that the cost of goods manufactured (€39,000) agrees with the amount transferred from Work in Process Inventory to Finished Goods Inventory in journal entry No. 7 in Illustration 2.15.

Under- or Overapplied Manufacturing Overhead

Recall that overhead is applied based on an estimate of total annual overhead costs. This estimate will rarely be exactly equal to actual overhead incurred. Therefore, at the end of the year, after overhead has been applied to specific jobs, the Manufacturing Overhead account will likely have a remaining balance (see **Decision Tools**).

DECISION TOOLS
The Manufacturing Overhead account helps managers determine if overhead applied exceeded or was less than actual overhead costs.

- When Manufacturing Overhead has a **debit balance**, overhead is said to be underapplied. **Underapplied overhead** means that the overhead applied to work in process is less than the overhead incurred.
- Conversely, when manufacturing overhead has a **credit balance**, overhead is overapplied. **Overapplied overhead** means that the overhead applied to work in process is greater than the overhead incurred.

Illustration 2.18 shows these concepts.

Manufacturing Overhead

Actual (Costs incurred)	Applied (Costs assigned)

If applied is **less** than actual, manufacturing overhead is underapplied.

If applied is **greater** than actual, manufacturing overhead is overapplied.

ILLUSTRATION 2.18 | Under- and overapplied overhead

Year-End Balance

At the end of the year, all manufacturing overhead transactions are complete. There is no further opportunity for offsetting events to occur. At this point, Martinez Electronics eliminates any balance in Manufacturing Overhead by an adjusting entry. It considers under- or overapplied overhead to be an **adjustment to cost of goods sold**.

- Martinez **debits underapplied overhead to Cost of Goods Sold**.
- **It credits overapplied overhead to Cost of Goods Sold**. (Service organizations use Cost of Completed Service Contracts.)

To illustrate, as noted earlier in the chapter and shown below, after overhead of €22,400 has been assigned, Martinez has a €1,400 debit balance in Manufacturing Overhead at January 31. This occurred because the amount of overhead applied was less than the amount actually incurred during the period.

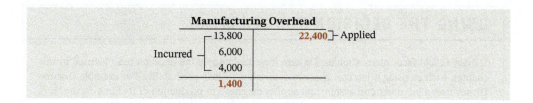

The adjusting entry for the underapplied overhead is:

Jan. 31	Cost of Goods Sold	1,400	
	Manufacturing Overhead		1,400
	(To transfer underapplied overhead to cost of goods sold)		

After Martinez posts this entry, Manufacturing Overhead has a zero balance. In preparing an income statement for the year, Martinez reports cost of goods sold **after adjusting it** for either under- or overapplied overhead.

Illustration 2.19 presents an income statement for Martinez after adjusting for the €1,400 of underapplied overhead.

Martinez Electronics
Income Statement (partial)
For the Month Ended January 31, 2023

Sales revenue		€50,000
Cost of goods sold		
Finished goods inventory, January 1	€ -0-	
Cost of goods manufactured (see Illustration 2.17)	39,000	
Cost of goods available for sale	39,000	
Less: Finished goods inventory, January 31	-0-	
Cost of goods sold—unadjusted	39,000	
Add: Adjustment for underapplied overhead	1,400	
Cost of goods sold—adjusted		40,400
Gross profit		€ 9,600

ILLUSTRATION 2.19 | Partial income statement

For more accurate costing, significant under- or overapplied overhead at the end of the year should be allocated among ending work in process, finished goods, and cost of goods sold. The discussion of this allocation approach is left to more advanced courses.

DO IT! 5 — Applied Manufacturing Overhead

For Schneider Manufacturing, the predetermined overhead rate is 140% of direct labor cost. During the month, Schneider incurred €90,000 of factory labor costs, of which €80,000 is direct labor and €10,000 is indirect labor. Actual overhead incurred (including indirect labor) was €119,000.

Compute the amount of manufacturing overhead applied during the month. Determine the amount of under- or overapplied manufacturing overhead.

Solution

Manufacturing overhead applied = (140% × €80,000) = €112,000
Underapplied manufacturing overhead = (€119,000 − €112,000) = €7,000

Related exercise material: **BE2.10, DO IT! 2.5, E2.4, E2.5, E2.9, and E2.13.**

ACTION PLAN
- Calculate the amount of overhead applied by multiplying the predetermined overhead rate by actual activity.
- If applied overhead is less than actual, overhead is underapplied.
- If applied overhead is greater than actual, overhead is overapplied.

USING THE DECISION TOOLS | Disney

Disney (USA) faces many situations where it needs to apply the decision tools learned in this chapter, such as using a job cost sheet to determine a film's profitability. For example, assume Disney uses a job order cost system and applies overhead to production of its films on the basis of direct labor cost. In computing a predetermined overhead rate for the year 2023, the company estimated film production overhead to be $24 million and direct labor costs to be $20 million. In addition, its accounting records included the following information.

Actual Costs Incurred During 2023

Direct materials used	$30,000,000
Direct labor cost incurred	21,000,000
Insurance, studio	500,000
Indirect labor costs incurred	7,500,000
Studio maintenance	1,000,000
Rent on studio building	11,000,000
Depreciation on studio equipment	2,000,000

Instructions

Answer each of the following:

a. Why is Disney using a job order cost system?

b. On what basis does Disney apply its film production overhead? Compute the predetermined overhead rate for 2023.

c. Compute the amount of the under- or overapplied overhead for 2023.

d. Disney had balances in the beginning and ending films in process and finished films accounts as follows:

	1/1/23	12/31/23
Films in process	$ 5,000,000	$ 4,000,000
Finished films	13,000,000	11,000,000

Determine the (1) cost of films completed and (2) cost of films sold for Disney during 2023. Assume that any under- or overapplied overhead is included in the cost of films sold.

e. During 2023, Film G408 (a short documentary film produced for a customer) was started and completed. Its cost sheet showed a total cost of $100,000, and Disney prices its film at 50% above its cost. What is the price to the customer if the company follows this pricing strategy?

Solution

a. Disney is using a job order cost system because it produces films. Each film is unique, with its own distinguishing characteristics; thus, the costs for each film should be tracked separately.

b. Disney applies its overhead on the basis of direct labor cost. The predetermined overhead rate is 120%, computed as follows: $24,000,000 ÷ 20,000,000 = 120%.

c.	Actual film production overhead		$ 22,000,000*
	Applied overhead cost ($21,000,000 × 120%)		25,200,000
	Overapplied overhead		$ 3,200,000

*$500,000 + $7,500,000 + $1,000,000 + $11,000,000 + $2,000,000

d. 1.	Films in process, 1/1/23			$ 5,000,000
	Direct materials used	$30,000,000		
	Direct labor	21,000,000		
	Film production overhead applied	25,200,000		
	Total film production costs			76,200,000
	Total cost of films in process			81,200,000
	Less: Films in process, 12/31/23			4,000,000
	Cost of films produced			$ 77,200,000
2.	Finished films, 1/1/23	$13,000,000		
	Cost of films produced (see above)	77,200,000		
	Cost of films available for sale	90,200,000		
	Finished films, 12/31/23	11,000,000		
	Cost of films sold (unadjusted)	79,200,000		
	Less: Overapplied overhead	3,200,000		
	Cost of films sold	$76,000,000		
e.	Film G408 cost		$ 100,000	
	Markup percentage		× 50%	
	Markup		$ 50,000	
	Price to customer: $150,000 ($100,000 + $50,000)			

REVIEW AND PRACTICE

Learning Objectives Review

LO 1 Describe cost systems and the flow of costs in a job order system.

Cost accounting focuses on the procedures for measuring, recording, and reporting product and service costs. From the data accumulated, companies determine the total production cost and the unit cost of each product. The two basic types of cost accounting systems are process cost and job order cost.

In job order costing, companies first accumulate manufacturing costs in three accounts: Raw Materials Inventory, Factory Labor, and Manufacturing Overhead. They then assign the accumulated costs to Work in Process Inventory and eventually to Finished Goods Inventory and Cost of Goods Sold.

LO 2 Use a job cost sheet to assign costs to work in process.

A job cost sheet is a form used to record the costs chargeable to a specific job and to determine the total and unit costs of the completed job. Job cost sheets constitute the subsidiary ledger for the Work in Process Inventory control account.

LO 3 Demonstrate how to determine and use the predetermined overhead rate.

The predetermined overhead rate is based on the relationship between estimated annual overhead costs and estimated annual operating activity. This is expressed in terms of a common activity base, such as direct labor cost, direct labor hours, or machine hours. Companies use this rate to assign overhead costs to work in process and to specific jobs.

LO 4 Prepare entries for manufacturing and service jobs completed and sold.

When jobs are completed, companies debit the cost to Finished Goods Inventory and credit it to Work in Process Inventory. When a job is sold, the entries are (a) debit Cash or Accounts Receivable and credit Sales Revenue for the selling price, and (b) debit Cost of Goods Sold and credit Finished Goods Inventory for the cost of the goods.

LO 5 Distinguish between under- and overapplied manufacturing overhead.

Underapplied manufacturing overhead indicates that the overhead assigned to work in process is less than the actual overhead costs incurred. Overapplied overhead indicates that the overhead assigned to work in process is greater than the actual overhead costs incurred.

Decision Tools Review

Decision Checkpoints	Info Needed for Decision	Tool to Use for Decision	How to Evaluate Results
What is the cost of a job?	Cost of direct materials, direct labor, and manufacturing overhead assigned to a specific job	Job cost sheet	Compare costs to those of previous periods to ensure that costs are in line. Compare costs to estimated selling price or service fees charged to determine overall profitability.
Has the company over- or underapplied overhead for the period?	Actual overhead costs and overhead applied	Manufacturing Overhead account	If the account balance is a credit, overhead applied exceeded actual overhead costs. If the account balance is a debit, overhead applied was less than actual overhead costs.

Glossary Review

Cost accounting An area of accounting that focuses on measuring, recording, and reporting product and service costs. (p. 2-3).

Cost accounting system Manufacturing and service cost accounts that are fully integrated into the general ledger of a company. (p. 2-3).

Job cost sheet A form used to record the costs chargeable to a specific job and to determine the total and unit costs of the completed job. (p. 2-8).

Job order cost system A cost accounting system in which costs are assigned to each job or batch. (p. 2-3).

Materials requisition slip A document authorizing the issuance of raw materials from the storeroom to production. (p. 2-8).

Overapplied overhead A situation in which overhead applied to work in process is greater than the actual overhead costs incurred. (p. 2-22).

Predetermined overhead rate A rate based on the relationship between estimated annual overhead costs and estimated annual operating activity, expressed in terms of a common activity base. (p. 2-13).

Process cost system A cost accounting system used when a company manufactures a large volume of similar products. (p. 2-3).

Time ticket A document that indicates the employee name, the hours worked, the account and job to be charged, and the total labor cost. (p. 2-10).

Underapplied overhead A situation in which overhead applied to work in process is less than the actual overhead costs incurred. (p. 2-22).

Practice Multiple-Choice Questions

1. **(LO 1)** Cost accounting focuses on the measuring, recording, and reporting of:
    a. product costs.
    b. future costs.
    c. manufacturing processes.
    d. managerial accounting decisions.

2. **(LO 1)** A company is more likely to use a job order cost system if:
    a. it manufactures a large volume of similar products.
    b. its production is continuous.
    c. it manufactures products with unique characteristics.
    d. it uses a periodic inventory system.

3. **(LO 1)** In accumulating raw materials costs, companies debit the cost of raw materials purchased in a perpetual inventory system to:
    a. Raw Materials Purchases.
    b. Raw Materials Inventory.
    c. Purchases.
    d. Work in Process.

4. **(LO 1)** When incurred, factory labor costs are debited to:
    a. Work in Process Inventory.
    b. Factory Wages Expense.
    c. Factory Labor.
    d. Payroll Liabilities.

5. **(LO 1)** The flow of costs in job order costing:
    a. begins with work in process inventory and ends with finished goods inventory.
    b. begins as soon as a sale occurs.
    c. parallels the physical flow of materials as they are converted into finished goods and then sold.
    d. is necessary to prepare the cost of goods manufactured schedule.

6. **(LO 2)** Raw materials are assigned to a job when:
    a. the job is sold.
    b. the materials are purchased.
    c. the materials are received from the vendor.
    d. the materials are issued by the materials storeroom.

7. (LO 2) The sources of information for assigning costs to job cost sheets are:
   a. invoices, time tickets, and the predetermined overhead rate.
   b. materials requisition slips, time tickets, and the actual overhead costs.
   c. materials requisition slips, payroll register, and the predetermined overhead rate.
   d. materials requisition slips, time tickets, and the predetermined overhead rate.

8. (LO 2) In recording the issuance of raw materials in a job order cost system, it would be **incorrect** to:
   a. debit Work in Process Inventory.
   b. debit Finished Goods Inventory.
   c. debit Manufacturing Overhead.
   d. credit Raw Materials Inventory.

9. (LO 2) The entry when direct factory labor is assigned to jobs is a debit to:
   a. Work in Process Inventory and a credit to Factory Labor.
   b. Manufacturing Overhead and a credit to Factory Labor.
   c. Factory Labor and a credit to Manufacturing Overhead.
   d. Factory Labor and a credit to Work in Process Inventory.

10. (LO 3) The equation for computing the predetermined manufacturing overhead rate is estimated annual overhead costs divided by estimated annual operating activity, expressed as:
   a. direct labor cost.
   b. direct labor hours.
   c. machine hours.
   d. Any of the answer choices is correct.

11. (LO 3) In Yuen Ltd., the predetermined overhead rate is 80% of direct labor cost. During the month, Yuen incurs HK$2,100,000 of factory labor costs, of which HK$1,800,000 is direct labor and HK$300,000 is indirect labor. Actual overhead incurred was HK$2,000,000. The amount of overhead debited to Work in Process Inventory should be:
   a. HK$2,000,000.
   b. HK$1,440,000.
   c. HK$1,680,000.
   d. HK$1,600,000.

12. (LO 4) Abella Dynamics completes Job No. 26 at a cost of €4,500 and later sells it for €7,000 cash. A **correct** entry is:
   a. debit Finished Goods Inventory €7,000 and credit Work in Process Inventory €7,000.
   b. debit Cost of Goods Sold €7,000 and credit Finished Goods Inventory €7,000.
   c. debit Finished Goods Inventory €4,500 and credit Work in Process Inventory €4,500.
   d. debit Accounts Receivable €7,000 and credit Sales Revenue €7,000.

13. (LO 5) At the end of an accounting period, a company using a job order cost system calculates the cost of goods manufactured:
   a. from the job cost sheet.
   b. from the Work in Process Inventory account.
   c. by adding direct materials used, direct labor incurred, and manufacturing overhead incurred.
   d. from the Cost of Goods Sold account.

14. (LO 4) Which of the following statements is **true**?
   a. Job order costing requires less data entry than process costing.
   b. Allocation of overhead is easier under job order costing than process costing.
   c. Job order costing provides more precise costing for custom jobs than process costing.
   d. The use of job order costing has declined because more companies have adopted automated accounting systems.

15. (LO 5) At end of the year, a company has a £1,200 debit balance in Manufacturing Overhead. The company:
   a. makes an adjusting entry by debiting Manufacturing Overhead Applied for £1,200 and crediting Manufacturing Overhead for £1,200.
   b. makes an adjusting entry by debiting Manufacturing Overhead Expense for £1,200 and crediting Manufacturing Overhead for £1,200.
   c. makes an adjusting entry by debiting Cost of Goods Sold for £1,200 and crediting Manufacturing Overhead for £1,200.
   d. makes no adjusting entry because differences between actual overhead and the amount applied are a normal part of job order costing and will average out over the next year.

16. (LO 5) Manufacturing overhead is underapplied if:
   a. actual overhead is less than applied.
   b. actual overhead is greater than applied.
   c. the predetermined rate equals the actual rate.
   d. actual overhead equals applied overhead.

Solutions

1. a. Cost accounting focuses on the measuring, recording, and reporting of product costs, not (b) future costs, (c) manufacturing processes, or (d) managerial accounting decisions.

2. c. A job costing system is more likely for products with unique characteristics. The other choices are incorrect because a process cost system is more likely for (a) large volumes of similar products or (b) if production is continuous. Choice (d) is incorrect because the choice of a costing system is not dependent on whether a periodic or perpetual inventory system is used.

3. b. In a perpetual inventory system, purchases of raw materials are debited to Raw Materials Inventory, not (a) Raw Materials Purchases, (c) Purchases, or (d) Work in Process.

4. c. When factory labor costs are incurred, they are debited to Factory Labor, not (a) Work in Process Inventory, (b) Factory Wages Expense, or (d) Payroll Liabilities (they are debited to Factory Labor and credited to Payroll Liabilities).

5. c. Job order costing parallels the physical flow of materials as they are converted into finished goods. The other choices are incorrect because job order costing begins (a) with raw materials, not work in process, and ends with cost of goods sold; and (b) as soon as raw materials are purchased, not when the sale occurs. Choice (d) is incorrect because the cost of goods manufactured schedule is prepared from the Work in Process Inventory account and is only a portion of the costs in a job order cost system.

6. d. Raw materials are assigned to a job when the materials are issued by the materials storeroom, not when (a) the job is sold, (b) the materials are purchased, or (c) the materials are received from the vendor.

7. **d.** Materials requisition slips are used to assign direct materials, time tickets are used to assign direct labor, and the predetermined overhead rate is used to assign manufacturing overhead to job cost sheets. The other choices are incorrect because (a) materials requisition slips, not invoices, are used to assign direct materials; (b) the predetermined overhead rate, not the actual overhead costs, is used to assign manufacturing overhead; and (c) time tickets, not the payroll register, are used to assign direct labor.

8. **b.** Finished Goods Inventory is debited when goods are transferred from work in process to finished goods, not when raw materials are issued for a job. Choices (a), (c), and (d) are true statements.

9. **a.** When direct factory labor is assigned to jobs, the entry is a debit to Work in Process Inventory and a credit to Factory Labor. The other choices are incorrect because (b) Work in Process Inventory, not Manufacturing Overhead, is debited; (c) Work in Process Inventory, not Factory Labor, is debited and Factory Labor, not Manufacturing Overhead, is credited; and (d) Work in Process Inventory, not Factory Labor, is debited and Factory Labor, not Work in Process Inventory, is credited.

10. **d.** Any of the activity bases mentioned can be used in computing the predetermined manufacturing overhead rate. Choices (a) direct labor cost, (b) direct labor hours, and (c) machine hours can all be used in computing the predetermined manufacturing overhead rate, but (d) is a better answer.

11. **b.** Work in Process Inventory should be debited for HK$1,440,000 (HK$1,800,000 × 80%), the amount of manufacturing overhead applied, not (a) HK$2,000,000, (c) HK$1,680,000, or (d) HK$1,600,000.

12. **c.** When a job costing €4,500 is completed, Finished Goods Inventory is debited and Work in Process Inventory is credited for €4,500.

Choices (a) and (b) are incorrect because the amounts should be for the cost of the job (€4,500), not the sale amount (€7,000). Choice (d) is incorrect because the debit should be to Cash, not Accounts Receivable.

13. **b.** At the end of an accounting period, a company using a job order cost system prepares the cost of goods manufactured schedule from the Work in Process Inventory account, not (a) from the job cost sheet; (c) by adding direct materials used, direct labor incurred, and manufacturing overhead incurred; or (d) from the Cost of Goods Sold Account.

14. **c.** Job order costing provides more precise costing for custom jobs than process costing. The other choices are incorrect because (a) job order costing often requires significant data entry, (b) overhead assignment is a problem for all costing systems, and (d) the use of job order costing has increased due to automated accounting systems.

15. **c.** The company would make an adjusting entry for the underapplied overhead by debiting Cost of Goods Sold for £1,200 and crediting Manufacturing Overhead for £1,200, not by debiting (a) Manufacturing Overhead Applied for £1,200 or (b) Manufacturing Overhead Expense for £1,200. Choice (d) is incorrect because at the end of the year, a company makes an entry to eliminate any balance in Manufacturing Overhead.

16. **b.** Manufacturing overhead is underapplied if actual overhead is greater than applied overhead. The other choices are incorrect because (a) if actual overhead is less than applied, then manufacturing overhead is overapplied; (c) if the predetermined rate equals the actual rate, the actual overhead costs incurred equal the overhead costs applied, neither over- nor underapplied; and (d) if the actual overhead equals the applied overhead, neither over- nor underapplied occurs.

Practice Exercises

Analyze a job cost sheet and prepare entries for manufacturing costs.

1. (LO 1, 2, 3, 4) A job cost sheet for Whitstable plc is shown below.

Job No. 92				For 2,000 Units
Date		Direct Materials	Direct Labor	Manufacturing Overhead
Beg. bal. Jan.	1	3,925	6,000	4,200
	8	6,000		
	12		8,500	6,375
	25	2,000		
	27		4,000	3,000
		11,925	18,500	13,575

Cost of completed job:	
Direct materials	£11,925
Direct labor	18,500
Manufacturing overhead	13,575
Total cost	£44,000
Unit cost (£44,000 ÷ 2,000)	£ 22.00

Instructions

a. Answer the following questions:
   1. What was the balance in Work in Process Inventory on January 1 if this was the only unfinished job?
   2. If manufacturing overhead is applied on the basis of direct labor cost, what overhead rate was used in each year?

b. Prepare summary entries at January 31 to record the current year's transactions pertaining to Job No. 92.

Solution

1. a. 1. £14,125, or (£3,925 + £6,000 + £4,200).

2. Last year 70%, or (£4,200 ÷ £6,000); this year 75% (either £6,375 ÷ £8,500 or £3,000 ÷ £4,000).

b.

Date	Account	Debit	Credit
Jan. 31	Work in Process Inventory	8,000	
	Raw Materials Inventory		8,000
	(£6,000 + £2,000)		
31	Work in Process Inventory	12,500	
	Factory Labor		12,500
	(£8,500 + £4,000)		
31	Work in Process Inventory	9,375	
	Manufacturing Overhead		9,375
	(£6,375 + £3,000)		
31	Finished Goods Inventory	44,000	
	Work in Process Inventory		44,000

2. (LO 3, 5) Charlie Kopy applies operating overhead to photocopying jobs on the basis of machine hours used. Overhead costs are estimated to total A$290,000 for the year, and machine usage is estimated at 125,000 hours.

For the year, A$295,000 of overhead costs are incurred and 130,000 hours are used.

Compute the overhead rate and under- or overapplied overhead.

Instructions

a. Compute the service overhead rate for the year.

b. What is the amount of under- or overapplied overhead at December 31?

c. Assuming the under- or overapplied overhead for the year is not allocated to inventory accounts, prepare the adjusting entry to assign the amount to cost of services provided.

Solution

2. a. A$2.32 per machine hour (A$290,000 ÷ 125,000).

b. (A$295,000) − (A$2.32 × 130,000 machine hours)

    A$295,000 − A$301,600 = A$6,600 overapplied

c.

Account	Debit	Credit
Operating Overhead	6,600	
Cost of Services Provided		6,600

Practice Problem

(LO 3, 5) Adriana AG applies overhead on the basis of direct labor costs. The company estimates annual overhead costs to be €760,000 and annual direct labor costs to be €950,000. During February, Adriana works on two jobs: A16 and B17. Summary data concerning these jobs are as follows:

Compute predetermined overhead rate, apply overhead, and calculate under- or overapplied overhead.

Manufacturing Costs Incurred

Purchased €54,000 of raw materials on account.

Factory labor €80,000.

Manufacturing overhead incurred exclusive of indirect materials and indirect labor €59,800. This was comprised of utilities €25,000, insurance €9,000, depreciation €10,000, and property taxes €15,800.

Assignment of Costs

Direct materials: Job A16 €27,000, Job B17 €21,000
Indirect materials: €3,000
Direct labor: Job A16 €52,000, Job B17 €26,000
Indirect labor: €2,000

The company completed Job A16 and sold it on account for €150,000. Job B17 was only partially completed.

Instructions

a. Compute the predetermined overhead rate.

b. Journalize the February transactions in the sequence presented in the chapter (use February 28 for all dates).

c. What was the amount of under- or overapplied manufacturing overhead?

Solution

a.

Estimated annual overhead costs	÷	Estimated annual operating activity	=	Predetermined overhead rate
€760,000	÷	€950,000	=	80%

b.

(1)

Feb. 28	Raw Materials Inventory	54,000	
	Accounts Payable		54,000
	(Purchase of raw materials on account)		

(2)

28	Factory Labor	80,000	
	Payroll Liabilities		80,000
	(To record factory labor costs)		

(3)

28	Manufacturing Overhead	59,800	
	Utilities Payable		25,000
	Prepaid Insurance		9,000
	Accumulated Depreciation		10,000
	Property Taxes Payable		15,800
	(To record overhead costs)		

(4)

Feb. 28	Work in Process Inventory	48,000*	
	Manufacturing Overhead	3,000	
	Raw Materials Inventory		51,000
	(To assign raw materials to production)		

*€27,000 + €21,000

(5)

28	Work in Process Inventory	78,000**	
	Manufacturing Overhead	2,000	
	Factory Labor		80,000
	(To assign factory labor to production)		

**€52,000 + €26,000

(6)

28	Work in Process Inventory	62,400	
	Manufacturing Overhead		62,400
	(To assign overhead to jobs— 80% × €78,000)		

(7)

28	Finished Goods Inventory	120,600	
	Work in Process Inventory		120,600
	(To record completion of Job A16: direct materials €27,000, direct labor €52,000, and manufacturing overhead €41,600)		

(8)

28	Accounts Receivable	150,000	
	Sales Revenue		150,000
	(To record sale of Job A16)		
28	Cost of Goods Sold	120,600	
	Finished Goods Inventory		120,600
	(To record cost of sale for Job A16)		

c. Manufacturing Overhead has a debit balance of €2,400 as shown below.

Manufacturing Overhead

(3)	59,800	(6)	62,400
(4)	3,000		
(5)	2,000		
Bal.	2,400		

Thus, manufacturing overhead is underapplied for the month.

Questions

1. **a.** Zahara Omari is not sure about the difference between cost accounting and a cost accounting system. Explain the difference to Zahara.
   b. What is an important feature of a cost accounting system?
2. **a.** Distinguish between the two types of cost accounting systems.
   b. Can a company use both types of cost accounting systems?
3. What type of industry is likely to use a job order cost system? Give some examples.
4. What type of industry is likely to use a process cost system? Give some examples.
5. Your roommate asks your help in understanding the major steps in the flow of costs in a job order cost system. Identify the steps for your roommate.
6. "Accumulation entries to Manufacturing Overhead normally are only made daily." Is this true? Explain why or why not.
7. Louis Müller is confused about the source documents used in assigning materials and labor costs. Identify the documents and give the entry for each document.
8. What is the purpose of a job cost sheet?
9. Indicate the source documents that are used in charging costs to specific jobs.
10. Explain the purpose and use of a "materials requisition slip" as used in a job order cost system.
11. Sam Bowden believes actual manufacturing overhead costs should be charged to jobs. Is this true? Explain why or why not.
12. What inputs are involved in computing a predetermined overhead rate?
13. How can the agreement of Work in Process Inventory and job cost sheets be verified?
14. Tarun Nair believes that the cost of goods manufactured schedule in job order cost accounting is the same as shown in Chapter 1. Is Tarun correct? Explain.
15. Zara Rashid is confused about under- and overapplied manufacturing overhead. Define the terms for Zara, and indicate the unadjusted balance in the manufacturing overhead account applicable to each term.
16. "At the end of the year, under- or overapplied overhead is closed to Income Summary." Is this correct? If not, indicate the customary treatment of this amount.

Brief Exercises

BE2.1 (LO 1), C Galli Group begins operations on January 1. Because all work is done to customer specifications, the company decides to use a job order cost system. Prepare a flowchart of a typical job order system with arrows showing the flow of costs. Identify the eight transactions.

Prepare a flowchart of a job order cost accounting system and identify transactions.

BE2.2 (LO 1), AP During January, its first month of operations, Galli Group accumulated the following manufacturing costs: raw materials purchased CHF4,000 on account, factory labor incurred CHF6,000, and factory utilities payable CHF2,000. Prepare separate journal entries for each type of manufacturing cost (use January 31 for all dates).

Prepare entries for accumulating manufacturing costs.

BE2.3 (LO 2), AP In January, Galli Group requisitions raw materials for production as follows: Job 1 CHF900, Job 2 CHF1,200, Job 3 CHF700, and general factory use CHF600. Prepare a summary journal entry to record raw materials used (use January 31 as the date).

Prepare entry for the assignment of raw materials costs.

BE2.4 (LO 2), AP Factory labor information for Galli Group is given in BE2.2. During January, time tickets show that the factory labor of CHF6,000 was used as follows: Job 1 CHF2,200, Job 2 CHF1,600, Job 3 CHF1,400, and general factory use CHF800. Prepare a summary journal entry to record factory labor used (use January 31 as the date).

Prepare entry for the assignment of factory labor costs.

BE2.5 (LO 2), AP Data pertaining to job cost sheets for Galli Group are given in BE2.3 and BE2.4. Prepare the job cost sheets for each of the three jobs using the format shown in Illustration 2.8 (use January 31 as the date). (*Note:* You may omit the column for Manufacturing Overhead.)

Prepare job cost sheets.

Compute predetermined overhead rates.

BE2.6 (LO 3), AP Dale Computers estimates that annual manufacturing overhead costs will be S$900,000. Estimated annual operating activity bases are direct labor cost S$500,000, direct labor hours 50,000, and machine hours 100,000. Compute the predetermined overhead rate for each activity base.

Assign manufacturing overhead to production.

BE2.7 (LO 3), AP During the first quarter, Xiaoping Ltd. incurs the following direct labor costs: January HK$400,000, February HK$300,000, and March HK$500,000. For each month, prepare the entry to assign overhead to production using a predetermined rate of 70% of direct labor cost (date journal entries as of the end of the month).

Prepare entries for completion and sale of completed jobs.

BE2.8 (LO 4), AP In March, Ghim Enterprises completes Jobs 10 and 11. Job 10 cost ₩20,000,000 and Job 11 ₩30,000,000. On March 31, Job 10 is sold to the customer for ₩35,000,000 in cash. Journalize the entries for the completion of the two jobs and the sale of Job 10 (date journal entries as of the end of the month).

Prepare entries for payroll liabilities and operating overhead.

BE2.9 (LO 4), AP Ruiz Engineering Contractors incurred employee payroll costs of R$360,000 (R$280,000 direct and R$80,000 indirect) on an engineering project. The company applies overhead at a rate of 25% of direct labor cost. Record the entries to assign payroll liabilities and to apply overhead. Assume journal entries are made at the end of the month.

Prepare adjusting entries for under- and overapplied overhead.

BE2.10 (LO 5), AP At December 31, balances in Manufacturing Overhead are Shimeca Company—debit $1,200, Garcia Company—credit $900. Prepare the adjusting entry for each company at December 31, assuming the adjustment is made to cost of goods sold.

DO IT! Exercises

Prepare entries for manufacturing costs.

DO IT! 2.1 (LO 1), AP During the current month, Lucas SA incurs the following manufacturing costs.

a. Purchased raw materials of R$180,000 on account.

b. Incurred factory labor of R$400,000.

c. Factory utilities of R$31,000 are payable, prepaid factory insurance of R$27,000 has expired, and depreciation on the factory building is R$95,000.

Prepare journal entries for each type of manufacturing cost. (Use a summary entry to record manufacturing overhead.)

Assign costs to work in process.

DO IT! 2.2 (LO 2), AP Tanaka Tech is working on two job orders. The job cost sheets show the following:

	Job 201	Job 202
Direct materials	¥720,000	¥900,000
Direct labor	400,000	800,000

Prepare the two summary entries to record the assignment of costs to Work in Process from the data on the job cost sheets.

Compute and apply the predetermined overhead rate.

DO IT! 2.3 (LO 3), AP Syed Company produces earbuds. During the year, manufacturing overhead costs are estimated to be ₹20,000,000. Estimated machine usage is 2,500 hours. The company assigns overhead based on machine hours. Job No. 551 used 90 machine hours. Compute the predetermined overhead rate, determine the amount of overhead to apply to Job No. 551, and prepare the entry to apply overhead to Job No. 551 on January 15.

Prepare entries for completion and sale of jobs.

DO IT! 2.4 (LO 4), AP During the current month, Standard Corporation completed Job 310 and Job 312. Job 310 cost NT$700,000 and Job 312 cost NT$500,000. Job 312 was sold on account for NT$900,000. Journalize the entries for the completion of the two jobs and the sale of Job 312 (use January 31 for the dates).

Apply manufacturing overhead and determine under- or overapplication.

DO IT! 2.5 (LO 5), AP For Rochester plc, the predetermined overhead rate is 130% of direct labor cost. During the month, Rochester incurred £100,000 of factory labor costs, of which £85,000 is direct labor and £15,000 is indirect labor. Actual overhead incurred was £115,000. Compute the amount of manufacturing overhead applied during the month. Determine the amount of under- or overapplied manufacturing overhead.

Exercises

Prepare entries for factory labor.

E2.1 (LO 1, 2), AP Total factory labor costs related to factory workers for Ahem A.S. during the month of January are ₺900,000. Of the total accumulated cost of factory labor, 85% is related to direct labor and 15% is attributable to indirect labor.

Instructions

a. Prepare the January 31 entry to record the factory labor costs for the month of January.

b. Prepare the January 31 entry to assign factory labor to production.

E2.2 (LO 1, 2, 3, 4), AP Junhong Ltd. uses a job order cost system. On May 1, the company has a balance in Work in Process Inventory of HK$35,000 and two jobs in process: Job No. 429 HK$20,000, and Job No. 430 HK$15,000. During May, a summary of source documents reveals the following:

Prepare entries for manufacturing costs.

Job Number	Materials Requisition Slips		Labor Time Tickets	
429	HK$25,000		HK$19,000	
430	35,000		30,000	
431	44,000	HK$104,000	76,000	HK$125,000
General use		8,000		12,000
		HK$112,000		HK$137,000

Junhong Ltd. applies manufacturing overhead to jobs at an overhead rate of 60% of direct labor cost. Job No. 429 is completed during the month.

Instructions

a. Prepare May 31 summary journal entries to record (1) the requisition slips, (2) the time tickets, (3) the assignment of manufacturing overhead to jobs, and (4) the completion of Job No. 429.

b. Post the entries to Work in Process Inventory, and prove the agreement of the control account with the job cost sheets. (Use a T-account.)

E2.3 (LO 1, 2, 3, 4), AP A job cost sheet for Koskinen SE is shown below.

Analyze a job cost sheet and prepare entries for manufacturing costs.

Job No. 92				For 2,000 Units
Date		Direct Materials	Direct Labor	Manufacturing Overhead
Beg. bal. Jan.	1	5,000	6,000	4,200
	8	6,000		
	12		8,000	6,400
	25	2,000		
	27		4,000	3,200
		13,000	18,000	13,800

Cost of completed job:	
Direct materials	€13,000
Direct labor	18,000
Manufacturing overhead	13,800
Total cost	€44,800
Unit cost (€44,800 ÷ 2,000)	€ 22.40

Instructions

a. On the basis of this data, answer the following questions:
   1. What was the balance in Work in Process Inventory on January 1 if this was the only unfinished job?
   2. If manufacturing overhead is applied on the basis of direct labor cost, what overhead rate was used in each year?

b. Prepare summary entries at January 31 to record the current year's transactions pertaining to Job No. 92.

Analyze costs of manufacturing and determine missing amounts.

E2.4 (LO 1, 5), AN Manufacturing cost data for Flock Hill plc, which uses a job order cost system, are presented below.

	Case A	Case B
Work in process 1/1/23	£ (a)	£ 15,500
Direct materials used	(b)	83,000
Direct labor	50,000	140,000
Manufacturing overhead applied	42,500	(d)
Total manufacturing costs	145,650	(e)
Total cost of work in process	201,500	(f)
Work in process 12/31/23	(c)	11,800
Cost of goods manufactured	192,300	(g)

Instructions

Determine the missing amount for each letter. Assume that in both cases manufacturing overhead is applied on the basis of direct labor cost and the rate is the same.

Compute the manufacturing overhead rate and under- or overapplied overhead.

E2.5 (LO 3, 5), AN Ikerd Company applies manufacturing overhead to jobs on the basis of machine hours used. Overhead costs are estimated to total $300,000 for the year, and machine usage is estimated at 125,000 hours.

For the year, $322,000 of overhead costs are incurred, and 130,000 machine hours are used.

Instructions

a. Compute the manufacturing overhead rate for the year.

b. What is the amount of under- or overapplied overhead at December 31?

c. Prepare the adjusting entry to assign the under- or overapplied overhead for the year to cost of goods sold.

Analyze job cost sheet and prepare entry for completed job.

E2.6 (LO 1, 2, 3, 4), AP A job cost sheet of Ingrid ASA is given below.

Job Cost Sheet

JOB NO. 469 Quantity 2,500
ITEM White Lion Cages Date Requested 7/2
FOR Todd Company Date Completed 7/31

Date	Direct Materials	Direct Labor	Manufacturing Overhead
7/10	690		
12	900		
15		440	550
22		380	475
24	1,600		
27	1,500		
31		540	675

Cost of completed job:
 Direct materials
 Direct labor
 Manufacturing overhead
Total cost
Unit cost

Instructions

a. Answer the following questions:

1. What are the source documents for direct materials, direct labor, and manufacturing overhead costs assigned to this job?

2. Overhead is applied on the basis of direct labor cost. What is the predetermined manufacturing overhead rate?

3. What are the total cost and the unit cost of the completed job?

b. Prepare the entry to record the completion of the job on July 31.

E2.7 (LO 1, 2, 3, 4), AP Hana Enterprises incurred the following transactions:

Prepare entries for manufacturing and nonmanufacturing costs.

1. Purchased raw materials on account ¥463,000.
2. Raw materials of ¥360,000 were requisitioned to the factory. An analysis of the materials requisition slips indicated that ¥68,000 was classified as indirect materials.
3. Factory labor costs incurred were ¥599,000.
4. Time tickets indicated that ¥540,000 was direct labor and ¥59,000 was indirect labor.
5. Manufacturing overhead costs incurred on account were ¥805,000.
6. Depreciation on the company's office building was ¥81,000.
7. Manufacturing overhead was applied at the rate of 150% of direct labor cost.
8. Goods costing ¥880,000 were completed and transferred to finished goods.
9. Finished goods costing ¥750,000 to manufacture were sold on account for ¥1,030,000.

Instructions

Journalize the transactions. (Omit explanations.)

E2.8 (LO 1, 2, 3, 4), AP Uranus Company uses a job order cost system. The following data summarize the operations related to the first quarter's production.

Prepare entries for manufacturing and nonmanufacturing costs.

1. Materials purchased on account £192,000, and factory wages incurred £87,300.
2. Materials requisitioned and factory labor used by job:

Job Number	Materials	Factory Labor
A20	£ 35,240	£18,000
A21	42,920	22,000
A22	36,100	15,000
A23	39,270	25,000
Indirect	4,470	7,300
	£158,000	£87,300

3. Manufacturing overhead costs incurred on account £49,500. (*Hint:* Use Accounts Payable.)
4. Depreciation on factory equipment £14,550.
5. Depreciation on the company's office building £14,300.
6. Manufacturing overhead rate is 90% of direct labor cost.
7. Jobs completed during the quarter: A20, A21, and A23.

Instructions

Prepare entries to record the operations summarized above. Prepare a schedule showing the individual cost elements and total cost for each job in item 7.

E2.9 (LO 1, 5), AP At May 31, 2023, the accounts of Lopez Company show the following:

Prepare a cost of goods manufactured schedule and partial financial statements.

1. May 1 inventories—finished goods $12,600, work in process $14,700, and raw materials $8,200.
2. May 31 inventories—finished goods $9,500, work in process $15,900, and raw materials $7,100.
3. Debit postings to work in process were direct materials $62,400, direct labor $50,000, and manufacturing overhead applied $40,000. (Assume that overhead applied was equal to overhead incurred.)
4. Sales revenue totaled $215,000.

Instructions

a. Prepare a condensed cost of goods manufactured schedule for May 2023.

b. Prepare an income statement for May 2023 through gross profit.

c. Prepare the balance sheet section of the manufacturing inventories at May 31, 2023.

Compute work in process and finished goods from job cost sheets.

E2.10 (LO 2, 4), AP Rossi AG begins operations on April 1. Information from job cost sheets shows the following:

	Manufacturing Costs Assigned			
Job Number	April	May	June	Month Completed
10	CHF5,200	CHF4,400		May
11	4,100	3,900	CHF2,000	June
12	1,200			April
13		4,700	4,500	June
14		5,900	3,600	Not complete

Job 12 was completed in April. Job 10 was completed in May. Jobs 11 and 13 were completed in June. Each job was sold for 25% above its cost in the month following completion.

Instructions

a. What is the balance in Work in Process Inventory at the end of each month?

b. What is the balance in Finished Goods Inventory at the end of each month?

c. What is the gross profit for May, June, and July?

Prepare entries for service organizations.

E2.11 (LO 1, 3, 4), AP **Service** The following are the job cost related accounts for the law firm of Caleb Associates and their manufacturing equivalents.

Law Firm Accounts	Manufacturing Company Accounts
Supplies	Raw Materials Inventory
Payroll Liabilities	Payroll Liabilities
Operating Overhead	Manufacturing Overhead
Service Contracts in Process	Work in Process Inventory
Cost of Completed Service Contracts	Finished Goods Inventory

Cost data for the month of March follow:

1. Purchased supplies on account S$1,800.
2. Issued supplies S$1,200 (60% direct and 40% indirect).
3. Assigned labor costs based on time tickets for the month which indicated labor costs of S$70,000 (80% direct and 20% indirect).
4. Operating overhead costs incurred for cash totaled S$40,000.
5. Operating overhead is applied at a rate of 90% of direct labor cost.
6. Work completed totaled S$75,000.

Instructions

a. Journalize the transactions for March. (Omit explanations.)

b. Determine the balance of the Service Contracts in Process account. (Use a T-account.)

Determine cost of jobs and ending balances of a service company's accounts.

E2.12 (LO 2, 3, 4), AP **Service** Cheuk and Associates uses job order costing to capture the costs of its audit jobs. There were no audit jobs in process at the beginning of November. Listed below are data concerning the three audit jobs worked on during November.

	Wing	Chi	Ying
Direct materials	HK$6,000	HK$4,000	HK$2,000
Auditor labor costs	HK$54,000	HK$66,000	HK$33,750
Auditor hours	72	88	45

Overhead costs are applied to jobs on the basis of auditor hours, and the predetermined overhead rate is HK$500 per auditor hour. The Wing job is the only incomplete job at the end of November. Actual overhead for the month was HK$110,000.

Instructions

a. Determine the cost assigned to each job.

b. Determine the balance of the Service Contracts in Process account at the end of November.

c. Calculate the ending balance of the Operating Overhead account for November.

E2.13 (LO 3, 5), AP **Service** Chia-hao Decorator uses a job order cost system to collect the costs of its interior decorating business. Each client's consultation is treated as a separate job. Overhead is applied to each job based on the number of decorator hours incurred. Listed below are data for the current year.

Determine predetermined overhead rate, apply overhead, and determine whether balance is under- or overapplied.

Estimated overhead costs	NT$9,600,000
Actual overhead costs	NT$9,828,000
Estimated decorator hours	40,000
Actual decorator hours	40,500

The company uses the account Operating Overhead in place of Manufacturing Overhead, and the account Service Contracts in Process in place of Work in Process Inventory.

Instructions

a. Compute the predetermined overhead rate.

b. Prepare the entry to apply the overhead for the year.

c. Determine whether the overhead was under- or overapplied and by how much.

Problems

P2.1 (LO 1, 2, 3, 4, 5), AP Apollo plc uses a job order cost system and applies overhead to production on the basis of direct labor costs. On January 1, 2023, Job 50 was the only job in process. The costs incurred prior to January 1 on this job were as follows: direct materials £20,000, direct labor £12,000, and manufacturing overhead £16,000. As of January 1, Job 49 had been completed at a cost of £90,000 and was part of finished goods inventory. There was a £15,000 balance in the Raw Materials Inventory account on January 1.

Prepare entries and postings to job cost sheets for a job order cost system.

During the month of January, Apollo plc began production on Jobs 51 and 52, and completed Jobs 50 and 51. Jobs 49 and 50 were sold on account during the month for £122,000 and £158,000, respectively. The following additional events occurred during the month.

1. Purchased additional raw materials of £90,000 on account.
2. Incurred factory labor costs of £70,000.
3. Incurred manufacturing overhead costs as follows: depreciation on equipment £12,000 and various other manufacturing overhead costs on account £16,000.
4. Assigned direct materials and direct labor to jobs as follows:

Job No.	Direct Materials	Direct Labor
50	£10,000	£ 5,000
51	39,000	25,000
52	30,000	20,000

5. Assigned indirect materials of £17,000 and indirect labor of £20,000.

Instructions

a. Calculate the predetermined overhead rate for 2023, assuming Apollo estimates total manufacturing overhead costs of £840,000, direct labor costs of £700,000, and direct labor hours of 20,000 for the year.

b. Open job cost sheets for Jobs 50, 51, and 52. Enter the January 1 balances on the job cost sheet for Job 50.

c. Prepare the journal entries to record the purchase of raw materials, the factory labor costs incurred, and the manufacturing overhead costs incurred during the month of January.

d. Prepare the journal entries to record the assignment of raw materials, factory labor, and manufacturing overhead costs to production. In assigning manufacturing overhead costs, use the overhead rate calculated in (a). Post all costs to the job cost sheets as necessary.

e. Job 50, £69,000
Job 51, £94,000

e. Total the job cost sheets for any job(s) completed during the month. Prepare the journal entry (or entries) to record the completion of any job(s) during the month.

f. Prepare the journal entry (or entries) to record the sale of any job(s) during the month.

g. What is the balance in the Finished Goods Inventory account at the end of the month? (*Hint*: Use a T-account for Finished Goods Inventory.) What does this balance consist of?

h. What is the amount of over- or underapplied overhead?

Prepare entries in a job order cost system and partial income statement.

P2.2 (LO 1, 2, 3, 4, 5), AP For the year ended December 31, 2023, the job cost sheets of Freya NV contained the following data.

Job Number	Explanation	Direct Materials	Direct Labor	Manufacturing Overhead	Total Costs
7640	Balance 1/1	€25,000	€24,000	€28,800	€ 77,800
	Current year's costs	30,000	36,000	43,200	109,200
7641	Balance 1/1	11,000	18,000	21,600	50,600
	Current year's costs	43,000	48,000	57,600	148,600
7642	Current year's costs	58,000	55,000	66,000	179,000

Other data:

1. Raw materials inventory totaled €15,000 on January 1. During the year, €140,000 of raw materials were purchased on account.
2. Finished goods on January 1 consisted of Job No. 7638 for €87,000 and Job No. 7639 for €92,000.
3. Job No. 7640 and Job No. 7641 were completed during the year.
4. Job Nos. 7638, 7639, and 7641 were sold on account for €530,000.
5. Manufacturing overhead incurred on account totaled €120,000.
6. Incurred depreciation on factory machinery €8,000.
7. Assigned indirect materials of €14,000 and indirect labor of €18,000.

Instructions

a. €179,000; Job 7642: €179,000

a. Prove the agreement of Work in Process Inventory with job cost sheets pertaining to unfinished work. (*Hint*: Use a single T-account for Work in Process Inventory.) Calculate each of the following, then post each to the T-account: (1) beginning balance, (2) direct materials, (3) direct labor, (4) manufacturing overhead, and (5) completed jobs.

b. Amount = €6,800

b. Prepare the adjusting entry for manufacturing overhead, assuming the balance is allocated entirely to Cost of Goods Sold.

c. €158,600

c. Prepare an income statement through gross profit for 2023.

Prepare entries in a job order cost system and cost of goods manufactured schedule.

P2.3 (LO 1, 2, 3, 4, 5), AP Case Inc. is a construction company specializing in custom patios. The patios are constructed of concrete, brick, fiberglass, and lumber, depending on customer preference. On June 1, 2023, the general ledger for Case Inc. contains the following data.

Raw Materials Inventory	$4,200	Manufacturing Overhead Applied	$32,640
Work in Process Inventory	$5,540	Manufacturing Overhead Incurred	$31,650

Subsidiary data for Work in Process Inventory on June 1 are as follows:

Job Cost Sheets

Cost Element	Customer Job		
	Rodgers	Stevens	Linton
Direct materials	$ 600	$ 800	$ 900
Direct labor	320	540	580
Manufacturing overhead	400	675	725
	$1,320	$2,015	$2,205

During June, raw materials purchased on account were $4,900, and $4,800 of factory wages were paid. Additional overhead costs consisted of depreciation on equipment $900 and miscellaneous costs of $400 incurred on account.

A summary of materials requisition slips and time tickets for June shows the following:

Customer Job	Materials Requisition Slips	Time Tickets
Rodgers	$ 800	$ 850
Koss	2,000	800
Stevens	500	360
Linton	1,300	1,200
Rodgers	300	390
	4,900	3,600
General use	1,500	1,200
	$6,400	$4,800

Overhead was assigned to jobs at the same rate of $1.25 per dollar of direct labor cost throughout the year. The patios for customers Rodgers, Stevens, and Linton were completed during June and sold for a total of $18,900. Each customer paid in full at the time of sale.

Instructions

a. Journalize the June transactions: (1) purchase of raw materials, factory labor costs incurred, and manufacturing overhead costs incurred; (2) assignment of direct materials, labor, and overhead to production; and (3) completion of jobs and sale of goods.

b. Post the entries to Work in Process Inventory.

c. Reconcile the balance in Work in Process Inventory with the costs of unfinished jobs.

d. Prepare a cost of goods manufactured schedule for June.

d. Cost of goods manufactured $14,740

P2.4 (LO 3, 5), AP Naidoo Company uses a job order cost system in each of its three manufacturing departments. Manufacturing overhead is applied to jobs on the basis of direct labor cost in Department D, direct labor hours in Department E, and machine hours in Department K.

In establishing the predetermined overhead rates for 2023, the following estimates were made for the year.

Compute predetermined overhead rates, apply overhead, and calculate under- or overapplied overhead.

	Department		
	D	E	K
Manufacturing overhead	R12,000,000	R15,000,000	R9,000,000
Direct labor costs	R15,000,000	R12,500,000	R4,500,000
Direct labor hours	100,000	125,000	40,000
Machine hours	400,000	500,000	120,000

The following information pertains to January 2023 for each manufacturing department.

	Department		
	D	E	K
Direct materials used	R1,400,000	R1,260,000	R780,000
Direct labor costs	R1,200,000	R1,100,000	R375,000
Manufacturing overhead incurred	R990,000	R1,240,000	R790,000
Direct labor hours	8,000	11,000	3,500
Machine hours	34,000	45,000	10,400

Instructions

a. Compute the predetermined overhead rate for each department.

b. Compute the total manufacturing costs assigned to jobs in January in each department.

c. Compute the under- or overapplied overhead for each department at January 31.

a. 80%, R120, R75
b. R3,560,000, R3,680,000, R1,935,000
c. R30,000, R(80,000), R(10,000)

Analyze manufacturing accounts and determine missing amounts.

P2.5 (LO 1, 2, 3, 4, 5), AN Hughes plc's fiscal year ends on November 30. The following accounts are found in its job order cost accounting system for the first month of the new fiscal year.

Raw Materials Inventory

Dec.	1	Beginning balance	(a)	Dec. 31	Requisitions	16,850
	31	Purchases	17,225			
Dec.	31	Ending balance	7,975			

Work in Process Inventory

Dec.	1	Beginning balance	(b)	Dec. 31	Jobs completed	(f)
	31	Direct materials	(c)			
	31	Direct labor	8,400			
	31	Overhead	(d)			
Dec.	31	Ending balance	(e)			

Finished Goods Inventory

Dec.	1	Beginning balance	(g)	Dec. 31	Cost of goods sold	(i)
	31	Jobs completed	(h)			
Dec.	31	Ending balance	(j)			

Factory Labor

| Dec. 31 | Factory wages | 12,025 | Dec. 31 | Wages assigned | (k) |

Manufacturing Overhead

Dec.	31	Indirect materials	2,900	Dec. 31	Overhead applied	(m)
	31	Indirect labor	(l)			
	31	Other overhead	1,245			

Other data:

1. On December 1, two jobs were in process: Job No. 154 and Job No. 155. These jobs had combined direct materials costs of £9,750 and combined direct labor costs of £15,000. Overhead was applied at a rate that was 75% of direct labor cost.

2. During December, Job Nos. 156, 157, and 158 were started. On December 31, Job No. 158 was unfinished. This job had charges for direct materials £3,800 and direct labor £4,800, plus manufacturing overhead. All jobs, except for Job No. 158, were completed in December.

3. On December 1, Job No. 153 was in the finished goods warehouse. It had a total cost of £5,000. On December 31, Job No. 157 was the only finished job that was not sold. It had a cost of £4,000.

4. Manufacturing overhead was £1,470 underapplied in December.

c. £13,950
f. £52,450
i. £53,450

Instructions

List the letters (a) through (m) and indicate the amount pertaining to each letter.

Continuing Case

Current Designs

CD2 Tranquillum House has ordered 20 rotomolded kayaks from **Current Designs** (USA). Each kayak will be formed in the rotomolded oven, cooled, and then have the excess plastic trimmed away. Then, the hatches, seat, ropes, and bungees will be attached to the kayak.

Dave Thill, the kayak factory manager, knows that manufacturing each kayak requires 54 pounds of polyethylene powder and a finishing kit (rope, seat, hardware, etc.). The polyethylene powder used in these kayaks costs $1.50 per pound, and the finishing kits cost $170 each. Each kayak will use two kinds of labor: 2 hours of more-skilled type I labor from people who run the oven and trim the plastic, and 3 hours of less-skilled type II labor from people who attach the hatches and seat and other hardware. The type I employees are paid $15 per hour, and the type II employees are paid $12 per hour. For purposes of this problem, assume that overhead is applied to all jobs at a rate of 150% of direct labor costs.

Instructions

Determine the total cost of the Tranquillum House order and the cost of each individual kayak in the order. Identify costs as direct materials, direct labor, or manufacturing overhead.

Data Analytics in Action

Using Data Visualization to Analyze Profitability

DA2.1 Data visualization can be used to review profitability.

Example: Recall the *Feature Story* "Profiting from the Silver Screen" presented at the beginning of the chapter. Data analytics can help movie executives understand industry performance. Industry experts track box office receipts, production costs, and estimated gross profit. From publicly available data, we can get an estimate of these amounts. Here are graphed data for comedy films derived from books. What do you observe?

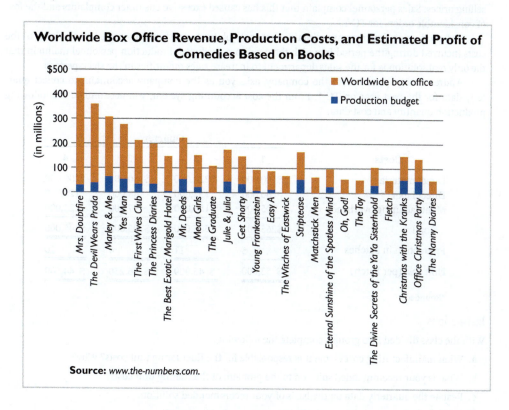

You can see that *Mrs. Doubtfire* has the highest box-office sales and relatively low production costs. But, does that mean it also has the highest gross profit? For this case, you will look closer at the costs and revenues for these movies by calculating gross profit and then graphing and analyzing the results.

Go to the book's product page on www.wiley.com for complete case details and instructions.

Data Analytics at the Movies

DA2.2 You are interested in the effect of production budget costs on the profitability of movies. For this case, you will use Excel pivot tables to summarize the production budget costs for worldwide box office receipts and the estimated gross profit, and then analyze the results.

Go to the book's product page on www.wiley.com for complete case details and instructions.

Data Analytics at HydroHappy

DA2.3 HydroHappy rents out giant water slides for parties and other events. HydroHappy has a team that loads and transports the requested slides on the company's trucks, assembles the slides at the customers' chosen locations, and dismantles, loads, and transports the slides back to HydroHappy's warehouse when the event is complete. In the past, HydroHappy has not kept job cost records due to having only two or three jobs per week. Now that demand is increasing, HydroHappy has purchased five new

Expand Your Critical Thinking

Decision-Making Across the Organization

CT2.1 Khan Products Company uses a job order cost system. For a number of months, there has been an ongoing rift between the sales department and the production department concerning a special-order product, TC-1. TC-1 is a seasonal product that is manufactured in batches of 1,000 units. TC-1 is sold at cost plus a markup of 40% of cost.

The sales department is unhappy because fluctuating unit production costs significantly affect selling prices. Sales personnel complain that this has caused excessive customer complaints and the loss of considerable orders for TC-1.

The production department maintains that each job order must be fully costed on the basis of the costs incurred during the period in which the goods are produced. Production personnel maintain that the only real solution is for the sales department to increase sales quantities in the slack periods.

Andrea Parley, president of the company, asks you as the company accountant to collect quarterly data for the past year on TC-1. From the cost accounting system, you accumulate the following production quantity and cost data:

| | Quarter | | | |
Costs	1	2	3	4
Direct materials	$100,000	$220,000	$80,000	$200,000
Direct labor	60,000	132,000	48,000	120,000
Manufacturing overhead	105,000	153,000	97,000	125,000
Total	$265,000	$505,000	$225,000	$445,000
Production in batches	5	11	4	10
Unit cost (per batch)	$53,000	$45,909*	$56,250	$44,500

*Rounded.

Instructions

With the class divided into groups, complete the following:

a. What manufacturing cost element is responsible for the fluctuating unit costs? Why?

b. What is your recommended solution to the problem of fluctuating unit costs?

c. Restate the quarterly data on the basis of your recommended solution.

Managerial Analysis

CT2.2 In the course of routine checking of all journal entries prior to preparing year-end reports, Yin Wang discovered several strange entries. She recalled that the president's son Jun had come in to help out during an especially busy time and that he had recorded some journal entries. She was relieved that there were only a few of his entries, and even more relieved that he had included rather lengthy explanations. The entries Jun made were:

(1)

Work in Process Inventory	250,000	
Cash		250,000

(This is for direct materials put into process. I don't find the record that we paid for these, so I'm crediting Cash because I know we'll have to pay for them sooner or later.)

(2)

Manufacturing Overhead	120,000	
Cash		120,000

(This is for bonuses paid to salespeople. I know they're part of overhead, and I can't find an account called "Non-Factory Overhead" or "Other Overhead" so I'm putting it in Manufacturing Overhead. I have the check stubs, so I know we paid these.)

	(3)		
Work in Process Inventory		30,000	
Raw Materials Inventory			30,000

(This is for the glue used in the factory. I know we used this to make the products, even though we didn't use very much on any one of the products. I got it out of inventory, so I credited an inventory account.)

Instructions

a. How should Jun have recorded each of the three events?

b. If the entry was not corrected, which financial statements (income statement or balance sheet) would be affected? What balances would be overstated or understated? (For events (2) and (3), assume the affected units were completed and sold.)

Real-World Focus

CT2.3 The **Institute of Management Accountants (IMA)** sponsors a certification for management accountants, allowing them to obtain the title of Certified Management Accountant.

Instructions

Go to the IMA website, choose **About IMA**, choose **CMA Certification**, and then **Getting Started**. Answer part (a) below. Next, choose **CMA Certification**, then **Current CMAs**, then **Maintain Your Certification**, and then click on **Download the CPE Requirements and Rules**. Answer part (b) below.

a. What is the experience qualification requirement?

b. How many hours of continuing education are required, and what types of courses qualify?

Communication Activity

CT2.4 You are the management accountant for Williams Company. Your company does custom carpentry work and uses a job order cost system. Williams sends detailed job cost sheets to its customers, along with an invoice. The job cost sheets show the date materials were used, the dollar cost of materials, and the hours and cost of labor. A predetermined overhead application rate is used, and the total overhead applied is also listed.

Nancy Kopay is a customer who recently had custom cabinets installed. Along with her check in payment for the work done, she included a letter. She thanked the company for including the detailed cost information but questioned why overhead was estimated. She stated that she would be interested in knowing exactly what costs were included in overhead, and she thought that other customers would, too.

Instructions

Prepare a letter to Ms. Kopay (address: 123 Cedar Lane, Altoona, KS 66651) and tell her why you did not send her information on exact costs of overhead included in her job. Respond to her suggestion that you provide this information.

Ethics Case

CT2.5 **Service** LRF Printing provides printing services to many different corporate clients. Although LRF bids most jobs, some jobs, particularly new ones, are negotiated on a "cost-plus" basis. Cost-plus means that the buyer is willing to pay the actual cost plus a return (profit) on these costs to LRF.

Hyejin Yoon, controller for LRF, has recently returned from a meeting where LRF's president stated that he wanted her to find a way to charge more costs to any project that was on a cost-plus basis. The president noted that the company needed more profits to meet its stated goals this period. By charging more costs to the cost-plus projects and therefore fewer costs to the jobs that were bid, the company should be able to increase its profit for the current year.

Hyejin knew why the president wanted to take this action. Rumors were that he was looking for a new position and if the company reported strong profits, the president's opportunities would be enhanced. Hyejin also recognized that she could probably increase the cost of certain jobs by changing the basis used to assign manufacturing overhead.

Instructions

a. Who are the stakeholders in this situation?

b. What are the ethical issues in this situation?

c. What would you do if you were Hyejin Yoon?

All About You

CT2.6 Many of you will work for a small business. Some of you will even own your own business. In order to operate a small business, you will need a good understanding of managerial accounting, as well as many other skills. Much information is available to assist people who are interested in starting a new business. A great place to start is the website provided by the **Small Business Administration**, which is an agency of the U.S. government whose purpose is to support small businesses.

Instructions

Go to *https://www.sba.gov/business-guide/10-steps-start-your-business/* and then list the 10 steps for starting a business.

Considering Your Costs and Benefits

CT2.7 After graduating, you might decide to start a small business. As discussed in this chapter, owners of any business need to know how to calculate the cost of their products. In fact, many small businesses fail because they don't accurately calculate their product costs, so they don't know whether they are making a profit or losing money—until it's too late.

Suppose that you decide to start a landscape business. You use an old pickup truck that you've fully paid for. You store the truck and other equipment in your parents' barn, and you store trees and shrubs on their land. Your parents will not charge you for the use of these facilities for the first two years, but beginning in the third year they will charge a reasonable rent. Your mother helps you by answering phone calls and providing customers with information. She doesn't charge you for this service, but she plans on doing it for only your first two years in business. In pricing your services, should you include charges for the truck, the barn, the land, and your mother's services when calculating your product cost? The basic arguments for and against are as follows:

- **YES:** If you don't include charges for these costs, your costs are understated and your profitability is overstated.
- **NO:** At this point, you are not actually incurring costs related to these activities; therefore, you shouldn't record charges.

Instructions

Write a response indicating your position regarding this situation. Provide support for your view.

CHAPTER 3

Process Costing

CHAPTER PREVIEW

As the following Feature Story describes, the cost accounting system used by companies such as **Back o' Bourke Cordials** (AUS) is **process cost accounting**. In contrast to job order cost accounting, which focuses on the individual job, process cost accounting focuses on the *processes* involved in mass-producing products that are identical or very similar in nature. The primary objective of this chapter is to explain and illustrate process costing.

FEATURE STORY

Famed Soft Drink in the Outback

It isn't easy for a small company to get a foothold in the bottled beverage business. The giants, such as **The Coca-Cola Company** (USA) and **Schweppes** (CHE), vigilantly defend their turf, constantly watching for new trends and opportunities. It is nearly impossible to get shelf space in stores, and consumer tastes can change faster than a bottle of soda can lose its fizz. But **Back o' Bourke Cordials Pty Ltd** (AUS) has overcome these and other obstacles to make a name for itself.

In the Australian vernacular, "back o-bourke" refers to any place a long way out or "in the sticks." If you go "back of beyond" and head 789 km northwest of Sydney, eventually you will hit the city of Bourke. Bourke was settled in 1835 as a log stockade on the banks of the Darling River; it was the hub of the far west of Australia. Camel wagons, horse teams, and bullock teams along with Cobb & Co. coaches used the bulldust and goat tracks for road travel into the largely uninhabited far west until they reached Bourke. In 1893, Henry Lawson, famed Australian writer and bush poet, claimed "you don't know Australia until you know Bourke."

Bourke has a number of things that it is known for, including Splashe's Back o' Bourke cola, which is sweet and syrupy with the nostalgic taste of old-fashioned sarsaparilla. This classic Outback drink is a taste of home or "liquid gold," as some locals have dubbed it. Back o' Bourke also produces numerous other soft drinks including club nectar, cream soda, lemonade, mandarin, raspberry, orange, mint freeze, lemon soda squash, and pineapple.

John Rice started the company in 1907, when he bought the Commercial Hotel and set up a lemonade factory in a converted stable. A modern factory was built in the 1950s, and eventually, the third-generation owner and grandson, Ted Rice, built an upgraded bottling plant. The company is currently owned by John Rice's great-grandsons, Daniel and Sam Rice.

Because Back o' Bourke has a large array of product flavors, keeping track of costs is of vital importance. As proof, when searching the Internet, you can see that Sam Rice is the contact for products that are being marketed in China. No matter how good your products are, if you don't keep your costs under control, you are likely to fail. The Rice family needs accurate cost information regarding each primary product to ensure profitability. So while its marketing approach may differ dramatically from the giant soft drink makers, Back o' Bourke needs essentially the same kind of cost information as the big guys.

Source: Back o' Bourke Cordials website, *http://www.splashe.com.au/link-hero*.

 Watch the *Jones Soda* video at https://wileyaccountingupdates.com/video/?p=57 to learn more about process costing in the real world.

CHAPTER OUTLINE

Learning Objectives	Review	Practice
LO 1 Discuss the uses of a process cost system and how it compares to a job order cost system.	• Uses of process cost systems • Process costing for service companies • Comparing job order and process cost systems	**DO IT! 1** Compare Job Order and Process Cost Systems
LO 2 Explain the flow of costs in a process cost system and the journal entries to assign manufacturing costs.	• Process cost flow • Assigning manufacturing costs	**DO IT! 2** Manufacturing Costs in Process Costing
LO 3 Compute equivalent units of production.	• Weighted-average method • Refinements on the method	**DO IT! 3** Equivalent Units of Production
LO 4 Complete the four steps to prepare a production cost report.	• Physical unit flow • Equivalent units of production • Unit production costs • Cost reconciliation schedule • Production cost report	**DO IT! 4** Cost Reconciliation Schedule

Go to the Review and Practice section at the end of the chapter for a targeted summary and practice applications with solutions.

OVERVIEW OF PROCESS COST SYSTEMS

Uses of Process Cost Systems

Companies use **process cost systems** to assign costs to similar products that are mass-produced in a continuous fashion. **Back o' Bourke Cordials Pty Ltd** (AUS) uses a process cost system as follows:

- Production of the soda, once it begins, continues until the completed bottles of soda emerge.
- The processing is the same for the entire production run—with precisely the same amount of materials, labor, and overhead.
- Each finished bottle of soda is indistinguishable from another.

A company such as **United States Steel** (USA) uses process costing in the manufacturing of steel. **Kellogg** (USA) and **General Mills** (USA) use process costing for cereal production; **Petro-China** (CHN) uses process costing for its oil refining. **Sherwin Williams** (USA) uses process costing for its paint products.

- At a bottling company like Back o' Bourke, the manufacturing process begins with the blending of ingredients.
- Next, automated machinery moves the bottles into position and fills them.
- The production process then caps, labels, packages, and forwards the bottles to the finished goods warehouse.

Illustration 3.1 shows this process.

> **LEARNING OBJECTIVE 1**
> Discuss the uses of a process cost system and how it compares to a job order cost system.

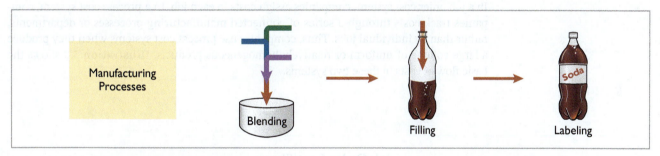

ILLUSTRATION 3.1 | **Manufacturing processes**

For Back o' Bourke, as well as the other companies just mentioned, once production begins, it continues until the finished product emerges. Each unit of finished product is like every other unit. In comparison, a job order cost system assigns costs to a *specific job*. Examples are the construction of a customized home, the making of a movie, or the manufacturing of a specialized machine. **Illustration 3.2** provides examples of companies that primarily use either a process cost system or a job order cost system.

Process Costing for Service Companies

When considering service companies, you might initially think of specific, nonroutine tasks, such as rebuilding an automobile engine, consulting on a business acquisition, or defending a major lawsuit. However, many service companies perform repetitive, routine work. For example, **Jiffy Lube** (USA) regularly performs oil changes. **H&R Block** (USA) focuses on the routine aspects of basic tax practice.

Process Cost System		Job Order Cost System	
Company	Product	Company	Product
Back o' Bourke, Coca-Cola	Soft drinks	Young & Rubicam, J. Walter Thompson	Advertising
ExxonMobil, Shell plc	Oil	Disney, Warner Bros.	Movies
Intel, Advanced Micro Devices	Computer chips	Center Ice Consultants, Ice Pro	Ice rinks
Dow Chemical, DuPont	Chemicals	Kaiser Permanente, Mayo Clinic	Patient health care

ILLUSTRATION 3.2 | Process cost and job order cost companies and products

- Service companies that perform individualized, nonroutine services will probably benefit from using a job order cost system.
- Those that perform routine, repetitive services would probably prefer a process cost system.

Similarities and Differences Between Job Order Cost and Process Cost Systems

In a job order cost system, companies assign costs to each job. In a process cost system, companies track costs through a series of connected manufacturing processes or departments, rather than by individual jobs. Thus, companies use process cost systems when they produce a large volume of uniform or relatively homogeneous products. **Illustration 3.3** shows the basic flow of costs in these two systems.

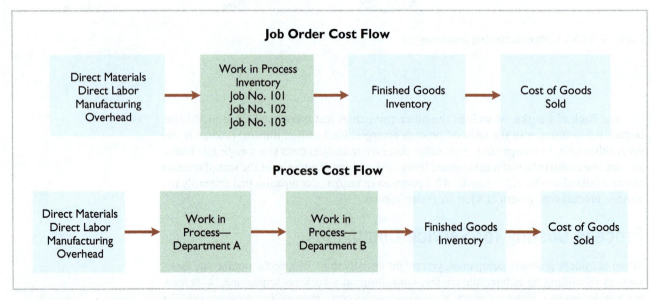

ILLUSTRATION 3.3 | Job order cost and process cost flow

The following analysis highlights the basic similarities and differences between these two systems.

Similarities

Job order cost and process cost systems are similar in three ways:

1. **The manufacturing cost components.** Both costing systems track three manufacturing cost components—direct materials, direct labor, and manufacturing overhead.
2. **The accumulation of the costs of materials, labor, and overhead.** Both costing systems record the acquisition of raw materials as a debit to Raw Materials Inventory, incurred factory labor as a debit to Factory Labor, and actual manufacturing overhead costs incurred as debits to Manufacturing Overhead.
3. **The flow of costs.** As noted above, both systems accumulate all manufacturing costs by debits to Raw Materials Inventory, Factory Labor, and Manufacturing Overhead. Both systems then assign these costs to the same accounts—Work in Process Inventory, Finished Goods Inventory, and Cost of Goods Sold. **The methods of assigning costs, however, differ significantly.** These differences are explained and illustrated later in the chapter.

Differences

The differences between a job order cost and a process cost system are as follows:

1. **The number of work in process inventory accounts used.** A job order cost system uses only one work in process inventory account. A process cost system uses multiple work in process inventory accounts.
2. **Documents used to track costs.** A job order cost system charges costs to individual jobs and summarizes them in a job cost sheet. A process cost system summarizes costs in a production cost report for each department; there are no job cost sheets.
3. **The point at which costs are totaled.** A job order cost system totals costs when the job is completed. A process cost system totals costs at the end of a period of time.
4. **Unit cost computations.** In a job order cost system, the unit cost is the total cost per job divided by the units produced for that job. In a process cost system, the unit cost is the sum of unit materials costs and unit conversion costs. This is determined as total materials costs and conversion costs divided by the equivalent units produced during the period for materials and conversion costs respectively.

Illustration 3.4 summarizes the major differences between a job order cost and a process cost system.

Feature	Job Order Cost System	Process Cost System
Work in process inventory accounts	One work in process inventory account	Multiple work in process inventory accounts
Documents used	Job cost sheets	Production cost reports
Determination of total manufacturing costs	Each job	Each period
Unit-cost computations	Cost of each job ÷ Units produced for the job	The sum of materials costs and conversion costs, each divided by their respective equivalent units

ILLUSTRATION 3.4 | **Job order versus process cost systems**

DO IT! 1 — Compare Job Order and Process Cost Systems

Indicate whether each of the following statements is true or false.

1. A law firm is likely to use process costing for major lawsuits.
2. A manufacturer of paintballs is likely to use process costing.
3. Both job order and process costing determine product costs at the end of a period of time, rather than when a product is completed.
4. Process costing does not keep track of manufacturing overhead.

Solution

1. False. 2. True. 3. False. 4. False.

Related exercise material: **DO IT! 3.1** and **E3.1**.

ACTION PLAN
- Use job order costing in situations where unit costs are high, unit volume is low, and products are unique.
- Use process costing when there is a large volume of relatively homogeneous products.

RECORDING COSTS

Process Cost Flow

LEARNING OBJECTIVE 2
Explain the flow of costs in a process cost system and the journal entries to assign manufacturing costs.

Illustration 3.5 shows the flow of costs in the process cost system for Ngg Wheels. Ngg manufactures roller blade and skateboard wheels that it sells to manufacturers and retail outlets. Manufacturing consists of two processes: machining and assembly. The Machining Department shapes, hones, and drills the raw materials. The Assembly Department assembles and packages the wheels.

As the flow of costs indicates, the company can assign direct materials, direct labor, and manufacturing overhead in both the Machining and Assembly Departments. When it finishes its work, the Machining Department transfers the partially completed units to the Assembly Department. The Assembly Department completes the goods and then transfers them to the finished goods inventory. Upon sale, Ngg removes the goods from the finished goods inventory. Within each department, a similar set of activities is performed on each unit processed.

Assigning Manufacturing Costs—Journal Entries

As indicated, the accumulation of the costs of direct materials, direct labor, and manufacturing overhead is the same in a process cost system as in a job order cost system. That is, both systems follow these procedures:

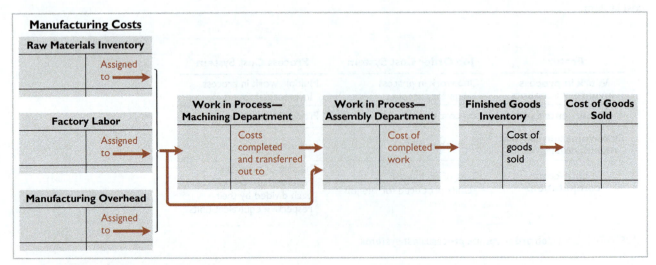

ILLUSTRATION 3.5 | Flow of costs in process cost system

- Debit all raw materials acquired to Raw Materials Inventory at the time of purchase.
- Debit all factory labor to Factory Labor as labor costs are incurred.
- Debit overhead costs to Manufacturing Overhead as these costs are incurred.

However, the assignment of the three manufacturing cost components to work in process inventory accounts in a process cost system is different from a job order cost system. Here, we look at how companies assign these manufacturing cost components in a process cost system.

Materials Costs

All direct materials issued for production are a materials cost to the producing department. A process cost system may use materials requisition slips, but **it generally requires fewer requisitions than in a job order cost system. The materials are used for processes rather than for specific jobs** and therefore typically are for larger quantities.

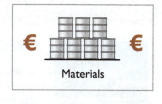
Materials

- At the beginning of the first process, a company usually adds most of the materials needed for production.
- However, other materials may be added at various points.

For example, in the manufacture of **Toblerone** (CHE) candy bars, the chocolate and other ingredients are added at the beginning of the first process, and the wrappers and cartons are added at the end of the packaging process.

Ngg Wheels adds materials at the beginning of each process. Suppose at the beginning of the current period that Ngg adds €50,000 of direct materials to the machining process and €20,000 of direct materials to the assembly process. Ngg makes the following entry to record the direct materials used.

Work in Process—Machining	50,000	
Work in Process—Assembly	20,000	
Raw Materials Inventory		70,000
(To record direct materials used)		

Factory Labor Costs

In a process cost system, as in a job order cost system, companies may use time tickets to determine the cost of labor assignable to production departments. Since they assign labor costs to a process rather than a job, they can obtain, from the payroll register or departmental payroll summaries, the labor cost chargeable to a process.

Factory Labor

Suppose that Ngg Wheels incurs factory labor charges of €20,000 in the machining process and €13,000 in the assembly process. The entry to assign direct labor costs to machining and assembly for Ngg is as follows:

Work in Process—Machining	20,000	
Work in Process—Assembly	13,000	
Factory Labor		33,000
(To assign direct labor to production)		

Manufacturing Overhead Costs

The objective in assigning overhead in a process cost system is to allocate the overhead costs to the production departments on an objective and equitable basis. That basis is the activity that "drives" or causes the costs.

Manufacturing Overhead

- A primary driver of overhead costs in continuous manufacturing operations is **machine time used**, not direct labor.
- Thus, companies **widely use machine hours** in assigning manufacturing overhead costs using predetermined overhead rates.

Assume that based on machine hours that Ngg Wheels assigns overhead of €45,000 to the machining process and €17,000 to the assembly process. Ngg's entry to assign overhead to the two processes is as follows:

Work in Process—Machining	45,000	
Work in Process—Assembly	17,000	
Manufacturing Overhead		62,000
(To assign overhead to production)		

MANAGEMENT INSIGHT Caterpillar

© SweetyMommy/iStockphoto

Choosing a Cost Driver

In one of its automated cost centers, **Caterpillar** (USA) inputs work into the cost center, where robotic machines process it and transfer the completed job to the next cost center without human intervention. One person tends all of the machines and spends more time maintaining machines than operating them. In such cases, overhead rates based on direct labor hours may be misleading. Surprisingly, some companies continue to assign manufacturing overhead on the basis of direct labor despite the fact that there is no cause-and-effect relationship between labor and overhead.

What is the result if a company uses the wrong "cost driver" to assign manufacturing overhead? (Answer is available in the book's product page on www.wiley.com)

Transfer to Next Department

When work in process items have received all the necessary inputs from one department, they progress to the next department. In our example, Ngg Wheels needs an entry to record the cost of the goods transferred out of the Machining Department. In this case, the transfer is to the Assembly Department. Suppose Ngg transfers goods with a recorded cost of €87,000 from machining to assembly. Ngg makes the following entry:

Work in Process—Assembly	87,000	
Work in Process—Machining		87,000
(To record transfer of units to the Assembly Department)		

Transfer to Finished Goods

Suppose the Assembly Department completes units with a recorded cost of €114,000 and then transfers them to the finished goods warehouse. The entry for this transfer is as follows:

Finished Goods Inventory	114,000	
Work in Process—Assembly		114,000
(To record transfer of completed units to finished goods)		

Transfer to Cost of Goods Sold

Suppose Ngg Wheels sells finished goods with a recorded cost of €27,000. It records the cost of goods sold as follows:

Cost of Goods Sold	27,000	
Finished Goods Inventory		27,000
(To record cost of units sold)		

DO IT! 2 ▶ Manufacturing Costs in Process Costing

White Cliff Company manufactures ZEBO through two processes: blending and bottling. In June, direct materials used were Blending €18,000 and Bottling €4,000. Direct labor costs were Blending €12,000 and Bottling €5,000. Manufacturing overhead costs assigned were Blending €6,000 and Bottling €2,500. The Blending Department transfers units completed at a cost of €19,000 to the Bottling Department. The Bottling Department transfers units completed at a cost of €11,000 to Finished Goods. Journalize the assignment of these costs to the two processes and the transfer of units as appropriate.

ACTION PLAN
- In process cost accounting, keep separate work in process inventory accounts for each process.
- When the costs are assigned to production, debit the separate work in process inventory accounts.
- Transfer cost of completed units to the next process or to Finished Goods.

Solution

The entries are:

Work in Process—Blending	18,000	
Work in Process—Bottling	4,000	
Raw Materials Inventory		22,000
(To record direct materials used)		
Work in Process—Blending	12,000	
Work in Process—Bottling	5,000	
Factory Labor		17,000
(To assign direct labor to production)		
Work in Process—Blending	6,000	
Work in Process—Bottling	2,500	
Manufacturing Overhead		8,500
(To assign overhead to production)		
Work in Process—Bottling	19,000	
Work in Process—Blending		19,000
(To record transfer of units to the Bottling Department)		
Finished Goods Inventory	11,000	
Work in Process—Bottling		11,000
(To record transfer of units to finished goods)		

Related exercise material: **BE3.1, BE3.2, BE3.3, DO IT! 3.2, E3.2,** and **E3.4.**

EQUIVALENT UNITS

Suppose you have a work-study job in the office of your college's president, and she asks you to compute the cost of instruction per full-time equivalent student at your college. The college's vice president for finance provides the information shown in **Illustration 3.6**.

LEARNING OBJECTIVE 3
Compute equivalent units of production.

Costs:	
Total annual cost of instruction	€9,000,000
Student population:	
Full-time students	900
Part-time students	1,000

ILLUSTRATION 3.6 | **Information for full-time student example**

Part-time students take 60% of the classes of full-time students during the year. **Illustration 3.7** shows how to compute the number of full-time equivalent students per year.

Full-Time Students	+	Equivalent Units of Part-Time Students	=	Full-Time Equivalent Students
900	+	(1,000 × 60%)	=	1,500

ILLUSTRATION 3.7 | **Full-time equivalent unit computation**

The cost of instruction per full-time equivalent student is therefore the total cost of instruction (€9,000,000) divided by the number of full-time equivalent students (1,500), which is €6,000 (€9,000,000 ÷ 1,500).

A process cost system uses the same idea, called equivalent units of production.

- **Equivalent units of production** measure the work done during the period, expressed in fully completed units.
- Companies use this measure to determine the cost per unit of a completed product.

Weighted-Average Method

The equation to compute equivalent units of production is shown in **Illustration 3.8**.

Units Completed and Transferred Out	+	Equivalent Units of Ending Work in Process	=	Equivalent Units of Production

ILLUSTRATION 3.8 | Equivalent units of production equation

To better understand this concept of equivalent units, consider the following two separate examples:

Example 1. In a specific period, the entire production efforts of Popov OAO's Blending Department resulted in ending work in process of 4,000 units that are 60% complete as to materials, labor, and overhead. The equivalent units of production for the Blending Department are therefore 2,400 units (4,000 × 60%).

Example 2. The production efforts of Kori Company's Packaging Department during the period resulted in 10,000 units completed and transferred out, and 5,000 units in ending work in process that are 70% completed. The equivalent units of production are therefore 13,500 [10,000 + (5,000 × 70%)].

This method of computing equivalent units is referred to as the **weighted-average method**. It considers the degree of completion (weighting) of the units completed and transferred out and the ending work in process.

Refinements on the Weighted-Average Method

Kellogg Company (USA) has produced Eggo® Waffles since 1970. Three departments produce these waffles: Mixing, Baking, and Freezing/Packaging. The Mixing Department combines dry ingredients, including flour, salt, and baking powder, with liquid ingredients, including eggs and vegetable oil, to make waffle batter. **Illustration 3.9** provides information related to the Mixing Department at the end of June. Note that separate unit cost computations are needed for materials and conversion costs whenever the two types of costs do not occur in the process at the same time.

Mixing Department			
		Percentage Complete	
	Physical Units	Direct Materials	Conversion Costs
Work in process, June 1	100,000	100%	70%
Started into production	800,000		
Total units to be accounted for	900,000		
Units completed and transferred out	700,000		
Work in process, June 30	200,000	100%	60%
Total units accounted for	900,000		

ILLUSTRATION 3.9 | Information for Mixing Department

Illustration 3.9 indicates that the beginning work in process is 100% complete as to materials cost and 70% complete as to conversion costs (see **Ethics Note**). **Conversion costs** are the sum of direct labor costs and manufacturing overhead costs. In other

ETHICS NOTE
An unethical manager might use incorrect completion percentages when determining equivalent units. This results in either raising or lowering costs. Since completion percentages are somewhat subjective, this form of income manipulation can be difficult to detect.

words, Kellogg adds both the dry and liquid ingredients (materials) at the beginning of the waffle-making process, and the conversion costs (labor and overhead) related to the mixing of these ingredients are incurred uniformly and are 70% complete. The ending work in process is 100% complete as to materials cost and 60% complete as to conversion costs.

We then use the Mixing Department information to determine equivalent units.

- **In computing equivalent units, the beginning work in process is not part of the equivalent units of production calculation.**
- The units transferred out to the Baking Department are fully complete as to both materials and conversion costs. The ending work in process is fully complete as to materials but only 60% complete as to conversion costs.
- We therefore need to make **two equivalent units computations**: one for direct materials and the other for conversion costs.

Illustration 3.10 shows these computations.

Mixing Department		
	Equivalent Units	
	Materials	Conversion Costs
Units completed and transferred out	700,000	700,000
Work in process, June 30		
200,000 × 100%	200,000	
200,000 × 60%		120,000
Total equivalent units	900,000	820,000

ILLUSTRATION 3.10 | Computation of equivalent units—Mixing Department

We can refine the earlier equation used to compute equivalent units of production (Illustration 3.8) to show the computations for materials and for conversion costs, as shown in **Illustration 3.11**.

Units Completed and Transferred Out— Materials	+	Equivalent Units of Ending Work in Process—Materials	=	Equivalent Units of Production— Materials
Units Completed and Transferred Out— Conversion Costs	+	Equivalent Units of Ending Work in Process—Conversion Costs	=	Equivalent Units of Production— Conversion Costs

ILLUSTRATION 3.11 | Refined equivalent units of production calculation

PEOPLE, PLANET, AND PROFIT INSIGHT — General Electric

Haven't I Seen That Before?

© Nicole Hofmann/ iStockphoto

For a variety of reasons, many companies, including **General Electric** (USA), are making a big push to remanufacture goods that have been thrown away. Items getting a second chance include cell phones, computers, home appliances, car parts, vacuum cleaners, and medical equipment. Businesses have figured out that profit margins on remanufactured goods are significantly higher than on new goods.

As prices of commodities such as copper and steel increase, reusing parts makes more sense. Also, as more local governments initiate laws requiring that electronics and appliances be recycled rather than thrown away, the cost of remanufacturing declines because the gathering of used goods becomes far more efficient.

Besides benefitting the manufacturer, remanufacturing provides goods at a much lower price to consumers, reduces waste going to landfills, saves energy, reuses scarce resources, and reduces emissions. For example, it was estimated that a remanufactured car starter results in about 50% less carbon dioxide emissions than making a new one.

Source: James R. Hagerty and Paul Glader, "From Trash Heap to Store Shelf," *Wall Street Journal Online* (January 24, 2011).

In what ways might the relative composition (direct materials, direct labor, and manufacturing overhead) of a remanufactured product's cost differ from that of a newly made product? (Answer is available in the book's product page on www.wiley.com)

DO IT! 3 ▶ Equivalent Units of Production

The Fabricating Department for Outdoor Essentials has the following production and cost data for the current month.

Beginning Work in Process	Units Completed and Transferred Out	Ending Work in Process
–0–	15,000	10,000

All direct materials are entered at the beginning of the process. The ending work in process units are 30% complete as to conversion costs. Compute the equivalent units of production for (a) materials and (b) conversion costs.

ACTION PLAN
- To measure the work done during the period, expressed in fully completed units, compute equivalent units of production.
- Use the appropriate equation: Units completed and transferred out + Equivalent units of ending work in process = Equivalent units of production.

Solution

a. Since direct materials are entered at the beginning of the process, ending work in process equals 10,000 equivalent units. Thus, 15,000 completed units + 10,000 equivalent units = 25,000 equivalent units of production for materials.

b. Since ending work in process is only 30% complete as to conversion costs, ending work in process equals 3,000 equivalent units (10,000 units × 30%). Thus, 15,000 completed units + 3,000 equivalent units = 18,000 equivalent units of production for conversion costs.

Related exercise material: **BE3.4, BE3.5, DO IT! 3.3, E3.5, E3.6, E3.8, E3.9, E3.10, E3.11, E3.13, E3.14, and E3.15.**

THE PRODUCTION COST REPORT

LEARNING OBJECTIVE 4
Complete the four steps to prepare a production cost report.

As mentioned earlier, companies using a process cost system prepare a production cost report for each department.

- A **production cost report** is the key document that management uses to understand the activities in a department.
- It shows the production quantity and cost data related to that department using process costing.

For example, in producing Eggo® Waffles, **Kellogg Company** uses three production cost reports: Mixing, Baking, and Freezing/Packaging. **Illustration 3.12** shows the flow of costs to make an Eggo® Waffle and the related production cost reports for each department.

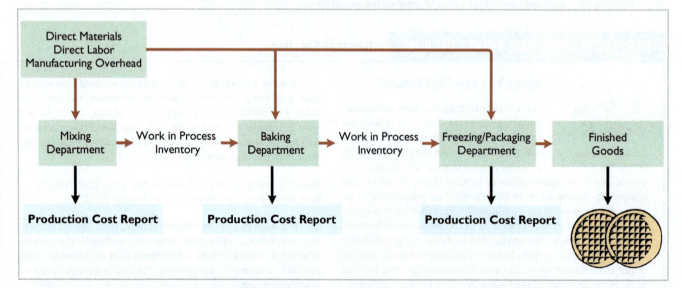

ILLUSTRATION 3.12 | Flow of costs in making Eggo® Waffles

In order to complete a production cost report, the company must perform four steps, which as a whole make up the process cost system.

1. Compute the physical unit flow.
2. Compute the equivalent units of production.
3. Compute unit production costs.
4. Prepare a cost reconciliation schedule.

Illustration 3.13 shows assumed data for the Mixing Department at **Kellogg Company** for the month of June. We will use this information to complete a production cost report for the Mixing Department.

Mixing Department	
Physical Units	
Work in process, June 1	100,000
Direct materials: 100% complete	
Conversion costs: 70% complete	
Units started into production during June	800,000
Units completed and transferred out to Baking Department	700,000
Work in process, June 30	200,000
Direct materials: 100% complete	
Conversion costs: 60% complete	
Costs	
Work in process, June 1	
Direct materials: 100% complete	$ 50,000
Conversion costs: 70% complete	35,000
Cost of work in process, June 1	$ 85,000
Costs incurred during production in June	
Direct materials	$400,000
Conversion costs	170,000
Costs incurred in June	$570,000

ILLUSTRATION 3.13 | **Unit and cost data—Mixing Department**

Compute the Physical Unit Flow (Step 1)

Physical units are the actual units to be accounted for during a period, irrespective of their state of completion. To keep track of these units, add the units started into production during the period to the units in process at the beginning of the period. This amount is referred to as the **total units to be accounted for**.

- The total units then are accounted for by the output of the period.
- The output consists of units completed and transferred out during the period and any units in process at the end of the period.
- This amount is referred to as the **total units accounted for**.

Illustration 3.14 shows the flow of physical units for Kellogg's Mixing Department for the month of June.

Mixing Department	
	Physical Units
Units to be accounted for	
Work in process, June 1	100,000
Started into production	800,000
Total units to be accounted for	**900,000**
Units accounted for	
Completed and transferred out	700,000
Work in process, June 30	200,000
Total units accounted for	**900,000**

ILLUSTRATION 3.14 | **Physical unit flow—Mixing Department**

The records indicate that the Mixing Department must account for 900,000 physical units. Of this sum, 700,000 units were completed and transferred to the Baking Department, and 200,000 units were still in process.

Compute the Equivalent Units of Production (Step 2)

Once the physical flow of the units is established, Kellogg must measure the Mixing Department's output in terms of equivalent units of production. The Mixing Department adds all direct materials at the beginning of the process, and it incurs conversion costs uniformly throughout the process (see **Helpful Hint**). Thus, we need two computations of equivalent units of production: one for materials and one for conversion costs. These computations are shown in **Illustration 3.15**. Recall that these computations ignore beginning work in process.

> **HELPFUL HINT**
> Materials are not always added at the beginning of the process. For example, materials are sometimes added uniformly during the process.

	Equivalent Units	
	Materials	Conversion Costs
Units completed and transferred out	700,000	700,000
Work in process, June 30		
200,000 × 100%	200,000	
200,000 × 60%		120,000
Total equivalent units	**900,000**	**820,000**

ILLUSTRATION 3.15 | Computation of equivalent units—Mixing Department

Compute Unit Production Costs (Step 3)

Armed with the knowledge of the equivalent units of production, we can now compute the unit production costs.

- **Unit production costs** are costs expressed in terms of equivalent units of production.
- When equivalent units of production are different for direct materials and conversion costs, we compute three unit costs: (1) materials, (2) conversion, and (3) total manufacturing.

The computation of total materials cost related to Eggo® Waffles is shown in **Illustration 3.16**.

Work in process, June 1	
Direct materials cost	$ 50,000
Costs added to production during June	
Direct materials cost	400,000
Total materials cost	**$450,000**

ILLUSTRATION 3.16 | Total materials cost computation

Illustration 3.17 shows the computation of unit materials cost.

Total Materials Cost	÷	Equivalent Units of Materials	=	Unit Materials Cost
$450,000	÷	900,000	=	$0.50

ILLUSTRATION 3.17 | Unit materials cost computation

Illustration 3.18 shows the computation of total conversion costs for June.

Work in process, June 1	
Conversion costs	$ 35,000
Costs added to production during June	
Conversion costs	170,000
Total conversion costs	**$205,000**

ILLUSTRATION 3.18 | Total conversion costs computation

The computation of unit conversion cost is shown in **Illustration 3.19**.

Total Conversion Costs	÷	Equivalent Units of Conversion Costs	=	Unit Conversion Cost
$205,000	÷	820,000	=	$0.25

ILLUSTRATION 3.19 | Unit conversion cost computation

Total manufacturing cost per unit is therefore computed as shown in **Illustration 3.20**.

Unit Materials Cost	+	Unit Conversion Cost	=	Total Manufacturing Cost per Unit
$0.50	+	$0.25	=	$0.75

ILLUSTRATION 3.20 | Total manufacturing cost per unit

Prepare a Cost Reconciliation Schedule (Step 4)

We are now ready to determine the cost of goods completed and transferred out of the Mixing Department to the Baking Department and the costs that remain in ending work in process inventory for the Mixing Department. Kellogg charged total costs of $655,000 to the Mixing Department in June, calculated as shown in **Illustration 3.21**.

Costs to be accounted for	
Work in process, June 1	$ 85,000
Started into production	570,000
Total costs to be accounted for	$655,000

ILLUSTRATION 3.21 | Costs charged to Mixing Department

The company then prepares a cost reconciliation schedule (see **Illustration 3.22**) to assign these costs to (a) units completed and transferred out to the Baking Department and (b) ending work in process.

Mixing Department
Cost Reconciliation Schedule

Costs accounted for			
Completed and transferred out (700,000 × $0.75)			$525,000
Work in process, June 30			
Materials (200,000 × $0.50)		$100,000	
Conversion costs (120,000 × $0.25)		30,000	130,000
Total costs accounted for			$655,000

ILLUSTRATION 3.22 | Cost reconciliation schedule—Mixing Department

Kellogg uses the total manufacturing cost per unit, $0.75, in costing the **units completed** and transferred to the Baking Department. In contrast, the unit materials cost and the unit conversion cost are needed in costing **units in process**. The **cost reconciliation schedule** shows that the **total costs accounted for** (Illustration 3.22) equal the **total costs to be accounted for** (Illustration 3.21).

Preparing the Production Cost Report

HELPFUL HINT

The four steps in preparing a production cost report:
1. Compute the physical unit flow.
2. Compute the equivalent units of production.
3. Compute unit production costs.
4. Prepare a cost reconciliation schedule.

DECISION TOOLS

A production cost report helps managers evaluate overall profitability by comparing costs to previous periods, competitors, and expected selling price.

At this point, Kellogg is ready to prepare the production cost report for the Mixing Department. As indicated earlier, this report is an internal document for management that shows production quantity and cost data for a production department. **Illustration 3.23** shows the completed production cost report for the Mixing Department and identifies the four steps used in preparing it (see **Helpful Hint**).

- Production cost reports provide a basis for evaluating the productivity of a department (see **Decision Tools**).
- In addition, managers can use the cost data to assess whether unit costs and total costs are reasonable.
- By comparing the quantity and cost data with predetermined goals, top management can also judge whether current performance is meeting planned objectives.

Mixing Department
Production Cost Report
For the Month Ended June 30, 2023

	Physical Units	Equivalent Units — Materials	Equivalent Units — Conversion Costs	
Quantities				
Units to be accounted for	Step 1	Step 2		
Work in process, June 1	100,000			
Started into production	800,000			
Total units to be accounted for	900,000			
Units accounted for				
Completed and transferred out	700,000	700,000	700,000	
Work in process, June 30	200,000	200,000	120,000	(200,000 × 60%)
Total units accounted for	900,000	900,000	820,000	

Costs		Materials	Conversion Costs	Total
Unit costs Step 3				
Total cost	(a)	$450,000	$205,000	$655,000
Equivalent units	(b)	900,000	820,000	
Unit costs [(a) ÷ (b)]		$0.50	$0.25	$0.75

Cost Reconciliation Schedule Step 4			
Costs to be accounted for			
Work in process, June 1			$ 85,000
Started into production			570,000
Total costs to be accounted for			$655,000
Costs accounted for			
Completed and transferred out (700,000 × $0.75)			$525,000
Work in process, June 30			
Materials (200,000 × $0.50)		$100,000	
Conversion costs (120,000 × $0.25)		30,000	130,000
Total costs accounted for			$655,000

ILLUSTRATION 3.23 | **Production cost report**

Costing Systems—Final Comments

Companies often use a combination of a process cost and a job order cost system.

- Called **operations costing**, this hybrid system is similar to process costing in its assumption that standardized methods are used to manufacture the product.
- At the same time, the product may have some customized, individual features that require the use of a job order cost system.

Consider, for example, **Hyundai Mobis** (KOR). Each vehicle at a given factory goes through the same assembly line, but Hyundai uses different materials (such as seat coverings, paint, and tinted glass) for different vehicles. Similarly, **Kellogg**'s (USA) Pop-Tarts® toaster pastries go through numerous standardized processes—mixing, filling, baking, frosting, and packaging. The pastry dough, though, comes in different flavors—plain, chocolate, and graham—and fillings include Smucker's® real fruit, chocolate fudge, vanilla creme, brown sugar cinnamon, and s'mores.

A cost-benefit trade-off occurs as a company decides which costing system to use (see **Decision Tools**). A job order cost system, for example, provides detailed information related to the cost of the product.

- Because each job has its own distinguishing characteristics, the system can provide an accurate cost per job.
- This information is useful in controlling costs and pricing products.
- However, the cost of implementing a job order cost system is often expensive because of the accounting costs involved.

On the other hand, for a company like **Intel** (USA), is there a benefit in knowing whether the cost of the one-hundredth computer chip produced is different from the one-thousandth chip produced? Probably not. An average cost of the product will suffice for control and pricing purposes.

In summary, when deciding to use one of these systems or a combination system, a company must weigh the costs of implementing the system against the benefits from the additional information provided.

> **DECISION TOOLS**
>
> A cost-benefit trade-off helps managers determine which costing system to use.

DO IT! 4 ▶ Cost Reconciliation Schedule

In March, Kelly Manufacturing had the following unit production costs in its Assembly Department: materials €6 and conversion costs €9. On March 1, it had no work in process. During March, the Assembly Department completed and transferred out 12,000 units. As of March 31, 800 units that were 25% complete as to conversion costs and 100% complete as to materials were in ending work in process in the Assembly Department. Assign the costs to the units completed and transferred out and to work in process at the end of the month.

Solution

The assignment of costs is as follows:

Costs accounted for			
Completed and transferred out (12,000 × €15)			€180,000
Work in process, March 31			
Materials (800 × €6)		€4,800	
Conversion costs (200* × €9)		1,800	6,600
Total costs accounted for			€186,600

*800 × 25%

Related exercise material: **BE3.6, BE3.7, BE3.8, BE3.9, DO IT! 3.4, E3.3, E3.5, E3.6, E3.7, E3.8, E3.9, E3.10, E3.11, E3.13, E3.14, and E3.15.**

> **ACTION PLAN**
>
> - Assign the total manufacturing cost of €15 per unit to the 12,000 units completed and transferred out.
> - Assign the materials cost and conversion costs based on equivalent units of production to units in ending work in process.

USING THE DECISION TOOLS | Back o' Bourke

Back o' Bourke Cordials Pty Ltd (AUS) faces many situations where it needs to apply the decision tools learned in this chapter, such as using a production cost report to evaluate profitability. For example, suppose Back o' Bourke manufactures a high-end organic fruit soda, called Eternity, in one-liter plastic bottles. Because the market for beverages is highly competitive, the company is very concerned about keeping its costs under control. Eternity is manufactured through three processes: blending, filling, and labeling. Materials are added at the beginning of the process, and labor and overhead are incurred uniformly throughout each process. The company uses a weighted-average method to cost its product. A partially completed production cost report for cases of Eternity soda for the month of May for the Blending Department is shown below.

Back o' Bourke
Blending Department
Production Cost Report
For the Month Ended May 31, 2023

		Physical Units	Equivalent Units — Materials	Equivalent Units — Conversion Costs
Quantities		**Step 1**	**Step 2**	
Units to be accounted for				
Work in process, May 1		1,000		
Started into production		2,000		
Total units		3,000		
Units accounted for				
Transferred out		2,200	?	?
Work in process, May 31		800	?	?
Total units		3,000	?	?

Costs		Materials	Conversion Costs	Total
Unit costs **Step 3**				
Total cost	(a)	?	?	?
Equivalent units	(b)	?	?	
Unit costs [(a) ÷ (b)]		?	?	?
Costs to be accounted for				
Work in process, May 1				A$ 56,300
Started into production				119,320
Total costs				A$175,620
Cost Reconciliation Schedule **Step 4**				
Costs accounted for				
Transferred out				?
Work in process, May 31				
Materials			?	
Conversion costs			?	?
Total costs				?

Additional information:
  Work in process, May 1, 1000 units
    Materials cost, 1,000 units (100% complete)   A$49,100
    Conversion costs, 1,000 units (70% complete)   7,200   A$ 56,300
  Materials cost for May, 2,000 units   A$100,000
  Work in process, May 31, 800 units, 100% complete as to materials and 50% complete as to conversion costs

Instructions

a. Prepare a production cost report for the Blending Department for the month of May.
b. Prepare the journal entry to record the transfer of goods from the Blending Department to the Filling Department.
c. Explain why Back o' Bourke is using a process cost system to account for its costs.

Solution

a. A completed production cost report for the Blending Department is shown below. Computations to support the amounts reported follow the report.

Back o' Bourke
Blending Department
Production Cost Report
For the Month Ended May 31, 2023

		Physical Units	Equivalent Units — Materials	Equivalent Units — Conversion Costs
Quantities		Step 1		Step 2
Units to be accounted for				
Work in process, May 1		1,000		
Started into production		2,000		
Total units		3,000		
Units accounted for				
Transferred out		2,200	2,200	2,200
Work in process, May 31		800	800	400 (800 × 50%)
Total units		3,000	3,000	2,600

Costs

		Materials	Conversion Costs	Total
Unit costs Step 3				
Total cost	(a)	A$149,100*	A$26,520**	A$175,620
Equivalent units	(b)	3,000	2,600	
Unit costs [(a) ÷ (b)]		A$49.70	A$10.20	A$59.90
Costs to be accounted for				
Work in process, May 1				A$ 56,300
Started into production				119,320
Total costs				A$175,620

*Materials cost—A$49,100 + A$100,000
**Conversion costs—A$7,200 + A$19,320 (A$119,320 − A$100,000)

Cost Reconciliation Schedule Step 4

Costs accounted for		
Transferred out (2,200 × A$59.90)		A$131,780
Work in process, May 31		
Materials (800 × A$49.70)	A$39,760	
Conversion costs (400 × A$10.20)	4,080	43,840
Total costs		A$175,620

b.
Work in Process—Filling	131,780	
Work in Process—Blending		131,780

c. Companies use process cost systems to apply costs to similar products that are mass-produced in a continuous fashion. Back o' Bourke uses a process cost system because production of the fruit soda, once it begins, continues until the soda emerges. The processing is the same for the entire run—with precisely the same amount of materials, labor, and overhead. Each bottle of Eternity soda is indistinguishable from another.

Appendix 3A | FIFO METHOD FOR EQUIVALENT UNITS

LEARNING OBJECTIVE *5
Compute equivalent units using the FIFO method.

In this chapter, we demonstrated the weighted-average method of computing equivalent units. Some companies use a different method, referred to as the **first-in, first-out (FIFO) method**, to compute equivalent units. The purpose of this appendix is to illustrate how companies use the FIFO method to prepare a production cost report.

Equivalent Units Under FIFO

Under the FIFO method, companies compute equivalent units on a first-in, first-out basis. Some companies favor the FIFO method because the FIFO cost assumption usually corresponds to the actual physical flow of the goods. Under the FIFO method, companies therefore assume that the beginning work in process is completed before new work is started.

Using the FIFO method, equivalent units are the sum of the work performed to:

1. Finish the units of beginning work in process inventory.
2. Complete the units started into production during the period (referred to as the **units started and completed**).
3. Start, but only partially complete, the units in ending work in process inventory.

Normally, in a process cost system, some units will always be in process at both the beginning and the end of the period.

Illustration

Illustration 3A.1 shows the physical flow of units for the Assembly Department of Closets Inc. In addition, it indicates the degree of completion of the work in process inventory accounts in regard to conversion costs.

Assembly Department	
	Physical Units
Units to be accounted for	
Work in process, June 1 (40% complete)	500
Started into production	8,000
Total units to be accounted for	**8,500**
Units accounted for	
Completed and transferred out	8,100
Work in process, June 30 (75% complete)	400
Total units accounted for	**8,500**

ILLUSTRATION 3A.1 | **Physical unit flow—Assembly Department**

In Illustration 3A.1, the units completed and transferred out (8,100) plus the units in ending work in process (400) equal the total units to be accounted for (8,500). Using FIFO, we then compute equivalent units of production for conversion costs for the Assembly Department as follows:

1. The 500 units of beginning work in process were 40% complete. Thus, 300 equivalent units (500 units × 60%) were required to complete the beginning inventory that was completed and transferred out.
2. The units started and completed during the current month are **the units transferred out minus the units in beginning work in process**. For the Assembly Department, units started and completed are 7,600 (8,100 − 500). These 7,600 physical units equate to 7,600 equivalent units.
3. The 400 units of ending work in process were 75% complete. Thus, equivalent units were 300 (400 × 75%).

Equivalent units for conversion costs for the Assembly Department are 8,200, computed as shown in **Illustration 3A.2**.

Assembly Department

Production Data	Work Added Physical Units	Equivalent This Period	Units
Work in process, June 1	500	60%	300
Started and completed	7,600	100%	7,600
Work in process, June 30	400	75%	300
Total	8,500		8,200

ILLUSTRATION 3A.2 | **Computation of equivalent units—FIFO method**

Comprehensive Example

To provide a complete illustration of the FIFO method, we will use the data for the Mixing Department at **Kellogg Company** for the month of June, as shown in **Illustration 3A.3**.

Mixing Department

Physical Units

Work in process, June 1	100,000
Direct materials: 100% complete	
Conversion costs: 70% complete	
Units started into production during June	800,000
Units completed and transferred out to Baking Department	700,000
Work in process, June 30	200,000
Direct materials: 100% complete	
Conversion costs: 60% complete	

Costs

Work in process, June 1	
Direct materials: 100% complete	$ 50,000
Conversion costs: 70% complete	35,000
Cost of work in process, June 1	$ 85,000
Costs incurred during production in June	
Direct materials	$400,000
Conversion costs	170,000
Costs incurred in June	$570,000

ILLUSTRATION 3A.3 | **Unit and cost data—Mixing Department**

Compute the Physical Unit Flow (Step 1)

Illustration 3A.4 shows the physical flow of units for Kellogg's Mixing Department for the month of June.

Mixing Department

	Physical Units
Units to be accounted for	
Work in process, June 1	100,000
Started into production	800,000
Total units to be accounted for	900,000
Units accounted for	
Completed and transferred out	700,000
Work in process, June 30	200,000
Total units accounted for	900,000

ILLUSTRATION 3A.4 | **Physical unit flow—Mixing Department**

Under the FIFO method, companies often expand the physical units schedule, as shown in **Illustration 3A.5**, to explain the completed and transferred-out section.

- As a result, this section reports the beginning work in process and the units started and completed.
- These two items further explain the completed and transferred-out section.

Mixing Department	
	Physical Units
Units to be accounted for	
Work in process, June 1	100,000
Started into production	800,000
Total units to be accounted for	**900,000**
Units accounted for	
Completed and transferred out	
Work in process, June 1	**100,000**
Started and completed	**600,000**
	700,000
Work in process, June 30	200,000
Total units accounted for	**900,000**

ILLUSTRATION 3A.5 | Physical unit flow (FIFO)—Mixing Department

The records indicate that the Mixing Department must account for 900,000 units. Of this sum, 700,000 units were completed and transferred to the Baking Department and 200,000 units were still in process.

Compute Equivalent Units of Production (Step 2)

As with the method presented in the chapter, once they determine the physical flow of the units, companies need to determine equivalent units of production. The Mixing Department adds materials at the beginning of the process, and it incurs conversion costs uniformly throughout the process (see **Helpful Hint**). Thus, Kellogg must make two computations of equivalent units: one for materials and one for conversion costs.

HELPFUL HINT
As noted earlier, materials are not always added at the beginning of the process. For example, companies sometimes add materials uniformly during the process.

Equivalent Units for Materials Since Kellogg adds materials at the beginning of the process, no additional materials costs are required to complete the beginning work in process. In addition, 100% of the materials costs has been incurred on the ending work in process. **Illustration 3A.6** shows the computation of equivalent units for materials.

Mixing Department—Materials			
Production Data	**Physical Units**	**Direct Materials Added This Period**	**Equivalent Units**
Work in process, June 1	100,000	–0–	–0–
Started and completed	600,000	100%	600,000
Work in process, June 30	200,000	100%	200,000
Total	900,000		800,000

ILLUSTRATION 3A.6 | Computation of equivalent units—materials

Equivalent Units for Conversion Costs The 100,000 units of beginning work in process were 70% complete in terms of conversion costs. Thus, the Mixing Department required 30,000 equivalent units [(100,000 units × (100% − 70%)] of conversion costs to complete the beginning inventory. In addition, the 200,000 units of ending work in process were 60% complete in terms of conversion costs. Thus, the equivalent units for conversion costs is 750,000, computed as shown in **Illustration 3A.7**.

Mixing Department—Conversion Costs			
Production Data	Physical Units	Work Added This Period	Equivalent Units
Work in process, June 1	100,000	30%	30,000
Started and completed	600,000	100%	600,000
Work in process, June 30	200,000	60%	120,000
Total	900,000		750,000

ILLUSTRATION 3A.7 | Computation of equivalent units—conversion costs

Compute Unit Production Costs (Step 3)

Armed with the knowledge of the equivalent units of production, Kellogg can now compute the unit production costs.

- Unit production costs are costs expressed in terms of equivalent units of production.
- When equivalent units of production are different for materials and conversion costs, companies compute three unit costs: (1) materials, (2) conversion, and (3) total manufacturing.

Under the FIFO method, the unit costs of production are based entirely on the production costs incurred during the month. Thus, the costs in the beginning work in process are not relevant because they were incurred on work done in the preceding month. As Illustration 3A.3 indicated, the costs incurred during production in June were as shown in **Illustration 3A.8**.

Direct materials	$400,000
Conversion costs	170,000
Total costs incurred during June	$570,000

ILLUSTRATION 3A.8 | Costs incurred during production in June

Illustration 3A.9 shows the computation of unit materials cost, unit conversion costs, and total unit cost related to Eggo® Waffles.

(1)	Total Materials Cost	÷	Equivalent Units of Materials	=	Unit Materials Cost
	$400,000	÷	800,000	=	$0.50
(2)	Total Conversion Costs	÷	Equivalent Units of Conversion Costs	=	Unit Conversion Cost
	$170,000	÷	750,000	=	$0.227 (rounded)*
(3)	Unit Materials Cost	+	Unit Conversion Cost	=	Total Manufacturing Cost per Unit
	$0.50	+	$0.227	=	$0.727

*For homework problems, round unit costs to three decimal places.

ILLUSTRATION 3A.9 | Unit cost computations—Mixing Department

As shown, the unit costs are $0.50 for materials, $0.227 for conversion costs, and $0.727 for total manufacturing costs.

Prepare a Cost Reconciliation Schedule (Step 4)

Kellogg is now ready to determine the cost of goods transferred out of the Mixing Department to the Baking Department and the costs in ending work in process. The total costs charged to the Mixing Department in June are $655,000, calculated as shown in **Illustration 3A.10** (see Illustration 3A.3 for further detail).

Costs to be accounted for	
Work in process, June 1	$ 85,000
Started into production	570,000
Total costs to be accounted for	$655,000

ILLUSTRATION 3A.10 | **Costs charged to Mixing Department**

Kellogg next prepares a cost reconciliation schedule to assign these costs to (1) units completed and transferred out to the Baking Department and (2) ending work in process. Under the FIFO method, the first goods to be completed during the period are the units in beginning work in process.

- Thus, the cost of the beginning work in process is always assigned to the goods transferred to the next department (or finished goods, if processing is complete).
- Under the FIFO method, ending work in process also will be assigned only the production costs incurred in the current period.

Illustration 3A.11 shows a cost reconciliation schedule for the Mixing Department.

Mixing Department
Cost Reconciliation Schedule

Costs accounted for		
Completed and transferred out		
Work in process, June 1		$ 85,000
Costs to complete beginning work in process		
Conversion costs (30,000 × $0.227)		6,810
Total costs		91,810
Units started and completed (600,000 × $0.727)*		435,950**
Total costs completed and transferred out		527,760
Work in process, June 30		
Materials (200,000 × $0.50)	$100,000	
Conversion costs (120,000 × $0.227)	27,240	127,240
Total costs accounted for		**$655,000**

*Any rounding errors should be adjusted in the "Units started and completed" calculation.
**Minus $250 rounding difference.

ILLUSTRATION 3A.11 | **Cost reconciliation report**

As you can see, the total costs accounted for ($655,000 from Illustration 3A.11) equal the total costs to be accounted for ($655,000 from Illustration 3A.10).

Preparing the Production Cost Report

At this point, Kellogg is ready to prepare the production cost report for the Mixing Department. This report is an internal document for management that shows production quantity and cost data for a production department.

As discussed previously, there are four steps in preparing a production cost report:

1. Compute the physical unit flow.
2. Compute the equivalent units of production.
3. Compute unit production costs.
4. Prepare a cost reconciliation schedule.

Illustration 3A.12 shows the production cost report for the Mixing Department, with the four steps identified in the report.

As indicated in the chapter, production cost reports provide a basis for evaluating the productivity of a department (see **Helpful Hint**). In addition, managers can use the cost data

HELPFUL HINT
The two self-checks in the report are (1) total physical units accounted for must equal the total units to be accounted for, and (2) total costs accounted for must equal the total costs to be accounted for.

to assess whether unit costs and total costs are reasonable. By comparing the quantity and cost data with predetermined goals, top management can also judge whether current performance is meeting planned objectives.

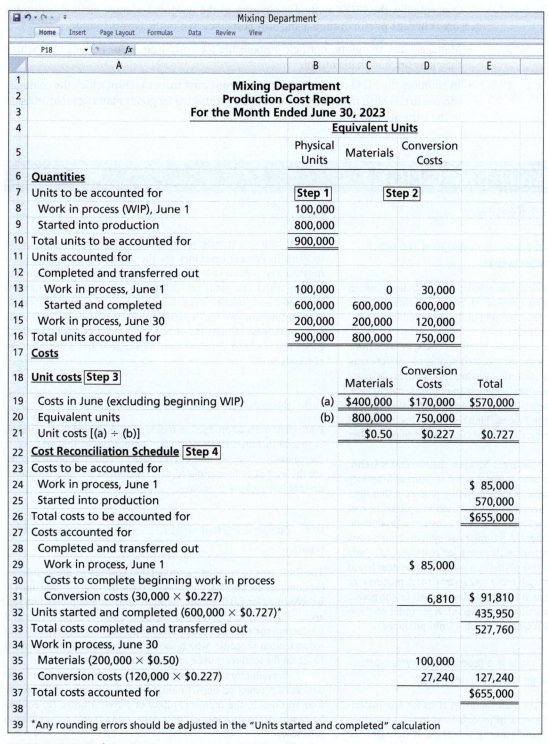

ILLUSTRATION 3A.12 | Production cost report—FIFO method

FIFO and Weighted-Average

The weighted-average method of computing equivalent units has **one major advantage**: It is simple to understand and apply.

- In cases where prices do not fluctuate significantly from period to period, the weighted-average method will be very similar to the FIFO method.

- In addition, companies that have been using just-in-time procedures effectively for inventory control purposes will have minimal inventory balances. In this case, differences between the weighted-average and the FIFO methods will not be material.

Conceptually, the FIFO method is superior to the weighted-average method because it measures **current performance** using only costs incurred in the current period.

- Managers are, therefore, not held responsible for costs from prior periods over which they may not have had control.
- In addition, the FIFO method **provides current cost information**, which the company can use to establish **more accurate pricing strategies** for goods manufactured and sold in the current period.

REVIEW AND PRACTICE

Learning Objectives Review

LO 1 Discuss the uses of a process cost system and how it compares to a job order cost system.

Companies that mass-produce similar products in a continuous fashion use process cost systems. Once production begins, it continues until the finished product emerges. Each unit of finished product is indistinguishable from every other unit.

Job order cost systems are similar to process cost systems in three ways. (1) Both systems track the same cost components—direct materials, direct labor, and manufacturing overhead. (2) Both accumulate costs in the same accounts—Raw Materials Inventory, Factory Labor, and Manufacturing Overhead. (3) Both assign accumulated costs to the same accounts—Work in Process, Finished Goods Inventory, and Cost of Goods Sold. However, the methods used to assign costs differ significantly.

There are four main differences between the two cost systems: (1) A process cost system uses separate work in process inventory accounts for each department or manufacturing process, rather than only one work in process inventory account used in a job order cost system. (2) A process cost system summarizes costs in a production cost report for each department. A job order cost system charges costs to individual jobs and summarizes them in a job cost sheet. (3) Costs are totaled at the end of a time period in a process cost system but at the completion of a job in a job order cost system. (4) A process cost system calculates unit cost as Total manufacturing costs for the period ÷ Equivalent units of production for the period. A job order cost system calculates unit cost as Total cost per job ÷ Units produced.

LO 2 Explain the flow of costs in a process cost system and the journal entries to assign manufacturing costs.

A process cost system assigns manufacturing costs for raw materials, labor, and overhead to work in process inventory accounts for various departments or manufacturing processes. It transfers the costs of partially completed units from one department to another as those units move through the manufacturing process. The system transfers the costs of completed work to Finished Goods Inventory. Finally, when inventory is sold, the system transfers the costs to Cost of Goods Sold.

Entries to assign the costs of direct materials, direct labor, and manufacturing overhead consist of credits to Raw Materials Inventory, Factory Labor, and Manufacturing Overhead, and debits to Work in Process Inventory for each department. Entries to record the cost of goods transferred to another department are a credit to Work in Process Inventory for the department whose work is finished and a debit to Work in Process Inventory for the department to which the goods are transferred. The entry to record units completed and transferred to the warehouse is a credit to Work in Process Inventory for the department whose work is finished and a debit to Finished Goods Inventory. The entry to record the sale of goods is a credit to Finished Goods Inventory and a debit to Cost of Goods Sold.

LO 3 Compute equivalent units of production.

Equivalent units of production measure work done during a period, expressed in fully completed units. Companies use this measure to determine the cost per unit of completed product. Equivalent units are the sum of units completed and transferred out plus equivalent units of ending work in process.

LO 4 Complete the four steps to prepare a production cost report.

The four steps to complete a production cost report are as follows: (1) Compute the physical unit flow—that is, the total physical units to be accounted for. (2) Compute the equivalent units of production separately for direct materials and conversion costs. (3) Compute the unit production costs per equivalent units of production. (4) Prepare a cost reconciliation schedule, which shows that the total costs accounted for equal the total costs to be accounted for.

The production cost report contains both quantity and cost data for a production department over a specific period. There are four sections in the report: (1) flow of physical units, (2) equivalent units determination, (3) unit costs, and (4) cost reconciliation schedule.

LO *5 Compute equivalent units using the FIFO method.

Equivalent units under the FIFO method are the sum of the work performed to (1) finish the units of beginning work in process inventory, if any; (2) complete some of the units started into production during the period; and (3) start, but only partially complete, the units in ending work in process inventory.

Decision Tools Review

Decision Checkpoints	Info Needed for Decision	Tool to Use for Decision	How to Evaluate Results
What is the cost of a product?	Cost of materials, labor, and overhead assigned to processes used to make the product	Production cost report	Compare costs to previous periods, to competitors, and to expected selling price to evaluate overall profitability.
What costing method should be used?	Type of good produced or service performed	Cost of accounting system; benefits of additional information	The benefits of providing the additional information should exceed the costs of the accounting system needed to develop the information.

Glossary Review

Conversion costs The sum of direct labor costs and manufacturing overhead costs. (p. 3-10)

Cost reconciliation schedule A schedule that shows that the total costs accounted for equal the total costs to be accounted for. (p. 3-15)

Equivalent units of production A measure of the work done during the period, expressed in fully completed units. (p. 3-10)

Operations costing A combination of a process cost and a job order cost system in which products are manufactured primarily by standardized methods, with some customization. (p. 3-17)

Physical units Actual units to be accounted for during a period, irrespective of their state of completion. (p. 3-13)

Process cost system An accounting system used to assign costs to similar products that are mass-produced in a continuous fashion. (p. 3-3)

Production cost report An internal report for management that shows both production quantity and cost data for a production department using process costing. (p. 3-12)

Total units accounted for The sum of the units completed and transferred out during the period plus the units in process at the end of the period. (p. 3-13)

Total units to be accounted for The sum of the units started into production during the period plus the units in process at the beginning of the period. (p. 3-13)

Unit production costs Costs expressed in terms of equivalent units of production. (p. 3-14)

Weighted-average method Method of computing equivalent units of production that considers the degree of completion (weighting) of the units completed and transferred out and the ending work in process. (p. 3-10)

Practice Multiple-Choice Questions

1. (LO 1) Which of the following items is **not** characteristic of a process cost system?
 a. Once production begins, it continues until the finished product emerges.
 b. The products produced are heterogeneous in nature.
 c. The focus is on continually producing homogeneous products.
 d. When the finished product emerges, all units have precisely the same amount of materials, labor, and overhead.

2. (LO 1) Indicate which of the following statements is **not** correct.
 a. Both a job order and a process cost system track the same three manufacturing cost components—direct materials, direct labor, and manufacturing overhead.
 b. A job order cost system uses only one work in process inventory account, whereas a process cost system uses multiple work in process inventory accounts.
 c. Manufacturing costs are accumulated the same way in a job order and in a process cost system.
 d. Manufacturing costs are assigned the same way in a job order and in a process cost system.

3. (LO 2) In a process cost system, the flow of costs is:
 a. work in process, cost of goods sold, finished goods.
 b. finished goods, work in process, cost of goods sold.
 c. finished goods, cost of goods sold, work in process.
 d. work in process, finished goods, cost of goods sold.

4. (LO 2) In making journal entries to assign direct materials costs, a company using process costing:
 a. debits Finished Goods Inventory.
 b. often debits two or more work in process inventory accounts.
 c. generally credits two or more work in process inventory accounts.
 d. credits Finished Goods Inventory.

5. (LO 2) In a process cost system, manufacturing overhead:
 a. is assigned to finished goods at the end of each accounting period.
 b. is assigned to a work in process inventory account for each job as the job is completed.
 c. is assigned to a work in process inventory account for each production department on the basis of a predetermined overhead rate.
 d. is assigned to a work in process inventory account for each production department as overhead costs are incurred.

6. (LO 3) Conversion costs are the sum of:
   a. fixed and variable overhead costs.
   b. direct labor costs and overhead costs.
   c. direct material costs and overhead costs.
   d. direct labor and indirect labor costs.

7. (LO 3) The Mixing Department's production efforts during the period resulted in 20,000 units completed and transferred out, and 5,000 units in ending work in process 60% complete as to materials and conversion costs. Beginning inventory is 1,000 units, 40% complete as to materials and conversion costs. The equivalent units of production for materials are:
   a. 22,600.
   b. 23,000.
   c. 24,000.
   d. 25,000.

8. (LO 3) In RYZ Company, there are zero units in beginning work in process, 7,000 units started into production, and 500 units in ending work in process 20% completed. The physical units to be accounted for are:
   a. 7,000.
   b. 7,360.
   c. 7,500.
   d. 7,340.

9. (LO 3) Kaya A.S. has 2,000 units in beginning work in process, 20% complete as to conversion costs, 23,000 units completed and transferred out to finished goods, and 3,000 units in ending work in process $33\frac{1}{3}$% complete as to conversion costs.

The beginning inventory and ending inventory are fully complete as to materials costs. Equivalent units for materials and conversion costs are, respectively:
   a. 22,000, 24,000.
   b. 24,000, 26,000.
   c. 26,000, 24,000.
   d. 26,000, 26,000.

10. (LO 4) Darcy Company has no beginning work in process; 9,000 units are completed and transferred out, and 3,000 units in ending work in process are one-third finished as to conversion costs and fully complete as to materials cost. If total materials cost is A$60,000, the unit materials cost is:
   a. A$5.00.
   b. A$5.45 (rounded).
   c. A$6.00.
   d. No correct answer is given.

11. (LO 4) Biarchi AG has unit costs of CHF10 for materials and CHF30 for conversion costs. If there are 2,500 units in ending work in process, 40% complete as to conversion costs and fully complete as to materials cost, the total cost assignable to the ending work in process inventory is:
   a. CHF45,000.
   b. CHF55,000.
   c. CHF75,000.
   d. CHF100,000.

12. (LO 4) A production cost report:
   a. is an external report.
   b. shows both the production quantity and cost data related to a department.
   c. shows equivalent units of production but not physical units.
   d. contains six sections.

13. (LO 4) In a production cost report, units to be accounted for are calculated as:
   a. Units started into production + Units in ending work in process.
   b. Units started into production − Units in beginning work in process.
   c. Units completed and transferred out + Units in beginning work in process.
   d. Units started into production + Units in beginning work in process.

*14. (LO 5) Ng Group uses the FIFO method to compute equivalent units. It has 2,000 units in beginning work in process, 20% complete as to conversion costs, 25,000 units started and completed, and 3,000 units in ending work in process, 30% complete as to conversion costs. All units are 100% complete as to materials. Equivalent units for materials and conversion costs are, respectively:
   a. 28,000 and 26,600.
   b. 28,000 and 27,500.
   c. 27,000 and 26,200.
   d. 27,000 and 29,600.

*15. (LO 5) KLM SpA uses the FIFO method to compute equivalent units. It has no beginning work in process; 9,000 units are started and completed and 3,000 units in ending work in process are one-third completed as to conversion costs. All material is added at the beginning of the process. If total materials cost is €60,000, the unit materials cost is:
   a. €5.00.
   b. €6.00.
   c. €6.67 (rounded).
   d. No correct answer is given.

*16. (LO 5) Wai Ltd. uses the FIFO method to compute equivalent units of production. It has unit costs of HK$100 for materials and HK$300 for conversion costs. If there are 2,500 units in ending work in process, 100% complete as to materials and 40% complete as to conversion costs, the total cost assignable to the ending work in process inventory is:
   a. HK$450,000
   b. HK$550,000
   c. HK$750,000
   d. HK$1,000,000

Solutions

1. b. The products produced are homogeneous, not heterogeneous, in nature. Choices (a), (c), and (d) are incorrect because they all represent characteristics of a process cost system.

2. d. Manufacturing costs are not assigned the same way in a job order and in a process cost system. Choices (a), (b), and (c) are true statements.

3. d. In a process cost system, the flow of costs is work in process, finished goods, cost of goods sold. Therefore, choices (a), (b), and (c) are incorrect.

4. b. The debit is often to two or more work in process inventory accounts, not (a) a debit to Finished Goods Inventory, (c) credits to two or more work in process inventory accounts, or (d) a credit to Finished Goods Inventory.

5. c. In a process cost system, manufacturing overhead is assigned to a work in process inventory account for each production department on the basis of a predetermined overhead rate, not (a) to a finished goods account, (b) as the job is completed, or (d) as overhead costs are incurred.

6. b. Conversion costs are the sum of labor costs and overhead costs, not the sum of (a) fixed and variable overhead costs, (c) direct material costs and overhead costs, or (d) direct labor and indirect labor costs.

7. b. For materials, the equivalent units of production is the sum of units completed and transferred out (20,000) and the equivalent units of ending work in process inventory (5,000 units × 60%), or 20,000 + 3,000 = 23,000 units, not (a) 22,600 units, (c) 24,000 units, or (d) 25,000 units.

8. a. There are 7,000 physical units to be accounted for (0 units in beginning inventory + 7,000 units started), not (b) 7,360, (c) 7,500, or (d) 7,340.

9. c. The equivalent units for materials are 26,000 (23,000 units completed and transferred out plus 3,000 in ending work in process inventory). The equivalent units for conversion costs are 24,000 (23,000 completed and transferred out plus $33\frac{1}{3}\%$ of the ending work in process inventory, or 1,000). Therefore, choices (a) 22,000, 24,000; (b) 24,000, 26,000; and (d) 26,000, 26,000 are incorrect.

10. a. A$60,000 ÷ (9,000 + 3,000 units) = A$5.00 per unit, not (b) A$5.45 (rounded), (c) A$6.00, or (d) no correct answer is given.

11. b. [(2,500 units × 100% complete) × CHF10] + [(2,500 units × 40% complete) × CHF30], or CHF25,000 + CHF30,000 = CHF55,000, not (a) CHF45,000, (c) CHF75,000, or (d) CHF100,000.

12. b. A production cost report shows the flow of units and costs assigned to a department and costs accounted for as well as the production quantity. The other choices are incorrect because a production cost report (a) is an internal, not external, report; (c) does show physical units; and (d) is prepared in four steps and does not contain six sections.

13. d. In a production cost report, units to be accounted for are calculated as Units started in production + Units in beginning work in process, not (a) Units in ending work in process, (b) minus Units in beginning work in process, or (c) Units completed and transferred out.

*14. b. The equivalent units for materials are 28,000 [25,000 started and completed + (3,000 × 100%)]. The equivalent units for conversion costs are 27,500 [(2,000 × 80%) + 25,000 + (3,000 × 30%)]. Therefore, choices (a) 28,000, 26,600; (c) 27,000, 26,200; and (d) 27,000, 29,600 are incorrect.

*15. a. Unit materials cost is €5.00 [€60,000 ÷ (9,000 + 3,000)]. Therefore, choices (b) €6.00, (c) €6.67 (rounded), and (d) no correct answer are incorrect.

*16. b. The total cost assignable to the ending work in process is HK$550,000 [(HK$100 × 2,500) + (HK$300 × 2,500 × 40%)]. Therefore, choices (a) HK$450,000, (c) HK$750,000, and (d) HK$1,000,000 are incorrect.

Practice Exercises

1. (LO 2) Tonino SpA manufactures pizza sauce through two production departments: Cooking and Canning. In each process, materials and conversion costs are incurred evenly throughout the process. For the month of April, the work in process inventory accounts show the following debits:

Journalize transactions.

	Cooking	Canning
Beginning work in process	€ -0-	€ 4,000
Direct materials	25,000	8,000
Direct labor	8,500	7,500
Manufacturing overhead	29,000	25,800
Costs transferred in		55,000

Instructions

Journalize the April transactions, using April 30 as the date.

Solution

1.

Date	Account	Debit	Credit
April 30	Work in Process—Cooking	25,000	
	Work in Process—Canning	8,000	
	Raw Materials Inventory		33,000
30	Work in Process—Cooking	8,500	
	Work in Process—Canning	7,500	
	Factory Labor		16,000
30	Work in Process—Cooking	29,000	
	Work in Process—Canning	25,800	
	Manufacturing Overhead		54,800
30	Work in Process—Canning	55,000	
	Work in Process—Cooking		55,000

2. (LO 3, 4) The Sanding Department of Kit Furnitures has the following production and manufacturing cost data for March 2023, the first month of operation.

Prepare a production cost report.

    Production: 15,000 units started in period; 11,000 units completed and transferred out; 4,000 units in ending work in process that are 100% complete as to materials and 25% complete as to conversion costs.

    Manufacturing costs: Materials HK$480,000; labor HK$420,000; and overhead HK$360,000.

Instructions

Prepare a production cost report for March 2023. All direct materials are added at the beginning of the process, and conversion costs are incurred uniformly throughout the process.

Solution

2.

Kit Furnitures
Sanding Department
Production Cost Report
For the Month Ended March 31, 2023

Quantities	Physical Units	Equivalent Units	
		Materials	Conversion Costs
Units to be accounted for			
Work in process, March 1	0		
Started into production	15,000		
Total units to be accounted for	15,000		
Units accounted for			
Completed and transferred out	11,000	11,000	11,000
Work in process, March 31	4,000	4,000	1,000 (4,000 × 25%)
Total units accounted for	15,000	15,000	12,000

Costs	Materials	Conversion Costs	Total
Unit costs			
Total cost	HK$480,000	HK$780,000*	HK$1,260,000
Equivalent units	15,000	12,000	
Unit costs	HK$32	HK$65	HK$97

Cost Reconciliation Schedule

Costs to be accounted for			
Work in process, March 1			HK$ 0
Started into production			1,260,000
Total costs to be accounted for			HK$1,260,000
Costs accounted for			
Completed and transferred out			HK$1,067,000
(11,000 × HK$97)			
Work in process, March 31			
Materials (4,000 × HK$32)		HK$128,000	
Conversion costs (1,000 × HK$65)		65,000	193,000
Total costs accounted for			HK$1,260,000

*HK$420,000 + HK$360,000

Practice Problem

Prepare a production cost report and journalize.

(LO 3, 4) Chin-lung Industries produces plastic ice cube trays in two processes: heating and stamping. All materials are added at the beginning of the Heating Department process, and conversion costs are incurred uniformly throughout the process. Chin-lung uses the weighted-average method to compute equivalent units of production.

On November 1, the Heating Department had in process 1,000 trays that were 70% complete. During November, it started into production 12,000 trays. On November 30, 2023, 2,000 trays that were 60% complete as to conversion costs were in process.

The following cost information for the Heating Department was also available.

Work in process, November 1:		Costs incurred in November:	
Materials	NT$ 6,400	Direct materials	NT$30,000
Conversion costs	3,600	Direct labor	23,000
Cost of work in process, Nov. 1	NT$10,000	Manufacturing overhead	40,500

Instructions

a. Prepare a production cost report for the Heating Department for the month of November 2023, using the weighted-average method.

b. Journalize the transfer of costs from the Heating Department to the Stamping Department.

Solution

a.

Chin-lung Industries
Heating Department
Production Cost Report
For the Month Ended November 30, 2023

	Physical Units	Equivalent Units	
		Materials	Conversion Costs
Quantities	Step 1	Step 2	
Units to be accounted for			
Work in process, November 1	1,000		
Started into production	12,000		
Total units to be accounted for	13,000		
Units accounted for			
Completed and transferred out	11,000*	11,000	11,000
Work in process, November 30	2,000	2,000	1,200**
Total units accounted for	13,000	13,000	12,200

*13,000 − 2,000; **2,000 × 60%

Costs		Materials	Conversion Costs	Total
Unit costs Step 3				
Total cost	(a)	NT$36,400*	NT$67,100**	NT$103,500
Equivalent units	(b)	13,000	12,200	
Unit costs [(a) ÷ (b)]		NT$2.80	NT$5.50	NT$8.30

Cost Reconciliation Schedule Step 4

Costs to be accounted for			
Work in process, November 1			NT$ 10,000
Started into production			93,500***
Total costs to be accounted for			NT$103,500
Costs accounted for			
Completed and transferred out			
(11,000 × NT$8.30)			NT$ 91,300
Work in process, November 30			
Materials (2,000 × NT$2.80)		NT$5,600	
Conversion costs (1,200 × NT$5.50)		6,600	12,200
Total costs accounted for			NT$103,500

*NT$6,400 + NT$30,000
**NT$3,600 + NT$23,000 + NT$40,500
***NT$30,000 + NT$23,000 + NT$40,500

b.
Work in Process—Stamping	91,300	
Work in Process—Heating		91,300
(To record transfer of units to the Stamping Department)		

Note: All asterisked Questions, Exercises, and Problems relate to material in the appendix to this chapter.

Questions

1. Identify which costing system—job order or process cost—the following companies would primarily use: (a) **Mars Foods (China) Co. Ltd.**, (b) **Jif Peanut Butter** (USA), (c) **Gulf Craft** (luxury yachts) (ARE), and (d) **Warner Bros. Motion Pictures** (USA).

2. Contrast the primary focus of job order cost accounting and of process cost accounting.

3. What are the similarities between a job order and a process cost system?

4. Your roommate is confused about the features of process cost accounting. Identify and explain the distinctive features for your roommate.

5. Zendaya Kofi believes there are no significant differences in the flow of costs between job order cost accounting and process cost accounting. Is Zendaya correct? Explain.

6. a. What source documents are used in assigning (1) materials and (2) labor to production in a process cost system?
   b. What criterion and basis are commonly used in assigning overhead to processes?

7. At Milton Company, overhead is assigned to production departments at the rate of £5 per machine hour. In July, machine hours were 3,000 in the Machining Department and 2,400 in the Assembly Department. Prepare the entry to assign overhead to production.

8. Priya Sen is uncertain about the steps used to prepare a production cost report. State the procedures that are required in the sequence in which they are performed.

9. John Harbeck is confused about computing physical units. Explain to John how physical units to be accounted for and physical units accounted for are determined.

10. What is meant by the term "equivalent units of production?"

11. How are equivalent units of production computed?

12. Song Ltd. had zero units of beginning work in process. During the period, 9,000 units were completed and transferred out, and there were 600 units of ending work in process. How many units were started into production?

13. Sanchez SA has zero units of beginning work in process. During the period, 12,000 units were completed and transferred out, and there were 500 units of ending work in process one-fifth complete as to conversion cost and 100% complete as to materials cost. What were the equivalent units of production for (a) materials and (b) conversion costs?

14. Dunder Co. started 3,000 units during the period. Its beginning inventory is 500 units one-fourth complete as to conversion costs and 100% complete as to materials costs. Its ending inventory is 300 units one-fifth complete as to conversion costs and 100% complete as to materials costs. How many units were completed and transferred out this period?

15. Zou Company completes and transfers out 14,000 units and has 2,000 units of ending work in process that are 25% complete as to conversion costs. Materials are entered at the beginning of the process, and there is no beginning work in process. Assuming unit materials costs of $3 and unit conversion costs of $5, what are the costs to be assigned to units (a) completed and transferred out and (b) in ending work in process?

16. a. Ann Quinn believes the production cost report is an external report for stockholders. Is Ann correct? Explain.
    b. Identify the sections in a production cost report.

17. What purposes are served by a production cost report?

18. At Zaire plc, there are 800 units of ending work in process that are 100% complete as to materials and 40% complete as to conversion costs. If the unit cost of materials is £3 and the total costs assigned to the 800 units is £6,000, what is the per unit conversion cost?

19. What is the difference between operations costing and a process cost system?

20. How does a company decide whether to use a job order or a process cost system?

*21. Kaan Company started and completed 2,000 units for the period. Its beginning inventory is 800 units 25% complete and its ending inventory is 400 units 20% complete. Kaan uses the FIFO method to compute equivalent units. How many units were completed and transferred out this period?

*22. Ava Ltd. completes and transfers out 12,000 units and has 2,000 units of ending work in process that are 25% complete as to conversion costs. Materials are entered at the beginning of the process, and there is no beginning work in process. Ava uses the FIFO method to compute equivalent units. Assuming unit materials costs of R30 and unit conversion costs of R70, what are the costs to be assigned to units (a) completed and transferred out and (b) in ending work in process?

Brief Exercises

Journalize entries for accumulating costs.

BE3.1 (LO 2), AP Changshan Ltd. purchases HK$500,000 of raw materials on account, and it incurs HK$600,000 of factory labor costs. Journalize the two transactions on March 31, assuming the labor costs are not paid until April.

Journalize the assignment of materials and labor costs.

BE3.2 (LO 2), AP Data for Changshan Ltd. are given in BE3.1. Supporting records show that (a) the Assembly Department used HK$240,000 of direct materials and HK$350,000 of direct labor, and (b) the Finishing Department used the remainder. Journalize the assignment of the costs to the processing departments on March 31.

Journalize the assignment of overhead costs.

BE3.3 (LO 2), AP Direct labor data for Changshan Ltd. are given in BE3.2. Manufacturing overhead is assigned to departments on the basis of 160% of direct labor costs. Journalize the assignment of overhead to the Assembly and Finishing Departments.

Compute equivalent units of production.

BE3.4 (LO 3), AP Ayaz Company has the following production data for selected months.

Month	Beginning Work in Process	Units Completed and Transferred Out	Ending Work in Process Units	% Complete as to Conversion Cost
January	-0-	35,000	10,000	40%
March	-0-	40,000	8,000	75
July	-0-	45,000	16,000	25

Compute equivalent units of production for materials and conversion costs, assuming that materials are entered at the beginning of the process and that conversion costs are incurred uniformly throughout the process.

BE3.5 (LO 3), AP The Smelting Department of Kato Enterprises has the following production data for November.

Compute equivalent units of production.

Beginning work in process 2,000 units that are 100% complete as to materials and 20% complete as to conversion costs; units completed and transferred out 9,000 units; and ending work in process 7,000 units that are 100% complete as to materials and 40% complete as to conversion costs.

Compute the equivalent units of production for (a) materials and (b) conversion costs for the month of November.

BE3.6 (LO 4), AP In Akira Manufacturing total materials costs are ¥3,300,000 and total conversion costs are ¥5,400,000 for June. Equivalent units of production are materials 10,000 and conversion costs 12,000. Compute the unit costs for materials, conversion costs, and total manufacturing costs.

Compute unit costs of production.

BE3.7 (LO 4), AP Bronte Company has the following production data for April: units completed and transferred out 40,000, and ending work in process 5,000 units that are 100% complete for materials and 40% complete for conversion costs. If unit materials cost is $4 and unit conversion cost is $7, determine the costs to be assigned to the units completed and transferred out and the units in ending work in process.

Assign costs to units completed and transferred out and to work in process.

BE3.8 (LO 4), AP Production costs of the Finishing Department in June in Hollins plc are materials £12,000, labor £29,500, and overhead £18,000. Equivalent units of production are materials 20,000 and conversion costs 19,000. Compute the unit costs for materials and conversion costs for June.

Compute unit costs.

BE3.9 (LO 4), AP Data for Hollins plc are given in BE3.8. Production records indicate that 18,000 units were completed and transferred out, and 2,000 units in ending work in process were 50% complete as to conversion costs and 100% complete as to materials. Prepare the "costs accounted for" section of a cost reconciliation schedule.

Prepare cost reconciliation schedule.

*BE3.10 (LO 5), AP Michel AG has the following production data for March 2023: no beginning work in process, units started and completed 30,000, and ending work in process 5,000 units that are 100% complete for materials and 40% complete for conversion costs. Michel uses the FIFO method to compute equivalent units. If unit materials cost is €6 and unit conversion cost is €10, determine the costs to be assigned to the units completed and transferred out and the units in ending work in process. The total costs to be assigned are €530,000.

Assign costs to units completed and transferred out and to work in process.

*BE3.11 (LO 5), AP Using the data in BE3.10, prepare the "costs accounted for" section of the production cost report for Michel AG using the FIFO method.

Prepare a partial production cost report using the FIFO method.

DO IT! Exercises

DO IT! 3.1 (LO 1), C Indicate whether each of the following statements is true or false.

Compare job order and process cost systems.

1. Many hospitals use job order costing for small, routine medical procedures.
2. A manufacturer of computer flash drives would use a job order cost system.
3. A process cost system uses multiple work in process inventory accounts.
4. A process cost system keeps track of costs on job cost sheets.

DO IT! 3.2 (LO 2), AP Kang Ltd. manufactures CH-21 through two processes: mixing and packaging. In July, the following costs were assigned.

Assign and journalize manufacturing costs.

	Mixing	Packaging
Direct materials used	₩10,000,000	₩28,000,000
Direct labor costs	8,000,000	36,000,000
Manufacturing overhead costs	12,000,000	54,000,000

Units completed at a cost of ₩21,000,000 in the Mixing Department are transferred to the Packaging Department. Units completed at a cost of ₩106,000,000 in the Packaging Department are transferred to Finished Goods. Journalize the assignment of these costs to the two processes and the transfer of units as appropriate.

Compute equivalent units.

DO IT! 3.3 (LO 3), AP The Assembly Department for Volga Group has the following production data for the current month.

Beginning Work in Process	Units Completed and Transferred Out	Ending Work in Process
–0–	20,000	10,000

Materials are entered at the beginning of the process. The ending work in process units are 70% complete as to conversion costs. Compute the equivalent units of production for (a) materials and (b) conversion costs.

Prepare cost reconciliation schedule.

DO IT! 3.4 (LO 4), AP In March, Olivia Company had the following unit production costs: materials S$10 and conversion costs S$8. On March 1, it had no work in process. During March, Olivia completed and transferred out 22,000 units. As of March 31, 4,000 units that were 40% complete as to conversion costs and 100% complete as to materials were in ending work in process.

a. Compute the total units to be accounted for.
b. Compute the equivalent units of production for materials and conversion costs.
c. Prepare a cost reconciliation schedule, including the costs of units completed and transferred out and the costs of units in work in process, for March 2023.

Exercises

Understand process cost accounting.

E3.1 (LO 1), C Akhtar Hussain has prepared the following list of statements about process cost accounting.

1. Process cost systems are used to apply costs to similar products that are mass-produced in a continuous fashion.
2. A process cost system is used when each finished unit is indistinguishable from another.
3. Companies that produce soft drinks, movies, and computer chips would all use process cost accounting.
4. In a process cost system, costs are tracked by individual jobs.
5. Job order costing and process costing track different manufacturing cost components.
6. Both job order costing and process costing account for direct materials, direct labor, and manufacturing overhead.
7. Costs flow through the accounts in the same basic way for both job order costing and process costing.
8. In a process cost system, only one work in process inventory account is used.
9. In a process cost system, costs are summarized in a job cost sheet.
10. In a process cost system, the unit cost is the sum of materials costs and conversion costs, each divided by their respective equivalent units.

Instructions

Identify each statement as true or false. If false, indicate how to correct the statement.

Journalize transactions.

E3.2 (LO 2), AP Miray Group manufactures pizza sauce through two production departments: Cooking and Canning. In each process, materials and conversion costs are incurred evenly throughout the process. For the month of April, the work in process inventory accounts show the following debits:

	Cooking	Canning
Beginning work in process	HK$ –0–	HK$ 40,000
Direct materials	210,000	90,000
Direct labor	85,000	70,000
Manufacturing overhead	315,000	258,000
Costs transferred in		530,000

Instructions

Journalize the April transactions, using April 30 as the date.

E3.3 (LO 2, 3, 4), AP The ledger of British Company has the following work in process inventory account.

Answer questions on costs and production.

Work in Process—Painting					
5/1	Balance	3,590	5/31	Completed and transferred out	?
5/31	Direct materials	5,160			
5/31	Direct labor	2,530			
5/31	Manufacturing overhead	1,380			
5/31	Balance	?			

Production records show that there were 400 units in the beginning inventory, 30% complete, 1,600 units started into production, and 1,700 units completed and transferred out. The beginning work in process had materials cost of £2,040 and conversion costs of £1,550. The units in ending inventory were 40% complete as to conversion costs. Materials are entered at the beginning of the painting process, and conversion costs are incurred uniformly throughout the process.

Instructions

a. How many units are in process at May 31?
b. What is the unit materials cost for May?
c. What is the unit conversion cost for May?
d. What is the total cost of units completed and transferred out in May?
e. What is the cost of the May 31 work in process inventory?

E3.4 (LO 2), AP Stella SA has two production departments: Cutting and Assembly. July 1 inventories are Raw Materials R$42,000, Work in Process—Cutting R$29,000, Work in Process—Assembly R$106,000 and Finished Goods R$310,000. During July, the following transactions occurred.

Journalize transactions for two processes.

1. Purchased R$625,000 of raw materials on account.
2. Incurred R$600,000 of factory labor. (Credit Wages Payable.)
3. Incurred R$700,000 of manufacturing overhead; R$400,000 was paid and the remainder is unpaid.
4. Requisitioned materials for Cutting R$157,000 and Assembly R$89,000.
5. Used factory labor for Cutting R$330,000 and Assembly R$270,000.
6. Applied overhead at the rate of R$180 per machine hour. Machine hours were Cutting 1,680 and Assembly 1,720.
7. Transferred goods costing R$676,000 from the Cutting Department to the Assembly Department.
8. Completed and transferred goods costing R$1,349,000 from Assembly to Finished Goods Inventory.
9. Sold goods costing R$1,500,000 for R$2,000,000 on account.

Instructions

Journalize the transactions. (Omit explanations and dates.)

E3.5 (LO 3, 4), AP In Samson Company, materials are entered at the beginning of each process, and conversion costs are incurred uniformly throughout the process. Work in process inventories, with the percentage of work done on conversion costs, and production data for its Sterilizing Department in selected months during 2023 are as follows:

Compute physical units and equivalent units of production.

	Beginning Work in Process		Units Completed and Transferred Out	Ending Work in Process	
Month	Units	Conversion Cost%		Units	Conversion Cost%
January	-0-	—	11,000	2,000	60
March	-0-	—	12,000	3,000	30
May	-0-	—	14,000	7,000	80
July	-0-	—	10,000	1,500	40

Instructions

a. For January and May, compute the physical units to be accounted for and the physical units accounted for.
b. Compute the equivalent units of production for (1) materials and (2) conversion costs for each month.

Determine equivalent units, unit costs, and assignment of costs.

E3.6 (LO 3, 4), AP The Cutting Department of Demir A.Ş. has the following production and cost data for July.

Production	Costs	
1. Completed and transferred out 12,000 units.	Beginning work in process	₺ -0-
2. 3,000 units in ending working in process are 60% complete as to conversion costs and 100% complete as to materials at July 31.	Direct materials	450,000
	Direct labor	162,000
	Manufacturing overhead	183,000

Materials are entered at the beginning of the process. Conversion costs are incurred uniformly throughout the process.

Instructions

a. Determine the equivalent units of production for (1) materials and (2) conversion costs.

b. Compute unit costs and prepare a cost reconciliation schedule.

Prepare a production cost report.

E3.7 (LO 3, 4), AP The Sanding Department of Quik Furniture Company has the following production and manufacturing cost data for March 2023, the first month of operation.

Production: 7,000 units completed and transferred out; 3,000 units in ending work in process are 100% complete as to materials and 20% complete as to conversion costs.

Manufacturing costs: Materials $33,000; labor $21,000; and overhead $36,000.

Instructions

Prepare a production cost report.

Determine equivalent units, unit costs, and assignment of costs.

E3.8 (LO 3, 4), AP The Blending Department of Luongo SpA has the following cost and production data for the month of April.

Costs:	
Work in process, April 1	
Direct materials: 100% complete	€100,000
Conversion costs: 20% complete	70,000
Cost of work in process, April 1	€170,000
Costs incurred during production in April	
Direct materials	€ 800,000
Conversion costs	365,000
Costs incurred in April	€1,165,000

Units completed and transferred out totaled 17,000. Ending work in process was 1,000 units that are 100% complete as to materials and 40% complete as to conversion costs.

Instructions

a. Compute the equivalent units of production for (1) materials and (2) conversion costs for the month of April.

b. Compute the unit costs for the month.

c. Determine the costs to be assigned to the units completed and transferred out and in ending work in process.

Determine equivalent units, unit costs, and assignment of costs.

E3.9 (LO 3, 4), AP Sakura Manufacturers has gathered the following information.

Units in beginning work in process	-0-
Units started into production	36,000
Units in ending work in process	6,000
Percent complete in ending work in process:	
Conversion costs	40%
Materials	100%
Costs incurred:	
Direct materials	¥7,200,000
Direct labor	¥6,100,000
Overhead	¥10,100,000

Instructions

a. Compute equivalent units of production for materials and for conversion costs.

b. Determine the unit costs of production.

c. Show the assignment of costs to units completed and transferred out and to work in process at the end of the period.

E3.10 (LO 3, 4), AP Shu-fen Ltd. has gathered the following information. All materials are added at the beginning of the process, and conversion costs are incurred uniformly throughout the process.

Determine equivalent units, unit costs, and assignment of costs.

Units in beginning work in process	20,000
Units started into production	164,000
Units in ending work in process	24,000
Percent complete in ending work in process:	
Conversion costs	60%
Materials	100%
Cost of beginning work in process, plus costs incurred during the period:	
Direct materials	NT$1,012,000
Direct labor	NT$1,648,000
Overhead	NT$1,840,000

Instructions

a. Compute equivalent units of production for materials and for conversion costs.

b. Determine the unit costs of production.

c. Show the assignment of costs to units completed and transferred out and to work in process at the end of the period.

E3.11 (LO 3, 4), AP The Polishing Department of Major Company has the following production and manufacturing cost data for September. All materials are added at the beginning of the process, and conversion costs are incurred uniformly throughout the process.

Compute equivalent units, unit costs, and costs assigned.

Excel

Production: Beginning inventory 1,600 units that are 100% complete as to materials and 30% complete as to conversion costs; units started during the period are 42,900; ending inventory of 5,000 units 10% complete as to conversion costs.

Manufacturing costs: Beginning inventory costs, comprised of $20,000 of materials and $43,180 of conversion costs; materials costs added in Polishing during the month, $175,800; labor and overhead applied in Polishing during the month, $125,680 and $257,140, respectively.

Instructions

a. Compute the equivalent units of production for materials and conversion costs for the month of September.

b. Compute the unit costs for materials and conversion costs for the month.

c. Determine the costs to be assigned to the units completed and transferred out and to work in process at the end of September.

E3.12 (LO 4), S Writing Kang Ting has recently been promoted to production manager. He has just started to receive various managerial reports, including the production cost report that you prepared. It showed that his department had 2,000 equivalent units in ending inventory. His department has had a history of not keeping enough inventory on hand to meet demand. He has come to you, very angry, and wants to know why you credited him with only 2,000 units when he knows he had at least twice that many on hand.

Explain the production cost report.

Instructions

Explain to him why his production cost report showed only 2,000 equivalent units in ending inventory. Write an informal memo. Be kind and explain very clearly why he is mistaken.

E3.13 (LO 3, 4), AP The Welding Department of PlasticWorks Company has the following production and manufacturing cost data for February 2023. All materials are added at the beginning of the process.

Prepare a production cost report.

Manufacturing Costs			Production Data	
Beginning work in process			Beginning work in process	15,000 units
Materials	A$18,000		Units completed and transferred out	55,000
Conversion costs	14,175	A$ 32,175	Units started in production	51,000
Costs added during month			Ending work in process	11,000 units
Direct materials		180,000		
Direct labor		67,380		
Manufacturing overhead		61,445		
		A$341,000		

Instructions

Beginning work in process and ending work in process were 10% and 20% complete with respect to conversion costs, respectively. Prepare a production cost report for the Welding Department for the month of February.

Determine equivalent units, unit costs, and assignment of costs.

*E3.14 (LO 5), AP The Cutting Department of Helium Group has the following production and cost data for August.

Production	Costs	
1. Started and completed 10,000 units.	Beginning work in process	S$ –0–
2. Started 2,000 units that are 40% complete at August 31.	Costs added during month	
	Direct materials	45,000
	Direct labor	13,600
	Manufacturing overhead	16,100

Materials are entered at the beginning of the process. Conversion costs are incurred uniformly during the process. Helium Group uses the FIFO method to compute equivalent units.

Instructions

a. Determine the equivalent units of production for (1) materials and (2) conversion costs.

b. Compute unit costs and prepare the cost reconciliation schedule at the end of August.

Compute equivalent units, unit costs, and costs assigned.

*E3.15 (LO 5), AP The Smelting Department of Polzin plc has the following production and cost data for September.

Production: Beginning work in process 2,000 units that are 100% complete as to materials and 20% complete as to conversion costs; units started and completed 9,000 units; and ending work in process 1,000 units that are 100% complete as to materials and 40% complete as to conversion costs.

Manufacturing costs: Work in process, September 1, £15,200; materials £60,000; conversion costs £132,000.

Polzin uses the FIFO method to compute equivalent units. All direct materials are added at the beginning of the process. Conversion costs are incurred uniformly throughout the process.

Instructions

a. Compute the equivalent units of production for (1) materials and (2) conversion costs for the month of September.

b. Compute the unit costs for the month.

c. Determine the costs to be assigned to the units completed and transferred out and to work in process units at the end of the month.

Answer questions on costs and production.

*E3.16 (LO 5), AP The ledger of Hasgrove Company has the following work in process inventory account.

	Work in Process—Painting				
3/1	Balance	3,680	3/31	Completed and transferred out	?
3/31	Direct materials	6,600			
3/31	Direct labor	2,400			
3/31	Manufacturing overhead	1,150			
3/31	Balance	?			

Production records show that there were 800 units in the beginning inventory, 30% complete, 1,100 units started, and 1,500 units completed and transferred out. The units in ending inventory were 40% complete. Materials are added at the beginning of the painting process, and conversion costs are incurred uniformly throughout the process. Hasgrove uses the FIFO method to compute equivalent units.

Instructions

Answer the following questions:

a. How many units are in process at March 31?
b. What is the unit materials cost for March?
c. What is the unit conversion cost for March?
d. What is the total cost of units started in February and completed in March?
e. What is the total cost of units started and completed in March?
f. What is the cost of the March 31 ending inventory?

*E3.17 (LO 5), AP The Welding Department of Liu Machinery has the following production and manufacturing cost data for February 2023. All materials are added at the beginning of the process, and conversion costs are incurred uniformly throughout the process. Liu uses the FIFO method to compute equivalent units of production.

Prepare a production cost report for a second process.

Manufacturing Costs		Production Data	
Beginning work in process	HK$ 321,750	Beginning work in process	15,000 units
Costs added during month		Units completed and transferred out	54,000
Direct materials	1,920,000	Units started in production	64,000
Direct labor	351,000	Ending work in process	25,000 units
Manufacturing overhead	684,000		

Instructions

Beginning work in process and ending work in process were 10% and 20% complete with respect to conversion costs, respectively. Prepare a production cost report for the Welding Department for February 2023.

Problems

P3.1 (LO 2), AP Biotique plc manufactures its product, Vitadrink, through two manufacturing processes: Mixing and Packaging. All materials are added at the beginning of each process, and conversion costs are incurred uniformly throughout the process. On October 1, 2023, inventories consisted of Raw Materials £26,000, Work in Process—Mixing £0, Work in Process—Packaging £250,000, and Finished Goods £289,000. The beginning inventory for Packaging consisted of 10,000 units that were 50% complete as to conversion costs and fully complete as to materials. During October, 50,000 units were started into production in the Mixing Department, and the following transactions were completed.

Journalize transactions.

1. Purchased £300,000 of raw materials on account.
2. Issued direct materials for production: Mixing £210,000 and Packaging £45,000.
3. Incurred labor costs of £278,900. (Use Wages Payable.)
4. Used factory labor: Mixing £182,500 and Packaging £96,400.
5. Incurred £810,000 of manufacturing overhead on account.
6. Applied manufacturing overhead on the basis of £23 per machine hour. Machine hours were 28,000 in Mixing and 6,000 in Packaging.
7. Transferred 45,000 units from Mixing to Packaging at a cost of £979,000.
8. Completed and transferred 53,000 units from Packaging to Finished Goods at a cost of £1,315,000.
9. Sold goods costing £1,604,000 for £2,500,000 on account.

Instructions

Journalize the October transactions.

P3.2 (LO 3, 4), AP Bautista Equipment manufactures bowling balls through two processes: Molding and Packaging. In the Molding Department, the urethane, rubber, plastics, and other materials are molded

Complete four steps necessary to prepare a production cost report.

into bowling balls. In the Packaging Department, the balls are placed in cartons and sent to the finished goods warehouse. All materials are added at the beginning of each process. Labor and manufacturing overhead are incurred uniformly throughout each process. Production and cost data for the Molding Department during June 2023 are presented below.

Production Data	June
Beginning work in process units	–0–
Units started into production	22,000
Ending work in process units	2,000
Percent complete as to conversion—ending inventory	40%

Cost Data	
Direct materials used in June	€198,000
Direct labor incurred in June	53,600
Manufacturing overhead assigned in June	112,800
Total	€364,400

Instructions

a. Prepare a schedule showing physical units of production.

b. Determine the equivalent units of production for materials and conversion costs.

c. Compute the unit costs of production.

d. Determine the costs to be assigned to the units completed and transferred out and to work in process for June.

e. Prepare a production cost report for the Molding Department for the month of June.

c. Materials €9.00
CC €8.00
d. Completed and transferred out €340,000
Ending WIP € 24,400

Complete four steps necessary to prepare a production cost report.

P3.3 (LO 3, 4), AP Hiranur Industries manufactures dorm furniture in separate processes. In each process, materials are added at the beginning, and conversion costs are incurred uniformly. Production and cost data for the first process in making a product are as follows:

Production Data—July	Cutting Department T12-Tables
Work in process units, July 1	–0–
Units started into production	20,000
Work in process units, July 31	3,000
Work in process percent complete as to conversion, July 31	60%

Cost Data—July	
Work in process, July 1	₺ –0–
Direct materials used in July	3,800,000
Direct labor incurred in July	2,344,000
Manufacturing overhead assigned in July	1,040,000
Total	₺7,184,000

Instructions

a. 1. Compute the physical units of production.

2. Compute equivalent units of production for materials and for conversion costs.

3. Determine the unit costs of production for July.

4. Show the assignment of costs to units completed and transferred out and to work in process for July.

b. Prepare the production cost report for July 2023.

a. 3. Materials ₺190
CC ₺180
4. Completed and transferred out ₺6,290,000
Ending WIP ₺894,000

Assign costs and prepare production cost report.

P3.4 (LO 3, 4), AP Amanda Industries Ltd. has several processing departments. Costs to be accounted for in the Assembly Department for November 2023 totaled S$2,280,000 as follows:

Work in process, November 1			
Materials		S$79,000	
Conversion costs		48,150	S$ 127,150
Direct materials added during November			1,589,000
Direct labor incurred during November			225,920
Manufacturing overhead assigned during November			337,930
			S$2,280,000

Production records show that 35,000 units were in beginning work in process 30% complete as to conversion costs, 660,000 units were started into production, and 25,000 units were in ending work in process 40% complete as to conversion costs. Materials are added at the beginning of each process, and conversion costs are incurred uniformly throughout the process.

Instructions

a. Determine the equivalent units of production and the unit production costs for the Assembly Department.

b. Determine the assignment of costs to goods completed and transferred out and to work in process for November.

c. Prepare a production cost report for the Assembly Department for November 2023.

b. Completed and transferred out S$2,211,000
Ending WIP S$ 69,000

P3.5 (LO 3, 4), AP Lin Sports Ltd. manufactures basketballs. The first step is the production of internal rubber bladders. Materials are added at the beginning of the production process, and conversion costs are incurred uniformly. Production and cost data for the Bladder Department for July 2023 are as follows:

Determine equivalent units and unit costs and assign costs.

Production Data—Basketballs	Units	Percentage Complete
Work in process units, July 1	500	60%
Units started into production	1,000	
Work in process units, July 31	600	40%

Cost Data—Basketballs		
Work in process, July 1		
Materials	HK$7,500	
Conversion costs	6,000	HK$13,500
Costs added during July		
Direct materials		24,000
Direct labor		15,800
Manufacturing overhead		12,400

Instructions

a. Calculate the following:
  1. The equivalent units of production for materials and conversion costs.
  2. The unit costs of production for materials and conversion costs.
  3. The assignment of costs to units completed and transferred out and to work in process at the end of the accounting period.

b. Prepare a production cost report for the month of July for the basketballs.

a. 2. Materials HK$21
3. Completed and transferred out HK$45,900
Ending WIP HK$19,800

P3.6 (LO 3, 4), AP Harry Processing Ltd. uses the weighted-average method and manufactures a single product—an industrial carpet shampoo used by many universities. The manufacturing activity for the month of October has just been completed. A partially completed production cost report for the month of October for the Mixing and Cooking Department is as follows. Beginning work in process is 100% complete for direct materials and 70% complete for conversion costs. Ending work in process is 60% complete for direct materials and 40% complete for conversion costs.

Compute equivalent units and complete production cost report.

Harry Processing Ltd.
Mixing and Cooking Department
Production Cost Report
For the Month Ended October 31, 2023

Quantities	Physical Units	Equivalent Units — Materials	Equivalent Units — Conversion Costs
Units to be accounted for			
Work in process, October 1 (100% materials, 70% conversion costs)	20,000		
Started into production	150,000		
Total units to be accounted for	170,000		
Units accounted for			
Completed and transferred out	120,000	?	?
Work in process, October 31 (60% materials, 40% conversion costs)	50,000	?	?
Total units accounted for	170,000	?	?

Costs

Unit costs	Materials	Conversion Costs	Total
Total cost	£240,000	£105,000	£345,000
Equivalent units	?	?	
Unit costs	£ ? +	£ ? =	£ ?

Cost Reconciliation Schedule	Physical Units	Equivalent Units — Materials	Equivalent Units — Conversion Costs	
Costs to be accounted for				
Work in process, October 1				£ 30,000
Started into production				315,000
Total costs to be accounted for				£345,000
Costs accounted for				
Completed and transferred out				£ ?
Work in process, October 31				
Materials		£ ?		
Conversion costs			?	?
Total costs accounted for				£ ?

Instructions

a. Prepare a schedule that shows how the equivalent units were computed so that you can complete the "Quantities: Units accounted for" equivalent units section shown in the production cost report, and compute October unit costs.

b. Complete the production cost report for October 2023.

a. Materials £1.60
b. Completed and transferred out £282,000
   Ending WIP £ 63,000

Determine equivalent units and unit costs and assign costs for processes; prepare production cost report.

*P3.7 (LO 5), AP Asahi Cycles manufactures bicycles and tricycles. For both products, materials are added at the beginning of the production process, and conversion costs are incurred uniformly. Asahi uses the FIFO method to compute equivalent units. Production and cost data for the Assembly Department for March are as follows:

Production Data—Bicycles	Units	Percentage Complete as to Conversion Costs
Work in process units, March 1	200	80%
Units started into production	1,000	
Work in process units, March 31	300	40%

Cost Data—Bicycles	
Work in process, March 1	¥1,928,000
Costs added during March	
Direct materials	5,000,000
Direct labor	2,590,000
Manufacturing overhead	3,000,000

Production Data—Tricycles	Units	Percentage Complete as to Conversion Costs
Work in process units, March 1	100	75%
Units started into production	1,000	
Work in process units, March 31	60	25%

Cost Data—Tricycles	
Work in process, March 1	¥ 612,500
Costs added during March	
Direct materials	3,000,000
Direct labor	1,430,000
Manufacturing overhead	2,000,000

Instructions

a. Calculate the following for both the bicycles and the tricycles.
   1. The equivalent units of production for materials and conversion costs.
   2. The unit costs of production for materials and conversion costs.
   3. The assignment of costs to units completed and transferred out and to work in process at the end of the accounting period.
b. Prepare a production cost report for March 2023 for the bicycles only.

a. Bicycles:
   1. Materials 1,000
   2. Materials ¥ 5,000
   3. Completed and transferred out ¥10,238,000
   Ending WIP ¥ 2,280,000

Continuing Case

Current Designs

CD3 Building a kayak using the composite method is a very labor-intensive process. In the Fabrication Department, the kayaks go through several steps as employees carefully place layers of Kevlar® in a mold and then use resin to fuse together the layers. The excess resin is removed with a vacuum process, and the upper shell and lower shell are removed from the molds and assembled. The seat, hatch, and other components are added in the Finishing Department.

At the beginning of April, **Current Designs** (USA) had 30 kayaks in process in the Fabrication Department. Rick Thrune, the production manager, estimated that about 80% of the materials costs had been added to these boats, which were about 50% complete with respect to the conversion costs. The cost of this inventory had been calculated to be $8,400 in materials and $9,000 in conversion costs.

During April, 72 boats were started into production. At the end of the month, the 35 kayaks in the ending inventory were 20% complete as to materials and 40% complete as to conversion costs.

A review of the accounting records for April showed that materials with a cost of $17,500 had been requisitioned by the Fabrication Department and that the conversion costs for the month were $39,600.

Instructions

Complete a production cost report for April 2023 for the Fabrication Department using the weighted-average method. Direct materials and conversion costs are incurred uniformly throughout the process.

Expand Your Critical Thinking

Decision-Making Across the Organization

CT3.1 Florida Beach Company manufactures sunscreen, called NoTan, in 11-ounce plastic bottles. NoTan is sold in a competitive market. As a result, management is very cost-conscious. NoTan is manufactured through two processes: mixing and filling. Materials are added at the beginning of each process, and labor and manufacturing overhead occur uniformly throughout each process. Unit costs are based on the cost per gallon of NoTan using the weighted-average method.

On June 30, 2023, Mary Ritzman, the chief accountant for the past 20 years, opted to take early retirement. Her replacement, Joe Benili, had extensive accounting experience with motels in the area but only limited contact with manufacturing accounting. During July, Joe correctly accumulated the following production quantity and cost data for the Mixing Department.

Production quantities: Work in process, July 1, 8,000 gallons 75% complete as to conversion costs; started into production 100,000 gallons; work in process, July 31, 5,000 gallons 20% complete. All materials are added at the beginning of the process.

Production costs: Beginning work in process $88,000, comprised of $21,000 of materials costs and $67,000 of conversion costs; incurred in July: materials $573,000, conversion costs $765,000.

Joe then prepared a production cost report on the basis of physical units started into production. His report showed a unit manufacturing cost of $14.26 per gallon of NoTan. The management of Florida Beach was surprised at the high unit cost. The president comes to you, as Mary's top assistant, to review Joe's report and prepare a correct report if necessary.

Instructions

With the class divided into groups, answer the following questions:

a. Show how Joe arrived at the unit manufacturing cost of $14.26 per gallon of NoTan.
b. What error(s) did Joe make in preparing his production cost report?
c. Prepare a correct production cost report for July.

Managerial Analysis

CT3.2 Moriarty Furniture Ltd. manufactures living room furniture through two departments: Framing and Upholstering. Materials are added at the beginning of each process, and conversion costs are incurred uniformly throughout the process. For May, the following cost data are obtained from the two work in process inventory accounts.

	Framing	Upholstering
Work in process, May 1	£ –0–	£ ?
Materials	450,000	?
Conversion costs	261,000	330,000
Costs transferred in	–0–	600,000
Costs completed and transferred out	600,000	?
Work in process, May 31	111,000	?

Instructions

Answer the following questions using the weighted-average method.

a. If 3,000 sofas were started into production in Framing on May 1 and 2,500 sofas were completed and transferred to Upholstering, what was the unit cost of materials for May in the Framing Department?
b. Using the data in part (a), what was the per unit conversion cost of the sofas completed and transferred to Upholstering?
c. Continuing the assumptions in (a) above, what is the percentage of completion as to conversion costs of the units in process at May 31 in the Framing Department?

Real-World Focus

CT3.3 Paintball is now played around the world. The process of making paintballs is actually quite similar to the process used to make certain medical pills. In fact, paintballs were previously often made at the same factories that made pharmaceuticals.

Instructions

Do an Internet search on "video of paintball production," view that video, and then complete the following:

a. Describe in sequence the primary steps used to manufacture paintballs.
b. Explain the costs incurred by the company that would fall into each of the following categories: materials, labor, and overhead. Of these categories, which do you think would be the greatest cost in making paintballs?
c. Discuss whether a paintball manufacturer would use job order costing or process costing.

Communication Activity

CT3.4 Qianyi Wu was a good friend of yours in high school and is from your home town. While you chose to major in accounting when you both went away to college, she majored in marketing and management. You are now the accounting manager for the Snack Foods Division of Li Enterprises. Your friend Qianyi was promoted to regional sales manager for the same division of Li. Qianyi recently telephoned you. She explained that she was familiar with job cost sheets, which had been used by the Special Projects Division where she had formerly worked. She was, however, very uncomfortable with the production cost reports prepared by your division. She emailed you a list of her particular questions:

1. Since Li occasionally prepares snack foods for special orders in the Snack Foods Division, why don't we track costs of the orders separately?
2. What is an equivalent unit of production?
3. Why am I getting four production cost reports? Isn't there one work in process inventory account?

Instructions

Prepare a memo to Qianyi. Answer her questions and include any additional information you think would be helpful. You may write informally but do use proper grammar and punctuation.

Ethics Case

CT3.5 Paek Electronics manufactures a high-tech component used in Bluetooth speakers that passes through two production processing departments, Molding and Assembly. Department managers are partially compensated on the basis of units of product completed and transferred out relative to units of product put into production. This was intended as encouragement to be efficient and to minimize waste.

Ki Rhim is the department head in the Molding Department, and Woonsup Choi is her quality control inspector. During the month of June, Ki hired three new employees who were not yet technically skilled. As a result, many of the units produced in June had minor molding defects. In order to maintain the department's normal high rate of completion, Ki told Woonsup to pass through inspection and on to the Assembly Department all units that had defects nondetectable to the human eye. "Company and industry tolerances on this product are too high anyway," says Ki. "Less than 2% of the units we produce are subjected in the market to the stress tolerance we've designed into them. The odds of those 2% being any of this month's units are even less. Anyway, we're saving the company money."

Instructions

a. Who are the potential stakeholders involved in this situation?
b. What alternatives does Woonsup have in this situation? What might the company do to prevent this situation from occurring?

Considering People, Planet, and Profit

CT3.6 When an oil refinery in Texas City, Texas, on the Houston Ship Channel exploded, it killed 15 people and sent a plume of smoke hundreds of feet into the air. The blast started as a fire in the section of the factory that increased the octane of the gasoline that was produced at the refinery. The Houston Ship Channel is the main waterway that allows commerce to flow from the Gulf of Mexico into Houston.

The Texas Commission on Environmental Quality expressed concern about the release of nitrogen oxides, benzene, and other known carcinogens as a result of the blast. Neighbors of the factory complained that the factory had been emitting carcinogens for years and that the regulators had ignored their complaints about emissions and unsafe working conditions.

Instructions

Answer the following questions:
a. What costs might the company face as a result of the accident?
b. How might the company have reduced the costs associated with the accident?

CHAPTER 4

Activity-Based Costing

CHAPTER PREVIEW

As indicated in the Feature Story below, traditional costing systems are not the best solution for every company. **Technogym SpA** (ITA) suspected that while a traditional costing system might perform well in one department, it could mask significant differences in cost structures in another department. The company sought solutions based on activities rather than traditional predetermined overhead allocations.

Similar searches by other companies for ways to improve operations and gather accurate data for decision-making have resulted in the development of powerful new management tools, including **activity-based costing (ABC)**. Simply put, activity-based costing allocates overhead to multiple activity cost pools and then assigns the activity cost pools to products and services by means of cost drivers.

FEATURE STORY

Wellness for Customers and the Company

The wellness movement can be thought of as a conscious, self-directed process of achieving a full harmonious balance among the mind, body, and spirit. It is a multifaceted, holistic concept. **Technogym SpA** (ITA), a manufacturer of gym equipment, has embraced this concept and is actively working to transform exercise facilities with their unique and elegantly designed wellness equipment and tools.

Ever since it made its first gym equipment in 1983, Technogym's mission has been to provide exercise equipment to wellness centers and homes around the world. The company, with sales of over $580 million, employs about 2,200 people worldwide and exports 90% of what is manufactured to over 100 countries. Headquartered in Cesena, Italy, its founder, Nerio Alessandri, an industrial designer by profession, pays particular attention to leveraging the company's technology to supply innovative services and equipment.

For example, the Technogym organization includes the After Sales Department, which provides parts and technical support for protecting the lifespan of the company's products. In order to reduce production and distribution costs, Technogym's After Sales Department analyzed its traditional system, which had become inadequate to satisfy customer needs. The company searched the market for a software solution that could achieve three activities: (1) integrate with its enterprise resource planning (ERP) system and internal management system, (2) personalize applications based on specific needs, and (3) allow the company to independently manage the database. Technogym's After Sales Department now has IT that offers the maximum integration with existing company IT systems, allows administrators to easily create and customize catalogs, and provides quick and flexible tailorization of global languages, shopping carts, and currency.

As a result of this investment, the functionality, flexibility, and usability of the new IT system cut time and errors, providing value-added activities and eliminating unnecessary activities and costs associated with the sale of spare parts. Tweaking activities and reducing overhead costs of the After Sales Department is just one way that Technogym safeguards its highly regarded reputation and maintains its revenue flow among the many companies within the competitive exercise equipment market.

Sources: D. Heitner, "How Wellness Helped Technogym Generate $581.2 Million in 2015," *Forbes* (June 6, 2016); and Interactive SPares staff, "Interactive SPares—The Case of Technogym S.p.A." (2016), http://interactivespares.com/technogym-story.html.

 Watch the *Precor* video at https://wileyaccountingupdates.com/video/?p=54 to learn more about activity-based costing.

CHAPTER OUTLINE

Learning Objectives	Review	Practice
LO 1 Discuss the difference between traditional costing and activity-based costing.	• Traditional costing systems • Illustration of a traditional system • Need for a new approach • Activity-based costing	**DO IT! 1** Costing Systems
LO 2 Apply activity-based costing to a manufacturer.	• Identify and classify activities and allocate overhead to cost pools • Identify cost drivers • Compute activity-based overhead rates • Assign overhead costs • Comparing unit costs	**DO IT! 2** Apply ABC to Manufacturer
LO 3 Explain the benefits and limitations of activity-based costing.	• Advantage of multiple cost pools • Advantage of enhanced cost control • Advantage of better management decisions • Limitations of ABC	**DO IT! 3** Classify Activity Levels
LO 4 Apply activity-based costing to service industries.	• Traditional costing example • ABC example	**DO IT! 4** Apply ABC to Service Company

Go to the Review and Practice section at the end of the chapter for a targeted summary and practice applications with solutions.

TRADITIONAL VS. ACTIVITY-BASED COSTING

Traditional Costing Systems

LEARNING OBJECTIVE 1
Discuss the difference between traditional costing and activity-based costing.

It is probably impossible to determine the *exact* cost of a product or service. However, in order to achieve improved management decisions, companies strive to provide decision-makers with the most accurate cost estimates they can.

- The most accurate estimate of product cost occurs when the costs are traced directly to the actual product or service.
- Direct materials and direct labor costs are the easiest to trace directly to the product through the use of material requisition forms and payroll time sheets.
- Overhead costs, on the other hand, are an indirect or common cost that generally cannot be easily or directly traced to individual products or services. Instead, companies use estimates to assign overhead costs to products and services.

Often, the most difficult part of computing accurate unit costs is determining the proper amount of **overhead cost** to assign to each product, service, or job.

- In our coverage of job order costing in Chapter 2 and of process costing in Chapter 3, we used a single or plantwide overhead rate throughout the year for the entire factory operation. That rate was called the **predetermined overhead rate**.
- For job order costing, we assumed that **direct labor (cost or hours)** was the relevant activity base for assigning all overhead costs to jobs. For process costing, we frequently assumed that **machine hours** was the relevant activity base for assigning all overhead to the process or department.

Illustration 4.1 displays a simplified (one-stage) traditional costing system relying on direct labor to assign overhead.

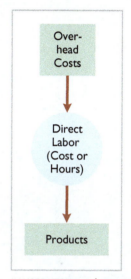

ILLUSTRATION 4.1 | Traditional one-stage costing system

Illustration of a Traditional Costing System

To illustrate a traditional costing system, assume that Odin AG produces two abdominal fitness products—the Ab Bench and the Ab Coaster. Each year, the company produces 25,000 Ab Benches but only 5,000 Ab Coasters (to simplify our example, we assume that all units manufactured in a year are sold in that same year). Each unit produced requires one hour of direct labor, for a total of 30,000 labor hours (25,000 + 5,000). The direct labor cost is €12 per unit for each product. Total direct labor costs are €360,000 [€12 × (25,000 + 5,000)].

The direct materials cost per unit is €40 for the Ab Bench and €30 for the Ab Coaster. Therefore, the per unit direct materials and direct labor costs are €52 for the Ab Bench and €42 for the Ab Coaster, as shown in **Illustration 4.2**. Total direct materials costs are €1,150,000 [(€40 × 25,000) + (€30 × 5,000)].

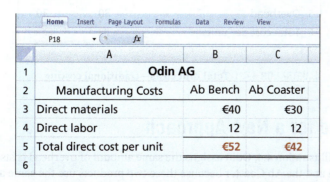

ILLUSTRATION 4.2 | Direct costs per unit—traditional costing

Odin expects to incur annual manufacturing overhead costs of €900,000. It sells the Ab Bench for €200 and the Ab Coaster for €170. Using this information, plus assumed data regarding selling and administrative expenses, a multiple-step income statement is provided in **Illustration 4.3**.

Odin AG
Income Statement
For the Year Ended December 31, 2023

Sales		€5,850,000
Cost of goods sold*		
Direct materials	€1,150,000	
Direct labor	360,000	
Manufacturing overhead	900,000	2,410,000
Gross profit		3,440,000
Selling and administrative expenses		
Administrative expenses	450,000	
Selling expenses	360,000	810,000
Net income		€2,630,000

*Because we have assumed that all goods produced during the period were sold, the cost of goods manufactured is equal to the cost of goods sold.

ILLUSTRATION 4.3 | **Income statement for Odin AG**

As discussed, the cost of direct materials and direct labor can be directly traced to each product. However, manufacturing overhead cannot be traced directly; instead, it must be assigned using a predetermined overhead rate in order to determine product cost.

Odin assigns overhead using a single predetermined overhead rate based on the 30,000 direct labor hours it expects to use this year. Thus, the predetermined overhead rate is €30 per direct labor hour (€900,000 ÷ 30,000 direct labor hours).

Since both products require one direct labor hour per unit, both products are assigned overhead costs of €30 per unit under traditional costing. **Illustration 4.4** shows the total unit costs for the Ab Bench and the Ab Coaster.

Odin AG

Manufacturing Costs	Ab Bench	Ab Coaster
Direct materials	€40	€30
Direct labor	12	12
Overhead	30	30
Total cost per unit	€82	€72

ILLUSTRATION 4.4 | **Total unit costs—traditional costing**

The Need for a New Approach

As shown in Illustration 4.4, Odin assigns the same amount of overhead costs per unit to both the Ab Bench and the Ab Coaster because these two products use the same amount of direct labor hours per unit.

- Historically, the use of direct labor as the activity base seemed to make sense as direct labor made up a large portion of total manufacturing cost.
- Also, there often was a correlation between direct labor and the incurrence of overhead cost.
- Direct labor thus became the most popular basis for allocating overhead.

However, using a single rate based on direct labor hours may not be the best approach for Odin to assign its overhead.

In recent years, manufacturers and service providers have experienced tremendous changes. Advances in computerized systems, technological innovations, global competition, and automation have altered the manufacturing environment drastically.

- As a result, the amount of direct labor used in many industries has greatly decreased, and total overhead costs resulting from depreciation on expensive equipment and machinery, utilities, repairs, and maintenance have significantly increased.
- When there is less (or no) correlation between direct labor and overhead costs incurred, plantwide predetermined overhead rates based on direct labor are misleading.

Companies that use overhead rates based on direct labor when this correlation does not exist experience significant product cost distortions.

To minimize such distortions, many companies began to use machine hours instead of labor hours as the basis to assign overhead in an automated manufacturing environment. But, even machine hours may not serve as a good basis for plantwide allocation of overhead costs. For example, product design and engineering costs are not correlated with machine hours but instead with the number of different items a company produces.

- Companies that have complex processes need to use multiple allocation bases to compute accurate product costs.
- An overhead cost allocation method that uses multiple bases is **activity-based costing**.

Activity-Based Costing

Activity-based costing (ABC) is an approach for allocating overhead costs. Specifically, ABC allocates overhead to multiple activity cost pools and then assigns the activity cost pools to products and services by means of cost drivers. In using ABC, you need to understand the following concepts:

Key Concepts

Activity. Any event, action, transaction, or work sequence that incurs costs when producing a product or performing a service.

Activity cost pool. The overhead cost attributed to a distinct activity (e.g., ordering materials or setting up machines).

Cost driver. Any factor or activity that has a direct cause-effect relationship with the resources consumed.

Activity-based costing involves the following four steps, as shown in **Illustration 4.5**.

- Step 1 allocates overhead costs to activity cost pools. Examples of overhead cost pools are ordering materials, setting up machines, assembling products, and inspecting products.
- Steps 2–4 assign the overhead in the activity cost pools to products, using cost drivers.

The cost drivers are activities undertaken to produce goods or perform services, which cause the company to consume resources. Examples are number of purchase orders, number of machine setups, labor hours, and number of inspections.

Illustration 4.6 shows examples of activities, and possible cost drivers to measure them, for a company that manufactures two types of equipment—lawn mowers and snow throwers.

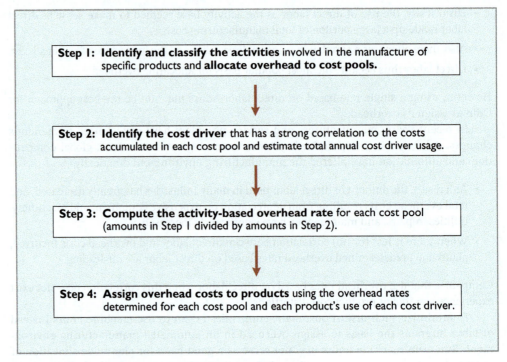

ILLUSTRATION 4.5 | The four steps of activity-based costing

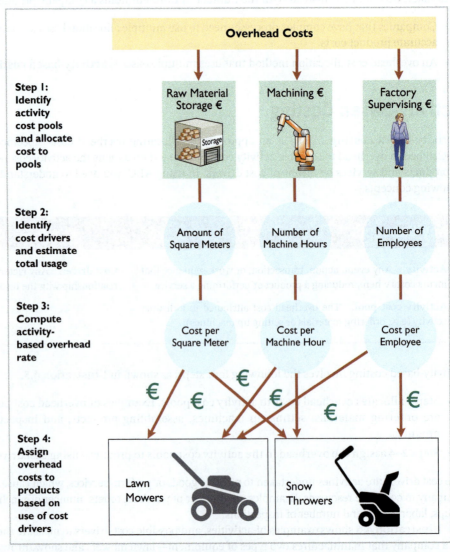

ILLUSTRATION 4.6 | Activities and related cost drivers

- In the first step, the company allocates overhead costs to activity cost pools. In this simplified example, the company has identified three activity cost pools: raw material storage, machining, and factory supervising.
- After the costs are allocated to the activity cost pools, the company uses cost drivers to determine the costs to assign to the individual products based on each product's use of each activity. For example, if lawn mowers require more activity by the machining department, as measured by the number of machine hours, then more of the overhead costs from the machining pool are assigned to the lawn mowers.
- The more complex a product's manufacturing operation, the more activities and cost drivers it is likely to have. If there is little or no correlation between changes in the cost driver and consumption of the overhead cost, inaccurate product costs are inevitable.

DO IT! 1 ▶ Costing Systems

Indicate whether the following statements are true or false.

1. A traditional costing system assigns overhead by means of multiple overhead rates.
2. Direct materials and direct labor costs are easier to trace to products than overhead.
3. As manufacturing processes have become more automated, more companies have chosen to assign overhead on the basis of direct labor costs.
4. In activity-based costing, an activity is any event, action, transaction, or work sequence that incurs cost when producing goods or performing services.

Solution

1. False.   2. True.   3. False.   4. True.

Related exercise material: **BE4.1, BE4.2, DO IT! 4.1, E4.1, and E4.2.**

ACTION PLAN
- Understand that a traditional costing system assigns overhead on the basis of a single predetermined overhead rate.
- Understand that an ABC system allocates overhead to identified activity cost pools and then assigns costs to products using related cost drivers that measure the resources consumed.

ABC AND MANUFACTURERS

In this section, we present a simple case example that compares activity-based costing with traditional costing. It illustrates how ABC eliminates the cost distortions that can occur in traditional overhead cost allocation.

- As you study this example, you should understand that ABC does not *replace* an existing job order or process cost system.
- What ABC does is to segregate overhead into various cost pools in an effort to provide more accurate cost information.

As a result, ABC supplements—rather than replaces—these cost systems.

Let's return to our Odin AG example. Using the information from Illustration 4.4, we can calculate unit costs under ABC. As shown earlier in Illustration 4.5, activity-based costing involves the following four steps:

1. **Identify and classify the activities** involved in the manufacture of specific products and **allocate overhead to cost pools**.
2. **Identify the cost driver** that has a strong correlation to the costs accumulated in each cost pool and estimate total annual cost driver usage.
3. **Compute the activity-based overhead rate** for each cost pool.
4. **Assign overhead costs to products** using the overhead rates determined for each cost pool and each product's use of each cost driver.

LEARNING OBJECTIVE 2
Apply activity-based costing to a manufacturer.

Identify and Classify Activities and Allocate Overhead to Cost Pools (Step 1)

Activity-based costing starts with an analysis of the activities needed to manufacture a product or perform a service.

- This analysis should identify all resource-consuming activities.
- It requires documenting every activity undertaken to accomplish a task.

Odin AG identifies four activity cost pools: manufacturing, machine setups, purchase ordering, and factory maintenance.

Next, the company allocates overhead costs directly to the appropriate activity cost pool. For example, Odin allocates all overhead costs directly associated with machine setups (such as salaries, supplies, and depreciation) to the setup cost pool. **Illustration 4.7** shows the four cost pools, along with the estimated overhead allocated to each cost pool. Note that the total estimated overhead is €900,000 under either traditional costing or ABC.

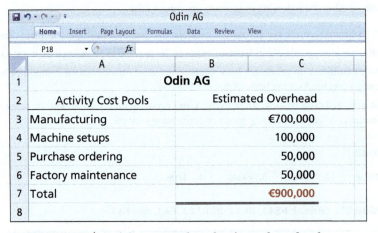

ILLUSTRATION 4.7 | Activity cost pools and estimated overhead

Identify Cost Drivers (Step 2)

After costs are allocated to the activity cost pools, the company must identify the cost drivers for each cost pool. The cost driver must accurately measure the actual consumption of the activity by the various products.

- To achieve accurate costing, a **high degree of correlation** must exist between the cost driver and the actual consumption of the overhead costs in the cost pool.
- This is an area that has benefited greatly from company data collection efforts at nearly every stage of the value chain.
- By applying analytics to this data, the company can increase the likelihood that cost drivers are closely related to resource consumption.

Availability and ease of obtaining data relating to the cost driver is an important factor that must be considered in its selection.

Illustration 4.8 shows the cost drivers that Odin AG identifies and their total estimated use per activity cost pool. For example, the cost driver for the machine setup cost pool is the number of setups. A product that requires more setups will cause more setup costs to be incurred, and it therefore should be assigned more overhead costs from the setup cost pool. The total number of setups is estimated to be 2,000 for the year.

Activity Cost Pools	Cost Drivers	Estimated Use of Cost Drivers per Activity
Manufacturing	Machine hours	50,000 machine hours
Machine setups	Number of setups	2,000 setups
Purchase ordering	Number of purchase orders	2,500 purchase orders
Factory maintenance	Square meters	25,000 square meters

ILLUSTRATION 4.8 | Cost drivers and their estimated use

Compute Activity-Based Overhead Rates (Step 3)

Next, the company computes an **activity-based overhead rate** per cost driver by dividing the estimated overhead per activity by the number of cost drivers estimated to be used per activity.

- This step is similar to calculating a predetermined overhead rate under the traditional costing approach except that instead of one rate for the company, there is one rate per cost pool.
- Illustration 4.9 shows the equation for this computation.

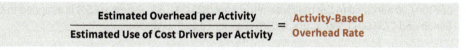

ILLUSTRATION 4.9 | Equation for computing activity-based overhead rate

Odin AG computes its activity-based overhead rates by using the estimated overhead per activity cost pool, shown in Illustration 4.7, and the estimated use of cost drivers per activity, shown in Illustration 4.8. These computations are presented in **Illustration 4.10**. For example, €100,000 was allocated to the machine setup pool, and the estimated number of annual setups is 2,000. The activity-based rate for machine setups is therefore €50 per setup (€100,000 ÷ 2,000 setups).

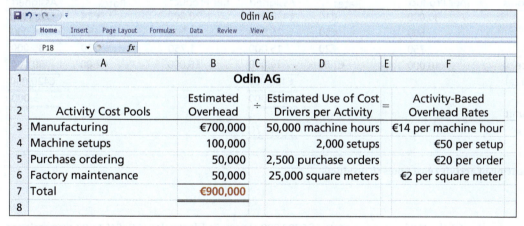

ILLUSTRATION 4.10 | Computation of activity-based overhead rates

Assign Overhead Costs to Products (Step 4)

In allocating overhead costs, the company must know the use of cost drivers **for each product**. Because of its low volume and higher number of components, the Ab Coaster requires more setups and purchase orders than the Ab Bench. **Illustration 4.11** shows the use of cost drivers per product for each of Odin AG's products. Note that of the 2,000 estimated total setups, 500 result from producing the Ab Bench and 1,500 result from the Ab Coaster.

Activity Cost Pools	Cost Drivers	Estimated Use of Cost Drivers per Activity	Use of Cost Drivers per Product	
			Ab Bench	Ab Coaster
Manufacturing	Machine hours	50,000 machine hours	30,000	20,000
Machine setups	Number of setups	2,000 setups	500	1,500
Purchase ordering	Number of purchase orders	2,500 purchase orders	750	1,750
Factory maintenance	Square meters	25,000 square meters	10,000	15,000

ILLUSTRATION 4.11 | **Use of cost drivers per product**

To assign overhead costs to each product, Odin multiplies the activity-based overhead rates per cost driver (Illustration 4.10) by the number of cost drivers used per product (Illustration 4.11). **Illustration 4.12** shows the overhead cost assigned to each product. For example, of the total of €100,000 allocated to the machine setup pool, €25,000 (500 setups × €50) is assigned to the Ab Bench and €75,000 (1,500 setups × €50) is assigned to the Ab Coaster.

Odin AG

	Ab Bench			Ab Coaster		
Activity Cost Pools	Use of Cost Drivers per Product	× Activity-Based Overhead Rates	= Cost Assigned	Use of Cost Drivers per Product	× Activity-Based Overhead Rates	= Cost Assigned
Manufacturing	30,000	€14	€420,000	20,000	€14	€280,000
Machine setups	500	€50	25,000	1,500	€50	75,000
Purchase ordering	750	€20	15,000	1,750	€20	35,000
Factory maintenance	10,000	€2.00	20,000	15,000	€2.00	30,000
Total costs assigned (a)			€480,000			€420,000
Units produced (b)			25,000			5,000
Overhead cost per unit [(a) ÷ (b)], rounded			€19.20			€84.00

ILLUSTRATION 4.12 | **Allocation of activity cost pools to products**

Of the total overhead costs of €900,000 shown in Illustration 4.7, €480,000 was assigned to the Ab Bench and €420,000 to the Ab Coaster. Under ABC, the overhead cost per unit is €19.20 (€480,000 ÷ 25,000) for the Ab Bench and €84.00 (€420,000 ÷ 5,000) for the Ab Coaster. We see next how this per unit amount substantially differs from that computed under a traditional costing system.

Comparing Unit Costs

Illustration 4.13 compares the unit costs for Odin AG's Ab Bench and Ab Coaster under traditional costing and ABC.

	Ab Bench		Ab Coaster	
Manufacturing Costs	Traditional Costing	ABC	Traditional Costing	ABC
Direct materials	€40.00	€40.00	€30.00	€ 30.00
Direct labor	12.00	12.00	12.00	12.00
Overhead	30.00	19.20	30.00	84.00
Total cost per unit	€82.00	€71.20	€72.00	€126.00
	Overstated €10.80		Understated €54.00	

ILLUSTRATION 4.13 | Comparison of unit product costs

The comparison shows that unit costs under traditional costing are different and often misleading.

- Traditional costing overstates the cost of producing the Ab Bench by €10.80 per unit and understates the cost of producing the Ab Coaster by €54 per unit.
- These differences are attributable to how Odin assigns manufacturing overhead across the two systems.

Using a traditional costing system, each product was assigned the same amount of overhead (€30) because both products use the same amount of the cost driver (direct labor hours). In contrast, ABC assigns overhead to products based on multiple cost drivers. For example, under ABC, Odin assigns 75% of the costs of equipment setups to Ab Coasters because Ab Coasters were responsible for 75% (1,500 ÷ 2,000) of the total number of setups.

Note that activity-based costing does not change the amount of total manufacturing overhead costs.

- Under both traditional costing and ABC, Odin spends the same amount of overhead—€900,000.
- However, ABC assigns manufacturing overhead costs in a more accurate manner.

Thus, ABC helps Odin avoid some negative consequences of a traditional costing system, such as overpricing its Ab Benches and thereby possibly losing market share to competitors. Odin has also been sacrificing profitability by underpricing the Ab Coaster.

Companies that move from traditional costing to ABC often have similar experiences as ABC shifts costs from high-volume products to low-volume products. This shift occurs because traditional overhead allocation uses volume-driven bases such as labor hours or machine hours. The traditional approach ignores the fact that many overhead costs are not correlated with volume. In addition, ABC recognizes products' use of resources, which also increases the accuracy of product costs.

MANAGEMENT INSIGHT

CGinspiration/ Getty Images

ABC Evaluated

Surveys of companies often show ABC usage of approximately 50%. Yet, in recent years, articles about ABC have expressed mixed opinions regarding its usefulness. To evaluate ABC practices and user satisfaction with ABC, a survey was conducted of 348 companies worldwide. Some of the interesting findings included the following: ABC methods are widely used across the entire value chain, rather than being primarily used to assign production-specific costs; only 25% of non-ABC companies think they are accurately tracing the costs of activities, while 70% of ABC companies think their company does this well; and respondents felt that ABC provides greater support for financial, operational, and strategic decisions. More than 87% of respondents said that their ideal costing system would include some form of ABC. Since this significantly exceeds the 50% of the respondents actually using it, ABC usage may well increase in the future.

Source: William Stratton, Denis Desroches, Raef Lawson, and Toby Hatch, "Activity-Based Costing: Is It Still Relevant?" *Management Accounting Quarterly* (Spring, 2009), pp. 31–39.

What might explain why so many companies say that ideally they would use ABC, but they haven't adopted it yet? (Answer is available in the book's product page on www.wiley.com)

DO IT! 2 — Apply ABC to Manufacturer

Florian Automobiles has five activity cost pools and two products. It estimates production of 200,000 units of its automobile scissors jack and 80,000 units of its truck hydraulic jack. Having identified its activity cost pools and the cost drivers for each cost pool, Florian accumulated the following data relative to those activity cost pools and cost drivers.

	Annual Overhead Data			Use of Cost Drivers per Product	
Activity Cost Pools	Cost Drivers	Estimated Overhead	Estimated Use of Cost Drivers per Activity	Scissors Jacks	Hydraulic Jacks
Ordering and receiving	Purchase orders	€ 200,000	2,500 orders	1,000	1,500
Machine setup	Setups	600,000	1,200 setups	500	700
Machining	Machine hours	2,000,000	800,000 machine hours	300,000	500,000
Assembling	Parts	1,800,000	3,000,000 parts	1,800,000	1,200,000
Inspecting and testing	Tests	700,000	35,000 tests	20,000	15,000
		€5,300,000			

Using the above data, do the following:

a. Prepare a schedule showing the computations of the activity-based overhead rates per cost driver.
b. Prepare a schedule assigning each activity's overhead cost to the two products.
c. Compute the overhead cost per unit for each product.
d. Comment on the comparative overhead cost per unit.

ACTION PLAN
- Determine the activity-based overhead rate by dividing the estimated overhead per activity by the estimated use of cost drivers per activity.

Solution

a. Computations of activity-based overhead rates per cost driver:

Activity Cost Pools	Estimated Overhead	÷	Estimated Use of Cost Drivers per Activity	=	Activity-Based Overhead Rates
Ordering and receiving	€ 200,000		2,500 purchase orders		€80 per order
Machine setup	600,000		1,200 setups		€500 per setup
Machining	2,000,000		800,000 machine hours		€2.50 per machine hour
Assembling	1,800,000		3,000,000 parts		€0.60 per part
Inspecting and testing	700,000		35,000 tests		€20 per test
	€5,300,000				

b. Assignment of each activity's overhead cost to products using ABC:

	Scissors Jacks			Hydraulic Jacks		
Activity Cost Pools	Use of Cost Drivers per Product ×	Activity-Based Overhead Rates	= Cost Assigned	Use of Cost Drivers per Product ×	Activity-Based Overhead Rates	= Cost Assigned
Ordering and receiving	1,000	€80	€ 80,000	1,500	€80	€ 120,000
Machine setup	500	€500	250,000	700	€500	350,000
Machining	300,000	€2.50	750,000	500,000	€2.50	1,250,000
Assembling	1,800,000	€0.60	1,080,000	1,200,000	€0.60	720,000
Inspecting and testing	20,000	€20	400,000	15,000	€20	300,000
Total assigned costs			€2,560,000			€2,740,000

c. Computation of overhead cost per unit:

	Scissors Jack	Hydraulic Jack
Total costs assigned (a)	€2,560,000	€2,740,000
Total units roduced (b)	200,000	80,000
Overhead cost per unit (a ÷ b)	€12.80	€34.25

d. These data show that the total overhead assigned to 80,000 hydraulic jacks exceeds the overhead assigned to 200,000 scissors jacks. The overhead cost per hydraulic jack is €34.25, but it is only €12.80 per scissors jack.

Related exercise material: **BE4.3, BE4.4, BE4.5, BE4.6, BE4.7, DO IT! 4.2, E4.3, E4.4, E4.5, E4.6, E4.7, and E4.8.**

ACTION PLAN
- Assign the overhead of each activity cost pool to the individual products by multiplying the use of cost driver per product times the activity-based overhead rate.
- Determine overhead cost per unit by dividing the overhead assigned to each product by the number of units of that product.

ABC BENEFITS AND LIMITATIONS

ABC has three primary benefits:

1. ABC employs more cost pools and therefore results in more accurate product costing.
2. ABC leads to enhanced control over overhead costs.
3. ABC supports better management decisions.

LEARNING OBJECTIVE 3
Explain the benefits and limitations of activity-based costing.

The Advantage of Multiple Cost Pools

The main mechanism by which ABC increases product cost accuracy is the use of multiple cost pools. Instead of one plantwide pool (or even several departmental pools) and a single cost driver, companies use numerous activity cost pools with more relevant cost drivers. Thus, costs are assigned more accurately on the basis of the cost drivers used to produce each product.

Note that in the Odin AG example, the *manufacturing* cost pool reflected multiple manufacturing activities, including machining, assembling, and painting. These activities were included in a single pool for simplicity.

- If we had instead broken the manufacturing pool into multiple pools, we would have used cost drivers specific to each pool.
- This would lead to more accurate overhead allocation.

In many companies, the number of activities—and thus the number of pools—can be substantial. For example, **Clark-Hurth** (a division of **Clark Equipment Company** [USA]), a manufacturer of axles and transmissions, identified over 170 activities. **Compumotor** (a division of **Parker Hannifin** [USA]) identified over 80 activities in just the procurement function of its Material Control Department. **Illustration 4.14** shows a more likely "split" of the activities that were included in Odin's manufacturing cost pool, reflecting separate pools and drivers for each of those activities.

Assigning Nonmanufacturing Overhead Costs

To simplify our presentation and to enable a direct comparison of overhead allocation under traditional costing versus activity-based costing, we assume that Odin AG only assigned manufacturing overhead costs to products. Consider again the multiple-step income statement presented for Odin AG, shown in **Illustration 4.15**.

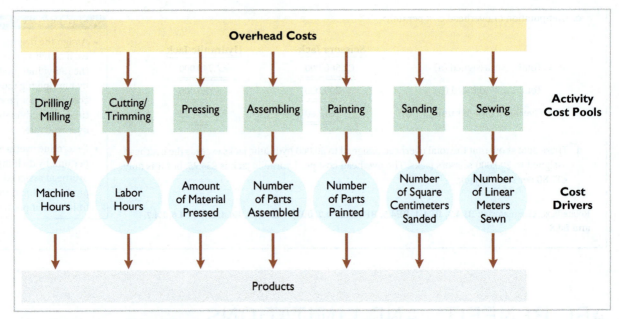

ILLUSTRATION 4.14 | A more detailed view of Odin's manufacturing activities

Odin AG
Income Statement
For the Year Ended December 31, 2023

Sales		€5,850,000
Cost of goods sold*		
Direct materials	€1,150,000	
Direct labor	360,000	
Manufacturing overhead	900,000	2,410,000
Gross profit		3,440,000
Selling and administrative expenses		
Administrative expenses	450,000	
Selling expenses	360,000	810,000
Net income		€2,630,000

*Because we have assumed that all goods produced during the period were sold, the cost of goods manufactured is equal to the cost of goods sold.

ILLUSTRATION 4.15 | Income statement for Odin AG showing manufacturing and nonmanufacturing costs

The nonmanufacturing overhead costs included in selling and administrative expenses represent a significant portion of the company's costs.

- Accounting standards require that these costs be expensed during the current period as period costs, rather than assigning these costs to products.
- However, to gain a better understanding of product and/or customer profitability, many companies use activity-based costing to assign some nonmanufacturing costs to products or customers.
- For example, if shipping costs are included in the selling expenses category, those costs can usually be directly traced to specific products. Note that the incurrence of other costs included in selling expenses can vary considerably across products or customers.

For example, suppose that Odin sells its products to three different types of customers: (1) "big box" stores, (2) workout facilities, and (3) individuals via online sales. The demands on the company's sales resources (e.g., order taking, order filling, sales calls, travel, and warranty costs) might vary considerably across these three sales channels. To evaluate the relative profitability of each of these three sales channels, Odin could use activity-based costing to allocate the sales costs to these three customer types for internal decision-making purposes.

Classification of Activity Levels

To gain the full advantage of having multiple cost pools, the costs within the pool must be correlated with the driver. To achieve this, a company's managers often characterize activities as belonging to one of the following four activity-level groups when designing an ABC system.

1. **Unit-level activities** are performed for each unit of production. For example, the assembly of cell phones is a unit-level activity because the amount of assembly the company performs increases with each additional cell phone assembled.

2. **Batch-level activities** are performed every time a company produces another batch of a product. For example, suppose that to start processing a new batch of ice cream, an ice cream producer needs to set up its machines. The amount of time spent setting up and cleaning up machines increases with the number of batches produced, not with the number of units produced.

3. **Product-level activities** are performed every time a company produces a new type of product. For example, before a pharmaceutical company can produce and sell a new type of medicine, it must undergo very substantial product tests to ensure the product is effective and safe. The amount of time spent on testing activities increases with the number of products the company produces.

4. **Facility-level activities** are required to support or sustain an entire production process. Consider, for example, a hospital. The hospital building must be insured and heated, and the property taxes must be paid, no matter how many patients the hospital treats. These costs do not vary as a function of the number of units, batches, or products.

Companies may achieve greater accuracy in overhead cost allocation to products by recognizing these four different levels of activities and, from them, developing specific activity cost pools and their related cost drivers. **Illustration 4.16** depicts this four-level activity hierarchy, along with the types of activities and examples of cost drivers for those activities at each level.

Note that sometimes the classification of an activity will depend on the context. For example, in some circumstances, inspection is a batch-level activity that is driven by the number of batches or setups. This is because the company will have to ensure that the setup was done properly and did not cause a deviation from product specifications. However, inspection can also be a unit-level activity that is driven by the number of units produced.

The Advantage of Enhanced Cost Control

Some companies experiencing the benefits of activity-based costing have applied it to a broader range of management activities. **Activity-based management (ABM)** extends the use of ABC from product costing to a comprehensive management tool that focuses on reducing costs and improving processes and decision-making.

For example, in developing an ABC system, managers increase their awareness of the activities performed by the company in its production and supporting processes.

- Many companies now employ lean manufacturing practices, which require that the companies review all business processes in an effort to increase productivity and eliminate waste.
- As part of this process, managers classify activities as value-added or non-valued-added.

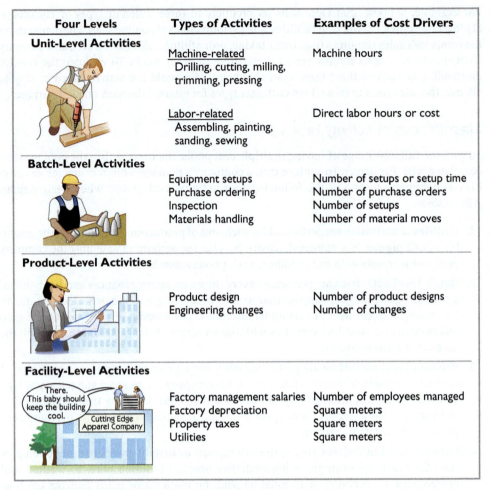

ILLUSTRATION 4.16 | Hierarchy of activity levels

Value-added activities are essential activities of **a company's operations** that increase the perceived value of a product or service to customers. Examples for the manufacture of **Technogym** (ITA) exercise equipment include engineering design, machining, assembly, assembly supervision, and painting. Supervision of a value-added activity is itself a value-added activity, as it coordinates and manages the value-added activity with a goal of improving operations. Thus, since assembly is a value-added activity, supervision of assembly is also value-added. Examples of value-added activities in a service company include performing surgery at a hospital, performing legal research at a law firm, and delivering packages by a freight company.

Non–value-added activities are nonessential activities that, if eliminated, would not reduce the perceived value of a company's product or service. These activities simply **add cost to, or increase the time spent on, a product or service without increasing its perceived value**. One example is inventory storage. If a company **eliminated the need** to store inventory, it would not reduce the value of its product, but it would decrease its product costs. Similarly, inspections are a non–value-added activity. A company can eliminate the need for inspections by improving its production process. Thus, the elimination of inspection would not reduce the value of the product. Other examples include moving materials, work in process, or finished goods from one location to another in the factory during the production process; waiting for manufacturing equipment to become available; and fixing defective goods under warranty.

Companies often use **activity flowcharts** to help identify the ABC activities, such as the one shown in **Illustration 4.17** (see **Decision Tools**). The top part of this flowchart identifies activities as value-added (highlighted in red) or non–value-added. Two rows in the lower part of the flowchart show the number of days spent on each activity. The first row shows the number of days spent on each activity under the current manufacturing process. The second row

DECISION TOOLS

The activity flowchart helps managers identify and reduce non–value-added activities.

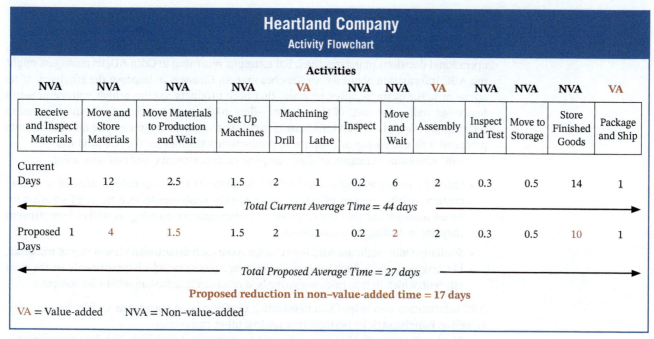

ILLUSTRATION 4.17 | **Analyzing non–value-added activities to improve operations**

shows the number of days estimated to be spent on each activity under management's proposed reengineered manufacturing process.

- The proposed changes would reduce time spent on non–value-added activities by 17 days.
- This 17-day improvement is due entirely to moving inventory more quickly through the non–value-added processes—that is, by reducing inventory time in moving, storage, and waiting.

Appendix 4A discusses a just-in-time inventory system, which some companies use to eliminate non–value-added activities related to inventory.

Not all activities labeled non–value-added are totally wasteful, nor can they be totally eliminated. For example, although inspection time is a non–value-added activity from a customer's perspective, few companies would eliminate their quality control functions. Similarly, moving and waiting time is non–value-added, but it would be impossible to completely eliminate in most instances. Nevertheless, when managers recognize the non–value-added characteristic of these activities, they are motivated to minimize them as much as possible. Attention to such matters is part of the growing practice of activity-based management, which helps managers concentrate on **continuous improvement** of operations and activities.

MANAGEMENT INSIGHT Orica

agnormark/Getty Images

Orica (AUS), which sells explosives to quarry companies, faced competition from a number of low-cost competitors. As these low-cost competitors penetrated the market, quarry companies tried to make up needed profits by ordering rationed amounts of explosives from inexpert discounters rather than from Orica. With Orica's financial bottom line nearly destroyed, the company examined the value-added activities of their customers and came up with a new profit model.

Orica chose to fight their low-cost rivals by expanding the catalog of products and services offered as an integrated package. Over time, this strategy prevailed because low-cost players, with limited product ranges and service capabilities, were unable to offer solutions that satisfied a diverse set of needs.

The result has been that customers do not look to the low-price competition that sells only explosives because they pay for activities rather than a physical product. Although Orica still sells explosives indirectly as part of a service (or set of activities), customers have become more dependent on Orica's enhanced competence and knowledge in blasting solutions and therefore invest less of their own money in the process.

Source: N. Kumar, "Strategies to Fight Low-Cost Rivals," *Harvard Business Review* (December 2016).

How has Orica benefited from the identification of value-added activities? (Answer is available in the book's product page on www.wiley.com)

The Advantage of Better Management Decisions

Managers extend the use of ABC via activity-based management (ABM) for both strategic and operational decisions or perspectives. For example, returning to Odin AG, its managers might use ABC information about its Ab Benches and Ab Coasters to improve the efficiency of its operations. For example, after realizing that both products require a high volume of setup hours—as well as the costs of these hours—they might want to reduce the hours required to set up production runs. Such information may lead managers to increase the number of units produced with each setup or to optimize production schedules for the two products.

ABC also helps managers evaluate employees, departments, and business units.

- Odin, for example, might use ABC information about salespeople's activities related to customer visits, number of orders, and post-sales customer service. Such information informs managers about how much effort salespeople are exerting, as well as how efficient they are in dealing with customers.
- Similarly, Odin might use ABC information about each department's use of shared resources, like inventory space. Such information lets managers know which departments are the most efficient, which in turn leads to sharing best-practices information within the company.

ABC information also helps Odin to establish **performance standards** within the company, as well as **benchmark** its performance against other companies.

The implications of ABC are not limited to operational decisions. The differences in profitability between the Ab Benches and Ab Coasters may suggest a need to change the company's product mix. Such considerations, in turn, have implications for Odin's marketing strategy. ABM may guide managers in considering different target customer markets for the two products. Or, managers might consider bundling the two products into a "home gym" set. As another, more extreme, example, managers might consider outsourcing production for one of the products or dropping one of the product lines altogether.

It is often the case that ABM for one perspective has implications for another perspective.

- For instance, the strategic decision to drop a product line is usually followed by operational decisions regarding what to do with employees' time or the machinery and equipment originally used to manufacture the dropped product.
- Similarly, increases in employees' efficiency following from operational decisions often lead to changes in employee hiring and compensation strategy.

The interrelated nature of the strategic and operational perspectives often means that a decision is not made until the cascading implications of that decision are also identified and considered.

Some Limitations and Knowing When to Use ABC

ABC can be very beneficial, but it is not without its limitations.

1. **ABC can be expensive to use.** The increased cost of identifying multiple activities and applying numerous cost drivers discourages many companies from using ABC.
2. **ABC systems are more complex than traditional systems.**
3. **Some arbitrary allocations remain.** Even though more overhead costs can be assigned directly to products through ABC, some overhead costs might still be assigned by fairly arbitrary cost drivers. For example, Odin AG allocated €50,000 of overhead pertaining to insurance and property taxes to the facility management cost pool. Odin assigned this €50,000 using square meters used by each product (10,000 square meters for Ab Benches and 15,000 square meters for Ab Coasters). A more accurate driver of insurance costs might be replacement costs of production equipment for each product type. However, such information may not be readily available, and Odin must make do with square meters.

So companies must ask, is the cost of implementation greater than the benefit of greater accuracy? For some companies, there may be no need to consider ABC at all because their existing system is sufficient.

In light of these limitations, how does a company know when to use ABC? The presence of one or more of the following factors would point to possible use:

1. Product lines differ greatly in volume and manufacturing complexity.
2. Product lines are numerous and diverse, requiring various degrees of support services.
3. Overhead costs constitute a significant portion of total costs.
4. The manufacturing process or the number of products has changed significantly, for example, from labor-intensive to capital-intensive due to automation.
5. Production or marketing managers are ignoring data provided by the existing system and are instead using "bootleg" costing data or other alternative data when pricing or making other product decisions.

Ultimately, it is important to realize that the redesign and installation of a product costing system is a significant decision that requires considerable cost and a major effort to accomplish (see **Decision Tools**).

- Financial managers need to be cautious and deliberate when initiating changes in costing systems, giving careful consideration to the relative costs and benefits.
- A key factor in implementing a successful ABC system is the support of top management, especially given that the benefits of ABC are not completely visible until *after* it has been implemented.

DECISION TOOLS

Companies replace traditional costing with ABC when ABC provides more accurate information at a reasonable cost.

DATA ANALYTICS INSIGHT

Istudioworkstock/Shutterstock.com

Delivering People and Packages

In the past, one of the main barriers to implementing ABC was the high cost of data collection needed to determine cost pools, cost drivers, and activity usage. But today's automated systems collect data on virtually every aspect of a company's operations, thus helping a company to more easily implement ABC and employ ABM. This data can also help companies employ ABM by reducing non–value-added activities.

For example, for airlines, nonscheduled maintenance and repairs is a significant non–value-added activity that causes many flight delays. In response, **General Electric** (USA), which makes many of the engines used in passenger jets, now equips its jet engines with sensors, which makes it possible to predict when parts are likely to fail. The airline can then preemptively schedule maintenance and preorder parts as needed.

Data analytics can also help to streamline operations and improve efficiency in package delivery. The goal of a package delivery company is to get packages to the destination in a cost-effective and timely fashion. And when these packages contain medical supplies, this goal can take on an added urgency as some medical supplies expire very quickly. **UPS** (USA) handles this issue by placing sensors on high-priority medical packages, which allows the company to continuously track the packages. UPS couples this with continuous data regarding weather patterns and other potential delivery disruptions to determine if the company should reroute any of these packages to avoid delays.

Sources: Sara Castellanos, "UPS to Use Sensors That Can Track Medical Packages at All Times," *Wall Street Journal Online* (November 20, 2019); and Bernard Marr, *Big Data in Practice* (Hoboken, N.J.: John Wiley & Sons, 2016), pp. 125–129.

How do big data and data analytics help companies implement and employ ABC and ABM? (Answer is available in the book's product page on www.wiley.com)

DO IT! 3 ▶ Classify Activity Levels

Merlin Toys manufactures six primary product lines of toys in its factory. As a result of an activity analysis, the accounting department has identified eight activity cost pools. Each of the toy products is produced in large batches, with the whole factory devoted to one product at a time. Classify each of the following activities as either unit-level, batch-level, product-level, or facility-level: (a) engineering design, (b) machine setup, (c) toy design, (d) interviews of prospective factory managers, (e) inspections after each setup, (f) polishing parts, (g) assembling parts, and (h) health and safety.

Solution

a. Product-level. b. Batch-level. c. Product-level. d. Facility-level. e. Batch-level.
f. Unit-level. g. Unit-level. h. Facility-level.

Related exercise material: **BE4.10, BE4.11, BE4.12, DO IT! 4.3, E4.12, and E4.3.**

ACTION PLAN

- You should use unit-level activities for each unit of product, batch-level activities for each batch of product, product-level activities for an entire product line, and facility-level activities for across the entire range of products.

ABC AND SERVICE INDUSTRIES

LEARNING OBJECTIVE 4
Apply activity-based costing to service industries.

Although initially developed and implemented by manufacturers, activity-based costing has been widely adopted in service industries as well. ABC is used by airlines, railroads, hotels, hospitals, banks, insurance companies, telephone companies, and financial services firms.

- The overall objective of ABC in service firms is no different than it is in a manufacturing company.
- That objective is to identify the key activities that generate costs and to keep track of how many of those activities are completed for each service performed (by job, service, contract, or customer).

The general approach to identifying activities, activity cost pools, and cost drivers is the same for service companies and for manufacturers. Also, the labeling of activities as value-added and non–value-added, and the attempt to reduce or eliminate non–value-added activities as much as possible, is just as valid in service industries as in manufacturing operations. What sometimes makes implementation of activity-based costing difficult in service industries is that, compared to manufacturers, **a larger proportion of overhead costs are company-wide costs** that cannot be easily traced to specific services performed by the company.

To illustrate the application of activity-based costing to a service company contrasted to traditional costing, we use a public accounting firm. This illustration is applicable to any service firm that performs numerous services for a client as part of a job, such as a law, consulting, or architectural firm.

Traditional Costing Example

Assume that the accounting firm of Friedman and Associates prepares the condensed annual budget shown in **Illustration 4.18**. The firm engages in a number of services, including audit, tax, and computer consulting.

The cost of the professional service performed is usually based on direct labor. Under traditional costing, direct labor is the basis for overhead application to each job. As shown in Illustration 4.18, the predetermined overhead rate of 50% is calculated by dividing the total estimated overhead cost by the total direct labor cost. To determine the operating income earned on any job, Friedman and Associates applies overhead at the rate of 50% of

Friedman and Associates		
Annual Budget		
Revenue		€4,000,000
Direct labor	€1,200,000	
Overhead (estimated)	600,000	
Total costs		1,800,000
Operating income		€2,200,000

$$\frac{\text{Estimated overhead}}{\text{Direct labor cost}} = \text{Predetermined overhead rate}$$

$$\frac{€600,000}{€1,200,000} = 50\%$$

ILLUSTRATION 4.18 | **Condensed annual budget of a service firm under traditional costing**

actual direct professional labor costs incurred. For example, assume that Friedman and Associates records €140,000 of actual direct professional labor cost during its audit of Sofia Molding, which was billed an audit fee of €260,000. Under traditional costing, using 50% as the rate for applying overhead to the job, Friedman and Associates would compute applied overhead and operating income related to the Sofia Molding audit as shown in **Illustration 4.19**.

Friedman and Associates
Sofia Molding Audit

Revenue		€260,000
Less: Direct professional labor	€140,000	
Applied overhead (50% × €140,000)	70,000	210,000
Operating income		€ 50,000

ILLUSTRATION 4.19 | Overhead applied under traditional costing system

This example, under traditional costing, uses only one cost driver (direct labor cost) to determine the overhead application rate.

Activity-Based Costing Example

Under *activity-based costing*, Friedman and Associates distributes its estimated annual overhead costs of €600,000 to three activity cost pools. The firm computes activity-based overhead rates per cost driver by dividing the amount allocated to each activity overhead cost pool by the estimated number of cost drivers used per activity. **Illustration 4.20** shows an annual overhead budget using an ABC system.

Friedman and Associates
Annual Overhead Budget

Activity Cost Pools	Cost Drivers	Estimated Overhead	÷	Estimated Use of Cost Drivers per Activity	=	Activity-Based Overhead Rates
Administration	Number of partner-hours	€335,000		3,350		€100 per partner-hour
Customer development	Revenue billed	160,000		€4,000,000		€0.04 per €1 of revenue
Recruiting and training	Direct professional hours	105,000		30,000		€3.50 per professional hour
		€600,000				

ILLUSTRATION 4.20 | Condensed annual budget of a service firm under activity-based costing

The assignment of the individual overhead activity rates to the actual number of activities used in the performance of Sofia Molding audit results in total overhead assigned of €57,200, as shown in **Illustration 4.21**.

Under activity-based costing, Friedman and Associates assigns overhead costs of €57,200 to the Sofia Molding audit, as compared to €70,000 under traditional costing. **Illustration 4.22** compares total costs and operating margins under the two costing systems.

Friedman and Associates
Sofia Molding Audit

Activity Cost Pools	Cost Drivers	Use of Drivers	Activity-Based Overhead Rates	Cost Assigned
Administration	Number of partner-hours	335	€100.00	€33,500
Customer development	Revenue billed	€260,000	€0.04	10,400
Recruiting and training	Direct professional hours	3,800	€3.50	13,300
				€57,200

ILLUSTRATION 4.21 | Assigning overhead in a service company

Friedman and Associates
Sofia Molding Audit

	Traditional Costing		ABC	
Revenue		€260,000		€260,000
Expenses				
Direct professional labor	€140,000		€140,000	
Applied overhead	70,000		57,200	
Total expenses		210,000		197,200
Operating income		€ 50,000		€ 62,800
Profit margin		**19.2%**		**24.2%**

ILLUSTRATION 4.22 | Comparison of traditional costing with ABC in a service company

Illustration 4.22 shows that the assignment of overhead costs under traditional costing and ABC is different.

- The total cost assigned to performing the audit of Sofia Modeling is greater under traditional costing by €12,800 (€70,000 − €57,200), and the profit margin is significantly lower.
- Traditional costing understates the profitability of the audit.

SERVICE COMPANY INSIGHT American Airlines

Image by tookapic from Pixabay

Traveling Light

Have you flown on **American Airlines** (USA) since baggage fees have been implemented? Did the fee make you so mad that you swore that the next time you flew, you would pack fewer clothes so you could use a carry-on bag instead? That is exactly how American Airlines (and the other airlines that charge baggage fees) hoped that you would react. Baggage handling is extremely labor-intensive. All that tagging, sorting, loading on carts, loading in planes, unloading, and sorting again add up to about $9 per bag. Baggage handling also involves equipment costs: sorters, carts, conveyors, tractors, and storage facilities. That's about another $4 of equipment-related overhead per bag. Finally, there is the additional fuel cost of a 40-pound item—about $2 in fuel for a 3-hour flight. These costs add up to $15 ($9 + $4 + $2).

Since airlines have implemented their baggage fees, fewer customers are checking bags. Not only does this save the airlines money, it also increases the amount of space available for hauling cargo. An airline can charge at least $80 for hauling a small parcel for same-day delivery service.

For those bags that do still get checked-in by customers, **Alaska Airlines** (USA) has reduced its costs by employing barcode scanning of every bag that goes on and off a plane to speed up its sorting process.

Source: Scott McCartney, "What It Costs an Airline to Fly Your Luggage," *Wall Street Journal* (November 25, 2008); and Scott McCartney, "The Best and Worst Airlines of 2016" *Wall Street Journal* (January 11, 2017).

Why do airlines charge even higher rates for heavier bags, bags that are odd shapes (e.g., ski bags), and bags with hazardous materials in them? (Answer is available in the book's product page on www.wiley.com)

DO IT! 4 ▶ Apply ABC to Service Company

Benito Logistics is a trucking company. It provides local, short-haul, and long-haul services. The company has developed the following three cost pools.

Activity Cost Pools	Cost Drivers	Estimated Overhead	Estimated Use of Cost Drivers per Activity
Loading and unloading	Number of pieces	€ 70,000	100,000 pieces
Travel	Kilometers driven	250,000	500,000 kilometers
Logistics	Hours	60,000	2,000 hours

a. Compute the activity-based overhead rate for each pool.

b. Determine the overhead assigned to Job A1027, which has 150 pieces and requires 200 kilometers of driving and 0.75 hours of logistics.

ACTION PLAN
- Divide the estimated overhead by the estimated use of cost driver per activity to determine activity-based overhead rate.
- Apply the activity-based overhead rate to jobs based on actual use of drivers.

Solution

a. The activity based overhead rates are as follows:

Activity Cost Pools	Estimated Overhead	÷	Estimated Use of Cost Drivers per Activity	=	Activity-Based Overhead Rate
Loading and unloading	€ 70,000		100,000 pieces		€0.70 per piece
Travel	250,000		500,000 kilometers		€0.50 per kilometer
Logistics	60,000		2,000 hours		€30 per hour

b. The overhead applied to job A1027 is (150 × €0.70) + (200 × €0.50) + (0.75 × €30) = €227.50

Related exercise material: **BE4.12**, **DO IT! 4.4**, **E4.14**, **E4.15**, and **E4.17**.

USING THE DECISION TOOLS | Technogym

Technogym SpA (ITA) faces many situations where it needs to apply the decision tools learned in this chapter. As mentioned in the Feature Story, Technogym manufactures a line of high-end exercise equipment of commercial quality. Assume that the chief accountant has proposed changing from a traditional costing system to an activity-based costing system. The financial vice president is not convinced, so she requests that the next large order for equipment be costed under both systems for purposes of comparison and analysis. A new order from Bellissima Salons for 150 low-impact treadmills is identified as the test case. The following cost data relate to the Bellissima order.

Data relevant to both costing systems

Direct materials	$55,500
Direct labor hours	820
Direct labor rate per hour	$ 18.00

Data relevant to the traditional costing system

Predetermined overhead rate is 300% of direct labor cost.

Data relevant to the activity-based costing system

Activity Cost Pools	Cost Drivers	Activity-Based Overhead Rate	Estimated Use of Cost Drivers for Treadmill Order
Engineering design	Engineering hours	$30 per hour	330
Machine setup	Setups	$200 per setup	22
Machining	Machine hours	$25 per hour	732
Assembly	Number of subassemblies	$8 per subassembly	1,500
Packaging and shipping	Packaging/shipping hours	$15 per hour	152
Building occupancy	Machine hours	$6 per hour	732

Instructions

Compute the total cost of the Bellissima Salons order under (a) the traditional costing system and (b) the activity-based costing system. (c) Evaluate the results.

Solution

a. Traditional costing system:

Direct materials	$ 55,500
Direct labor (820 × $18)	14,760
Overhead assigned ($14,760 × 300%)	44,280
Total costs assigned to Bellissima order	$114,540
Number of low-impact treadmills	150
Cost per unit	$ 763.60

b. Activity-based costing system:

Direct materials		$ 55,500
Direct labor (820 × $18)		14,760
Overhead activities costs:		
Engineering design (330 hours @ $30)	$ 9,900	
Machine setup (22 setups @ $200)	4,400	
Machining (732 machine hours @ $25)	18,300	
Assembly (1,500 subassemblies @ $8)	12,000	
Packaging and shipping (152 hours @ $15)	2,280	
Building occupancy (732 hours @ $6)	4,392	51,272
Total costs assigned to Bellissima order		$121,532
Number of low-impact treadmills		150
Cost per unit		$ 810.21

c. Technogym will likely adopt ABC because of the difference in the cost per unit (which ABC found to be higher). More importantly, ABC provides greater insight into the sources and causes of the cost per unit. Managers are given greater insight into which activities to control in order to reduce costs. ABC will provide better product costing and greater profitability for the company.

Appendix 4A — JUST-IN-TIME PROCESSING

LEARNING OBJECTIVE *5
Explain just-in-time (JIT) processing.

Traditionally, continuous process manufacturing has been based on a **just-in-case** philosophy: Inventories of raw materials are maintained *just in case* some items are of poor quality or a key supplier is shut down by a strike. Similarly, subassembly parts are manufactured and stored *just in case* they are needed later in the manufacturing process. Finished goods are completed and stored *just in case* unexpected and rush customer orders are received. This philosophy often results in a "**push approach**," in which raw materials and subassembly parts are pushed through each process. Traditional processing often results in the buildup of extensive manufacturing inventories.

Primarily in response to foreign competition, many firms have switched to **just-in-time (JIT) processing**.

- JIT manufacturing is dedicated to having the right amounts of materials, parts, or products just as they are needed.
- JIT first hit the United States in the early 1980s when automobile companies adopted it to compete with foreign automakers. Many U.S. companies, including **Dell**, **Caterpillar**, and **Harley-Davidson**, now successfully use JIT.
- Under JIT processing, companies receive raw materials **just in time** for use in production, they complete subassembly parts **just in time** for use in finished goods, and they complete finished goods **just in time** to be sold.

Illustration 4A.1 shows the sequence of activities in just-in-time processing.

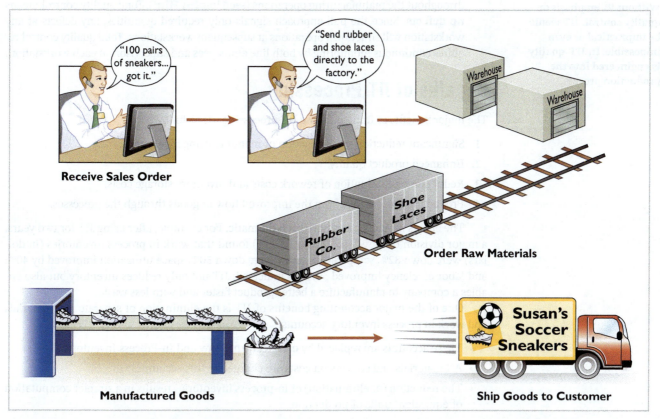

ILLUSTRATION 4A.1 | Just-in-time processing

Objective of JIT Processing

An ultimate objective of JIT is to eliminate manufacturing inventories. Inventories have an adverse effect on net income because they tie up funds and storage space that could be put to more productive uses. JIT strives to eliminate inventories by using a **"pull approach"** in manufacturing.

- This approach begins with the customer placing an order with the company, which starts the process of pulling the product through the manufacturing process.
- A computer at the final workstation sends a signal to the preceding workstation.
- This signal indicates the exact materials (parts and subassemblies) needed to complete the production of a specified product for a specified time period, such as an eight-hour shift.
- The next-preceding process, in turn, sends its signal to other processes back up the line.

The goal is a smooth, continuous flow in the manufacturing process, with no buildup of inventories at any point.

Elements of JIT Processing

There are three important elements in JIT processing:

1. **Dependable suppliers.** Suppliers must be willing to deliver on short notice exact quantities of raw materials according to precise quality specifications (even including multiple deliveries within the same day) (see **Helpful Hint**). Suppliers must also be willing to deliver the raw materials at specified workstations rather than at a central receiving department. This type of purchasing requires constant and direct communication. Such communication is facilitated by an online computer linkage between the company and its suppliers.

2. **A multiskilled work force.** Under JIT, machines are often strategically grouped into work cells or workstations. Much of the work is automated. As a result, one worker may operate and maintain several different types of machines.

HELPFUL HINT

Buyer leverage is important in finding dependable suppliers. U.S. companies like GM and Apple have more success than smaller companies.

HELPFUL HINT

Without its emphasis on quality control, JIT would be impractical or even impossible. In JIT, quality is engineered into the production process.

3. **A total quality control system.** The company must establish total quality control throughout the manufacturing operations (see **Helpful Hint**). Total quality control means **no defects**. Since the pull approach signals only required quantities, any defects at any workstation will shut down operations at subsequent workstations. Total quality control requires continuous monitoring by both line employees and supervisors at each workstation.

Benefits of JIT Processing

The major benefits of implementing JIT processing are as follows:

1. Significant reduction or elimination of manufacturing inventories.
2. Enhanced product quality.
3. Reduction or elimination of rework costs and inventory storage costs.
4. Production cost savings from the improved flow of goods through the processes.

The effects in many cases have been dramatic. For example, after using JIT for two years, a major division of **Hewlett-Packard** (USA) found that work in process inventories (in dollars) were down 82%, scrap/rework costs were down 30%, space utilization improved by 40%, and labor efficiency improved 50%. As indicated, JIT not only reduces inventory but also enables a company to manufacture a better product faster and with less waste.

One of the major accounting benefits of JIT is the elimination of separate raw materials and work in process inventory accounts.

- These accounts are replaced by **one account**, Raw and In-Process Inventory.
- All materials and conversion costs are charged to this account.
- The reduction (or elimination) of in-process inventories results in a simpler computation of equivalent units of production.

A significant potential downside of JIT is the higher risk of not having materials when they are needed. As noted above, JIT requires dependable suppliers. But even dependable suppliers cannot overcome unexpected situations, such as natural disasters, that disrupt the supply chain.

REVIEW AND PRACTICE

Learning Objectives Review

LO 1 Discuss the difference between traditional costing and activity-based costing.

A traditional costing system assigns overhead to products on the basis of predetermined plantwide or departmentwide rates such as direct labor or machine hours. An ABC system allocates overhead to identified activity cost pools and then assigns costs to products using related cost drivers that measure the activities (resources) consumed.

The development of an activity-based costing system involves the following four steps: (1) Identify and classify the major activities involved in the manufacture of specific products and allocate overhead to cost pools. (2) Identify the cost driver that has a strong correlation to the costs accumulated in each cost pool and estimate total annual cost driver usage. (3) Compute the activity-based overhead rate for each cost pool. (4) Assign overhead costs to products using the overhead rates determined for each cost pool and each product's use of each cost driver.

LO 2 Apply activity-based costing to a manufacturer.

To identify activity cost pools, a company must perform an analysis of each operation or process, documenting and timing every task, action, or transaction. Cost drivers identified for assigning activity cost pools must (a) accurately measure the actual consumption of the activity by the various products and (b) have related data easily available. The overhead allocated to each activity cost pool is divided by the estimated use of cost drivers to determine the activity-based overhead rate for each pool. Overhead is assigned to products by multiplying a particular product's estimated use of a cost driver by the activity-based overhead rate. This is done for each activity cost pool and then summed.

LO 3 Explain the benefits and limitations of activity-based costing.

Features of ABC that make it a more accurate product costing system include (1) the increased number of cost pools used to assign overhead (including use of the activity-level hierarchy), (2) the enhanced control over overhead costs (including identification of non–value-added activities), and (3) the better management decisions it makes possible. The limitations of ABC are (1) the higher analysis and measurement costs that accompany multiple activity centers and cost drivers, and (2) the necessity still to assign some costs arbitrarily.

LO 4 Apply activity-based costing to service industries.

The overall objective of using ABC in service industries is no different than for manufacturing industries—that is, improved costing of services performed (by job, service, contract, or customer). The general approach to costing is the same: analyze operations, identify activities, accumulate overhead costs by activity cost pools, and identify and use cost drivers to assign the cost pools to the services.

LO *5 Explain just-in-time (JIT) processing.

JIT is a processing system dedicated to having on hand the right materials and products just at the time they are needed, thereby reducing the amount of inventory and the time inventory is held. One of the principal accounting effects is that one account, Raw and In-Process Inventory, replaces both the raw materials and work in process inventory accounts.

Decision Tools Review

Decision Checkpoints	Info Needed for Decision	Tool to Use for Decision	How to Evaluate Results
How can activity-based management help managers?	Activities classified as value-added and non–value-added	Activity flowchart	The flowchart should motivate managers to minimize non–value-added activities. Managers should better understand the relationship between activities and the resources they consume.
When should we use ABC?	Knowledge of the products or product lines, manufacturing process, and overhead costs	A detailed and accurate cost accounting system; cooperation between accountants and operating managers	Compare the results under both costing systems. If managers are better able to understand and control their operations using ABC and the costs are not prohibitive, the use of ABC would be beneficial.

Glossary Review

Activity Any event, action, transaction, or work sequence that incurs costs when producing a product or performing a service. (p. 4-5).

Activity-based costing (ABC) A costing system that allocates overhead to multiple activity cost pools and assigns the activity cost pools to products or services by means of cost drivers. (p. 4-5).

Activity-based management (ABM) Extends ABC from product costing to a comprehensive management tool that focuses on reducing costs and improving processes and decision-making. (p. 4-15).

Activity cost pool The overhead cost attributed to a distinct type of activity or related activities. (p. 4-5).

Batch-level activities Activities performed for each batch of products rather than for each unit. (p. 4-15).

Cost driver Any factor or activity that has a direct cause-effect relationship with the resources consumed. In ABC, cost drivers are used to assign activity cost pools to products or services. (p. 4-5).

Facility-level activities Activities required to support or sustain an entire production process. (p. 4-15).

*__Just-in-time (JIT) processing__ A processing system dedicated to having the right amount of materials, parts, or products arrive as they are needed, thereby reducing the amount of inventory. (p. 4-24).

Non–value-added activity A nonessential activity that, if eliminated, would not reduce the perceived value of a company's product or service. (p. 4-16).

Product-level activities Activities performed in support of an entire product line but not always performed every time a new unit or batch of products is produced. (p. 4-15).

Unit-level activities Activities performed for each unit of production. (p. 4-15).

Value-added activity An essential activity that increases the perceived value of a product or service to a customer. (p. 4-16).

Practice Multiple-Choice Questions

1. **(LO 1)** Activity-based costing (ABC):
    a. can be used only in a process cost system.
    b. focuses on units of production.
    c. focuses on activities needed to produce a good or perform a service.
    d. uses only a single basis of allocation.

2. **(LO 1)** Activity-based costing:
    a. is the initial phase of converting to a just-in-time operating environment.
    b. can be used only in a job order costing system.
    c. is a two-stage overhead cost allocation system that identifies activity cost pools and cost drivers.
    d. uses direct labor as its primary cost driver.

3. **(LO 1)** Any activity that causes resources to be consumed is called a:
   a. just-in-time activity.
   b. facility-level activity.
   c. cost driver.
   d. non–value-added activity.

4. **(LO 2)** Which of the following would be the **best** cost driver for the assembling cost pool?
   a. Number of product lines.
   b. Number of parts.
   c. Number of orders.
   d. Amount of square meters.

5. **(LO 2)** The overhead rate for machine setups is €100 per setup. Products A and B have 80 and 60 setups, respectively. The overhead assigned to each product is:
   a. Product A €8,000, Product B €8,000.
   b. Product A €8,000, Product B €6,000.
   c. Product A €6,000, Product B €6,000.
   d. Product A €6,000, Product B €8,000.

6. **(LO 2)** Marvel Ltd. has identified inspections as an activity cost pool to which it has allocated estimated overhead of £1,920,000. It has estimated use of cost drivers for that activity to be 160,000 inspections. Widgets require 40,000 inspections, gadgets 30,000 inspections, and targets 90,000 inspections. The overhead assigned to each product is:
   a. Widgets £40,000, gadgets £30,000, targets £90,000.
   b. Widgets £640,000, gadgets £640,000, targets £640,000.
   c. Widgets £360,000, gadgets £480,000, targets £1,080,000.
   d. Widgets £480,000, gadgets £360,000, targets £1,080,000.

7. **(LO 3)** A frequently cited limitation of activity-based costing is:
   a. ABC results in more cost pools being used to assign overhead costs to products.
   b. certain overhead costs remain to be assigned by means of some arbitrary volume-based cost driver such as labor or machine hours.
   c. ABC leads to poorer management decisions.
   d. ABC results in less control over overhead costs.

8. **(LO 3)** A company should consider using ABC if:
   a. overhead costs constitute a small portion of total product costs.
   b. it has only a few product lines that require similar degrees of support services.
   c. direct labor constitutes a significant part of the total product cost and a high correlation exists between direct labor and changes in overhead costs.
   d. its product lines differ greatly in volume and manufacturing complexity.

9. **(LO 3)** A nonessential activity that adds costs to the product but does not increase its perceived value is a:
   a. value-added activity.
   b. cost driver.
   c. cost/benefit activity.
   d. non–value-added activity.

10. **(LO 3)** The following activity is value-added:
    a. storage of raw materials.
    b. moving parts from machine to machine.
    c. producing a necessary product component on a machine.
    d. All of the above.

11. **(LO 3)** A relevant facility-level cost driver for factory heating costs is:
    a. machine hours.
    b. direct materials.
    c. floor space.
    d. direct labor cost.

12. **(LO 4)** The first step in the development of an activity-based costing system for a service company is:
    a. identify and classify activities and allocate overhead to cost pools.
    b. assign overhead costs to products.
    c. identify cost drivers.
    d. compute overhead rates.

*13. **(LO 5)** Under just-in-time processing:
    a. raw materials are received just in time for use in production.
    b. subassembly parts are completed just in time for use in assembling finished goods.
    c. finished goods are completed just in time to be sold.
    d. All of the answer choices are correct.

*14. **(LO 5)** The primary objective of just-in-time processing is to:
    a. accumulate overhead in activity cost pools.
    b. eliminate or reduce all manufacturing inventories.
    c. identify relevant activity cost drivers.
    d. identify value-added activities.

Solutions

1. c. Focusing on activities needed to produce a good or perform a service is an accurate statement about activity-based costing. The other choices are incorrect because ABC (a) can be used in either a process cost or a job order cost system; (b) focuses on activities performed to produce a product, not on units of production; and (d) uses multiple bases of allocation, not just a single basis of allocation.

2. c. ABC is a two-stage overhead cost allocation system that identifies activity cost pools and cost drivers. The other choices are incorrect because ABC (a) is not necessarily part of the conversion to a just-in-time operating environment, (b) can be used in either a process cost or a job order cost system, and (d) uses other activities in addition to direct labor as cost drivers.

3. c. Activities that cause resources to be consumed are called cost drivers, not (a) just-in-time activities, (b) facility-level activities, or (d) non–value-added activities.

4. b. The number of parts would be the best cost driver for the assembling cost pool as it has a higher degree of correlation with the actual consumption of the overhead costs, that is, the assembling of parts, than (a) number of product lines, (c) number of orders, or (d) amount of square meters.

5. b. The overhead assigned to Product A is €8,000 (€100 × 80) and to Product B is €6,000 (€100 × 60), not (a) €8,000, €8,000; (c) €6,000, €6,000; or (d) €6,000, €8,000.

6. **d.** The overhead assigned to widgets is £480,000 [(£1,920,000 ÷ 160,000) × 40,000], to gadgets is £360,000 [(£1,920,000 ÷ 160,000) × 30,000], and to targets is £1,080,000 [(£1,920,000 ÷ 160,000) × 90,000]. Therefore, choices (a) £40,000, £30,000, and £90,000; (b) £640,000, £640,000, and £640,000; and (c) £360,000, £480,000, and £1,080,000 are incorrect.

7. **b.** A limitation of ABC is that certain overhead costs remain to be assigned by means of some arbitrary volume-based cost driver. The other choices are incorrect because (a) more cost pools is an advantage of ABC, (c) ABC can lead to better management decisions, and (d) ABC results in more control over overhead costs.

8. **d.** A company should consider using ABC if its product lines differ greatly in volume and manufacturing complexity. For choices (a), (b), and (c), a traditional costing system should be sufficient and less expensive to implement.

9. **d.** Non–value-added activities add costs to a product but do not increase its perceived value, not (a) value-added activities, (b) cost drivers, or (c) cost/benefit activities.

10. **c.** Producing a necessary product component on a machine is a value-added activity as it is an integral part of manufacturing a product. Choices (a) and (b) are non–value-added activities, so therefore choice (d) is incorrect as well.

11. **c.** Floor space is a relevant facility-level cost driver for factory heating costs as a larger space will result in higher heating costs. The other choices are incorrect because (a) machine hours, (b) direct materials, and (d) direct labor cost are all unit-level cost drivers.

12. **a.** The first step in developing an ABC system is to identify and classify activities and allocate overhead to cost pools. The other choices are incorrect because (b) is Step 4, (c) is Step 2, and (d) is Step 3.

*13. **d.** All of the choices are accurate statements about just-in-time processing.

*14. **b.** Eliminating or reducing all manufacturing inventories is the primary objective of just-in-time processing. The other choices are incorrect because choices (a), (c), and (d) are part of the process of implementing an ABC system.

Practice Exercises

1. **(LO 1, 2)** Chic Fabrics has budgeted overhead costs of €955,000. It has assigned overhead on a plant-wide basis to its two products (wool and cotton) using direct labor hours which are estimated to be 477,500 for the current year. The company has decided to experiment with activity-based costing and has created two activity cost pools and related activity cost drivers. These two cost pools are cutting (cost driver is machine hours) and machine setups (cost driver is number of machine setups). Overhead allocated to the cutting cost pool is €400,000, and €555,000 is allocated to the machine setups cost pool. Additional information regarding cost driver usage related to these pools is as follows:

Assign overhead using traditional costing and ABC.

	Wool	Cotton	Total
Machine hours	100,000	100,000	200,000
Number of machine setups	1,000	500	1,500

Instructions

a. Determine the amount of overhead assigned to the wool product line and the cotton product line using activity-based costing.

b. What is the difference between the allocation of overhead to the wool and cotton product lines using activity-based costing versus the traditional approach, assuming direct labor hours were incurred evenly between the wool and cotton?

Solution

1. a.

Activity Cost Pools	Cost Drivers	Estimated Overhead
Cutting	Machine hours	€400,000
Machine setups	Number of machine setups	555,000

Activity-based overhead rates:

Cutting	Machine Setups
$\dfrac{€400,000}{200,000} = €2$ per machine hour	$\dfrac{€555,000}{1,500} = €370$ per setup

	Wool	Cotton
Activity-based costing		
Cutting		
100,000 × €2	€200,000	
100,000 × €2		€200,000
Machine setups		
1,000 × €370	370,000	
500 × €370		185,000
Total cost assigned	€570,000	€385,000

b. $\dfrac{\text{Estimated overhead}}{\text{Direct labors hours}} = \dfrac{\text{€955,000}}{477,500} = $ €2 per direct labor hour

	Wool	Cotton
Traditional costing		
238,750* × €2	€477,500	
238,750 × €2		€477,500

*477,500 ÷ 2

The wool product line is assigned €92,500 (€570,000 − €477,500) more overhead cost when an activity-based costing system is used. As a result, the cotton product line is assigned €92,500 (€477,500 − €385,000) less.

Assign overhead using traditional costing and ABC.

2. **(LO 1, 2, 3)** Ginger Products Corporation uses a traditional product costing system to assign overhead costs uniformly to all products. To assure its customers of safe, sanitary, and nutritious food, Ginger engages in a high level of quality control. Ginger assigns its quality-control overhead costs to all products at a rate of 20% of direct labor costs. Its direct labor cost for the month of June for its low-calorie dessert line is £55,000. In response to repeated requests from its financial vice president, Ginger management agrees to adopt activity-based costing. Data relating to the low-calorie dessert line for the month of June are as follows:

Activity Cost Pools	Cost Drivers	Overhead Rate	Cost Drivers Used per Activity
Inspections of material received	Number of kilograms	£ 0.70 per kilogram	6,000 kilograms
In-process inspections	Number of servings	£ 0.35 per serving	10,000 servings
Final certification	Customer orders	£13.00 per order	450 orders

Instructions

a. Compute the quality-control overhead cost to be assigned to the low-calorie dessert product line for the month of June using (1) the traditional product costing system (direct labor cost is the cost driver), and (2) activity-based costing.

b. By what amount does the traditional product costing system undercost or overcost the low-calorie dessert line?

Solution

2. a. 1. Traditional product costing system:

£55,000 × .20 = £11,000. Quality-control overhead costs assigned in June to the low-calorie dessert line are £11,000.

2. Activity-based costing system:

Activity Cost Pools	Cost Drivers Used	×	Activity-Based Overhead Rate	=	Overhead Cost Assigned
Inspections of material received	6,000		£ 0.70		£ 4,200
In-process inspections	10,000		0.35		3,500
Final certification	450		13.00		5,850
Total assigned cost for June					£13,550

b. As compared to ABC, the traditional costing system undercosts the quality-control overhead cost assigned to the low-calorie dessert product line by £2,550 (£13,550 − £11,000) in the month of June. That is a 23.2% (£2,550 ÷ £11,000) understatement.

Practice Problem

Assign overhead and compute unit costs.

(LO 2) Liau Paint manufactures two high-quality base paints: an *oil-based* paint and a *latex* paint. Both are housepaints and are manufactured only in a neutral white color. Liau sells the white base paints to franchised retail paint and decorating stores where pigments are added to tint (color) the paint as the customer desires. The oil-based paint is made with organic solvents (petroleum products) such as mineral spirits or turpentine. The latex paint is made with water; synthetic resin particles are suspended in the water, and dry and harden when exposed to air.

Liau uses the same processing equipment to produce both paints in different production runs. Between batches, the vats and other processing equipment must be washed and cleaned.

After analyzing the company's entire operations, Liau's accountants and production managers have identified activity cost pools and accumulated annual budgeted overhead costs by pool as follows:

Activity Cost Pools	Estimated Overhead
Purchasing	HK$ 2,400,000
Processing (weighing and mixing, grinding, thinning and drying, straining)	14,000,000
Packaging (1/2-liter, 1-liter, and 5-liter)	5,800,000
Testing	2,400,000
Storage and inventory control	1,800,000
Washing and cleaning equipment	5,600,000
Total annual budgeted overhead	HK$32,000,000

Following further analysis, activity cost drivers were identified, and their estimated use by activity, as well as use by product, were scheduled as follows:

Activity Cost Pools	Cost Drivers	Estimated Cost Drivers per Activity	Use of Drivers per Product	
			Oil-Based	Latex
Purchasing	Purchase orders	1,500 orders	800	700
Processing	Liters processed	1,000,000 liters	400,000	600,000
Packaging	Containers filled	400,000 containers	180,000	220,000
Testing	Number of tests	4,000 tests	2,100	1,900
Storing	Avg. liters on hand	18,000 liters	10,400	7,600
Washing	Number of batches	800 batches	350	450

Liau has budgeted 400,000 liters of oil-based paint and 600,000 liters of latex paint for processing during the year.

Instructions

a. Prepare a schedule showing the computations of the activity-based overhead rates.
b. Prepare a schedule assigning each activity's overhead cost pool to each product.
c. Compute the overhead cost per unit for each product.

Solution

a. Computations of activity-based overhead rates:

Activity Cost Pools	Estimated Overhead	÷	Estimated Use of Cost Drivers	=	Activity-Based Overhead Rates
Purchasing	HK$ 2,400,000		1,500 orders		HK$1,600 per order
Processing	14,000,000		1,000,000 liters		HK$14.0 per liter
Packaging	5,800,000		400,000 containers		HK$14.5 per container
Testing	2,400,000		4,000 tests		HK$600 per test
Storing	1,800,000		18,000 liters		HK$100 per liter
Washing	5,600,000		800 batches		HK$7,000 per batch
	HK$32,000,000				

b. Assignment of activity cost pools to products:

Activity Cost Pools	Oil-Based Paint			Latex Paint		
	Use of Drivers	Overhead Rates	Cost Assigned	Use of Drivers	Overhead Rates	Cost Assigned
Purchasing	800	HK$1,600	HK$ 1,280,000	700	HK$1,600	HK$ 1,120,000
Processing	400,000	HK$14.0	5,600,000	600,000	HK$14.0	8,400,000
Packaging	180,000	HK$14.5	2,610,000	220,000	HK$14.5	3,190,000
Testing	2,100	HK$600	1,260,000	1,900	HK$600	1,140,000
Storing	10,400	HK$100	1,040,000	7,600	HK$100	760,000
Washing	350	HK$7,000	2,450,000	450	HK$7,000	3,150,000
Total overhead assigned			HK$14,240,000			17,760,000

c. Computation of overhead cost assigned per unit:

	Oil-Based Paint	Latex Paint
Total overhead cost assigned	HK$14,240,000	HK$17,760,000
Total liters produced	400,000	600,000
Overhead cost per liter	HK$35.6	HK$29.6

Note: All asterisked Questions, Exercises, and Problems relate to material in the appendix to the chapter.

Questions

1. Under what conditions is direct labor a valid basis for allocating overhead?
2. What has happened in recent industrial history to reduce the usefulness of direct labor as the primary basis for allocating overhead to products?
3. In an automated manufacturing environment, what basis of overhead allocation is frequently more relevant than direct labor hours?
4. What is generally true about overhead allocation to high-volume products versus low-volume products under a traditional costing system?
5. What are the principal differences between activity-based costing (ABC) and traditional product costing?
6. What is the equation for computing activity-based overhead rates?
7. What steps are involved in developing an activity-based costing system?
8. Explain the preparation and use of a value-added/non–value-added activity flowchart in an ABC system.
9. What is an activity cost pool?
10. What is a cost driver?
11. What makes a cost driver accurate and appropriate?
12. What is the calculation for assigning activity cost pools to products?
13. What are the primary benefits of activity-based costing?
14. What are the limitations of activity-based costing?
15. Under what conditions is ABC generally the superior overhead costing system?
16. What refinement has been made to enhance the efficiency and effectiveness of ABC for use in managing costs?
17. Of what benefit is classifying activities as value-added or non–value-added?
18. In what ways is the application of ABC to service industries the same as its application to manufacturing companies?
19. What is the relevance of the classification of levels of activity to ABC?
*20. a. Describe the philosophy and approach of just-in-time processing.
    b. Identify the major elements of JIT processing.

Brief Exercises

Identify differences between costing systems.

BE4.1 (LO 1), AP Service Lauwita Ltd. sells a high-speed retrieval system for mining information. It provides the following information for the year.

	Budgeted	Actual
Overhead cost	Rp9,750,000,000	Rp9,500,000,000
Machine hours	50,000	45,000
Direct labor hours	100,000	92,000

Overhead is applied on the basis of direct labor hours. (a) Compute the predetermined overhead rate. (b) Determine the amount of overhead applied for the year. (c) Explain how an activity-based costing system might differ in terms of computing a predetermined overhead rate.

Identify differences between costing systems.

BE4.2 (LO 1), AP Pretorius Ltd. has conducted an analysis of overhead costs related to one of its product lines using a traditional costing system (volume-based) and an activity-based costing system. Here are its results:

	Traditional Costing	ABC
Sales revenue	R6,000,000	R6,000,000
Overhead costs:		
Product RX3	R 340,000	R 500,000
Product Y12	360,000	200,000
	R 700,000	R 700,000

Explain how a difference in the overhead costs between the two systems may have occurred.

BE4.3 (LO 2), AP Splash Co. identifies the following activities that pertain to manufacturing overhead for its production of water polo balls: materials handling, machine setups, factory machine maintenance, factory supervision, and quality control. For each activity, identify an appropriate cost driver.

Identify cost drivers.

BE4.4 (LO 2), AP Tseng Company manufactures four products in a single production facility. The company uses activity-based costing. The following activities have been identified through the company's activity analysis: (a) inventory control, (b) machine setups, (c) employee training, (d) quality inspections, (e) materials orderings, (f) drilling operations, and (g) factory maintenance.

For each activity, name a cost driver that might be used to assign overhead costs to products.

Identify cost drivers.

BE4.5 (LO 2), AP Lixun Ltd. identifies three activities in its manufacturing process: machine set-ups, machining, and inspections. Estimated annual overhead cost for each activity is HK$1,500,000, HK$3,750,000, and HK$875,000, respectively. The cost driver for each activity and the estimated annual usage are number of setups 2,500, machine hours 25,000, and number of inspections 1,750. Compute the overhead rate for each activity.

Compute activity-based overhead rates.

BE4.6 (LO 2), AP Spencer Ltd. uses activity-based costing as the basis for information to set prices for its six lines of seasonal coats. Compute the activity-based overhead rates using the following budgeted data for each of the activity cost pools:

Compute activity-based overhead rates.

Activity Cost Pools	Estimated Overhead	Estimated Use of Cost Drivers per Activity
Sizing and cutting	£ 4,000,000	160,000 machine hours
Stitching and trimming	1,440,000	80,000 labor hours
Wrapping and packing	336,000	32,000 finished units

BE4.7 (LO 2), AP Baker's Street, a manufacturer of snacks, employs activity-based costing. The budgeted data for each of the activity cost pools is provided below for the year 2023.

Compute overhead applied.

Activity Cost Pools	Estimated Overhead	Estimated Use of Cost Drivers per Activity
Ordering and receiving	$ 84,000	12,000 orders
Food processing	480,000	60,000 machine hours
Packaging	1,760,000	40,000 labor hours

For 2023, the company had 7,000 orders for its snacks and used 40,000 machine hours; labor hours totaled 25,000. What is the total overhead applied?

BE4.8 (LO 3), AP Takahashi Company identified the following activities in its production and support operations. Classify each of these activities as either value-added or non–value-added.

Classify activities as value- or non–value-added.

a. Machine setup.
b. Design engineering.
c. Storing inventory.
d. Moving work in process.
e. Inspecting and testing.
f. Painting and packing.

BE4.9 (LO 3, 4), AN `Service` Masood and Sons is an architectural firm that is contemplating the implementation of activity-based costing. The following activities are performed daily by staff architects. Classify these activities as value-added or non–value-added: (a) designing and drafting, 3 hours; (b) staff meetings, 1 hour; (c) on-site supervision, 2 hours; (d) lunch, 1 hour; (e) consultation with client on specifications, 1.5 hours; and (f) entertaining a prospective client for dinner, 2 hours.

Classify service company activities as value- or non–value-added.

BE4.10 (LO 3, 4), AN `Service` Kwik Pix is a large digital processing center that serves 130 outlets in grocery stores, service stations, camera and photo shops, and drug stores in 16 nearby towns. Kwik Pix operates 24 hours a day, 6 days a week. Classify each of the following activity costs of Kwik Pix as either unit-level, batch-level, product-level, or facility-level.

Classify activities according to level.

a. Color printing materials.
b. Photocopy paper.
c. Depreciation of machinery (assume units-of-activity depreciation).
d. Setups for enlargements.
e. Supervisor's salary.
f. Ordering materials.
g. Pickup and delivery.
h. Commission to dealers.
i. Insurance on building.
j. Loading developing machines.

BE4.11 (LO 3), AP Blue Kite Ltd. operates 20 injection molding machines in the production of tool boxes of four different sizes, named the Apprentice, the Handyman, the Journeyman, and the Professional. Classify each of the following costs as unit-level, batch-level, product-level, or facility-level.

Classify activities according to level.

a. First-shift supervisor's salary.
b. Powdered raw plastic.

c. Dies for casting plastic components.
d. Depreciation on injection molding machines (assume units-of-activity depreciation).
e. Changing dies on machines.
f. Moving components to assembly department.
g. Engineering design.
h. Employee health and medical insurance coverage.

Compute rates and activity levels.

BE4.12 (LO 3, 4), AP Spin Cycle Architecture uses three activity pools to apply overhead to its projects. Each activity has a cost driver used to assign the overhead costs to the projects. The activities and related overhead costs are as follows: initial concept formation S$40,000, design S$300,000, and construction oversight S$100,000. The cost drivers and estimated use are as follows:

Activities	Cost Drivers	Estimated Use of Cost Drivers per Activity
Initial concept formation	Number of project changes	20
Design	Square meters	150,000
Construction oversight	Number of months	100

a. Compute the predetermined overhead rate for each activity.
b. Classify each of these activities as unit-level, batch-level, product-level, or facility-level.

DO IT! Exercises

Identify characteristics of traditional and ABC systems.

DO IT! 4.1 (LO 1), K Indicate whether the following statements are true or false.

a. The reasoning behind ABC cost allocation is that products consume activities and activities consume resources.
b. Activity-based costing is an approach for allocating direct labor to products.
c. In today's increasingly automated environment, direct labor is never an appropriate basis for allocating costs to products.
d. A cost driver is any factor or activity that has a direct cause-effect relationship with resources consumed.
e. Activity-based costing segregates overhead into various cost pools in an effort to provide more accurate cost information.

Compute activity-based overhead rates and assign overhead using ABC.

DO IT! 4.2 (LO 2), AP Harlow Industries has three activity cost pools and two products. It estimates production of 3,000 units of Product BC113 and 1,500 of Product AD908. Having identified its activity cost pools and the cost drivers for each pool, Harlow accumulated the following data relative to those activity cost pools and cost drivers.

	Annual Overhead Data			Use of Cost Drivers per Product	
Activity Cost Pools	Cost Drivers	Estimated Overhead	Estimated Use of Cost Drivers per Activity	Product BC113	Product AD908
Machine setup	Setups	A$ 16,000	40	25	15
Machining	Machine hours	110,000	5,000	1,000	4,000
Packing	Orders	30,000	500	150	350

Using the above data, do the following:
a. Prepare a schedule showing the computations of the activity-based overhead rates per cost driver.
b. Prepare a schedule assigning each activity's overhead cost to the two products.
c. Compute the overhead cost per unit for each product. (Round to nearest cent.)
d. Comment on the comparative overhead cost per product.

Classify activities according to level.

DO IT! 4.3 (LO 3), C Singh Machine Tools manufactures four lines of garden tools. As a result of an activity analysis, the accounting department has identified eight activity cost pools. Each of the product lines is produced in large batches, with the whole factory devoted to one product at a time. Classify each of the following activities or costs as either unit-level, batch-level, product-level, or facility-level.

a. Machining parts.
b. Product design.
c. Factory maintenance.
d. Machine setup.

e. Assembling parts.
f. Purchasing raw materials.
g. Factory property taxes.
h. Painting garden tools.

DO IT! 4.4 (LO 4), AP Service Wan Ride is a trucking company. It provides local, short-haul, and long-haul services. It has developed the following three cost pools.

Apply ABC to service company.

Activity Cost Pools	Cost Drivers	Estimated Overhead	Estimated Use of Cost Driver per Activity
Loading and unloading	Number of pieces	HK$ 900,000	900,000
Travel	Kilometers driven	450,000	600,000
Logistics	Hours	75,000	3,000

a. Compute the activity-based overhead rates for each pool.
b. Determine the overhead assigned to Job XZ3275, which has 150 pieces and requires 200 kilometers of driving and 0.75 hours of logistics.

Exercises

E4.1 (LO 1, 2), AP Chul Ltd. has two types of handbags: standard and custom. The controller has decided to use a plantwide overhead rate based on direct labor costs. The president has heard of activity-based costing and wants to see how the results would differ if this system were used. Two activity cost pools were developed: machining (machine hours) and machine setup (number of setups). The total estimated machine hours is 2,000, and the total estimated number of setups is 500. Presented below is information related to each product's use of cost drivers.

Assign overhead using traditional costing and ABC.

	Standard	Custom
Direct labor costs	₩50,000,000	₩100,000,000
Machine hours	1,000	1,000
Number of setups	100	400

Total estimated overhead costs are ₩240,000,000. Overhead cost allocated to the machining activity cost pool is ₩140,000,000, and ₩100,000,000 is allocated to the machine setup activity cost pool.

Instructions

a. Compute the overhead rate using the traditional (plantwide) approach.
b. Compute the overhead rates using the activity-based costing approach.
c. Determine the difference in allocation between the two approaches.

E4.2 (LO 1), AP Thomson Ltd. has conducted the following analysis related to its product lines, using a traditional costing system (volume-based) and an activity-based costing system. The traditional and the activity-based costing systems assign the same amount of direct materials and direct labor costs.

Explain difference between traditional and activity-based costing.

		Total Costs	
Products	Sales Revenue	Traditional	ABC
Product 540X	£180,000	£55,000	£50,000
Product 137Y	160,000	50,000	35,000
Product 249S	70,000	15,000	35,000

Instructions

a. For each product line, compute operating income using the traditional costing system.
b. For each product line, compute operating income using the activity-based costing system.
c. Using the following calculation, compute the percentage difference in operating income for each of the product lines of Thomson: [Operating Income (ABC) − Operating Income (traditional cost)] ÷ Operating Income (traditional cost). (Round to two decimals.)
d. Provide a rationale as to why the costs for Product 540X are approximately the same using either the traditional or activity-based costing system.

E4.3 (LO 1, 2), AN EcoFabrics has budgeted overhead costs of ₤9,450,000. It has assigned overhead on a plantwide basis to its two products (wool and cotton) using direct labor hours which are estimated to be 450,000 for the current year. The company has decided to experiment with activity-based costing and has created two activity cost pools and related activity cost drivers. These two cost pools are cutting (cost

Assign overhead using traditional costing and ABC.

driver is machine hours) and design (cost driver is number of setups). Total estimated machine hours is 200,000, and total estimated number of setups is 1,500. Overhead allocated to the cutting cost pool is ₺3,600,000, and ₺5,850,000 is allocated to the design cost pool. Additional information related to product usage by these pools is as follows:

	Wool	Cotton
Machine hours	100,000	100,000
Number of setups	1,000	500

Instructions

a. Determine the amount of overhead assigned to the wool product line and the cotton product line using activity-based costing.

b. What amount of overhead would be assigned to the wool and cotton product lines using the traditional approach, assuming direct labor hours were incurred evenly between the wool and cotton? How does this compare with the amount assigned using ABC in part (a)?

E4.4 (LO 1, 2), AN Altex Wheels manufactures two products: car wheels and truck wheels. To determine the amount of overhead to assign to each product line, the controller, Jun Tsai, has developed the following information.

	Car	Truck
Estimated wheels produced	40,000	10,000
Direct labor hours per wheel	1	3

Total estimated overhead costs for the two product lines are NT$7,700,000.

Instructions

a. Compute the overhead cost assigned to the car wheels and truck wheels, assuming that direct labor hours is used to assign overhead costs.

b. Tsai is not satisfied with the traditional method of allocating overhead because he believes that most of the overhead costs relate to the truck wheels product line because of its complexity. He therefore develops the following three activity cost pools and related cost drivers to better understand these costs.

Activity Cost Pools	Estimated Overhead Costs	Estimated Use of Cost Drivers
Setting up machines	NT$2,200,000	1,000 setups
Assembling	2,800,000	70,000 labor hours
Inspection	2,700,000	1,200 inspections

Compute the activity-based overhead rates for these three cost pools.

c. Compute the cost that is assigned to the car wheels and truck wheels product lines using an activity-based costing system, given the following information.

Use of Cost Drivers per Product		
	Car	Truck
Number of setups	200	800
Direct labor hours	40,000	30,000
Number of inspections	100	1,100

d. What do you believe Tsai should do?

E4.5 (LO 1, 2), AN Tagus SpA manufactures safes—large mobile safes, and large walk-in stationary bank safes. As part of its annual budgeting process, Tagus is analyzing the profitability of its two products. Part of this analysis involves estimating the amount of overhead to be assigned to each product line. The information shown below relates to overhead.

	Mobile Safes	Walk-In Safes
Units planned for production	200	50
Material moves per product line	300	200
Purchase orders per product line	450	350
Direct labor hours per product line	800	1,700

Instructions

a. The total estimated manufacturing overhead was €260,000. Under traditional costing (which assigns overhead on the basis of direct labor hours), what amount of manufacturing overhead costs are assigned to:
   1. One mobile safe?
   2. One walk-in safe?

b. The total estimated manufacturing overhead of €260,000 was comprised of €160,000 for materials handling costs and €100,000 for purchasing activity costs. Under activity-based costing (ABC):
   1. What amount of materials handling costs are assigned to:
      a. One mobile safe?
      b. One walk-in safe?
   2. What amount of purchasing activity costs are assigned to:
      a. One mobile safe?
      b. One walk-in safe?

c. Compare the amount of overhead assigned to one mobile safe and to one walk-in safe under the traditional costing approach versus under ABC.

E4.6 (LO 2), AN Bouchard Corporation manufactures snowmobiles in its Canada plant. The following costs are budgeted for the first quarter's operations.

Identify activity cost pools and cost drivers.

Machine setup, indirect materials	$ 4,000
Inspections	16,000
Tests	4,000
Insurance, factory	110,000
Engineering design	140,000
Depreciation, machinery	520,000
Machine setup, indirect labor	20,000
Property taxes on factory	29,000
Factory heating	19,000
Electricity, factory lighting	21,000
Engineering prototypes	60,000
Depreciation, factory	210,000
Electricity, machinery	36,000
Machine maintenance wages	19,000

Instructions

Classify the above costs of Bouchard Corporation into activity cost pools using the following: engineering, machinery, machine setup, quality control, factory costs. Next, identify a cost driver that may be used to assign each cost pool to each line of snowmobiles.

E4.7 (LO 2), AN Toulon Vineyards in produces three varieties of wine: merlot, viognier, and pinot noir. The winemaster, Russel Durand, has identified the following activities as cost pools for accumulating overhead and assigning it to products.

Identify activity cost drivers.

1. Spraying. The vines are sprayed with organic pesticides for protection against insects and fungi.
2. Harvesting. The grapes are hand-picked, placed in carts, and transported to the crushers.
3. Stemming and crushing. Cartfuls of bunches of grapes of each variety are separately loaded into machines that remove stems and gently crush the grapes.
4. Pressing and filtering. The crushed grapes are transferred to presses that mechanically remove the juices and filter out bulk and impurities.
5. Fermentation. The grape juice, by variety, is fermented in either stainless-steel tanks or oak barrels.
6. Aging. The wines are aged in either stainless-steel tanks or oak barrels for one to three years depending on variety.
7. Bottling and corking. Bottles are machine-filled and corked.
8. Labeling and boxing. Each bottle is labeled, as is each nine-bottle case, with the name of the vintner, vintage, and variety.
9. Storing. Packaged and boxed bottles are stored awaiting shipment.
10. Shipping. The wine is shipped to distributors and private retailers.

11. Heating and air-conditioning of plant and offices.
12. Maintenance of production equipment. Repairs, replacements, and general maintenance are performed in the off-season.

Instructions

For each of Toulon Vineyards' activity cost pools, identify a probable cost driver that might be used to assign overhead costs to its three wine varieties.

E4.8 (LO 2), AN Singhal Machines manufactures five models of kitchen appliances. The company is installing activity-based costing and has identified the following activities performed at its Delhi plant.

1. Designing new models.
2. Purchasing raw materials and parts.
3. Storing and managing inventory.
4. Receiving and inspecting raw materials and parts.
5. Interviewing and hiring new personnel.
6. Machine forming sheet steel into appliance parts.
7. Manually assembling parts into appliances.
8. Training all employees of the company.
9. Insuring all tangible fixed assets.
10. Supervising production.
11. Maintaining and repairing machinery and equipment.
12. Painting and packaging finished appliances.

Having analyzed its Delhi plant operations for purposes of installing activity-based costing, Singhal Machines identified its activity cost centers. It now needs to identify relevant activity cost drivers in order to assign overhead costs to its products.

Instructions

Using the activities listed above, identify for each activity one or more cost drivers that might be used to assign overhead to Singhal's five products.

E4.9 (LO 2, 3), AP Writing Hiu Technologies manufactures two products: missile range instruments and space pressure gauges. During April, 50 range instruments and 300 pressure gauges were produced, and overhead costs of HK$945,000 were estimated. An analysis of estimated overhead costs reveals the following activities:

Activities	Cost Drivers	Total Cost
1. Materials handling	Number of requisitions	HK$400,000
2. Machine setups	Number of setups	215,000
3. Quality inspections	Number of inspections	330,000
		HK$945,000

The cost driver volume for each product was as follows:

Cost Drivers	Instruments	Gauges	Total
Number of requisitions	400	600	1,000
Number of setups	200	300	500
Number of inspections	200	400	600

Instructions

a. Determine the overhead rate for each activity.
b. Assign the manufacturing overhead costs for April to the two products using activity-based costing.
c. Write a memorandum to the president of Hiu Technologies explaining the benefits of activity-based costing.

E4.10 (LO 1, 2, 3), AP Kragan Clothing Company manufactures its own designed and labeled athletic wear and sells its products through catalog sales and retail outlets. While Kragan has for years used activity-based costing in its manufacturing activities, it has always used traditional costing in assigning its selling costs to its product lines. Selling costs have traditionally been assigned to Kragan's product lines at a rate of 70% of direct materials costs. Its direct materials costs for the month of March for Kragan's "high-intensity" line of athletic wear are $400,000. The company has decided to extend activity-based costing to its selling costs (for internal decision-making only). Data relating to the "high-intensity" line of products for the month of March are as follows:

Activity Cost Pools	Cost Drivers	Overhead Rate	Number of Cost Drivers Used per Activity
Sales commissions	Dollar sales	$0.05 per dollar sales	$900,000
Advertising—TV	Minutes	$300 per minute	250
Advertising—Internet	Column inches	$10 per column inch	2,000
Catalogs	Catalogs mailed	$2.50 per catalog	60,000
Cost of catalog sales	Catalog orders	$1 per catalog order	9,000
Credit and collection	Dollar sales	$0.03 per dollar sales	900,000

Instructions

a. Compute the selling costs to be assigned to the "high-intensity" line of athletic wear for the month of March (1) using the traditional product costing system (direct materials cost is the cost driver), and (2) using activity-based costing.

b. By what amount does the traditional product costing system undercost or overcost the "high-intensity" product line relative to costing under ABC?

E4.11 (LO 1, 2, 3), AP Health & Taste Ltd. uses a traditional product costing system to assign overhead costs uniformly to all its packaged multigrain products. To assure its customers of safe, sanitary, and nutritious food, Health & Taste engages in a high level of quality control. Health & Taste assigns its quality-control overhead costs to all products at a rate of 17% of direct labor costs. Its direct labor cost for the month of June for its low-calorie breakfast line is £70,000. In response to repeated requests from its financial vice president, Health & Taste's management agrees to adopt activity-based costing. Data relating to the low-calorie breakfast line for the month of June are as follows:

Assign overhead using traditional costing and ABC.

Activity Cost Pools	Cost Drivers	Overhead	Number of Cost Drivers Used per Activity
Inspections of material received	Number of kilograms	£0.90 per kilogram	6,000 kilograms
In-process inspections	Number of servings	£0.33 per serving	10,000 servings
Final certification	Customer orders	£12.00 per order	420 orders

Instructions

a. Compute the quality-control overhead cost to be assigned to the low-calorie breakfast product line for the month of June (1) using the traditional product costing system (direct labor cost is the cost driver), and (2) using activity-based costing.

b. By what amount does the traditional product costing system undercost or overcost the low-calorie breakfast line relative to costing under ABC?

E4.12 (LO 3), AN Having itemized its costs for the first quarter of next year's budget, Bouchard Corporation desires to install an activity-based costing system. First, it identified the activity cost pools in which to accumulate factory overhead. Second, it identified the relevant cost drivers. (This was done in E4.6.)

Classify activities by level.

Instructions

Using the activity cost pools identified in E4.6, classify each of those cost pools as either unit-level, batch-level, product-level, or facility-level.

E4.13 (LO 3), AN Khiw Ltd. is a small manufacturing company in Taiwan that uses activity-based costing. Khiw accumulates overhead in the following activity cost pools.

Classify activities by level.

1. Hiring personnel.
2. Managing parts inventory.
3. Purchasing.
4. Testing prototypes.
5. Designing products.
6. Setting up equipment.
7. Training employees.
8. Inspecting machined parts after each setup.
9. Machining.
10. Assembling.

Instructions

For each activity cost pool, indicate whether the activity cost pool would be unit-level, batch-level, product-level, or facility-level.

Assign overhead using traditional costing and ABC.

E4.14 (LO 4), AP `Service` Astrid Creations sells window treatments (shades, blinds, and awnings) to both commercial and residential customers. The following information relates to its budgeted operations for the current year.

	Commercial		Residential	
Revenues		CHF 300,000		CHF 480,000
Direct materials costs	CHF 30,000		CHF 50,000	
Direct labor costs	100,000		300,000	
Overhead costs	85,000	215,000	150,000	500,000
Operating income (loss)		CHF 85,000		(CHF 20,000)

The controller, Erik Fischer, is concerned about the residential product line. He cannot understand why this line is not more profitable given that the installations of window coverings are less complex for residential customers. In addition, the residential client base resides in close proximity to the company office, so travel costs are not as expensive on a per client visit for residential customers. As a result, he has decided to take a closer look at the overhead costs assigned to the two product lines to determine whether a more accurate product costing model can be developed. Here are the three activity cost pools and related information he developed:

Activity Cost Pools	Estimated Overhead	Cost Drivers
Scheduling and travel	CHF 85,000	Hours of travel
Setup time	90,000	Number of setups
Supervision	60,000	Direct labor cost

	Use of Cost Drivers per Product	
	Commercial	Residential
Scheduling and travel	750 hours	500 hours
Setup time	350 setups	250 setups

Instructions

a. Compute the activity-based overhead rates for each of the three cost pools, and determine the overhead cost assigned to each product line.

b. Compute the operating income for each product line, using the activity-based overhead rates.

c. What do you believe Erik Fischer should do?

Identify activity cost pools.

E4.15 (LO 4), AP `Service` Office Depot Company is a small printing and copying firm with three high-speed offset printing presses, five copiers (two color and three black-and-white), one collator, one cutting and folding machine, and one fax machine. To improve its pricing practices, owner-manager Erin Morton is installing activity-based costing. Additionally, Erin employs five employees: two printers/designers, one receptionist/bookkeeper, one salesperson/copy-machine operator, and one janitor/delivery clerk. Erin can operate any of the machines and, in addition to managing the entire operation, she performs the training, designing, selling, and marketing functions.

Instructions

As Office Depot's independent accountant who prepares tax forms and quarterly financial statements, you have been asked to identify the activities that would be used to accumulate overhead costs for assignment to jobs and customers. Using your knowledge of a small printing and copying firm (and some imagination), identify at least 12 activity cost pools as the start of an activity-based costing system for Office Depot Company.

E4.16 (LO 3, 4), AN Service Winsdor and Merkel Associates is a law firm that is initiating an activity-based costing system. Harry Winsdor, the senior partner and strong supporter of ABC, has prepared the following list of activities performed by a typical attorney in a day at the firm.

Classify service company activities as value-added or non–value-added.

Activities	Hours
Writing contracts and letters	1.5
Attending staff meetings	0.5
Taking depositions	1.0
Doing research	1.0
Traveling to/from court	1.0
Contemplating legal strategy	1.0
Eating lunch	1.0
Litigating a case in court	2.5
Entertaining a prospective client	1.5

Instructions

Classify each of the activities listed by Harry Winsdor as value-added or non–value-added, and defend your classification. How much was value-added time and how much was non–value-added?

E4.17 (LO 4), AP Service Manzeck Company operates a snow-removal service. The company owns five trucks, each of which has a snow plow in the front to plow driveways and a snow thrower in the back to clear sidewalks. Because plowing snow is very tough on trucks, the company incurs significant maintenance costs. Truck depreciation and maintenance represents a significant portion of the company's overhead. The company removes snow at residential locations, in which case the drivers spend the bulk of their time walking behind the snow-thrower machine to clear sidewalks. On commercial jobs, the drivers spend most of their time plowing. Manzeck assigns overhead based on labor hours. Total estimated overhead costs for the year are $42,000. Total estimated labor hours are 1,500 hours. The average residential property requires 0.5 hours of labor, while the average commercial property requires 2.5 hours of labor. The following additional information is available.

Apply ABC to service company.

Activity Cost Pools	Cost Drivers	Estimated Overhead	Estimated Use of Cost Drivers per Activity
Plowing	Square yards of surface plowed	$38,000	200,000
Snow throwing	Linear feet of sidewalk cleared	$ 4,000	50,000

Instructions

a. Determine the predetermined overhead rate under traditional costing.

b. Determine the amount of overhead assigned to the average residential job using traditional costing based on labor hours.

c. Determine the activity-based overhead rates for each cost pool.

d. Determine the amount of overhead assigned to the average residential job using activity-based costing. Assume that the average residential job has 20 square yards of plowing and 60 linear feet of snow throwing.

e. Discuss your findings from parts (b) and (d).

Problems

P4.1 (LO 1, 2, 3), AP Steve Fire Safety Ltd. manufactures steel cylinders and nozzles for two models of fire extinguishers: (1) a home fire extinguisher and (2) a commercial fire extinguisher. The *home model* is a high-volume (54,000 units), half-gallon cylinder that holds 2 1/2 pounds of multi-purpose dry chemical at 480 PSI. The *commercial model* is a low-volume (10,200 units), two-gallon cylinder that holds 10 pounds of multi-purpose dry chemical at 390 PSI. Both products require 1.5 hours of direct labor for completion. Therefore, total annual direct labor hours are 96,300 or [1.5 hours × (54,000 + 10,200)]. Estimated annual manufacturing overhead is $1,584,280. Thus, the predetermined overhead rate is

Assign overhead using traditional costing and ABC; compute unit costs; classify activities as value- or non–value-added.

$16.45 or ($1,584,280 ÷ 96,300) per direct labor hour. The direct materials cost per unit is $18.50 for the home model and $26.50 for the commercial model. The direct labor cost is $19 per unit for both the home and the commercial models.

The company's managers identified six activity cost pools and related cost drivers and accumulated overhead by cost pool as follows:

Activity Cost Pools	Cost Drivers	Estimated Overhead	Estimated Use of Cost Drivers	Use of Drivers by Product	
				Home	Commercial
Receiving	Pounds	$ 80,400	335,000	215,000	120,000
Forming	Machine hours	150,500	35,000	27,000	8,000
Assembling	Number of parts	412,300	217,000	165,000	52,000
Testing	Number of tests	51,000	25,500	15,500	10,000
Painting	Gallons	52,580	5,258	3,680	1,578
Packing and shipping	Pounds	837,500	335,000	215,000	120,000
		$1,584,280			

Instructions

a. Unit cost—H.M. $62.18

a. Under traditional product costing, compute the total unit cost of each product. Prepare a simple comparative schedule of the individual costs by product (similar to Illustration 4.4).

b. Under ABC, prepare a schedule showing the computations of the activity-based overhead rates (per cost driver).

c. Cost assigned—H.M. $1,086,500

c. Prepare a schedule assigning each activity's overhead cost pool to each product based on the use of cost drivers. (Include a computation of overhead cost per unit, rounding to the nearest cent.)

d. Cost/unit—H.M. $57.62

d. Compute the total cost per unit for each product under ABC.

e. Classify each of the activities as a value-added activity or a non–value-added activity.

f. Comment on (1) the comparative overhead cost per unit for the two products under ABC, and (2) the comparative total costs per unit under traditional costing and ABC.

Assign overhead to products using ABC and evaluate decision.

P4.2 (LO 2), AP Writing Aurelio Electronics manufactures two ultra-high-definition television models: the Royale, which sells for R$16,000, and a new model, the Majestic, which sells for R$13,000. The production cost computed per unit under traditional costing for each model in 2023 was as follows:

Traditional Costing	Royale	Majestic
Direct materials	R$ 7,000	R$4,200
Direct labor (R$200 per hour)	1,200	1,000
Manufacturing overhead (R$380 per DLH)	2,280	1,900
Total per unit cost	R$10,480	R$7,100

In 2023, Aurelio manufactured 25,000 units of the Royale and 10,000 units of the Majestic. The overhead rate of R$380 per direct labor hour was determined by dividing total estimated manufacturing overhead of R$76,000,000 by the total direct labor hours (200,000) for the two models.

Under traditional costing, the gross profit on the models was Royale R$5,520 (R$16,000 − R$10,480) and Majestic R$5,900 (R$13,000 − R$7,100). Because of this difference, management is considering phasing out the Royale model and increasing the production of the Majestic model.

Before finalizing its decision, management asks Aurelio's controller to prepare an analysis using activity-based costing (ABC). The controller accumulates the following information about overhead for the year ended December 31, 2023.

Activity Cost Pools	Cost Drivers	Estimated Overhead	Estimated Use of Cost Drivers	Activity Based Overhead Rate
Purchasing	Number of orders	R$12,000,000	40,000	R$300/order
Machine setups	Number of setups	9,000,000	18,000	R$500/setup
Machining	Machine hours	48,000,000	120,000	R$400/hour
Quality control	Number of inspections	7,000,000	28,000	R$250/inspection

The cost drivers used for each product were:

Cost Drivers	Royale	Majestic	Total
Purchase orders	17,000	23,000	40,000
Machine setups	5,000	13,000	18,000
Machine hours	75,000	45,000	120,000
Inspections	11,000	17,000	28,000

Instructions

a. Assign the total 2023 manufacturing overhead costs to the two products using activity-based costing (ABC) and determine the overhead cost per unit.

b. What was the cost per unit and gross profit of each model using ABC?

c. Are management's future plans for the two models sound? Explain.

a. Royale R$ 40,350,000

b. Cost/unit—Royale R$ 9,814

P4.3 (LO 1, 2), AN **Writing** Fuji Woodworks designs and builds factory-made premium wooden stairways for homes. The manufactured stairway components (spindles, risers, hangers, hand rails) permit installation of stairways of varying lengths and widths. All are of white oak wood. Budgeted manufacturing overhead costs for the year 2023 are as follows:

Assign overhead costs using traditional costing and ABC; compare results.

Overhead Cost Pools	Amount
Purchasing	¥ 7,500,000
Handling materials	8,200,000
Production (cutting, milling, finishing)	21,000,000
Setting up machines	10,500,000
Inspecting	9,000,000
Inventory control (raw materials and finished goods)	12,600,000
Utilities	18,000,000
Total budgeted overhead costs	¥86,800,000

For the last four years, Fuji Woodworks has been charging overhead to products on the basis of machine hours. For the year 2023, 100,000 machine hours are budgeted.

Hiroto Wakui, owner-manager of Fuji Woodworks, recently directed his accountant, Kiato Watanabe, to implement the activity-based costing system that he has repeatedly proposed. At Hiroto's request, Kiato and the production foreman identify the following cost drivers and their usage for the previously budgeted overhead cost pools.

Activity Cost Pools	Cost Drivers	Estimated Use of Cost Drivers
Purchasing	Number of orders	600
Handling materials	Number of moves	8,000
Production (cutting, milling, finishing)	Direct labor hours	100,000
Setting up machines	Number of setups	1,250
Inspecting	Number of inspections	6,000
Inventory control (raw materials and finished goods)	Number of components	168,000
Utilities	Square meters occupied	90,000

Itsuki Nakano, sales manager, has received an order for 250 stairways from Akaishi Builders, a large housing development contractor. At Itsuki's request, Kiato prepares cost estimates for producing components for 250 stairways so Itsuki can submit a contract price per stairway to Akaishi Builders. He accumulates the following data for the production of 250 stairways.

Direct materials	¥10,360,000
Direct labor	¥11,200,000
Machine hours	14,500
Direct labor hours	5,000
Number of purchase orders	60
Number of material moves	800
Number of machine setups	100
Number of inspections	450
Number of components	16,000
Number of square meters occupied	8,000

Instructions

a. Compute the predetermined overhead rate using traditional costing with machine hours as the basis.

b. What is the manufacturing cost per stairway under traditional costing?

c. What is the manufacturing cost per stairway under the proposed activity-based costing? (Prepare all of the necessary schedules.)

d. Which of the two costing systems is preferable in pricing decisions and why?

P4.4 (LO 1, 2), AN Alzbeta Corporation produces two grades of non-alcoholic wine from grapes that it buys from Scotland growers. It produces and sells roughly 3,000,000 liters per year of a low-cost, high-volume product called CoolDay. It sells this in 600,000 5-liter jugs. Alzbeta also produces and sells roughly 300,000 liters per year of a low-volume, high-cost product called LiteMist. LiteMist is sold in 1-liter bottles. Based on recent data, the CoolDay product has not been as profitable as LiteMist. Management is considering dropping the inexpensive CoolDay line so it can focus more attention on the LiteMist product. The LiteMist product already demands considerably more attention than the CoolDay line.

Ross Miller, president and founder of Alzbeta, is skeptical about this idea. He points out that for many decades the company produced only the CoolDay line and that it was always quite profitable. It wasn't until the company started producing the more complicated LiteMist wine that the profitability of CoolDay declined. Prior to the introduction of LiteMist, the company had basic equipment, simple production procedures, and virtually no need for quality control. Because LiteMist is bottled in 1-liter bottles, it requires considerably more time and effort, both to bottle and to label and box than does CoolDay. The company must bottle and handle five times as many bottles of LiteMist to sell the same quantity as CoolDay. CoolDay requires one month of aging; LiteMist requires one year. CoolDay requires cleaning and inspection of equipment every 10,000 liters; LiteMist requires such maintenance every 600 liters.

Ross has asked the accounting department to prepare an analysis of the cost per liter using the traditional costing approach and using activity-based costing. The following information was collected.

	CoolDay	LiteMist
Direct materials per liter	£0.40	£1.20
Direct labor cost per liter	£0.50	£0.90
Direct labor hours per liter	0.05	0.09
Total direct labor hours	150,000	27,000

Activity Cost Pools	Cost Drivers	Estimated Overhead	Estimated Use of Cost Drivers	Use of Cost Drivers per Product	
				CoolDay	LiteMist
Grape processing	Cart of grapes	£ 145,860	6,600	6,000	600
Aging	Total months	396,000	6,600,000	3,000,000	3,600,000
Bottling and corking	Number of bottles	270,000	900,000	600,000	300,000
Labeling and boxing	Number of bottles	189,000	900,000	600,000	300,000
Maintain and inspect equipment	Number of inspections	240,800	800	350	450
		£1,241,660			

Instructions

Answer each of the following questions. (Round all calculations to three decimal places.)

a. Under traditional product costing using direct labor hours, compute the total manufacturing cost per **liter** of both products.

b. Under ABC, prepare a schedule showing the computation of the activity-based overhead rates (per cost driver).

c. Prepare a schedule assigning each activity's overhead cost pool to each product, based on the use of cost drivers. Include a computation of overhead cost per liter.

d. Compute the total manufacturing cost per liter for both products under ABC.

e. Write a memo to Ross Miller discussing the implications of your analysis for the company's plans. In this memo, provide a brief description of ABC as well as an explanation of how the traditional approach can result in distortions.

P4.5 (LO 1, 2, 3, 4), AN Service Lewis and Stark is a public accounting firm that offers two primary services, auditing and tax-return preparation. A controversy has developed between the partners of the two service lines as to who is contributing the greater amount to the bottom line. The area of contention is the assignment of overhead. The tax partners argue for assigning overhead on the basis of 40% of direct labor dollars, while the audit partners argue for implementing activity-based costing. The partners agree to use next year's budgeted data for purposes of analysis and comparison. The following overhead data are collected to develop the comparison.

Assign overhead costs to services using traditional costing and ABC; compute overhead rates and unit costs; compare results.

Activity Cost Pools	Cost Drivers	Estimated Overhead	Estimated Use of Cost Drivers	Use of Cost Drivers per Service	
				Audit	Tax
Employee training	Direct labor dollars	$216,000	$1,800,000	$1,100,000	$700,000
Typing and secretarial	Number of reports/forms	76,200	2,500	800	1,700
Computing	Number of minutes	204,000	60,000	27,000	33,000
Facility rental	Number of employees	142,500	40	22	18
Travel	Per expense reports	81,300	Trace directly	56,000	25,300
		$720,000			

Instructions

a. Using traditional product costing as proposed by the tax partners, compute the total overhead cost assigned to both services (audit and tax) of Lewis and Stark.

b. 1. Using activity-based costing, prepare a schedule showing the computations of the activity-based overhead rates (per cost driver). (*Hint:* As a result of breaking out travel costs as a separate cost pool, travel costs can now be traced directly to services provided. Thus, an overhead rate is not needed.)

   2. Prepare a schedule assigning each activity's overhead cost pool to each accounting service based on the use of the cost drivers.

c. Comment on the comparative overhead cost for the two services under both traditional costing and ABC.

b. (2) Cost assigned—Tax $337,441

c. Difference—Audit $57,441

Continuing Case

Current Designs

CD4 As you learned in the previous chapters, **Current Designs** (USA) has two main product lines—composite kayaks, which are handmade and very labor-intensive, and rotomolded kayaks, which require less labor but employ more expensive equipment. Current Designs' controller, Diane Buswell, is now evaluating several different methods of assigning overhead to these products. It is important to ensure

Current Designs Activity Cost Pools

	A	B
1		
2	Activities	Cost
3	Designing new models	$121,100
4	Creating and testing prototypes	152,000
5	Creating molds for kayaks	188,500
6	Operating oven for the rotomolded kayaks	40,000
7	Operating the vacuum line for the composite kayaks	28,000
8	Supervising production employees	180,000
9	Curing time (the time that is needed for the chemical processes to finish before the next step in the production process; many of these costs are related to the space required in the building)	190,400
10	Total	$900,000

Current Designs Cost Drivers

Activity Cost Pools	Cost Drivers	Driver Amount for Composite Kayaks	Driver Amount for Rotomolded Kayaks
Designing new models	Number of models	3	1
Creating and testing prototypes	Number of prototypes	6	2
Creating molds for kayaks	Number of molds	12	1
Supervising production employees	Number of employees	12	12
Curing time	Number of days of curing time	15,000	2,000

that costs are appropriately assigned to the company's products. At the same time, the system that is used must not be so complex that its costs are greater than its benefits.

Diane has decided to use the following activities and costs to evaluate the methods of assigning overhead.

As Diane examines the data, she decides that the cost of operating the oven for the rotomolded kayaks and the cost of operating the vacuum line for the composite kayaks can be directly assigned to each of these product lines and do not need to be assigned with the other costs.

Instructions

For purposes of this analysis, assume that Current Designs uses $234,000 in direct labor costs to produce 1,000 composite kayaks and $286,000 in direct labor costs to produce 4,000 rotomolded kayaks each year.

a. One method of assigning overhead would assign the common costs to each product line by using an assignment basis such as the number of employees working on each type of kayak or the amount of factory space used for the production of each type of kayak. Diane knows that about 50% of the area of the factory and 50% of the employees work on the composite kayaks, and the remaining space and other employees work on the rotomolded kayaks. Using this information and remembering that the costs of operating the oven and vacuum line have been directly assigned, determine the total amount to be assigned to the composite kayak line and the rotomolded kayak line, and the amount to be assigned to each of the units in each line.

b. Another method of assigning overhead is to use direct labor dollars as an assignment basis. Remembering that the costs of the oven and the vacuum line have been assigned directly to the product lines, allocate the remaining costs using direct labor dollars as the allocation basis. Then, determine the amount of overhead that should be assigned to each unit of each product line using this method.

c. Activity-based costing requires a cost driver for each cost pool. Use the following information to assign the costs to the product lines using the activity-based costing approach.

What amount of overhead should be assigned to each composite kayak using this method? What amount of overhead should be assigned to each rotomolded kayak using this method?

d. Which of the three methods do you think Current Designs should use? Why?

Expand Your Critical Thinking

Decision-Making Across the Organization

CT4.1 **Service** East Valley Hospital is a primary medical care facility and trauma center that serves 11 small, rural communities within a 50-km radius. The hospital offers all the medical/surgical services of a typical small hospital. It has a staff of 18 full-time doctors and 20 part-time visiting specialists. East Valley has a payroll of 150 employees consisting of technicians, nurses, therapists, managers, directors, administrators, dieticians, secretaries, data processors, and janitors.

Instructions

With the class divided into groups, discuss and answer the following:

a. Using your (limited, moderate, or in-depth) knowledge of a hospital's operations, identify as many **activities** as you can that would serve as the basis for implementing an activity-based costing system.

b. For each of the activities listed in (a), identify a **cost driver** that would serve as a valid measure of the resources consumed by the activity.

Managerial Analysis

CT4.2 Real Manufacturing Company has supported a research and development (R&D) department that has for many years been the sole contributor to the company's new farm machinery products. The R&D activity is an overhead cost center that performs services only to in-house manufacturing departments (four different product lines), all of which produce agricultural or farm-related machinery products.

The department has never sold its services to outside companies. But, because of its long history of success, larger manufacturers of agricultural products have approached Real to hire its R&D department for special projects. Because the costs of operating the R&D department have been spiraling uncontrollably, Real's management is considering entertaining these outside approaches to absorb the increasing costs. However, (1) management doesn't have any cost basis for charging R&D services to outsiders, and (2) it needs to gain control of its R&D costs. Management decides to implement an activity-based costing system in order to determine the charges for both outsiders and in-house users of the department's services.

R&D activities fall into four pools with the following annual costs:

Market analysis	€1,050,000
Product design	2,350,000
Product development	3,600,000
Prototype testing	1,400,000

Activity analysis determines that the appropriate cost drivers and their usage for the four activities are:

Activities	Cost Drivers	Total Estimated Drivers
Market analysis	Hours of analysis	15,000 hours
Product design	Number of designs	2,500 designs
Product development	Number of products	90 products
Prototype testing	Number of tests	500 tests

Instructions

a. Compute the activity-based overhead rate for each activity cost pool.
b. How much cost would be charged to an in-house manufacturing department that consumed 1,800 hours of market analysis time, was provided 280 designs relating to 10 products, and requested 92 engineering tests?
c. How much cost would serve as the basis for pricing an R&D bid with an outside company on a contract that would consume 800 hours of analysis time, require 178 designs relating to three products, and result in 70 engineering tests?
d. What is the benefit to Real Manufacturing of applying activity-based costing to its R&D activity for both in-house and outside charging purposes?

Real-World Focus

CT4.3 **Service** An article in *Cost Management*, by Kocakulah, Bartlett, and Albin entitled "ABC for Calculating Mortgage Loan Servicing Expenses" (July/August 2009, p. 36), discusses a use of ABC in the financial services industry.

Instructions

Read the article (obtain online or at your library) and then answer the following questions:

a. What are some of the benefits of ABC that relate to the financial services industry?
b. What are three things that the company's original costing method did not take into account?
c. What were some of the cost drivers used by the company in the ABC approach?

Ethics Case

CT4.4 Riz Ansari, the cost accountant for Lawn-Power Company, recently installed activity-based costing at Lawn-Power's lawn tractor (riding mower) factory where three models—the 8-horsepower Bladerunner, the 12-horsepower Quickcut, and the 18-horsepower Supercut—are manufactured. Riz's new product costs for these three models show that the company's traditional costing system had been significantly undercosting the 18-horsepower Supercut. This was due primarily to the lower sales volume of the Supercut compared to the Bladerunner and the Quickcut.

Before completing his analysis and reporting these results to management, Riz is approached by his friend Rachel Holmes who is the production manager for the 18-horsepower Supercut model. Rachel has heard from one of Riz's staff about the new product costs and is upset and worried for her job because the new costs show the Supercut to be losing, rather than making, money.

At first, Rachel condemns the new cost system, whereupon Riz explains the practice of activity-based costing and why it is more accurate than the company's present system. Even more worried now, Rachel begs Riz, "Massage the figures just enough to save the line from being discontinued. You don't want me to lose my job, do you? Anyway, nobody will know."

Riz holds firm but agrees to recompute all his calculations for accuracy before submitting his costs to management.

Instructions

a. Who are the stakeholders in this situation?
b. What, if any, are the ethical considerations in this situation?
c. What are Riz's ethical obligations to the company? To his friend?

All About You

CT4.5 There are many resources available on the Internet to assist people in time management. Some of these resources are designed specifically for college students.

Instructions

Do an Internet search of Dartmouth College's time-management video. Watch the video and then answer the following questions:

a. What are the main tools of time management for students, and what is each used for?
b. At what time of day are students most inclined to waste time? What time of day is the best for studying complex topics?
c. How can employing time-management practices be a "liberating" experience?
d. Why is goal-setting important? What are the characteristics of good goals, and what steps should you take to help you develop your goals?

Considering Your Costs and Benefits

CT4.6 As discussed in the chapter, the principles underlying activity-based costing have evolved into the broader approach known as *activity-based management*. One of the common practices of activity-based management is to identify all business activities, classify each activity as either a value-added or a non–value-added activity, and then try to reduce or eliminate the time spent on non–value-added activities. Consider the implications of applying this same approach to your everyday life, at work and at school. How do you spend your time each day? How much of your day is spent on activities that help you accomplish your objectives, and how much of your day is spent on activities that do not add value?

Many self-help books and websites offer suggestions on how to improve your time management. Should you minimize the "non–value-added" hours in your life by adopting the methods suggested by these sources? The basic arguments for and against are as follows:

YES: There are a limited number of hours in a day. You should try to maximize your chances of achieving your goals by eliminating the time that you waste.

NO: Life is about more than working yourself to death. Being an efficiency expert doesn't guarantee that you will be happy. Schedules and daily planners are too constraining.

Instructions

Write a response indicating your position regarding this situation. Provide support for your view.

CHAPTER 5

Cost-Volume-Profit

CHAPTER PREVIEW

As the following Feature Story indicates, to manage any size business you must understand how costs respond to changes in sales volume (quantity sold) and the effect of costs and revenues on profits. A prerequisite to understanding cost-volume-profit (CVP) relationships is knowledge of how costs behave. In this chapter, we first explain the considerations involved in cost behavior analysis. Then, we discuss and illustrate CVP analysis.

FEATURE STORY

Don't Worry—Just Get Big

It wasn't that Jeff didn't have a good job. He was a vice president at a Wall Street firm. But, despite his good position, he quit his job, moved to Seattle, and started an online retailer, which he named **Amazon.com** (USA). Like any good entrepreneur, Jeff Bezos kept his initial investment small. Operations were run out of his garage. And, to avoid the need for a warehouse, he took orders for books and had them shipped from other distributors' warehouses.

By its fourth month, Amazon was selling 100 books a day. In its first full year, it had $15.7 million in sales. The next year, sales increased eightfold. Two years later, sales were $1.6 billion.

Although its sales growth was impressive, Amazon's ability to lose money was equally amazing. One analyst nicknamed it *Amazon.bomb*, while another, predicting its demise, called it *Amazon.toast*. Why was it losing money?

The company used every available dollar to reinvest in itself. It built massive warehouses and bought increasingly sophisticated (and expensive) computers and equipment to improve its distribution system. This desire to grow as fast as possible was captured in a T-shirt slogan at its company picnic, which read "Eat another hot dog, get big fast." This buying binge was increasing the company's fixed costs at a rate that exceeded its sales growth. Skeptics predicted that Amazon would soon run out of cash. It didn't.

At the end of one year, even as it announced record profits, Amazon's share price fell by 9%. Why? Because although the company was predicting that its sales revenue in the next quarter would increase by at least 28%, it predicted that its operating profit would fall by at least 2% and perhaps by as much as 34%. The company made no apologies. It explained that it was in the process of expanding from 39 distribution centers to 52. As Amazon's finance chief noted, "You're not as productive on those assets for some time. I'm very pleased with the investments we're making and we've shown over our history that we've been able to make great returns on the capital we invest in." Or, in the words of Jeff Bezos, "It's a fixed cost business and so what I could see from the internal metrics at a certain volume level we would cover our fixed costs, and we would **be profitable**." In other words, eat another hot dog.

Sources: Christine Frey and John Cook, "How Amazon.com Survived, Thrived and Turned a Profit," *Seattle Post* (January 28, 2008); Stu Woo, "Sticker Shock Over Amazon Growth," *Wall Street Journal* (January 28, 2011); Miriam Guttfried, "Amazon's Never-Ending Story," *Wall Street Journal* (April 25, 2014); and John Stoll, "Why Investors Don't Care That Snap and Lyft Are Hemorrhaging Money," *Wall Street Journal* (April 26, 2019).

 Watch the *Southwest Airlines* video at https://wileyaccountingupdates.com/video/?p=39 to learn more about cost-volume-profit analysis in the real world.

CHAPTER OUTLINE

Learning Objectives	Review	Practice
LO 1 Explain variable, fixed, and mixed costs and the relevant range.	• Variable costs • Fixed costs • Relevant range • Mixed costs	**DO IT! 1** Types of Costs
LO 2 Apply the high-low method to determine the components of mixed costs.	• High-low method • Identifying variable and fixed costs	**DO IT! 2** High-Low Method
LO 3 Prepare a CVP income statement to determine contribution margin.	• Basic components • CVP income statement	**DO IT! 3** CVP Income Statement
LO 4 Compute the break-even point using three approaches.	• Mathematical equation • Contribution margin techniques • Graphic presentation	**DO IT! 4** Break-Even Analysis
LO 5 Determine the sales required to earn target net income and determine margin of safety.	• Target net income • Margin of safety • CVP and data analytics	**DO IT! 5** Break-Even Point, Margin of Safety, and Target Net Income

Go to the Review and Practice section at the end of the chapter for a targeted summary and practice applications with solutions.

COST BEHAVIOR ANALYSIS

Cost behavior analysis is the study of how specific costs respond to changes in the level of business activity.

> **LEARNING OBJECTIVE 1**
> Explain variable, fixed, and mixed costs and the relevant range.

- Some costs change when activity changes, and others remain the same. For example, for an airline company such as **British Airways** (GBR) or **Singapore Airlines** (SGP), the longer the flight, the higher the fuel costs. On the other hand, **Karolinska University Hospital**'s (SWE) costs to staff the emergency room on any given night are relatively constant regardless of the number of patients treated.
- A knowledge of cost behavior helps management plan operations and decide between alternative courses of action.
- Cost behavior analysis applies to all types of entities.

The starting point in cost behavior analysis is measuring the key business activities. Activity levels may be expressed in terms of sales euros (in a retail company), kilometers driven (in a trucking company), room occupancy (in a hotel), or dance classes taught (by a dance studio). Many companies use more than one measurement base. A manufacturer, for example, may use direct labor hours or units of output for manufacturing costs, and sales revenue or units sold for selling expenses.

For an activity level to be useful in cost behavior analysis, changes in the level or volume of activity should be correlated with changes in costs.

- The activity level selected is referred to as the activity index or driver.
- The **activity index** identifies the activity that causes changes in the behavior of costs.
- With an appropriate activity index, companies can classify the behavior of costs in response to changes in activity levels into three categories: variable, fixed, or mixed.

Unless specifically stated otherwise, our examples and end-of-chapter material use the volume (quantity) of output (e.g., goods produced or services provided) as the activity index.

Variable Costs

Variable costs are costs that vary **in total** directly and proportionately with changes in the activity level.

- If the level increases 10%, total variable costs will increase 10%. If the level of activity decreases by 25%, variable costs will decrease 25%.
- Examples of variable costs include direct materials and direct labor for a manufacturer; cost of goods sold, sales commissions, and freight-out for a merchandiser; and gasoline in airline and trucking companies.
- A variable cost may also be defined as a cost that **remains the same *per unit* at every level of activity**. This means that the unit variable cost is constant.

To illustrate the behavior of a variable cost, assume that Silva SpA manufactures cell phones that contain cameras. Silva purchases the cameras, a direct material, from a supplier for €10 each. **The activity index is the number of cell phones produced**. As Silva manufactures each phone, the total cost of cameras installed in phones increases by €10. As part (a) of **Illustration 5.1** shows, total cost of the cameras will be €20,000 (2,000 × €10) if Silva produces 2,000 phones, and €100,000 when it produces 10,000 phones. We can also see that the unit variable costs remain the same as the level of activity changes. As part (b) of Illustration 5.1 shows, the unit variable cost of €10 for the cameras is the same whether Silva produces 2,000 or 10,000 phones.

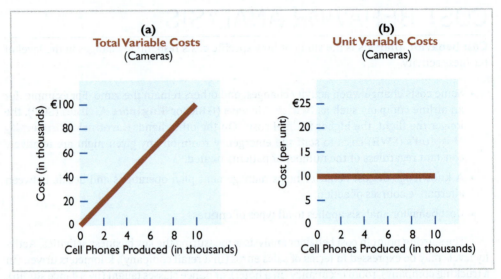

ILLUSTRATION 5.1 | Behavior of total and unit variable costs; unit variable costs remain constant

Companies that rely heavily on labor either to manufacture a product or perform a service, such as **Gritti Palace** (ITA) and **Hilton Garden** (USA), are likely to have a high percentage of variable costs related to direct labor. In contrast, companies that use a high proportion of machinery and equipment in producing revenue, such as **Telstra** (AUS) and **Eni Energy** (ITA), may have a lower percentage of variable costs related to direct labor.

Fixed Costs

Fixed costs are costs that **remain the same in total** regardless of changes in the activity level.

- Examples include property taxes, insurance, rent, supervisory salaries, and straight-line depreciation on buildings and equipment.
- Because total fixed costs remain constant as activity changes, it follows that **fixed costs *per unit* vary inversely with activity: As volume increases, unit cost declines, and vice versa.**

To illustrate the behavior of fixed costs, assume that Silva SpA leases its productive facilities at a rental cost of €10,000 per month. Total fixed costs of the facilities remain a constant €10,000 at every level of activity, as part (a) of **Illustration 5.2** shows. But, **on a per unit basis, the cost of rent declines as activity increases**, as part (b) of

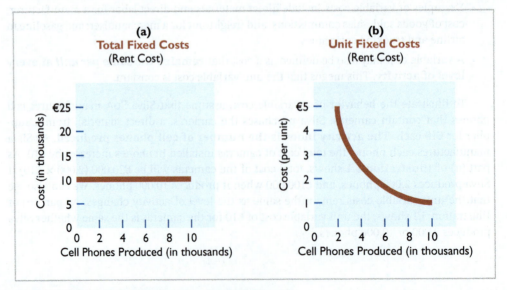

ILLUSTRATION 5.2 | Behavior of total and unit fixed costs

Illustration 5.2 shows. At 2,000 units, the unit cost per cell phone is €5 (€10,000 ÷ 2,000). When Silva produces 10,000 cell phones, the unit cost of the rent is only €1 per phone (€10,000 ÷ 10,000).

The trend for many manufacturers is to have more fixed costs and fewer variable costs. This trend is the result of increased use of automation and less use of employee direct labor. As a result, depreciation and rent charges (fixed costs) increase, whereas direct labor costs (variable costs) decrease.

PEOPLE, PLANET, AND PROFIT INSIGHT — Synergy

Between a Rock and a Hard Place

Alessandro2802/Getty Images

Households in Western Australia that install solar panels sometimes generate several times the amount of energy that they use. For these surplus kilowatts generated that can be fed back into the grid, their electric company **Synergy** (AUS) pays them a rebate (referred to as a feedback tariff). However, the amount recently paid by Synergy has been cut to a third of what imported electricity costs, so household users (and electricity producers) have to export a lot to break even. This rebate or feed-in tariff was reduced considerably because the surplus uptake due to renewables has been so great.

What this means is that when the initial customers that installed solar panels signed up for a 10-year contract under "The Premium Feed-In Tariff Scheme," Synergy agreed to pay customers 40 cents per unit of power they fed back into the grid. The tariff was then reduced to 20 cents, and now new customers are paid just 7.135 cents per unit under the Renewable Energy Buyback plan and have to buy electricity back at night for 26 cents per unit.

Customers, who wanted the greatest return on their investment, installed the maximum-size solar system (five-kilowatt equipment). These customers are now investigating the use of batteries to reduce the amount of power they purchase—their overnight costs—while looking to pay off their equipment investment.

Source: K. Diss, "Solar Panel Owners Caught Between a Rock and a Hard Place," *ABC News* (October 22, 2016).

If a five-kilowatt solar system costs A$24,000 to install, how many units of power were required to break even under the original Premium Feed-In Tariff Scheme? How many units are currently required? (Answer is available in the book's product page on www.wiley.com)

Relevant Range

In Illustration 5.1 part (a), a straight line is drawn throughout the entire range of the activity index for total variable costs. In essence, the assumption is that the costs are **linear**.

- If a relationship is linear (that is, straight-line), then changes in the activity index will result in a direct, proportional change in the total variable costs.
- For example, if the activity level doubles, the total variable costs double.

It is now necessary to ask: Is the straight-line relationship realistic? In most business situations, a straight-line relationship **does not exist** for variable costs throughout the entire range of possible activity.

- At abnormally low levels of activity, it may be impossible to be cost-efficient. Small-scale operations may not allow the company to obtain quantity discounts for raw materials or to use specialized labor.
- At abnormally high levels of activity, unit labor costs may increase sharply because of overtime pay. Also, at high activity levels, unit materials costs may jump significantly because of excess spoilage caused by worker fatigue.

As a result, in the real world, the relationship between the behavior of variable costs and changes in the activity level is often **curvilinear**, as shown in part (a) of **Illustration 5.3**. In the curved sections of the line, a change in the activity index will **not** result in a direct, proportional change in the total variable costs. That is, a doubling of the activity index will not result in an exact doubling of the total variable costs. The total variable costs may be more than double, or they may be less than double.

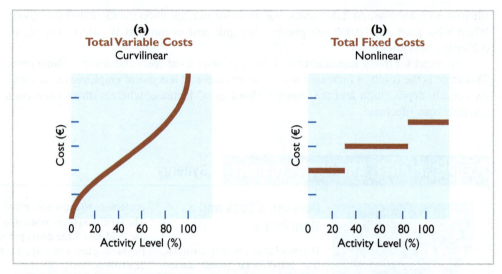

ILLUSTRATION 5.3 | Nonlinear behavior of variable and fixed costs

Total fixed costs also do not have a straight-line relationship over the entire range of activity. Some fixed costs will not change. But it is possible for management to change other fixed costs (see **Helpful Hint**). For example, in some instances, salaried employees (fixed) are replaced with freelance workers (variable). Some costs are step costs. For example, once a company exceeds certain levels of activity, it may have to add an additional warehouse or more machinery. Illustration 5.3 part (b) shows an example of step-cost behavior of total fixed costs through all potential levels of activity.

For most companies, operating at almost zero or at 100% capacity is the exception rather than the rule. Instead, companies often operate over a somewhat narrower range, such as 40–80% of capacity. For example, the average occupancy rate for hotels is between 50% and 80%. Airlines calculate their capacity using a measure called a load factor (which combines the number of available seats and the kilometers flown); this measure has risen to an average of 80% or higher for some airlines in recent years.

HELPFUL HINT
Fixed costs that may be changed by managers include research, such as new product development, and management training programs.

- The range over which a company expects to operate during a year is called the **relevant range** of the activity index (see **Alternative Terminology**).
- Within the relevant range, as both diagrams in **Illustration 5.4** show, a straight-line relationship generally exists for both variable and fixed costs between 40% and 80% of capacity.

ALTERNATIVE TERMINOLOGY
The relevant range is also called the *normal* or *practical range.*

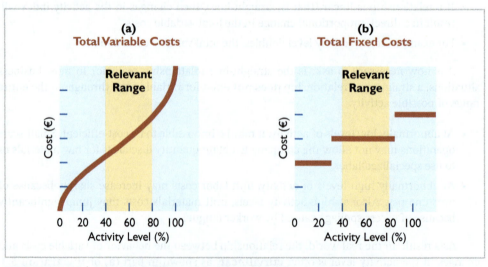

ILLUSTRATION 5.4 | Linear behavior within relevant range

As you can see, although the linear (straight-line) relationship may not be completely realistic, **the linear assumption produces useful data for CVP analysis as long as the level of activity remains within the relevant range.**

Mixed Costs

Mixed costs are costs that contain both variable-cost and fixed-cost components. **Mixed costs, therefore, change in total but not proportionately with changes in the activity level.** For example, each month the electric bill includes a flat service fee plus a usage charge.

The rental of a **Buchbinder** (DEU) truck is another good example of a mixed cost. Assume that local rental terms for a 5-meter truck, including insurance, are €50 per day plus €0.50 per kilometer. When determining the cost of a one-day rental:

- The fixed-cost component is the cost of having the truck available (€50 per day charge).
- The variable-cost component is the cost of actually using the truck (€0.50 per kilometer driven).

The graphic presentation of the rental cost for a one-day rental is shown in **Illustration 5.5**.

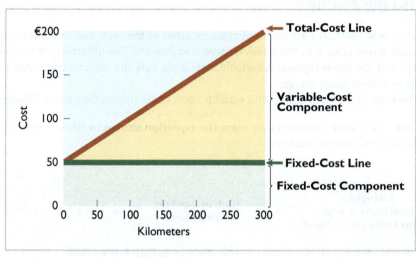

ILLUSTRATION 5.5 | Behavior of a mixed cost

DO IT! 1 ▶ Types of Costs

Anderson SA reports the following total costs at two levels of production.

	10,000 Units	20,000 Units
Direct materials	€20,000	€40,000
Maintenance	8,000	10,000
Direct labor	17,000	34,000
Indirect materials	1,000	2,000
Depreciation (straight-line)	4,000	4,000
Utilities	3,000	5,000
Rent	6,000	6,000

Classify each cost as variable, fixed, or mixed.

ACTION PLAN
- Recall that a variable cost varies in total directly and proportionately with each change in activity level.
- Recall that a fixed cost remains the same in total with each change in activity level.
- Recall that a mixed cost changes in total but not proportionately with each change in activity level.

Solution

Direct materials, direct labor, and indirect materials are variable costs because the total cost doubles with the doubling in activity.

Depreciation and rent are fixed costs because the total cost does not vary with the change in activity.

Maintenance and utilities are mixed costs because the total cost changes, but the change is not proportional to the change in activity.

Related exercise material: **BE5.1, BE5.2, BE5.3, DO IT! 5.1, E5.1, E5.2, E5.4, and E5.6.**

MIXED COSTS ANALYSIS

LEARNING OBJECTIVE 2
Apply the high-low method to determine the components of mixed costs.

For purposes of cost-volume-profit analysis, **mixed costs must be classified into their fixed and variable components**. How does management make the classification?

- One possibility is to determine the variable and fixed components each time a mixed cost is incurred. But because of time and cost constraints, this approach is rarely followed.
- Instead, the usual approach is to collect data on the behavior of the mixed costs at various levels of activity.
- Analysts then identify the fixed-cost and variable-cost components.

Companies use various types of analysis. One type of analysis, called the **high-low method**, is discussed next.

High-Low Method

The **high-low method** uses the total costs incurred at the high and low levels of activity to classify mixed costs into fixed and variable components. The difference in costs between the high and low levels represents variable costs since only the variable-cost component can change as activity levels change.

The steps in computing fixed and variable costs under this method are as follows:

1. **Determine unit variable costs from the equation shown in Illustration 5.6.** This is the slope of the cost function.

Change in Total Costs at High versus Low Activity Level	÷	High minus Low Activity Level	=	Unit Variable Costs

ILLUSTRATION 5.6 | Equation for unit variable costs using high-low method

To illustrate, assume that Metro Transit has the maintenance costs and distance data for its fleet of buses over a six-month period shown in **Illustration 5.7**.

Month	Kilometers Driven	Total Cost	Month	Kilometers Driven	Total Cost
January	20,000	€30,000	April	50,000	€63,000
February	40,000	48,000	May	30,000	42,000
March	35,000	49,000	June	43,000	61,000

ILLUSTRATION 5.7 | Assumed maintenance costs and distance data

The high level of activity is 50,000 kilometers in April, and the low level of activity is 20,000 kilometers in January. The maintenance costs at these two levels are €63,000 and €30,000, respectively. The difference in maintenance costs is €33,000 (€63,000 − €30,000), and the difference in kilometers is 30,000 (50,000 − 20,000). Therefore, for Metro Transit, unit variable costs are €1.10, computed as follows:

Change in Total Costs at High versus Low Activity Level		High minus Low Activity Level		Unit Variable Costs
€33,000	÷	30,000 kilometers	=	€1.10 per kilometer

2. **Determine the total fixed costs by subtracting the total variable costs at either the high or the low activity level from the total cost at that activity level.**

Illustration 5.8 shows the computations for Metro Transit.

		Activity Level	
		High	**Low**
Total cost		€63,000	€30,000
Less:	Variable costs		
	50,000 × €1.10	55,000	
	20,000 × €1.10		22,000
Total fixed costs		€ 8,000	€ 8,000

ILLUSTRATION 5.8 | **High-low method computation of fixed costs**

For example, at the 50,000-kilometer level of activity, variable costs are 50,000 × €1.10 = €55,000. To determine the fixed costs of €8,000, we subtract the variable costs of €55,000 from the total cost of €63,000. **Total maintenance costs are therefore €8,000 per month of fixed costs plus €1.10 per kilometer of variable costs.** This is represented by the following total cost equation:

For example, at 45,000 kilometers, estimated maintenance costs would be €8,000 fixed and €49,500 variable (€1.10 × 45,000), for a total of €57,500.

The graph in **Illustration 5.9** plots the six-month data for Metro Transit.

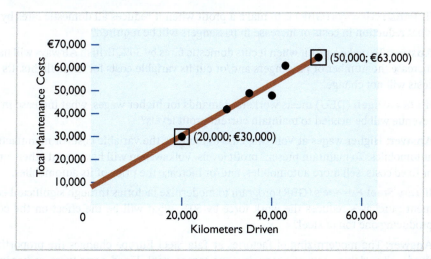

ILLUSTRATION 5.9 | **Scatter plot for Metro Transit**

- The red line drawn in the graph connects the high and low data points (in squares) and therefore represents the equation that we just solved using the high-low method.
- The red, "high-low" line intersects the y-axis at €8,000 (the fixed-cost level), and it rises by its slope of €1.10 per unit (the unit variable costs).

- Note that not all data points fall exactly on the plotted line. A completely different line would result if we chose to draw a line through any two of the other data points. That is, by choosing two other data points, we would end up with a different estimate of fixed costs and different unit variable costs.
- Thus, from this scatter plot, we can see that while the high-low method is simple, the result is rather arbitrary.

A better approach, which uses information from all the data points to estimate fixed and variable costs, is called *regression analysis*. A discussion of regression analysis is provided in Appendix 5A.

MANAGEMENT INSIGHT   **Kroger**

Are Robotic Workers More Humane?

phonlamaiphoto/Adobe Stock Photos

Warehouse distribution centers for large retailers and grocers employ more than 800,000 people in the United States. But many companies, such as grocer **Kroger** (USA), have a hard time finding and retaining warehouse workers. One reason? Studies have shown that some warehouse workers walk up to 20 miles and lift 50,000 pounds during a single day. As a result, as the needs for storage increase and companies are faced with the proposition of building massive new warehouses, some companies are choosing instead to invest in robotic warehousing systems.

Robots can provide many advantages over their human counterparts. Robots need aisles that are less than 30 inches wide, as opposed to traditional warehouse aisles that are 10 to 12 feet wide. Moving at speeds of up to 25 miles per hour, robots can drop off and retrieve warehouse cases about five times as fast as a human. Robotic systems cut labor costs by about 80%, and they cut warehouse size anywhere from 25% to 40%. However, a fully automated system costs between $40 to $80 million, so the switch to robotic systems is not a trivial decision.

Source: Robbie Whelan, "Fully Autonomous Robots: The Warehouse Workers of the Near Future," *Wall Street Journal* (September 20, 2016).

How would a company's variable and fixed costs change if it adopts a robotic system? (Answer is available in the book's product page on www.wiley.com)

Importance of Identifying Variable and Fixed Costs

Why is it important to identify costs as either variable or fixed components? The answer may become apparent if we look at the following four business decisions:

1. If **British Airways** (GBR) is to make a profit when it reduces all domestic fares by 30%, what reduction in costs or increase in passengers will be required?

   Answer: To make a profit when it cuts domestic fares by 30%, British Airways will have to increase the number of passengers and/or cut its variable costs for those flights. Its fixed costs will not change.

2. If **Volkswagen** (DEU) meets workers' demands for higher wages, what increase in sales revenue will be needed to maintain current profit levels?

   Answer: Higher wages at Volkswagen will increase the variable costs of manufacturing automobiles. To maintain present profit levels, Volkswagen will have to cut other variable or fixed costs, sell more automobiles, and/or increase the price of its automobiles.

3. If **Tata Steel Europe**'s (GBR) program to modernize factories through significant equipment purchases reduces the work force by 50%, what will be the effect on the cost of producing one ton of steel?

   Answer: The modernizing of factories at Tata Steel Europe changes the proportion of fixed and variable costs of producing one ton of steel. Fixed costs increase because of higher depreciation charges, whereas variable costs decrease due to the reduction in the number of steelworkers and related direct labor costs.

4. What happens if **Nestle** (CHE) increases its advertising expenses but cannot increase prices because of competitive pressure?

   Answer: Sales volume must be increased to cover the increase in fixed advertising costs.

> **DO IT! 2** ▶ **High-Low Method**
>
> Thomson SpA accumulates the following data concerning a mixed cost, using units produced as the activity level.
>
> | | Units Produced | Total Cost |
> |-------|---------------:|-----------:|
> | March | 9,800 | €14,740 |
> | April | 8,500 | 13,250 |
> | May | 7,000 | 11,100 |
> | June | 7,600 | 12,000 |
> | July | 8,100 | 12,460 |
>
> a. Compute the variable-cost and fixed-cost components using the high-low method.
> b. Using the information from your answer to part (a), write the cost equation.
> c. Estimate the total cost if the Thomson produces 8,000 units.
>
> **Solution**
>
> a. Unit variable cost: (€14,740 − €11,100) ÷ (9,800 − 7,000) = €1.30
>   Fixed cost: €14,740 − (€1.30 × 9,800 units) = €2,000
>   OR €11,100 − (€1.30 × 7,000 units) = €2,000
> b. Cost = €2,000 + (€1.30 × units produced)
> c. Total cost to produce 8,000 units: €2,000 + €10,400 (€1.30 × 8,000 units) = €12,400
>
> Related exercise material: **BE5.4, BE5.5, DO IT! 5.2, E5.3,** and **E5.5.**

ACTION PLAN
- Determine the highest and lowest levels of activity.
- Compute unit variable cost as Change in total costs ÷ Change in activity level = Unit variable cost.
- Compute fixed cost as Total cost − (Unit variable cost × Units produced) = Total fixed cost.

CVP ANALYSIS

Cost-volume-profit (CVP) analysis is the study of the effects of changes in costs and volume (quantity) on a company's profits.

- CVP analysis is important in profit planning.
- It is also a critical factor in management decisions such as setting selling prices, determining product mix, and maximizing use of production facilities.

LEARNING OBJECTIVE 3
Prepare a CVP income statement to determine contribution margin.

Basic Components

CVP analysis considers the interrelationships among the components—production/sales quantity, unit selling price, unit variable costs, total fixed costs, and sales mix—shown in **Illustration 5.10**. Note that management can modify operations to impact these components. But, it needs to do so with a solid understanding of how any operational changes will impact net income. This is CVP analysis.

The following assumptions underlie each CVP analysis.

1. The behavior of both costs and revenues is linear throughout the relevant range of the activity index.
2. Costs can be classified accurately as either variable or fixed.
3. Changes in activity are the only factors that affect costs.
4. All units produced are sold.

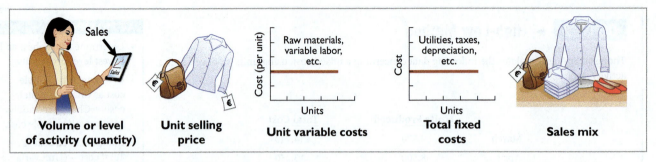

ILLUSTRATION 5.10 | **Components of CVP analysis**

5. When more than one type of product is sold, the sales mix will remain constant. That is, the percentage that each product represents of total sales will stay the same. Sales mix complicates CVP analysis because different products will have different cost relationships. In this chapter, we assume a single product. In Chapter 6, however, we examine the sales mix more closely.

When these assumptions are not valid, the CVP analysis may be inaccurate.

CVP Income Statement

Because CVP is so important for decision-making, management often wants this information reported in a **cost-volume-profit (CVP) income statement** format for internal use.

- The CVP income statement classifies costs as variable or fixed and computes a contribution margin.
- **Contribution margin (CM)** is the amount of revenue remaining after deducting variable costs. It is often stated both as a total amount and on a per unit basis.

We use Laurel Electronics to illustrate a CVP income statement and to contrast it with an income statement reported under traditional income statement. Laurel Electronics produces tablet computers. **Illustration 5.11** presents relevant data for the tablets sold by this company in June 2023.

Unit selling price per tablet		€500
Unit variable costs		
Direct materials	€185	
Direct labor	100	
Sales personnel commissions	15	
Total unit variable costs		€300
Monthly fixed costs		
Manufacturing overhead	€ 40,000	
CEO salary	150,000	
Sales salaries	10,000	
Total monthly fixed costs		€200,000
Units sold		1,600

ILLUSTRATION 5.11 | **Selling and cost data for Laurel Electronics**

Note that in Illustration 5.11, as well as in the applications and assignment material of CVP analysis that follow, **we assume that the term "costs" includes all costs and expenses related to production and sale of the product. That is, costs include manufacturing product costs plus selling and administrative period expenses.**

Illustration 5.12 compares the traditional income statement for Laurel Electronics with its CVP income statement.

(a)
Laurel Electronics
Traditional Income Statement
For the Month Ended June 30, 2023

Sales (1,600 × €500)		€800,000
Cost of goods sold		
Direct materials (1,600 × €185)	€296,000	
Direct labor (1,600 × €100)	160,000	
Manufacturing overhead	40,000	496,000
Gross profit		**304,000**
Operating expenses		
Sales commissions (1,600 × €15)	24,000	
Sales personnel salaries	10,000	
CEO salary	150,000	184,000
Net income		**€120,000**

(b)
Laurel Electronics
CVP Income Statement
For the Month Ended June 30, 2023

Sales (1,600 × €500)		€800,000
Variable costs		
Direct materials (1,600 × €185)	€296,000	
Direct labor (1,600 × €100)	160,000	
Sales commissions (1,600 × €15)	24,000	480,000
Contribution margin		**320,000**
Fixed costs		
Manufacturing overhead	40,000	
Sales personnel salaries	10,000	
CEO salary	150,000	200,000
Net income		**€120,000**

ILLUSTRATION 5.12 | Traditional income statement versus CVP income statement

While both income statements arrive at the same net income of €120,000, the components of each income statement are grouped differently to emphasize different aspects of the company's operations.

- The traditional income statement differentiates between **product costs** (those included in cost of goods sold) and **period costs** (those listed in operating expenses). The CVP statement differentiates between **variable costs** and **fixed costs**.
- The traditional income statement emphasizes **gross profit** (the difference between the amount received for goods sold and the cost of producing/purchasing these goods). Gross profit represents the net amount available to cover the company's operating expenses.
- The CVP income statement highlights **contribution margin** (the difference between the amount received for goods sold and the company's variable costs). Contribution margin represents the net amount available to cover fixed costs.

Subsequent illustrations show that sometimes per unit amounts and percentage of sales amounts are included in separate columns in a CVP statement to facilitate CVP analysis. *Homework assignments specify which columns to present.*

Unit Contribution Margin

Illustration 5.13 shows the equation for **unit contribution margin** and the computation for Laurel Electronics.

Unit Selling Price	−	Unit Variable Costs	=	Unit Contribution Margin
€500	−	€300	=	€200

ILLUSTRATION 5.13 | Equation for unit contribution margin

Unit contribution margin indicates that for every tablet sold, the selling price exceeds the unit variable costs by €200.

- Laurel generates €200 of contribution margin per unit to cover fixed costs and contribute to net income.
- Because Laurel has fixed costs of €200,000, it must sell 1,000 tablets (€200,000 ÷ €200) to cover its fixed costs.

- At the point where total contribution margin exactly equals fixed costs (sale of 1,000 tablets), Laurel will report net income of zero.
- At this point, referred to as the **break-even point**, total costs (variable plus fixed) exactly equal total revenue.

Illustration 5.14 shows Laurel's condensed CVP income statement, which assumes that June sales were at the point where net income equals zero. For Laurel, this point occurs when sales volume is 1,000 units. It shows a contribution margin of €200,000. A separate per unit column was added, which shows a unit contribution margin of €200 (€500 − €300).

Laurel Electronics
CVP Income Statement
For the Month Ended June 30, 2023

	Total	Per Unit
Sales (1,000 × €500)	€500,000	€500
Variable costs (1,000 × €300)	300,000	300
Contribution margin	200,000	**€200**
Fixed costs	200,000	
Net income	€ –0–	

ILLUSTRATION 5.14 | CVP income statement, with zero net income (1,000 tablets sold)

It follows that for every tablet sold above the break-even point of 1,000 units, **net income increases by the amount of the unit contribution margin, €200** (see **Decision Tools**). For example, assume that Laurel sold one more tablet, for a total of 1,001 tablets sold. In this case, Laurel reports net income of €200, as shown in **Illustration 5.15**.

DECISION TOOLS
The unit contribution margin indicates the increase in net income that results from every additional unit sold after the break-even point.

Laurel Electronics
CVP Income Statement
For the Month Ended June 30, 2023

	Total	Per Unit
Sales (1,001 × €500)	€500,500	€500
Variable costs (1,001 × €300)	300,300	300
Contribution margin	200,200	**€200**
Fixed costs	200,000	
Net income	€ 200	

ILLUSTRATION 5.15 | CVP income statement, with net income and per unit data (1,001 tablets sold)

Contribution Margin Ratio

Many managers use the contribution margin ratio in CVP analysis. The contribution margin ratio is the contribution margin expressed as a percentage of sales. **Illustration 5.16** presents the same information as Illustration 5.14 but with a column added that presents percentage of sales information.

Laurel Electronics
CVP Income Statement
For the Month Ended June 30, 2023

	Total	Per Unit	Percent of Sales	
Sales (1,000 × €500)	€500,000	€500	100%	
Variable costs (1,000 × €300)	300,000	300	60	← Variable cost ratio
Contribution margin	200,000	**€200**	40%	← Contribution margin ratio
Fixed costs	200,000			
Net income	€ –0–			

ILLUSTRATION 5.16 | CVP income statement, with net income and percent of sales data (1,000 tablets sold)

- This column shows that Laurel has a **variable cost ratio**, that is, variable costs expressed as a percentage of sales, of 60%. This tells us that for every euro of sales, Laurel incurs variable costs of €0.60.
- When this percentage is subtracted from 100%, we arrive at Laurel's contribution margin ratio of 40%. This tells us that for every euro of sales, Laurel earns a contribution margin of €0.40.

Alternatively, the **contribution margin ratio** can be determined by dividing the unit contribution margin by the unit selling price. **Illustration 5.17** shows the ratio for Laurel Electronics.

Unit Contribution Margin	÷	Unit Selling Price	=	Contribution Margin Ratio
€200	÷	€500	=	40%

ILLUSTRATION 5.17 | Equation for contribution margin ratio

- The contribution margin ratio of 40% means that Laurel generates 40 cents of contribution margin with each euro of sales. That is, €0.40 of each sales euro (40% × €1) is available to apply to fixed costs and to contribute to net income (see **Decision Tools**).
- This expression of contribution margin is very helpful in determining the effect of changes in sales on net income. For example, if Laurel's sales increase €100,000, net income will increase €40,000 (40% × €100,000).
- Thus, by using the contribution margin ratio, managers can quickly determine increases in net income from any change in sales.

> **DECISION TOOLS**
>
> The contribution margin ratio indicates by how much every euro of sales will increase income after the break-even point.

We can also see this effect through a CVP income statement. Assume that Laurel's current sales are €500,000 and it wants to know the effect of a €100,000 (200-unit) increase in sales. Laurel prepares the comparative CVP income statement analysis shown in **Illustration 5.18**.

Laurel Electronics
CVP Income Statement
For the Month Ended June 30, 2023

	No Change			With €100,000 Increase in Sales		
	Total	Per Unit	Percent of Sales	Total	Per Unit	Percent of Sales
Sales	€500,000	€500	100%	€600,000	€500	100%
Variable costs	300,000	300	60%	360,000	300	60%
Contribution margin	200,000	€200	40%	240,000	€200	40%
Fixed costs	200,000			200,000		
Net income	€ –0–			€ 40,000		

ILLUSTRATION 5.18 | Comparative CVP income statements

As sales increase, variable costs also increase.

- We can employ Laurel's variable cost ratio of 60% to determine that the €100,000 increase in sales results in a €60,000 (60% × €100,000) increase in variable costs.
- Since fixed costs do not increase, the resulting increase in net income is the difference between the increase in sales and the increase in variable costs of €40,000 (€100,000 − €60,000).
- Alternatively, the €40,000 increase in net income can be calculated on either a unit contribution margin basis (200 units × €200 per unit) or using the contribution margin ratio times the increase in sales euros (40% × €100,000).
- Note that the unit contribution margin and contribution margin as a percentage of sales (that is, the contribution margin ratio) remain unchanged by the increase in sales.

Study these CVP income statements carefully. The concepts presented in these statements are used extensively in this and later chapters.

DO IT! 3 | CVP Income Statement

Lansdowne Industries produces and sells a cell phone-operated thermostat. Information regarding the costs and sales of thermostats during September 2023 are provided below.

Unit selling price of thermostat	€85
Unit variable costs	€32
Total monthly fixed costs	€190,000
Units sold	4,000

Prepare a CVP income statement for Lansdowne Industries for the month of September. Provide total, per unit, and percent of sales values.

Solution

Lansdowne Industries
CVP Income Statement
For the Month Ended September 30, 2023

	Total	Per Unit	Percent of Sales
Sales	€340,000	€85	100.00%
Variable costs	128,000	32	37.65
Contribution margin	212,000	€53	62.35%
Fixed costs	190,000		
Net income	€ 22,000		

Related exercise material: **BE5.6, BE5.7, DO IT! 5.3, and E5.7.**

ACTION PLAN
- Provide a heading with the name of the company, name of statement, and period covered.
- Subtract variable costs from sales to determine contribution margin. Subtract fixed costs from contribution margin to determine net income.
- Express sales, variable costs, and contribution margin on a per unit basis.
- Express sales, variable costs, and contribution margin as a percentage of sales.

BREAK-EVEN ANALYSIS

LEARNING OBJECTIVE 4
Compute the break-even point using three approaches.

DECISION TOOLS
Break-even analysis indicates the amount of sales units or sales euros that a company needs to cover all of its costs.

A key relationship in CVP analysis is the level of activity at which total revenues equal total costs (both fixed and variable)—the **break-even point**. At this volume of sales, the company will realize no income but will suffer no loss. The process of finding the break-even point is called **break-even analysis**. Knowledge of the break-even point is useful to management when it considers decisions such as whether to introduce new product lines, change sales prices on established products, or enter new market areas (see **Decision Tools**).

The break-even point can be:

1. Computed from a mathematical equation.
2. Computed by using contribution margin techniques.
3. Derived from a cost-volume-profit (CVP) graph.

The break-even point can be expressed either in **sales units** (quantity) or **sales euros**.

Mathematical Equation

Illustration 5.19 shows a common profit equation used as the basis for CVP analysis. This equation expresses net income as sales minus variable and fixed costs.

- Sales is expressed as the unit selling price (€500) times the quantity of units sold (Q).
- Variable costs are determined by multiplying the unit variable costs (€300) by the quantity of units sold (Q).

Sales	−	Variable Costs	−	Fixed Costs	=	Net Income
€500Q	−	€300Q	−	€200,000	=	€0

ILLUSTRATION 5.19 | Profit equation for break-even point

- When net income is set to zero, as it is in this illustration, this equation can be used to calculate the break-even point.

As shown in Illustration 5.14, net income equals zero when the contribution margin (sales minus variable costs) is equal to fixed costs. To reflect this, **Illustration 5.20** rewrites the equation with contribution margin (sales minus variable costs) on the left side, and fixed costs and net income of zero on the right. We can then compute the break-even point **in sales units** by **using the unit selling price** and **unit variable costs** and solving for the quantity (Q).

$$\text{Sales} - \text{Variable Costs} - \text{Fixed Costs} = \text{Net Income}$$

$$€500Q - €300Q - €200{,}000 = €0 \quad \leftarrow \text{Profit equation set to zero}$$

$$€500Q - €300Q = €200{,}000 + €0 \quad \leftarrow \text{Total contribution margin} = \text{Fixed costs}$$

$$€200Q = €200{,}000 \quad \leftarrow \text{Solve for Q to determine break-even quantity}$$

$$Q = \frac{€200{,}000}{€200} = \frac{\text{Fixed Costs}}{\text{Unit Contribution Margin}} \quad \leftarrow \text{Equation for break-even point in sales units}$$

$$Q = 1{,}000 \text{ units}$$

where

- Q = quantity of units sold
- €500 = unit selling price
- €300 = unit variable costs
- €200,000 = total fixed costs

ILLUSTRATION 5.20 | Computation of break-even point in sales units

Thus, Laurel Electronics must sell 1,000 tablets to break even.

To find the amount of **sales euros** required to break even, we multiply the units sold at the break-even point times the unit selling price, as shown below.

$$1{,}000 \times €500 = €500{,}000 \text{ (break-even point in sales euros)}$$

Contribution Margin Techniques

Many managers employ contribution margin analysis to compute the break-even point. This can be a shortcut to the mathematical equation method discussed above.

Unit Contribution Margin: Break-Even Point in Sales Units

The final step in Illustration 5.20 divides fixed costs by the unit contribution margin (highlighted in red). Thus, rather than walk through all of the steps of the equation approach, we can simply employ the equation shown in **Illustration 5.21**.

Fixed Costs	÷	Unit Contribution Margin	=	Break-Even Point in Sales Units
€200,000	÷	€200	=	1,000 units

ILLUSTRATION 5.21 | Equation for break-even point in sales units using unit contribution margin

Why does this equation work?

- The unit contribution margin is the net amount by which the unit selling price exceeds the unit variable costs.
- Every sale generates this much (in this case, €200 per unit) to cover fixed costs (in this case, €200,000).

- Consequently, if we divide fixed costs (€200,000) by the unit contribution margin (€200), we know how many units we need to sell to break even (1,000 units).

Contribution Margin Ratio: Break-Even Point in Sales Euros

When a company has numerous products, it is not practical to determine the unit contribution margin for each product. In this case, we instead use the contribution margin ratio to determine the break-even point in total sales euros (rather than sales units).

- Recall that the contribution margin ratio is the **percentage** of each euro of sales that is available to cover fixed costs and generate net income.
- Therefore, **to determine the sales euros needed to cover fixed costs,** we divide fixed costs by the contribution margin ratio, as shown in **Illustration 5.22**.

Fixed Costs	÷	Contribution Margin Ratio	=	Break-Even Point in Sales Euros
€200,000	÷	40%	=	€500,000

ILLUSTRATION 5.22 | Equation for break-even point in sales euros using contribution margin ratio

To apply this equation to Laurel Electronics, consider that its 40% contribution margin ratio means that for every euro sold, it generates 40 cents of contribution margin. The question is, how many sales euros does Laurel need in order to generate total contribution margin of €200,000 to pay off fixed costs?

- We divide the fixed costs of €200,000 by the 40 cents of contribution margin generated by each euro of sales to arrive at €500,000 (€200,000 ÷ 40%).
- To prove this result, if we generate 40 cents of contribution margin for each euro of sales, then the total contribution margin generated by €500,000 in sales is €200,000 (€500,000 × 40%), just enough to cover the total fixed costs.

SERVICE COMPANY INSIGHT   Sina

Portal Advertising Bolstered by Social Media

Lemberg Vector studio/Shutterstock

The social media giant of **Sina** (CHN) has market penetration similar to Twitter and YouTube in the United States. On average, 100 million messages are posted each day on Sina Weibo.

Advertising revenues for Sina include portal advertising, or revenues generated from online brand advertising on Sina.com, mobile value-added services (MVAS), and fee-based services for data licensing, company accounts, and gaming-related services. Weibo earns advertising revenue generated by advertising and marketing on its microblogging and social media platform. Weibo has been instrumental in driving growth for the consolidated company while portal advertising revenues on Sina's platforms have struggled.

Over the last five years, Sina's advertising revenues have grown by a compounded annual growth rate of 20%. During the first three quarters of 2016, advertising revenues continued to grow by 16% to $602 million, while its MVAS revenues for the same period grew 11% to $116 million. Weibo, on the other hand, saw advertising gross margins of just under 70% in 2015 which improved to 72.5% in 2016, when compared to non-advertising segments whose gross margins were less than 60%.

Despite the slowdown in portal advertising growth, Sina is hoping to turn things around with new projects like the National Football League (NFL) deal. The NFL is hoping to expand its presence in China by giving Sina's social media platform the rights to live stream select games, including the Super Bowl, on its network. The deal marks the first time a sports league will live stream games on the service, the NFL says. Additionally, Sina will gain the rights to non-game, video-on-demand clips, highlights, and other NFL content.

Sources: Trefis Team, "How Sina's Ad Revenues Are Primarily Dependent on Weibo as Portal Advertising Struggles," *Nasdaq.com* (December 13, 2016); and S. Perez, "NFL Games Are Now Live Streaming on China's Sina Weibo Network," *TechCrunch.com* (December 29, 2016).

If the fixed costs associated with Sina's advertising segment are equal to those of its non-advertising segment, which segment has a higher break-even point in dollars? (Answer is available in the book's product page on www.wiley.com)

Graphic Presentation

An effective way to understand the break-even point is to prepare a break-even graph. Because this graph also shows costs, volume, and profits, it is referred to as a **cost-volume-profit (CVP) graph**.

- Sales volume is represented along the horizontal axis.
- This axis should extend to the maximum level of expected sales.
- Both total revenues (sales) and total costs (fixed plus variable) are represented on the vertical axis (in euros).

An example of a CVP graph is shown in **Illustration 5.23**.

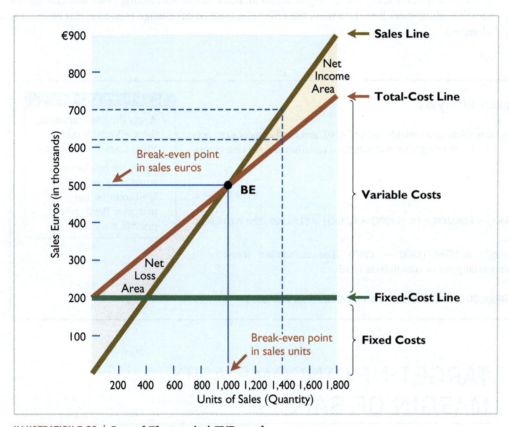

ILLUSTRATION 5.23 | Laurel Electronics' CVP graph

The construction of the graph, using the data for Laurel Electronics, is as follows:

1. Plot the sales line (shown in brown), starting at the zero activity level. For every tablet sold, total revenue increases by €500. For example, at 200 units, sales are €100,000. At the upper level of activity (1,800 units), sales are €900,000. The sales line is assumed to be linear through the full range of activity. **It has a slope equal to the unit selling price**.

2. Plot the total fixed costs using a horizontal line (shown in green). For the tablets, this line is plotted at €200,000. The fixed costs are the same at every level of activity.

3. Plot the total-cost line (shown in red). This starts at the fixed-cost line at zero activity. It increases by the variable costs at each level of activity. For each tablet, variable costs are €300. Thus, at 200 units, total variable costs are €60,000 (€300 × 200) and the total cost is €260,000 (€60,000 + €200,000). At 1,800 units, total variable costs are €540,000 (€300 × 1,800) and total cost is €740,000 (€540,000 + €200,000). On the graph, the amount of the variable costs can be

derived from the difference between the total-cost and fixed-cost lines at each level of activity. **The total-cost line has a slope equal to the unit variable costs. It has a *y*-intercept, at the point of zero units sold, equal to the fixed costs of €200,000.**

4. Determine the break-even point from the intersection of the total-cost line and the sales line at point BE. The break-even point in sales euros is found by drawing a horizontal line from the break-even point to the vertical axis. The break-even point in sales units is found by drawing a vertical line from the break-even point to the horizontal axis. For the tablets, the break-even point is €500,000 of sales, or 1,000 units. At this sales level, Laurel will cover costs but make no profit.

The CVP graph also shows both the net income and net loss areas. Thus, the amount of net income or net loss at each level of sales can be derived from the sales and total-cost lines.

A CVP graph is useful because the effects of a change in any component in the CVP analysis can be quickly seen. For example, a 10% increase in the unit selling price will change the location of the sales line. Likewise, the effects on total costs of wage increases can be quickly observed.

DO IT! 4 ▶ Break-Even Analysis

Lombardi NV has a unit selling price of €400, unit variable costs of €240, and fixed costs of €180,000. Compute the break-even point in sales units using (a) a mathematical equation and (b) unit contribution margin.

Solution

a. The equation is €400Q − €240Q − €180,000 = €0; (€400Q − €240Q) = €180,000. The break-even point in sales units is 1,125.

b. The unit contribution margin is €160 (€400 − €240). The calculation therefore is €180,000 ÷ €160, and the break-even point in sales units is 1,125.

Related exercise material: **BE5.8, BE5.9, DO IT! 5.4, E5.8, E5.9, E5.10, E5.11, E5.12, and E5.13.**

ACTION PLAN
- Apply the profit equation: Sales − Variable costs − Fixed costs = Net income.
- Apply the break-even equation: Fixed costs ÷ Unit contribution margin = Break-even point in sales units.

TARGET NET INCOME AND MARGIN OF SAFETY

LEARNING OBJECTIVE 5
Determine the sales required to earn target net income and determine margin of safety.

Target Net Income

Rather than simply striving to "breaking even," management usually sets an income objective often called **target net income**. It then determines the sales necessary to achieve this specified level of income by using one of the three approaches discussed earlier.

Mathematical Equation

We know that at the break-even point no profit or loss results for the company. By adding an amount for target net income to the same basic equation, we obtain the equation shown in **Illustration 5.24** for determining required sales.

| Sales | − | Variable Costs | − | Fixed Costs | = | Target Net Income |

ILLUSTRATION 5.24 | Equation for sales to meet target net income

Recall that once the break-even point has been reached so that fixed costs are covered, each additional unit sold increases net income by the amount of the unit contribution margin. We can rewrite the equation with contribution margin (sales minus variable costs) on the left-hand side, and fixed costs and target net income on the right. Assuming that target net income is €120,000 for Laurel Electronics, the computation of required sales in units is as shown in **Illustration 5.25**.

$$\text{Sales} - \text{Variable Costs} - \text{Fixed Costs} = \text{Target Net Income}$$

$$€500Q - €300Q - €200,000 = €120,000$$

$$€500Q - €300Q = €200,000 + €120,000$$

$$€200Q = €200,000 + €120,000$$

$$Q = \frac{€200,000 + €120,000}{€200} = \frac{\text{Fixed Costs} + \text{Target Net Income}}{\text{Unit Contribution Margin}}$$

$$Q = 1,600$$

where
- Q = quantity of units sold
- €500 = unit selling price
- €300 = unit variable costs
- €200,000 = total fixed costs
- €120,000 = target net income

ILLUSTRATION 5.25 | Computation of required sales units to achieve target net income

Laurel must sell 1,600 units to achieve target net income of €120,000. The sales euros required to achieve the target net income is found by multiplying the units sold by the unit selling price [(1,600 × €500) = €800,000].

Contribution Margin Techniques

As in the case of the break-even point, we can compute the sales units or sales euros required to meet a target net income. The calculation to compute required sales in units for Laurel Electronics using the unit contribution margin can be seen in the final step of the approach in Illustration 5.25 (shown in red). We simply divide the sum of fixed costs and target net income by the unit contribution margin. **Illustration 5.26** shows this for Laurel.

(Fixed Costs + Target Net Income)	÷	Unit Contribution Margin	=	Sales Units
(€200,000 + €120,000)	÷	€200	=	1,600 units

ILLUSTRATION 5.26 | Equation for sales units required to achieve target net income using unit contribution margin

To achieve its desired target net income of €120,000, Laurel must sell 1,600 tablets.

Illustration 5.27 presents the equation to compute the required sales euros for Laurel using the contribution margin ratio.

(Fixed Costs + Target Net Income)	÷	Contribution Margin Ratio	=	Sales Euros
(€200,000 + €120,000)	÷	40%	=	€800,000

ILLUSTRATION 5.27 | Equation for sales euros required to achieve target net income using contribution margin ratio

To achieve its desired target net income of €120,000, Laurel must generate sales of €800,000.

Graphic Presentation

We also can use the CVP graph in Illustration 5.23 to find the sales required to meet target net income.

- In the net income area of the graph, the distance between the sales line and the total-cost line at any point equals net income.
- We can find required sales by analyzing the differences between the two lines until the desired net income is found.

For example, suppose Laurel Electronics sells 1,400 tablets. Illustration 5.23 shows that a vertical line drawn at 1,400 units intersects the sales line at €700,000 and the total-cost line at €620,000. The difference between the two amounts represents the net income (profit) of €80,000.

Margin of Safety

Suppose that your company has been operating at a profit, but you are concerned that business might slow down in the coming year. You would like to know how far your sales could fall before you begin losing money. **Margin of safety** is the difference between actual or expected sales, and sales at the break-even point.

- It measures the "cushion" that a particular level of sales provides above the break-even point.
- It tells us how far sales could fall before the company begins operating at a loss.
- The margin of safety is expressed in euros or as a ratio.

The equation for stating the **margin of safety in euros** is actual (or expected) sales minus break-even sales. **Illustration 5.28** shows the computation for Laurel Electronics, assuming that actual (or expected) sales are €750,000.

Actual (or Expected) Sales	−	Break-Even Sales	=	Margin of Safety in Euros
€750,000	−	€500,000	=	€250,000

ILLUSTRATION 5.28 | Equation for margin of safety in euros

Laurel's margin of safety is €250,000. Its sales could fall by €250,000 before it operates at a loss.

The **margin of safety ratio** is the margin of safety in euros divided by actual (or expected) sales. **Illustration 5.29** shows the equation and computation for determining the margin of safety ratio.

Margin of Safety in Euros	÷	Actual (or Expected) Sales	=	Margin of Safety Ratio
€250,000	÷	€750,000	=	33%

ILLUSTRATION 5.29 | Equation for margin of safety ratio

This means that the company's sales could fall by 33% before it operates at a loss.

The higher the margin of safety in euros or the margin of safety ratio, the lower the risk that the company will operate at a loss. Management evaluates the adequacy of the margin of safety in terms of such factors as the vulnerability of the product to competitive pressures or a potential downturn in the economy.

CVP and Data Analytics

Data analytics plays an important role in CVP analysis. Consider that to perform CVP analysis meaningfully, you need to collect data that you have confidence is accurate. For example, the shipping company **DHL Express** (USA), a competitor to **UPS** (USA) and **FedEx** (USA), at one point lacked data of sufficient quality to accurately distinguish between fixed and variable costs, information crucial to performing CVP analysis.

- The company then made a big investment in data collection and analysis, which enabled it to determine the cost and profitability of every shipment.
- Over time, the company was able to refine its abilities to use this data so that it can now link the profitability of what is being shipped to the cost of shipping it.
- This helps DHL Express determine what size airplanes it should use for particular shipments, which leads to better cost control and profitability.

SERVICE COMPANY INSIGHT Rolling Stones

Yael/Retna

How a Rolling Stones' Tour Makes Money

Computations of break-even and margin of safety are important for service companies. Consider how the promoter for the **Rolling Stones**' tour used the break-even point and margin of safety. For example, say one outdoor show should bring 70,000 individuals for a gross of £2.45 million. The promoter guarantees £1.2 million to the Rolling Stones. In addition, 20% of gross goes to the stadium in which the performance is staged.

Add another £400,000 for other expenses such as ticket takers, parking attendants, advertising, and so on. The promoter also shares in sales of T-shirts and memorabilia for which the promoter will net over £7 million during the tour. From a successful Rolling Stones' tour, the promoter could make £35 million!

What amount of sales are required for the promoter to break even? (Answer is available in the book's product page on www.wiley.com)

DO IT! 5 ▶ Break-Even Point, Margin of Safety, and Target Net Income

Zootsuit SpA makes travel bags that sell for €56 each. For the coming year, management expects fixed costs to total €320,000 and variable costs to be €42 per unit. Compute the following: (a) break-even point in sales euros using the contribution margin (CM) ratio; (b) the margin of safety and margin of safety ratio assuming actual sales are €1,382,400; and (c) the sales euros required to earn net income of €410,000.

Solution

a. Contribution margin ratio = [(€56 − €42) ÷ €56] = 25%

   Break-even point in sales euros = €320,000 ÷ 25% = €1,280,000

b. Margin of safety = €1,382,400 − €1,280,000 = €102,400

   Margin of safety ratio = €102,400 ÷ €1,382,400 = 7.4%

c. Sales euros = (€320,000 + €410,000) ÷ 25% = €2,920,000

Related exercise material: **BE5.10, BE5.11, BE5.12, DO IT! 5.5, E5.14, E5.15, E5.16, and E5.17.**

ACTION PLAN

- Apply the equation for the break-even point in sales euros.
- Apply the equations for the margin of safety in euros and the margin of safety ratio.
- Apply the equation for the sales euros to achieve target net income.

USING THE DECISION TOOLS | Amazon.com

Amazon.com (USA) faces many situations where it needs to apply the decision tools presented in this chapter, such as calculating the break-even point to determine a product's profitability. Amazon's dominance of the online retail space, selling other company's products, is well known. But not everyone may realize that Amazon also sells its own private-label electronics, including USB cables, mice, keyboards, and audio cables, under the brand name AmazonBasics. Assume that Amazon's management was provided with the following information regarding the production and sales of Bluetooth keyboards for tablet computers for 2023.

Cost Schedules

Variable costs	
Direct labor per keyboard	$ 8.00
Direct materials per keyboard	4.00
Variable overhead per keyboard	3.00
Variable cost per keyboard	$15.00
Fixed costs (per year)	
Manufacturing	$ 25,000
Selling	40,000
Administrative	70,000
Total fixed costs	$135,000
Selling price per keyboard	$25.00
Sales, 2023 (20,000 keyboards)	$500,000

Instructions

(Ignore any income tax considerations.)

a. What is the operating income for 2023?

b. What is the unit contribution margin for 2023?

c. What is the break-even point in sales units for 2023?

d. Assume that management set the sales target for the year 2024 at a level of $550,000 (22,000 keyboards at the same unit selling price). Amazon's management believes that to attain the sales target in 2024, the company must incur an additional selling expense of $10,000 for advertising in 2024, with all other unit variable costs and fixed costs remaining constant. What will be the break-even point in sales dollars for 2024 if the company spends the additional $10,000?

e. If the company spends the additional $10,000 for advertising in 2024 and unit variable costs, unit selling price, and all other fixed costs remain at 2023 levels, what is the sales level in dollars required to equal 2023 operating income?

Solution

a.

Sales		$500,000
Less:		
Variable costs (20,000 keyboards × $15)		300,000
Fixed costs		135,000
Operating income		$ 65,000

b.

Selling price per keyboard	$25
Variable cost per keyboard	15
Unit contribution margin	$10

c. Fixed costs ÷ Unit contribution margin = Break-even point in sales units: $135,000 ÷ $10 = 13,500 units

d. Fixed costs ÷ Contribution margin ratio = Break-even point in sales dollars: $145,000* ÷ 40%** = $362,500

*Current fixed costs	$135,000
Additional advertising expense	10,000
Revised fixed costs	$145,000

**Unit contribution margin remains $10, as unit variable cost and unit selling price did not change.
Contribution margin ratio = Unit contribution margin ÷ Unit selling price: 40% = $10 ÷ $25

e. Sales = (Fixed costs + Target net income) ÷ Contribution margin ratio

$525,000 = ($145,000 + $65,000) ÷ 40%

| Appendix 5A | REGRESSION ANALYSIS |

The high-low method is often used to estimate fixed and variable costs for a mixed-cost situation.

- An advantage of the high-low method is that it is easy to apply.
- But, how accurate and reliable is the estimated cost equation that it produces?

For example, consider the example shown in **Illustration 5A.1**, which indicates the cost equation line produced by the high-low method for Metro Transit's maintenance costs. How well does the high-low method represent the relationship between kilometers driven and total cost? This line is close to nearly all of the data points. Therefore, in this case, the high-low method provides a cost equation that is a very good fit for this data set. It identifies fixed and variable costs in an accurate and reliable way.

While the high-low method works well for the Metro Transit data set, a weakness of this method is that it employs only two data points and ignores the rest.

- If those two data points are representative of the entire data set, then the high-low method provides reasonable results (as seen in Illustration 5A.1).

LEARNING OBJECTIVE *6
Apply regression analysis to determine the components of mixed costs.

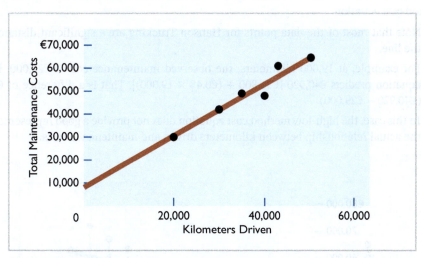

ILLUSTRATION 5A.1 | **Scatter plot for Metro Transit (total maintenance costs as a function of kilometers driven)**

- But, if the high and low data points are not representative of the rest of the data set, then the results are misleading.

To illustrate, assume that Hanson Trucking Ltd. has 12 months of maintenance cost data, as shown in **Illustration 5A.2**.

Month	Kilometers Driven	Total Cost	Month	Kilometers Driven	Total Cost
January	20,000	€30,000	July	15,000	€39,000
February	40,000	49,000	August	28,000	41,000
March	35,000	46,000	September	60,000	72,000
April	50,000	63,000	October	55,000	67,000
May	30,000	42,000	November	19,000	29,000
June	43,000	52,000	December	65,000	63,000

ILLUSTRATION 5A.2 | **Maintenance costs and distance data for Hanson Trucking Ltd.**

The high and low activities are 65,000 kilometers in December and 15,000 kilometers in July. The maintenance costs at these two levels are €63,000 and €39,000, respectively. The difference in maintenance costs is €24,000 (€63,000 − €39,000), and the difference in kilometers is 50,000 (65,000 − 15,000). Therefore, for Hanson Trucking, unit variable costs under the high-low method are €0.48 (€24,000 ÷ 50,000). To determine total variable costs, we multiply the number of kilometers by cost per kilometer. For example, at the low activity level of 15,000 kilometers, total variable costs are €7,200 (15,000 × €0.48). To determine fixed costs, we subtract total variable costs at the low activity level from the total cost at the low activity level (€39,000) as follows:

$$\text{Fixed costs} = €39,000 − (€0.48 × 15,000) = €31,800$$

Therefore, the cost equation based on the high-low method for this data produces the following calculation:

		Fixed Costs		Variable Costs
Maintenance costs	=	Intercept	+	Slope × Quantity
	=	€31,800	+	(€0.48 × Kilometers driven)

Illustration 5A.3 shows a scatter plot of the data with a line representing the high-low method cost equation.

- Note that most of the data points for Hanson Trucking are a significant distance from the line.
- For example, at 19,000 kilometers, the observed maintenance cost is €29,000, but the equation predicts €40,920 [€31,800 + (€0.48 × 19,000)]. That is a difference of €11,920 (€40,920 − €29,000).
- In this case, the high-low method cost equation does not provide a good representation of the actual relationship between kilometers driven and maintenance costs.

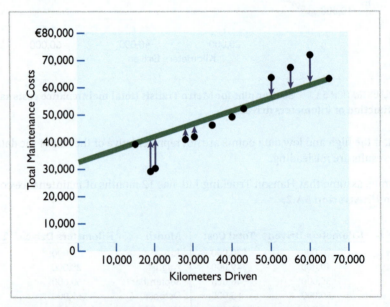

ILLUSTRATION 5A.3 | Scatter plot for Hanson Trucking Ltd. (total maintenance costs as a function of kilometers driven)

To derive a more representative cost equation, the company should employ regression analysis.

Regression analysis is a statistical approach that estimates the cost equation by employing information from **all** data points, not just the highest and lowest ones. While it involves mathematical analysis taught in statistics courses (which we will not address here), we can provide you with a basic understanding of how regression analysis works.

Consider Illustration 5A.3, which highlights the distance that each data point is from the high-low cost equation line. Regression analysis determines a cost equation that results in a line that minimizes the sum of the squared distances from the line to the data points.

Many software packages perform regression analysis. In **Illustration 5A.4**, we use the **Intercept** and **Slope** functions in Excel to estimate the regression equation for the Hanson Trucking Ltd. data.[1]

	A	B	C	D
1	Month	Kilometers Driven	Total Maintenance Costs	
2	January	20,000	30,000	
3	February	40,000	49,000	
4	March	35,000	46,000	
5	April	50,000	63,000	
6	May	30,000	42,000	
7	June	43,000	52,000	
8	July	15,000	39,000	
9	August	28,000	41,000	
10	September	60,000	72,000	
11	October	55,000	67,000	
12	November	19,000	29,000	
13	December	65,000	63,000	
14				
15		Formula		
16	Intercept	=INTERCEPT(C2:C13,B2:B13)	18,502	
17	Slope	=SLOPE(C2:C13,B2:B13)	0.81	
18				

ILLUSTRATION 5A.4 | **Excel spreadsheet for Hanson Trucking Ltd. (total maintenance costs)**

The cost equation based on the regression results is:

		Fixed Costs		Variable Costs
Total maintenance costs	=	Intercept	+	Slope × Quantity
	=	€18,502	+	(€0.81 × Kilometers driven)

Compare this to the cost equation based on the use of the high-low cost approach:

		Fixed Costs		Variable Costs
Total maintenance costs	=	Intercept	+	Slope × Quantity
	=	€31,800	+	(€0.48 × Kilometers driven)

---

[1] To use the Intercept and Slope functions in Excel, enter your data in two columns in an Excel spreadsheet. The first column should be your "X" independent variable (kilometers driven, cells B2 to B13 in our example). The second column should be your "Y" dependent variable (maintenance costs, cells C2 to C13 in our example). Next, in a separate cell, choosing from Excel's statistical functions, enter =Intercept(C2:C13,B2:B13) and in a different cell enter =Slope(C2:C13,B2:B13).

As **Illustration 5A.5** shows, the intercept and slope differ significantly between the regression equation (green) and the high-low equation (red).[2]

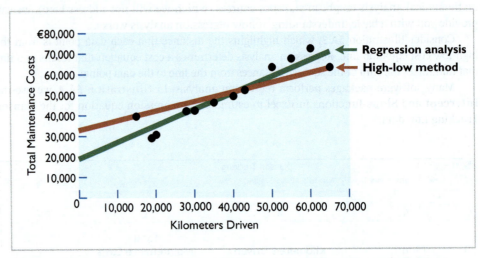

ILLUSTRATION 5A.5 | **Comparison of cost equation lines from regression analysis versus high-low method**

- The regression cost equation line does not include the high and low data points but instead follows a path that minimizes the cumulative distance from all of the data points.
- By doing so, it provides a cost equation that is more representative of the relationship between kilometers driven and total maintenance costs than the high-low method.

Why should managers care about the accuracy of the cost equation? Managers make many decisions that require that mixed costs be separated into fixed and variable components. Inaccurate classifications of these costs might cause a manager to make an inappropriate decision. For example, Hanson Trucking's break-even point differs significantly depending on which of these two cost equations was used. If Hanson Trucking relies on the high-low method, it would have a distorted view of the level of sales it would need in order to break even. In addition, misrepresentation for fixed and variable costs could result in inappropriate decisions, such as whether to discontinue a product line. It would also result in inaccurate product costing under activity-based costing.

While regression analysis usually provides more reliable estimates of the cost equation, it does have its limitations.

1. The regression approach that we applied above assumes a linear relationship between the variables (that is, an increase or decrease in one variable results in a proportional increase or decrease in the other). If the actual relationship differs significantly from linearity, then linear regression can provide misleading results. (Nonlinear regression is addressed in advanced statistics courses.)

2. Regression estimates can be severely influenced by "outliers"—data points that differ significantly from the rest of the observations. It is therefore good practice to plot data points in a scatter graph to identify outliers and then investigate the reasons why they differ. In some cases, outliers must be adjusted for or eliminated.

3. Regression estimation is most accurate when it is based on a large number of data points. However, collecting data can be time-consuming and costly. In some cases, there simply are not enough observable data points to arrive at a reliable estimate.

---

[2] To plot a scatter graph in Excel, highlight the data and then click on Scatter under the Insert tab. To draw the cost equation line, click on the scatter plot, then select Layout and Trendline. In order to get the cost equation line to intercept the Y-axis, under Trendline Options in the Backward field, enter the lowest value of your X variable. For example, for Hanson Trucking, we entered 15,000.

REVIEW AND PRACTICE

Learning Objectives Review

LO 1 Explain variable, fixed, and mixed costs and the relevant range.

Variable costs are costs that vary in total directly and proportionately with changes in the activity index. Fixed costs are costs that remain the same in total regardless of changes in the activity index.

The relevant range is the range of activity in which a company expects to operate during a year. It is important in CVP analysis because the behavior of costs is assumed to be linear throughout the relevant range.

Mixed costs change in total but not proportionately with changes in the activity level. For purposes of CVP analysis, mixed costs must be classified into their fixed and variable components.

LO 2 Apply the high-low method to determine the components of mixed costs.

Determine the unit variable costs by dividing the change in total costs at the highest and lowest levels of activity by the difference in activity at those levels. Then, determine fixed costs by subtracting total variable costs from the amount of total costs at either the highest or lowest level of activity.

LO 3 Prepare a CVP income statement to determine contribution margin.

The five components of CVP analysis are (1) volume or level of activity (quantity), (2) unit selling price, (3) unit variable costs, (4) total fixed costs, and (5) sales mix. Contribution margin is the amount of revenue remaining after deducting variable costs. It is identified in a CVP income statement, which classifies costs as variable or fixed. It can be expressed as a total amount, as a per unit amount, or as a ratio.

LO 4 Compute the break-even point using three approaches.

At the break-even point, sales revenue equals total costs, resulting in a net income of zero. The break-even point can be (a) computed from a mathematical equation, (b) computed by using a contribution margin technique, and (c) derived from a CVP graph.

LO 5 Determine the sales required to earn target net income and determine margin of safety.

The general equation for required sales is Sales − Variable costs − Fixed costs = Target net income. Two other equations are (1) Sales in units = (Fixed costs + Target net income) ÷ Unit contribution margin, and (2) Sales euros = (Fixed costs + Target net income) ÷ Contribution margin ratio.

Margin of safety is the difference between actual or expected sales and sales at the break-even point. The equations for margin of safety metrics are (1) Actual (or expected) sales − Break-even sales = Margin of safety in euros, and (2) Margin of safety in euros ÷ Actual (expected) sales = Margin of safety ratio.

LO *6 Apply regression analysis to determine the components of mixed costs.

The high-low method provides a quick estimate of the cost equation for a mixed cost. However, the high-low method is based on only the highest and lowest data points. Regression analysis provides an estimate of the cost equation based on all data points. The cost equation line that results from regression analysis minimizes the sum of the (squared) distances of all of the data points from the cost equation line. Computer programs such as Excel enable easy estimation of the cost equation with regression.

Decision Tools Review

Decision Checkpoints	Info Needed for Decision	Tool to Use for Decision	How to Evaluate Results
What was the contribution toward fixed costs and net income from each unit sold?	Selling price per unit and unit variable costs	Unit contribution margin = Unit selling price − Unit variable cost	Every unit sold will increase net income by the contribution margin.
What would be the increase in net income as a result of an increase in sales?	Unit contribution margin and unit selling price	Contribution margin ratio = Unit contribution margin ÷ Unit selling price	Every euro of sales will increase net income by the contribution margin ratio.
At what amount of sales does a company cover its total costs?	Unit selling price, unit variable cost, and total fixed costs	Break-even analysis *In sales units:* $$\text{Break-even point} = \frac{\text{Fixed costs}}{\text{Unit contribution margin}}$$ *In sales euros:* $$\text{Break-even point} = \frac{\text{Fixed costs}}{\text{Contribution margin ratio}}$$	Below the break-even point, the company is unprofitable.

Glossary Review

Activity index The activity that causes changes in the behavior of costs. (p. 5-3).

Break-even point The level of activity at which total revenue equals total costs, yielding a net income of zero. (p. 5-14).

Contribution margin (CM) The amount of revenue remaining after deducting variable costs. (p. 5-12).

Contribution margin ratio The percentage of each euro of sales that is available to apply to fixed costs and contribute to net income; calculated as unit contribution margin divided by unit selling price, or as total contribution margin divided by total sales. (p. 5-15).

Cost behavior analysis The study of how specific costs respond to changes in the level of business activity. (p. 5-3).

Cost-volume-profit (CVP) analysis The study of the effects of changes in costs and volume (quantity) on a company's profits. (p. 5-11).

Cost-volume-profit (CVP) graph A graph showing the relationship between costs, volume, and profits. (p. 5-19).

Cost-volume-profit (CVP) income statement A statement for internal use that classifies costs as fixed or variable and reports contribution margin in the body of the statement. (p. 5-12).

Fixed costs Costs that remain the same in total regardless of changes in the activity level. (p. 5-4).

High-low method A mathematical calculation that uses the total costs incurred at the high and low levels of activity to classify mixed costs into fixed and variable components. (p. 5-8).

Margin of safety The difference between actual or expected sales, and sales at the break-even point. (p. 5-22).

Mixed costs Costs that contain both a variable-cost and a fixed-cost component and change in total but not proportionately with changes in the activity level. (p. 5-7).

*****Regression analysis** A statistical approach that estimates the cost equation by employing information from all data points to find the cost equation line that minimizes the sum of the squared distances from the line to all the data points. (p. 5-27).

Relevant range The range of the activity index over which the company expects to operate during the year. (p. 5-6).

Target net income The income objective set by management. (p. 5-20).

Unit contribution margin The amount of revenue remaining per unit after deducting variable costs; calculated as unit selling price minus unit variable costs. (p. 5-13).

Variable cost ratio Variable costs expressed as a percentage of sales. (p. 5-15).

Variable costs Costs that vary in total directly and proportionately with changes in the activity level. (p. 5-3).

Practice Multiple-Choice Questions

1. **(LO 1)** Variable costs are costs that:
   a. vary in total directly and proportionately with changes in the activity level but do not remain the same per unit at every activity level.
   b. remain the same per unit and in total at every activity level.
   c. neither vary in total directly and proportionately with changes in the activity level nor remain the same per unit at every activity level.
   d. both vary in total directly and proportionately with changes in the activity level and remain the same per unit at every activity level.

2. **(LO 2)** The relevant range is:
   a. the range of activity in which variable costs will be curvilinear.
   b. the range of activity in which fixed costs will be curvilinear.
   c. the range over which the company expects to operate during a year.
   d. usually from zero to 100% of operating capacity.

3. **(LO 1, 2)** Mixed costs consist of a:
   a. variable-cost component and a fixed-cost component.
   b. fixed-cost component and a product-cost component.
   c. period-cost component and a product-cost component.
   d. variable-cost component and a period-cost component.

4. **(LO 1, 2)** Your cell phone service provider offers a plan that is classified as a mixed cost. The cost for 1,000 minutes in a month is €50. If you use 2,000 minutes this month, your cost will be:

   a. €50.
   b. €100.
   c. more than €100.
   d. between €50 and €100.

5. **(LO 2)** Yunxuan Group's total utility costs during the past year were HK$12,000 during its highest month and HK$6,000 during its lowest month. These costs corresponded with 10,000 units of production during the high month and 2,000 units during the low month. What are the fixed cost and unit variable cost of its utility costs using the high-low method?
   a. HK$0.75 variable and HK$4,500 fixed.
   b. HK$1.20 variable and HK$0 fixed.
   c. HK$3.00 variable and HK$0 fixed.
   d. HK$0.60 variable and HK$6,000 fixed.

6. **(LO 3)** Which of the following is **not** involved in CVP analysis?
   a. Sales mix.
   b. Unit selling price.
   c. Fixed costs per unit.
   d. Volume or level of activity (quantity).

7. **(LO 3)** When comparing a traditional income statement to a CVP income statement:
   a. net income will always be greater on the traditional statement.
   b. net income will always be less on the traditional statement.
   c. net income will always be identical on both.
   d. net income will be greater or less depending on the sales volume.

8. **(LO 3)** Contribution margin:
   a. is revenue remaining after deducting fixed and variable costs.
   b. may not be expressed as unit contribution margin.
   c. is sales less cost of goods sold.
   d. is revenue remaining after deducting variable costs and may be expressed as unit contribution margin.

9. **(LO 3)** Pelham plc sells 100,000 wrenches for £12 a unit. Fixed costs are £300,000, and net income is £200,000. What should be reported as variable costs in the CVP income statement?
   a. £700,000.
   b. £900,000.
   c. £500,000.
   d. £1,000,000.

10. **(LO 4)** Gossen SA is planning to sell 200,000 pliers for €4 per unit. The contribution margin ratio is 25%. If Gossen will break even at this level of sales, what are the fixed costs?
    a. €100,000.
    b. €160,000.
    c. €200,000.
    d. €300,000.

11. **(LO 4)** Tanaya Company's contribution margin ratio is 30%. If Tanaya's sales revenue is Rp1,000,000 greater than its break-even sales rupiah, its net income:
    a. will be Rp1,000,000.
    b. will be Rp700,000.
    c. will be Rp300,000.
    d. cannot be determined without knowing fixed costs.

12. **(LO 5)** The mathematical equation for computing required sales to obtain target net income is:
    a. Variable costs + Target net income.
    b. Variable costs + Fixed costs + Target net income.
    c. Fixed costs + Target net income.
    d. No correct answer is given.

13. **(LO 5)** Margin of safety is computed as:
    a. Actual sales − Break-even sales.
    b. Contribution margin − Fixed costs.
    c. Break-even point in sales euros − Variable costs.
    d. Actual sales − Contribution margin.

14. **(LO 5)** Marshall Company had actual sales of $600,000 when the break-even point in sales dollars was $420,000. What is the margin of safety ratio?
    a. 25%.
    b. 30%.
    c. $33\frac{1}{3}$%.
    d. 45%.

Solutions

1. **d.** Variable costs vary in total directly and proportionately with changes in the activity level and remain the same per unit at every activity level. Choices (a) and (b) are only partially correct. Choice (c) is incorrect as it is the opposite of (d).

2. **c.** The relevant range is the range over which the company expects to operate during a year. The other choices are incorrect because the relevant range is the range over which (a) variable costs are expected to be linear, not curvilinear, and (b) the company expects fixed costs to remain the same. Choice (d) is incorrect because this answer does not specifically define relevant range.

3. **a.** Mixed costs consist of a variable-cost component and a fixed-cost component, not (b) a product-cost component, (c) a period-cost component or a product-cost component, or (d) a period-cost component.

4. **d.** Your cost will include the fixed-cost component (flat service fee), which does not increase, plus the variable-cost component (usage charge) for the additional 1,000 minutes, which will increase your cost to between €50 and €100. Therefore, choices (a) €50, (b) €100, and (c) more than €100 are incorrect.

5. **a.** Unit variable cost is HK$0.75 [(HK$12,000 − HK$6,000) ÷ (10,000 − 2,000)] and fixed is HK$4,500 [(HK$12,000 − (HK$0.75 × 10,000)]. Therefore, choices (b) HK$1.20 variable and HK$0 fixed, (c) HK$3.00 variable and HK$0 fixed, and (d) HK$0.60 variable and HK$6,000 fixed are incorrect.

6. **c.** Total fixed costs, not fixed costs per unit, are involved in CVP analysis. Choices (a) sales mix, (b) unit selling price, and (d) volume or level of activity are all involved in CVP analysis.

7. **c.** Net income will always be identical on both a traditional income statement and a CVP income statement. Therefore, choices (a), (b), and (d) are incorrect statements.

8. **d.** Contribution margin is revenue remaining after deducting variable costs and it may be expressed on a per unit basis. Choices (a) and (b) are incorrect because (a) includes fixed costs and (b) contribution margin can be expressed on a per unit basis. Choice (c) is incorrect because it defines gross profit, not contribution margin.

9. **a.** Contribution margin is equal to fixed costs plus net income (£300,000 + £200,000 = £500,000). Since variable costs are the difference between total sales (£1,200,000) and contribution margin (£500,000), £700,000 must be the amount of variable costs in the CVP income statement. Therefore, choices (b) £900,000, (c) £500,000, and (d) £1,000,000 are incorrect.

10. **c.** Fixed costs ÷ Contribution margin ratio = Break-even point in sales euros. Solving for fixed costs, (200,000 × €4) × .25 = €200,000, not (a) €100,000, (b) €160,000, or (d) €300,000.

11. **c.** If Tanaya's sales revenue is Rp1,000,000 greater than its break-even sales rupiah, its net income will be Rp300,000 or (Rp1,000,000 × 30%), not (a) Rp1,000,000 or (b) Rp700,000. Choice (d) is incorrect because net income can be determined without knowing fixed costs.

12. **b.** The correct equation is Sales = Variable costs + Fixed costs + Target net income. The other choices are incorrect because (a) needs fixed costs added, (c) needs variable costs added, and (d) there is a correct answer given (b).

13. **a.** Margin of safety is computed as Actual sales − Break-even point in sales euros. Therefore, choices (b) Contribution margin − Fixed costs, (c) Break-even sales − Variable costs, and (d) Actual sales − Contribution margin are incorrect.

14. **b.** The margin of safety ratio is computed by dividing the margin of safety in dollars of $180,000 ($600,000 − $420,000) by actual sales of $600,000. The result is 30% ($180,000 ÷ $600,000), not (a) 25%, (c) $33\frac{1}{3}$%, or (d) 45%.

Practice Exercises

Determine fixed-cost and variable-cost components using the high-low method and prepare graph.

1. (LO 1, 2) The controller of Sahin Industries A.S. has collected the following monthly cost data for use in analyzing the behavior of maintenance costs.

Month	Total Maintenance Costs	Total Machine Hours
January	₺29,000	300
February	30,000	400
March	36,000	600
April	43,000	790
May	32,000	500
June	45,000	800

Instructions

a. Determine the fixed-cost and unit variable-cost components using the high-low method.

b. Prepare a graph showing the behavior of maintenance costs, and identify the fixed-cost and variable-cost components. Use 200 unit increments and ₺10,000 cost increments.

Solution

1. a. Total Maintenance Costs:

$$\frac{₺45{,}000 - ₺29{,}000}{800 - 300} = \frac{₺16{,}000}{500} = ₺32 \text{ unit variable costs per machine hour}$$

	800 Machine Hours	300 Machine Hours
Total costs	₺45,000	₺29,000
Less: Variable costs		
800 × ₺32	25,600	
300 × ₺32		9,600
Total fixed costs	₺19,400	₺19,400

Thus, total maintenance costs are ₺19,400 per month plus ₺32 per machine hour.

The cost equation is:
Total maintenance costs = ₺19,400 + (₺32 × Machine hours)

b.

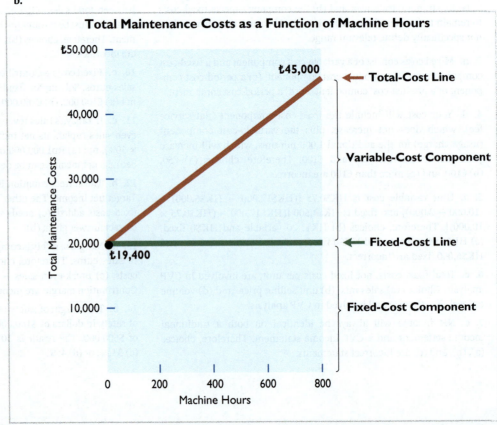

2. **(LO 3, 4, 5)** Zion Seating, a manufacturer of chairs, had the following data for the year ended December 31, 2023.

Determine contribution margin ratio, break-even point in sales euros, and margin of safety.

Sales	2,400 chairs
Unit selling price	€40 per chair
Unit variable costs	€15 per chair
Fixed costs	€19,500

Instructions

a. Prepare a CVP income statement with columns for per unit and percent of sales information.
b. What is the contribution margin ratio?
c. What is the break-even point in sales euros?
d. What is the margin of safety in euros and the margin of safety ratio?
e. If the company wishes to increase its total euro contribution margin by 40% in 2024, by how much will it need to increase its sales if unit contribution margin remains constant?

Solution

2. a.

Zion Seating
CVP Income Statement
For the Month Ended December 31, 2023

	Total	Per Batch	Percent of Sales
Sales (2,400 × €40)	€96,000	€40	100.0%
Variable costs (2,400 × €15)	36,000	15	37.5
Contribution margin	60,000	€25	62.5%
Fixed costs	19,500		
Net income	€40,500		

b. Contribution margin ratio = Unit contribution margin ÷ Unit selling price
   (€40 − €15) ÷ €40 = 62.5%

c. Break-even point in sales euros: €19,500 ÷ 62.5% = €31,200

d. Margin of safety in euros = (2,400 × €40) − €31,200 = €64,800
   Margin of safety ratio = €64,800 ÷ (2,400 × €40) = 67.5%

e. Current contribution margin is €40 − €15 = €25
   Current total contribution margin is €25 × 2,400 = €60,000
   40% increase in contribution margin is €60,000 × 40% = €24,000
   Total increase in sales required is €24,000 ÷ 62.5% = €38,400

Practice Problem

(LO 4, 5) Vargo NV makes calculators that sell for €20 each. For the coming year, management expects fixed costs to total €220,000 and unit variable costs to be €9 per unit.

Compute break-even point, contribution margin ratio, margin of safety, and sales for target net income.

Instructions

a. Compute the break-even point in sales units using the mathematical equation.
b. Compute the break-even point in sales euros using the contribution margin (CM) ratio.
c. Compute the margin of safety ratio assuming actual sales are €500,000.
d. Compute the sales required in euros to earn net income of €165,000.

Solution

a. Sales − Variable costs − Fixed costs = Net income
   €20Q − €9Q − €220,000 = €0
   €11Q = €220,000
   Q = 20,000 calculators

b. Unit contribution margin = Unit selling price − Unit variable costs
   €11 = €20 − €9

Contribution margin ratio = Unit contribution margin ÷ Unit selling price
$$55\% = €11 ÷ €20$$
Break-even point in sales euros = Fixed costs ÷ Contribution margin ratio
$$= €220{,}000 ÷ 55\%$$
$$= €400{,}000$$

c. Margin of safety ratio = $\dfrac{\text{Actual sales} - \text{Break-even sales}}{\text{Actual sales}}$

$$= \dfrac{€500{,}000 - €400{,}000}{€500{,}000}$$

$$= 20\%$$

d. Sales − Variable costs − Fixed costs = Net income
$$€20Q − €9Q − €220{,}000 = €165{,}000$$
$$€11Q = €385{,}000$$
$$Q = 35{,}000 \text{ calculators}$$

35,000 calculators × €20 = €700,000 required sales

OR

(Fixed costs + Target net income) ÷ Contribution margin ratio = Sales in euros
(€220,000 + €165,000) ÷ 0.55 = €700,000

Note: All asterisked Questions, Exercises, and Problems relate to material in the appendix to this chapter.

Questions

1. **a.** What is cost behavior analysis?
   b. Why is cost behavior analysis important to management?
2. **a.** Ke Liu asks your help in understanding the term "activity index." Explain the meaning and importance of this term for Liu.
   b. State the two ways that variable costs may be defined.
3. Contrast the effects of changes in the activity level on total fixed costs and on unit fixed costs.
4. J.P. Alexander claims that the relevant range concept is important only for variable costs.
   a. Explain the relevant range concept.
   b. Is J.P.'s claim correct? Explain why or why not.
5. "The relevant range is indispensable in cost behavior analysis." Is this true? Why or why not?
6. Rezaul Karim is confused. He does not understand why rent on his apartment is a fixed cost and rent on a Hertz rental truck is a mixed cost. Explain the difference to Rezaul.
7. How should mixed costs be classified in CVP analysis? What approach is used to effect the appropriate classification?
8. At the high and low levels of activity during the month, direct labor hours are 90,000 and 40,000, respectively. The related costs are $165,000 and $100,000. What are the fixed costs and unit variable costs?
9. "Cost-volume-profit (CVP) analysis is based entirely on unit costs." Is this true? Explain why or why not.
10. Yoko Kawamura defines contribution margin as the amount of profit available to cover operating expenses. Is there any truth in this definition? Discuss.
11. Marshall plc's GWhiz calculator sells for A$40. Unit variable costs are estimated to be A$26. What are the unit contribution margin and the contribution margin ratio?
12. "Break-even analysis is of limited use to management because a company cannot survive by just breaking even." Is this true? Explain why or why not.
13. Total fixed costs are €26,000 for Daz SA. It has a unit contribution margin of €15 and a contribution margin ratio of 25%. Compute the break-even point in sales euros.
14. Peggy Turnbull asks your help in constructing a CVP graph. Explain to Peggy (a) how the break-even point is plotted, and (b) how the level of activity and sales euros at the break-even point are determined.
15. Define the term "margin of safety." If Yunxuan Group expects to sell 1,250 units of its product at HK$120 per unit, and break-even sales for the product are HK$132,000, what is the margin of safety ratio?
16. Huang Company's break-even point in sales dollars is $500,000. Assuming fixed costs are $180,000, what sales revenue is needed to achieve a target net income of $90,000?
17. The traditional income statement for Pace Industries for the year ended December 31, 2023, shows sales £900,000, cost of goods sold £600,000, and operating expenses £200,000. Assuming all costs and expenses are 70% variable and 30% fixed, prepare a CVP income statement through contribution margin.
*18. Harry Brooks estimated the unit variable-cost and fixed-cost components of his company's utility costs using the high-low method. He is concerned that the cost equation that resulted from the high-low method might not provide an accurate representation of his company's utility costs. What is the inherent weakness of the high-low method? What alternative approach might Brooks use, and what are its advantages?
*19. Adam Webster owns and manages a company that provides trenching services. His clients are companies that need to lay power lines, gas lines, and fiber optic cable. Because trenching machines require considerable maintenance due to the demanding nature of the work, Adam has created a scatter plot that displays his monthly maintenance costs. If Adam were to estimate a cost equation line using regression analysis for the data in his scatter plot, what primary characteristic would that line display?
*20. What are some of the limitations of regression analysis?

Brief Exercises

BE5.1 (LO 1), C Monthly production costs in Paek Ltd. for two levels of production are as follows:

Cost	2,000 Units	4,000 Units
Indirect labor	₩10,000,000	₩20,000,000
Supervisory salaries	5,000,000	5,000,000
Maintenance	4,000,000	6,000,000

Classify costs as variable, fixed, or mixed.

Indicate which costs are variable, fixed, and mixed, and give the reason for each answer.

BE5.2 (LO 1), AN For Lodes SpA, the relevant range of production is 40–80% of capacity. At 40% of capacity, variable costs are €4,000 and fixed costs are €6,000. At 80% capacity, the same variable and fixed costs are €8,000 and €6,000, respectively. Diagram the behavior of each cost within the relevant range assuming the behavior is linear.

Diagram the behavior of costs within the relevant range.

BE5.3 (LO 1), AN For Wesland Ltd., a mixed cost is £15,000 plus £18 per direct labor hour. Diagram the behavior of the fixed cost and total cost using increments of 500 hours up to 2,500 hours on the horizontal axis and increments of £15,000 up to £60,000 on the vertical axis.

Diagram the behavior of a mixed cost.

BE5.4 (LO 2), AP Victoria Group accumulates the following data concerning a mixed cost, using kilometers as the activity level.

Determine unit variable costs and fixed costs using the high-low method.

	Kilometers Driven	Total Cost		Kilometers Driven	Total Cost
January	8,000	A$14,150	March	8,500	A$15,000
February	7,500	13,500	April	8,200	14,490

Compute the unit variable costs and fixed costs using the high-low method for this mixed cost.

BE5.5 (LO 2), AP Markowis Corp. has collected the following data concerning its maintenance costs for the past six months.

Determine unit variable costs and fixed costs using the high-low method.

	Units Produced	Total Maintenance Costs
July	18,000	$36,000
August	32,000	48,000
September	36,000	55,000
October	22,000	38,000
November	40,000	74,500
December	38,000	62,000

Compute the unit variable costs and fixed costs using the high-low method for this mixed cost.

BE5.6 (LO 3), AN Determine the missing amounts.

Determine missing amounts for contribution margin.

	Unit Selling Price	Unit Variable Costs	Unit Contribution Margin	Contribution Margin Ratio
1.	NT$6,400	NT$3,520	(a)	(b)
2.	NT$3,000	(c)	NT$930	(d)
3.	(e)	(f)	NT$3,250	25%

BE5.7 (LO 3), AP Russell Inc. had sales of $2,200,000 for the first quarter of 2023 (it sold 220,000 units). In making the sales, the company incurred the following costs and expenses:

Prepare CVP income statement.

	Variable	Fixed
Cost of goods sold	$920,000	$440,000
Selling expenses	70,000	45,000
Administrative expenses	88,000	98,000

Prepare a CVP income statement for the quarter ended March 31, 2023. Include columns for per unit and percent of sales information.

Compute the break-even point in sales units.

BE5.8 (LO 4), AP Rice Company has a unit selling price of HK$5,200, unit variable costs of HK$2,860, and fixed costs of HK$1,638,000. Compute the break-even point in sales units using (a) the mathematical equation and (b) unit contribution margin.

Compute the break-even point in sales euros.

BE5.9 (LO 4), AP Presto Industries had total variable costs of €180,000, total fixed costs of €110,000, and total revenues of €300,000. Compute the required sales euros to break even.

Compute sales for target net income.

BE5.10 (LO 5), AP For Flynn Manufacturing, variable costs are 70% of sales, and fixed costs are £195,000. Management's net income goal is £75,000. Compute the required sales pounds needed to achieve management's target net income of £75,000. (Use the contribution margin technique.)

Compute the margin of safety in dollars and the margin of safety ratio.

BE5.11 (LO 5), AP For Xin Industries, actual sales are HK$10,000,000, and break-even sales are HK$8,000,000. Compute (a) the margin of safety in dollars and (b) the margin of safety ratio.

Compute the required sales in units for target net income.

BE5.12 (LO 5), AP Yamamoto Enterprises has fixed costs of ¥48,000,000. It has a unit selling price of ¥600, unit variable costs of ¥440, and a target net income of ¥150,000,000. Compute the required sales in units to achieve its target net income.

Compute unit variable costs and fixed costs using regression analysis.

*BE5.13 (LO 6), AP Stiever Corporation's maintenance costs are shown here.

	Units Produced	Total Cost
July	18,000	$32,000
August	32,000	48,000
September	36,000	55,000
October	22,000	38,000
November	40,000	66,100
December	38,000	62,000

Compute the unit variable costs and fixed costs using regression analysis for this mixed cost. Present your solution in the form of a cost equation. (We recommend that you use the Intercept and Slope functions in Excel.)

DO IT! Exercises

DO IT! 5.1 (LO 1), C Huang Ltd. reports the following total costs at two levels of production.   *Classify types of costs.*

	5,000 Units	10,000 Units
Indirect labor	HK$ 30,000	HK$ 60,000
Property taxes	70,000	70,000
Direct labor	280,000	560,000
Direct materials	220,000	440,000
Depreciation (straight-line)	40,000	40,000
Utilities	50,000	80,000
Maintenance	90,000	110,000

Classify each cost as variable, fixed, or mixed.

DO IT! 5.2 (LO 2), AP Damon Company accumulates the following data concerning a mixed cost, using units produced as the activity level.   *Compute costs using high-low method and estimate total cost.*

	Units Produced	Total Cost
March	10,000	A$18,000
April	9,000	16,650
May	10,500	18,580
June	8,800	16,200
July	9,500	17,100

a. Compute the unit variable costs and fixed costs using the high-low method.
b. Using the information from your answer to part (a), write the cost equation.
c. Estimate the total cost if the company produces 9,200 units.

DO IT! 5.3 (LO 3), AP Cedar Grove plc produces and sells cell phone-operated home security systems.   *Prepare CVP income statement.*
Information regarding the costs and sales during May 2023 is as follows:

Unit selling price	£45.00
Unit variable costs	£21.60
Total monthly fixed costs	£120,000
Units sold	8,000

Prepare a CVP income statement for Cedar Grove plc for the month of May. Provide total, per unit, and percent of sales values.

DO IT! 5.4 (LO 4), AP Zhou Bicycles has a unit selling price of HK$2,500, unit variable costs of HK$1,700, and fixed costs of HK$1,600,000. Compute the break-even point in sales units using (a) the mathematical equation and (b) unit contribution margin.

Compute break-even point in sales units.

DO IT! 5.5 (LO 4, 5), AP Lika AG makes radios that sell for €30 each. For the coming year, management expects fixed costs to total €220,000 and unit variable costs to be €18.

Compute break-even point, margin of safety ratio, and sales for target net income.

a. Compute the break-even point in sales euros using the contribution margin (CM) ratio.
b. Compute the margin of safety ratio assuming actual sales are €800,000.
c. Compute the sales euros required to earn net income of €140,000.

Exercises

E5.1 (LO 1), C Chen Bucket Ltd. manufactures a single product. Annual production costs incurred in the manufacturing process are shown here for two levels of production.

Define and classify variable, fixed, and mixed costs.

	Costs Incurred			
Production in Units	5,000		10,000	
Production Costs	Total Cost	Unit Cost	Total Cost	Unit Cost
Direct materials	HK$80,000	HK$16.00	HK$160,000	HK$16.00
Direct labor	95,000	19.00	190,000	19.00
Utilities	20,000	4.00	33,000	3.30
Rent	40,000	8.00	40,000	4.00
Maintenance	8,000	1.60	14,000	1.40
Supervisory salaries	10,000	2.00	10,000	1.00

Instructions

a. Define the terms variable costs, fixed costs, and mixed costs.
b. Classify each cost above as either variable, fixed, or mixed.

E5.2 (LO 1), AP Shingle Enterprises is considering manufacturing a new product. It projects the cost of direct materials and rent for a range of output as follows:

Diagram cost behavior, determine relevant range, and classify costs.

Output in Units	Rent Cost	Direct Materials
1,000	£ 5,000	£ 4,000
2,000	5,000	7,200
3,000	8,000	9,000
4,000	8,000	12,000
5,000	8,000	15,000
6,000	8,000	18,000
7,000	8,000	21,000
8,000	8,000	24,000
9,000	10,000	29,300
10,000	10,000	35,000
11,000	10,000	44,000

Instructions

a. Diagram the anticipated behavior of each cost for outputs ranging from 1,000 to 11,000 units.
b. Determine the relevant range of activity for this product based on the cost behavior of each input.
c. Calculate the unit variable costs within the relevant range.
d. Indicate the fixed cost within the relevant range.

Determine fixed costs and unit variable costs using the high-low method and prepare graph.

E5.3 (LO 1, 2), AN The controller of Daritan Industries has collected the following monthly cost data for use in analyzing the behavior of maintenance costs.

Month	Total Maintenance Costs	Total Machine Hours
January	Rp27,000,000	300
February	30,000,000	350
March	36,000,000	500
April	45,000,000	690
May	32,000,000	400
June	55,000,000	700

Instructions

a. Determine the fixed costs and unit variable costs using the high-low method for this mixed cost.

b. Prepare a graph showing the behavior of maintenance costs, and identify the fixed-cost and unit variable-cost components. Use 100-hour increments and Rp10,000,000-cost increments.

Classify variable, fixed, and mixed costs.

E5.4 (LO 1), C Rustic Style Furniture incurred the following costs.

1. Wood used in the production of furniture.
2. Fuel used in delivery trucks.
3. Straight-line depreciation on factory building.
4. Screws used in the production of furniture.
5. Sales staff salaries.
6. Sales commissions.
7. Property taxes.
8. Insurance on buildings.
9. Hourly wages of furniture craftsmen.
10. Salaries of factory supervisors.
11. Utilities expense.
12. Telephone bill.

Instructions

Identify the costs above as variable, fixed, or mixed.

Determine fixed costs and unit variable costs using the high-low method and prepare graph.

E5.5 (LO 1, 2), AP The controller of Hall Industries has collected the following monthly cost data for use in analyzing the behavior of maintenance costs.

Month	Total Maintenance Costs	Total Machine Hours
January	$2,640	3,500
February	3,000	4,000
March	3,600	6,000
April	4,500	7,900
May	3,200	5,000
June	4,620	8,000

Instructions

a. Determine the fixed costs and unit variable costs using the high-low method for this mixed cost.

b. Prepare a graph showing the behavior of maintenance costs and identify the fixed-cost and variable-cost components. Use 2,000-hour increments and $1,000-cost increments.

Determine fixed, variable, and mixed costs.

E5.6 (LO 1), AP PCB Technology Ltd. manufactures a single product. Monthly production costs incurred in the manufacturing process are shown below for the production of 3,000 units.

Direct materials	HK$ 75,000
Direct labor	180,000
Utilities	21,000
Property taxes	10,000
Indirect labor	45,000
Supervisory salaries	19,000
Maintenance	11,000
Depreciation (straight-line)	24,000

The utilities and maintenance costs are mixed costs. The fixed components of these costs are HK$3,000 and HK$2,000, respectively.

Instructions

a. Identify the above costs as variable, fixed, or mixed.

b. Calculate the expected costs when production is 5,000 units.

E5.7 (LO 3), K **Writing** Yun-Ting Hung wants Hung Ltd. to use CVP analysis to study the effects of changes in costs and volume on the company. Yun has heard that certain assumptions must be valid in order for CVP analysis to be useful.

Explain assumptions underlying CVP analysis.

Instructions

Prepare a memo to Yun-Ting concerning the assumptions that underlie CVP analysis.

E5.8 (LO 3, 4), AP **Service** All That Blooms provides environmentally friendly lawn services for homeowners. Its operating costs are as follows:

Compute break-even point in sales units and in sales pounds.

Depreciation (straight-line)	£1,400 per month
Advertising	£200 per month
Insurance	£2,000 per month
Weed and feed materials	£12 per lawn
Direct labor	£10 per lawn
Fuel	£2 per lawn

All That Blooms charges £60 per treatment for the average single-family lawn. For the month ended July 31, 2023, the company had total sales of £7,200.

Instructions

a. Prepare a CVP income statement for the month ended July 31, 2023. Include columns for per unit and percent of sales information.

b. Determine the company's break-even point in (1) number of lawns serviced per month and (2) sales pounds.

E5.9 (LO 3, 4), AP **Service** The Palmer Acres Inn is trying to determine its break-even point during its off-peak season. The inn has 50 rooms that it rents at $60 a night. Operating costs are as follows:

Compute break-even point in sales units and in sales dollars.

Salaries	$5,900 per month
Property tax	$1,100 per month
Depreciation (straight-line)	$1,000 per month
Maintenance	$100 per month
Maid service	$14 per room
Other costs	$28 per room

Instructions

Determine the inn's break-even point in (a) number of rented rooms per month and (b) sales dollars.

E5.10 (LO 3, 4), AP **Service** In the month of March, Style Salon serviced 560 clients at an average price of A$120. During the month, fixed costs were A$21,024 and variable costs were 60% of sales.

Compute contribution margin and break-even point.

Instructions

a. Determine the total contribution margin in dollars, the unit contribution margin, and the contribution margin ratio.

b. Using the contribution margin technique, compute the break-even point in sales dollars and in sales units.

E5.11 (LO 3, 4), AP **Service** Hiroki Tsuji provides shuttle service between four hotels near a medical center and an international airport. Tsuji uses two 10-passenger vans to offer 12 round trips per day. A recent month's activity in the form of a CVP income statement is as follows:

Compute break-even point.

Sales (1,500 passengers)		¥3,600,000
Variable costs		
Fuel	¥ 504,000	
Tolls and parking	310,000	
Maintenance	86,000	900,000
Contribution margin		2,700,000
Fixed costs		
Salaries	1,570,000	
Depreciation (straight-line)	130,000	
Insurance	100,000	1,800,000
Net income		¥ 900,000

Instructions

a. Calculate the break-even point in (1) sales (yen) and (2) number of passengers.

b. Without calculations, determine the contribution margin at the break-even point.

Compute unit variable costs, contribution margin ratio, and increase in fixed costs.

E5.12 (LO 3, 4), AP In 2022, Silva SA had a break-even point of R$3,500,000 based on a unit selling price of R$50 and fixed costs of R$1,120,000. In 2023, the unit selling price and the unit variable costs did not change, but the break-even point increased to R$4,200,000.

Instructions

a. Compute the unit variable costs and the contribution margin ratio for 2022.

b. Compute the increase in fixed costs for 2023.

Prepare CVP income statements.

E5.13 (LO 3, 4), AP Choh Electronics has the following information available for September 2023.

Unit selling price of video game consoles	HK$4,000
Unit variable costs	HK$2,800
Total fixed costs	HK$540,000
Units sold	600

Instructions

a. Compute the unit contribution margin.

b. Prepare a CVP income statement. Include columns for per unit and percent of sales information.

c. Compute Choh's break-even point in sales units.

d. Prepare a CVP income statement for the break-even point. Include columns for per unit and percent of sales information.

Prepare traditional income statement and CVP income statement.

E5.14 (LO 3), AP Durand Music had sales of €3,000,000 for the year ended December 31, 2023. The unit selling price was €15. In making the sales, the company incurred the following costs and expenses:

	Variable	Fixed
Cost of goods sold	€600,000	€800,000
Selling expenses	120,000	60,000
Administrative expenses	240,000	80,000

Instructions

a. Prepare a traditional income statement.

b. Prepare a CVP income statement. Include columns for per unit and percent of sales information.

Compute various components to derive target net income under different assumptions.

E5.15 (LO 4, 5), AP Naylor Company had $210,000 of net income in 2022 when the unit selling price was $140, the unit variable costs were $90, and the fixed costs were $570,000. Management expects per unit data and total fixed costs to remain the same in 2023. The president of Naylor Company is under pressure from stockholders to increase net income by $62,400 in 2023.

Instructions

a. Compute the number of units sold in 2022.

b. Compute the number of units that would have to be sold in 2023 to reach the stockholders' desired net income.

c. Assume that Naylor Company sells the same number of units in 2023 as it did in 2022. What would the selling price have to be in order to reach the stockholders' desired net income, assuming the unit variable costs and fixed costs remain at 2022 levels?

Compute net income under different alternatives.

E5.16 (LO 5), AP Yams Company reports the following operating results for the month of August: sales $400,000 (5,000 units), variable costs $240,000, and fixed costs $90,000. Management is considering the following independent courses of action to increase net income.

1. Increase the unit selling price by 10% with no change in total variable costs, fixed costs, or units sold.

2. Reduce variable costs to 55% of sales while holding fixed costs, quantity, and unit selling price constant.

Instructions

Compute the net income to be earned under each alternative. Which course of action will produce the higher net income?

E5.17 (LO 4, 5), AP Glacial plc estimates that variable costs will be 62.5% of sales, and fixed costs will total £600,000. The unit selling price of the product is £4.

Prepare a CVP graph and compute break-even point and margin of safety.

Instructions

a. Compute the break-even point in (1) sales units and (2) sales pounds.

b. Prepare a CVP graph, assuming maximum sales of £3,200,000. (*Note:* Use £400,000 increments for sales and costs and 100,000 increments for units.)

c. Assuming actual sales are £2 million, compute the margin of safety (1) in pounds and (2) as a ratio.

E5.18 (LO 3, 4, 5), AP Felde Bucket, a manufacturer of rain barrels, had the following data for 2022.

Determine contribution margin ratio, break-even point in sales euros, and margin of safety.

Sales quantity	2,500 barrels
Unit selling price	€40 per barrel
Unit variable costs	€24 per barrel
Fixed costs	€19,500

Instructions

a. What is the contribution margin ratio?

b. What is the break-even point in sales euros?

c. What is the margin of safety in sales euros and as a ratio?

d. If the company wishes to increase its total euro contribution margin by 30% in 2023, by how much will it need to increase its sales euros if all other factors (other than sales quantity) remain constant?

***E5.19 (LO 6), AP** The controller of Standard Industries has collected the following monthly cost data for analyzing the behavior of electricity costs.

Determine fixed costs and unit variable costs using regression analysis, prepare scatter plot, and estimate cost at particular level of activity.

	Total Electricity Costs	Total Machine Hours
January	$2,500	300
February	3,000	350
March	3,600	500
April	4,500	690
May	3,200	400
June	4,900	700
July	4,100	650
August	3,800	520
September	5,100	680
October	4,200	630
November	3,300	350
December	6,100	720

Instructions

a. Determine the fixed costs and unit variable costs using regression analysis. (We recommend the use of Excel.)

b. Prepare a scatter plot using Excel. Present the cost equation line estimated in part (a).

c. What electricity cost does the cost equation estimate for a level of activity of 500 machine hours? By what amount does this differ from March's observed cost for 500 machine hours?

Problems

Determine fixed costs and unit variable costs using high-low method, and estimate cost at particular level of activity.

P5.1 (LO 1, 2), AP The controller of Helena Company has collected the following monthly cost data for analyzing the behavior of electricity costs.

	Total Electricity Costs	Total Machine Hours
January	£2,500	300
February	3,000	350
March	3,600	500
April	4,500	690
May	3,200	400
June	4,900	700
July	4,100	650
August	3,800	520
September	5,100	680
October	4,200	630
November	3,300	350
December	5,860	720

Instructions

a. VC £8

a. Determine the fixed costs and unit variable costs using the high-low method.

b. What electricity cost does the cost equation estimate for a level of activity of 500 machine hours? By what amount does this differ from March's observed cost for 500 machine hours?

c. What electricity cost does the cost equation estimate for a level of activity of 700 machine hours? By what amount does this differ from June's observed cost for 700 machine hours?

Determine unit variable costs and fixed costs, compute break-even point, prepare a CVP graph, and determine net income.

P5.2 (LO 1, 2, 3, 4), AN Service Juan Perez owns the Hogsfeet Barber Shop. He employs four barbers and pays each a base salary of €1,250 per month. One of the barbers serves as the manager and receives an extra €500 per month. In addition to the base salary, each barber also receives a commission of €4.50 per haircut.

Other costs are as follows:

Advertising	€200 per month
Rent	€1,100 per month
Barber supplies	€0.30 per haircut
Utilities	€175 per month plus €0.20 per haircut
Magazines	€25 per month

Juan currently charges €10 per haircut.

Instructions

a. VC €5

a. Determine the unit variable costs per haircut and the total monthly fixed costs.

b. Compute the break-even point in sales units and in sales euros.

c. Prepare a CVP graph, assuming a maximum of 1,800 haircuts in a month. Use increments of 300 haircuts on the horizontal axis and €3,000 on the vertical axis.

d. Determine net income, assuming 1,600 haircuts are given in a month.

Prepare a CVP income statement and compute break-even point, contribution margin ratio, margin of safety ratio, and sales for target net income.

P5.3 (LO 3, 4, 5), AP Jorge Company bottles and distributes B-Lite, a diet soft drink. The beverage is sold for 50 cents per 16-ounce bottle to retailers. For the year 2023, management estimates the following revenues and costs:

Sales	$1,800,000	Selling expenses—variable	$70,000
Direct materials	430,000	Selling expenses—fixed	65,000
Direct labor	360,000	Administrative expenses—	
Manufacturing overhead—		variable	20,000
variable	380,000	Administrative expenses—	
Manufacturing overhead—		fixed	60,000
fixed	280,000		

Instructions

a. Prepare a CVP income statement for 2023 based on management's estimates. Include columns for per unit and percent of sales information.

b. (1) 2,700,000 units

b. Compute the break-even point in (1) sales units and (2) sales dollars.

c. Compute the contribution margin ratio and the margin of safety ratio. (Round to nearest full percent.)

d. Determine the sales dollars required to earn net income of $180,000.

c. CM ratio 30%

P5.4 (LO 4), E Wong Corp.'s sales slumped badly in 2023. For the first time in its history, it operated at a loss. The company's income statement showed the following results from selling 500,000 units of product: sales S$2,500,000, total costs and expenses S$2,590,000, and net loss S$90,000. Costs and expenses consisted of the following amounts:

Compute break-even point under alternative courses of action.

	Total	Variable	Fixed
Cost of goods sold	S$2,140,000	S$1,590,000	S$550,000
Selling expenses	250,000	92,000	158,000
Administrative expenses	200,000	68,000	132,000
	S$2,590,000	S$1,750,000	S$840,000

Management is considering the following independent alternatives for 2024.

1. Increase the unit selling price 20% with no change in total costs, total expenses, and sales volume.
2. Change the compensation of sales personnel from fixed annual salaries totaling S$140,000 to total salaries of S$60,000 plus a 5% commission on sales. All other total costs, total expenses, and total sales remain unchanged.

Instructions

a. Compute the break-even point in sales dollars for 2023.

b. Compute the break-even point in sales dollars under each of the alternative courses of action. (Round all ratios to nearest full percent.) Which course of action do you recommend?

b. Alternative 1 S$2,000,000

P5.5 (LO 3, 4, 5), E Mary Willis is the advertising manager for Bargain Shoe Store. She is currently working on a major promotional campaign. Her ideas include the installation of a new lighting system and increased display space that will add $29,000 in fixed costs to the $270,000 currently spent. In addition, Mary is proposing that a 5% price decrease ($40 to $38) will produce a 25% increase in sales volume (20,000 to 25,000). Variable costs will remain at $25 per pair of shoes. Management is impressed with Mary's ideas but concerned about the effects that these changes will have on the break-even point and the margin of safety.

Compute break-even point and margin of safety ratio, and prepare a CVP income statement before and after changes in business environment.

Instructions

a. Prepare a CVP income statement for current operations and after Mary's changes are introduced. (Show column for total amounts only.) Would you make the changes suggested?

b. Compute the current break-even point in sales units, and compare it to the break-even point in sales units if Mary's ideas are implemented.

c. Compute the margin of safety ratio for current operations and after Mary's changes are introduced. (Round to nearest full percent.)

c. Current margin of safety ratio 10%

P5.6 (LO 3, 4, 5), AN Zhenhao Ltd. has collected the following information after its first year of operations. Sales were HK$1,600,000 on 100,000 units, selling expenses HK$250,000 (40% variable and 60% fixed), direct materials HK$490,000, direct labor HK$290,000, administrative expenses HK$270,000 (20% variable and 80% fixed), and manufacturing overhead HK$380,000 (70% variable and 30% fixed). Top management has asked you to do a CVP analysis so that it can make plans for the coming year. It has projected that unit sales will increase by 10% next year.

Compute contribution margin, fixed costs, break-even point, sales for target net income, and margin of safety ratio.

Instructions

a. Compute (1) the contribution margin for the current year and the projected year, and (2) the fixed costs for the current year and the projected year. Unit selling price, unit variable costs, and fixed costs are estimated to remain unchanged.

b. Compute the break-even point in sales units and sales dollars for the current year.

b. 120,000 units

c. The company has a target net income of HK$145,000. What is the required sales in dollars for the company to meet its target?

d. If the company meets its target net income number, by what percentage could its sales fall before it is operating at a loss? That is, what is its margin of safety ratio?

P5.7 (LO 1, 3, 5), E Kaiser Industries carries no inventories. Its product is manufactured only when a customer's order is received. It is then shipped immediately after it is made. For its fiscal year ended October 31, 2023, Kaiser's break-even point was £1.5 million. On sales of £1.5 million, its traditional income statement showed a gross profit of £242,500, direct materials cost of £500,000, and direct labor costs of £625,000. The contribution margin was £180,000, and variable manufacturing overhead was £62,500.

Determine variable and fixed costs.

5-44 CHAPTER 5 Cost-Volume-Profit

a. 2. £70,000

Instructions

a. Calculate the following:
  1. Variable selling and administrative expenses.
  2. Fixed manufacturing overhead.
  3. Fixed selling and administrative expenses.

b. Ignoring your answer to part (a), assume that fixed manufacturing overhead was £100,000 and the fixed selling and administrative expenses were £80,000. The marketing vice president feels that if the company increased its advertising, sales could be increased by 20%. What is the maximum increased advertising cost the company can incur and still report the same income as before the advertising expenditure, assuming that the contribution margin ratio remains unchanged?

Determine fixed costs and unit variable costs using regression analysis, and estimate cost at particular level of activity.

*P5.8 (LO 1, 2, 6), AP The controller of Brokaw Production has collected the following monthly cost data for analyzing the behavior of utility costs.

	Total Utility Costs	Total Machine Hours
January	$3,200	400
February	4,700	550
March	4,000	500
April	2,100	790
May	3,600	450
June	5,300	700
July	5,500	690
August	5,100	620
September	7,400	880
October	4,600	610
November	3,000	350
December	6,700	820

Instructions

a. VC $5.7343

a. Determine the fixed costs and unit variable costs using regression analysis. (We recommend the use of Excel.)

b. Prepare a scatter plot using Excel. Present the cost equation line estimated in part (a).

c. What utility cost does the cost equation estimate for a level of activity of 500 machine hours? By what amount does this differ from March's observed cost for 500 machine hours?

d. What utility cost does the cost equation estimate for a level of activity of 700 machine hours? By what estimate does this differ from June's observed cost for 700 machine hours?

Continuing Case

Current Designs

CD5 Bill Johnson, sales manager, and Diane Buswell, controller, at Current Designs are beginning to analyze the cost considerations for one of the composite models of the kayak division. They have provided the following production and operational costs necessary to produce one composite kayak.

	A	B
1	Kevlar®	$250 per kayak
2	Resin and supplies	$100 per kayak
3	Finishing kit (seat, rudder, ropes, etc.)	$170 per kayak
4	Direct labor	$420 per kayak
5	Selling and administrative expenses—variable	$400 per kayak
6	Selling and administrative expenses—fixed	$119,700 per year
7	Manufacturing overhead—fixed	$240,000 per year

Current Designs—Cost Information

Bill and Diane have asked you to provide a cost-volume-profit analysis, to help them finalize the budget projections for the upcoming year. Bill has informed you that the selling price of the composite kayak will be $2,000.

Instructions

a. Calculate unit variable costs.

b. Determine the unit contribution margin.

c. Using the unit contribution margin, determine the break-even point in sales units for this product line.

d. Assume that Current Designs would like to earn net income of $270,600 on this product line. Using the unit contribution margin, calculate the number of units that need to be sold to achieve this goal.

e. Based on the most recent sales forecast, Current Designs expects to sell 1,000 units of this model. Using your results from part (c), calculate the margin of safety in dollars and the margin of safety ratio.

Data Analytics in Action

Using Data Visualization to Analyze Costs

DA5.1 Data visualization can be used to compare options.

Example: Consider the *Management Insight* box "Are Robotic Workers More Humane?" presented in the chapter. Data analytics can help **Kroger** (USA) determine if using robots in its warehouse would be a cost-effective decision. Consider the following chart, which compares income effects in both a manual and a robotic system. When using human labor in a manual system, we see that labor costs are substantial. When a robotic system is utilized, we see that depreciation is a larger cost item, and labor is much less.

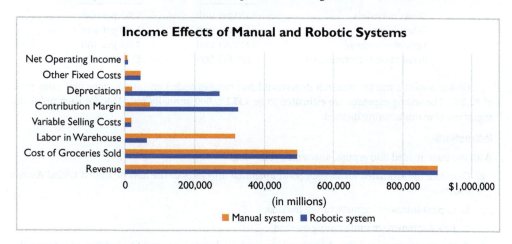

If we assume that revenues will increase 40% due to an increased sales volume, what effect will we see on net operating income? As shown in the following chart, the increase in net operating income is larger in an automated system. This is because the labor increase was a smaller dollar amount than the respective increase in a manual system, coupled with no increase in total fixed costs. This effect is often referred to as **operating leverage**, which is discussed further in Chapter 6.

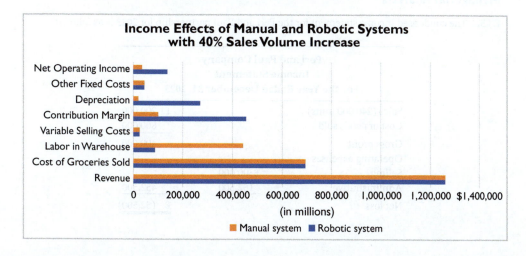

For this case, you will use an approach similar to that used in the example just presented. You will help a fast food restaurant evaluate the benefits of installing a kiosk in the lobby to automate customer orders, thus reducing the need for cashiers. This case requires you to compare income statement data for traditional and digital ordering for the restaurant, and then create and analyze a bar chart.

Go to the book's product page on www.wiley.com for complete case details and instructions.

Data Analytics at HydroHappy

DA5.2 HydroHappy management wants to examine its largest non–value-added cost, selling costs, to see if it can identify a better cost driver in an effort to lower its total selling costs. The company currently uses the number of sales calls as its cost driver. For this case, you will generate scatter charts, as well as use Excel's Slope and Intercept functions, to help HydroHappy determine the best cost driver for selling costs.

Go to the book's product page on www.wiley.com for complete case details and instructions.

Expand Your Critical Thinking

Decision-Making Across the Organization

CT5.1 Global Ascent has decided to introduce a new product. The new product can be manufactured by either a capital-intensive method or a labor-intensive method. The manufacturing method will not affect the quality of the product. The estimated manufacturing costs by the two methods are as follows:

	Capital-Intensive	Labor-Intensive
Direct materials	₹350 per unit	₹385 per unit
Direct labor	₹420 per unit	₹560 per unit
Variable overhead	₹210 per unit	₹315 per unit
Fixed manufacturing costs	₹176,680,000	₹108,500,000

Global Ascent's market research department has recommended an introductory unit sales price of ₹2,240. The selling expenses are estimated to be ₹35,140,000 annually plus ₹140 for each unit sold, regardless of manufacturing method.

Instructions

With the class divided into groups, answer the following:

a. Calculate the estimated break-even point in annual unit sales of the new product if Global Ascent uses the:
   1. Capital-intensive manufacturing method.
   2. Labor-intensive manufacturing method.

b. Determine the annual unit sales volume at which Global Ascent would be indifferent between the two manufacturing methods.

c. Explain the circumstance under which Global Ascent should employ each of the two manufacturing methods.

Managerial Analysis

CT5.2 The condensed income statement for the Peri and Paul partnership for 2023 is as follows:

Peri and Paul Company
Income Statement
For the Year Ended December 31, 2023

Sales (240,000 units)		£1,200,000
Cost of goods sold		800,000
Gross profit		400,000
Operating expenses		
Selling	£300,000	
Administrative	152,500	452,500
Net loss		£ (52,500)

A cost behavior analysis indicates that 75% of the cost of goods sold are variable and 40% of the selling expenses are variable. Administrative expenses are £92,500 fixed.

Instructions

(Round to nearest unit, cent, and percentage, where necessary. Use the CVP income statement format in computing net income.)

a. Compute the break-even point in sales pounds and in sales units for 2023.

b. Peri has proposed a plan to get the partnership "out of the red" and improve its profitability. She feels that the quality of the product could be substantially improved by spending £0.32 more per unit on better raw materials. The unit selling price could be increased to £5.25. Peri estimates that sales volume would increase by 25%. Compute net income under Peri's proposal and the break-even point in sales pounds.

c. Paul was a marketing major in college. He believes that sales volume can be increased only by intensive advertising and promotional campaigns. He therefore proposed the following plan as an alternative to Peri's: (1) increase unit variable selling expenses to £0.575, (2) lower the unit selling price by £0.25, and (3) increase fixed selling expenses by £51,000. Paul quoted an old marketing research report that said that sales volume would increase by 60% if these changes were made. Compute net income under Paul's proposal and the break-even point in sales pounds.

d. Which plan should be accepted? Explain your answer.

Real-World Focus

CT5.3 **The Coca-Cola Company** (USA) hardly needs an introduction. A line taken from the cover of a recent annual report says it all: If you measured time in servings of Coca-Cola, "a billion Coca-Cola's ago was yesterday morning." On average, every U.S. citizen drinks 363 8-ounce servings of Coca-Cola products each year. Coca-Cola's primary line of business is the making and selling of syrup to bottlers. These bottlers then sell the finished bottles and cans of Coca-Cola to retailers.

In the annual report of Coca-Cola, the following information was provided.

The Coca-Cola Company
Management Discussion

Our gross margin declined to 61 percent this year from 62 percent in the prior year, primarily due to costs for materials such as sweeteners and packaging.

The increases [in selling expenses] in the last two years were primarily due to higher marketing expenditures in support of our Company's volume growth.

We measure our sales volume in two ways: (1) gallon shipments of concentrates and syrups and (2) unit cases of finished product (bottles and cans of Coke sold by bottlers).

Instructions

Answer the following questions:

a. Are sweeteners and packaging a variable cost or a fixed cost? What is the impact on the contribution margin of an increase in the per unit cost of sweeteners or packaging? What are the implications for profitability?

b. In your opinion, are Coca-Cola's marketing expenditures a fixed cost, variable cost, or mixed cost? Give justification for your answer.

c. Which of the two measures cited for measuring volume represents the activity index as defined in this chapter? Why might Coca-Cola use two different measures?

Communication Activity

CT5.4 Your roommate asks for your help on the following questions about CVP analysis equations.

a. How can the mathematical equation for the break-even point provide a result for units sold and sales dollars?

b. How do the equations differ for unit contribution margin and contribution margin ratio?

c. How can contribution margin techniques be used to determine the break-even point in sales units and in sales dollars?

Instructions

Write a memo to your roommate stating the relevant equations and answering each question.

Ethics Case

CT5.5 Hao Zhang is an accountant for Wu Ltd. Early this year, Hao made a highly favorable projection of sales and net income over the next three years for Wu's hot-selling computer PLEX. Based on the projections Hao presented to senior management, the company decided to expand production in this area. This decision led to dislocations of some factory personnel, who were reassigned to one of the company's newer factories in another city. However, no one was fired, and in fact the company expanded its workforce slightly.

Unfortunately, Hao rechecked his projection computations a few months later and found that he had made an error that would have reduced his projections substantially. Luckily, sales of PLEX have exceeded projections so far, and management is satisfied with its decision. Hao, however, is not sure what to do. Should he confess his honest mistake and jeopardize his possible promotion? He suspects that no one will catch the error because PLEX sales have exceeded his projections, and it appears that net income will materialize close to his projections.

Instructions

a. Who are the stakeholders in this situation?

b. Identify the ethical issues involved in this situation.

c. What are the possible alternative actions for Hao? What would you do in Hao's position?

All About You

CT5.6 Cost-volume-profit analysis can also be used in making personal financial decisions. For example, the purchase of a new car is one of your biggest personal expenditures. It is important that you carefully analyze your options.

Suppose that you are considering the purchase of a hybrid vehicle. Let's assume the following facts. The hybrid will initially cost an additional $4,500 above the cost of a traditional vehicle. On average, the hybrid will get 50 miles per gallon of gas, and the traditional car will get 30 miles per gallon. Also, assume that the cost of gas is $2.50 per gallon.

Instructions

Using the facts above, answer the following questions:

a. For gasoline, what is the unit variable cost of going one mile in the hybrid car? What is the unit variable cost of going one mile in the traditional car?

b. Using the information in part (a), if "miles" is your unit of measure, what is the differential between the hybrid vehicle and the traditional vehicle? That is, express the variable cost savings on a per-mile basis.

c. How many miles would you have to drive in order to break even on your investment in the hybrid car?

d. What other factors might you want to consider?

CHAPTER 6

Cost-Volume-Profit Analysis: Additional Issues

CHAPTER PREVIEW

As the following Feature Story about **Aldi** (DEU) suggests, the relationship between a company's fixed and variable costs can have a huge impact on its profitability. In particular, the trend toward cost structures dominated by fixed costs has significantly increased the volatility of many companies' net income. The purpose of this chapter is to demonstrate additional uses of cost-volume-profit analysis in making sound business decisions.

FEATURE STORY

The Secret to Supermarket Profitability

With slim profit margins in the supermarket industry, how do huge international discount chains **Aldi** (DEU) and **Lidl** (DEU) survive and flourish? In 2015, Aldi and Lidl accounted for 10% of the total discount supermarket industry. Since then, they continue to grow in their native Germany, as well as in the United Kingdom and around the world.

One of the reasons for the chains' continued success is due to their business models of quality products at low prices for shoppers on a budget. Both chains carry a limited range of products, which results in both fixed- and variable-cost reductions. So although some of their rivals may have tens of thousands of products in their stores, Aldi and Lidl are more likely to have only one or two thousand. In terms of variable costs that means a lot less money tied up in stock. Their relatively small stores also mean lower fixed costs of operation as well as fewer variable costs to staff the stores.

Aldi and Lidl do not buy brand-name merchandise, which eliminates premium costs of getting products onto their shelves. These lesser-known or generic product markups tend to be a lot higher as well, leading to greater profitability.

In addition, the chains have lowered variable costs by investing in capital assets like conveyor belts that drop items straight into carts, with bar codes on both sides of products to save workers' time. Being so efficient lets these supermarkets extract every possible cost savings from the business.

Source: C. Hutchison, "What's Behind the Rise of Discount Supermarkets Aldi and Lidl?" *Evening Standard* (November 17, 2015).

 Watch the *Whole Foods Market* video at https://wileyaccountingupdates.com/video/?p=80 to learn more about the use of cost-volume-profit analysis in a changing business environment.

CHAPTER OUTLINE

Learning Objectives	Review	Practice
LO 1 Apply basic CVP concepts.	• Basic concepts • Business environment	**DO IT! 1** CVP Analysis
LO 2 Explain the term sales mix and its effects on break-even sales.	• Break-even in units • Break-even in euros	**DO IT! 2** Sales Mix Break-Even
LO 3 Determine sales mix when a company has limited resources.	• Contribution margin per unit • Theory of constraints	**DO IT! 3** Sales Mix with Limited Resources
LO 4 Indicate how operating leverage affects profitability.	• Contribution margin ratio • Break-even point • Margin of safety ratio • Operating leverage	**DO IT! 4** Operating Leverage

Go to the Review and Practice section at the end of the chapter for a targeted summary and practice applications with solutions.

BASIC CVP CONCEPTS

LEARNING OBJECTIVE 1
Apply basic CVP concepts.

As indicated in Chapter 5, cost-volume-profit (CVP) analysis is the study of the effects of changes in costs and volume on a company's profit.

- CVP analysis is important to profit planning.
- It is also a critical factor in determining product mix, maximizing use of production facilities, and setting selling prices.

Basic Concepts

Before we introduce additional issues of CVP analysis, let's review some of the basic concepts that you learned in Chapter 5—specifically, break-even analysis, target net income, and margin of safety. As in Chapter 5, we use Laurel Electronics to illustrate these concepts.

Break-Even Analysis

Laurel Electronics' CVP income statement (**Illustration 6.1**) shows that total contribution margin (sales minus variable expenses) is €320,000, and the company's unit contribution margin is €200. Recall that contribution margin can also be expressed in the form of the

contribution margin ratio (contribution margin divided by sales), which in the case of Laurel is 40% (€200 ÷ €500).

Laurel Electronics
CVP Income Statement
For the Month Ended June 30, 2023

	Total		Per Unit	Percent of Sales
Sales		€800,000	€500	100%
Variable expenses				
Cost of goods sold	€400,000			
Selling expenses	60,000			
Administrative expenses	20,000			
Total variable expenses		480,000	300	60
Contribution margin		**320,000**	**€200**	**40%**
Fixed expenses				
Cost of goods sold	120,000			
Selling expenses	40,000			
Administrative expenses	40,000			
Total fixed expenses		200,000		
Net income		**€120,000**		

ILLUSTRATION 6.1 | Detailed CVP income statement

Illustration 6.2 demonstrates how to compute Laurel's break-even point in sales units (using unit contribution margin).

Fixed Costs	÷	Unit Contribution Margin	=	Break-Even Point in Sales Units
€200,000	÷	€200	=	1,000 units

ILLUSTRATION 6.2 | Break-even point in sales units

Illustration 6.3 shows the computation for the break-even point in sales euros (using contribution margin ratio).

Fixed Costs	÷	Contribution Margin Ratio	=	Break-Even Point in Sales Euros
€200,000	÷	.40	=	€500,000

ILLUSTRATION 6.3 | Break-even point in sales euros

When a company is in its early stages of operation, its primary goal is to break even. Failure to break even will lead eventually to financial failure.

Target Net Income

Once a company achieves its break-even point, it then sets a sales goal that will generate a target net income. For example, assume that Laurel's management has a target net income of €250,000. **Illustration 6.4** shows the required sales in units to achieve its target net income.

(Fixed Costs + Target Net Income)	÷	Unit Contribution Margin	=	Sales in Units
(€200,000 + €250,000)	÷	€200	=	2,250 units

ILLUSTRATION 6.4 | Target net income in units

Illustration 6.5 uses the contribution margin ratio to compute the required sales in euros.

(Fixed Costs + Target Net Income)	÷	Contribution Margin Ratio	=	Sales in Euros
(€200,000 + €250,000)	÷	.40	=	€1,125,000

ILLUSTRATION 6.5 | **Target net income in euros**

In order to achieve net income of €250,000, Laurel has to sell 2,250 tablets, for a total price of €1,125,000.

Margin of Safety

Another measure managers use to assess profitability is the margin of safety.

- The **margin of safety** tells us **how far sales can drop** before the company will be operating at a loss.
- Managers like to have a sense of how much cushion they have between their current situation and operating at a loss.
- The margin of safety can be expressed in euros or as a ratio.

In Illustration 6.1, for example, Laurel reported sales of €800,000. At that sales level, its margin of safety in euros and as a ratio are as shown in **Illustrations 6.6** and 6.7.

Actual (Expected) Sales	−	Break-Even Sales	=	Margin of Safety in Euros
€800,000	−	€500,000	=	€300,000

ILLUSTRATION 6.6 | **Margin of safety in euros**

As **Illustration 6.7** indicates (as does Illustration 6.6), Laurel's sales could drop by €300,000, or 37.5%, before the company would operate at a loss.

Margin of Safety in Euros	÷	Actual (Expected) Sales	=	Margin of Safety as a Ratio
€300,000	÷	€800,000	=	37.5%

ILLUSTRATION 6.7 | **Margin of safety as a ratio**

CVP and Changes in the Business Environment

To better understand how CVP analysis works, let's look at three independent cases that might occur at Laurel Electronics. Each case uses the original tablet sales and cost data, shown in **Illustration 6.8**.

Unit selling price	€500
Unit variable costs	€300
Total fixed costs	€200,000
Break-even sales	€500,000 or 1,000 units

ILLUSTRATION 6.8 | **Original tablet sales and cost data**

Case I

A competitor is offering a 10% discount on the selling price of its tablets. Management must decide whether to offer a similar discount.

Question: What effect will a 10% discount on selling price have on the break-even point for tablets?

Answer: A 10% discount on selling price reduces the unit selling price to €450 [€500 − (€500 × 10%)]. Unit variable costs remain unchanged at €300. Thus, the unit contribution margin is €150 (€450 − €300). Assuming no change in fixed costs, break-even sales are 1,333 units, computed as shown in **Illustration 6.9**.

Fixed Costs	÷	Unit Contribution Margin	=	Break-Even Sales
€200,000	÷	€150	=	1,333 units (rounded)

ILLUSTRATION 6.9 | Computation of break-even sales in units

For Laurel, this change requires monthly sales to increase by 333 units, or 33⅓%, in order to break even. In reaching a conclusion about offering a 10% discount to customers, management must determine how likely it is to achieve the increased sales. Also, management should estimate the possible loss of sales if the competitor's discount price is not matched.

Case II

To meet the threat of foreign competition, management invests in new robotic equipment that will lower the amount of direct labor required to make tablets. The company estimates that total fixed costs will increase by 30% and that unit variable costs will decrease by 30%.

Question: What effect will the new equipment have on the sales volume required to break even?

Answer: Total fixed costs become €260,000 [€200,000 + (€200,000 × 30%)]. The unit variable costs become €210 [€300 − (€300 × 30%)]. Thus, the unit contribution margin is €290 (€500 − €210). The new break-even point is approximately 897 units, computed as shown in **Illustration 6.10**.

Fixed Costs	÷	Unit Contribution Margin	=	Break-Even Sales
€260,000	÷	(€500 − €210)	=	897 units (rounded)

ILLUSTRATION 6.10 | Computation of break-even sales in units

These changes appear to be advantageous for Laurel. The break-even point is reduced by 103 units (1,000 − 897).

Case III

Laurel's principal supplier of raw materials has just announced a price increase. The higher cost is expected to increase the unit variable costs of tablets by €25. Management decides that it does not want to increase the selling price of the tablets. It plans a cost-cutting program that will save €17,500 in fixed costs per month. Laurel is currently realizing monthly net income of €80,000 on sales of 1,400 tablets.

Question: What increase in units sold will be needed to maintain the same level of net income?

Answer: The unit variable costs increase to €325 (€300 + €25). Fixed costs are reduced to €182,500 (€200,000 − €17,500). Because of the change in variable costs, the unit contribution margin becomes €175 (€500 − €325). **Illustration 6.11** shows the computation of the required number of units sold to achieve the target net income.

(Fixed Costs + Target Net Income)	÷	Unit Contribution Margin	=	Sales in Units
(€182,500 + €80,000)	÷	€175	=	1,500

ILLUSTRATION 6.11 | Computation of required sales

To achieve the required sales, Laurel Electronics will have to sell 1,500 tablets, an increase of 100 units. If this does not seem to be a reasonable expectation, management will either have to make further cost reductions or accept less net income if the selling price remains unchanged.

We hope that the concepts reviewed in this section are now familiar to you. We are now ready to examine additional ways that companies use CVP analysis to assess profitability and to help in making effective business decisions.

MANAGEMENT INSIGHT — Amazon.com

Don't Just Look—Buy Something

Warchi/Getty Images

When analyzing an Internet business such as **Amazon.com** (USA), analysts closely watch the so-called "conversion rate." This rate is calculated by dividing the number of people who actually take a desired action at an Internet site (e.g., buy something) by the total number of people who visit the site. Average conversion rates are from 3% to 5%. A rate below 2% is poor, while a rate above 10% is great.

Conversion rates have an obvious effect on the break-even point. Suppose you spend $10,000 on your site, which then attracts 5,000 visitors. If you get a 2% conversion rate (100 purchases), your site costs $100 per purchase ($10,000 ÷ 100). A 4% conversion rate lowers your cost to $50 per transaction, and an 8% conversion rate gets you down to $25. One recent study estimates that the average conversion rate for e-commerce is 1.6% but that it can vary considerably. Other studies show that conversion rates increase if the site has an easy-to-use interface, fast-performing screens, a convenient ordering process, and advertising that is both clever and clear.

Sources: J. William Gurley, "The One Internet Metric That Really Counts," *Fortune* (March 6, 2000), p. 392; Milind Mody, "Chief Mentor: How Startups Can Win Customers Online," *Wall Street Journal* (May 11, 2011); and Neil Patel, "What Is a Good Conversion Rate? The Answer Might Surprise You," *The Daily Egg* (updated October 23, 2018).

Besides increasing their conversion rates, what steps can online merchants use to lower their break-even points? (Answer is available in the book's product page on www.wiley.com)

DO IT! 1 ▶ CVP Analysis

ACTION PLAN
- Apply the equation for the break-even point in sales units.
- Apply the equation for the break-even point in sales euros.
- Apply the equation for the margin of safety in euros.

Ramsay SpA reports the following operating results for the month of June.

Ramsay SpA
CVP Income Statement
For the Month Ended June 30, 2023

	Total	Per Unit	Percent of Sales
Sales (5,000 units)	€300,000	€60	100%
Variable costs	180,000	36	60
Contribution margin	120,000	€24	40%
Fixed expenses	100,000		
Net income	€ 20,000		

To increase net income, management is considering reducing the selling price by 10%, with no changes to unit variable costs or fixed costs. Management is confident that this change will increase unit sales by 25%.

Using the contribution margin technique, compute the break-even point in sales units and sales euros and the margin of safety in euros (a) assuming no changes to sales price or costs, and (b) assuming changes to sales price and volume as described above. (c) Comment on your findings.

Solution

a. Assuming no changes to sales price or costs:

Break-even point in sales units = 4,167 units (rounded) (€100,000 ÷ €24)

Break-even point in sales euros = €250,000 (€100,000 ÷ .40ᵃ)

Margin of safety in euros = €50,000 (€300,000 − €250,000)

ᵃ€24 ÷ €60

b. Assuming changes to sales price and volume:

Break-even point in sales units = 5,556 units (rounded) (€100,000 ÷ €18^b)

Break-even point in sales euros = €300,000 (€100,000 ÷ (€18 ÷ €54^c))

Margin of safety in euros = €37,500 (€337,500^d − €300,000)

^{b}€60 − (.10 × €60) − €36 = €18

^{c}€60 − (.10 × €60)

^{d}5,000 + (.25 × 5,000) = 6,250 units, 6,250 units × €54 = €337,500

c. The increase in the break-even point and the decrease in the margin of safety indicate that management should not implement the proposed change. The increase in sales volume will result in contribution margin of €112,500 (6,250 × €18), which is €7,500 (€120,000 − €112,500) less than the current amount.

Related exercise material: **BE6.3, BE6.4, BE6.5, BE6.6, DO IT! 6.1, E6.1, E6.2, E6.3, E6.4, and E6.5.**

SALES MIX AND BREAK-EVEN SALES

To this point, our discussion of CVP analysis has assumed that a company sells only one product. However, most companies sell multiple products.

LEARNING OBJECTIVE 2
Explain the term sales mix and its effects on break-even sales.

- When a company sells multiple products, it is important that management understands the financial implications of its sales mix.
- **Sales mix** is the relative percentage in which a company sells its products.

For example, suppose 80% of **Lenovo**'s (HKG) unit sales are printers and the other 20% are PCs. Its sales mix is 80% printers to 20% PCs.

Sales mix is important to managers because different products often have substantially different contribution margins. For example, **ISUZU**'s (JPN) SUVs and Taga pickup trucks have higher contribution margins compared to its economy cars. Similarly, first-class tickets sold by **British Airways** (GBR) provide substantially higher contribution margins than coach-class tickets.

Break-Even Sales in Units

Companies can compute break-even sales for a mix of two or more products by determining the **weighted-average unit contribution margin of all the products**. Returning to our example from Chapter 5, assume that Laurel Electronics sells not only tablets but high-definition TVs as well. Laurel sells its two products in the following amounts: 1,500 tablets and 500 TVs, for a total of 2,000 units. **Illustration 6.12** shows the sales mix, expressed as a percentage of the 2,000 total units sold.

Tablets	TVs
1,500 units ÷ 2,000 units = 75%	500 units ÷ 2,000 units = 25%

ILLUSTRATION 6.12 | Sales mix as a percentage of units sold

That is, 75% of the 2,000 units sold are tablets, and 25% of the 2,000 units sold are TVs.

Illustration 6.13 shows additional information related to Laurel. The unit contribution margin for tablets is €200; for TVs, it is €500. Laurel's fixed costs in total are €275,000.

Unit Data	Tablets	TVs
Selling price	€500	€1,000
Variable costs	300	500
Contribution margin	€200	€ 500
Sales mix—units	75%	25%
Fixed costs = €275,000		

ILLUSTRATION 6.13 | **Per unit data—sales mix**

To compute break-even for Laurel, we must determine the weighted-average unit contribution margin for the two products.

- We use the **weighted-average**, as opposed to a simple average, because Laurel sells three times as many tablets as TVs.
- As a result, in determining an average unit contribution margin, three times as much weight should be placed on the contribution margin of the tablets as on the TVs.

The weighted-average contribution margin for a sales mix of 75% tablets and 25% TVs is €275, which is computed as shown in **Illustration 6.14**.

Tablets				TVs				
(Unit Contribution Margin	×	Sales Mix Percentage)	+	(Unit Contribution Margin	×	Sales Mix Percentage)	=	Weighted-Average Unit Contribution Margin
(€200	×	.75)	+	(€500	×	.25)	=	€275

ILLUSTRATION 6.14 | **Weighted-average unit contribution margin**

Similar to our calculation in the single-product setting, we can compute the break-even point in sales units by dividing the fixed costs by the weighted-average unit contribution margin of €275. **Illustration 6.15** shows the computation of break-even sales in units for Laurel, assuming €275,000 of fixed costs.

Fixed Costs	÷	Weighted-Average Unit Contribution Margin	=	Break-Even Point in Sales Units
€275,000	÷	€275	=	1,000 units

ILLUSTRATION 6.15 | **Break-even point in sales units**

DECISION TOOLS

The break-even point in sales units helps managers determine how many units of each product need to be sold to avoid a loss.

Illustration 6.15 shows the break-even point for Laurel is 1,000 units—tablets and TVs combined (see **Decision Tools**). Management needs to know how many of the 1,000 units sold are tablets and how many are TVs. Applying the sales mix percentages that we computed previously of 75% for tablets and 25% for TVs, these 1,000 units would be comprised of 750 tablets (.75 × 1,000 units) and 250 TVs (.25 × 1,000). This is verified by the computations in **Illustration 6.16**, which shows that the total contribution margin is €275,000 when 1,000 units are sold. As required at the break-even point, this contribution margin equals the fixed costs of €275,000.

Product	Unit Sales	×	Unit Contribution Margin	=	Total Contribution Margin
Tablets	750	×	€200	=	€150,000
TVs	250	×	500	=	125,000
	1,000				€275,000

ILLUSTRATION 6.16 | **Break-even proof—sales units**

Management should continually review and update the company's sales mix.

- At any level of units sold, **net income will be greater if higher contribution margin units are sold rather than lower contribution margin units**.
- For Laurel, TVs produce a higher contribution margin.
- Consequently, if Laurel sells 700 tablets instead of 750, and 300 TVs instead of 250 (a sales mix of 70% tablets and 30% TVs), net income would be higher than in the current sales mix even though total units sold (1,000 units) are the same.

An analysis of these relationships shows that a shift from low-margin sales to high-margin sales may increase net income even though there is a decline in total units sold. Likewise, a shift from high- to low-margin sales may result in a decrease in net income even though there is an increase in total units sold.

> ### DATA ANALYTICS INSIGHT   Caesars Entertainment
>
>
>
> Maz Day/Shutterstock.com
>
> **Taking No Chances with Its Profits**
>
> To navigate in a constantly changing casino environment, many casinos rely heavily on data analytics to improve profitability. For example, **Caesars Entertainment** (USA) says it can trace and collect data on 85% of the dollars spent in its casinos. This helps the company optimize its sale mix while also gaining a precise understanding of its customer base.
>
> Optimizing the sales mix is vital in this business. In fact, data analytics provides evidence that refutes the popular view that casinos make significant profits from wealthy "high-rollers" losing big money at the gaming tables. Instead, it's the sales from food, beverages, lodging, and concerts that help the casinos rake in the money. Further, through data analysis, Caesars has determined that it gets 80% of its revenues and nearly 100% of its profits from "normal" as opposed to "high-roller" customers. With that in mind, the company can then also use data analytics to determine what types of incentives are the most effective in motivating targeted customer types to spend more money on specific goods and services. For Caesars, chance is limited to its gaming tables, not its profits.
>
> Source: Berbard Marr, *Big Data in Practice* (Hoboken, N.J.: John Wiley and Sons, 2016), pp. 181–187.
>
> **How does big data correct management's view on two misconceptions about where today's casinos make their money? (Answer is available in the book's product page on www.wiley.com)**

Break-Even Sales in Euros

The calculation of the break-even point presented for Laurel Electronics in the previous section works well if a company has only a *small number* of products. In contrast, consider **3M** (USA), the maker of Post-it Notes, which has more than 30,000 products. In order to calculate the break-even point for 3M using a weighted-average unit contribution margin, we would need to calculate 30,000 different unit contribution margins. That is not realistic.

- Therefore, for a company with many products, we calculate the break-even point in terms of sales euros (rather than units sold), using sales information for divisions or product lines (rather than individual products) (see **Decision Tools**).
- This requires that we compute both sales mix as a percentage of total euro sales (rather than units sold) and the contribution margin ratio (rather than unit contribution margin).

To illustrate, suppose that Kale Garden Supply has two divisions—Indoor Plants and Outdoor Plants. Each division has hundreds of different types of plants and plant-care products. **Illustration 6.17** provides the information necessary for determining the sales mix percentages for the two divisions of Kale Garden Supply.

> **DECISION TOOLS**
>
> The break-even point in sales euros helps managers determine the sales euros required from each division to avoid a loss.

	Indoor Plant Division	Percent of Sales	Outdoor Plant Division	Percent of Sales	Company Total	Percent of Sales
Sales	€ 200,000	100%	€ 800,000	100%	€1,000,000	100%
Variable costs	120,000	60	560,000	70	680,000	68
Contribution margin	€ 80,000	40%	€ 240,000	30%	€ 320,000	32%
Sales mix percentage (in sales euros) (Division sales ÷ Total sales)	$\frac{€\,200,000}{€1,000,000} = .20$		$\frac{€\,800,000}{€\,1,000,000} = .80$			

ILLUSTRATION 6.17 | **Cost-volume-profit data for Kale Garden Supply**

Illustration 6.18 shows the contribution margin ratio for each division (40% and 30%) and for the combined company (32%), which is computed by dividing the total contribution margin by total sales. (These amounts are also listed in Illustration 6.17.)

	Indoor Plant Division	Outdoor Plant Division	Company Total
Contribution margin ratio (Contribution margin ÷ Sales)	$\frac{€80,000}{€200,000} = .40$	$\frac{€240,000}{€800,000} = .30$	$\frac{€320,000}{€1,000,000} = .32$

ILLUSTRATION 6.18 | **Contribution margin ratio for each division**

Note that the contribution margin ratio of 32% for the total company is a weighted average of the individual contribution margin ratios of the two divisions (40% and 30%).

- To illustrate, in **Illustration 6.19** we multiply each division's contribution margin ratio by its sales mix percentage, based on sales euros, and then total these amounts.
- The calculation in Illustration 6.19 is useful because it enables us to determine how the break-even point changes when the sales mix changes.

Indoor Plant Division		Outdoor Plant Division		
(Contribution Margin Ratio × Sales Mix Percentage)	+	(Contribution Margin Ratio × Sales Mix Percentage)	=	Weighted-Average Contribution Margin Ratio
(.40 × .20)	+	(.30 × .80)	=	.32

ILLUSTRATION 6.19 | **Calculation of weighted-average contribution margin**

Kale Garden Supply's break-even point in sales euros is computed by dividing its fixed costs of €300,000 by the weighted-average contribution margin ratio of 32%, as shown in **Illustration 6.20**.

Fixed Costs	÷	Weighted-Average Contribution Margin Ratio	=	Break-Even Point in Sales Euros
€300,000	÷	.32	=	€937,500

ILLUSTRATION 6.20 | **Calculation of break-even point in sales euros**

This break-even point is based on the sales mix of 20% to 80%. We can determine the amount of sales contributed by each division by multiplying the sales mix percentage of each division by the total sales figure. Of the company's total break-even sales of €937,500, a total of €187,500 (.20 × €937,500) will come from the Indoor Plant Division, and €750,000 (.80 × €937,500) will come from the Outdoor Plant Division.

What would be the impact on the break-even point if a higher percentage of Kale Garden Supply's sales were to come from the Indoor Plant Division?

- Because the Indoor Plant Division enjoys a higher contribution margin ratio, this change in the sales mix would result in a higher weighted-average contribution margin ratio and consequently a lower break-even point in sales euros.
- For example, if the sales mix changes to 50% for the Indoor Plant Division and 50% for the Outdoor Plant Division, the weighted-average contribution margin ratio would be 35% [(.40 × .50) + (.30 × .50)]. The new, lower, break-even point is €857,143 (€300,000 ÷ .35).
- The opposite would occur if a higher percentage of sales were expected from the Outdoor Plant Division.

As you can see, the information provided using CVP analysis can help managers better understand the impact of sales mix on profitability.

SERVICE COMPANY INSIGHT   Falfish

Monty Rakusen/Cultura/Getty Images

Weatherproofing Profits

Seafood processor **Falfish** (GBR) saw its profit margin and bottom-line profit fall for the year ended March 31, 2016, even though the company experienced an increase in sales. This was the second year in a row that this had happened. Although the company continued to see savings in its production-processing initiatives, the change in sales mix, due to extreme winter storms, resulted in decreased overall gross profits margins. While sales rose 15% during the past year, cost of sales rose 20.2%. To combat these changes, the firm said its business strategy remains to maximize value from investments made over the past four years and focus on its key skill sets and sourcing capability, to support both U.K. and international customers. As a result, Falfish invested in a new subsidiary and a new joint venture to diversify its product range to help ensure the supply of seafood products.

Source: N. Ramsden, "Falfish Sees Profits Fall on Changed Product Mix," *Undercurrent News* (January 9, 2017).

When sales rose 15% and cost of sales rose 20.2%, did Falfish's contribution margin ratio increase or decrease? How did this change in the contribution margin ratio affect break-even sales? (Answer is available in the book's product page on www.wiley.com)

DO IT! 2 ▶ Sales Mix Break-Even

Manchester Bicycles International produces and sells three different types of mountain bikes. Information regarding the three models is shown below.

	Pro	Intermediate	Standard	Total
Units sold	5,000	10,000	25,000	40,000
Selling price	€800	€500	€350	
Variable costs	€500	€300	€250	

The company's total fixed costs to produce the bicycles are €7,500,000.

a. Determine the sales mix as a function of units sold for the three products.
b. Determine the weighted-average unit contribution margin.
c. Determine the total number of units that the company must sell to break even.
d. Determine the number of units of each model that the company must sell to break even.

Solution

a. The sales mix percentages as a function of units sold are:

Pro	Intermediate	Standard
$\frac{5,000}{40,000} = 12.5\%$	$\frac{10,000}{40,000} = 25\%$	$\frac{25,000}{40,000} = 62.5\%$

b. The weighted-average unit contribution margin is:

[.125 × (€800 − €500)] + [.25 × (€500 − €300)] + [.625 × (€350 − €250)] = €150

ACTION PLAN

- The sales mix is the relative percentage of each product sold in units.
- The weighted-average unit contribution margin is the sum of the unit contribution margins multiplied by the respective sales mix percentage.
- Determine the break-even point in sales units by dividing the fixed costs by the weighted-average unit contribution margin.
- Determine the number of units of each model to sell by multiplying the total break-even units by the respective sales mix percentage for each product.

c. The break-even point in sales units is:

$$\frac{€7,500,000}{€150} = 50,000 \text{ units}$$

d. The break-even units to sell for each product are:

Pro:	50,000 units × 12.5%	=	6,250 units
Intermediate:	50,000 units × 25%	=	12,500 units
Standard:	50,000 units × 62.5%	=	31,250 units
			50,000 units

Related exercise material: **BE6.7, BE6.8, BE6.9, BE6.10, DO IT! 6.2, E6.6, E6.7, E6.8, E6.9, and E6.10.**

SALES MIX WITH LIMITED RESOURCES

LEARNING OBJECTIVE 3
Determine sales mix when a company has limited resources.

In the previous discussion, we assumed a certain sales mix and then determined the break-even point given that sales mix. We now discuss how limited resources influence the sales-mix decision.

- All companies have resource limitations.
- The limited resource may be floor space in a retail department store, raw materials, direct labor hours, or machine capacity in a manufacturing company.
- When a company has limited resources, management must decide which products to make and sell in order to maximize net income (see **Decision Tools**).

DECISION TOOLS
Determining the unit contribution margin of limited resource helps managers decide which product should receive any additional capacity of the limited resource.

To illustrate, recall that Laurel Electronics manufactures tablet computers and TVs. The limiting resource is machine capacity, which is 3,600 hours per month. **Illustration 6.21** shows that each TV requires more than three times as many machine hours as one tablet.

	Tablets	TVs
Unit contribution margin	€200	€500
Machine hours required per unit	.2	.625

ILLUSTRATION 6.21 | Contribution margin and machine hours

The TVs may appear to be more profitable since they have a higher unit contribution margin (€500) than the tablets (€200). However, the tablets take fewer machine hours to produce than the TVs.

- Therefore, it is necessary to find the **contribution margin per unit of limited resource**—in this case, contribution margin per machine hour (see **Helpful Hint**).
- This is obtained by dividing the unit contribution margin of each product by the number of units of the limited resource required for each product, as shown in **Illustration 6.22**.

HELPFUL HINT
CM alone is not enough to make this decision. The key factor is CM per unit of limited resource.

	Tablets	TVs
Unit contribution margin (a)	€ 200	€500
Machine hours required (b)	0.2	0.625
Contribution margin per unit of limited resource [(a) ÷ (b)]	€1,000	€800

ILLUSTRATION 6.22 | Contribution margin per unit of limited resource

The computation shows that the tablets have a higher contribution margin per unit of limited resource. This would suggest that, given sufficient demand for tablets, Laurel should shift the sales mix to produce more tablets or increase machine capacity.

As indicated in Illustration 6.22, the constraint for the production of the TVs is the number of machine hours available to produce them.

- In addressing this problem, we have taken the limited number of machine hours as a given and have attempted to maximize the contribution margin given the constraint.
- One question that Laurel should ask, however, is whether this constraint can be reduced or eliminated.
- If Laurel is able to increase machine capacity from 3,600 hours to 4,200 hours, the additional 600 hours could be used to produce either the tablets or TVs.

The total contribution margin that results from producing more tablets versus more TVs is found by multiplying the additional machine hours by the contribution margin per unit of limited resource, as shown in **Illustration 6.23**.

	Tablets	TVs
Machine hours (a)	600	600
Contribution margin per unit of limited resource (b)	€ 1,000	€ 800
Contribution margin [(a) × (b)]	**€600,000**	**€480,000**

ILLUSTRATION 6.23 | Incremental analysis—computation of total contribution margin

From this analysis, we can see that to maximize net income, all of the increased capacity should be used to make and sell the tablets (assuming sufficient demand exists for the tablets).

Laurel's manufacturing constraint might be due to a bottleneck in production or to poorly trained machine operators.

- In addition to finding ways to solve those problems, the company should consider other possible solutions, such as outsourcing part of the production, acquiring additional new equipment (discussed in Chapter 12), or striving to eliminate any non–value-added activities (see Chapter 4).
- As discussed in Chapter 1, this approach is referred to as the **theory of constraints**, which is a specific approach used to identify and manage constraints in order to achieve the company's goals.
- According to this theory, a company must continually identify its constraints and find ways to reduce or eliminate them, where appropriate.

MANAGEMENT INSIGHT   Aurobindo Pharma

Generic Drugs Boost Financial Health

smartboy 10/Getty Images

Aurobindo Pharma (IND) is among the top five listed pharmaceutical companies in India. The company met investor expectations for the first quarter of 2016–2017, indicating that revenue growth was 14% higher than the same time a year earlier, with net profit increasing by 24% and a strong contribution margin. Between 2012–2013 and 2015–2016, its revenue and net profit reported a compound annual growth rate of 33% and 89%, respectively.

Approximately 90% of Aurobindo's sales come from the international markets, spread across 150 countries, with the majority from the United States and Europe. Since the penetration of generic drugs is low in the European countries of France, Spain, and Italy, Aurobindo sees this as a good opportunity and is also focusing on the emerging markets of Brazil, South Africa, Ukraine, and Mexico. By setting up a plant in Brazil, Aurobindo plans to improve its profit margin as a result of this change in sales mix and penetration through local manufacturing facilities.

Source: N. Nathan, "Improved Margins, Better Sales Mix Make Aurobindo Pharma Stock Analysts' Top Pick," *Economic Times* (September 5, 2016).

If Aurobindo Pharma's sales mix is trending toward a larger percentage of generic drugs, do the generics have a higher or lower contribution margin ratio than other product lines? (Answer is available in the book's product page on www.wiley.com)

DO IT! 3 ▶ Sales Mix with Limited Resources

Mount Hebron NV manufactures and sells three different types of high-quality sealed ball bearings for mountain bike wheels. The bearings vary in terms of their quality specifications—primarily with respect to their smoothness and roundness. They are referred to as Fine, Extra-Fine, and Super-Fine bearings. Machine time is limited. More machine time is required to manufacture the Extra-Fine and Super-Fine bearings. The following information is also provided.

	Product		
	Fine	Extra-Fine	Super-Fine
Selling price	€6.00	€10.00	€16.00
Variable costs and expenses	4.00	6.50	11.00
Contribution margin	€2.00	€ 3.50	€ 5.00
Machine hours required	0.02	0.04	0.08

ACTION PLAN
- Calculate the contribution margin per unit of limited resource for each product.
- Apply the equation for the contribution margin per unit of limited resource.
- To maximize net income, shift sales mix to the product with the highest contribution margin per unit of limited resource.

a. Ignoring the machine time constraint, what strategy would appear optimal?
b. What is the contribution margin per unit of limited resource for each type of bearing?
c. If additional machine time could be obtained, how should the additional capacity be used?

Solution

a. The Super-Fine bearings have the highest unit contribution margin. Thus, ignoring any manufacturing constraints, it would appear that the company should shift toward production of more Super-Fine units.

b. The contribution margin per unit of limited resource (machine hours) is calculated as:

$$\frac{\text{Unit contribution margin}}{\text{Limited resource consumed per unit}}$$

Fine: $\frac{€2}{.02} = €100$ Extra-Fine: $\frac{€3.5}{.04} = €87.50$ Super-Fine: $\frac{€5}{.08} = €62.50$

c. The Fine bearings have the highest contribution margin per unit of limited resource (machine time) even though they have the lowest unit contribution margin. Given the resource constraint, any additional capacity should be used to make Fine bearings, assuming that the market can absorb additional units.

Related exercise material: **BE6.11, BE6.12, DO IT! 6.3, E6.11, E6.12, and E6.13**.

OPERATING LEVERAGE AND PROFITABILITY

LEARNING OBJECTIVE 4
Indicate how operating leverage affects profitability.

Cost structure refers to the relative proportion of fixed versus variable costs that a company incurs. Cost structure can have a significant effect on profitability. For example, computer equipment manufacturer **Cisco Systems** (USA) substantially reduced its fixed costs by outsourcing much of its production. By minimizing its fixed costs, Cisco is now less susceptible to economic swings. However, as the following discussion shows, its reduced reliance on fixed costs reduced its ability to experience the incredible profitability that it used to have during economic booms.

The choice of cost structure should be carefully considered as there are many ways that companies can influence it.

- By acquiring sophisticated robotic equipment, many companies have reduced their use of manual labor.
- Similarly, by investing heavily in computers and online technology, some brokerage firms, such as **E*Trade** (USA), have reduced their reliance on human brokers. In so doing, they have increased their reliance on fixed costs (through depreciation on the robotic equipment or computer equipment) and reduced their reliance on variable costs (the variable employee labor cost).

- Alternatively, by outsourcing their production, some companies have reduced their fixed costs and increased their variable costs. **Nike** (USA), for example, does very little manufacturing but instead outsources the manufacture of nearly all of its shoes and clothing. It has consequently converted many of its fixed costs into variable costs and therefore changed its cost structure.

Consider the following example of Laurel Electronics and one of its competitors, New Wave Company. Both make consumer electronics. Laurel uses a traditional, labor-intensive manufacturing process. New Wave has invested in a completely automated system. The factory employees are involved only in setting up, adjusting, and maintaining the machinery. **Illustration 6.24** shows CVP income statements for each company.

	Laurel Electronics	Percent of Sales	New Wave Company	Percent of Sales
Sales	€800,000	100%	€800,000	100%
Variable costs	480,000	60	160,000	20
Contribution margin	320,000	40%	640,000	80%
Fixed costs	200,000		520,000	
Net income	€120,000		€120,000	

ILLUSTRATION 6.24 | CVP income statements for two companies

Both companies have the same sales and the same net income.

- But, notice that Laurel has much higher variable costs (€480,000) than New Wave (€160,000).
- Conversely, Laurel has much lower fixed costs (€200,000) than New Wave (€520,000).
- Because of these differences in cost structures, Laurel and New Wave differ greatly in how their net income is affected by sales increases or decreases.

Let's evaluate the impact of cost structure on the profitability of the two companies.

Effect on Contribution Margin Ratio

First let's look at the contribution margin ratio. **Illustration 6.25** shows the computation of the contribution margin ratio for each company (which can also be seen in Illustration 6.24).

	Contribution Margin	÷	Sales	=	Contribution Margin Ratio
Laurel Electronics	€320,000	÷	€800,000	=	40%
New Wave	€640,000	÷	€800,000	=	80%

ILLUSTRATION 6.25 | Contribution margin ratio for two companies

Because of its lower variable costs, New Wave has a contribution margin ratio of 80% versus only 40% for Laurel Electronics.

- That means that with every euro of sales, New Wave generates 80 cents of contribution margin (and thus an 80-cent increase in net income), versus only 40 cents for Laurel.
- However, it also means that for every euro that sales decline, New Wave loses 80 cents in net income, whereas Laurel will lose only 40 cents.
- New Wave's cost structure, which relies more heavily on fixed costs, makes its net income more sensitive to changes in sales revenue.

Effect on Break-Even Point

The difference in cost structure also affects the break-even point. The break-even point for each company is calculated in **Illustration 6.26**.

	Fixed Costs	÷	Contribution Margin Ratio	=	Break-Even Point in Sales Euros
Laurel Electronics	€200,000	÷	.40	=	€500,000
New Wave	€520,000	÷	.80	=	€650,000

ILLUSTRATION 6.26 | **Computation of break-even point for two companies**

New Wave's break-even point is €650,000 versus only €500,000 for Laurel Electronics. That means that New Wave needs to generate €150,000 (€650,000 − €500,000) more in sales than Laurel before it breaks even. This higher break-even point makes New Wave riskier than Laurel. A company cannot survive for very long unless it at least breaks even.

Effect on Margin of Safety Ratio

We can also evaluate the relative impact that changes in sales would have on the two companies by computing the margin of safety ratio. **Illustration 6.27** shows the computation of the **margin of safety ratio** for the two companies.

	(Actual Sales	−	Break-Even Sales)	÷	Actual Sales	=	Margin of Safety Ratio
Laurel Electronics	(€800,000	−	€500,000)	÷	€800,000	=	38%
New Wave	(€800,000	−	€650,000)	÷	€800,000	=	19%

ILLUSTRATION 6.27 | **Computation of margin of safety ratio for two companies**

The difference in the margin of safety ratio reflects the difference in risk between the two companies. Laurel Electronics could sustain a 38% decline in sales before it would be operating at a loss. New Wave could sustain only a 19% decline in sales before it would be operating "in the red."

Operating Leverage

Operating leverage refers to the extent to which a company's net income reacts to a given change in sales (see **Decision Tools**).

> **DECISION TOOLS**
>
> Calculating the degree of operating leverage helps managers determine how sensitive the company's net income is to changes in sales.

- Companies that have higher fixed costs relative to variable costs have higher operating leverage.
- When a company's sales revenue is increasing, high operating leverage is a good thing because it means that profits will increase rapidly.
- But when sales are declining, too much operating leverage can have devastating consequences.

Degree of Operating Leverage

How can we compare operating leverage between two companies?

- The **degree of operating leverage** provides a measure of a company's potential for volatile earnings and can be used to compare companies.
- Degree of operating leverage is computed by dividing contribution margin by net income.

This equation is presented in **Illustration 6.28** and applied to our two manufacturers of tablets.

	Contribution Margin	÷	Net Income	=	Degree of Operating Leverage
Laurel Electronics	€320,000	÷	€120,000	=	2.67
New Wave	€640,000	÷	€120,000	=	5.33

ILLUSTRATION 6.28 | **Computation of degree of operating leverage**

Laurel Electronics' degree of operating leverage is 2.67 versus 5.33 for New Wave. Its higher degree of operating leverage means that New Wave's net income reacts more to changes in sales. In fact, New Wave's earnings would go up (or down) by two times (5.33 ÷ 2.67 = 2.00) as much as Laurel Electronics' with an equal increase (or decrease) in sales. For example, suppose both companies experience a 10% decrease in sales. Laurel's net income will decrease by 26.7% (2.67 × 10%), while New Wave's will decrease by 53.3% (5.33 × 10%). Thus, New Wave's higher operating leverage exposes it to greater earnings volatility risk.

You should be careful not to conclude from this analysis that a cost structure that relies on higher fixed costs, and consequently has higher operating leverage, is necessarily bad.

- Internet music companies **Pandora** (USA) and **Spotify** (SWE) have very little operating leverage. Some have suggested that they have limited potential for net income growth. When their revenues grow, their variable costs (very significant fees for the right to use music) grow proportionally.
- When used carefully, operating leverage can add considerably to a company's profitability.

For example, computer equipment manufacturer **Komag** (USA) enjoyed a 66% increase in net income when its sales increased by only 8%. As one commentator noted, "Komag's fourth quarter illustrates the company's significant operating leverage; a small increase in sales leads to a big profit rise." However, as our illustration demonstrates, increased reliance on fixed costs increases a company's risk.

PEOPLE, PLANET, AND PROFIT INSIGHT

Solar Power Generates More Than Electricity

Alessandro2802/ Getty Images

When homeowners first began to put solar panels on their homes, electric utility companies encouraged them to do so. The power companies saw this as an opportunity to reduce their fixed investment in power-generating equipment. When a homeowner generated more electricity than the household needed, the extra electricity went into the grid, and the homeowner was compensated by the power company. It seemed to be a win-win situation.

But, now that solar power has become so widespread, power companies are concerned that they might have excess power-generating capacity and that they won't be able to charge customers enough to cover their fixed costs. So the power companies have been reducing the amount that they pay homeowners for excess electricity generated by solar power. They are arguing that a larger portion of customers' bills should be fixed charges, as opposed to charges that vary with use. The power companies say that since so much of their costs are fixed costs, they need a dependable income stream to cover their fixed costs. Environmentalists worry that if a large percentage of a customer's bill is fixed (that is, doesn't vary with usage), then the customer won't have an incentive to conserve energy.

How do the homeowner solar panels represent a form of outsourcing? At what point did this create a dilemma for power companies? (Answer is available in the book's product page on www.wiley.com)

DO IT! 4 ▶ Operating Leverage

Rexfield Ltd., a company specializing in crime scene investigations, is contemplating an investment in automated mass-spectrometers. Its current process relies on a high number of lab technicians. The new equipment would employ a computerized expert system. The company's CEO has requested a comparison of the old technology versus the new technology. The accounting department has prepared the following CVP income statements for use in your analysis.

	CSI Equipment	
	Old	New
Sales	€2,000,000	€2,000,000
Variable costs	1,400,000	600,000
Contribution margin	600,000	1,400,000
Fixed costs	400,000	1,200,000
Net income	€ 200,000	€ 200,000

ACTION PLAN
- Divide contribution margin by net income to determine degree of operating leverage.
- A higher degree of operating leverage will result in a greater change in net income with a given change in sales.

Use the information provided above to do the following:

a. Compute the degree of operating leverage for the company under each scenario.

b. Discuss your results.

Solution

a.

	Contribution Margin	÷	Net Income	=	Degree of Operating Leverage
Old	€600,000	÷	€200,000	=	3.00
New	€1,400,000	÷	€200,000	=	7.00

b. The degree of operating leverage measures the company's sensitivity to changes in sales. By switching to a cost structure dominated by fixed costs, the company would significantly increase its operating leverage. As a result, with a percentage change in sales, its percentage change in net income would be 2.33 (7.00 ÷ 3.00) times as much with the new technology as it would under the old.

Related exercise material: **BE6.13, BE6.14, BE6.15, DO IT! 6.4, E6.14, E6.15, and E6.16.**

USING THE DECISION TOOLS | Aldi

Aldi (DEU) faces many decisions where it needs to apply the decision tools learned in this chapter, such as determining its cost structure. For example, suppose that Aldi has been approached by a robotics company with a proposal to significantly automate one of its stores. All stocking of shelves and bagging of groceries would be done by robots. Customers would check out through self-service scanners and point-of-sale terminals. Any assistance would be provided by robots. Assume management has compiled the following comparative data for one average-sized store.

	Old	New
Sales	€3,600,000	€3,600,000
Variable costs	2,800,000	2,000,000
Contribution margin	800,000	1,600,000
Fixed costs	480,000	1,280,000
Net income	€ 320,000	€ 320,000

Instructions

Use the information provided above to do the following:

a. Compute the degree of operating leverage for the company under each scenario and discuss your results.

b. Compute the break-even sales and margin of safety ratio for the company under each scenario and discuss your results.

Solution

a.

	Contribution Margin	÷	Net Income	=	Degree of Operating Leverage
Old	€800,000	÷	€320,000	=	2.5
New	€1,600,000	÷	€320,000	=	5.0

The degree of operating leverage measures the company's sensitivity to changes in sales. By switching to a cost structure with higher fixed costs, Aldi would significantly increase its operating leverage. As a result, with a percentage change in sales, its percentage change in net income would be two times as much (5 ÷ 2.5) under the new structure as it would under the old.

b. To compute the break-even sales, we first need to compute the contribution margin ratio under each scenario. Under the old structure, the contribution margin ratio would be .22 (€800,000 ÷ €3,600,000), and under the new it would be .44 (€1,600,000 ÷ €3,600,000).

	Fixed Costs	÷	Contribution Margin Ratio	=	Break-Even Sales
Old	€480,000	÷	.22	=	€2,181,818
New	€1,280,000	÷	.44	=	€2,909,091

Because Aldi's fixed costs would be substantially higher under the new cost structure, its break-even point would increase significantly, from €2,181,818 to €2,909,091. A higher break-even point is riskier because it means that the company must generate higher sales to be profitable.

The margin of safety ratio tells how far sales can fall before Aldi is operating at a loss.

	(Actual Sales	−	Break-Even Sales)	÷	Actual Sales	=	Margin of Safety Ratio
Old	(€3,600,000	−	€2,181,818)	÷	€3,600,000	=	.39
New	(€3,600,000	−	€2,909,091)	÷	€3,600,000	=	.19

Under the old structure, sales could fall by 39% before the company would be operating at a loss. Under the new structure, sales could fall by only 19%.

On the one hand, grocery store sales are more stable than most products. Sales are less inclined to fluctuate with changes in the economy. However, if Aldi's sales are subject to significant swings, then changes in its cost structure could significantly affect its risk profile.

Appendix 6A ABSORPTION COSTING VERSUS VARIABLE COSTING

In earlier chapters, we classified both variable and fixed manufacturing costs as product costs. In job order costing, for example, a job is assigned the costs of direct materials, direct labor, and **both** variable and fixed manufacturing overhead.

- This costing approach is referred to as **full** or **absorption costing**.
- It is so named because all manufacturing costs are charged to, or absorbed by, the product.
- Absorption costing is the approach required for external reporting under accounting standards.

LEARNING OBJECTIVE *5
Explain the differences between absorption costing and variable costing.

In this appendix, we now present an alternative approach, **variable costing**, which is consistent with the cost-volume-profit material presented in Chapters 5 and 6, and therefore readily supports CVP analysis.

- Under **variable costing**, only direct materials, direct labor, and variable manufacturing overhead costs are considered product costs.
- Companies using variable costing recognize fixed manufacturing overhead costs as period costs (expenses) when incurred.
- Companies may not use variable costing for external financial reports because accounting standards require that fixed manufacturing overhead be accounted for as a product cost.

Illustration 6A.1 shows the difference between absorption costing and variable costing. Under both absorption and variable costing, selling and administrative expenses are period costs.

ILLUSTRATION 6A.1 | Difference between absorption costing and variable costing

Example Comparing Absorption Costing with Variable Costing

To illustrate absorption and variable costing, assume that Premium Products manufactures a polyurethane sealant, called Fix-It, for car windshields. Relevant data for Fix-It in January 2023, the first month of production, are shown in **Illustration 6A.2**.

Selling price	€20 per unit.
Units	Produced 30,000; sold 20,000; beginning inventory zero.
Unit variable costs	Manufacturing €9 (direct materials €5, direct labor €3, and variable overhead €1).
	Selling and administrative expenses €2.
Fixed costs	Manufacturing overhead €120,000.
	Selling and administrative expenses €15,000.

ILLUSTRATION 6A.2 | Sealant sales and cost data for Premium Products

The per unit manufacturing cost under each costing approach is computed in **Illustration 6A.3**.

Type of Cost	Absorption Costing	Variable Costing
Direct materials	€ 5	€5
Direct labor	3	3
Variable manufacturing overhead	1	1
Fixed manufacturing overhead (€120,000 ÷ 30,000 units produced)	4	0
Manufacturing cost per unit	**€13**	**€9**

ILLUSTRATION 6A.3 | Computation of per unit manufacturing cost

The manufacturing cost per unit is €4 higher (€13 − €9) for absorption costing.

- This occurs because fixed manufacturing overhead costs are a product cost under absorption costing.
- Under variable costing, they are, instead, a period cost, and so they are expensed.

Based on these data, each unit sold and each unit remaining in inventory on the balance sheet is costed under absorption costing at €13 and under variable costing at €9.

Absorption Costing Example

Illustration 6A.4 shows the income statement for Premium Products using absorption costing. It shows that cost of goods manufactured is €390,000, computed by multiplying the 30,000 units produced times the manufacturing cost per unit of €13 (see Illustration 6A.3). Cost of goods sold is €260,000, after subtracting ending inventory of €130,000.

- Notice that the ending inventory of €130,000 includes fixed manufacturing overhead costs of €40,000 (10,000 × €4).
- Under absorption costing, €40,000 of the fixed manufacturing overhead is deferred to a future period as part of the cost of ending inventory.
- We will see that this is the primary difference between absorption costing and variable costing.

Premium Products
Income Statement
For the Month Ended January 31, 2023
Absorption Costing

Sales (20,000 units × €20)		€400,000
Cost of goods sold		
Inventory, January 1	€ -0-	
Cost of goods manufactured (30,000 units × €13)	390,000*	
Cost of goods available for sale	390,000	
Less: Inventory, January 31 (10,000 units × €13)	130,000	
Cost of goods sold (20,000 units × €13)		260,000
Gross profit		140,000
Variable selling and administrative expenses		
(20,000 × €2)	40,000	
Fixed selling and administrative expenses	15,000	55,000
Net income		**€ 85,000**

*(30,000 units × €9) variable + €120,000 fixed

ILLUSTRATION 6A.4 | Absorption costing income statement

Variable Costing Example

As **Illustration 6A.5** shows, companies use the cost-volume-profit format in preparing a variable costing income statement. The variable manufacturing cost of €270,000 is computed by multiplying the 30,000 units produced times variable manufacturing cost of €9 per unit (see Illustration 6A.3). As in absorption costing, both variable and fixed selling and administrative expenses are treated as period costs.

Premium Products
Income Statement
For the Month Ended January 31, 2023
Variable Costing

Sales (20,000 units × €20)		€400,000
Variable cost of goods sold		
Inventory, January 1	€ -0-	
Variable cost of goods manufactured		
(30,000 units × €9)	270,000	
Variable cost of goods available for sale	270,000	
Less: Inventory, January 31 (10,000 units × €9)	90,000	
Variable cost of goods sold	180,000	
Variable selling and administrative expenses		
(20,000 units × €2)	40,000	220,000
Contribution margin		180,000
Fixed manufacturing overhead	120,000	
Fixed selling and administrative expenses	15,000	135,000
Net income		**€ 45,000**

ILLUSTRATION 6A.5 | Variable costing income statement

There is one primary difference between variable and absorption costing: Under variable costing, companies charge the fixed manufacturing overhead as an expense in the current period.

- Fixed manufacturing overhead costs of the current period, therefore, are not deferred to future periods through the ending inventory.
- As a result, absorption costing will show a **higher net income number** than variable costing **whenever units produced exceed units sold**.

This difference can be seen in the income statements in Illustrations 6A.4 and 6A.5. Note the difference in the computation of the January 31 ending inventory: €9 per unit times 10,000 units in Illustration 6A.5, €13 per unit times 10,000 units in Illustration 6A.4. This translates into a €40,000 difference in the ending inventories (€130,000 under absorption costing versus €90,000 under variable costing), which results in the €40,000 difference in net income. Under absorption costing, expensing €40,000 of the fixed overhead costs (10,000 units × €4) has been deferred (delayed) to a future period as part of inventory on the balance sheet. In contrast, under variable costing, all fixed manufacturing costs are expensed in the current period.

- As shown, when units produced exceed units sold, income under absorption costing is *higher*.
- When units produced are less than units sold, income under absorption costing is *lower*.
- When units produced and sold are the same, net income will be *equal* under the two costing approaches. In this case, there is no increase in ending inventory. So fixed overhead costs of the current period are not deferred to future periods through the ending inventory.

Net Income Effects

To further illustrate the concepts underlying absorption and variable costing, we will look at an extended example using OverSky Ltd., a manufacturer of small flying drones. We assume that production volume stays the same each year over the three-year period, but the number of units sold varies each year.

2022 Results

As indicated in **Illustration 6A.6**, the variable manufacturing cost per drone is €240,000, and the fixed manufacturing overhead cost per drone is €60,000 (assuming 10 drones). Total manufacturing cost per drone under absorption costing is therefore €300,000 (€240,000 + €60,000). OverSky also has variable selling and administrative expenses of €5,000 per drone. The fixed selling and administrative expenses are €80,000.

	2022	2023	2024
Volume information			
Drones in beginning inventory	0	0	2
Drones produced	10	10	10
Drones sold	10	8	12
Drones in ending inventory	0	2	0
Financial information			
Selling price per drone	€400,000		
Variable manufacturing cost per drone	€240,000		
Fixed manufacturing overhead for the year	€600,000		
Fixed manufacturing overhead per drone	€ 60,000 (€600,000 ÷ 10)		
Variable selling and administrative expenses per drone	€ 5,000		
Fixed selling and administrative expenses	€ 80,000		

ILLUSTRATION 6A.6 | Information for OverSky Ltd.

An absorption costing income statement for 2022 for OverSky Ltd. is shown in **Illustration 6A.7**.

OverSky Ltd.
Income Statement
For the Year Ended December 31, 2022
Absorption Costing

Sales (10 drones × €400,000)		€4,000,000
Cost of goods sold (10 drones × €300,000)		3,000,000
Gross profit		1,000,000
Variable selling and administrative expenses		
(10 drones × €5,000)	€50,000	
Fixed selling and administrative expenses	80,000	130,000
Net income		€ 870,000

ILLUSTRATION 6A.7 | Absorption costing income statement—2022

OverSky reports net income of €870,000 under absorption costing.

Under a variable costing system, the income statement follows a cost-volume-profit (CVP) format. In this case, the manufacturing cost is comprised solely of the variable manufacturing costs of €240,000 per drone. The entire amount of fixed manufacturing overhead costs of €600,000 for the year are expensed in 2022. As in absorption costing, the fixed and variable selling and administrative expenses are period costs expensed in 2022. A variable costing income statement for OverSky Ltd. for 2022 is shown in **Illustration 6A.8**.

OverSky Ltd.
Income Statement
For the Year Ended December 31, 2022
Variable Costing

Sales (10 drones × €400,000)		€4,000,000
Variable cost of goods sold		
(10 drones × €240,000)	€2,400,000	
Variable selling and administrative expenses		
(10 drones × €5,000)	50,000	2,450,000
Contribution margin		1,550,000
Fixed manufacturing overhead	600,000	
Fixed selling and administrative expenses	80,000	680,000
Net income		€ 870,000

ILLUSTRATION 6A.8 | Variable costing income statement—2022

As shown in Illustration 6A.8, the variable costing net income of €870,000 is the same as the absorption costing net income computed in Illustration 6A.7.

- **When the numbers of units produced and sold are the same, net income is equal under the two costing approaches.**
- Because no increase in ending inventory occurs, no fixed manufacturing overhead costs incurred in 2022 are deferred to future periods as part of ending inventory using absorption costing.

2023 Results

In 2023, OverSky produced 10 drones but sold only eight drones. As a result, there are two drones in ending inventory. The absorption costing income statement for 2023 is shown in **Illustration 6A.9**.

OverSky Ltd.
Income Statement
For the Year Ended December 31, 2023
Absorption Costing

Sales (8 drones × €400,000)		€3,200,000
Cost of goods sold (8 drones × €300,000)		2,400,000
Gross profit		800,000
Variable selling and administrative expenses		
(8 drones × €5,000)	€40,000	
Fixed selling and administrative expenses	80,000	120,000
Net income		€ 680,000

ILLUSTRATION 6A.9 | Absorption costing income statement—2023

Under absorption costing, the ending inventory of two drones is €600,000 (€300,000 × 2). As shown in Illustration 6A.6, each unit of ending inventory includes €60,000 (€600,000 ÷ 10) of fixed manufacturing overhead. Therefore, fixed manufacturing overhead costs of €120,000 (€60,000 × 2 drones) are deferred until a future period.

The variable costing income statement for 2023 is shown in **Illustration 6A.10**.

OverSky Ltd.
Income Statement
For the Year Ended December 31, 2023
Variable Costing

Sales (8 drones × €400,000)		€3,200,000
Variable cost of goods sold		
(8 drones × €240,000)	€1,920,000	
Variable selling and administrative expenses		
(8 drones × €5,000)	40,000	1,960,000
Contribution margin		1,240,000
Fixed manufacturing overhead	600,000	
Fixed selling and administrative expenses	80,000	680,000
Net income		€ 560,000

ILLUSTRATION 6A.10 | Variable costing income statement—2023

As shown in Illustrations 6A.9 and 6A.10, because the number of units produced (10) exceeds units sold (8), net income under absorption costing (€680,000) is higher than net income under variable costing (€560,000).

- The reason: The cost of the ending inventory is higher under absorption costing than under variable costing because fixed manufacturing overhead cost is retained in ending inventory.
- In 2023, under absorption costing, fixed manufacturing overhead of €120,000 is deferred and carried to future periods as part of inventory.
- Under variable costing, the €120,000 is expensed in the current period, and therefore the difference in the two net income numbers is €120,000 (€680,000 − €560,000).

2024 Results

In 2024, OverSky produced 10 drones and sold 12 (10 drones from the current year's production and 2 drones from the beginning inventory). As a result, there are no drones in ending inventory. The absorption costing income statement for 2024 is shown in **Illustration 6A.11**.

Fixed manufacturing costs of €720,000 (€60,000 × 12 drones) are expensed as part of cost of goods sold in 2024. This €720,000 includes €120,000 of fixed manufacturing costs incurred during 2023 and included in beginning inventory, plus €600,000 of fixed manufacturing costs incurred during 2024. Given this result for the absorption costing statement, what would you now expect the result to be under variable costing? Let's take a look.

OverSky Ltd.
Income Statement
For the Year Ended December 31, 2024
Absorption Costing

Sales (12 drones × €400,000)		€4,800,000
Cost of goods sold (12 drones × €300,000)		3,600,000
Gross profit		1,200,000
Variable selling and administrative expenses		
(12 drones × €5,000)	€60,000	
Fixed selling and administrative expenses	80,000	140,000
Net income		€1,060,000

ILLUSTRATION 6A.11 | **Absorption costing income statement—2024**

The variable costing income statement for 2024 is shown in **Illustration 6A.12**.

OverSky Ltd.
Income Statement
For the Year Ended December 31, 2024
Variable Costing

Sales (12 drones × €400,000)		€4,800,000
Variable cost of goods sold		
(12 drones × €240,000)	€2,880,000	
Variable selling and administrative expenses		
(12 drones × €5,000)	60,000	2,940,000
Contribution margin		1,860,000
Fixed manufacturing overhead	600,000	
Fixed selling and administrative expenses	80,000	680,000
Net income		€1,180,000

ILLUSTRATION 6A.12 | **Variable costing income statement—2024**

When drones produced (10) are less than drones sold (12), net income under absorption costing (€1,060,000) is less than net income under variable costing (€1,180,000).

- This difference of €120,000 (€1,180,000 − €1,060,000) results because €120,000 of fixed manufacturing overhead costs in beginning inventory are charged to 2024 under absorption costing, in addition to the €600,000 of fixed manufacturing overhead incurred during the current period.
- Under variable costing, there is no fixed manufacturing overhead cost in beginning or ending inventory.

Illustration 6A.13 summarizes the results of the three years.

	Net Income Under Two Costing Approaches		
	2022 Units Produced = Units Sold	2023 Units Produced > Units Sold	2024 Units Produced < Units Sold
Absorption costing	€870,000	€680,000	€1,060,000
Variable costing	870,000	560,000	1,180,000
Difference	€ –0–	€120,000	€ (120,000)

ILLUSTRATION 6A.13 | **Comparison of net income under two costing approaches**

This relationship between production and sales and its effect on net income under the two costing approaches is shown in **Illustration 6A.14**.

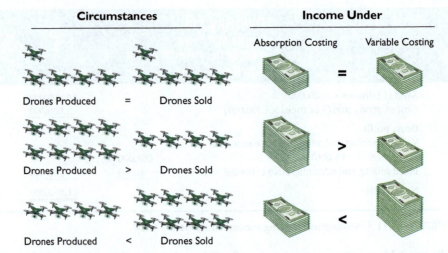

ILLUSTRATION 6A.14 | Summary of income effects under absorption costing and variable costing

Decision-Making Concerns

Accounting standards require that absorption costing be used for the costing of inventory for external reporting purposes.

- Net income measured under absorption costing is often used internally to evaluate performance, justify cost reductions, or evaluate new projects.
- Some companies, however, have recognized that net income calculated using absorption costing does not highlight differences between variable and fixed costs and may lead to poor business decisions. These companies use variable costing for internal reporting purposes.

The following discussion and example highlight a significant problem related to the use of absorption costing for decision-making purposes.

When production exceeds sales, absorption costing reports a higher net income than variable costing. The reason is that some fixed manufacturing costs are not expensed in the current period but are deferred to future periods as part of inventory. As a result, **management may be tempted to overproduce in a given period in order to increase net income**. Although net income will increase, this decision to overproduce may not be in the company's best interest.

- Suppose, for example, a division manager's compensation is based on the division's net income. In such a case, the manager may decide to meet the net income targets by producing more units than will be sold.
- While this overproduction may increase the manager's compensation, the buildup of inventories in the long run will lead to additional costs to the company.
- Variable costing avoids this situation because net income under variable costing is unaffected by changes in production levels, as the following illustration shows.

For example, say that Sheldon Kramer, a division manager of Star Enterprises, is under pressure to boost the performance of the Lighting Division in 2023. Unfortunately, recent profits have not met expectations. The expected sales for this year are 20,000 units. As he plans for the year, Sheldon has to decide whether to produce 20,000 or 30,000 units. **Illustration 6A.15** presents the facts available for the division.

Illustration 6A.16 shows the division's results based on the two possible levels of output under absorption costing.

If the Lighting Division produces and sells 20,000 units, its net income under absorption costing is €85,000. If it produces 30,000 units but sells only 20,000 units, its net income is €105,000. By producing 30,000 units, the division has inventory of 10,000 units. This excess inventory causes net income to increase €20,000 because €20,000 of fixed costs (10,000 units × €2) are not charged to the current year, but are deferred to future periods.

Beginning inventory	0
Expected sales in units	20,000
Selling price per unit	€15
Variable manufacturing cost per unit	€6
Fixed manufacturing overhead cost (total)	€60,000
Fixed manufacturing overhead costs per unit	
Based on 20,000 units produced	€3 per unit (€60,000 ÷ 20,000 units)
Based on 30,000 units produced	€2 per unit (€60,000 ÷ 30,000 units)
Total manufacturing cost per unit	
Based on 20,000 units produced	€9 per unit (€6 variable + €3 fixed)
Based on 30,000 units produced	€8 per unit (€6 variable + €2 fixed)
Selling and administrative expenses	
Variable selling and administrative expenses per unit	€1
Fixed selling and administrative expenses	€15,000

ILLUSTRATION 6A.15 | Variable costing income statement—2023

Lighting Division
Income Statement
For the Year Ended December 31, 2023
Absorption Costing

	20,000 Produced	30,000 Produced
Sales (20,000 units × €15)	€300,000	€300,000
Cost of goods sold	180,000*	160,000**
Gross profit	120,000	140,000
Variable selling and administrative expenses (20,000 units × €1)	20,000	20,000
Fixed selling and administrative expenses	15,000	15,000
Net income	€ 85,000	€105,000

*20,000 units × €9; see red content in Illustration 6A.15.
**20,000 units × €8; see red content in Illustration 6A.15.

ILLUSTRATION 6A.16 | Absorption costing income statement—2023

What do you think Sheldon Kramer might do in this situation?

- Given his concern about the profit numbers of the Lighting Division, he may be tempted to produce more units than are needed.
- Although this increased production will increase 2023 net income, it may be costly to the company in the long run because holding excess inventory is costly.

Now let's evaluate the same situation under variable costing. **Illustration 6A.17** shows a variable costing income statement for production at both 20,000 and 30,000 units, using the information from Illustration 6A.15.

From this example, we see that under variable costing, net income is not affected by the number of units produced. Net income is €85,000 whether the division produces 20,000 or 30,000 units. Why? Because fixed manufacturing overhead is treated as a period expense.

- Unlike absorption costing, no fixed manufacturing overhead is deferred through inventory buildup.
- Therefore, under variable costing, production does not increase income; sales do.
- As a result, if the company uses variable costing, managers like Sheldon Kramer cannot affect profitability by increasing production.

Lighting Division
Income Statement
For the Year Ended December 31, 2023
Variable Costing

	20,000 Produced	30,000 Produced
Sales (20,000 units × €15)	€300,000	€300,000
Variable cost of goods sold (20,000 units × €6)	120,000	120,000
Variable selling and administrative expenses (20,000 units × €1)	20,000	20,000
Contribution margin	160,000	160,000
Fixed manufacturing overhead	60,000	60,000
Fixed selling and administrative expenses	15,000	15,000
Net income	€ 85,000	€ 85,000

ILLUSTRATION 6A.17 | Variable costing income statement—2023

Potential Advantages of Variable Costing

Variable costing has a number of potential advantages relative to absorption costing:

1. Net income computed under variable costing is unaffected by changes in production levels. As a result, it is much easier to understand the impact of fixed and variable costs on the computation of net income when variable costing is used.

2. The use of variable costing is consistent with the cost-volume-profit material presented in Chapters 5 and 6 and therefore readily supports CVP analysis.

3. Net income computed under variable costing is closely tied to changes in sales levels (not production levels) and therefore provides a more realistic assessment of the company's success or failure during a period.

4. The presentation of fixed-cost and variable-cost components on the face of the variable costing income statement makes it easier to identify these costs and understand their effect on the business. Under absorption costing, the allocation of fixed costs to inventory makes it difficult to evaluate the impact of fixed costs on the company's results.

Companies that use just-in-time processing techniques to minimize their inventories will not have significant differences between absorption and variable costing net income.

DO IT! 5 ▶ Variable Costing

Francis Sports produces and sells cricket balls. The following costs are available for the year ended December 31, 2023. The company has no beginning inventory. In 2023, 8,000,000 units were produced, but only 7,500,000 units were sold. The unit selling price was €0.50 per ball. Costs and expenses were as follows:

Unit variable costs	
Direct materials	€0.10
Direct labor	0.05
Variable manufacturing overhead	0.08
Variable selling and administrative expenses	0.02
Annual fixed costs and expenses	
Manufacturing overhead	€500,000
Selling and administrative expenses	100,000

a. Compute the manufacturing cost of one unit of product using variable costing.
b. Prepare a 2023 income statement for Francis Sports using variable costing.

ACTION PLAN
- Recall that under variable costing, only variable manufacturing costs are treated as manufacturing (product) costs.
- Subtract all fixed costs, both manufacturing overhead and selling and administrative expenses, as period costs.

Solution

a. The cost of one unit of product under variable costing would be:

Direct materials	€0.10
Direct labor	0.05
Variable manufacturing overhead	0.08
	€0.23

b. The variable costing income statement would be as follows:

Francis Sports
Income Statement
For the Year Ended December 31, 2023
Variable Costing

Sales (7,500,000 × €0.50)		€3,750,000
Variable cost of goods sold (7,500,000 × €0.23)	€1,725,000	
Variable selling and administrative expenses (7,500,000 × .02)	150,000	1,875,000
Contribution margin		1,875,000
Fixed manufacturing overhead	500,000	
Fixed selling and administrative expenses	100,000	600,000
Net income		€1,275,000

Related exercise material: **BE6.16, BE6.17, BE6.18, BE6.19, E6.17, E6.18, and E6.19.**

REVIEW AND PRACTICE

Learning Objectives Review

LO 1 Apply basic CVP concepts.

The CVP income statement classifies costs and expenses as variable or fixed and reports contribution margin in the body of the statement. Contribution margin is the amount of revenue remaining after deducting variable costs. It can be expressed as a per unit amount or as a ratio. The break-even point in sales units is fixed costs divided by unit contribution margin. The break-even point in sales euros is fixed costs divided by the contribution margin ratio. These equations can also be used to determine sales units or sales euros needed to achieve target net income, simply by adding target net income to fixed costs before dividing by the contribution margin. Margin of safety indicates how much sales can decline before the company is operating at a loss. It can be expressed in euro terms or as a percentage.

LO 2 Explain the term sales mix and its effects on break-even sales.

Sales mix is the relative proportion in which each product is sold when a company sells more than one product. For a company with a small number of different products, break-even sales in units is determined by using the weighted-average unit contribution margin of all the products. If the company sells many different products, then calculating the break-even point using unit information is not practical. Instead, in a company with many products, break-even sales in euros is calculated using the weighted-average contribution margin ratio.

LO 3 Determine sales mix when a company has limited resources.

When a company has limited resources, it is necessary to find the contribution margin per unit of limited resource. This amount is then multiplied by the units of limited resource to determine which product maximizes net income.

LO 4 Indicate how operating leverage affects profitability.

Operating leverage refers to the degree to which a company's net income reacts to a change in sales. Operating leverage is determined by a company's relative use of fixed versus variable costs. Companies with high fixed costs relative to variable costs have high operating leverage. A company with high operating leverage experiences a sharp increase (decrease) in net income with a given increase (decrease) in sales. The degree of operating leverage is measured by dividing contribution margin by net income.

LO *5 Explain the differences between absorption costing and variable costing.

Under absorption costing, fixed manufacturing costs are product costs. Under variable costing, fixed manufacturing costs are period costs.

If production volume exceeds sales volume, net income under absorption costing will exceed net income under variable costing by the amount of fixed manufacturing costs included in ending inventory that results from units produced but not sold during the period. If production volume is less than sales volume, net income under absorption costing will be less than under variable costing by the amount of fixed manufacturing costs included in the units sold during the period that were not produced during the period.

The use of variable costing is consistent with cost-volume-profit analysis. Net income under variable costing is unaffected by changes in production levels. Instead, it is closely tied to changes in sales. The presentation of fixed costs in the variable costing approach makes it easier to identify fixed costs and to evaluate their impact on the company's profitability.

Decision Tools Review

Decision Checkpoints	Info Needed for Decision	Tool to Use for Decision	How to Evaluate Results
How many units of product A and product B do we need to sell to break even?	Fixed costs, weighted-average unit contribution margin, sales mix	Break-even point in sales units = $\dfrac{\text{Fixed costs}}{\text{Weighted-average unit contribution margin}}$	To determine number of units of products A and B, allocate total break-even units based on unit sales mix.
How many euros of sales are required from each division in order to break even?	Fixed costs, weighted-average contribution margin ratio, sales mix	Break-even point in sales euros = $\dfrac{\text{Fixed costs}}{\text{Weighted-average contribution margin ratio}}$	To determine the sales euros required from each division, allocate the total break-even sales using the sales revenue mix.
How many units of products A and B should we produce in light of a limited resource?	Unit contribution margin, limited resource required per unit	Contribution margin per unit of limited resource = $\dfrac{\text{Unit contribution margin}}{\text{Limited resource per unit}}$	Any additional capacity of limited resource should be applied toward the product with higher contribution margin per unit of limited resource.
How sensitive is the company's net income to changes in sales?	Contribution margin and net income	Degree of operating leverage = $\dfrac{\text{Contribution margin}}{\text{Net income}}$	Reports the change in net income that occurs with a given change in sales. A high degree of operating leverage means that the company's net income is very sensitive to changes in sales.

Glossary Review

*__Absorption costing__ A costing approach in which all manufacturing costs are charged to the product. (p. 6-19).

__Cost structure__ The relative proportion of fixed versus variable costs that a company incurs. (p. 6-14).

__Degree of operating leverage__ A measure of the extent to which a company's net income reacts to a change in sales. It is calculated by dividing contribution margin by net income. (p. 6-16).

__Operating leverage__ The extent to which a company's net income reacts to a change in sales. Operating leverage is determined by a company's relative use of fixed versus variable costs. (p. 6-16).

__Sales mix__ The relative percentage in which a company sells its multiple products. It can be calculated based on unit sales or sales revenue. (p. 6-7).

__Theory of constraints__ A specific approach used to identify and manage constraints in order to achieve the company's goals. (p. 6-13).

*__Variable costing__ A costing approach in which only variable manufacturing costs are product costs, and fixed manufacturing costs are period costs (expenses). (p. 6-19).

Practice Multiple-Choice Questions

1. (LO 1) Which one of the following is the format of a CVP income statement?

   a. Sales − Variable costs = Fixed costs + Net income.
   b. Sales − Fixed costs − Variable costs − Operating expenses = Net income.
   c. Sales − Cost of goods sold − Operating expenses = Net income.
   d. Sales − Variable costs − Fixed costs = Net income.

2. (LO 1) Croc Catchers calculates its contribution margin to be less than zero. Which statement is **true**?

   a. Its fixed costs are less than the unit variable costs.
   b. Its profits are greater than its total costs.
   c. The company should sell more units.
   d. Its selling price is less than its variable costs.

3. **(LO 1)** Which one of the following describes the break-even point?
   a. It is the point where total sales equal total variable plus total fixed costs.
   b. It is the point where the contribution margin equals zero.
   c. It is the point where total variable costs equal total fixed costs.
   d. It is the point where total sales equal total fixed costs.

4. **(LO 1)** The following information is available for Edward Company.

Sales	€350,000
Cost of goods sold	€120,000
Total fixed expenses	€60,000
Total variable expenses	€100,000

   Which amount would you find on Edward's CVP income statement?
   a. Contribution margin of €250,000.
   b. Contribution margin of €190,000.
   c. Gross profit of €230,000.
   d. Gross profit of €190,000.

5. **(LO 1)** Gabriel Group has fixed costs of £180,000 and unit variable costs of £8.50. It has a target income of £268,000. How many units must it sell at £12 per unit to achieve its target net income?
   a. 51,429 units.
   b. 128,000 units.
   c. 76,571 units.
   d. 21,176 units.

6. **(LO 1)** Lopez Corporation has fixed costs of $150,000 and unit variable costs of $9. If sales price per unit is $12, what is break-even sales in dollars?
   a. $200,000.
   b. $450,000.
   c. $480,000.
   d. $600,000.

7. **(LO 2)** Sales mix is:
   a. important to sales managers but not to accountants.
   b. easier to analyze on absorption costing income statements.
   c. a measure of the relative percentage of a company's variable costs to its fixed costs.
   d. a measure of the relative percentage in which a company's products are sold.

8. **(LO 2)** Net income will be:
   a. greater if more higher-contribution margin units are sold than lower-contribution margin units.
   b. greater if more lower-contribution margin units are sold than higher-contribution margin units.
   c. equal as long as total sales remain equal, regardless of which products are sold.
   d. unaffected by changes in the mix of products sold.

9. **(LO 3)** If the unit contribution margin is A$15 and it takes 3.0 machine hours to produce the unit, the contribution margin per unit of limited resource is:
   a. A$25.
   b. A$5.
   c. A$4.
   d. None of the answer choices are correct.

10. **(LO 3)** Jun Ltd. manufactures two products. Product X has a contribution margin of HK$260 and requires 4 hours of machine time. Product Y has a contribution margin of HK$140 and requires 2 hours of machine time. Assuming that machine time is limited to 3,000 hours, how should Jun allocate the machine time to maximize its income?
    a. Use 1,500 hours to produce X and 1,500 hours to produce Y.
    b. Use 2,250 hours to produce X and 750 hours to produce Y.
    c. Use 3,000 hours to produce only X.
    d. Use 3,000 hours to produce only Y.

11. **(LO 3)** When a company has a limited resource, it should apply additional capacity of that resource to providing more units of the product or service that has:
    a. the highest contribution margin.
    b. the highest selling price.
    c. the highest gross profit.
    d. the highest unit contribution margin of that limited resource.

12. **(LO 4)** The degree of operating leverage:
    a. can be computed by dividing total contribution margin by net income.
    b. provides a measure of the company's earnings volatility.
    c. affects a company's break-even point.
    d. All of the answer choices are correct.

13. **(LO 4)** A high degree of operating leverage:
    a. indicates that a company has a larger percentage of variable costs relative to its fixed costs.
    b. is computed by dividing fixed costs by contribution margin.
    c. exposes a company to greater earnings volatility risk.
    d. exposes a company to less earnings volatility risk.

14. **(LO 4)** Huang Company has a degree of operating leverage of 3.5 at a sales level of NT$12,000,000 and net income of NT$2,000,000. If Huang's sales fall by 10%, Huang can be expected to experience a:
    a. decrease in net income of NT$700,000.
    b. decrease in contribution margin of NT$70,000.
    c. decrease in operating leverage of 35%.
    d. decrease in net income of NT$1,750,000.

*15. **(LO 5)** Fixed manufacturing overhead costs are recognized as:
    a. period costs under absorption costing.
    b. product costs under absorption costs.
    c. product costs under variable costing.
    d. part of ending inventory costs under both absorption and variable costing.

*16. **(LO 5)** Net income computed under absorption costing will be:
    a. higher than net income computed under variable costing in all cases.
    b. equal to net income computed under variable costing in all cases.
    c. higher than net income computed under variable costing when units produced are greater than units sold.
    d. higher than net income computed under variable costing when units produced are less than units sold.

Solutions

1. d. The format of a CVP income statement is Sales − Variable costs − Fixed costs = Net income. Therefore, choices (a), (b), and (c) are incorrect.

2. d. If contribution margin is less than zero, selling price is less than variable costs. The other choices are incorrect because if contribution margin is less than zero (a) selling price, not fixed costs, is less than variable costs; (b) neither profits nor total costs can be determined from the contribution margin amount; and (c) selling more units will only increase the negativity of the contribution margin.

3. a. The break-even point is the point where total sales equal total variable costs plus total fixed costs. Choices (b), (c), and (d) are therefore incorrect.

4. a. The CVP income statement would show Sales (€350,000) − Total variable expenses (€100,000) = Contribution margin (€250,000), not (b) contribution margin of €190,000. Choices (c) and (d) are incorrect because gross profit does not appear on a CVP income statement.

5. b. Required sales in units to achieve net income = (£180,000 + £268,000)/(£12 − £8.50) = 128,000 units, not (a) 51,429 units, (c) 76,571 units, or (d) 21,176 units.

6. d. Fixed costs ($150,000) ÷ Contribution margin ratio ($3 ÷ $12) = $600,000, not (a) $200,000, (b) $450,000, or (c) $480,000.

7. d. Sales mix is the relative percentage in which a company sells its multiple products. The other choices are incorrect because (a) sales mix is also important to accountants, and (b) absorption costing income statements are not needed. Choice (c) is an incorrect definition of sales mix.

8. a. Net income will be greater if more higher contribution margin units are sold than lower contribution units. Choices (b), (c), and (d) are therefore incorrect statements.

9. b. The contribution margin per unit of limited resource is Unit contribution margin (A$15) ÷ Units of limited resource (3.0 machine hours) = A$5, not (a) A$25, (c) A$4, or (d) none of the above.

10. d. Unit contribution margin of Product X (HK$260 ÷ 4) < unit contribution margin of Product Y (HK$140 ÷ 2), so the machine time should be applied toward the product with the higher unit contribution margin. Choices (a), (b), and (c) are incorrect because these options will not maximize Jun's income.

11. d. The company should apply additional capacity of the limited resource to providing more units of the product or service that has the highest unit contribution margin of that limited resource, not (a) the highest contribution margin, (b) the highest selling price, or (c) the highest gross profit.

12. d. All of the above statements about operating leverage are true. So while choices (a), (b), and (c) are true statements, choice (d) is the better answer.

13. c. A high degree of operating leverage exposes a company to greater earnings volatility risk. The other choices are incorrect because a high degree of operating leverage (a) means a company has higher fixed costs relative to variable costs, not vice versa; (b) is computed by dividing contribution margin by net income, not fixed costs by contribution margin; and (d) exposes a company to greater, not less, earnings volatility risk.

14. a. Net income (NT$2,000,000) × Operating leverage (3.5) × Decrease in sales (10%) = decrease in net income of NT$700,000, not (b) decrease in contribution margin of NT$70,000, (c) decrease in operating leverage of 35%, or (d) decrease in net income of NT$1,750,000.

*15. b. Under absorption costing, fixed manufacturing overhead costs and variable manufacturing overhead costs are both product costs. The other choices are incorrect because (a) fixed manufacturing overhead costs are recognized as product costs under absorption costing, not period costs; (c) under variable costing, fixed manufacturing costs are recognized as period costs; and (d) fixed manufacturing costs are part of ending inventory under absorption costing only.

*16. c. Net income is higher under absorption costing than under variable costing when units produced exceed units sold, not (a) higher in all cases, (b) equal to net income under variable costing in all cases, or (d) higher when units produced are less than units sold.

Practice Exercises

Compute break-even point in sales units for a company with more than one product.

1. (LO 2) Yard-King manufactures lawnmowers, weed-trimmers, and chainsaws. Its sales mix and unit contribution margins are as follows:

	Sales Mix	Unit Contribution Margin
Lawnmowers	30%	£35
Weed-trimmers	50	25
Chainsaws	20	50

Yard-King has fixed costs of £4,620,000.

Instructions

Compute the number of units of each product that Yard-King must sell in order to break even under this product mix.

Solution

1.

	Sales Mix Percentage	Unit Contribution Margin	Weighted-Average Contribution Margin
Lawnmowers	30%	£35	£10.50
Weed-trimmers	50	25	12.50
Chainsaws	20	50	10.00
			£33.00

Total break-even sales in units = £4,620,000 ÷ £33.00 = 140,000 units

	Sales Mix Percentage		Total Break-Even Sales		Sales Needed per Product
Lawnmowers	30%	×	140,000 units	=	42,000 units
Weed-trimmers	50	×	140,000	=	70,000
Chainsaws	20	×	140,000	=	28,000
Total units					140,000 units

2. (LO 3) Rene Company manufactures and sells three products. Relevant per unit data concerning each product are given below.

	Product		
	A	B	C
Selling price	$12	$13	$15
Variable costs and expenses	$ 4	$ 8	$ 9
Machine hours to produce	2	1	2

Compute contribution margin and determine the product to be manufactured.

Instructions

a. Compute the contribution margin per unit of limited resource (machine hours) for each product.

b. Assuming 4,500 additional machine hours are available, which product should be manufactured and why?

c. Prepare an analysis showing the total contribution margin if the additional hours are (1) divided equally among the products, and (2) allocated entirely to the product identified in (b) above.

Solution

2. a.

	Product		
	A	B	C
Unit contribution margin (a)	$8	$5	$6
Machine hours required (b)	2	1	2
Contribution margin per unit of limited resource (a) ÷ (b)	$4	$5	$3

b. Product B should be manufactured because it results in the highest contribution margin per machine hour.

c. 1.

	Product		
	A	B	C
Machine hours (a) (4,500 ÷ 3)	1,500	1,500	1,500
Contribution margin per unit of limited resource (b)	$ 4	$ 5	$ 3
Total contribution margin [(a)] × [(b)]	$6,000	$7,500	$4,500

The total contribution margin is $18,000 ($6,000 + $7,500 + $4,500).

2.

	Product B
Machine hours (a)	4,500
Contribution margin per unit of limited resource (b)	$ 5
Total contribution margin [(a) × (b)]	$22,500

3. (LO 4) The CVP income statements shown below are available for Vericelli SpA and Boone Enterprises.

	Vericelli SpA	Boone Enterprises
Sales revenue	€600,000	€600,000
Variable costs	320,000	120,000
Contribution margin	280,000	480,000
Fixed costs	180,000	380,000
Net income	€100,000	€100,000

Compute degree of operating leverage and evaluate impact of alternative cost structures on net income.

Instructions

a. Compute the degree of operating leverage for each company and interpret your results.

b. Assuming that sales revenue increases by 10%, prepare a variable costing income statement for each company.

c. Discuss how the cost structure of these two companies affects their operating leverage and profitability.

Solution

3. a.

	Contribution Margin	÷	Net Income	=	Degree of Operating Leverage
Vericelli	€280,000	÷	€100,000	=	2.8
Boone	480,000	÷	100,000	=	4.8

Boone has a higher degree of operating leverage. Its earnings would increase (decrease) by a greater amount than Vericelli if each experienced an equal increase (decrease) in sales.

b.

	Vericelli SpA	Boone Enterprises
Sales revenue	€660,000*	€660,000
Variable costs	352,000**	132,000***
Contribution margin	308,000	528,000
Fixed costs	180,000	380,000
Net income	€128,000	€148,000

*€600,000 × 1.1   **€320,000 × 1.1   ***€120,000 × 1.1

c. Each company experienced a €60,000 increase in sales. However, because of Boone's higher operating leverage, it experienced a €48,000 (€148,000 − €100,000) increase in net income while Vericelli experienced only a €28,000 (€128,000 − €100,000) increase. This is what we would have expected since Boone's degree of operating leverage exceeds that of Vericelli.

Practice Problem

Determine sales mix with limited resources.

(LO 3) Ying Sports manufactures and sells three different types of water-sport wakeboards. The boards vary in terms of their quality specifications—primarily with respect to their smoothness and finish. They are referred to as Smooth, Extra-Smooth, and Super-Smooth boards. Machine time is limited. More machine time is required to manufacture the Extra-Smooth and Super-Smooth boards. Additional information on a per unit basis is provided below.

	Product		
	Smooth	Extra-Smooth	Super-Smooth
Selling price	HK$600	HK$1,000	HK$1,600
Variable costs and expenses	500	750	1,300
Contribution margin	HK$100	HK$250	HK$300
Machine hours required	0.25	0.40	0.60

Total fixed costs: HK$2,340,000

Instructions

Answer each of the following questions:

a. Ignoring the machine time constraint, what strategy would appear optimal?

b. What is the contribution margin per unit of limited resource for each type of board?

c. If additional machine time could be obtained, how should the additional capacity be used?

Solution

a. The Super-Smooth boards have the highest unit contribution margin. Thus, ignoring any manufacturing constraints, it would appear that the company should shift toward production of more Super-Smooth units.

b. The contribution margin per unit of limited resource is calculated as follows:

	Smooth	Extra-Smooth	Super-Smooth
$\dfrac{\text{Unit contribution margin}}{\text{Limited resource consumed per unit}}$	$\dfrac{\text{HK\$100}}{.25} = \text{HK\$400}$	$\dfrac{\text{HK\$250}}{.40} = \text{HK\$625}$	$\dfrac{\text{HK\$300}}{.60} = \text{HK\$500}$

c. The Extra-Smooth boards have the highest contribution margin per unit of limited resource. Given the resource constraint, any additional capacity should be used to make Extra-Smooth boards.

Note: All asterisked Questions, Exercises, and Problems relate to material in the appendix to this chapter.

Questions

1. What is meant by CVP analysis?
2. Provide three examples of management decisions that benefit from CVP analysis.
3. Distinguish between a traditional income statement and a CVP income statement.
4. Describe the features of a CVP income statement that make it more useful for management decision-making than the traditional income statement that is prepared for external users.
5. The traditional income statement for Wheat Company shows sales $900,000, cost of goods sold $500,000, and operating expenses $200,000. Assuming all costs and expenses are 75% variable and 25% fixed, prepare a CVP income statement through contribution margin.
6. If management chooses to reduce its selling price to match that of a competitor, how will the break-even point be affected?
7. What is meant by the term sales mix? How does sales mix affect the calculation of the break-even point?
8. Performance Company sells two types of performance tires. The lower-priced model is guaranteed for only 50,000 kilometers; the higher-priced model is guaranteed for 150,000 kilometers. The unit contribution margin on the higher-priced tire is twice as high as that of the lower-priced tire. If the sales mix shifts so that the company begins to sell more units of the lower-priced tire, explain how the company's break-even point in units will change.
9. What approach should be used to calculate the break-even point of a company that has many products?
10. How is the contribution margin per unit of limited resource computed?
11. What is the theory of constraints? Provide some examples of possible constraints for a manufacturer.
12. What is meant by "cost structure"? Explain how a company's cost structure affects its break-even point.
13. What is operating leverage? How does a company increase its operating leverage?
14. How does the replacement of manual labor with automated equipment affect a company's cost structure? What implications does this have for its operating leverage and break-even point?
15. What is a measure of operating leverage, and how is it calculated?
16. Pine Company has a degree of operating leverage of 8. Fir Company has a degree of operating leverage of 4. Interpret these measures.
*17. Distinguish between absorption costing and variable costing.
*18. a. What is the major rationale for the use of variable costing?
    b. Discuss why variable costing cannot be used for financial reporting purposes.
*19. Schulz SE sells one product, its waterproof hiking boot. It began operations in the current year and had an ending inventory of 8,500 units. The company sold 20,000 units throughout the year. Fixed manufacturing overhead is €5 per unit, and total manufacturing cost per unit is €20 (including fixed manufacturing overhead costs). What is the difference in net income between absorption and variable costing?
*20. If production equals sales, what, if any, is the difference between net income under absorption costing versus under variable costing?
*21. If production is greater than sales, how does absorption costing net income differ from variable costing net income?
*22. In the long run, will net income be higher or lower under variable costing compared to absorption costing?

Brief Exercises

BE6.1 (LO 1), AN Determine the missing amounts.

Determine missing amounts for contribution margin.

	Unit Selling Price	Unit Variable Costs	Unit Contribution Margin	Contribution Margin Ratio
1.	¥25,000	¥18,000	(a)	(b)
2.	¥50,000	(c)	¥20,000	(d)
3.	(e)	(f)	¥33,000	30%

BE6.2 (LO 1), AP Hamby Inc. has sales of $2,000,000 for the first quarter of 2023. In making the sales, the company incurred the following costs and expenses:

Prepare CVP income statement.

	Variable	Fixed
Cost of goods sold	$760,000	$600,000
Selling expenses	95,000	60,000
Administrative expenses	79,000	66,000

Prepare a CVP income statement for the quarter ended March 31, 2023.

Compute the break-even point.

BE6.3 (LO 1), AP Pak Ltd. had total variable costs of ₩150,000,000, total fixed costs of ₩120,000,000, and total revenues of ₩250,000,000. Compute the required sales to break even.

Compute the break-even point.

BE6.4 (LO 1), AP Xin Ltd. has a unit selling price of NT$4,000, unit variable costs of NT$2,500, and fixed costs of NT$2,100,000. Compute the break-even point in sales units using (a) the mathematical equation and (b) unit contribution margin.

Compute sales for target net income.

BE6.5 (LO 1), AP For Rivera SpA, variable costs are 70% of sales, and fixed costs are €210,000. Management's net income goal is €60,000. Compute the required sales needed to achieve management's target net income of €60,000. (Use the mathematical equation approach.)

Compute the margin of safety and the margin of safety ratio.

BE6.6 (LO 1), AP For Kosko Company, actual sales are A$1,200,000 and break-even sales are A$960,000. Compute (a) the margin of safety in dollars and (b) the margin of safety ratio.

Compute weighted-average unit contribution margin based on sales mix.

BE6.7 (LO 2), AP Seto Company sells three different models of an electrical bulb. Model A12 sells for Rp500,000 and has variable costs of Rp350,000. Model B22 sells for Rp1,000,000 and has variable costs of Rp700,000. Model C124 sells for Rp4,000,000 and has variable costs of Rp3,000,000. The sales mix of the three models is A12, 60%; B22, 15%; and C124, 25%. What is the weighted-average unit contribution margin?

Compute break-even point in sales units for company with multiple products.

BE6.8 (LO 2), AP Information for Seto Company is given in BE6.7. If the company has fixed costs of Rp2,695,000,000, how many units of each model must the company sell in order to break even?

Compute break-even point in sales pounds for company with multiple product lines.

BE6.9 (LO 2), AP Finn Candle Supply makes candles. The sales mix (as a percentage of total pound sales) of its three product lines is birthday candles 30%, standard tapered candles 50%, and large scented candles 20%. The contribution margin ratio of each candle type is shown below.

Candle Type	Contribution Margin Ratio
Birthday	20%
Standard tapered	30%
Large scented	45%

a. What is the weighted-average contribution margin ratio?

b. If the company's fixed costs are £450,000 per year, what is the sales amount of each type of candle that must be sold to break even?

Determine weighted-average contribution margin.

BE6.10 (LO 2), AP Faune Furniture Co. consists of two divisions, Bedroom Division and Dining Room Division. The results of operations for the most recent quarter are:

	Bedroom Division	Dining Room Division	Total
Sales	$500,000	$750,000	$1,250,000
Variable costs	225,000	450,000	675,000
Contribution margin	$275,000	$300,000	$ 575,000

a. Determine the company's sales mix based on sales revenue.

b. Determine the company's weighted-average contribution margin ratio.

Show allocation of limited resources.

BE6.11 (LO 3), AP In Kumar & Sons, data concerning two products are unit contribution margin—Product A ₹1,000, Product B ₹1,200; machine hours required for one unit—Product A 2, Product B 3. Compute the contribution margin per unit of limited resource for each product.

Show allocation of limited resources.

BE6.12 (LO 3), AP Sage SpA manufactures two products with the following characteristics.

	Unit Contribution Margin	Machine Hours Required for Production
Product 1	€42	.15 hours
Product 2	€32	.10 hours

If Sage's machine hours are limited to 2,000 per month, determine which product it should produce.

Compute degree of operating leverage.

BE6.13 (LO 4), AP Demir A.Ş. is considering the purchase of a new automated shingle-cutting machine. The new machine will reduce variable labor costs but will increase depreciation expense. Contribution margin is expected to increase from ₺2,000,000 to ₺2,400,000. Net income is expected to be the same at ₺400,000. Compute the degree of operating leverage before and after the purchase of the new equipment. Interpret your results.

BE6.14 (LO 4), AP Presented below are variable costing income statements for Fung Ltd. and Kai Ltd. They are in the same industry, with the same net incomes, but different cost structures.

Compute break-even point with change in operating leverage.

	Fung Ltd.	Kai Ltd.
Sales	HK$2,000,000	HK$2,000,000
Variable costs	800,000	500,000
Contribution margin	1,200,000	1,500,000
Fixed costs	750,000	1,050,000
Net income	HK$ 450,000	HK$ 450,000

Compute the break-even point for each company and comment on your findings.

BE6.15 (LO 4), AP The degree of operating leverage for Natan Ltd. and Wono Ltd. are 1.6 and 5.4, respectively. Both have net incomes of Rp500,000,000. Determine their respective contribution margins.

Determine contribution margin from degree of operating leverage.

*BE6.16 (LO 5), AP The Rock Company produces basketballs. It incurred the following costs during the year.

Compute product costs under variable costing.

Direct materials	A$14,400
Direct labor	A$25,600
Fixed manufacturing overhead	A$12,000
Variable manufacturing overhead	A$29,400
Selling costs	A$21,000

What are the total product costs for the company under variable costing?

*BE6.17 (LO 5), AP Information concerning The Rock Company is provided in BE6.16. What are the total product costs for the company under absorption costing?

Compute product costs under absorption costing.

*BE6.18 (LO 5), AP Burns plc incurred the following costs during the year: direct materials £20 per unit; direct labor £14 per unit; variable manufacturing overhead £15 per unit; variable selling and administrative costs £8 per unit; fixed manufacturing overhead £128,000; and fixed selling and administrative costs £10,000. Burns produced 8,000 units and sold 6,000 units. Determine the manufacturing cost per unit under (a) absorption costing and (b) variable costing.

Determine manufacturing cost per unit under absorption and variable costing.

*BE6.19 (LO 5), AP `Writing` Harris Company's fixed overhead costs are $4 per unit, and its variable overhead costs are $8 per unit. In the first month of operations, 50,000 units are produced, and 46,000 units are sold. Write a short memo to the chief financial officer explaining which costing approach will produce the higher income and what the difference will be.

DO IT! Exercises

DO IT! 6.1 (LO 1), AP Victoria plc reports the following operating results for the month of April.

Compute the break-even point and margin of safety under different alternatives.

Victoria plc
CVP Income Statement
For the Month Ended April 30, 2023

	Total	Per Unit	Percent of Sales
Sales (9,000 units)	£450,000	£50	100%
Variable costs	270,000	30	60
Contribution margin	180,000	£20	40%
Fixed expenses	150,000		
Net income	£ 30,000		

Management is considering the following course of action to increase net income: Reduce the selling price by 4%, with no changes to unit variable costs or fixed costs. Management is confident that this change will increase unit sales by 20%.

Using the contribution margin technique, compute the break-even point in sales units and sales pounds and margin of safety in pounds:

a. Assuming no changes to selling price or costs, and

b. Assuming changes to sales price and volume as described above.

Comment on your findings.

Compute sales mix, weighted-average contribution margin, and break-even point.

DO IT! 6.2 (LO 2), AP Snow Cap Springs produces and sells water filtration systems for homeowners. Information regarding its three models is shown below.

	Basic	Basic Plus	Premium	Total
Units sold	750	450	300	1,500
Selling price	CHF250	CHF400	CHF800	
Variable costs	CHF195	CHF285	CHF415	

The company's total fixed costs to produce the filtration systems are CHF180,700.

a. Determine the sales mix as a function of units sold for the three products.
b. Determine the weighted-average unit contribution margin.
c. Determine the total number of units that the company must produce to break even.
d. Determine the number of units of each model that the company must produce to break even.

Determine sales mix with limited resources.

DO IT! 6.3 (LO 3), AP Zhou Group manufactures and sells three different types of binoculars. They are referred to as Good, Better, and Best binoculars. Grinding and polishing time is limited. More time is required to grind and polish the lenses used in the Better and Best binoculars. Additional information is provided below.

	Product		
	Good	Better	Best
Selling price	HK$900	HK$3,300	HK$9,000
Variable costs and expenses	500	1,800	4,800
Contribution margin	HK$400	HK$1,500	HK$4,200
Grinding and polishing time required	0.5 hrs	1.5 hrs	6 hrs

a. Ignoring the time constraint, what strategy would appear to be optimal?
b. What is the contribution margin per unit of limited resource for each type of binocular?
c. If additional grinding and polishing time could be obtained, how should the additional capacity be used?

Determine operating leverage.

DO IT! 6.4 (LO 4), AP Bergen Hospital is contemplating an investment in an automated surgical system. Its current process relies on the a number of skilled physicians. The new equipment would employ a computer robotic system operated by a technician. The company requested an analysis of the old technology versus the new technology. The accounting department has prepared the following CVP income statements for use in your analysis.

	Old	New
Sales	$3,000,000	$3,000,000
Variable costs	1,600,000	700,000
Contribution margin	1,400,000	2,300,000
Fixed costs	1,000,000	1,900,000
Net income	$ 400,000	$ 400,000

a. Compute the degree of operating leverage for the company under each scenario.
b. Discuss your results.

Exercises

Compute break-even point and margin of safety.

E6.1 (LO 1), AP Service The Como Inn is trying to determine its break-even point. The inn has 75 rooms that are rented at €60 a night. Operating costs are as follows:

Salaries	€10,600 per month
Utilities	2,400 per month
Depreciation	1,500 per month
Maintenance	800 per month
Maid service	8 per room
Other costs	34 per room

Instructions

a. Determine the inn's break-even point in (1) number of rented rooms per month and (2) sales euros.

b. If the inn plans on renting an average of 50 rooms per day (assuming a 30-day month), what is (1) the monthly margin of safety in euros and (2) the margin of safety ratio?

E6.2 (LO 1), AP `Service` In the month of June, Good Hand's Beauty Salon gave 4,000 haircuts, shampoos, and hair colorings at an average price of £30 each. During the month, fixed costs were £16,800 and variable costs were 75% of sales.

Compute contribution margin, break-even point, and margin of safety.

Instructions

a. Determine the contribution margin in pounds, per unit and as a ratio.

b. Using the contribution margin technique, compute the break-even point in sales pounds and in sales units.

c. Compute the margin of safety in pounds and as a ratio.

E6.3 (LO 1), AP Lim Ltd. reports the following operating results for the month of August: sales ₩325,000,000 (units 5,000); variable costs ₩210,000,000; and fixed costs ₩75,000,000. Management is considering the following independent courses of action to increase net income.

Compute net income under different alternatives.

1. Increase selling price by 10% with no change in total variable costs or sales volume.
2. Reduce variable costs to 58% of sales.
3. Reduce fixed costs by ₩15,000,000.

Instructions

Compute the net income to be earned under each alternative. Which course of action will produce the highest net income?

E6.4 (LO 1), AP `Service` Comfi Airways, Inc., a small two-plane passenger airline, has asked for your assistance in some basic analysis of its operations. Both planes seat 10 passengers each, and they fly commuters from Comfi's base airport to a major city in the state of Texas, USA. Each month, 40 round-trip flights are made. The following is a recent month's activity in the form of a cost-volume-profit income statement.

Compute break-even point and prepare CVP income statement.

Fare revenues (400 passenger flights)		$48,000
Variable costs		
Fuel	$14,000	
Snacks and drinks	800	
Landing fees	2,000	
Supplies and forms	1,200	18,000
Contribution margin		30,000
Fixed costs		
Depreciation	3,000	
Salaries	15,000	
Advertising	500	
Airport hangar fees	1,750	20,250
Net income		$ 9,750

Instructions

a. Calculate the break-even point in (1) sales dollars and (2) number of passenger flights.

b. Without calculations, determine the contribution margin at the break-even point.

c. If ticket prices were decreased by 10%, passenger flights would increase by 25%. However, total variable costs would increase by the same percentage as passenger flights. Should the ticket price decrease be adopted?

E6.5 (LO 1), AP Zhenhao Ltd. had sales in 2022 of HK$15,000,000 on 60,000 units. Variable costs totaled HK$9,000,000, and fixed costs totaled HK$5,000,000.

Prepare a CVP income statement before and after changes in business environment.

A new raw material is available that will decrease the unit variable costs by 20% (or HK$30). However, to process the new raw material, fixed operating costs will increase by HK$1,000,000. Management feels that one-half of the decline in the unit variable costs should be passed on to customers in the form of a sales price reduction. The marketing department expects that this sales price reduction will result in a 5% increase in the number of units sold.

Instructions

Prepare a projected CVP income statement for 2023 (a) assuming the changes have not been made, and (b) assuming that changes are made as described.

Compute break-even point in sales units for a company with more than one product.

E6.6 (LO 2), AP Garden Tools manufactures lawnmowers, weed-trimmers, and chainsaws. Its sales mix and unit contribution margin are as follows:

	Sales Mix	Unit Contribution Margin
Lawnmowers	20%	£30
Weed-trimmers	50%	£20
Chainsaws	30%	£40

Garden Tools has fixed costs of £4,200,000.

Instructions

Compute the number of units of each product that Garden Tools must sell in order to break even under this product mix.

Compute service line break-even point and target net income in dollars for a company with more than one service.

E6.7 (LO 2), AN Service PDQ Repairs has 200 auto-maintenance service outlets nationwide. It performs primarily two lines of service: oil changes and brake repair. Oil change–related services represent 70% of its sales and provide a contribution margin ratio of 20%. Brake repair represents 30% of its sales and provides a 40% contribution margin ratio. The company's fixed costs are $15,600,000 (that is, $78,000 per service outlet).

Instructions

a. Calculate the dollar amount of each type of service that the company must provide in order to break even.

b. The company has a desired net income of $52,000 per service outlet. What is the dollar amount of each type of service that must be performed by each service outlet to meet its target net income per outlet?

Compute break-even point in sales dollars for a company with more than one service.

E6.8 (LO 2), AN Service Express Shipping is a rapidly growing delivery service. Last year, 80% of its revenue came from the delivery of mailing "pouches" and small, standardized delivery boxes (which provides a 20% contribution margin). The other 20% of its revenue came from delivering non-standardized boxes (which provides a 70% contribution margin). With the rapid growth of Internet retail sales, Express believes that there are great opportunities for growth in the delivery of non-standardized boxes. The company has fixed costs of A$12,000,000.

Instructions

a. What is the company's break-even point in total sales dollars? At the break-even point, how much of the company's sales are provided by each type of service?

b. The company's management would like to hold its fixed costs constant but shift its sales mix so that 60% of its revenue comes from the delivery of non-standardized boxes and the remainder from pouches and small boxes. If this were to occur, what would be the company's break-even sales, and what amount of sales would be provided by each service type?

Compute break-even point in sales units for a company with multiple products.

E6.9 (LO 2), AP Lion Golf Accessories sells golf shoes, gloves, and a laser-guided range-finder that measures distance. Shown below are unit cost and sales data.

	Pairs of Shoes	Pairs of Gloves	Range-Finder
Unit sales price	€100	€30	€260
Unit variable costs	60	10	200
Unit contribution margin	€ 40	€20	€ 60
Sales mix	35%	55%	10%

Fixed costs are €620,000.

Instructions

a. Compute the break-even point in sales units for the company.

b. Determine the number of units to be sold at the break-even point for each product line.

c. Verify that the mix of sales units determined in (b) will generate a zero net income.

E6.10 (LO 2), AP Fandi Electronics sells TVs and MP3 players. The business is divided into two divisions along product lines. CVP income statements for a recent quarter's activity are presented below.

Determine break-even point for two divisions.

	TV Division	MP3 Player Division	Total
Sales	£600,000	£400,000	£1,000,000
Variable costs	420,000	260,000	680,000
Contribution margin	£180,000	£140,000	320,000
Fixed costs			120,000
Net income			£ 200,000

Instructions

a. Determine the sales mix percentage based on sales revenue and contribution margin ratio for each division.
b. Calculate the company's weighted-average contribution margin ratio.
c. Calculate the company's break-even point.
d. Determine the sales level for each division at the break-even point.

E6.11 (LO 3), AN Weimiao Ltd. manufactures and sells three products. Relevant per unit data concerning each product are given below.

Compute contribution margin and determine the product to be manufactured.

	Product		
	A	B	C
Selling price	HK$90	HK$120	HK$150
Variable costs and expenses	HK$30	HK$100	HK$120
Machine hours to produce	2	1	2

Instructions

a. Compute the contribution margin per unit of limited resource (machine hours) for each product.
b. Assuming 3,000 additional machine hours are available, which product should be manufactured?
c. Prepare an analysis showing the total contribution margin if the additional hours are (1) divided equally among the products, and (2) allocated entirely to the product identified in (b) above.

E6.12 (LO 3), AN Venter Ltd. produces and sells three products. Unit data concerning each product are shown below.

Compute contribution margin and determine the products to be manufactured.

	Product		
	D	E	F
Selling price	R2,000	R3,000	R2,500
Direct labor costs	300	800	350
Other variable costs	950	800	1,450

The company has 2,000 hours of labor available to build inventory in anticipation of the company's peak season. Management is trying to decide which product should be produced. The direct labor hourly rate is R100.

Instructions

a. Determine the number of direct labor hours per unit.
b. Determine the contribution margin per direct labor hour.
c. Determine which product should be produced and the total contribution margin for that product.

E6.13 (LO 3), AN Chiu Ltd. manufactures and sells two products. Relevant per unit data concerning each product follow:

Compute contribution margin and determine the products to be manufactured.

	Product	
	Basic	Deluxe
Selling price	NT$400	NT$520
Variable costs	NT$220	NT$240
Machine hours	0.5	0.8

Instructions

a. Compute the contribution margin per machine hour for each product.
b. If 1,000 additional machine hours are available, which product should Chiu manufacture?

c. Prepare an analysis showing the total contribution margin if the additional hours are:
  1. Divided equally between the products.
  2. Allocated entirely to the product identified in part (b).

Compute degree of operating leverage and evaluate impact of alternative cost structures on net income.

E6.14 (LO 4), AN The single-column CVP income statements shown below are available for Armstrong Company and Contador Company.

	Armstrong Co.	Contador Co.
Sales	$500,000	$500,000
Variable costs	240,000	50,000
Contribution margin	260,000	450,000
Fixed costs	160,000	350,000
Net income	$100,000	$100,000

Instructions

a. Compute the degree of operating leverage for each company and interpret your results.
b. Assuming that sales revenue increases by 10%, restate the single-column CVP income statement from above for each company.
c. Discuss how the cost structure of these two companies affects their operating leverage and profitability.

Compute degree of operating leverage and evaluate impact of alternative cost structures on net income and margin of safety.

E6.15 (LO 4), AN **Service** Casas Modernas of Juarez, Mexico, is contemplating a major change in its cost structure. Currently, all of its drafting work is performed by skilled draftsmen. Rafael Jiminez, Casas' owner, is considering replacing the draftsmen with a computerized drafting system. However, before making the change, Rafael would like to know the consequences of the change, since the volume of business varies significantly from year to year. Shown below are CVP income statements for each alternative.

	Manual System	Computerized System
Sales	$1,500,000	$1,500,000
Variable costs	1,200,000	600,000
Contribution margin	300,000	900,000
Fixed costs	100,000	700,000
Net income	$ 200,000	$ 200,000

Instructions

a. Determine the degree of operating leverage for each alternative.
b. Which alternative would produce the higher net income if sales increased by $150,000?
c. Using the margin of safety ratio, determine which alternative could sustain the greater decline in sales before operating at a loss.

Compute degree of operating leverage and impact on net income of alternative cost structures.

E6.16 (LO 4), AN An investment banker is analyzing two companies that specialize in the production and sale of candied yams. Traditional Yams uses a labor-intensive approach, and Auto-Yams uses a mechanized system. CVP income statements for the two companies are shown below.

	Traditional Yams	Auto-Yams
Sales	R$4,000,000	R$4,000,000
Variable costs	3,200,000	1,600,000
Contribution margin	800,000	2,400,000
Fixed costs	300,000	1,900,000
Net income	R$ 500,000	R$ 500,000

The investment banker is interested in acquiring one of these companies. However, she is concerned about the impact that each company's cost structure might have on its profitability.

Instructions

a. Calculate each company's degree of operating leverage. Determine which company's cost structure makes it more sensitive to changes in sales volume.

b. Determine the effect on each company's net income if sales decrease by 15% and if sales increase by 10%. Do not prepare income statements.

c. Which company should the investment banker acquire? Discuss.

*E6.17 (LO 5), AP Siren Company builds custom fishing lures for sporting goods stores. In its first year of operations, 2023, the company incurred the following costs:

Compute product cost and prepare an income statement under variable and absorption costing.

Unit Variable Costs	
Direct materials	$7.50
Direct labor	$3.45
Variable manufacturing overhead	$5.80
Variable selling and administrative expenses	$3.90
Annual Fixed Costs	
Fixed manufacturing overhead	$225,000
Fixed selling and administrative expenses	$210,100

Siren Company sells the fishing lures for $25. During 2023, the company sold 80,000 lures and produced 90,000 lures.

Instructions

a. Assuming the company uses variable costing, calculate Siren's manufacturing cost per unit for 2023.

b. Prepare a variable costing income statement for 2023.

c. Assuming the company uses absorption costing, calculate Siren's manufacturing cost per unit for 2023.

d. Prepare an absorption costing income statement for 2023.

*E6.18 (LO 5), AN Preston Ltd. produced 9,000 units during the past year, but only 8,200 of the units were sold. The following additional information is also available.

Determine ending inventory under variable costing and determine whether absorption or variable costing would result in higher net income.

Direct materials used	£79,000
Direct labor incurred	£30,000
Variable manufacturing overhead	£21,500
Fixed manufacturing overhead	£45,000
Fixed selling and administrative expenses	£70,000
Variable selling and administrative expenses	£10,000

There was no work in process inventory at the beginning and end of the year, nor did Preston have any beginning finished goods inventory.

Instructions

a. What would be Preston Company's finished goods inventory cost on December 31 under variable costing?

b. Which costing method, absorption or variable costing, would show a higher net income for the year? By what amount?

*E6.19 (LO 5), AN Trunk Express produces wooden trunks used for shipping products by ocean liner. In 2023, Trunk Express incurred the following costs:

Compute manufacturing cost under absorption and variable costing and explain difference.

Wood used in trunk production	€54,000
Nails (considered insignificant and a variable expense)	350
Direct labor	43,000
Utilities for the factory:	
€1,500 each month,	
plus €0.50 for each kilowatt-hour used each month	
Rent expense for the factory for the year	21,400

Assume Trunk Express used an average 500 kilowatt-hours each month over the past year.

Instructions

a. What is Trunk Express's total manufacturing cost if it uses a variable costing approach?

b. What is Trunk Express's total manufacturing cost if it uses an absorption costing approach?

c. What accounts for the difference in manufacturing costs between these two costing approaches?

Problems

Compute break-even point under alternative courses of action.

P6.1 (LO 1), AN Lanza SA had a bad year in 2022. For the first time in its history, it operated at a loss. The company's income statement showed the following results from selling 80,000 units of product: net sales R$20,000,000; total costs and expenses R$22,350,000; and net loss R$2,350,000. Costs and expenses consisted of the following:

	Total	Variable	Fixed
Cost of goods sold	R$15,680,000	R$10,500,000	R$5,180,000
Selling expenses	5,170,000	920,000	4,250,000
Administrative expenses	1,500,000	580,000	920,000
	R$22,350,000	R$12,000,000	R$10,350,000

Management is considering the following independent alternatives for 2023.

1. Increase unit selling price 25% with no change in costs and expenses.
2. Change the compensation of salespersons from fixed annual salaries totaling R$2,000,000 to total salaries of R$400,000 plus a 5% commission on net sales.
3. Purchase new high-tech factory machinery that will change the proportion between variable and fixed cost of goods sold to 50:50.

Instructions

b. (2) R$25,000,000

a. Compute the break-even point in sales (Brazilian real) for 2022.
b. Compute the break-even point in sales (Brazilian real) under each of the alternative courses of action for 2023. (Round to the nearest real.) Which course of action do you recommend?

Compute break-even point and margin of safety ratio, and prepare a CVP income statement before and after changes in business environment.

P6.2 (LO 1), AN Yoris Ltd. has collected the following information after its first year of sales. Sales were €1,500,000 on 100,000 units; selling expenses €250,000 (40% variable and 60% fixed); direct materials €511,000; direct labor €290,000; administrative expenses €270,000 (20% variable and 80% fixed); and manufacturing overhead €350,000 (70% variable and 30% fixed). Top management has asked you to do a CVP analysis so that it can make plans for the coming year. It has projected that unit sales will increase by 10% next year.

Instructions

a. Compute (1) the contribution margin for the current year and the projected year, and (2) the fixed costs for the current year. (Assume that fixed costs will remain the same in the projected year.)

b. 157,000 units

b. Compute the break-even point in sales units and sales euros for the first year.
c. The company has a target net income of €200,000. What is the required sales in euros for the company to meet its target?
d. If the company meets its target net income number, by what percentage could its sales fall before it is operating at a loss? That is, what is its margin of safety ratio?

e. (3) €1,735,714

e. The company is considering a purchase of equipment that would reduce its direct labor costs by €104,000 and would change its manufacturing overhead costs to 30% variable and 70% fixed (assume total manufacturing overhead cost is €350,000, as above). It is also considering switching to a pure commission basis for its sales staff. This would change selling expenses to 90% variable and 10% fixed (assume total selling expense is €250,000, as above). Compute (1) the contribution margin and (2) the contribution margin ratio, and recompute (3) the break-even point in sales euros. Comment on the effect each of management's proposed changes has on the break-even point.

Determine break-even sales under alternative sales strategies and evaluate results.

P6.3 (LO 2), AN Service The Harbour Inn is a restaurant in Sydney. It specializes in southwestern style cuisine in a moderate price range. Paul Weld, the manager of Harbour, has determined that during the last two years the sales mix and contribution margin ratio of its offerings are as follows:

	Percent of Total Sales	Contribution Margin Ratio
Appetizers	15%	50%
Main entrees	50%	25%
Desserts	10%	50%
Beverages	25%	80%

Paul is considering a variety of options to try to improve the profitability of the restaurant. His goal is to generate a target net income of A$117,000. The company has fixed costs of A$1,053,000 per year.

Instructions

a. Calculate the total restaurant sales and the sales of each product line that would be necessary to achieve the desired target net income.

b. Paul believes the restaurant could greatly improve its profitability by reducing the complexity and selling price of its entrees to increase the number of clients that it serves. It would then more heavily market its appetizers and beverages. He is proposing to reduce the contribution margin ratio on the main entrees to 10% by dropping the average selling price. He envisions an expansion of the restaurant that would increase fixed costs by A$585,000. At the same time, he is proposing to change the sales mix to the following:

	Percent of Total Sales	Contribution Margin Ratio
Appetizers	25%	50%
Main entrees	25%	10%
Desserts	10%	50%
Beverages	40%	80%

Compute the total restaurant sales, and the sales of each product line that would be necessary to achieve the desired target net income of A$117,000.

c. Suppose that Paul reduces the selling price on entrees and increases fixed costs as proposed in part (b), but customers are not swayed by the marketing efforts and the sales mix remains what it was in part (a). Compute the total restaurant sales and the sales of each product line that would be necessary to achieve the desired target net income. Comment on the potential risks and benefits of this strategy.

a. Total sales A$2,600,000

b. Total sales A$3,375,000

P6.4 (LO 3), AN Yu Industries manufactures and sells three different models of wet-dry shop vacuum cleaners. Although the vacuum cleaners vary in terms of quality and features, all are good sellers. Yu is currently operating at full capacity with limited machine time.
Sales and production information relevant to each model follows:

Determine sales mix with limited resources.

	Product		
	Economy	Standard	Deluxe
Selling price	HK$300	HK$500	HK$1,000
Variable costs and expenses	HK$160	HK$200	HK$ 460
Machine hours required	0.5	0.8	1.6

Instructions

a. Ignoring the machine time constraint, which single product should Yu Industries produce?

b. What is the contribution margin per unit of limited resource for each product?

c. If additional machine time could be obtained, how should the additional time be used?

b. Economy HK$280

P6.5 (LO 4), AN Writing The following single-column CVP income statements are available for Torino SpA and Augusta SpA.

Compute degree of operating leverage and evaluate impact of operating leverage on financial results.

	Torino SpA	Augusta SpA
Sales	€500,000	€500,000
Variable costs	280,000	180,000
Contribution margin	220,000	320,000
Fixed costs	170,000	270,000
Net income	€ 50,000	€ 50,000

Instructions

a. Compute the break-even point in sales euros and the margin of safety ratio (round to 3 places) for each company.

b. Compute the degree of operating leverage for each company and interpret your results.

a. BE, Torino €386,364
BE, Augusta €421,875

b. DOL, Torino 4.4
DOL, Augusta 6.4

c. Assuming that sales revenue increases by 20%, restate the CVP income statement for each company.

d. Assuming that sales revenue decreases by 20%, restate the CVP income statement for each company.

e. Discuss how the cost structure of these two companies affects their operating leverage and profitability.

Determine contribution margin, break-even point, target sales, and degree of operating leverage.

P6.6 (LO 1, 4), AN Bonita Beauty Corporation manufactures cosmetic products that are sold through a network of sales agents. The agents are paid a commission of 18% of sales. The income statement for the year ending December 31, 2023, is as follows:

Bonita Beauty Corporation
Income Statement
For the Year Ended December 31, 2023

Sales		$75,000,000
Cost of goods sold		
Variable	$31,500,000	
Fixed	8,610,000	40,110,000
Gross margin		34,890,000
Selling and marketing expenses		
Commissions	13,500,000	
Fixed costs	10,260,000	23,760,000
Operating income		$11,130,000

The company is considering hiring its own sales staff to replace the network of agents. It will pay its salespeople a commission of 8% and incur additional fixed costs of $7.5 million.

Instructions

a. $47,175,000

a. Under the current policy of using a network of sales agents, calculate the Bonita Beauty Corporation's break-even point in sales dollars for the year 2023.

b. Calculate the company's break-even point in sales dollars for the year 2023 if it hires its own sales force to replace the network of agents.

c. (2) 3.37

c. Calculate the degree of operating leverage at sales of $75 million if (1) Bonita Beauty uses sales agents, and (2) Bonita Beauty employs its own sales staff. Describe the advantages and disadvantages of each alternative.

d. Calculate the estimated sales volume in sales dollars that would generate an identical net income for the year ending December 31, 2023, regardless of whether Bonita Beauty Corporation employs its own sales staff and pays them an 8% commission or continues to use the independent network of agents. (*Hint:* Set up an equation, with the net income formula employing independent agents as one side of the equation and the net income formula employing the company's own sales staff as the other side of the equation. Before solving, eliminate those aspects that are the same on each side of the equation as they do not vary under the two alternatives.)

Prepare income statements under absorption costing and variable costing for a company with beginning inventory, and reconcile differences.

*** P6.7 (LO 5), AN Writing** Rafael SA produces plastic that is used for injection-molding applications such as gears for small motors. In 2022, the first year of operations, Rafael produced 4,000 tons of plastic and sold 3,500 tons. In 2023, the production and sales results were exactly reversed. In each year, the selling price per ton was €2,000, variable manufacturing costs were 15% of the sales price of units produced, variable selling expenses were 10% of the selling price of units sold, fixed manufacturing costs were €2,800,000, and fixed administrative expenses were €500,000.

Instructions

a. 2023 €2,700,000

a. Prepare income statements for each year using variable costing. (Use the format from Illustration 6A.5.)

b. 2023 €2,350,000

b. Prepare income statements for each year using absorption costing. (Use the format from Illustration 6A.4.)

c. Comment on the effects of production and sales on net income under the two costing approaches.

Prepare absorption and variable costing income statements and reconcile differences between absorption and variable costing income statements when sales level and production level change. Discuss relative usefulness of absorption costing versus variable costing.

*** P6.8 (LO 5), AN Writing** Dilithium Batteries is a division of Paragon Corporation. The division manufactures and sells a long-life battery used in a wide variety of applications. During the coming year, it expects to sell 60,000 units for £30 per unit. Margaret Lipscomb is the division manager. She is considering producing either 60,000 or 90,000 units during the period. Other information is presented in the schedule.

Division Information for 2023

Beginning inventory	0
Expected sales in units	60,000
Selling price per unit	£30
Variable manufacturing costs per unit	£12
Fixed manufacturing overhead costs (total)	£540,000
Fixed manufacturing overhead costs per unit:	
Based on 60,000 units	£9 per unit (£540,000 ÷ 60,000)
Based on 90,000 units	£6 per unit (£540,000 ÷ 90,000)
Manufacturing costs per unit:	
Based on 60,000 units	£21 per unit (£12 variable + £9 fixed)
Based on 90,000 units	£18 per unit (£12 variable + £6 fixed)
Variable selling and administrative expenses	£2
Fixed selling and administrative expenses (total)	£50,000

Instructions

a. Prepare an absorption costing income statement, with one column showing the results if 60,000 units are produced and one column showing the results if 90,000 units are produced.

b. Prepare a variable costing income statement, with one column showing the results if 60,000 units are produced and one column showing the results if 90,000 units are produced.

c. Reconcile the difference in net incomes under the two approaches and explain what accounts for this difference.

d. Discuss the relative usefulness of the variable costing income statements versus the absorption costing income statements for decision making and for evaluating the manager's performance.

a. 90,000 units: NI £550,000

b. 90,000 units: NI £370,000

Continuing Case

Current Designs

CD6 Current Designs (USA) manufactures two different types of kayaks, rotomolded kayaks and composite kayaks. The following information is available for each product line.

	Rotomolded	Composite
Unit selling price	$950	$2,000
Unit variable costs	$570	$1,340

The company's fixed costs are $820,000. An analysis of the sales mix identifies that rotomolded kayaks make up 80% of the total units sold.

Instructions

a. Determine the weighted-average unit contribution margin for Current Designs.

b. Determine the break-even point in sales units for Current Designs and identify how many units of each type of kayak will be sold at the break-even point. (Round to the nearest whole number.)

c. Assume that the sales mix changes, and rotomolded kayaks now make up 70% of total units sold. Calculate the total number of units that would need to be sold to earn a net income of $2,000,000 and identify how many units of each type of kayak will be sold at this level of income. (Round to the nearest whole number.)

d. Assume that Current Designs will have sales of $3,000,000 with two-thirds of the sales dollars in rotomolded kayaks and one-third of the sales dollars in composite kayaks. Assuming $660,000 of fixed costs are allocated to the rotomolded kayaks and $160,000 to the composite kayaks, prepare a CVP income statement for each product line.

e. Using the information in part (d), calculate the degree of operating leverage for each product line and interpret your findings. (Round to two decimal places.)

Data Analytics in Action

Using Data Visualization to Analyze Revenues

DA6.1 Data visualization can be used to identify business expansion opportunities.

Example: Recall the *Data Analytics Insight* box "Taking No Chances with Its Profits" presented in the chapter. Data analytics can help companies know where opportunities lie. For example, while **Caesars Entertainment** (USA) uses data analytics to maximize its in-house profitability, other gaming companies may look to expand through outside operations. For example, consider the following chart, which shows gaming revenue by state in 2018, 2009, and 2001.

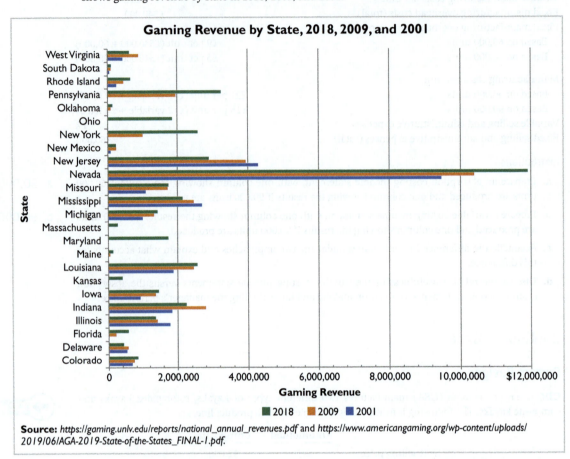

You can see that some states have grown their gaming revenue significantly, while other states show a declining gaming revenue. Managers look for states that have growth potential when deciding where to expand.

For this case, you will take a closer look at this data, to identify which states hold potential for further expansion of gaming revenue. This case requires you to create and analyze a column chart.

Go to the book's product page on www.wiley.com for complete case details and instructions.

Data Analytics at HydroHappy

DA6.2 HydroHappy management wants to examine the profitability of its small retail shop near the beach in St. Thomas, Virgin Islands. The shop rents and sells two unique products, boogie boards and skim boards, referred to by the locals as a "Boogie" and a "Skimmy." Even though the rental operations are profitable, the retail operations may not be covering the related costs. On average, the company sells two Skimmy boards for every one Boogie. For this case, you will prepare a break-even analysis for HydroHappy's two products by using data for forecasted sales. You will also create a CVP graph to forecast the company's total sales revenue, fixed costs, and total variable costs in order to determine the profitability of HydroHappy's retail sales operation.

Go to the book's product page on www.wiley.com for complete case details and instructions.

Expand Your Critical Thinking

Decision-Making Across the Organization

CT6.1 E-Z Seats manufactures swivel seats for customized vans. It currently manufactures 10,000 seats per year, which it sells for €500 per seat. It incurs unit variable costs of €200 per seat and fixed costs of

€2,000,000. It is considering automating the upholstery process, which is now largely manual. It estimates that if it does so, its fixed costs will be €3,000,000, and its unit variable costs will decline to €100 per seat.

Instructions

With the class divided into groups, complete the following activities:

a. Prepare a single-column CVP income statement based on current activity.

b. Compute the contribution margin ratio, break-even point in sales euros, margin of safety ratio, and degree of operating leverage based on current activity.

c. Prepare a single-column CVP income statement assuming that the company invests in the automated upholstery system.

d. Compute the contribution margin ratio, break-even point in sales euros, margin of safety ratio, and degree of operating leverage assuming the new upholstery system is implemented.

e. Discuss the implications of adopting the new system.

Managerial Analysis

CT6.2 For nearly 20 years, Indigo Paints has provided painting and galvanizing services for manufacturers in its region. Manufacturers of various metal products have relied on the quality and quick turnaround time provided by Indigo Paints and its 20 skilled employees. During the last year, as a result of a sharp upturn in the economy, the company's sales have increased by 30% relative to the previous year. The company has not been able to increase its capacity fast enough, so Indigo Paints has had to turn work away because it cannot keep up with customer requests.

Top management is considering the purchase of a sophisticated robotic painting booth. The booth would represent a considerable move in the direction of automation versus manual labor. If Indigo Paints purchases the booth, it would most likely lay off 15 of its skilled painters. To analyze the decision, the company compiled production information from the most recent year and then prepared a parallel compilation assuming that the company would purchase the new equipment and lay off the workers. Those data are shown below. As you can see, the company projects that during the last year it would have been far more profitable if it had used the automated approach.

	Current Approach	Automated Approach
Sales	£2,000,000	£2,000,000
Variable costs	1,500,000	1,000,000
Contribution margin	500,000	1,000,000
Fixed costs	380,000	800,000
Net income	£ 120,000	£ 200,000

Instructions

a. Compute and interpret the contribution margin ratio under each approach.

b. Compute the break-even point in sales pounds under each approach. Discuss the implications of your findings.

c. Using the current level of sales, compute the margin of safety ratio under each approach and interpret your findings.

d. Determine the degree of operating leverage for each approach at current sales levels. How much would the company's net income decline under each approach with a 10% decline in sales?

e. At what level of sales would the company's net income be the same under either approach?

f. Discuss the issues that the company must consider in making this decision.

Real-World Focus

CT6.3 At one time, **Del Monte Foods Company** (USA) reported three separate operating segments: consumer products (which includes a variety of canned foods including tuna, fruit, and vegetables); pet products (which includes pet food and snacks and veterinary products); and soup and infant-feeding products (which includes soup, broth, and infant feeding and pureed products).

In its annual report, Del Monte uses absorption costing. As a result, information regarding the relative composition of its fixed and variable costs is not available. We have assumed that $860.3 million of its total operating expenses of $1,920.3 million are fixed and have allocated the remaining variable costs across the three divisions. Sales data, along with assumed expense data, are provided below.

	(in millions)	
	Sales	Variable Costs
Consumer products	$1,031.8	$ 610
Pet products	837.3	350
Soup and infant-feeding products	302.0	100
	$2,171.1	$1,060

Instructions

a. Compute each segment's contribution margin ratio and the sales mix.

b. Using the information computed in part (a), compute the company's break-even point in sales dollars, and then determine the amount of sales that would be generated by each division at the break-even point.

CT6.4 **Service** The external financial statements published by publicly traded companies are based on absorption cost accounting. As a consequence, it is very difficult to gain an understanding of the relative composition of the companies' fixed and variable costs. It is possible, however, to learn about a company's sales mix and the relative profitability of its various divisions. This exercise looks at the financial statements of **FedEx Corporation** (USA).

Instructions

Go to the FedEx website to access the company's 2019 annual report and then use it to answer the following questions:

a. Read page 64 of the report under the heading "Reportable Segments." What are the four reportable segments of the company?

b. Page 69 of the report shows an income statement for the FedEx Ground segment, which lists the operating expenses. Assuming that rentals, depreciation, and "other" are all fixed costs, prepare a variable costing income statement for 2019.

c. Using the information from part (b), compute the segment's contribution margin ratio and the break-even point in sales dollars.

Communication Activity

CT6.5 Swedex AG makes two different boat anchors—a traditional fishing anchor and a high-end yacht anchor—using the same production machinery. The contribution margin of the yacht anchor is three times as high as that of the other product. The company is currently operating at full capacity and has been doing so for nearly two years. Bjorn Borg, the company's CEO, wants to cut back on production of the fishing anchor so that the company can make more yacht anchors. He says that this is a "no-brainer" because the contribution margin of the yacht anchor is so much higher.

Instructions

Write a short memo to Bjorn Borg describing the analysis that the company should do before it makes this decision and any other considerations that would affect the decision.

Ethics Case

*CT6.6 Nishit Pravin was hired during January 2023 to manage the home products division of Hi-Tech Products. As part of his employment contract, he was told that he would get £5,000 of additional bonus for every 1% increase that the division's profits exceeded those of the previous year.

Soon after coming on board, Nishit met with his factory managers and explained that he wanted the factory to be run at full capacity. Previously, the factory had employed just-in-time inventory practices and had consequently produced units only as they were needed. Nishit stated that under previous management the company had missed out on too many sales opportunities because it didn't have enough inventory on hand. Because previous management had employed just-in-time inventory practices, when Nishit came on board there was virtually no beginning inventory. The unit selling price and unit variable costs remained the same from 2022 to 2023. The following additional information is also provided.

	2022	2023
Net income (based on absorption costing)	£ 300,000	£ 525,000
Units produced	25,000	30,000
Units sold	25,000	25,000
Fixed manufacturing overhead costs	£1,350,000	£1,350,000
Fixed manufacturing overhead costs per unit	£ 54	£ 45

Instructions

a. Calculate Nishit's bonus based on the net income shown above.
b. Recompute the 2022 and 2023 results using variable costing.
c. Recompute Nishit's 2023 bonus under variable costing.
d. Were Nishit's actions unethical? Do you think any actions need to be taken by the company?

All About You

CT6.7 **Service** Many of you will some day own your own business. One rapidly growing opportunity is no-frills workout centers. Such centers attract customers who want to take advantage of state-of-the-art fitness equipment but do not need the other amenities of full-service health clubs. One way to own your own fitness business is to buy a franchise. **Snap Fitness** (USA) is a Minnesota-based business that offers franchise opportunities. For a very low monthly fee ($26, without an annual contract), customers can access a Snap Fitness center 24 hours a day.

The Snap Fitness website indicates that start-up costs range from $60,000 to $184,000. This initial investment covers the following pre-opening costs: franchise fee, grand opening marketing, leasehold improvements, utility/rent deposits, and training.

Instructions

a. Suppose that Snap Fitness estimates that each location incurs $4,000 per month in fixed operating expenses plus $1,460 to lease equipment. A recent newspaper article describing no-frills fitness centers indicated that a Snap Fitness site might require only 300 members to break even. Using the information provided above and your knowledge of CVP analysis, estimate the amount of variable costs. (When performing your analysis, assume that the only fixed costs are the estimated monthly operating expenses and the equipment lease.)
b. Using the information from part (a), what would monthly sales in members and dollars have to be to achieve a target net income of $3,640 for the month?
c. Provide five examples of variable costs for a fitness center.
d. Go to a fitness-business website, such as **Snap Fitness** or **Anytime Fitness** (USA), and find information about purchasing a franchise. Summarize the franchise information needed to decide whether entering into a franchise agreement would be a good idea.

Considering People, Planet, and Profit

CT6.8 Many politicians, scientists, economists, and businesspeople have become concerned about the potential implications of global warming. The largest source of the emissions thought to contribute to global warming is from coal-fired power plants. The cost of alternative energy has declined, but it is still higher than coal. In 1980, wind-powered electricity cost 80 cents per kilowatt hour. Using today's highly efficient turbines with rotor diameters of up to 125 meters, the cost can be as low as 4 cents (about the same as coal), or as much as 20 cents in places with less wind.

Some people have recently suggested that conventional cost comparisons are not adequate because they do not take environmental costs into account. For example, while coal is a very cheap energy source, it is also a significant contributor of greenhouse gases. Should environmental costs be incorporated into decision calculations when planners evaluate new power plants? The basic arguments for and against are as follows:

> **YES:** As long as environmental costs are ignored, renewable energy will appear to be too expensive relative to coal.
> **NO:** If one country decides to incorporate environmental costs into its decision-making process but other countries do not, the country that does so will be at a competitive disadvantage because its products will cost more to produce.

Instructions

Write a response indicating your position regarding this situation. Provide support for your view.

CHAPTER 7

Incremental Analysis

CHAPTER PREVIEW

An important purpose of management accounting is to provide managers with relevant information for decision-making. Companies of all sorts must make product decisions. **Unilever** (GBR), the world's largest supplier of teas, considered exiting the tea industry in the developed world. **Little Caesars** (USA) decided to team up with **DoorDash** (USA) to deliver its pizzas. **Quaker Oats** (USA) decided to sell off a line of beverages, at a price more than $1 billion less than it paid for that product line only a few years before.

This chapter explains management's decision-making process and a decision-making approach called incremental analysis. The use of incremental analysis is demonstrated in a variety of situations.

FEATURE STORY

Keeping It Clean

When you think of new, fast-growing, San Francisco companies, you probably think of fun products like smartphones, social networks, and game apps. You don't tend to think of soap. In fact, given that some of the biggest, most powerful companies in the world dominate the soap market (e.g., **Procter & Gamble** (USA), **Clorox** (USA), and **Unilever** (GBR), starting a new soap company seems like an outrageously bad idea. But that didn't dissuade Adam Lowry and Eric Ryan from giving it a try. The long-time friends and former roommates combined their skills (Adam's chemical engineering and Eric's design and marketing) to start **Method Products** (USA). Their goal: selling environmentally friendly soaps that actually remove dirt.

Within a year of its formation, the company had products on the shelves at **Target** stores (USA). Within five years, Method was cited by numerous business publications as one of the fastest-growing companies in the country. It was easy—right? Wrong. Running a company is never easy. In addition, because of Method's commitment to sustainability, all of its business decisions are just a little more complex than usual. For example, the company wanted to use solar power to charge the batteries for the forklifts used in its factories. No problem, just put solar panels on the buildings. But because Method outsources its manufacturing, it doesn't actually own factory buildings. In fact, the company that does Method's manufacturing doesn't own the buildings either. Solution—Method parked old semi-trailers next to the factories and installed solar panels on those.

Since Method insists on using natural products and sustainable production practices, its production costs are higher than those of companies that don't adhere to these standards. Adam and Eric insist, however, that this actually benefits them because they have to be far more careful about controlling costs and far more innovative in solving problems. Consider Method's laundry detergent. It is eight times stronger than normal detergent, so it can be sold in a substantially smaller package. This reduces both its packaging and shipping costs. In fact, when the cost of the raw materials used for soap production jumped by as much as 40%, Method actually viewed it as an opportunity to grab market share. It determined that it could offset the cost increases in other places in its supply chain, thus absorbing the cost much easier than its big competitors.

In these and other instances, Adam and Eric identified their alternative courses of action, determined what was relevant to each choice and what wasn't, and then carefully evaluated the incremental costs and revenues of each alternative. When you are small and your competitors have some of the biggest marketing budgets in the world, you can't afford to make very many mistakes.

 Watch the *Method Products* video at https://wileyaccountingupdates.com/video/?p=45 learn more about incremental analysis in the real world.

CHAPTER OUTLINE

Learning Objectives	Review	Practice
LO 1 Describe management's decision-making process and incremental analysis.	• Incremental analysis approach • How incremental analysis works • Qualitative factors • Relationship of incremental analysis and activity-based costing • Types of incremental analysis	**DO IT! 1** Incremental Analysis
LO 2 Analyze the relevant costs in accepting an order at a special price.	• Special price • Available capacity	**DO IT! 2** Special Orders
LO 3 Analyze the relevant costs in a make-or-buy decision.	• Make or buy • Opportunity cost	**DO IT! 3** Make or Buy
LO 4 Analyze the relevant costs and revenues in determining whether to sell or process materials further.	• Single-product case • Multiple-product case	**DO IT! 4** Sell or Process Further
LO 5 Analyze the relevant costs to be considered in repairing, retaining, or replacing equipment.	• Repair, retain, or replace equipment • Sunk costs	**DO IT! 5** Repair or Replace Equipment
LO 6 Analyze the relevant costs in deciding whether to eliminate an unprofitable segment or product.	• Unprofitable segments • Avoidable fixed costs • Effect of contribution margin	**DO IT! 6** Unprofitable Segments

Go to the Review and Practice section at the end of the chapter for a targeted summary and practice applications with solutions.

DECISION-MAKING AND INCREMENTAL ANALYSIS

Making decisions is an important management function.

- However, management's decision-making process does not always follow a set pattern because decisions vary significantly in their scope, urgency, and importance.
- It is possible, though, to identify some steps that are frequently involved in the process. These steps are shown in **Illustration 7.1**.

> **LEARNING OBJECTIVE 1**
> Describe management's decision-making process and incremental analysis.

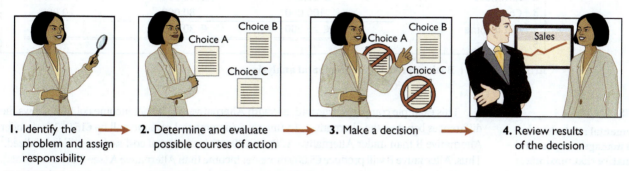

1. Identify the problem and assign responsibility
2. Determine and evaluate possible courses of action
3. Make a decision
4. Review results of the decision

ILLUSTRATION 7.1 | Steps in management's decision-making process

Accounting's contribution to the decision-making process occurs primarily in Steps 2 and 4—evaluating possible courses of action and reviewing results.

- In Step 2, for each possible course of action, relevant revenue and cost data are provided. These show the expected overall effect on net income.
- In Step 4, internal reports are prepared that review the actual impact of the decision.

In making business decisions, management ordinarily considers both financial and nonfinancial information. **Financial** information is related to revenues and costs and their effect on the company's overall profitability. **Nonfinancial** information relates to such factors as the effect of the decision on employee turnover, the environment, or the overall image of the company in the community. (These are considerations that we touched on in our Chapter 1 discussion of corporate social responsibility.)

Incremental Analysis Approach

Decisions involve a choice among alternative courses of action. Suppose you face the personal financial decision of whether to purchase or lease a car. The financial data relate to the cost of leasing versus the cost of purchasing. For example, leasing involves periodic lease payments; purchasing requires "upfront" payment of the purchase price. In other words, the financial information relevant to the decision are the data that vary in the future among the possible alternatives.

- The process used to identify the financial data that change under alternative courses of action is called **incremental analysis** (see **Alternative Terminology**).
- In some cases, you will find that when you use incremental analysis, both costs **and** revenues vary.
- In other cases, only costs **or** revenues vary.

Just as your decision to buy or lease a car affects your future financial situation, similar decisions, on a larger scale, affect a company's future. Incremental analysis identifies the probable effects of those decisions on future earnings. Such analysis inevitably involves estimates and uncertainty. Gathering data for incremental analyses may involve market analysts, engineers, and accountants. In quantifying the data, the accountant must produce the most reliable information available.

> **ALTERNATIVE TERMINOLOGY**
>
> Incremental analysis is also called *differential analysis* because the analysis focuses on differences.

How Incremental Analysis Works

The basic approach in incremental analysis is shown in **Illustration 7.2**.

	Alternative A	Alternative B	Net Income Increase (Decrease)
Revenues	€125,000	€110,000	€ (15,000)
Costs	100,000	80,000	20,000
Net income	€ 25,000	€ 30,000	€ 5,000

ILLUSTRATION 7.2 | Basic approach in incremental analysis

DECISION TOOLS

Incremental analysis helps managers choose the alternative that maximizes net income.

This example compares Alternative B with Alternative A. The net income column shows the differences between the alternatives. In this case, incremental revenue will be €15,000 less under Alternative B than under Alternative A. But a €20,000 incremental cost savings will be realized.[1] Thus, Alternative B will produce €5,000 more net income than Alternative A (see **Decision Tools**).

In the following pages, you will encounter three important cost concepts used in incremental analysis:

1. **Relevant cost and revenues.** In incremental analysis, the only factors to be considered are those costs and revenues that differ across alternatives. Those factors are called **relevant costs and revenues**. Costs and revenues that do not differ across alternatives can be ignored when trying to choose between alternatives.

2. **Opportunity cost.** Often in choosing one course of action, the company must give up the opportunity to benefit from some other course of action. For example, if a machine is used to make one type of product, the benefit of making another type of product with that machine is lost. This lost potential benefit is referred to as **opportunity cost**.

3. **Sunk cost.** Costs that have already been incurred and will not be changed or avoided by any present or future decisions are referred to as **sunk costs**. For example, the amount you spent in the past to purchase or repair a laptop should have no bearing on your decision whether to buy a new laptop. **Sunk costs are not relevant costs.**

Incremental analysis sometimes involves changes that at first glance might seem contrary to your intuition.

- Sometimes variable costs **do not change** under the alternative courses of action. For example, direct labor, normally a variable cost, is not a relevant cost in deciding between the acquisition of two new factory machines if each asset requires the same amount of direct labor.

- Sometimes fixed costs **do change**. For example, rent expense, normally a fixed cost, is a relevant cost in a decision whether to continue occupancy of a building or to purchase or lease a new building.

It is also important to understand that **the approaches to incremental analysis discussed in this chapter do not take into consideration the time value of money**. That is, amounts to be paid or received in future years are not discounted for the cost of interest in this chapter. The effect of the time value of money on decisions is addressed in Chapter 12 and Appendix A.

---

[1] Although income taxes are sometimes important in incremental analysis, they are ignored in the chapter for simplicity's sake.

PEOPLE, PLANET, AND PROFIT INSIGHT

Joseph Clark/ Digital Vision/GettyImages

Water: Liquid Gold of the Future

Currently, finding ground water in some places is becoming cost prohibitive. Because of this, some companies and governments are banking on desalination. In some areas, it is thought that these desalination plants may provide more than 10% of the fresh water that is needed by 2020 to sustain life and growth around the world. But at what cost?

Some view the expensive desalination process as an investment that can be written off as a sunk cost in the future. As with any new technology, supporters believe that the costs will come down, modularity of the plants will occur, and new cost-effective membrane processes will be developed.

During the drought period from 1997 to 2009, Australia invested in the sunk-cost line of thinking. When rain levels hit record lows, roughly $11 billion was funneled into desalination. The Australian government also began a reframing of peoples' thinking about the drought, calling it a policy issue rather than a natural disaster. In the case of Australia, water experts believe that individuals learned and applied water innovations, such as adopting "greywater" measures that use dishwater or water from laundry machines to water lawns along with the use of the desalination. The result? An average Melbourne resident uses just 25% of the water used by a person in Los Angeles.

Sources: M. Jackson, "Can Lessons from Australia's 'Big Dry' Save California?" *The Christian Science Monitor* (December 1, 2015); and L. Williams, "Desalination Is No Longer a Pipe Dream in Southern California," *Los Angeles Daily News* (January 22, 2017).

Should sunk costs be treated as relevant costs when applying incremental analysis? (Answer is available in the book's product page on www.wiley.com)

Qualitative Factors

In this chapter, we focus primarily on the quantitative factors that affect a decision—those attributes that can be easily expressed in terms of numbers or euros. However, many of the decisions involving incremental analysis have important qualitative features. Though not easily measured, they should not be ignored.

- Consider, for example, the potential effects of the make-or-buy decision or of the decision to eliminate a line of business on existing employees and the community in which the plant is located.
- The cost savings that may be obtained from outsourcing or from eliminating a plant should be weighed against these qualitative attributes.
- One example would be the cost of lost morale that might result.

For example, Al "Chainsaw" Dunlap was a so-called "turnaround" artist who went into many companies, identified inefficiencies (using incremental analysis techniques), and tried to correct these problems to improve corporate profitability. Along the way, he laid off thousands of employees at numerous companies. As head of **Sunbeam** (USA), it was Al Dunlap who lost his job because his Draconian approach failed to improve Sunbeam's profitability. It was reported that Sunbeam's employees openly rejoiced for days after his departure. Clearly, qualitative factors can matter.

Relationship of Incremental Analysis and Activity-Based Costing

In Chapter 4, we noted that many companies have shifted to activity-based costing to allocate overhead costs to products. The primary reason for using activity-based costing is that it results in a more accurate allocation of overhead.

- The concepts presented in this chapter are completely consistent with the use of activity-based costing.
- In fact, activity-based costing results in more accurate costing and, therefore, improved incremental analysis.

Types of Incremental Analysis

A number of different types of decisions involve incremental analysis. The more common types of decisions are whether to:

1. Accept an order at a special price.
2. Make or buy component parts or finished products.
3. Sell products or process them further.
4. Repair, retain, or replace equipment.
5. Eliminate an unprofitable business segment or product.

We consider each of these types of decisions in the following pages.

DO IT! 1 ▶ Incremental Analysis

Wilson O Corporation is comparing two different options. The company currently operates under Option 1, with revenues of €80,000 per year, maintenance expenses of €5,000 per year, and operating expenses of €38,000 per year. Option 2 provides revenues of €80,000 per year, maintenance expenses of €12,000 per year, and operating expenses of €32,000 per year. Option 1 employs a piece of equipment that was upgraded two years ago at a cost of €22,000. If Option 2 is chosen, it will free up resources that will increase revenues by €3,000.

Complete the following table to show the change in income from choosing Option 2 versus Option 1. Designate any sunk costs with an "S."

	Option 1	Option 2	Net Income Increase (Decrease)	Sunk (S)
Revenues				
Maintenance expenses				
Operating expenses				
Equipment upgrade				
Opportunity cost				

ACTION PLAN
- Past costs that cannot be changed as a result of any present or future action are sunk costs.
- Benefits lost by choosing one option over another are opportunity costs.

Solution

	Option 1	Option 2	Net Income Increase (Decrease)	Sunk (S)
Revenues	€80,000	€80,000	€ 0	
Maintenance expenses	5,000	12,000	(7,000)	
Operating expenses	38,000	32,000	6,000	
Cost of past equipment upgrade	22,000	0	0	S
Opportunity cost	3,000	0	3,000	
			€ 2,000	

Related exercise material: **BE7.1, BE7.2, DO IT! 7.1, E7.1, and E7.18.**

SPECIAL ORDERS

LEARNING OBJECTIVE 2
Analyze the relevant costs in accepting an order at a special price.

Sometimes a company has an opportunity to obtain additional business if it is willing to make a price concession to a specific customer or make a special accommodation for a potential new customer. **In this case, the basic decision rule is to accept the special order if the incremental price exceeds the incremental costs to complete the order.**

To illustrate, assume that Natalya SA produces 100,000 smoothie blenders per month, which is 80% of plant capacity. Variable manufacturing costs are €8 per unit. Fixed manufacturing costs are €400,000, or €4 per unit. The smoothie blenders are normally sold directly to retailers at €20 each. Kensington Co. (a foreign wholesaler) has offered to purchase an additional 2,000 blenders from Natalya at €11 per unit. Management has determined that acceptance of the offer would not affect normal sales of the product, and the additional units can be manufactured without increasing plant capacity. What should management do?

If management makes its decision on the basis of the total cost per unit of €12 (€8 variable + €4 fixed), the order would be rejected because costs per unit (€12) exceed revenues per unit (€11) by €1 per unit. However, since the units can be produced within existing plant capacity, the special order **will not increase fixed costs**. Let's identify the relevant data for the decision.

- The variable manufacturing costs increase €16,000 (€8 × 2,000).
- The expected revenue increases €22,000 (€11 × 2,000).

Thus, as shown in **Illustration 7.3**, Natalya increases its net income by €6,000 by accepting this special order (see **Helpful Hint**).

> **HELPFUL HINT**
>
> This is a good example of different costs for different purposes. In the long run all costs are relevant, but for this decision only costs that change are relevant.

Incremental Analysis - Accepting an order at a special price

	A	B	C	D
1		Reject Order	Accept Order	Net Income Increase (Decrease)
2	Revenues	€0	€22,000	€ 22,000
3	Costs	0	16,000	(16,000)
4	Net income	€0	€ 6,000	€ 6,000

ILLUSTRATION 7.3 | Incremental analysis—accepting an order at a special price

Additional Considerations

Decisions regarding special orders often need to take into account other factors beyond costs and revenues. For example, consider the following:

- We assume that sales of the product in other markets **would not be affected by this special order**. If other sales were affected, then Natalya would have to consider the change in profit due to lost sales in making the decision.
- If Natalya is operating **at full capacity**, it is likely that the special order would be rejected. Under such circumstances, the company would have to expand plant capacity. In that case, the special order would have to absorb these additional fixed manufacturing costs as well as the variable manufacturing costs.

DO IT! 2 ▶ **Special Orders**

Origin Company incurs costs of €28 per unit (€18 variable and €10 fixed) to make a product that normally sells for €42. A foreign wholesaler offers to buy 5,000 units at €25 each. The special order results in additional shipping costs of €1 per unit. Compute the increase or decrease in net income Origin realizes by accepting the special order, assuming Origin has excess operating capacity. Should Origin Company accept the special order?

> **ACTION PLAN**
>
> - Identify all revenues that would change as a result of accepting the order.
> - Identify all costs that would change as a result of accepting the order, and net this amount against the change in revenues.

Solution

	Reject	Accept	Net Income Increase (Decrease)
Revenues	€-0-	€125,000*	€125,000
Costs	-0-	95,000**	(95,000)
Net income	€-0-	€ 30,000	€ 30,000

*5,000 × €25
**(5,000 × €18) + (5,000 × €1)

The analysis indicates net income increases by €30,000; therefore, Origin Company should accept the special order.

Related exercise material: **BE7.3, DO IT! 7.2, E7.2, E7.3, and E7.4.**

MAKE OR BUY

LEARNING OBJECTIVE 3
Analyze the relevant costs in a make-or-buy decision.

When a manufacturer assembles component parts to produce a finished product, management must decide whether to make or buy the components. The decision to buy parts or services is often referred to as outsourcing. For example, as discussed in the Feature Story, a company such as **Method Products** (USA) may either make or buy the soaps used in its products. Similarly, **Hewlett-Packard Corporation** (USA) may make or buy the electronic circuitry, cases, and printer heads for its printers. At one time, **Boeing** (USA) sold some of its commercial aircraft factories in an effort to cut production costs and focus on engineering and final assembly rather than manufacturing. The decision to make or buy components should be made on the basis of incremental analysis.

Viscount Bikes makes motorcycles. **Illustration 7.4** shows the annual costs it incurs in producing 25,000 ignition switches for motorcycles.

Direct materials	€ 50,000
Direct labor	75,000
Variable manufacturing overhead	40,000
Fixed manufacturing overhead	60,000
Total manufacturing costs	€225,000
Total cost per unit (€225,000 ÷ 25,000)	**€ 9.00**

ILLUSTRATION 7.4 | Annual product cost data

Instead of making its own switches at a cost of €9, Viscount Bikes might purchase the ignition switches from Ignition, Inc. at a price of €8 per unit. Should management do this?

- A review of operations indicates that if the ignition switches are purchased from Ignition, Inc., *all* of Viscount's variable costs but only €10,000 of its fixed manufacturing costs will be eliminated (avoided).
- Thus, €50,000 of the fixed manufacturing costs remain if the ignition switches are purchased.

The relevant costs for incremental analysis are shown in **Illustration 7.5**.

This analysis indicates that Viscount Bikes incurs €25,000 of additional costs by buying the ignition switches rather than making them. Therefore, Viscount should continue to make the ignition switches even though the total manufacturing cost is €1 higher per unit than the purchase price. The primary cause of this result is that, even if the company purchases the ignition switches, it will still have fixed costs of €50,000 to absorb.

	A	B	C	D
1		Make	Buy	Net Income Increase (Decrease)
2	Direct materials	€ 50,000	€ 0	€ 50,000
3	Direct labor	75,000	0	75,000
4	Variable manufacturing costs	40,000	0	40,000
5	Fixed manufacturing costs	60,000	50,000	10,000
6	Purchase price (25,000 × €8)	0	200,000	(200,000)
7	Total annual cost	€225,000	€250,000	€ (25,000)

ILLUSTRATION 7.5 | Incremental analysis—make or buy

Opportunity Cost

The previous make-or-buy analysis is complete only if it is assumed that the productive capacity used to make the ignition switches cannot be converted to another purpose. If there is an opportunity to use this productive capacity in some other manner, then this opportunity cost must be considered. As indicated earlier, **opportunity cost** is the lost potential benefit that could have been obtained by following an alternative course of action.

To illustrate, assume that through buying the switches, Viscount Bikes can use the released productive capacity to generate additional income of €38,000 from producing a different product.

- This lost income is an additional cost of continuing to make the switches in the make-or-buy decision.
- This €38,000 opportunity cost is therefore added to the "Make" column for comparison.

As shown in **Illustration 7.6**, it is now advantageous to buy the ignition switches because the company's income would increase by €13,000.

	A	B	C	D
1		Make	Buy	Net Income Increase (Decrease)
2	Total annual cost*	€225,000	€250,000	€(25,000)
3	Opportunity cost	38,000	0	38,000
4	Total cost	€263,000	€250,000	€ 13,000
5	*From Illustration 7.5.			

ILLUSTRATION 7.6 | Incremental analysis—make or buy, with opportunity cost

Additional Considerations

In the make-or-buy decision, it is important for management to also take into account qualitative factors.

- For instance, buying may be the most economically feasible solution, but such action could result in the closing of a manufacturing plant and laying off many good workers.
- In addition, management must assess the supplier's ability to satisfy the company's quality control standards at the quoted price per unit on a timely basis.

SERVICE COMPANY INSIGHT — Amazon.com

Giving Away the Store?

iStock.com/klenger

In an earlier chapter, we discussed **Amazon.com**'s (USA) incredible growth. However, some analysts have questioned whether some of the methods that Amazon uses to increase its sales make good business sense. For example, a few years ago, Amazon initiated a "Prime" free-shipping subscription program. For an annual fee, Amazon's customers get free shipping on as many goods as they want to buy. At the time, CEO Jeff Bezos promised that the program would be costly in the short-term but benefit the company in the long-term. Six years later, it was true that Amazon's sales had grown considerably. It was also estimated that its Prime customers buy two to three times as much as non-Prime customers. But its shipping costs rose from 2.8% of sales to 4% of sales, which is remarkably similar to the drop in its gross margin from 24% to 22.3%. Amazon's order fulfillment center uses 30,000 robots and more than 100 million square feet of space. It generates significant fees from merchants that sell on its site and rely on its fulfillment services.

Sources: Martin Peers, "Amazon's Prime Numbers," *Wall Street Journal Online* (February 3, 2011); and Evan Niu, "Ever Wonder How Amazon.com Pays for All of That Free Shipping?" *The Motley Fool* (October 26, 2015).

What are the relevant revenues and costs that Amazon should consider relative to the decision whether to offer the Prime free-shipping subscription? (Answer is available in the book's product page on www.wiley.com)

DO IT! 3 ▶ Make or Buy

Santiago SA must decide whether to make or buy some of its components for the appliances it produces. The costs of producing 166,000 electrical cords for its appliances are as follows:

Direct materials	€90,000	Variable overhead	€32,000
Direct labor	20,000	Fixed overhead	24,000

Instead of making the electrical cords at an average cost per unit of €1.00 (€166,000 ÷ 166,000), the company has an opportunity to buy the cords at €0.90 per unit. If the company purchases the cords, all variable costs and one-fourth of the fixed costs are eliminated.

a. Prepare an incremental analysis showing whether the company should make or buy the electrical cords.

b. Will your answer be different if the released productive capacity of the production facility will generate additional income of €5,000?

ACTION PLAN
- Look for the costs that change.
- Ignore the costs that do not change.
- Use the format in the chapter for your answer.
- Recognize that opportunity cost can make a difference.

Solution

a.

	Make	Buy	Net Income Increase (Decrease)
Direct materials	€ 90,000	€ –0–	€ 90,000
Direct labor	20,000	–0–	20,000
Variable manufacturing costs	32,000	–0–	32,000
Fixed manufacturing costs	24,000	18,000*	6,000
Purchase price	–0–	149,400**	(149,400)
Total cost	€166,000	€167,400	€ (1,400)

*€24,000 × .75
**166,000 × €0.90

This analysis indicates that Santiago SA will incur €1,400 of additional costs if it buys the electrical cords rather than making them.

b.

	Make	Buy	Net Income Increase (Decrease)
Total cost	€166,000	€167,400	€(1,400)
Opportunity cost	5,000	–0–	5,000
Total cost	€171,000	€167,400	€ 3,600

Yes, the answer is different. The analysis shows that net income increases by €3,600 if Santiago SA purchases the electrical cords rather than making them.

Related exercise material: **BE7.4, DO IT! 7.3, E7.5, E7.6, E7.7, and E7.8.**

SELL OR PROCESS FURTHER

Many manufacturers have the option of selling products at a given point in the production cycle or continuing to process with the expectation of selling them at a later point at a higher price. For example, a bicycle manufacturer such as **Great Go Cycles** (TWN) could sell its bicycles to retailers either unassembled or assembled. A furniture manufacturer such as **IKEA** (SWE) could sell its furniture to stores either unfinished or finished. The sell-or-process-further decision should be made on the basis of incremental analysis. The basic decision rule is: **Process further as long as the incremental revenue from such processing exceeds the incremental processing costs.**

> **LEARNING OBJECTIVE 4**
> Analyze the relevant costs and revenues in determining whether to sell or process materials further.

Single-Product Case

Assume, for example, that Bosco SpA makes tables. It sells unfinished tables for €50. The cost to manufacture an unfinished table is €35, computed as shown in **Illustration 7.7**.

Direct materials	€15
Direct labor	10
Variable manufacturing overhead	6
Fixed manufacturing overhead	4
Manufacturing cost per unit	**€35**

ILLUSTRATION 7.7 | Per unit cost of unfinished table

Bosco currently has unused productive capacity that is expected to continue indefinitely. Some of this capacity could be used to finish the tables and sell them at €60 per unit.

- For a finished table, direct materials will increase €2 and direct labor costs will increase €4.
- Variable manufacturing overhead costs will increase by €2.40 (60% of direct labor).
- No increase is anticipated in fixed manufacturing overhead.

Should the company sell the unfinished tables, or should it process them further (see **Helpful Hint**)? **Illustration 7.8** shows the incremental analysis on a per unit basis.

> **HELPFUL HINT**
> Current net income is known. Net income from processing further is an estimate. In making its decision, management could add a "risk" factor for the estimate.

Incremental Analysis - Sell or process further

	Sell Unfinished	Process Further	Net Income Increase (Decrease)
Unit selling price	€50.00	€60.00	€10.00
Cost per unit			
Direct materials	15.00	17.00	(2.00)
Direct labor	10.00	14.00	(4.00)
Variable manufacturing overhead	6.00	8.40	(2.40)
Fixed manufacturing overhead	4.00	4.00	0.00
Total	35.00	43.40	(8.40)
Net income per unit	€15.00	€16.60	€ 1.60

ILLUSTRATION 7.8 | Incremental analysis—sell or process further

It would be advantageous for Bosco to process the tables further. The incremental revenue of €10.00 from the additional processing is €1.60 higher than the incremental processing costs of €8.40. This results in an increase to net income of €1.60 per unit.

Multiple-Product Case

Sell-or-process-further decisions are particularly applicable to processes that produce multiple products simultaneously.

- In many industries, a number of end-products are produced from a single raw material and a common production process.
- These multiple end-products are commonly referred to as **joint products**.

For example, in the meat-packing industry, **Armour** (USA) processes a cow or pig into meat, internal organs, hides, bones, and fat products. In the petroleum industry, **Shell plc** (GBR) refines crude oil to produce gasoline, lubricating oil, kerosene, paraffin, and ethylene.

Illustration 7.9 presents a joint product situation for Marais Laiterie involving a decision **to sell or process further** cream and skim milk. Cream and skim milk are joint products that result from the processing of raw milk. The company must decide whether to sell the cream or process it further into cottage cheese. It must also decide whether to sell the skim milk or process it further into condensed milk.

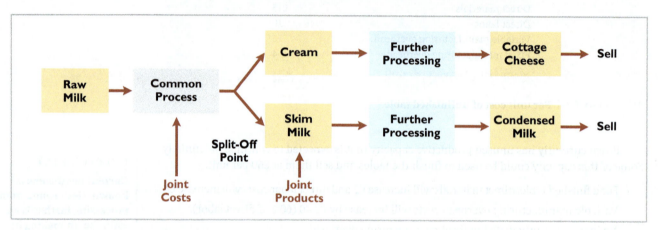

ILLUSTRATION 7.9 | Joint production process—Laiterie

Marais incurs many costs prior to the manufacture of the cream and skim milk. All costs incurred prior to the point at which the two products are separately identifiable (the **split-off point**) are called **joint costs**.

- For purposes of determining the cost of each product, joint product costs must be allocated to the individual products.
- This is frequently done based on the relative sales value of the joint products.
- While this allocation is important for determination of product cost, **it is irrelevant for any sell-or-process-further decisions; joint product costs are sunk costs**. That is, they have already been incurred, and they cannot be changed or avoided by any subsequent decision.

Should Marais sell the cream or process it further into cottage cheese? **Illustration 7.10** provides the daily cost and revenue data for Marais Laiterie related to this decision.

Costs (per day)	
Joint cost allocated to cream	€ 9,000
Cost to process cream into cottage cheese	10,000
Revenues from Products (per day)	
Cream	€19,000
Cottage cheese	27,000

ILLUSTRATION 7.10 | Cost and revenue data per day for cream

From this information, we can determine whether the company should simply sell the cream or process it further into cottage cheese. **Illustration 7.11** shows the necessary analysis.

	Incremental Analysis - Sell or process further - Cream or cottage cheese		
A	B	C	D
1	Sell	Process Further	Net Income Increase (Decrease)
2 Sales per day	€19,000	€ 27,000	€ 8,000
3 Cost per day to process cream into cottage cheese	0	10,000	(10,000)
4 Net income per day	€19,000	€ 17,000	€ (2,000)

ILLUSTRATION 7.11 | **Analysis of whether to sell cream or process into cottage cheese**

- Note that the joint cost of €9,000 that is allocated to the cream is not included in this decision.
- It is not relevant to the decision because it is a sunk cost.
- It has been incurred in the past and will remain the same no matter whether the cream is subsequently processed into cottage cheese or not.

From this analysis, we can see that Marais should not process the cream further because it will sustain an incremental loss of €2,000.

Should Marais sell the skim milk or process it further into condensed milk? **Illustration 7.12** provides the daily cost and revenue data for the company related to this decision.

Costs (per day)	
Joint cost allocated to skim milk	€ 5,000
Cost to process skim milk into condensed milk	8,000
Revenues from Products (per day)	
Skim milk	€11,000
Condensed milk	26,000

ILLUSTRATION 7.12 | **Cost and revenue data per day for skim milk**

Illustration 7.13 shows that Marais should process the skim milk into condensed milk, as it will increase net income by €7,000.

	Incremental Analysis - Sell or process further - Skim milk or condensed milk		
A	B	C	D
1	Sell	Process Further	Net Income Increase (Decrease)
2 Sales per day	€11,000	€26,000	€15,000
3 Cost per day to process skim milk into condensed milk	0	8,000	(8,000)
4 Net income per day	€11,000	€18,000	€ 7,000

ILLUSTRATION 7.13 | **Analysis of whether to sell skim milk or process into condensed milk**

- Again, note that the €5,000 of joint cost allocated to the skim milk is irrelevant in deciding whether to sell or process further.
- The joint cost remains the same, whether or not further processing is performed.

Additional Considerations

The decision on whether to sell or process further needs to be reevaluated as market conditions change. For example, if the price of skim milk increases relative to the price of condensed milk, it may become more profitable to sell the skim milk rather than process it into condensed milk.

- Consider French food company **Danone SA**, which was heavily invested in organic milk production. As consumers of organic milk shifted to milk substitutes (e.g., almond milk), Danone chose to process more of its organic milk into organic cheese, yogurt, and creamer.
- Similarly, oil refineries, such as the **Port Arthur Refinery** in Texas, USA, must also constantly reassess which products to produce from the oil they receive at their plants as market conditions change.

DO IT! 4 ▶ Sell or Process Further

Assemble It manufactures unpainted furniture for the do-it-yourself (DIY) market. It currently sells a child's rocking chair for €25. Production costs per unit are €12 variable and €8 fixed. Assemble It is considering painting the rocking chair and selling it for €35. Variable costs to paint each chair are expected to be €9, and fixed costs are expected to be €2.

Prepare an analysis showing whether Assemble It should sell unpainted or painted chairs.

ACTION PLAN
- Identify the revenues that change as a result of painting the rocking chair.
- Identify all costs that change as a result of painting the rocking chair, and net the amount against the revenues.

Solution

	Sell	Process Further	Net Income Increase (Decrease)
Revenues	€25	€35	€10
Variable costs	12	21[a]	(9)
Fixed costs	8	10[b]	(2)
Net income	€ 5	€ 4	€(1)

[a]€12 + €9; [b]€8 + €2

The analysis indicates that the rocking chair should be sold unpainted because net income per chair will be €1 greater.

Related exercise material: **BE7.5, BE7.6, DO IT! 7.4, E7.9, E7.10, E7.11, and E7.12.**

REPAIR, RETAIN, OR REPLACE EQUIPMENT

LEARNING OBJECTIVE 5
Analyze the relevant costs to be considered in repairing, retaining, or replacing equipment.

Management often has to decide whether to continue using an asset, repair it, or replace it. For example, **Lufthansa** (DEU) must decide whether to replace old jets with new, more fuel-efficient ones. **The basic decision rule is that the company should choose the option that results in the lowest cost (and thus the highest income) over the relevant time period.**

To illustrate, assume that Hollander Company has a factory machine that originally cost €110,000. It has a balance in Accumulated Depreciation of €70,000, so the machine's book value is €40,000. It has a remaining useful life of four years. The company is considering replacing this machine with a new machine.

- A new machine is available that costs €120,000. It is expected to have zero salvage value at the end of its four-year useful life.

- If the new machine is acquired, variable manufacturing costs are expected to decrease from €160,000 to €125,000 annually (that is, €640,000 versus €500,000 over the four-year period). The old unit could be sold for €5,000.
- The costs that are relevant to this decision are the four-year variable manufacturing costs (€640,000 versus €500,000), the cost of the new machine (€120,000), and the amount that could be received from the sale of the old machine (€5,000).

Illustration 7.14 shows the incremental analysis for the **four-year period**.

	A	B	C	D	E	F
1		Retain Equipment		Replace Equipment		Net Income Increase (Decrease)
2	Variable manufacturing costs	€640,000	a	€500,000	b	€140,000
3	New machine cost			120,000		(120,000)
4	Sale of old machine			(5,000)		5,000
5	Total	€640,000		€615,000		€ 25,000
6						
7	a4 years × €160,000					
8	b4 years × €125,000					
9						

ILLUSTRATION 7.14 | **Incremental analysis—retain or replace equipment**

In this case, it would be to the company's advantage to replace the equipment.

- The lower variable manufacturing costs due to replacement more than offset the cost of the new equipment.
- Note that the €5,000 received from the sale of the old machine is relevant to the decision because it will only be received if the company chooses to replace its equipment.

In general, any trade-in allowance or cash disposal value of existing assets is relevant to the decision to retain or replace equipment.

One other point should be mentioned regarding Hollander's decision: **The book value of the old machine does not affect the decision.**

- Book value is a **sunk cost**, which is a cost that cannot be changed by any present or future decision.
- **Sunk costs are not relevant in incremental analysis.**

Additional Considerations

Sometimes, decisions regarding whether to replace equipment are clouded by behavioral decision-making errors. For example, suppose a manager spent €90,000 repairing a machine two months ago. Suppose that the machine now breaks down again.

- The manager might be inclined to think that because the company recently spent a large amount of money to repair the machine, the machine should be repaired again rather than replaced.
- However, the amount spent in the past to repair the machine is irrelevant to the current decision. It is a sunk cost.

Similarly, suppose a manager spent €5,000,000 to purchase a machine. Six months later, a new machine comes on the market that is significantly more efficient than the one recently purchased. The manager might be inclined to think that he or she should not buy the new machine because of the recent purchase. In fact, the manager might fear that buying a different machine so quickly might call into question the merit of the previous decision.

- Again, the fact that the company recently bought a machine is not relevant.
- Instead, the manager should use incremental analysis to determine whether the savings generated by the efficiencies of the new machine would justify its purchase.

DO IT! 5 ▶ Repair or Replace Equipment

Capital Roofing is faced with a decision. The company relies very heavily on the use of its 20-meter extension lift for work on large homes and commercial properties. Last year, the company spent €60,000 refurbishing the lift. It has just determined that another €40,000 of repair work is required. Alternatively, Capital Roofing has found a newer used lift that is for sale for €170,000. The company estimates that both the old and new lifts would have useful lives of six years. However, the new lift is more efficient and thus would reduce operating expenses from €70,000 to €50,000 each year. The company could also rent the new lift to other contractors for about €2,000 per year. The old lift is not suitable for rental. The old lift could currently be sold for €25,000 if the new lift is purchased. The new lift and old lift are estimated to have salvage values of zero if used for another six years. Prepare an incremental analysis that shows whether the company should repair or replace the equipment.

ACTION PLAN
- Those costs and revenues that differ across the alternatives are relevant to the decision.
- Past costs that cannot be changed are sunk costs.

Solution

	Retain Equipment	Replace Equipment	Net Income Increase (Decrease)
Operating expenses	€420,000*	€300,000**	€120,000
Repair costs	40,000		40,000
Rental revenue		€(12,000)***	12,000
New machine cost		170,000	(170,000)
Sale of old machine		(25,000)	25,000
Total cost	€460,000	€433,000	€ 27,000

*6 years × €70,000
**6 years × €50,000
***6 years × €2,000

The analysis indicates that purchasing the new machine would increase net income for the six-year period by €27,000.

Related exercise material: **BE7.7, DO IT! 7.5, E7.13, and E7.14.**

ELIMINATE UNPROFITABLE SEGMENT OR PRODUCT

LEARNING OBJECTIVE 6
Analyze the relevant costs in deciding whether to eliminate an unprofitable segment or product.

HELPFUL HINT
A decision to discontinue a segment based solely on the bottom line—net loss—is inappropriate.

Management sometimes must decide whether to eliminate an unprofitable business segment or product. For example, airlines such as **British Airways** (GBR) sometimes stop servicing certain cities or cut back on the number of flights. **Goodyear** (USA) quit producing several brands in the low-end tire market, and **adidas** (USA) eliminated its **Rockport** (USA) division. Again, the key is to **focus on the relevant costs—the data that change under the alternative courses of action** (see Helpful Hint).

To illustrate, assume that Jupiter Sports manufactures tennis racquets in three models: Pro, Master, and Champ. Pro and Master are profitable lines. Champ (highlighted in red in the table below) operates at a loss. Condensed income statement data are as shown in **Illustration 7.15.**

	Pro	Master	Champ	Total
Sales	€800,000	€300,000	€100,000	€1,200,000
Variable costs	520,000	210,000	90,000	820,000
Contribution margin	280,000	90,000	10,000	380,000
Fixed costs	80,000	50,000	30,000	160,000
Net income	€200,000	€ 40,000	€(20,000)	€ 220,000

ILLUSTRATION 7.15 | **Segment income data**

You might think that total net income will increase by €20,000 to €240,000 if the unprofitable Champ line of racquets is eliminated. However, **net income may actually decrease if the Champ line is discontinued**.

- The reason is that the company's total fixed costs will be the same whether or not the Champ line is discontinued.
- That is, the fixed costs allocated to the Champ racquets cannot be eliminated, so they will have to be absorbed by the other products.

To illustrate, assume that the €30,000 of fixed costs applicable to the unprofitable segment are instead allocated $\frac{2}{3}$ to the Pro model and $\frac{1}{3}$ to the Master model if the Champ model is eliminated. Fixed costs will increase to €100,000 (€80,000 + €20,000) in the Pro line and to €60,000 (€50,000 + €10,000) in the Master line. **Illustration 7.16** shows the revised income statement.

	Pro	Master	Total
Sales	€800,000	€300,000	€1,100,000
Variable costs	520,000	210,000	730,000
Contribution margin	280,000	90,000	370,000
Fixed costs	100,000	60,000	160,000
Net income	€180,000	€ 30,000	€ 210,000

ILLUSTRATION 7.16 | **Income data after eliminating unprofitable product line**

Total net income would decrease €10,000 (€220,000 − €210,000). This result is also obtained in the incremental analysis of the Champ racquets shown in **Illustration 7.17**.

A	B	C	D
	Continue	Eliminate	Net Income Increase (Decrease)
Sales	€100,000	€ 0	€(100,000)
Variable costs	90,000	0	90,000
Contribution margin	10,000	0	(10,000)
Fixed costs	30,000	30,000	0
Net income	€(20,000)	€(30,000)	€ (10,000)

ILLUSTRATION 7.17 | **Incremental analysis—eliminating unprofitable segment with no reduction in fixed costs**

The loss in net income is attributable to the Champ line's €10,000 contribution margin (€220,000 − €210,000), which will not be realized if the segment is discontinued.

Assume the same facts as above, except now assume that €22,000 of the fixed costs attributed to the Champ line can be eliminated if the line is discontinued. **Illustration 7.18** presents the incremental analysis based on this revised assumption.

Incremental Analysis – Eliminating an unprofitable segment

	Continue	Eliminate	Net Income Increase (Decrease)
Sales	€100,000	€ 0	€(100,000)
Variable costs	90,000	0	90,000
Contribution margin	10,000	0	(10,000)
Fixed costs	30,000	8,000	22,000
Net income	€(20,000)	€(8,000)	€ 12,000

ILLUSTRATION 7.18 | Incremental analysis—eliminating unprofitable segment with reduction in fixed costs

In this case, because the company is able to eliminate some of its fixed costs by eliminating the division, it can increase its net income by €12,000. **This occurs because the €22,000 savings that results from the eliminated fixed costs exceeds the €10,000 in lost contribution margin by €12,000 (€22,000 – €10,000).**

Additional Considerations

In deciding on the future status of an unprofitable segment, management should consider the effect of elimination on related product lines. For example, companies might retain high-quality product lines that are individually unprofitable because of the reputational benefits that carry over to lower-end products. In our previous tennis racquet example, the Pro and Master lines might benefit from the fact that the Champ line is used by recognized tennis professionals. Other considerations are as follows:

- It may be possible for continuing product lines to obtain some or all of the sales lost by the discontinued product line.
- In some businesses, services or products may be linked—for example, free checking accounts at a bank, or coffee at a donut shop.
- In addition, management should consider the effect of eliminating the product line on employees who may have to be discharged or retrained.

DO IT! 6 ▶ Unprofitable Segments

Heinrich AG manufactures several types of accessories. For the year, the knit hats and scarves line had sales of €400,000, variable expenses of €310,000, and fixed expenses of €120,000. Therefore, the knit hats and scarves line had a net loss of €30,000. If Heinrich eliminates the knit hats and scarves line, €20,000 of fixed costs will remain. Prepare an analysis showing whether the company should eliminate the knit hats and scarves line.

ACTION PLAN
- Identify the revenues that change as a result of eliminating a product line.
- Identify all costs that change as a result of eliminating a product line, and net the amount against the revenues.

Solution

	Continue	Eliminate	Net Income Increase (Decrease)
Sales	€400,000	€ 0	€(400,000)
Variable costs	310,000	0	310,000
Contribution margin	90,000	0	(90,000)
Fixed costs	120,000	20,000	100,000
Net income	€(30,000)	€(20,000)	€ 10,000

The analysis indicates that Heinrich should eliminate the knit hats and scarves line because net income will increase €10,000.

Related exercise material: **BE7.8, DO IT! 7.6, E7.15, E7.16, and E7.17.**

USING THE DECISION TOOLS | Method Products

Method Products (USA) faces many situations where it needs to apply the decision tool learned in this chapter. For example, assume that in order to have control over the creative nature of its packaging, Method decides to manufacture (instead of outsourcing) some of its more creative soap dispensers. Suppose that the company has been approached by a plastic container manufacturer with a proposal to provide 500,000 Mickey and Minnie Mouse hand wash dispensers. Assume Method's cost of producing 500,000 of the dispensers is $110,000, broken down as follows:

| Direct materials | $60,000 | Variable manufacturing overhead | $12,000 |
| Direct labor | 30,000 | Fixed manufacturing overhead | 8,000 |

Instead of making the dispensers at an average cost per unit of $0.22 ($110,000 ÷ 500,000), Method has an opportunity to buy the dispensers at $0.215 per unit. If the dispensers are purchased, all variable costs and one-half of the fixed costs will be eliminated.

Instructions

a. Prepare an incremental analysis showing whether Method should make or buy the dispensers.
b. Will your answer be different if the released productive capacity resulting from the purchase of the dispensers will generate additional income of $25,000?
c. What additional qualitative factors might Method need to consider?

Solution

a.

	Make	Buy	Net Income Increase (Decrease)
Direct materials	$ 60,000	$ -0-	$ 60,000
Direct labor	30,000	-0-	30,000
Variable manufacturing costs	12,000	-0-	12,000
Fixed manufacturing costs	8,000	4,000*	4,000
Purchase price	-0-	107,500**	(107,500)
Total cost	$110,000	$111,500	$ (1,500)

*$8,000 × .50; **$0.215 × 500,000

This analysis indicates that Method will incur $1,500 of additional costs if it buys the dispensers. Method therefore would choose to make the dispensers.

b.

	Make	Buy	Net Income Increase (Decrease)
Total cost	$110,000	$111,500	$ (1,500)
Opportunity cost	25,000	-0-	25,000
Total cost	$135,000	$111,500	$23,500

Yes, the answer is different. The analysis shows that if additional capacity is released, net income will be increased by $23,500 if the dispensers are purchased. In this case, Method would choose to purchase the dispensers.

c. Method is very concerned about the image of its products. It charges a higher price for many of its products than those of its larger competitors. It therefore wants to ensure that the functionality of the dispenser, as well as the appearance, are up to its standards. Also, because of Method's commitment to sustainability, it would consider numerous qualitative issues. For example, is this supplier going to use sustainable manufacturing practices? Method currently requires that its suppliers meet its expectations regarding sustainability.

REVIEW AND PRACTICE

Learning Objectives Review

LO 1 Describe management's decision-making process and incremental analysis.

Management's decision-making process consists of (a) identifying the problem and assigning responsibility for the decision, (b) determining and evaluating possible courses of action, (c) making the decision, and (d) reviewing the results of the decision. Incremental analysis identifies financial data that change under alternative courses of action. These data are relevant to the decision because they vary across the possible alternatives.

LO 2 Analyze the relevant costs in accepting an order at a special price.

The relevant costs are those that change if the order is accepted. The relevant information in accepting an order at a special price is the difference between the variable manufacturing costs to produce the special order and expected revenues. Any changes in fixed costs, opportunity cost, or other incremental costs or savings (such as additional shipping) should be considered.

LO 3 Analyze the relevant costs in a make-or-buy decision.

In a make-or-buy decision, the relevant costs are (a) the variable manufacturing costs that will be saved as well as changes to fixed manufacturing costs, (b) the purchase price, and (c) opportunity cost.

LO 4 Analyze the relevant costs and revenues in determining whether to sell or process materials further.

The decision rule for whether to sell or process materials further is: Process further as long as the incremental revenue from processing exceeds the incremental processing costs.

LO 5 Analyze the relevant costs to be considered in repairing, retaining, or replacing equipment.

The relevant costs to be considered in determining whether equipment should be repaired, retained, or replaced are the effects on variable costs and the cost of the new equipment. Also, any disposal value of the existing asset must be considered.

LO 6 Analyze the relevant costs in deciding whether to eliminate an unprofitable segment or product.

In deciding whether to eliminate an unprofitable segment or product, the relevant costs are the variable costs that drive the contribution margin, if any, produced by the segment or product. Opportunity cost and reduction of fixed expenses must also be considered.

Decision Tools Review

Decision Checkpoints	Info Needed for Decision	Tool to Use for Decision	How to Evaluate Results
Which alternative should the company choose?	All relevant costs including opportunity cost	Compare the relevant cost of each alternative.	Choose the alternative that maximizes net income.

Glossary Review

Incremental analysis The process of identifying the financial data that change under alternative courses of action. (p. 7-3).

Joint costs For joint products, all costs incurred prior to the point at which the two products are separately identifiable (known as the split-off point). (p. 7-12).

Joint products Multiple end-products produced from a single raw material and a common production process. (p. 7-12).

Opportunity cost The potential benefit that is lost when one course of action is chosen rather than an alternative course of action. (p. 7-4).

Relevant costs and revenues Those costs and revenues that differ across alternatives. (p. 7-4).

Sunk cost A cost incurred in the past that cannot be changed or avoided by any present or future decision. (p. 7-4).

Practice Multiple-Choice Questions

1. (LO 1) Three of the steps in management's decision-making process are (1) review results of decision, (2) determine and evaluate possible courses of action, and (3) make the decision. The steps are carried out in the following order:

    a. (1), (2), (3).   **c.** (2), (1), (3).
    b. (3), (2), (1).   **d.** (2), (3), (1).

2. (LO 1) Incremental analysis is the process of identifying the financial data that:

    a. do not change under alternative courses of action.
    b. change under alternative courses of action.
    c. are mixed under alternative courses of action.
    d. No correct answer is given.

3. (LO 1) In making business decisions, management ordinarily considers:
   a. quantitative factors but not qualitative factors.
   b. financial information only.
   c. both financial and nonfinancial information.
   d. relevant costs, opportunity cost, and sunk costs.

4. (LO 1) A company is considering the following alternatives:

	Alternative A	Alternative B
Revenues	€50,000	€50,000
Variable costs	24,000	24,000
Fixed costs	12,000	15,000

Which of the following are relevant in choosing between these alternatives?
   a. Revenues, variable costs, and fixed costs.
   b. Variable costs and fixed costs.
   c. Variable costs only.
   d. Fixed costs only.

5. (LO 2) It costs a company £14 of variable costs and £6 of fixed costs to produce product Z200, which sells for £30. A foreign buyer offers to purchase 3,000 units at £18 each. If the special offer is accepted and produced with unused capacity, net income will:
   a. decrease £6,000.   c. increase £12,000.
   b. increase £6,000.   d. increase £9,000.

6. (LO 2) It costs a company R140 of variable costs and R60 of fixed costs to produce product Z200. Product Z200 sells for R300. A buyer offers to purchase 3,000 units at R180 each. The seller will incur special shipping costs of R50 per unit. If the special offer is accepted and produced with unused capacity, net income will:
   a. increase R30,000.   c. decrease R120,000.
   b. increase R120,000.   d. decrease R30,000.

7. (LO 3) Edward plc is currently operating at full capacity. It is considering buying a part from an outside supplier rather than making it in-house. If Edward purchases the part, it can use the released productive capacity to generate additional income of £30,000 from producing a different product. When conducting incremental analysis in this make-or-buy decision, the company should:
   a. ignore the £30,000.
   b. add £30,000 to other costs in the "Make" column.
   c. add £30,000 to other costs in the "Buy" column.
   d. subtract £30,000 from the other costs in the "Make" column.

8. (LO 3) In a make-or-buy decision, relevant costs are:
   a. manufacturing costs that will be saved.
   b. the purchase price of the units.
   c. the opportunity cost.
   d. All of the answer choices are correct.

9. (LO 3) Yanzhi Ltd. is performing incremental analysis in a make-or-buy decision for Item X. If Yanzhi buys Item X, he can use its released productive capacity to produce Item Z. Yanzhi will sell Item Z for HK$120,000 and incur production costs of HK$80,000. Yanzhi's incremental analysis should include an opportunity cost of:
   a. HK$120,000.
   b. HK$80,000.
   c. HK$40,000.
   d. HK$0.

10. (LO 4) The decision rule in a sell-or-process-further decision is: Process further as long as the incremental revenue from processing exceeds:
   a. incremental processing costs.
   b. variable processing costs.
   c. fixed processing costs.
   d. No correct answer is given.

11. (LO 4) Dubois SA makes an unassembled product that it currently sells for €55. Production costs are €20. Dubois is considering assembling the product and selling it for €68. The cost to assemble the product is estimated at €12. What decision should Dubois make?
   a. Sell before assembly; net income per unit will be €12 greater.
   b. Sell before assembly; net income per unit will be €1 greater.
   c. Process further; net income per unit will be €13 greater.
   d. Process further; net income per unit will be €1 greater.

12. (LO 5) In a decision to retain or replace equipment, the book value of the old equipment is a (an):
   a. opportunity cost.   c. incremental cost.
   b. sunk cost.   d. marginal cost.

13. (LO 6) If an unprofitable segment is eliminated:
   a. net income will always increase.
   b. variable costs of the eliminated segment will have to be absorbed by other segments.
   c. fixed costs allocated to the eliminated segment will have to be absorbed by other segments.
   d. net income will always decrease.

14. (LO 6) A segment of Hazard Inc. has the following data:

Sales	$200,000
Variable expenses	140,000
Fixed expenses	100,000

If this segment is eliminated, what will be the effect on the remaining company? Assume that 50% of the fixed expenses will be eliminated and the rest will be allocated to the segments of the remaining company.
   a. $120,000 increase.   c. $50,000 increase.
   b. $10,000 decrease.   d. $10,000 increase.

Solutions

1. d. The order of the steps in the decision process is (2) determine and evaluate possible courses of action, (3) make the decision, and (1) review the results of decision. Choices (a), (b), and (c) list the steps in the incorrect order.

2. b. Incremental analysis is the process of identifying the financial data that change under alternative courses of action, not the financial data that (a) do not change or (c) are mixed. Choice (d) is wrong as there is a correct answer given.

3. c. Management ordinarily considers both financial and nonfinancial information in making business decisions. The other choices are incorrect because they are all limited to financial data and do not consider nonfinancial information.

4. d. Fixed costs are the only relevant factor, that is, the only factor that differs across Alternatives A and B. The other choices are incorrect because they list either revenues, variable costs, or both, which are the same amounts for both alternatives.

5. **c.** If the special offer is accepted and produced with unused capacity, unit variable costs = £14 and income per unit = (£18 − £14), so net income will increase by £12,000 (3,000 × £4), not (a) decrease £6,000, (b) increase £6,000, or (d) increase £9,000.

6. **d.** If the special offer is accepted and produced with unused capacity, unit variable costs = R190 (R140 variable + R50 shipping costs) and income per unit = −R10 (R180 − R190), so net income will decrease by R30,000 (3,000 × −R10), not (a) increase R30,000 (b) increase R120,000 or (c) decrease R120,000.

7. **b.** Edward plc should add £30,000 to other costs in the "Make" column as it represents lost income of continuing to make the part in-house. The other choices are incorrect because the £30,000 (a) should not be ignored as it is an opportunity cost, (c) represents potential lost income if the company continues to make the part instead of buying it so therefore should not be placed in the "Buy" column, and (d) should be added to, not subtracted from, the other costs in the "Make" column.

8. **d.** All the costs in choices (a), (b), and (c) are relevant in a make-or-buy decision. So although choices (a), (b), and (c) are true statements, choice (d) is a better answer.

9. **c.** Yanzhi's opportunity cost in its make-or-buy decision is HK$120,000 (revenue for Item Z) − HK$80,000 (production costs for Item Z) = HK$40,000, not (a) HK$120,000, (b) HK$80,000, or (d) HK$0.

10. **a.** The decision rule in a sell-or-process-further decision is to process further as long as the incremental revenue from such processing exceeds incremental processing costs, not (b) variable processing costs or (c) fixed processing costs. Choice (d) is wrong as there is a correct answer given.

11. **d.** If Dubois processes further, net income per unit will increase €13 (€68 − €55), which is €1 more than its additional production costs (€12). The other choices are therefore incorrect.

12. **b.** In the decision to retain or replace equipment, the book value of the old equipment is a sunk cost (it reflects the original cost less accumulated depreciation, neither of which is relevant to the decision), not (a) an opportunity cost, (c) an incremental cost, or (d) a marginal cost.

13. **c.** Even though the segment is eliminated, the fixed costs allocated to that segment will still have to be covered. This is done by having other segments absorb the fixed costs of that segment. Choices (a) and (d) are incorrect because net income can either increase or decrease if a segment is eliminated. Choice (b) is incorrect because when a segment is eliminated, the variable costs of that segment will also be eliminated and will not need to be absorbed by other segments.

14. **b.** If the segment continues, net income = −$40,000 ($200,000 − $140,000 − $100,000). If the segment is eliminated, the contribution margin will also be eliminated but $50,000 ($100,000 × .50) of the fixed costs will remain. Therefore, the effect of eliminating the segment will be a $10,000 decrease not (a) a $120,000 increase, (c) a $50,000 increase, or (d) a $10,000 increase.

Practice Exercises

Use incremental analysis for make-or-buy decision.

1. (LO 3) Maningly Inc. has been manufacturing its own lampshades for its table lamps. The company is currently operating at 100% of capacity. Variable manufacturing overhead is charged to production at the rate of 50% of direct labor cost. The direct materials and direct labor cost per unit to make the lampshades are $4 and $6, respectively. Normal production is 50,000 table lamps per year.

A supplier offers to make the lampshades at a price of $13.50 per unit. If Maningly accepts the supplier's offer, all variable manufacturing costs will be eliminated. But, the $50,000 of fixed manufacturing overhead currently being charged to the lampshades will have to be absorbed by other products.

Instructions

a. Prepare the incremental analysis for the decision to make or buy the lampshades.
b. Should Maningly buy the lampshades?
c. Would your answer be different in (b) if the productive capacity released by not making the lampshades could be used to produce income of $40,000?

Solution

1. a.

	Make	Buy	Net Income Increase (Decrease)
Direct materials (50,000 × $4.00)	$200,000	$ -0-	$ 200,000
Direct labor (50,000 × $6.00)	300,000	-0-	300,000
Variable manufacturing costs ($300,000 × 50%)	150,000	-0-	150,000
Fixed manufacturing costs	50,000	50,000	-0-
Purchase price (50,000 × $13.50)	-0-	675,000	(675,000)
Total annual cost	$700,000	$725,000	$ (25,000)

b. No, Maningly should not purchase the lampshades. As indicated by the incremental analysis, it would cost the company $25,000 more to purchase the lampshades.

c. Yes, by purchasing the lampshades, a total cost saving of $15,000 will result as shown below.

	Make	Buy	Net Income Increase (Decrease)
Total annual cost (from (a))	$700,000	$725,000	$(25,000)
Opportunity cost	40,000	-0-	40,000
Total cost	$740,000	$725,000	$ 15,000

2. **(LO 4)** A company manufactures three products using the same production process. The costs incurred up to the split-off point are £200,000. These costs are allocated to the products on the basis of their sales value at the split-off point. The number of units produced, the selling prices per unit of the three products at the split-off point and after further processing, and the additional processing costs are as follows:

Use incremental analysis for whether to sell or process materials further.

Product	Number of Units Produced	Selling Price at Split-Off	Selling Price after Processing	Additional Processing Costs
D	3,000	£11.00	£15.00	£14,000
E	6,000	12.00	16.20	16,000
F	2,000	19.40	24.00	9,000

Instructions

a. Which information is relevant to the decision on whether or not to process the products further? Explain why this information is relevant.

b. Which product(s) should be processed further and which should be sold at the split-off point?

c. Would your decision be different if the company was using the quantity of output to allocate joint costs? Explain.

Solution

2. a. The costs that are relevant in this decision are the incremental revenues and the incremental costs associated with processing the material past the split-off point. Any costs incurred up to the split-off point are sunk costs and therefore irrelevant to this decision.

b. Revenue after further processing:
Product D: £45,000 (3,000 units × £15.00 per unit)
Product E: £97,200 (6,000 units × £16.20 per unit)
Product F: £48,000 (2,000 units × £24.00 per unit)

Revenue at split-off:
Product D: £33,000 (3,000 units × £11.00 per unit)
Product E: £72,000 (6,000 units × £12.00 per unit)
Product F: £38,800 (2,000 units × £19.40 per unit)

	D	E	F
Incremental revenue	£ 12,000[a]	£ 25,200[b]	£ 9,200[c]
Incremental cost	(14,000)	(16,000)	(9,000)
Increase (decrease) in profit	£ (2,000)	£ 9,200	£ 200

[a]£45,000 − £33,000; [b]£97,200 − £72,000; [c]£48,000 − £38,800

Products E and F should be processed further, but Product D should not be processed further.

c. The decision would remain the same. It does not matter how the joint costs are allocated because joint costs are irrelevant to this decision.

3. **(LO 5)** Kang Enterprises uses a computer to process its payroll. Lately, business has been so good that it takes an extra 3 hours per night, plus every third Saturday, to process. Management is considering updating its computer with a faster model that would eliminate all of the overtime processing.

Use incremental analysis for retaining or replacing equipment.

	Current Machine	New Machine
Original purchase cost	₩9,000,000	₩12,000,000
Accumulated depreciation	2,000,000	—
Estimated annual operating costs	16,000,000	12,000,000
Useful life	6 years	6 years

If sold now, the current machine would have a salvage value of ₩3,000,000. If operated for the remainder of its useful life, the current machine would have zero salvage value. The new machine is expected to have zero salvage value after six years.

Instructions

Should the current machine be replaced? (Ignore the time value of money.)

Solution

3.

	Retain Machine	Replace Machine	Net Income Increase (Decrease)
Operating costs	₩96,000,000*	₩72,000,000**	₩24,000,000
New machine cost	-0-	12,000,000	(12,000,000)
Salvage value (old)	-0-	(3,000,000)	3,000,000
Total	₩96,000,000	₩81,000,000	₩15,000,000

*₩16,000,000 × 6
**₩12,000,000 × 6

The current machine should be replaced. The incremental analysis shows that net income for the six-year period will be ₩15,000,000 higher by replacing the current machine.

Use incremental analysis for elimination of division.

4. (LO 6) Nancy Leathers, a recent graduate of Bonita's accounting program, evaluated the operating performance of Watson Group's six divisions. Nancy made the following presentation to the Watson board of directors and suggested the Ortiz Division be eliminated. "If the Ortiz Division is eliminated," she said, "our total profits would increase by €23,870."

	The Other Five Divisions	Ortiz Division	Total
Sales	€1,664,200	€ 96,200	€1,760,400
Cost of goods sold	978,520	76,470	1,054,990
Gross profit	685,680	19,730	705,410
Operating expenses	527,940	43,600	571,540
Net income	€ 157,740	€(23,870)	€ 133,870

In the Ortiz Division, cost of goods sold is €70,000 variable and €6,470 fixed, and operating expenses are €15,000 variable and €28,600 fixed. None of the Ortiz Division's fixed costs will be eliminated if the division is discontinued.

Instructions

Is Nancy right about eliminating the Ortiz Division? Prepare an incremental analysis schedule to support your answer.

Solution

4.

	Continue	Eliminate	Net Income Increase (Decrease)
Sales	€ 96,200	€ -0-	€(96,200)
Variable expenses			
Cost of goods sold	70,000	-0-	70,000
Operating expenses	15,000	-0-	15,000
Total variable	85,000	-0-	85,000
Contribution margin	11,200	-0-	(11,200)
Fixed expenses			
Cost of goods sold	6,470	6,470	-0-
Operating expenses	28,600	28,600	-0-
Total fixed	35,070	35,070	-0-
Net income (loss)	€(23,870)	€(35,070)	€(11,200)

Nancy is incorrect. The incremental analysis shows that net income will be €11,200 less if the Ortiz Division is eliminated. This amount equals the contribution margin that would be lost by discontinuing the division.

Practice Problem

(LO 2) Western Company produces kitchen cabinets for homebuilders across the western United States. The cost of producing 5,000 cabinets is as follows:

Use incremental analysis for a special order.

Materials	$ 500,000
Labor	250,000
Variable overhead	100,000
Fixed overhead	400,000
Total	$1,250,000

Western also incurs selling expenses of $20 per cabinet. Wellington Corp. has offered Western $165 per cabinet for a special order of 1,000 cabinets. The cabinets would be sold to homebuilders in the eastern United States and thus would not conflict with Western's current sales. Selling expenses per cabinet would be only $5 per cabinet. Western has available capacity to do the work.

Instructions

a. Prepare an incremental analysis for the special order.
b. Should Western accept the special order? Why or why not?

Solution

a. Relevant costs per unit would be:

Materials	$500,000 ÷ 5,000 =	$100
Labor	250,000 ÷ 5,000 =	50
Variable overhead	100,000 ÷ 5,000 =	20
Selling expenses		5
Total relevant cost per unit		$175

	Reject Order	Accept Order	Net Income Increase (Decrease)
Revenues	$-0-	$165,000*	$ 165,000
Costs	-0-	175,000**	(175,000)
Net income	$-0-	$ (10,000)	$ (10,000)

*$165 × 1,000; **$175 × 1,000

b. Western should reject the offer. The incremental benefit of $165 per cabinet is less than the incremental cost of $175. By accepting the order, Western's net income would actually decline by $10,000.

Questions

1. What steps are frequently involved in management's decision-making process?

2. Your roommate, Evan Martin, contends that accounting contributes to most of the steps in management's decision-making process. Is your roommate correct? Explain.

3. "Incremental analysis involves the accumulation of information concerning a single course of action." Is this true? Explain why or why not.

4. Oskar Hirsch asks for your help concerning the relevance of variable and fixed costs in incremental analysis. Help Oskar with his problem.

5. What data are relevant in deciding whether to accept an order at a special price?

6. Emil SA has an opportunity to buy parts at €9 each that currently cost €12 to make. What manufacturing costs are relevant to this make-or-buy decision?

7. Define the term "opportunity cost." How may this cost be relevant in a make-or-buy decision?

8. What is the decision rule in deciding whether to sell a product or process it further?

9. What are joint products? What accounting issue results from the production process that creates joint products?

10. How are allocated joint costs treated when making a sell-or-process-further decision?

11. Your roommate, Noha Ahlat, is confused about sunk costs. Explain to your roommate the meaning of sunk costs and their relevance to a decision to retain or replace equipment.

12. Huang Ltd. has one product line that is unprofitable. What circumstances may cause overall company net income to be lower if the unprofitable product line is eliminated?

Brief Exercises

Identify the steps in management's decision-making process.

BE7.1 (LO 1), K The steps in management's decision-making process are listed in random order below. Indicate the order in which the steps should be executed.

_____ Make a decision.
_____ Identify the problem and assign responsibility.
_____ Review results of the decision.
_____ Determine and evaluate possible courses of action.

Determine incremental changes.

BE7.2 (LO 1), AP Binbin Ltd. is considering two alternatives. Alternative A will have revenues of ¥1,600,000 and costs of ¥1,000,000. Alternative B will have revenues of ¥1,800,000 and costs of ¥1,250,000. Compare Alternative A to Alternative B showing incremental revenues, costs, and net income.

Determine whether to accept a special order.

BE7.3 (LO 2), AP At Clemenza SpA, it costs €30 per unit (€20 variable and €10 fixed) to make an MP3 player that normally sells for €45. A foreign wholesaler offers to buy 3,000 units at €25 each. Clemenza will incur special shipping costs of €3 per unit. Assuming that Clemenza has excess operating capacity, indicate the net income (loss) Clemenza would realize by accepting the special order.

Determine whether to make or buy a part.

BE7.4 (LO 3), AP Hoanita Industries incurs unit costs of Rp80,000 (Rp50,000 variable and Rp30,000 fixed) in making an assembly part for its finished product. A supplier offers to make 10,000 of the assembly part at Rp60,000 per unit. If the offer is accepted, Hoanita will save all variable costs but no fixed costs. Prepare an analysis showing the total cost saving, if any, that Hoanita will realize by buying the part.

Determine whether to sell or process further.

BE7.5 (LO 4), AP Oak Street Ltd. makes unfinished bookcases that it sells for HK$620. Production costs are HK$360 variable and HK$100 fixed. Because it has unused capacity, Oak Street is considering finishing the bookcases and selling them for HK$700. Variable finishing costs are expected to be HK$60 per unit with no increase in fixed costs. Prepare an analysis on a per unit basis showing whether Oak Street should sell unfinished or finished bookcases.

Determine whether to sell or process further, joint products.

BE7.6 (LO 4), AP Each day, Lixia Ltd. processes 1 ton of a secret raw material into two resulting products, AB1 and XY1. When it processes 1 ton of the raw material, the company incurs joint processing costs of NT$600,000. It allocates NT$250,000 of these costs to AB1 and NT$350,000 of these costs to XY1. The resulting AB1 can be sold for NT$1,000,000. Alternatively, it can be processed further to make AB2 at an additional processing cost of NT$450,000, and sold for NT$1,500,000. Each day's batch of XY1 can be sold for NT$950,000. Or, it can be processed further to create XY2, at an additional processing cost of NT$500,000, and sold for NT$1,300,000. Discuss what products Lixia Ltd. should make.

Determine whether to retain or replace equipment.

BE7.7 (LO 5), AP Esposito SpA has a factory machine with a book value of €90,000 and a remaining useful life of five years. It can be sold for €30,000. A new machine is available at a cost of €400,000. This machine will have a five-year useful life with no salvage value. The new machine will lower annual variable manufacturing costs from €600,000 to €500,000. Prepare an analysis showing whether the old machine should be retained or replaced.

Determine whether to eliminate an unprofitable segment.

BE7.8 (LO 6), AP Lisah, Inc., manufactures golf clubs in three models. For the year, the Big Bart line has a net loss of $10,000 from sales $200,000, variable costs $180,000, and fixed costs $30,000. If the Big Bart line is eliminated, $20,000 of fixed costs will remain. Prepare an analysis showing whether the Big Bart line should be eliminated.

DO IT! Exercises

Determine incremental costs.

DO IT! 7.1 (LO 1), AN Davies plc is comparing two different options. Davies plc currently uses Option 1, with revenues of £65,000 per year, maintenance expenses of £5,000 per year, and operating expenses of £26,000 per year. Option 2 provides revenues of £60,000 per year, maintenance expenses of £5,000 per year, and operating expenses of £22,000 per year. Option 1 employs a piece of equipment which was upgraded two years ago at a cost of £17,000. If Option 2 is chosen, it will free up resources that will bring in an additional £4,000 of revenue. Complete the following table to show the change in income from choosing Option 2 versus Option 1. Designate sunk costs with an "S."

	Option 1	Option 2	Net Income Increase (Decrease)	Sunk (S)
Revenues				
Maintenance expenses				
Operating expenses				
Equipment upgrade				
Opportunity cost				

DO IT! 7.2 (LO 2), AN Alba SA incurs a cost of €35 per unit, of which €20 is variable, to make a product that normally sells for €58. A foreign wholesaler offers to buy 6,000 units at €30 each. Alba will incur additional costs of €4 per unit to imprint a logo and to pay for shipping. Compute the increase or decrease in net income Alba will realize by accepting the special order, assuming Alba has sufficient excess operating capacity. Should Alba accept the special order?

Evaluate special order.

DO IT! 7.3 (LO 3), AN Baek Ltd. must decide whether to make or buy some of its components. The costs of producing 60,000 switches for its generators are as follows:

Direct materials	₩30,000,000	Variable overhead	₩45,000,000
Direct labor	42,000,000	Fixed overhead	60,000,000

Evaluate make-or-buy opportunity.

Instead of making the switches at an average cost of ₩2,950 (₩177,000,000 ÷ 60,000), the company has an opportunity to buy the switches at ₩2,700 per unit. If the company purchases the switches, all the variable costs and one-fourth of the fixed costs will be eliminated. (a) Prepare an incremental analysis showing whether the company should make or buy the switches. (b) Would your answer be different if the released productive capacity will generate additional income of ₩34,000,000?

DO IT! 7.4 (LO 4), AP Royal National manufactures unpainted furniture for the do-it-yourself (DIY) market. It currently sells a table for A$75. Production costs per unit are A$40 variable and A$10 fixed. Royal National is considering staining and sealing the table to sell it for A$100. Unit variable costs to finish each table are expected to be an additional A$19 per table, and fixed costs are expected to be an additional A$3 per table. Prepare an analysis showing whether Royal National should sell stained or finished tables.

Sell or process further.

DO IT! 7.5 (LO 5), AP Darcy Roofing is faced with a decision. The company relies very heavily on the use of its 20-meter extension lift for work on large homes and commercial properties. Last year, Darcy Roofing spent £60,000 refurbishing the lift. It has just determined that another £50,000 of repair work is required. Alternatively, it has found a newer used lift that is for sale for £170,000. The company estimates that both lifts would have useful lives of five years. The new lift is more efficient and thus would reduce operating expenses from £90,000 to £60,000 each year. Darcy Roofing could also rent out the new lift for about £10,000 per year. The old lift is not suitable for rental. The old lift could currently be sold for £15,000 if the new lift is purchased. The new lift and old lift are estimated to have salvage values of zero if used for another six years. Prepare an incremental analysis showing whether the company should repair or replace the equipment.

Repair or replace equipment.

DO IT! 7.6 (LO 6), AP Madeira SA manufactures several types of accessories. For the year, the gloves and mittens line had sales of R$5,000,000, variable expenses of R$3,700,000, and fixed expenses of R$1,500,000. Therefore, the gloves and mittens line had a net loss of R$200,000. If Madeira eliminates the line, R$380,000 of fixed costs will remain. Prepare an analysis showing whether the company should eliminate the gloves and mittens line.

Analyze whether to eliminate unprofitable segment.

Exercises

E7.1 (LO 1), C As a study aid, your classmate Jia Feng has prepared the following list of statements about decision-making and incremental analysis.

Analyze statements about decision-making and cincremental analysis.

1. The first step in management's decision-making process is, "Determine and evaluate possible courses of action."
2. The final step in management's decision-making process is to actually make the decision.
3. Accounting's contribution to management's decision-making process occurs primarily in evaluating possible courses of action and in reviewing the results.
4. In making business decisions, management ordinarily considers only financial information because it is objectively determined.
5. Decisions involve a choice among alternative courses of action.
6. The process used to identify the financial data that change under alternative courses of action is called incremental analysis.
7. Costs that are the same under all alternative courses of action sometimes affect the decision.
8. When using incremental analysis, some costs will always change under alternative courses of action, but revenues will not.
9. Variable costs will change under alternative courses of action, but fixed costs will not.

Use incremental analysis for special-order decision.

Instructions

Identify each statement as true or false. If false, indicate how to correct the statement.

E7.2 (LO 2), AN Olympic Ltd. produces golf discs which it normally sells to retailers for £7 each. The cost of manufacturing 20,000 golf discs is:

Materials	£ 10,000
Labor	30,000
Variable overhead	20,000
Fixed overhead	40,000
Total	£100,000

Olympic also incurs 5% sales commission (£0.35) on each disc sold.

Limanto Ltd. offers Olympic £4.80 per disc for 5,000 discs. Limanto would sell the discs under its own brand name in foreign markets not yet served by Olympic. If Olympic accepts the offer, it will incur a one-time fixed cost of £6,000 due to the rental of an imprinting machine. No sales commission will result from the special order.

Instructions

a. Prepare an incremental analysis for the special order.

b. Should Olympic accept the special order? Why or why not?

c. What assumptions underlie the decision made in part (b)?

Use incremental analysis for special order.

E7.3 (LO 2), AN Moonbeam Ltd. manufactures toasters. For the first eight months of 2023, the company reported the following operating results while operating at 75% of plant capacity.

Sales (350,000 units)	HK$43,750,000
Cost of goods sold	26,000,000
Gross profit	17,750,000
Operating expenses	8,400,000
Net income	HK$ 9,350,000

Cost of goods sold was 70% variable and 30% fixed; operating expenses were 80% variable and 20% fixed.

In September, Moonbeam receives a special order for 15,000 toasters at HK$76 each from Luna Company. Acceptance of the order would result in an additional HK$30,000 of shipping costs but no increase in fixed costs.

Instructions

a. Prepare an incremental analysis for the special order.

b. Should Moonbeam accept the special order? Why or why not?

Use incremental analysis for special order.

E7.4 (LO 2), AN Klean Fiber Company is the creator of Y-Go, a technology that weaves silver into its fabrics to kill bacteria and odor on clothing while managing heat. Y-Go has become very popular in undergarments for sports activities. Operating at capacity, the company can produce 1,000,000 Y-Go undergarments a year. The per unit and the total costs for an individual garment when the company operates at full capacity are as follows:

	Per Undergarment	Total
Direct materials	$2.00	$2,000,000
Direct labor	0.75	750,000
Variable manufacturing overhead	1.00	1,000,000
Fixed manufacturing overhead	1.50	1,500,000
Variable selling expenses	0.25	250,000
Totals	$5.50	$5,500,000

The U.S. Army has approached Klean Fiber and expressed an interest in purchasing 250,000 Y-Go undergarments for soldiers in extremely warm climates. The Army would pay the unit cost for direct materials, direct labor, and variable manufacturing overhead costs. In addition, the Army has agreed to pay an additional $1 per undergarment to cover all other costs and provide a profit. Presently, Klean Fiber is operating at 70% capacity and does not have any other potential buyers for Y-Go. If Klean Fiber accepts the Army's offer, it will not incur any variable selling expenses related to this order.

Instructions

Using incremental analysis, determine whether Klean Fiber should accept the Army's offer.

E7.5 (LO 3), AN Rehan Pottery has been manufacturing its own finials for its curtain rods. The company is currently operating at 100% of capacity, and variable manufacturing overhead is charged to production at the rate of 70% of direct labor cost. The direct materials and direct labor cost per unit to make a pair of finials are ₹400 and ₹500, respectively. Normal production is 30,000 curtain rods per year.

A supplier offers to make a pair of finials at a price of ₹1,295 per unit. If Rehan Pottery accepts the supplier's offer, all variable manufacturing costs will be eliminated, but the ₹4,500,000 of fixed manufacturing overhead currently being charged to the finials will have to be absorbed by other products.

Use incremental analysis for make-or-buy decision.

Instructions

a. Prepare the incremental analysis for the decision to make or buy the finials.
b. Should Rehan Pottery buy the finials?
c. Would your answer be different in (b) if the productive capacity released by not making the finials could be used to produce income of ₹2,000,000?

E7.6 (LO 3), E O'Brien Ltd. has recently started the manufacture of Tri-Robo, a three-wheeled robot that can scan a home for fires and gas leaks and then transmit this information to a smartphone. The cost structure to manufacture 20,000 Tri-Robos is as follows:

Use incremental analysis for make-or-buy decision.

	Cost
Direct materials (€50 per robot)	€1,000,000
Direct labor (€40 per robot)	800,000
Variable overhead (€6 per robot)	120,000
Allocated fixed overhead (€30 per robot)	600,000
Total	€2,520,000

O'Brien is approached by Tiny Ltd., which offers to make Tri-Robo for €115 per unit or €2,300,000.

Instructions

a. Using incremental analysis, determine whether O'Brien should accept this offer under each of the following independent assumptions.
 1. Assume that €405,000 of the fixed overhead cost can be avoided.
 2. Assume that none of the fixed overhead can be avoided. However, if the robots are purchased from Tiny Ltd., O'Brien can use the released productive resources to generate additional income of €375,000.
b. Describe the qualitative factors that might affect the decision to purchase the robots from an outside supplier.

E7.7 (LO 3), E Riggs Company purchases sails and produces sailboats. It currently produces 1,200 sailboats per year, operating at normal capacity, which is about 80% of full capacity. Riggs purchases sails at $250 each, but the company is considering using the excess capacity to manufacture the sails instead. The manufacturing cost per sail would be $100 for direct materials, $80 for direct labor, and $90 for overhead. The $90 overhead is based on $78,000 of annual fixed overhead that is allocated using normal capacity.

The president of Riggs has come to you for advice. "It would cost me $270 to make the sails," she says, "but only $250 to buy them. Should I continue buying them, or have I missed something?"

Prepare incremental analysis for make-or-buy decision.

Instructions

a. Prepare a per unit analysis of the differential costs. Briefly explain whether Riggs should make or buy the sails.
b. If Riggs suddenly finds an opportunity to rent out the unused capacity of its factory for $77,000 per year, would your answer to part (a) change? Briefly explain.
c. Identify three qualitative factors that should be considered by Riggs in this make-or-buy decision.

E7.8 (LO 3), E Innova uses 1,000 units of the component IMC2 every month to manufacture one of its products. The unit costs incurred to manufacture the component are as follows:

Prepare incremental analysis concerning make-or-buy decision.

Direct materials	$ 65.00
Direct labor	45.00
Overhead	126.50
Total	$236.50

Overhead costs include variable material handling costs of $6.50, which are applied to products on the basis of direct material costs. The remainder of the overhead costs are applied on the basis of direct labor dollars and consist of 60% variable costs and 40% fixed costs.

A vendor has offered to supply the IMC2 component at a price of $200 per unit.

Instructions

a. Should Innova purchase the component from the outside vendor if Innova's unused facilities remain idle?

b. Should Innova purchase the component from the outside vendor if it can use its facilities to manufacture another product? What information will Innova need to make an accurate decision? Show your calculations.

c. What are the qualitative factors that Innova will have to consider when making this decision?

Use incremental analysis for further processing of materials decision.

E7.9 (LO 4), AN Mei Yang recently opened her own basketweaving studio. She sells finished baskets in addition to selling the raw materials needed by customers to weave baskets of their own. Unfortunately, owing to space limitations, Mei is unable to carry all the varieties of kits originally assembled and must choose between two basic packages.

The Basic Kit includes undyed, uncut reeds (with dye included) for weaving one basket. This basic package costs Mei HK$160 and sells for HK$300. The second kit, called Stage 2, includes cut reeds that have already been dyed. With this kit the customer need only soak the reeds and weave the basket. Mei produces the Stage 2 kit by using the materials included in the Basic Kit. Because she is more efficient at cutting and dying reeds than her average customer, Mei is able to produce two Stage 2 kits in one hour from one Basic Kit. (She values her time at HK$180 per hour.) The Stage 2 kit sells for HK$360.

Instructions

Determine whether Mei's basketweaving studio should carry the Basic Kit with undyed and uncut reeds or the Stage 2 kit with reeds already dyed and cut. Prepare an incremental analysis to support your answer.

Determine whether to sell or process further, joint products.

E7.10 (LO 4), AN Moreau SA produces three separate products from a common process costing €100,000. Each of the products can be sold at the split-off point or can be processed further and then sold for a higher price. Shown here are cost and selling price data for a recent period.

	Sales Value at Split-Off Point	Cost to Process Further	Sales Value after Further Processing
Product 10	€60,000	€100,000	€190,000
Product 12	15,000	30,000	35,000
Product 14	55,000	150,000	215,000

Instructions

a. Determine total net income if all products are sold at the split-off point.

b. Determine total net income if all products are sold after further processing.

c. Using incremental analysis, determine which products should be sold at the split-off point and which should be processed further.

d. Determine total net income using the results from (c) and explain why the net income is different from that determined in (b).

Determine whether to sell or process further, joint products.

E7.11 (LO 4), AN Kirk Minerals processes materials extracted from mines. The most common raw material that it processes results in three joint products: Spock, Uhura, and Sulu. Each of these products can be sold as is, or each can be processed further and sold for a higher price. The company incurs joint costs of $180,000 to process one batch of the raw material that produces the three joint products. The following cost and sales information is available for one batch of each product.

	Sales Value at Split-Off Point	Allocated Joint Costs	Cost to Process Further	Sales Value of Processed Product
Spock	$210,000	$40,000	$110,000	$300,000
Uhura	300,000	60,000	85,000	400,000
Sulu	455,000	80,000	250,000	800,000

Instructions

Determine whether each of the three joint products should be sold as is, or processed further.

E7.12 (LO 4), E A company manufactures three products using the same production process. The costs incurred up to the split-off point are ¥20,000,000. These costs are allocated to the products on the basis of their sales value at the split-off point. The number of units produced, the selling prices per unit of the three products at the split-off point and after further processing, and the additional processing costs are as follows:

Prepare incremental analysis for whether to sell or process materials further.

Product	Number of Units Produced	Selling Price at Split-Off	Selling Price after Processing	Additional Processing Costs
D	4,000	¥1,000	¥1,500	¥1,400,000
E	6,000	1,160	1,620	2,000,000
F	2,000	1,940	2,260	900,000

Instructions

a. Which information is relevant to the decision on whether or not to process the products further? Explain why this information is relevant.
b. Which product(s) should be processed further and which should be sold at the split-off point?
c. Would your decision be different if the company was using the quantity of output to allocate joint costs? Explain.

E7.13 (LO 5), E Service On January 2, 2022, Assisi Hospital purchased a €100,000 special radiology scanner from Bella SpA. The scanner had a useful life of four years and was estimated to have no disposal value at the end of its useful life. The straight-line method of depreciation is used on this scanner. Annual operating costs with this scanner are €105,000.

Use incremental analysis for retaining or replacing equipment decision.

Approximately one year later, the hospital is approached by Dyno Technology salesperson, Anthony Ricci, who indicated that purchasing the scanner in 2022 from Bella SpA was a mistake. He points out that Dyno has a scanner that will save Assisi Hospital €25,000 a year in operating expenses over its three-year useful life. Anthony notes that the new scanner will cost €110,000 and has the same capabilities as the scanner purchased last year. The hospital agrees that both scanners are of equal quality. The new scanner will have no disposal value. Anthony agrees to buy the old scanner from Assisi Hospital for €50,000.

Instructions

a. If Assisi Hospital sells its old scanner on January 2, 2023, compute the gain or loss on the sale.
b. Using incremental analysis, determine if Assisi Hospital should purchase the new scanner on January 2, 2023.
c. Explain why Assisi Hospital might be reluctant to purchase the new scanner, regardless of the results indicated by the incremental analysis in (b).

E7.14 (LO 5), AN Jackson plc uses a computer to handle its sales invoices. Lately, business has been so good that it takes an extra 3 hours per night, plus every third Saturday, to keep up with the volume of sales invoices. Management is considering updating its computer with a faster model that would eliminate all of the overtime processing.

Use incremental analysis for retaining or replacing equipment decision.

	Current Machine	New Machine
Original purchase cost	£15,000	£25,000
Accumulated depreciation	£ 6,000	—
Estimated annual operating costs	£25,000	£20,000
Remaining useful life	5 years	5 years

If sold now, the current machine would have a salvage value of £6,000. If operated for the remainder of its useful life, the current machine would have zero salvage value. The new machine is expected to have zero salvage value after five years.

Instructions

Prepare an incremental analysis to determine whether the current machine should be replaced.

E7.15 (LO 6), AN Ian Edward, a recent graduate of Australian National University, evaluated the operating performance of Dunn Company's six divisions. Ian made the following presentation to Dunn's board of directors and suggested the Percy Division be eliminated. "If the Percy Division is eliminated," he said, "our total profits would increase by A$26,000."

Use incremental analysis concerning elimination of division.

	The Other Five Divisions	Percy Division	Total
Sales	A$1,664,200	A$100,000	A$1,764,200
Cost of goods sold	978,520	76,000	1,054,520
Gross profit	685,680	24,000	709,680
Operating expenses	527,940	50,000	577,940
Net income	A$ 157,740	A$(26,000)	A$ 131,740

In the Percy Division, cost of goods sold is A$61,000 variable and A$15,000 fixed, and operating expenses are A$30,000 variable and A$20,000 fixed. None of the Percy Division's fixed costs will be eliminated if the division is discontinued.

Instructions

Is Ian right about eliminating the Percy Division? Prepare a schedule to support your answer.

Use incremental analysis for elimination of a product line.

E7.16 (LO 6), AN Cawley Company makes three models of tasers. Information on the three products is given here.

	Tingler	Shocker	Stunner
Sales	$300,000	$500,000	$200,000
Variable expenses	150,000	200,000	145,000
Contribution margin	150,000	300,000	55,000
Fixed expenses	120,000	230,000	95,000
Net income	$ 30,000	$ 70,000	$(40,000)

Fixed expenses consist of $300,000 of common costs allocated to the three products based on relative sales, as well as direct fixed expenses unique to each model of $30,000 (Tingler), $80,000 (Shocker), and $35,000 (Stunner). The common costs will be incurred regardless of how many models are produced. The direct fixed expenses would be eliminated if that model is phased out.

James Watt, an executive with the company, feels the Stunner line should be discontinued to increase the company's net income.

Instructions

a. Compute current net income for Cawley Company.

b. Compute net income by product line and in total for Cawley Company if the company discontinues the Stunner product line. (*Hint:* Allocate the $300,000 common costs to the two remaining product lines based on their relative sales.)

c. Should Cawley eliminate the Stunner product line? Why or why not?

Prepare incremental analysis concerning keeping or dropping a product to maximize operating income.

E7.17 (LO 6), AN Maharaja Industries operates a small factory in which it manufactures two products: C and D. Production and sales results for last year were as follows:

	C	D
Units sold	9,000	20,000
Unit selling price	₹9,500	₹7,500
Unit variable costs	5,000	4,000
Unit fixed costs	2,400	2,400

For purposes of simplicity, the firm averages total fixed costs over the total number of units of C and D produced and sold.

The research department has developed a new product (E) as a replacement for product D. Market studies show that Maharaja Industries could sell 10,000 units of E next year at a price of ₹11,500; unit variable costs of E are ₹4,500. The introduction of product E will lead to a 10% increase in demand for product C and discontinuation of product D. If the company does not introduce the new product, it expects next year's results to be the same as last year's.

Instructions

Should Maharaja Industries introduce product E next year? Explain why or why not. Show calculations to support your decision.

E7.18 (LO 1, 2, 3, 4, 5, 6), C The following costs relate to a variety of different decision situations.

Identify relevant costs for different decisions.

Cost	Decision
1. Unavoidable fixed overhead	Eliminate an unprofitable segment
2. Direct labor	Make or buy
3. Original cost of old equipment	Equipment replacement
4. Joint production costs	Sell or process further
5. Opportunity cost	Accepting a special order
6. Segment manager's salary	Eliminate an unprofitable segment (manager will be terminated)
7. Cost of new equipment	Equipment replacement
8. Incremental production costs	Sell or process further
9. Direct materials	Equipment replacement (the amount of materials required does not change)
10. Rent expense	Purchase or lease a building

Instructions

For each cost listed above, indicate if it is relevant or not to the related decision. For those costs determined to be irrelevant, briefly explain why.

Problems

P7.1 (LO 2), E **Writing** ThreePoint Sports manufactures basketballs for the Women's National Basketball Association (WNBA). For the first six months of 2023, the company reported the following operating results while operating at 80% of plant capacity and producing 120,000 units.

Use incremental analysis for special order and identify nonfinancial factors in the decision.

	Amount
Sales	€4,800,000
Cost of goods sold	3,600,000
Selling and administrative expenses	405,000
Net income	€ 795,000

Fixed costs for the period were cost of goods sold €960,000, and selling and administrative expenses €225,000.

In July, normally a slack manufacturing month, ThreePoint Sports receives a special order for 10,000 basketballs at €28 each from the Greek Basketball Association (GBA). Acceptance of the order would increase variable selling and administrative expenses €0.75 per unit because of shipping costs but would not increase fixed costs and expenses.

Instructions

a. Prepare an incremental analysis for the special order.

b. Should ThreePoint Sports accept the special order? Explain your answer.

c. What is the minimum selling price on the special order to produce net income of €5.00 per ball?

d. What nonfinancial factors should management consider in making its decision?

a. NI increase €37,500

P7.2 (LO 3), E **Writing** The management of Zhou Manufacturing is trying to decide whether to continue manufacturing a part or to buy it from an outside supplier. The part, called CISCO, is a component of the company's finished product.

Use incremental analysis related to make or buy, consider opportunity cost, and identify nonfinancial factors.

The following information was collected from the accounting records and production data for the year ended December 31, 2023.

1. 8,000 units of CISCO were produced in the Machining Department.

2. Variable manufacturing costs applicable to the production of each CISCO unit were: direct materials HK$48, direct labor HK$43, indirect labor HK$4.30, utilities HK$4.00.

3. Fixed manufacturing costs applicable to the production of CISCO were:

Cost Item	Direct	Allocated	Total
Depreciation	HK$21,000	HK$ 9,000	HK$30,000
Property taxes	5,000	2,000	7,000
Insurance	9,000	6,000	15,000
	HK$35,000	HK$17,000	HK$52,000

All variable manufacturing and direct fixed costs will be eliminated if CISCO is purchased. Allocated costs will not be eliminated if CISCO is purchased. So if CISCO is purchased, the fixed manufacturing costs allocated to CISCO will have to be absorbed by other production departments.

4. The lowest quotation for 8,000 CISCO units from a supplier is HK$800,000.
5. If CISCO units are purchased, freight and inspection costs would be HK$3.50 per unit, and receiving costs totaling HK$13,000 per year would be incurred by the Machining Department.

Instructions

a. NI (decrease) HK$(11,600)

a. Prepare an incremental analysis for CISCO. Your analysis should have columns for (1) Make CISCO, (2) Buy CISCO, and (3) Net Income Increase/(Decrease).

b. Based on your analysis, what decision should management make?

c. NI increase HK$18,400

c. Would the decision be different if Zhou has the opportunity to produce HK$30,000 of net income with the facilities currently being used to manufacture CISCO? Show computations.

d. What nonfinancial factors should management consider in making its decision?

Determine if product should be sold or processed further.

P7.3 (LO 4), AN Robin Industrial Products (RIPI) is a diversified industrial-cleaner processing company. The company's Liverpool plant produces two products, a table cleaner and a floor cleaner, from a common set of chemical inputs (CDG). Each week, 900,000 ounces of chemical input are processed at a cost of £210,000 into 600,000 ounces of floor cleaner and 300,000 ounces of table cleaner. The floor cleaner has no market value until it is converted into a polish with the trade name FloorShine. The additional processing costs for this conversion amount to £240,000.

FloorShine sells at £20 per 30-ounce bottle. The table cleaner can be sold for £17 per 25-ounce bottle. However, the table cleaner can be converted into two other products by adding 300,000 ounces of another compound (TCP) to the 300,000 ounces of table cleaner. This joint process will yield 300,000 ounces each of table stain remover (TSR) and table polish (TP). The additional processing costs for this process amount to £100,000. Both table products can be sold for £14 per 25-ounce bottle.

The company decided not to process the table cleaner into TSR and TP based on the following analysis:

	Table Cleaner	Process Further Table Stain Remover (TSR)	Table Polish (TP)	Total
Production in ounces	300,000	300,000	300,000	
Revenues	£204,000	£168,000	£168,000	£336,000
Costs:				
CDG costs	70,000*	52,500	52,500	105,000**
TCP costs	-0-	50,000	50,000	100,000
Total costs	70,000	102,500	102,500	205,000
Weekly gross profit	£134,000	£ 65,500	£ 65,500	£131,000

*If table cleaner is not processed further, it is allocated ⅓ of the £210,000 of CDG cost, which is equal to ⅓ of the total physical output.

**If table cleaner is processed further, total physical output is 1,200,000 ounces. TSR and TP combined account for 50% of the total physical output and are each allocated 25% of the CDG cost.

Instructions

a. Determine if management made the correct decision to not process the table cleaner further by doing the following:

1. Calculate the company's total weekly gross profit assuming the table cleaner is not processed further.

a. 2. Gross profit £186,000

2. Calculate the company's total weekly gross profit assuming the table cleaner is processed further.
3. Compare the resulting net incomes and comment on management's decision.

b. Using incremental analysis, determine if the table cleaner should be processed further.

Compute gain or loss, and determine if equipment should be replaced.

P7.4 (LO 5), S Service Writing At the beginning of last year (2022), Richter Condos installed a mechanized elevator for its tenants. The owner of the company, Ron Richter, recently returned from an industry equipment exhibition where he watched a computerized elevator demonstrated. He was impressed with the elevator's speed, comfort of ride, and cost efficiency. Upon returning from the exhibition, he asked his purchasing agent to collect price and operating cost data on the new elevator. In addition, he asked the company's accountant to provide him with cost data on the company's elevator. This information is presented here.

	Old Elevator	New Elevator
Purchase price	$120,000	$160,000
Estimated salvage value	-0-	-0-
Estimated useful life	5 years	4 years
Depreciation method	Straight-line	Straight-line
Annual operating costs other than depreciation:		
Variable	$35,000	$10,000
Fixed	23,000	8,500

Annual revenues are $240,000, and selling and administrative expenses are $29,000, regardless of which elevator is used. If the old elevator is replaced now, at the beginning of 2023, Richter Condos will be able to sell it for $25,000.

Instructions

a. Determine any gain or loss if the old elevator is replaced.

b. Prepare a four-year summarized income statement for each of the following assumptions:
   1. The old elevator is retained.
   2. The old elevator is replaced.

c. Using incremental analysis, determine if the old elevator should be replaced.

d. Write a memo to Ron Richter explaining why any gain or loss should be ignored in the decision to replace the old elevator.

b. 2. NI $539,000

c. NI increase $23,000

P7.5 (LO 6), AN Yi Tower has four operating divisions. During the first quarter of 2023, the company reported aggregate income from operations of ₩213,000,000 and the following divisional results:

Prepare incremental analysis concerning elimination of divisions.

	Division			
	I	II	III	IV
Sales	₩250,000,000	₩200,000,000	₩500,000,000	₩450,000,000
Cost of goods sold	200,000,000	192,000,000	300,000,000	250,000,000
Selling and administrative expenses	75,000,000	60,000,000	60,000,000	50,000,000
Income (loss) from operations	₩(25,000,000)	₩(52,000,000)	₩140,000,000	₩150,000,000

Analysis reveals the following percentages of variable costs in each division.

	I	II	III	IV
Cost of goods sold	70%	90%	80%	75%
Selling and administrative expenses	40	60	50	60

Discontinuance of any division would save 50% of the fixed costs and expenses for that division.

Top management is very concerned about the unprofitable divisions (I and II). Consensus is that one or both of the divisions should be discontinued.

Instructions

a. Compute the contribution margin for Divisions I and II.

b. Prepare an incremental analysis concerning the possible discontinuance of (1) Division I and (2) Division II. What course of action do you recommend for each division?

c. Prepare a columnar condensed income statement for Yi Tower, assuming Division II is eliminated. (Use the CVP format.) Division II's unavoidable fixed costs are allocated equally to the continuing divisions.

d. Reconcile the total income from operations (₩213,000,000) with the total income from operations without Division II.

a. Contribution margin I ₩80,000,000

c. Income III ₩132,800,000

Continuing Case

Current Designs

CD7 **Current Designs** (USA) faces a number of important decisions that require incremental analysis. Consider each of the following situations independently.

Situation 1

Recently, Mike Cichanowski, owner and CEO of Current Designs, received a phone call from the president of a brewing company. He was calling to inquire about the possibility of Current Designs producing "floating coolers" for a promotion his company was planning. These coolers resemble kayaks but are about one-third the size. They are used to float food and beverages while paddling down the river on a weekend leisure trip. The company would be interested in purchasing 100 coolers for the upcoming summer. It is willing to pay $250 per cooler. The brewing company would pick up the coolers upon completion of the order.

Mike met with Diane Buswell, controller, to identify how much it would cost Current Designs to produce the coolers. After careful analysis, the following costs were identified.

Direct materials	$80/unit
Direct labor	$60/unit
Variable overhead	$20/unit

Current Designs would be able to modify an existing mold to produce the coolers. The cost of these modifications would be approximately $3,000.

Instructions

a. Assuming that the company has available capacity, prepare an incremental analysis to determine whether Current Designs should accept this special order to produce the coolers.

b. Discuss additional factors that Mike and Diane should consider if Current Designs is currently operating at full capacity.

Situation 2

Current Designs is always working to identify ways to increase efficiency while becoming more environmentally conscious. During a recent brainstorming session, one employee suggested to Diane Buswell, controller, that the company should consider replacing the current rotomold oven as a way to realize savings from reduced energy consumption. The oven operates on natural gas, using 17,000 therms of natural gas for an entire year. A new, energy-efficient rotomold oven would operate on 15,000 therms of natural gas for an entire year. After seeking out price quotes from a few suppliers, Diane determined that it would cost approximately $250,000 to purchase a new, energy-efficient rotomold oven. She determines that the expected useful life of the new oven would be 10 years, and it would have no salvage value at the end of its useful life. Current Designs would be able to sell the current oven for $10,000.

Instructions

a. Prepare an incremental analysis to determine if Current Designs should purchase the new rotomold oven, assuming that the average price for natural gas over the next 10 years will be $0.65 per therm.

b. Diane is concerned that natural gas prices might increase at a faster rate over the next 10 years. If the company projects that the average natural gas price of the next 10 years could be as high as $0.85 per therm, discuss how that might change your conclusion in (a).

Situation 3

One of Current Designs' competitive advantages is found in the ingenuity of its owner and CEO, Mike Cichanowski. His involvement in the design of kayak molds and production techniques has led to Current Designs being recognized as an industry leader in the design and production of kayaks. This ingenuity was evident in an improved design of one of the most important components of a kayak, the seat. The "Revolution Seating System" is a one-of-a-kind, rotating axis seat that gives unmatched, full-contact, under-leg support. It is quickly adjustable with a lever-lock system that allows for a customizable seat position that maximizes comfort for the rider.

Having just designed the "Revolution Seating System," Current Designs must now decide whether to produce the seats internally or buy them from an outside supplier. The costs for Current Designs to produce the seats are as follows:

Direct materials	$20/unit		Direct labor	$15/unit
Variable overhead	$12/unit		Fixed overhead	$20,000

Current Designs will need to produce 3,000 seats this year; 25% of the fixed overhead will be avoided if the seats are purchased from an outside vendor. After soliciting prices from outside suppliers, the company determined that it will cost $50 to purchase a seat from an outside vendor.

Instructions

a. Prepare an incremental analysis showing whether Current Designs should make or buy the "Revolution Seating System."

b. Would your answer in (a) change if the productive capacity released by not making the seats could be used to produce income of $20,000?

Expand Your Critical Thinking

Decision-Making Across the Organization

CT7.1 Aurora Company is considering the purchase of a new machine. The invoice price of the machine is $140,000, freight charges are estimated to be $4,000, and installation costs are expected to be $6,000. Salvage value of the new equipment is expected to be zero after a useful life of 5 years. Existing equipment could be retained and used for an additional 5 years if the new machine is not purchased. At that time, the salvage value of the equipment would be zero. If the new machine is purchased now, the existing machine would have to be scrapped. Aurora's accountant, Lisah Huang, has accumulated the following data regarding annual sales and expenses with and without the new machine.

1. Without the new machine, Aurora can sell 12,000 units of product annually at a per unit selling price of $100. If the new machine is purchased, the number of units produced and sold would increase by 10%, and the selling price would remain the same.

2. The new machine is faster than the old machine, and it is more efficient in its usage of materials. With the old machine the gross profit rate will be 25% of sales, whereas the rate will be 30% of sales with the new machine.

3. Annual selling expenses are $180,000 with the current equipment. Because the new equipment would produce a greater number of units to be sold, annual selling expenses are expected to increase by 10% if it is purchased.

4. Annual administrative expenses are expected to be $100,000 with the old machine, and $113,000 with the new machine.

5. The current book value of the existing machine is $36,000. Aurora uses straight-line depreciation.

Instructions

With the class divided into groups, prepare an incremental analysis for the five years showing whether Aurora should keep the existing machine or buy the new machine. (Ignore income tax effects.)

Managerial Analysis

CT7.2 MiniTek manufactures private-label small electronic products, such as alarm clocks, calculators, kitchen timers, stopwatches, and automatic pencil sharpeners. Some of the products are sold as sets, and others are sold individually. Products are studied as to their sales potential, and then cost estimates are made. The Engineering Department develops production plans, and then production begins. The company has generally had very successful product introductions. Only two products introduced by the company have been discontinued.

One of the products currently sold is a multi-alarm clock. The clock has four alarms that can be programmed to sound at various times and for varying lengths of time. The company has experienced a great deal of difficulty in making the circuit boards for the clocks. The production process has never operated smoothly. The product is unprofitable at the present time, primarily because of warranty repairs and product recalls. Two models of the clocks were recalled, for example, because they sometimes caused an electric shock when the alarms were being shut off. The Engineering Department is attempting to revise the manufacturing process, but the revision will take another six months at least.

The clocks were very popular when they were introduced, and since they are private-label, the company has not suffered much from the recalls. Presently, the company has a very large order for several items from BigMart. The order includes 5,000 of the multi-alarm clocks. When the company suggested that BigMart purchase the clocks from another manufacturer, BigMart threatened to rescind the entire order unless the clocks were included.

The company has therefore investigated the possibility of having another company make the clocks for them. The clocks were bid for the BigMart order based on an estimated $6.90 cost to manufacture:

Circuit board, 1 each @ $2.00	$2.00
Plastic case, 1 each @ $0.80	0.80
Alarms, 4 @ $0.15 each	0.60
Labor, 15 minutes @ $12/hour	3.00
Overhead, $2.00 per labor hour	0.50

MiniTek could purchase clocks to fill the BigMart order for $10 from Trans-Tech Asia, a Korean manufacturer with a very good quality record. Trans-Tech has offered to reduce the price to $7.50 after MiniTek has been a customer for six months, placing an order of at least 1,000 units per month. If MiniTek becomes a "preferred customer" by purchasing 15,000 units per year, the price would be reduced still further to $4.50.

Omega Products, a local manufacturer, has also offered to make clocks for MiniTek. They have offered to sell 5,000 clocks for $5 each. However, Omega Products has been in business for only six months. They have experienced significant turnover in their labor force, and the local press has reported that the owners may face tax evasion charges soon. The owner of Omega Products is an electronics engineer, however, and the quality of the clocks is likely to be good.

If MiniTek decides to purchase the clocks from either Trans-Tech or Omega, all the costs to manufacture could be avoided, except a total of $1,000 in overhead costs for machine depreciation. The machinery is fairly new, and has no alternate use.

Instructions

a. What is the difference in profit under each of the alternatives if the clocks are to be sold for $14.50 each to BigMart?

b. What are the most important nonfinancial factors that MiniTek should consider when making this decision?

c. What do you think MiniTek should do in regard to the BigMart order? What should it do in regard to continuing to manufacture the multi-alarm clocks? Be prepared to defend your answer.

Real-World Focus

CT7.3 Founded in 1983 and foreclosed in 1996, **Beverly Hills Fan Company** (USA) was located in Woodland Hills, California. With 23 employees and sales of less than $10 million, the company was relatively small. Management felt that there was potential for growth in the upscale market for ceiling fans and lighting. They were particularly optimistic about growth in Mexican and Canadian markets.

Presented here is information from the president's letter in one of the company's last annual reports.

Beverly Hills Fan Company
President's Letter

An aggressive product development program was initiated during the past year resulting in new ceiling fan models planned for introduction this year. Award winning industrial designer Ron Rezek created several new fan models for the Beverly Hills Fan and L.A. Fan lines, including a new Showroom Collection, designed specifically for the architectural and designer markets. Each of these models has received critical acclaim, and order commitments for this year have been outstanding. Additionally, our Custom Color and special order fans continued to enjoy increasing popularity and sales gains as more and more customers desire fans that match their specific interior decors. Currently, Beverly Hills Fan Company offers a product line of over 100 models of contemporary, traditional, and transitional ceiling fans.

Instructions

a. What points did the company management need to consider before deciding to offer the special-order fans to customers?

b. How would have incremental analysis been employed to assist in this decision?

Communication Activity

CT7.4 Hao Yang is a production manager at a metal fabricating factory. Last night, he read an article about a new piece of equipment that would dramatically reduce his division's costs. Hao was very excited about the prospect, and the first thing he did this morning was to bring the article to his supervisor, Jun Lai, the factory manager. The following conversation occurred:

Hao: Jun, I thought you would like to see this article on the new PDD1130; they've made some fantastic changes that could save us significantly money.

Jun: I appreciate your interest, Hao, but I actually have been aware of the new machine for two months. The problem is that we just bought a new machine last year. We spent NT$20 million on that machine, and it was supposed to last us 12 years. If we replace it now, we would have to write its book value off of the books for a huge loss. If I go to top management now and say that I want a new machine, they will fire me. I think we should use our existing machine for a couple of years, and then when it becomes obvious that we have to have a new machine, I will make the proposal.

Instructions

Hao just completed a course in managerial accounting, and he believes that Jun is making a big mistake. Write a memo from Hao to Jun explaining Jun's decision-making error.

Ethics Case

CT7.5 Samir Ansari became Chief Executive Officer of Delta Enterprises two years ago. At the time, the company was reporting lagging profits, and Samir was brought in to "stir things up." The company has three divisions: electronics, fiber optics, and plumbing supplies. Samir has no interest in plumbing supplies, and one of the first things he did was to put pressure on his accountants to reallocate some of the company's fixed costs away from the other two divisions to the plumbing division. This had the effect of causing the plumbing division to report losses during the last two years; in the past it had always reported low, but acceptable, net income. Samir felt that this reallocation would shine a favorable light on him in front of the board of directors because it meant that the electronics and fiber optics divisions would look like they were improving. Given that these are "businesses of the future," he believed that the stock market would react favorably to these increases, while not penalizing the poor results of the plumbing division. Without this shift in the allocation of fixed costs, the profits of the electronics and fiber optics divisions would not have improved. But now the board of directors has suggested that the plumbing division be closed because it is reporting losses. This would mean that nearly 500 employees, many of whom have worked for Delta their whole lives, would lose their jobs.

Instructions

a. If a division is reporting losses, does that necessarily mean that it should be closed?
b. Was the reallocation of fixed costs across divisions unethical?
c. What should Samir do?

All About You

CT7.6 Managerial accounting techniques can be used in a wide variety of settings. As we have frequently pointed out, you can use them in many personal situations. They also can be useful in trying to find solutions for societal issues that appear to be hard to solve.

Instructions

Read the *Fortune* article, "The Toughest Customers: How Hardheaded Business Metrics Can Help the Hard-Core Homeless," by Cait Murphy (do an Internet search on the title), and then answer the following questions:

a. How does the article define "chronic" homelessness?
b. In what ways does homelessness cost a city money? What are the estimated costs of a chronic homeless person to various cities?
c. What are the steps suggested to address the problem?
d. What is the estimated cost of implementing this program in New York? What results have been seen?
e. In terms of incremental analysis, frame the relevant costs in this situation.

Considering Your Costs and Benefits

CT7.7 School costs money. Is this an expenditure that you should have avoided? On average, a year of tuition in the USA at a public four-year college costs about $10,000, and a year of tuition at a public two-year college costs about $5,000. If you did not go to college, you might avoid mountains of school-related debt. In fact, each year, about 600,000 students decide to drop out of school. Many of them never return. Suppose that you are working two jobs and going to college, and that you are not making ends meet. Your grades are suffering due to your lack of available study time. You feel depressed. Should you drop out of school?

YES: You can always go back to school. If your grades are bad and you are depressed, what good is school doing you anyway?

NO: Once you drop out, it is very hard to get enough momentum to go back. Dropping out will dramatically reduce your long-term opportunities. It is better to stay in school, even if you take only one class per semester. While you cannot go back and redo your initial decision, you can look at some facts to evaluate the wisdom of your decision.

Instructions

Write a response indicating your position regarding this situation. Provide support for your view.

CHAPTER 8

Pricing

CHAPTER PREVIEW

As the following Feature Story about **Zappos.com** (USA) indicates, few management decisions are more important than setting prices. **Samsung** (KOR), for example, must sell computer chips at a price that is high enough to cover its costs and ensure a reasonable profit. But if the price is too high, the chips will not sell. In this chapter, we examine two types of pricing situations. The first part of the chapter addresses pricing for goods sold or services provided to external parties. The second part of the chapter addresses pricing decisions managers face when they sell goods to other divisions within the company.

FEATURE STORY

They've Got Your Size—and Color

Nick Swinmurn was shopping for a pair of shoes. He found a store with the right style, but not the right color. The next store had the right color, but not the right size. After visiting numerous stores, he went home, figuring he would buy them online. After all, it was 1999, so you could buy everything online, right? Well, apparently not shoes. After an exhaustive search, Nick still came up shoeless.

Nick lived in San Francisco, where in 1999 everybody with even half an idea started an Internet company and became a millionaire. Or so it seemed. So Nick started **Zappos.com** (USA). The company is dedicated to providing the best selection in shoes in terms of brands, styles, colors, size, and, most importantly, service.

8-1

To make sure that Zappos had a fighting chance of evolving from a half-baked idea to a thriving business, Nick brought in Tony Hsieh. At the age of 24, Tony had developed and recently sold a business to **Microsoft** (USA) for $265 million. Tony then brought in Alfred Lin to manage the company's finances. Tony and Alfred first met when Tony was running a pizza business and Alfred was Tony's best pizza customer. Together, Tony and Alfred have run Zappos based on 10 basic principles:

1. Deliver WOW through service.
2. Embrace and drive change.
3. Create fun and a little weirdness.
4. Be adventurous, creative, and open-minded.
5. Pursue growth and learning.
6. Build open and honest relationships with communication.
7. Build a positive team and family spirit.
8. Do more with less.
9. Be passionate and determined.
10. Be humble.

Are you looking for a pair of size 6 Giuseppe Zanotti heels for $1,295 or a pair of Keen size 17 sandals for $95? Zappos is committed to having what you want and getting it to you as fast as possible. Providing this kind of service is not cheap, however. It means having vast warehouses and sophisticated order processing systems. The company's price has to cover its costs and provide a reasonable profit yet still be competitive. If the price is too high, Zappos loses business. Too low and the company could lose its shirt (or in this case, shoes).

Source: *www.zappos.com.*

Video Watch the *Zappos.com* video at https://wileyaccountingupdates.com/video/?p=27 to learn more about how the company sets prices.

CHAPTER OUTLINE

Learning Objectives	Review	Practice
LO 1 Compute a target cost when the market determines a product price.	• Establishing a target cost	**DO IT! 1** Target Costing
LO 2 Compute a target selling price using cost-plus pricing.	• Cost-plus pricing • Limitations of cost-plus pricing • Variable-cost pricing	**DO IT! 2** Target Selling Price
LO 3 Use time-and-material pricing to determine the cost of services provided.	• Calculate labor rate • Calculate material loading charge • Calculate charges for a particular job	**DO IT! 3** Time-and-Material Pricing
LO 4 Determine a transfer price using the negotiated, cost-based, and market-based approaches.	• Negotiated transfer prices • Cost-based transfer prices • Market-based transfer prices • Effect of outsourcing on transfer pricing • Transfers between divisions in different countries	**DO IT! 4** Transfer Pricing

Go to the Review and Practice section at the end of the chapter for a targeted summary and practice applications with solutions.

TARGET COSTING

Establishing the price for any good or service is affected by many factors. Take the pharmaceutical industry as an example. Its approach to profitability has been to:

- Spend heavily on research and development in an effort to find and patent a few new drugs.
- Price them high.
- Market them aggressively.

> **LEARNING OBJECTIVE 1**
> Compute a target cost when the market determines a product price.

Individuals in the United States sometimes question whether these prices are too high. For example, the price of EpiPens® received considerable criticism. The drug companies counter that they need to set these prices high to cover their substantial financial risks to develop these products. **Illustration 8.1** indicates the many factors that can affect pricing decisions.

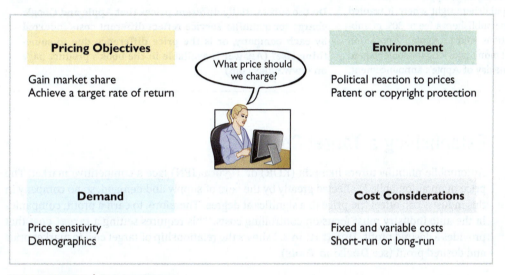

ILLUSTRATION 8.1 | Pricing factors

In the long run, a company must price its product to cover its costs and earn a reasonable profit.

- But to price its product appropriately, it must have a good understanding of market forces at work.
- In most cases, a company does not set the prices.
- Instead, the price is set by the competitive market (the laws of supply and demand).

For example, a company such as **Chevron** (USA) or **ExxonMobil** (USA) cannot set the price of gasoline by itself. These companies are called **price takers** because the price of gasoline is set by market forces (the supply of oil and the demand by customers). This is the case for any product that is not easily differentiated from competing products, such as farm products (corn or wheat) or minerals (coal or sand).

In other situations, the company sets the prices:

- When the product is specially made for a customer. An example would be a unique dress designed by **Chanel** (GBR) or **Armani** (ITA).
- When there are few or no other producers capable of manufacturing a similar item. An example would be a company that has a patent or copyright on a unique process, such as computer chips by **Intel** (USA).

- When it effectively differentiates its product or service from others. For example, even in a competitive market like coffee, **Starbucks** (USA) has been able to differentiate its product and charge a premium for a cup of java.

> **MANAGEMENT INSIGHT** | **Google**
>
> ### The Only Game in Town?
>
>
> Frank Gärtner/iStockphoto
>
> Pricing plays a critical role in company strategy. For example, almost 50% of tablet computer users say that they use them to read newspapers and magazines. And since **Apple**'s (USA) iPad tablet computer at one time represented 75% of the tablets being sold, Apple felt like it had the newspaper and magazine publishers right where it wanted them. So it decided to charge the publishers a fee of 30% of subscription revenue for subscriptions sold at Apple's App Store. Publishers were outraged, but it didn't take long for somebody to come to their rescue. Within one day of Apple's announcement, **Google** (USA) announced that it would only charge a fee of about 10% of subscription revenue for users of its Android system. That might at least partially explain why *Sports Illustrated* provided an app to run on Android tablets before it provided one for iPads, even though at that time Android tablets only had a small share of the market.
>
> **Source:** Martin Peers, "Apple Risks App-lash on iPad," *Wall Street Journal Online* (February 17, 2011).
>
> **Do the substantially different prices that Apple and Google charge for a similar service reflect different costs incurred by each company, or is the price difference due to something else? (Answer is available in the book's product page on www.wiley.com)**

Establishing a Target Cost

Automobile manufacturers like **Kia** (KOR) or **Toyota** (JPN) face a competitive market. The price of an automobile is affected greatly by the laws of supply and demand, so no company in this industry can affect the price to a significant degree. Therefore, to earn a profit, companies in the auto industry must focus on controlling costs. This requires setting a **target cost** that provides a desired profit. **Illustration 8.2** shows the relationship of target cost to market price and desired profit (see **Decision Tools**).

> **DECISION TOOLS**
>
> Managers use the target cost equation in Illustration 8.2 to make decisions about manufacturing products or performing services.

| Market Price | − | Desired Profit | = | Target Cost |

ILLUSTRATION 8.2 | Target cost as related to price and profit

Assuming it reaches sales targets, if **General Motors** (USA) can produce its automobiles for its target cost (or less), it will meet its profit goal. If it cannot achieve its target cost, it will fail to achieve the desired profit, which will disappoint its stockholders.

In a competitive market, a company generally establishes and uses a target cost as follows:

1. **Chooses the segment of the market it wants to compete in—that is, its market niche.** For example, it may choose between selling luxury goods or economy goods in order to focus its efforts on one segment or the other.
2. **Conducts market research.** This determines the features its product should have, and what the market price is for a product with those features.
3. **Determines its target cost by setting a desired profit.** The difference between the market price and the desired profit is the target cost of the product (shown in Illustration 8.2).
4. **Assembles a team of employees with expertise in a variety of areas (production and operations, marketing, and finance).** The team's task is to design and develop a product that can meet quality specifications while not exceeding the target cost.

Thus, the target cost includes all product and period costs necessary to make and market the product or service.

SERVICE COMPANY INSIGHT Disney

How Much Did You Pay for That Seat?

Tomas Abad/Alamy Stock Photo

Pricing decisions are now frequently made by sophisticated computer algorithms. This is true for airlines, hotels, and even Broadway shows. Pricing for these service businesses is particularly important because no revenue is earned on an unused airplane seat, hotel room, or theater seat. These algorithms, which are based on models derived from vast amounts of data from previous customer experiences, strive to determine the best price to charge to fill the seats and maximize revenue. Prices are very dynamic, changing daily or hourly.

As a result, it is not unusual to sit directly next to somebody that paid significantly more (or less) than you did on an airplane.

Experts says that the algorithm that **Disney** (USA) employs to determine ticket prices for its Broadway show *The Lion King* is among the best in the business. Disney's pricing model enabled *The Lion King* to nearly double its revenues within six years. As a consequence, the company is very reluctant to reveal specific information about its formulas.

Source: Patrick Healy, "Ticket Pricing Puts 'Lion King' Atop Broadway's Circle of Life," *The New York Times* (March 17, 2014).

What factors must the managers of a Broadway show consider when setting prices? (Answer is available in the book's product page on www.wiley.com)

DO IT! 1 ▶ Target Costing

Durable Covers is considering introducing a fashion cover for its mobile phones. Market research indicates that 200,000 units can be sold if the price is no more than €20. If Durable Covers decides to produce the covers, it will need to invest €1,000,000 in new production equipment. Durable Covers requires a minimum rate of return of 25% on all investments.

Determine the target cost per unit for the cover.

ACTION PLAN
- Recall that Market price − Desired profit = Target cost.
- The minimum rate of return is a company's desired profit.

Solution

The desired profit for this new product line is as follows:

Invested assets	×	Minimum rate of return	=	Desired profit
€1,000,000	×	25%	=	€250,000

Each cover must therefore result in €1.25 of profit (€250,000 ÷ 200,000 units). The target cost per unit for the cover can then be calculated as follows:

Market price	−	Desired profit	=	Target cost per unit
€20	−	€1.25	=	€18.75 per unit

Related exercise material: **BE8.1, DO IT! 8.1, E8.1, and E8.2.**

COST-PLUS AND VARIABLE-COST PRICING

Cost-Plus Pricing

LEARNING OBJECTIVE 2
Compute a target selling price using cost-plus pricing.

As discussed, in a competitive product environment, the price of a product is set by the market. In order to achieve its desired profit, the company focuses on achieving a target cost.

- In a less competitive environment, companies have a greater ability to set the product price.
- Commonly, when a company sets a product price, it does so as a function of, or relative to, the cost of the product or service. This is referred to as **cost-plus pricing**.

- Under cost-plus pricing, a company first determines a cost base and then adds a **markup** to the cost base to determine the **target selling price**.

If the cost base includes all of the costs required to produce and sell the product, then the markup represents the desired profit.

- The size of the markup (profit) depends on the return the company hopes to generate on the amount it has invested.
- In determining the optimal markup, the company must also consider competitive and market conditions, political and legal issues, and other relevant factors.
- Once the company has determined its cost base and its desired markup, it can add the two together to determine the target selling price.

Illustration 8.3 presents the basic cost-plus pricing equation (see **Decision Tools**).

DECISION TOOLS

The equation in Illustration 8.3 represents how managers use cost-plus pricing to achieve the desired profit.

$$\text{Cost} + \text{Markup} = \text{Target Selling Price}$$

ILLUSTRATION 8.3 | Cost-plus pricing equation

To illustrate, assume that PenCam Products is in the process of setting a selling price on its new video camera pen. It is a functioning pen that records up to 2 hours of audio and video. The unit variable cost estimates for the video camera pen are as shown in **Illustration 8.4**.

	Per Unit
Direct materials	€23
Direct labor	17
Variable manufacturing overhead	12
Variable selling and administrative expenses	8
Unit variable cost	**€60**

ILLUSTRATION 8.4 | Unit variable cost

To produce and sell its product, PenCam incurs fixed manufacturing overhead of €350,000 and fixed selling and administrative expenses of €300,000. To determine the unit cost, we divide total fixed costs by the number of units the company expects to produce. **Illustration 8.5** shows the computation of unit fixed cost for PenCam assuming the production of 10,000 units.

	Total Costs	÷	Budgeted Volume	=	Unit Cost
Fixed manufacturing overhead	€350,000	÷	10,000	=	€35
Fixed selling and administrative expenses	300,000	÷	10,000	=	30
Unit fixed cost (at 10,000 units)					**€65**

ILLUSTRATION 8.5 | Unit fixed cost, 10,000 units

Management is ultimately evaluated based on its ability to generate a high return on the company's investment. This is frequently expressed as a return on investment (ROI) percentage, calculated as income divided by the average amount invested in a product or service. A higher percentage reflects a greater success in generating profits from the investment in a product or service. Chapter 10 provides a more in-depth discussion of the use of ROI to evaluate the performance of investment center managers.

- To achieve a desired ROI percentage, a product's markup should be determined by calculating the desired ROI per unit.
- This is calculated by multiplying the desired ROI percentage times the amount invested to produce the product, and then dividing this by the number of units produced.

Illustration 8.6 shows the computation used to determine a markup amount based on a desired ROI per unit for PenCam, assuming that the company expects to produce 10,000 units, desires a 20% ROI, and invests €2,000,000.

$$\frac{\text{Desired ROI Percentage} \times \text{Amount Invested}}{\text{Units Produced}} = \text{Markup (Desired ROI per Unit)}$$

$$\frac{20\% \times €2,000,000}{10,000 \text{ units}} = €40$$

ILLUSTRATION 8.6 | Calculation of markup based on desired ROI per unit

PenCam expects to receive income of €400,000 (20% × €2,000,000) on its €2,000,000 investment. On a per unit basis, the markup based on the desired ROI per unit is €40 (€400,000 ÷ 10,000 units). Given the unit costs shown above, **Illustration 8.7** computes the sales price to be €165.

	Per Unit
Variable cost	€ 60
Fixed cost	65
Total cost	125
Markup (desired ROI per unit)	40
Unit selling price (at 10,000 units)	**€165**

ILLUSTRATION 8.7 | Computation of selling price, 10,000 units

In most cases, companies like PenCam use a markup percentage on cost to determine the selling price. **Illustration 8.8** presents the equation to compute the markup percentage to achieve a desired ROI of €40 per unit.

$$\text{Markup (Desired ROI per Unit)} \div \text{Total Unit Cost} = \text{Markup Percentage}$$

$$€40 \div €125 = 32\%$$

ILLUSTRATION 8.8 | Computation of markup percentage

Using a 32% markup on cost, PenCam would compute the target selling price as shown in **Illustration 8.9**.

$$\text{Total Unit Cost} + (\text{Total Unit Cost} \times \text{Markup Percentage}) = \text{Target Selling Price}$$

$$€125 + (€125 \times 32\%) = €165$$

ILLUSTRATION 8.9 | Computation of selling price—markup approach

PenCam should set the selling price for its video camera pen at €165.

Limitations of Cost-Plus Pricing

The cost-plus pricing approach has a major advantage: It is simple to compute.

- However, the cost model does not give consideration to the demand side. That is, will customers pay the price PenCam Products computed for its video camera pen?

- In addition, sales volume plays a large role in determining unit costs. The lower the sales volume, for example, the higher the price PenCam must charge to meet its desired ROI.

To illustrate, if the budgeted sales volume was 5,000 instead of 10,000, PenCam's unit variable costs would remain the same. However, the unit fixed cost would change as shown in **Illustration 8.10**.

	Total Costs	÷	Budgeted Volume	=	Unit Cost
Fixed manufacturing overhead	€350,000	÷	5,000	=	€ 70
Fixed selling and administrative expenses	300,000	÷	5,000	=	60
Unit fixed cost (at 5,000 units)					€130

ILLUSTRATION 8.10 | **Unit fixed cost, 5,000 units**

As indicated in Illustration 8.5, the unit fixed cost for 10,000 units was €65. However, at a lower sales volume of 5,000 units, the unit fixed cost increases to €130. PenCam's desired 20% ROI now results in a €80 ROI per unit [(20% × €2,000,000) ÷ 5,000]. PenCam computes the selling price at 5,000 units as shown in **Illustration 8.11**.

	Per Unit
Variable cost	€ 60
Fixed cost	130
Total cost	190
Markup (desired ROI per unit)	80
Unit selling price (at 5,000 units)	€270

ILLUSTRATION 8.11 | **Computation of selling price, 5,000 units**

As shown, the lower the budgeted volume, the higher the unit price. The reason: Fixed costs and ROI are spread over fewer units, and therefore the fixed cost and ROI per unit increase. In this case, at 5,000 units, PenCam would have to mark up its total unit costs 42.11% to earn a desired ROI of €80 per unit, as shown below.

$$42.11\% = \frac{€80 \text{ (desired ROI per unit)}}{€190 \text{ (total unit cost)}}$$

The target selling price would then be €270, as indicated earlier:

$$€190 + (€190 \times 42.11\%) = €270$$

The opposite effect will occur if budgeted volume is higher (say, 12,000 units) because fixed costs and ROI can be spread over more units. As a result, the cost-plus model of pricing will achieve its desired ROI only when PenCam sells the quantity it budgeted. If actual volume is much less than budgeted volume, PenCam may sustain losses unless it can raise its prices.

Variable-Cost Pricing

In determining the target price for PenCam Products' video camera pen, we calculated the cost base by including all costs incurred. This approach is referred to as **full-cost pricing**.

- Instead of using full costs to set prices, some companies simply add a markup to their variable costs (thus excluding fixed manufacturing and fixed selling and administrative costs).

- Using **variable-cost pricing** as the basis for setting prices avoids the problem of using uncertain cost information (as discussed above for PenCam) related to unit fixed cost computations.
- Variable-cost pricing also is helpful in pricing special orders or when excess capacity exists.

The major disadvantage of variable-cost pricing is that managers may set the price too low and consequently fail to cover their fixed costs. In the long run, failure to cover fixed costs will lead to losses. As a result, companies that use variable-cost pricing must adjust their markups to make sure that the price set will provide a fair return. The use of variable costs as the basis for setting prices is discussed in Appendix 8A.

DO IT! 2 ▶ Target Selling Price

Big Sky Ltd. produces air purifiers. The following unit cost information is available: direct materials €16, direct labor €18, variable manufacturing overhead €11, variable selling and administrative expenses €6. Fixed selling and administrative expenses are €50,000, and fixed manufacturing overhead is €150,000. Using a 45% markup percentage on total unit cost and assuming 10,000 units, compute the target selling price.

ACTION PLAN
- Calculate the unit total cost.
- Multiply the unit total cost by the markup percentage, then add this amount to the unit total cost to determine the target selling price.

Solution

Direct materials	€16
Direct labor	18
Variable manufacturing overhead	11
Variable selling and administrative expenses	6
Fixed selling and administrative expenses	5*
Fixed manufacturing overhead	15**
Total unit cost	€71

$$\text{Total unit cost} + (\text{Total unit cost} \times \text{Markup percentage}) = \text{Target selling price}$$

$$€71 + (€71 \times 45\%) = €102.95$$

*€50,000 ÷ 10,000; **€150,000 ÷ 10,000

Related exercise material: **BE8.2, BE8.3, BE8.4, BE8.5, DO IT! 8.2, E8.3, E8.4, E8.5, E8.6, and E8.7.**

TIME-AND-MATERIAL PRICING

Another variation on cost-plus pricing is **time-and-material pricing**.

LEARNING OBJECTIVE 3
Use time-and-material pricing to determine the cost of services provided.

- Under this approach, the company sets two pricing rates—one for the **labor** used on a job and another for the **material**.
- The labor rate includes the hourly rate paid for direct labor time and other employee costs.
- The material charge is based on the cost of direct parts and materials used and a **material loading charge** for related overhead costs.

Time-and-material pricing is widely used in service industries, especially professional firms such as public accounting, law, engineering, and consulting firms, as well as construction companies, repair shops, and printers.

To illustrate a time-and-material pricing situation, assume the data shown in **Illustration 8.12** for Orion Ocean Park, a boat and motor repair shop.

Orion Ocean Park
Budgeted Costs for the Year 2023

	Time Charges	Material Loading Charges*
Mechanics' wages and benefits	€103,500	—
Parts manager's salary and benefits	—	€11,500
Office employee's salary and benefits	20,700	2,300
Other overhead (supplies, depreciation, property taxes, advertising, utilities)	26,800	14,400
Total budgeted costs	€151,000	€28,200

*The material loading charges exclude the invoice cost of the materials.

ILLUSTRATION 8.12 | Total annual budgeted time and material costs

Using time-and-material pricing involves three steps:

1. Calculate the per hour labor charge.
2. Calculate the charge for obtaining and holding materials.
3. Calculate the charges for a particular job.

Step 1: Calculate the Labor Rate The first step for time-and-material pricing is to determine a charge for labor time. The charge for labor time is expressed as a rate per hour of labor. This rate includes:

1. The direct labor cost of the employees, including hourly pay rate plus fringe benefits.
2. Selling, administrative, and similar overhead costs.
3. An allowance for a desired profit or ROI per hour of employee time.

In some industries, such as repair shops for autos and boats, the same hourly labor rate is charged regardless of which employee performs the work. In other industries, the rate that is charged is adjusted according to classification or level of the employee. A public accounting firm, for example, would charge different rates for the services of an assistant, senior manager, or partner. A law firm would charge different rates for the work of a paralegal, associate, or partner.

Illustration 8.13 shows computation of the hourly charges for Orion Ocean Park during 2023. The park budgets 5,000 annual labor hours in 2023, and it desires a profit margin of €8 per hour of labor.

Orion Ocean Park

	A Per Hour	B Total Cost	C	D Total Hours	E	F Per Hour Charge
2	Hourly labor rate for repairs					
3	Mechanics' wages and benefits	€103,500	÷	5,000	=	€20.70
4	Overhead costs					
5	Office employee's salary and benefits	20,700	÷	5,000	=	4.14
6	Other overhead	26,800	÷	5,000	=	5.36
7	Total hourly cost	€151,000	÷	5,000	=	30.20
8	Profit margin					8.00
9	Rate charged per hour of labor					€38.20

ILLUSTRATION 8.13 | Computation of hourly time-charge rate

To determine the labor charge for a job, the park multiplies this rate of €38.20 by the number of hours of labor used.

Step 2: Calculate the Material Loading Charge The charge for materials typically includes the invoice price of any materials used on the job plus a material loading charge.

- The **material loading charge** covers the costs of purchasing, receiving, handling, and storing materials, plus any desired profit margin on the materials themselves.
- The material loading charge is expressed as a **percentage** of the total estimated costs of parts and materials for the year.
- To determine this percentage, the company:

    1. Estimates its total annual costs for purchasing, receiving, handling, and storing materials.
    2. Divides this amount by the total estimated cost of parts and materials.
    3. Adds a desired profit margin on the materials themselves.

Illustration 8.14 shows the computation of the material loading charge used by Orion Ocean Park during 2023. The park estimates that the total invoice cost of parts and materials used

	A	B	C	D	E	F
1		Material Loading Charges	÷	Total Invoice Cost, Parts and Materials	=	Material Loading Percentage
2	Overhead costs					
3	Parts manager's salary and benefits	€11,500				
4	Office employee's salary	2,300				
5		13,800	÷	€120,000	=	11.50%
6						
7	Other overhead	14,400	÷	120,000	=	12.00%
8		€28,200	÷	120,000	=	23.50%
9	Profit margin					20.00%
10	Material loading percentage					43.50%

ILLUSTRATION 8.14 | Computation of material loading charge

in 2023 will be €120,000. The park desires a 20% profit margin on the invoice cost of parts and materials.

The park's material loading charge on any particular job is 43.50% multiplied by the cost of materials used on the job. For example, if the park used €100 of parts, the additional material loading charge would be €43.50.

Step 3: Calculate Charges for a Particular Job The charges for any particular job are the sum of:

1. The labor charge.
2. The charge for the materials.
3. The material loading charge.

For example, suppose that Orion Ocean Park prepares a price quotation to estimate the cost to refurbish a used 8-meter pontoon boat. Orion Ocean Park estimates the job will require 50 hours of labor and €3,600 in parts and materials. **Illustration 8.15** shows the park's price quotation.

Orion Ocean Park
Time-and-Material Price Quotation

Job: Orion Perino, repair of 8-meter pontoon boat		
Labor charges: 50 hours @ €38.20		€1,910
Material charges		
Cost of parts and materials	€3,600	
Material loading charge (43.5% × €3,600)	1,566	5,166
Total price of labor and material		€7,076

ILLUSTRATION 8.15 | Price quotation for time and material

DECISION TOOLS

The time-and-material price quotation covers costs for parts and labor as well as the desired profit margins on parts and labor.

Included in the €7,076 price quotation for the boat repair are charges for labor costs, overhead costs, materials costs, materials handling and storage costs, and a profit margin on both labor and parts (see **Decision Tools**). Orion Ocean Park used labor hours as a basis for computing the time rate. Other companies, such as machine shops, plastic molding shops, and printers, might use machine hours.

SERVICE COMPANY INSIGHT Button Worldwide

Don Bayley/iStockphoto

It Ain't Like It Used to Be

In the United States, for many decades, professionals in most service industries used some form of hourly based price, regardless of the outcome. But the financial crisis of 2008 brought an end to that practice. Many customers now demand that bills be tied to actual performance, rather than to the amount of hours worked.

For example, communications company **Button Worldwide** (USA), which used to charge about $15,000 or more per month as its "retainer fee," now instead charges based on achieving particular outcomes. For example, the company might charge $10,000 if it obtains a desirable public speaking engagement for a company executive. Similarly, a digital marketing agency reduced its hourly fee from $135 to $80, but it gets a bonus if it achieves specified increases in the sales volume on a customer's website.

Source: Simona Covel, "Firms Try Alternative to Hourly Fees," *Wall Street Journal Online* (April 2, 2009).

What implications does this have for a service company's need for managerial accounting? (Answer is available in the book's product page on www.wiley.com)

DO IT! 3 ▶ Time-and-Material Pricing

Presented below are data for Andrea Electrical Repair Shop for next year.

Repair-technicians' wages	€130,000
Fringe benefits	30,000
Overhead	20,000

The desired profit margin per labor hour is €10. The material loading charge is 40% of invoice cost. Andrea estimates that 8,000 labor hours will be worked next year. If Andrea repairs a TV that takes 4 hours to repair and uses parts costing €50, compute the bill for this job.

ACTION PLAN
- Calculate the labor charge.
- Calculate the material loading charge.
- Compute the bill for specific repair.

Solution

	Total Cost	÷	Total Hours	=	Per Hour Charge
Repair-technicians' wages	€130,000	÷	8,000	=	€16.25
Fringe benefits	30,000	÷	8,000	=	3.75
Overhead	20,000	÷	8,000	=	2.50
	€180,000	÷	8,000	=	22.50
Profit margin					10.00
Rate charged per hour of labor					€32.50

> Job: Repair TV
> Labor charges: 4 hours @ €32.50   €130
> Material charges
>   Cost of parts and materials   €50
>   Material loading charge (40% × €50)   20   70
> Total price of labor and material   €200
>
> Related exercise material: **BE8.6, DO IT! 8.3, E8.8, E8.9, and E8.10.**

TRANSFER PRICES

In today's global economy, growth is often vital to survival. Some companies grow "vertically," meaning they expand in the direction of either their suppliers or customers. For example, a manufacturer of bicycles like **Trek** (USA) may acquire a bicycle component manufacturer or a chain of bicycle shops. A movie production company like **Walt Disney** (USA) or **Sony Pictures Entertainment** (USA) may acquire a movie theater chain or a cable television company.

LEARNING OBJECTIVE 4
Determine a transfer price using the negotiated, cost-based, and market-based approaches.

- Divisions within vertically integrated companies often transfer goods or services to other divisions in the company.
- When goods are transferred between divisions of the same company, the price used to record the transaction is the **transfer price**.

Illustration 8.16 shows transfers between divisions for Aerobic Bicycle Company. As shown, the Component Division sells goods to the Company's Assembly Division, as well as to outside parties. Units sold to the Assembly Division are recorded at the transfer price.

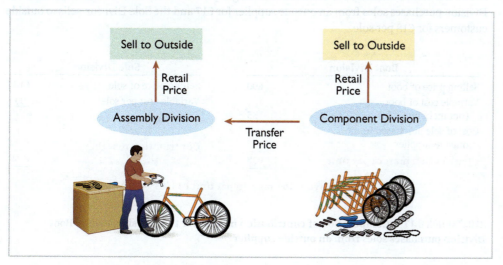

ILLUSTRATION 8.16 | Transfer pricing example

The primary objective of transfer pricing is the same as that of pricing a product to an outside party.

- The objective is to maximize the return to the company.
- An additional objective of transfer pricing is to measure divisional performance accurately.

Setting a transfer price is complicated because of competing interests among divisions within the company. For example, in the case of the bicycle company shown in Illustration 8.16, setting the transfer price high will benefit the Component Division (the selling division) but will hurt the Assembly Division (the purchasing division).

There are three possible approaches for determining a transfer price:

1. Negotiated transfer prices.
2. Cost-based transfer prices.
3. Market-based transfer prices.

Conceptually, a negotiated transfer price should work best, but due to practical considerations, companies often use the other two methods.

Negotiated Transfer Prices

A **negotiated transfer price** is determined through agreement of division managers. To illustrate negotiated transfer pricing, we examine Dover Outfitters. Until recently, Dover focused exclusively on making rubber soles for work boots and hiking boots. It sold these rubber soles to boot manufacturers for €18 per sole and had a variable cost of €11 per sole.

- Last year, the company decided to take advantage of its strong reputation by expanding into the business of making hiking boots.
- As a consequence of this expansion, the company is now structured as two independent divisions, the Boot Division and the Sole Division.
- The company compensates the manager of each division based on achievement of profitability targets for that division.

The Boot Division manufactures leather uppers for hiking boots and attaches these uppers to rubber soles. Its variable costs, not including the sole, are €35 per boot. During its first year, the Boot Division purchased its rubber soles from an outside supplier for €17 per sole so as not to disrupt the operations of the Sole Division. However, top management now wants the Sole Division to provide at least some of the soles used by the Boot Division. **Illustration 8.17** shows the computation of the contribution margin per unit for each division when the Boot Division purchases soles from an outside supplier for €17 and the Sole Division sells to outside customers for €18 per sole.

Boot Division		Sole Division	
Selling price of boot	€90	Selling price of sole	€18
Variable cost of boot (not including sole)	35	Variable cost per sole	11
Cost of sole purchased from outside supplier	17		
Contribution margin per unit	**€38**	**Contribution margin per unit**	**€ 7**
	Total contribution margin per unit €45 (€38 + €7)		

ILLUSTRATION 8.17 | Computation of contribution margin for two divisions, when Boot Division purchases soles from an outside supplier

This information indicates that the contribution margin per unit for the Boot Division is €38 and for the Sole Division is €7. The total contribution margin per unit is €45 (€38 + €7).

Now let's ask the question, "What would be a fair transfer price if the Sole Division sold 10,000 soles to the Boot Division?" The answer depends on how busy the Sole Division is—that is, whether it has excess capacity.

No Excess Capacity

Assume that the Sole Division has no excess capacity and produces and sells 80,000 soles to outside customers. As indicated in Illustration 8.17, the Sole Division charges outside customers €18 and has a variable cost of €11, so its contribution margin on units sold to outside customers is €7 (€18 − €11). Since the Sole Division has no excess capacity, if it chooses to sell 10,000 units to the Boot Division, it would have to forgo sales of 10,000 units to outside customers.

- The contribution margin on sales to outside customers that would be forgone as a result of an internal transfer is referred to as the **opportunity cost**.
- Therefore, the Sole Division must receive from the Boot Division a payment that will at least cover its variable cost of €11 per sole **plus** its contribution margin—opportunity cost— of €7 per sole.
- The sum of the variable cost and the opportunity cost is referred to as the **minimum transfer price**.
- If the Sole Division cannot recover the minimum transfer price, it should not sell its soles to the Boot Division.

The minimum transfer price that would be acceptable to the Sole Division is €18, as shown in **Illustration 8.18** (see **Decision Tools**).

> **DECISION TOOLS**
>
> The equation in Illustration 8.18 helps managers set prices for the transfer of goods between a company's divisions.

Variable Cost	+	Opportunity Cost	=	Minimum Transfer Price
€11	+	€7	=	€18

ILLUSTRATION 8.18 | Minimum transfer price equation—no excess capacity

From the perspective of the Boot Division (the buyer), the most it will pay is what the sole would cost from an outside supplier. In this case, therefore, the Boot Division would pay no more than €17. As shown in **Illustration 8.19**, an acceptable transfer price is not available in this situation.

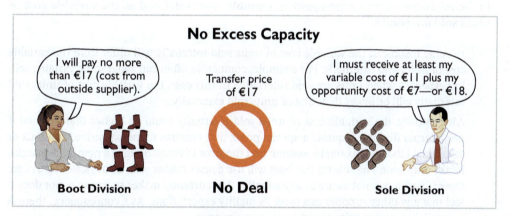

ILLUSTRATION 8.19 | Transfer price negotiations—no excess capacity

Excess Capacity

What happens if the Sole Division **has excess capacity**? For example, assume the Sole Division can produce 80,000 soles but can sell only 70,000 soles in the open market. As a result, it has available capacity of 10,000 units. Because it has excess capacity, the Sole Division could provide 10,000 units to the Boot Division without losing its €7 contribution margin on these units. Therefore, as **Illustration 8.20** shows, the minimum price it would now accept is €11.

Variable Cost	+	Opportunity Cost	=	Minimum Transfer Price
€11	+	€0	=	€11

ILLUSTRATION 8.20 | Minimum transfer price equation—excess capacity

In this case, the Boot Division and the Sole Division should negotiate a transfer price within the range of €11 to €17, as shown in **Illustration 8.21**.

Given excess capacity, Dover Outfitters will increase its overall net income if the Boot Division purchases the 10,000 soles internally. This is true as long as the Sole Division's variable cost is less than the outside price of €17.

ILLUSTRATION 8.21 | Transfer pricing negotiations—excess capacity

- The Sole Division will receive a positive contribution margin from any transfer price above its variable cost of €11.
- The Boot Division will benefit from any price below €17.
- At any transfer price above €17, the Boot Division will go to an outside supplier, a solution that would be undesirable to both divisions as well as to the company as a whole.

Variable Costs

In the minimum transfer price equation, **variable cost is defined as the variable cost of units sold** *internally*.

- In some instances, the variable cost of units sold internally will differ from the variable cost of units sold externally. For example, companies often can avoid some variable selling expenses when units are sold internally. In this case, the variable cost of units sold internally will be lower than that of units sold externally.
- Alternatively, the variable cost of units sold internally could be higher than normal if the internal division requests a special order that requires more expensive materials or additional labor. For example, assume that the Boot Division designs a new high-margin, heavy-duty boot. The sole for this boot will use denser rubber with an intricate lug design. Dover Outfitters is not aware of any supplier that currently makes such a sole, nor does it feel that any other supplier can meet its quality expectations. As a consequence, there is no available market price to use as the transfer price.

We can, however, employ the equation for the minimum transfer price to assist in arriving at a reasonable solution. After evaluating the special sole, the Sole Division determines that its variable cost would be €19 per sole. The Sole Division is at full capacity. The Sole Division's opportunity cost at full capacity is the €7 (€18 − €11) per sole that it earns producing the standard sole and selling it to an outside customer. Therefore, the minimum transfer price that the Sole Division would be willing to accept for the special-order sole is as shown in **Illustration 8.22**.

Variable Cost	+	Opportunity Cost	=	Minimum Transfer Price
€19	+	€7	=	€26

ILLUSTRATION 8.22 | Minimum transfer price equation—special order

The transfer price of €26 provides the Sole Division with enough revenue to cover its increased variable cost and its opportunity cost (contribution margin on its standard sole).

Units Transferred Are Unequal to Units Forgone

In some situations, when the division has no excess capacity, the number of units transferred internally differs from the number of units forgone on sales to outside parties. This occurs if characteristics of the units transferred internally differ from standard units, and thus differ in terms of the amount of manufacturing resources required for production. For example, suppose that the Boot Division requests 7,000 units of a special, high-endurance sole that requires more manufacturing resources than a standard sole. To produce 7,000 units of the special sole for the Boot Division, the Sole Division will have to forgo sales of 10,000 units of its standard sole to outside customers.

- When the number of units transferred internally differs from the number of units of external sales forgone, a company must compute the opportunity cost per unit transferred internally.
- This is accomplished by first computing the total contribution margin on all units forgone and then dividing by the number of units transferred internally.

The calculation for the opportunity cost, applied to the special order from the Boot Division, is shown in **Illustration 8.23**.

[(Selling Price − Variable Cost) × Units Forgone] ÷	Units Transferred Internally	=	Opportunity Cost
[(€18 − €11) × 10,000] ÷	7,000	=	€10

ILLUSTRATION 8.23 | Opportunity cost if units sold are unequal to units forgone

Notice that, because the number of units forgone exceeds the number of units that will be transferred internally, the opportunity cost per unit of €10 exceeds the opportunity cost per unit of €7 that we computed previously on a standard unit.

Summary of Negotiated Transfer Pricing

Under negotiated transfer pricing, the selling division establishes a minimum transfer price, and the purchasing division establishes a maximum transfer price. This system provides a sound basis for establishing a transfer price because both divisions are better off if the proper decision-making rules are used. However, companies often do not use negotiated transfer pricing because:

- Market price information is sometimes not easily obtainable.
- A lack of trust between the two negotiating divisions may lead to a breakdown in the negotiations.
- Negotiations often lead to different pricing strategies from division to division, which is cumbersome and sometimes costly to implement.

Many companies, therefore, often use simple systems based on cost or market information to develop transfer prices.

Cost-Based Transfer Prices

An alternative to negotiated transfer pricing is cost-based pricing.

- A **cost-based transfer price** is based on the costs incurred by the division producing the goods or services.
- A cost-based transfer price can be based on variable costs alone, or on variable costs plus fixed costs.
- In some cases, the selling division may add a markup.

The cost-based approach sometimes results in improper transfer prices. Improper transfer prices can reduce company profits and provide unfair evaluations of division performance. To illustrate, assume that Dover Outfitters requires the division to use a transfer price based on the variable cost of the sole. With no excess capacity, the contribution margins per unit for the two divisions are as shown in **Illustration 8.24**.

	Boot Division		Sole Division	
Selling price of boot		€90	Selling price of sole	€11
Variable cost of boot (not including sole)		35	Variable cost per sole	11
Cost of sole purchased from sole division		11		
Contribution margin per unit		**€44**	**Contribution margin per unit**	**€ 0**
	Total contribution margin per unit	**€44**	(€44 + €0)	

ILLUSTRATION 8.24 | **Cost-based transfer price—10,000 units**

This cost-based transfer system is a bad deal for the Sole Division as it reports no profit on the transfer of 10,000 soles to the Boot Division.

- If the Sole Division could sell these soles to an outside customer, it would make €70,000 [10,000 × (€18 − €11)].
- The Boot Division, on the other hand, is delighted. Its contribution margin per unit increases from €38 to €44, or €6 per boot.
- Thus, this transfer price results in an unfair evaluation of these two divisions.

Further examination of this example reveals that this transfer price reduces the company's overall profits. The Sole Division lost a contribution margin per unit of €7 (Illustration 8.17), and the Boot Division experiences only a €6 increase in its contribution margin per unit. Overall, Dover Outfitters loses €10,000 [10,000 boots × (€7 − €6)]. **Illustration 8.25** illustrates this deficiency.

ILLUSTRATION 8.25 | **Cost-based transfer price results—no excess capacity**

The overall results change if the Sole Division **has excess capacity**. In this case, the Sole Division continues to report a zero profit on these 10,000 units but does not lose the €7 per unit of contribution margin (because it had excess capacity). The Boot Division gains €6. So overall, the company is better off by €60,000 (10,000 × €6). However, with a cost-based system, the Sole Division continues to report a zero profit on these 10,000 units.

The cost-based approach has disadvantages:

- A cost-based system does not reflect the division's true profitability.
- **It does not provide adequate incentive for the Sole Division to control costs**. The division's costs are simply passed on to the next division.

Despite these disadvantages, the cost system is simple to understand and easy to use because the information is already available in the accounting system. In addition, market information is sometimes not available, so the only alternative is some type of cost-based system. As a result, cost-based transfer prices are the most common method used by companies to establish transfer prices.

Market-Based Transfer Prices

The **market-based transfer price** is based on existing market prices of competing goods or services.

- A market-based system is often considered the best approach because it is objective and generally provides the proper economic incentives.
- For example, if the Sole Division can charge the market price, it is indifferent as to whether soles are sold to outside customers or internally to the Boot Division—it does not lose any contribution margin.
- Similarly, the Boot Division pays a price for the soles that is at or reasonably close to market.

When the Sole Division has no excess capacity, the market-based system works reasonably well. The Sole Division receives market price, and the Boot Division pays market price.

If the Sole Division has excess capacity, however, the market-based system can lead to actions that are not in the best interest of the company. The minimum transfer price that the Sole Division should receive is its variable cost plus its opportunity cost. If the Sole Division has excess capacity, its opportunity cost is zero. However, under the market-based system, the Sole Division transfers the goods at the market price of €18, for a contribution margin per unit of €7 (€18 − €11). The Boot Division manager has to accept the €18 sole price. This price may not accurately reflect a fair cost of the sole, given that the Sole Division had excess capacity. As a result, the Boot Division may overprice its boots in the market if it uses the market price of the sole plus a markup in setting the price of the boot. This action can lead to losses for Dover Outfitters overall.

As indicated earlier, in many cases, there simply is not a well-defined market for the good or service being transferred. When this is the case, a reasonable market value cannot be developed, so companies often resort to a cost-based system.

Effect of Outsourcing on Transfer Pricing

An increasing number of companies rely on **outsourcing**.

- Outsourcing involves contracting with an external party to provide a good or service, rather than performing the work internally.
- Some companies have taken outsourcing to the extreme by outsourcing all of their production. Many of these so-called **virtual companies** have well-established brand names though they do not manufacture any of their own products.

Companies use incremental analysis (Chapter 7) to determine whether outsourcing is profitable. When companies outsource, fewer components are transferred internally between divisions. This reduces the need for transfer prices.

Transfers Between Divisions in Different Countries

As more companies "globalize" their operations, an increasing number of intercompany transfers are between divisions that are located in different countries. One estimate suggests that 60% of trade between countries is simply transfers between company divisions. Differences in tax rates across countries can complicate the determination of the appropriate transfer price.

- A company pays income tax in the country in which it generates revenue.
- Some companies intentionally shift income from divisions located in countries with high tax rates to divisions located in countries with low tax rates.

Appendix 8B discusses in more detail transfer pricing issues that occur when goods are exchanged between divisions in different countries.

DATA ANALYTICS INSIGHT Big Data Pricing

Setting the Optimal Price

Studio Romantic/ Shutterstock.com

Product pricing has benefitted greatly from the use of big data and data analytics. One example is dynamic pricing, where companies rapidly adjust a product's prices across customers or across time based on changing market conditions. Dynamic pricing has been used by ride-sharing services such as **Uber** (USA), hotel chains such as **Marriott** (USA), and sports teams such as the **San Francisco Giants** (USA).

As you might expect, the concept of dynamic pricing ties in very well with data analytics. For example, consider **Big Data Pricing** (USA), which provides consulting services to assist companies in obtaining optimal pricing. In its promotional materials, Big Data Pricing advertises that it helps companies to "gain access to deep pricing and technical expertise to help drive ROI, pricing process improvement, business adoption and optimize performance." To accomplish this, employees at Big Data Pricing employ a variety of software platforms, including Salesforce CPQ, Vendavo, Price f(x), Vistex, Tableau, and Lumira.

Finally, consider that a recent job opening at Big Data Pricing required the following qualifications: "deep analytical skills, critical thinking, excellent communication skills, work collaboratively, willingness to learn." So, a combination of data analytical skills and an understanding of pricing models could very well be your ticket to a good job!

Sources: *www.bigdatapricing.com* (March 2020).

What is dynamic pricing, and why would the use of dynamic pricing require data analytics? (Answer is available in the book's product page on www.wiley.com)

DO IT! 4 ▶ Transfer Pricing

The clock division of Flavio Clocks Company manufactures clocks and then sells them to customers for €10 per unit. Its unit variable cost is €4, and its unit fixed cost is €2.50. Management would like the clock division to transfer 8,000 of these clocks to another division within the company at a price of €5. The clock division could avoid €0.50 per clock of variable packaging costs by selling internally.

a. Determine the minimum transfer price, assuming the clock division is not operating at full capacity.

b. Determine the minimum transfer price, assuming the clock division is operating at full capacity.

ACTION PLAN
- Determine whether the company is at full capacity or not.
- Determine variable cost and opportunity cost.
- Apply minimum transfer price equation.

Solution

a. If the clock division is not operating at full capacity, the opportunity cost for the clocks is €0. Since internal sales will eliminate €0.50 of packaging costs, the variable cost per clock is €3.50 (€4 − €0.50).

$$\text{Minimum transfer price} = \text{Variable cost} + \text{Opportunity cost}$$
$$€3.50 = €3.50 + €0$$

b. If the clock division is already operating at full capacity, the opportunity cost for the clocks is €6 (€10 − €4). Since internal sales will eliminate €0.50 of packaging costs, the variable cost per clock is €3.50 (€4 − €0.50).

$$\text{Minimum transfer price} = \text{Variable cost} + \text{Opportunity cost}$$
$$€9.50 = €3.50 + €6$$

Related exercise material: **BE8.7, BE8.8, BE8.9, DO IT! 8.4, E8.11, E8.12, E8.13, E8.14, and E8.15.**

USING THE DECISION TOOLS | Zappos.com

As mentioned in the Feature Story, **Zappos.com** (USA) faces many situations where it needs to apply the decision tools learned in this chapter. For example, suppose that Zappos is considering the idea of manufacturing a fun, low-cost "energy" shoe and selling it under its own name. It has estimated the following information based on a budgeted volume of 100,000 units.

	Per Unit	Total
Direct materials	$8.40	
Direct labor	$1.90	
Variable manufacturing overhead	$0.80	
Fixed manufacturing overhead		$940,000
Variable selling and administrative expenses	$0.90	
Fixed selling and administrative expenses		$320,000

Assume Zappos uses cost-plus pricing to set its selling price. Management also directs that the target price be set to provide a 25% return on investment (ROI) on invested assets of $4,200,000.

Instructions

a. Compute the markup percentage and target selling price on this new shoe.

b. Assuming that the volume is 50,000 units instead of 100,000 units, compute the markup percentage and target selling price that will allow Zappos to earn its desired ROI of 25%.

Solution

a.

Unit variable cost

	Per Unit
Direct materials	$ 8.40
Direct labor	1.90
Variable manufacturing overhead	0.80
Variable selling and administrative expenses	0.90
Unit variable cost	$12.00

Unit fixed cost

	Total Costs	÷	Budgeted Volume	=	Unit Cost
Fixed manufacturing overhead	$ 940,000	÷	100,000	=	$ 9.40
Fixed selling and administrative expenses	320,000	÷	100,000	=	3.20
Unit fixed cost	$1,260,000				$12.60

Computation of unit selling price (100,000 units)

Unit variable cost	$12.00
Unit fixed cost	12.60
Total unit cost	24.60
Desired ROI per unit*	10.50
Unit selling price	$35.10

*($4,200,000 × .25) ÷ 100,000

The markup percentage is:

$$\frac{\text{Desired ROI per unit}}{\text{Total unit cost}} = \frac{\$10.50}{\$24.60} = 42.68\%$$

b. If the company produces 50,000 units, its selling price and markup percentage would be:

Computation of unit selling price (50,000 units)

Unit variable cost	$12.00
Unit fixed cost ($1,260,000 ÷ 50,000)	25.20
Total unit cost	37.20
Desired ROI per unit*	21.00
Unit selling price	$58.20

*($4,200,000 × .25) ÷ 50,000

The markup percentage would be:

$$\frac{\text{Desired ROI per unit}}{\text{Total unit cost}} = \frac{\$21.00}{\$37.20} = 56.45\%$$

Appendix 8A | ABSORPTION-COST AND VARIABLE-COST PRICING

LEARNING OBJECTIVE *5
Determine prices using absorption-cost pricing and variable-cost pricing.

In determining the target price for PenCam Products' video camera pen in the chapter, we calculated the cost base **by including all costs incurred**. This approach is referred to as **full-cost pricing**.

- Using total cost as the basis of the markup makes sense conceptually. In the long run, the price must cover all costs and provide a reasonable profit.
- However, total cost is difficult to determine in practice. This is because period costs (selling and administrative expenses) are difficult to trace to a specific product.
- Activity-based costing can be used to overcome this difficulty to some extent.

In practice, companies sometimes use two other cost approaches: (1) absorption-cost pricing or (2) variable-cost pricing. Absorption-cost pricing is more popular than variable-cost pricing.[1] We illustrate both approaches because both have merit.

Absorption-Cost Pricing

Absorption-cost pricing is consistent with accounting standards. The reason: It includes both variable and fixed manufacturing costs as product costs.

- **Absorption-cost pricing excludes from this cost base both variable and fixed selling and administrative costs.**
- Thus, companies must somehow provide for selling and administrative costs plus the target ROI. They do this through the markup.

The **first step** in absorption-cost pricing is to compute the unit **manufacturing cost**. For PenCam Products, this amounts to €87 per unit at a volume of 10,000 units, as shown in **Illustration 8A.1**.

	Per Unit
Direct materials	€23
Direct labor	17
Variable manufacturing overhead	12
Fixed manufacturing overhead (€350,000 ÷ 10,000)	35
Total unit manufacturing cost (absorption cost)	€87

ILLUSTRATION 8A.1 | Computation of unit manufacturing cost

In addition, PenCam provides the information given in **Illustration 8A.2** regarding selling and administrative expenses per unit and desired ROI per unit.

Variable selling and administrative expenses	€ 8
Fixed selling and administrative expenses (€300,000 ÷ 10,000)	30
Total selling and administrative expenses per unit	€38
Desired ROI per unit (see Illustration 8.6)	€40

ILLUSTRATION 8A.2 | Other selling and administrative expense information

The **second step** in absorption-cost pricing is to compute the markup percentage using the equation in **Illustration 8A.3**. Note that when companies use manufacturing cost per unit as the cost base to compute the markup percentage, the **percentage must cover the desired ROI and also the selling and administrative expenses**.

---
[1]For a discussion of cost-plus pricing, see Eunsup Skim and Ephraim F. Sudit, "How Manufacturers Price Products," *Management Accounting* (February 1995), pp. 37–39; and V. Govindarajan and R.N. Anthony, "How Firms Use Cost Data in Pricing Decisions," *Management Accounting* (65, no. 1), pp. 30–36.

Desired ROI per Unit	+	Selling and Administrative Expenses per Unit	=	Markup Percentage	×	Manufacturing Cost per Unit
€40	+	€38	=	MP	×	€87

ILLUSTRATION 8A.3 | Markup percentage—absorption-cost pricing

Solving, we find:

$$MP = (€40 + €38) \div €87 = 89.66\%$$

The **third** and final **step** is to set the target selling price. Using a markup percentage of 89.66% and absorption-cost pricing, PenCam computes the target selling price as shown in **Illustration 8A.4**.

Manufacturing Cost per Unit	+	(Markup Percentage	×	Manufacturing Cost per Unit)	=	Target Selling Price
€87	+	(89.66%	×	€87)	=	€165

ILLUSTRATION 8A.4 | Computation of target price—absorption-cost pricing

Using a target price of €165 will produce the desired 20% return on investment for PenCam on its video camera pen at a volume level of 10,000 units, as shown in **Illustration 8A.5**.

PenCam Products
Budgeted Absorption-Cost Income Statement

Revenue (10,000 camera pens × €165)	€1,650,000
Cost of goods sold (10,000 camera pens × €87)	870,000
Gross profit	780,000
Selling and administrative expenses	
[10,000 camera pens × (€8 + €30)]	380,000
Net income	**€ 400,000**

Budgeted ROI

$$\frac{\text{Net income}}{\text{Invested assets}} = \frac{€400,000}{€2,000,000} = \underline{\underline{20\%}}$$

Markup Percentage

$$\frac{\text{Net income + Selling and administrative expenses}}{\text{Cost of goods sold}} = \frac{€400,000 + €380,000}{€870,000} = \underline{\underline{89.66\%}}$$

ILLUSTRATION 8A.5 | Proof of 20% ROI—absorption-cost pricing

Because of the fixed-cost component, if PenCam sells more than 10,000 units, the ROI will be greater than 20%. If it sells fewer than 10,000 units, the ROI will be less than 20%. The markup percentage is also verified by adding €400,000 (the net income) and €380,000 (selling and administrative expenses) and then dividing by €870,000 (the cost of goods sold or the cost base).

Most companies that use cost-plus pricing use either absorption cost or full cost as the basis. The reasons for this tendency are as follows:

1. Absorption-cost information is most readily provided by a company's cost accounting system. Because absorption-cost data already exist in general ledger accounts, it is cost-effective to use the data for pricing.

2. Basing the cost-plus calculation on only variable costs could encourage managers to set too low a price to boost sales. There is the fear that if managers use only variable costs, they will substitute variable costs for full costs, which can lead to repeated price cutting.
3. Absorption-cost or full-cost pricing provides the most defensible base for justifying prices to all interested parties—managers, customers, and government.

Variable-Cost Pricing

Under **variable-cost pricing**, the cost base consists of all of the **variable costs** associated with a product, including variable selling and administrative costs.

- **Because fixed costs are not included in the base, the markup must provide for all fixed costs (manufacturing, and selling and administrative) and the target ROI.**
- Variable-cost pricing is more useful for making short-run decisions because it considers variable-cost and fixed-cost behavior patterns separately.

The **first step** in variable-cost pricing is to compute the unit variable cost. For PenCam Products, this amounts to €60 per unit, as shown in **Illustration 8A.6**.

	Per Unit
Direct materials	€23
Direct labor	17
Variable manufacturing overhead	12
Variable selling and administrative expense	8
Total unit variable cost	€60

ILLUSTRATION 8A.6 | Computation of unit variable cost

The **second step** in variable-cost pricing is to compute the markup percentage. **Illustration 8A.7** shows the calculation for the markup percentage. For PenCam, fixed costs include fixed manufacturing overhead of €35 per unit (€350,000 ÷ 10,000) and fixed selling and administrative expenses of €30 per unit (€300,000 ÷ 10,000).

Desired ROI per Unit	+	Unit Fixed Cost	=	Markup Percentage	×	Unit Variable Cost
€40	+	(€35 + €30)	=	MP	×	€60

ILLUSTRATION 8A.7 | Computation of markup percentage—variable-cost pricing

Solving, we find:

$$MP = \frac{€40 + (€35 + €30)}{€60} = 175\%$$

The **third step** is to set the target selling price. Using a markup percentage of 175% and the variable-cost approach, PenCam computes the selling price as shown in **Illustration 8A.8**.

Unit Variable Cost	+	(Markup Percentage	×	Unit Variable Cost)	=	Target Selling Price
€60	+	(175%	×	€60)	=	€165

ILLUSTRATION 8A.8 | Computation of target price—variable-cost pricing

Using a target price of €165 will produce the desired 20% return on investment for PenCam on its video camera pen at a volume level of 10,000 units, as shown in **Illustration 8A.9**.

PenCam Products
Budgeted Variable-Cost Income Statement

Revenue (10,000 camera pens × €165)		€1,650,000
Variable costs (10,000 camera pens × €60)		600,000
Contribution margin		1,050,000
Fixed manufacturing overhead	€350,000	
Fixed selling and administrative expenses	300,000	650,000
Net income		**€ 400,000**

Budgeted ROI

$$\frac{\text{Net income}}{\text{Invested assets}} = \frac{€400,000}{€2,000,000} = \mathbf{20\%}$$

Markup Percentage

$$\frac{\text{Net income} + \text{Fixed costs}}{\text{Variable costs}} = \frac{€400,000 + €650,000}{€600,000} = \mathbf{175\%}$$

ILLUSTRATION 8A.9 | **Proof of 20% ROI—variable-cost approach**

Under any of the three pricing approaches we have looked at (full-cost, absorption-cost, and variable-cost), the desired ROI will be attained only if the budgeted sales volume for the period is attained.

- None of these approaches guarantees a profit or a desired ROI.
- Achieving a desired ROI is the result of many factors, some of which are beyond the company's control, such as market conditions, political and legal issues, customers' tastes, and competitive actions.

Because absorption-cost pricing includes allocated fixed costs, it does not make clear how the company's costs will change as volume changes. To avoid blurring the effects of cost behavior on net income, some managers therefore prefer variable-cost pricing. The specific reasons for using variable-cost pricing, even though the basic accounting data are less accessible, are as follows:

1. Variable-cost pricing, being based on variable cost, is more consistent with cost-volume-profit analysis used by managers to measure the profit implications of changes in price and volume.
2. Variable-cost pricing provides the type of data managers need for pricing special orders. It reveals the incremental effect of accepting one more order.
3. Variable-cost pricing avoids arbitrary allocation of common fixed costs (such as executive salaries) to individual product lines.

Appendix 8B | TRANSFERS BETWEEN DIVISIONS IN DIFFERENT COUNTRIES

LEARNING OBJECTIVE *6
Explain issues involved in transferring goods between divisions in different countries.

Companies must pay income tax in the country where they generate the income.

- In order to maximize income and minimize income tax, some companies attempt to report more income in countries with low tax rates, and less income in countries with high tax rates.
- They accomplish this by adjusting the transfer prices they use on internal transfers between divisions located in different countries.

- They allocate more contribution margin to the division in the low-tax-rate country, and allocate less to the division in the high-tax-rate country.

To illustrate, suppose that Dover Outfitters' Boot Division is located in a country with a corporate tax rate of 10%, and the Sole Division is located in a country with a tax rate of 30%. To maximize the company's combined after-tax profit, it would want to shift income from the Sole Division to the Boot Division because the Boot Division is taxed at a lower rate. **Illustration 8B.1** compares the after-tax contribution margin to the company using a transfer price of €18 versus a transfer price of €11.

Note that the **before-tax** total contribution margin to Dover Outfitters is €44 regardless of whether the transfer price is €18 or €11. However, the **after-tax** total contribution margin to Dover is €38.20 using the €18 transfer price and €39.60 using the €11 transfer price. The reason: When Dover uses the €11 transfer price, more of the contribution margin is attributed to the division that is in the country with the lower tax rate, so the company pays €1.40 less per unit in taxes [(€3.70 + €2.10) − €4.40].

At €18 Transfer Price

Boot Division		Sole Division	
Selling price of boot	€90.00	Selling price of sole	€18.00
Variable cost of boot (not including sole)	35.00	Variable cost per sole	11.00
Cost of sole purchased internally	18.00		
Before-tax contribution margin	37.00	Before-tax contribution margin	7.00
Tax at 10%	3.70	Tax at 30%	2.10
After-tax contribution margin	€33.30	After-tax contribution margin	€ 4.90

Before-tax total contribution margin per unit to company = €37 + €7 = **€44**
After-tax total contribution margin per unit to company = €33.30 + €4.90 = **€38.20**

At €11 Transfer Price

Boot Division		Sole Division	
Selling price of boot	€90.00	Selling price of sole	€11.00
Variable cost of boot (not including sole)	35.00	Variable cost per sole	11.00
Cost of sole purchased internally	11.00		
Before-tax contribution margin	44.00	Before-tax contribution margin	0.00
Tax at 10%	4.40	Tax at 30%	0.00
After-tax contribution margin	€39.60	After-tax contribution margin	€ 0.00

Before-tax total contribution margin per unit to company = €44 + €0 = **€44**
After-tax total contribution margin per unit to company = €39.60 + €0 = **€39.60**

ILLUSTRATION 8B.1 | After-tax contribution margin per unit under alternative transfer prices

As this analysis shows, Dover Outfitters would be better off using the €11 transfer price. However, this presents some concerns.

- The Sole Division manager will not be happy with an €11 transfer price. This price may lead to unfair evaluations of the Sole Division's manager.
- The company must ask whether it is legal and ethical to use an €11 transfer price when the market price clearly is higher than that.

Additional consideration of international transfer pricing is discussed in advanced accounting courses.

REVIEW AND PRACTICE

Learning Objectives Review

LO 1 Compute a target cost when the market determines a product price.

To compute a target cost, the company determines its target selling price. Once the target selling price is set, it determines its target cost by setting a desired profit. The difference between the target price and desired profit is the target cost of the product.

LO 2 Compute a target selling price using cost-plus pricing.

Cost-plus pricing involves establishing a cost base and adding to this cost base a markup to determine a target selling price. The cost-plus pricing equation is expressed as follows: Target selling price = Cost + (Markup percentage × Cost).

LO 3 Use time-and-material pricing to determine the cost of services provided.

Under time-and-material pricing, two pricing rates are set—one for the labor used on a job and another for the material. The labor rate includes direct labor time and other employee costs. The material charge is based on the cost of direct parts and materials used and a material loading charge for related overhead costs.

LO 4 Determine a transfer price using the negotiated, cost-based, and market-based approaches.

The negotiated price is determined through agreement of division managers. Under a cost-based approach, the transfer price may be based on variable cost alone or on variable costs plus fixed costs. Companies may add a markup to these numbers. The cost-based approach often leads to poor performance evaluations and purchasing decisions. The advantage of the cost-based system is its simplicity. A market-based transfer price is based on existing competing market prices and services. A market-based system is often considered the best approach because it is objective and generally provides the proper economic incentives.

LO *5 Determine prices using absorption-cost pricing and variable-cost pricing.

Absorption-cost pricing uses total manufacturing cost as the cost base and provides for selling and administrative costs plus the target ROI through the markup. The target selling price is computed as: Manufacturing cost per unit + (Markup percentage × Manufacturing cost per unit).

Variable-cost pricing uses all of the variable costs, including selling and administrative costs, as the cost base and provides for fixed costs and target ROI through the markup. The target selling price is computed as: Unit variable cost + (Markup percentage × Unit variable cost).

LO *6 Explain issues involved in transferring goods between divisions in different countries.

Companies must pay income tax in the country where they generate the income. In order to maximize income and minimize income tax, many companies prefer to report more income in countries with low tax rates, and less income in countries with high tax rates. This is accomplished by adjusting the transfer prices they use on internal transfers between divisions located in different countries.

Decision Tools Review

Decision Checkpoints	Info Needed for Decision	Tool to Use for Decision	How to Evaluate Results
How does management use target costs to make decisions about manufacturing products or performing services?	Target selling price, desired profit, target cost	Target selling price less desired profit equals target cost	If actual cost exceeds target cost, the company will not earn desired profit. If desired profit is not achieved, company must evaluate whether to manufacture the product or perform the service.
What factors should be considered in determining selling price in a less competitive environment?	Total unit cost and desired profit (cost-plus pricing)	Total unit cost plus desired profit equals target selling price	Does company make its desired profit? If not, does the profit shortfall result from less volume?
How do we set prices for service jobs that require separate cost estimates for service labor and parts used?	Two pricing rates needed: one for labor use and another for materials	Compute labor rate charge and materials rate charge; in each of these calculations, add a profit margin	Is the company profitable under this pricing approach? Are employees earning reasonable wages?
What price should be charged for transfer of goods between divisions of a company?	Variable cost, opportunity cost, market prices	Variable cost plus opportunity cost provides minimum transfer price for seller	If income of division provides fair evaluation of managers, then transfer price is useful. Also, income of the company overall should not be reduced due to the transfer pricing approach.

Glossary Review

*Absorption-cost pricing An approach to pricing that defines the cost base as the manufacturing cost; it excludes both variable and fixed selling and administrative costs. (p. 8-22).

Cost-based transfer price A transfer price that uses as its foundation the costs incurred by the division producing the goods. (p. 8-17).

Cost-plus pricing A process whereby a product's selling price is determined by adding a markup to a cost base. (p. 8-5).

Full-cost pricing An approach to pricing that defines the cost base as all costs incurred. (p. 8-8).

Market-based transfer price A transfer price that is based on existing market prices of competing products. (p. 8-19).

Markup The amount added to a product's cost base to determine the product's selling price. (p. 8-6).

Material loading charge A charge added to cover the cost of purchasing, receiving, handling, and storing materials, plus any desired profit margin on the materials themselves. (p. 8-11).

Negotiated transfer price A transfer price that is determined by the agreement of the division managers. (p. 8-14).

Opportunity cost The contribution margin on sales to outside customers that would be forgone as a result of an internal transfer. (p. 8-15).

Outsourcing Contracting with an external party to provide a good or service, rather than performing the work internally. (p. 8-19).

Target cost The cost that will provide the desired profit on a product when the seller does not have control over the product's price. (p. 8-4).

Target selling price The selling price that will provide the desired profit on a product when the seller has the ability to determine the product's price. (p. 8-6).

Time-and-material pricing An approach to cost-plus pricing in which the company uses two pricing rates, one for the labor used on a job and another for the material. (p. 8-9).

Transfer price The price used to record the transfer of goods between two divisions of a company. (p. 8-13).

Variable-cost pricing An approach to pricing that defines the cost base as all variable costs; it excludes both fixed manufacturing and fixed selling and administrative costs. (pp. 8-9, 8-24).

Practice Multiple-Choice Questions

1. **(LO 1)** Target cost related to price and profit means that:
   a. cost and desired profit must be determined before selling price.
   b. cost and selling price must be determined before desired profit.
   c. price and desired profit must be determined before costs.
   d. costs can be achieved only if the company is at full capacity.

2. **(LO 1)** Taan Classic Toys has examined the market for toy train locomotives. It believes there is a market niche in which it can sell locomotives at NT$800 each. It estimates that it could sell 10,000 of these locomotives annually. Variable costs to make a locomotive are expected to be NT$250. Taan anticipates a profit of NT$150 per locomotive. The target cost for the locomotive is:
   a. NT$800.   c. NT$400.
   b. NT$650.   d. NT$250.

3. **(LO 1, 2)** In a competitive, common-product environment, a seller would most likely use:
   a. time-and-material pricing.   c. target costing.
   b. variable costing.   d. cost-plus pricing.

4. **(LO 2)** Cost-plus pricing means that:
   a. Selling price = Variable cost + (Markup percentage + Variable cost).
   b. Selling price = Cost + (Markup percentage × Cost).
   c. Selling price = Manufacturing cost + (Markup percentage + Manufacturing cost).
   d. Selling price = Fixed cost + (Markup percentage × Fixed cost).

5. **(LO 2)** Jiawei Ltd. is considering developing a new product. The company has gathered the following information on this product.

Expected total unit cost	HK$250
Estimated investment for new product	HK$5,000,000
Desired ROI	10%
Expected number of units to be produced and sold	1,000

   Given this information, the desired markup percentage and selling price are:
   a. markup percentage 10%; selling price HK$550.
   b. markup percentage 200%; selling price HK$750.
   c. markup percentage 10%; selling price HK$500.
   d. markup percentage 100%; selling price HK$550.

6. **(LO 2)** Limawan Tools provides the following information for the new product it recently introduced.

Total unit cost	Rp3,000,000
Desired ROI per unit	Rp1,000,000
Target selling price	Rp4,000,000

   What would be Limawan's percentage markup on cost?
   a. 125%.   c. 33⅓%.
   b. 75%.   d. 25%.

7. **(LO 3)** Harmon Electrical Repair has decided to price its work on a time-and-material basis. It estimates the following costs for the year related to labor.

Technician wages and benefits	€100,000
Office employee's salary and benefits	€ 40,000
Other overhead	€ 80,000

   Harmon desires a profit margin of €10 per labor hour and budgets 5,000 hours of repair time for the year. The office employee's salary, benefits, and other overhead costs should be divided evenly between time charges and material loading charges. Harmon labor charge per hour would be:
   a. €42.   c. €32.
   b. €34.   d. €30.

8. **(LO 3)** Time-and-material pricing would most likely be used by a:
   a. garden-fertilizer producer.
   b. lawn-mower manufacturer.
   c. tree farm.
   d. lawn-care provider.

9. (LO 3) When a company uses time-and-material pricing, the material loading charge is expressed as a percentage of:
   a. the total estimated labor costs for the year.
   b. the total estimated costs of parts and materials for the year.
   c. the total estimated overhead costs for the year.
   d. the total estimated costs of parts, materials, and labor for the year.

10. (LO 4) The Plastics Division of Weston Ltd. manufactures plastic molds and then sells them to customers for £70 per unit. Its unit variable cost is £30, and its unit fixed cost is £10. Management would like the Plastics Division to transfer 10,000 of these molds to another division within the company at a price of £40. The Plastics Division is operating at full capacity. What is the minimum transfer price that the Plastics Division should accept?
   a. £10.
   b. £30.
   c. £40.
   d. £70.

11. (LO 4) Assume the same information as Question 10, except that the Plastics Division has available capacity of 10,000 units for plastic moldings. What is the minimum transfer price that the Plastics Division should accept?
   a. £10.
   b. £30.
   c. £40.
   d. £70.

12. (LO 4) The most common method used to establish transfer prices is the:
   a. negotiated transfer pricing approach.
   b. opportunity costing transfer pricing approach.
   c. cost-based transfer pricing approach.
   d. market-based transfer pricing approach.

*13. (LO 5) AST Electrical provides the following cost information related to its production of electronic circuit boards.

	Per Unit
Variable manufacturing cost	€40
Fixed manufacturing cost	€30
Variable selling and administrative expenses	€ 8
Fixed selling and administrative expenses	€12
Desired ROI per unit	€15

What is its markup percentage assuming that AST Electrical uses absorption-cost pricing?
   a. 16.67%.
   b. 50%.
   c. 54.28%.
   d. 118.75%.

*14. (LO 5) Assume the same information as Question 13 and determine AST Electrical's markup percentage using variable-cost pricing.
   a. 16.67%.
   b. 50%.
   c. 54.28%.
   d. 118.75%.

*15. (LO 6) Global Industries transfers parts between divisions in two countries, Eastland and Westland. Eastland's tax rate is 8%, and Westland's tax rate is 16%. If Global desired to minimize tax payments and maximize net income, it might consider establishing transfer prices that:
   a. allocate contribution margin equally between Eastland and Westland.
   b. allocate more contribution margin to Eastland.
   c. allocate more contribution margin to Westland.
   d. allocate half as much contribution margin to Eastland as it does to Westland.

Solutions

1. c. The selling price and the desired profit must be decided before costs are determined. Therefore, the other choices are incorrect.

2. b. The target cost for the locomotive is selling price less desired profit or NT$800 − NT$150 = NT$650, not (a) NT$800, (c) NT$400, or (d) NT$250.

3. c. A seller would most likely use target costing in a competitive common-product environment as the price is set by the market. In a less competitive environment, companies have a greater ability to set the product price and therefore could use (a) time-and-material pricing, (b) variable costing, or (d) cost-plus pricing.

4. b. In cost-plus pricing, Selling price = Cost + (Markup percentage × Cost). The other choices are therefore incorrect.

5. b. The desired markup percentage = [(.10 × HK$5,000,000) ÷ 1,000] ÷ HK$250 = 200%. The selling price = HK$250 + HK$500 = HK$750. The other choices are therefore incorrect.

6. c. The percentage markup on cost = (Rp1,000,000 ÷ Rp3,000,000) = 33⅓%, not (a) 125%, (b) 75%, or (d) 25%.

7. a. The labor charge per hour = €10 + {[€100,000 + .5(€40,000) +.5(€80,000)] ÷ 5,000} = €42, not (b) €34, (c), €32, or (d) €30.

8. d. A lawn-care provider would be most likely to use time-and-material pricing as it is a service company. The other choices provide products rather than services.

9. b. In time-and-material pricing, the material loading charge is expressed as a percentage of the total estimated costs of parts and materials for the year. Therefore, the other choices are incorrect.

10. d. The minimum transfer price the Plastics Division should accept = Unit variable cost + Opportunity cost per unit. Since the Plastics Division is operating at full capacity, the opportunity cost per unit is equal to the contribution margin per unit of £40 (selling price of £70 − unit variable cost of £30). The minimum transfer price is therefore £30 + £40 = £70, not (a) £10, (b) £30, or (c) £40.

11. b. Since we assume the Plastics Division has excess capacity of 10,000 units, the minimum transfer price is equal to the unit variable cost of £30, not (a) £10, (c) £40, or (d) £70.

12. c. The most common method to establish transfer prices is the cost-based transfer pricing approach as it is simple to use, easy to understand, and has available cost data. Negotiated transfer pricing and market-based transfer pricing are considered better approaches but often are not used because of lack of market price information or other considerations.

*13. b. Using the absorption-cost approach, add the desired ROI per unit (€15) and selling and administrative expenses per unit (€20) = €35 per unit, then divide that by the manufacturing cost per unit (€70), which equals the markup percentage of 50%, not (a) 16.67%, (c) 54.28%, or (d) 118.75%.

*14. d. Using variable-cost pricing, add the desired ROI per unit (€15), fixed manufacturing costs per unit (€30) and fixed selling and administrative expenses per unit (€12) = €57, then divide that by the total unit variable costs (€40 + €8) = €57 ÷ €48 = 118.75%, not (a) 16.67%, (b) 50%, or (c) 54.28%.

*15. b. To minimize tax payments and maximize net income, Global's transfer prices might allocate more contribution margin to Eastland as it has a lower tax rate. (Note that the legal and ethical ramifications of this action would need to be considered.) The other choices are therefore incorrect.

Practice Exercises

Use cost-plus pricing to determine various amounts.

1. (LO 2) Choi Recording Studio rents studio time to musicians in 2-hour blocks. Each session includes the use of the studio facilities, a digital recorded CD of the performance, and a professional music producer/mixer. Anticipated annual volume is 1,000 sessions. The company has invested ₩2,300,000,000 in the studio and expects a return on investment (ROI) of 15%. Budgeted costs for the coming year are as follows:

	Per Session	Total
Direct materials (CDs, etc.)	₩ 20,000	
Direct labor	400,000	
Variable overhead	50,000	
Fixed overhead		₩950,000,000
Variable selling and administrative expenses	40,000	
Fixed selling and administrative expenses		540,000,000

Instructions

a. Determine the total cost per session.
b. Determine the desired ROI per session.
c. Calculate the markup percentage on the total cost per session.
d. Calculate the target price per session.

Solution

1. a. Total cost per session:

	Per Session
Direct materials	₩ 20,000
Direct labor	400,000
Variable overhead	50,000
Fixed overhead (₩950,000,000 ÷ 1,000)	950,000
Variable selling & administrative expenses	40,000
Fixed selling & administrative expenses (₩540,000,000 ÷ 1,000)	540,000
Total cost per session	₩2,000,000

b. Desired ROI per session = (15% × ₩2,300,000,000) ÷ 1,000 = ₩345,000

c. Markup percentage on total cost per session = ₩345,000 ÷ ₩2,000,000 = 17.25%

d. Target price per session = ₩2,000,000 + (₩2,000,000 × 17.25%) = ₩2,345,000

Determine minimum transfer price.

2. (LO 4) Mercury Sound manufactures car audio systems. It is a division of Universal Motors, which manufactures vehicles. Mercury sells car audio systems to other divisions of Universal, as well as to other vehicle manufacturers and retail stores. The following information is available for Mercury's standard unit: unit variable cost ¥3,100, unit fixed cost ¥2,300, and unit selling price to outside customer ¥8,500. Universal currently purchases a standard unit from an outside supplier for ¥8,000. Because of quality concerns and to ensure a reliable supply, the top management of Universal has ordered Mercury to provide 200,000 units per year at a transfer price of ¥3,000 per unit. Mercury is already operating at full capacity. Mercury can avoid ¥200 per unit of variable selling costs by selling the unit internally.

Instructions

a. What is the minimum transfer price that Mercury should accept?
b. What is the potential loss to the corporation as a whole resulting from this forced transfer?
c. How should the company resolve this situation?

Solution

2. a. The minimum transfer price that Mercury should accept is:

Minimum transfer price = (¥3,100 − ¥200) + (¥8,500 − ¥3,100) = ¥8,300

b. The lost contribution margin per unit to the company is:

Contribution margin lost by Mercury {(¥8,500 − ¥3,100) − [¥3,000 − (¥3,100 − ¥200)]}	¥5,300
Increased contribution margin to vehicle division (¥8,000 − ¥3,000)	5,000
Net loss in contribution margin	¥ 300

Total lost contribution margin is ¥300 × 200,000 units = ¥60,000,000

c. If management insists that it wants Mercury to provide the car audio systems and Mercury is operating at full capacity, then it must be willing to pay the minimum transfer price for those units. Otherwise, it will penalize the managers of Mercury by not giving them adequate credit for their contribution to the corporation's contribution margin.

Practice Problem

Determine minimum transfer price under different situations.

(LO 4) Revco Electronics is a division of International Motors, an automobile manufacturer. Revco produces car radio/CD players. Revco sells its products to other divisions of International Motors, as well as to other car manufacturers and electronics distributors. The following information is available regarding Revco's car radio/CD player.

Selling price of car radio/CD player to external customers	$49
Unit variable cost	$28
Capacity	200,000 units

Instructions

Determine whether the goods should be transferred internally or purchased externally and what the appropriate transfer price should be under each of the following **independent** situations:

a. Revco Electronics is operating at full capacity. There is a saving of $4 per unit for variable cost if the car radio is made for internal sale. International Motors can purchase a comparable car radio from an outside supplier for $47.

b. Revco Electronics has sufficient existing capacity to meet the needs of International Motors. International Motors can purchase a comparable car radio from an outside supplier for $47.

c. International Motors wants to purchase a special-order car radio/CD player with additional features. It needs 15,000 units. Revco Electronics has determined that the additional unit variable cost would be $12. Revco Electronics has no spare capacity. It will have to forgo sales of 15,000 units to external parties in order to provide this special order.

Solution

a. Revco Electronics' opportunity cost (its lost contribution margin) would be $21 ($49 − $28). Using the equation for minimum transfer price, we determine:

Minimum transfer price	=	Variable cost	+	Opportunity cost
$45	=	($28 − $4)	+	$21

Since this minimum transfer price is less than the $47 it would cost if International Motors purchases from an external party, internal transfer should take place. Revco Electronics and International Motors should negotiate a transfer price between $45 and $47.

b. Since Revco Electronics has available capacity, its opportunity cost (its lost contribution margin) would be $0. Using the equation for minimum transfer price, we determine the following:

Minimum transfer price	=	Variable cost	+	Opportunity cost
$28	=	$28	+	$0

Since International Motors can purchase the unit for $47 from an external party, the most it would be willing to pay would be $47. It is in the best interest of the company as a whole, as well as the two divisions, for a transfer to take place. The two divisions must reach a negotiated transfer price between $28 and $47 that recognizes the costs and benefits to each party and is acceptable to both.

c. Revco Electronics' opportunity cost (its lost contribution margin per unit) would be $21 ($49 − $28). Its variable cost would be $40 ($28 + $12). Using the equation for minimum transfer price, we determine the following:

Minimum transfer price	=	Variable cost	+	Opportunity cost
$61	=	$40	+	$21

Note that in this case Revco Electronics has no available capacity. Its management may decide that it does not want to provide this special order because to do so will require that it cut off the supply of the standard unit to some of its existing customers. This may anger those customers and result in the loss of customers.

Questions

1. What are the two types of pricing environments for sales to external parties?

2. In what situation does a company place the greatest focus on its target cost? How is the target cost determined?

3. What is the basic equation to determine the target selling price in cost-plus pricing?

4. Fungestu Air produces a filter that has a unit cost of Rp180,000. The company would like a 30% markup. Using cost-plus pricing, determine the unit selling price.

5. What is the basic equation for the markup percentage?

6. Devon Electronics manufactures an electronic switch for dishwashers. The unit cost base, excluding selling and administrative expenses, is £60. The unit cost of selling and administrative expenses is £15. The company's desired ROI per unit is £6. Calculate its markup percentage on total unit cost.

7. Fei Ltd. manufactures a standard cabinet for a Blu-ray player. The unit variable cost is HK$160. The unit fixed cost is HK$90. The desired ROI per unit is HK$60. Compute the markup percentage on total unit cost and the target selling price for the cabinet.

8. In what circumstances is time-and-material pricing most often used?

9. What is the material loading charge? How is it expressed?

10. What is a transfer price? Why is determining a fair transfer price important to division managers?

11. When setting a transfer price, what objective(s) should the company have in mind?

12. What are the three approaches for determining transfer prices?

13. Describe the cost-based approach to transfer pricing. What is the strength of this approach? What are the weaknesses of this approach?

14. What is the general equation for determining the minimum transfer price that the selling division should be willing to accept?

15. When determining the minimum transfer price, what is meant by the "opportunity cost"?

16. In what circumstances will a negotiated transfer price be used instead of a market-based price?

*17. What costs are excluded from the cost base when absorption-cost pricing is used to determine the markup percentage?

*18. Bernasconi AG manufactures a fiber optic connector. The unit variable cost is CHF16. The unit fixed cost is CHF9. The company's desired ROI per unit is CHF3. Compute the markup percentage using variable-cost pricing.

*19. Explain how companies use transfer pricing between divisions located in different countries to reduce tax payments, and discuss the propriety of this approach.

Brief Exercises

Compute target cost.

BE8.1 (LO 1), AP Olivera Industries manufactures computer hard drives. The market for hard drives is very competitive. The current market price for a computer hard drive is R$450. Olivera would like a profit of R$100 per drive. How can Olivera accomplish this objective?

Use cost-plus pricing to determine selling price.

BE8.2 (LO 2), AP Mussatto Outdoors produces snowboards. The following unit cost information is available: direct materials €12, direct labor €8, variable manufacturing overhead €6, fixed manufacturing overhead €14, variable selling and administrative expenses €4, and fixed selling and administrative expenses €12. Using a 30% markup percentage on total unit cost, compute the target selling price.

Compute ROI per unit.

BE8.3 (LO 2), AP Kirti Industries produces high-performance rotors. It expects to produce 50,000 rotors in the coming year. It has invested ₹1,000,000,000 to produce rotors. The company has a required return on investment of 12%. What is its ROI per unit?

Compute markup percentage.

BE8.4 (LO 2), AP Morales Corporation produces microwave ovens. The following unit cost information is available: direct materials $36, direct labor $24, variable manufacturing overhead $18, fixed manufacturing overhead $40, variable selling and administrative expenses $14, and fixed selling and administrative expenses $28. Its desired ROI per unit is $30. Compute its markup percentage using a total-cost approach.

Compute ROI and markup percentage.

BE8.5 (LO 2), AP During the current year, Schmidt AG expects to produce 10,000 units and has budgeted the following: net income €300,000, variable costs €1,100,000, and fixed costs €100,000. It has invested assets of €1,500,000. The company's budgeted ROI was 20%. What was its budgeted markup percentage using a full-cost approach?

Use time-and-material pricing to determine bill.

BE8.6 (LO 3), AP `Service` Henry Small Engine Repair charges A$42 per hour of labor. It has a material loading percentage of 40%. On a recent job replacing the engine of a riding lawnmower, Henry worked 10.5 hours and used parts with a cost of A$700. Calculate Henry's total bill.

Determine minimum transfer price.

BE8.7 (LO 4), AP The Heating Division of Smith International produces a heating element that it sells to its customers for £45 per unit. Its unit variable cost is £25, and its unit fixed cost is £10. Top management of Smith International would like the Heating Division to transfer 15,000 heating units to another division within the company at a price of £29. The Heating Division is operating at full capacity. What is the minimum transfer price that the Heating Division should accept?

BE8.8 (LO 4), AP Use the data from BE8.7 but assume that the Heating Division has sufficient excess capacity to provide the 15,000 heating units to the other division. What is the minimum transfer price that the Heating Division should accept?

Determine minimum transfer price with excess capacity.

BE8.9 (LO 4), AP Use the data from BE8.7 but assume that the units being requested are special high-performance units, and the division's unit variable cost would be £27 (rather than £25). What is the minimum transfer price that the Heating Division should accept?

Determine minimum transfer price for special order.

*****BE8.10 (LO 5), AP** Using the data in BE8.4, compute the markup percentage using absorption-cost pricing.

Compute markup percentage using absorption-cost pricing.

*****BE8.11 (LO 5), AP** Using the data in BE8.4, compute the markup percentage using variable-cost pricing.

Compute markup percentage using variable-cost pricing.

DO IT! Exercises

DO IT! 8.1 (LO 1), AP Yilmaz Water is considering introducing a water filtration device for its one-liter water bottles. Market research indicates that 1,000,000 units can be sold if the price is no more than ₺30. If Yilmaz Water decides to produce the filters, it will need to invest ₺20,000,000 in new production equipment. Yilmaz Water requires a minimum rate of return of 16% on all investments.

Determine the target cost for the filter.

Determine target cost.

DO IT! 8.2 (LO 2), AP Dewsbury Ltd. produces area rugs. The following unit cost information is available: direct materials £18, direct labor £9, variable manufacturing overhead £5, fixed manufacturing overhead £6, variable selling and administrative expenses £3, and fixed selling and administrative expenses £7.

Using a 30% markup on total per unit cost, compute the target selling price.

Use cost-plus pricing to determine various amounts.

DO IT! 8.3 (LO 3), AP `Service` The following information relates to labor for Chen Appliance Repair Shop.

Use time-and-material pricing to determine bill.

Repair-technicians' wages	HK$1,100,000
Fringe benefits	400,000
Overhead	500,000

The desired profit margin per hour is HK$200. The material loading charge is 60% of invoice cost. Chen estimates that 5,000 labor hours will be worked next year. If Chen repairs a dishwasher that takes 1.5 hours to repair and uses parts that cost HK$700, compute the bill for the job.

DO IT! 8.4 (LO 4), AP The fastener division of Kyoto Fasteners manufactures zippers and then sells them to customers for ¥800 per unit. Its unit variable cost is ¥300, and its unit fixed cost is ¥150. Management would like the fastener division to transfer 12,000 of these zippers to another division within the company at a price of ¥300. The fastener division could avoid ¥20 per zipper of variable packaging costs by selling internally.

Determine the minimum transfer price (a) assuming the fastener division is not operating at full capacity, and (b) assuming the fastener division is operating at full capacity.

Determine transfer prices.

Exercises

E8.1 (LO 1), AP Mesa Cheese Company has developed a new cheese slicer called Slim Slicer. The company plans to sell this slicer through its online website. Given market research, Mesa believes that it can charge $20 for the Slim Slicer. Prototypes of the Slim Slicer, however, are costing $22. By using cheaper materials and gaining efficiencies in mass production, Mesa believes it can reduce Slim Slicer's cost substantially. Mesa wishes to earn a return of 40% of the selling price.

Compute target cost.

Instructions

a. Compute the target cost for the Slim Slicer.

b. When is target costing particularly helpful in deciding whether to produce a given product?

E8.2 (LO 1), AP Eckert Ltd. is involved in producing and selling high-end golf equipment. The company has recently been involved in developing various types of laser guns to measure yardages on the golf course. One small laser gun, called LittleLaser, appears to have a very large potential market. Because of competition, Eckert does not believe that it can charge more than £90 for LittleLaser. At this price, Eckert believes it can sell 100,000 of these laser guns. Eckert will require an investment of £8,000,000 to manufacture, and the company wants an ROI of 20%.

Compute target cost.

Compute target cost and cost-plus pricing.

Instructions

Determine the target cost for one LittleLaser.

E8.3 (LO 1, 2), AP Leno AG makes swimsuits and sells these suits directly to retailers. Although Leno has a variety of suits, it does not make the Performance suit used by highly skilled swimmers. The market research department believes that a strong market exists for this type of suit. The department indicates that the Performance suit would sell for approximately €100. Given its experience, Leno believes the Performance suit would have the following manufacturing costs:

Direct materials	€ 25
Direct labor	30
Manufacturing overhead	45
Total costs	€100

Instructions

a. Assume that Leno uses cost-plus pricing, setting the selling price 25% above its costs. (1) What would be the price charged for the Performance swimsuit? (2) Under what circumstances might Leno consider manufacturing the Performance swimsuit given this approach?

b. Assume that Leno uses target costing. What is the price that Leno would charge the retailer for the Performance swimsuit?

c. What is the highest acceptable manufacturing cost Leno would be willing to incur to produce the Performance swimsuit, if it desired a profit of €25 per unit? (Assume target costing.)

Use cost-plus pricing to determine selling price.

E8.4 (LO 2), AP Yun Kitchen makes a commercial-grade cooking griddle. The following information is available for Yun Kitchen's anticipated annual volume of 30,000 units.

	Per Unit	Total
Direct materials	₩17,000	
Direct labor	8,000	
Variable manufacturing overhead	11,000	
Fixed manufacturing overhead		₩300,000,000
Variable selling and administrative expenses	4,000	
Fixed selling and administrative expenses		150,000,000

The company uses a 40% markup percentage on total cost.

Instructions

a. Compute the total unit cost.

b. Compute the target selling price.

Use cost-plus pricing to determine various amounts.

E8.5 (LO 2), AP Schopp Corporation makes a mechanical stuffed alligator that sings the Martian national anthem. The following information is available for Schopp Corporation's anticipated annual volume of 500,000 units.

	Per Unit	Total
Direct materials	$ 7	
Direct labor	11	
Variable manufacturing overhead	15	
Fixed manufacturing overhead		$3,000,000
Variable selling and administrative expenses	14	
Fixed selling and administrative expenses		1,500,000

The company has a desired ROI of 25%. It has invested assets of $28,000,000.

Instructions

a. Compute the total unit cost.

b. Compute the desired ROI per unit.

c. Compute the markup percentage using total unit cost.

d. Compute the target selling price.

Use cost-plus pricing to determine various amounts.

E8.6 (LO 2), AP **Service** Aiden's Recording Studio rents studio time to musicians in 2-hour blocks. Each session includes the use of the studio facilities, a digital recording of the performance, and a professional music producer/mixer. Anticipated annual volume is 1,000 sessions. The company has invested S$2,352,000 in the studio and expects a return on investment (ROI) of 20%. Budgeted costs for the coming year are as follows:

	Per Session	Total
Direct materials (CDs, etc.)	S$ 20	
Direct labor	400	
Variable overhead	50	
Fixed overhead		S$950,000
Variable selling and administrative expenses	40	
Fixed selling and administrative expenses		500,000

Instructions

a. Determine the total cost per session.
b. Determine the desired ROI per session.
c. Calculate the markup percentage on the total cost per session.
d. Calculate the target price per session.

E8.7 (LO 2), AP Weber AG produces industrial robots for high-precision manufacturing. The following information is given for Weber.

Use cost-plus pricing to determine various amounts.

	Per Unit	Total
Direct materials	€380	
Direct labor	290	
Variable manufacturing overhead	72	
Fixed manufacturing overhead		€1,500,000
Variable selling and administrative expenses	55	
Fixed selling and administrative expenses		324,000

The company has a desired ROI of 20%. It has invested assets of €54,000,000. It anticipates production of 3,000 units per year.

Instructions

a. Compute the unit cost of the fixed manufacturing overhead and the fixed selling and administrative expenses.
b. Compute the desired ROI per unit. (Round to the nearest euro.)
c. Compute the target selling price.

E8.8 (LO 3), AP **Service** Second Chance Welding rebuilds spot welders for manufacturers. The following budgeted cost data for 2023 is available for Second Chance.

Use time-and-material pricing to determine bill.

	Time Charges	Material Loading Charges
Technicians' wages and benefits	£228,000	—
Parts manager's salary and benefits	—	£42,500
Office employee's salary and benefits	38,000	9,000
Other overhead	15,200	24,000
Total budgeted costs	£281,200	£75,500

The company desires a £30 profit margin per hour of labor and a 20% profit margin on parts. It has budgeted for 7,600 hours of repair time in the coming year, and estimates that the total invoice cost of parts and materials in 2023 will be £400,000.

Instructions

a. Compute the rate charged per hour of labor.
b. Compute the material loading percentage. (Round to three decimal places.)
c. Pace plc has requested an estimate to rebuild its spot welder. Second Chance estimates that it would require 40 hours of labor and £2,000 of parts. Compute the total estimated bill.

Use time-and-material pricing to determine bill.

E8.9 (LO 3), AP **Service** Govender Custom Electronics (GCE) sells and installs complete security, computer, audio, and video systems for homes. On newly constructed homes it provides bids using time-and-material pricing. The following budgeted cost data are available.

	Time Charges	Material Loading Charges
Technicians' wages and benefits	R1,500,000	—
Parts manager's salary and benefits	—	R340,000
Office employee's salary and benefits	300,000	150,000
Other overhead	150,000	420,000
Total budgeted costs	R1,950,000	R910,000

The company has budgeted for 6,250 hours of technician time during the coming year. It desires a R380 profit margin per hour of labor and an 80% profit on parts. It estimates the total invoice cost of parts and materials in 2023 will be R7,000,000.

Instructions

a. Compute the rate charged per hour of labor.

b. Compute the material loading percentage.

c. GCE has just received a request for a bid on a security and home entertainment system from Nel Builders on a R12,000,000 new home. The company estimates that the job would require 80 hours of labor and R400,000 of parts. Compute the total estimated bill.

Use time-and-material pricing to determine bill.

E8.10 (LO 3), AP **Service** Wyatt's Classic Cars restores classic automobiles to showroom status. Budgeted data for the current year are as follows:

	Time Charges	Material Loading Charges
Restorers' wages and fringe benefits	€270,000	—
Purchasing agent's salary and fringe benefits	—	€ 67,500
Administrative salaries and fringe benefits	54,000	21,960
Other overhead costs	24,000	77,490
Total budgeted costs	€348,000	€166,950

The company anticipated that the restorers would work a total of 12,000 hours this year. Expected parts and materials were €1,260,000.

In late January, the company experienced a fire in its facilities that destroyed most of the accounting records. The accountant remembers that the hourly labor rate was €70.00 and that the material loading charge was 83.25%.

Instructions

a. Determine the profit margin per hour on labor.

b. Determine the profit margin on materials.

c. Determine the total price of labor and materials on a job that was completed after the fire that required 150 hours of labor and €60,000 in parts and materials.

Determine minimum transfer price.

E8.11 (LO 4), AP **Writing** Noah Company's Small Motor Division manufactures a number of small motors used in household and office appliances. The Household Division of Noah then assembles and packages such items as blenders and juicers. Both divisions are free to buy and sell any of their components internally or externally. The following costs relate to small motor LN233 on a per unit basis.

Unit fixed cost	A$ 5
Unit variable cost	11
Unit selling price	35

Instructions

a. Assuming that the Small Motor Division has excess capacity, compute the minimum acceptable price for the transfer of small motor LN233 to the Household Division.

b. Assuming that the Small Motor Division does not have excess capacity, compute the minimum acceptable price for the transfer of the small motor to the Household Division.

c. Explain why the level of capacity in the Small Motor Division has an effect on the transfer price.

E8.12 (LO 4), AN The Cycle Division of Fit Athletics has the following unit data related to its most recent cycle, the Roadbuster.

Determine effect on income from transfer price.

Selling price		£2,200
Variable cost of goods sold		
Body frame	£300	
Other variable costs	900	1,200
Contribution margin		£1,000

Presently, the Cycle Division buys its body frames from an outside supplier. However, Fit Athletics has another division, FrameBody, that makes body frames for other cycle companies. The Cycle Division believes that FrameBody's product is suitable for its new Roadbuster cycle. Presently, FrameBody sells its frames for £350 per frame. The variable cost for FrameBody is £270. The Cycle Division is willing to pay £280 to purchase the frames from FrameBody.

Instructions

a. Assume that FrameBody has excess capacity and is able to meet all of the Cycle Division's needs. If the Cycle Division buys 1,000 frames from FrameBody, determine the following: (1) effect on the income of the Cycle Division, (2) effect on the income of FrameBody, and (3) effect on the income of Fit Athletics.

b. Assume that FrameBody does not have excess capacity and therefore would lose sales if the frames were sold to the Cycle Division. If the Cycle Division buys 1,000 frames from FrameBody, determine the following: (1) effect on the income of the Cycle Division, (2) effect on the income of FrameBody, and (3) effect on the income of Fit Athletics.

E8.13 (LO 4), AP Lee Audio manufactures car stereos. It is a division of Im Motors, which manufactures vehicles. Lee sells car stereos to Im, as well as to other vehicle manufacturers and retail stores. The following information is available for Lee's standard unit: unit variable cost ₩37,000, unit fixed cost ₩23,000, and unit selling price to outside customer ₩86,000. Im currently purchases a standard unit from an outside supplier for ₩80,000. Because of quality concerns and to ensure a reliable supply, the top management of Im has ordered Lee to provide 200,000 units per year at a transfer price of ₩35,000 per unit. Lee is already operating at full capacity. Lee can avoid ₩3,000 per unit of variable selling costs by selling the unit internally.

Determine minimum transfer price.

Instructions

Answer each of the following questions:

a. What is the minimum transfer price that Lee should accept?

b. What is the potential loss to the corporation as a whole resulting from this forced transfer?

c. How should the company resolve this situation?

E8.14 (LO 4), AP The Bathtub Division of Winarto Plumbing has recently approached the Faucet Division with a proposal. The Bathtub Division would like to make a special "ivory" tub with gold-plated fixtures for the company's 50-year anniversary. It would make only 5,000 of these units. It would like the Faucet Division to make the fixtures and provide them to the Bathtub Division at a transfer price of €160. If sold externally, the estimated unit variable cost would be €140. However, by selling internally, the Faucet Division would save €6 per unit on variable selling expenses. The Faucet Division is currently operating at full capacity. Its standard unit sells for €50 per unit and has variable costs of €29.

Compute minimum transfer price.

Instructions

Compute the minimum transfer price that the Faucet Division should be willing to accept, and discuss whether it should accept this offer.

E8.15 (LO 4), AP **Service** The Appraisal Department of Jean Bank performs appraisals of business properties for loans being considered by the bank and appraisals for home buyers that are financing their purchase through some other financial institution. The department charges $160 per home appraisal, and its variable costs are $130 per appraisal.

Determine minimum transfer price.

Recently, Jean Bank has opened its own Home-Loan Department and wants the Appraisal Department to perform 1,200 appraisals on all Jean Bank–financed home loans. Bank management feels that the cost of these appraisals to the Home-Loan Department should be $150. The variable cost per appraisal to the Home-Loan Department would be $8 less than those performed for outside customers due to savings in administrative costs.

Instructions

a. Determine the minimum transfer price, assuming the Appraisal Department has excess capacity.

b. Determine the minimum transfer price, assuming the Appraisal Department has no excess capacity.

c. Assuming the Appraisal Department has no excess capacity, should management force the department to charge the Home-Loan Department only $150? Discuss.

Determine minimum transfer price under different situations.

E8.16 (LO 4), AP Modern Furnishings has two divisions. Division A makes and sells student desks. Division B manufactures and sells reading lamps.

Each desk has a reading lamp as one of its components. Division A can purchase reading lamps at a cost of £10 from an outside vendor. Division A needs 10,000 lamps for the coming year.

Division B has the capacity to manufacture 50,000 lamps annually. Sales to outside customers are estimated at 40,000 lamps for the next year. Reading lamps are sold at £12 each. Variable costs are £7 per lamp and include £1 of variable sales costs that are not incurred if lamps are sold internally to Division A. The total amount of fixed costs for Division B is £80,000.

Instructions

Consider the following independent situations:

a. What should be the minimum transfer price accepted by Division B for the 10,000 lamps and the maximum transfer price paid by Division A? Justify your answer.

b. Suppose Division B could use the excess capacity to produce and sell externally 15,000 units of a new product at a unit selling price of £7. The unit variable cost for this new product is £5. What should be the minimum transfer price accepted by Division B for the 10,000 lamps and the maximum transfer price paid by Division A? Justify your answer.

c. If Division A needs 15,000 lamps instead of 10,000 during the next year, what should be the minimum transfer price accepted by Division B and the maximum transfer price paid by Division A? Justify your answer.

Determine minimum transfer price under different situations.

E8.17 (LO 4), AP Ramos Industries is a multidivisional company. Its managers have full responsibility for profits and complete autonomy to accept or reject transfers from other divisions. Division A produces a subassembly part for which there is a competitive market. Division B currently uses this subassembly for a final product that is sold outside at A$2,400. Division A charges Division B market price for the part, which is A$1,500 per unit. Variable costs are A$1,100 and A$1,200 for Divisions A and B, respectively.

The manager of Division B feels that Division A should transfer the part at a lower price than market because at market, Division B is unable to make a profit.

Instructions

a. Calculate Division B's contribution margin if transfers are made at the market price, and calculate the company's total contribution margin.

b. Assume that Division A can sell all its production in the open market. Should Division A transfer the goods to Division B? If so, at what price?

c. Assume that Division A can sell in the open market only 500 units at A$1,500 per unit out of the 1,000 units that it can produce every month. Assume also that a 20% reduction in price is necessary to sell all 1,000 units each month. Should transfers be made? If so, how many units should the division transfer and at what price? To support your decision, submit a schedule that compares the total company contribution margins under the following three different alternatives. Alternative 1: maintain price, no transfers; Alternative 2: cut price, no transfers; and Alternative 3: maintain price and transfers.

Compute total unit cost, ROI, and markup percentages using absorption-cost pricing and variable-cost pricing.

*****E8.18 (LO 5), AP** Information for Schopp Corporation is given in E8.5.

Instructions

Using the information given in E8.5, complete the following:

a. Compute the total unit cost.

b. Compute the desired ROI per unit.

c. Using absorption-cost pricing, compute the markup percentage.

d. Using variable-cost pricing, compute the markup percentage.

*E8.19 (LO 5), AP** Rap Corporation produces outdoor portable fireplace units. The following unit cost information is available: direct materials $20, direct labor $25, variable manufacturing overhead $14, fixed manufacturing overhead $21, variable selling and administrative expenses $9, and fixed selling and administrative expenses $11. The company's ROI per unit is $24.

Compute markup percentage using absorption-cost pricing and variable-cost pricing.

Instructions

Compute Rap Corporation's markup percentage using (a) absorption-cost pricing and (b) variable-cost pricing.

*E8.20 (LO 5), AP** Information for Weber AG is given in E8.7.

Compute various amounts using absorption-cost pricing and variable-cost pricing.

Instructions

Using the information given in E8.7, answer the following:

a. Compute the cost per unit of the fixed manufacturing overhead and the fixed selling and administrative expenses.

b. Compute the desired ROI per unit. (Round to the nearest euro.)

c. Compute the markup percentage and target selling price using absorption-cost pricing. (Round the markup percentage to three decimal places.)

d. Compute the markup percentage and target selling price using variable-cost pricing. (Round the markup percentage to three decimal places.)

Problems

P8.1 (LO 2), AP National Corporation needs to set a target price for its newly designed product M14–M16. The following data relate to this new product.

Use cost-plus pricing to determine various amounts.

	Per Unit	Total
Direct materials	$25	
Direct labor	40	
Variable manufacturing overhead	10	
Fixed manufacturing overhead		$1,440,000
Variable selling and administrative expenses	5	
Fixed selling and administrative expenses		960,000

These costs are based on a budgeted volume of 80,000 units produced and sold each year. National uses cost-plus pricing methods to set its target selling price. The markup percentage on total unit cost is 40%.

Instructions

a. Compute the total unit variable cost, total unit fixed cost, and total unit cost for M14–M16.

b. Compute the desired ROI per unit for M14–M16.

c. Compute the target selling price for M14–M16.

d. Compute unit variable cost, unit fixed cost, and unit total cost assuming that 60,000 M14–M16s are produced and sold during the year.

a. Unit variable cost $80

P8.2 (LO 2), AP Lyon Computer Parts is in the process of setting a selling price on a new component it has just designed and developed. The following cost estimates for this new component have been provided by the accounting department for a budgeted volume of 50,000 units.

Use cost-plus pricing to determine various amounts.

	Per Unit	Total
Direct materials	€50	
Direct labor	26	
Variable manufacturing overhead	20	
Fixed manufacturing overhead		€600,000
Variable selling and administrative expenses	19	
Fixed selling and administrative expenses		400,000

Lyon Computer Parts management requests that the total unit cost be used in cost-plus pricing its products. On this particular product, management also directs that the target price be set to provide a 25% return on investment (ROI) on invested assets of €1,000,000.

Instructions

(Round all calculations to two decimal places.)

a. Compute the markup percentage and target selling price that will allow Lyon Computer Parts to earn its desired ROI of 25% on this new component.

b. Assuming that the volume is 40,000 units, compute the markup percentage and target selling price that will allow Lyon Computer Parts to earn its desired ROI of 25% on this new component.

b. Target selling price €146.25

Use time-and-material pricing to determine bill.

P8.3 (LO 3), AP Service Marin's Electronic Repair Shop has budgeted the following time and material for 2023.

	Time Charges	Material Loading Charges
Marin's Electronic Repair Shop		
Budgeted Costs for the Year 2023		
Shop employees' wages and benefits	£108,000	—
Parts manager's salary and benefits	—	£25,400
Office employee's salary and benefits	23,500	13,600
Overhead (supplies, depreciation, advertising, utilities)	26,000	16,000
Total budgeted costs	£157,500	£55,000

Marin's budgets 5,000 hours of repair time in 2023 and will bill a profit of £10 per labor hour along with a 25% profit markup on the invoice cost of parts. The estimated invoice cost for parts to be used is £100,000.

On January 5, 2023, Marin's is asked to submit a price estimate to fix a 72-inch flat-screen TV. Marin's estimates that this job will consume 4 hours of labor and £200 in parts.

Instructions

a. Compute the labor rate for Marin's Electronic Repair Shop for the year 2023.

b. Compute the material loading charge percentage for Marin's Electronic Repair Shop for the year 2023.

c. Prepare a time-and-material price quotation for fixing the flat-screen TV.

c. £526

Determine minimum transfer price with no excess capacity and with excess capacity.

P8.4 (LO 4), AP Service Writing Wisanto Word Wizard is a publishing company with a number of different book lines. Each line has contracts with a number of different authors. The company also owns a printing operation called Quick Press. The book lines and the printing operation each operate as a separate profit center. The printing operation earns revenue by printing books by authors under contract with the book lines owned by Wisanto Word Wizard, as well as authors under contract with other companies. The printing operation bills out at Rp100 per page, and a typical book requires 500 pages of print. A manager from Business Books, one of Wisanto Word Wizard's lines, has approached the manager of the printing operation offering to pay Rp70 per page for 1,500 copies of a 500-page book. The book line pays outside printers Rp90 per page. The printing operation's variable cost per page is Rp40.

Instructions

Determine whether the printing should be done internally or externally, and the appropriate transfer price, under each of the following situations.

a. Assume that the printing operation is booked solid for the next two years, and it would have to cancel an obligation with an outside customer in order to meet the needs of the internal division.

b. Assume that the printing operation has available capacity.

c. The top management of Wisanto Word Wizard believes that the printing operation should always do the printing for the company's authors. On a number of occasions, it has forced the printing operation to cancel jobs with outside customers in order to meet the needs of its own lines. Discuss the pros and cons of this approach.

d. Calculate the change in contribution margin to each division, and to the company as a whole, if top management forces the printing operation to accept the Rp70 per page transfer price when it has no available capacity.

d. Loss to company Rp (7,500,000)

P8.5 (LO 4), AP Mehmet A.S. makes various electronic products. The company is divided into a number of autonomous divisions that can either sell to internal units or sell externally. All divisions are located in buildings on the same piece of property. The Board Division has offered the Chip Division ₺210 per unit to supply it with chips for 40,000 boards. It has been purchasing these chips for ₺220 per unit from outside suppliers. The Chip Division receives ₺225 per unit for sales made to outside customers on this type of chip. The variable cost of chips sold externally by the Chip Division is ₺145. It estimates that it will save ₺45 per chip of selling expenses on units sold internally to the Board Division. The Chip Division has no excess capacity.

Determine minimum transfer price with no excess capacity.

Instructions

a. Calculate the minimum transfer price that the Chip Division should accept. Discuss whether it is in the Chip Division's best interest to accept the offer.

b. Suppose that the Chip Division decides to reject the offer. What are the financial implications for each division, and for the company as a whole, of this decision?

b. Total loss to company
₺(1,600,000)

P8.6 (LO 4), AP Comm Devices (CD) is a division of Pacific Communications. CD produces restaurant pagers and other personal communication devices. These devices are sold to other Pacific divisions, as well as to other communication companies. CD was recently approached by the manager of the Personal Communications Division regarding a request to make a special emergency-response pager designed to receive signals from anywhere in the world. The Personal Communications Division has requested that CD produce 12,000 units of this special pager. The following facts are available regarding the Comm Devices Division.

Determine minimum transfer price under different situations.

Selling price of standard pager	HK$950
Variable cost of standard pager	500
Additional variable cost of special pager	300

Instructions

For each of the following independent situations, calculate the minimum transfer price, and discuss whether the internal transfer should take place or whether the Personal Communications Division should purchase the pager externally.

a. The Personal Communications Division has offered to pay the CD Division HK$1,050 per pager. The CD Division has no available capacity. The CD Division would have to forgo sales of 10,000 pagers to existing customers in order to meet the request of the Personal Communications Division. (*Note:* The number of special pagers to be produced does not equal the number of existing pagers that would be forgone.)

b. The Personal Communications Division has offered to pay the CD Division HK$1,500 per pager. The CD Division has no available capacity. The CD Division would have to forgo sales of 16,000 pagers to existing customers in order to meet the request of the Personal Communications Division. (*Note:* The number of special pagers to be produced does not equal the number of existing pagers that would be forgone.)

b. Minimum transfer price HK$1,400

c. The Personal Communications Division has offered to pay the CD Division HK$1,000 per pager. The CD Division has available capacity.

*****P8.7 (LO 5), AP** Stent Corporation needs to set a target price for its newly designed product EverReady. The following data relate to this new product.

Compute the target price using absorption-cost pricing and variable-cost pricing.

	Per Unit	Total
Direct materials	$20	
Direct labor	40	
Variable manufacturing overhead	10	
Fixed manufacturing overhead		$1,600,000
Variable selling and administrative expenses	5	
Fixed selling and administrative expenses		1,120,000

The costs shown above are based on a budgeted volume of 80,000 units produced and sold each year. Stent uses cost-plus pricing methods to set its target selling price. Because some managers prefer absorption-cost pricing and others prefer variable-cost pricing, the accounting department provides information under both approaches using a markup of 50% on absorption cost and a markup of 80% on variable cost.

Instructions

a. Compute the target price for one unit of EverReady using absorption-cost pricing.

b. Compute the target price for one unit of EverReady using variable-cost pricing.

a. Markup $45
b. Markup $60

Compute various amounts using absorption-cost pricing and variable-cost pricing.

*P8.8 (LO 5), AP **Writing** Pritchett Windows is in the process of setting a target price on its newly designed tinted window. Cost data relating to the window at a budgeted volume of 4,000 units are as follows:

	Per Unit	Total
Direct materials	€100	
Direct labor	70	
Variable manufacturing overhead	20	
Fixed manufacturing overhead		€120,000
Variable selling and administrative expenses	10	
Fixed selling and administrative expenses		102,000

Pritchett Windows uses cost-plus pricing methods that are designed to provide the company with a 25% ROI on its tinted window line. A total of €1,016,000 in assets is committed to production of the new tinted window.

Instructions

a. Compute the markup percentage under absorption-cost pricing that will allow Pritchett Windows to realize its desired ROI.

b. Compute the target price of the window under absorption-cost pricing, and show proof that the desired ROI is realized.

c. Compute the markup percentage under variable-cost pricing that will allow Pritchett Windows to realize its desired ROI. (Round to three decimal places.)

d. Compute the target price of the window under variable-cost pricing, and show proof that the desired ROI is realized.

e. Since both absorption-cost pricing and variable-cost pricing produce the same target price and provide the same desired ROI, why do both methods exist? Isn't one method clearly superior to the other?

a. 45%

Continuing Case

Current Designs

CD8 As a service to its customers, **Current Designs** (USA) repairs damaged kayaks. This is especially valuable to customers that have made a significant investment in the composite kayaks. To price the repair jobs, Current Designs uses time-and-material pricing with a desired profit margin of $20 per labor hour and a 50% materials loading charge.

Recently, Bill Johnson, Vice President of Sales and Marketing, received a phone call from a dealer in Brainerd, Minnesota. The dealer has a customer who recently damaged his composite kayak and would like an estimate of the cost to repair it. After the dealer emailed pictures of the damage, Bill reviewed the pictures with the repair technician and determined that the total materials charges for the repair would be $100. Bill estimates that the job will take 3 labor hours to complete. Following is the budgeted cost data for Current Designs:

Repair-technician wages	$30,000
Fringe benefits	10,000
Overhead	10,000

Current Designs has allocated 2,000 hours of repair time for the upcoming year. The customer has agreed to transport the kayak to the Winona production facility for the repairs.

Instructions

Determine the price that Current Designs would charge to complete the repairs for the customer.

Data Analytics in Action

Using Data Visualization to Analyze Trends

DA8 Data visualization can help Broadway theatre analysts to understand ticket prices.
Example: Recall the *Service Company Insight* box "How Much Did You Pay for That Seat?" presented in the chapter. As discussed, ticket prices are dynamic and respond quickly to changes in demand. For example, take a look at the following chart. How might you explain some of the biggest drops in ticket prices in the first week of 2020?

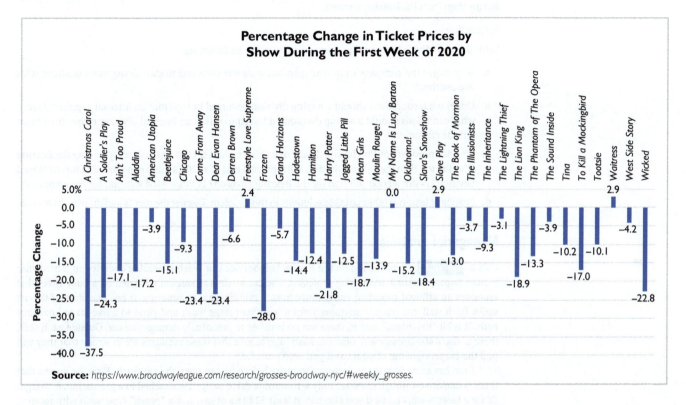

Source: *https://www.broadwayleague.com/research/grosses-broadway-nyc/#weekly_grosses.*

You can see that *A Christmas Carol* has the biggest average weekly price drop. However, we would expect this drop. The show would have had its highest sales and prices in November and December, during the holiday season.

Using data analytics to get big-picture results often leads to additional analysis. In this case, you will use tree map visualizations and a combo chart to delve deeper into the possible causes and effects of dynamic Broadway ticket prices.

Go to the book's product page on www.wiley.com for complete case details and instructions.

Expand Your Critical Thinking

Decision-Making Across the Organization

CT8.1 Li Manufacturing has multiple divisions that make a wide variety of products. Recently, the Bearing Division and the Wheel Division argued over a transfer price. The Wheel Division needed bearings for garden tractor wheels. It normally buys its bearings from an outside supplier for ¥250 per set. However, the company's top management just initiated a campaign to persuade the different divisions to buy their materials from within the company whenever possible. As a result, Hao Zhang, the purchasing manager for the Wheel Division, received a letter from the vice president of Purchasing, ordering him to contact the Bearing Division to discuss buying bearings from this division.

To comply with this request, Hao from the Wheel Division called Ying Wang of the Bearing Division, to request the price for 15,000 bearings. Ying responded that the bearings normally sell for ¥360 per set. However, Ying noted that the Bearing Division would save ¥30 on marketing costs by selling internally and would pass this cost savings on to the Wheel Division. She further commented that the

Bearing Division was at full capacity and therefore would not be able to provide any bearings presently. In the future, if the Bearing Division had available capacity, it would be happy to provide bearings.

Hao responded indignantly, "Thanks but no thanks." He said, "We can get all the bearings we need from Feng Manufacturing for ¥250 per set, and its quality is acceptable for our product." Ying snorted back, "Feng makes low-quality bearings. We incur a total unit cost of ¥220 unit for units we sell externally. Our bearings can withstand heat of 2,000 degrees centigrade and are good to within .00001 centimeters. If you guys are happy buying low-quality bearings, then go ahead and buy from Feng."

Two weeks later, Hao's boss from the central office stopped in to find out whether he had placed an order with the Bearing Division. Hao responded that he would sooner buy his bearings from his worst enemy than from the Bearing Division.

Instructions

With the class divided into groups, prepare answers to the following:

a. Why might the company's top management want the divisions to start doing more business with one another?

b. Under what conditions should a buying division be forced to buy from an internal supplier? Under what conditions should a selling division be forced to sell to an internal division rather than to an outside customer?

c. The vice president of Purchasing thinks that this problem should be resolved by forcing the Bearing Division to sell to the Wheel Division at its internal cost of ¥220. Is this a good solution for the Wheel Division? Is this a good solution for the Bearing Division? Is this a good solution for the company?

d. Provide at least two other possible solutions to this problem. Discuss the merits and drawbacks of each.

Managerial Analysis

CT8.2 **Service** Construction on the Bonita Full-Service Car Wash is nearing completion. The owner is Juan Lopez, a retired accounting professor. The car wash is strategically located on a busy street that separates an affluent suburban community from a middle-class community. It has two state-of-the-art stalls. Each stall can provide anything from a basic two-stage wash and rinse to a five-stage luxurious bath. It is all "touchless," that is, there are no brushes to potentially damage the car. Outside each stall, there is also a 400-horsepower vacuum. Juan likes to joke that these vacuums are so strong that they will pull the carpet right out of your car if you aren't careful.

Juan has some important decisions to make before he can open the car wash. First, he knows that there is one drive-through car wash only a 10-minute drive away. It is attached to a gas station; it charges €5 for a basic wash, and €4 if you also buy at least 32 liters of gas. It is a "brush"-type wash with rotating brush heads. There is also a self-serve "stand outside your car and spray until you are soaked" car wash a 15-minute drive away from Juan's location. He went over and tried this out. He went through €3 in quarters to get the equivalent of a basic wash. He knows that both of these locations always have long lines, which is one reason why he decided to build a new car wash.

Juan is planning to offer three levels of wash service—Basic, Deluxe, and Premium. The Basic is all automated; it requires no direct intervention by employees. The Deluxe is all automated except that at the end an employee will wipe down the car and will put a window treatment on the windshield that reduces glare and allows rainwater to run off more quickly. The Premium level is a "pampered" service. This will include all the services of the Deluxe, plus a special wax after the machine wax, and an employee will vacuum the car, wipe down the entire interior, and wash the inside of the windows. To provide the Premium service, Juan will have to hire a couple of "car wash specialists" to do the additional pampering.

Juan has pulled together the following estimates, based on data he received from the local Chamber of Commerce and information from a trade association.

	Per Unit	Total
Direct materials per Basic wash	€0.30	
Direct materials per Deluxe wash	0.80	
Direct materials per Premium wash	1.10	
Direct labor per Basic wash	na	
Direct labor per Deluxe wash	0.40	
Direct labor per Premium wash	2.40	
Variable overhead per Basic wash	0.10	
Variable overhead per Deluxe and Premium washes	0.20	
Fixed overhead		€117,000
Variable selling and administrative expenses all washes	0.10	
Fixed selling and administrative expenses		130,500

The total estimated number of washes of any type is 45,000. Juan has invested assets of €393,750. He would like a return on investment (ROI) of 20%.

Instructions

Complete the following:

a. Identify the issues that Juan must consider in deciding on the price of each level of service of his car wash. Also discuss what issues he should consider in deciding on what levels of service to provide.

b. Juan estimates that of the total 45,000 washes, 20,000 will be Basic, 20,000 will be Deluxe, and 5,000 will be Premium. Calculate the selling price, using cost-plus pricing, that Juan should use for each type of wash to achieve his desired ROI of 20%.

c. During the first year, instead of selling 45,000 washes, Juan sold 43,000 washes. He was quite accurate in his estimate of first-year sales, but he was way off on the types of washes that he sold. He sold 3,000 Basic, 31,000 Deluxe, and 9,000 Premium. His actual total fixed expenses were as he expected, and his unit variable cost was as estimated. Calculate Juan's actual net income and his actual ROI. (Round to two decimal places.)

d. Juan is using a traditional approach to allocate overhead. As a consequence, he is allocating overhead equally to all three types of washes, even though the Basic wash is considerably less complicated and uses very little of the technical capabilities of the machinery. What should Juan do to determine more accurate unit costs? How will this affect his pricing and, consequently, his sales?

Real-World Focus

CT8.3 **Merck & Co., Inc.** (USA) is a global, research-driven pharmaceutical company that discovers, develops, manufactures, and markets a broad range of human and animal health products. The following are excerpts from the financial review section of the company's annual report.

Merck & Co., Inc.
Financial Review Section (partial)

In the United States, the Company has been working with private and governmental employers to slow the increase of health care costs.

Outside of the United States, in difficult environments encumbered by government cost containment actions, the Company has worked with payers to help them allocate scarce resources to optimize health care outcomes, limiting potentially detrimental effects of government actions on sales growth.

Several products face expiration of product patents in the near term.

The Company, along with other pharmaceutical manufacturers, received a notice from the Federal Trade Commission (FTC) that it was conducting an investigation into pricing practices.

Instructions

Complete the following:

a. Based on the above excerpts from Merck's annual report, discuss some unique pricing issues faced by companies that operate in the pharmaceutical industry.

b. What are some reasons why the same company often sells identical drugs for dramatically different prices in different countries? How can the same drug used for both humans and animals cost significantly different prices?

c. Suppose that Merck has just developed a revolutionary new drug. Discuss the steps it would go through in setting a price. Include a discussion of the information it would need to gather, and the issues it would need to consider.

Communication Activity

CT8.4 **Service** Romila Prasad recently graduated from college with a degree in landscape architecture. Her father runs a tree, shrub, and perennial-flower nursery, and her brother has a business delivering topsoil, mulch, and compost. Romila has decided that she would like to start a landscape business. She believes that she can generate a nice profit for herself, while providing an opportunity for both her brother's and father's businesses to grow.

One potential problem that Romila is concerned about is that her father and brother tend to charge the highest prices of any local suppliers for their products. She is hoping that she can demonstrate that it would be in her interest, as well as theirs, for them to sell to her at a discounted price.

Instructions

Write a memo to Romila explaining what information she must gather, and what issues she must consider, in working out an arrangement with her father and brother. In your memo, discuss how this situation differs from a "standard" transfer pricing problem, but also how it has many of the characteristics of a transfer pricing problem.

Ethics Case

CT8.5 **Service** Jumbo Airlines operates out of three main "hub" airports in India. Recently, Econo Airlines began operating a flight from Bangalore to Mumbai, which is Jumbo's Metropolis hub, for ₹19,000. Jumbo Airlines offers a price of ₹42,500 for the same route. The management of Jumbo is not happy about Econo invading its turf. In fact, Jumbo has driven off nearly every other competing airline from its hub, so that today 90% of flights into and out of Metropolis are Jumbo Airline flights. Econo is able to offer a lower fare because its pilots are paid less, it uses older planes, and it has lower overhead costs. Econo has been in business for only six months, and it services only two other cities. It expects the Metropolis route to be its most profitable.

Jumbo estimates that it would have to charge ₹21,000 just to break even on this flight. It estimates that Econo can break even at a price of ₹16,000. Within one day of Econo's entry into the market, Jumbo dropped its price to ₹14,000, whereupon Econo matched its price. They both maintained this fare for a period of nine months, until Econo went out of business. As soon as Econo went out of business, Jumbo raised its fare back to ₹42,500.

Instructions

Answer each of the following questions:

a. Who are the stakeholders in this case?

b. What are some of the reasons why Econo's break-even point is lower than that of Jumbo?

c. What are the likely reasons why Jumbo was able to offer this price for this period of time, while Econo could not?

d. What are some of the possible courses of action available to Econo in this situation?

e. Do you think that this kind of pricing activity is ethical? What are the implications for the stakeholders in this situation?

Considering Your Costs and Benefits

CT8.6 The January 2011 issue of *Strategic Finance* includes an article by J. Lockhart, A. Taylor, K. Thomas, B. Levetsovitis, and J. Wise entitled "When a Higher Price Pays Off."

Instructions

Read the article and then complete the following:

a. Explain what is meant by a "low-cost" supplier versus a "low-priced" supplier.

b. **Clarus Technologies**' (USA) products are typically priced significantly higher than its competitors' products. How is it able to overcome the initial "sticker shock"?

c. List the five categories of costs that the authors used to compare the Tornado to competing products. Give examples of specific types of costs in each category.

d. The article discusses full-cost accounting as developed by the U.S. Environmental Protection Agency (EPA). What are the characteristics of this approach, and what implications does the approach used in this article have for corporate social responsibility?

CHAPTER 9

Budgetary Planning

CHAPTER PREVIEW

As the following Feature Story about **Erin McKenna's Bakery NYC** (USA) (formerly **BabyCakes NYC**) indicates, budgeting is critical to financial well-being. As a student, you budget your study time and your money. Families budget income and expenses. Governmental agencies budget revenues and expenditures. Businesses use budgets in planning and controlling their operations.

Our primary focus in this chapter is the use of budgeting as a planning tool by management. Through budgeting, it should be possible for management to maintain enough cash to pay creditors as well as have sufficient raw materials to meet production requirements and adequate finished goods to meet expected sales.

FEATURE STORY

What's in Your Cupcake?

The best business plans often result from meeting a basic human need. Many people would argue that cupcakes aren't necessarily essential to support life. But if you found out that allergies were going to deprive you forever of cupcakes, you might view baked goods in a whole new light. Such was the dilemma faced by Erin McKenna. When she found that her wheat allergies prevented her from consuming most baked sweets, she decided to open a bakery that met her needs. Her vegan and kosher bakery, **Erin McKenna's Bakery NYC** (USA), advertises that it is refined-sugar-free, gluten-free, wheat-free, soy-free, dairy-free, and egg-free. So if you're one of the more than 10 million Americans with a food allergy or some other dietary constraint, this is probably the bakery for you.

Those of you that have spent a little time in the kitchen might wonder what kind of ingredients Erin McKenna's Bakery uses. To avoid the gluten in wheat, the company uses Bob's Red Mill (USA) rice flour, a garbanzo/fava bean mix, or oat flours. How does Erin McKenna's Bakery get all those great frosting colors without artificial dyes? The company achieves pink with beets, green with chlorophyll, yellow with turmeric, and blue/purple with red cabbage. To eliminate dairy and soy, the bakers use rice and coconut milk. And finally, to accomplish over-the-top deliciousness without refined sugar, the company uses agave nectar (a sweetener derived from cactus) and evaporated cane juice (often referred to as organic or unrefined sugar).

With cupcakes priced at over $3 per item and a brisk business, you might think that making money is easy for Erin McKenna's Bakery. But all of these specialty ingredients don't come cheap. In addition, the company's shops are located in Manhattan, Los Angeles, and Orlando, so rent isn't exactly inexpensive either. Despite these costs, Erin's first store made a profit its first year and did even better in later years.

To achieve this profitability, Erin relies on careful budgeting. First, she estimates sales. Then, she determines her needs for materials, labor, and overhead. Prices for raw materials can fluctuate significantly, so Erin needs to update her budget accordingly. Finally, she has to budget for other products such as her cookbooks, baking kits, and T-shirts. Without a budget, Erin's business might not be so sweet.

 Watch the *BabyCakes NYC* video at https://wileyaccountingupdates.com/video/?p=4 to learn more about real-world budgetary planning.

CHAPTER OUTLINE

Learning Objectives	Review	Practice
LO 1 State the essentials of effective budgeting and the components of the master budget.	• Budgeting and accounting • Benefits of budgeting • Effective budgeting essentials • Master budget	**DO IT! 1** Budget Terminology
LO 2 Prepare budgets for sales, production, and direct materials.	• Sales budget • Production budget • Direct materials budget	**DO IT! 2** Sales, Production, and Direct Materials Budgets
LO 3 Prepare budgets for direct labor, manufacturing overhead, and selling and administrative expenses, and a budgeted income statement.	• Direct labor budget • Manufacturing overhead budget • Selling and administrative expense budget • Budgeted income statement	**DO IT! 3** Budgeted Income Statement
LO 4 Prepare a cash budget and a budgeted balance sheet.	• Cash budget • Budgeted balance sheet	**DO IT! 4** Cash Budget
LO 5 Apply budgeting principles to nonmanufacturing companies.	• Merchandisers • Service companies • Not-for-profit organizations	**DO IT! 5** Merchandise Purchases Budget

Go to the Review and Practice section at the end of the chapter for a targeted summary and practice applications with solutions.

EFFECTIVE BUDGETING AND THE MASTER BUDGET

As explained in Chapter 1, **planning** is the process of establishing company-wide objectives. A successful organization makes both long-term and short-term plans. These plans establish the objectives of the company and the proposed approach to accomplish them.

A **budget** is a formal written statement of management's plans for a specified future time period, expressed in financial terms.

- It represents the primary method of communicating agreed-upon objectives throughout the organization.
- Once adopted, a budget becomes an important basis for evaluating performance.
- It promotes efficiency and serves as a deterrent to waste and inefficiency.

We consider the role of budgeting as a **control device** in Chapter 10.

> **LEARNING OBJECTIVE 1**
> State the essentials of effective budgeting and the components of the master budget.

Budgeting and Accounting

Accounting information makes major contributions to the budgeting process. From the accounting records, companies obtain historical data on revenues, costs, and expenses. These data are helpful in formulating future budget goals.

Accountants are responsible for presenting management's budgeting goals in financial terms.

- Accountants translate management's plans and communicate the budget to employees throughout the company.
- They prepare periodic budget reports that provide the basis for measuring performance and comparing actual results with planned objectives.

The budget itself and the administration of the budget, however, are entirely management responsibilities.

The Benefits of Budgeting

The primary benefits of budgeting are as follows:

1. It requires all levels of management to **plan ahead** and to formalize goals on a recurring basis.
2. It provides **definite objectives** for evaluating performance at each level of responsibility.
3. It creates an **early warning system** for potential problems so that management can make changes before things get out of hand.
4. It facilitates the **coordination of activities** within the business. It does this by correlating the goals of each segment with overall company objectives. Thus, the company can integrate production and sales promotion with expected sales.
5. It results in greater **management awareness** of the entity's overall operations and the impact on operations of external factors, such as economic trends.
6. It **motivates personnel** throughout the organization to meet planned objectives.

A budget is an aid to management; it is not a *substitute* for management. A budget cannot operate or enforce itself. Companies can realize the benefits of budgeting only when managers carefully administer budgets.

Essentials of Effective Budgeting

Effective budgeting depends on a **sound organizational structure**. In such a structure, authority and responsibility for all phases of operations are clearly defined. Budgets based on **research and analysis** are more likely to result in realistic goals that will contribute to the growth and profitability of a company. And, the effectiveness of a budget program is directly related to its **acceptance by all levels of management**.

Once adopted, the budget is an important tool for evaluating performance. Managers should systematically and periodically review variations between actual and expected results to determine their cause(s). However, individuals should not be held responsible for variations that are beyond their control.

Length of the Budget Period

The budget period is not necessarily one year in length. **A budget may be prepared for any period of time.** Various factors influence the length of the budget period:

- The type of budget.
- The nature of the organization.
- The need for periodic appraisal.
- Prevailing business conditions.

The budget period should be long enough to provide an attainable goal under normal business conditions. Ideally, the time period should minimize the impact of seasonal or cyclical fluctuations. On the other hand, the budget period should not be so long that reliable estimates are impossible.

The **most common budget period is one year**. The annual budget, in turn, is often supplemented by monthly and quarterly budgets. Many companies use **continuous 12-month budgets**. These budgets drop the month just ended and add a future month. One benefit of continuous budgeting is that it keeps management planning a full year ahead.

ACCOUNTING ACROSS THE ORGANIZATION

Thinkstock/Stockbyte/Getty Images

Businesses Often Feel Too Busy to Plan for the Future

A study by Willard & Shullman Group Ltd. found that less than 14% of businesses with fewer than 500 employees do an annual budget or have a written business plan. For many small businesses, the basic assumption is that, "As long as I sell as much as I can, and keep my employees paid, I'm doing OK."

A few small business owners even say that they see no need for budgeting and planning. Most small business owners, though, say that they understand that budgeting and planning are critical for survival and growth. But given the long hours that they already work addressing day-to-day challenges, they also say that they are "just too busy to plan for the future."

Describe a situation in which a business "sells as much as it can" but cannot "keep its employees paid." (Answer is available in the book's product page on www.wiley.com)

The Budgeting Process

The development of the budget for the coming year generally starts several months before the end of the current year. The budgeting process usually begins with the collection of data from each organizational unit of the company. Past performance is often the starting point from which future budget goals are formulated.

The budget is developed within the framework of a **sales forecast**.

- This forecast shows potential sales for the industry and the company's expected share of such sales.
- Sales forecasting involves a consideration of various factors:
    1. General economic conditions.
    2. Industry trends.
    3. Market research studies.
    4. Anticipated advertising and promotion.
    5. Previous market share.
    6. Changes in prices.
    7. Technological developments.
- The input of sales personnel and top management is essential to the sales forecast.

In small companies like **Erin McKenna's Bakery NYC** (USA), the budgeting process is often informal. In larger companies, a **budget committee** has responsibility for coordinating the preparation of the budget.

- The committee ordinarily includes the president, treasurer, chief accountant (controller), and management personnel from each of the major areas of the company, such as sales, production, and research.
- The budget committee serves as a review board where managers can defend their budget goals and requests. Differences are reviewed, modified if necessary, and reconciled.
- The budget is then put in its final form by the budget committee, approved, and distributed.

Budgeting and Human Behavior

A budget can have a significant impact on human behavior. If done well, it can inspire managers to higher levels of performance. However, if done poorly, budgets can discourage additional effort and pull down the morale of managers. Why do these diverse effects occur? The answer is found in how the budget is developed and administered.

In developing the budget, each level of management should be invited to participate. This "bottom-to-top" approach is referred to as **participative budgeting**.

- One benefit of participative budgeting is that lower-level managers have more detailed knowledge of their specific area and thus are able to provide more accurate budgetary estimates.
- When lower-level managers participate in the budgeting process, they are more likely to perceive the resulting budget as fair.
- The overall goal is to reach agreement on a budget that the managers consider fair and achievable, but which also meets the corporate goals set by top management. When this goal is met, the budget will provide positive motivation for the managers.

In contrast, if managers view the budget as unfair and unrealistic, they may feel discouraged and uncommitted to budget goals. The risk of having unrealistic budgets is generally greater when the budget is developed from top management down to lower management than vice versa. **Illustration 9.1** shows the flow of budget data from bottom to top under participative budgeting.

At one time, in an effort to revive its plummeting stock price, **WarnerMedia**'s (USA) top management determined and publicly announced bold (and ultimately unattainable) new financial goals for the coming year. Unfortunately, these goals were not reached. The next year, the company hired a new CEO who said the company would now set reasonable goals. The new budgets were developed with participative budgeting. Each operating unit set what it felt were optimistic but attainable goals. In the words of one manager, using this approach created a sense of teamwork.

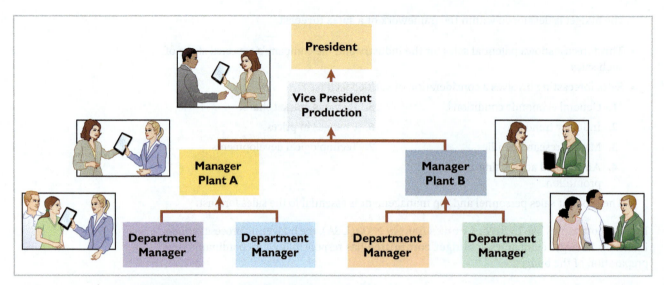

ILLUSTRATION 9.1 | Flow of budget data under participative budgeting

Participative budgeting does, however, have potential disadvantages.

1. The "give and take" of participative budgeting is time-consuming (and thus more costly). Under a "top-down" approach, the budget can be more quickly developed by top management and then dictated to lower-level managers.
2. Participative budgeting can foster budgetary "gaming" through **budgetary slack**, which occurs when managers intentionally underestimate budgeted revenues or overestimate budgeted expenses in order to make it easier to achieve budgetary goals for their division.

To minimize budgetary slack, higher-level managers must carefully review and thoroughly question the budget projections provided to them by employees whom they supervise.

For the budget to be effective, top management must completely support the budget. The budget is an important tool for evaluating performance. It also can be used as a positive aid in achieving projected goals. The effect of an evaluation is positive when top management tempers criticism with advice and assistance. In contrast, a manager is likely to respond negatively if top management uses the budget exclusively to assess blame. A budget should not be used as a pressure device to force improved performance (see **Ethics Note**). In sum, a budget can be a manager's friend or foe.

ETHICS NOTE
Unrealistic budgets can lead to unethical employee behavior such as cutting corners on the job or distorting internal financial reports.

HELPFUL HINT
A budget has more detail and is more concerned with short-term goals than a long-range plan.

Budgeting and Long-Range Planning

Budgeting and long-range planning have three significant differences:

1. **The time period involved.** The maximum length of a budget is usually one year, and budgets are often prepared for shorter periods of time, such as a month or a quarter. In contrast, long-range planning usually encompasses a period of at least five years (see **Helpful Hint**).
2. **Emphasis.** Budgeting focuses on achieving specific short-term goals, such as meeting annual profit objectives. **Long-range planning**, on the other hand:
   - Identifies long-term goals.
   - Selects strategies to achieve those goals.
   - Develops policies and plans to implement the strategies.

   In long-range planning, management also considers anticipated trends in the economic and political environment and how the company should cope with them.

3. **The amount of detail presented.** Budgets, as you will see in this chapter, can be very detailed. Long-range plans contain considerably less detail as the data are intended more for a review of progress toward long-term goals than as a basis of control for achieving specific results. The primary objective of long-range planning is to develop the best strategy to maximize the company's performance over an extended future period.

The Master Budget

The term "budget" is actually a shorthand term to describe a variety of budget documents. All of these documents are combined into a master budget. The **master budget** is a set of interrelated budgets that constitutes a plan of action for a specified time period (see **Decision Tools**).

The master budget contains two classes of budgets:

1. **Operating budgets**, which are the individual budgets that result in the preparation of the budgeted income statement. These budgets establish goals for the company's sales and production personnel.
2. **Financial budgets**, which focus primarily on the cash resources needed to fund expected operations and planned capital expenditures. Financial budgets include the capital expenditure budget, the cash budget, and the budgeted balance sheet.

DECISION TOOLS

Managers use the master budget to determine if the company met its targets for such things as sales, production expenses, selling and administrative expenses, and net income.

Illustration 9.2 shows the individual budgets included in a master budget and the sequence in which they are prepared. The company first develops the operating budgets, beginning with the sales budget. Then, it prepares the financial budgets. In this chapter, we explain and illustrate each budget shown in Illustration 9.2 except the capital expenditure budget. That budget is discussed under the topic of capital budgeting in Chapter 12.

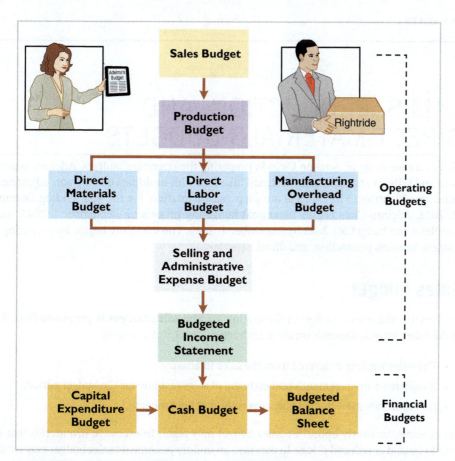

ILLUSTRATION 9.2 | Components of the master budget

DO IT! 1 ▶ Budget Terminology

Use this list of terms to complete the sentences that follow:

>   Long-range planning   Participative budgeting
>   Sales forecast   Operating budgets
>   Master budget   Financial budgets

1. A _____ shows potential sales for the industry and a company's expected share of such sales.
2. _____ are used as the basis for the preparation of the budgeted income statement.
3. The _____ is a set of interrelated budgets that constitutes a plan of action for a specified time period.
4. _____ identifies long-term goals, selects strategies to achieve these goals, and develops policies and plans to implement the strategies.
5. Lower-level managers are more likely to perceive results as fair and achievable under a _____ approach.
6. _____ focus primarily on the cash resources needed to fund expected operations and planned capital expenditures.

ACTION PLAN
- Understand the budgeting process, including the importance of the sales forecast.
- Understand the difference between an operating budget and a financial budget.
- Differentiate budgeting from long-range planning.
- Realize that the master budget is a set of interrelated budgets.

Solution

1. Sales forecast.
2. Operating budgets.
3. Master budget.
4. Long-range planning.
5. Participative budgeting.
6. Financial budgets.

Related exercise material: **BE9.1, DO IT! 9.1, and E9.1.**

SALES, PRODUCTION, AND DIRECT MATERIALS BUDGETS

LEARNING OBJECTIVE 2
Prepare budgets for sales, production, and direct materials.

We use a case study of Adelmo Ciclo in preparing the operating budgets. Adelmo manufactures and sells an ergonomically designed bike seat with multiple customizable adjustments, called the Rightride. The budgets are prepared by quarters for the year ending December 31, 2023. Adelmo Ciclo begins its annual budgeting process on September 1, 2022, and it completes the budget for 2023 by December 1, 2022. The company begins by preparing the budgets for sales, production, and direct materials.

Sales Budget

As shown in the master budget in Illustration 9.2, **the sales budget is prepared first**. Each of the other budgets depends on the sales budget (see **Helpful Hint**).

HELPFUL HINT
For a retail or manufacturing company, the sales budget is the starting point for the master budget. It sets the level of activity for other functions such as production and purchasing.

- The **sales budget** is derived from the sales forecast.
- It represents management's best estimate of sales revenue for the budget period.
- An inaccurate sales budget may adversely affect net income.

For example, an overly optimistic sales budget may result in excessive inventories that may have to be sold at reduced prices. In contrast, an unduly pessimistic sales budget may result in loss of sales revenue due to inventory shortages.

For example, at one time **Amazon.com** (USA) significantly underestimated demand for its e-book reader, the Kindle. As a consequence, it did not produce enough Kindles and was completely sold out well before the holiday shopping season. Not only did this represent a huge lost opportunity for Amazon, but it exposed the company to potential competitors, who were eager to provide customers with alternatives to the Kindle.

Forecasting sales is challenging. For example, consider the forecasting challenges faced by major sports arenas, whose revenues depend on the success of the home team. **Madison Square Garden**'s (USA) revenues from April to June were $193 million during a year when the New York Knicks made the NBA playoffs. But revenues were only $133.2 million a couple of years later when the team did not make the playoffs. Or, consider the challenges faced by Hollywood movie producers in predicting the complicated revenue stream produced by a new movie. Movie theater ticket sales represent only 20% of total revenue. The bulk of revenue comes from global sales, video-on-demand streaming, television rights, merchandising products, and videogames, all of which are difficult to forecast.

The sales budget is prepared by multiplying the expected unit sales volume for each product by its anticipated unit selling price. Adelmo Ciclo expects sales volume to be 3,000 units in the first quarter, with 500-unit increases in each succeeding quarter. **Illustration 9.3** shows the sales budget for the year, by quarter, based on a unit selling price of €60.

Adelmo Ciclo
Sales Budget
For the Year Ending December 31, 2023

	Quarter				
	1	2	3	4	Year
Expected sales units	3,000	3,500	4,000	4,500	15,000
Unit selling price	× €60	× €60	× €60	× €60	× €60
Total sales	€180,000	€210,000	€240,000	€270,000	€900,000

ILLUSTRATION 9.3 | Sales budget

Some companies classify the anticipated sales revenue as cash or credit sales and by geographic regions, territories, or salespersons.

SERVICE COMPANY INSIGHT

MarsBars/iStock/
Getty Images Plus/
Getty Images

The Implications of Budgetary Optimism

Companies aren't the only ones that need to estimate revenues. Governments at all levels (e.g., local, state, and federal) prepare annual budgets. Most are required to submit balanced budgets, that is, estimated revenues are required to cover anticipated expenditures. Estimating government revenues can be very difficult. For example, at one time, the median state government overestimated revenues by 10.2%, with four state governments missing by more than 25%.

What makes estimation so difficult for governments? Most states rely on income taxes, which fluctuate widely with economic gyrations. Some states rely on sales taxes, which are problematic because the laws regarding sales taxes haven't fully adjusted for the shift from manufacturing to service companies and from brick-and-mortar stores to online sales.

Sources: Conor Dougherty, "States Fumble Revenue Forecasts," *Wall Street Journal Online* (March 2, 2011); and Elizabeth McNichol, "Improving State Revenue Forecasting: Best Practices for a More Trusted and Reliable Revenue Estimate," *Center on Budget and Policy Priorities* (September 4, 2014).

Why is it important that government budgets accurately estimate future revenues during economic downturns? (Answer is available in the book's product page on www.wiley.com)

Production Budget

The **production budget** shows the number of units of a product to produce to meet anticipated sales demand. Production requirements are determined from the equation shown in **Illustration 9.4**.[1]

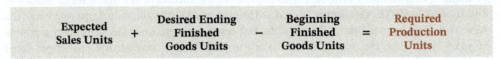

ILLUSTRATION 9.4 | Production requirements equation

Illustration 9.5 shows the production budget for Adelmo Ciclo, which is based on the equation shown in Illustration 9.4.

Adelmo Ciclo Production Budget

Adelmo Ciclo
Production Budget
For the Year Ending December 31, 2023

	Quarter				
	1	2	3	4	Year
Expected sales units (Illustration 9.3)	3,000	3,500	4,000	4,500	
Add: Desired ending finished goods units[a]	700	800	900	1,000[b]	
Total required units	3,700	4,300	4,900	5,500	
Less: Beginning finished goods units[c]	600	700	800	900	
Required production units	**3,100**	**3,600**	**4,100**	**4,600**	**15,400**

[a] 20% of next quarter's sales
[b] Expected 2024 first-quarter sales, 5,000 units × .20
[c] 20% of estimated first-quarter 2023 sales units

ILLUSTRATION 9.5 | Production budget

- In the first quarter, expected sales are 3,000 units.
- Adelmo Ciclo believes it should maintain an ending inventory equal to 20% of the next quarter's budgeted sales volume to ensure a continuous supply. The ending finished goods inventory for the first quarter is 700 units (.20 × anticipated second-quarter sales of 3,500 units).
- If we then subtract the beginning finished goods units of 600 units (20% of first-quarter sales), we arrive at required production of 3,100 units.

An accurate estimate of the amount of ending inventory required to meet demand is essential in scheduling production requirements. Excessive inventories in one quarter may lead to cutbacks in production and employee layoffs in a subsequent quarter. On the other hand, inadequate inventories may result either in added costs for overtime work or in lost sales.

---

[1] This equation ignores any work in process inventories, which are assumed to be nonexistent in Adelmo Ciclo.

The production budget, in turn, provides the basis for the budgeted costs for each manufacturing cost component, as explained in the following discussion.

Direct Materials Budget

The **direct materials budget** shows both the quantity and cost of direct materials to be purchased. The first step toward computing the cost of direct materials purchases is to compute the direct materials units required for production. **Illustration 9.6** shows the equation for this amount.

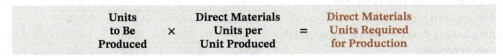

ILLUSTRATION 9.6 | Equation for direct materials units required for production

Employing this equation, Illustration 9.9 shows the following:

- For Adelmo Ciclo's first quarter of production, there are 3,100 units to be produced.
- Each unit produced requires two kilograms of raw materials.
- Therefore, the units of direct materials required for production is 6,200 kilograms (3,100 × 2).

Next we can compute the direct materials units to be purchased using the equation shown in **Illustration 9.7**.

Direct Materials Units Required for Production	+	Desired Ending Direct Materials Units	−	Beginning Direct Materials Units	=	Direct Materials Units to Be Purchased

ILLUSTRATION 9.7 | Equation for direct materials units to be purchased

Employing this equation, Illustration 9.9 shows the following:

- For Adelmo Ciclo's first quarter of production, the direct materials units required for production is 6,200 kilograms (computed above).
- To that we add the desired ending direct materials units. For Adelmo, this is assumed to be 10% of the next quarter's production requirements, or 720 kilograms (.10 × 7,200).
- Then, we subtract the beginning direct materials units of 620 kilograms (10% of this quarter's production requirements of 6,200) to arrive at the direct materials units to be purchased of 6,300 kilograms.

Finally, to arrive at the cost of direct materials purchases, we employ the equation shown in **Illustration 9.8**.

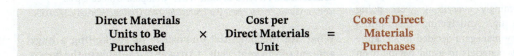

ILLUSTRATION 9.8 | Equation for cost of direct materials purchases

Adelmo Ciclo's direct materials cost is €4 per kilogram. Employing this equation, **Illustration 9.9** shows that for Adelmo's first quarter of production, the cost of direct

Adelmo Ciclo
Direct Materials Budget
For the Year Ending December 31, 2023

	Quarter				
	1	2	3	4	Year
Units to be produced (Illustration 9.5)	3,100	3,600	4,100	4,600	
Direct materials units per unit produced	× 2	× 2	× 2	× 2	
Direct materials units required for production	6,200	7,200	8,200	9,200	
Add: Desired ending direct materials (kilograms)[a]	720	820	920	1,020[c]	
Total materials required	6,920	8,020	9,120	10,220	
Less: Beginning direct materials (kilograms)	620[b]	720	820	920	
Direct materials units to be purchased (kilograms)	6,300	7,300	8,300	9,300	
Cost per kilogram	× €4	× €4	× €4	× €4	
Cost of direct materials purchases	**€25,200**	**€29,200**	**€33,200**	**€37,200**	**€124,800**

[a]10% of next quarter's production requirements
[b]10% of estimated first-quarter kilograms needed for production
[c]Total kilograms needed for production is assumed to be 10,200 for the first quarter of 2024

ILLUSTRATION 9.9 | Direct materials budget

materials purchases is computed by multiplying the units to be purchased of 6,300 kilograms by the cost per direct materials unit of €4 per kilogram, to arrive at €25,200 (6,300 × €4).

The desired ending inventory is again a key component in the budgeting process. For example, inadequate inventories could result in temporary shutdowns of production. Adelmo Ciclo is located in close proximity to its suppliers. It therefore believes that an ending inventory of raw materials equal to 10% of the next quarter's production requirements is adequate to meet its needs.

MANAGEMENT INSIGHT

Betting That Prices Won't Fall

WilliamWang/Getty Images

Sometimes things happen that cause managers to reevaluate their normal purchasing patterns. Consider, for example, the predicament that businesses faced when the price of many raw materials skyrocketed. Rubber, cotton, oil, corn, wheat, steel, copper, and spices—prices for seemingly everything were going straight up. Anticipating that prices might continue to go up, many managers decided to stockpile much larger quantities of raw materials to avoid paying even higher prices in the future.

For example, after cotton prices rose 92%, one manager of a printed T-shirt manufacturer decided to stockpile a huge supply of plain T-shirts in anticipation of additional price increases. While he normally has about 30 boxes of T-shirts in inventory, he purchased 2,500 boxes. Similarly, the supply chain disruptions caused by COVID-19 created many difficult purchasing decisions for companies.

Source: Liam Pleven and Matt Wirz, "Companies Stock Up as Commodities Prices Rise," *Wall Street Journal Online* (February 3, 2011).

What are the potential downsides of stockpiling a huge amount of raw materials? (Answer is available in the book's product page on www.wiley.com)

DO IT! 2 — Sales, Production, and Direct Materials Budgets

Ramon SpA is preparing its master budget for 2023. Relevant data pertaining to its sales, production, and direct materials budgets are as follows:

Sales. Sales for the year are expected to total 1,200,000 units. Quarterly sales, as a percentage of total sales, are 20%, 25%, 30%, and 25%, respectively. The unit selling price is expected to be €50 for the first three quarters and €55 beginning in the fourth quarter. Sales in the first quarter of 2024 are expected to be 10% higher than the budgeted sales for the first quarter of 2023.

Production. Management desires to maintain the ending finished goods inventories at 25% of the next quarter's budgeted sales volume.

Direct materials. Each unit requires 3 kilograms of raw materials at a cost of €5 per kilogram. Management desires to maintain raw materials inventories at 5% of the next quarter's production requirements. Assume the production requirements for the first quarter of 2024 are 810,000 kilograms.

Prepare the sales, production, and direct materials budgets by quarters for 2023.

ACTION PLAN

- Know the form and content of the sales budget.
- Prepare the sales budget first, as the basis for the other budgets.
- Determine the units that must be produced to meet anticipated sales.
- Know how to compute the beginning and ending finished goods units.
- Determine the materials required to meet production needs.
- Know how to compute the beginning and ending direct materials units.

Solution

Ramon SpA
Sales Budget
For the Year Ending December 31, 2023

	Quarter				
	1	2	3	4	Year
Expected unit sales[a]	240,000	300,000	360,000	300,000	1,200,000
Unit selling price	× €50	× €50	× €50	× €55	
Total sales	**€12,000,000**	**€15,000,000**	**€18,000,000**	**€16,500,000**	**€61,500,000**

[a]Specified quarterly percentage times annual units, e.g., first quarter of .20 × 1,200,000

Ramon SpA
Production Budget
For the Year Ending December 31, 2023

	Quarter				
	1	2	3	4	Year
Expected unit sales	240,000	300,000	360,000	300,000	
Add: Desired ending finished goods units[a]	75,000	90,000	75,000	66,000[b]	
Total required units	315,000	390,000	435,000	366,000	
Less: Beginning finished goods units	60,000[c]	75,000	90,000	75,000	
Required production units	**255,000**	**315,000**	**345,000**	**291,000**	**1,206,000**

[a]25% of next quarter's unit sales
[b]Estimated first-quarter 2024 sales units: 240,000 + (240,000 × .10) = 264,000; 264,000 × .25
[c]25% of estimated first-quarter 2023 sales units (240,000 × .25)

Ramon SpA
Direct Materials Budget
For the Year Ending December 31, 2023

	Quarter 1	Quarter 2	Quarter 3	Quarter 4	Year
Units to be produced	255,000	315,000	345,000	291,000	
Direct materials per unit	× 3	× 3	× 3	× 3	
Total kilograms needed for production	765,000	945,000	1,035,000	873,000	
Add: Desired ending direct materials (kilograms)	47,250	51,750	43,650	40,500[a]	
Total materials required	812,250	996,750	1,078,650	913,500	
Less: Beginning direct materials (kilograms)	38,250[b]	47,250	51,750	43,650	
Direct materials purchases	774,000	949,500	1,026,900	869,850	
Cost per kilogram	× €5	× €5	× €5	× €5	
Total cost of direct materials purchases	**€3,870,000**	**€4,747,500**	**€5,134,500**	**€4,349,250**	**€18,101,250**

[a]Estimated first-quarter 2024 production requirements: 810,000 × .05 = 40,500
[b]5% of estimated first-quarter kilograms needed for production

Related exercise material: **BE9.2, BE9.3, BE9.4, DO IT! 9.2, E9.2, E9.3, E9.4, E9.5, E9.6, E9.7, and E9.8.**

DIRECT LABOR, MANUFACTURING OVERHEAD, AND S&A EXPENSE BUDGETS

LEARNING OBJECTIVE 3
Prepare budgets for direct labor, manufacturing overhead, and selling and administrative expenses, and a budgeted income statement.

As shown in Illustration 9.2, the operating budgets culminate with preparation of the budgeted income statement. Before we can do that, we need to prepare budgets for direct labor, manufacturing overhead, and selling and administrative expenses.

Direct Labor Budget

Like the direct materials budget, the **direct labor budget** contains the quantity (hours) and cost of direct labor necessary to meet production requirements. The total direct labor cost is derived from the equation shown in **Illustration 9.10**.

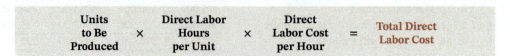

ILLUSTRATION 9.10 | Equation for direct labor cost

Direct labor hours are determined based on the units to be produced as reported in the production budget. For example, in the first quarter, 3,100 units are to be produced. At Adelmo Ciclo, 2 hours of direct labor are required to produce each unit of finished goods. The anticipated hourly wage rate is €10. **Illustration 9.11** employs the equation in Illustration 9.10 using these data.

Adelmo Ciclo
Direct Labor Budget
For the Year Ending December 31, 2023

	Quarter				
	1	2	3	4	Year
Units to be produced (Illustration 9.5)	3,100	3,600	4,100	4,600	
Direct labor time (hours) per unit	× 2	× 2	× 2	× 2	
Total required direct labor hours	6,200	7,200	8,200	9,200	
Direct labor cost per hour	× €10	× €10	× €10	× €10	
Total direct labor cost	**€62,000**	**€72,000**	**€82,000**	**€92,000**	**€308,000**

ILLUSTRATION 9.11 | **Direct labor budget**

- Each of the 3,100 units produced in the first quarter requires 2 hours of labor per unit, for a total of 6,200 hours (3,100 × 2).
- Each hour of labor costs €10, for a total cost of €62,000 (6,200 × €10).

The direct labor budget is critical in maintaining a labor force that can meet the expected levels of production (see **Helpful Hint**). Maintaining steady employment levels benefits employers because it reduces hiring and training costs. A steady employment level also keeps employees' morale high since it reduces their income concerns.

HELPFUL HINT
An important assumption in Illustration 9.11 is that the company can add to and subtract from its work force as needed so that the €10 per hour labor cost applies to a wide range of possible production activity.

Manufacturing Overhead Budget

The **manufacturing overhead budget** shows the expected manufacturing overhead costs for the budget period. As **Illustration 9.12** shows, **this budget distinguishes between variable and fixed overhead costs**.

Adelmo Ciclo
Manufacturing Overhead Budget
For the Year Ending December 31, 2023

	Quarter				
	1	2	3	4	Year
Direct labor hours (Illustration 9.11)	6,200	7,200	8,200	9,200	30,800
Variable costs					
Indirect materials (€1.00/hour)	€ 6,200	€ 7,200	€ 8,200	€ 9,200	€ 30,800
Indirect labor (€1.40/hour)	8,680	10,080	11,480	12,880	43,120
Utilities (€0.40/hour)	2,480	2,880	3,280	3,680	12,320
Maintenance (€0.20/hour)	1,240	1,440	1,640	1,840	6,160
Total variable costs	18,600	21,600	24,600	27,600	92,400
Fixed costs					
Supervisory salaries	20,000	20,000	20,000	20,000	80,000
Depreciation	3,800	3,800	3,800	3,800	15,200
Property taxes and insurance	9,000	9,000	9,000	9,000	36,000
Maintenance	5,700	5,700	5,700	5,700	22,800
Total fixed costs	38,500	38,500	38,500	38,500	154,000
Total manufacturing overhead	**€57,100**	**€60,100**	**€63,100**	**€66,100**	**€246,400**
Manufacturing overhead rate per direct labor hour (€246,400 ÷ 30,800)					**€8**

ILLUSTRATION 9.12 | **Manufacturing overhead budget**

- Adelmo Ciclo expects variable costs to fluctuate with production volume on the basis of the following rates per direct labor hour: indirect materials €1.00, indirect labor €1.40, utilities €0.40, and maintenance €0.20.
- Thus, for the 6,200 direct labor hours needed to produce 3,100 units, budgeted indirect materials are €6,200 (6,200 × €1), and budgeted indirect labor is €8,680 (6,200 × €1.40).
- Adelmo also recognizes that some maintenance is fixed (the amounts reported for fixed costs are assumed for our example).

At Adelmo Ciclo, overhead is applied to production on the basis of direct labor hours. Thus, as Illustration 9.12 shows, the budgeted annual rate is €8 per hour (€246,400 ÷ 30,800). Note that the accuracy of budgeted overhead cost estimates can be greatly improved by employing activity-based costing.

Selling and Administrative Expense Budget

Adelmo Ciclo combines its operating expenses into one budget, the **selling and administrative expense budget**. This budget (**Illustration 9.13**) projects anticipated selling and administrative expenses for the budget period. It also classifies expenses as either variable or fixed.

Adelmo Ciclo
Selling and Administrative Expense Budget
For the Year Ending December 31, 2023

	Quarter				
	1	2	3	4	Year
Budgeted sales in units (Illustration 9.3)	3,000	3,500	4,000	4,500	15,000
Variable expenses					
Sales commissions (€3 per unit)	€ 9,000	€10,500	€12,000	€13,500	€ 45,000
Freight-out (€1 per unit)	3,000	3,500	4,000	4,500	15,000
Total variable expenses	12,000	14,000	16,000	18,000	60,000
Fixed expenses					
Advertising	5,000	5,000	5,000	5,000	20,000
Sales salaries	15,000	15,000	15,000	15,000	60,000
Office salaries	7,500	7,500	7,500	7,500	30,000
Depreciation	1,000	1,000	1,000	1,000	4,000
Property taxes and insurance	1,500	1,500	1,500	1,500	6,000
Total fixed expenses	30,000	30,000	30,000	30,000	120,000
Total selling and administrative expenses	€42,000	€44,000	€46,000	€48,000	€180,000

ILLUSTRATION 9.13 | Selling and administrative expense budget

- In this case, the variable expense rates per unit of sales are sales commissions €3 and freight-out €1.
- Variable expenses per quarter are based on the unit sales from the sales budget (see Illustration 9.3).

Adelmo expects sales in the first quarter to be 3,000 units. Sales commissions expense is therefore €9,000 (3,000 × €3), and freight-out is €3,000 (3,000 × €1) (fixed expenses are based on assumed data).

Budgeted Income Statement

The **budgeted income statement** is the important end-product of the operating budgets.

- This budget indicates the expected profitability of operations for the budget period.
- The budgeted income statement provides the basis for evaluating company performance.

Budgeted income statements often act as a call to action. For example, a board member at **XM Satellite Radio** (USA) felt that budgeted costs were too high relative to budgeted revenues. When management refused to cut its marketing and programming costs, the board member resigned. He felt that without the cuts, the company risked financial crisis.

As you would expect, the budgeted income statement is prepared from the various operating budgets. For example, to find the cost of goods sold, Adelmo Ciclo must first determine the total unit cost of producing one Rightride bicycle seat, as shown in **Illustration 9.14**.

Cost Component	Illustration	Quantity	Unit Cost	Total
Direct materials	9.9	2 kilograms	€ 4.00	€ 8.00
Direct labor	9.11	2 hours	€10.00	20.00
Manufacturing overhead	9.12	2 hours	€ 8.00	16.00
Total unit cost				**€44.00**

Cost of One Rightride

ILLUSTRATION 9.14 | **Computation of total unit cost**

Adelmo then determines cost of goods sold by multiplying the units sold by the unit cost. Its budgeted cost of goods sold is €660,000 (15,000 × €44). All data for the income statement come from the individual operating budgets except the following: (1) interest expense is expected to be €100, and (2) income taxes are estimated to be €12,000. **Illustration 9.15** shows the budgeted multiple-step income statement.

Adelmo Ciclo
Budgeted Income Statement
For the Year Ending December 31, 2023

Sales (Illustration 9.3)	€900,000
Cost of goods sold (15,000 × €44)	660,000
Gross profit	240,000
Selling and administrative expenses (Illustration 9.13)	180,000
Income from operations	60,000
Interest expense	100
Income before income taxes	59,900
Income tax expense	12,000
Net income	€ 47,900

ILLUSTRATION 9.15 | **Budgeted multiple-step income statement**

DATA ANALYTICS INSIGHT | Dickey's Barbecue Pit

mphillips007/Getty Images

That's Some Tasty Data!

What could be better than big data covered in luscious barbecue sauce? Consider Dickey's Barbecue Pit (USA), which operates more than 500 restaurants in the United States. The company employs a sophisticated data collection and analysis system that helps it to choose the best menu options to meet customer tastes in specific locations, create budgets, and make rapid adjustments on a daily basis so that individual restaurants as well as the company as a whole can hit budgeted targets. If the data indicate that results at a specific restaurant are subpar, the company can quickly implement training or operational support, tailored to the particular aspects of operations that need to change, to get that location back on track.

Further, if sales at a specific restaurant have been low and inventory is accumulating, the system can text known customers in that restaurant's area with promotions that will spur sales until inventory returns to desired levels. Of particular importance is that the system's dashboard is easily understood and used by employees at all levels of the company. This creates a more participative environment where employees feel like they are contributing to the success of the company.

Source: Bernard Marr, *Big Data in Practice* (Hoboken, N.J.: John Wiley and Sons, 2016), pp. 175–180.

Why are flexibility and ease of use important to this application of big data and data analytics? (Answer is available in the book's product page on www.wiley.com)

DO IT! 3 ▶ Budgeted Income Statement

Ramon SpA is preparing its budgeted income statement for 2023. Relevant data pertaining to its sales, production, and direct materials budgets can be found in **DO IT! 2**.

In addition, Ramon budgets 0.5 hours of direct labor per unit, labor costs at €15 per hour, and manufacturing overhead at €25 per direct labor hour. Its budgeted selling and administrative expenses for 2023 are €12,000,000.

a. Calculate the budgeted total unit cost.

b. Prepare the budgeted multiple-step income statement for 2023. (Ignore income taxes.)

ACTION PLAN
- Recall that total unit cost consists of direct materials, direct labor, and manufacturing overhead.
- Recall that direct materials costs are included in the direct materials budget.
- Know the form and content of the income statement.
- Use the total unit sales information from the sales budget to compute annual sales and cost of goods sold.

Solution

a.

Cost Component	Quantity	Unit Cost	Total
Direct materials	3.0 kilograms	€ 5	€15.00
Direct labor	0.5 hours	15	7.50
Manufacturing overhead	0.5 hours	25	12.50
Total unit cost			**€35.00**

b.

Ramon SpA
Budgeted Income Statement
For the Year Ending December 31, 2023

Sales (1,200,000 units from sales budget)	€61,500,000
Cost of goods sold (1,200,000 × €35.00/unit)	42,000,000
Gross profit	19,500,000
Selling and administrative expenses	12,000,000
Net income	€ 7,500,000

Related exercise material: **BE9.8, DO IT! 9.3, E9.11, and E9.13**.

CASH BUDGET AND BUDGETED BALANCE SHEET

As shown in Illustration 9.2, the financial budgets consist of the capital expenditure budget, the cash budget, and the budgeted balance sheet. We will discuss the capital expenditure budget in Chapter 12.

LEARNING OBJECTIVE 4
Prepare a cash budget and a budgeted balance sheet.

Cash Budget

The **cash budget** shows anticipated cash flows.

- Because cash is so vital, this budget is often considered to be the most important financial budget (see **Decision Tools**).
- The cash budget contains three sections (cash receipts, cash disbursements, and financing) and the beginning and ending cash balances, as shown in **Illustration 9.16** (see **Helpful Hint**).
  1. The **cash receipts section** includes expected receipts from the company's principal source(s) of revenue. These are usually cash sales and collections from customers on credit sales. This section also shows anticipated receipts of interest and dividends, and proceeds from planned sales of investments, plant assets, and the company's capital stock.

DECISION TOOLS

Managers use the cash budget to determine if the company needs to borrow funds in the coming period.

HELPFUL HINT

The cash budget is prepared after the other budgets because the information generated by the other budgets dictates the expected inflows and outflows of cash.

Any Company Cash Budget	
	B
Any Company **Cash Budget**	
Beginning cash balance	€X,XXX
Add: Cash receipts (itemized)	X,XXX
Total available cash	X,XXX
Less: Cash disbursements (itemized)	X,XXX
Excess (deficiency) of available cash over cash disbursements	X,XXX
Financing	X,XXX
Ending cash balance	€X,XXX

ILLUSTRATION 9.16 | Basic form of a cash budget

  2. The **cash disbursements section** shows expected cash payments. Such payments include direct materials, direct labor, manufacturing overhead, and selling and administrative expenses. This section also includes projected payments for income taxes, dividends, investments, and plant assets.
  3. The **financing section** shows expected borrowings and the repayment of the borrowed funds plus interest. Companies need this section when there is a cash deficiency or when the cash balance is below management's minimum required balance.

Data in the cash budget are prepared in sequence. The ending cash balance of one period becomes the beginning cash balance for the next period. Companies obtain data for preparing the cash budget from other budgets and from information provided by management. In practice, cash budgets are often prepared for the year on a monthly basis.

To minimize detail, we assume that Adelmo Ciclo prepares an annual cash budget by quarters. To prepare the cash budget, it is useful to prepare a schedule for collections from customers. This schedule is based on the following assumption:

Sales (Illustration 9.3): 60% are collected in the quarter sold and 40% are collected in the following quarter. Accounts receivable of €60,000 at December 31, 2022, are expected to be collected in full in the first quarter of 2023.

The schedule of cash collections from customers in **Illustration 9.17** applies this assumption.

- In the first quarter, Adelmo collects the €60,000 that was outstanding at the beginning of the quarter, as well as an additional €108,000 (.60 × €180,000), which is 60% of the first-quarter sales of €180,000.
- Total receipts in the first quarter are €168,000 (€60,000 + €108,000).
- In the second quarter, the company collects the remaining 40% of first-quarter sales of €72,000 (.40 × €180,000) as well as €126,000 (.60 × €210,000), which is 60% of second-quarter sales of €210,000.
- Second-quarter receipts are €198,000 (€72,000 + €126,000).

Next, it is useful to prepare a schedule of expected cash payments for direct materials, based on this second assumption:

Direct materials (Illustration 9.9): 50% are paid in the quarter purchased and 50% are paid in the following quarter. Accounts payable of €10,600 at December 31, 2022, are expected to be paid in full in the first quarter of 2023.

Adelmo Ciclo
Schedule of Expected Collections from Customers
For the Year Ending December 31, 2023

	Sales[a]	Collections by Quarter			
		1	2	3	4
Accounts receivable, 12/31/22		€ 60,000			
First quarter	€180,000	108,000[b]	€ 72,000[c]		
Second quarter	210,000		126,000	€ 84,000	
Third quarter	240,000			144,000	€ 96,000
Fourth quarter	270,000				162,000
Total collections		€168,000	€198,000	€228,000	€258,000

[a]Per Illustration 9.3; [b]€180,000 × .60; [c]€180,000 × .40

ILLUSTRATION 9.17 | **Collections from customers**

The schedule of cash payments for direct materials in **Illustration 9.18** applies this second assumption.

- In the first quarter, Adelmo pays the balance of its beginning accounts payable balance of €10,600 as well as pays €12,600, which is 50% of its first-quarter purchases of €25,200.

Adelmo Ciclo
Schedule of Expected Payments for Direct Materials
For the Year Ending December 31, 2023

	Purchases[a]	Payments by Quarter			
		1	2	3	4
Accounts payable, 12/31/22		€10,600			
First quarter	€25,200	12,600[b]	€12,600[c]		
Second quarter	29,200		14,600	€14,600	
Third quarter	33,200			16,600	€16,600
Fourth quarter	37,200				18,600
Total payments		€23,200	€27,200	€31,200	€35,200

[a]Per Illustration 9.9; [b]€25,200 × .50; [c]€25,200 × .50

ILLUSTRATION 9.18 | Payments for direct materials

- The total payments in the first quarter are €23,200 (€10,600 + €12,600).
- In the second quarter, it pays €12,600 (.50 × €25,200) for the remaining 50% of its first-quarter purchases as well as €14,600 (.50 × €29,200) for 50% of the second-quarter purchases.
- Total payments in the second quarter are €27,200 (€12,600 + €14,600).

The preparation of Adelmo Ciclo's cash budget is based on the following additional assumptions:

1. The January 1, 2023, cash balance is expected to be €38,000. Adelmo wishes to maintain a balance of at least €15,000.
2. Short-term investment securities are expected to be sold for €2,000 cash in the first quarter.
3. Direct labor (Illustration 9.11): 100% is paid in the quarter incurred.
4. Manufacturing overhead (Illustration 9.12) and selling and administrative expenses (Illustration 9.13): All items except depreciation are paid in the quarter incurred.
5. Management plans to purchase a truck in the second quarter for €10,000 cash.
6. Adelmo makes equal quarterly payments of its estimated €12,000 annual income taxes.
7. Loans are repaid in the earliest quarter in which there is sufficient cash (that is, when the cash on hand exceeds the €15,000 minimum required balance).

Illustration 9.19 shows the cash budget for Adelmo Ciclo. The budget indicates that Adelmo will need €3,000 of financing in the second quarter to maintain a minimum cash balance of €15,000. Since there is an excess of available cash over disbursements of €22,500 at the end of the third quarter, the borrowing, plus €100 interest, is repaid in this quarter.

A cash budget contributes to more effective cash management. It shows managers when additional financing is necessary well before the actual need arises. And, it indicates when excess cash is available for investments or other purposes.

9-22 CHAPTER 9 Budgetary Planning

Adelmo Ciclo
Cash Budget
For the Year Ending December 31, 2023

	Quarter			
	1	2	3	4
Beginning cash balance	€ 38,000	€ 25,500	€ 15,000	€ 19,400
Add: Receipts				
Collections from customers	168,000	198,000	228,000	258,000
Sale of investment securities	2,000	0	0	0
Total receipts	170,000	198,000	228,000	258,000
Total available cash	208,000	223,500	243,000	277,400
Less: Disbursements				
Direct materials	23,200	27,200	31,200	35,200
Direct labor	62,000	72,000	82,000	92,000
Manufacturing overhead	53,300[a]	56,300	59,300	62,300
Selling and administrative expenses	41,000[b]	43,000	45,000	47,000
Purchase of truck	0	10,000	0	0
Income tax expense	3,000	3,000	3,000	3,000
Total disbursements	182,500	211,500	220,500	239,500
Excess (deficiency) of available cash over cash disbursements	25,500	12,000	22,500	37,900
Financing				
Add: Borrowings	0	3,000	0	0
Less: Repayments including interest	0	0	3,100	0
Ending cash balance	€ 25,500	€ 15,000	€ 19,400	€ 37,900

[a]€57,100 − €3,800 depreciation; [b]€42,000 − €1,000 depreciation

ILLUSTRATION 9.19 | Cash budget

SERVICE COMPANY INSIGHT — Olympic Games

Marianna Day Massey/ZumaPress/NewsCom

Without a Budget, Can the Games Begin?

Behind the grandeur of the Olympic Games lies a huge financial challenge—how to keep budgeted costs in line with revenues. Tokyo Olympics, which was originally scheduled for 2020, was postponed to 2021 due to the COVID-19 pandemic. As a result, the organizers of the Tokyo Olympics faced several financial challenges. The decision to postpone the Olympics by a year due to the pandemic incurred significant additional costs. As per reports, the budget for the delayed Tokyo Olympics and Paralympics ballooned to ¥1.42 trillion, nearly twice the original estimate. Thus, the delay of the Olympics resulted in additional expenses and led to the draining of the budgets of the organizing committee and the host city.

Since the Japan Government imposed restrictions to mitigate the spread of COVID-19 and the games were held mostly without spectators, this led to a revenue loss to the tune of ¥90 billion ($800 million). We can infer from the above that Olympics costs are notoriously difficult to track, and there is always debate about what are and are not Olympic costs.

Source: Hisashi Tsutsui and Junichiro Sato, "Tokyo Olympics Cost Doubles to $13bn on COVID and Overruns," *NIKKEI Asia* (June 22, 2022).

Why does it matter whether the Olympic Games meet their budget? (The answer is available in the book's product page on www.wiley.com)

Budgeted Balance Sheet

The **budgeted balance sheet** is a projection of financial position at the end of the budget period. This budget is developed from the budgeted balance sheet for the preceding year and the budgets for the current year. For Adelmo Ciclo, pertinent data from the budgeted balance sheet at December 31, 2022, are as follows:

Buildings and equipment	€182,000	Common stock	€225,000
Accumulated depreciation	28,800	Retained earnings	46,480

Illustration 9.20 shows Adelmo Ciclo's budgeted classified balance sheet at December 31, 2023.

Adelmo Ciclo
Budgeted Balance Sheet
December 31, 2023

Assets

Current assets		
Cash		€ 37,900
Accounts receivable		108,000
Finished goods inventory		44,000
Raw materials inventory		4,080
Total current assets		193,980
Property, plant, and equipment		
Buildings and equipment	€192,000	
Less: Accumulated depreciation	48,000	144,000
Total assets		€337,980

Liabilities and Stockholders' Equity

Liabilities		
Accounts payable		€ 18,600
Stockholders' equity		
Common stock	€225,000	
Retained earnings	94,380	
Total stockholders' equity		319,380
Total liabilities and stockholders' equity		€337,980

ILLUSTRATION 9.20 | **Budgeted classified balance sheet**

The computations and sources of the amounts are explained as follows:

- **Cash:** Ending cash balance €37,900, shown in the cash budget (Illustration 9.19).
- **Accounts receivable:** 40% of fourth-quarter sales €270,000, shown in the schedule of expected collections from customers (Illustration 9.17).
- **Finished goods inventory:** Desired ending inventory 1,000 units, shown in the production budget (Illustration 9.5) times the total unit cost €44 (shown in Illustration 9.14).
- **Raw materials inventory:** Desired ending inventory 1,020 kilograms, times the cost per kilogram €4, shown in the direct materials budget (Illustration 9.9).
- **Buildings and equipment:** December 31, 2022, balance €182,000, plus purchase of truck for €10,000 (Illustration 9.19).
- **Accumulated depreciation:** December 31, 2022, balance €28,800, plus €15,200 depreciation shown in manufacturing overhead budget (Illustration 9.12) and €4,000 depreciation shown in selling and administrative expense budget (Illustration 9.13).
- **Accounts payable:** 50% of fourth-quarter purchases €37,200, shown in schedule of expected payments for direct materials (Illustration 9.18).
- **Common stock:** Unchanged from the beginning of the year.
- **Retained earnings:** December 31, 2022, balance €46,480, plus net income €47,900, shown in budgeted income statement (Illustration 9.15).

After budget data are entered into the computer, Adelmo prepares the various budgets (sales, cash, etc.), as well as the budgeted financial statements. Using spreadsheets, management can also perform "what if" (sensitivity) analyses based on different hypothetical assumptions. For example, suppose that sales managers project that sales will be 10% higher in the coming quarter. What impact does this change have on the rest of the budgeting process and the financing needs of the business? The impact of the various assumptions on the budget is quickly determined by the spreadsheet. Armed with these analyses, managers make more informed decisions about the impact of various projects. They also anticipate future problems and business opportunities. As seen in this chapter, budgeting is an excellent use of computer spreadsheets.

DO IT! 4 ▶ Cash Budget

Harlyn SA management wants to maintain a minimum monthly cash balance of €15,000. At the beginning of March, the cash balance is €16,500, expected cash receipts for March are €210,000, and cash disbursements are expected to be €220,000. How much cash, if any, must be borrowed to maintain the desired minimum monthly balance?

Solution

Harlyn SA
Cash Budget
For the Month Ending March 31, 2023

	B
Beginning cash balance	€ 16,500
Add: Cash receipts for March	210,000
Total available cash	226,500
Less: Cash disbursements for March	220,000
Excess (deficiency) of available cash over cash disbursements	6,500
Financing	8,500
Ending cash balance	**€ 15,000**

To maintain the desired minimum cash balance of €15,000, Harlyn SA must borrow €8,500 of cash.

Related exercise material: **BE9.9, DO IT! 9.4, E9.14, E9.15, and E9.16.**

ACTION PLAN
- Write down the basic form of the cash budget, starting with the beginning cash balance, adding cash receipts for the period, deducting cash disbursements, and identifying the needed financing to achieve the desired minimum ending cash balance.
- Insert the data given into the outlined form of the cash budget.

BUDGETING IN NONMANUFACTURING COMPANIES

LEARNING OBJECTIVE 5
Apply budgeting principles to nonmanufacturing companies.

Budgeting is not limited to manufacturers. Budgets are also used by merchandisers, service companies, and not-for-profit organizations.

Merchandisers

As in manufacturing operations, the sales budget for a merchandiser is both the starting point and the key factor in the development of the master budget. The major differences between the master budgets of a merchandiser and a manufacturer are as follows:

1. A merchandiser **uses a merchandise purchases budget instead of a production budget**.
2. A merchandiser **does not use the manufacturing budgets (direct materials, direct labor, and manufacturing overhead)**.

The **merchandise purchases budget** shows the estimated cost of goods to be purchased to meet expected sales. The equation for determining budgeted merchandise purchases is as shown in **Illustration 9.21.**

| Budgeted Cost of Goods Sold | + | Desired Ending Merchandise Inventory | − | Beginning Merchandise Inventory | = | Required Merchandise Purchases |

ILLUSTRATION 9.21 | **Merchandise purchases equation**

To illustrate, assume that the budget committee of Lima Fashions is preparing the merchandise purchases budget for July 2023. It estimates that budgeted sales will be €300,000 in July and €320,000 in August. Cost of goods sold is expected to be 70% of sales—that is, €210,000 in July (.70 × €300,000) and €224,000 in August (.70 × €320,000). The company's desired ending inventory is 30% of the following month's cost of goods sold. Required merchandise purchases for July are €214,200, computed as shown in **Illustration 9.22**.

Lima Fashions
Merchandise Purchases Budget
For the Month Ending July 31, 2023

Budgeted cost of goods sold (€300,000 × .70)	€210,000
Add: Desired ending merchandise inventory (€224,000 × .30)	67,200
Total	277,200
Less: Beginning merchandise inventory (€210,000 × .30)	63,000
Required merchandise purchases for July	**€214,200**

ILLUSTRATION 9.22 | **Merchandise purchases budget**

When a merchandiser is departmentalized, it prepares separate budgets for each department (see infographic).

- For example, a grocery store prepares sales budgets and purchases budgets for each of its major departments, such as meats, dairy, and produce.
- The store then combines these budgets into a master budget for the store.

When a retailer has branch stores, it prepares a separate master budget for each store. Then, it incorporates these budgets into master budgets for the company as a whole.

Service Companies

In a service company, such as a public accounting firm, a law office, or a medical practice, the critical factor in budgeting is **coordinating professional staff needs with anticipated services**.

- If a firm is overstaffed, labor costs may be disproportionately high, profits may be lower because of the additional salaries, and staff turnover sometimes increases because of lack of challenging work.
- If a service company is understaffed, it may lose revenue because existing and prospective client needs for service cannot be met, and professional staff may seek other jobs because of excessive workloads.

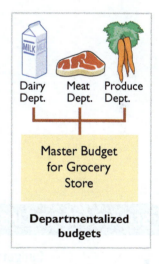

Departmentalized budgets

Suppose that Boris Lawn and Plowing Service estimates that it will service 300 small lawns, 200 medium lawns, and 100 large lawns during the month of July. It estimates its direct labor needs as 1 hour per small lawn, 1.75 hours for a medium lawn, and 2.75 hours for a large lawn. Its average cost for direct labor is €15 per hour. Boris prepares a direct labor budget as shown in **Illustration 9.23**.

Service companies can obtain budget data for service revenue from **expected output** or **expected input**.

- When output is used, it is necessary to determine the expected billings of clients for services performed. In a public accounting firm, for example, output is the sum of its billings in auditing, tax, and consulting services.

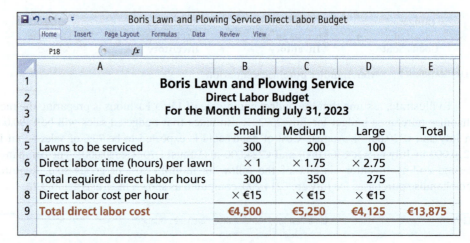

ILLUSTRATION 9.23 | **Direct labor budget for service company**

- When input data are used, each professional staff member projects his or her billable time. The firm then applies billing rates to billable time to produce expected service revenue.

Not-for-Profit Organizations

Budgeting is just as important for not-for-profit organizations as for profit-oriented businesses. The budget process, however, is different. In most cases, not-for-profit entities budget **on the basis of cash flows (expenditures and receipts), rather than on a revenue and expense basis**.

- The starting point in the process is usually expenditures, not receipts. Management's task generally is to find the receipts needed to support the planned expenditures.

- The activity index is also likely to be significantly different. For example, in a not-for-profit entity, such as a university, budgeted faculty positions may be based on full-time equivalent students or credit hours expected to be taught in a department.

For some governmental units, voters approve the budget. In other cases, such as state governments and the federal government, legislative approval is required. After the budget is adopted, it must be followed. Overspending is often illegal. In governmental budgets, authorizations tend to be on a line-by-line basis. That is, the budget for a municipality may have a specified authorization for police and fire protection, garbage collection, street paving, and so on. The line-item authorization of governmental budgets significantly limits the amount of discretion management can exercise. The city manager often cannot use savings from one line item, such as street paving, to cover increased spending in another line item, such as snow removal.

SERVICE COMPANY INSIGHT   Museum of Contemporary Art

ZUMA Press, Inc./ Alamy Stock Photo

Budget Shortfalls as Far as the Eye Can See

All organizations need to stick to budgets. The **Museum of Contemporary Art** (USA) in Los Angeles learned this the hard way. Over a 10-year period, its endowment shrunk from $50 million to $6 million as its newly hired director strove to build the museum's reputation through spending. The director consistently ran budget deficits, which eventually threatened the museum's survival.

The most recent recession created budgeting challenges for nearly all governmental agencies. Tax revenues dropped rapidly as earnings declined and unemployment skyrocketed. At the same time, sources of debt financing dried up. Even **Princeton University** (USA), with the largest endowment per student of any U.S. university ($2 million per student), experienced a 25% drop in the value of its endowment when the financial markets plunged. Because the endowment supports 45% of the university's $1.25 billion budget, when the endowment fell the university had to make cuts. Many raises were capped at $2,000, administrative budgets were cut by 5%, and major construction projects were put on hold.

Sources: Edward Wyatt and Jori Finkel, "Soaring in Art, Museum Trips Over Finances," *Wall Street Journal Online* (December 4, 2008); Stu Woo, "California's Plans to Close Gap Become More Drastic," *Wall Street Journal Online* (January 8, 2009); and John Hechinger, "Princeton Cuts Budget as Endowment Slides," *Wall Street Journal Online* (January 9, 2009).

Why would a university's budgeted scholarships probably fall when the stock market suffers a serious drop? (Answer is available in the book's product page on www.wiley.com)

DO IT! 5 ▶ Merchandise Purchases Budget

Beckett Market estimates that 2023 sales will be €15,000 in quarter 1, €20,000 in quarter 2, and €25,000 in quarter 3. Cost of goods sold is 80% of sales. Management desires to have ending finished goods inventory equal to 15% of the next quarter's expected cost of goods sold. Prepare a merchandise purchases budget by quarter for the first six months of 2023.

ACTION PLAN
- Begin with budgeted cost of goods sold.
- Add desired ending merchandise inventory.
- Subtract beginning merchandise inventory.

Solution

Beckett Market
Merchandise Purchases Budget
For the Six Months Ending June 30, 2023

	Quarter 1	Quarter 2	Six Months
Budgeted cost of goods sold (sales × .80)	€12,000	€16,000	
Add: Desired ending merchandise inventory (15% of next quarter's cost of goods sold)	2,400	3,000	
Total	14,400	19,000	
Less: Beginning merchandise inventory (15% this quarter's cost of goods sold)	1,800	2,400	
Required merchandise purchases	€12,600	€16,600	€29,200

Related exercise material: **BE9.10, DO IT! 9.5, E9.19, E9.20, and E9.21.**

USING THE DECISION TOOLS | Erin McKenna's Bakery NYC

As discussed in the Feature Story, **Erin McKenna's Bakery NYC** (USA) relies on budgeting to aid in the management of its cupcake operations. Assume that the company prepares monthly cash budgets. Relevant data from assumed operating budgets for 2023 are as follows:

	January	February
Sales	$460,000	$412,000
Direct materials purchases	185,000	210,000
Direct labor	70,000	85,000
Manufacturing overhead	50,000	65,000
Selling and administrative expenses	85,000	95,000

Assume that Erin McKenna's Bakery sells its cupcakes in its own shops as well as to other stores. Collections are expected to be 75% in the month of sale, and 25% in the month following sale. The company pays 60% of direct materials purchases in cash in the month of purchase, and the balance due in the month following the purchase. All other items above are paid in the month incurred. (Depreciation has been excluded from manufacturing overhead and selling and administrative expenses.)

Other data:

1. Sales: December 2022, $320,000
2. Purchases of direct materials: December 2022, $175,000
3. Other receipts: January—Sale of used equipment, $2,000
   February—Sale of used equipment, $4,000

4. Other disbursements: February—Purchased equipment, $10,000
5. Repaid debt: January, $30,000

The company's cash balance on January 1, 2023, is expected to be $50,000. The company wants to maintain a minimum cash balance of $45,000.

Instructions

a. Prepare schedules for (1) expected collections from customers and (2) expected payments for direct materials purchases for January and February.

b. Prepare a cash budget for January and February in columnar form.

Solution

a. 1.

Expected Collections from Customers

	Sales	January	February
December	$320,000	$ 80,000	$ 0
January	460,000	345,000	115,000
February	412,000	0	309,000
Totals		$425,000	$424,000

2.

Expected Payments for Direct Materials

	Purchases	January	February
December	$175,000	$ 70,000	$ 0
January	185,000	111,000	74,000
February	210,000	0	126,000
Totals		$181,000	$200,000

b.

Erin McKenna's Bakery NYC
Cash Budget
For the Two Months Ending February 28, 2023

	January	February
Beginning cash balance	$ 50,000	$ 61,000
Add: Receipts		
Collections from customers	425,000	424,000
Sale of used equipment	2,000	0
Sale of used equipment	0	4,000
Total receipts	427,000	428,000
Total available cash	477,000	489,000
Less: Disbursements		
Direct materials	181,000	200,000
Direct labor	70,000	85,000
Manufacturing overhead	50,000	65,000
Selling and administrative expenses	85,000	95,000
Purchase of equipment	0	10,000
Total disbursements	386,000	455,000
Excess (deficiency) of available cash over cash disbursements	91,000	34,000
Financing		
Add: Borrowings	0	11,000
Less: Repayments	30,000	0
Ending cash balance	$ 61,000	$ 45,000

REVIEW AND PRACTICE

Learning Objectives Review

LO 1 State the essentials of effective budgeting and the components of the master budget.

The primary benefits of budgeting are that it (a) requires management to plan ahead, (b) provides definite objectives for evaluating performance, (c) creates an early warning system for potential problems, (d) facilitates coordination of activities, (e) results in greater management awareness, and (f) motivates personnel to meet planned objectives. The essentials of effective budgeting are (a) sound organizational structure, (b) research and analysis, and (c) acceptance by all levels of management.

The master budget consists of the following budgets: (a) sales, (b) production, (c) direct materials, (d) direct labor, (e) manufacturing overhead, (f) selling and administrative expense, (g) budgeted income statement, (h) capital expenditure budget, (i) cash budget, and (j) budgeted balance sheet.

LO 2 Prepare budgets for sales, production, and direct materials.

The sales budget is derived from sales forecasts. The production budget starts with budgeted sales units, adds desired ending finished goods inventory, and subtracts beginning finished goods inventory to arrive at the required number of units to be produced. The direct materials budget starts with the direct materials units (e.g., kilograms) required for budgeted production, adds desired ending direct materials units, and subtracts beginning direct materials units to arrive at required direct materials units to be purchased. This amount is multiplied by the direct materials cost (e.g., cost per kilogram) to arrive at the total cost of direct materials purchases.

LO 3 Prepare budgets for direct labor, manufacturing overhead, and selling and administrative expenses, and a budgeted income statement.

The direct labor budget starts with the units to be produced as determined in the production budget. This amount is multiplied by the direct labor hours per unit and the direct labor cost per hour to arrive at the total direct labor cost. The manufacturing overhead budget lists all of the individual types of overhead costs, distinguishing between fixed and variable costs. The selling and administrative expense budget lists all of the individual types of selling and administrative expense items, distinguishing between fixed and variable costs. The budgeted income statement is prepared from the various operating budgets. Cost of goods sold is determined by calculating the budgeted cost to produce one unit, then multiplying this amount by the number of units sold.

LO 4 Prepare a cash budget and a budgeted balance sheet.

The cash budget has three sections (receipts, disbursements, and financing) and the beginning and ending cash balances. Receipts and payments sections are determined after preparing separate schedules for collections from customers and payments to suppliers. The budgeted balance sheet is developed from the budgeted balance sheet from the preceding year and the various budgets for the current year.

LO 5 Apply budgeting principles to nonmanufacturing companies.

Budgeting may be used by merchandisers for development of a merchandise purchases budget. In service companies, budgeting is a critical factor in coordinating staff needs with anticipated services. In not-for-profit organizations, the starting point in budgeting is usually expenditures, not receipts.

Decision Tools Review

Decision Checkpoints	Info Needed for Decision	Tool to Use for Decision	How to Evaluate Results
Has the company met its targets for sales, production expenses, selling and administrative expenses, and net income?	Sales forecasts, inventory levels, projected materials, labor, overhead, and selling and administrative requirements	Master budget—a set of interrelated budgets including sales, production, materials, labor, overhead, and selling and administrative expense budgets	Results are favorable if revenues exceed budgeted amounts, or if expenses are less than budgeted amounts.
Is the company going to need to borrow funds in the coming period?	Beginning cash balance, cash receipts, cash disbursements, and desired ending cash balance	Cash budget	The company will need to borrow money if the cash budget indicates a projected cash deficiency.

Glossary Review

Budget A formal written statement of management's plans for a specified future time period, expressed in financial terms. (p. 9-3).

Budgetary slack The amount by which a manager intentionally underestimates budgeted revenues or overestimates budgeted expenses in order to make it easier to achieve budgetary goals. (p. 9-6).

Budget committee A group responsible for coordinating the preparation of the budget. (p. 9-5).

Budgeted balance sheet A projection of financial position at the end of the budget period. (p. 9-22).

Budgeted income statement An estimate of the expected profitability of operations for the budget period. (p. 9-17).

Cash budget A projection of anticipated cash flows. (p. 9-19).

Direct labor budget A projection of the quantity and cost of direct labor necessary to meet production requirements. (p. 9-14).

Direct materials budget An estimate of the quantity and cost of direct materials to be purchased. (p. 9-11).

Financial budgets Individual budgets that focus primarily on the cash resources needed to fund expected operations and planned capital expenditures. (p. 9-7).

Long-range planning A formalized process of identifying long-term goals, selecting strategies to achieve those goals, and developing policies and plans to implement the strategies. (p. 9-6).

Manufacturing overhead budget An estimate of expected manufacturing overhead costs for the budget period. (p. 9-15).

Master budget A set of interrelated budgets that constitutes a plan of action for a specific time period. (p. 9-7).

Merchandise purchases budget The estimated cost of goods to be purchased by a merchandiser to meet expected sales. (p. 9-24).

Operating budgets Individual budgets that result in a budgeted income statement. (p. 9-7).

Participative budgeting A budgetary approach that starts with input from lower-level managers and works upward so that managers at all levels participate. (p. 9-5).

Production budget A projection of the units that must be produced to meet anticipated sales. (p. 9-10).

Sales budget An estimate of expected sales revenue for the budget period. (p. 9-8).

Sales forecast The projection of potential sales for the industry and the company's expected share of such sales. (p. 9-5).

Selling and administrative expense budget A projection of anticipated selling and administrative expenses for the budget period. (p. 9-16).

Practice Multiple-Choice Questions

1. **(LO 1)** Which of the following is **not** a benefit of budgeting?
   a. Management can plan ahead.
   b. An early warning system is provided for potential problems.
   c. It enables disciplinary action to be taken at every level of responsibility.
   d. The coordination of activities is facilitated.

2. **(LO 1)** A budget:
   a. is the responsibility of management accountants.
   b. is the primary method of communicating agreed-upon objectives throughout an organization.
   c. ignores past performance because it represents management's plans for a future time period.
   d. may promote efficiency but has no role in evaluating performance.

3. **(LO 1)** The essentials of effective budgeting do **not** include:
   a. top-down budgeting.
   b. management acceptance.
   c. research and analysis.
   d. sound organizational structure.

4. **(LO 1)** Compared to budgeting, long-range planning generally has the:
   a. same amount of detail.
   b. longer time period.
   c. same emphasis.
   d. same time period.

5. **(LO 2)** A sales budget is:
   a. derived from the production budget.
   b. management's best estimate of sales revenue for the year.
   c. not the starting point for the master budget.
   d. prepared only for credit sales.

6. **(LO 2)** The equation for the production budget is budgeted sales in units plus:
   a. desired ending merchandise inventory less beginning merchandise inventory.
   b. beginning finished goods units less desired ending finished goods units.
   c. desired ending direct materials units less beginning direct materials units.
   d. desired ending finished goods units less beginning finished goods units.

7. **(LO 2)** Direct materials inventories are kept in kilograms in Bautista Company, and the total kilograms of direct materials needed for production is 9,500. If the beginning inventory is 1,000 kilograms and the desired ending inventory is 2,200 kilograms, the total number of kilograms to be purchased is:
   a. 9,400.
   b. 9,500.
   c. 9,700.
   d. 10,700.

8. **(LO 3)** The equation for computing the direct labor budget is to multiply the direct labor cost per hour by the:
   a. total required direct labor hours.
   b. physical units to be produced.
   c. equivalent units to be produced.
   d. No correct answer is given.

9. **(LO 3)** Each of the following budgets is used in preparing the budgeted income statement **except** the:
   a. sales budget.
   b. selling and administrative expense budget.
   c. capital expenditure budget.
   d. direct labor budget.

10. **(LO 3)** The budgeted income statement is:
    a. the end-product of the operating budgets.
    b. the end-product of the financial budgets.
    c. the starting point of the master budget.
    d. dependent on cash receipts and cash disbursements.

11. **(LO 4)** The budgeted balance sheet is:
    a. developed from the budgeted balance sheet for the preceding year and the budgets for the current year.
    b. the last operating budget prepared.
    c. used to prepare the cash budget.
    d. All of the answer choices are correct.

12. **(LO 4)** The format of a cash budget is:
    a. Beginning cash balance + Cash receipts + Cash from financing − Cash disbursements = Ending cash balance.
    b. Beginning cash balance + Cash receipts − Cash disbursements +/− Financing = Ending cash balance.
    c. Beginning cash balance + Net income − Cash dividends = Ending cash balance.
    d. Beginning cash balance + Cash revenues − Cash expenses = Ending cash balance.

13. **(LO 4)** Expected direct materials purchases in Paul SA are €70,000 in the first quarter and €90,000 in the second quarter. Forty percent of the purchases are paid in cash as incurred, and the balance is paid in the following quarter. The budgeted cash payments for purchases in the second quarter are:

   a. €96,000.   c. €78,000.
   b. €90,000.   d. €72,000.

14. **(LO 5)** The budget for a merchandiser differs from a budget for a manufacturer because:
   a. a merchandise purchases budget replaces the production budget, and the other manufacturing budgets are not used.
   b. the manufacturing budgets are not applicable, except the production budget is still used.
   c. a merchandise purchases budget replaces the production budget (and the other manufacturing budgets are not used), and the manufacturing budgets are not applicable (except the production budget is still used).
   d. None of the answer choices is correct.

15. **(LO 5)** In most cases, not-for-profit entities:
   a. prepare budgets using the same steps as those used by profit-oriented businesses.
   b. know budgeted cash receipts at the beginning of a time period, so they budget only for expenditures.
   c. begin the budgeting process by budgeting expenditures rather than receipts.
   d. can ignore budgets because they are not expected to generate net income.

Solutions

1. **c.** Budgeting does not necessarily enable disciplinary action to be taken at every level of responsibility. The other choices are all benefits of budgeting.

2. **b.** A budget is the primary method of communicating agreed-upon objectives throughout an organization. The other choices are incorrect because (a) a budget is the responsibility of all levels of management, not management accountants; (c) past performance is not ignored in the budgeting process but instead is the starting point from which future budget goals are formulated; and (d) the budget not only may promote efficiency but is an important tool for evaluating performance.

3. **a.** Top-down budgeting is not one of the essentials of effective budgeting. The other choices are true statements.

4. **b.** Long-range planning generally encompasses a period of at least five years whereas budgeting usually covers a period of one year. The other choices are incorrect because budgeting and long-range planning (a) do not have the same amount of detail, (c) do not have the same emphasis, and (d) do not cover the same time period.

5. **b.** A sales budget is management's best estimate of sales revenue for the year. The other choices are incorrect because a sales budget (a) is the first budget prepared and is the one budget that is not derived from any other budget, (c) is the starting point for the master budget, and (d) is prepared for both cash and credit sales.

6. **d.** The equation for the production budget is budgeted sales in units plus desired ending finished goods units less beginning finished goods units. The other choices are therefore incorrect.

7. **d.** Kilograms to be purchased = Amount needed for production (9,500) + Desired ending inventory (2,200) − Beginning inventory (1,000) = 10,700, not (a) 9,400, (b) 9,500, or (c) 9,700.

8. **a.** Direct labor cost = Direct labor cost per hour × Total required direct labor hours. The other choices are therefore incorrect.

9. **c.** The capital expenditure budget is not used in preparing the budgeted income statement. The other choices are true statements.

10. **a.** The budgeted income statement is the end-product of the operating budgets, not (b) the end-product of the financial budgets, (c) the starting point of the master budget, or (d) dependent on cash receipts and cash disbursements.

11. **a.** The budgeted balance sheet is developed from the budgeted balance sheet for the preceding year and the budgets for the current year. The other choices are therefore incorrect.

12. **b.** The format of a cash budget is Beginning cash balance + Cash receipts − Cash disbursements +/− Financing = Ending cash balance. The other choices are therefore incorrect.

13. **c.** Budgeted cash payments for the second quarter = Purchases for the first quarter (€42,000; €70,000 × .60) + 40% of the purchases for the second quarter (€36,000; €90,000 × .40) = €78,000, not (a) €96,000, (b) €90,000, or (d) €72,000.

14. **a.** The budget for a merchandiser uses a merchandise purchases budget in place of a production budget, and the other manufacturing budgets are not used. It is true the manufacturing budgets are not applicable for a merchandiser, but it is not true the production budget is still used, so choice (b) is not correct.

15. **c.** In most cases, not-for-profit entities begin the budgeting process by budgeting expenditures rather than receipts. The other choices are incorrect because in most cases not-for-profit entities (a) prepare budgets using different, not the same, steps as those used by profit-oriented enterprises; (b) budget for both expenditures and receipts; and (d) cannot ignore budgets.

Practice Exercises

Prepare production and direct materials budgets by quarter for six months.

1. **(LO 2)** On January 1, 2023, the Colton plc budget committee has reached agreement on the following data for the six months ending June 30, 2023.

   Sales units: First quarter 5,000; second quarter 6,000; third quarter 7,000
   Ending raw materials inventory: 40% of the next quarter's production requirements
   Ending finished goods inventory: 30% of the next quarter's expected sales units
   Third-quarter 2023 production: 7,500 units

The ending raw materials and finished goods inventories at December 31, 2022, follow the same percentage relationships to production and sales that are desired for 2023. Two kilograms of raw materials are required to make each unit of finished goods. Raw materials purchased are expected to cost £5 per kilogram.

Instructions

a. Prepare a production budget by quarters for the six-month period ended June 30, 2023.
b. Prepare a direct materials budget by quarters for the six-month period ended June 30, 2023.

Solution

1. a.

Colton plc
Production Budget
For the Six Months Ending June 30, 2023

	Quarter 1	Quarter 2	Six Months
Expected unit sales	5,000	6,000	
Add: Desired ending finished goods units	1,800[1]	2,100[2]	
Total required units	6,800	8,100	
Less: Beginning finished goods units	1,500[3]	1,800	
Required production units	5,300	6,300	11,600

[1] .30 × 6,000; [2] .30 × 7,000; [3] .30 × 5,000

b.

Colton plc
Direct Materials Budget
For the Six Months Ending June 30, 2023

	Quarter 1	Quarter 2	Six Months
Units to be produced	5,300	6,300	
Direct materials per unit	× 2	× 2	
Total kilograms needed for production	10,600	12,600	
Add: Desired ending direct materials (kilograms)	5,040[1]	6,000[2]	
Total materials required	15,640	18,600	
Less: Beginning direct materials (kilograms)	4,240[3]	5,040	
Direct materials purchase	11,400	13,560	
Cost per kilogram	× £5	× £5	
Total cost of direct materials purchase	£57,000	£67,800	£124,800

[1] .40 × 12,600; [2] .40 × (7,500 × 2); [3] .40 × 10,600

Prepare a cash budget for two months.

2. **(LO 4)** Fletcher Company expects to have a cash balance of A$45,000 on January 1, 2023. Relevant monthly budget data for the first two months of 2023 are as follows:

Collections from customers: January A$100,000, February A$160,000.
Payments for direct materials: January A$60,000, February A$80,000.
Direct labor: January A$30,000, February A$45,000. Wages are paid in the month they are incurred.
Manufacturing overhead: January A$26,000, February A$31,000. These costs include depreciation of A$1,000 per month. All other overhead costs are paid as incurred.

Selling and administrative expenses: January A$15,000, February A$20,000. These costs are exclusive of depreciation. They are paid as incurred.

Sales of marketable securities in January are expected to realize A$10,000 in cash. Fletcher Company has a line of credit at a local bank that enables it to borrow up to A$25,000. The company wants to maintain a minimum monthly cash balance of A$25,000.

Instructions

Prepare a cash budget for January and February.

Solution

2.

Fletcher Company
Cash Budget
For the Two Months Ending February 28, 2023

	January	February
Beginning cash balance	A$ 45,000	A$ 25,000
Add: Receipts		
Collections from customers	100,000	160,000
Sale of marketable securities	10,000	0
Total receipts	110,000	160,000
Total available cash	155,000	185,000
Less: Disbursements		
Direct materials	60,000	80,000
Direct labor	30,000	45,000
Manufacturing overhead	25,000*	30,000
Selling and administrative expenses	15,000	20,000
Total disbursements	130,000	175,000
Excess (deficiency) of available cash over cash Disbursements	25,000	10,000
Financing		
Borrowings	0	15,000
Repayments	0	0
Ending cash balance	**A$ 25,000**	**A$ 25,000**

*A$26,000 − A$1,000

Practice Problems

1. (LO 2) Henshall Company is preparing its master budget for 2023. Relevant data pertaining to its sales and production budgets are as follows:

Prepare sales and production budgets.

Sales. Sales for the year are expected to total 2,100,000 units. Quarterly sales, as a percentage of total sales, are 15%, 25%, 35%, and 25%, respectively. The unit selling price is expected to be €70 for the first three quarters and €75 beginning in the fourth quarter. Sales in the first quarter of 2024 are expected to be 10% higher than the budgeted sales volume for the first quarter of 2023.

Production. Management desires to maintain ending finished goods inventories at 20% of the next quarter's budgeted sales volume.

Instructions

Prepare the sales budget and production budget by quarters for 2023.

Solution

1.

Henshall Company Sales Budget and Production Budget

Henshall Company
For the Year Ending December 31, 2023
Sales Budget

	Quarter				
	1	2	3	4	Year
Expected unit sales[a]	315,000	525,000	735,000	525,000	2,100,000
Unit selling price	× €70	× €70	× €70	× €75	
Total sales	€22,050,000	€36,750,000	€51,450,000	€39,375,000	€149,625,000

Production Budget

	1	2	3	4	
Expected unit sales	315,000	525,000	735,000	525,000	
Add: Desired ending finished goods units	105,000	147,000	105,000	69,300[b]	
Total required units	420,000	672,000	840,000	594,300	
Less: Beginning finished goods units	63,000[c]	105,000	147,000	105,000	
Required production units	**357,000**	**567,000**	**693,000**	**489,300**	**2,106,300**

[a] Expected first-quarter unit sales 2,100,000 × .15; second and fourth quarters 2,100,000 × .25; third quarter 2,100,000 × .35

[b] Estimated first-quarter 2024 sales volume 315,000 + (315,000 × .10) = 346,500; 346,500 × .20

[c] 20% of estimated first-quarter 2023 sales units (315,000 × .20)

Prepare budgeted cost of goods sold, income statement, and balance sheet.

2. (LO 3, 4) Huimin Ltd. has completed all operating budgets other than the income statement for 2023. Selected data from these budgets follow:

Sales: HK$3,000,000
Purchases of raw materials: HK$1,450,000
Ending inventory of raw materials: HK$150,000
Direct labor: HK$400,000
Manufacturing overhead: HK$730,000, including HK$30,000 of depreciation expense
Selling and administrative expenses: HK$360,000 including depreciation expense of HK$10,000
Interest expense: HK$10,000
Principal payment on note: HK$20,000
Dividends declared: HK$20,000
Income tax rate: 30%

Other information:

Assume that there are no work-in-process or finished goods inventories.
Year-end accounts receivable: 4% of 2023 sales.
Year-end accounts payable: 50% of ending inventory of raw materials.
Interest, direct labor, manufacturing overhead, and selling and administrative expenses other than depreciation are paid as incurred.
Dividends declared and income taxes for 2023 will not be paid until 2024.

Huimin Ltd.
Balance Sheet
December 31, 2022

Assets

Current assets		
Cash		HK$200,000
Raw materials inventory		100,000
Total current assets		300,000
Property, plant, and equipment		
Equipment	HK$400,000	
Less: Accumulated depreciation	40,000	360,000
Total assets		HK$660,000

Liabilities and Stockholders' Equity

Liabilities		
Accounts payable	HK$ 50,000	
Notes payable	220,000	
Total liabilities		HK$270,000
Stockholders' equity		
Common stock	250,000	
Retained earnings	140,000	
Total stockholders' equity		390,000
Total liabilities and stockholders' equity		HK$660,000

Instructions

a. Calculate budgeted cost of goods sold.

b. Prepare a budgeted multiple-step income statement for the year ending December 31, 2023.

c. Prepare a budgeted classified balance sheet as of December 31, 2023.

Solution

2. a. Beginning raw materials + Purchases − Ending raw materials = Cost of direct materials used
(HK$100,000 + HK$1,450,000 − HK$150,000 = HK$1,400,000)
Direct materials used + Direct labor + Manufacturing overhead = Cost of goods sold (HK$1,400,000 + HK$400,000 + HK$730,000 = HK$2,530,000)

b.

Huimin Ltd.
Budgeted Income Statement
For the Year Ending December 31, 2023

Sales		HK$3,000,000
Cost of goods sold		2,530,000
Gross profit		470,000
Selling and administrative expenses		360,000
Income from operations		110,000
Interest expense		10,000
Income before income tax expense		100,000
Income tax expense (30%)		30,000*
Net income		HK$ 70,000

*HK$100,000 × .30

c.

Huimin Ltd.
Budgeted Balance Sheet
December 31, 2023

Assets

Current assets		
Cash[1]		HK$175,000
Accounts receivable (.04 × HK$3,000,000)		120,000
Raw materials inventory		150,000
Total current assets		445,000
Property, plant, and equipment		
Equipment	HK$400,000	
Less: Accumulated depreciation[2]	80,000	320,000
Total assets		HK$765,000

Liabilities and Stockholders' Equity

Liabilities		
Accounts payable (.50 × HK$150,000)	HK$ 75,000	
Income taxes payable (see income statement)	30,000	
Dividends payable	20,000	
Note payable (HK$220,000 − HK$20,000)	200,000	
Total liabilities		HK$ 325,000
Stockholders' equity		
Common stock	250,000	
Retained earnings[3]	190,000	
Total stockholders' equity		440,000
Total liabilities and stockholders' equity		HK$765,000

[1]Beginning cash balance		HK$ 200,000
Add: Receipts		
Collections from customers [(1 − .04) × HK$3,000,000 sales)]		2,880,000
Total available cash		3,080,000
Less: Disbursements		
Direct materials (HK$50,000 + HK$1,450,000 − HK$75,000)	HK$1,425,000	
Direct labor	400,000	
Manufacturing overhead (HK$730,000 − HK$30,000)	700,000	
Selling and administrative expenses (HK$360,000 − HK$10,000)	350,000	
Total disbursements		2,875,000
Excess of available cash over cash disbursements		205,000
Financing		
Less: Repayment of principal and interest		30,000
Ending cash balance		HK$ 175,000

[2]HK$40,000 + HK$30,000 + HK$10,000

[3]Beginning retained earnings + Net income − Dividends declared = Ending retained earnings (HK$140,000 + HK$70,000 − HK$20,000 = HK$190,000)

Questions

1. **a.** What is a budget?
   b. How does a budget contribute to good management?

2. Shih Bo and Hong Yu are discussing the benefits of budgeting. They ask you to identify the primary benefits of budgeting. Comply with their request.

3. Jugal Ghai asks your help in understanding the essentials of effective budgeting. Identify the essentials for Jugal.

4. **a.** "Accounting plays a relatively unimportant role in budgeting." Is this true? Explain why or why not.
   b. What responsibilities does management have in budgeting?

5. What criteria are helpful in determining the length of the budget period? What is the most common budget period?

6. Nitin Mittal maintains that the only difference between budgeting and long-range planning is time. Is this true? Explain why or why not.

7. What is participative budgeting? What are its potential benefits? What are its potential disadvantages?

8. What is budgetary slack? What incentive do managers have to create budgetary slack?

9. Distinguish between a master budget and a sales forecast.

10. What budget is the starting point in preparing the master budget? What may result if this budget is inaccurate?

11. "The production budget shows both unit production data and unit cost data." Is this true? Explain why or why not.

12. Popov OAO has 20,000 beginning finished goods units. Budgeted sales units are 160,000. If management desires 15,000 ending finished goods units, what are the required units of production?

13. In preparing the direct materials budget for Quan Company, management concludes that required purchases are 64,000 units. If 52,000 direct materials units are required in production and there are 9,000 units of beginning direct materials, what are the desired units of ending direct materials?

14. The production budget of Rojas SA calls for 80,000 units to be produced. If it takes 45 minutes to make one unit and the direct labor rate is R$160 per hour, what is the total budgeted direct labor cost?

15. Ortiz Appliances' manufacturing overhead budget shows total variable costs of S$198,000 and total fixed costs of S$162,000. Total production in units is expected to be 150,000. It takes 20 minutes to make one unit, and the direct labor rate is S$15 per hour. Express the manufacturing overhead rate as (a) a percentage of direct labor cost, and (b) an amount per direct labor hour.

16. Newcastle Boots' variable selling and administrative expenses are 12% of net sales. Fixed expenses are £50,000 per quarter. The sales budget shows expected sales of £200,000 and £240,000 in the first and

second quarters, respectively. What are the total budgeted selling and administrative expenses for each quarter?

17. For Haruki Ltd., the budgeted cost for one unit of product is direct materials ¥1,000, direct labor ¥2,000, and manufacturing overhead 80% of direct labor cost. If 25,000 units are expected to be sold at ¥6,500 each, what is the budgeted gross profit?

18. Indicate the supporting schedules used in preparing a budgeted income statement through gross profit for a manufacturer.

19. Identify the three sections of a cash budget. What balances are also shown in this budget?

20. Elif A.S. has credit sales of ₺6,000,000 in January. Past experience suggests that 40% is collected in the month of sale, 50% in the month following the sale, and 10% in the second month following the sale. Compute the cash collections from January sales in January, February, and March.

21. What is the equation for determining required merchandise purchases for a merchandiser?

22. How might expected revenues in a service company be computed?

Brief Exercises

BE9.1 (LO 1), AN Iskandar Electronics uses the following budgets: balance sheet, capital expenditure, cash, direct labor, direct materials, income statement, manufacturing overhead, production, sales, and selling and administrative expense. Prepare a diagram of the interrelationships of the budgets in the master budget. Indicate whether each budget is an operating or a financial budget.

Prepare a diagram of a master budget.

BE9.2 (LO 2), AP Chin Ltd. estimates that unit sales will be 10,000 in quarter 1, 14,000 in quarter 2, 15,000 in quarter 3, and 18,000 in quarter 4. Using a unit selling price of HK$700, prepare the sales budget by quarters for the year ending December 31, 2023.

Prepare a sales budget.

BE9.3 (LO 2), AP Chin Ltd. estimates that unit sales will be 10,000 in quarter 1, 14,000 in quarter 2, 15,000 in quarter 3, and 18,000 in quarter 4. The unit selling price is HK$700. Management desires to have an ending finished goods inventory equal to 25% of the next quarter's expected unit sales. Prepare a production budget by quarters for the first six months of 2023.

Prepare a production budget for two quarters.

BE9.4 (LO 2), AP Princeton Company has 2,000 kilograms of raw materials in its December 31, 2022, ending inventory. Required production for January and February of 2023 are 4,000 and 5,000 units, respectively. Two kilograms of raw materials are needed for each unit, and the estimated cost per kilogram is A$6. Management desires an ending inventory equal to 25% of next month's materials requirements. Prepare the direct materials budget for January.

Prepare a direct materials budget for one month.

BE9.5 (LO 3), AP For Shu-fen Ltd., units to be produced are 5,000 in quarter 1 and 7,000 in quarter 2. It takes 1.6 hours to make a finished unit, and the expected hourly wage rate is NT$150 per hour. Prepare a direct labor budget by quarters for the six months ending June 30, 2023.

Prepare a direct labor budget for two quarters.

BE9.6 (LO 3), AP For Mandarin Company, variable manufacturing overhead costs are expected to be S$20,000 in the first quarter of 2023, with S$5,000 increments in each of the remaining three quarters. Fixed overhead costs are estimated to be S$40,000 in each quarter. Prepare the manufacturing overhead budget by quarters and in total for the year.

Prepare a manufacturing overhead budget.

BE9.7 (LO 3), AP Echuca Autos classifies its selling and administrative expense budget into variable and fixed components. Variable expenses are expected to be €24,000 in the first quarter, and €4,000 increments are expected in the remaining quarters of 2023. Fixed expenses are expected to be €40,000 in each quarter. Prepare the selling and administrative expense budget by quarters and in total for 2023.

Prepare a selling and administrative expense budget.

BE9.8 (LO 3), AP Crivelli AG has completed all of its operating budgets. The sales budget for the year shows 50,000 units and total sales of CHF2,250,000. The total cost of producing one unit is CHF25. Selling and administrative expenses are expected to be CHF300,000. Interest is estimated to be CHF10,000. Income taxes are estimated to be CHF200,000. Prepare a budgeted multiple-step income statement for the year ending December 31, 2023.

Prepare a budgeted income statement for the year.

BE9.9 (LO 4), AP Kaspar Industries expects credit sales for January, February, and March to be $220,000, $260,000, and $300,000, respectively. It is expected that 75% of the sales will be collected in the month of sale, and 25% will be collected in the following month. Compute cash collections from customers for each month.

Prepare data for a cash budget.

BE9.10 (LO 5), AP Zuri Wholesalers is preparing its merchandise purchases budget. Budgeted sales are R4,000,000 for April and R4,800,000 for May. Cost of goods sold is expected to be 65% of sales. The company's desired ending inventory is 20% of the following month's cost of goods sold. Compute the required purchases for April.

Determine required merchandise purchases for one month.

DO IT! Exercises

Identify budget terminology.

DO IT! 9.1 (LO 1), K Use this list of terms to complete the sentences that follow:

- Long-range plans
- Sales forecast
- Master budget
- Participative budgeting
- Operating budgets
- Financial budgets

1. _____ establish goals for the company's sales and production personnel.
2. The _____ is a set of interrelated budgets that constitutes a plan of action for a specified time period.
3. _____ reduces the risk of having unrealistic budgets.
4. _____ include the cash budget and the budgeted balance sheet.
5. The budget is formed within the framework of a _____.
6. _____ contain considerably less detail than budgets.

Prepare sales, production, and direct materials budgets.

DO IT! 9.2 (LO 2), AP Harper Ltd. is preparing its master budget for 2023. Relevant data pertaining to its sales, production, and direct materials budgets are as follows:

Sales. Sales for the year are expected to total 1,000,000 units. Quarterly sales are 20%, 25%, 25%, and 30%, respectively. The unit selling price is expected to be £40 for the first three quarters and £45 beginning in the fourth quarter. Sales in the first quarter of 2024 are expected to be 20% higher than the budgeted sales for the first quarter of 2023.

Production. Management desires to maintain the ending finished goods inventories at 25% of the next quarter's budgeted sales volume.

Direct materials. Each unit requires 2 kilograms of raw materials at a cost of £12 per kilogram. Management desires to maintain raw materials inventories at 10% of the next quarter's production requirements. Assume the production requirements for first quarter of 2024 are 450,000 kilograms.

Prepare the sales, production, and direct materials budgets by quarters for 2023.

Calculate budgeted total unit cost and prepare budgeted income statement.

DO IT! 9.3 (LO 3), AP Harper Ltd. is preparing its budgeted income statement for 2023. Relevant data pertaining to its sales, production, and direct materials budgets can be found in **DO IT! 9.2**.

In addition, Harper budgets 0.3 hours of direct labor per unit, labor costs at £15 per hour, and manufacturing overhead at £20 per direct labor hour. Its budgeted selling and administrative expenses for 2023 are £6,000,000.

a. Calculate the budgeted total unit cost.
b. Prepare the budgeted multiple-step income statement for 2023. (Ignore income taxes.)

Determine amount of financing needed.

DO IT! 9.4 (LO 4), AP Wing Ltd. management wants to maintain a minimum monthly cash balance of HK$250,000. At the beginning of April, the cash balance is HK$250,000, expected cash receipts for April are HK$2,450,000, and cash disbursements are expected to be HK$2,550,000. How much cash, if any, must be borrowed to maintain the desired minimum monthly balance?

Prepare merchandise purchases budget.

DO IT! 9.5 (LO 5), AP SanTin Ltd. estimates that 2023 sales will be NT$400,000 in quarter 1, NT$480,000 in quarter 2, and NT$580,000 in quarter 3. Cost of goods sold is 50% of sales. Management desires to have ending merchandise inventory equal to 10% of the next quarter's expected cost of goods sold. Prepare a merchandise purchases budget by quarter for the first six months of 2023.

Exercises

Explain the concept of budgeting.

E9.1 (LO 1), C **Writing** Thanjavur Toys has always done some planning for the future, but the company has never prepared a formal budget. Now that the company is growing larger, it is considering preparing a budget.

Instructions

Write a memo to Jiya Verghese, the president of Thanjavur Toys, in which you define budgeting, identify the budgets that comprise the master budget, identify the primary benefits of budgeting, and discuss the essentials of effective budgeting.

E9.2 (LO 2), AP Asuka Electronics produces and sells two models of calculators, XQ-103 and XQ-104. The calculators sell for ¥1,500 and ¥2,500, respectively. Because of the intense competition Asuka faces, management budgets sales semiannually. Its projections for the first two quarters of 2023 are as follows:

Prepare a sales budget for two quarters.

	Unit Sales	
Product	Quarter 1	Quarter 2
XQ-103	2,000,000	2,200,000
XQ-104	1,200,000	1,500,000

No changes in selling prices are anticipated.

Instructions

Prepare a sales budget for the two quarters ending June 30, 2023. List the products and show units, selling price, and total sales by product and in total for each quarter and for the six months.

E9.3 (LO 2), AP **Service** Harrison Associates is preparing its service revenue (sales) budget for the coming year (2024). The practice is divided into three departments: auditing, tax, and consulting. Billable hours for each department, by quarter, are provided here:

Prepare a sales budget for four quarters.

Department	Quarter 1	Quarter 2	Quarter 3	Quarter 4
Auditing	2,300	1,600	2,000	2,400
Tax	3,000	2,200	2,000	2,500
Consulting	1,500	1,500	1,500	1,500

Average hourly billing rates are auditing €80, tax €90, and consulting €110.

Instructions

Prepare the service revenue (sales) budget for 2024 by listing the departments and showing billable hours, billable rate, and total revenue for each quarter and the year in total.

E9.4 (LO 2), AP Suharto Automobiles produces and sells automobile batteries, the heavy-duty HD-240. The 2023 sales forecast is as follows:

Prepare quarterly production budgets.

Quarter	HD-240
1	5,000
2	7,000
3	8,000
4	10,000

The January 1, 2023, inventory of HD-240 is 2,000 units. Management desires an ending inventory each quarter equal to 40% of the next quarter's sales. Sales in the first quarter of 2024 are expected to be 25% higher than sales in the same quarter in 2023.

Instructions

Prepare quarterly production budgets for each quarter and in total for 2023.

E9.5 (LO 2), AP Demir Industries has adopted the following production budget for the first four months of 2023.

Prepare a direct materials purchases budget.

Month	Units	Month	Units
January	10,000	March	5,000
February	8,000	April	4,000

Each unit requires 2 kilograms of raw materials costing ₺30 per kilogram. On December 31, 2022, the ending raw materials inventory was 4,000 kilograms. Management wants to have a raw materials inventory at the end of the month equal to 20% of next month's production requirements.

Instructions

Prepare a direct materials purchases budget by month for the first quarter.

E9.6 (LO 2), AP On January 1, 2023, the Pok Goods budget committee has reached agreement on the following data for the six months ending June 30, 2023.

Prepare production and direct materials budgets by quarters for six months.

Sales units: First quarter 5,000, second quarter 6,000, third quarter 7,000.

Ending raw materials inventory: 40% of the next quarter's production requirements.

Ending finished goods inventory: 25% of the next quarter's expected sales units.

Third-quarter production: 7,200 units.

The ending raw materials and finished goods inventories at December 31, 2022, follow the same percentage relationships to production and sales that occur in 2023. Three kilograms of raw materials are required to make each unit of finished goods. Raw materials purchased are expected to cost HK$40 per kilogram.

Instructions

a. Prepare a production budget by quarters for the six-month period ended June 30, 2023.

b. Prepare a direct materials budget by quarters for the six-month period ended June 30, 2023.

Calculate raw materials purchases in euros.

E9.7 (LO 2), AP Rensing Ltd. estimates sales for the second quarter of 2023 will be as follows:

Month	Units
April	2,550
May	2,675
June	2,390

The target ending inventory of finished products is as follows:

March 31	2,000
April 30	2,230
May 31	2,200
June 30	2,310

Two units of materials are required for each unit of finished product. Production for July is estimated at 2,700 units to start building inventory for the fall sales period. Rensing's policy is to have an inventory of raw materials at the end of each month equal to 50% of the following month's production requirements.

Raw materials are expected to cost €4 per unit throughout the period.

Instructions

Calculate the May raw materials purchases in euros.

Prepare a production and a direct materials budget.

E9.8 (LO 2), AP Fuqua SA's sales budget projects unit sales of part 198Z of 10,000 units in January, 12,000 units in February, and 13,000 units in March. Each unit of part 198Z requires 4 kilograms of materials, which cost €2 per kilogram. Fuqua desires its ending raw materials inventory to equal 40% of the next month's production requirements, and its ending finished goods inventory to equal 20% of the next month's expected unit sales. These goals were met at December 31, 2022.

Instructions

a. Prepare a production budget for January and February 2023.

b. Prepare a direct materials budget for January 2023.

Prepare a direct labor budget.

E9.9 (LO 3), AP Sanchez Enterprises is preparing its direct labor budget for 2023 from the following production budget based on a calendar year.

Quarter	Units	Quarter	Units
1	20,000	3	35,000
2	25,000	4	30,000

Each unit requires 1.5 hours of direct labor.

Instructions

Prepare a direct labor budget for 2023. Wage rates are expected to be R$160 for the first two quarters and R$180 for quarters 3 and 4.

Prepare production and direct labor budgets.

E9.10 (LO 2, 3), AP Adisa ASA makes and sells artistic frames for pictures. The controller is responsible for preparing the master budget and has accumulated the following information for 2023.

	January	February	March	April	May
Estimated unit sales	12,000	14,000	13,000	11,000	11,000
Unit selling price	R500	R475	R475	R475	R475
Direct labor hours per unit	20	20	15	15	15
Direct labor cost per hour	R80	R80	R80	R90	R90

Adisa has a labor contract that calls for a wage increase to R90 per hour on April 1. New labor-saving machinery has been installed and will be fully operational by March 1.

Adisa expects to begin the year with 17,600 frames on hand and has a policy of carrying an end-of-month inventory of 100% of the following month's sales, plus 40% of the second following month's sales.

Instructions

Prepare a production budget and a direct labor budget for Adisa ASA by month and for the first quarter of the year. The direct labor budget should include direct labor hours.

E9.11 (LO 3), AP Grand Coast Company is preparing its manufacturing overhead budget for 2023. Relevant data consist of the following:

Prepare a manufacturing overhead budget for the year.

Units to be produced (by quarters): 10,000, 12,000, 14,000, 16,000.

Direct labor: time is 1.5 hours per unit.

Variable overhead costs per direct labor hour: indirect materials A$0.80, indirect labor A$1.20, and maintenance A$0.50.

Fixed overhead costs per quarter: supervisory salaries A$41,250, depreciation A$15,000, and maintenance A$12,000.

Instructions

Prepare the manufacturing overhead budget for the year, showing quarterly data.

E9.12 (LO 3), AP Leicester Art combines its operating expenses for budget purposes in a selling and administrative expense budget. For the first six months of 2023, the following data are available.

Prepare a selling and administrative expense budget for two quarters.

1. Sales: 20,000 units quarter 1; 22,000 units quarter 2.
2. Variable costs per pound of sales: sales commissions 5%, delivery expense 2%, and advertising 3%.
3. Fixed costs per quarter: sales salaries £12,000, office salaries £8,000, depreciation £4,200, insurance £1,500, utilities £800, and repairs expense £500.
4. Unit selling price: £20.

Instructions

Prepare a selling and administrative expense budget by quarters for the first six months of 2023.

E9.13 (LO 3), AP Dusseldorf SE has accumulated the following budget data for the year 2023.

Prepare a budgeted income statement for the year.

1. Sales: 30,000 units, unit selling price €85.
2. Cost of one unit of finished goods: direct materials 1 kilogram at €5 per kilogram, direct labor 3 hours at €15 per hour, and manufacturing overhead €5 per direct labor hour.
3. Inventories (raw materials only): beginning, 10,000 kilograms; ending, 15,000 kilograms.
4. Selling and administrative expenses: €170,000; interest expense: €30,000.
5. Income taxes: 20% of income before income taxes.

Instructions

a. Prepare a schedule showing the computation of cost of goods sold for 2023.

b. Prepare a budgeted multiple-step income statement for 2023.

E9.14 (LO 4), AP Tigris A.S. expects to have a cash balance of ₺450,000 on January 1, 2023. Relevant monthly budget data for the first two months of 2023 are as follows:

Prepare a cash budget for two months.

Collections from customers: January ₺850,000, February ₺1,500,000.

Payments for direct materials: January ₺500,000, February ₺750,000.

Direct labor: January ₺300,000, February ₺450,000. Wages are paid in the month they are incurred.

Manufacturing overhead: January ₺210,000, February ₺250,000. These costs include depreciation of ₺15,000 per month. All other overhead costs are paid as incurred.

Selling and administrative expenses: January ₺150,000, February ₺200,000. These costs are exclusive of depreciation. They are paid as incurred.

Sales of marketable securities in January are expected to realize ₺120,000 in cash. Tigris A.S. has a line of credit at a local bank that enables it to borrow up to ₺250,000. The company wants to maintain a minimum monthly cash balance of ₺200,000.

Instructions

Prepare a cash budget for January and February.

E9.15 (LO 4), AP Yi-chun Corporation is projecting a cash balance of NT$300,000 in its December 31, 2022, balance sheet. Yi-chun's schedule of expected collections from customers for the first quarter of 2023 shows total collections of NT$1,850,000. The schedule of expected payments for direct materials

Prepare a cash budget.

for the first quarter of 2023 shows total payments of NT$430,000. Other information gathered for the first quarter of 2023 is sale of equipment NT$30,000, direct labor NT$700,000, manufacturing overhead NT$350,000, selling and administrative expenses NT$450,000, and purchase of securities NT$140,000. Yi-chun wants to maintain a balance of at least NT$250,000 cash at the end of each quarter.

Instructions

Prepare a cash budget for the first quarter.

E9.16 (LO 4), AN The controller of Tanandar Apparel wants to improve the company's control system by preparing a month-by-month cash budget. The following information is for the month ending July 31, 2023.

June 30, 2023, cash balance	Rp450,000,000
Dividends to be declared on July 15*	120,000,000
Cash expenditures to be paid in July for operating expenses	408,000,000
Amortization expense in July	45,000,000
Cash collections to be received in July	900,000,000
Merchandise purchases to be paid in cash in July	562,000,000
Equipment to be purchased for cash in July	200,000,000

*Dividends are payable 30 days after declaration to shareholders of record on the declaration date.

Tanandar Apparel wants to keep a minimum cash balance of Rp250,000,000.

Instructions

a. Prepare a cash budget for the month ended July 31, 2023, and indicate how much money, if any, Tanandar Apparel will need to borrow to meet its minimum cash requirement.

b. Explain how cash budgeting can reduce the cost of short-term borrowing.

E9.17 (LO 4), AP National Company's budgeted sales and direct materials purchases are as follows:

	Budgeted Sales	Budgeted D.M. Purchases
January	A$200,000	A$30,000
February	220,000	36,000
March	250,000	38,000

National's sales are 30% cash and 70% credit. Credit sales are collected 10% in the month of sale, 50% in the month following sale, and 36% in the second month following sale; 4% are uncollectible. National's purchases are 50% cash and 50% on account. Purchases on account are paid 40% in the month of purchase, and 60% in the month following purchase.

Instructions

a. Prepare a schedule of expected collections from customers for March.

b. Prepare a schedule of expected payments for direct materials for March.

E9.18 (LO 4, 5), AP **Service** Green Landscaping is preparing its budget for the first quarter of 2023. The next step in the budgeting process is to prepare a cash receipts schedule and a cash payments schedule. To that end, the following information has been collected.

Clients usually pay 60% of their fee in the month that service is performed, 30% the month after, and 10% the second month after receiving service.

Actual service revenue for 2022 and expected service revenues for 2023 are November 2022, $80,000; December 2022, $90,000; January 2023, $100,000; February 2023, $120,000; and March 2023, $140,000.

Purchases of landscaping supplies (direct materials) are paid 60% in the month of purchase and 40% the following month. Actual purchases for 2022 and expected purchases for 2023 are December 2022, $14,000; January 2023, $12,000; February 2023, $15,000; and March 2023, $18,000.

Instructions

a. Prepare the following schedules for each month in the first quarter of 2023 and for the quarter in total:
   1. Expected collections from clients.
   2. Expected payments for landscaping supplies.

b. Determine the following balances at March 31, 2023:
   1. Accounts receivable.
   2. Accounts payable.

E9.19 (LO 4, 5), AP **Service** Murugan Dental Clinic is a medium-sized dental service specializing in family dental care. The clinic is currently preparing the master budget for the first two quarters of 2023. All that remains in this process is the cash budget. The following information has been collected from other portions of the master budget and elsewhere.

Prepare a cash budget for two quarters.

Beginning cash balance	S$ 30,000
Required minimum cash balance	25,000
Payment of income taxes (2nd quarter)	4,000
Professional salaries:	
1st quarter	140,000
2nd quarter	140,000
Interest from investments (2nd quarter)	7,000
Overhead costs:	
1st quarter	77,000
2nd quarter	100,000
Selling and administrative costs, including S$2,000 depreciation:	
1st quarter	50,000
2nd quarter	70,000
Purchase of equipment (2nd quarter)	50,000
Sale of equipment (1st quarter)	12,000
Collections from patients:	
1st quarter	235,000
2nd quarter	380,000
Interest payments (2nd quarter)	200

Instructions

Prepare a cash budget for each of the first two quarters of 2023.

E9.20 (LO 5), AP **Service** In May 2023, the budget committee of Grand Stores assembles the following data in preparation of budgeted merchandise purchases for the month of June.

Prepare a purchases budget and budgeted income statement for a merchandiser.

1. Expected sales: June A$500,000, July A$600,000.
2. Cost of goods sold is expected to be 75% of sales.
3. Desired ending merchandise inventory is 30% of the following (next) month's cost of goods sold.
4. The beginning inventory at June 1 will be the desired amount.

Instructions

a. Compute the budgeted merchandise purchases for June.
b. Prepare the budgeted multiple-step income statement for June through gross profit.

E9.21 (LO 5), AP Emine and Emir's Painting Service estimates that it will paint 10 small homes, 5 medium homes, and 2 large homes during the month of June 2023. The company estimates its direct labor needs as 40 hours per small home, 70 hours for a medium home, and 120 hours for a large home. Its average cost for direct labor is ₺180 per hour.

Prepare a direct labor budget for a service company.

Instructions

Prepare a direct labor budget for Emine and Emir's Painting Service for June 2023.

Problems

P9.1 (LO 2, 3), AP Cornwall Farm Supply Company manufactures and sells a pesticide called Snare. The following data are available for preparing budgets for Snare for the first two quarters of 2023.

Prepare budgeted income statement and supporting budgets.

1. Sales: quarter 1, 40,000 bags; quarter 2, 56,000 bags. Selling price is £60 per bag.
2. Direct materials: each bag of Snare requires 4 kilograms of Gumm at a cost of £3.80 per kilogram and 6 kilograms of Tarr at £1.50 per kilogram.
3. Desired inventory levels:

Type of Inventory	January 1	April 1	July 1
Snare (bags)	8,000	15,000	18,000
Gumm (kilograms)	9,000	10,000	13,000
Tarr (kilograms)	14,000	20,000	25,000

4. Direct labor: direct labor time is 15 minutes per bag at an hourly rate of £16 per hour.
5. Selling and administrative expenses are expected to be 15% of sales plus £175,000 per quarter.
6. Interest expense is £100,000 for the two quarters.
7. Income taxes are expected to be 20% of income before income taxes.

Your assistant has prepared two budgets: (1) the manufacturing overhead budget shows expected costs to be 125% of direct labor cost, and (2) the direct materials budget for Tarr shows the cost of Tarr purchases to be £297,000 in quarter 1 and £439,500 in quarter 2.

Instructions

Prepare the budgeted multiple-step income statement for the first six months and all required operating budgets by quarters. (*Note:* Use variable and fixed in the selling and administrative expense budget.) Do not prepare the manufacturing overhead budget or the direct materials budget for Tarr.

Net income £1,007,040
Cost per bag £33.20

Prepare sales, production, direct materials, direct labor, and income statement budgets.

P9.2 (LO 2, 3), AP Madison SpA is preparing its annual budgets for the year ending December 31, 2023. Accounting assistants furnish the following data.

	Product JB 50	Product JB 60
Sales budget:		
Anticipated volume in units	400,000	200,000
Unit selling price	€20	€25
Production budget:		
Desired ending finished goods units	30,000	15,000
Beginning finished goods units	25,000	10,000
Direct materials budget:		
Direct materials per unit (kilograms)	2	3
Desired ending direct materials kilograms	30,000	10,000
Beginning direct materials kilograms	40,000	15,000
Cost per kilogram	€3	€4
Direct labor budget:		
Direct labor time per unit	0.4	0.6
Direct labor rate per hour	€12	€12
Budgeted income statement:		
Total unit cost	€13	€20

An accounting assistant has prepared the detailed manufacturing overhead budget and the selling and administrative expense budget. The latter shows selling expenses of €560,000 for product JB 50 and €360,000 for product JB 60, and administrative expenses of €540,000 for product JB 50 and €340,000 for product JB 60. Interest expense is €150,000 (not allocated to products). Income taxes are expected to be 20%.

Instructions

Prepare the following budgets for the year. Show data for each product. Quarterly budgets should not be prepared.

a. Sales.
b. Production.
c. Direct materials.
d. Direct labor.
e. Multiple-step income statement (*Note:* income taxes are not allocated to the products).

a. Total sales €13,000,000
b. Required production units:
   JB 50, 405,000
   JB 60, 205,000
c. Total cost of direct materials purchases €4,840,000
d. Total direct labor cost €3,420,000
e. Net income €1,480,000

Prepare sales and production budgets and compute cost per unit under two plans.

P9.3 (LO 2), E Lucerne Industries had sales in 2022 of CHF6,800,000 and gross profit of CHF1,100,000. Management is considering two alternative budget plans to increase its gross profit in 2023.

Plan A would increase the unit selling price from CHF8.00 to CHF8.40. Sales volume would decrease by 125,000 units from its 2022 level. Plan B would decrease the unit selling price by CHF0.50. The marketing department expects that the sales volume would increase by 130,000 units.

At the end of 2022, Lucerne has 40,000 units of inventory on hand. If Plan A is accepted, the 2023 ending inventory should be 35,000 units. If Plan B is accepted, the ending inventory should be 60,000 units. Each unit produced will cost CHF1.50 in direct labor, CHF1.30 in direct materials, and CHF1.20 in variable overhead. The fixed overhead for 2023 should be CHF1,895,000.

Instructions

a. Prepare a sales budget for 2023 under each plan.
b. Prepare a production budget for 2023 under each plan.
c. Compute the production cost per unit under each plan. Why is the cost per unit different for the two plans? (Round to two decimals.)
d. Which plan should be accepted? (*Hint:* Compute the gross profit under each plan.)

c. Unit cost: Plan A CHF6.63
   Plan B CHF5.90
d. Gross profit:
   Plan A CHF1,283,250
   Plan B CHF1,568,000

P9.4 (LO 4), AP Colter Company prepares monthly cash budgets. Relevant data from operating budgets for 2023 are as follows:

Prepare cash budget for two months.

	January	February
Sales	$360,000	$400,000
Direct materials purchases	120,000	125,000
Direct labor	90,000	100,000
Manufacturing overhead	70,000	75,000
Selling and administrative expenses	79,000	85,000

All sales are on account. Collections are expected to be 50% in the month of sale, 30% in the first month following the sale, and 20% in the second month following the sale. Sixty percent (60%) of direct materials purchases are paid in cash in the month of purchase, and the balance due is paid in the month following the purchase. All other items above are paid in the month incurred except for selling and administrative expenses, which include $1,000 of depreciation per month.

Other data:

1. Credit sales: November 2022, $250,000; December 2022, $320,000.
2. Purchases of direct materials: December 2022, $100,000.
3. Other receipts: January—collection of December 31, 2022, notes receivable $15,000; February—proceeds from sale of securities $6,000.
4. Other disbursements: February—payment of $6,000 cash dividend.

The company's cash balance on January 1, 2023, is expected to be $60,000. The company wants to maintain a minimum cash balance of $50,000.

Instructions

a. Prepare schedules for (1) expected collections from customers and (2) expected payments for direct materials purchases for January and February.
b. Prepare a cash budget for January and February in columnar form.

a. January: collections $326,000; payments $112,000
b. Ending cash balance:
   January $51,000
   February $50,000

P9.5 (LO 5), AP The budget committee of Jinsung Industries collects the following data in preparing budgeted income statements for May and June 2023.

Prepare purchases and income statement budgets for a merchandiser.

1. Sales for May are expected to be HK$8,000,000. Sales in June and July are expected to be 5% higher than the preceding month.
2. Cost of goods sold is expected to be 75% of sales.
3. Company policy is to maintain ending merchandise inventory at 10% of the following month's cost of goods sold.
4. Operating expenses are estimated to be as follows:

Sales salaries	HK$350,000 per month
Advertising	6% of monthly sales
Delivery expense	2% of monthly sales
Sales commissions	5% of monthly sales
Rent expense	HK$50,000 per month
Depreciation	HK$8,000 per month
Utilities	HK$6,000 per month
Insurance	HK$5,000 per month

5. Interest expense is HK$20,000 per month. Income taxes are estimated to be 20% of income before income taxes.

Instructions

a. Prepare the merchandise purchases budget for each month in columnar form.
b. Prepare budgeted multiple-step income statements for each month in columnar form. Show in the statements the details of cost of goods sold.

a. Purchases:
   May HK$6,030,000
   June HK$6,331,500
b. Net income:
   May HK$416,800
   June HK$455,200

Prepare budgeted cost of goods sold, income statement, retained earnings, and balance sheet.

P9.6 (LO 3, 4), AP Kimje Industries' balance sheet at December 31, 2022, is presented here.

Kimje Industries
Balance Sheet
December 31, 2022

Assets

Current assets		
Cash		₩ 7,500,000
Accounts receivable		73,500,000
Finished goods inventory (1,500 units)		24,000,000
Total current assets		105,000,000
Property, plant, and equipment		
Equipment	₩40,000,000	
Less: Accumulated depreciation	10,000,000	30,000,000
Total assets		₩135,000,000

Liabilities and Stockholders' Equity

Liabilities		
Notes payable		₩25,000,000
Accounts payable		45,000,000
Total liabilities		70,000,000
Stockholders' equity		
Common stock	₩40,000,000	
Retained earnings	25,000,000	
Total stockholders' equity		65,000,000
Total liabilities and stockholders' equity		₩135,000,000

Budgeted data for the year 2023 include the following:

	2023	
	Quarter 4	Total
Sales budget (8,000 units at ₩32,000)	₩76,800,000	₩256,000,000
Direct materials used	17,000,000	62,500,000
Direct labor	12,500,000	50,900,000
Manufacturing overhead applied	10,000,000	48,600,000
Selling and administrative expenses	18,000,000	75,000,000

    To meet sales requirements and to have 2,500 units of finished goods on hand at December 31, 2023, the production budget shows 9,000 required units of output. The total unit cost of production is expected to be ₩18,000. Kimje uses the first-in, first-out (FIFO) inventory costing method. Interest expense is expected to be ₩3,500,000 for the year. Income taxes are expected to be 20% of income before income taxes. In 2023, the company expects to declare and pay an ₩8,000,000 cash dividend.

    The company's cash budget shows an expected cash balance of ₩13,180,000 at December 31, 2023. All sales and purchases are on account. It is expected that 60% of quarterly sales are collected in cash within the quarter and the remainder is collected in the following quarter. Direct materials purchased from suppliers are paid 50% in the quarter incurred and the remainder in the following quarter. Purchases in the fourth quarter were the same as the materials used. In 2023, the company expects to purchase additional equipment costing ₩9,000,000. A total of ₩4,000,000 of depreciation expense on equipment is included in the budget data and split equally between manufacturing overhead and selling and administrative expenses. Kimje expects to pay ₩8,000,000 on the outstanding notes payable balance plus all interest due and payable to December 31 (included in interest expense ₩3,500,000, above). Accounts payable at December 31, 2023, includes amounts due suppliers (see above) plus other accounts payable relating to manufacturing overhead of ₩7,200,000. Unpaid income taxes at December 31 will be ₩5,000,000.

Instructions

Prepare a budgeted statement of cost of goods sold, budgeted multiple-step income statement, and retained earnings statement for 2023, and a budgeted classified balance sheet at December 31, 2023.

Net income ₩29,200,000
Total assets ₩123,900,000

Continuing Case

Current Designs

CD9 Diane Buswell is preparing the 2023 budget for one of **Current Designs**' (USA) rotomolded kayaks. Extensive meetings with members of the sales department and executive team have resulted in the following unit sales projections for 2023.

Quarter 1	1,000 kayaks
Quarter 2	1,500 kayaks
Quarter 3	750 kayaks
Quarter 4	750 kayaks

Current Designs' policy is to have finished goods ending inventory in a quarter equal to 20% of the next quarter's anticipated sales. Preliminary sales projections for 2024 are 1,100 units for the first quarter and 1,500 units for the second quarter. Ending inventory of finished goods at December 31, 2022, will be 200 rotomolded kayaks.

Production of each kayak requires 54 pounds of polyethylene powder and a finishing kit (rope, seat, hardware, etc.). Company policy is that the ending inventory of polyethylene powder should be 25% of the amount needed for production in the next quarter. Assume that the ending inventory of polyethylene powder on December 31, 2022, is 19,400 pounds. The finishing kits can be assembled as they are needed. As a result, Current Designs does not maintain a significant inventory of the finishing kits.

The polyethylene powder used in these kayaks costs $1.50 per pound, and the finishing kits cost $170 each. Production of a single kayak requires 2 hours of time by more experienced, type I employees and 3 hours of finishing time by type II employees. The type I employees are paid $15 per hour, and the type II employees are paid $12 per hour.

Selling and administrative expenses for this line are expected to be $45 per unit sold plus $7,500 per quarter. Manufacturing overhead is assigned at 150% of labor costs.

Instructions

Prepare the production budget, direct materials budget, direct labor budget, manufacturing overhead budget, and selling and administrative budget for this product line by quarter and in total for 2023.

Data Analytics in Action

Data Analytics at HydroHappy

DA9 HydroHappy has developed a new marketing plan that looks very promising for increased sales for the upcoming summer months. The biggest concern is that the production facility will not have the capacity to handle the additional production needed. For this case, you will generate Excel pivot tables and pivot line charts to analyze company capacity for estimated increased production levels.

Go to the book's product page on www.wiley.com for complete case details and instruction.

Expand Your Critical Thinking

Decision-Making Across the Organization

CT9.1 Palmer Corporation operates on a calendar-year basis. It begins the annual budgeting process in late August when the president establishes targets for the total dollar sales and net income before taxes for the next year.

The sales target is given first to the marketing department. The marketing manager formulates a sales budget by product line in both units and dollars. From this budget, sales quotas by product line in units and dollars are established for each of the corporation's sales districts. The marketing manager also estimates the cost of the marketing activities required to support the target sales volume and prepares a tentative marketing expense budget.

The executive vice president uses the sales and profit targets, the sales budget by product line, and the tentative marketing expense budget to determine the dollar amounts that can be devoted to manufacturing and corporate office expense. The executive vice president prepares the budget for corporate expenses. She then forwards to the production department the product-line sales budget in units and the total dollar amount that can be devoted to manufacturing.

The production manager meets with the factory managers to develop a manufacturing plan that will produce the required units when needed within the cost constraints set by the executive vice president. The budgeting process usually comes to a halt at this point because the production department does not consider the financial resources allocated to be adequate.

When this standstill occurs, the vice president of finance, the executive vice president, the marketing manager, and the production manager meet together to determine the final budgets for each of the areas. This normally results in a modest increase in the total amount available for manufacturing costs and cuts in the marketing expense and corporate office expense budgets. The total sales and net income figures proposed by the president are seldom changed. Although the participants are seldom pleased with the compromise, these budgets are final. Each executive then develops a new detailed budget for the operations in his or her area.

None of the areas has achieved its budget in recent years. Sales often run below the target. When budgeted sales are not achieved, each area is expected to cut costs so that the president's profit target can be met. However, the profit target is seldom met because costs are not cut enough. In fact, costs often run above the original budget in all functional areas (marketing, production, and corporate office).

The president is disturbed that Palmer has not been able to meet the sales and profit targets. He hires a consultant with considerable experience with companies in Palmer's industry. The consultant reviews the budgets for the past four years. He concludes that the product line sales budgets were reasonable and that the cost and expense budgets were adequate for the budgeted sales and production levels.

Instructions

With the class divided into groups, complete the following:

a. Discuss how the budgeting process employed by Palmer Corporation contributes to the failure to achieve the president's sales and profit targets.

b. Suggest how Palmer Corporation's budgeting process could be revised to correct the problems.

c. Should the functional areas be expected to cut their costs when sales volume falls below budget? Explain your answer.

Managerial Analysis

CT9.2 Hanjaya Industries manufactures ergonomic devices for computer users. Some of its more popular products include anti-glare filters and privacy filters (for computer monitors) and keyboard stands with wrist rests. Over the past five years, it experienced rapid growth, with sales of all products increasing 20% to 50% each year.

Last year, some of the primary manufacturers of computers began introducing new products with some of the ergonomic designs, such as anti-glare filters and wrist rests, already built in. As a result, sales of Hanjaya Industries' accessory devices have declined somewhat. The company believes that the privacy filters will probably continue to show growth, but that the other products will probably continue to decline. When the next year's budget was prepared, increases were built into research and development so that replacement products could be developed or the company could expand into some other product line. Some product lines being considered are general-purpose ergonomic devices including back supports, foot rests, and sloped writing pads.

The most recent results have shown that sales decreased more than was expected for the anti-glare filters. As a result, the company may have a shortage of funds. Top management has therefore asked that all expenses be reduced 10% to compensate for these reduced sales. Summary budget information is as follows:

Direct materials	Rp240,000,000
Direct labor	110,000,000
Insurance	50,000,000
Depreciation	90,000,000
Machine repairs	30,000,000
Sales salaries	50,000,000
Office salaries	80,000,000
Factory salaries (indirect labor)	50,000,000
Total	Rp700,000,000

Instructions

Using the information above, answer the following questions:

a. What are the implications of reducing each of the costs? For example, if the company reduces direct materials costs, it may have to do so by purchasing lower-quality materials. This may affect sales in the long run.

b. Based on your analysis in (a), what do you think is the best way to obtain the Rp70,000,000 in cost savings requested? Be specific. Are there any costs that cannot or should not be reduced? Why?

Real-World Focus

CT9.3 Information regarding many approaches to budgeting can be found online. The following activity investigates the merits of "zero-based" budgeting, as discussed by Michael LaFaive, Director of Fiscal Policy of the **Mackinac Center for Public Policy** (USA).

Instructions

Read the article at the Mackinac website and then answer the following questions:

a. How does zero-based budgeting differ from standard budgeting procedures?
b. What are some potential advantages of zero-based budgeting?
c. What are some potential disadvantages of zero-based budgeting?
d. How often do departments in Oklahoma undergo zero-based budgeting?

Communication Activity

CT9.4 **Service** In order to better serve their rural patients, Drs. Hao and Jun Zhang (brothers) began giving safety seminars. Especially popular were their "emergency-preparedness" talks given to farmers. Many people asked whether the "kit" of materials the doctors recommended for common farm emergencies was commercially available.

After checking with several suppliers, the doctors realized that no other company offered the supplies they recommended in their seminars, packaged in the way they described. Their wives, Tian and Qing, agreed to make a test package by ordering supplies from various medical supply companies and assembling them into a "kit" that could be sold at the seminars. When these kits proved a runaway success, the sisters-in-law decided to market them. At the advice of their accountant, they organized this venture as a separate company, called Life Protection Products (LPP), with Tian Zhang as CEO and Qing Zhang as Secretary-Treasurer.

LPP soon started receiving requests for the kits from all over the country, as word spread about their availability. Even without advertising, LPP was able to sell its full inventory every month. However, the company was becoming financially strained. Tian and Qing had about HK$1,000,000 in savings, and they invested about half that amount initially. They believed that this venture would allow them to make money. However, at the present time, only about HK$300,000 of the cash remains, and the company is constantly short of cash.

Tian has come to you for advice. She does not understand why the company is having cash flow problems. She and Qing have not even been withdrawing salaries. However, they have rented a local building and have hired two more full-time workers to help them cope with the increasing demand. They do not think they could handle the demand without this additional help.

Tian is also worried that the cash problems mean that the company may not be able to support itself. She has prepared the cash budget that follows. All seminar customers pay for their products in full at the time of purchase. In addition, several large companies have ordered the kits for use by employees who work in remote sites. They have requested credit terms and have been allowed to pay in the month following the sale. These large purchasers amount to about 25% of the sales at the present time. LPP purchases the materials for the kits about two months ahead of time. Tian and Qing are considering slowing the growth of the company by simply purchasing less materials, which will mean selling fewer kits.

The workers are paid weekly. Tian and Qing need about HK$150,000 cash on hand at the beginning of the month to pay for purchases of raw materials. Right now they have been using cash from their savings, but as noted, only HK$300,000 is left.

Life Protection Products
Cash Budget
For the Quarter Ending June 30, 2023

	April	May	June
Cash balance, beginning	HK$150,000	HK$150,000	HK$150,000
Cash received			
From prior month sales	50,000	75,000	125,000
From current sales	150,000	225,000	375,000
Total available cash	350,000	450,000	650,000
Cash payments			
To employees	30,000	30,000	30,000
For products	250,000	350,000	450,000
Miscellaneous expenses	50,000	60,000	70,000
Postage	10,000	10,000	10,000
Total cash payments	340,000	450,000	560,000
Cash balance	HK$ 10,000	HK$ 0	HK$ 90,000
Borrow from savings	HK$140,000	HK$150,000	HK$ 10,000
Borrow from bank?	HK$ 0	HK$ 0	HK$ 50,000

Instructions

Write a response to Tian Zhang. Explain why LPP is short of cash. Will this company be able to support itself? Explain your answer. Make any recommendations you deem appropriate.

Ethics Case

CT9.5 You are an accountant in the budgetary, projections, and special projects department of Goel Conductor Ltd., a large manufacturing company. The president, Samira Malik, asks you on very short notice to prepare some sales and income projections covering the next two years of the company's much-heralded new product lines. She wants these projections for a series of speeches she is making while on a two-week trip to eight brokerage firms. The president hopes to bolster Goel's stock sales and price.

You work 23 hours in two days to compile the projections, hand-deliver them to the president, and are swiftly but graciously thanked as she departs. A week later, you find time to go over some of your computations and discover a miscalculation that makes the projections grossly overstated. You quickly inquire about the president's itinerary and learn that she has made half of her speeches and has half yet to make. You are in a quandary as to what to do.

Instructions

a. What are the consequences of telling the president of your gross miscalculations?
b. What are the consequences of not telling the president of your gross miscalculations?
c. What are the ethical considerations to you and the president in this situation?

All About You

CT9.6 In order to get your personal finances under control, you need to prepare a personal budget. Assume that you have compiled the following information regarding your expected cash flows for a typical month.

Rent payment	€ 500	Miscellaneous costs	€210
Interest income	50	Savings	50
Income tax withheld	300	Eating out	150
Electricity bill	85	Telephone and Internet costs	125
Groceries	100	Student loan payments	375
Wages earned	2,500	Entertainment costs	250
Insurance	100	Transportation costs	150

Instructions

Using the information above, prepare a personal budget. In preparing this budget, use the format included in the "Steps to Creating a Household Budget" article available at **the balance**'s website (go to the site and do a search for the article). Just skip any unused line items.

Considering Your Costs and Benefits

CT9.7 You might hear people say that they "need to learn to live within a budget." The funny thing is that most people who say this haven't actually prepared a personal budget, nor do they intend to. Instead, what they are referring to is a vaguely defined, poorly specified collection of rough ideas of how much they should spend on various aspects of their lives. However, you can't live within or even outside of something that doesn't exist. With that in mind, let's take a look at one aspect of personal-budget templates.

Many personal-budget worksheet templates that are provided for college students treat student loans as an income source. See, for example, the template included in the "Steps to Creating a Household Budget" article available at **the balance**'s website. Based on your knowledge of accounting, is this correct?

> **YES:** Student loans provide a source of cash, which can be used to pay costs. As the saying goes, "It all spends the same." Therefore, student loans are income.
>
> **NO:** Student loans must eventually be repaid; therefore, they are not income. As the name indicates, they are loans.

Instructions

Write a response indicating your position regarding this situation. Provide support for your view.

CHAPTER 10

Budgetary Control and Responsibility Accounting

CHAPTER PREVIEW

In Chapter 9, we discussed the use of budgets for planning. We now consider how budgets are used by management to control operations. In the following Feature Story on **The Roxy Hotel Tribeca** (USA), we see that management uses the budget to adapt to the business environment. This chapter focuses on two aspects of management control: (1) budgetary control and (2) responsibility accounting.

FEATURE STORY

Pumpkin Madeleines and a Movie

Perhaps no place in the world has a wider variety of distinctive, high-end accommodations than New York City. It's tough to set yourself apart in the Big Apple, but unique is what **The Roxy Hotel Tribeca** (USA) is all about.

When you walk through the doors of this triangular-shaped building, nestled in one of Manhattan's most affluent neighborhoods, you immediately encounter a striking eight-story atrium. Although the hotel was completely renovated, it still maintains its funky mid-century charm. Just consider the always hip hotel bar. Besides serving up cocktails until 2 a.m., the bar also provides food. These are not the run-of-the-mill, chain-hotel, borderline edibles. The chef is famous for tantalizing delectables such as duck rillettes, sea salt baked branzino, housemade pappardelle, and pumpkin madeleines.

Another thing that really sets the hotel apart is its private screening room. As a guest, you can enjoy plush leather seating, state-of-the-art projection, and digital surround sound, all while viewing a cult classic from the hotel's film series. In fact, on Sundays, free screenings are available to guests and non-guests alike on a first-come-first-served basis.

To attract and satisfy a discerning clientele, The Roxy Hotel Tribeca's management incurs higher and more unpredictable costs than those of a standard hotel. As fun as it might be to run a high-end hotel, management cannot be cavalier about spending money. To maintain profitability, management closely monitors costs and revenues to make sure that they track with budgeted amounts. Further, because of unexpected fluctuations in demand for rooms (think hurricanes or bitterly cold winter weather), management must sometimes revise forecasts and budgets and adapt quickly. To evaluate performance and identify when changes need to be made, the budget needs to be flexible.

CHAPTER OUTLINE

Learning Objectives	Review	Practice
LO 1 Describe budgetary control and static budget reports.	• Budgetary control • Static budget reports	**DO IT! 1** Static Budget Reports
LO 2 Prepare flexible budget reports.	• Why flexible budgets? • Developing the flexible budget • Flexible budget—a case study • Flexible budget reports	**DO IT! 2** Flexible Budgets
LO 3 Apply responsibility accounting to cost and profit centers.	• Controllable vs. noncontrollable revenues and costs • Principles of performance evaluation • Responsibility reporting system • Types of responsibility centers	**DO IT! 3** Profit Center Responsibility Report
LO 4 Evaluate performance in investment centers.	• Return on investment (ROI) • Responsibility report • Alternative measures of ROI inputs • Improving ROI	**DO IT! 4** Performance Evaluation

Go to the Review and Practice section at the end of the chapter for a targeted summary and practice applications with solutions.

BUDGETARY CONTROL AND STATIC BUDGET REPORTS

Budgetary Control

One of management's responsibilities is to control company operations. Control consists of the steps taken by management to see that planned objectives are met. We now ask: How do budgets contribute to control of operations?

The use of budgets in controlling operations is known as **budgetary control**.

- Such control takes place by means of **budget reports** that compare actual results with planned objectives.
- The use of budget reports is based on the belief that planned objectives lose much of their potential value without some monitoring of progress along the way.
- Just as your professors give midterm exams to evaluate your progress, top management requires periodic reports on the progress of department managers toward planned objectives.

Budget reports provide management with feedback on operations and are prepared as frequently as needed.

- The feedback for a crucial objective, such as having enough cash on hand to pay bills, may be made daily.
- For other objectives, such as meeting budgeted annual sales and operating expenses, monthly budget reports may suffice.

From these reports, management analyzes any differences between actual and planned results and determines their causes. Management then takes corrective action, or it decides to modify future plans. Budgetary control involves the activities shown in **Illustration 10.1**.

> **LEARNING OBJECTIVE 1**
> Describe budgetary control and static budget reports.

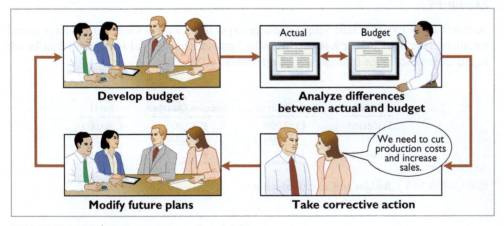

ILLUSTRATION 10.1 | **Budgetary control activities**

Budgetary control works best when a company has a formalized reporting system. The reporting system does the following:

1. Identifies the name of the budget report, such as the sales budget or the manufacturing overhead budget.
2. States the frequency of the report, such as weekly or monthly.
3. Specifies the purpose of the report.
4. Indicates the primary recipient(s) of the report.

Illustration 10.2 provides a partial budgetary control system for a manufacturing company. Note the frequency of the reports and their emphasis on control. For example, there is a daily report on scrap and a weekly report on labor.

Name of Report	Frequency	Purpose	Primary Recipient(s)
Sales	Weekly	Determine whether sales goals are met	Top management and sales manager
Labor	Weekly	Control direct and indirect labor costs	Vice president of production and production department managers
Scrap	Daily	Determine efficient use of materials	Production manager
Departmental overhead costs	Monthly	Control overhead costs	Department manager
Selling expenses	Monthly	Control selling expenses	Sales manager
Income statement	Monthly and quarterly	Determine whether income goals are met	Top management

ILLUSTRATION 10.2 | **Budgetary control reporting system**

Static Budget Reports

You learned in Chapter 9 that the master budget formalizes management's planned objectives for the coming year. When used in budgetary control, each budget included in the master budget is considered to be static.

- A **static budget** is a projection of budget data **at a single level of activity before actual activity occurs**.
- These budgets do not consider data for different levels of activity.
- As a result, companies compare actual results with budget data at the activity level that was used in developing the master budget.

Examples

To illustrate the role of a static budget in budgetary control, we will use selected data prepared for Adelmo Ciclo in Chapter 9. **Illustration 10.3** provides budget and actual sales data for the Rightride product in the first and second quarters of 2023.

Sales	First Quarter	Second Quarter	Total
Budgeted	€180,000	€210,000	€390,000
Actual	179,000	199,500	378,500
Difference	€ 1,000	€ 10,500	€ 11,500

ILLUSTRATION 10.3 | **Budget and actual sales data**

The sales budget report for Adelmo's first quarter is shown in **Illustration 10.4**. The rightmost column reports the difference between the budgeted and actual amounts (see **Alternative Terminology**).

The report shows that sales are €1,000 under budget—an unfavorable result.

ALTERNATIVE TERMINOLOGY

The difference between budget and actual is sometimes called a *budget variance*.

- This difference is less than 1% of budgeted sales (€1,000 ÷ €180,000 = .0056, or 0.56%).
- Top management's reaction to differences is often influenced by the materiality (significance) of the difference.
- Since the difference of €1,000 is immaterial in this case, we assume that Adelmo management takes no specific corrective action.

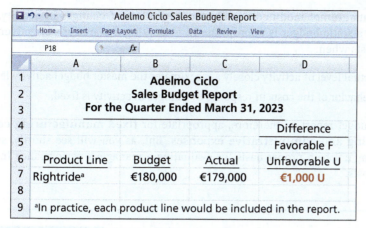

ILLUSTRATION 10.4 | Sales budget report—first quarter

Illustration 10.5 shows the sales budget report for the second quarter. It contains one new feature: cumulative year-to-date information. This report indicates that sales for the second quarter are €10,500 below budget. This is 5% of budgeted sales (€10,500 ÷ €210,000). Top management may now conclude that the difference between budgeted and actual sales requires investigation.

		Second Quarter			Year-to-Date		
				Difference			Difference
				Favorable F			Favorable F
Product Line	Budget	Actual		Unfavorable U	Budget	Actual	Unfavorable U
Rightride	€210,000	€199,500		€10,500 U	€390,000	€378,500	€11,500 U

Adelmo Ciclo Sales Budget Report
For the Quarter Ended June 30, 2023

ILLUSTRATION 10.5 | Sales budget report—second quarter

Management's analysis should start by:
- Asking the sales manager the cause(s) of the shortfall.
- Considering the need for corrective action.

For example, management may attempt to increase sales by offering sales incentives to customers or by increasing the advertising of Rightrides. Or, if management concludes that a downturn in the economy is responsible for the lower sales, it may modify planned sales and profit goals for the remainder of the year.

Uses and Limitations

From these examples, you can see that a master sales budget is useful in evaluating the performance of a sales manager. It is now necessary to ask: Is the master budget appropriate for evaluating a manager's performance in controlling costs? Recall that in a static

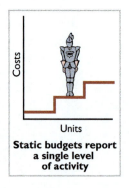

Static budgets report a single level of activity

budget, data are not modified or adjusted, regardless of changes in activity. It follows, then, that a static budget is appropriate in evaluating a manager's effectiveness in controlling costs when:

1. The actual level of activity closely approximates the master budget activity level, and/or
2. The behavior of the costs in response to changes in activity is fixed.

A static budget report is, therefore, appropriate for **fixed manufacturing costs** and for **fixed selling and administrative expenses**. But, as you will see shortly, static budget reports may not be a proper basis for evaluating a manager's performance in controlling variable costs.

DO IT! 1 ▶ Static Budget Reports

Trawler Company expects to produce 5,000 units of product CV93 during the current month. Budgeted variable manufacturing costs per unit are direct materials €6, direct labor €15, and overhead €24. Monthly budgeted fixed manufacturing overhead costs are €10,000 for depreciation and €5,000 for supervision.

In the current month, Trawler actually produced 5,500 units and incurred the following costs: direct materials €33,900, direct labor €74,200, variable overhead €120,500, depreciation €10,000, and supervision €5,000.

Prepare a static budget report. (*Hint:* The Budget column is based on estimated production of 5,000 units while the Actual column is the actual costs incurred during the period.) Were costs controlled? Discuss limitations of this budget.

ACTION PLAN

- Classify each cost as variable or fixed
- Determine the difference as favorable or unfavorable.
- Determine the difference in total variable costs, total fixed costs, and total costs.

Solution

Trawler Company

A	B	C	D	
			Difference Favorable - F Unfavorable - U	
	Budget	Actual		
Production in units	5,000	5,500		
Variable costs				
Direct materials (€6)	€ 30,000	€ 33,900	€3,900	U
Direct labor (€15)	75,000	74,200	800	F
Overhead (€24)	120,000	120,500	500	U
Total variable costs	225,000	228,600	3,600	U
Fixed costs				
Depreciation	10,000	10,000	0	
Supervision	5,000	5,000	0	
Total fixed costs	15,000	15,000	0	
Total costs	€240,000	€243,600	€3,600	U

The static budget indicates that actual variable costs exceeded budgeted amounts by €3,600. Fixed costs were exactly as budgeted. The static budget gives the impression that the company did not control its variable costs. However, the static budget does not give consideration to the fact that the company produced 500 more units than planned. As a result, the static budget is not a good tool to evaluate variable costs. It is, however, a good tool to evaluate fixed costs as those should not vary with changes in production volume.

Related exercise material: **BE10.1, BE10.2, DO IT! 10.1,** and **E10.2.**

FLEXIBLE BUDGET REPORTS

In contrast to a static budget, which is based on one level of activity, a **flexible budget** projects budget data for various levels of activity.

- In essence, **the flexible budget is a series of static budgets at different levels of activity**.
- The flexible budget recognizes that the budgetary process is more useful if it is adaptable to changed operating conditions.

Flexible budgets can be prepared for each of the types of budgets included in the master budget. For example, **Motel One** (DEU) can budget revenues and net income on the basis of 60%, 80%, and 100% of room occupancy. Similarly, **American Van Lines** (USA) can budget its operating expenses on the basis of various levels of truck-miles driven. **Energy Australia** (AUS) can budget revenue and net income on the basis of estimated billions of kwh (kilowatt hours) of residential, commercial, and industrial electricity generated. In the following pages, we will illustrate a flexible budget for manufacturing overhead.

LEARNING OBJECTIVE 2
Prepare flexible budget reports.

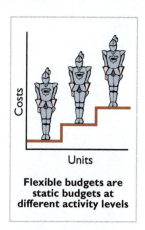

Flexible budgets are static budgets at different activity levels

Why Flexible Budgets?

Assume that you are the manager in charge of manufacturing overhead in the Assembly Department of Silvan Robotics. In preparing the manufacturing overhead budget for 2023, you prepare the static budget shown in **Illustration 10.6** based on a production volume of 10,000 units of robotic controls (see **Helpful Hint**).

HELPFUL HINT

The master budget described in Chapter 9 is based on a static budget.

Silvan Robotics
Manufacturing Overhead Budget (Static)
Assembly Department
For the Year Ended December 31, 2023

Budgeted production in units (robotic controls)	10,000
Budgeted costs	
Indirect materials	€ 250,000
Indirect labor	260,000
Utilities	190,000
Depreciation	280,000
Property taxes	70,000
Supervision	50,000
	€1,100,000

ILLUSTRATION 10.6 | **Static overhead budget**

Fortunately for the company, the demand for robotic controls has increased, and Silvan produces and sells 12,000 units during the year rather than 10,000. You are elated! Increased sales means increased profitability, which should mean a bonus or a raise for you and the employees in your department. Unfortunately, a comparison of Assembly Department actual and budgeted costs has put you on the spot. **Illustration 10.7** shows the budget report.

Silvan Robotics
Manufacturing Overhead Static Budget Report
For the Year Ended December 31, 2023

	Budget	Actual	Difference Favorable - F Unfavorable - U	
Production in units	10,000	12,000		
Costs				
Indirect materials	€ 250,000	€ 295,000	€ 45,000	U
Indirect labor	260,000	312,000	52,000	U
Utilities	190,000	225,000	35,000	U
Depreciation	280,000	280,000	0	
Property taxes	70,000	70,000	0	
Supervision	50,000	50,000	0	
	€1,100,000	€1,232,000	€132,000	U

ILLUSTRATION 10.7 | **Overhead static budget report**

This comparison uses budgeted cost data based on the original activity level (10,000 robotic controls).

- It indicates that the costs incurred by the Assembly Department are significantly **over budget** for three of the six overhead costs.
- There is a total unfavorable difference of €132,000, which is 12% over budget (€132,000 ÷ €1,100,000).

Your supervisor is very unhappy. Instead of sharing in the company's success, you may find yourself looking for another job. What went wrong?

When you calm down and carefully examine the manufacturing overhead budget, you identify the problem: The budget data are not relevant!

- At the time the budget was developed, the company anticipated that only 10,000 units would be produced. Instead, 12,000 units were actually produced.
- Comparing actual costs incurred at a production level of 12,000 units with budgeted variable costs at an expected production level of 10,000 units is meaningless (see **Helpful Hint**).
- As production increases, the budget allowances for variable costs should increase proportionately. The variable costs in this example are indirect materials, indirect labor, and utilities.

HELPFUL HINT

A static budget is not useful for performance evaluation if a company has substantial variable costs.

Analyzing the budget data for these costs at 10,000 units, you arrive at the unit variable cost results shown in **Illustration 10.8**.

Item	Budgeted Cost	÷	Budgeted Number of Units	=	Unit Variable Cost
Indirect materials	€250,000		10,000		€25
Indirect labor	260,000		10,000		26
Utilities	190,000		10,000		19
	€700,000				€70

ILLUSTRATION 10.8 | **Unit variable costs**

Using these unit variable costs, **Illustration 10.9** calculates the budgeted variable costs at 12,000 units.

Item	Unit Variable Cost × Actual Units	=	Budgeted Variable Costs
Indirect materials	€25 × 12,000		€300,000
Indirect labor	€26 × 12,000		312,000
Utilities	€19 × 12,000		228,000
			€840,000

ILLUSTRATION 10.9 | Budgeted variable costs, 12,000 units

Because fixed costs do not change in total as activity changes, the budgeted amounts for these costs remain the same. **Illustration 10.10** shows the budget report based on the flexible budget for **12,000 units** of production. (Compare this with Illustration 10.7.)

Silvan Robotics
Manufacturing Overhead Flexible Budget Report
For the Year Ended December 31, 2023

	Budget	Actual	Difference Favorable - F Unfavorable - U	
Production in units	12,000	12,000		
Variable costs				
Indirect materials (€25)	€ 300,000	€ 295,000	€5,000	F
Indirect labor (€26)	312,000	312,000	0	
Utilities (€19)	228,000	225,000	3,000	F
Total variable costs	840,000	832,000	8,000	F
Fixed costs				
Depreciation	280,000	280,000	0	
Property taxes	70,000	70,000	0	
Supervision	50,000	50,000	0	
Total fixed costs	400,000	400,000	0	
Total costs	€1,240,000	€1,232,000	€8,000	F

ILLUSTRATION 10.10 | Overhead flexible budget report

This flexible budget report indicates that the Assembly Department's costs are **under budget**—a favorable difference. Instead of worrying about being fired, you may be in line for a bonus or a raise after all! As this analysis shows, the only appropriate comparison is between actual costs at 12,000 units of production and budgeted costs at 12,000 units. Flexible budget reports provide this comparison (see **Decision Tools**).

> **DECISION TOOLS**
> The flexible budget helps management evaluate whether cost changes resulting from different production volumes are reasonable.

Developing the Flexible Budget

The flexible budget uses the master budget as its basis. To develop the flexible budget, management uses the following steps:

1. Identify the activity index and the relevant range of activity.
2. Identify the variable costs, and determine the budgeted variable cost per unit of activity for each cost.
3. Identify the fixed costs, and determine the budgeted amount for each cost.
4. Prepare the budget for selected increments of activity within the relevant range.

The activity index chosen should have a strong relationship with the costs being budgeted. That is, an increase in the activity index should coincide with an increase in costs. For manufacturing overhead costs, for example, the activity index is usually the same as the index used in developing the predetermined overhead rate—that is, direct labor hours or machine hours. For selling and administrative expenses, the activity index usually is sales or net sales.

The choice of the increment of activity is largely a matter of judgment. For example, if the relevant range is 8,000 to 12,000 direct labor hours, increments of 1,000 hours may be selected. The flexible budget is then prepared for each increment within the relevant range.

SERVICE COMPANY INSIGHT NBCUniversal

KlaraBstock/Shutterstock.com

Just What the Doctor Ordered?

Nobody is immune from the effects of declining revenues—not even movie stars. When the number of viewers of a popular medical drama declined by almost 20%, **Fox Broadcasting** (USA) said it wanted to cut the license fee that it paid to **NBCUniversal** (USA) by 20%.

What would NBCUniversal do in response? It might cut the size of the show's cast, which would reduce the payroll costs associated with the show. Or, it could reduce the number of episodes that take advantage of the full cast. Alternatively, it might threaten to quit providing the show to Fox altogether and instead present the show on its own NBC-affiliated channels. As consumers continue to shift to alternative entertainment sources, television executives will need to make creative adjustments in order to maintain profitability.

Sources: Sam Schechner, "Media Business Shorts: NBCU, Fox Taking Scalpel to 'House'," *Wall Street Journal Online* (April 17, 2011); and Rick Porter, "TV LongView: Five Years of Network Ratings Declines in Context," *The Hollywood Reporter* (September 21, 2019).

How might the use of flexible budgets help to identify the best solution to this problem? (Answer is available in the book's product page on www.wiley.com)

Flexible Budget—A Case Study

To illustrate the flexible budget, we use Orris Industries. Orris's management uses a **flexible budget for monthly comparisons** of actual and budgeted manufacturing overhead costs of the Finishing Department. The master budget for the year ending December 31, 2023, shows expected **annual** operating capacity of 120,000 direct labor hours and the overhead costs shown in **Illustration 10.11**.

Variable Costs		Fixed Costs	
Indirect materials	€180,000	Depreciation	€180,000
Indirect labor	240,000	Supervision	120,000
Utilities	60,000	Property taxes	60,000
Total	€480,000	Total	€360,000

ILLUSTRATION 10.11 | Master budget data

The four steps for developing the flexible budget are applied as follows:

Step 1 **Identify the activity index and the relevant range of activity.** Management has found that there is a strong relationship between direct labor hours and variable manufacturing overhead costs. Thus, the activity index is direct labor hours. The relevant range is 8,000–12,000 direct labor hours per **month**.

Step 2 **Identify the variable costs, and determine the budgeted variable cost per unit of activity for each cost.** A cost is variable if total costs vary directly as a result of a change in the activity index, which is direct labor in this case. In this example, indirect materials, indirect labor, and utilities are variable costs. The variable cost per unit is found by dividing each total budgeted cost by the direct labor hours used in preparing the annual master budget (120,000 hours). **Illustration 10.12** shows the computations for Orris Industries.

Variable Costs	Total Budgeted Cost ÷ Budgeted Direct Labor Hours	=	Variable Cost per Direct Labor Hour
Indirect materials	€180,000 ÷ 120,000		€1.50
Indirect labor	€240,000 ÷ 120,000		2.00
Utilities	€60,000 ÷ 120,000		0.50
Total			€4.00

ILLUSTRATION 10.12 | Computation of variable cost per direct labor hour

Step 3 **Identify the fixed costs, and determine the budgeted amount for each cost.** A cost is fixed if the total cost does not vary as a result of changes in the activity index. In this example, depreciation, supervision, and property taxes are fixed costs. Since Orris desires **monthly budget data**, it divides each annual budgeted cost by 12 to find the monthly amounts. Therefore, the monthly budgeted fixed costs are depreciation €15,000 (€180,000 ÷ 12), supervision €10,000 (€120,000 ÷ 12), and property taxes €5,000 (€60,000 ÷ 12).

Step 4 **Prepare the budget for selected increments of activity within the relevant range.** Management prepares the budget in increments of 1,000 direct labor hours.

Illustration 10.13 shows Orris's flexible budget.

Orris Industries
Monthly Manufacturing Overhead Flexible Budget
Finishing Department
For Months During the Year 2023

Activity level					
Direct labor hours	8,000	9,000	10,000	11,000	12,000
Variable costs					
Indirect materials (€1.50)[a]	€12,000[b]	€13,500	€15,000	€16,500	€18,000
Indirect labor (€2.00)[a]	16,000[c]	18,000	20,000	22,000	24,000
Utilities (€0.50)[a]	4,000[d]	4,500	5,000	5,500	6,000
Total variable costs	32,000	36,000	40,000	44,000	48,000
Fixed costs					
Depreciation	15,000	15,000	15,000	15,000	15,000
Supervision	10,000	10,000	10,000	10,000	10,000
Property taxes	5,000	5,000	5,000	5,000	5,000
Total fixed costs	30,000	30,000	30,000	30,000	30,000
Total costs	€62,000	€66,000	€70,000	€74,000	€78,000

[a]Cost per direct labor hour; [b]8,000 × €1.50; [c]8,000 × €2.00; [d]8,000 × €0.50

ILLUSTRATION 10.13 | Monthly overhead flexible budget

Orris uses the cost equation shown in **Illustration 10.14** to determine total budgeted costs at any level of activity.

$$\text{Fixed Costs} + \text{Variable Costs*} = \text{Total Budgeted Costs}$$

*Total variable cost per unit of activity × Activity level.

ILLUSTRATION 10.14 | Cost equation for total budgeted costs

HELPFUL HINT

Using the data given for Orris, the amount of total costs to be budgeted for 10,600 direct labor hours would be €30,000 fixed + €42,400 variable (10,600 × €4) = €72,400 total.

For Orris, fixed costs are €30,000 per month, and total variable cost per direct labor hour is €4 (€1.50 + €2.00 + €0.50).

- At 9,000 direct labor hours, total budgeted costs are €66,000 [€30,000 + (€4 × 9,000)].
- At 8,622 direct labor hours, total budgeted costs are €64,488 [€30,000 + (€4 × 8,622)] (see **Helpful Hint**).

Total budgeted costs can also be shown graphically, as in **Illustration 10.15**.

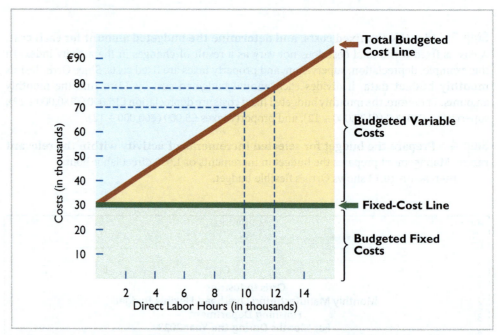

ILLUSTRATION 10.15 | Graphic flexible budget data highlighting 10,000 and 12,000 activity levels

- In the graph, the horizontal axis represents the activity index, and costs are indicated on the vertical axis.
- The graph highlights two activity levels (10,000 and 12,000).
- As shown, total budgeted costs at these activity levels are €70,000 [€30,000 + (€4 × 10,000)] and €78,000 [€30,000 + (€4 × 12,000)], respectively.

Flexible Budget Reports

Flexible budget reports are another type of internal report. The flexible budget report consists of two sections:

1. Production data for a selected activity index, such as direct labor hours.
2. Cost data for variable and fixed costs.

The report provides a basis for evaluating a manager's performance in two areas: production control and cost control. Flexible budget reports are widely used in production and service departments.

Illustration 10.16 shows a flexible budget report for the Finishing Department of Orris Industries for the month of January. In this month, 9,000 hours are worked. The budget data are therefore based on the flexible budget for 9,000 hours in Illustration 10.13. The actual cost data are assumed.

How appropriate is this report in evaluating the Finishing Department manager's performance in controlling overhead costs? The report clearly provides a more reliable basis than a static budget.

Orris Industries
Manufacturing Overhead Flexible Budget Report
Finishing Department
For the Month Ended January 31, 2023

	Budget at 9,000 DLH	Actual costs at 9,000 DLH	Difference Favorable - F Unfavorable - U	
Direct labor hours (DLH)				
Variable costs				
Indirect materials (€1.50)[a]	€13,500	€14,000	€ 500	U
Indirect labor (€2.00)[a]	18,000	17,000	1,000	F
Utilities (€0.50)[a]	4,500	4,600	100	U
Total variable costs	36,000	35,600	400	F
Fixed costs				
Depreciation	15,000	15,000	0	
Supervision	10,000	10,000	0	
Property taxes	5,000	5,000	0	
Total fixed costs	30,000	30,000	0	
Total costs	€66,000	€65,600	€ 400	F

[a]Cost per direct labor hour

ILLUSTRATION 10.16 | Overhead flexible budget report

- Both actual and budget costs are based on the activity level worked during January.
- Since variable costs generally are incurred directly by the department, the difference between the budget allowance for those hours and the actual costs is the responsibility of the department manager.

In subsequent months, Orris Industries will prepare other flexible budget reports. For each month, the budget data are based on the actual activity level attained. In February, that level may be 11,000 direct labor hours, in July 10,000, and so on.

Note that this flexible budget is based on a single cost driver. A more accurate budget often can be developed using activity-based costing (see Chapter 4).

DATA ANALYTICS INSIGHT

These Forecasts Move with the Times!

Solarbeamk/Shutterstock.com

Many companies now supplement their annual static budgets with rolling forecasts. Although budgets are detailed documents, they are typically only prepared annually and thus can quickly lose usefulness as business conditions change. In contrast, rolling forecasts are less detailed, focus on those elements that management believes are the most important, and are usually updated monthly. As a result, rolling forecasts can help improve management's ability to respond to changing business conditions and enable creation of scenarios where management can experiment with "what if" questions.

Forecasts are forward-looking, covering a period of time anywhere from 4 to 18 months. And while long-term forecasts might provide more insight, shorter-term forecasts are more accurate. To create and update these short-term rolling forecasts, companies rely heavily on big data. For example, companies must identify the most significant value-drivers in creating rolling forecasts; data analytics can help to verify the accuracy of the data used. For many companies, a well-developed rolling forecast system, based on data analytics, is invaluable.

Source: Robert Freedman, "How to Transition from a Static to a Rolling Forecast," *CFO Dive* (December 4, 2019).

In what ways are budgets and rolling forecasts similar, and in what ways do they differ? (Answer is available in the book's product page on www.wiley.com)

DO IT! 2 ▶ Flexible Budgets

In Gabrielle Company's flexible budget graph, the fixed-cost line and the total budgeted cost line intersect the vertical axis at €36,000. The total budgeted cost line is €186,000 at an activity level of 50,000 direct labor hours. Compute total budgeted costs at 30,000 direct labor hours.

ACTION PLAN
- Apply the equation: Fixed costs + Variable costs (Total variable cost per unit × Activity level) = Total budgeted costs.

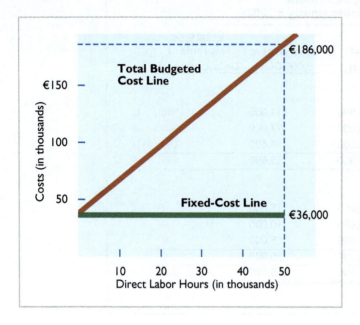

Solution

Using the graph, fixed costs are €36,000, and variable costs are €3 per direct labor hour [(€186,000 − €36,000) ÷ 50,000]. Thus, at 30,000 direct labor hours, total budgeted costs are €126,000 [€36,000 + (€3 × 30,000)].

Related exercise material: **BE10.4, DO IT! 10.2, E10.3, and E10.5.**

RESPONSIBILITY ACCOUNTING AND RESPONSIBILITY CENTERS

LEARNING OBJECTIVE 3
Apply responsibility accounting to cost and profit centers.

Like budgeting, responsibility accounting is an important part of management accounting.

- **Responsibility accounting** involves identifying and reporting costs (and revenues, where relevant) on the basis of the manager who has the authority to make the day-to-day decisions about the items.
- Under responsibility accounting, a manager's performance is evaluated on matters directly under that manager's control.

Responsibility accounting can be used at every level of management in which the following conditions exist.

1. Costs and revenues can be directly associated with the specific level of management responsibility.

2. The costs and revenues can be controlled by employees at the level of responsibility with which they are associated.
3. Budget data can be developed for evaluating the manager's effectiveness in controlling the costs and revenues.

Illustration 10.17 depicts levels of responsibility for controlling costs.

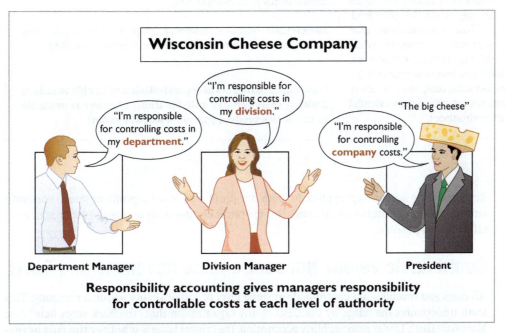

ILLUSTRATION 10.17 | **Responsibility for controllable costs at varying levels of management**

Under responsibility accounting, any individual who controls a specified set of activities can be a responsibility center. Thus, responsibility accounting may extend from the lowest level of control to the top strata of management. Once responsibility is established, the company first measures and reports the effectiveness of the individual's performance for the specified activity. It then reports that measure upward throughout the organization (see **Helpful Hint**).

Responsibility accounting is especially valuable in a decentralized company.

- **Decentralization** means that the control of operations is delegated to many managers throughout the organization.
- The term **segment** (or **division**) is sometimes used to identify an area of responsibility in decentralized operations.

Under responsibility accounting, companies prepare segment reports periodically, such as monthly, quarterly, and annually, to evaluate managers' performance.

Responsibility accounting is an essential part of any effective system of budgetary control. The reporting of costs and revenues under responsibility accounting differs from budgeting in two respects:

1. A distinction is made between controllable and noncontrollable items.
2. Performance reports either emphasize or include only items controllable by the individual manager.

HELPFUL HINT

All companies use responsibility accounting. Without some form of responsibility accounting, there would be chaos in discharging management's control function.

MANAGEMENT INSIGHT — Procter & Gamble

Competition versus Collaboration

Khuong Hoang/iStockphoto

Many compensation and promotion programs encourage competition among employees for pay raises. To get ahead, you have to perform better than your fellow employees. While this may encourage hard work, it does not foster collaboration, and it can lead to distrust and disloyalty. Such negative effects have led some companies to believe that cooperation and collaboration, not competition, are essential in order to succeed in today's work environment.

As a consequence, many companies now explicitly include measures of collaboration in their performance measures. For example, **Procter & Gamble** (USA) measures collaboration in employees' annual performance reviews. At **Cisco Systems** (USA), the assessment of an employee's teamwork can affect the annual bonus by as much as 20%.

Source: Carol Hymowitz, "Rewarding Competitors Over Collaboration No Longer Makes Sense," *Wall Street Journal* (February 13, 2006).

How might managers of separate divisions be able to reduce division costs through collaboration? (Answer is available in the book's product page on www.wiley.com)

Responsibility accounting applies to both for-profit and not-for-profit entities. For-profit entities seek to maximize net income. Not-for-profit entities wish to provide services as cost-efficiently as possible.

Controllable versus Noncontrollable Revenues and Costs

HELPFUL HINT
There are more, not fewer, controllable costs as you move to higher levels of management.

HELPFUL HINT
The longer the time span, the more likely that the cost becomes controllable since it is more likely that managers' requested changes can be implemented.

All costs and revenues are controllable at some level of responsibility within a company. This truth underscores the adage by the CEO of any organization that "the buck stops here" (see **Helpful Hint**). Under responsibility accounting, the critical issue is **whether the cost or revenue is controllable at the level of responsibility with which it is associated**. A cost over which a manager has control is called a **controllable cost**. From this definition, it follows that:

1. All costs are controllable by top management because of the broad range of its authority.
2. Fewer costs are controllable as one moves down to each lower level of managerial responsibility because of the manager's decreasing authority.

In general, **costs incurred directly by a level of responsibility are controllable at that level** (see **Helpful Hint**). In contrast, costs incurred indirectly and allocated to a responsibility level are **noncontrollable costs** at that level.

Principles of Performance Evaluation

Performance evaluation is at the center of responsibility accounting. It is a management function that compares actual results with budget goals. It involves both behavioral and reporting principles.

Management by Exception

Management by exception means:

- Top management's review of a budget report is focused either entirely or primarily on significant differences between actual results and planned objectives.
- This approach enables top management to focus on problem areas.

For example, many companies now use online reporting systems for employees to file their travel and entertainment expense reports. In addition to significantly reducing reporting time, the online system enables managers to quickly analyze variances from travel budgets. This cuts down on expense account "padding" such as spending too much on meals or falsifying documents for costs that were never actually incurred.

Under management by exception, top management does not investigate every difference. For this approach to be effective, there must be guidelines for identifying which differences to investigate. The usual criteria are materiality and controllability.

Materiality Without quantitative guidelines, management would have to investigate every budget difference regardless of the amount.

- Materiality is usually expressed as a percentage difference from budget. For example, management may set the percentage difference at 5% for important items and 10% for other items.
- Managers will investigate all differences either over or under budget by the specified percentage. Costs over budget warrant investigation to determine why they were not controlled. Likewise, costs under budget merit investigation to determine whether costs critical to profitability are being curtailed.

For example, if maintenance costs are budgeted at €80,000 but only €40,000 is spent, major unexpected breakdowns in productive facilities may occur in the future. Or, as discussed in Chapter 9, cost might be under budget due to budgetary slack.

Alternatively, a company may specify a single percentage difference from budget for all items and supplement this guideline with a minimum limit. For example, the exception criteria may be stated at 5% of budget or more than €10,000.

Controllability of the Item Exception guidelines are more restrictive for controllable items than for items the manager cannot control.

- In fact, there may be no guidelines for noncontrollable items.
- For example, a large unfavorable difference between actual and budgeted property tax expense may not be flagged for investigation because the only possible causes are an unexpected increase in the tax rate or in the assessed value of the property.
- An investigation into the difference would be useless: The manager cannot control either cause.

Behavioral Principles

The human factor is critical in evaluating performance. Behavioral principles include the following:

1. **Managers of responsibility centers should have direct input into the process of establishing budget goals of their area of responsibility.** Without such input, managers may view the goals as unrealistic or arbitrarily set by top management. Such views adversely affect the managers' motivation to meet the targeted objectives.
2. **The evaluation of performance should be based entirely on matters that are controllable by the manager being evaluated.** Criticism of a manager on matters outside his or her control reduces the effectiveness of the evaluation process. It leads to negative reactions by the manager and to doubts about the fairness of the company's evaluation policies.
3. **Top management should support the evaluation process.** As explained earlier, the evaluation process begins at the lowest level of responsibility and extends upward to the highest level of management. Managers quickly lose faith in the process when top management ignores, overrules, or bypasses established procedures for evaluating a manager's performance.
4. **The evaluation process must allow managers to respond to their evaluations.** Evaluation is not a one-way street. Managers should have the opportunity to defend their performance. Evaluation without feedback is both impersonal and ineffective.
5. **The evaluation should identify both good and poor performance.** Praise for good performance is a powerful motivating factor for a manager. This is especially true when a manager's compensation includes rewards for meeting budget goals.

Reporting Principles

Performance evaluation under responsibility accounting should be based on certain reporting principles. These principles pertain primarily to the internal reports that provide the basis for evaluating performance. Performance reports should:

- Contain only data that are controllable by the manager of the responsibility center.
- Provide accurate and reliable budget data to measure performance.
- Highlight significant differences between actual results and budget goals.
- Be tailor-made for the intended evaluation by ensuring only controllable costs are included.
- Be prepared at reasonable time intervals.

In recent years, companies have come under increasing pressure from influential shareholder groups to do a better job of linking executive pay to corporate performance. For example, at one time software maker **Siebel Systems** (USA) unveiled an incentive plan after lengthy discussions with the California Public Employees' Retirement System. One unique feature of the plan is that managers' targets will be publicly disclosed at the beginning of each year for investors to evaluate.

DATA ANALYTICS INSIGHT

chombosan / Alamy Stock Photo

Hitting the Road with Zero-Based Budgeting

The automotive industry has enjoyed a relatively stable business model for almost 100 years. But now it is threatened by changes coming from multiple fronts. Managers at auto manufacturers must decide whether they are going to expend massive investments in electric vehicles, autonomous vehicles, and mobility as a service. Such large outlays of company resources would necessitate diverting funds away from some current activities. How will these managers determine what to invest in and what to drop?

One possible tool these managers might use is zero-based budgeting. This approach requires that "all costs and expenses be reassessed and justified in terms of their contribution to the business' overall value." This determination relies heavily on data analytic models that employ large amounts of data from a wide variety of sources to predict future business trends. Proponents of "zero-basing" argue that it enables companies to rapidly redeploy limited resources when the business environment is constantly changing. But, zero-based budgeting has been criticized by some as being unnecessarily disruptive, time-consuming, and expensive. Zero-based budgeting might be especially problematic in the automotive industry, where a company culture is well-established. Big changes can stir up big emotions.

Source: Global Strategy Group, KPMG International Cooperative, "Zero Basing in Automotive," *Realizing Value Series* (2018).

What are some of the pros and cons of employing zero-based budgeting? (Answer is available in the book's product page on www.wiley.com)

Responsibility Reporting System

DECISION TOOLS

Responsibility reports help to hold individual managers accountable for the costs and revenues under their control.

A **responsibility reporting system** involves the preparation of a report for each level of responsibility in the company's organization chart (see **Decision Tools**). To illustrate such a system, we use the partial organization chart and production departments of Empire Furniture Company in **Illustration 10.18**.

The responsibility reporting system begins with the lowest level of responsibility for controlling costs and moves upward to each higher level. (Illustration 10.19 details the connections between levels.) A brief description of the four reports for Empire Furniture is as follows:

1. **Report D** is typical of reports that go to department managers. Similar reports are prepared for the managers of the Assembly and Enameling Departments.

2. **Report C** is an example of reports that are sent to factory managers. It shows the costs of the Berlin factory that are controllable at the second level of responsibility. In addition, Report C shows summary data for each department that is controlled by the factory manager. Similar reports are prepared for the Hamburg and Frankfurt factory managers.

3. **Report B** illustrates the reports at the third level of responsibility. It shows the controllable costs of the vice president of production and summary data on the three assembly factories for which this officer is responsible. Similar reports are prepared for the vice presidents of sales and finance.

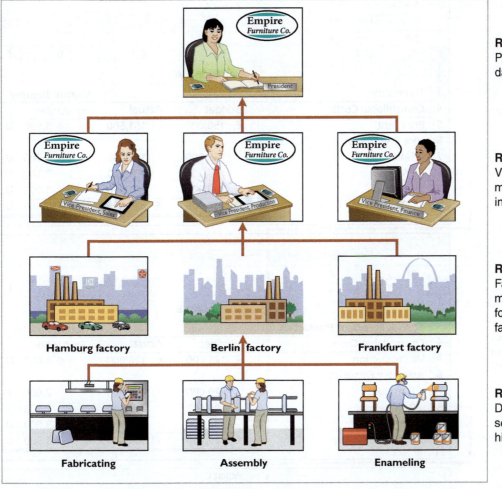

ILLUSTRATION 10.18 | Partial organization chart

Report A
President sees summary data of vice presidents.

Report B
Vice president sees summary of controllable costs in his/her functional area.

Report C
Factory manager sees summary of controllable costs for each department in the factory.

Report D
Department manager sees controllable costs of his/her department.

4. **Report A** is typical of reports that go to the top level of responsibility—the president. It shows the controllable costs and expenses of this office and summary data on the vice presidents that are accountable to the president.

A responsibility reporting system permits management by exception at each level of responsibility. And, each higher level of responsibility can obtain the detailed report for each lower level of responsibility. For example, the vice president of production in Empire Furniture may request the Berlin factory manager's report because this factory is €5,300 over budget.

This type of reporting system also permits comparative evaluations. In **Illustration 10.19**, the Berlin factory manager can easily rank the department managers' effectiveness in controlling manufacturing costs. Comparative rankings provide further incentive for a manager to control costs.

Types of Responsibility Centers

There are three basic types of responsibility centers: cost centers, profit centers, and investment centers. These classifications indicate the nature of the responsibility the manager has for the performance of the center.

1. A **cost center** incurs costs (and expenses) but does not directly generate revenues.
   - Managers of cost centers have the authority to incur costs.
   - They are evaluated on their ability to control costs.
   - **Cost centers are usually either production departments or service departments.**

Report A
President sees summary data of vice presidents.

Report B
Vice president sees summary of controllable costs in his/her functional area.

Report C
Factory manager sees summary of controllable costs for each department in the factory.

Report D
Department manager sees controllable costs of his/her department.

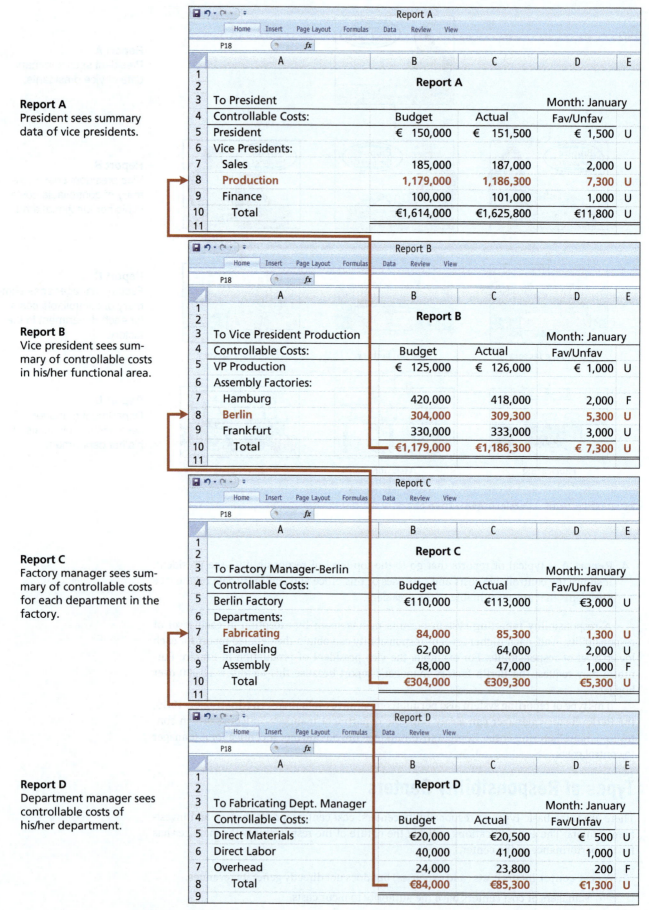

ILLUSTRATION 10.19 | Responsibility reporting system

Production departments participate directly in making the product. Service departments provide only support services. In a **Ford Motor Company** (USA) manufacturing facility, the welding, painting, and assembling departments are production departments. Ford's maintenance and human resources departments are service departments. Both the production departments and service departments are cost centers.

2. A **profit center** incurs costs (and expenses) and also generates revenues.
   - Managers of profit centers are judged on the profitability of their centers.
   - Examples of profit centers include the individual departments of a retail store, such as clothing, furniture, and automotive products, and branch offices of banks (see **Helpful Hint**).

3. Like a profit center, an **investment center** incurs costs (and expenses) and generates revenues. In addition, an investment center has control over decisions regarding the assets available for use.
   - Investment center managers are evaluated on both the profitability of the center and the rate of return earned on the assets used.
   - Investment centers are often associated with subsidiary companies.

> **HELPFUL HINT**
> The jewelry department of **Harrods'** (GBR) department store is a profit center, while the makeup department of a movie studio is a cost center.

Utility company **Duke Energy** (USA) has operating divisions such as electric utility, energy trading, and natural gas. Investment center managers control or significantly influence investment decisions related to such matters as plant expansion and entry into new market areas.

Illustration 10.20 depicts the three types of responsibility centers.

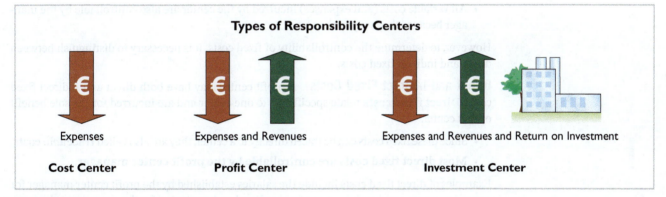

ILLUSTRATION 10.20 | **Types of responsibility centers**

Responsibility Accounting for Cost Centers

The evaluation of a manager's performance for cost centers is based on his or her ability to meet budgeted goals for controllable costs. **Responsibility reports for cost centers compare actual controllable costs with flexible budget data.**

Illustration 10.21 shows a responsibility report. The report is adapted from the flexible budget report for Orris Industries in Illustration 10.16. It assumes that the Finishing Department manager is able to control all manufacturing overhead costs except depreciation, property taxes, and his own monthly salary of €6,000. The remaining €4,000 (€10,000 − €6,000) of supervision costs are assumed to apply to other supervisory personnel within the Finishing Department, whose salaries are controllable by the manager.

- The report in Illustration 10.21 includes **only controllable costs**, and no distinction is made between variable and fixed costs.
- The responsibility report continues the concept of management by exception.
- In this case, top management may request an explanation of the €1,000 favorable difference in indirect labor and/or the €500 unfavorable difference in indirect materials if considered significant.

Orris Industries
Finishing Department
Responsibility Report
For the Month Ended January 31, 2023

Controllable Costs	Budget	Actual	Difference Favorable - F Unfavorable - U	
Indirect materials	€13,500	€14,000	€ 500	U
Indirect labor	18,000	17,000	1,000	F
Utilities	4,500	4,600	100	U
Supervision	4,000	4,000	0	
Total	€40,000	€39,600	€ 400	F

ILLUSTRATION 10.21 | Responsibility report for a cost center

Responsibility Accounting for Profit Centers

To evaluate the performance of a profit center manager, upper management needs detailed information about both controllable revenues and controllable costs.

- The operating revenues earned by a profit center, such as sales, are controllable by the manager.
- All variable costs (and expenses) incurred by the center are also controllable by the manager because they vary with sales.

However, to determine the controllability of fixed costs, it is necessary to distinguish between direct and indirect fixed costs.

Direct and Indirect Fixed Costs
A profit center may have both direct and indirect fixed costs. **Direct fixed costs** relate specifically to one center and are incurred for the sole benefit of that center.

- Since these fixed costs can be traced directly to a center, they are also called **traceable costs**.
- **Most direct fixed costs are controllable by the profit center manager**.

Examples of direct fixed costs include the salaries established by the profit center manager for supervisory personnel and the cost of a timekeeping department for the center's employees.

In contrast, **indirect fixed costs** pertain to a company's overall operating activities and are incurred for the benefit of more than one profit center.

- When preparing budgets, a company allocates indirect fixed costs to profit centers on some type of equitable basis.
- Because these fixed costs apply to more than one center, they are also called **common costs**.
- **Most indirect fixed costs are not controllable by the profit center manager and are therefore not reported in the responsibility report.**

For example, property taxes on a building occupied by more than one center may be allocated on the basis of square yards of floor space used by each center. Or, the costs of a company's human resources department may be allocated to profit centers on the basis of the number of employees in each center.

Responsibility Report
The responsibility report for a profit center shows budgeted and actual **controllable revenues and costs**. The report is prepared using the cost-volume-profit income statement explained in Chapter 5 (see **Helpful Hint**). In the report:

1. Controllable fixed costs are deducted from contribution margin.
2. The excess of contribution margin over controllable fixed costs is identified as **controllable margin**.
3. Noncontrollable fixed costs, such as indirect fixed costs, are not reported.

HELPFUL HINT
Recognize that we are emphasizing *financial* measures of performance. Companies are now making an effort to also stress *nonfinancial* performance measures such as product quality, labor productivity, market growth, materials' yield, manufacturing flexibility, and technological capability.

Illustration 10.22 shows the responsibility report for the manager of the Marine Division, a profit center of Peerless Group. For the year, the Marine Division also had €60,000 of indirect fixed costs that were not controllable by the profit center manager and therefore were omitted from the report.

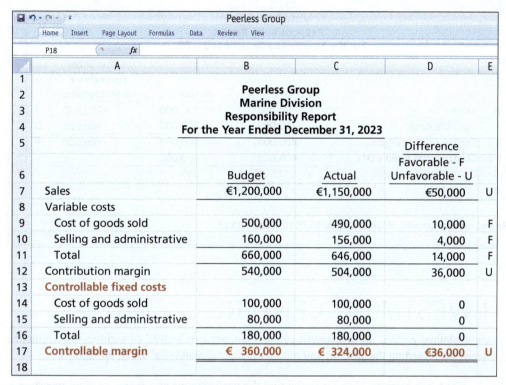

ILLUSTRATION 10.22 | **Responsibility report for profit center**

Controllable margin is considered to be the best measure of the manager's performance **in controlling revenues and costs**.

- The report in Illustration 10.22 shows that the manager's performance was below budgeted expectations by 10% (€36,000 ÷ €360,000) of the budgeted controllable margin.
- Top management would likely investigate the causes of this unfavorable result.
- Note that the responsibility report for the division manager does not show the Marine Division's noncontrollable indirect fixed costs of €60,000 because the manager cannot control these costs.

Management also may choose to see **monthly** responsibility reports for profit centers. In addition, responsibility reports may include cumulative year-to-date results.

DO IT! 3 ▶ **Profit Center Responsibility Report**

Victoria Division operates as a profit center. It reports the following for the year.

	Budget	Actual
Sales	€1,500,000	€1,700,000
Variable costs	700,000	800,000
Controllable fixed costs	400,000	400,000
Noncontrollable fixed costs	200,000	200,000

Prepare a responsibility report for the Victoria Division for December 31, 2023.

ACTION PLAN
- Deduct variable costs from sales to show contribution margin.
- Deduct controllable fixed costs from the contribution margin to show controllable margin.
- Do not report noncontrollable fixed costs.

Solution

Victoria Division Responsibility Report
For the Year Ended December 31, 2023

	Budget	Actual	Difference Favorable F Unfavorable U	
Sales	€1,500,000	€1,700,000	€200,000	F
Variable costs	700,000	800,000	100,000	U
Contribution margin	800,000	900,000	100,000	F
Controllable fixed costs	400,000	400,000	0	
Controllable margin	**€ 400,000**	**€ 500,000**	**€100,000**	**F**

Related exercise material: **BE10.7, BE10.8, DO IT! 10.3,** and **E10.15.**

INVESTMENT CENTERS

LEARNING OBJECTIVE 4
Evaluate performance in investment centers.

As explained earlier, an investment center manager can control or significantly influence decisions regarding the amount and nature of assets available for use in operations.

- Thus, the primary basis for evaluating the performance of a manager of an investment center is **return on investment (ROI)**.
- The return on investment is considered to be a useful performance measurement because it shows the **effectiveness of the manager in utilizing the assets at his or her disposal**.

Return on Investment (ROI)

The equation for computing ROI for an investment center, together with assumed illustrative data, is shown in **Illustration 10.23**.

Controllable Margin	÷	Average Operating Assets	=	Return on Investment (ROI)
€1,000,000	÷	€5,000,000	=	20%

ILLUSTRATION 10.23 | ROI equation

The two factors that determine ROI are controllable margin and average operating assets. Both factors in the equation are controllable by the investment center manager (see **Decision Tools**).

DECISION TOOLS
The ROI equation helps managers determine if the investment center has used its assets effectively.

- Operating assets consist of current assets and factory assets used in operations by the center and controlled by the manager.
- Nonoperating assets such as idle factory assets and land held for future use are excluded.

- Average operating assets are usually based on the cost or book value of the assets at the beginning and end of the year.

Based on these assigned values, the ROI of 20% indicates that, on average, the segment generates 20 cents of profit for every euro invested in assets.

Responsibility Report

The scope of the investment center manager's responsibility significantly affects the content of the performance report.

- Since an investment center is an independent entity for operating purposes, **all fixed costs are controllable by its manager**. For example, the manager is responsible for depreciation on investment center assets.
- Therefore, more fixed costs are identified as controllable in the performance report for an investment center manager than in a performance report for a profit center manager.
- The report also shows budgeted and actual ROI below controllable margin.

To illustrate this responsibility report, we will now assume that the Marine Division of Peerless Group is an investment center. It has budgeted and actual average operating assets of €2,000,000. The manager can control €60,000 of additional fixed costs that were not controllable when the division was a profit center. **Illustration 10.24** shows the division's responsibility report.

Peerless Group
Marine Division
Responsibility Report
For the Year Ended December 31, 2023

	Budget	Actual	Difference Favorable - F Unfavorable - U	
Sales	€ 1,200,000	€ 1,150,000	€ 50,000	U
Variable costs				
Cost of goods sold	500,000	490,000	10,000	F
Selling and administrative	160,000	156,000	4,000	F
Total	660,000	646,000	14,000	F
Contribution margin	540,000	504,000	36,000	U
Controllable fixed costs				
Cost of goods sold	100,000	100,000	0	
Selling and administrative	80,000	80,000	0	
Other fixed costs	60,000	60,000	0	
Total	240,000	240,000	0	
Controllable margin	€ 300,000	€ 264,000	€ 36,000	U
Return on investment	15.0%	13.2%	1.8%	U
	(a)	(b)	(c)	
	(a) € 300,000 / € 2,000,000	(b) € 264,000 / € 2,000,000	(c) € 36,000 / € 2,000,000	

ILLUSTRATION 10.24 | **Responsibility report for investment center**

The report shows that the manager's performance based on ROI was below budget expectations by 1.8% (15.0% versus 13.2%). Top management would likely want explanations for this unfavorable result.

Alternative Measures of ROI Inputs

The inputs to ROI can be measured in a variety of ways.

1. **Valuation of operating assets.**
   - Operating asset measures include acquisition cost, book value, appraised value, or fair value. The first two bases are readily available from the accounting records.
   - Each of the alternative values for operating assets can provide a reliable basis for evaluating a manager's performance as long as it is consistently applied between reporting periods.

2. **Margin (income) measure.**
   - Possible income measures include controllable margin, income from operations, or net income.
   - When computing ROI for a responsibility report, the best option is to use controllable margin since it is computed using only controllable costs. Income from operations and net income include noncontrollable costs in their computation.

Improving ROI

The manager of an investment center can improve ROI by increasing controllable margin, and/or reducing average operating assets. To illustrate, we use the assumed data for the Laser Division of Bence Equipment shown in **Illustration 10.25**.

Sales	€2,000,000
Variable costs	1,100,000
Contribution margin (45%)	900,000
Controllable fixed costs	300,000
Controllable margin (a)	€ 600,000
Average operating assets (b)	€5,000,000
Return on investment (a) ÷ (b)	12%

ILLUSTRATION 10.25 | Assumed data for Laser Division

Increasing Controllable Margin

Controllable margin can be increased by increasing sales or by reducing variable and controllable fixed costs as follows:

1. **Increase sales 10%.** Sales will increase €200,000 (€2,000,000 × .10). Assuming no change in the contribution margin percentage of 45% (€900,000 ÷ €2,000,000), contribution margin will increase €90,000 (€200,000 × .45). Controllable margin will also increase by €90,000 because controllable fixed costs will not change. Thus, controllable margin becomes €690,000 (€600,000 + €90,000). The new ROI is 13.8%, computed as shown in **Illustration 10.26**.

$$\text{ROI} = \frac{\text{Controllable margin}}{\text{Average operating assets}} = \frac{€690,000}{€5,000,000} = 13.8\%$$

ILLUSTRATION 10.26 | ROI computation—increase in sales

- An increase in sales benefits both the investment center and the company if it results in new business.
- It would not benefit the company if the increase was achieved at the expense of other investment centers.

2. **Decrease variable and fixed costs 10%.** Total costs decrease €140,000 [(€1,100,000 + €300,000) × .10]. This reduction results in a corresponding increase in controllable margin. Thus, controllable margin becomes €740,000 (€600,000 + €140,000). The new ROI is 14.8%, computed as shown in **Illustration 10.27**.

$$\text{ROI} = \frac{\text{Controllable margin}}{\text{Average operating assets}} = \frac{€740{,}000}{€5{,}000{,}000} = 14.8\%$$

ILLUSTRATION 10.27 | **ROI computation—decrease in costs**

- This course of action is clearly beneficial when the reduction in costs is the result of eliminating waste and inefficiency.
- But, a reduction in costs that results from cutting expenditures on vital activities, such as required maintenance and inspections, is not likely to be acceptable to top management.

Reducing Average Operating Assets

Assume that average operating assets are reduced 10% or €500,000 (€5,000,000 × .10). Average operating assets become €4,500,000 (€5,000,000 − €500,000). Since controllable margin remains unchanged at €600,000, the new ROI is 13.3%, computed as shown in **Illustration 10.28**.

$$\text{ROI} = \frac{\text{Controllable margin}}{\text{Average operating assets}} = \frac{€600{,}000}{€4{,}500{,}000} = 13.3\%$$

ILLUSTRATION 10.28 | **ROI computation—decrease in operating assets**

Reductions in operating assets may or may not be prudent.

- It is beneficial to eliminate overinvestment in inventories and to dispose of excessive factory assets.
- However, it is unwise to reduce inventories below expected needs or to dispose of essential factory assets.

ACCOUNTING ACROSS THE ORGANIZATION   Hollywood

brentmelissa/iStockphoto

Does Hollywood Look at ROI?

If Hollywood were run like a real business, where things like return on investment mattered, there would be one unchallenged, sacred principle that studio chieftains would never violate: Make lots of G-rated movies.

No matter how you slice the movie business—by star vehicles, by budget levels, or by sequels or franchises—by far the best return on investment comes from the not-so-glamorous world of G-rated films. The problem is, these movies represent only 3% of the total films made in a typical year.

On the flip side are the R-rated films, which dominate the total releases and yet yield the worst return on investment. A whopping 646 R-rated films were released in a recent year—69% of the total output—but only four of the top-20 grossing movies of the year were R-rated films.

This trend—G-rated movies are good for business but underproduced, R-rated movies are bad for business and yet overdone—is something that has been driving economists batty for the past several years.

Source: David Grainger, "The Dysfunctional Family-Film Business," *Fortune* (January 10, 2005), pp. 20–21.

What might be the reason that movie studios do not produce G-rated movies as much as R-rated ones? (Answer is available in the book's product page on www.wiley.com)

DO IT! 4 ▶ Performance Evaluation

Metro Industries reported the following results for 2023.

Sales	€400,000
Variable costs	320,000
Controllable fixed costs	40,800
Average operating assets	280,000

Management is considering the following two independent courses of action in 2024 in order to maximize the return on investment for this division.

1. Reduce average operating assets by €80,000, with no change in controllable margin.
2. Increase sales €80,000, with no change in the contribution margin percentage.

ACTION PLAN

Recall key equations:
- Sales − Variable costs = Contribution margin.
- Contribution margin − Controllable fixed costs = Controllable margin.
- Return on investment = Controllable margin ÷ Average operating assets.

For each proposed course of action:

a. Compute the controllable margin and the return on investment for 2023.
b. Compute the controllable margin and the expected return on investment for 2024.

Solution

a. Return on investment for 2023:

Sales	€400,000
Variable costs	320,000
Contribution margin	80,000
Controllable fixed costs	40,800
Controllable margin	€ 39,200

$$\text{Return on investment} \quad \frac{€39{,}200}{€280{,}000} = 14\%$$

b. Expected return on investment for alternative 1:

$$\frac{€39{,}200}{€280{,}000 - €80{,}000} = 19.6\%$$

Expected return on investment for alternative 2:

Sales (€400,000 + €80,000)	€480,000
Variable costs (€320,000 ÷ €400,000 × €480,000)	384,000
Contribution margin	96,000
Controllable fixed costs	40,800
Controllable margin	€ 55,200

$$\text{Return on investment} \quad \frac{€55{,}200}{€280{,}000} = 19.7\%$$

Related exercise material: **BE10.9, BE10.10, DO IT! 10.4, E10.16,** and **E10.17.**

USING THE DECISION TOOLS | The Roxy Hotel Tribeca

The Roxy Hotel Tribeca (USA), which was discussed in the Feature Story, faces many situations where it needs to apply the decision tools learned in this chapter. For example, assume that the hotel's housekeeping budget contains the following items:

Variable costs	
Direct labor	$37,000
Laundry service	10,000
Supplies	6,000
Total variable	$53,000
Fixed costs	
Supervision	$17,000
Inspection costs	1,000
Insurance expenses	2,000
Depreciation	15,000
Total fixed	$35,000

The budget was based on an estimated 4,000-room rental for the month. During November, 3,000 rooms were actually rented, with the following costs incurred.

Variable costs	
Direct labor	$38,700
Laundry service	8,200
Supplies	5,100
Total variable	$52,000
Fixed costs	
Supervision	$19,300
Inspection costs	1,200
Insurance expenses	2,200
Depreciation	14,700
Total fixed	$37,400

Instructions

a. Determine which items would be controllable by the housekeeping manager. (Assume "supervision" excludes the housekeeping manager's own salary.)
b. How much should have been spent during the month for providing rental of 3,000 rooms?
c. Prepare a flexible housekeeping budget report for the housekeeping manager.
d. Prepare a responsibility report. Include only the costs that would have been controllable by the housekeeping manager.

Solution

a. The housekeeping manager should be able to control all the variable costs and the fixed costs of supervision and inspection. Insurance and depreciation ordinarily are not the responsibility of the housekeeping manager.

b. The total variable cost per unit is $13.25 ($53,000 ÷ 4,000). The total budgeted cost during the month to provide 3,000 room rentals is variable costs $39,750 (3,000 × $13.25) plus fixed costs ($35,000), for a total of $74,750 ($39,750 + $35,000).

c.

The Roxy Hotel Tribeca
Housekeeping Department
Housekeeping Budget Report (Flexible)
For the Month Ended November 30, 2023

	Budget at 3,000 Rooms	Actual at 3,000 Rooms	Difference Favorable F Unfavorable U
Variable costs			
Direct labor ($9.25)*	$27,750	$38,700	$10,950 U
Laundry service ($2.50)	7,500	8,200	700 U
Supplies ($1.50)	4,500	5,100	600 U
Total variable ($13.25)	39,750	52,000	12,250 U
Fixed costs			
Supervision	17,000	19,300	2,300 U
Inspection	1,000	1,200	200 U
Insurance	2,000	2,200	200 U
Depreciation	15,000	14,700	300 F
Total fixed	35,000	37,400	2,400 U
Total costs	$74,750	$89,400	$14,650 U

*Original budgeted amount divided by original budgeted units, e.g., $37,000 ÷ 4,000

d. Because a housekeeping department is a cost center, the responsibility report should include only the costs that are controllable by the housekeeping manager. In this type of report, no distinction is made between variable and fixed costs. Budget data in the report should be based on the rooms actually rented.

The Roxy Hotel Tribeca
Housekeeping Department
Housekeeping Responsibility Report
For the Month Ended November 30, 2023

Controllable Costs	Budget	Actual	Difference Favorable F Unfavorable U
Direct labor	$27,750	$38,700	$10,950 U
Laundry service	7,500	8,200	700 U
Supplies	4,500	5,100	600 U
Supervision	17,000	19,300	2,300 U
Inspection	1,000	1,200	200 U
Total	$57,750	$72,500	$14,750 U

LEARNING OBJECTIVE *5
Explain the difference between ROI and residual income.

Appendix 10A: ROI VERSUS RESIDUAL INCOME

Although most companies use ROI to evaluate investment performance, ROI has a significant disadvantage. To illustrate, let's look at the Electronics Division of Poels Manufacturing. It has an ROI of 20%, computed as shown in **Illustration 10A.1**.

Controllable Margin	÷	Average Operating Assets	=	Return on Investment (ROI)
€1,000,000	÷	€5,000,000	=	20%

ILLUSTRATION 10A.1 | **ROI computation**

The Electronics Division is considering producing a new product, a GPS device (hereafter referred to as Tracker) for its boats. To produce Tracker, operating assets will have to increase €2,000,000. Tracker is expected to generate an additional €260,000 of controllable margin. **Illustration 10A.2** shows how Tracker will affect ROI.

	Without Tracker	Tracker	With Tracker
Controllable margin (a)	€1,000,000	€260,000	€1,260,000
Average operating assets (b)	€5,000,000	€2,000,000	€7,000,000
Return on investment [(a) ÷ (b)]	20%	13%	18%

ILLUSTRATION 10A.2 | **ROI comparison**

The investment in Tracker reduces ROI from 20% to 18%.

Let's suppose that you are the manager of the Electronics Division and must make the decision to produce or not produce Tracker.

- If you were evaluated using ROI, you probably would not produce Tracker because your ROI would drop from 20% to 18%.
- The problem with this ROI analysis is that it ignores an important variable: the minimum rate of return on a company's operating assets.
- The **minimum rate of return** is the rate at which the Electronics Division can cover its costs and earn a profit.

Assuming that the Electronics Division has a minimum rate of return of 10%, it should probably invest in Tracker because its ROI of 13% is greater than 10%.

Residual Income Compared to ROI

To evaluate performance using the minimum rate of return, companies use the residual income approach. **Residual income** is the income that remains after subtracting from the controllable margin the minimum rate of return on a company's average operating assets. The residual income for Tracker would be computed as shown in **Illustration 10A.3**.

Controllable Margin	−	(Minimum Rate of Return × Average Operating Assets)	=	Residual Income
€260,000	−	(10% × €2,000,000)	=	€60,000

ILLUSTRATION 10A.3 | **Residual income computation**

As shown, the residual income related to the Tracker investment is €60,000. **Illustration 10A.4** indicates how the division's residual income changes as the additional investment in Tracker is made.

	Without Tracker	Tracker	With Tracker
Controllable margin (a)	€1,000,000	€260,000	€1,260,000
Average operating assets × 10% (b)	500,000	200,000	700,000
Residual income [(a) − (b)]	€ 500,000	€ 60,000	€ 560,000

ILLUSTRATION 10A.4 | **Residual income comparison**

This example illustrates how performance evaluation based on ROI can be misleading and can even cause managers to reject projects that would actually increase income for the company. As a result, many companies such as **Coca-Cola** (USA), **Briggs & Stratton** (USA), **Eli Lilly** (USA), and **Siemens AG** (DEU) use residual income (or a variant often referred to as economic value added) to evaluate investment alternatives and measure company performance.

Residual Income Weakness

It might appear from the above discussion that the goal of any company should be to maximize the total amount of residual income in each division. This goal, however, ignores the fact that one division might use substantially fewer assets to attain the same level of residual income as another division. For example, we know that to produce Tracker, the Electronics Division of Poels Manufacturing used €2,000,000 of average operating assets to generate €260,000 of controllable margin. Now let's say a different division produced a product called SeaDog, which used €4,000,000 to generate €460,000 of controllable margin, as shown in **Illustration 10A.5**.

	Tracker	SeaDog
Controllable margin (a)	€260,000	€460,000
Average operating assets × 10% (b)	200,000	400,000
Residual income [(a) − (b)]	€ 60,000	€ 60,000

ILLUSTRATION 10A.5 | **Comparison of two products**

If the performance of these two investments were evaluated using residual income, they would be considered equal:

- Both products have the same total residual income.
- This ignores, however, the fact that SeaDog required **twice** as many operating assets to achieve the same level of residual income.

REVIEW AND PRACTICE

Learning Objectives Review

LO 1 **Describe budgetary control and static budget reports.**

Budgetary control consists of (a) preparing periodic budget reports that compare actual results with planned objectives, (b) analyzing the differences to determine their causes, (c) taking appropriate corrective action, and (d) modifying future plans, if necessary.

Static budget reports are useful in evaluating the progress toward planned sales and profit goals. They are also appropriate in assessing a manager's effectiveness in controlling costs when (a) actual activity closely approximates the master budget activity level, and/or (b) the behavior of the costs in response to changes in activity is fixed.

LO 2 **Prepare flexible budget reports.**

To develop the flexible budget, it is necessary to do the following: (a) Identify the activity index and the relevant range of activity. (b) Identify the variable costs, and determine the budgeted variable cost per unit of activity for each cost. (c) Identify the fixed costs, and determine the budgeted amount for each cost. (d) Prepare the budget for selected increments of activity within the relevant range. Flexible budget reports permit an evaluation of a manager's performance in controlling production and costs.

LO 3 Apply responsibility accounting to cost and profit centers.

Responsibility accounting involves accumulating and reporting revenues and costs on the basis of the individual manager who has the authority to make the day-to-day decisions about the items. The evaluation of a manager's performance is based on the matters directly under the manager's control. In responsibility accounting, it is necessary to distinguish between controllable and noncontrollable fixed costs and to identify three types of responsibility centers: cost, profit, and investment.

Responsibility reports for cost centers compare actual costs with flexible budget data. The reports show only controllable costs, and no distinction is made between variable and fixed costs. Responsibility reports show contribution margin, controllable fixed costs, and controllable margin for each profit center.

LO 4 Evaluate performance in investment centers.

The primary basis for evaluating performance in investment centers is return on investment (ROI). The equation for computing ROI for investment centers is Controllable margin ÷ Average operating assets.

LO *5 Explain the difference between ROI and residual income.

ROI is controllable margin divided by average operating assets. Residual income is the income that remains after subtracting the minimum rate of return on a company's average operating assets. ROI sometimes provides misleading results because profitable investments are often rejected when the investment reduces ROI but increases overall profitability.

Decision Tools Review

Decision Checkpoints	Info Needed for Decision	Tool to Use for Decision	How to Evaluate Results
Are the cost changes resulting from changed production levels reasonable?	Variable costs projected at different levels of production	Flexible budget	After taking into account different production levels, results are favorable if actual expenses are less than budgeted amounts at the actual activity level.
Have the individual managers been held accountable for the costs and revenues under their control?	Relevant costs and revenues, where the individual manager has authority to make day-to-day decisions about the items	Responsibility reports focused on cost centers, profit centers, and investment centers as appropriate	Compare budget to actual costs and revenues for controllable items.
Has the investment center performed up to expectations?	Controllable margin (contribution margin minus controllable fixed costs), and average investment center operating assets	Return on investment	Compare actual ROI to expected ROI based on the company's minimum required rate of return.

Glossary Review

Budgetary control The use of budgets to control operations. (p. 10-3).

Controllable cost A cost over which a manager has control. (p. 10-16).

Controllable margin Contribution margin less controllable fixed costs. (p. 10-22).

Cost center A responsibility center that incurs costs but does not directly generate revenues. (p. 10-19).

Decentralization Organizational structure in which control of operations is delegated to many managers throughout the organization. (p. 10-15).

Direct fixed costs Costs that relate specifically to a responsibility center and are incurred for the sole benefit of the center. (p. 10-22).

Flexible budget A projection of budget data for various levels of activity. (p. 10-7).

Indirect fixed costs Costs that are incurred for the benefit of more than one profit center. (p. 10-22).

Investment center A responsibility center that incurs costs, generates revenues, and has control over decisions regarding the assets available for use. (p. 10-21).

Management by exception The review of budget reports by top management focused entirely or primarily on significant differences between actual results and planned objectives. (p. 10-16).

Noncontrollable costs Costs incurred indirectly and allocated to a responsibility level that are not controllable at that level. (p. 10-16).

Profit center A responsibility center that incurs costs and also generates revenues. (p. 10-21).

*****Residual income** The income that remains after subtracting from the controllable margin the minimum rate of return on a company's average operating assets. (p. 10-30).

Responsibility accounting A part of management accounting that involves identifying and reporting revenues and costs on the basis of the manager who has the authority to make the day-to-day decisions about the items. (p. 10-14).

Responsibility reporting system The preparation of reports for each level of responsibility in the company's organization chart. (p. 10-18).

Return on investment (ROI) A measure of management's effectiveness in utilizing assets at its disposal in an investment center. (p. 10-24).

Segment (or division) An area of responsibility in decentralized operations. (p. 10-15).

Static budget A projection of budget data at one level of activity. (p. 10-4).

Practice Multiple-Choice Questions

1. **(LO 1)** Budgetary control involves all but one of the following:
   a. modifying future plans.
   b. analyzing differences.
   c. using static budgets but **not** flexible budgets.
   d. determining differences between actual and planned results.

2. **(LO 1)** Depending on the nature of the report, budget reports are prepared:
   a. daily.
   b. weekly.
   c. monthly.
   d. All of the answer choices are correct.

3. **(LO 1)** A production manager in a manufacturing company would most likely receive a:
   a. sales report.
   b. income statement.
   c. scrap report.
   d. shipping department overhead report.

4. **(LO 1)** A static budget is:
   a. a projection of budget data at several levels of activity within the relevant range of activity.
   b. a projection of budget data at a single level of activity.
   c. compared to a flexible budget in a budget report.
   d. never appropriate in evaluating a manager's effectiveness in controlling costs.

5. **(LO 1)** A static budget is useful in controlling costs when cost behavior is:
   a. mixed.
   b. fixed.
   c. variable.
   d. linear.

6. **(LO 2)** At zero direct labor hours in a flexible budget graph, the total budgeted cost line intersects the vertical axis at £30,000. At 10,000 direct labor hours, a horizontal line drawn from the total budgeted cost line intersects the vertical axis at £90,000. Fixed and variable costs may be expressed as:
   a. £30,000 fixed plus £6 per direct labor hour variable.
   b. £30,000 fixed plus £9 per direct labor hour variable.
   c. £60,000 fixed plus £3 per direct labor hour variable.
   d. £60,000 fixed plus £6 per direct labor hour variable.

7. **(LO 2)** At 9,000 direct labor hours, the flexible budget for indirect materials (a variable cost) is €27,000. If €28,000 of indirect materials costs are incurred at 9,200 direct labor hours, the flexible budget report should show the following difference for indirect materials:
   a. €1,000 unfavorable.
   b. €1,000 favorable.
   c. €400 favorable.
   d. €400 unfavorable.

8. **(LO 3)** Under responsibility accounting, the evaluation of a manager's performance is based on matters that the manager:
   a. directly controls.
   b. directly and indirectly controls.
   c. indirectly controls.
   d. has shared responsibility for with another manager.

9. **(LO 3)** Responsibility centers include:
   a. cost centers.
   b. profit centers.
   c. investment centers.
   d. All of the answer choices are correct.

10. **(LO 3)** Responsibility reports for cost centers:
    a. distinguish between fixed and variable costs.
    b. use static budget data.
    c. include both controllable and noncontrollable costs.
    d. include only controllable costs.

11. **(LO 3)** The accounting department of a manufacturing company is an example of:
    a. a cost center.
    b. a profit center.
    c. an investment center.
    d. a contribution center.

12. **(LO 3)** To evaluate the performance of a profit center manager, upper management needs detailed information about:
    a. controllable costs.
    b. controllable revenues.
    c. controllable costs and revenues.
    d. controllable costs and revenues and average operating assets.

13. (LO 3) In a responsibility report for a profit center, controllable fixed costs are deducted from contribution margin to show:

   a. profit center margin.
   b. controllable margin.
   c. net income.
   d. income from operations.

14. (LO 4) In the equation for return on investment (ROI), the factors for controllable margin and operating assets are, respectively:

   a. controllable margin percentage and total operating assets.
   b. controllable margin amounts and average operating assets.
   c. controllable margin amounts and total assets.
   d. controllable margin percentage and average operating assets.

15. (LO 4) A manager of an investment center can improve ROI by:

   a. increasing average operating assets.
   b. reducing sales.
   c. increasing variable costs.
   d. reducing variable and/or controllable fixed costs.

Solutions

1. c. Budgetary control involves using flexible budgets and sometimes static budgets. The other choices are all part of budgetary control.

2. d. Budget reports are prepared daily, weekly, or monthly. The other choices are correct, but choice (d) is the better answer.

3. c. A production manager in a manufacturing company would most likely receive a scrap report. The other choices are incorrect because (a) top management or a sales manager would most likely receive a sales report, (b) top management would most likely receive an income statement, and (d) a department manager would most likely receive a shipping department overhead report.

4. b. A static budget is a projection of budget data at a single level of activity. The other choices are incorrect because a static budget (a) is a projection of budget data at a single level of activity, not at several levels of activity within the relevant range of activity; (c) is not compared to a flexible budget in a budget report; and (d) is appropriate in evaluating a manager's effectiveness in controlling fixed costs.

5. b. A static budget is useful for controlling fixed costs. The other choices are incorrect because a static budget is not useful for controlling (a) mixed costs, (c) variable costs, or (d) linear costs.

6. a. The intersection point of £90,000 is total budgeted costs, or budgeted fixed costs plus budgeted variable costs. Fixed costs are £30,000 (amount at zero direct labor hours), so budgeted variable costs are £60,000 [£90,000 (Total costs) − £30,000 (Fixed costs)]. Budgeted variable costs (£60,000) divided by total activity level (10,000 direct labor hours) gives the variable cost per unit of £6 per direct labor hour. The other choices are therefore incorrect.

7. d. Budgeted indirect materials per direct labor hour (DLH) is €3 (€27,000 ÷ 9,000). At an activity level of 9,200 direct labor hours, budgeted indirect materials are €27,600 (9,200 × €3 per DLH) but actual indirect materials costs are €28,000, resulting in a €400 unfavorable difference. The other choices are therefore incorrect.

8. a. The evaluation of a manager's performance is based only on matters that the manager directly controls. The other choices are therefore incorrect as they include indirect controls and shared responsibility.

9. d. Cost centers, profit centers, and investment centers are all responsibility centers. The other choices are correct, but choice (d) is the better answer.

10. d. Responsibility reports for cost centers report only controllable costs; they (a) do not distinguish between fixed and variable costs; (b) use flexible budget data, not static budget data; and (c) do not include noncontrollable costs.

11. a. The accounting department of a manufacturing company is an example of a cost center, not (b) a profit center, (c) an investment center, or (d) contribution center.

12. c. To evaluate the performance of a profit center manager, upper management needs detailed information about controllable costs and revenues, not just (a) controllable costs or (b) controllable revenues. Choice (d) is incorrect because upper management does not need information about average operating assets.

13. b. Contribution margin less controllable fixed costs is the controllable margin, not (a) the profit center margin, (c) net income, or (d) income from operations.

14. b. The factors in the equation for ROI are controllable margin amounts and average operating assets. The other choices are therefore incorrect.

15. d. Reducing variable or controllable fixed costs will cause the controllable margin to increase, which is one way a manager of an investment center can improve ROI. The other choices are incorrect because (a) increasing average operating assets will lower ROI; (b) reducing sales will cause contribution margin to go down, thereby decreasing controllable margin since there will be less contribution margin to cover controllable fixed costs and resulting in lower ROI; and (c) increasing variable costs will cause the contribution margin to be lower, thereby decreasing controllable margin and resulting in lower ROI.

Practice Exercises

Prepare flexible manufacturing overhead budget.

1. (LO 2) Dylan Ltd. uses a flexible budget for manufacturing overhead based on direct labor hours. Variable manufacturing overhead costs per direct labor hour are as follows:

Indirect labor	£0.70
Indirect materials	0.50
Utilities	0.40

Budgeted fixed overhead costs per month are supervision £4,000, depreciation £3,000, and property taxes £800. The company believes it will normally operate in a range of 7,000–10,000 direct labor hours per month.

Instructions

Prepare a monthly flexible manufacturing overhead budget for 2023 for the expected range of activity, using increments of 1,000 direct labor hours.

Solution

1.

Dylan Ltd.
Monthly Flexible Manufacturing Overhead Budget
For the Year 2023

Activity level				
Direct labor hours	7,000	8,000	9,000	10,000
Variable costs				
Indirect labor (£.70)	£ 4,900	£ 5,600	£ 6,300	£ 7,000
Indirect materials (£.50)	3,500	4,000	4,500	5,000
Utilities (£.40)	2,800	3,200	3,600	4,000
Total variable costs (£1.60)	11,200	12,800	14,400	16,000
Fixed costs				
Supervision	4,000	4,000	4,000	4,000
Depreciation	3,000	3,000	3,000	3,000
Property taxes	800	800	800	800
Total fixed costs	7,800	7,800	7,800	7,800
Total costs	£19,000	£20,600	£22,200	£23,800

2. (LO 4) The White Division of Ready Textiles reported the following data for the current year.

Compute ROI for current year and for possible future changes.

Sales	€3,000,000
Variable costs	2,400,000
Controllable fixed costs	400,000
Average operating assets	5,000,000

Top management is unhappy with the investment center's return on investment (ROI). It asks the manager of the White Division to submit plans to improve ROI in the next year. The manager believes it is feasible to consider the following independent courses of action.

1. Increase sales by €300,000 with no change in the contribution margin percentage.
2. Reduce variable costs by €100,000.
3. Reduce average operating assets by 4%.

Instructions

a. Compute the return on investment (ROI) for the current year.
b. Using the ROI equation, compute the ROI under each of the proposed courses of action. (Round to one decimal.)

Solution

2. a. Controllable margin = (€3,000,000 − €2,400,000 − €400,000) = €200,000
   ROI = €200,000 ÷ €5,000,000 = 4%

   b. 1. Contribution margin percentage is 20%, or [(€3,000,000 − €2,400,000) ÷ €3,000,000]
      Increase in controllable margin = €300,000 × 20% = €60,000
      ROI = (€200,000 + €60,000) ÷ €5,000,000 = 5.2%

      2. (€200,000 + €100,000) ÷ €5,000,000 = 6%
      3. €200,000 ÷ [€5,000,000 − (€5,000,000 × .04)] = 4.2%

Practice Problem

(LO 2) Hank Group uses a flexible budget for manufacturing overhead based on direct labor hours. For 2023, the master overhead budget for the Packaging Department based on 300,000 direct labor hours was as follows:

Prepare flexible budget report.

Variable Costs		Fixed Costs	
Indirect labor	A$360,000	Supervision	A$ 60,000
Supplies and lubricants	150,000	Depreciation	24,000
Maintenance	210,000	Property taxes	18,000
Utilities	120,000	Insurance	12,000
	A$840,000		A$114,000

During July, 24,000 direct labor hours were worked. The company incurred the following variable costs in July: indirect labor A$30,200, supplies and lubricants A$11,600, maintenance A$17,500, and utilities A$9,200. Actual fixed overhead costs were the same as monthly budgeted fixed costs.

Instructions
Prepare a flexible budget report for the Packaging Department for July.

Solution

Hank Group
Manufacturing Overhead Budget Report (Flexible)
Packaging Department
For the Month Ended July 31, 2023

Direct labor hours (DLH)	Budget 24,000 DLH	Actual Costs 24,000 DLH	Difference Favorable F Unfavorable U
Variable costs			
Indirect labor (A$1.20[a])	A$28,800	A$30,200	A$1,400 U
Supplies and lubricants (A$0.50[a])	12,000	11,600	400 F
Maintenance (A$0.70[a])	16,800	17,500	700 U
Utilities (A$0.40[a])	9,600	9,200	400 F
Total variable	67,200	68,500	1,300 U
Fixed costs			
Supervision	5,000[b]	5,000	-0-
Depreciation	2,000[b]	2,000	-0-
Property taxes	1,500[b]	1,500	-0-
Insurance	1,000[b]	1,000	-0-
Total fixed	9,500	9,500	-0-
Total costs	A$76,700	A$78,000	A$1,300 U

[a] A$360,000 ÷ 300,000; A$150,000 ÷ 300,000; A$210,000 ÷ 300,000; A$120,000 ÷ 300,000
[b] Annual cost divided by 12

Note: All asterisked Questions, Exercises, and Problems relate to material in the appendix to the chapter.

Questions

1. **a.** What is budgetary control?
   b. Kabir Lal is describing budgetary control. What steps should be included in Kabir's description?

2. The following purposes are part of a budgetary reporting system: (a) Determine efficient use of materials. (b) Control overhead costs. (c) Determine whether income objectives are being met. For each purpose, indicate the name of the report, the frequency of the report, and the primary recipient(s) of the report.

3. How may a budget report for the second quarter differ from a budget report for the first quarter?

4. Razia Azen questions the usefulness of a master sales budget in evaluating sales performance. Is there justification for Razia's concern? Explain.

5. Under what circumstances may a static budget be an appropriate basis for evaluating a manager's effectiveness in controlling costs?

6. "A flexible budget is really a series of static budgets." Is this true? Explain why or why not.

7. The static manufacturing overhead budget based on 40,000 direct labor hours shows budgeted indirect labor costs of HK$540,000. During March, the department incurs HK$640,000 of indirect labor

while working 45,000 direct labor hours. Is this a favorable or unfavorable performance? Why?

8. A static overhead budget based on 40,000 direct labor hours shows Factory Insurance NT$65,000 as a fixed cost. At the 50,000 direct labor hours worked in March, factory insurance costs were NT$63,000. Is this a favorable or unfavorable performance? Why?

9. Georgi Petrov is confused about how a flexible budget is prepared. Identify the steps for Georgi.

10. Yildiz A.S. has prepared a graph of flexible budget data. At zero direct labor hours, the total budgeted cost line intersects the vertical axis at ₺200,000. At 10,000 direct labor hours, the line drawn from the total budgeted cost line intersects the vertical axis at ₺850,000. How may the fixed and variable costs be expressed?

11. The flexible budget calculation is fixed costs ¥5,000,000 plus variable costs of ¥400 per direct labor hour. What is the total budgeted cost at (a) 9,000 hours and (b) 12,345 hours?

12. What is management by exception? What criteria may be used in identifying exceptions?

13. What is responsibility accounting? Explain the purpose of responsibility accounting.

14. Kalyani Rai is studying for an accounting examination. Describe for Kalyani what conditions are necessary for responsibility accounting to be used effectively.

15. Distinguish between controllable and noncontrollable costs.

16. How do responsibility reports differ from budget reports?

17. What is the relationship, if any, between a responsibility reporting system and a company's organization chart?

18. Distinguish among the three types of responsibility centers.

19. (a) What costs are included in a performance report for a cost center? (b) In the report, are variable and fixed costs identified?

20. How do direct fixed costs differ from indirect fixed costs? Are both types of fixed costs controllable?

21. Ojas Namjoshi is confused about controllable margin reported in an income statement for a profit center. How is this margin computed, and what is its primary purpose?

22. What is the primary basis for evaluating the performance of the manager of an investment center? Indicate the equation for this basis.

23. Explain the ways in which ROI can be improved.

24. Indicate two behavioral principles that pertain to (a) the manager being evaluated and (b) top management.

*25. What is a major disadvantage of using ROI to evaluate investment and company performance?

*26. What is residual income, and what is one of its major weaknesses?

Brief Exercises

BE10.1 (LO 1), AP For the quarter ended March 31, 2023, Crowe Music Factory accumulates the following sales data for its newest guitar, The Edge: €315,000 budget; €305,000 actual. Prepare a static budget report for the quarter.

Prepare static budget report.

BE10.2 (LO 1), AP For the quarter ended March 31, 2023, Crowe Music Factory accumulates the following sales data for its newest guitar, The Edge: €315,000 budget; €305,000 actual. In the second quarter, budgeted sales were €380,000, and actual sales were €384,000. Prepare a static budget report for the second quarter and for the year to date.

Prepare static budget report for two quarters.

BE10.3 (LO 2), E In Emerson plc, direct labor is £20 per hour. The company expects to operate at 10,000 direct labor hours each month. In January 2023, direct labor totaling £206,000 is incurred in working 10,400 hours. Prepare (a) a static budget report and (b) a flexible budget report. Evaluate the usefulness of each report.

Show usefulness of flexible budgets in evaluating performance.

BE10.4 (LO 2), AP Fizah Manufacturing expects to produce 1,200,000 units of Product XX in 2023. Monthly production is expected to range from 80,000 to 120,000 units. Budgeted variable manufacturing costs per unit are direct materials S$5, direct labor S$6, and overhead S$8. Budgeted fixed manufacturing costs per unit for depreciation are S$2 and for supervision are S$1. Prepare a flexible manufacturing budget for the relevant range value using 20,000 unit increments.

Prepare a flexible budget for variable costs.

BE10.5 (LO 2), AN Fizah Manufacturing expects to produce 1,200,000 units of Product XX in 2023. Monthly production is expected to range from 80,000 to 120,000 units. Budgeted variable manufacturing costs per unit are direct materials S$5, direct labor S$6, and overhead S$8. Budgeted fixed manufacturing costs per unit for depreciation are S$2 and for supervision are S$1. In March 2023, the company incurs the following costs in producing 100,000 units: direct materials S$520,000, direct labor S$596,000, and variable overhead S$805,000. Actual fixed costs were equal to budgeted fixed costs. Prepare a flexible budget report for March. Were costs controlled?

Prepare flexible budget report.

BE10.6 (LO 3), AP In the Assembly Department of Hongsong Toys, budgeted and actual manufacturing overhead costs for the month of April 2023 were as follows:

Prepare a responsibility report for a cost center.

	Budget	Actual
Indirect materials	₩16,000,000	₩14,300,000
Indirect labor	20,000,000	20,600,000
Utilities	10,000,000	10,850,000
Supervision	5,000,000	5,000,000

All costs are controllable by the department manager. Prepare a responsibility report for April for the cost center.

Prepare a responsibility report for a profit center.

BE10.7 (LO 3), AP Thomas plc accumulates the following summary data for the year ending December 31, 2023, for its Water Division, which it operates as a profit center: sales—£2,000,000 budget, £2,080,000 actual; variable costs—£1,000,000 budget, £1,050,000 actual; and controllable fixed costs—£300,000 budget, £305,000 actual. Prepare a responsibility report for the Water Division for the year ending December 31, 2023.

Prepare a responsibility report for an investment center.

BE10.8 (LO 4), AP For the year ending December 31, 2023, Corum Industries accumulates the following data for the Plastics Division, which it operates as an investment center: contribution margin—€700,000 budget, €710,000 actual; controllable fixed costs—€300,000 budget, €302,000 actual. Average operating assets for the year were €2,000,000. Prepare a responsibility report for the Plastics Division beginning with contribution margin for the year ending December 31, 2023.

Compute return on investment using the ROI equation.

BE10.9 (LO 4), AP For its three investment centers, Croix AG accumulates the following data:

	I	II	III
Sales	CHF2,000,000	CHF4,000,000	CHF 4,000,000
Controllable margin	1,400,000	2,000,000	3,600,000
Average operating assets	5,000,000	8,000,000	10,000,000

Compute the return on investment (ROI) for each center.

Compute return on investment under changed conditions.

BE10.10 (LO 4), AP For its three investment centers, Croix AG accumulates the following data:

	I	II	III
Sales	CHF2,000,000	CHF4,000,000	CHF 4,000,000
Controllable margin	1,400,000	2,000,000	3,600,000
Average operating assets	5,000,000	8,000,000	10,000,000

The company expects the following changes for investment centers I, II, and III in the next year: investment center I to increase sales 15%, investment center II to decrease controllable fixed costs CHF400,000, and investment center III to decrease average operating assets CHF400,000. Compute the expected return on investment (ROI) for each center. Assume investment center I has a contribution margin percentage of 70%.

Compute ROI and residual income.

*BE10.11 (LO 5), AP Cape Sports reports the following financial information for its sports clothing segment.

Average operating assets	R30,000,000
Controllable margin	R6,300,000
Minimum rate of return	10%

Compute the return on investment and the residual income for the segment.

Compute ROI and residual income.

*BE10.12 (LO 5), AP Presented here is information related to the Southern Division of Porto Alegro SA.

Contribution margin	R$12,000,000
Controllable margin	R$8,000,000
Average operating assets	R$40,000,000
Minimum rate of return	15%

Compute the Southern Division's return on investment and residual income.

DO IT! Exercises

Prepare and evaluate a static budget report.

DO IT! 10.1 (LO 1), AP Liou Ltd. estimates that it will produce 6,000 units of product IOA during the current month. Budgeted variable manufacturing costs per unit are direct materials NT$70, direct labor NT$130, and overhead NT$180. Monthly budgeted fixed manufacturing overhead costs are NT$80,000 for depreciation and NT$38,000 for supervision.

In the current month, Liou actually produced 6,500 units and incurred the following costs: direct materials NT$388,500, direct labor NT$764,400, variable overhead NT$1,166,400, depreciation NT$80,000, and supervision NT$40,000.

Prepare a static budget report. *Hint:* The Budget column is based on estimated production while the Actual column is the actual cost incurred during the period. (*Note:* You do not need to prepare the heading.) Were costs controlled? Discuss limitations of the budget.

Compute total budgeted costs in flexible budget.

DO IT! 10.2 (LO 2), AP In Luda Company's flexible budget graph, the fixed-cost line and the total budgeted cost line intersect the vertical axis at ¥900,000. The total budgeted cost line is ¥3,500,000 at an activity level of 50,000 direct labor hours. Compute total budgeted costs at 65,000 direct labor hours.

DO IT! 10.3 (LO 3), AP The Rockies Division operates as a profit center. It reports the following for the year ending December 31, 2023.

Prepare a responsibility report.

	Budget	Actual
Sales	$2,000,000	$1,890,000
Variable costs	800,000	760,000
Controllable fixed costs	550,000	550,000
Noncontrollable fixed costs	250,000	250,000

Prepare a responsibility report for the Rockies Division at December 31, 2023.

DO IT! 10.4 (LO 4), AP The service division of Sarah Industries reported the following results for 2023.

Compute ROI and expected return on investments.

Sales	₤5,000,000
Variable costs	3,000,000
Controllable fixed costs	750,000
Average operating assets	6,250,000

Management is considering the following independent courses of action in 2024 in order to maximize the return on investment for this division.

1. Reduce average operating assets by ₤1,250,000, with no change in controllable margin.
2. Increase sales ₤1,000,000, with no change in the contribution margin percentage.
a. Compute the controllable margin and the return on investment for 2023.
b. Compute the controllable margin and the expected return on investment for 2024 for each proposed alternative.

Exercises

E10.1 (LO 1, 2), K Yun Bai has prepared the following list of statements about budgetary control.

Understand the concept of budgetary control.

1. Budget reports compare actual results with planned objectives.
2. All budget reports are prepared on a weekly basis.
3. Management uses budget reports to analyze differences between actual and planned results and to determine their causes.
4. As a result of analyzing budget reports, management may either take corrective action or modify future plans.
5. Budgetary control works best when a company has an informal reporting system.
6. The primary recipients of the sales report are the sales manager and the production supervisor.
7. The primary recipient of the scrap report is the production manager.
8. A static budget is a projection of budget data at a single level of activity.
9. Top management's reaction to unfavorable differences is not influenced by the materiality of the difference.
10. A static budget is not appropriate in evaluating a manager's effectiveness in controlling costs unless the actual activity level approximates the static budget activity level or the behavior of the costs is fixed.

Instructions

Identify each statement as true or false. If false, indicate how to correct the statement.

E10.2 (LO 1), AN Mitchell Industries budgeted selling expenses of A$30,000 in January, A$35,000 in February, and A$40,000 in March. Actual selling expenses were A$31,200 in January, A$34,525 in February, and A$46,000 in March. The company considers any difference that is less than 5% of the budgeted amount to be immaterial.

Prepare and evaluate static budget report.

Instructions

a. Prepare a selling expense report that compares budgeted and actual amounts by month and for the year to date.
b. What is the purpose of the report prepared in (a), and who would be the primary recipient?
c. What would be the likely result of management's analysis of the report?

Prepare flexible manufacturing overhead budget.

E10.3 (LO 2), AP Cheung Equipment uses a flexible budget for manufacturing overhead based on direct labor hours. Variable manufacturing overhead costs per direct labor hour are as follows:

Indirect labor	HK$10.0
Indirect materials	7.0
Utilities	4.0

Fixed overhead costs per month are supervision HK$40,000, depreciation HK$12,000, and property taxes HK$8,000. The company believes it will normally operate in a range of 7,000–10,000 direct labor hours per month.

Instructions

Prepare a monthly manufacturing overhead flexible budget for 2023 for the expected range of activity, using increments of 1,000 direct labor hours.

Prepare flexible budget reports for manufacturing overhead costs, and comment on findings.

E10.4 (LO 2), AN Writing Using the information in E10.3, assume that in July 2023, Cheung Equipment incurs the following manufacturing overhead costs:

Variable Costs		Fixed Costs	
Indirect labor	HK$88,000	Supervision	HK$40,000
Indirect materials	58,000	Depreciation	12,000
Utilities	32,000	Property taxes	8,000

Instructions

a. Prepare a flexible budget performance report, assuming that the company worked 9,000 direct labor hours during the month.

b. Prepare a flexible budget performance report, assuming that the company worked 8,500 direct labor hours during the month.

c. Comment on your findings.

Prepare flexible selling expense budget.

E10.5 (LO 2), AP Moscavide Publishers uses flexible budgets to control its selling expenses. Monthly sales are expected to range from €170,000 to €200,000. Variable costs and their percentage relationship to sales are sales commissions 6%, advertising 4%, travel 3%, and delivery 2%. Fixed selling expenses will consist of sales salaries €35,000, depreciation on delivery equipment €7,000, and insurance on delivery equipment €1,000.

Instructions

Prepare a monthly selling expense flexible budget for each €10,000 increment of sales within the relevant range for the year ending December 31, 2023.

Prepare flexible budget reports for selling expenses.

E10.6 (LO 2), AN Writing The actual selling expenses incurred in March 2023 by Moscavide Publishers are as follows:

Variable Expenses		Fixed Expenses	
Sales commissions	€11,000	Sales salaries	€35,000
Advertising	6,900	Depreciation	7,000
Travel	5,100	Insurance	1,000
Delivery	3,450		

Instructions

a. Prepare a flexible budget performance report for March using the budget data in E10.5, assuming that March sales were €170,000.

b. Prepare a flexible budget performance report, assuming that March sales were €180,000.

c. Comment on the importance of using flexible budgets in evaluating the performance of the sales manager.

Prepare flexible budget.

E10.7 (LO 2), AP AppleWare (AW) is a manufacturer of toaster ovens. To improve control over operations, the president of AW wants to begin using a flexible budgeting system, rather than using only the current master budget. The following data are available for AW's expected costs at production levels of 90,000, 100,000, and 110,000 units.

Variable costs	
Manufacturing	£6 per unit
Administrative	£4 per unit
Selling	£3 per unit
Fixed costs	
Manufacturing	£160,000
Administrative	£80,000

Instructions

a. Prepare a flexible budget for each of the possible production levels: 90,000, 100,000, and 110,000 units.

b. If AW sells the toaster ovens for £16 each, how many units will it have to sell to make a profit of £60,000 before taxes?

E10.8 (LO 1, 2), E Service Writing Rensing Groomers is in the dog-grooming business. Its operating costs are described by the following equations:

Prepare flexible budget report; compare flexible and static budgets.

Grooming supplies (variable)	y = R0 + R50x
Direct labor (variable)	y = R0 + R140x
Overhead (mixed)	y = R100,000 + R10x

Roel Darvishi, the owner, has determined that direct labor is the cost driver for all three categories of costs.

Instructions

a. Prepare a flexible budget for activity levels of 550, 600, and 700 direct labor hours.

b. Explain why the flexible budget is more informative than the static budget.

c. Calculate the total cost per direct labor hour at each of the activity levels specified in part (a).

d. The groomers at Rensing normally work a total of 650 direct labor hours during each month. Each grooming job normally takes a groomer 1.3 hours. Roel wants to earn a profit equal to 40% of the costs incurred. Determine what he should charge each pet owner for grooming.

E10.9 (LO 1, 2), E As sales manager, Hans Keller was given the following static budget report for selling expenses in the Clothing Department of Lugano Textiles for the month of October.

Prepare flexible budget report, and answer question.

Lugano Textiles
Clothing Department
Budget Report
For the Month Ended October 31, 2023

	Budget	Actual	Difference Favorable F Unfavorable U
Sales in units	8,000	10,000	2,000 F
Variable expenses			
Sales commissions	CHF 2,400	CHF 2,600	CHF 200 U
Advertising expense	720	850	130 U
Travel expense	3,600	4,100	500 U
Free samples given out	1,600	1,400	200 F
Total variable	8,320	8,950	630 U
Fixed expenses			
Rent	1,500	1,500	–0–
Sales salaries	1,200	1,200	–0–
Office salaries	800	800	–0–
Depreciation—autos (sales staff)	500	500	–0–
Total fixed	4,000	4,000	–0–
Total expenses	CHF12,320	CHF12,950	CHF 630 U

As a result of this budget report, Hans was called into the president's office and congratulated on his fine sales performance. He was reprimanded, however, for allowing his costs to get out of control. Hans knew something was wrong with the performance report that he had been given. However, he was not sure what to do, and comes to you for advice.

Instructions

a. Prepare a budget report based on flexible budget data to help Hans.

b. Should Hans have been reprimanded? Explain.

Prepare flexible budget and responsibility report for manufacturing overhead.

E10.10 (LO 2, 3), AP Gold Coast Company's manufacturing overhead budget for the first quarter of 2023 contained the following data:

Variable Costs		Fixed Costs	
Indirect materials	A$12,000	Supervisory salaries	A$36,000
Indirect labor	10,000	Depreciation	7,000
Utilities	8,000	Property taxes and insurance	8,000
Maintenance	6,000	Maintenance	5,000

Actual variable costs were indirect materials A$13,500, indirect labor A$9,500, utilities A$8,700, and maintenance A$5,000. Actual fixed costs equaled budgeted costs except for property taxes and insurance, which were A$8,300. The actual activity level equaled the budgeted level.

All costs are considered controllable by the production department manager except for depreciation, property taxes, and insurance.

Instructions

a. Prepare a manufacturing overhead flexible budget report for the first quarter.

b. Prepare a responsibility report for the first quarter.

Prepare and discuss a responsibility report.

E10.11 (LO 2, 3), AP **Service** **Writing** UrLink Solutions is a newly formed company specializing in high-speed Internet service for home and business. The owner, Juan Bell, divided the company into two segments: Home Internet Service and Business Internet Service. Each segment is run by its own supervisor, while basic selling and administrative services are shared by both segments.

Juan has asked you to help him create a performance reporting system that will allow him to measure each segment's performance in terms of its profitability. To that end, the following information has been collected on the Home Internet Service segment for the first quarter of 2023.

	Budget	Actual
Service revenue	£25,000	£26,200
Allocated portion of:		
Building depreciation	11,000	11,000
Advertising	5,000	4,200
Billing	3,500	3,000
Property taxes	1,200	1,000
Material and supplies	1,600	1,200
Supervisory salaries	9,000	9,500
Insurance	4,000	3,900
Wages	3,000	3,250
Gas and oil	2,800	3,400
Equipment depreciation	1,500	1,300

Instructions

a. Prepare a responsibility report for the first quarter of 2023 for the Home Internet Service segment.

b. Write a memo to Juan Bell discussing the principles that should be used when preparing performance reports.

State total budgeted cost equations, and prepare flexible budget graph.

E10.12 (LO 2), AP Adriel Windows has two production departments, Fabricating and Assembling. At a department managers' meeting, the controller uses flexible budget graphs to explain total budgeted costs. A separate graph based on direct labor hours is used for each department. The graphs show the following:

1. At zero direct labor hours, the total budgeted cost line and the fixed-cost line intersect the vertical axis at S$50,000 in the Fabricating Department and S$40,000 in the Assembling Department.

2. At normal capacity of 50,000 direct labor hours, the line drawn from the total budgeted cost line intersects the vertical axis at S$150,000 in the Fabricating Department and S$120,000 in the Assembling Department.

Instructions

a. State the total budgeted cost equation for each department.

b. Compute the total budgeted cost for each department, assuming actual direct labor hours worked were 53,000 and 47,000, in the Fabricating and Assembling Departments, respectively.

c. Prepare the flexible budget graph for the Fabricating Department, assuming the maximum direct labor hours in the relevant range is 100,000. Use increments of 10,000 direct labor hours on the horizontal axis and increments of S$50,000 on the vertical axis.

E10.13 (LO 3), AP Ilya SA's organization chart includes the president; the vice president of production; three assembly factories—Samara, Kazan, and Omsk; and two departments within each factory—Machining and Finishing. Budget and actual manufacturing cost data for July 2023 are as follows:

Prepare reports in a responsibility reporting system.

Finishing Department—Samara: direct materials R$425,000 actual, R$440,000 budget; direct labor R$834,000 actual, R$820,000 budget; manufacturing overhead R$510,000 actual, R$492,000 budget.

Machining Department—Samara: total manufacturing costs R$2,200,000 actual, R$2,190,000 budget.

Kazan Factory: total manufacturing costs R$4,240,000 actual, R$4,200,000 budget.

Omsk Factory: total manufacturing costs R$4,942,000 actual, R$4,965,000 budget.

The Samara factory manager's office costs were R$950,000 actual and R$920,000 budget. The vice president of production's office costs were R$1,320,000 actual and R$1,300,000 budget. Office costs are not allocated to departments and factories.

Instructions

Using the format shown in Illustration 10.19, prepare the reports in a responsibility system for:

a. The Finishing Department—Samara.

b. The factory manager—Samara.

c. The vice president of production.

E10.14 (LO 3), AN The Mixing Department manager of Viuu Group is able to control all overhead costs except rent, property taxes, and salaries. Budgeted monthly overhead costs for the Mixing Department, in alphabetical order, are:

Prepare a responsibility report for a cost center.

Indirect labor	NT$120,000	Property taxes	NT$ 10,000
Indirect materials	77,000	Rent	18,000
Lubricants	16,750	Salaries	100,000
Maintenance	35,000	Utilities	50,000

Actual costs incurred for January 2023 are indirect labor NT$122,500, indirect materials NT$102,000, lubricants NT$16,500, maintenance NT$35,000, property taxes NT$11,000, rent NT$18,000, salaries NT$100,000, and utilities NT$64,000.

Instructions

a. Prepare a responsibility report for January 2023.

b. What would be the likely result of management's analysis of the report?

E10.15 (LO 3), AN Chang Company has three divisions which are operated as profit centers. Actual operating data for the divisions listed alphabetically are as follows:

Compute missing amounts in responsibility reports for three profit centers, and prepare a report.

Operating Data	Women's Shoes	Men's Shoes	Children's Shoes
Contribution margin	S$270,000	(3)	S$180,000
Controllable fixed costs	100,000	(4)	(5)
Controllable margin	(1)	S$ 90,000	95,000
Sales	600,000	450,000	(6)
Variable costs	(2)	320,000	250,000

Instructions

a. Compute the missing amounts. Show computations.

b. Prepare a responsibility report for the Women's Shoes Division assuming (1) the data are for the month ended June 30, 2023, and (2) all data equal budget except variable costs which are S$5,000 over budget.

Prepare a responsibility report for a profit center, and compute ROI.

E10.16 (LO 3, 4), AP The Sports Equipment Division of Almeria SpA is operated as a profit center. Sales for the division were budgeted for 2023 at €900,000. The only variable costs budgeted for the division were cost of goods sold (€440,000) and selling and administrative (€60,000). Fixed costs were budgeted at €100,000 for cost of goods sold, €90,000 for selling and administrative, and €70,000 for noncontrollable fixed costs. Actual results for these items were:

Sales	€880,000
Cost of goods sold	
Variable	408,000
Fixed	105,000
Selling and administrative	
Variable	61,000
Fixed	66,000
Noncontrollable fixed	90,000

Instructions

a. Prepare a responsibility report for the Sports Equipment Division for 2023.

b. Assume the division is an investment center, and average operating assets were €1,000,000. The noncontrollable fixed costs are controllable at the investment center level. Compute ROI using the actual amounts.

Compute ROI for current year and for possible future changes.

E10.17 (LO 4), AP The South Division of Ethan Electrical reported the following data for the current year.

Sales	£3,000,000
Variable costs	1,950,000
Controllable fixed costs	600,000
Average operating assets	5,000,000

Top management is unhappy with the investment center's return on investment (ROI). It asks the manager of the South Division to submit plans to improve ROI in the next year. The manager believes it is feasible to consider the following independent courses of action.

1. Increase sales by £300,000 with no change in the contribution margin percentage.
2. Reduce variable costs by £150,000.
3. Reduce average operating assets by 6.25%.

Instructions

a. Compute the return on investment (ROI) for the current year.

b. Using the ROI equation, compute the ROI under each of the proposed courses of action. (Round to one decimal.)

Prepare a responsibility report for an investment center.

E10.18 (LO 4), AP **Service** **Writing** The Dinkle and Frizell Dental Clinic provides both preventive and orthodontic dental services. The two owners, Reese Dinkle and Anita Frizell, operate the clinic as two separate investment centers: Preventive Services and Orthodontic Services. Each of them is in charge of one of the centers: Reese for Preventive Services and Anita for Orthodontic Services. Each month, they prepare an income statement for the two centers to evaluate performance and make decisions about how to improve the operational efficiency and profitability of the clinic.

Recently, they have been concerned about the profitability of the Preventive Services operations. For several months, it has been reporting a loss. The responsibility report for the month of May 2023 is shown here:

	Actual	Difference from Budget
Service revenue	$40,000	$1,000 F
Variable costs		
Filling materials	5,000	100 U
Novocain	3,900	100 U
Supplies	1,900	350 F
Dental assistant wages	2,500	0
Utilities	500	110 U
Total variable costs	13,800	40 F

	Actual	Difference from Budget
Fixed costs		
Allocated portion of receptionist's salary	$ 3,000	$ 200 U
Dentist salary	9,800	400 U
Equipment depreciation	6,000	0
Allocated portion of building depreciation	15,000	1,000 U
Total fixed costs	33,800	1,600 U
Operating income (loss)	$(7,600)	$ 560 U

In addition, the owners know that the investment in operating assets at the beginning of the month was $82,400, and it was $77,600 at the end of the month. They have asked for your assistance in evaluating their current performance reporting system.

Instructions

a. Prepare an investment center responsibility report for the Preventative Services segment for May 2023.

b. Write a memo to the owners discussing the deficiencies of their current reporting system.

E10.19 (LO 4), AN `Service` Li Transportation uses a responsibility reporting system to measure the performance of its three investment centers: Planes, Taxis, and Limos. Segment performance is measured using a system of responsibility reports and return on investment calculations. The allocation of resources within the company and the segment managers' bonuses are based in part on the results shown in these reports.

Recently, the company was the victim of a computer virus that deleted portions of the company's accounting records. This was discovered when the current period's responsibility reports were being prepared. The printout of the actual operating results, with question marks for missing amounts, appeared as follows:

Prepare missing amounts in responsibility reports for three investment centers.

	Planes	Taxis	Limos
Service revenue	HK$?	HK$5,000,000	HK$?
Variable costs	55,000,000	?	3,000,000
Contribution margin	?	2,500,000	4,800,000
Controllable fixed costs	15,000,000	?	?
Controllable margin	?	800,000	2,100,000
Average operating assets	250,000,000	?	15,000,000
Return on investment	12%	10%	?

Instructions

Determine the missing pieces of information above.

*E10.20 (LO 5), AN Presented here is selected information for three regional divisions of Limyadi Machinery.

Compare ROI and residual income.

	Divisions		
	North	West	South
Contribution margin	Rp3,000,000,000	Rp5,000,000,000	Rp4,000,000,000
Controllable margin	Rp1,400,000,000	Rp3,600,000,000	Rp2,100,000,000
Average operating assets	Rp10,000,000,000	Rp20,000,000,000	Rp15,000,000,000
Minimum rate of return	13%	16%	10%

Instructions

a. Compute the return on investment for each division.

b. Compute the residual income for each division.

c. Assume that each division has an investment opportunity that would provide a rate of return of 16%.

   1. If ROI is used to measure performance, which division or divisions will probably make the additional investment?

   2. If residual income is used to measure performance, which division or divisions will probably make the additional investment?

Fill in information related to ROI and residual income.

*E10.21 (LO 5), AN The following is selected financial information for two divisions of Deniz Brewery.

	Lager	Lite Lager
Contribution margin	₺5,000,000	₺ 3,000,000
Controllable margin	2,000,000	(c)
Average operating assets	(a)	₺12,000,000
Minimum rate of return	(b)	11%
Return on investment	16%	(d)
Residual income	₺1,000,000	₺ 1,560,000

Instructions

Supply the missing information for the lettered items.

Problems

Prepare flexible budget and budget report for manufacturing overhead.

P10.1 (LO 2), AN Writing Robin NE estimates that 300,000 direct labor hours will be worked during the coming year, 2023, in the Packaging Department. On this basis, the following budgeted manufacturing overhead cost data are computed for the year.

Fixed Overhead Costs		Variable Overhead Costs	
Supervision	€ 96,000	Indirect labor	€126,000
Depreciation	72,000	Indirect materials	90,000
Insurance	30,000	Repairs	69,000
Rent	24,000	Utilities	72,000
Property taxes	18,000	Lubricants	18,000
	€240,000		€375,000

It is estimated that direct labor hours worked each month will range from 27,000 to 36,000 hours.

During October, 27,000 direct labor hours were worked, and the following overhead costs were incurred.

Fixed overhead costs: supervision €8,000, depreciation €6,000, insurance €2,460, rent €2,000, and property taxes €1,500.

Variable overhead costs: indirect labor €12,432, indirect materials €7,680, repairs €6,100, utilities €6,840, and lubricants €1,920.

Instructions

a. Prepare a monthly manufacturing overhead flexible budget for each increment of 3,000 direct labor hours over the relevant range for the year ending December 31, 2023.

b. Prepare a flexible budget report for October.

c. Comment on management's efficiency in controlling manufacturing overhead costs in October.

a. Total costs: DLH 27,000, €53,750; DLH 36,000, €65,000
b. Total cost €1,182 U

Prepare flexible budget, budget report, and graph for manufacturing overhead.

P10.2 (LO 2), E Jaffery and Sons manufactures tablecloths. Sales have grown rapidly over the past two years. As a result, the president has installed a budgetary control system for 2023. The following data were used in developing the master manufacturing overhead budget for the Ironing Department, which is based on an activity index of direct labor hours.

Variable Costs	Rate per Direct Labor Hour	Annual Fixed Costs	
Indirect labor	£0.40	Supervision	£48,000
Indirect materials	0.50	Depreciation	18,000
Factory utilities	0.30	Insurance	12,000
Factory repairs	0.20	Rent	30,000

The master overhead budget was prepared in the expectation that 480,000 direct labor hours will be worked during the year. In June, 41,000 direct labor hours were worked. At that level of activity, actual costs were as shown below.

Variable—per direct labor hour: indirect labor £0.44, indirect materials £0.48, factory utilities £0.32, and factory repairs £0.25.

Fixed: same as budgeted.

Instructions

a. Prepare a monthly manufacturing overhead flexible budget for the year ending December 31, 2023, assuming production levels range from 35,000 to 50,000 direct labor hours. Use increments of 5,000 direct labor hours.

b. Prepare a budget report for June comparing actual results with budget data based on the flexible budget.

c. Were costs effectively controlled? Explain.

d. State the equation for computing the total budgeted costs for the Ironing Department.

e. Prepare the flexible budget graph, showing total budgeted costs at 35,000 and 45,000 direct labor hours. Use increments of 5,000 direct labor hours on the horizontal axis and increments of £10,000 on the vertical axis.

a. Total costs: 35,000 DLH, £58,000; 50,000 DLH, £79,000

b. Total cost:
Budget £66,400
Actual £70,090

P10.3 (LO 1, 2), AN Nicole Company uses budgets in controlling costs. The August 2023 budget report for the company's Assembling Department is as follows:

State total budgeted cost equation, and prepare flexible budget reports for two time periods.

Nicole Company
Budget Report
Assembling Department
For the Month Ended August 31, 2023

Manufacturing Costs	Budget	Actual	Difference Favorable F Unfavorable U
Variable costs			
Direct materials	S$ 48,000	S$ 47,000	S$1,000 F
Direct labor	54,000	51,200	2,800 F
Indirect materials	24,000	24,200	200 U
Indirect labor	18,000	17,500	500 F
Utilities	15,000	14,900	100 F
Maintenance	12,000	12,400	400 U
Total variable	171,000	167,200	3,800 F
Fixed costs			
Rent	12,000	12,000	-0-
Supervision	17,000	17,000	-0-
Depreciation	6,000	6,000	-0-
Total fixed	35,000	35,000	-0-
Total costs	S$206,000	S$202,200	S$3,800 F

The monthly budget amounts in the report were based on an expected production of 60,000 units per month or 720,000 units per year. The Assembling Department manager is pleased with the report and expects a raise, or at least praise for a job well done. The company president, however, is unhappy with the results for August because only 58,000 units were produced.

Instructions

a. State the total monthly budgeted cost equation.

b. Prepare a budget report for August using flexible budget data. Why does this report provide a better basis for evaluating performance than the report based on static budget data?

c. In September, 64,000 units were produced. Prepare the budget report using flexible budget data, assuming (1) each variable cost was 10% higher than its actual cost in August, and (2) fixed costs were the same in September as in August.

b. Total budgeted cost S$200,300

c. Total cost:
Budget S$217,400
Actual S$218,920

P10.4 (LO 3), AN Writing Sydney Furnitures operates the Patio Furniture Division as a profit center. Operating data for this division for the year ended December 31, 2023 are shown here.

Prepare responsibility report for a profit center.

	Budget	Difference from Budget
Sales	A$2,500,000	A$50,000 F
Cost of goods sold		
Variable	1,300,000	41,000 F
Controllable fixed	200,000	3,000 U
Selling and administrative		
Variable	220,000	6,000 U
Controllable fixed	50,000	2,000 U
Noncontrollable fixed costs	70,000	4,000 U

In addition, Sydney incurs A$180,000 of indirect fixed costs that were budgeted at A$175,000. Twenty percent (20%) of these costs are allocated to the Patio Furniture Division.

Instructions

a. Prepare a responsibility report for the Patio Furniture Division for the year.
b. Comment on the manager's performance in controlling revenues and costs.
c. Identify any costs excluded from the responsibility report and explain why they were excluded.

a. Contribution margin A$85,000 F
Controllable margin A$80,000 F

Prepare responsibility report for an investment center, and compute ROI.

P10.5 (LO 4), E Elijah Equipment manufactures a variety of tools and industrial equipment. The company operates through three divisions. Each division is an investment center. Operating data for the Home Division for the year ended December 31, 2023, and relevant budget data are as follows:

	Actual	Comparison with Budget
Sales	CHF1,400,000	CHF100,000 favorable
Variable cost of goods sold	665,000	45,000 unfavorable
Variable selling and administrative expenses	125,000	25,000 unfavorable
Controllable fixed cost of goods sold	170,000	On target
Controllable fixed selling and administrative expenses	80,000	On target

Average operating assets for the year for the Home Division were CHF2,000,000, which was also the budgeted amount.

Instructions

a. Prepare a responsibility report for the Home Division.
b. Evaluate the manager's performance. Which items will likely be investigated by top management?
c. Compute the expected ROI in 2023 for the Home Division, assuming the following independent changes to actual data.
   1. Variable selling and administrative expenses are decreased by 4%.
   2. Average operating assets are decreased by 10%.
   3. Sales are increased by CHF200,000, and this increase is expected to increase contribution margin by CHF80,000.

a. Controllable margin: Budget CHF330 Actual CHF360

Prepare reports for cost centers under responsibility accounting, and comment on performance of managers.

P10.6 (LO 3), AN Chao Ltd. uses a responsibility reporting system. It has divisions in Beijing, Shanghai, and Xi An. Each division has three production departments: Cutting, Shaping, and Finishing. The responsibility for each department rests with a manager who reports to the division production manager. Each division manager reports to the vice president of production. There are also vice presidents for marketing and finance. All vice presidents report to the president.

In January 2023, controllable actual and budget manufacturing overhead cost data for the departments and divisions were as shown here:

Manufacturing Overhead	Actual	Budget
Individual costs—Cutting Department—Shanghai		
Indirect labor	¥ 730,000	¥ 700,000
Indirect materials	479,000	460,000
Maintenance	205,000	180,000
Utilities	201,000	170,000
Supervision	220,000	200,000
	¥1,835,000	¥1,710,000
Total costs		
Shaping Department—Shanghai	¥1,580,000	¥1,480,000
Finishing Department—Shanghai	2,100,000	2,050,000
Beijing division	6,780,000	6,730,000
Xi An division	7,220,000	7,150,000

Additional overhead costs were incurred as follows: Shanghai division production manager—actual costs ¥525,000, budget ¥510,000; vice president of production—actual costs ¥650,000, budget ¥640,000; president—actual costs ¥764,000, budget ¥742,000. These expenses are not allocated.

The vice presidents who report to the president, other than the vice president of production, had the following expenses:

Vice President	Actual	Budget
Marketing	¥1,336,000	¥1,300,000
Finance	1,090,000	1,040,000

Instructions

Using the format in Illustration 10.19, prepare the following responsibility reports:

a. Manufacturing overhead—Cutting Department manager—Shanghai division.

b. Manufacturing overhead—Shanghai division manager.

c. Manufacturing overhead—vice president of production.

d. Manufacturing overhead and expenses—president.

a. ¥125,000 U
b. ¥290,000 U
c. ¥420,000 U
d. ¥528,000 U

*P10.7 (LO 5), AN Writing Sentinel Industries has manufactured prefabricated houses for over 20 years. The houses are constructed in sections to be assembled on customers' lots. Sentinel expanded into the precut housing market when it acquired Jensen Company, one of its suppliers. In this market, various types of lumber are precut into the appropriate lengths, banded into packages, and shipped to customers' lots for assembly. Sentinel designated the Jensen Division as an investment center.

Compare ROI and residual income.

Sentinel uses return on investment (ROI) as a performance measure with investment defined as average operating assets. Management bonuses are based in part on ROI. All investments are expected to earn a minimum rate of return of 18%. Jensen's ROI has ranged from 20.1% to 23.5% since it was acquired. Jensen had an investment opportunity in 2023 that had an estimated ROI of 19%. Jensen management decided against the investment because it believed the investment would decrease the division's overall ROI.

Selected financial information for Jensen is presented here. The division's average operating assets were $12,300,000 for the year 2023.

Sentinel Industries
Jensen Division
Selected Financial Information
For the Year Ended December 31, 2023

Sales	$24,000,000
Contribution margin	9,100,000
Controllable margin	2,460,000

Instructions

a. Calculate the following performance measures for 2023 for the Jensen Division.

1. Return on investment (ROI).
2. Residual income.

a. ROI 20%

b. Would the management of Jensen Division have been more likely to accept the investment opportunity it had in 2023 if residual income were used as a performance measure instead of ROI? Explain your answer.

Continuing Case

Current Designs

CD10 The **Current Designs** (USA) staff has prepared the annual manufacturing budget for the roto-molded line based on an estimated annual production of 4,000 kayaks during 2023. Each kayak will require 54 pounds of polyethylene powder and a finishing kit (rope, seat, hardware, etc.). The polyethylene powder used in these kayaks costs $1.50 per pound, and the finishing kits cost $170 each. Each kayak will use two kinds of labor—2 hours of type I labor from people who run the oven and trim the plastic, and 3 hours of work from type II workers who attach the hatches and seat and other hardware. The type I employees are paid $15 per hour, and the type II are paid $12 per hour.

Manufacturing overhead is budgeted at $396,000 for 2023, broken down as follows:

Variable costs		
Indirect materials	$ 40,000	
Manufacturing supplies	53,800	
Maintenance and utilities	88,000	
		181,800
Fixed costs		
Supervision	90,000	
Insurance	14,400	
Depreciation	109,800	
		214,200
Total		$396,000

During the first quarter, ended March 31, 2023, 1,050 units were actually produced with the following costs:

Polyethylene powder	$ 87,000
Finishing kits	178,840
Type I labor	31,500
Type II labor	39,060
Indirect materials	10,500
Manufacturing supplies	14,150
Maintenance and utilities	26,000
Supervision	20,000
Insurance	3,600
Depreciation	27,450
Total	$438,100

Instructions

a. Prepare the annual manufacturing budget for 2023, assuming that 4,000 kayaks will be produced.

b. Prepare the flexible budget for manufacturing for the quarter ended March 31, 2023. Assume activity levels of 900, 1,000, and 1,050 units.

c. Assuming the rotomolded line is treated as a cost center, prepare a flexible budget report for manufacturing for the quarter ended March 31, 2023, when 1,050 units were produced. (Round all budgeted amounts to the nearest dollar.)

Data Analytics in Action

Using Data Visualization for Budgeting

DA10.1 Data visualization can be used to help improve forecasts.

Example: Recall the section "Flexible Budget—A Case Study" presented in the chapter. Flexible budgeting is useful because it enables managers to evaluate performance in light of changing conditions. But the ability to react quickly to changing conditions is even more important. For example, consider the following charts, which present quarterly data for Honda sales in four regional markets.

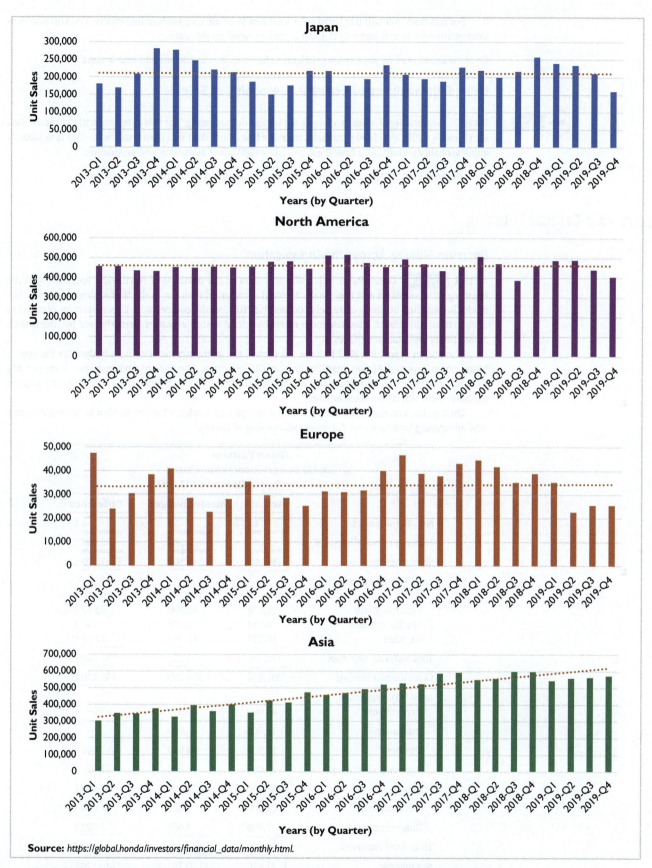

Source: *https://global.honda/investors/financial_data/monthly.html*.

While the number of vehicles sold differs by region, the trends shown are used in forecasting sales and accompanying budgets. In examining the above charts, it appears that some regions will likely be more difficult to budget than others. For example, sales in Europe are the most volatile, as shown by the changing heights of the columns, and Japan is somewhat erratic. On the other hand, North America's and Asia's upward trends are much more consistent, making it easier to forecast sales in those regions.

Using Data Analytics to Evaluate Seasonality of Sales

DA10.2 Seasonality of sales can have a big impact on budgeting. For this case, you will use recent data for **Honda**'s (JPN) worldwide unit sales to create line charts. You will then analyze the charts to identify any seasonality patterns and how these patterns might affect budgeting and production.

Go to the book's product page on www.wiley.com for complete case details and instructions.

Expand Your Critical Thinking

Decision-Making Across the Organization

CT10.1 **Service** Green Pastures is a 400-acre farm on the outskirts of Northwich, specializing in the boarding of broodmares and their foals. A recent economic downturn in the thoroughbred industry has made the boarding business extremely competitive. To meet the competition, Green Pastures planned in 2023 to entertain clients, advertise more extensively, and absorb expenses formerly paid by clients such as veterinary and blacksmith fees.

The budget report for 2023 follows. As shown, the static income statement budget for the year is based on an expected 21,900 boarding days at £25 per mare. The variable expenses per mare per day were budgeted: feed £5, veterinary fees £3, blacksmith fees £0.25, and supplies £0.55. All other budgeted expenses were either semifixed or fixed.

During the year, management decided not to replace a worker who quit in March, but it did issue a new advertising brochure and did more entertaining of clients.[1]

Green Pastures
Static Budget Income Statement
For the Year Ended December 31, 2023

	Actual	Master Budget	Difference
Number of mares	52	60	8 U
Number of boarding days	19,000	21,900	2,900 U
Service revenue	£380,000	£547,500	£167,500 U
Less: Variable expenses			
Feed	104,390	109,500	5,110 F
Veterinary fees	58,838	65,700	6,862 F
Blacksmith fees	4,984	5,475	491 F
Supplies	10,178	12,045	1,867 F
Total variable expenses	178,390	192,720	14,330 F
Contribution margin	201,610	354,780	153,170 U
Less: Fixed expenses			
Depreciation	40,000	40,000	–0–
Insurance	11,000	11,000	–0–
Utilities	12,000	14,000	2,000 F
Repairs and maintenance	10,000	11,000	1,000 F
Labor	88,000	95,000	7,000 F
Advertisement	12,000	8,000	4,000 U
Entertainment	7,000	5,000	2,000 U
Total fixed expenses	180,000	184,000	4,000 F
Net income	£ 21,610	£170,780	£149,170 U

---

[1] Data for this case are based on Hans Sprohge and John Talbott, "New Applications for Variance Analysis," *Journal of Accountancy* (AICPA, New York), April 1989, pp. 137–141.

Instructions

With the class divided into groups, answer the following:

a. Based on the static budget report:
   1. What was the primary cause(s) of the decline in net income?
   2. Did management do a good, average, or poor job of controlling expenses?
   3. Were management's decisions to stay competitive sound?
b. Prepare a flexible budget report for the year.
c. Based on the flexible budget report, answer the three questions in part (a) above.
d. What course of action do you recommend for the management of Green Pastures?

Managerial Analysis

CT10.2 Lumbrein Luggage manufactures expensive watch cases sold as souvenirs. Three of its sales departments are Retail Sales, Wholesale Sales, and Outlet Sales. The Retail Sales Department is a profit center. The Wholesale Sales Department is a cost center. Its managers merely take orders from customers who purchase through the company's wholesale catalog. The Outlet Sales Department is an investment center because each manager is given full responsibility for an outlet store location. The manager can hire and discharge employees, purchase, maintain, and sell equipment, and in general is fairly independent of company control.

Marie Cavadini is a manager in the Retail Sales Department. Luis Fontana manages the Wholesale Sales Department. Antoni Michel manages the LeMont outlet store. The following are the budget responsibility reports for each of the three departments.

Budget

	Retail Sales	Wholesale Sales	Outlet Sales
Sales	CHF 750,000	CHF 400,000	CHF 200,000
Variable costs			
Cost of goods sold	150,000	100,000	25,000
Advertising	100,000	30,000	5,000
Sales salaries	75,000	15,000	3,000
Printing	10,000	20,000	5,000
Travel	20,000	30,000	2,000
Fixed costs			
Rent	50,000	30,000	10,000
Insurance	5,000	2,000	1,000
Depreciation	75,000	100,000	40,000
Investment in assets	1,000,000	1,200,000	800,000

Actual Results

	Retail Sales	Wholesale Sales	Outlet Sales
Sales	CHF 750,000	CHF 400,000	CHF 200,000
Variable costs			
Cost of goods sold	192,000	122,000	26,500
Advertising	100,000	30,000	5,000
Sales salaries	75,000	15,000	3,000
Printing	10,000	20,000	5,000
Travel	14,000	21,000	1,500
Fixed costs			
Rent	40,000	50,000	12,300
Insurance	5,000	2,000	1,000
Depreciation	80,000	90,000	56,000
Investment in assets	1,000,000	1,200,000	800,000

Instructions

a. Determine which of the items should be included in the responsibility report for each of the three managers.
b. Compare the budgeted measures with the actual results. Decide which results should be called to the attention of each manager.

Real-World Focus

CT10.3 CA Technologies (USA), the world's leading business software company, delivers the end-to-end infrastructure to enable e-business through innovative technology, services, and education. Recently, CA Technologies had 19,000 employees worldwide and revenue of over $6 billion.

The following information is from the company's annual report.

CA Technologies
Management Discussion

The Company has experienced a pattern of business whereby revenue for its third and fourth fiscal quarters reflects an increase over first- and second-quarter revenue. The Company attributes this increase to clients' increased spending at the end of their calendar year budgetary periods and the culmination of its annual sales plan. Since the Company's costs do not increase proportionately with the third- and fourth-quarters' increase in revenue, the higher revenue in these quarters results in greater profit margins and income. Fourth-quarter profitability is traditionally affected by significant new hirings, training, and education expenditures for the succeeding year.

Instructions

a. Why don't the company's costs increase proportionately as the revenues increase in the third and fourth quarters?

b. What type of budgeting seems appropriate for the CA Technologies situation?

Communication Activity

CT10.4 The manufacturing overhead budget for Huang Sunglasses contains the following items:

Variable costs		Fixed costs	
Indirect materials	HK$220,000	Supervision	HK$170,000
Indirect labor	120,000	Inspection costs	10,000
Maintenance expense	100,000	Insurance expense	20,000
Manufacturing supplies	60,000	Depreciation	150,000
Total variable	HK$500,000	Total fixed	HK$350,000

The budget was based on an estimated 2,000 units being produced. During the past month, 1,500 units were produced, and the following costs incurred.

Variable costs		Fixed costs	
Indirect materials	HK$225,000	Supervision	HK$184,000
Indirect labor	135,000	Inspection costs	12,000
Maintenance expense	82,000	Insurance expense	22,000
Manufacturing supplies	50,000	Depreciation	147,000
Total variable	HK$492,000	Total fixed	HK$365,000

Instructions

a. Determine which items would be controllable by Jun Chen, the production manager.

b. How much should have been spent during the month for the manufacture of the 1,500 units?

c. Prepare a flexible manufacturing overhead budget report for Mr. Chen.

d. Prepare a responsibility report. Include only the costs that would have been controllable by Mr. Chen. Assume that the supervision cost above includes Mr. Chen's monthly salary of HK$100,000, both at budget and actual. In an attached memo, describe clearly for Mr. Chen the areas in which his performance needs to be improved.

Ethics Case

CT10.5 World Wide Production Ltd. participates in a highly competitive industry. In order to meet this competition and achieve profit goals, the company has chosen the decentralized form of organization. Each manager of a decentralized investment center is measured on the basis of profit contribution, market penetration, and return on investment. Failure to meet the objectives established by corporate management for these measures has not been acceptable and usually has resulted in demotion or dismissal of an investment center manager.

An anonymous survey of managers in the company revealed that the managers feel the pressure to compromise their personal ethical standards to achieve the corporate objectives. For example, at certain factory locations there was pressure to reduce quality control to a level which could not assure that all unsafe products would be rejected. Also, sales personnel were encouraged to use questionable sales tactics to obtain orders, including gifts and other incentives to purchasing agents.

The chief executive officer is disturbed by the survey findings. In his opinion, such behavior cannot be condoned by the company. He concludes that the company should do something about this problem.

Instructions

a. Who are the stakeholders (the affected parties) in this situation?
b. Identify the ethical implications, conflicts, or dilemmas in the above described situation.
c. What might the company do to reduce the pressures on managers and to decrease the ethical conflicts?

All About You

CT10.6 It is one thing to prepare a personal budget; it is another thing to stick to it. Financial planners have suggested various mechanisms to provide support for enforcing personal budgets. One approach is called "envelope budgeting."

Instructions

Do an Internet search on "envelope system money management" and then complete the following:

a. Summarize the process of envelope budgeting.
b. Evaluate whether you think you would benefit from envelope budgeting. What do you think are its strengths and weaknesses relative to your situation?

Considering Your Costs and Benefits

CT10.7 Preparing a personal budget is a great first step toward control over your personal finances. It is especially useful to prepare a budget when you face a big decision. For most people, the biggest decision they will ever make is whether to purchase a house. The percentage of people in the United States who own a home is high compared to many other countries. This is partially the result of U.S. government programs and incentives that encourage home ownership. For example, the interest on a home mortgage is tax-deductible, subject to some limitations.

Before purchasing a house, you should first consider whether buying it is the best choice for you. Suppose you just graduated from college and are moving to a new community. Should you immediately buy a new home?

YES: If I purchase a home, I am making my housing cost more like a "fixed cost," thus minimizing increases in my future housing costs. Also, I benefit from the appreciation in my home's value. Although recent turbulence in the economy has caused home prices in many communities to decline, I know that over the long term, home prices have increased across the country.

NO: I just moved to a new town, so I don't know the housing market. I am new to my job, so I don't know whether I will like it or my new community. Also, if my job does go well, it is likely that my income will increase in the next few years, so I will able to afford a better house if I wait. Therefore, the flexibility provided by renting is very valuable to me at this point in my life.

Instructions

Write a response indicating your position regarding this situation. Provide support for your view.

CHAPTER 11

Standard Costs and Balanced Scorecard

CHAPTER PREVIEW

Standards are a fact of life. You met the admission standards for the school you are attending. The vehicle that you drive had to meet certain governmental emissions standards. The hamburgers and salads that you eat in a restaurant have to meet certain health and nutritional standards before they can be sold. As described in the following Feature Story, **Starbucks** (USA) has standards for the costs of its materials, labor, and overhead. The reason for standards in these cases is very simple: They help to ensure that overall product quality is high while keeping costs under control.

In this chapter, we continue the study of controlling costs. You will learn how to evaluate performance using standard costs and a balanced scorecard.

CHAPTER 11
Standard Costs and Balanced Scorecard

FEATURE STORY

80,000 Different Caffeinated Combinations

When Howard Schultz purchased a small Seattle coffee-roasting business in 1987, he set out to create a new kind of company. He also saw the store as a place where you could order a beverage, custom-made to your unique tastes, in an environment that would give you the sense that you had escaped, if only momentarily, from the chaos we call life. Schultz believed that the company would prosper if employees shared in its success.

In a little more than 20 years, Howard Schultz's company, **Starbucks** (USA), grew from that one store to over 17,000 locations in 54 countries. That is an incredible rate of growth, and it didn't happen by accident. While Starbucks does everything it can to maximize the customer's experience, behind the scenes it needs to control costs. Consider the almost infinite options of beverage combinations and variations at Starbucks. The company must determine the most efficient way to make each beverage, it must communicate these methods in the form of standards to its employees, and it must then evaluate whether those standards are being met.

Schultz's book, *Onward: How Starbucks Fought for Its Life Without Losing Its Soul*, describes a painful period in which Starbucks had to close 600 stores and lay off thousands of employees. When a prominent shareholder suggested that the company eliminate its employee healthcare plan, as so many other companies had done, Schultz refused. Schultz feels that providing health care to the company's employees is an essential part of the standard cost of a cup of Starbucks' coffee.

At https://wileyaccountingupdates.com/video/?p=50, watch the *Starbucks* video to learn more about how the company sets standards, and watch the *Southwest Airlines* video at https://wileyaccountingupdates.com/video/?p=61 to learn more about the real-world use of the balanced scorecard.

CHAPTER OUTLINE

Learning Objectives	Review	Practice
LO 1 Describe standard costs.	• Distinguishing between standards and budgets • Setting standard costs	**DO IT! 1** Standard Costs
LO 2 Determine direct materials variances.	• Analyzing and reporting variances • Calculating direct materials variances	**DO IT! 2** Direct Materials Variances
LO 3 Determine direct labor and total manufacturing overhead variances.	• Direct labor variances • Manufacturing overhead variances	**DO IT! 3** Labor and Manufacturing Overhead Variances
LO 4 Prepare variance reports and balanced scorecards.	• Reporting variances • Income statement presentation of variances • Balanced scorecard	**DO IT! 4** Reporting Variances

Go to the Review and Practice section at the end of the chapter for a targeted summary and practice applications with solutions.

STANDARD COSTS

Standards are common in business.

> **LEARNING OBJECTIVE 1**
> Describe standard costs.

- Standards established internally by a company may extend to personnel matters, such as employee absenteeism and ethical codes of conduct, quality control standards for products, and standard costs for goods and services.
- In managerial accounting, **standard costs** are predetermined unit costs, which companies use as measures of performance.

We focus on manufacturing operations in this chapter. But you should recognize that standard costs also apply to many types of service businesses as well. For example, a fast-food restaurant such as **McDonald's** (USA) knows the price it should pay for pickles, beef, buns, and other ingredients. It also knows how much time it should take an employee to prepare and serve hamburgers. If the company pays too much for pickles or if employees take too much time to prepare Big Macs, McDonald's notices the deviations from standards and takes corrective action. Not-for-profit entities, such as universities, charitable organizations, and governmental agencies, also may use standard costs as measures of performance.

Standard costs offer a number of advantages to an organization, as shown in **Illustration 11.1**.

- The organization will realize these advantages only when standard costs are carefully established and prudently used.
- Using standards as a way to place blame can have a negative effect on managers and employees.
- To minimize this effect, many companies offer wage incentives to those who meet the standards.

Advantages of Standard Costs

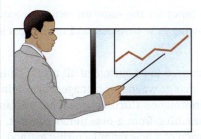

Facilitate management planning

Promote greater economy by making employees more "cost-conscious"

Useful in setting selling prices

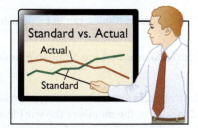

Contribute to management control by providing basis for evaluation of cost control

Useful in highlighting variances in management by exception

Simplify costing of inventories and reduce clerical costs

ILLUSTRATION 11.1 | **Advantages of standard costs**

Distinguishing Between Standards and Budgets

Both **standards** and **budgets** are predetermined costs, and both contribute to management planning and control. There is a difference, however, in the way the terms are expressed.

- A standard is a **unit** amount.
- A budget is a **total** amount.

Thus, it is customary to state that the **standard cost** of direct labor for a unit of product is, say, €10. If the company produces 5,000 units of the product, the €50,000 of direct labor is the **budgeted** labor cost. A standard is the budgeted **cost per unit** of product. A standard is therefore concerned with each individual cost component that makes up the entire budget.

There are important accounting differences between budgets and standards.

- Except in the application of manufacturing overhead to jobs and processes, budget data are not journalized in cost accounting systems.
- In contrast, as we illustrate in the appendix to this chapter, standard costs may be incorporated into cost accounting systems.
- A company may report its inventories at standard cost in its financial statements, but it would not report inventories at budgeted costs.

Setting Standard Costs

The setting of standard costs to produce a unit of product is a difficult task. It requires input from all persons who have responsibility for costs and quantities.

- To determine the standard cost of direct materials, management consults purchasing agents, product managers, quality control engineers, and production supervisors.
- In setting the standard cost for direct labor, managers obtain pay rate data from the payroll department.
- Industrial engineers generally determine the labor time requirements.
- The managerial accountant provides important input for the standard-setting process by accumulating historical cost data and by knowing how costs respond to changes in activity levels.

To be effective in controlling costs, standard costs need to be current at all times. Thus, standards are under continuous review. They should change whenever managers determine that the existing standard is not a good measure of performance. Circumstances that warrant revision of a standard include changed wage rates resulting from a new union contract, a change in product specifications, and the implementation of a new manufacturing method.

Ideal versus Normal Standards

Companies set standards at one of two levels: ideal or normal.

- **Ideal standards** represent optimum levels of performance under perfect operating conditions.
- **Normal standards** represent efficient levels of performance that are attainable under expected operating conditions.

Some managers believe ideal standards will stimulate workers to ever-increasing improvement. However, most managers believe that ideal standards lower the morale of the workforce because they are difficult, if not impossible, to meet (see **Ethics Note**). Very few companies use ideal standards.

Most companies that use standards set them at a normal level. Properly set, normal standards should be **rigorous but attainable**. Normal standards allow for rest periods, machine breakdowns, and other "normal" contingencies in the production process. In the remainder of this chapter, we will assume that standard costs are set at a normal level.

ETHICS NOTE

When standards are set too high, employees sometimes feel pressure to consider unethical practices to meet these standards.

ACCOUNTING ACROSS THE ORGANIZATION — U.S. Navy

SpotX/iStockphoto.com

How Do Standards Help a Business?

A number of organizations, including corporations, consultants, and governmental agencies, share information regarding performance standards in an effort to create a standard set of measures for thousands of business processes. The group, referred to as the Open Standards Benchmarking Collaborative, includes the U.S. companies such as **IBM** and **Procter and Gamble**; the **U.S. Navy**; and the **World Bank**. Companies that are interested in participating can go to the group's website and enter their information.

Sources: Becky Partida, "Benchmark Your Manufacturing Performance," *Control Engineering* (February 4, 2013); and American Productivity and Quality Center, *APQC.org* (accessed April 3, 2020).

How will the creation of such standards help a business or organization? (Answer is available in the book's product page on www.wiley.com)

A Case Study

To establish the standard cost of producing a product:

- Determine standards for each manufacturing cost component—direct materials, direct labor, and manufacturing overhead.
- Derive the standard for each component from the standard price to be paid and the standard quantity to be used.

To illustrate, we use an extended example. Spark Drinks uses standard costs to measure performance at the production facility of its caffeinated energy drink, Spark Tonic. Spark produces one-liter containers of concentrated syrup that it sells to coffee and smoothie shops, and other retail outlets. The syrup is mixed with ice water or ice "slush" before serving. The potency of the beverage varies depending on the amount of concentrated syrup used.

Direct Materials The **direct materials price standard** is the cost per finished unit of product of direct materials that should be incurred.

- This standard is based on the purchasing department's best estimate of the **cost of raw materials**.
- This cost is frequently based on current purchase prices.
- The price standard also includes an amount for related costs such as receiving, storing, and handling.

Illustration 11.2 shows the materials price standard per kilogram of material for Spark Tonic.

Item	Price
Purchase price, net of discounts	€2.70
Freight	0.20
Receiving and handling	0.10
Standard direct materials price per kilogram	**€3.00**

ILLUSTRATION 11.2 | Setting direct materials price standard

The **direct materials quantity standard** is the quantity of direct materials that management determines should be used per unit of finished goods.

- This standard is expressed as a physical measure, such as kilograms, barrels, or cubic meters.
- In setting the standard, management considers both the quality and quantity of materials required to manufacture the product.
- The standard includes allowances for unavoidable waste and normal spoilage.

The standard quantity per unit for Spark Tonic is shown in **Illustration 11.3**.

Item	Quantity (Kilograms)
Required materials	3.5
Allowance for waste	0.4
Allowance for spoilage	0.1
Standard direct materials quantity per unit	**4.0**

ILLUSTRATION 11.3 | Setting direct materials quantity standard

The standard direct materials cost per unit is the standard direct materials price times the standard direct materials quantity. For Spark, the standard direct materials cost per liter of Spark Tonic is €12 (€3 × 4 kilograms), as follows:

Standard Direct Materials Cost per Liter

Standard Direct Materials Price (SP)	×	Standard Direct Materials Quantity (SQ)	=	Standard Direct Materials Cost
€3 per kg	×	4 kg per liter	=	€12 per liter

Direct Labor The **direct labor price standard** is the rate per hour that should be incurred for direct labor (see **Alternative Terminology**).

> **ALTERNATIVE TERMINOLOGY**
> The direct labor price standard is also called the *direct labor rate standard.*

- This standard is based on current wage rates, adjusted for anticipated changes such as cost of living adjustments (COLAs).
- The price standard also generally includes employer payroll taxes and fringe benefits, such as paid holidays and vacations.

For Spark, the direct labor price standard is as shown in **Illustration 11.4**.

Item	Price
Hourly wage rate	€12.50
COLA	0.25
Payroll taxes	0.75
Fringe benefits	1.50
Standard direct labor rate per hour	**€15.00**

ILLUSTRATION 11.4 | Setting direct labor price standard

The **direct labor quantity standard** is the time that management determines should be required to make one unit of the product (see **Alternative Terminology**).

> **ALTERNATIVE TERMINOLOGY**
> The direct labor quantity standard is also called the *direct labor efficiency standard.*

- This standard is especially critical in labor-intensive companies.
- Allowances should be made in this standard for rest periods, cleanup, machine setup, and machine downtime.

Illustration 11.5 shows the direct labor quantity standard for Spark.

Item	Quantity (Hours)
Actual production time	1.5
Rest periods and cleanup	0.2
Setup and downtime	0.3
Standard direct labor hours per unit	**2.0**

ILLUSTRATION 11.5 | Setting direct labor quantity standard

The standard direct labor cost per unit of finished product is the standard direct labor rate times the standard direct labor hours. For Spark, the standard direct labor cost per liter is €30 (€15 × 2 hours), as follows:

Standard Direct Labor Cost per Liter			
Standard Direct Labor Rate (SP)	×	Standard Direct Labor Hours (SQ)	= Standard Direct Labor Cost
€15 per hour	×	2 hours per liter	= €30 per liter

Manufacturing Overhead For manufacturing overhead, companies use a **standard predetermined overhead rate** in setting the standard.

- This overhead rate is determined by dividing budgeted overhead costs by an expected standard activity index.
- For example, the index may be standard direct labor hours or standard machine hours.

As discussed in Chapter 4, many companies employ activity-based costing (ABC) to allocate overhead costs. Because ABC uses multiple activity indices to allocate overhead costs, it results in a better correlation between activities and costs incurred than do other methods. As a result, the use of ABC can significantly improve the usefulness of standard costing for management decision-making.

Spark uses standard direct labor hours as the activity index. The company expects to produce 13,200 liters of Spark Tonic during the year at normal capacity. **Normal capacity** is the average activity output that a company should experience over the long run. Since it takes two direct labor hours for each liter, total standard direct labor hours are 26,400 (13,200 liters × 2 hours).

At normal capacity of 26,400 direct labor hours, overhead costs are budgeted to be €132,000. Of that amount, €79,200 are variable and €52,800 are fixed. **Illustration 11.6** shows computation of the standard predetermined overhead rates for Spark.

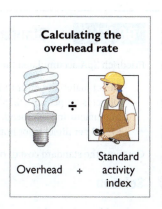

Calculating the overhead rate

Overhead ÷ Standard activity index

Budgeted Overhead Costs	Amount	÷	Standard Direct Labor Hours	=	Overhead Rate per Direct Labor Hour
Variable	€ 79,200		26,400		€3.00
Fixed	52,800		26,400		2.00
Total	€132,000		26,400		€5.00

ILLUSTRATION 11.6 | Computing predetermined overhead rates

The standard manufacturing overhead cost per unit is the predetermined overhead rate times the activity index quantity standard. For Spark, which uses direct labor hours as its activity index, the standard manufacturing overhead cost per liter of Spark Tonic is €10 (€5 × 2 hours), as follows:

Standard Manufacturing Overhead Cost per Liter			
Predetermined Overhead Rate (SP)	×	Standard Direct Labor Hours (SQ)	= Overhead Rate per Direct Labor Hour
€5	×	2 hours	= €10

Total Standard Cost per Unit After a company has established the standard quantity and price per unit of finished product for each cost component, it can determine the total standard cost. The total standard cost per unit is the sum of the standard costs of direct materials, direct labor, and manufacturing overhead. The total standard cost per liter of Spark Tonic is €52, as the standard cost card in **Illustration 11.7** shows.

Product: Spark Tonic		Unit Measure: Liter		
Manufacturing Cost Components	Quantity ×	**Standard** Price =	Cost	
Direct materials	4 kilograms	€3.00	€12.00	
Direct labor	2 hours	€15.00	30.00	
Manufacturing overhead	2 hours*	€5.00	10.00	
			€52.00	

*Overhead assigned based on direct labor hours

ILLUSTRATION 11.7 | Standard cost per liter of Spark Tonic

The company prepares a standard cost card for each product. This card provides the basis for determining variances from standards.

DO IT! 1 ▶ Standard Costs

Friedrich SpA accumulated the following standard cost data concerning product Cty31.

Direct materials per unit: 1.5 kilograms at €4 per kilogram
Direct labor per unit: 0.25 hours at €13 per hour.
Manufacturing overhead: allocated based on direct labor hours at a predetermined rate of €15.60 per direct labor hour.

Compute the standard cost of one unit of product Cty31.

Solution

Manufacturing Cost Components	Quantity ×	**Standard** Price =	Cost
Direct materials	1.5 kilograms	€ 4.00	€ 6.00
Direct labor	0.25 hours	€13.00	3.25
Manufacturing overhead	0.25 hours	€15.60	3.90
Total			€13.15

Related exercise material: **BE11.2, BE11.3, DO IT! 11.1, E11.1, E11.2,** and **E11.3.**

ACTION PLAN
- Know that standard costs are predetermined unit costs.
- To establish the standard cost of producing a product, establish the standard for each manufacturing cost component—direct materials, direct labor, and manufacturing overhead.
- Compute the standard cost for each component from the standard price to be paid and the standard quantity to be used.

DIRECT MATERIALS VARIANCES

LEARNING OBJECTIVE 2
Determine direct materials variances.

ALTERNATIVE TERMINOLOGY
In business, the term *variance* is also used to indicate differences between total budgeted and total actual costs.

Analyzing and Reporting Variances

One of the major management uses of standard costs is to identify variances from standards. **Variances** are the differences between total actual costs and total standard costs (see **Alternative Terminology**).

To illustrate, assume that in producing 1,000 liters of Spark Tonic in the month of June, Spark incurred the costs listed in **Illustration 11.8.**

Direct materials	€13,020
Direct labor	31,080
Variable overhead	6,500
Fixed overhead	4,400
Total actual costs	€55,000

ILLUSTRATION 11.8 | **Actual production costs**

Companies determine total standard costs by multiplying the units produced by the standard cost per unit. The total standard cost of Spark Tonic is €52,000 (1,000 liters × €52). Thus, the total variance is €3,000, as shown in **Illustration 11.9**.

Actual costs	€55,000
Less: Standard costs	52,000
Total variance	**€ 3,000**

ILLUSTRATION 11.9 | **Computation of total variance**

Note that the variance is expressed in total euros, not on a per unit basis.
When actual costs exceed standard costs, the variance is **unfavorable**.

- The €3,000 variance in June for Spark Tonic is unfavorable.
- An unfavorable variance has a negative connotation as it reduces profit. It suggests that the company paid too much for one or more of the manufacturing cost components or that it used the components inefficiently.

If actual costs are less than standard costs, the variance is **favorable**.

- A favorable variance has a positive connotation as it increases profit.
- It suggests efficiencies in incurring manufacturing costs and in using direct materials, direct labor, and manufacturing overhead.

However, be careful: A favorable variance could be obtained by using inferior materials. In printing wedding invitations, for example, a favorable variance could result from using an inferior grade of paper. Or, a favorable variance might be achieved in installing tires on an automobile assembly line by tightening only half of the lug bolts. A variance is not favorable if the company has sacrificed quality control standards.

- To interpret a variance, you must analyze its components.
- A variance can result from differences related to the cost of materials, labor, or overhead.

Illustration 11.10 shows that the total variance is the sum of the materials, labor, and overhead variances.

Materials Variance	+	Labor Variance	+	Overhead Variance	=	**Total Variance**

ILLUSTRATION 11.10 | **Components of total variance**

In the following discussion, you will see that the materials variance and the labor variance are the sum of variances resulting from price differences and quantity differences. **Illustration 11.11** shows a format for computing the price and quantity variances.

```
                    Total Materials or Labor Variance
                    ↑                              ↑
    Actual Cost              Actual Quantity              Standard Cost
    Actual Quantity                 ×                     Standard Quantity
         ×                    Standard Price                   ×
    Actual Price                                          Standard Price
         ↓           ↓                        ↓                 ↓
              Price Variance              Quantity Variance
```

ILLUSTRATION 11.11 | Breakdown of materials or labor variance into price and quantity variances

Note that the left side of the matrix is actual cost (actual quantity times actual price). The right hand is standard cost (standard quantity times standard price). The difference between these two amounts (shown in the blue box in Illustration 11.11) is the total materials or labor variance. The only additional component you need in order to compute the price and quantity variances is the middle component, the actual quantity at the standard price.

- To compute the price variance, we hold the quantity constant (at the actual quantity) but vary the price (actual versus standard).
- Similarly, to compute the quantity variance, we hold the price constant (at the standard price) but vary the quantity (actual versus standard).

Calculating Direct Materials Variances

DECISION TOOLS

The materials price and materials quantity variances help managers determine if they have met their price and quantity objectives regarding materials.

Part of Spark's total variance of €3,000 is due to a materials variance (see **Decision Tools**).

- In completing the order for 1,000 liters of Spark Tonic, the company used 4,200 kilograms of direct materials. From Illustration 11.3, we know that Spark's standards require it to use 4 kilograms of materials per liter produced, so it should have only used 4,000 (4 × 1,000) kilograms of direct materials to produce 1,000 liters.
- The direct materials were purchased at a price of €3.10 per unit. Illustration 11.2 shows that the standard cost of each kilogram of direct materials is €3 instead of the €3.10 actually paid.

Illustration 11.12 shows that the **total materials variance** is computed as the difference between the amount paid (actual quantity times actual price) and the amount that should have been paid based on standards (standard quantity times standard price of materials).

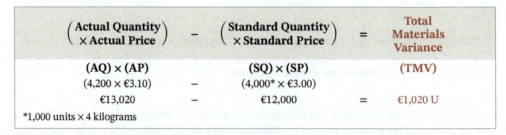

$\begin{pmatrix} \text{Actual Quantity} \\ \times \text{ Actual Price} \end{pmatrix}$	−	$\begin{pmatrix} \text{Standard Quantity} \\ \times \text{ Standard Price} \end{pmatrix}$	=	Total Materials Variance
(AQ) × (AP)		(SQ) × (SP)		(TMV)
(4,200 × €3.10)	−	(4,000* × €3.00)		
€13,020	−	€12,000	=	€1,020 U

*1,000 units × 4 kilograms

ILLUSTRATION 11.12 | Equation for total materials variance

Thus, for Spark, the total materials variance is €1,020 (€13,020 − €12,000) unfavorable (abbreviated as "U"). It is unfavorable because the actual cost exceeded the standard cost.

The total materials variance could be caused by differences in the price paid (price variance) for the materials or by differences in the amount of materials used (quantity variance). **Illustration 11.13** shows that the total materials variance is the sum of the materials price variance and the materials quantity variance.

Materials Price Variance + Materials Quantity Variance = Total Materials Variance

ILLUSTRATION 11.13 | **Components of total materials variance**

The materials price variance results from a difference between the actual price and the standard price. **Illustration 11.14** shows that the **materials price variance** is computed as the difference between the actual amount paid (actual quantity of materials times actual price) and the standard amount that should have been paid for the materials used (actual quantity of materials times standard price).[1]

$\begin{pmatrix} \text{Actual Quantity} \\ \times \text{Actual Price} \end{pmatrix}$	−	$\begin{pmatrix} \text{Actual Quantity} \\ \times \text{Standard Price} \end{pmatrix}$	=	Materials Price Variance
(AQ) × (AP)		(AQ) × (SP)		(MPV)
(4,200 × €3.10)	−	(4,200 × €3.00)		
€13,020	−	€12,600	=	€420 U

ILLUSTRATION 11.14 | **Equation for materials price variance**

For Spark, the materials price variance is €420 (€13,020 − €12,600) unfavorable.

Another way of thinking about the price variance is that we are holding the quantity constant at the actual quantity and varying the price. Thus, the price variance can also be computed by multiplying the actual quantity purchased by the difference between the actual and standard price per unit (see **Helpful Hint**). The computation in this case is 4,200 × (€3.10 − €3.00) = €420 U.

- As seen in Illustration 11.13, the other component of the materials variance is the quantity variance.
- The quantity variance results from differences between the amount of material actually used and the amount that should have been used.

HELPFUL HINT
The alternative equation is:
$\boxed{\text{AQ}} \times \boxed{\text{AP} - \text{SP}} = \boxed{\text{MPV}}$

As shown in **Illustration 11.15**, the **materials quantity variance** is computed as the difference between the standard cost of the actual quantity (actual quantity times standard price) and the standard cost of the amount that should have been used (standard quantity times standard price for materials).

$\begin{pmatrix} \text{Actual Quantity} \\ \times \text{Standard Price} \end{pmatrix}$	−	$\begin{pmatrix} \text{Standard Quantity} \\ \times \text{Standard Price} \end{pmatrix}$	=	Materials Quantity Variance
(AQ) × (SP)		(SQ) × (SP)		(MQV)
(4,200 × €3.00)	−	(4,000 × €3.00)		
€12,600	−	€12,000	=	€600 U

ILLUSTRATION 11.15 | **Equation for materials quantity variance**

Thus, for Spark, the materials quantity variance is €600 (€12,600 − €12,000) unfavorable.

The quantity variance can also be computed by applying the standard price to the difference between actual and standard quantities used (see **Helpful Hint**). The computation in this example is €3.00 × (4,200 − 4,000) = €600 U.

Illustration 11.16 summarizes the total materials variance of €1,020 U.

HELPFUL HINT
The alternative equation is:
$\boxed{\text{SP}} \times \boxed{\text{AQ} - \text{SQ}} = \boxed{\text{MQV}}$

---

[1] Assume that all materials purchased during the period are used in production and that no units remain in inventory at the end of the period.

	Materials price variance	€ 420 U
	Materials quantity variance	600 U
	Total materials variance	**€1,020 U**

ILLUSTRATION 11.16 | Summary of materials variances

Companies sometimes use a matrix to analyze a variance.

- **When the matrix is used, a company computes the amounts using the equations for each cost component first and then computes the variances.**
- The matrix provides a convenient structure for determining each variance.

Illustration 11.17 shows the completed matrix for the direct materials variance for Spark.

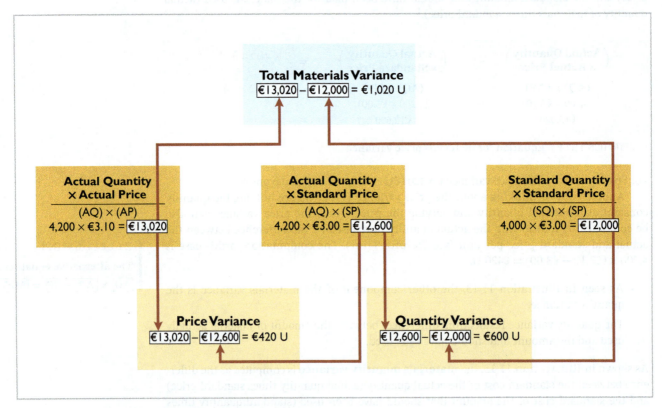

ILLUSTRATION 11.17 | Matrix for direct materials variances

Causes of Materials Variances

What are the causes of a variance? The causes may relate to both internal and external factors.

Materials Price Variances The investigation of a **materials price variance usually begins in the purchasing department**.

- Many factors affect the price paid for raw materials, such as the availability of quantity and cash discounts, the quality of the materials requested, and the delivery method used.
- To the extent that these factors are considered in setting the price standard, the purchasing department is responsible for any variances.
- However, a variance may be beyond the control of the purchasing department. Sometimes, for example, prices may rise faster than expected, or actions by groups over which the company has no control, such as the OPEC nations' oil price increases, may cause an unfavorable variance.

For example, during a recent year, **Kraft Foods** (USA) and **Kellogg Company** (USA) both experienced unfavorable materials price variances when the cost of dairy and wheat products jumped unexpectedly. There are also times when a production department may be responsible for the price variance. This may occur when a rush order forces the company to pay a higher price for the materials.

Materials Quantity Variances The starting point for determining the cause(s) of a significant **materials quantity variance is in the production department**.

- If the variances are due to inexperienced workers, faulty machinery, or carelessness, the production department is responsible.
- However, if the materials obtained by the purchasing department were of inferior quality, then the purchasing department is responsible.

DO IT! 2 ▶ Direct Materials Variances

The standard cost of Wonder Walkers includes two units of direct materials at €8.00 per unit. During July, the company buys 22,000 units of direct materials at €7.50 and uses those materials to produce 10,000 Wonder Walkers. Compute the total, price, and quantity variances for materials.

Solution

Standard quantity = 10,000 × 2 = 20,000
Substituting amounts into the equations, the variances are:

Total materials variance = (22,000 × €7.50) − (20,000 × €8.00) = €5,000 unfavorable
Materials price variance = (22,000 × €7.50) − (22,000 × €8.00) = €11,000 favorable
Materials quantity variance = (22,000 × €8.00) − (20,000 × €8.00) = €16,000 unfavorable

Related exercise material: **BE11.4, DO IT! 11.2, and E11.5.**

ACTION PLAN

Use the equations for computing each of the materials variances:
- Total materials variance = (AQ × AP) − (SQ × SP)
- Materials price variance = (AQ × AP) − (AQ × SP)
- Materials quantity variance = (AQ × SP) − (SQ × SP)

DIRECT LABOR AND MANUFACTURING OVERHEAD VARIANCES

Direct Labor Variances

The process of determining direct labor variances is the same as for determining the direct materials variances (see **Decision Tools**). In completing the Spark Tonic order, the company incurred 2,100 direct labor hours. The standard hours allowed for the units produced were 2,000 hours (1,000 liters × 2 hours). The standard labor rate was €15 per hour, and the actual labor rate was €14.80.

- The total labor variance is the difference between the amount actually paid for labor versus the amount that should have been paid.
- Illustration 11.18 shows that the **total labor variance** is computed as the difference between the amount actually paid for labor (actual hours times actual rate) and the amount that should have been paid (standard hours times standard rate for labor).

The total labor variance is €1,080 (€31,080 − €30,000) unfavorable.

LEARNING OBJECTIVE 3
Determine direct labor and total manufacturing overhead variances.

DECISION TOOLS

Labor price and labor quantity variances help managers to determine if they have met their price and quantity objectives regarding labor.

(Actual Hours × Actual Rate)	−	(Standard Hours × Standard Rate)	=	Total Labor Variance
(AH) × (AR)		(SH) × (SR)		(TLV)
(2,100 × €14.80)	−	(2,000 × €15.00)		
€31,080	−	€30,000	=	€1,080 U

ILLUSTRATION 11.18 | Equation for total labor variance

The total labor variance is caused by differences in the labor rate (labor price variance) or differences in labor hours (labor quantity variance). **Illustration 11.19** shows that the total labor variance is the sum of the labor price variance and the labor quantity variance.

| Labor Price Variance | + | Labor Quantity Variance | = | Total Labor Variance |

ILLUSTRATION 11.19 | Components of total labor variance

- The labor price variance results from the difference between the rate paid to workers and the rate that was supposed to be paid.
- **Illustration 11.20** shows that the **labor price variance** is computed as the difference between the actual amount paid (actual hours times actual rate) and the amount that should have been paid for the number of hours worked (actual hours times standard rate for labor).

$\begin{pmatrix} \text{Actual Hours} \\ \times \text{Actual Rate} \end{pmatrix}$	−	$\begin{pmatrix} \text{Actual Hours} \\ \times \text{Standard Rate} \end{pmatrix}$	=	Labor Price Variance
(AH) × (AR)		(AH) × (SR)		(LPV)
(2,100 × €14.80)	−	(2,100 × €15.00)		
€31,080	−	€31,500	=	€420 F

ILLUSTRATION 11.20 | Equation for labor price variance

For Spark, the labor price variance is €420 (€31,080 − €31,500) favorable.

The labor price variance can also be computed by multiplying actual hours worked by the difference between the actual pay rate and the standard pay rate (see **Helpful Hint**). The computation in this example is 2,100 × (€15.00 − €14.80) = €420 F.

The other component of the total labor variance is the labor quantity variance.

HELPFUL HINT
The alternative equation is:
$\boxed{AH} \times \boxed{AR - SR} = \boxed{LPV}$

- The labor quantity variance results from the difference between the actual number of labor hours and the number of hours that should have been worked for the quantity produced.
- **Illustration 11.21** shows that the **labor quantity variance** is computed as the difference between the amount that should have been paid for the hours worked (actual hours times standard rate) and the amount that should have been paid for the amount of hours that should have been worked (standard hours times standard rate for labor).

$\begin{pmatrix} \text{Actual Hours} \\ \times \text{Standard Rate} \end{pmatrix}$	−	$\begin{pmatrix} \text{Standard Hours} \\ \times \text{Standard Rate} \end{pmatrix}$	=	Labor Quantity Variance
(AH) × (SR)		(SH) × (SR)		(LQV)
(2,100 × €15.00)	−	(2,000 × €15.00)		
€31,500	−	€30,000	=	€1,500 U

ILLUSTRATION 11.21 | Equation for labor quantity variance

Thus, for Spark, the labor quantity variance is €1,500 (€31,500 − €30,000) unfavorable.

The same result can be obtained by multiplying the standard rate by the difference between actual hours worked and standard hours allowed (see **Helpful Hint**). In this case, the computation is €15.00 × (2,100 − 2,000) = €1,500 U.

Illustration 11.22 summarizes the total direct labor variance of €1,080 U.

HELPFUL HINT
The alternative equation is:
$\boxed{SR} \times \boxed{AH - SH} = \boxed{LQV}$

Labor price variance	€ 420 F
Labor quantity variance	1,500 U
Total direct labor variance	**€1,080 U**

ILLUSTRATION 11.22 | Summary of labor variances

These results can also be obtained from the matrix in **Illustration 11.23**.

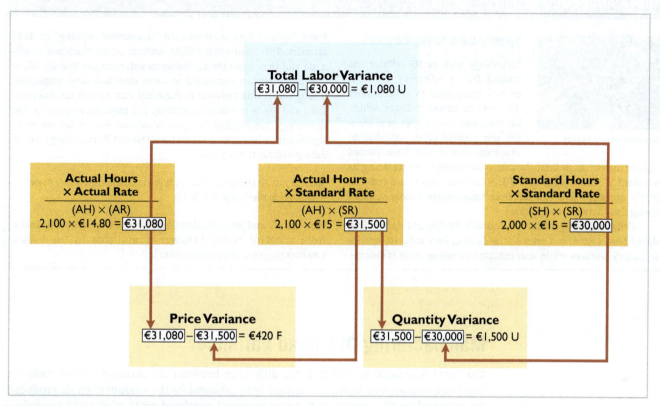

ILLUSTRATION 11.23 | Matrix for direct labor variances

Causes of Labor Variances

Labor variances can result from a variety of factors.

Labor Price Variances
Labor price variances usually result from two factors:

1. Paying workers **different wages than expected**.
2. **Misallocation of workers**.

In companies where pay rates are determined by union contracts, labor price variances should be infrequent. When workers are not unionized, there is a much higher likelihood of such variances. The responsibility for these variances rests with the manager who authorized the wage change.

Misallocation of the workforce refers to using skilled workers in place of unskilled workers and vice versa.

- The use of an inexperienced worker instead of an experienced one will result in a favorable price variance because of the lower pay rate of the unskilled worker.
- An unfavorable price variance would result if a skilled worker were substituted for an inexperienced one.

The production department generally is responsible for labor price variances resulting from misallocation of the workforce.

Labor Quantity Variances
Labor quantity variances relate to the **efficiency of workers**. The cause of a quantity variance generally can be traced to the production department.

- The causes of an unfavorable variance may be poor training, worker fatigue, faulty machinery, or carelessness, and are the responsibility of the **production department**.
- However, if the excess time is due to inferior materials, the responsibility falls outside the production department and resides instead with the purchasing department.

DATA ANALYTICS INSIGHT Whirlpool

Iaremenko/Getty Images

Speedy Data to the Rescue!

Technology such as 5G cellular has boosted factory efficiency. How? It enables companies to collect more data, and to collect it faster, which has often allowed companies to identify and provide quick remedies to situations that would have caused significant variances from standards. For example, by replacing its standard Wi-Fi network with 5G, **Whirlpool** (USA) has reduced costly stoppages that resulted from autonomous factory vehicles losing their network connection.

Other technologies, such as wearable devices and sensors that detect heat, sound, and even worker fatigue, have reduced injuries to factory workers while also reducing variances from standards.

Some factories have even adopted "unattended running" in their factories. This means that skilled workers set up machines to run a job and then leave the machines to automatically operate, often overnight. Sensors connected to these machines alert employees through their smart phones in the event that a batch run has gone awry and needs human intervention. For example, employing this technology has enabled **Wagner Machine Inc.** (USA) to avoid significant variances that would have resulted from leaking coolant during overnight batch runs.

Source: Austen Hufford, "How 5G Will Transform the Factory Floor," *Wall Street Journal* (March 5, 2020).

How do 5G and other technologies reduce specific variances from standard costs? (Answer is available in the book's product page on www.wiley.com)

Manufacturing Overhead Variances

The **total overhead variance** is the difference between the actual overhead costs and overhead costs applied based on standard hours allowed for the amount of goods produced. As indicated in Illustration 11.8, Spark incurred overhead costs of €10,900 to produce 1,000 liters of Spark Tonic in June. The computation of the actual overhead is comprised of a variable and a fixed component. **Illustration 11.24** shows this computation.

Variable overhead	€ 6,500
Fixed overhead	4,400
Total actual overhead	**€10,900**

ILLUSTRATION 11.24 | Actual overhead costs

DECISION TOOLS

The total manufacturing overhead variance helps managers to determine if they have met their objectives regarding manufacturing overhead.

To find the total overhead variance in a standard costing system, we determine the overhead costs applied based on standard hours allowed (see **Decision Tools**).

- **Standard hours allowed** are the hours that *should* have been worked for the units produced.
- Overhead costs for Spark Tonic are applied based on direct labor hours. Because it takes 2 hours of direct labor to produce one liter of Spark Tonic, for the 1,000-liter Spark Tonic order, the standard hours allowed are 2,000 hours (1,000 liters × 2 hours).
- We then apply the predetermined overhead rate to the 2,000 standard hours allowed.

Recall from Illustration 11.6 that the amount of budgeted overhead costs at normal capacity of €132,000 was divided by normal capacity of 26,400 direct labor hours, to arrive at a predetermined overhead rate of €5 (€132,000 ÷ 26,400). The predetermined rate of €5 is then multiplied by the 2,000 standard hours allowed, to determine the overhead costs applied.

Illustration 11.25 shows the equation for the total overhead variance and the calculation for Spark for the month of June.

Actual Overhead	−	Overhead Applied*	=	Total Overhead Variance
€10,900 (€6,500 + €4,400)	−	€10,000 (€5 × 2,000 hours)	=	€900 U

*Based on standard hours allowed.

ILLUSTRATION 11.25 | **Equation for total overhead variance**

Thus, for Spark, the total overhead variance is €900 unfavorable.

The overhead variance is generally analyzed through a price and a quantity variance.

- The name usually given to the price variance is the **overhead controllable variance**.
- The quantity variance is referred to as the **overhead volume variance**.

Appendix 11B discusses how the total overhead variance can be broken down into these two variances.

Causes of Manufacturing Overhead Variances

One reason for an overhead variance relates to over- or underspending on overhead items. For example, overhead may include indirect labor for which a company paid wages higher than the standard labor price allowed. Or, the price of electricity to run the company's machines increased, and the company did not anticipate this additional cost.

- Companies should investigate any spending variances to determine whether they will continue in the future.
- Generally, the responsibility for these variances rests with the production department.

The overhead variance can also result from the inefficient use of overhead.

- For example, the flow of materials through the production process may be impeded because of a lack of skilled labor to perform the necessary production tasks, due to a lack of planning. In this case, the production department is responsible for the cause of the variance.
- On the other hand, overhead can also be underutilized because of a lack of sales orders. When the cause is a lack of sales orders, the responsibility rests outside the production department and resides instead with the sales department.

For example, at one point **Chrysler** (USA) experienced a very significant unfavorable overhead variance because factory capacity was maintained at excessively high levels, due to overly optimistic sales forecasts.

PEOPLE, PLANET, AND PROFIT INSIGHT   **Starbucks**

Archer Colin/SIPA/NewsCom

What's Brewing at Starbucks?

It's easy for a company to say it's committed to corporate social responsibility. But **Starbucks** (USA) actually spells out measurable goals. In its annual *Global Social Impact Report*, the company describes its goals, its achievements, and even its shortcomings related to corporate social responsibility. For example, Starbucks discussed its goal of getting 100% of its electricity from renewable sources. It also has numerous goals related to purchasing coffee from sources that are certified as responsibly grown and ethically traded, providing funds for loans to coffee farmers, and fostering partnerships to provide training to 200,000 farmers on ecologically friendly growing.

In those instances where it didn't achieve its goals, Starbucks set new goals and described steps it would take to achieve them. You can view the company's *Global Social Impact Report* at the Starbucks website.

Source: "2018 Global Social Impact Report," *Starbucks.com*.

What implications does Starbucks' commitment to corporate social responsibility have for the standard cost of a cup of coffee? (Answer is available in the book's product page on www.wiley.com)

DO IT! 3 ▶ Labor and Manufacturing Overhead Variances

The standard cost of Product YY includes 3 hours of direct labor at €12.00 per hour. The predetermined overhead rate is €20.00 per direct labor hour. During July, the company incurred 3,500 hours of direct labor at an average rate of €12.40 per hour and €71,300 of manufacturing overhead costs. It produced 1,200 units.

a. Compute the total, price, and quantity variances for labor.
b. Compute the total overhead variance.

Solution

Substituting amounts into the equations, the variances are:

Total labor variance = (3,500 × €12.40) − (3,600 × €12.00) = €200 unfavorable
Labor price variance = (3,500 × €12.40) − (3,500 × €12.00) = €1,400 unfavorable
Labor quantity variance = (3,500 × €12.00) − (3,600 × €12.00) = €1,200 favorable
Total overhead variance = €71,300 − €72,000* = €700 favorable

*(1,200 × 3 hours) × €20.00

Related exercise material: **BE11.5, BE11.6, DO IT! 11.3, E11.4, E11.6, E11.7, E11.8, and E11.11.**

ACTION PLAN
- Use the equations for computing each of the variances.
- Total labor variance = (AH × AR) − (SH × SR)
- Labor price variance = (AH × AR) − (AH × SR)
- Labor quantity variance = (AH × SR) − (SH × SR)
- Total overhead variance = Actual overhead − Overhead applied*

*Based on standard hours allowed.

VARIANCE REPORTS AND BALANCED SCORECARDS

LEARNING OBJECTIVE 4
Prepare variance reports and balanced scorecards.

Reporting Variances

All variances should be reported to appropriate levels of management as soon as possible. The sooner managers are informed, the sooner they can evaluate problems and take corrective action.

- The form, content, and frequency of variance reports vary considerably among companies.
- One approach is to prepare a weekly report for each department that has primary responsibility for cost control.
- Under this approach, materials price variances are reported to the purchasing department, and all other variances are reported to the production department that did the work.

The report for Spark shown in **Illustration 11.26**, with the materials for the Spark Tonic order listed first, illustrates this approach.

Spark
Variance Report—Purchasing Department
For Week Ended June 8, 2023

Type of Materials	Quantity Purchased	Actual Price	Standard Price	Price Variance	Explanation
X100	4,200 lbs.	€3.10	€3.00	€420 U	Rush order
X142	1,200 units	2.75	2.80	60 F	Quantity discount
A85	600 doz.	5.20	5.10	60 U	Regular supplier on strike
Total price variance				**€420 U**	

ILLUSTRATION 11.26 | **Materials price variance report**

The explanation column is completed after consultation with the purchasing department manager.

Variance reports facilitate the principle of "management by exception" explained in Chapter 10. For example, the vice president of purchasing can use the report shown above to evaluate the effectiveness of the purchasing department manager. Or, the vice president of production can use production department variance reports to determine how well each production manager is controlling costs.

- In using variance reports, top management normally looks for **significant variances**.
- These may be judged on the basis of some quantitative measure, such as more than 10% of the standard or more than €1,000.

Income Statement Presentation of Variances

In income statements **prepared for management** under a standard cost accounting system, **cost of goods sold is stated at standard cost and the variances are disclosed separately**. Unfavorable variances increase cost of goods sold. Favorable variances decrease cost of goods sold, thus increasing gross profit. **Illustration 11.27** shows the presentation of variances in an income statement. This income statement is based on the production and sale of 1,000 units of Spark Tonic at €70 per unit. It also assumes selling and administrative costs of €3,000. Observe that each variance is shown, as well as the total net variance. In this example, variations from standard costs reduced net income by €3,000.

Standard costs may be used in financial statements prepared for stockholders and other external users.

- The costing of inventories at standard costs is in accordance with accounting standards when there are no significant differences between actual costs and standard costs. **Hewlett-Packard** (USA) and **Jostens, Inc.** (USA), for example, report their inventories at standard costs.
- However, if there are significant differences between actual and standard costs, the financial statements must report inventories and cost of goods sold at actual costs.

It is also possible to show the variances in an income statement prepared in the variable costing (CVP) format. To do so, it is necessary to analyze the overhead variances into variable and fixed components. This type of analysis is explained in cost accounting texts.

Spark
Income Statement
For the Month Ended June 30, 2023

Sales revenue		€70,000
Cost of goods sold (at standard)		52,000
Gross profit (at standard)		18,000
Variances		
Materials price	€ 420 U	
Materials quantity	600 U	
Labor price	420 F	
Labor quantity	1,500 U	
Overhead	900 U	
Total variance unfavorable		3,000
Gross profit (actual)		15,000
Selling and administrative expenses		3,000
Net income		€12,000

ILLUSTRATION 11.27 | **Variances in income statement for management**

Balanced Scorecard

Financial measures, such as variance analysis and return on investment (ROI), are useful tools for evaluating performance. However, many companies now supplement these financial measures with nonfinancial measures to better assess performance and anticipate future results. For example, airlines like **Delta** (USA) and **United** (USA) use capacity utilization as an important measure to understand and predict future performance. Companies that publish the *New York Times* and the *Chicago Tribune* newspapers use circulation figures as another measure by which to assess performance. **Penske Automotive Group** (USA), the owner of 300 dealerships, rewards executives for meeting employee retention targets. **Illustration 11.28** lists some key nonfinancial measures used in various industries.

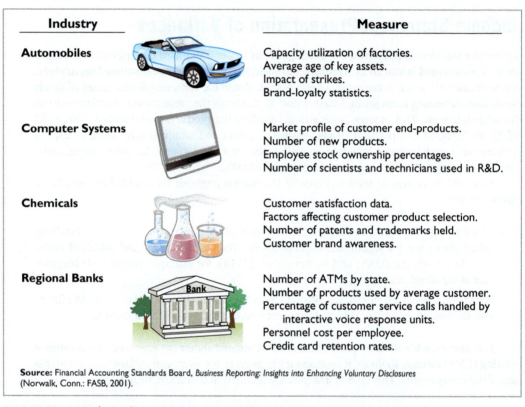

Industry	Measure
Automobiles	Capacity utilization of factories. Average age of key assets. Impact of strikes. Brand-loyalty statistics.
Computer Systems	Market profile of customer end-products. Number of new products. Employee stock ownership percentages. Number of scientists and technicians used in R&D.
Chemicals	Customer satisfaction data. Factors affecting customer product selection. Number of patents and trademarks held. Customer brand awareness.
Regional Banks	Number of ATMs by state. Number of products used by average customer. Percentage of customer service calls handled by interactive voice response units. Personnel cost per employee. Credit card retention rates.

Source: Financial Accounting Standards Board, *Business Reporting: Insights into Enhancing Voluntary Disclosures* (Norwalk, Conn.: FASB, 2001).

ILLUSTRATION 11.28 | Nonfinancial measures used in various industries

Most companies recognize that both financial and nonfinancial measures can provide useful insights into what is happening in the company.

- As a result, many companies now use a broad-based measurement approach, called the **balanced scorecard**, to evaluate performance.
- The **balanced scorecard** incorporates financial and nonfinancial measures in an integrated system that links performance measurement with a company's strategic goals.

Nearly 50% of the largest companies in the United States, including **Unilever**, **Chase**, and **Walmart**, are using the balanced scorecard approach.

The balanced scorecard evaluates company performance from a series of "perspectives." The four most commonly employed perspectives are as follows:

1. The **financial perspective** is the most traditional view of the company. It employs financial measures of performance used by most firms.
2. The **customer perspective** evaluates the company from the viewpoint of those people who buy its products or services. This view compares the company to competitors in terms of price, quality, product innovation, customer service, and other dimensions.

3. The **internal process perspective** evaluates the internal operating processes critical to success. All critical aspects of the value chain—including product development, production, delivery, and after-sale service—are evaluated to ensure that the company is operating effectively and efficiently.
4. The **learning and growth perspective** evaluates how well the company develops and retains its employees. This would include evaluation of such things as employee skills, employee satisfaction, training programs, and information dissemination.

Within each perspective, the balanced scorecard identifies objectives that contribute to attainment of strategic goals. **Illustration 11.29** shows examples of objectives within each perspective.

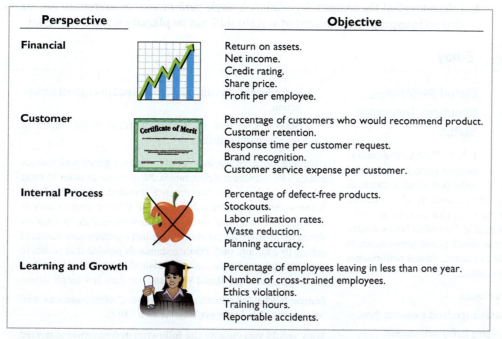

ILLUSTRATION 11.29 | **Examples of objectives within the four perspectives of balanced scorecard**

The objectives are linked across perspectives in order to tie performance measurement to company goals. The financial-perspective objectives are normally set first, and then objectives are set in the other perspectives in order to accomplish the financial goals. For example, within the financial perspective, a common goal is to increase profit per euro invested as measured by ROI.

- In order to increase ROI, a customer-perspective objective might be to increase customer satisfaction as measured by the percentage of customers who would recommend the product to a friend.
- In order to increase customer satisfaction, an internal-process-perspective objective might be to increase product quality as measured by the percentage of defect-free units.
- Finally, in order to increase the percentage of defect-free units, the learning-and-growth-perspective objective might be to reduce factory employee turnover as measured by the percentage of employees leaving in under one year.

Illustration 11.30 illustrates this linkage across perspectives.

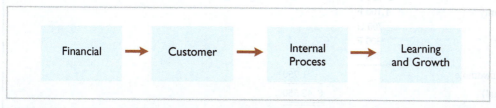

ILLUSTRATION 11.30 | **Linked process across balanced scorecard perspectives**

Through this linked process, the company can better understand how to achieve its goals and what measures to use to evaluate performance.

In summary, the balanced scorecard does the following:

1. Employs both **financial and nonfinancial measures**. (For example, ROI is a financial measure; employee turnover is a nonfinancial measure.)
2. **Creates linkages** so that high-level corporate goals can be communicated all the way down to the shop floor.
3. **Provides measurable objectives for nonfinancial measures** such as product quality, rather than vague statements such as "We would like to improve quality."
4. Integrates all of the company's goals into a single performance measurement system, so that **an inappropriate amount of weight will not be placed on any single goal**.

MANAGEMENT INSIGHT E-bay

rvlsoft/Shutterstock

Global Performance Standards Determine Status

E-bay (USA), the online auction giant, has set global seller performance standards to highlight the efforts of sellers that consistently offer excellent service in both their U.S. and international transactions. In particular, for sellers that sell to buyers outside the United States, United Kingdom, or Germany, information about global performance is available on the seller's standards dashboard. Theses performance standards rate seller commitments toward:

- Promptly resolving customer issues.
- Shipping items on time, within a specified handling time.
- Managing inventory and keeping items well stocked.
- Having reasonable shipping and handling charges.
- Specifying shipping costs and handling time in the listing.
- Following through on a stated return policy.
- Responding to buyers' questions promptly.

- Being helpful, friendly, and professional throughout a transaction.
- Making sure that an item is delivered to the buyers as described in the listing.

All transactions with defects count toward the global performance rating. The minimum defect rate is 2% or lower in order to meet minimum global seller performance standards and a Top-Rated Seller standard requires a defect rate of 0.5% or lower. Cases or returns found in favor of the seller or those decided as "no fault" of the buyer or seller are not counted against a performance standard rating. In addition, performance standards provide that sellers in the global program must maintain a late shipment rate of less than 5% for status as a Top-Rated Seller and less than 10% for all sellers.

Source: "Global Seller Performance Standards," http://pages.ebay.com/help/policies/global-seller-performance.html (2017).

How would you classify the following performance standard objectives—promptly resolving customer issues, shipping items on time, managing inventory and keeping items well stocked, and responding to buyers' questions promptly—using the four balanced scorecard perspectives? (Answer is available in the book's product page on www.wiley.com)

DO IT! 4 ▶ Reporting Variances

Peyton Corporation experienced the following variances: materials price €250 F, materials quantity €1,100 F, labor price €700 U, labor quantity €300 F, and overhead €800 F. Sales revenue was €102,700, and cost of goods sold (at standard) was €61,900. Determine the actual gross profit.

ACTION PLAN
- Gross profit at standard is sales revenue less cost of goods sold at standard.
- Adjust standard gross profit by adding a net favorable variance or subtracting a net unfavorable variance.

Solution

Sales revenue		€102,700
Cost of goods sold (at standard)		61,900
Standard gross profit		40,800
Variances		
Materials price	€ 250 F	
Materials quantity	1,100 F	
Labor price	700 U	
Labor quantity	300 F	
Overhead	800 F	
Total variance favorable		1,750
Gross profit (actual)		€ 42,550

Related exercise material: **DO IT! 11.4, E11.10, E11.14, and E11.15.**

USING THE DECISION TOOLS | Starbucks

Starbucks (USA) faces many situations where it needs to apply the decision tools learned in this chapter. Assume that during the past month, Starbucks produced 10,000 50-pound sacks of dark roast Sumatra coffee beans, with the standard cost for one 50-pound sack of dark roast Sumatra as follows:

Manufacturing Cost Components	Standard Quantity	×	Price	=	Cost
Direct materials (unroasted beans)	60 lbs.	×	$ 2.00	=	$120.00
Direct labor	0.25 hours	×	$16.00	=	4.00
Overhead	0.25 hours	×	$48.00	=	12.00
					$136.00

During the month, the following transactions occurred in manufacturing the 10,000 50-pound sacks of Sumatra coffee.

1. Purchased 620,000 pounds of unroasted beans at a price of $1.90 per pound for a total cost of $1,178,000.
2. All materials purchased during the period were used to make coffee during the period.
3. 2,300 direct labor hours were worked at a total labor cost of $36,340 (an average hourly rate of $15.80).
4. Variable manufacturing overhead incurred was $34,600, and fixed overhead incurred was $84,000.

The manufacturing overhead rate of $48.00 is based on a normal capacity of 2,600 direct labor hours. The total overhead budget at this capacity is $83,980 fixed and $40,820 variable.

Instructions

Determine whether Starbucks met its price and quantity objectives relative to materials, labor, and overhead.

Solution

To determine whether Starbucks met its price and quantity objectives, compute the total variance and the variances for direct materials and direct labor, and calculate the total variance for manufacturing overhead.

Total Variance

Actual cost incurred:	
Direct materials	$1,178,000
Direct labor	36,340
Overhead	118,600
Total actual costs	1,332,940
Less: Standard cost (10,000 × $136.00)	1,360,000
Total variance	$ 27,060 F

Direct Materials Variances

Total	= $1,178,000	− $1,200,000 (600,000 × $2.00)	=	$22,000 F
Price	= $1,178,000 (620,000 × $1.90)	− $1,240,000 (620,000 × $2.00)	=	$62,000 F
Quantity	= $1,240,000 (620,000 × $2.00)	− $1,200,000 (600,000 × $2.00)	=	$40,000 U

Direct Labor Variances

Total	= $36,340 (2,300 × $15.80)	− $40,000 (2,500* × $16.00)	=	$ 3,660 F
Price	= $36,340 (2,300 × $15.80)	− $36,800 (2,300 × $16.00)	=	$ 460 F
Quantity	= $36,800 (2,300 × $16.00)	− $40,000 (2,500* × $16.00)	=	$ 3,200 F

*10,000 × .25

Overhead Variance		
Total	= $118,600 ($84,000 + $34,600) − $120,000 (2,500 × $48)	= $ 1,400 F

Starbucks' total variance was a favorable $27,060. The total materials, labor, and overhead variances were favorable. The company did have an unfavorable materials quantity variance, but this was outweighed by the favorable materials price variance.

Appendix 11A   STANDARD COST ACCOUNTING SYSTEM

LEARNING OBJECTIVE *5
Identify the features of a standard cost accounting system.

A **standard cost accounting system** is a double-entry system of accounting.

- In this system, companies use standard costs in making entries, and they formally recognize variances in the accounts.
- Companies may use a standard cost system with either job order or process costing.

In this appendix, we will explain and illustrate a **standard cost, job order cost accounting system**. The system is based on two important assumptions:

1. Variances from standards are recognized at the earliest opportunity.
2. The Work in Process account is maintained exclusively on the basis of standard costs.

In practice, there are many variations among standard cost systems. The system described here should prepare you for systems you see in the "real world."

Journal Entries

We will use the transactions of Spark to illustrate the journal entries. Note as you study the entries that the major difference between the entries here and those for the job order cost accounting system in Chapter 2 is the **variance accounts**.

1. Purchase raw materials on account for €13,020 when the standard cost is €12,600.

Raw Materials Inventory	12,600	
Materials Price Variance	420	
Accounts Payable		13,020
(To record purchase of materials)		

Spark debits the inventory account for actual quantities at standard cost. This enables the perpetual materials records to show actual quantities. Spark debits the price variance, which is unfavorable, to Materials Price Variance.

2. Incur direct labor costs of €31,080 when the standard labor cost is €31,500.

Factory Labor	31,500	
Labor Price Variance		420
Factory Wages Payable		31,080
(To record direct labor costs)		

Like the raw materials inventory account, Spark debits Factory Labor for actual hours worked at the standard hourly rate of pay. In this case, the labor variance is favorable. Thus, Spark credits Labor Price Variance.

3. Incur actual manufacturing overhead costs of €10,900.

Manufacturing Overhead	10,900	
Accounts Payable/Cash/Acc. Depreciation		10,900
(To record overhead incurred)		

The controllable overhead variance (see Appendix 11B) is not recorded at this time. It depends on standard hours applied to work in process. This amount is not known at the time overhead is incurred.

4. Issue raw materials for production at a cost of €12,600 when the standard cost is €12,000.

Work in Process Inventory	12,000	
Materials Quantity Variance	600	
Raw Materials Inventory		12,600
(To record issuance of raw materials)		

Spark debits Work in Process Inventory for standard materials quantities used at standard prices. It debits the variance account because the variance is unfavorable. The company credits Raw Materials Inventory for actual quantities at standard prices.

5. Assign factory labor to production at a cost of €31,500 when standard cost is €30,000.

Work in Process Inventory	30,000	
Labor Quantity Variance	1,500	
Factory Labor		31,500
(To assign factory labor to jobs)		

Spark debits Work in Process Inventory for standard labor hours at standard rates. It debits the unfavorable variance to Labor Quantity Variance. The credit to Factory Labor produces a zero balance in this account.

6. Apply manufacturing overhead to production €10,000.

Work in Process Inventory	10,000	
Manufacturing Overhead		10,000
(To assign overhead to jobs)		

Spark debits Work in Process Inventory for standard hours allowed multiplied by the standard overhead rate.

7. Transfer completed work to finished goods €52,000.

Finished Goods Inventory	52,000	
Work in Process Inventory		52,000
(To record transfer of completed work to finished goods)		

In this example, both inventory accounts are at standard cost.

8. Sell the 1,000 liters of Spark Tonic for €70,000.

Accounts Receivable	70,000	
Cost of Goods Sold	52,000	
Sales		70,000
Finished Goods Inventory		52,000
(To record sale of finished goods and the cost of goods sold)		

The company debits Cost of Goods Sold at standard cost. Gross profit, in turn, is the difference between sales and the standard cost of goods sold.

9. Recognize unfavorable total overhead variance:

Overhead Variance	900	
Manufacturing Overhead		900
(To recognize overhead variances)		

Prior to this entry, a debit balance of €900 existed in Manufacturing Overhead because overhead of €10,900 was incurred but only €10,000 of overhead was applied. This entry therefore adjusts the account to a zero balance in the Manufacturing Overhead account. The information needed for this entry is often not available until the end of the accounting period.

CHAPTER 11 Standard Costs and Balanced Scorecard

HELPFUL HINT

Each debit balance in variance accounts indicates an unfavorable variance; each credit balance indicates a favorable variance.

Ledger Accounts

Illustration 11A.1 shows the cost accounts for Spark after posting the entries. Note that five variance accounts, highlighted in red, are included in the ledger (see **Helpful Hint**). The six other accounts are the same as those illustrated for a job order cost system in Chapter 2, in which only actual costs were used.

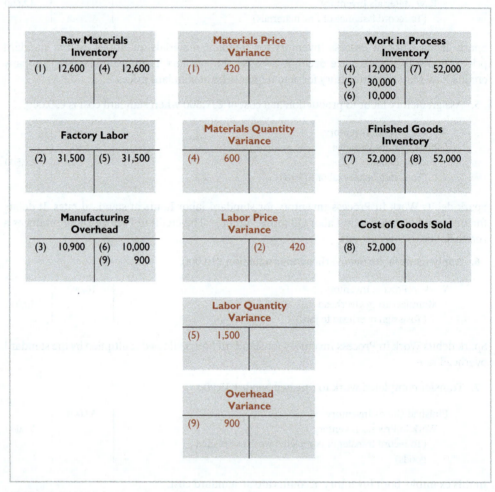

ILLUSTRATION 11A.1 | Cost accounts with variances

Appendix 11B | # OVERHEAD CONTROLLABLE AND VOLUME VARIANCES

LEARNING OBJECTIVE *6
Compute overhead controllable and volume variances.

As indicated in the chapter, the total overhead variance is generally analyzed through a price variance and a quantity variance. The name usually given to the price variance is the **overhead controllable variance**; the quantity variance is referred to as the **overhead volume variance**.

Overhead Controllable Variance

The **overhead controllable variance** shows whether overhead costs are effectively controlled.

- To compute this variance, the company compares actual overhead costs incurred with budgeted costs for the **standard hours allowed**.

- The budgeted costs are determined from a flexible manufacturing overhead budget. (The concepts related to a flexible budget were discussed in Chapter 10.)

For Spark, the budget computation for manufacturing overhead is variable manufacturing overhead cost of €3 per hour of labor plus fixed manufacturing overhead costs of €4,400 (€52,800 ÷ 12, per Illustration 11.6). **Illustration 11B.1** shows the monthly flexible budget for Spark.

	Spark Flexible Manufacturing Overhead Monthly Budget			
Activity Index				
Standard direct labor hours	1,800	2,000	2,200	2,400
Costs				
Variable costs				
Indirect materials	€1,800	€ 2,000	€ 2,200	€ 2,400
Indirect labor	2,700	3,000	3,300	3,600
Utilities	900	1,000	1,100	1,200
Total variable costs	5,400	6,000	6,600	7,200
Fixed costs				
Supervision	3,000	3,000	3,000	3,000
Depreciation	1,400	1,400	1,400	1,400
Total fixed costs	4,400	4,400	4,400	4,400
Total costs	€9,800	€10,400	€11,000	€11,600

ILLUSTRATION 11B.1 | **Flexible budget using standard direct labor hours**

As shown, the budgeted costs for 2,000 standard hours are €10,400 (€6,000 variable and €4,400 fixed).

Illustration 11B.2 shows the equation for the overhead controllable variance and the calculation for Spark at 1,000 units of output (2,000 standard labor hours).

Actual Overhead	−	Overhead Budgeted*	=	Overhead Controllable Variance
€10,900 (€6,500 + €4,400)	−	€10,400 (€6,000 + €4,400)	=	€500 U

*Based on standard hours allowed.

ILLUSTRATION 11B.2 | **Equation for overhead controllable variance**

The overhead controllable variance for Spark is €500 unfavorable.

- Most controllable variances are associated with variable costs, which are controllable costs.
- Fixed costs are often known at the time the budget is prepared and are therefore not as likely to deviate from the budgeted amount.

In Spark's case, all of the overhead controllable variance is due to the difference between the actual variable overhead costs (€6,500) and the budgeted variable costs (€6,000).

Management can compare actual and budgeted overhead for each manufacturing overhead cost that contributes to the controllable variance. In addition, management can develop cost and quantity variances for each overhead cost, such as indirect materials and indirect labor.

Overhead Volume Variance

The **overhead volume variance** is the difference between normal capacity hours and standard hours allowed times the fixed overhead rate.

- The overhead volume variance relates to whether fixed costs were under- or overapplied during the year.
- For example, the overhead volume variance answers the question of whether Spark effectively used its factory assets.
- If Spark produces less Spark Tonic than normal capacity would allow, an unfavorable variance results. Conversely, if Spark produces more Spark Tonic than what is considered normal capacity, a favorable variance results.

Illustration 11B.3 provides the equation for computing the overhead volume variance.

Fixed Overhead Rate	×	(Normal Capacity Hours	−	Standard Hours Allowed)	=	Overhead Volume Variance

ILLUSTRATION 11B.3 | Equation for overhead volume variance

To illustrate the fixed overhead rate computation, recall that Spark budgeted fixed overhead cost for the year of €52,800 (Illustration 11.6). At normal capacity, 26,400 standard direct labor hours are required. The fixed overhead rate is therefore €2 per hour (€52,800 ÷ 26,400 hours).

Spark produced 1,000 units of Spark Tonic in June. The standard hours allowed for the 1,000 liters produced in June is 2,000 (1,000 liters × 2 hours). For Spark, normal capacity for June is 1,100, so standard direct labor hours for June at normal capacity is 2,200 (26,400 annual hours ÷ 12 months). The computation of the overhead volume variance in this case is as shown in **Illustration 11B.4**.

Fixed Overhead Rate	×	(Normal Capacity Hours	−	Standard Hours Allowed)	=	Overhead Volume Variance
€2	×	(2,200	−	2,000)	=	€400 U

ILLUSTRATION 11B.4 | Computation of overhead volume variance for Spark

In Spark's case, a €400 unfavorable volume variance results. The volume variance is unfavorable because Spark produced only 1,000 liters rather than the normal capacity of 1,100 liters in the month of June. As a result, it underapplied fixed overhead for that period.

In computing the overhead variances, it is important to remember the following:

1. Standard hours allowed are used in each of the variances.
2. Budgeted costs for the controllable variance are derived from the flexible budget.
3. The controllable variance generally pertains to variable costs.
4. The volume variance pertains solely to fixed costs. Often, these volume variances arise because productive capacity exceeds what is needed to satisfy sales. This is usually beyond the control of the production manager.

REVIEW AND PRACTICE

Learning Objectives Review

LO 1 Describe standard costs.

Both standards and budgets are predetermined costs. The primary difference is that a standard is a unit amount, whereas a budget is a total amount. A standard may be regarded as the budgeted cost per unit of product.

Standard costs offer a number of advantages. They (a) facilitate management planning, (b) promote greater economy, (c) are useful in setting selling prices, (d) contribute to management control, (e) permit "management by exception," and (f) simplify the costing of inventories and reduce clerical costs.

The direct materials price standard should be based on the delivered cost of raw materials plus an allowance for receiving and handling. The direct materials quantity standard should establish the required quantity plus an allowance for waste and spoilage.

The direct labor price standard should be based on current wage rates and anticipated adjustments such as COLAs. It also generally includes payroll taxes and fringe benefits. Direct labor quantity standards should be based on required production time plus an allowance for rest periods, cleanup, machine setup, and machine downtime.

For manufacturing overhead, a standard predetermined overhead rate is used. It is based on an expected standard activity index such as standard direct labor hours or standard machine hours.

LO 2 Determine direct materials variances.

The equations for the direct materials variances are as follows:

$$\begin{pmatrix} \text{Actual quantity} \\ \times \text{ Actual price} \end{pmatrix} - \begin{pmatrix} \text{Standard quantity} \\ \times \text{ Standard price} \end{pmatrix} = \text{Total materials variance}$$

$$\begin{pmatrix} \text{Actual quantity} \\ \times \text{ Actual price} \end{pmatrix} - \begin{pmatrix} \text{Actual quantity} \\ \times \text{ Standard price} \end{pmatrix} = \text{Materials price variance}$$

$$\begin{pmatrix} \text{Actual quantity} \\ \times \text{ Standard price} \end{pmatrix} - \begin{pmatrix} \text{Standard quantity} \\ \times \text{ Standard price} \end{pmatrix} = \text{Materials quantity variance}$$

LO 3 Determine direct labor and total manufacturing overhead variances.

The equations for the direct labor variances are as follows:

$$\begin{pmatrix} \text{Actual hours} \\ \times \text{ Actual rate} \end{pmatrix} - \begin{pmatrix} \text{Standard hours} \\ \times \text{ Standard rate} \end{pmatrix} = \text{Total labor variance}$$

$$\begin{pmatrix} \text{Actual hours} \\ \times \text{ Actual rate} \end{pmatrix} - \begin{pmatrix} \text{Actual hours} \\ \times \text{ Standard rate} \end{pmatrix} = \text{Labor price variance}$$

$$\begin{pmatrix} \text{Actual hours} \\ \times \text{ Standard rate} \end{pmatrix} - \begin{pmatrix} \text{Standard hours} \\ \times \text{ Standard rate} \end{pmatrix} = \text{Labor quantity variance}$$

The equation for the total manufacturing overhead variance is as follows:

$$\begin{pmatrix} \text{Actual} \\ \text{overhead} \end{pmatrix} - \begin{pmatrix} \text{Overhead} \\ \text{applied at} \\ \text{standard hours} \\ \text{allowed} \end{pmatrix} = \text{Total overhead variance}$$

LO 4 Prepare variance reports and balanced scorecards.

Variances are reported to management in variance reports. The reports facilitate management by exception by highlighting significant differences. Under a standard costing system, an income statement prepared for management will report cost of goods sold at standard cost and then disclose each variance separately.

The balanced scorecard incorporates financial and nonfinancial measures in an integrated system that links performance measurement and a company's strategic goals. It employs four perspectives: financial, customer, internal process, and learning and growth. Objectives are set within each of these perspectives that link to objectives within the other perspectives.

LO *5 Identify the features of a standard cost accounting system.

In a standard cost accounting system, companies journalize and post standard costs, and they maintain separate variance accounts in the ledger.

LO *6 Compute overhead controllable and volume variances.

The total overhead variance is generally analyzed through a price variance and a quantity variance. The name usually given to the price variance is the overhead controllable variance. The quantity variance is referred to as the overhead volume variance.

Decision Tools Review

Decision Checkpoints	Info Needed for Decision	Tool to Use for Decision	How to Evaluate Results
Has management accomplished its price and quantity objectives regarding materials?	Actual cost and standard cost of materials	Materials price and materials quantity variances	Favorable (positive) variances suggest that price and quantity objectives have been met.

(Continued)

(Continued)

Decision Checkpoints	Info Needed for Decision	Tool to Use for Decision	How to Evaluate Results
Has management accomplished its price and quantity objectives regarding labor?	Actual cost and standard cost of labor	Labor price and labor quantity variances	Favorable (positive) variances suggest that price and quantity objectives have been met.
Has management accomplished its objectives regarding manufacturing overhead?	Actual cost and standard cost of manufacturing overhead	Total manufacturing overhead variance	Favorable (positive) variances suggest that manufacturing overhead objectives have been met.

Glossary Review

Balanced scorecard An approach that incorporates financial and non-financial measures in an integrated system that links performance measurement and a company's strategic goals. (p. 11-20).

Customer perspective A viewpoint employed in the balanced scorecard to evaluate the company from the perspective of those people who buy and use its products or services. (p. 11-20).

Direct labor price standard The rate per hour that management determines should be incurred for direct labor to produce one unit of product. (p. 11-6).

Direct labor quantity standard The time that management determines should be required to produce one unit of product. (p. 11-6).

Direct materials price standard The cost per unit of direct materials that management determines should be incurred to produce one unit of product. (p. 11-5).

Direct materials quantity standard The quantity of direct materials that management determines should be used per unit of finished goods. (p. 11-5).

Financial perspective A viewpoint employed in the balanced scorecard to evaluate a company's performance using financial measures. (p. 11-20).

Ideal standards Standards based on the optimum level of performance under perfect operating conditions. (p. 11-4).

Internal process perspective A viewpoint employed in the balanced scorecard to evaluate the effectiveness and efficiency of a company's value chain, including product development, production, delivery, and after-sale service. (p. 11-21).

Labor price variance The difference between the actual hours times the actual rate and the actual hours times the standard rate for labor. (p. 11-14).

Labor quantity variance The difference between actual hours times the standard rate and standard hours times the standard rate for labor. (p. 11-14).

Learning and growth perspective A viewpoint employed in the balanced scorecard to evaluate how well a company develops and retains its employees. (p. 11-21).

Materials price variance The difference between the actual quantity times the actual price and the actual quantity times the standard price for materials. (p. 11-11).

Materials quantity variance The difference between the actual quantity times the standard price and the standard quantity times the standard price for materials. (p. 11-11).

Normal capacity The average activity output that a company should experience over the long run. (p. 11-7).

Normal standards Standards based on an efficient level of performance that is attainable under expected operating conditions. (p. 11-4).

*__Overhead controllable variance__ The difference between actual overhead incurred and overhead budgeted for the standard hours allowed. (p. 11-26).

*__Overhead volume variance__ The difference between normal capacity hours and standard hours allowed times the fixed overhead rate. (p. 11-28).

*__Standard cost accounting system__ A double-entry system of accounting in which standard costs are used in making entries, and variances are recognized in the accounts. (p. 11-24).

Standard costs Predetermined unit costs which companies use as measures of performance. (p. 11-3).

Standard hours allowed The hours that should have been worked for the units produced. (p. 11-16).

Standard predetermined overhead rate An overhead rate determined by dividing budgeted overhead costs by an expected standard activity index. (p. 11-7).

Total labor variance The difference between actual hours times the actual rate and standard hours times the standard rate for labor. (p. 11-13).

Total materials variance The difference between the actual quantity times the actual price and the standard quantity times the standard price of materials. (p. 11-10).

Total overhead variance The difference between actual overhead costs and overhead costs applied to work done, based on standard hours allowed. (p. 11-16).

Variance The difference between total actual costs and total standard costs. (p. 11-8).

Practice Multiple-Choice Questions

1. **(LO 1)** Standards differ from budgets in that:
   a. budgets but not standards may be used in valuing inventories.
   b. budgets but not standards may be journalized and posted.
   c. budgets are a total amount and standards are a unit amount.
   d. only budgets contribute to management planning and control.

2. **(LO 1)** Standard costs:
   a. are imposed by governmental agencies.
   b. are predetermined unit costs which companies use as measures of performance.
   c. can be used by manufacturing companies but not by service or not-for-profit companies.
   d. All of the answer choices are correct.

3. **(LO 1)** The advantages of standard costs include all of the following **except**:
   a. management by exception may be used.
   b. management planning is facilitated.
   c. they may simplify the costing of inventories.
   d. management must use a static budget.

4. **(LO 1)** Normal standards:
   a. allow for rest periods, machine breakdowns, and setup time.
   b. represent levels of performance under perfect operating conditions.
   c. are rarely used because managers believe they lower workforce morale.
   d. are more likely than ideal standards to result in unethical practices.

5. **(LO 1)** The setting of standards is:
   a. a managerial accounting decision.
   b. a management decision.
   c. a worker decision.
   d. preferably set at the ideal level of performance.

6. **(LO 2)** Each of the following equations is correct **except**:
   a. Labor price variance = (Actual hours × Actual rate) − (Actual hours × Standard rate).
   b. Total overhead variance = Actual overhead − Overhead applied.
   c. Materials price variance = (Actual quantity × Actual price) − (Standard quantity × Standard price).
   d. Labor quantity variance = (Actual hours × Standard rate) − (Standard hours × Standard rate).

7. **(LO 2)** In producing product AA, 6,300 kilograms of direct materials were used at a cost of €1.10 per kilogram. The standard was 6,000 kilograms at €1.00 per kilogram. The direct materials quantity variance is:
   a. €330 unfavorable.
   b. €300 unfavorable.
   c. €600 unfavorable.
   d. €630 unfavorable.

8. **(LO 3)** In producing product ZZ, 14,800 direct labor hours were used at a rate of £8.20 per hour. The standard was 15,000 hours at £8.00 per hour. Based on these data, the direct labor:
   a. quantity variance is £1,600 favorable.
   b. quantity variance is £1,600 unfavorable.
   c. price variance is £3,000 favorable.
   d. price variance is £3,000 unfavorable.

9. **(LO 3)** Which of the following is **correct** about the total overhead variance?
   a. Budgeted overhead and overhead applied are the same.
   b. Total actual overhead is composed of variable overhead, fixed overhead, and period costs.
   c. Standard hours actually worked are used in computing the variance.
   d. Standard hours allowed for the work done is the measure used in computing the variance.

10. **(LO 3)** The equation for computing the total overhead variance is:
    a. actual overhead less overhead applied.
    b. overhead budgeted less overhead applied.
    c. actual overhead less overhead budgeted.
    d. No correct answer is given.

11. **(LO 4)** Which of the following is **incorrect** about variance reports?
    a. They facilitate "management by exception."
    b. They should only be sent to the top level of management.
    c. They should be prepared as soon as possible.
    d. They may vary in form, content, and frequency among companies.

12. **(LO 4)** In using variance reports to evaluate cost control, management normally looks into:
    a. all variances.
    b. favorable variances only.
    c. unfavorable variances only.
    d. both favorable and unfavorable variances that exceed a predetermined quantitative measure such as a percentage or amount (in euros).

13. **(LO 4)** Accounting standards allow a company to:
    a. report inventory at standard cost but cost of goods sold must be reported at actual cost.
    b. report cost of goods sold at standard cost but inventory must be reported at actual cost.
    c. report inventory and cost of goods sold at standard cost as long as there are no significant differences between actual and standard cost.
    d. report inventory and cost of goods sold only at actual costs; standard costing is never permitted.

14. (LO 4) Which of the following would **not** be an objective used in the customer perspective of the balanced scorecard approach?

   a. Percentage of customers who would recommend product to a friend.
   b. Customer retention.
   c. Brand recognition.
   d. Earnings per share.

*15. **(LO 5)** Which of the following is **incorrect** about a standard cost accounting system?

   a. It is applicable to job order costing.
   b. It is applicable to process costing.
   c. It reports only favorable variances.
   d. It keeps separate accounts for each variance.

*16. **(LO 6)** The equation to compute the overhead volume variance is:

   a. Fixed overhead rate × (Standard hours − Actual hours).
   b. Fixed overhead rate × (Normal capacity hours − Actual hours).
   c. Fixed overhead rate × (Normal capacity hours − Standard hours allowed).
   d. (Variable overhead rate + Fixed overhead rate) × (Normal capacity hours − Standard hours allowed).

Solutions

1. **c.** Budgets are expressed in total amounts, and standards are expressed in unit amounts. The other choices are incorrect because (a) standards, not budgets, may be used in valuing inventories; (b) standards, not budgets, may be journalized and posted; and (d) both budgets and standards contribute to management planning and control.

2. **b.** Standard costs are predetermined units costs which companies use as measures of performance. The other choices are incorrect because (a) only those that are called regulations are imposed by governmental agencies, (c) standard costs can be used by all types of companies, and (d) choices (a) and (c) are incorrect.

3. **d.** Standard costs are separate from a static budget. The other choices are all advantages of using standard costs.

4. **a.** Normal standards allow for rest periods, machine breakdowns, and setup time. The other choices are incorrect because they describe ideal standards, not normal standards.

5. **b.** Standards are set by management. The other choices are incorrect because setting standards requires input from (a) managerial accountants and (c) sometimes workers, but the final decision is made by management. Choice (d) is incorrect because setting standards at the ideal level of performance is uncommon because of the perceived negative effect on worker morale.

6. **c.** Materials price variance = (Actual quantity × Actual price) − (Actual quantity (not Standard quantity) × Standard price). The other choices are correct equations.

7. **b.** The direct materials quantity variance is (6,300 × €1.00) − (6,000 × €1.00) = €300. This variance is unfavorable because more material was used than prescribed by the standard. The other choices are therefore incorrect.

8. **a.** The direct labor quantity variance is (14,800 × £8) − (15,000 × £8) = £1,600. This variance is favorable because fewer labor hours were used than prescribed by the standard. The other choices are therefore incorrect.

9. **d.** Standard hours allowed for work done is the measure used in computing the variance. The other choices are incorrect because (a) budgeted overhead is used to calculate the predetermined overhead rate while overhead applied is equal to standard hours allowed times the predetermined overhead rate, (b) overhead is a product cost and does not include period costs, and (c) standard hours allowed, not hours actually worked, are used in computing the overhead variance.

10. **a.** Total overhead variance equals actual overhead less overhead applied. The other choices are therefore incorrect.

11. **b.** Variance reports should be sent to the level of management responsible for the area in which the variance occurred so it can be remedied as quickly as possible. The other choices are correct statements.

12. **d.** In using variance reports to evaluate cost control, management normally looks into both favorable and unfavorable variances that exceed a predetermined quantitative measure such as percentage or amount (in euros). The other choices are therefore incorrect.

13. **c.** Accounting standards allow a company to report both inventory and cost of goods sold at standard cost as long as there are no significant differences between actual and standard cost. The other choices are therefore incorrect.

14. **d.** Earnings per share is not an objective used in the customer perspective of the balanced scorecard approach. The other choices are all true statements.

*15. **c.** A standard cost accounting system reports both favorable and unfavorable variances. The other choices are all correct statements.

*16. **c.** The equation to compute the overhead volume variance is Fixed overhead rate × (Normal capacity hours − Standard hours allowed). The other choices are therefore incorrect.

Practice Exercises

Compute materials and labor variances.

1. (LO 2, 3) Apollo plc, which produces a single product, has prepared the following standard cost sheet for one unit of the product.

Direct materials (6 kilograms at £2.50 per kilogram)	£15.00
Direct labor (3.1 hours at £12.00 per hour)	£37.20

During the month of April, the company manufactures 250 units and incurs the following actual costs:

Direct materials purchased and used (1,600 kilograms)	£4,192
Direct labor (760 hours)	£8,740

Instructions
Compute the total, price, and quantity variances for materials and labor.

Solution

1. Total materials variance:

(AQ × AP)	−	(SQ × SP)	=	TMV
(1,600 × £2.62*)	−	(1,500** × £2.50)		
£4,192	−	£3,750	=	£442 U

*£4,192 ÷ 1,600; **250 × 6

Materials price variance:

(AQ × AP)	−	(AQ × SP)	=	MPV
(1,600 × £2.62)	−	(1,600 × £2.50)		
£4,192	−	£4,000	=	£192 U

Materials quantity variance:

(AQ × SP)	−	(SQ × SP)	=	MQV
(1,600 × £2.50)	−	(1,500 × £2.50)		
£4,000	−	£3,750	=	£250 U

Total labor variance:

(AH × AR)	−	(SH × SR)	=	TLV
(760 × £11.50*)	−	(775** × £12.00)		
£8,740	−	£9,300	=	£560 F

*£8,740 ÷ 760; **250 × 3.1

Labor price variance:

(AH × AR)	−	(AH × SR)	=	LPV
(760 × £11.50)	−	(760 × £12.00)		
£8,740	−	£9,120	=	£380 F

Labor quantity variance:

(AH × SR)	−	(SH × SR)	=	LQV
(760 × £12.00)	−	(775 × £12.00)		
£9,120	−	£9,300	=	£180 F

2. **(LO 3)** Manufacturing overhead data for the production of Product H by Yi Hsuan Ltd. are as follows: *Compute overhead variances.*

Overhead incurred for 35,000 actual direct labor hours worked	NT$1,400,000
Overhead rate (variable NT$30; fixed NT$10) at normal capacity of 36,000 direct labor hours	NT$40
Standard hours allowed for work done	34,000

Instructions
Compute the total overhead variance.

Solution

2. Total overhead variance:

Actual Overhead	−	Overhead Applied	=	Overhead Variance
NT$1,400,000	−	NT$1,360,000	=	NT$40,000 U
		(34,000 × NT$40)		

Practice Problem

(LO 2, 3) BioKing Company sells bottles of organic saffron capsules. The standard cost for one bottle is as follows: *Compute variances.*

	Standard			
Manufacturing Cost Components	Quantity	× Price	=	Cost
Direct materials	6 gms	× € 0.90	=	€ 5.40
Direct labor	0.5 hrs.	× €12.00	=	6.00
Manufacturing overhead	0.5 hrs.	× € 4.80	=	2.40
				€13.80

During the month, the following transactions occurred in manufacturing 10,000 bottles.

1. 58,000 grams of materials were purchased at €1.00 per gram.
2. All the materials purchased were used to produce the 10,000 bottles.
3. 4,900 direct labor hours were worked at a total labor cost of €56,350.
4. Variable manufacturing overhead incurred was €15,000 and fixed overhead incurred was €10,400.

The manufacturing overhead rate of €4.80 is based on a normal capacity of 5,200 direct labor hours. The total budget at this capacity is €10,400 fixed and €14,560 variable.

Instructions

a. Compute the total variance and the variances for direct materials and direct labor components.
b. Compute the total variance for manufacturing overhead.

Solution

a.

Total Variance

Actual costs incurred	
Direct materials	€ 58,000
Direct labor	56,350
Manufacturing overhead	25,400
	139,750
Standard cost (10,000 × €13.80)	138,000
Total variance	€ 1,750 U

Direct Materials Variances

Total	= €58,000 (58,000 × €1.00)	−	€54,000 (60,000* × €0.90)	=	€4,000 U
Price	= €58,000 (58,000 × €1.00)	−	€52,200 (58,000 × €0.90)	=	€5,800 U
Quantity	= €52,200 (58,000 × €0.90)	−	€54,000 (60,000 × €0.90)	=	€1,800 F

*10,000 × 6

Direct Labor Variances

Total	= €56,350 (4,900 × €11.50*)	−	€60,000 (5,000** × €12.00)	=	€3,650 F
Price	= €56,350 (4,900 × €11.50)	−	€58,800 (4,900 × €12.00)	=	€2,450 F
Quantity	= €58,800 (4,900 × €12.00)	−	€60,000 (5,000 × €12.00)	=	€1,200 F

*56,350 ÷ 4,900; **10,000 × 0.5

b.

Overhead Variance

Total	= €25,400 (€15,000 + €10,400)	−	€24,000 (5,000 × €4.80)	=	€1,400 U

Note: All asterisked Questions, Exercises, and Problems relate to material in the appendices to the chapter.

Questions

1. **a.** "Standard costs are the expected total cost of completing a job." Is this correct? Explain why or why not.
   b. "A standard imposed by a governmental agency is known as a regulation." Is this correct? Explain why or why not.

2. **a.** Explain the similarities and differences between standards and budgets.
   b. Contrast the accounting for standards and budgets.

3. Standard costs facilitate management planning. What are the other advantages of standard costs?

4. Contrast the roles of the management accountant and management in setting standard costs.

5. Distinguish between an ideal standard and a normal standard.

6. What factors should be considered in setting (a) the direct materials price standard and (b) the direct materials quantity standard?

7. "The objective in setting the direct labor quantity standard is to determine the aggregate time required to make one unit of product." Is this correct? Explain why or why not. What allowances should be made in setting this standard?

8. How is the predetermined overhead rate determined when standard costs are used?

9. What is the difference between a favorable cost variance and an unfavorable cost variance?

10. In each of the following equations, supply the words that should be inserted for each number in parentheses.
    a. (Actual quantity × (1)) − (Standard quantity × (2)) = Total materials variance
    b. ((3) × Actual price) − (Actual quantity × (4)) = Materials price variance
    c. (Actual quantity × (5)) − ((6) × Standard price) = Materials quantity variance

11. In the direct labor variance matrix, there are three factors: (1) Actual hours × Actual rate, (2) Actual hours × Standard rate, and (3) Standard hours × Standard rate. Using the numbers, indicate the equations for each of the direct labor variances.

12. Hazel Company's standard predetermined overhead rate is A$9 per direct labor hour. For the month of June, 26,000 actual hours were worked, and 27,000 standard hours were allowed. How much overhead was applied?

13. How often should variances be reported to management? What principle may be used with variance reports?

14. What circumstances may cause the purchasing department to be responsible for both an unfavorable materials price variance and an unfavorable materials quantity variance?

15. What are the four perspectives used in the balanced scorecard? Discuss the nature of each, and how the perspectives are linked.

16. Ayan Nigam says that the balanced scorecard was created to replace financial measures as the primary mechanism for performance evaluation. He says that it uses only nonfinancial measures. Is this true?

17. What are some examples of nonfinancial measures used by companies to evaluate performance?

18. (a) How are variances reported in income statements prepared for management? (b) Can standard costs be used in preparing financial statements for stockholders? Explain.

*19. (a) Explain the basic features of a standard cost accounting system. (b) What type of balance will exist in the variance account when (1) the materials price variance is unfavorable and (2) the labor quantity variance is favorable?

*20. If the A$9 per hour overhead rate in Question 12 includes A$5 variable, and actual overhead costs were A$248,000, what is the overhead controllable variance for June? The normal capacity hours were 28,000. Is the variance favorable or unfavorable?

*21. What is the purpose of computing the overhead volume variance? What is the basic equation for this variance?

*22. Abdul Qadir does not understand why the overhead volume variance indicates that fixed overhead costs are either underapplied or overapplied. Clarify this matter for Abdul.

*23. Jun Wang is attempting to outline the important points about overhead variances on a class examination. List four points that Jun should include in his outline.

Brief Exercises

BE11.1 (LO 1), AP Xu Zhu Ltd. uses both standards and budgets. For the year, estimated production of Product X is 500,000 units. Total estimated cost for materials and labor are HK$14,000,000 and HK$17,000,000, respectively. Compute the estimates for (a) a standard cost and (b) a budgeted cost.

Distinguish between a standard and a budget.

BE11.2 (LO 1), AP Celik Cleaners accumulates the following data concerning raw materials in making its finished product. (1) Price per kilogram of raw materials is net purchase price ₺23, freight-in ₺2.0, and receiving and handling ₺1.0. (2) Quantity per liter of finished product is required materials 3.6 kilograms and allowance for waste and spoilage 0.4 kilograms. Compute the following:

a. Standard direct materials price per kilogram of raw materials.
b. Standard direct materials quantity per liter.
c. Total standard materials cost per liter.

Set direct materials standard.

BE11.3 (LO 1), AP Labor data for making one liter of finished product in Waugh Company are as follows: (1) Price—hourly wage rate A$14.00, payroll taxes A$0.80, and fringe benefits A$1.20. (2) Quantity—actual production time 1.1 hours, rest periods and cleanup 0.25 hours, and setup and downtime 0.15 hours. Compute the following:

a. Standard direct labor rate per hour.
b. Standard direct labor hours per liter.
c. Standard labor cost per liter.

Set direct labor standard.

BE11.4 (LO 2), AP Eric Wong Ltd.'s standard materials cost per unit of output is HK$100 (2 kilograms × HK$50). During July, the company purchases and uses 3,200 kilograms of materials costing HK$161,920 in making 1,500 units of finished product. Compute the total, price, and quantity materials variances.

Compute direct materials variances.

BE11.5 (LO 3), AP Nilsen Papers' standard labor cost per unit of output is €22 (2 hours × €11 per hour). During August, the company incurs 2,150 hours of direct labor at an hourly cost of €10.80 per hour in making 1,000 units of finished product. Compute the total, price, and quantity labor variances.

Compute direct labor variances.

BE11.6 (LO 3), AP In October, Redmond plc reports 21,000 actual direct labor hours, and it incurs £118,000 of manufacturing overhead costs. Standard hours allowed for the work done is 20,600 hours. The predetermined overhead rate is £6 per direct labor hour. Compute the total overhead variance.

Compute total overhead variance.

BE11.7 (LO 4), AP The four perspectives in the balanced scorecard are (1) financial, (2) customer, (3) internal process, and (4) learning and growth. Match each of the following objectives with the perspective it is most likely associated with: (a) factory capacity utilization, (b) employee work days missed due to injury, (c) return on assets, and (d) brand recognition.

Match balanced scorecard perspectives.

***BE11.8 (LO 5), AP** Journalize the following transactions for Buhle Company.

a. Purchased 6,000 units of raw materials on account for R115,000. The standard cost was R120,000.
b. Issued 5,600 units of raw materials for production. The standard units were 5,800.

Journalize materials variances.

Journalize labor variances.

*BE11.9 (LO 5), AP Journalize the following transactions for Woo Industries.

a. Incurred direct labor costs of NT$240,000 for 3,000 hours. The standard labor cost was NT$249,000.

b. Assigned 3,000 direct labor hours costing NT$240,000 to production. Standard hours were 3,150.

Compute the overhead controllable variance.

*BE11.10 (LO 6), AP Some overhead data for Redmond plc are given in BE11.6. In addition, the flexible manufacturing overhead budget shows that budgeted costs are £4 variable per direct labor hour and £50,000 fixed. Compute the overhead controllable variance.

Compute overhead volume variance.

*BE11.11 (LO 6), AP Using the data in BE11.6 and BE11.10, compute the overhead volume variance. Normal capacity was 25,000 direct labor hours.

DO IT! Exercises

Compute standard cost.

DO IT! 11.1 (LO 1), AP Wai Ltd. accumulated the following standard cost data concerning product I-Tal.

Direct materials per unit: 2 kilograms at HK$50 per kilogram.
Direct labor per unit: 0.2 hours at HK$160 per hour
Manufacturing overhead: Allocated based on direct labor hours at a predetermined rate of HK$200 per direct labor hour
Compute the standard cost of one unit of product I-Tal.

Compute materials variance.

DO IT! 11.2 (LO 2), AP The standard cost of product 777 includes 2 units of direct materials at €6.00 per unit. During August, the company bought 29,000 units of materials at €6.30 and used those materials to produce 16,000 units. Compute the total, price, and quantity variances for materials.

Compute labor and manufacturing overhead variances.

DO IT! 11.3 (LO 3), AP The standard cost of product 5252 includes 1.9 hours of direct labor at R$140 per hour. The predetermined overhead rate is R$220 per direct labor hour. During July, the company incurred 4,000 hours of direct labor at an average rate of R$143 per hour and R$813,000 of manufacturing overhead costs. It produced 2,000 units.

a. Compute the total, price, and quantity variances for labor.

b. Compute the total overhead variance.

Prepare variance report.

DO IT! 11.4 (LO 4), AP Tropic Zone Corporation experienced the following variances: materials price A$350 U, materials quantity A$1,700 F, labor price A$800 F, labor quantity A$500 F, and total overhead A$1,200 U. Sales revenue was A$92,100, and cost of goods sold (at standard) was A$51,600. Determine the actual gross profit.

Exercises

Compute budget and standard.

E11.1 (LO 1), AP **Writing** Ceyhun A.S. is planning to produce 2,000 units of product in 2023. Each unit requires 3 kilograms of materials at ₺50 per kilogram and a half-hour of labor at ₺160 per hour. The overhead rate is 70% of direct labor.

Instructions

a. Compute the budgeted amounts for 2023 for direct materials to be used, direct labor, and applied overhead.

b. Compute the standard cost of one unit of product.

c. What are the potential advantages to a corporation of using standard costs?

Compute standard materials costs.

E11.2 (LO 1), AP Hank Itzek manufactures and sells homemade wine, and he wants to develop a standard cost per gallon. The following are required for production of a 50-gallon batch.

3,000 ounces of grape concentrate at $0.06 per ounce
54 pounds of granulated sugar at $0.30 per pound
60 lemons at $0.60 each
50 yeast tablets at $0.25 each
50 nutrient tablets at $0.20 each
2,600 ounces of water at $0.005 per ounce

Hank estimates that 4% of the grape concentrate is wasted, 10% of the sugar is lost, and 25% of the lemons cannot be used.

Instructions

Compute the standard cost of the ingredients for one gallon of wine. (Carry computations to two decimal places.)

E11.3 (LO 1), AP Sabatini Ltd. has gathered the following information about its product.

Compute standard cost per unit.

Direct materials. Each unit of product contains 4.5 kilograms of materials. The average waste and spoilage per unit produced under normal conditions is 0.5 kilograms. Materials cost €5 per kilogram, but Sabatini always takes the 2% cash discount all of its suppliers offer. Freight costs average €0.25 per kilogram.

Direct labor. Each unit requires 2 hours of labor. Setup, cleanup, and downtime average 0.4 hours per unit. The average hourly pay rate of Sabatini's employees is €12. Payroll taxes and fringe benefits are an additional €3 per hour.

Manufacturing overhead. Overhead is applied at a rate of €7 per direct labor hour.

Instructions

Compute Sabatini's total standard cost per unit.

E11.4 (LO 1, 3), AP Service Braganza Services is trying to establish the standard labor cost of a typical brake repair. The following data have been collected from time and motion studies conducted over the past month.

Compute labor cost and labor quantity variance.

Actual time spent on the brake repair	1.0 hour
Hourly wage rate	R$120
Payroll taxes	10% of wage rate
Setup and downtime	20% of actual labor time
Cleanup and rest periods	30% of actual labor time
Fringe benefits	25% of wage rate

Instructions

a. Determine the standard direct labor hours per brake repair.
b. Determine the standard direct labor hourly rate.
c. Determine the standard direct labor cost per brake repair.
d. If a brake repair took 1.6 hours at the standard hourly rate, what was the direct labor quantity variance?

E11.5 (LO 2), AP The standard cost of Product B manufactured by Louis Company includes three units of direct materials at A$5.00 per unit. During June, 29,000 units of direct materials are purchased at a cost of A$4.70 per unit, and 29,000 units of direct materials are used to produce 9,400 units of Product B.

Compute materials price and quantity variances.

Instructions

a. Compute the total materials variance and the price and quantity variances.
b. Repeat (a), assuming the purchase price is A$5.15 and the quantity purchased and used is 28,000 units.

E11.6 (LO 3), AP Ryan Manufacturing Ltd.'s standard labor cost of producing one unit of Product DD is 4 hours at the rate of S$12 per hour. During August, 40,600 hours of labor are incurred at a cost of S$12.15 per hour to produce 10,000 units of Product DD.

Compute labor price and quantity variances.

Instructions

a. Compute the total labor variance.
b. Compute the labor price and quantity variances.
c. Repeat (b), assuming the standard is 4.1 hours of direct labor at S$12.25 per hour.

E11.7 (LO 2, 3), AP Levine Inc., which produces a single product, has prepared the following standard cost sheet for one unit of the product.

Compute materials and labor variances.

Direct materials (8 pounds at $2.50 per pound)	$20
Direct labor (3 hours at $12.00 per hour)	$36

During the month of April, the company manufactures 230 units and incurs the following actual costs:

Direct materials purchased and used (1,900 pounds)	$5,035
Direct labor (700 hours)	$8,120

Compute the materials and labor variances and list reasons for unfavorable variances.

Instructions

Compute the total, price, and quantity variances for materials and labor.

E11.8 (LO 2, 3), AN Writing The following direct materials and direct labor data pertain to the operations of Jack Sports for the month of August.

Costs		Quantities	
Actual labor rate	£13 per hour	Actual hours incurred and used	4,150 hours
Actual materials price	£128 per ton	Actual quantity of materials purchased and used	1,220 tons
Standard labor rate	£12.50 per hour	Standard hours used	4,300 hours
Standard materials price	£130 per ton	Standard quantity of materials used	1,200 tons

Instructions

a. Compute the total, price, and quantity variances for materials and labor.

b. Provide two possible explanations for each of the unfavorable variances calculated above, and suggest where responsibility for the unfavorable result might be placed.

Determine amounts from variance report.

E11.9 (LO 2, 3), AN You have been given the following information about the production of Yamato Ltd., and are asked to provide the factory manager with information for a meeting with the vice president of operations.

	Standard Cost Card
Direct materials (5 kilograms at ¥400 per kilogram)	¥2,000
Direct labor (0.8 hours at ¥1,000)	800
Variable overhead (0.8 hours at ¥300 per hour)	240
Fixed overhead (0.8 hours at ¥700 per hour)	560
	¥3,600

The following is a variance report for the most recent period of operations.

			Variances	
Costs	Total Standard Cost		Price	Quantity
Direct materials	¥41,000,000		¥209,500 F	¥ 900,000 U
Direct labor	16,400,000		390,600 U	2,200,000 U

Instructions

a. How many units were produced during the period?
b. How many kilograms of raw materials were purchased and used during the period?
c. What was the actual cost per kilogram of raw materials?
d. How many actual direct labor hours were worked during the period?
e. What was the actual rate paid per direct labor hour?

Prepare a variance report for direct labor.

E11.10 (LO 3, 4), AP During March 2023, Roy Tools & Accessories worked on four jobs. A review of direct labor costs reveals the following summary data:

Job Number	Actual Hours	Actual Costs	Standard Hours	Standard Costs	Total Variance
A257	221	A$4,420	225	A$4,500	A$ 80 F
A258	450	9,450	430	8,600	850 U
A259	300	6,180	300	6,000	180 U
A260	116	2,088	110	2,200	112 F
Total variance					A$838 U

Analysis reveals that Job A257 was a repeat job. Job A258 was a rush order that required overtime work at premium rates of pay. Job A259 required a more experienced replacement worker on one shift. Work on Job A260 was done for one day by a new trainee when a regular worker was absent.

Instructions

Prepare a report for the factory supervisor on direct labor cost variances for March. The report should have columns for (1) Job No., (2) Actual Hours, (3) Standard Hours, (4) Quantity Variance, (5) Actual Rate, (6) Standard Rate, (7) Price Variance, and (8) Explanation.

E11.11 (LO 3), AP Manufacturing overhead data for the production of Product H by Javier Company, assuming the company uses a standard cost system, are as follows:

Compute overhead variance.

Overhead incurred for 52,000 actual direct labor hours worked	S$263,000
Overhead rate (variable S$3; fixed S$2) at normal capacity of 54,000 direct labor hours	S$5
Standard hours allowed for work done	52,000

Instructions

Compute the total overhead variance.

E11.12 (LO 3), AP Dilara A.S. produces one product, a putter called GO-Putter. Dilara uses a standard cost system and determines that it should take one hour of direct labor to produce one GO-Putter. The normal production capacity for this putter is 100,000 units per year. The total budgeted overhead at normal capacity is ₺8,500,000 comprising of ₺2,500,000 of variable costs and ₺6,000,000 of fixed costs. Dilara applies overhead on the basis of direct labor hours.

Compute overhead variances.

During the current year, Dilara produced 95,000 putters, worked 94,000 direct labor hours, and incurred variable overhead costs of ₺2,560,000 and fixed overhead costs of ₺6,000,000.

Instructions

a. Compute the predetermined variable overhead rate and the predetermined fixed overhead rate.
b. Compute the applied overhead for Dilara for the year.
c. Compute the total overhead variance.

E11.13 (LO 2, 3), AP `Writing` Ceelo SE purchased (at a cost of €10,200) and used 2,400 kilograms of materials during May. Ceelo's standard cost of materials per unit produced is based on 2 kilograms per unit at a cost €5 per kilogram. Production in May was 1,050 units.

Compute variances for materials.

Instructions

a. Compute the total, price, and quantity variances for materials.
b. Assume Ceelo also had an unfavorable labor quantity variance. What is a possible scenario that would provide one cause for the variances computed in (a) and the unfavorable labor quantity variance?

E11.14 (LO 2, 4), AP `Service` Picard Landscaping plants grass seed as the basic landscaping for business campuses. During a recent month, the company worked on three projects (Remington, Chang, and Wyco). The company is interested in controlling the materials costs, namely the grass seed, for these plantings projects.

Prepare a variance report.

In order to provide management with useful cost control information, the company uses standard costs and prepares monthly variance reports. Analysis reveals that the purchasing agent mistakenly purchased poor-quality seed for the Remington project. The Chang project, however, received higher-than-standard-quality seed that was on sale. The Wyco project received standard-quality seed. However, the price had increased and a new employee was used to spread the seed.

Shown below are quantity and cost data for each project.

	Actual		Standard		Total
Project	Quantity	Costs	Quantity	Costs	Variance
Remington	500 lbs.	$1,200	460 lbs.	$1,150	$ 50 U
Chang	400	920	410	1,025	105 F
Wyco	550	1,430	480	1,200	230 U
Total variance					$175 U

Instructions

a. Prepare a variance report for the purchasing department with the following columns: (1) Project, (2) Actual Pounds Purchased, (3) Actual Price per Pound, (4) Standard Price per Pound, (5) Price Variance, and (6) Explanation.
b. Prepare a variance report for the production department with the following columns: (1) Project, (2) Actual Pounds, (3) Standard Pounds, (4) Standard Price per Pound, (5) Quantity Variance, and (6) Explanation.

Complete variance report.

E11.15 (LO 4), AN Urban Corporation prepared the following variance report:

Urban Corporation
Variance Report—Purchasing Department
For the Week Ended January 9, 2023

Type of Materials	Quantity Purchased	Actual Price	Standard Price	Price Variance	Explanation
Rogue11	? lbs.	$5.20	$5.00	$5,500 ?	Price increase
Storm17	7,000 oz.	?	3.30	1,050 U	Rush order
Beast29	22,000 units	0.40	?	660 F	Bought larger quantity

Instructions

Fill in the appropriate amounts or letters for the question marks in the report.

Prepare income statement for management.

E11.16 (LO 4), AP Hekou Ltd. uses a standard cost accounting system. During January, the company reported the following manufacturing variances:

Materials price variance	HK$12,000 U	Labor quantity variance	HK$7,500 U
Materials quantity variance	8,000 F	Overhead variance	8,000 U
Labor price variance	5,500 U		

In addition, 8,000 units of product were sold at HK$80 per unit. Each unit sold had a standard cost of HK$50. Selling and administrative expenses were HK$80,000 for the month.

Instructions

Prepare an income statement for management for the month ended January 31, 2023.

Identify performance evaluation terminology.

E11.17 (LO 1, 4), C The following is a list of terms related to performance evaluation.

1. Balanced scorecard
2. Variance
3. Learning and growth perspective
4. Nonfinancial measures
5. Customer perspective
6. Internal process perspective
7. Ideal standards
8. Normal standards

Instructions

Match each of the following descriptions with one of the terms above.

a. The difference between total actual costs and total standard costs.

b. An efficient level of performance that is attainable under expected operating conditions.

c. An approach that incorporates financial and nonfinancial measures in an integrated system that links performance measurement and a company's strategic goals.

d. A viewpoint employed in the balanced scorecard to evaluate how well a company develops and retains its employees.

e. An evaluation tool that is not based on dollars.

f. A viewpoint employed in the balanced scorecard to evaluate the company from the perspective of those people who buy its products or services.

g. An optimum level of performance under perfect operating conditions.

h. A viewpoint employed in the balanced scorecard to evaluate the efficiency and effectiveness of the company's value chain.

Identify balanced scorecard perspectives.

E11.18 (LO 4), C Indicate which of the four perspectives in the balanced scorecard is most likely associated with the objectives that follow:

1. Percentage of repeat customers.
2. Number of suggestions for improvement from employees.
3. Contribution margin.
4. Brand recognition.
5. Number of cross-trained employees.
6. Amount of setup time.

E11.19 (LO 4), C Indicate which of the four perspectives in the balanced scorecard is most likely associated with the objectives that follow:

1. Ethics violations.
2. Credit rating.
3. Customer retention.
4. Stockouts.
5. Reportable accidents.
6. Brand recognition.

Identify balanced scorecard perspectives.

*E11.20 (LO 5), AP Redstone Electric installed a standard cost system on January 1. Selected transactions for the month of January are as follows:

1. Purchased 18,000 units of raw materials on account at a cost of €4.50 per unit. Standard cost was €4.40 per unit.
2. Issued 18,000 units of raw materials for jobs that required 17,500 standard units of raw materials.
3. Incurred 15,300 actual hours of direct labor at an actual rate of €5.00 per hour. The standard rate is €5.50 per hour. (Credit Factory Wages Payable.)
4. Performed 15,300 hours of direct labor on jobs when standard hours were 15,400.
5. Applied overhead to jobs at the rate of 100% of direct labor cost for standard hours allowed.

Journalize entries in a standard cost accounting system.

Instructions

Journalize the January transactions.

*E11.21 (LO 2, 3, 5), AN Lynx Manufacturing uses a standard cost accounting system. Some of the ledger accounts have been destroyed in a fire. The controller asks your help in reconstructing some missing entries and balances.

Answer questions concerning missing entries and balances.

Instructions

Answer the following questions:

a. Materials Price Variance shows a A$2,000 unfavorable balance. Accounts Payable shows A$138,000 of raw materials purchases. What was the amount debited to Raw Materials Inventory for raw materials purchased?

b. Materials Quantity Variance shows a A$3,000 favorable balance. Raw Materials Inventory shows a zero balance. What was the amount debited to Work in Process Inventory for direct materials used?

c. Labor Price Variance shows a A$1,500 favorable balance. Factory Labor shows a debit of A$145,000 for wages incurred. What was the amount credited to Factory Wages Payable?

d. Factory Labor shows a credit of A$145,000 for direct labor used. Labor Quantity Variance shows a A$900 favorable balance. What was the amount debited to Work in Process for direct labor used?

e. Overhead applied to Work in Process totaled A$165,000. If the total overhead variance was A$1,200 favorable, what was the amount of overhead costs debited to Manufacturing Overhead?

*E11.22 (LO 5), AP Data for Levine Inc. are given in E11.7.

Journalize entries for materials and labor variances.

Instructions

Journalize the entries to record the materials and labor variances.

*E11.23 (LO 6), AN Writing The information shown below was taken from the annual manufacturing overhead cost budget of Itanagar Ltd.

Compute manufacturing overhead variances and interpret findings.

Variable manufacturing overhead costs	₹3,465,000
Fixed manufacturing overhead costs	₹1,980,000
Normal production level in labor hours	16,500
Normal production level in units	4,125
Standard labor hours per unit	4

During the year, 4,050 units were produced, 16,100 hours were worked, and the actual manufacturing overhead was ₹555,000. Actual fixed manufacturing overhead costs equaled budgeted fixed manufacturing overhead costs. Overhead is applied on the basis of direct labor hours.

Instructions

a. Compute the total, fixed, and variable predetermined manufacturing overhead rates.
b. Compute the total, controllable, and volume overhead variances.
c. Briefly interpret the overhead controllable and volume variances computed in (b).

Compute overhead variances.

*E11.24 (LO 6), AN Service The loan department of Cayman Bank uses standard costs to determine the overhead cost of processing loan applications. During the current month, a fire occurred, and the accounting records for the department were mostly destroyed. The following data were salvaged from the ashes.

Standard variable overhead rate per hour	£9
Standard hours per application	2
Standard hours allowed	2,000
Standard fixed overhead rate per hour	£6
Actual fixed overhead cost	£12,600
Variable overhead budget based on standard hours allowed	£18,000
Fixed overhead budget	£12,600
Overhead controllable variance	£1,200 U

Instructions

a. Determine the following:
   1. Total actual overhead cost.
   2. Actual variable overhead cost.
   3. Variable overhead costs applied.
   4. Fixed overhead costs applied.
   5. Overhead volume variance.

b. Determine how many loans were processed.

Compute variances.

*E11.25 (LO 6), AP Kiyan SA's overhead rate was based on estimates of R$2,400,000 for overhead costs and 24,000 direct labor hours. Kiyan's standards allow 2 hours of direct labor per unit produced. Production in May was 900 units, and actual overhead incurred in May was R$195,000. The overhead budgeted for 1,800 standard direct labor hours is R$186,000 (R$60,000 fixed and R$126,000 variable).

Instructions

a. Compute the total, controllable, and volume variances for overhead.

b. What are possible causes of the variances computed in part (a)?

Problems

Compute variances.

P11.1 (LO 2, 3), AP Freyja Corporation manufactures a single product. The standard cost per unit of product is shown below.

Direct materials—1 kilogram plastic at CHF7.00 per kilogram	CHF 7.00
Direct labor—1.6 hours at CHF12.00 per hour	19.20
Variable manufacturing overhead	12.00
Fixed manufacturing overhead	4.00
Total standard cost per unit	CHF42.20

The predetermined manufacturing overhead rate is CHF10 per direct labor hour (CHF16.00 ÷ 1.6). It was computed from a master manufacturing overhead budget based on normal production of 8,000 direct labor hours (5,000 units) for the month. The master budget showed total variable costs of CHF60,000 (CHF7.50 per hour) and total fixed overhead costs of CHF20,000 (CHF2.50 per hour). Actual costs for October in producing 4,800 units were as follows:

Direct materials (5,100 kilograms)	CHF 36,720
Direct labor (7,400 hours)	92,500
Variable overhead	59,700
Fixed overhead	21,000
Total manufacturing costs	CHF209,920

The purchasing department buys the quantities of raw materials that are expected to be used in production each month. Raw materials inventories, therefore, can be ignored.

Instructions

a. MPV CHF1,020 U

a. Compute all of the materials and labor variances.

b. Compute the total overhead variance.

P11.2 (LO 2, 3, 4), AP Hinata Corporation accumulates the following data relative to jobs started and finished during the month of June 2023.

Compute variances, and prepare income statement.

Costs and Production Data	Actual	Standard
Raw materials unit cost	¥225	¥210
Raw materials units	10,600	10,000
Direct labor payroll	¥12,096,000	¥12,000,000
Direct labor hours	14,400	15,000
Manufacturing overhead incurred	¥18,950,000	
Manufacturing overhead applied		¥19,350,000
Machine hours expected to be used at normal capacity		42,500
Budgeted fixed overhead for June		¥5,525,000
Variable overhead rate per machine hour		¥300
Fixed overhead rate per machine hour		¥130

Overhead is applied on the basis of standard machine hours. Three hours of machine time are required for each direct labor hour. The jobs were sold for ¥40,000,000. Selling and administrative expenses were ¥4,000,000. Assume that the amount of raw materials purchased equaled the amount used.

Instructions

a. Compute all of the variances for (1) direct materials and (2) direct labor.

b. Compute the total overhead variance.

c. Prepare an income statement for management. (Ignore income taxes.)

a. LQV ¥480,000 F

P11.3 (LO 2, 3, 4), AN *Writing* Rudd Clothiers is a small company that manufactures tall-men's suits. The company has used a standard cost accounting system. In May 2023, 11,250 suits were produced. The following standard and actual cost data applied to the month of May, when normal capacity was 14,000 direct labor hours. All materials purchased were used.

Compute and identify significant variances.

Cost Component	Standard (per unit)	Actual
Direct materials	8 yards at $4.40 per yard	$375,575 for 90,500 yards ($4.15 per yard)
Direct labor	1.2 hours at $13.40 per hour	$200,925 for 14,250 hours ($14.10 per hour)
Overhead	1.2 hours at $6.10 per hour (fixed $3.50; variable $2.60)	$49,000 fixed overhead $37,000 variable overhead

Overhead is applied on the basis of direct labor hours. At normal capacity, budgeted fixed overhead costs were $49,000, and budgeted variable overhead was $36,400.

Instructions

a. Compute the total, price, and quantity variances for (1) materials and (2) labor.

b. Compute the total overhead variance.

c. Which of the materials and labor variances should be investigated if management considers a variance of more than 4% from standard to be significant?

a. MPV $22,625 F

P11.4 (LO 2, 3), AN Anahita Company uses a standard cost accounting system. In 2023, the company produced 28,000 units. Each unit took several kilograms of direct materials and 1.6 standard hours of direct labor at a standard hourly rate of £12.00. Normal capacity was 50,000 direct labor hours. During the year, 117,000 kilograms of raw materials were purchased at £0.92 per kilogram. All materials purchased were used during the year.

Answer questions about variances.

Instructions

a. If the materials price variance was £3,510 favorable, what was the standard materials price per kilogram?

b. If the materials quantity variance was £4,750 unfavorable, what was the standard materials quantity per unit?

b. 4.0 kilograms

c. What were the standard hours allowed for the units produced?

d. If the labor quantity variance was £7,200 unfavorable, what were the actual direct labor hours worked?

e. If the labor price variance was £9,080 favorable, what was the actual rate per hour?

f. £7.20 per DLH

f. If total budgeted manufacturing overhead was £360,000 at normal capacity, what was the predetermined overhead rate?
g. What was the standard cost per unit of product?
h. How much overhead was applied to production during the year?
i. Using one or more answers above, what were the total costs assigned to work in process?

Compute variances, prepare an income statement, and explain unfavorable variances.

P11.5 (LO 2, 3, 4), AP Service Writing Hans Labs provides mad cow disease testing for governmental agricultural agencies. Because the company's customers are governmental agencies, prices are strictly regulated. Therefore, Hans Labs must constantly monitor and control its testing costs. Shown below are the standard costs for a typical test.

Direct materials (2 test tubes @ €1.46 per tube)	€ 2.92
Direct labor (1 hour @ €24 per hour)	24.00
Variable overhead (1 hour @ €6 per hour)	6.00
Fixed overhead (1 hour @ €10 per hour)	10.00
Total standard cost per test	€42.92

The lab does not maintain an inventory of test tubes. As a result, the tubes purchased each month are used that month. Actual activity for the month of November 2023, when 1,475 tests were conducted, resulted in the following:

Direct materials (3,050 test tubes)	€ 4,270
Direct labor (1,550 hours)	35,650
Variable overhead	7,400
Fixed overhead	15,000

Monthly budgeted fixed overhead is €14,000. Revenues for the month were €75,000, and selling and administrative expenses were €5,000.

Instructions

a. LQV €1,800 U

a. Compute the price and quantity variances for direct materials and direct labor.
b. Compute the total overhead variance.
c. Prepare an income statement for management.
d. Provide possible explanations for each unfavorable variance.

Journalize and post standard cost entries, and prepare income statement.

*P11.6 (LO 2, 3, 4, 5), AP Limyadi Company uses standard costs with its job order cost accounting system. In January, an order (Job No. 12) for 1,900 units of Product B was received. The standard cost of one unit of Product B is as follows:

Direct materials	3 kilograms at Rp10,000 per kilogram	Rp 30,000
Direct labor	1 hour at Rp80,000 per hour	80,000
Overhead	2 hours (variable Rp40,000 per machine hour; fixed Rp22,500 per machine hour)	125,000
Standard cost per unit		Rp235,000

Normal capacity for the month was 4,200 machine hours. During January, the following transactions applicable to Job No. 12 occurred.

1. Purchased 6,200 kilograms of raw materials on account at Rp10,500 per kilogram.
2. Requisitioned 6,200 kilograms of raw materials for Job No. 12.
3. Incurred 2,000 hours of direct labor at a rate of Rp78,000 per hour.
4. Worked 2,000 hours of direct labor on Job No. 12.
5. Incurred manufacturing overhead on account Rp250,000,000.
6. Applied overhead to Job No. 12 on basis of standard machine hours allowed.
7. Completed Job No. 12.
8. Billed customer for Job No. 12 at a selling price of Rp650,000,000.

Instructions

a. Journalize the transactions.

b. Post to the job order cost accounts.

c. Prepare the entry to recognize the total overhead variance.

d. Prepare the January 2023 income statement for management. Assume selling and administrative expenses were Rp20,000,000.

d. NI Rp158,900,000

*P11.7 (LO 6), AP** Using the information in P11.1, compute the overhead controllable variance and the overhead volume variance.

Compute overhead controllable and volume variances.

*P11.8 (LO 6), AP** Using the information in P11.2, compute the overhead controllable variance and the overhead volume variance.

Compute overhead controllable and volume variances.

*P11.9 (LO 6), AP** Using the information in P11.3, compute the overhead controllable variance and the overhead volume variance.

Compute overhead controllable and volume variances.

*P11.10 (LO 6), AP** Using the information in P11.5, compute the overhead controllable variance and the overhead volume variance.

Compute overhead controllable and volume variances.

Continuing Case

Current Designs

CD11 The executive team at **Current Designs** (USA) has gathered to evaluate the company's operations for the last month. One of the topics on the agenda is the special order from Huegel Hollow, which was presented in CD2. Recall that Current Designs had a special order to produce a batch of 20 kayaks for a client, and you were asked to determine the cost of the order and the cost per kayak.

Mike Cichanowski asked the others if the special order caused any particular problems in the production process. Dave Thill, the production manager, made the following comments: "Since we wanted to complete this order quickly and make a good first impression on this new customer, we had some of our most experienced type I workers run the rotomold oven and do the trimming. They were very efficient and were able to complete that part of the manufacturing process even more quickly than the regular crew. However, the finishing on these kayaks required a different technique than what we usually use, so our type II workers took a little longer than usual for that part of the process."

Deb Welch, who is in charge of the purchasing function, said, "We had to pay a little more for the polyethylene powder for this order because the customer wanted a color that we don't usually stock. We also ordered a little extra since we wanted to make sure that we had enough to allow us to calibrate the equipment. The calibration was a little tricky, and we used all of the powder that we had purchased. Since the number of kayaks in the order was fairly small, we were able to use some rope and other parts that were left over from last year's production in the finishing kits. We've seen a price increase for these components in the last year, so using the parts that we already had in inventory cut our costs for the finishing kits."

Instructions

a. Based on the comments above, predict whether each of the following variances will be favorable or unfavorable. If you don't have enough information to make a prediction, use "NEI" to indicate "Not Enough Information."

  1. Quantity variance for polyethylene powder.
  2. Price variance for polyethylene powder.
  3. Quantity variance for finishing kits.
  4. Price variance for finishing kits.
  5. Quantity variance for type I workers.
  6. Price variance for type I workers.
  7. Quantity variance for type II workers.
  8. Price variance for type II workers.

b. Diane Buswell examined some of the accounting records and reported that Current Designs purchased 1,200 pounds of pellets for this order at a total cost of $2,040. Twenty finishing kits were assembled at a total cost of $3,240. The payroll records showed that the type I employees worked 38 hours on this project at a total cost of $570. The type II finishing employees worked 65 hours at a total cost of $796.25. A total of 20 kayaks were produced for this order.

The standards that had been developed for this model of kayak were used in CD2 and are reproduced here. For each kayak:

  54 pounds of polyethylene powder at $1.50 per pound

  1 finishing kit (rope, seat, hardware, etc.) at $170

  2 hours of type I labor from people who run the oven and trim the plastic at a standard wage rate of $15 per hour

  3 hours of type II labor from people who attach the hatches and seat and other hardware at a standard wage rate of $12 per hour.

Calculate the eight variances that are listed in part (a) of this problem.

Data Analytics in Action

Data Analytics at HydroHappy

DA11 HydroHappy's management want to see a visual comparison of its materials variances to better illustrate trends over time. For this case, you will use materials price and quantity variance data to create and analyze stacked area charts.

Go to the book's product page on www.wiley.com for complete case details and instructions.

Expand Your Critical Thinking

Decision-Making Across the Organization

CT11.1 **Service** Jiarong Professionals, a management consulting firm, specializes in strategic planning for financial institutions. Hoang Le and Qilin Jian, partners in the firm, are assembling a new strategic planning model for use by clients. The model is designed for use on most personal computers and replaces a rather lengthy manual model currently marketed by the firm. To market the new model, Hoang and Qilin will need to provide clients with an estimate of the number of labor hours and computer time needed to operate the model. The model is currently being test-marketed at five small financial institutions. These financial institutions are listed below, along with the number of combined computer/labor hours used by each institution to run the model one time.

Financial Institutions	Computer/Labor Hours Required
Midland National	25
First State	45
Financial Federal	40
Pacific Coast	30
Lakeview National	30
Total	170
Average	34

Any company that purchases the new model will need to purchase user manuals for the system. User manuals will be sold to clients in cases of 20, at a cost of HK$3,200 per case. One manual must be used each time the model is run because each manual includes a nonreusable computer-accessed password for operating the system. Also required are specialized computer forms that are sold only by Jiarong. The specialized forms are sold in packages of 250, at a cost of HK$600 per package. One application of the model requires the use of 50 forms. This amount includes two forms that are generally wasted in each application due to printer alignment errors. The overall cost of the strategic planning model to clients is HK$120,000. Most clients will use the model four times annually.

Jiarong must provide its clients with estimates of ongoing costs incurred in operating the new planning model, and would like to do so in the form of standard costs.

Instructions

With the class divided into groups, answer the following:

a. What factors should be considered in setting a standard for computer/labor hours?

b. What alternatives for setting a standard for computer/labor hours might be used?

c. What standard for computer/labor hours would you select? Justify your answer.

d. Determine the standard materials cost associated with the user manuals and computer forms for each application of the strategic planning model.

Managerial Analysis

*CT11.2 Lys Carillo and Associates is a medium-sized company located near a large metropolitan area. The company manufactures cabinets of mahogany, oak, and other fine woods for use in expensive homes, restaurants, and hotels. Although some of the work is custom, many of the cabinets are a standard size.

One non-custom model is called Luxury Base Frame. Normal production is 1,000 units. Each unit has a direct labor hour standard of 5 hours. Overhead is applied to production based on standard direct labor hours. During the most recent month, only 900 units were produced; 4,500 direct labor hours were allowed for standard production, but only 4,000 hours were used. Standard and actual overhead costs were as follows:

	Standard (1,000 units)	Actual (900 units)
Indirect materials	€ 12,000	€ 12,300
Indirect labor	43,000	51,000
(Fixed) Manufacturing supervisors salaries	22,500	22,000
(Fixed) Manufacturing office employees salaries	13,000	12,500
(Fixed) Engineering costs	27,000	25,000
Computer costs	10,000	10,000
Electricity	2,500	2,500
(Fixed) Manufacturing building depreciation	8,000	8,000
(Fixed) Machinery depreciation	3,000	3,000
(Fixed) Trucks and forklift depreciation	1,500	1,500
Small tools	700	1,400
(Fixed) Insurance	500	500
(Fixed) Property taxes	300	300
Total	€144,000	€150,000

Instructions

a. Determine the overhead application rate.
b. Determine how much overhead was applied to production.
c. Calculate the total overhead variance, controllable variance, and volume variance.
d. Decide which overhead variances should be investigated.
e. Discuss causes of the overhead variances. What can management do to improve its performance next month?

Real-World Focus

CT11.3 Glassmaster Company (USA) is organized as two divisions and one subsidiary. One division focuses on the manufacture of filaments such as fishing line and sewing thread; the other division manufactures antennas and specialty fiberglass products. Its subsidiary manufactures flexible steel wire controls and molded control panels.

The annual report of Glassmaster provides the following information:

Glassmaster Company
Management Discussion

Gross profit margins for the year improved to 20.9% of sales compared to last year's 18.5%. All operations reported improved margins due in large part to improved operating efficiencies as a result of cost reduction measures implemented during the second and third quarters of the fiscal year and increased manufacturing throughout due to higher unit volume sales. Contributing to the improved margins was a favorable materials price variance due to competitive pricing by suppliers as a result of soft demand for petrochemical-based products. This favorable variance is temporary and will begin to reverse itself as stronger worldwide demand for commodity products improves in tandem with the economy. Partially offsetting these positive effects on profit margins were competitive pressures on sales prices of certain product lines. The company responded with pricing strategies designed to maintain and/or increase market share.

Instructions

a. Is it apparent from the information whether Glassmaster utilizes standard costs?

b. Do you think the price variance experienced should lead to changes in standard costs for the next fiscal year?

CT11.4 **Service** The **Balanced Scorecard Institute** (USA) is a great resource for information about implementing the balanced scorecard. One item of interest provided at its website is an example of a balanced scorecard for a regional airline.

Instructions

Go to the Balanced Scorecard Institute website, do a search on "Examples and Success Stories," scroll down to select the Regional Airline example under Commercial Organizations, and then answer the following questions:

a. What are the objectives identified for the airline for each perspective?

b. What measures are used for the objectives in the customer perspective?

c. What initiatives are planned to achieve the objective in the learning perspective?

Communication Activity

CT11.5 The setting of standards is critical to the effective use of standards in evaluating performance.

Instructions

Explain the following in a memo to your instructor.

a. The comparative advantages and disadvantages of ideal versus normal standards.

b. The factors that should be included in setting the price and quantity standards for direct materials, direct labor, and manufacturing overhead.

Ethics Case

CT11.6 At Kanpur Company, production workers in the Painting Department are paid on the basis of productivity. The labor time standard for a unit of production is established through periodic time studies conducted by Pradesh Management Consultants. In a time study, the actual time required to complete a specific task by a worker is observed. Allowances are then made for preparation time, rest periods, and cleanup time. Guneet Singh is one of several veterans in the Painting Department.

Guneet is informed by Pradesh that he will be used in the time study for the painting of a new product. The findings will be the basis for establishing the labor time standard for the next six months. During the test, Guneet deliberately slows his normal work pace in an effort to obtain a labor time standard that will be easy to meet. Because it is a new product, the Pradesh representative who conducted the test is unaware that Guneet did not give the test his best effort.

Instructions

a. Who was benefited and who was harmed by Guneet's actions?

b. Was Guneet ethical in the way he performed the time study test?

c. What measure(s) might the company take to obtain valid data for setting the labor time standard?

All About You

CT11.7 From the time you first entered school many years ago, instructors have been measuring and evaluating you by imposing standards. In addition, many of you will pursue professions that administer professional examinations to attain recognized certification. A federal commission presented proposals suggesting all public colleges and universities should require standardized tests to measure their students' learning.

Instructions

Answer the following questions:

a. What are possible advantages of standard testing?

b. What are possible disadvantages of standard testing?

c. Would you be in favor of standardized tests?

Considering Your Costs and Benefits

CT11.8 **Writing** Do you think that standard costs are used only in making products like wheel bearings and hamburgers? Think again. Standards influence virtually every aspect of our lives. For example, the next time you call to schedule an appointment with your doctor, ask the receptionist how many minutes the appointment is scheduled for. Doctors are under increasing pressure to see more patients each day, which means the time spent with each patient is shorter. As insurance companies and employers push for reduced medical costs, every facet of medicine has been standardized and analyzed. Doctors, nurses, and other medical staff are evaluated in every part of their operations to ensure maximum efficiency. While keeping medical treatment affordable seems like a worthy goal, what are the potential implications for the quality of health care? Does a focus on the bottom line result in a reduction in the quality of health care?

A simmering debate has centered on a very basic question: To what extent should accountants, through financial measures, influence the type of medical care that you receive? Suppose that your local medical facility is in danger of closing because it has been losing money. Should the facility put in place incentives that provide bonuses to doctors if they meet certain standard-cost targets for the cost of treating specific ailments?

> **YES:** If the facility is in danger of closing, then someone should take steps to change the medical practices to reduce costs. A closed medical facility is of no use to me, my family, or the community.
>
> **NO:** I don't want an accountant deciding the right medical treatment for me. My family and I deserve the best medical care.

Instructions

Write a response indicating your position regarding this situation. Provide support for your view.

CHAPTER 12

Planning for Capital Investments

CHAPTER PREVIEW

Companies like **Holland America Line** (USA) (as discussed in the following Feature Story) must constantly determine how to invest their resources. Other examples: **Dell** (USA) announced plans to spend $1 billion on data centers for cloud computing. **ExxonMobil** (USA) announced that two wells off the Brazilian coast, which it had spent hundreds of millions of dollars to drill, would produce no oil. **Renault** (FRA) and **Nissan** (JPN) spent over $5 billion during a nearly 20-year period to develop electric cars, such as the Leaf.

The process of making such capital expenditure decisions is referred to as **capital budgeting**. Capital budgeting involves choosing among various capital projects to find those that will maximize a company's return on its financial investment. The purpose of this chapter is to discuss the various techniques used to make effective capital budgeting decisions.

CHAPTER 12
Planning for Capital Investments

FEATURE STORY

Floating Hotels

Do you own a boat? Maybe you think it's a nice boat, but how many swimming pools, movie theaters, shopping malls, or restaurants does it have on board? If you are in the cruise-line business, like **Holland America Line** (USA), you need all of these amenities and more just to stay afloat. Holland America Line is considered by many to be the leader of the premium luxury-liner segment.

Carnival Corporation (USA/GBR), which owns Holland America Line and other cruise lines, is one of the largest vacation companies in the world. During one recent three-year period, Carnival spent more than $3 billion per year on capital expenditures. That's a big number, but keep in mind that Carnival estimates that at any given time there are 270,000 people (200,000 customers and 70,000 crew) on its 100 ships somewhere in the world.

The cruise industry is a tricky business. When times are good, customers are looking for ways to splurge. But when times get tough, people are more inclined to take a trip in a minivan than a luxury yacht. So, if you are a cruise-line executive, it's important to time your investments properly. For example, during one stretch of solid global economic growth, many cruise lines decided to add capacity. The industry built 14 new ships at a total price of $4.7 billion. (That's an average price of about $330 million.) But, it takes up to three years to build one of these giant vessels. Unfortunately, by the time the ships were completed, the economy was in a nosedive.

To maintain passenger numbers during the recession, cruise prices had to be cut by up to 40%. While the lower prices attracted lots of customers, that wasn't enough to offset an overall decline in revenue of 10%. The industry had added capacity at exactly the wrong time.

 Watch the *Holland America Line* video at https://wileyaccountingupdates.com/video/?p=66 to learn more about real-world capital budgeting.

CHAPTER OUTLINE

Learning Objectives	Review	Practice
LO 1 Describe capital budgeting inputs and apply the cash payback technique.	• Cash flow information • Cash payback	**DO IT! 1** Cash Payback Period
LO 2 Use the net present value method.	• Equal annual cash flows • Unequal annual cash flows • Choosing a discount rate • Simplifying assumptions • Comprehensive example	**DO IT! 2** Net Present Value
LO 3 Identify capital budgeting challenges and refinements.	• Intangible benefits • Profitability index for mutually exclusive projects • Risk analysis • Post-audit of investment projects	**DO IT! 3** Profitability Index
LO 4 Use the internal rate of return method.	• Comparing discounted cash flow methods	**DO IT! 4** Internal Rate of Return
LO 5 Use the annual rate of return method.	• Based on accrual-accounting data	**DO IT! 5** Annual Rate of Return

Go to the Review and Practice section at the end of the chapter for a targeted summary and practice applications with solutions.

CAPITAL BUDGETING AND CASH PAYBACK

Many companies follow a carefully prescribed process for capital expenditure decisions, known as **capital budgeting**. **Illustration 12.1** shows this general process.

The involvement of top management and the board of directors in the process demonstrates the importance of capital budgeting decisions.

> **LEARNING OBJECTIVE 1**
> Describe capital budgeting inputs and apply the cash payback technique.

1. Project proposals are requested from departments, factories, and authorized personnel.
2. Proposals are screened by a capital budget committee.
3. Company officers determine which projects are worthy of funding.
4. Board of directors approves capital budget.

ILLUSTRATION 12.1 | Corporate capital budget authorization process

- These decisions often have a significant impact on a company's future profitability.
- Poor capital budgeting decisions can cost a lot of money and have even led to the bankruptcy of some companies.

Cash Flow Information

In this chapter, we look at several methods that help companies make effective capital budgeting decisions. Most of these methods employ **cash flow numbers**, rather than accrual accounting revenues and expenses.

- Remember from your financial accounting course that accrual accounting records **revenues** and **expenses**, rather than cash inflows and cash outflows. In fact, revenues and expenses measured during a period often differ significantly from their cash flow counterparts.
- Accrual accounting has advantages over cash accounting in many contexts.
- **For purposes of capital budgeting, though, estimated cash inflows and outflows are the preferred inputs.**
- Ultimately, the value of all financial investments is determined by the value of cash flows received and paid.

Sometimes cash flow information is not available. In this case, companies can make adjustments to accrual accounting numbers to estimate cash flow. Often, they estimate net annual cash flow by adding back depreciation expense to net income.

- Depreciation expense is added back because it is an expense that does not require an outflow of cash.
- By adding depreciation expense back to net income, companies approximate net annual cash flow.

Suppose, for example, that Epic Designs' net income of €13,000 includes a charge for depreciation expense of €26,000. Its estimated net annual cash flow would be €39,000 (€13,000 + €26,000).

Illustration 12.2 lists some typical cash outflows and inflows related to equipment purchase and replacement.

Cash Outflows
Initial investment
Repairs and maintenance
Increased operating costs
Overhaul of equipment

Cash Inflows
Proceeds from sale of old equipment
Increased cash received from customers
Reduced cash outflows related to operating costs
Salvage value of equipment

ILLUSTRATION 12.2 | **Typical cash flows relating to capital budgeting decisions**

These cash flows are the inputs that are considered relevant in capital budgeting decisions.

The capital budgeting decision, under any technique, depends in part on a variety of considerations:

- **The availability of funds:** Does the company have unlimited funds, or will it have to ration capital investments?
- **Relationships among proposed projects:** Are proposed projects independent of each other, or does the acceptance or rejection of one depend on the acceptance or rejection of another?
- **The company's basic decision-making approach:** Does the company want to produce an accept-reject decision or a ranking of desirability among possible projects?
- **The risk associated with a particular project:** How certain are the projected returns? The certainty of estimates varies with such issues as market considerations or the length of time before returns are expected.

Illustrative Data

To compare the results of the various capital budgeting techniques, we use a continuing example. Assume that Soren Shipping Company is considering an investment of €130,000 in new equipment. The new equipment is expected to last 10 years. It is estimated to have a zero salvage value at the end of its useful life. The expected annual cash inflows are €200,000, and the annual cash outflows are €176,000. **Illustration 12.3** summarizes these data.

Initial investment	€130,000
Estimated useful life	10 years
Estimated salvage value	–0–
Estimated annual cash flows	
Cash inflows from customers	€200,000
Cash outflows for operating costs	176,000
Net annual cash flow	€ 24,000

ILLUSTRATION 12.3 | **Investment information for Soren Shipping example**

In the following two sections, we examine two popular techniques for evaluating capital investments: the cash payback technique and the net present value method.

Cash Payback

The **cash payback technique** identifies the time period required to recover the cost of the capital investment from the net annual cash flow produced by the investment. **Illustration 12.4** presents the equation for computing the cash payback period **assuming equal net annual cash flows.**

| Cost of Capital Investment | ÷ | Net Annual Cash Flow | = | Cash Payback Period |

ILLUSTRATION 12.4 | **Cash payback equation**

The cash payback period in the Soren Shipping example is 5.42 years, computed as follows (see **Helpful Hint**).

$$€130,000 ÷ €24,000 = 5.42 \text{ years}$$

The evaluation of the payback period is often tied to the expected useful life of the asset. For example, assume that at Soren Shipping a project is unacceptable if the payback period is longer than 60% of the asset's expected useful life. The 5.42-year payback period is 54.2% (5.42 ÷ 10) of the project's expected useful life. Thus, the project is acceptable.

It follows that when the payback technique is used to decide among acceptable alternative projects, **the shorter the payback period, the more attractive the investment**. This is true for two reasons:

1. The earlier the investment is recovered, the sooner the company can use the cash funds for other purposes.
2. The risk of loss from obsolescence and changed economic conditions is less in a shorter payback period.

> **HELPFUL HINT**
>
> Net annual cash flow can also be approximated by "Net cash provided by operating activities" from the statement of cash flows.

The preceding computation of the cash payback period assumes **equal net annual cash flows** in each year of the investment's life. In many cases, this assumption is not valid. In the case of **uneven** net annual cash flows, the company determines the cash payback period **when the cumulative net cash flows from the investment equal the cost of the investment**.

To illustrate unequal cash flows, assume that Chen Enterprises proposes an investment in new equipment that is estimated to cost €300,000. **Illustration 12.5** shows how to use the proposed investment data to calculate the cash payback period.

Investment data:

Year	Investment	Net Annual Cash Flow	Cumulative Net Cash Flow
0	€300,000		
1		€ 60,000	€ 60,000
2		90,000	150,000
3		90,000	240,000
4		120,000	360,000
5		100,000	460,000

Determining the cash payback period:

We can first visualize the investment data as follows:

Year	1	2	3	4	5
Net Annual Cash Flow	€60,000	€90,000	€90,000	€120,000	€100,000
Cumulative Value	€60,000	€150,000	**€240,000**	**€360,000**	€460,000

Because the €300,000 investment falls between the cumulative values for years 3 (€240,000) and 4 (€360,000), we next need to calculate the fraction of the year needed beyond year 3, as follows:

Investment cost	€300,000
Year 3 cumulative value	240,000
Additional cash flow needed during year 4	€ 60,000

$$\text{Fractional year} = \frac{\text{Additional cash flow needed during year 4}}{\text{Year 4 net annual cash flow}} = \frac{€60,000}{€120,000} = .5$$

Total cash payback period = 3 years + .5 years = **3.5 years**

ILLUSTRATION 12.5 | **Computation of cash payback period—unequal cash flows**

As Illustration 12.5 shows, at the end of year 3, cumulative net cash flow of €240,000 is less than the investment cost of €300,000, but at the end of year 4 the cumulative cash inflow of €360,000 exceeds the investment cost. The cash flow needed in year 4 to equal the investment cost is €60,000 (€300,000 − €240,000). Assuming the cash inflow occurred evenly during year 4, we divide €60,000 by the net annual cash flow in year 4 (€120,000) to determine the point during the year when the cash payback occurs. Thus, we get 0.50 (€60,000 ÷ €120,000), or half of the year, and the cash payback period is 3.5 years.

The cash payback technique may be a useful initial screening tool. It may be the most critical factor in the capital budgeting decision for a company that desires a fast turnaround of its investment because of a weak cash position. It also is relatively easy to compute and understand.

However, cash payback should not be the only basis for the capital budgeting decision.

- **It ignores the expected profitability of the project**. To illustrate, assume that Projects A and B have the same payback period, but Project A's useful life is double the useful life of Project B. Project A's earning power, therefore, is twice that of Project B's.
- A further—and major—disadvantage of this technique is that **it ignores the time value of money**. We address time value of money with the approach described in the next section.

DO IT! 1 ▶ Cash Payback Period

Dublin Paper Corporation is considering adding another machine for the manufacture of corrugated cardboard. The machine would cost €900,000. It would have an estimated life of six years and no salvage value. The company estimates that annual cash inflows would increase by €400,000 and that annual cash outflows would increase by €190,000. Compute the cash payback period.

Solution

Estimated annual cash inflows	€400,000
Estimated annual cash outflows	190,000
Net annual cash flow	€210,000

Cash payback period = €900,000 ÷ €210,000 = 4.3 years

Related exercise material: **BE12.1 and DO IT! 12.1.**

ACTION PLAN
- Annual cash inflows − Annual cash outflows = Net annual cash flow.
- Cash payback period = Cost of capital investment ÷ Net annual cash flow.

NET PRESENT VALUE METHOD

LEARNING OBJECTIVE 2
Use the net present value method.

The time value of money can have a significant impact on a capital budgeting decision. Cash flows that occur early in the life of an investment are worth more than those that occur later—because of the time value of money. Therefore, it is useful to recognize the timing of cash flows when evaluating projects.

Capital budgeting techniques that take into account both the time value of money and the estimated net cash flows from an investment are called **discounted cash flow techniques**.

- They are generally recognized as the most informative and best conceptual approaches to making capital budgeting decisions.
- The expected net cash flow used in discounting cash flows consists of the annual net cash flows plus the estimated liquidation proceeds (salvage value) when the asset is sold for salvage at the end of its useful life.

The primary discounted cash flow technique is the **net present value method**. A second method, discussed later in the chapter, is the **internal rate of return**. At this point, we recommend that you examine **Appendix A** to review the time value of money concepts upon which these methods are based.

The **net present value (NPV) method** involves discounting net cash flows to their present value and then comparing that present value with the capital outlay required by the investment (see **Decision Tools**).

- The difference between these two amounts is referred to as **net present value (NPV)**.
- Company management determines what interest rate to use in discounting the future net cash flows. This rate, often referred to as the **discount rate** or **required rate of return**, is management's minimum acceptable rate of return on investments (discussed in a later section).
- The NPV decision rule is this: **A proposal is acceptable when net present value is zero or positive**. A zero or positive NPV indicates that the rate of return on the investment equals or exceeds (respectively) the required rate of return. When net present value is negative, the project is unacceptable.

Illustration 12.6 shows the net present value decision criteria.

When making a selection among acceptable proposals, **the higher the positive net present value, the more attractive the investment**. The application of this method to two cases is described in the next two sections. In each case, we assume that the investment has no salvage value at the end of its useful life.

> **DECISION TOOLS**
>
> Using the net present value method helps companies to determine whether or not to invest in proposed projects.

Equal Annual Cash Flows

In our Soren Shipping Company example, the company's net annual cash flows are €24,000 (€200,000 cash inflows − €176,000 cash outflows). If we assume this amount **is uniform over the asset's useful life**, we can compute the present value of the net annual cash flows by using the present value of an annuity of 1 for 10 payments (from Table 4, Appendix A). Assuming a discount rate of 12%, the present value of net cash flows is as shown in **Illustration 12.7** (rounded to the nearest euro) (see **Helpful Hint**).

> **HELPFUL HINT**
>
> The ABC Co. expects equal cash flows over an asset's five-year useful life. The discount factor it should use in determining present values if management wants a 12% return is 3.60478 (using Table 4, Appendix A).

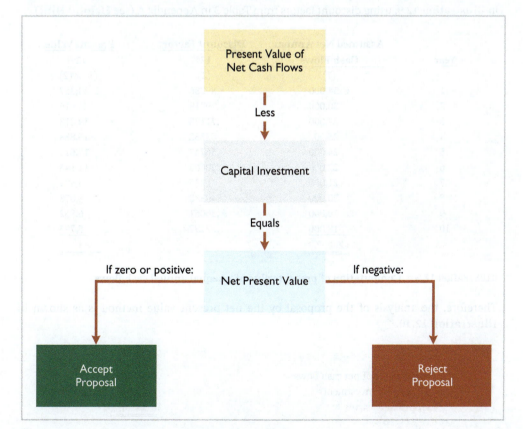

ILLUSTRATION 12.6 | **Net present value decision criteria**

	Present Value at 12%
Discount factor for 10 periods	5.65022
Present value of net cash flows: €24,000 × 5.65022	€135,605

ILLUSTRATION 12.7 | Computation of present value of equal net annual cash flows

Illustration 12.8 shows the analysis of the proposal by the net present value method.

	12%
Present value of net cash flows	€135,605
Less: Capital investment	130,000
Net present value	€ 5,605

ILLUSTRATION 12.8 | Computation of net present value—equal net annual cash flows

The proposed capital expenditure is acceptable at a required rate of return of 12% because the net present value is positive. The positive NPV indicates that the expected return on the investment exceeds 12%.

Unequal Annual Cash Flows

When net annual cash flows are unequal, we cannot use annuity tables to calculate present value. Instead, we use tables showing the **present value of a single future amount for each annual cash flow**.

To illustrate, assume that Soren Shipping Company expects the same total net cash flows of €240,000 over the life of the investment. But, because of a declining market demand for the product over the life of the equipment, the net annual cash flows are higher in the early years and lower in the later years. The present value of the net annual cash flows is calculated as shown in **Illustration 12.9**, using discount factors from Table 3 in Appendix A (see **Helpful Hint**).

HELPFUL HINT
Appendix A demonstrates the use of a financial calculator to solve time value of money problems.

Year	Assumed Net Annual Cash Flows (1)	Discount Factor 12% (2)	Present Value 12% (1) × (2)
1	€ 34,000	.89286	€ 30,357
2	30,000	.79719	23,916
3	27,000	.71178	19,218
4	25,000	.63552	15,888
5	24,000	.56743	13,618
6	22,000	.50663	11,146
7	21,000	.45235	9,499
8	20,000	.40388	8,078
9	19,000	.36061	6,852
10	18,000	.32197	5,795
	€240,000		€144,367

ILLUSTRATION 12.9 | Computation of present value of unequal annual cash flows

Therefore, the analysis of the proposal by the net present value method is as shown in **Illustration 12.10**.

	12%
Present value of net cash flows	€144,367
Less: Capital investment	130,000
Net present value	€ 14,367

ILLUSTRATION 12.10 | Computation of net present value—unequal annual cash flows

In this example, the present value of the net cash flows is greater than the €130,000 capital investment. Thus, the project is acceptable at a 12% required rate of return.

- The difference between the present values using the 12% rate under **equal** cash flows (€135,605) and **unequal** cash flows (€144,367) is due to the pattern of the flows.
- Since more money is received sooner under this particular uneven cash flow scenario, its present value is greater.

MANAGEMENT INSIGHT

Can You Hear Me—Better?

7506417745/
Shutterstock.com

With speeds up to 100 times faster than 4G, 5G cellular technology promises great potential. In fact, many factory applications that rely on connected machines require 5G speed. But delivering 5G means that the top U.S. telecom operators such as **Verizon**, **AT&T**, and **T-Mobile US** must make massive capital investments.

Investments in 5G have additional risks because companies must make choices regarding which airwave spectrum to operate in. Choosing to operate in the high-frequency range will offer superfast speeds. But, this range has significant limitations in terms of how far the signal will travel (thus requiring investing in more towers) and what it will travel through. By contrast, if a company chooses the low-band spectrum, its signal will travel long distances, but the speeds are about the same as 4G. With so much at stake, these decisions have huge implications.

A big question that nobody has answered yet is why will customers be willing to pay more for 5G than for 4G? Use of 5G will require consumers to purchase new phones—not a trivial personal investment. And if consumers do not switch quickly, telecom companies might not get the payback they need for their huge investments. In the meantime, 6G technology, which will be 10 times faster than 5G, is already being designed. This additional speed will be needed in order for autonomous cars to operate safely.

Sources: Sarah Krouse, "U.S. Telecom Giants Take Different Paths to 5G," *Wall Street Journal* (April 12, 2020); and River Davis, "Forget 5G for a Moment. Instead, Imagine 6G," *Wall Street Journal* (April 12, 2020).

Why is the capital investment in 5G technology particularly risky for telecom carriers? (Answer is available in the book's product page on www.wiley.com)

Choosing a Discount Rate

Now that you understand how companies apply the net present value method, it is logical to ask a related question: How is a discount rate (required rate of return) determined in real capital budgeting decisions?

- In many instances, a company uses a required rate of return equal to its **cost of capital**—that is, the rate that it must pay to obtain funds from creditors and stockholders.
- The cost of capital is a weighted average of the rates paid on borrowed funds as well as on funds provided by investors in the company's common stock and preferred stock (see **Helpful Hint**).
- If management believes a project is riskier than the company's usual line of business, the discount rate should be increased.

That is, the discount rate has two components, a cost of capital component and a risk component. Often, companies assume the risk component is equal to zero.

Using an incorrect discount rate can lead to incorrect capital budgeting decisions. Consider again the Soren Shipping example in Illustration 12.8, where we used a discount rate of 12%. Suppose that this rate does not take into account the fact that this project is riskier than most of the company's investments. A more appropriate discount rate, given the risk, might be 15%. **Illustration 12.11** compares the net present values at the two rates. At the higher, more appropriate discount rate of 15%, the net present value is negative. The negative NPV indicates that the expected rate of return on the investment is less than the required rate of return of 15%. The company should reject the project (discount factors from Appendix A, Table 4).

The discount rate is often referred to by alternative names, including the **required rate of return**, the **hurdle rate**, and the **cutoff rate**. Determination of the cost of capital varies

> **HELPFUL HINT**
>
> Cost of capital is the rate that management expects to pay on all borrowed and equity funds. It does not relate to the cost of funding a *specific* project.

	Present Values at Different Discount Rates	
	12%	15%
Discount factor for 10 payments	5.65022	5.01877
Present value of net cash flows:		
€24,000 × 5.65022	€135,605	
€24,000 × 5.01877		€120,450
Less: Capital investment	130,000	130,000
Positive (negative) net present value	€ 5,605	€ (9,550)

ILLUSTRATION 12.11 | **Comparison of net present values at different discount rates**

somewhat depending on whether the entity is a for-profit or not-for-profit business. Calculation of the cost of capital is discussed more fully in advanced accounting and finance courses.

Simplifying Assumptions

In our examples of the net present value method, we made a number of simplifying assumptions:

- **All cash flows occur at the end of each year.** In reality, cash flows will occur at uneven intervals throughout the year. However, it is far simpler to assume that all cash flows come at the end (or in some cases the beginning) of the year. In fact, this assumption is frequently made in practice.
- **All cash flows are immediately reinvested in another project that has a similar return.** In most capital budgeting situations, companies receive cash flows during each year of a project's life. In order to determine the return on the investment, some assumption must be made about how the cash flows are reinvested in the year that they are received. It is customary to assume that cash flows received are reinvested in some other project of similar return until the end of the project's life.
- **All cash flows can be predicted with certainty.** The outcomes of business investments are full of uncertainty, as the **Holland America Line** (USA) Feature Story shows. There is no way of knowing how popular a new product will be, how long a new machine will last, or what competitors' reactions might be to changes in a product. But, in order to make investment decisions, analysts must estimate future outcomes. In this chapter, we have assumed that future amounts are known with certainty.[1] In reality, little is known with certainty. More advanced capital budgeting techniques deal with uncertainty by considering the probability that various outcomes will occur.

Comprehensive Example

Good Taste Foods is considering investing in new equipment to produce fat-free snack foods. Management believes that although demand for fat-free foods has leveled off, fat-free foods are here to stay. The estimated costs, cost of capital, and cash flows shown in **Illustration 12.12** were determined in consultation with the marketing, production, and finance departments.

Initial investment	€1,000,000
Cost of equipment overhaul in 5 years	€200,000
Salvage value of equipment in 10 years	€20,000
Cost of capital (discount rate)	15%
Estimated annual cash flows	
Cash inflows received from sales	€500,000
Cash outflows for cost of goods sold	€200,000
Maintenance costs	€30,000
Other direct operating costs	€40,000

ILLUSTRATION 12.12 | **Investment information for Good Taste Foods example**

---

[1] One exception is a brief discussion of sensitivity analysis later in the chapter.

- Remember that we are using cash flows in our analysis, not accrual revenues and expenses.
- Thus, for example, the direct operating costs would not include depreciation expense since depreciation expense does not use cash.

Illustration 12.13 presents the computation of the net annual cash flows of this project.

Cash inflows received from sales	€ 500,000
Cash outflows for cost of goods sold	(200,000)
Maintenance costs	(30,000)
Other direct operating costs	(40,000)
Net annual cash flow	**€ 230,000**

ILLUSTRATION 12.13 | Computation of net annual cash flow

Illustration 12.14 shows computation of the net present value for this proposed investment (discount factors from Appendix A, Tables 3 and 4).

Event	Time Period	Cash Flow	×	15% Discount Factor	=	Present Value
Net annual cash flow	1–10	€ 230,000		5.01877		€1,154,317
Salvage value	10	20,000		.24719		4,944
Less: Equipment purchase	0	1,000,000		1.00000		1,000,000
Less: Equipment overhaul	5	200,000		.49718		99,436
Net present value						**€ 59,825**

ILLUSTRATION 12.14 | Computation of net present value for Good Taste Foods investment

Because the net present value of the project is positive, Good Taste should accept the project.

DO IT! 2 ▶ Net Present Value

Dublin Paper Corporation is considering adding another machine for the manufacture of corrugated cardboard. The machine would cost €900,000. It would have an estimated life of six years and no salvage value. The company estimates that annual cash inflows would increase by €400,000 and that annual cash outflows would increase by €190,000. Management has a required rate of return of 9%. Calculate the net present value on this project and discuss whether it should be accepted.

Solution

Estimated annual cash inflows	€400,000
Estimated annual cash outflows	190,000
Net annual cash flow	€210,000

	Cash Flow		9% Discount Factor		Present Value
Present value of net annual cash flows	€210,000	×	4.48592[a]	=	€942,043
Less: Capital investment					900,000
Net present value					€ 42,043

[a]Table 4, Appendix A, 9%, 6 years

Since the net present value is greater than zero, Dublin should accept the project.

Related exercise material: **BE12.2, BE12.3, DO IT! 12.2, E12.1, E12.2, and E12.3.**

ACTION PLAN
- Recall that Estimated annual cash inflows − Estimated annual cash outflows = Net annual cash flow.
- Use the NPV technique to calculate the difference between net cash flows and the initial investment.
- Accept the project if the net present value is positive.

CAPITAL BUDGETING CHALLENGES AND REFINEMENTS

LEARNING OBJECTIVE 3
Identify capital budgeting challenges and refinements.

Now that you understand how the net present value method works, we can add some "additional wrinkles." Specifically, these are the impact of intangible benefits, a way to compare mutually exclusive projects, refinements that take risk into account, and the need to conduct post-audits of investment projects.

Intangible Benefits

The NPV evaluation techniques employed thus far rely on tangible costs and benefits that can be relatively easily quantified. Some investment projects, especially high-tech projects, fail to make it through initial capital budget screens because only the project's tangible benefits are considered.

- **Intangible benefits** might include increased quality, improved safety, or enhanced employee loyalty.
- By ignoring intangible benefits, capital budgeting techniques might incorrectly eliminate projects that could be financially beneficial to the company.

To avoid rejecting projects that actually should be accepted, analysts suggest two possible approaches:

1. Calculate net present value ignoring intangible benefits. Then, if the NPV is negative, ask whether the project offers any intangible benefits that are worth at least the amount of the negative NPV.
2. Project conservative estimates of the value of the intangible benefits, and incorporate these values into the NPV calculation.

Example

Assume that Selmer Electronics is considering the purchase of a new mechanical robot to be used for soldering electrical connections. **Illustration 12.15** shows the estimates related to this proposed purchase (discount factor from Appendix A, Table 4).

Initial investment	€200,000	
Annual cash inflows	€ 50,000	
Annual cash outflows	20,000	
Net annual cash flow	**€ 30,000**	
Estimated life of equipment	10 years	
Discount rate	12%	

	Cash Flows		12% Discount Factor		Present Value
Present value of net annual cash flows	€30,000	×	5.65022	=	€ 169,507
Less: Initial investment					200,000
Net present value					**€ (30,493)**

ILLUSTRATION 12.15 | **Investment information for Selmer Electronics example**

Based on the negative net present value of €30,493, the proposed project is not acceptable. This calculation, however, ignores important information.

- The company's engineers believe that purchasing this machine will improve the quality of electrical connections in the company's products. As a result, future warranty costs may be reduced.

- This higher quality may translate into higher future sales.
- The new machine will be safer than the current machine.

The managers at Selmer Electronics do not have confidence in their ability to accurately estimate these potentially higher revenues and lower costs. But Selmer can incorporate this new information into the capital budgeting decision in the two ways discussed earlier.

1. Management might simply ask whether the reduced warranty costs, increased sales, and improved safety benefits have an estimated total present value to the company of at least €30,493. If yes, then the project is acceptable.
2. Analysts can estimate the annual cash flows of these benefits. In our initial calculation, we assumed each of these benefits to have a value of zero. It seems likely that their actual values are much higher than zero. Given the difficulty of estimating these benefits, however, conservative values should be assigned to them. If, after using conservative estimates, the net present value is positive, Selmer should accept the project.

To illustrate, assume that Selmer estimates that improved sales will increase cash inflows by €10,000 annually as a result of an increase in perceived quality. Selmer also estimates that annual cost outflows would be reduced by €5,000 as a result of lower warranty claims, reduced injury claims, and fewer missed work days. Consideration of the intangible benefits results in the revised NPV calculation shown in **Illustration 12.16** (discount factor from Appendix A, Table 4).

Initial investment	€200,000			
Annual cash inflows (revised)	€ 60,000 (€50,000 + €10,000)			
Annual cash outflows (revised)	15,000 (€20,000 − €5,000)			
Net annual cash flow	**€ 45,000**			
Estimated life of equipment	10 years			
Discount rate	12%			
	Cash Flows	12% Discount Factor		Present Value
Present value of net annual cash flows	€45,000	× 5.65022	=	€254,260
Less: Initial investment				200,000
Net present value				**€ 54,260**

ILLUSTRATION 12.16 | Revised investment information for Selmer Electronics example, including intangible benefits

Using these conservative estimates of the value of the additional benefits, Selmer should accept the project.

ETHICS INSIGHT Coal & Allied

Investments in Safety

Courtesy of SmartCap Technologies

Operators at **Coal & Allied**'s (AUS) Hunter Valley Operations mine in Australia wear a piece of technology called a "SmartCap." The sophisticated technology uses electroencephalogram (EEG), the gold standard in sleep science, to measure fatigue levels and reduce fatigue-related incidents. This investment by Coal & Allied provides operators with real-time information about their alertness levels and allows them to understand and manage their own fatigue.

Not only did the SmartCap capture more than 4,200 hours of data in its first year, it also added to the number of fatigue-management measures that the company implemented onsite. Other measures included improvements in diet, exercise, and educating operators about other causes of fatigue including medication. Coal & Allied has been part of the Hunter Valley community for nearly 170 years and sees this investment as part of its efforts to build stronger, smarter, and more sustainable communities around the three open-cut coal mines that it manages.

Source: "Hi-Tech Cap Helps Coal & Allied Truck Drivers Work Smarter to Manage Fatigue," *Rio Tinto Global Home media release* (May 20, 2013).

In addition to the obvious humanitarian benefit of reducing serious injuries, how else might the manufacturer of this product convince potential customers of its worth? (Answer is available in the book's product page on www.wiley.com)

Profitability Index for Mutually Exclusive Projects

In theory, companies should accept all projects with positive NPVs. However, companies rarely are able to adopt all positive-NPV proposals.

1. Proposals often are **mutually exclusive**.

   - This means that if the company adopts one proposal, it would be impossible or impractical to also adopt the other proposal.
   - For example, a company may be considering the purchase of a new packaging machine and is looking at various brands and models.
   - Once the company has determined which brand and model to purchase, the others will not be purchased—even though they also may have positive net present values.

2. Managers often must choose between various positive-NPV projects because of **limited resources**.

   - For example, the company might have ideas for two new lines of business, each of which has a projected positive NPV.
   - However, both of these proposals require skilled personnel, and the company determines that it will not be able to find enough skilled personnel to staff both projects.
   - Management will have to choose the project it thinks is the better option.

When choosing between alternative proposals, it is tempting simply to choose the project with the higher NPV. Consider the following example of two mutually exclusive projects. Each is assumed to have a 10-year life and a 12% discount rate (discount factors from Appendix A, Tables 3 and 4). **Illustration 12.17** shows the estimates for each project and the computation of the present value of the net cash flows.

	Project A	Project B
Initial investment	€40,000	€ 90,000
Net annual cash inflow	10,000	19,000
Salvage value	5,000	10,000
Present value of net cash flows		
(€10,000 × 5.65022) + (€5,000 × .32197)	58,112	
(€19,000 × 5.65022) + (€10,000 × .32197)		110,574

ILLUSTRATION 12.17 | **Investment information for mutually exclusive projects**

Illustration 12.18 computes the net present values of Project A and Project B by subtracting the initial investment from the present value of the net cash flows.

	Project A	Project B
Present value of net cash flows	€58,112	€110,574
Less: Initial investment	40,000	90,000
Net present value	€18,112	€ 20,574

ILLUSTRATION 12.18 | **Net present value computation**

As Project B has the higher NPV, it would seem that the company should adopt it. However, Project B also requires more than twice the original investment of Project A (€90,000 versus €40,000). In choosing between the two projects, the company should also include in its calculations the amount of the original investment.

One relatively simple method of comparing alternative projects is the **profitability index**.

- This method takes into account both the size of the original investment and the discounted cash flows.
- The profitability index is calculated by dividing the present value of net cash flows that occur after the initial investment by the amount of the initial investment, as **Illustration 12.19** shows.

| Present Value of Net Cash Flows | ÷ | Initial Investment | = | **Profitability Index** |

ILLUSTRATION 12.19 | Equation for profitability index

- The profitability index allows comparison of the relative desirability of projects that require differing initial investments (see **Decision Tools**).
- Note that any project with a positive NPV will have a profitability index above 1.

The profitability index for each of the mutually exclusive projects is calculated in **Illustration 12.20**.

> **DECISION TOOLS**
>
> The profitability index helps a company determine which investment proposal to accept.

$$\text{Profitability Index} = \frac{\text{Present Value of Net Cash Flows}}{\text{Initial Investment}}$$

Project A	Project B
$\dfrac{€58{,}112}{€40{,}000} = 1.45$	$\dfrac{€110{,}574}{€90{,}000} = 1.23$

ILLUSTRATION 12.20 | Calculation for profitability index

In this case, the profitability index of Project A exceeds that of Project B. Thus, Project A is more desirable. Again, if these were not mutually exclusive projects and if resources were not limited, then the company should invest in both projects since both have positive NPVs. Additional considerations related to preference decisions are discussed in more advanced courses.

Risk Analysis

A simplifying assumption made by many financial analysts is that projected results are known with certainty. In reality, projected results are only estimates based on the forecaster's belief as to the most probable outcome.

- One approach for dealing with such uncertainty is **sensitivity analysis**.
- Sensitivity analysis uses a number of outcome estimates to get a sense of the variability among potential returns.

An example of sensitivity analysis was presented in Illustration 12.11, where we illustrated the impact on NPV of different discount rate assumptions. A higher-risk project would be evaluated using a higher discount rate.

Similarly, to take into account that more distant cash flows are often more uncertain, a higher discount rate can be used to discount more distant cash flows. Other techniques to address uncertainty are discussed in advanced courses.

PEOPLE, PLANET, AND PROFIT INSIGHT

Big Spenders

Elnur/Shutterstock.com

Investments in electricity production and transmission represent some of society's biggest capital budgeting decisions. For example, billionaire Philip Anschutz is backing a project to build a 3,000-megawatt Wyoming wind farm as well as a 730-mile transmission line that would efficiently transfer the electricity to Las Vegas, where it could then travel on existing lines to locations in California. Total cost: $9 billion. This would be the biggest wind farm in the United States except that an even bigger, 4,000-megawatt wind farm is being planned by a different group of investors. In the past, these investments were made by regulated utility companies, which were allowed to pass on their costs to customers and thus essentially guaranteed a steady revenue stream. Today, many of the biggest projects are instead being financed by private investors. These investors will be selling their electricity in energy markets driven by market demand. This provides for more potential upside on their investment but also more uncertainty regarding revenue flows.

Source: Russell Gold, "Investors Are Building Their Own Green-Power Lines," *Wall Street Journal* (April 6, 2017).

How does the financing of today's big energy investments differ from big energy capital investments of the past, and what are the implications? (Answer is available in the book's product page on www.wiley.com)

Post-Audit of Investment Projects

Well-run organizations perform post-audits of investment projects after their completion. A **post-audit** is a thorough evaluation of how well a project's actual performance matches the original projections. An example of a post-audit is seen in a situation that occurred at **Campbell Soup** (USA). The company made the original decision to invest in the Intelligent Quisine line based on management's best estimates of future cash flows. During the development phase of the project, Campbell hired an outside consulting firm to evaluate the project's potential for success. Because actual results during the initial years were far below the estimated results and because the future also did not look promising, the project was terminated.

Performing a post-audit is important for a variety of reasons.

1. If managers know that the company will compare their estimates to actual results, they will be more likely to submit reasonable and accurate data when they make investment proposals. This reduces overly optimistic estimates by managers hoping to get pet projects approved.
2. As seen with Campbell Soup, a post-audit provides a formal mechanism by which the company can determine whether existing projects should be supported or terminated.
3. Post-audits improve future investment proposals because, by evaluating past successes and failures, managers improve their estimation techniques.

A post-audit involves the same evaluation techniques used in making the original capital budgeting decision—for example, use of the NPV method. The difference is that, in the post-audit, analysts insert actual figures, where known, and they revise estimates of future amounts based on new information. The managers responsible for the estimates used in the original proposal must explain the reasons for any significant differences between their estimates and actual results.

Post-audits are not foolproof. In the case of Campbell Soup, some observers suggested that the company was too quick to abandon the project. Industry analysts suggested that with more time and more advertising expenditures, Intelligent Quisine might have enjoyed success.

DO IT! 3 ▶ Profitability Index

Tasmin Industries has decided to invest in renewable energy sources to meet part of its energy needs for production. It is considering solar power versus wind power. After considering cost savings as well as incremental revenues from selling excess electricity into the power grid, it has determined the following:

	Solar	Wind
Present value of annual cash flows	€78,580	€168,450
Initial investment	€45,500	€125,300

Determine the net present value and profitability index of each project. Which energy source should it choose?

ACTION PLAN
- Determine the present value of annual cash flows of each mutually exclusive project.
- Determine profitability index by dividing the present value of annual cash flows by the amount of the initial investment.
- Choose project with highest profitability index.

Solution

	Solar	Wind
Present value of annual cash flows	€78,580	€168,450
Less: Initial investment	45,500	125,300
Net present value	€33,080	€ 43,150
Profitability index	1.73*	1.34**

*€78,580 ÷ €45,500
**€168,450 ÷ €125,300

While the investment in wind power generates the higher net present value, it also requires a substantially higher initial investment. The profitability index favors solar power, which suggests that the additional net present value of wind is outweighed by the cost of the initial investment. The company should choose solar power.

Related exercise material: **BE12.5, DO IT! 12.3, and E12.4.**

INTERNAL RATE OF RETURN

The **internal rate of return method** differs from the net present value method in that it finds the **interest yield of the potential investment**.

> **LEARNING OBJECTIVE 4**
> Use the internal rate of return method.

- The **internal rate of return (IRR)** is the interest rate that causes the present value of the proposed capital expenditure to equal the present value of the expected net annual cash flows (that is, NPV equal to zero).
- Because it recognizes the time value of money, the internal rate of return method is (like the NPV method) a discounted cash flow technique (see **Decision Tools**).

> **DECISION TOOLS**
> The IRR helps a company determine if it should invest in a proposed project.

How do we determine the internal rate of return? One way is to use a financial calculator (see Appendix A) or electronic spreadsheet to solve for this rate. Or, we can use a trial-and-error procedure searching for a discount rate that results in an NPV equal to zero.

To illustrate, assume that Soren Shipping Company is considering the purchase of a new front-end loader at a cost of €244,371. Net annual cash flows from this loader are estimated to be €100,000 a year for three years. To determine the internal rate of return on this front-end loader, the company finds the discount rate that results in a net present value of zero. **Illustration 12.21** shows that at a rate of return of 10%, Soren Shipping has a positive net present value of €4,315. At a rate of return of 12%, it has a negative net present value of €4,188. At an 11% rate, the net present value is zero. Therefore, 11% is the internal rate of return for this investment (discount factors from Appendix A, Table 3).

Year	Net Annual Cash Flows	Discount Factor 10%	Present Value 10%	Discount Factor 11%	Present Value 11%	Discount Factor 12%	Present Value 12%
1	€100,000	.90909	€ 90,909	.90090	€ 90,090	.89286	€ 89,286
2	€100,000	.82645	82,645	.81162	81,162	.79719	79,719
3	€100,000	.75132	75,132	.73119	73,119	.71178	71,178
			248,686		244,371		240,183
Less: Initial investment			244,371		244,371		244,371
Net present value			€ 4,315		€ -0-		€ (4,188)

ILLUSTRATION 12.21 | Estimation of internal rate of return

An easier approach to solving for the internal rate of return can be used if the net annual cash flows are **equal**, as in the Soren Shipping example. In this special case, we can find the internal rate of return using the equation provided in **Illustration 12.22**.

$$\text{Capital Investment} \div \text{Net Annual Cash Flows} = \text{Internal Rate of Return Factor}$$

ILLUSTRATION 12.22 | Equation for internal rate of return—even cash flows

Applying this equation to the Soren Shipping example, we find:

$$€244,371 \div 100,000 = 2.44371$$

We then look up the factor 2.44371 in Table 4 of Appendix A in the three-payment row and find it under 11%. Row 3 is reproduced here for your convenience.

	Table 4 Present Value of an Annuity of 1									
(n) Payments	4%	5%	6%	7%	8%	9%	10%	11%	12%	15%
3	2.77509	2.72325	2.67301	2.62432	2.57710	2.53130	2.48685	2.44371	2.40183	2.28323

Recognize that if the cash flows are **uneven**, then a trial-and-error approach or a financial calculator or computerized spreadsheet must be used.

Once managers know the internal rate of return, they compare it to the company's required rate of return (the discount rate). The IRR decision rule is as follows:

- **Accept the project when the internal rate of return is equal to or greater than the required rate of return.**
- **Reject the project when the internal rate of return is less than the required rate of return.**

Illustration 12.23 shows these relationships. The internal rate of return method is widely used in practice, largely because most managers find the internal rate of return easy to interpret.

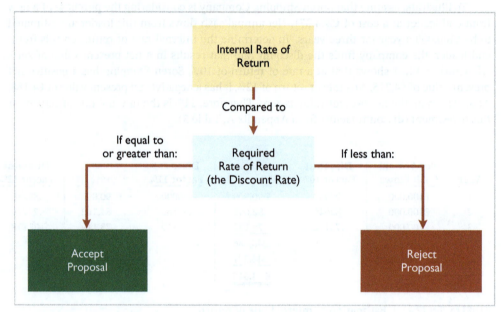

ILLUSTRATION 12.23 | Internal rate of return decision criteria

Comparing Discounted Cash Flow Methods

Illustration 12.24 compares the two discounted cash flow methods—net present value and internal rate of return. When properly used, either method will provide management with relevant quantitative data for making capital budgeting decisions.

	Net Present Value	**Internal Rate of Return**
1. Objective	Compute net present value (a euro amount).	Compute internal rate of return (a percentage).
2. Decision Rule	If net present value is zero or positive, accept the proposal.	If internal rate of return is equal to or greater than the required rate of return, accept the proposal.
	If net present value is negative, reject the proposal.	If internal rate of return is less than the required rate of return, reject the proposal.

ILLUSTRATION 12.24 | Comparison of discounted cash flow methods

Finally, note that these capital budgeting calculations can also be performed using Excel. A big benefit of using Excel is the ability to quickly experiment with different input variables such as the number of payments, interest rates, or payment amounts.

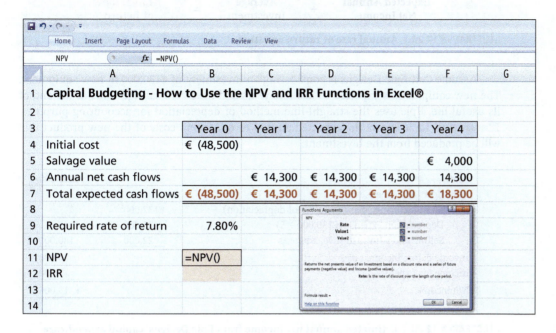

DO IT! 4 ▶ Internal Rate of Return

Dublin Paper Corporation is considering adding another machine for the manufacture of corrugated cardboard. The machine would cost €900,000. It would have an estimated life of six years and no salvage value. The company estimates that annual cash inflows would increase by €400,000 and that annual cash outflows would increase by €190,000. Management has a required rate of return of 9%. Calculate the internal rate of return on this project and discuss whether it should be accepted.

Solution

Estimated annual cash inflows	€400,000
Estimated annual cash outflows	190,000
Net annual cash flow	€210,000

€900,000 ÷ €210,000 = 4.285714. Using Table 4 of Appendix A and the factors that correspond with the six-payment row, 4.285714 is between the factors for 10% and 11%. Since the project has an internal rate that is greater than 10% and the required rate of return is only 9%, the project should be accepted.

Related exercise material: **BE12.7, BE12.8, DO IT! 12.4, E12.5, E12.6, and E12.7.**

ACTION PLAN
- Estimated annual cash inflows − Estimated annual cash outflows = Net annual cash flow.
- Capital investment ÷ Net annual cash flows = Internal rate of return factor.
- Look up the factor in the present value of an annuity table to find the internal rate of return.
- Accept the project if the internal rate of return is equal to or greater than the required rate of return.

ANNUAL RATE OF RETURN

The final capital budgeting technique we discuss is the **annual rate of return method**.

- It employs accrual accounting data rather than cash flows.
- It indicates **the profitability of a capital expenditure** by dividing expected annual net income by the average investment.

LEARNING OBJECTIVE 5
Use the annual rate of return method.

Illustration 12.25 shows the equation for computing annual rate of return.

| Expected Annual Net Income | ÷ | Average Investment | = | Annual Rate of Return |

ILLUSTRATION 12.25 | Annual rate of return equation

Assume that Epic Designs is considering an investment of €130,000 in new equipment. The new equipment is expected to last five years and have zero salvage value at the end of its useful life. Epic uses the straight-line method of depreciation for accounting purposes. **Illustration 12.26** shows the expected annual revenues and costs of the new product that will be produced from the investment.

Sales		€200,000
Less: Costs and expenses		
Manufacturing costs (exclusive of depreciation)	€132,000	
Depreciation expense (€130,000 ÷ 5)	26,000	
Selling and administrative expenses	22,000	180,000
Income before income taxes		20,000
Income tax expense		7,000
Net income		€ 13,000

ILLUSTRATION 12.26 | Estimated annual net income from Epic Designs' capital expenditure

Epic's expected annual net income is €13,000. Average investment is derived from the equation shown in **Illustration 12.27**.

$$\frac{\text{Original Investment} + \text{Value at End of Useful Life}}{2} = \text{Average Investment}$$

ILLUSTRATION 12.27 | Equation for computing average investment

The value at the end of useful life is equal to the asset's salvage value, if any. For Epic, average investment is €65,000 [(€130,000 + €0) ÷ 2]. The expected annual rate of return for Epic's investment in new equipment is therefore 20%, computed as follows:

$$€13,000 ÷ €65,000 = 20\%$$

Management then compares the annual rate of return with its **required rate of return** for investments of similar risk. The required rate of return is generally based on the company's cost of capital. The decision rule is:

- **A project is acceptable if its rate of return is greater than management's required rate of return.**
- **It is unacceptable when the reverse is true.**
- When companies use the rate of return technique in deciding among several acceptable projects, **the higher the rate of return for a given risk, the more attractive the investment.**

The principal advantages of this method are the simplicity of its calculation and management's familiarity with the accounting terms used in the computation. Two limitations of the annual rate of return method are:

1. It does not consider the time value of money. For example, no consideration is given to whether cash inflows will occur early or late in the life of the investment.

As explained in Appendix A, recognition of the time value of money can make a significant difference between the future value and the discounted present value of an investment.

2. This method relies on accrual accounting numbers rather than expected cash flows. This is potentially problematic because valuation theories employed in finance are based on cash flows. Also, some people feel that accrual accounting numbers are more susceptible to manipulation by management (see **Helpful Hint**).

HELPFUL HINT

A capital budgeting decision based on only one technique may be misleading. It is often wise to analyze an investment from a number of different perspectives.

DATA ANALYTICS INSIGHT Electronic Arts

Chris Willson/Alamy Stock Photo

Increasing the Chances of Gaming Wins

Today's video games are infinitely more sophisticated than the games produced 25 years ago, and the costs required to develop them have skyrocketed. In 1994, **Electronic Arts** (USA) spent an unheard of $5 million developing a new game. These days, game development requires a two-year commitment by hundreds of employees and costs around $500 million. And if the game fails to attract buyers, then all of that money is gone.

How does Electronic Arts increase the likelihood of success? Big data. Because today's games are nearly all played online, the company collects data about which features of a game that players engage with the most. The company does not have to ask survey questions to collect this data but instead obtains the information from the usage data. However, when Electronic Arts first switched to this big-data approach, it quickly found out that it had more data than it could handle. Over time, the company has learned to collect only a fraction of the available data and then use it wisely.

The company's data analysis now guides the design and development of new games as well as the subsequent marketing. This dramatically reduces the risks associated with the giant capital investments involved.

Source: Bernard Marr, *Big Data in Practice* (Hoboken, NJ: John Wiley and Sons, 2016), pp. 273–279.

In what ways do the capital investments of Electronic Arts benefit from data analytics? (Answer is available in the book's product page on www.wiley.com)

DO IT! 5 Annual Rate of Return

Dublin Paper Corporation is considering adding another machine for the manufacture of corrugated cardboard. The machine would cost €900,000. It would have an estimated life of six years and no salvage value. The company estimates that annual revenues would increase by €400,000 and that annual expenses excluding depreciation would increase by €190,000. It uses the straight-line method to compute depreciation expense. Management has a required rate of return of 9%. Compute the annual rate of return.

Solution

Revenues		€400,000
Less:		
Expenses (excluding depreciation)	€190,000	
Depreciation (€900,000 ÷ 6 years)	150,000	340,000
Annual net income		€ 60,000

Average investment = (€900,000 + €0) ÷ 2 = €450,000
Annual rate of return = €60,000 ÷ €450,000 = 13.3%

Since the annual rate of return (13.3%) is greater than Dublin's required rate of return (9%), the proposed project is acceptable.

Related exercise material: **BE12.9, DO IT! 12.5, E12.8, E12.9, E12.10, and E12.11.**

ACTION PLAN

- Expected annual net income = Annual revenues − Annual expenses (including depreciation expense).
- Average investment = (Original investment + Value at end of useful life) ÷ 2.
- Annual rate of return = Expected annual net income ÷ Average investment.

USING THE DECISION TOOLS | Holland America Line

As noted in the Feature Story, **Holland America Line** (USA) must continually make significant capital investments in ships. Some of these decisions require comparisons of strategic alternatives. For example, not all of the company's ships are the same size. Different-sized ships offer alternative advantages and disadvantages. Suppose the company engages in ferrying activities and is trying to decide between two investment options. It is weighing the purchase of three larger ships for a total of $2,500,000 versus five smaller ships for a total of $1,400,000. Information regarding these two alternatives is provided here:

	Three Larger Ships	Five Smaller Ships
Initial investment	$2,500,000	$1,400,000
Estimated useful life	20 years	20 years
Annual revenues (accrual)	$500,000	$380,000
Annual expenses (accrual)	$200,000	$180,000
Annual cash inflows	$550,000	$430,000
Annual cash outflows	$222,250	$206,350
Estimated salvage value	$500,000	$0
Discount rate	9%	9%

Instructions

Evaluate each of these mutually exclusive proposals employing (a) cash payback, (b) net present value, (c) profitability index, (d) internal rate of return, and (e) annual rate of return. Discuss the implications of your findings.

Solution

	Three Larger Ships	Five Smaller Ships
a. Cash payback	$\frac{\$2,500,000}{\$327,750^*}$ = 7.63 years	$\frac{\$1,400,000}{\$223,650^{**}}$ = 6.26 years

*$550,000 − $222,250; **$430,000 − $206,350

b. Net present value

Present value of net cash flows

$327,750 × 9.12855 =	$2,991,882	$223,650 × 9.12855 =	$2,041,600
$500,000 × 0.17843 =	89,215		
	3,081,097		
Less: Initial investment	2,500,000		1,400,000
Net present value	$ 581,097		$ 641,600

c. Profitability index	$\frac{\$3,081,097}{\$2,500,000}$ = 1.23	$\frac{\$2,041,600}{\$1,400,000}$ = 1.46

d. The internal rate of return can be approximated by experimenting with different discount rates to see which one comes the closest to resulting in a net present value of zero. Doing this, we find that the larger ships have an internal rate of return of approximately 12%, while the internal rate of return of the smaller ships is approximately 15% as shown below.

Internal rate of return

Cash Flows	×	12% Discount Factor	=	Present Value	Cash Flows	×	15% Discount Factor	=	Present Value
$327,750	×	7.46944	=	$2,448,109	$223,650	×	6.25933	=	$1,399,899
$500,000	×	0.10367	=	51,835					
				$2,499,944					
Less: Capital investment				2,500,000					1,400,000
Net present value				$ (56)					$ (101)

e. Annual rate of return

Three Larger Ships	Five Smaller Ships

Average investment

$$\frac{(\$2,500,000 + \$500,000)}{2} = \$1,500,000 \qquad \frac{(\$1,400,000 + \$0)}{2} = \$700,000$$

$$\text{Annual rate of return } \frac{\$300,000^*}{\$1,500,000} = .20 = 20\% \qquad \frac{\$200,000^{**}}{\$700,000} = .286 = 28.6\%$$

*$500,000 − $200,000; **$380,000 − $180,000

Although the annual rate of return is higher for the smaller ships, annual rate of return has the disadvantage of ignoring time value of money, as well as using accrual numbers rather than cash flows. The cash payback of the smaller ships is also shorter, but this method also ignores the time value of money. Thus, while these two methods can be used for a quick assessment, neither should be relied upon as the sole evaluation tool.

From the net present value calculation, it would appear that the two alternatives are nearly identical in their acceptability. However, the profitability index indicates that the small-ship investment is far more desirable because it generates its cash flows with a much smaller initial investment. A similar result is found by using the internal rate of return. Overall, assuming that the company will select only one alternative, it would appear that the small-ship option should be chosen.

REVIEW AND PRACTICE

Learning Objectives Review

LO 1 Describe capital budgeting inputs and apply the cash payback technique.

Management gathers project proposals from each department; a capital budget committee screens the proposals and recommends worthy projects. Company officers decide which projects to fund, and the board of directors approves the capital budget. In capital budgeting, estimated cash inflows and outflows, rather than accrual-accounting numbers, are the preferred inputs.

The cash payback technique identifies the time period required to recover the cost of the investment. The equation when net annual cash flows are equal is: Cost of capital investment ÷ Estimated net annual cash flow = Cash payback period. The shorter the payback period, the more attractive the investment.

LO 2 Use the net present value method.

The net present value method compares the present value of future cash inflows with the capital investment to determine net present value. The NPV decision rule is: Accept the project if net present value is zero or positive. Reject the project if net present value is negative.

LO 3 Identify capital budgeting challenges and refinements.

Intangible benefits are difficult to quantify and thus are often ignored in capital budgeting decisions. This can result in incorrectly rejecting some projects. One method for considering intangible benefits is to calculate the NPV, ignoring intangible benefits. If the resulting NPV is below zero, evaluate whether the benefits are worth at least the amount of the negative net present value. Alternatively, intangible benefits can be incorporated into the NPV calculation, using conservative estimates of their value.

The profitability index is a tool for comparing the relative merits of alternative capital investment opportunities. It is computed as Present value of net cash flows ÷ Initial investment. The higher the index, the more desirable the project.

A post-audit is an evaluation of a capital investment's actual performance. Post-audits create an incentive for managers to make accurate estimates. Post-audits also are useful for determining whether a company should continue, expand, or terminate a project. Finally, post-audits provide feedback that is useful for improving estimation techniques.

LO 4 Use the internal rate of return method.

The objective of the internal rate of return method is to find the interest yield of the potential investment, which is expressed as a percentage rate. The IRR decision rule is: Accept the project when the internal rate of return is equal to or greater than the required rate of return. Reject the project when the internal rate of return is less than the required rate of return.

LO 5 Use the annual rate of return method.

The annual rate of return uses accrual accounting data to indicate the profitability of a capital investment. It is calculated as Expected annual net income ÷ Amount of the average investment. The higher the rate of return, the more attractive the investment.

Decision Tools Review

Decision Checkpoints	Info Needed for Decision	Tool to Use for Decision	How to Evaluate Results
Should the company invest in a proposed project?	Cash flow estimates, discount rate	Net present value = Present value of net cash flows less capital investment	The investment is financially acceptable if net present value is zero or positive.
Which investment proposal should a company accept?	Estimated cash flows and discount rate for each proposal	Profitability index = $\dfrac{\text{Present value of net cash flows}}{\text{Initial investment}}$	The investment proposal with the highest profitability index should be accepted.
Should the company invest in a proposed project?	Estimated cash flows and the required rate of return (hurdle rate)	Internal rate of return = Interest rate that results in a net present value of zero	If the internal rate of return exceeds the required rate of return for the project, then the project is financially acceptable.

Glossary Review

Annual rate of return method The determination of the profitability of a capital expenditure, computed by dividing expected annual net income by the average investment. (p. 12-19).

Capital budgeting The process of making capital expenditure decisions in business. (p. 12-3).

Cash payback technique A capital budgeting technique that identifies the time period required to recover the cost of a capital investment from the net annual cash flow produced by the investment. (p. 12-4).

Cost of capital The weighted-average rate of return that the firm must pay to obtain funds from creditors and stockholders. (p. 12-9).

Discounted cash flow technique A capital budgeting technique that considers both the estimated net cash flows from the investment and the time value of money. (p. 12-6).

Discount rate The interest rate used in discounting the future net cash flows to determine present value. (p. 12-7).

Internal rate of return (IRR) The interest rate that will cause the present value of the proposed capital expenditure to equal the present value of the expected net annual cash flows. (p. 12-17).

Internal rate of return (IRR) method A method used in capital budgeting that results in finding the interest yield of the potential investment. (p. 12-17).

Net present value (NPV) The difference that results when the original capital outlay is subtracted from the discounted net cash flows. (p. 12-7).

Net present value (NPV) method A method used in capital budgeting in which net cash flows are discounted to their present value and then compared to the capital outlay required by the investment. (p. 12-7).

Post-audit A thorough evaluation of how well a project's actual performance matches the original projections. (p. 12-16).

Profitability index A method of comparing alternative projects that takes into account both the size of the investment and its discounted net cash flows. It is computed by dividing the present value of net cash flows by the initial investment. (p. 12-14).

Required rate of return Management's minimum acceptable rate of return on investments, sometimes called the discount rate or cost of capital. (p. 12-7).

Sensitivity analysis An approach that uses a number of outcome estimates to get a sense of the variability among potential returns. (p. 12-15).

Practice Multiple-Choice Questions

1. (LO 1) Which of the following is **not** an example of a capital budgeting decision?

   a. Decision to build a new factory.
   b. Decision to renovate an existing facility.
   c. Decision to buy a piece of machinery.
   d. All of the answer choices are capital budgeting decisions.

2. (LO 1) What is the order of involvement of the following parties in the capital budgeting authorization process?

   a. Factory managers, officers, capital budget committee, board of directors.
   b. Board of directors, factory managers, officers, capital budget committee.
   c. Factory managers, capital budget committee, officers, board of directors.
   d. Officers, factory managers, capital budget committee, board of directors.

3. **(LO 1)** What is a weakness of the cash payback approach?
   a. It uses accrual-based accounting numbers.
   b. It ignores the time value of money.
   c. It ignores the expected profitability of the project.
   d. It ignores both the time value of money and the expected profitability of the project.

4. **(LO 1)** Sutton Industries is considering two capital budgeting projects. Project A requires an initial investment of £48,000. It is expected to produce net annual cash flows of £7,000. Project B requires an initial investment of £75,000 and is expected to produce net annual cash flows of £12,000. Using the cash payback technique to evaluate the two projects, Sutton should accept:
   a. Project A because it has a shorter cash payback period.
   b. Project B because it has a shorter cash payback period.
   c. Project A because it requires a smaller initial investment.
   d. Project B because it produces a larger net annual cash flow.

5. **(LO 2)** Which is a **true** statement regarding using a higher discount rate to calculate the net present value of a project?
   a. It will make it less likely that the project will be accepted.
   b. It will make it more likely that the project will be accepted.
   c. It is appropriate to use a higher rate if the project is perceived as being less risky than other projects being considered.
   d. It is appropriate to use a higher rate if the project will have a short useful life relative to other projects being considered.

6. **(LO 2)** A positive net present value means that the:
   a. project's rate of return is less than the cutoff rate.
   b. project's rate of return exceeds the required rate of return.
   c. project's rate of return equals the required rate of return.
   d. project is unacceptable.

7. **(LO 2)** Which of the following is **not** an alternative name for the discount rate?
   a. Hurdle rate.
   b. Required rate of return.
   c. Cutoff rate.
   d. All of the answer choices are alternative names for the discount rate.

8. **(LO 3)** If a project has intangible benefits whose value is hard to estimate, the best thing to do is:
   a. ignore these benefits since any estimate of their value will most likely be wrong.
   b. include a conservative estimate of their value.
   c. ignore their value in your initial net present value calculation, but then estimate whether their potential value is worth at least the amount of the net present value deficiency.
   d. either include a conservative estimate of their value or ignore their value in your initial net present value calculation, but then estimate whether their potential value is worth at least the amount of the net present value deficiency.

9. **(LO 3)** An example of an intangible benefit provided by a capital budgeting project is:
   a. the salvage value of the capital investment.
   b. a positive net present value.
   c. a decrease in customer complaints regarding poor quality.
   d. an internal rate of return greater than zero.

10. **(LO 3)** The following information is available for a potential capital investment.

Initial investment	S$80,000
Salvage value	10,000
Net annual cash flow	14,820
Present value of net annual cash flows	98,112
Net present value	18,112
Useful life	10 years

    The potential investment's profitability index (rounded to two decimals) is:
    a. 5.40.
    b. 1.19.
    c. 1.23.
    d. 1.40.

11. **(LO 3)** A post-audit of an investment project should be performed:
    a. on all significant capital expenditure projects.
    b. on all projects that management feels might be financial failures.
    c. on randomly selected projects.
    d. only on projects that enjoy tremendous success.

12. **(LO 4)** A project should be accepted if its internal rate of return exceeds:
    a. zero.
    b. the rate of return on a government bond.
    c. the company's required rate of return.
    d. the rate the company pays on borrowed funds.

13. **(LO 4)** The following information is available for a potential capital investment.

Initial investment	€60,000
Net annual cash flow	15,400
Net present value	3,143
Useful life	5 years

    The potential investment's internal rate of return is approximately:
    a. 5%.
    b. 10%.
    c. 4%.
    d. 9%.

14. **(LO 5)** Which of the following is **incorrect** about the annual rate of return technique?
    a. The calculation is simple.
    b. The accounting terms used are familiar to management.
    c. The timing of the cash inflows is not considered.
    d. The time value of money is considered.

15. **(LO 5)** The following information is available for a potential capital investment.

Initial investment	A$120,000
Annual net income	15,000
Net annual cash flow	27,500
Salvage value	20,000
Useful life	8 years

    The potential investment's annual rate of return is approximately:
    a. 21%.
    b. 15%.
    c. 30%.
    d. 39%.

Solutions

1. **d.** Choices (a), (b), and (c) are all examples of capital budgeting decisions, so choice (d) is the best answer.

2. **c.** The process of authorizing capital budget expenditures starts with factory managers, moves on to the capital budgeting committee, goes next to the officers of the firm and finally is acted upon by the board of directors. The other choices are therefore incorrect.

3. **d.** Choices (b) and (c) are both correct; therefore, choice (d) is the best answer. Choice (a) is incorrect as the use of accrual-based accounting numbers is not a weakness of the cash payback approach.

4. **b.** Project B (£75,000 ÷ £12,000) has a shorter cash payback period than Project A (£48,000 ÷ £7,000). The other choices are therefore incorrect.

5. **a.** If a higher discount rate is used in calculating the net present value of a project, the resulting net present value will be lower and the project will be less likely to be accepted. The other choices are therefore incorrect.

6. **b.** A positive net present value means that the project's rate of return exceeds the required rate of return. The other choices are therefore incorrect.

7. **d.** Choices (a), (b), and (c) are all alternative names for the discount rate; therefore, choice (d) is the best answer.

8. **d.** Choices (b) and (c) are both reasonable approaches to including intangible benefits in the capital budgeting process; therefore, choice (d) is the best answer. Choice (a) is incorrect because even though these intangible benefits may be hard to quantify, they should not be ignored in the capital budgeting process.

9. **c.** A decrease in customer complaints regarding poor quality is one example of an intangible benefit provided by a capital budgeting project. The other choices are incorrect because (a) salvage value, (b) net present value, and (d) internal rate of return are all quantitative measures, i.e., tangible.

10. **c.** (S$18,112 + S$80,000) ÷ S$80,000 = 1.23, not (a) 5.40, (b) 1.19, or (d) 1.40.

11. **a.** A post-audit should be performed on all significant capital expenditure projects, not just on (b) financial failures, (c) randomly selected projects, or (d) tremendous successes, because the feedback gained will help to improve the process in the future and also will give managers an incentive to be more realistic in preparing capital expenditure proposals.

12. **c.** A project should be accepted if its internal rate of return exceeds the company's required rate of return, not (a) zero, (b) the rate of return on a government bond, or (d) the rate the company pays on borrowed funds.

13. **d.** (€60,000 ÷ €15,400) equals 3.8961, which corresponds with approximately 9% in Table 4 of Appendix A, not (a) 5%, (b) 10%, or (c) 4%.

14. **d.** The time value of money is not considered when applying the annual rate of return method. The other choices are correct statements.

15. **a.** A$15,000 ÷ [(A$120,000 + A$20,000) ÷ 2] = 21%, not (b) 15%, (c) 30%, or (d) 39%.

Practice Exercises

Calculate payback period and internal rate of return, and apply decision rules.

1. (LO 1, 4) Witty Enterprises wants to purchase a new machine for €30,000. Installation costs are €1,500. The old machine was bought five years ago and had an expected economic life of 10 years without salvage value. This old machine now has a book value of €2,000, and Witty Enterprises expects to sell it for that amount. The new machine would decrease operating costs by €8,000 each year of its economic life. The straight-line depreciation method would be used for the new machine, for a five-year period with no salvage value.

Instructions

a. Determine the cash payback period.

b. Determine the approximate internal rate of return.

c. Assuming the company has a required rate of return of 10%, state your conclusion on whether the new machine should be purchased.

Solution

1. a. Total net investment = €30,000 + €1,500 − €2,000 = €29,500

   Annual net cash flow = €8,000

   Payback period = €29,500 ÷ €8,000 = 3.7 years

   b. Net present value approximates zero when discount rate is 11%.

Item	Amount	Years	PV Factor	Present Value
Net annual cash flows	€8,000	1–5	3.69590	€29,567
Less: Capital investment				29,500
Net present value				€ 67

   c. Because the approximate internal rate of return of 11% exceeds the required rate of return of 10%, the investment should be accepted.

2. (LO 1, 2, 5) BTS Ltd. is reviewing an investment proposal. The initial cost is £105,000. Estimates of the book value of the investment at the end of each year, the net cash flows for each year, and the net income for each year are presented in the schedule below. All cash flows are assumed to take place at the end of the year. The salvage value of the investment at the end of each year is equal to its book value. There would be no salvage value at the end of the investment's life.

Calculate payback, annual rate of return, and net present value

Investment Proposal

Year	Book Value	Annual Cash Flows	Annual Net Income
1	£70,000	£45,000	£16,000
2	42,000	40,000	18,000
3	21,000	35,000	20,000
4	7,000	30,000	22,000
5	0	25,000	24,000

BTS Ltd. uses a 15% target rate of return for new investment proposals.

Instructions

a. What is the cash payback period for this proposal?
b. What is the annual rate of return for the investment?
c. What is the net present value of the investment?

Solution

2. a.

	Year	Amount	Balance
Initial investment	0	£(105,000)	£(105,000)
Less: Cash flow	1	45,000	(60,000)
	2	40,000	(20,000)
	3	35,000	15,000

Payback period = 2 + (£20,000 ÷ £35,000) = 2.57 years

b. Average annual net income = (£16,000 + £18,000 + £20,000 + £22,000 + £24,000) ÷ 5 = £20,000

Average investment = (£105,000 + £0) ÷ 2 = £52,500

Annual rate of return = £20,000 ÷ £52,500 = 38.10%

c.

	Year	Discount Factor, 15%	×	Amount	=	Present Value
Net cash flows	1	0.86957		£45,000		£ 39,131
	2	0.75614		40,000		30,246
	3	0.65752		35,000		23,013
	4	0.57175		30,000		17,153
	5	0.49718		25,000		12,430

Present value of cash inflows	121,973
Less: Initial investment	105,000
Net present value	£ 16,973

Practice Problem

(LO 1, 2, 5) Sienna Company is considering a long-term capital investment project in laser equipment. This will require an investment of A$280,000, and it will have a useful life of five years. Annual net income is expected to be A$16,000 a year. Depreciation is computed by the straight-line method with no salvage value. The company's cost of capital is 10%, and it desires a cash payback of 60% of a project's useful life or less. (*Hint:* Assume cash flows can be computed by adding back depreciation expense.)

Compute annual rate of return, cash payback, and net present value.

Instructions

(Round all computations to two decimal places unless directed otherwise.)

a. Compute the cash payback period for the project.
b. Compute the net present value for the project. (Round to nearest dollar.)
c. Compute the annual rate of return for the project.
d. Should the project be accepted? Why or why not?

Solution

a. A$280,000 ÷ A$72,000 (A$16,000 + A$56,000) = 3.89 years

b.

		Present Value at 10%
Discount factor for five payments		3.79079
Present value of net cash flows:		
A$72,000 × 3.79079		A$272,937
Less: Capital investment		280,000
Negative net present value		A$ (7,063)

c. A$16,000 ÷ A$140,000 (A$280,000 ÷ 2) = 11.4%

d. The annual rate of return of 11.4% is reasonable. However, the cash payback period is 78% of the project's useful life, and net present value is negative. The recommendation is to reject the project.

Questions

1. Describe the process a company may use in screening and approving the capital expenditure budget.

2. What are the advantages and disadvantages of the cash payback technique?

3. Ethan Wills claims the equation for the cash payback technique is the same as the equation for the annual rate of return technique. Is Ethan correct? What is the equation for the cash payback technique?

4. Two types of present value tables may be used with the discounted cash flow techniques. Identify the tables and the circumstance(s) when each table should be used.

5. What is the decision rule under the net present value method?

6. Discuss the factors that determine the appropriate discount rate to use when calculating the net present value.

7. What simplifying assumptions were made in the chapter regarding the calculation of net present value?

8. What are some examples of potential intangible benefits of investment proposals? Why do these intangible benefits complicate the capital budgeting evaluation process? What might happen if intangible benefits are ignored in a capital budgeting decision?

9. What steps can be taken to incorporate intangible benefits into the capital budget evaluation process?

10. What advantages does the profitability index provide over direct comparison of net present value when comparing two projects?

11. What is a post-audit? What are the potential benefits of a post-audit?

12. Identify the steps required in using the internal rate of return method when the net annual cash flows are equal.

13. Sato Medical uses the internal rate of return method. What is the decision rule for this method?

14. What are the strengths of the annual rate of return approach? What are its weaknesses?

15. Your classmate, Ahana Nath, is confused about the factors that are included in the annual rate of return technique. What is the equation for this technique?

16. Sveta Pace is trying to understand the term "cost of capital." Define the term and indicate its relevance to the decision rule under the internal rate of return technique.

Brief Exercises

Compute the cash payback period for a capital investment.

BE12.1 (LO 1), AP Hsung Industries is considering purchasing new equipment for HK$4,500,000. It is expected that the equipment will produce net annual cash flows of HK$600,000 over its 10-year useful life. Annual depreciation will be HK$450,000. Compute the cash payback period.

Compute net present value of an investment.

BE12.2 (LO 2), AN Hamza A.S. accumulates the following data concerning a proposed capital investment: cash cost ₺2,150,000, net annual cash flows ₺400,000, and present value factor of cash inflows for 10 years 5.65 (rounded). Determine the net present value, and indicate whether the investment should be made.

Compute net present value of an investment.

BE12.3 (LO 2), AP Huang Capital, an amusement park, is considering a capital investment in a new exhibit. The exhibit would cost NT$1,360,000 and have an estimated useful life of five years. It can be sold for NT$600,000 at the end of that time. (Amusement parks need to rotate exhibits to keep people interested.) It is expected to increase net annual cash flows by NT$250,000. The company's borrowing rate is 8%. Its cost of capital is 10%. Calculate the net present value of this project to the company.

Compute net present value of an investment and consider intangible benefits.

BE12.4 (LO 2, 3), AN City Corporation is considering the purchase of a new bottling machine. The machine would cost A$200,000 and has an estimated useful life of eight years with zero salvage value. Management estimates that the new bottling machine will provide net annual cash flows of A$34,000.

Management also believes that the new bottling machine will save the company money because it is expected to be more reliable than other machines, and thus will reduce downtime. How much would the reduction in downtime have to be worth in order for the project to be acceptable? Assume a discount rate of 9%. (*Hint:* Calculate the net present value.)

BE12.5 (LO 2, 3), AN Viera plc is considering two different, mutually exclusive capital expenditure proposals. Project A will cost £400,000, has an expected useful life of 10 years and a salvage value of zero, and is expected to increase net annual cash flows by £70,000. Project B will cost £310,000, has an expected useful life of 10 years and a salvage value of zero, and is expected to increase net annual cash flows by £55,000. A discount rate of 9% is appropriate for both projects. Compute the net present value and profitability index of each project. Which project should be accepted?

Compute net present value and profitability index.

BE12.6 (LO 3), AN Baichun Group is performing a post-audit of a project completed one year ago. The initial estimates were that the project would cost ₩250,000,000, would have a useful life of nine years and zero salvage value, and would result in net annual cash flows of ₩46,000,000 per year. Now that the investment has been in operation for 1 year, revised figures indicate that it actually cost ₩260,000,000, will have a total useful life of 11 years (including the year just completed), and will produce net annual cash flows of ₩39,000,000 per year. Evaluate the success of the project. Assume a discount rate of 10%.

Perform a post-audit.

BE12.7 (LO 4), AP Adolfus Group is evaluating the purchase of a rebuilt spot-welding machine to be used in the manufacture of a new product. The machine will cost CHF176,000, has an estimated useful life of seven years and a salvage value of zero, and will increase net annual cash flows by CHF35,000. What is its approximate internal rate of return?

Calculate internal rate of return.

BE12.8 (LO 4), AN Jingga Industries is considering investing in a new facility. The estimated cost of the facility is Rp20,450,000,000. It will be used for 12 years, then sold for Rp7,160,000,000. The facility will generate annual cash inflows of Rp4,000,000,000 and will need new annual cash outflows of Rp1,500,000,000. The company has a required rate of return of 7%. Calculate the internal rate of return on this project, and discuss whether the project should be accepted.

Calculate internal rate of return.

BE12.9 (LO 5), AP Swift Oil Company is considering investing in a new oil well. It is expected that the oil well will increase annual revenues by $130,000 and will increase annual expenses by $70,000 including depreciation. The oil well will cost $490,000 and will have a $10,000 salvage value at the end of its 10-year useful life. Calculate the annual rate of return.

Compute annual rate of return.

DO IT! Exercises

DO IT! 12.1 (LO 1), AP Yuet Ltd. is considering a long-term investment project called ZIP. ZIP will require an investment of HK$1,400,000. It will have a useful life of four years and no salvage value. Annual cash inflows would increase by HK$800,000, and annual cash outflows would increase by HK$400,000. Compute the cash payback period.

Compute the cash payback period for an investment.

DO IT! 12.2 (LO 2), AN Yuet Ltd. is considering a long-term investment project called ZIP. ZIP will require an investment of HK$1,200,000. It will have a useful life of four years and no salvage value. Annual cash inflows would increase by HK$800,000, and annual cash outflows would increase by HK$400,000. The company's required rate of return is 12%. Calculate the net present value on this project and discuss whether it should be accepted.

Calculate net present value of an investment.

DO IT! 12.3 (LO 3), AP New Energy Corporation has decided to invest in renewable energy sources to meet part of its energy needs for production. It is considering solar power versus wind power. After considering cost savings as well as incremental revenues from selling excess electricity into the power grid, it has determined the following:

Compute profitability index.

	Solar	Wind
Present value of annual cash flows	A$52,580	A$128,450
Capital investment	A$39,500	A$105,300

Determine the net present value and profitability index of each project. Which energy source should it choose?

DO IT! 12.4 (LO 4), AN Yuet Ltd. is considering a long-term investment project called ZIP. ZIP will require an investment of HK$1,200,000. It will have a useful life of four years and no salvage value. Annual cash inflows would increase by HK$800,000, and annual cash outflows would increase by HK$400,000. The company's required rate of return is 12%. Calculate the internal rate of return on this project and discuss whether it should be accepted.

Calculate internal rate of return.

Calculate annual rate of return.

DO IT! 12.5 (LO 5), AP Yuet Ltd. is considering a long-term investment project called ZIP. ZIP will require an investment of HK$1,200,000. It will have a useful life of four years and no salvage value. Annual revenues would increase by HK$800,000, and annual expenses (excluding depreciation) would increase by HK$410,000. Yuet uses the straight-line method to compute depreciation expense. The company's required rate of return is 12%. Compute the annual rate of return.

Exercises

Compute cash payback and net present value.

E12.1 (LO 1, 2), AN Linkin Corporation is considering purchasing a new delivery truck. The truck has many advantages over the company's current truck (not the least of which is that it runs). The new truck would cost A$56,000. Because of the increased capacity, reduced maintenance costs, and increased fuel economy, the new truck is expected to generate cost savings of A$8,000. At the end of eight years, the company will sell the truck for an estimated A$27,000. Traditionally the company has used a rule of thumb that a proposal should not be accepted unless it has a payback period that is less than 50% of the asset's estimated useful life. Larry Newton, a new manager, has suggested that the company should not rely solely on the payback approach, but should also employ the net present value method when evaluating new projects. The company's cost of capital is 8%.

Instructions

a. Compute the cash payback period and net present value of the proposed investment.

b. Does the project meet the company's cash payback criteria? Does it meet the net present value criteria for acceptance? Discuss your results.

Compute cash payback period and net present value.

E12.2 (LO 1, 2), AN Hifang Construction Ltd. is considering three new projects, each requiring an equipment investment of NT$220,000. Each project will last for three years and produce the following net annual cash flows:

Year	AA	BB	CC
1	NT$ 70,000	NT$100,000	NT$130,000
2	90,000	100,000	120,000
3	120,000	100,000	110,000
Total	NT$280,000	NT$300,000	NT$360,000

The equipment's salvage value is zero, and Hifang uses straight-line depreciation. Hifang will not accept any project with a cash payback period over two years. Hifang's required rate of return is 12%.

Instructions

a. Compute each project's payback period, indicating the most desirable project and the least desirable project using this method. (Round to two decimals and assume in your computations that cash flows occur evenly throughout the year.)

b. Compute the net present value of each project. Does your evaluation change? (Round to nearest dollar.)

Calculate net present value and apply decision rule.

E12.3 (LO 2), AN Alpine Clothing manufactures snowsuits. Alpine is considering purchasing a new sewing machine at a cost of €2.45 million. Its existing machine was purchased five years ago at a price of €1.8 million; six months ago, Alpine spent €55,000 to keep it operational. The existing sewing machine can be sold today for €250,000. The new sewing machine would require a one-time, €85,000 training cost. Operating costs would decrease by the following amounts for years 1 to 7:

Year	
1	€390,000
2	400,000
3	411,000
4	426,000
5	434,000
6	435,000
7	436,000

The new sewing machine would be depreciated according to the declining-balance method at a rate of 20%. The salvage value is expected to be €400,000. This new equipment would require maintenance costs of €100,000 at the end of the fifth year. The cost of capital is 9%.

Instructions

Compute cash payback period and annual rate of return.

Use the net present value method to determine whether Alpine should purchase the new machine to replace the existing machine, and state the reason for your conclusion.

E12.4 (LO 2, 3), AN Oleg Medical is considering purchasing one of two new diagnostic machines. Either machine would make it possible for the company to bid on jobs that it currently isn't equipped to do. Estimates regarding each machine are provided here.

Compute net present value and profitability index.

	Machine A	Machine B
Original cost	R$755,000	R$1,800,000
Estimated life	8 years	8 years
Salvage value	-0-	-0-
Estimated annual cash inflows	R$200,000	R$400,000
Estimated annual cash outflows	R$50,000	R$100,000

Instructions

Calculate the net present value and profitability index of each machine. Assume a 9% discount rate. Which machine should be purchased?

E12.5 (LO 4), AN Kohima Ltd. is involved in the business of injection molding of plastics. It is considering the purchase of a new computer-aided design and manufacturing machine for ₹43,000,000. The company believes that with this new machine it will improve productivity and increase quality, resulting in an increase in net annual cash flows of ₹10,100,000 for the next six years. Management requires a 10% rate of return on all new investments.

Determine internal rate of return.

Instructions

Calculate the internal rate of return on this new machine. Should the investment be accepted?

E12.6 (LO 1, 4), AN Diego's Custom Construction wants to purchase a new machine for €29,300, excluding €1,500 of installation costs. The old machine was purchased five years ago and had an expected economic life of 10 years with no salvage value. The old machine has a book value of €2,000, and Diego expects to sell it for that amount. The new machine will decrease operating costs by €7,000 each year of its economic life. The straight-line depreciation method will be used for the new machine for a six-year period with no salvage value.

Calculate cash payback period and internal rate of return, and apply decision rules.

Instructions

a. Determine the cash payback period.
b. Determine the approximate internal rate of return.
c. Assuming the company has a required rate of return of 10%, state your conclusion on whether the new machine should be purchased.

E12.7 (LO 4), AN Desmond Company is considering three capital expenditure projects. Relevant data for the projects are as follows:

Determine internal rate of return.

Project	Investment	Annual Net Income	Life of Project
22A	S$240,000	S$15,500	6 years
23A	270,000	20,600	9 years
24A	280,000	15,700	7 years

Annual net income is constant over the life of the project. Each project is expected to have zero salvage value at the end of the project. Desmond Company uses the straight-line method of depreciation.

Instructions

a. Determine the internal rate of return for each project. Round the internal rate of return factor to three decimals.
b. If Desmond Company's required rate of return is 10%, which projects are acceptable?

E12.8 (LO 5), AP **Service** Altan's Hair Salon is considering opening a new location. The cost of building a new salon is ₺3,000,000. A new salon will normally generate annual revenues of ₺700,000, with annual expenses (including depreciation) of ₺415,000. At the end of 15 years, the salon will have a salvage value of ₺800,000.

Calculate annual rate of return.

Instructions

Calculate the annual rate of return on the project.

E12.9 (LO 1, 5), AP **Service** Legend Service Center just purchased an automobile hoist for R324,000. The hoist has an eight-year life and an estimated salvage value of R30,000. Installation costs and freight charges were R33,000 and R7,000, respectively. Legend uses straight-line depreciation.

The new hoist will be used to replace mufflers and tires on automobiles. Legend estimates that the new hoist will enable its mechanics to replace five extra mufflers per week. Each muffler sells for R720 installed. The cost of a muffler is R360, and the labor cost to install a muffler is R160.

Instructions

a. Compute the cash payback period for the new hoist.

b. Compute the annual rate of return for the new hoist. (Round to one decimal.)

Compute annual rate of return, cash payback period, and net present value.

E12.10 (LO 1, 2, 5), AP Denzel Company is considering a capital investment of $190,000 in additional productive facilities. The new machinery is expected to have a useful life of five years with no salvage value. Depreciation is by the straight-line method. During the life of the investment, annual net income and net annual cash flows are expected to be $12,000 and $50,000, respectively. Denzel has a 12% cost of capital rate, which is the required rate of return on the investment.

Instructions

(Round to two decimals.)

a. Compute (1) the cash payback period and (2) the annual rate of return on the proposed capital expenditure.

b. Using the discounted cash flow technique, compute the net present value.

Calculate payback, annual rate of return, and net present value.

E12.11 (LO 1, 2, 5), AP Sapporo Enterprises is reviewing an investment proposal. The initial cost is ¥10,500,000. Estimates of the book value of the investment at the end of each year, the net cash flows for each year, and the net income for each year are presented in the following schedule. All cash flows are assumed to take place at the end of the year. The salvage value of the investment at the end of each year is assumed to equal its book value. There would be no salvage value at the end of the investment's life.

Investment Proposal

Year	Book Value	Annual Cash Flows	Annual Net Income
1	¥7,000,000	¥4,500,000	¥1,000,000
2	4,200,000	4,000,000	1,200,000
3	2,100,000	3,500,000	1,400,000
4	700,000	3,000,000	1,600,000
5	0	2,500,000	1,800,000

Sapporo Enterprises uses an 11% target rate of return for new investment proposals.

Instructions

a. What is the cash payback period for this proposal?

b. What is the annual rate of return for the investment?

c. What is the net present value of the investment?

Problems

Compute annual rate of return, cash payback, and net present value.

P12.1 (LO 1, 2, 5), AN T3 Tools is considering three long-term capital investment proposals. Each investment has a useful life of five years. Relevant data on each project are as follows:

	Project Bono	Project Edge	Project Clayton
Capital investment	€160,000	€175,000	€200,000
Annual net income:			
Year 1	14,000	18,000	27,000
2	14,000	17,000	23,000
3	14,000	16,000	21,000
4	14,000	12,000	13,000
5	14,000	9,000	12,000
Total	€ 70,000	€ 72,000	€ 96,000

Depreciation is computed by the straight-line method with no salvage value. The company's cost of capital is 15%. (Assume that cash flows occur evenly throughout the year.)

Instructions

a. Compute the cash payback period for each project. (Round to two decimals.)

b. Compute the net present value for each project. (Round to nearest euro.)

c. Compute the annual rate of return for each project. (Round to two decimals.) (*Hint:* Use average annual net income in your computation.)

d. Rank the projects on each of the foregoing bases. Which project do you recommend?

b. E €(7,312); C €2,163

P12.2 (LO 1, 2, 5), AN `Service` `Writing` Lon Timur is an accounting major at a state university located approximately 60 miles from a major city. Many of the students attending the university are from the metropolitan area and visit their homes regularly on the weekends. Lon, an entrepreneur at heart, realizes that few good commuting alternatives are available for students doing weekend travel. He believes that a weekend commuting service could be organized and run profitably from several suburban and downtown shopping mall locations. Lon has gathered the following investment information.

Compute annual rate of return, cash payback, and net present value.

1. Five used vans would cost a total of $75,000 to purchase and would have a three-year useful life with negligible salvage value. Lon plans to use straight-line depreciation.

2. Ten drivers would have to be employed at a total payroll expense of $48,000.

3. Other annual out-of-pocket expenses associated with running the commuter service would include gasoline $16,000, maintenance $3,300, repairs $4,000, insurance $4,200, and advertising $2,500.

4. Lon has visited several financial institutions to discuss funding. The best interest rate he has been able to negotiate is 15%. Use this rate for cost of capital.

5. Lon expects each van to make 10 round trips weekly and carry an average of six students each trip. The service is expected to operate 30 weeks each year, and each student will be charged $12.00 for a round-trip ticket.

Instructions

a. Determine the annual (1) net income and (2) net annual cash flows for the commuter service.

b. Compute (1) the cash payback period and (2) the annual rate of return. (Round to two decimals.)

c. Compute the net present value of the commuter service. (Round to the nearest dollar.)

d. What should Lon conclude from these computations?

a. (1) $5,000

b. (1) 2.5 years

P12.3 (LO 2, 3, 4), AN `Service` Joel Clinic is considering investing in new heart-monitoring equipment. It has two options. Option A would have an initial lower cost but would require a significant expenditure for rebuilding after four years. Option B would require no rebuilding expenditure, but its maintenance costs would be higher. Since the Option B machine is of initial higher quality, it is expected to have a salvage value at the end of its useful life. The following estimates were made of the cash flows. The company's cost of capital is 8%.

Compute net present value, profitability index, and internal rate of return.

	Option A	Option B
Initial cost	CHF160,000	CHF227,000
Annual cash inflows	CHF71,000	CHF80,000
Annual cash outflows	CHF30,000	CHF31,000
Cost to rebuild (end of year 4)	CHF50,000	CHF0
Salvage value	CHF0	CHF8,000
Estimated useful life	7 years	7 years

Instructions

a. Compute the (1) net present value, (2) profitability index, and (3) internal rate of return for each option. (*Hint:* To solve for internal rate of return, experiment with alternative discount rates to arrive at a net present value of zero.)

b. Which option should be accepted?

a. (1) NPV A CHF16,709
(3) IRR B 12%

P12.4 (LO 2, 3), E `Service` Xiao's Auto Care is considering the purchase of a new tow truck. The garage doesn't currently have a tow truck, and the HK$600,000 price tag for a new truck would represent a major expenditure. Xiao Chan, owner of the garage, has compiled the following estimates in trying to determine whether the tow truck should be purchased.

Compute net present value considering intangible benefits.

Initial cost	HK$600,000
Estimated useful life	8 years
Net annual cash flows from towing	HK$80,000
Overhaul costs (end of year 4)	HK$60,000
Salvage value	HK$120,000

Xiao's good friend, Kai Tang, stopped by. He is trying to convince Xiao that the tow truck will have other benefits that Xiao hasn't even considered. First, he says, cars that need towing need to be fixed. Thus, when Xiao tows them to his facility, his repair revenues will increase. Second, he notes that the tow truck could have a plow mounted on it, thus saving Xiao the cost of plowing his parking lot. (Kai will give him a used plow blade for free if Xiao will plow Kai's driveway.) Third, he notes that the truck will generate goodwill; people who are rescued by Xiao's tow truck will feel grateful and might be more inclined to use his service station in the future or buy gas there. Fourth, the tow truck will have "Xiao's Auto Care" on its doors, hood, and back tailgate—a form of free advertising wherever the tow truck goes. Kai estimates that, at a minimum, these benefits would be worth the following:

Additional annual net cash flows from repair work	HK$30,000
Annual savings from plowing	7,500
Additional annual net cash flows from customer "goodwill"	10,000
Additional annual net cash flows resulting from free advertising	7,500

The company's cost of capital is 9%.

Instructions

a. NPV HK$(139,500)

a. Calculate the net present value, ignoring the additional benefits described by Kai. Should the tow truck be purchased?

b. NPV HK$164,910

b. Calculate the net present value, incorporating the additional benefits suggested by Kai. Should the tow truck be purchased?

c. Suppose Kai has been overly optimistic in his assessment of the value of the additional benefits. At a minimum, how much would the additional benefits have to be worth in order for the project to be accepted?

Compute net present value and internal rate of return with sensitivity analysis.

P12.5 (LO 2, 3, 4), E Service SummerPlay Camps is thinking about opening a soccer camp. To start the camp, SummerPlay would need to purchase land and build four soccer fields and a sleeping and dining facility to house 150 soccer players. Each year, the camp would be run for eight sessions of one week each. The company would hire college soccer players as coaches. The camp attendees would be male and female soccer players ages 12–18. Property values in the area have enjoyed a steady increase in value. It is expected that after using the facility for 20 years, SummerPlay can sell the property for more than it was originally purchased for. The following amounts have been estimated.

Cost of land	€300,000
Cost to build soccer fields, dorm, and dining facility	€600,000
Annual cash inflows assuming 150 players and 8 weeks	€920,000
Annual cash outflows	€840,000
Estimated useful life	20 years
Salvage value	€1,500,000
Discount rate	8%

Instructions

a. NPV €207,277

a. Calculate the net present value of the project.

b. To gauge the sensitivity of the project to these estimates, assume that if only 125 players attend each week, annual cash inflows will be €805,000 and annual cash outflows will be €750,000. What is the net present value using these alternative estimates? Discuss your findings.

c. Assuming the original facts, what is the net present value if the project is actually riskier than first assumed and a 10% discount rate is more appropriate?

d. IRR 12%

d. Assume that during the first five years, the annual net cash flows each year were only €40,000. At the end of the fifth year, the company is running low on cash, so management decides to sell the property for €1,332,000. What was the actual internal rate of return on the project? Explain how this return was possible given that the camp did not appear to be successful.

Continuing Case

Current Designs

CD12 A company that manufactures recreational pedal boats has approached Mike Cichanowski to ask if he would be interested in using **Current Designs'** (USA) rotomold expertise and equipment to produce some of the pedal boat components. Mike is intrigued by the idea and thinks it would be an interesting way of complementing the present product line.

One of Mike's hesitations about the proposal is that the pedal boats are a different shape than the kayaks that Current Designs produces. As a result, the company would need to buy an additional roto-mold oven in order to produce the pedal boat components. This project clearly involves risks, and Mike wants to make sure that the returns justify the risks. In this case, since this is a new venture, Mike thinks that a 15% discount rate is appropriate to use to evaluate the project.

As an intern at Current Designs, Mike has asked you to prepare an initial evaluation of this proposal. To aid in your analysis, he has provided the following information and assumptions.

1. The new rotomold oven will have a cost of $256,000, a salvage value of $0, and an eight-year useful life. Straight-line depreciation will be used.

2. The projected revenues, costs, and results for each of the eight years of this project are as follows:

Sales		$220,000
Less:		
Manufacturing costs	$140,000	
Depreciation	32,000	
Shipping and administrative costs	22,000	194,000
Income before income taxes		26,000
Income tax expense		10,800
Net income		$ 15,200

Instructions

a. Compute the annual rate of return. (Round to two decimal places.)

b. Compute the payback period. (Round to two decimal places.)

c. Compute the net present value using a discount rate of 9%. (Round to nearest dollar.) Should the proposal be accepted using this discount rate?

d. Compute the net present value using a discount rate of 15%. (Round to nearest dollar.) Should the proposal be accepted using this discount rate?

Data Analytics in Action

Using Data Visualization for Capital Budgeting Decisions

DA12.1 Data visualization can be used to help analyze investment decisions.

Example: Recall the *People, Planet, and Profit Insight* box "Big Spenders" presented in the chapter. However, not all upgrades to clean energy need to be quite so large. For example, consider the following chart, which shows an investment in solar panels for a factory in Australia. The chart shows that the company will recover its solar-panel investment during 2025, during the investment's sixth year of its expected 16-year life. With an estimate of $0.12 per kilowatt hour, the annual savings will be around $6,500.

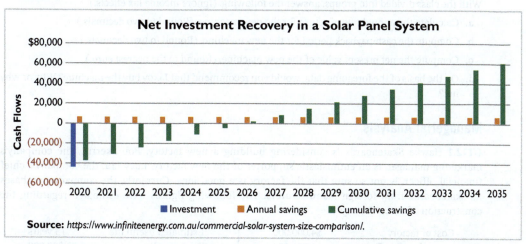

Source: https://www.infiniteenergy.com.au/commercial-solar-system-size-comparison/.

For this case, you will create line charts to analyze the present value of the solar-panel investment at different rates of return. You will also consider what other sensitivity analyses might be used with the data provided.

Go to the book's product page on www.wiley.com for complete case details and instructions.

Data Analytics at HydroHappy

DA12.2 HydroHappy's management believes the net present value (NPV) method provides the best information to make capital budgeting decisions. NPV analysis indicates that purchasing new forklifts will result in a higher return than retaining and overhauling the old forklifts. For this case, you will create and analyze clustered column and bar charts that will help management easily visualize which new forklift model will provide the best option for the company.

Go to the book's product page on www.wiley.com for complete case details and instructions.

Expand Your Critical Thinking

Decision-Making Across the Organization

CT12.1 Jakov Textiles is considering the purchase of a new machine. Its invoice price is €122,000, freight charges are estimated to be €3,000, and installation costs are expected to be €5,000. Salvage value of the new machine is expected to be zero after a useful life of four years. Existing equipment could be retained and used for an additional four years if the new machine is not purchased. At that time, the salvage value of the equipment would be zero. If the new machine is purchased now, the existing machine would be scrapped. Jakov's accountant, Marta Babic, has accumulated the following data regarding annual sales and expenses with and without the new machine.

1. Without the new machine, Jakov can sell 10,000 units of product annually at a per unit selling price of €100. If the new unit is purchased, the number of units produced and sold would increase by 25%, and the selling price would remain the same.

2. The new machine is faster than the old machine, and it is more efficient in its usage of materials. With the old machine, the gross profit rate will be 28.5% of sales, whereas the rate will be 30% of sales with the new machine. (*Note*: These gross profit rates do not include depreciation on the machines. For purposes of determining net income, treat depreciation expense as a separate line item.)

3. Annual selling expenses are €160,000 with the current equipment. Because the new equipment would produce a greater number of units to be sold, annual selling expenses are expected to increase by 10% if it is purchased.

4. Annual administrative expenses are expected to be €100,000 with the old machine, and €112,000 with the new machine.

5. The current book value of the existing machine is €40,000. Jakov uses straight-line depreciation.

6. Jakov's management has a required rate of return of 15% on its investment and a cash payback period of no more than three years.

Instructions

With the class divided into groups, answer the following. (Ignore income tax effects.)

a. Calculate the annual rate of return for the new machine. (Round to two decimals.)
b. Compute the cash payback period for the new machine. (Round to two decimals.)
c. Compute the net present value of the new machine. (Round to the nearest euro.)
d. On the basis of the foregoing data, would you recommend that Jakov buy the machine? Why or why not?

Managerial Analysis

CT12.2 Hawke Skateboards is considering building a new factory. Bob Skerritt, the company's marketing manager, is an enthusiastic supporter of the new factory. Lucy Liu, the company's chief financial officer, is not so sure that the factory is a good idea. Currently, the company purchases its skateboards from foreign manufacturers. The following figures were estimated regarding the construction of a new factory.

Cost of factory	$4,000,000		Estimated useful life	15 years
Annual cash inflows	4,000,000		Salvage value	$2,000,000
Annual cash outflows	3,540,000		Discount rate	11%

Bob Skerritt believes that these figures understate the true potential value of the factory. He suggests that by manufacturing its own skateboards the company will benefit from a "buy American" patriotism that he believes is common among skateboarders. He also notes that the firm has had numerous quality problems with the skateboards manufactured by its suppliers. He suggests that the inconsistent quality has resulted in lost sales, increased warranty claims, and some costly lawsuits. Overall, he believes sales will be $200,000 higher than projected above, and that the savings from lower warranty costs and legal costs will be $60,000 per year. He also believes that the project is not as risky as assumed above, and that a 9% discount rate is more reasonable.

Instructions

Complete the following:

a. Compute the net present value of the project based on the original projections.

b. Compute the net present value incorporating Bob's estimates of the value of the intangible benefits, but still using the 11% discount rate.

c. Compute the net present value using the original estimates, but employing the 9% discount rate that Bob suggests is more appropriate.

d. Comment on your findings.

Real-World Focus

CT12.3 Tecumseh Products Company (USA) has its headquarters in Ann Arbor, Michigan. It describes itself as "a global multinational corporation producing mechanical and electrical components essential to industries creating end-products for health, comfort, and convenience." The following was excerpted from the management discussion and analysis section of a recent annual report.

> **Tecumseh Products Company**
> **Management Discussion and Analysis**
>
> The company has invested approximately $50 million in a scroll compressor manufacturing facility in Tecumseh, Michigan. After experiencing setbacks in developing a commercially acceptable scroll compressor, the Company is currently testing a new generation of scroll product. The Company is unable to predict when, or if, it will offer a scroll compressor for commercial sale, but it does anticipate that reaching volume production will require a significant additional investment. Given such additional investment and current market conditions, management is currently reviewing its options with respect to scroll product improvement, cost reductions, joint ventures, and alternative new products.

Instructions

Discuss issues the company should consider and techniques the company should employ to determine whether to continue pursuing this project.

CT12.4 Campbell Soup Company (USA) is an international provider of soup products. Management is very interested in continuing to grow the company in its core business, while "spinning off" those businesses that are not part of its core operation.

Instructions

Go to the home page of Campbell Soup Company and access its current annual report. Review the financial statements and management's discussion and analysis, and answer the following questions:

a. What was the total amount of capital expenditures in the current year, and how does this amount compare with the previous year? In your response, note what year you are using.

b. What interest rate did the company pay on new borrowings in the current year?

c. Assume that this year's capital expenditures are expected to increase cash flows by $60 million. What is the expected internal rate of return (IRR) for these capital expenditures? (Assume a 10-year period for the cash flows.)

Communication Activity

CT12.5 Refer to E12.9 to address the following:

Instructions

Prepare a memo to Pari Raman, your supervisor. Show your calculations from E12.9 (a) and (b). In one or two paragraphs, discuss important nonfinancial considerations. Make any assumptions you believe to be necessary. Make a recommendation based on your analysis.

Ethics Case

CT12.6 NuComp Company operates in a state in the United States where corporate taxes and workers' compensation insurance rates have recently doubled. NuComp's president has just assigned you the task of preparing an economic analysis and making a recommendation relative to moving the entire operation to Missouri. The president is slightly in favor of such a move because Missouri is his boyhood home and he also owns a fishing lodge there.

You have just completed building your dream house, moved in, and sodded the lawn. Your children are all doing well in school and sports and, along with your spouse, want no part of a move to Missouri. If the company does move, so will you because the town is a one-industry community and you and your spouse will have to move to have employment. Moving when everyone else does will cause you to take a big loss on the sale of your house. The same hardships will be suffered by your coworkers, and the town will be devastated.

In compiling the costs of moving versus not moving, you have latitude in the assumptions you make, the estimates you compute, and the discount rates and time periods you project. You are in a position to influence the decision singlehandedly.

Instructions

a. Who are the stakeholders in this situation?

b. What are the ethical issues in this situation?

c. What would you do in this situation?

All About You

CT12.7 Numerous articles have been written that identify early warning signs that you might be getting into trouble with your personal debt load. You can find many good articles on this topic on the Web.

Instructions

Find an article that identifies early warning signs of personal debt trouble. Write a summary of the article and bring your summary and the article to class to share.

Considering Your Costs and Benefits

CT12.8 The March 31, 2011, edition of the *Wall Street Journal* included an article by Russell Gold entitled "Solar Gains Traction—Thanks to Subsidies."

Instructions

Read the article and then answer the following questions:

a. What was the total cost of the solar panels installed? What was the "out-of-pocket" cost to the couple?

b. Using the total annual electricity bill of $5,000 mentioned in the story, what is the cash payback of the project using the total cost? What is the cash payback based on the "out-of-pocket" cost?

c. Solar panel manufacturers estimate that solar panels can last up to 40 years with only minor maintenance costs. Assuming no maintenance costs, a 6% rate of interest, a more conservative 20-year life, and zero salvage value, what is the net present value of the project based on the total cost? What is the net present value of the project based on the "out-of-pocket" cost?

d. What was the wholesale price of panels per watt at the time the article was written? At what price per watt does the article say that subsidies will no longer be needed? Does this price appear to be achievable?

CHAPTER 13

Statement of Cash Flows

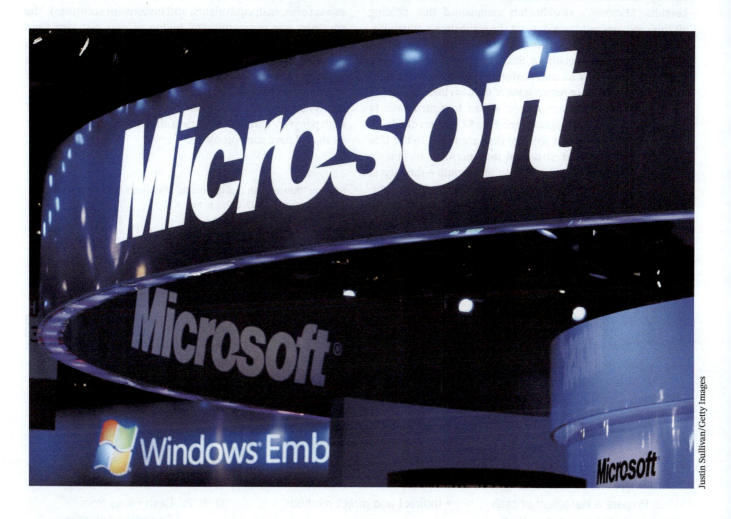

CHAPTER PREVIEW

The balance sheet, income statement, and retained earnings statement do not always show the whole picture of the financial condition of a company or institution. In fact, looking at the financial statements of some well-known companies, a thoughtful investor might ask questions like these: How did **Eastman Kodak** (USA) finance cash dividends of $649 million in a year in which it earned only $17 million? How could **United Air Lines** (USA) purchase new planes that cost $1.9 billion in a year in which it reported a net loss of over $2 billion? How did the companies that spent a combined fantastic $4.1 trillion on mergers and acquisitions in a recent year finance those deals? Answers to these and similar questions can be found in this chapter, which presents the statement of cash flows.

FEATURE STORY

Got Cash?

Companies must be ready to respond to changes quickly in order to survive and thrive. This requires careful management of cash. One company that managed cash successfully in its early years was **Microsoft** (USA). During those years, the company paid much of its payroll with stock options (rights to purchase company stock in the future at a given price) instead of cash. This conserved cash and turned more than a thousand of its employees into millionaires.

Eventually, Microsoft had a different kind of cash problem. It reached a more "mature" stage in life, generating so much cash—roughly $1 billion per month—that it could not always figure out what to do with it. At one time, Microsoft had accumulated $60 billion.

The company said it was accumulating cash to invest in new opportunities, buy other companies, and pay off pending lawsuits. Microsoft's stockholders complained that holding all this cash was putting a drag on the company's profitability. Why? Because Microsoft had the cash invested in very low-yielding government securities. Stockholders felt that the company either should find new investment projects that would bring higher returns, or return some of the cash to stockholders.

Finally, Microsoft announced a plan to return cash to stockholders by paying a special one-time $32 billion dividend. This special dividend was so large that, according to the U.S. Commerce Department, it caused total personal income in the United States to rise by 3.7% in one month—the largest increase ever recorded by the agency. (It also made the holiday season brighter, especially for retailers in the Seattle area.)

Microsoft also doubled its regular annual dividend to $3.50 per share. Further, it announced that it would spend another $30 billion buying treasury stock.

Apple (USA) also has encountered this cash "problem." Recently, Apple had approximately $100 billion in liquid assets (cash, cash equivalents, and investment securities). The company was generating $69 billion of cash per year from its operating activities but spending only about $10 billion on plant assets. In response to shareholder pressure, Apple announced that it would begin to pay a quarterly dividend of $2.65 per share and buy back up to $10 billion of its stock. Analysts noted that the dividend consumes only $10 billion of cash per year. This leaves Apple wallowing in cash. The rest of us should have such problems.

Source: "Business: An End to Growth? Microsoft's Cash Bonanza," *The Economist* (July 23, 2005), p. 61.

CHAPTER OUTLINE

Learning Objectives	Review	Practice
LO 1 Discuss the usefulness and format of the statement of cash flows.	• Usefulness of the statement of cash flows • Classification of cash flows • Significant noncash activities • Format of the statement of cash flows	**DO IT! 1** Classification of Cash Flows
LO 2 Prepare a statement of cash flows using the indirect method.	• Indirect and direct methods • Indirect method—Computer Services International • Step 1: Operating activities • Summary of conversion to net cash provided by operating activities • Step 2: Investing and financing activities • Step 3: Net change in cash	**DO IT! 2a** Cash Flows from Operating Activities **DO IT! 2b** Indirect Method
LO 3 Analyze the statement of cash flows.	• Free cash flow	**DO IT! 3** Free Cash Flow

Go to the Review and Practice section at the end of the chapter for a review of key concepts and practice applications with solutions.

STATEMENT OF CASH FLOWS: USEFULNESS AND FORMAT

The balance sheet, income statement, and retained earnings statement provide only limited information about a company's cash flows (cash receipts and cash payments).

- Comparative balance sheets show the net increase in property, plant, and equipment during the year. But, they do not show how the additions were financed or paid for.
- The income statement shows net income based on the accrual basis of accounting. But, it does not indicate the amount of cash generated by operating activities.
- The retained earnings statement shows cash dividends declared but not the cash dividends paid during the year.

None of these statements presents a detailed summary of where cash came from and how it was used (see **Helpful Hint**).

LEARNING OBJECTIVE 1
Discuss the usefulness and format of the statement of cash flows.

HELPFUL HINT
In this chapter, when we refer to cash, we are also including cash equivalents (short-term, highly liquid, very low-risk securities).

Usefulness of the Statement of Cash Flows

The **statement of cash flows** reports the cash receipts, cash payments, and net change in cash resulting from operating, investing, and financing activities during a period. The information in a statement of cash flows helps investors, creditors, and others assess the following:

1. **The entity's ability to generate future cash flows.** By examining relationships between items in the statement of cash flows, investors can better predict the amounts, timing, and uncertainty of future cash flows than they can from accrual-basis data.
2. **The entity's ability to pay dividends and meet obligations.** If a company does not have adequate cash, it cannot pay employees, settle debts, or pay dividends. Employees, creditors, and stockholders should be particularly interested in this statement because it alone shows the flows of cash in a business.
3. **The reasons for the difference between net income and net cash provided (used) by operating activities.** Net income provides information on the success or failure of a business. However, some financial statement users are critical of accrual-basis net income because it requires many estimates (see **Ethics Note**). As a result, users often challenge the reliability of the number. Such is not the case with cash. Many readers of the statement of cash flows want to know the reasons for the difference between net income and net cash provided by operating activities. Then, they can assess for themselves the reliability of the net income number.
4. **The cash investing and financing transactions during the period.** By examining a company's investing and financing transactions, a financial statement reader can better understand why assets and liabilities changed during the period.

ETHICS NOTE
Though we discourage reliance on cash flows to the exclusion of accrual accounting, comparing net cash provided by operating activities to net income can reveal important information about the "quality" of reported net income. Such a comparison can reveal the extent to which net income provides a good measure of actual performance.

Classification of Cash Flows

The statement of cash flows classifies cash receipts and cash payments as operating, investing, and financing activities. Transactions and other events characteristic of each kind of activity are as follows:

1. **Operating activities** include the cash effects of transactions that generate revenues and expenses. They thus enter into the determination of net income.
2. **Investing activities** include (a) acquiring and disposing of investments and property, plant, and equipment, and (b) lending money and collecting the loans.
3. **Financing activities** include (a) obtaining cash from issuing debt and repaying the amounts borrowed, and (b) obtaining cash from stockholders, repurchasing shares, and paying dividends.

The operating activities category is the most important. It shows the cash provided by company operations. This source of cash is generally considered to be the best measure of a company's ability to generate sufficient cash to continue as a going concern.

Illustration 13.1 lists typical cash receipts and cash payments within each of the three classifications. *Study the list carefully; it will prove very useful in solving homework exercises and problems.*

ILLUSTRATION 13.1 | **Typical receipt and payment classifications**

Types of Cash Inflows and Outflows

Operating activities—Income statement items
Cash inflows:
  From sale of goods or services.
  From interest received and dividends received.
Cash outflows:
  To suppliers for inventory.
  To employees for wages.
  To government for taxes.
  To lenders for interest.
  To others for expenses.

Investing activities—Changes in investments and long-term assets
Cash inflows:
  From sale of property, plant, and equipment.
  From sale of investments in debt or equity securities of other entities.
  From collection of principal on loans to other entities.
Cash outflows:
  To purchase property, plant, and equipment.
  To purchase investments in debt or equity securities of other entities.
  To make loans to other entities.

Financing activities—Changes in long-term liabilities and stockholders' equity
Cash inflows:
  From sale of common and preferred stock.
  From issuance of debt (bonds and notes).
Cash outflows:
  To stockholders as dividends.
  To redeem long-term debt or reacquire capital stock (treasury stock).

Note the following general guidelines:

1. Operating activities involve income statement items.
2. Investing activities involve cash flows resulting from changes in investments and long-term asset items.
3. Financing activities involve cash flows resulting from changes in long-term liability and stockholders' equity items.

Companies classify as operating activities some cash flows related to investing or financing activities. For example, receipts of investment revenue (interest and dividends) are classified as operating activities. So are payments of interest to lenders. Why are these considered operating activities? **Because companies report these items in the income statement, where results of operations are shown.**

Significant Noncash Activities

Not all of a company's significant activities involve cash. Examples of significant noncash activities are as follows:

1. Direct issuance of common stock to purchase assets.
2. Conversion of bonds into common stock.

3. Direct issuance of debt to purchase assets.
4. Exchanges of plant assets.

Companies do not report in the body of the statement of cash flows significant financing and investing activities that do not affect cash. Instead, they report these activities in either a **separate schedule** at the bottom of the statement of cash flows or in a **separate note or supplementary schedule** to the financial statements (see **Helpful Hint**). The reporting of these noncash activities in a separate schedule satisfies the **full disclosure principle**.

In solving homework assignments, you should present significant noncash investing and financing activities in a separate schedule at the bottom of the statement of cash flows (see the last item in Illustration 13.2 below).

> **HELPFUL HINT**
> Do not include noncash investing and financing activities in the body of the statement of cash flows. Report this information in a separate schedule.

ACCOUNTING ACROSS THE ORGANIZATION   Nestle

Net What?

Net income is not the same as net cash provided by operating activities. The table shows some results from recent annual reports of FMCG companies operating in Europe (FY 2022, currency in millions), including Nestle A.G. Note how the numbers differ greatly across the list even though all these companies engage in FMCG sector.

Company	Net Income	Net Cash Provided by Operating Activities
Unilever plc (GBR)	€8,269	€10,755
Reckitt and Benckiser A.G. (GBR)	£2,330	£3,249
Nestle A.G. (CHE)	CHF9,270	CHF11,907
L'Oréal SA (FRA)	€6,054	€7,456
Associated British Foods plc (GBR)	£700	£1,457

In general, why do differences exist between net income and net cash provided by operating activities? (Answer is available in the book's product page on www.wiley.com)

Format of the Statement of Cash Flows

The general format of the statement of cash flows presents the results of the three activities discussed previously—operating, investing, and financing—plus the significant noncash investing and financing activities. **Illustration 13.2** shows a widely used form of the statement of cash flows.

Company Name		
Statement of Cash Flows		
For the Period Covered		
Cash flows from operating activities		
(List of individual items)	XX	
Net cash provided (used) by operating activities		XXX
Cash flows from investing activities		
(List of individual inflows and outflows)	XX	
Net cash provided (used) by investing activities		XXX
Cash flows from financing activities		
(List of individual inflows and outflows)	XX	
Net cash provided (used) by financing activities		XXX
Net increase (decrease) in cash		XXX
Cash at beginning of period		XXX
Cash at end of period		XXX
Noncash investing and financing activities		
(List of individual noncash transactions)		XXX

ILLUSTRATION 13.2 | **Format of statement of cash flows**

- The cash flows from operating activities section always appears first, followed by the investing activities section and then the financing activities section.
- The sum of the operating, investing, and financing sections equals the net increase or decrease in cash for the period.
- This amount is added to the beginning cash balance to arrive at the ending cash balance—the same amount reported on the balance sheet.

The IFRS requires that an entity disclose the components of cash and cash equivalents and present a reconciliation of the amounts in its statement of cash flows with the equivalent items reported in the statement of financial position.

DO IT! 1 ▶ Classification of Cash Flows

During its first week, Schmidt & Martin Company had these transactions:

1. Issued 100,000 shares of common stock at par for €800,000 cash.
2. Borrowed €200,000 from Castle Bank, signing a five-year note bearing 8% interest.
3. Purchased two semi-trailer trucks for €170,000 cash.
4. Paid employees €12,000 for salaries and wages.
5. Collected €20,000 cash for services performed.

Classify each of these transactions by type of cash flow activity. (*Hint:* Refer to Illustration 13.1.)

Solution

1. Financing activity.
2. Financing activity.
3. Investing activity.
4. Operating activity.
5. Operating activity.

Related exercise material: **BE13.1, BE13.2, BE13.3, DO IT! 13.1, E13.1, E13.2, and E13.3.**

ACTION PLAN
- Identify the three types of activities used to report all cash inflows and outflows.
- Report as operating activities the cash effects of transactions that generate revenues and expenses and enter into the determination of net income.
- Report as investing activities transactions that (a) acquire and dispose of investments and long-term assets and (b) lend money and collect loans.
- Report as financing activities transactions that (a) obtain cash from issuing debt and repay the amounts borrowed and (b) obtain cash from stockholders and pay them dividends.

PREPARING THE STATEMENT OF CASH FLOWS—INDIRECT METHOD

LEARNING OBJECTIVE 2
Prepare a statement of cash flows using the indirect method.

Companies prepare the statement of cash flows differently from the three other basic financial statements. First, it is not prepared from an adjusted trial balance. It requires detailed information concerning the changes in account balances that occurred between two points in time. An adjusted trial balance will not provide the necessary data. Second, the statement of cash flows deals with cash receipts and payments. As a result, the company **adjusts** the effects of the use of accrual accounting **to determine cash flows**.

The information to prepare this statement usually comes from three sources:

- **Comparative balance sheets.** Information in the comparative balance sheets indicates the amount of the changes in assets, liabilities, and stockholders' equity from the beginning to the end of the period.
- **Current income statement.** Information in this statement helps determine the amount of net cash provided or used by operating activities during the period.

- **Additional information.** Such information includes transaction data that are needed to determine how cash was provided or used during the period.

Preparing the statement of cash flows from these data sources involves three major steps, explained in **Illustration 13.3**.

Step 1: Determine net cash provided/used by operating activities by converting net income from an accrual basis to a cash basis.

This step involves analyzing not only the current year's income statement but also comparative balance sheets and selected additional data.

Step 2: Analyze changes in noncurrent asset and liability accounts and stockholders' equity accounts and report as investing and financing activities, or disclose as noncash transactions.

This step involves analyzing comparative balance sheet data and selected additional information for their effects on cash.

Step 3: Compare the net change in cash on the statement of cash flows with the change in the Cash account reported on the balance sheet to make sure the amounts agree.

The difference between the beginning and ending cash balances can be easily computed from comparative balance sheets.

ILLUSTRATION 13.3 | Three major steps in preparing the statement of cash flows

Indirect and Direct Methods

In order to perform Step 1, a company **must convert net income from an accrual basis to a cash basis**. This conversion may be done by either of two methods: (1) the indirect method or (2) the direct method. **Both methods arrive at the same amount** for "Net cash provided by operating activities." They differ in **how** they arrive at the amount.

- The **indirect method** adjusts net income for items that do not affect cash. A great majority of companies (98%) use this method. Companies favor the indirect method for two reasons:
    1. It is easier and less costly to prepare.
    2. It focuses on the differences between net income and net cash flow from operating activities.
- The **direct method** shows operating cash receipts and payments. It is prepared by adjusting each item in the income statement from the accrual basis to the cash basis.

The IASB has expressed a preference for the direct method but allows the use of either method.

The next section illustrates the more popular indirect method. Appendix 13A illustrates the direct method.

Indirect Method—Computer Services International

To explain how to prepare a statement of cash flows using the indirect method, we use financial information from Computer Services International. **Illustration 13.4** presents Computer Services' current- and previous-year balance sheets, its current-year income statement, and related financial information for the current year.

Computer Services International
Comparative Balance Sheets
December 31

	2023	2022	Change in Account Balance Increase/Decrease
Assets			
Current assets			
Cash	€ 55,000	€ 33,000	€ 22,000 Increase
Accounts receivable	20,000	30,000	10,000 Decrease
Inventory	15,000	10,000	5,000 Increase
Prepaid expenses	5,000	1,000	4,000 Increase
Property, plant, and equipment			
Land	130,000	20,000	110,000 Increase
Buildings	160,000	40,000	120,000 Increase
Accumulated depreciation—buildings	(11,000)	(5,000)	6,000 Increase
Equipment	27,000	10,000	17,000 Increase
Accumulated depreciation—equipment	(3,000)	(1,000)	2,000 Increase
Total assets	€398,000	€138,000	
Liabilities and Stockholders' Equity			
Current liabilities			
Accounts payable	€ 28,000	€ 12,000	€ 16,000 Increase
Income taxes payable	6,000	8,000	2,000 Decrease
Long-term liabilities			
Bonds payable	130,000	20,000	110,000 Increase
Stockholders' equity			
Common stock	70,000	50,000	20,000 Increase
Retained earnings	164,000	48,000	116,000 Increase
Total liabilities and stockholders' equity	€398,000	€138,000	

Computer Services International
Income Statement
For the Year Ended December 31, 2023

Sales revenue		€507,000
Cost of goods sold	€150,000	
Operating expenses (excluding depreciation)	111,000	
Depreciation expense	9,000	
Loss on disposal of plant assets	3,000	
Interest expense	42,000	315,000
Income before income tax		192,000
Income tax expense		47,000
Net income		€145,000

Additional information for 2023:
1. Depreciation expense was comprised of €6,000 for building and €3,000 for equipment.
2. The company sold equipment with a book value of €7,000 (cost €8,000, less accumulated depreciation €1,000) for €4,000 cash.
3. Issued €110,000 of long-term bonds in direct exchange for land.
4. A building costing €120,000 was purchased for cash. Equipment costing €25,000 was also purchased for cash.
5. Issued common stock at par for €20,000 cash.
6. The company declared and paid a €29,000 cash dividend.

ILLUSTRATION 13.4 | **Comparative balance sheets, income statement, and additional information for Computer Services International**

We now apply the three steps for preparing a statement of cash flows to the information provided for Computer Services International.

Step 1: Operating Activities

Determine Net Cash Provided/Used by Operating Activities by Converting Net Income from an Accrual Basis to a Cash Basis

To determine net cash provided by operating activities under the indirect method, companies **adjust net income in numerous ways**. A useful starting point is to understand **why** net income must be converted to net cash provided by operating activities.

Under IFRS, most companies use the accrual basis of accounting.

- This basis requires that companies record revenue when a performance obligation is satisfied and record expenses when incurred.
- Revenues include credit sales for which the company has not yet collected cash.
- Expenses incurred include some items that have not yet been paid in cash.

Thus, under the accrual basis, net income is not the same as net cash provided by operating activities.

Therefore, under the **indirect method**, companies must adjust net income to convert certain items to the cash basis. The indirect method (or reconciliation method) starts with net income and converts it to net cash provided by operating activities. **Illustration 13.5** lists the three types of adjustments.

Net Income	+/−	Adjustments	=	Net Cash Provided/Used by Operating Activities
		• **Add back noncash expenses**, such as depreciation expense and amortization expense.		
		• **Deduct gains and add losses** that resulted from investing and financing activities.		
		• **Analyze changes** to noncash current asset and current liability accounts.		

ILLUSTRATION 13.5 | Three types of adjustments to convert net income to net cash provided by operating activities

We explain the three types of adjustments in the next three sections.

Depreciation Expense

Computer Services' income statement reports depreciation expense of €9,000.

- Although depreciation expense reduces net income, it does not reduce cash. In other words, depreciation expense is a noncash charge.
- The company must add it back to net income to negate the effect of the expense to arrive at net cash provided by operating activities (see **Helpful Hint**).

Computer Services reports depreciation expense in the statement of cash flows as in **Illustration 13.6**.

Cash flows from operating activities	
Net income	€145,000
Adjustments to reconcile net income to net cash provided by operating activities:	
Depreciation expense	9,000
Net cash provided by operating activities	€154,000

ILLUSTRATION 13.6 | Adjustment for depreciation

Companies frequently list depreciation and similar noncash charges, such as amortization of intangible assets and bad debt expense, as the first adjustment to net income in the statement of cash flows.

> **HELPFUL HINT**
> Depreciation is similar to any other expense in that it reduces net income. It differs in that it does not involve a current cash outflow. That is why it must be *added back* to net income to arrive at net cash provided by operating activities.

Loss on Disposal of Plant Assets

Illustration 13.1 states that cash received from the sale (disposal) of plant assets is reported in the investing activities section. Because of this, **companies eliminate from net income all gains and losses related to the disposal of plant assets, to arrive at net cash provided by operating activities.**

In our example, Computer Services' income statement reports a €3,000 loss on the disposal of plant assets (book value €7,000, less €4,000 cash received from disposal of plant assets). The journal entry to record this transaction would have been as follows:

Cash	4,000	
Accumulated Depreciation—Equipment	1,000	
Loss on Disposal of Plant Assets	3,000	
Equipment		8,000

- The company's loss of €3,000 should be added to net income in order to determine net cash provided by operating activities.
- The loss reduced net income but did not reduce cash.

Illustration 13.7 shows that the €3,000 loss is eliminated by adding €3,000 back to net income to arrive at net cash provided by operating activities. (The cash received of €4,000 will be reported in the investing activities section, as discussed later.)

Cash flows from operating activities		
Net income		€145,000
Adjustments to reconcile net income to net cash provided by operating activities:		
Depreciation expense	€9,000	
Loss on disposal of plant assets	**3,000**	12,000
Net cash provided by operating activities		€157,000

ILLUSTRATION 13.7 | **Adjustment for loss on disposal of plant assets**

- If a gain on disposal occurs, the company deducts the gain from net income in order to determine net cash provided by operating activities.
- **In the case of either a gain or a loss, companies report the actual amount of cash received from the sale in the investing activities section of the statement of cash flows.**

Changes to Noncash Current Asset and Current Liability Accounts

A final adjustment in reconciling net income to net cash provided by operating activities involves examining all changes in current asset and current liability accounts. The accrual-accounting process records revenues in the period in which the performance obligation is satisfied and expenses as incurred.

- Accounts Receivable reflects amounts owed to the company for sales that have been made but for which cash collections have not yet been received.
- Prepaid Insurance reflects insurance that has been paid for but has not yet expired (therefore has not been expensed).
- Salaries and Wages Payable reflects salaries and wages expense that has been incurred but has not been paid.

As a result, companies need to adjust net income for these accruals and prepayments to determine net cash provided by operating activities. Thus, they must analyze the change in each current asset and current liability account to determine its impact on net income and cash.

Changes in Noncash Current Assets The adjustments required for changes in noncash current asset accounts are as follows: **Deduct from net income increases in current asset accounts, and add to net income decreases in current asset accounts, to arrive at net cash provided by operating activities.** We observe these relationships by analyzing the accounts of Computer Services.

Decrease in Accounts Receivable Computer Services' accounts receivable decreased by €10,000 (from €30,000 to €20,000) during the period. For Computer Services, this means that cash receipts were €10,000 higher than sales revenue. The Accounts Receivable account in **Illustration 13.8** shows that Computer Services had €507,000 in sales revenue (as reported on the income statement), but it collected €517,000 in cash.

		Accounts Receivable		
1/1/23	Balance	30,000	Receipts from customers	517,000
	Sales revenue	507,000		
12/31/23	Balance	20,000		

ILLUSTRATION 13.8 | **Analysis of accounts receivable**

As shown in Illustration 13.9, to adjust net income to net cash provided by operating activities, the company **adds** to net income the decrease of €10,000 in accounts receivable.

- When the Accounts Receivable balance increases, cash receipts are lower than sales revenue earned under the accrual basis.
- Therefore, the company **deducts** from net income the amount of the increase in accounts receivable, to arrive at net cash provided by operating activities.

Increase in Inventory Computer Services' inventory increased €5,000 (from €10,000 to €15,000) during the period. The change in the Inventory account reflects the difference between the amount of inventory purchased and the cost of inventory sold. For Computer Services, this means that the cost of merchandise purchased exceeded the cost of goods sold by €5,000.

- As a result, cost of goods sold does not reflect €5,000 of cash payments made for merchandise.
- The company **deducts** from net income this inventory increase of €5,000 during the period, to arrive at net cash provided by operating activities (see Illustration 13.9).
- If inventory decreases, the company **adds** to net income the amount of the change, to arrive at net cash provided by operating activities.

Increase in Prepaid Expenses Computer Services' prepaid expenses increased during the period by €4,000. This means that cash paid for prepaid expenses is greater than the actual expenses reported on an accrual basis.

- In other words, the company has made cash payments in the current period that will not be charged to expenses until future periods.
- To adjust net income to net cash provided by operating activities, the company **deducts** from net income the €4,000 increase in prepaid expenses (see **Illustration 13.9**).

Cash flows from operating activities		
Net income		€145,000
Adjustments to reconcile net income to net cash provided by operating activities:		
Depreciation expense	€ 9,000	
Loss on disposal of plant assets	3,000	
Decrease in accounts receivable	10,000	
Increase in inventory	(5,000)	
Increase in prepaid expenses	(4,000)	13,000
Net cash provided by operating activities		€158,000

ILLUSTRATION 13.9 | **Adjustments for changes in current asset accounts**

If prepaid expenses decrease, reported expenses are greater than the expenses paid. Therefore, the company **adds** to net income the decrease in prepaid expenses, to arrive at net cash provided by operating activities.

Changes in Current Liabilities The adjustments required for changes in current liability accounts are as follows: **Add to net income increases in current liability accounts and deduct from net income decreases in current liability accounts, to arrive at net cash provided by operating activities.**

Increase in Accounts Payable For Computer Services, Accounts Payable increased by €16,000 (from €12,000 to €28,000) during the period.

- That means the company received €16,000 more in goods than it actually paid for.
- As shown in **Illustration 13.10**, to adjust net income to determine net cash provided by operating activities, the company adds to net income the €16,000 increase in Accounts Payable.

Decrease in Income Taxes Payable When a company incurs income tax expense but has not yet paid its taxes, it records income taxes payable. A change in the Income Taxes Payable account reflects the difference between income tax expense incurred and income tax actually paid. Computer Services' Income Taxes Payable account decreased by €2,000.

- That means the €47,000 of income tax expense reported on the income statement was €2,000 less than the amount of taxes paid during the period of €49,000.
- As shown in Illustration 13.10, to adjust net income to a cash basis, the company must reduce net income by €2,000.

Illustration 13.10 shows that after starting with net income of €145,000, the sum of all of the adjustments to net income was €27,000. This resulted in net cash provided by operating activities of €172,000.

Cash flows from operating activities		
Net income		€145,000
Adjustments to reconcile net income to net cash provided by operating activities:		
Depreciation expense	€ 9,000	
Loss on disposal of plant assets	3,000	
Decrease in accounts receivable	10,000	
Increase in inventory	(5,000)	
Increase in prepaid expenses	(4,000)	
Increase in accounts payable	**16,000**	
Decrease in income taxes payable	**(2,000)**	27,000
Net cash provided by operating activities		€172,000

ILLUSTRATION 13.10 | **Adjustments for changes in current liability accounts**

Summary of Conversion to Net Cash Provided by Operating Activities—Indirect Method

As shown in the previous illustrations, the statement of cash flows prepared by the indirect method starts with net income. It then adds or deducts items to arrive at net cash provided by operating activities. The required adjustments are of three types:

1. Noncash charges such as depreciation and amortization.
2. Gains and losses on the disposal of plant assets.
3. Changes in noncash current asset and current liability accounts.

Illustration 13.11 provides a summary of these changes and required adjustments.

		Adjustments Required to Convert Net Income to Net Cash Provided by Operating Activities
Noncash Charges	Depreciation expense	Add
	Amortization expense	Add
Gains and Losses	Loss on disposal of plant assets	Add
	Gain on disposal of plant assets	Deduct
Changes in Current Assets and Current Liabilities	Increase in noncash current asset account	Deduct
	Decrease in noncash current asset account	Add
	Increase in current liability account	Add
	Decrease in current liability account	Deduct

ILLUSTRATION 13.11 | **Adjustments required to convert net income to net cash provided by operating activities**

ANATOMY OF A FRAUD

On June 15, 2022, **Allianz Australia Insurance Limited** (AUS) and **AWP Australia** (AUS) (which marketed and sold policies) pleaded guilty to seven criminal charges of misleading and fraudulent conduct.

Background

Three companies Allianz, AWP, and **Expedia** (USA) entered into a comprehensive agreement and a set of local arrangements to offer insurance products on Expedia's websites. Allianz and AWP were accused of mis-selling domestic and international travel insurance products between 2016 and 2018 and terminated their relationships with Expedia to minimize the penalties and consequences.

Violations

Premium calculation. Allianz/AWP misled customers by giving the impression of a customized insurance product. Only the cost and duration of the journey determined the insurance cost.

Journey criterion. The regulatory disclosure and website content stated that the insured journey must start or end in Australia. The companies needed to ensure Expedia's websites had a mechanism to prevent ineligible customers from purchasing insurance.

Age criterion. The regulatory disclosure says a maximum age limit of 61 for insurance coverage. Allianz/AWP should have monitored Expedia websites to ensure a checkbox confirming the full age was included.

Smart traveler. Customers had three options during the insurance booking process—cancellation, essentials, and opt-out. The Expedia website opt-out option displayed a statement misquoting the Department of Foreign Affairs Smart Traveler website. The misquotation wrongly suggested that travel insurance was as essential as a passport, even for policies that didn't cover hospital or medical expenses.

The above violations highlight that the main concern and catalysts were the actions of Allianz, AWP, and Expedia when interacting with customers in Australia. Australian Securities and Investment Commission collected A$10 million from Allianz to compensate more than 31,500 customers who were mis-sold the travel insurance. Australian court fined Allianz and AWP A$1.5 million for selling travel insurance to ineligible customers and not disclosing how premiums were calculated.

Source: https://www.wfw.com/articles/australian-civil-and-criminal-convictions-for-online-travel-insurance-products-what-do-you-need-to-know/ (accessed June 30, 2023).

DO IT! 2a ▶ Cash Flows from Operating Activities

Ivanov's PhotoPlus reported net income of €73,000 for 2023. Included in the income statement were depreciation expense of €7,000 and a gain on disposal of plant assets of €2,500. Ivanov's comparative balance sheets show the following balances:

	12/31/22	12/31/23
Accounts receivable	€17,000	€21,000
Accounts payable	6,000	2,200

Calculate net cash provided by operating activities for Ivanov's PhotoPlus.

Solution

Cash flows from operating activities		
Net income		€73,000
Adjustments to reconcile net income to net cash provided by operating activities:		
Depreciation expense	€ 7,000	
Gain on disposal of plant assets	(2,500)	
Increase in accounts receivable	(4,000)	
Decrease in accounts payable	(3,800)	(3,300)
Net cash provided by operating activities		€69,700

Related exercise material: **BE13.4, BE13.5, BE13.6, DO IT! 13.2a, E13.4, E13.5, E13.6, and E13.7.**

ACTION PLAN

- Add noncash charges such as depreciation back to net income to compute net cash provided by operating activities.
- Deduct from net income gains on the disposal of plant assets, or add losses back to net income, to compute net cash provided by operating activities.
- Use changes in noncash current asset and current liability accounts to compute net cash provided by operating activities.

Step 2: Investing and Financing Activities

Analyze Changes in Noncurrent Asset and Liability Accounts and Stockholders' Equity Accounts and Report as Investing and Financing Activities, or as Noncash Investing and Financing Activities

Increase in Land As indicated from the change in the Land account and the additional information, Computer Services purchased land for €110,000. This activity is generally classified as an investing activity. However, by directly exchanging bonds for land, the issuance of bonds payable for land has no effect on cash. But, it is a significant noncash investing and financing activity that merits disclosure in a separate schedule (see Illustration 13.14).

Increase in Buildings As the additional data indicate, Computer Services acquired an office building for €120,000 cash. This is a cash outflow reported in the investing activities section (see Illustration 13.14).

Increase in Equipment The Equipment account increased €17,000. The additional information explains that this net increase resulted from two transactions: (1) a purchase of equipment for €25,000, and (2) the sale for €4,000 of equipment costing €8,000. These transactions are investing activities (see **Helpful Hint**). The company should report each transaction separately. Thus, it reports the purchase of equipment as an outflow of cash for €25,000. It reports the sale as an inflow of cash for €4,000. The T-account in **Illustration 13.12** shows the reasons for the change in this account during the year.

> **HELPFUL HINT**
> The investing and financing activities are measured and reported the same way under both the direct and indirect methods.

		Equipment		
1/1/23	Balance	10,000	Cost of equipment sold	8,000
	Purchase of equipment	**25,000**		
12/31/23	Balance	27,000		

ILLUSTRATION 13.12 | Analysis of equipment

The following entry shows the details of the equipment sale transaction.

Cash	4,000	
Accumulated Depreciation—Equipment	1,000	
Loss on Disposal of Plant Assets	3,000	
Equipment		8,000

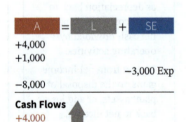

Increase in Bonds Payable The Bonds Payable account increased €110,000. As indicated in the additional information, the company acquired land from the issuance of these bonds. It reports this noncash transaction in a separate schedule at the bottom of the statement.

> **HELPFUL HINT**
> When companies issue stocks or bonds for cash, the actual proceeds will appear in the statement of cash flows as a financing inflow (rather than the par value of the stocks or face value of bonds).

Increase in Common Stock The balance sheet reports an increase in Common Stock of €20,000. The additional information section notes that this increase resulted from the issuance of new shares of stock for cash at par. This is a cash inflow reported in the financing activities section (see **Helpful Hint**).

Increase in Retained Earnings Retained earnings increased €116,000 during the year. This increase can be explained by two factors: (1) net income of €145,000 increased retained earnings, and (2) dividends declared of €29,000 decreased retained earnings. The company adjusts net income to net cash provided by operating activities in the operating activities section. The T-account shown in **Illustration 13.13** shows the reasons for the change in this account during the year.

Retained Earnings				
Dividends declared	29,000	1/1/23	Balance	48,000
			Net income	145,000
		12/31/23	Balance	164,000

ILLUSTRATION 13.13 | Analysis of retained earnings

Payment of the dividends (not the declaration) is a **cash outflow that the company reports as a financing activity**. Since the balance sheet does not report a Cash Dividends Payable account, the declared cash dividends of €29,000 must have been paid.

Statement of Cash Flows—2023

Using the previous information, we can now prepare a statement of cash flows for 2023 for Computer Services International as shown in **Illustration 13.14** (see **Helpful Hint**).

HELPFUL HINT

Note that in the investing and financing activities sections, positive numbers indicate cash inflows (receipts), and negative numbers indicate cash outflows (payments).

Computer Services International
Statement of Cash Flows—Indirect Method
For the Year Ended December 31, 2023

Cash flows from operating activities		
Net income		€145,000
Adjustments to reconcile net income to net cash provided by operating activities:		
Depreciation expense	€ 9,000	
Loss on disposal of plant assets	3,000	
Decrease in accounts receivable	10,000	
Increase in inventory	(5,000)	
Increase in prepaid expenses	(4,000)	
Increase in accounts payable	16,000	
Decrease in income taxes payable	(2,000)	27,000
Net cash provided by operating activities		172,000
Cash flows from investing activities		
Purchase of building	(120,000)	
Purchase of equipment	(25,000)	
Sale of equipment	4,000	
Net cash used by investing activities		(141,000)
Cash flows from financing activities		
Issuance of common stock	20,000	
Payment of cash dividends	(29,000)	
Net cash used by financing activities		(9,000)
Net increase in cash		22,000
Cash at beginning of period		33,000
Cash at end of period		€ 55,000
Noncash investing and financing activities		
Issuance of bonds payable to purchase land		€110,000

ILLUSTRATION 13.14 | Statement of cash flows, 2023—indirect method

Step 3: Net Change in Cash

Compare the Net Change in Cash on the Statement of Cash Flows with the Change in the Cash Account Reported on the Balance Sheet to Make Sure the Amounts Agree

Illustration 13.14 indicates that the net change in cash during the period was an increase of €22,000. This agrees with the change in Cash account reported on the comparative balance sheets in Illustration 13.4.

DO IT! 2b ▶ Indirect Method

Use the following information to prepare a statement of cash flows using the indirect method.

Horvat SpA
Comparative Balance Sheets
December 31

	2023	2022	Change Increase/Decrease
Assets			
Cash	€ 54,000	€ 37,000	€ 17,000 Increase
Accounts receivable	68,000	26,000	42,000 Increase
Inventory	54,000	–0–	54,000 Increase
Prepaid expenses	4,000	6,000	2,000 Decrease
Land	45,000	70,000	25,000 Decrease
Buildings	200,000	200,000	–0–
Accumulated depreciation—buildings	(21,000)	(11,000)	10,000 Increase
Equipment	193,000	68,000	125,000 Increase
Accumulated depreciation—equipment	(28,000)	(10,000)	18,000 Increase
Totals	€569,000	€386,000	
Liabilities and Stockholders' Equity			
Accounts payable	€ 23,000	€ 40,000	€ 17,000 Decrease
Accrued expenses payable	10,000	–0–	10,000 Increase
Bonds payable	110,000	150,000	40,000 Decrease
Common stock (€1 par)	220,000	60,000	160,000 Increase
Retained earnings	206,000	136,000	70,000 Increase
Totals	€569,000	€386,000	

Horvat SpA
Income Statement
For the Year Ended December 31, 2023

Sales revenue		€890,000
Cost of goods sold	€465,000	
Operating expenses	221,000	
Interest expense	12,000	
Loss on disposal of plant assets	2,000	700,000
Income before income taxes		190,000
Income tax expense		65,000
Net income		€125,000

Additional information:

1. Operating expenses include depreciation expense of €33,000, €10,000 for the building and €23,000 for the equipment.
2. Land was sold at its book value for cash.
3. Cash dividends of €55,000 were declared and paid in 2023.
4. Equipment with a cost of €166,000 was purchased for cash. Equipment with a cost of €41,000 and a book value of €36,000 was sold for €34,000 cash.
5. Bonds of €40,000 were redeemed at their face value for cash.
6. Common stock (€1 par) was issued at par for €160,000 cash.

ACTION PLAN

- Determine net cash provided/used by operating activities by adjusting net income for items that did not affect cash.
- Determine net cash provided/used by investing activities and financing activities.
- Determine the net increase/decrease in cash.

Solution

Horvat SpA
Statement of Cash Flows—Indirect Method
For the Year Ended December 31, 2023

Cash flows from operating activities		
Net income		€ 125,000
Adjustments to reconcile net income to net cash provided by operating activities:		
Depreciation expense	€ 33,000	
Loss on disposal of plant assets	2,000	
Increase in accounts receivable	(42,000)	
Increase in inventory	(54,000)	
Decrease in prepaid expenses	2,000	
Decrease in accounts payable	(17,000)	
Increase in accrued expenses payable	10,000	(66,000)
Net cash provided by operating activities		59,000
Cash flows from investing activities		
Sale of land	25,000	
Sale of equipment	34,000	
Purchase of equipment	(166,000)	
Net cash used by investing activities		(107,000)
Cash flows from financing activities		
Redemption of bonds	(40,000)	
Issuance of common stock	160,000	
Payment of cash dividends	(55,000)	
Net cash provided by financing activities		65,000
Net increase in cash		17,000
Cash at beginning of period		37,000
Cash at end of period		€ 54,000

Related exercise material: **BE13.4, BE13.5, BE13.6, BE13.7, DO IT! 13.2b, E13.4, E13.5, E13.6, E13.7, E13.8, and E13.9.**

ANALYZING THE STATEMENT OF CASH FLOWS

Traditionally, investors and creditors used ratios based on accrual accounting. These days, cash-based ratios are gaining increased acceptance among analysts.

LEARNING OBJECTIVE 3
Analyze the statement of cash flows.

Free Cash Flow

In the statement of cash flows, net cash provided by operating activities is intended to indicate the cash-generating capability of a company. Analysts have noted, however, that **net cash provided by operating activities fails to take into account that a company must invest in new fixed assets** just to maintain its current level of operations. Companies also must at least **maintain dividends at current levels** to satisfy investors.

DECISION TOOLS

Free cash flow helps users determine the amount of cash the company generated to expand operations or pay dividends.

- The measurement of free cash flow provides additional insight regarding a company's cash-generating ability.
- **Free cash flow** describes the net cash provided by operating activities after adjustment for capital expenditures and dividends (see **Decision Tools**).

Consider the following example. Suppose that MPC produced and sold 10,000 personal computers this year. It reported €100,000 net cash provided by operating activities. In order to maintain production at 10,000 computers, MPC invested €15,000 in equipment. It chose to pay €5,000 in dividends. Its free cash flow was €80,000 (€100,000 − €15,000 − €5,000). The company could use this €80,000 either to purchase new assets to expand the business or to pay an €80,000 dividend and continue to produce 10,000 computers. In practice, free cash flow is often calculated with the equation in **Illustration 13.15**. (Alternative definitions also exist.)

| Free Cash Flow | = | Net Cash Provided by Operating Activities | − | Capital Expenditures | − | Cash Dividends |

ILLUSTRATION 13.15 | **Free cash flow**

Illustration 13.16 provides basic information excerpted from the 2019 statement of cash flows of **Apple Inc.** (USA).

Real World

Apple Inc.
Statement of Cash Flows (partial)
2019

Net cash provided by operating activities	$69,391
Cash flows from investing activities	
Purchases of marketable securities	$(39,630)
Proceeds from maturities of marketable securities	40,102
Proceeds from sales of marketable securities	56,988
Payments for acquisition of property, plant, and equipment	(10,495)
Payment made in connection with business acquisitions, net	(624)
Purchases of non-marketable securities	(1,001)
Proceeds from non-marketable securities	1,634
Other	(1,078)
Cash generated by/(used in) investing activities	$45,896
Cash paid for dividends	$(14,119)

ILLUSTRATION 13.16 | **Apple's cash flow information ($ in millions)**

Apple's free cash flow is calculated as shown in **Illustration 13.17** (in millions). Apple generated approximately $45 billion of free cash flow. This is a significant amount of cash generated in a single year. It is available for the acquisition of new assets, the buyback and retirement of stock or debt, or the payment of dividends.

Net cash provided by operating activities	$69,391
Less: Expenditures on property, plant, and equipment	10,495
Dividends paid	14,119
Free cash flow	$44,777

ILLUSTRATION 13.17 | **Calculation of Apple's free cash flow ($ in millions)**

Apple's cash from operations of $69.4 billion exceeds its 2019 net income of $55.3 billion by $14.1 billion. This lends additional credibility to Apple's income number as an indicator of potential future performance. If anything, Apple's net income might understate its actual performance.

DO IT! 3 ▶ Free Cash Flow

Budapest Corporation issued the following statement of cash flows for 2023.

Budapest Corporation
Statement of Cash Flows—Indirect Method
For the Year Ended December 31, 2023

Cash flows from operating activities		
Net income		€ 19,000
Adjustments to reconcile net income to net cash provided by operating activities:		
Depreciation expense	€ 8,100	
Loss on disposal of plant assets	1,300	
Decrease in accounts receivable	6,900	
Increase in inventory	(4,000)	
Decrease in accounts payable	(2,000)	10,300
Net cash provided by operating activities		29,300
Cash flows from investing activities		
Sale of investments	1,100	
Purchase of equipment	(19,000)	
Net cash used by investing activities		(17,900)
Cash flows from financing activities		
Issuance of common stock	10,000	
Payment on long-term note payable	(5,000)	
Payment of cash dividends	(9,000)	
Net cash used by financing activities		(4,000)
Net increase in cash		7,400
Cash at beginning of year		10,000
Cash at end of year		€ 17,400

ACTION PLAN
- Compute free cash flow as Net cash provided by operating activities − Capital expenditures − Cash dividends.

(a) Compute free cash flow for Budapest Corporation. (b) Explain why free cash flow often provides better information than "Net cash provided by operating activities."

Solution

a. Free cash flow = €29,300 − €19,000 − €9,000 = €1,300

b. Net cash provided by operating activities fails to take into account that a company must invest in new plant assets just to maintain the current level of operations. Companies must also maintain dividends at current levels to satisfy investors. The measurement of free cash flow provides additional insight regarding a company's cash-generating ability.

Related exercise material: **BE13.8, BE13.9, BE13.10, BE13.11, DO IT! 13.3, E13.8, and E13.10.**

> ### USING THE DECISION TOOLS | Intel Corporation
>
> **Intel Corporation** (USA) is the leading producer of computer chips for personal computers. A primary competitor is **Qualcomm** (USA). Financial statement data for Intel are provided below.
>
> **Intel Corporation**
> **Statement of Cash Flows**
> **For the Year Ended December 28, 2019 (in millions)**
>
> | | 2019 |
> |---|---|
> | Net cash provided by operating activities | $ 33,145 |
> | Net cash used for investing activities | (14,405) |
> | Net cash used for financing activities | (17,565) |
> | Net increase (decrease) in cash and cash equivalents | $ 1,175 |
>
> **Note.** Cash spent on property, plant, and equipment in 2019 was $16,213. Cash paid for dividends was $5,576.
>
> #### Instructions
>
> Calculate free cash flow for Intel and compare it with that of Qualcomm ($3,431 million).
>
> #### Solution
>
> Intel's free cash flow is $11,356 million ($33,145 − $16,213 − $5,576). Qualcomm's is $3,431 million. This gives Intel an advantage in the ability to move quickly to invest in new projects.

Appendix 13A   STATEMENT OF CASH FLOWS— DIRECT METHOD

LEARNING OBJECTIVE *4
Prepare a statement of cash flows using the direct method.

To explain and illustrate the direct method for preparing a statement of cash flows, we use the transactions of Computer Services International for 2023. **Illustration 13A.1** presents information related to 2023 for the company.

To prepare a statement of cash flows under the direct method, we apply the three steps outlined in Illustration 13.3 for the indirect method.

Step 1: Operating Activities

Determine Net Cash Provided/Used by Operating Activities by Converting Net Income Components from an Accrual Basis to a Cash Basis

Under the **direct method**, companies compute net cash provided by operating activities by **adjusting each item in the income statement** from the accrual basis to the cash basis.

- To simplify and condense the operating activities section, companies **report only major classes of operating cash receipts and cash payments**.
- For these major classes, the difference between cash receipts and cash payments is the net cash provided by operating activities.

These relationships are as shown in **Illustration 13A.2**.
   An efficient way to apply the direct method is to analyze the items reported in the income statement in the order in which they are listed. We then determine cash receipts and cash payments related to these revenues and expenses. The following presents the adjustments required to prepare a statement of cash flows for Computer Services International using the direct method.

Computer Services International
Comparative Balance Sheets
December 31

Assets	2023	2022	Change in Account Balance Increase/Decrease
Current assets			
Cash	€ 55,000	€ 33,000	€ 22,000 Increase
Accounts receivable	20,000	30,000	10,000 Decrease
Inventory	15,000	10,000	5,000 Increase
Prepaid expenses	5,000	1,000	4,000 Increase
Property, plant, and equipment			
Land	130,000	20,000	110,000 Increase
Buildings	160,000	40,000	120,000 Increase
Accumulated depreciation—buildings	(11,000)	(5,000)	6,000 Increase
Equipment	27,000	10,000	17,000 Increase
Accumulated depreciation—equipment	(3,000)	(1,000)	2,000 Increase
Total assets	€398,000	€138,000	

Liabilities and Stockholders' Equity	2023	2022	Change
Current liabilities			
Accounts payable	€ 28,000	€ 12,000	€ 16,000 Increase
Income taxes payable	6,000	8,000	2,000 Decrease
Long-term liabilities			
Bonds payable	130,000	20,000	110,000 Increase
Stockholders' equity			
Common stock	70,000	50,000	20,000 Increase
Retained earnings	164,000	48,000	116,000 Increase
Total liabilities and stockholders' equity	€398,000	€138,000	

Computer Services International
Income Statement
For the Year Ended December 31, 2023

Sales revenue		€507,000
Cost of goods sold	€150,000	
Operating expenses (excluding depreciation)	111,000	
Depreciation expense	9,000	
Loss on disposal of plant assets	3,000	
Interest expense	42,000	315,000
Income before income tax		192,000
Income tax expense		47,000
Net income		€145,000

Additional information for 2023:

1. Depreciation expense was comprised of €6,000 for building and €3,000 for equipment.
2. The company sold equipment with a book value of €7,000 (cost €8,000, less accumulated depreciation €1,000) for €4,000 cash.
3. Issued €110,000 of long-term bonds in direct exchange for land.
4. A building costing €120,000 was purchased for cash. Equipment costing €25,000 was also purchased for cash.
5. Issued common stock at par for €20,000 cash.
6. The company declared and paid a €29,000 cash dividend.

ILLUSTRATION 13A.1 | Comparative balance sheets, income statement, and additional information for Computer Services International

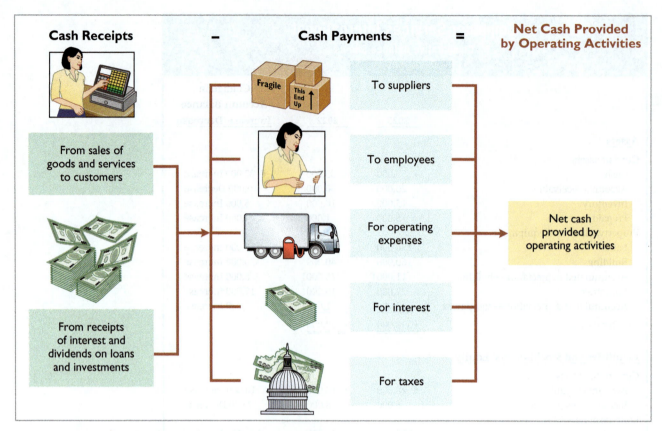

ILLUSTRATION 13A.2 | Major classes of cash receipts and payments

Cash Receipts from Customers The income statement for Computer Services reported sales revenue from customers of €507,000. How much of that was cash receipts? To answer that, a company considers the change in accounts receivable during the year. When accounts receivable increase during the year, revenues on an accrual basis are higher than cash receipts from customers. Operations led to revenues, but not all of those revenues resulted in cash receipts.

- To determine the amount of cash receipts, a company deducts from sales revenue the increase in accounts receivable.
- On the other hand, there may be a decrease in accounts receivable. That would occur if cash receipts from customers exceeded sales revenue. In that case, a company adds to sales revenue the decrease in accounts receivable.

For Computer Services, accounts receivable decreased €10,000. Thus, cash receipts from customers were €517,000, computed as shown in **Illustration 13A.3**.

Sales revenue	€507,000
Add: Decrease in accounts receivable	10,000
Cash receipts from customers	**€517,000**

ILLUSTRATION 13A.3 | Computation of cash receipts from customers

Computer Services can also determine cash receipts from customers from an analysis of the Accounts Receivable account, as shown in **Illustration 13A.4**.

Accounts Receivable				
1/1/23	Balance	30,000	Receipts from customers	517,000
	Sales revenue	507,000		
12/31/23	Balance	20,000		

ILLUSTRATION 13A.4 | Analysis of accounts receivable

Illustration 13A.5 shows the relationships among cash receipts from customers, sales revenue, and changes in accounts receivable (see **Helpful Hint**).

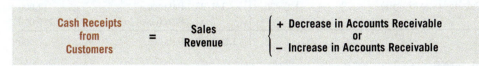

ILLUSTRATION 13A.5 | Equation to compute cash receipts from customers—direct method

HELPFUL HINT

The T-account in Illustration 13A.4 shows that sales revenue plus decrease in accounts receivable equals cash receipts.

Cash Payments to Suppliers Computer Services reported cost of goods sold of €150,000 on its income statement. How much of that was cash payments to suppliers? To answer that, it is first necessary to find purchases for the year.

- To find purchases, a company adjusts cost of goods sold for the change in inventory.
- When inventory increases during the year, purchases for the year have exceeded cost of goods sold.
- As a result, to determine the amount of purchases, a company adds to cost of goods sold the increase in inventory.

In 2023, Computer Services' inventory increased €5,000. It computes purchases as shown in **Illustration 13A.6**.

Cost of goods sold	€150,000
Add: Increase in inventory	5,000
Purchases	**€155,000**

ILLUSTRATION 13A.6 | Computation of purchases

Computer Services can also determine purchases from an analysis of the Inventory account, as shown in **Illustration 13A.7**.

Inventory				
1/1/23	Balance	10,000	Cost of goods sold	150,000
	Purchases	**155,000**		
12/31/23	Balance	15,000		

ILLUSTRATION 13A.7 | Analysis of inventory

After computing purchases, a company can determine cash payments to suppliers. This is done by adjusting purchases for the change in accounts payable. When accounts payable increase during the year, purchases on an accrual basis are higher than they are on a cash basis.

- As a result, to determine cash payments to suppliers, a company deducts from purchases the increase in accounts payable.
- On the other hand, if cash payments to suppliers exceed purchases, there will be a decrease in accounts payable. In that case, a company adds to purchases the decrease in accounts payable.

For Computer Services, cash payments to suppliers were €139,000, computed as shown in **Illustration 13A.8**.

Purchases	€155,000
Deduct: Increase in accounts payable	16,000
Cash payments to suppliers	**€139,000**

ILLUSTRATION 13A.8 | Computation of cash payments to suppliers

Computer Services also can determine cash payments to suppliers from an analysis of the Accounts Payable account, as shown in **Illustration 13A.9**.

Accounts Payable

Payments to suppliers	139,000	1/1/23	Balance	12,000
			Purchases	155,000
		12/31/23	Balance	28,000

ILLUSTRATION 13A.9 | **Analysis of accounts payable**

HELPFUL HINT

The T-account in Illustration 13A.9 shows that purchases less increase in accounts payable equals payments to suppliers.

Illustration 13A.10 shows the relationships among cash payments to suppliers, cost of goods sold, changes in inventory, and changes in accounts payable (see **Helpful Hint**).

Cash Payments to Suppliers	=	Cost of Goods Sold	+ Increase in Inventory or − Decrease in Inventory	+ Decrease in Accounts Payable or − Increase in Accounts Payable

ILLUSTRATION 13A.10 | **Equation to compute cash payments to suppliers—direct method**

Cash Payments for Operating Expenses Computer Services reported on its income statement operating expenses of €111,000. How much of that amount was cash paid for operating expenses? To answer that, we need to adjust this amount for any changes in prepaid expenses and accrued expenses payable.

Adjustments for Prepaid Expenses If prepaid expenses increase during the year, cash paid for operating expenses is higher than operating expenses reported on the income statement.

- To convert operating expenses to cash payments for operating expenses, a company adds the increase in prepaid expenses to operating expenses.
- On the other hand, if prepaid expenses decrease during the year, it deducts the decrease from operating expenses.

Adjustments for Accrued Expenses When accrued expenses payable increase during the year, operating expenses on an accrual basis are higher than they are on a cash basis.

- As a result, to determine cash payments for operating expenses, a company deducts from operating expenses an increase in accrued expenses payable.
- On the other hand, a company adds to operating expenses a decrease in accrued expenses payable because cash payments exceed operating expenses.

Computer Services' cash payments for operating expenses were €115,000, computed as shown in **Illustration 13A.11**.

Operating expenses	€111,000
Add: Increase in prepaid expenses	4,000
Cash payments for operating expenses	**€115,000**

ILLUSTRATION 13A.11 | **Computation of cash payments for operating expenses**

Illustration 13A.12 shows the relationships among cash payments for operating expenses, changes in prepaid expenses, and changes in accrued expenses payable.

Cash Payments for Operating Expenses	=	Operating Expenses	+ Increase in Prepaid Expenses or − Decrease in Prepaid Expenses	+ Decrease in Accrued Expenses Payable or − Increase in Accrued Expenses Payable

ILLUSTRATION 13A.12 | **Equation to compute cash payments for operating expenses—direct method**

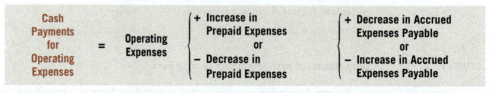

Depreciation Expense and Loss on Disposal of Plant Assets Computer Services' depreciation expense in 2023 was €9,000.

- Depreciation expense is not shown on a statement of cash flows under the direct method because it is a noncash charge.
- If the amount for operating expenses includes depreciation expense, operating expenses must be reduced by the amount of depreciation to determine cash payments for operating expenses.

The loss on disposal of plant assets of €3,000 is also a noncash charge.

- The loss on disposal of plant assets reduces net income, but it does not reduce cash.
- Thus, the loss on disposal of plant assets is not shown on the statement of cash flows under the direct method.

Other charges to expense that do not require the use of cash, such as the amortization of intangible assets and bad debt expense, are treated in the same manner as depreciation.

Cash Payments for Interest Computer Services reported on the income statement interest expense of €42,000. Since the balance sheet did not report interest payable for 2022 or 2023, the amount reported as interest expense is the same as the amount of interest paid.

Cash Payments for Income Taxes Computer Services reported income tax expense of €47,000 on the income statement. Income taxes payable, however, decreased €2,000. This decrease means that income taxes paid were more than income tax expense reported in the income statement. Cash payments for income taxes were therefore €49,000 as shown in **Illustration 13A.13**.

Income tax expense	€47,000
Add: Decrease in income taxes payable	2,000
Cash payments for income taxes	**€49,000**

ILLUSTRATION 13A.13 | Computation of cash payments for income taxes

Computer Services can also determine cash payments for income taxes from an analysis of the Income Taxes Payable account, as shown in **Illustration 13A.14**.

Income Taxes Payable

Cash payments for income taxes	49,000	1/1/23	Balance	8,000
			Income tax expense	47,000
		12/31/23	Balance	6,000

ILLUSTRATION 13A.14 | Analysis of income taxes payable

Illustration 13A.15 shows the relationships among cash payments for income taxes, income tax expense, and changes in income taxes payable.

$$\text{Cash Payments for Income Taxes} = \text{Income Tax Expense} \begin{cases} + \text{ Decrease in Income Taxes Payable} \\ \quad \text{or} \\ - \text{ Increase in Income Taxes Payable} \end{cases}$$

ILLUSTRATION 13A.15 | Equation to compute cash payments for income taxes—direct method

The operating activities section of the statement of cash flows of Computer Services is shown in **Illustration 13A.16**.

Cash flows from operating activities		
Cash receipts from customers		€517,000
Less: Cash payments:		
To suppliers	€139,000	
For operating expenses	115,000	
For interest expense	42,000	
For income taxes	49,000	345,000
Net cash provided by operating activities		€172,000

ILLUSTRATION 13A.16 | Operating activities section of the statement of cash flows

When a company uses the direct method, it must also provide in a **separate schedule** (not shown here) the net cash flows from operating activities as computed under the indirect method. Note that whether a company uses the indirect or direct method, the net cash provided by operating activities is the same.

Step 2: Investing and Financing Activities

Analyze Changes in Noncurrent Asset and Liability Accounts and Stockholders' Equity Accounts and Record as Investing and Financing Activities, or Disclose as Noncash Transactions

Increase in Land As indicated from the change in the Land account and the additional information, Computer Services purchased land for €110,000 by directly exchanging bonds for the land. The exchange of bonds payable for land has no effect on cash. But, it is a significant noncash investing and financing activity that merits disclosure in a separate schedule (see Illustration 13A.18).

Increase in Buildings As the additional data indicate, Computer Services acquired an office building for €120,000 cash. This is a cash outflow reported in the investing activities section (see Illustration 13A.18).

Increase in Equipment The Equipment account increased €17,000. The additional information explains that this was a net increase that resulted from two transactions: (1) a purchase of equipment of €25,000, and (2) the sale for €4,000 of equipment costing €8,000. These transactions are investing activities (see **Helpful Hint**). The company should report each transaction separately. The statement in Illustration 13A.18 reports the purchase of equipment as an outflow of cash for €25,000. It reports the sale as an inflow of cash for €4,000. The T-account in **Illustration 13A.17** shows the reasons for the change in this account during the year.

HELPFUL HINT
The investing and financing activities are measured and reported the same under both the direct and indirect methods.

	Equipment		
1/1/23 Balance	10,000	Cost of equipment sold	8,000
Purchase of equipment	25,000		
12/31/23 Balance	27,000		

ILLUSTRATION 13A.17 | Analysis of equipment

The following entry shows the details of the equipment sale transaction.

Cash	4,000	
Accumulated Depreciation—Equipment	1,000	
Loss on Disposal of Plant Assets	3,000	
Equipment		8,000

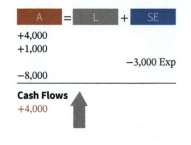

Increase in Bonds Payable The Bonds Payable account increased €110,000. As indicated in the additional information, the company acquired land by directly exchanging bonds for land. Illustration 13A.18 reports this noncash transaction in a separate schedule at the bottom of the statement.

Increase in Common Stock The balance sheet reports an increase in Common Stock of €20,000. The additional information section notes that this increase resulted from the issuance of new shares of stock. This is a cash inflow reported in the financing activities section in Illustration 13A.18 (see **Helpful Hint**).

Increase in Retained Earnings Retained earnings increased €116,000 during the year. This increase can be explained by two factors: (1) net income of €145,000 increased retained earnings, and (2) dividends of €29,000 decreased retained earnings. **Payment of the dividends (not the declaration) is a cash outflow that the company reports as a financing activity in Illustration 13A.18.**

HELPFUL HINT

When companies issue stocks or bonds for cash, the actual proceeds will appear in the statement of cash flows as a financing inflow (rather than the par value of the stocks or face value of bonds).

Statement of Cash Flows—2023

Illustration 13A.18 shows the statement of cash flows for Computer Services International.

Computer Services International
Statement of Cash Flows—Direct Method
For the Year Ended December 31, 2023

Cash flows from operating activities		
Cash receipts from customers		€ 517,000
Less: Cash payments:		
To suppliers	€ 139,000	
For operating expenses	115,000	
For income taxes	49,000	
For interest expense	42,000	345,000
Net cash provided by operating activities		172,000
Cash flows from investing activities		
Sale of equipment	4,000	
Purchase of building	(120,000)	
Purchase of equipment	(25,000)	
Net cash used by investing activities		(141,000)
Cash flows from financing activities		
Issuance of common stock	20,000	
Payment of cash dividends	(29,000)	
Net cash used by financing activities		(9,000)
Net increase in cash		22,000
Cash at beginning of period		33,000
Cash at end of period		€ 55,000
Noncash investing and financing activities		
Issuance of bonds payable to purchase land		€ 110,000

ILLUSTRATION 13A.18 | Statement of cash flows, 2023—direct method

Step 3: Net Change in Cash

Compare the Net Change in Cash on the Statement of Cash Flows with the Change in the Cash Account Reported on the Balance Sheet to Make Sure the Amounts Agree

Illustration 13A.18 indicates that the net change in cash during the period was an increase of €22,000. This agrees with the change in balances in the Cash account reported on the balance sheets in Illustration 13A.1.

Appendix 13B STATEMENT OF CASH FLOWS—T-ACCOUNT APPROACH

Many people like to use T-accounts to provide structure to the preparation of a statement of cash flows. The use of T-accounts is based on the accounting equation:

LEARNING OBJECTIVE *5
Use the T-account approach to prepare a statement of cash flows.

$$\text{Assets} = \text{Liabilities} + \text{Stockholders' Equity}$$

Now, let's rewrite the left-hand side as:

> **Cash + Noncash Assets = Liabilities + Stockholders' Equity**

Next, rewrite the equation by subtracting Noncash Assets from each side to isolate Cash on the left-hand side:

> **Cash = Liabilities + Stockholders' Equity − Noncash Assets**

Finally, if we insert the Δ symbol (which means "change in"), we have:

> **Δ Cash = Δ Liabilities + Δ Stockholders' Equity − Δ Noncash Assets**

What this means is that the change in cash is equal to the change in all of the other balance sheet accounts. Another way to think about this is that if we analyze the changes in all of the noncash balance sheet accounts, we will explain the change in the Cash account. This, of course, is exactly what we are trying to do with the statement of cash flows.

To implement this approach:

- Prepare a large Cash T-account with sections for operating, investing, and financing activities.
- Then, prepare smaller T-accounts for all of the other noncash balance sheet accounts. Insert the beginning and ending balances for each of these accounts.
- Once you have done this, then walk through the steps outlined in Illustration 13.3.

As you walk through the steps, enter debit and credit amounts into the affected accounts. When all of the changes in the T-accounts have been explained, you are done. To demonstrate, we apply this approach to the example of Computer Services International that is presented in the chapter. Each of the adjustments in **Illustration 13B.1** is numbered so you can follow them through the T-accounts.

1. Post net income as a debit to the operating section of the Cash T-account and a credit to Retained Earnings. Make sure to label all adjustments to the Cash T-account. It also helps to number each adjustment so you can trace all of them if you make an error.
2. Post depreciation expense as a debit to the operating section of Cash and a credit to each of the appropriate accumulated depreciation accounts.
3. Post any gains or losses on the sale of property, plant, and equipment. To do this, it is best to first prepare the journal entry that was recorded at the time of the sale and then post each component of the journal entry. For example, for Computer Services the entry was as follows:

Cash	4,000	
Accumulated Depreciation—Equipment	1,000	
Loss on Disposal of Plant Assets	3,000	
Equipment		8,000

The €4,000 cash entry is a source of cash in the investing section of the Cash account. Accumulated Depreciation—Equipment is debited for €1,000. The Loss on Disposal of Plant Assets (equipment) is a debit to the operating section of the Cash T-account. Finally, Equipment is credited for €8,000.

4–8. Next, post each of the changes to the noncash current asset and current liability accounts. For example, to explain the €10,000 decline in Computer Services' accounts receivable, credit Accounts Receivable for €10,000 and debit the operating section of the Cash T-account for €10,000.

		Cash			
Operating					
(1)	Net income	145,000	5,000	Inventory (5)	
(2)	Depreciation expense	9,000	4,000	Prepaid expenses (6)	
(3)	Loss on equipment	3,000	2,000	Income taxes payable (8)	
(4)	Accounts receivable	10,000			
(7)	Accounts payable	16,000			
	Net cash provided by operating activities	172,000			
Investing					
(3)	Sold equipment	4,000	120,000	Purchased building (10)	
			25,000	Purchased equipment (11)	
			141,000	Net cash used by investing activities	
Financing					
(12)	Issued common stock	20,000	29,000	Dividend paid (13)	
			9,000	Net cash used by financing activities	
	Net increase in cash	22,000			

Accounts Receivable		Inventory		Prepaid Expenses		Land	
30,000		10,000		1,000		20,000	
	10,000 (4)	(5) 5,000		(6) 4,000		(9) 110,000	
20,000		15,000		5,000		130,000	

Buildings		Accumulated Depreciation—Buildings		Equipment		Accumulated Depreciation—Equipment	
40,000			5,000	10,000			1,000
(10) 120,000			6,000 (2)	(11) 25,000	8,000 (3)	(3) 1,000	3,000 (2)
160,000			11,000	27,000			3,000

Accounts Payable		Income Taxes Payable		Bonds Payable		Common Stock		Retained Earnings	
	12,000		8,000		20,000		50,000		48,000
	16,000 (7)	(8) 2,000			110,000 (9)		20,000 (12)		145,000 (1)
	28,000		6,000		130,000		70,000	(13) 29,000	
									164,000

ILLUSTRATION 13B.1 | **T-account approach**

9. Analyze the changes in the noncurrent accounts. Land was purchased by issuing bonds payable. This requires a debit to Land for €110,000 and a credit to Bonds Payable for €110,000. Note that this is a significant noncash event that requires disclosure at the bottom of the statement of cash flows.

10. Buildings is debited for €120,000, and the investing section of the Cash T-account is credited for €120,000 as a use of cash from investing.

11. Equipment is debited for €25,000 and the investing section of the Cash T-account is credited for €25,000 as a use of cash from investing.

12. Common Stock is credited for €20,000 for the issuance of shares of stock, and the financing section of the Cash T-account is debited for €20,000.

13. Retained Earnings is debited to reflect the payment of the €29,000 dividend, and the financing section of the Cash T-account is credited to reflect the use of Cash.

At this point, all of the changes in the noncash accounts have been explained. All that remains is to subtotal each section of the Cash T-account and compare the total change in cash with the change shown on the balance sheet. Once this is done, the information in the Cash T-account can be used to prepare a statement of cash flows.

REVIEW AND PRACTICE

Learning Objectives Review

LO 1 Discuss the usefulness and format of the statement of cash flows.

The statement of cash flows provides information about the cash receipts, cash payments, and net change in cash resulting from the operating, investing, and financing activities of a company during the period. Operating activities include the cash effects of transactions that enter into the determination of net income. Investing activities involve cash flows resulting from changes in investments and long-term asset items. Financing activities involve cash flows resulting from changes in long-term liability and stockholders' equity items.

LO 2 Prepare a statement of cash flows using the indirect method.

The preparation of a statement of cash flows involves three major steps. (1) Determine net cash provided/used by operating activities by converting net income from an accrual basis to a cash basis. (2) Analyze changes in noncurrent asset and liability accounts and stockholders' equity accounts and report as investing and financing activities, or disclose as noncash transactions. (3) Compare the net change in cash on the statement of cash flows with the change in the Cash account reported on the balance sheet to make sure the amounts agree.

LO 3 Analyze the statement of cash flows.

Free cash flow indicates the amount of cash a company generated during the current year that is available for the payment of additional dividends or for expansion.

LO*4 Prepare a statement of cash flows using the direct method.

The preparation of the statement of cash flows involves three major steps. (1) Determine net cash provided/used by adjusting each item in the income statement from the accrual basis to the cash basis. (2) Analyze changes in noncurrent asset and liability accounts and stockholders' equity accounts and record as investing and financing activities, or disclose as noncash transactions. (3) Compare the net change in cash on the statement of cash flows with the change in the Cash account reported on the balance sheet to make sure the amounts agree. The direct method reports cash receipts less cash payments to arrive at net cash provided by operating activities.

LO*5 Use the T-account approach to prepare a statement of cash flows.

To use T-accounts to prepare the statement of cash flows: (1) prepare a large Cash T-account with sections for operating, investing, and financing activities; (2) prepare smaller T-accounts for all other noncash accounts; (3) insert beginning and ending balances for all balance sheet accounts; and (4) follows the steps in Illustration 13B.1, entering debit and credit amounts as needed.

Decision Tools Review

Decision Checkpoints	Info Needed for Decision	Tool to Use for Decision	How to Evaluate Results
How much cash did the company generate to either expand operations or pay dividends?	Net cash provided by operating activities, cash spent on fixed assets, and cash dividends	Free cash flow = Net cash provided by operating activities − Capital expenditures − Cash dividends	Significant free cash flow indicates greater potential to finance new investment and pay additional dividends.

Glossary Review

*Direct method A method of preparing a statement of cash flows that shows operating cash receipts and payments. It is prepared by adjusting each item in the income statement from the accrual basis to the cash basis. (pp. 13-7, 13-20).

Financing activities Cash flow activities that include (a) obtaining cash from issuing debt and repaying the amounts borrowed and (b) obtaining cash from stockholders, repurchasing shares, and paying dividends. (p. 13-3).

Free cash flow Net cash provided by operating activities adjusted for capital expenditures and cash dividends paid. (p. 13-18).

Indirect method A method of preparing a statement of cash flows in which net income is adjusted for items that do not affect cash, to determine net cash provided by operating activities. (p. 13-7).

Investing activities Cash flow activities that include (a) purchasing and disposing of investments and property, plant, and equipment using cash and (b) lending money and collecting the loans. (p. 13-3).

Operating activities Cash flow activities that include the cash effects of transactions that generate revenues and expenses and thus enter into the determination of net income. (p. 13-3).

Statement of cash flows A basic financial statement that provides information about the cash receipts, cash payments, and net change in cash during a period, resulting from operating, investing, and financing activities. (p. 13-3).

Practice Multiple-Choice Questions

1. **(LO 1)** Which of the following is **incorrect** about the statement of cash flows?
   a. It is a fourth basic financial statement.
   b. It provides information about cash receipts and cash payments of an entity during a period.
   c. It reconciles the ending Cash account balance to the balance per the bank statement.
   d. It provides information about the operating, investing, and financing activities of the business.

2. **(LO 1)** Which of the following is **not** reported in the statement of cash flows?
   a. The net change in stockholders' equity during the year.
   b. Cash payments for plant assets during the year.
   c. Cash receipts from sales of plant assets during the year.
   d. How acquisitions of plant assets during the year were financed.

3. **(LO 1)** The statement of cash flows classifies cash receipts and cash payments into these activities:
   a. operating and nonoperating.
   b. investing, financing, and operating.
   c. financing, operating, and nonoperating.
   d. investing, financing, and nonoperating.

4. **(LO 1)** Which is an example of a cash flow from an operating activity?
   a. Payment of cash to lenders for interest.
   b. Receipt of cash from the sale of common stock.
   c. Payment of cash dividends to the company's stockholders.
   d. None of the answer choices is correct.

5. **(LO 1)** Which is an example of a cash flow from an investing activity?
   a. Receipt of cash from the issuance of bonds payable.
   b. Payment of cash to repurchase outstanding common stock.
   c. Receipt of cash from the sale of equipment.
   d. Payment of cash to suppliers for inventory.

6. **(LO 1)** Cash dividends paid to stockholders are classified on the statement of cash flows as:
   a. an operating activity.
   b. an investing activity.
   c. a combination of an operating activity and an investing activity.
   d. a financing activity.

7. **(LO 1)** Which is an example of a cash flow from a financing activity?
   a. Receipt of cash from sale of land.
   b. Issuance of debt for cash.
   c. Purchase of equipment for cash.
   d. None of the answer choices is correct.

8. **(LO 1)** Which of the following is **incorrect** about the statement of cash flows?
   a. The direct method may be used to report net cash provided by operating activities.
   b. The statement shows the net cash provided (used) for three categories of activity.
   c. The operating section is the last section of the statement.
   d. The indirect method may be used to report net cash provided by operating activities.

Use the indirect method to solve Questions 9 through 11.

9. **(LO 2)** Net income is €132,000, accounts payable increased €10,000 during the year, inventory decreased €6,000 during the year, and accounts receivable increased €12,000 during the year. Under the indirect method, what is net cash provided by operating activities?
   a. €102,000.
   b. €112,000.
   c. €124,000.
   d. €136,000.

10. **(LO 2)** Items that are added back to net income in determining net cash provided by operating activities under the indirect method do **not** include:
    a. depreciation expense.
    b. an increase in inventory.
    c. amortization expense.
    d. loss on disposal of plant assets.

11. **(LO 2)** The following data are available for Allen Graf Group.

Net income	€200,000
Depreciation expense	40,000
Dividends paid	60,000
Gain on sale of land	10,000
Decrease in accounts receivable	20,000
Decrease in accounts payable	30,000

    Net cash provided by operating activities is:
    a. €160,000.
    b. €220,000.
    c. €240,000.
    d. €280,000.

12. **(LO 2)** The following data are available for White Castles Ltd.

Proceeds from sale of land	£100,000
Proceeds from sale of equipment	50,000
Issuance of common stock	70,000
Purchase of equipment	30,000
Payment of cash dividends	60,000

    Net cash provided by investing activities is:
    a. £120,000.
    b. £130,000.
    c. £150,000.
    d. £190,000.

13. **(LO 2)** The following data are available for Iconic!

Increase in accounts payable	A$ 40,000
Increase in bonds payable	100,000
Sale of investment	50,000
Issuance of common stock	60,000
Payment of cash dividends	30,000

    Net cash provided by financing activities is:
    a. A$90,000.
    b. A$130,000.
    c. A$160,000.
    d. A$170,000.

14. **(LO 3)** The statement of cash flows should **not** be used to evaluate an entity's ability to:
    a. generate net income.
    b. generate future cash flows.
    c. pay dividends.
    d. meet obligations.

15. (LO 3) Free cash flow provides an indication of a company's ability to:

   a. manage inventory.
   b. generate cash to pay additional dividends.
   c. generate cash to invest in new capital expenditures.
   d. both generate cash to pay additional dividends and invest in new capital expenditures.

Use the direct method to solve Questions 16 and 17.

*16. (LO 4) The beginning balance in accounts receivable is HK$440,000, the ending balance is HK$420,000, and sales during the period are HK$1,290,000. What are cash receipts from customers?

   a. HK$1,270,000.
   b. HK$1,290,000.
   c. HK$1,310,000.
   d. HK$1,410,000.

*17. (LO 4) Which of the following items is reported on a statement of cash flows prepared by the direct method?

   a. Loss on sale of building.
   b. Increase in accounts receivable.
   c. Depreciation expense.
   d. Cash payments to suppliers.

Solutions

1. c. The statement of cash flows does not reconcile the ending cash balance to the balance per the bank statement. The other choices are true statements.

2. a. The net change in stockholders' equity during the year is not reported in the statement of cash flows. The other choices are true statements.

3. b. Operating, investing, and financing activities are the three classifications of cash receipts and cash payments used in the statement of cash flows. The other choices are therefore incorrect.

4. a. Payment of cash to lenders for interest is an operating activity. The other choices are incorrect because (b) receipt of cash from the sale of common stock is a financing activity, (c) payment of cash dividends to the company's stockholders is a financing activity, and (d) there is a correct answer.

5. c. Receipt of cash from the sale of equipment is an investing activity. The other choices are incorrect because (a) the receipt of cash from the issuance of bonds payable is a financing activity, (b) payment of cash to repurchase outstanding common stock is a financing activity, and (d) payment of cash to suppliers for inventory is an operating activity.

6. d. Cash dividends paid to stockholders are classified as a financing activity, not (a) an operating activity, (b) an investing activity, or (c) a combination of an operating and an investing activity.

7. b. Issuance of debt for cash is a financing activity. The other choices are incorrect because (a) the receipt of cash from the sale of land is an investing activity, (c) the purchase of equipment for cash is an investing activity, and (d) there is a correct answer.

8. c. The operating section of the statement of cash flows is the first, not the last, section of the statement. The other choices are true statements.

9. d. Net cash provided by operating activities is computed by adjusting net income for the changes in the three current asset/current liability accounts listed. An increase in accounts payable (€10,000) and a decrease in inventory (€6,000) are added to net income (€132,000), while an increase in accounts receivable (€12,000) is subtracted from net income, or €132,000 + €10,000 + €6,000 − €12,000 = €136,000, not (a) €102,000, (b) €112,000, or (c) €124,000.

10. b. An increase in inventory is subtracted, not added, to net income in determining net cash provided by operating activities. The other choices are incorrect because (a) depreciation expense, (c) amortization expense, and (d) loss on disposal of plant assets are all added back to net income in determining net cash provided by operating activities.

11. b. Net cash provided by operating activities is €220,000 (Net income €200,000 + Depreciation expense €40,000 − Gain on sale of land €10,000 + Decrease in accounts receivable €20,000 − Decrease in accounts payable €30,000), not (a) €160,000, (c) €240,000, or (d) €280,000.

12. a. Net cash provided by investing activities is £120,000 (Sale of land £100,000 + Sale of equipment £50,000 − Purchase of equipment £30,000), not (b) £130,000, (c) £150,000, or (d) £190,000. Issuance of common stock and payment of cash dividends are financing activities.

13. b. Net cash provided by financing activities is A$130,000 (Increase in bonds payable A$100,000 + Issuance of common stock A$60,000 − Payment of cash dividends A$30,000), not (a) A$90,000, (c) A$160,000, or (d) A$170,000. Increase in accounts payable is an operating activity, and sale of investment is an investing activity.

14. a. The statement of cash flows is not used to evaluate an entity's ability to generate net income. The other choices are true statements.

15. d. Free cash flow provides an indication of a company's ability to generate cash to pay additional dividends and invest in new capital expenditures. Choice (a) is incorrect because other measures besides free cash flow provide the best measure of a company's ability to manage inventory. Choices (b) and (c) are true statements, but (d) is the better answer.

*16. c. Cash from customers amount to HK$1,310,000 (HK$1,290,000 + a decrease in accounts receivable of HK$20,000). The other choices are therefore incorrect.

*17. d. Cash payments to suppliers are reported on a statement of cash flows prepared by the direct method. The other choices are incorrect because (a) loss on sale of building, (b) increase in accounts receivable, and (c) depreciation expense are reported in the operating activities section of the statement of cash flows when the indirect, not direct, method is used.

Practice Exercises

Prepare journal entries to determine effect on statement of cash flows.

1. (LO 2) Keiko Ltd. had the following transactions:

   1. Paid salaries of ¥1,400,000.
   2. Issued 1,000 shares of ¥100 par value common stock for equipment worth ¥1,600,000.
   3. Sold equipment (cost ¥1,000,000, accumulated depreciation ¥600,000) for ¥300,000.

4. Sold land (cost ¥1,200,000) for ¥1,600,000.
5. Issued another 1,000 shares of ¥100 par value common stock for ¥1,800,000.
6. Recorded depreciation of ¥2,000,000.

Instructions

For each transaction above, (a) prepare the journal entry, and (b) indicate how it would affect the statement of cash flows. Assume the indirect method.

Solution

1. 1. a. Salaries and Wages Expense 1,400,000
      Cash 1,400,000

   b. Salaries and wages expense is not reported separately on the statement of cash flows. It is part of the computation of net income in the income statement and is included in the net income amount on the statement of cash flows.

   2. a. Equipment 1,600,000
      Common Stock 100,000
      Paid-in Capital in Excess of Par—Common Stock 1,500,000

   b. The issuance of common stock for equipment (¥1,600,000) is reported as a noncash financing and investing activity at the bottom of the statement of cash flows.

   3. a. Cash 300,000
      Loss on Disposal of Plant Assets 100,000
      Accumulated Depreciation—Equipment 600,000
      Equipment 1,000,000

   b. The cash receipt (¥300,000) is reported in the investing section. The loss (¥100,000) is added to net income in the operating section.

   4. a. Cash 1,600,000
      Land 1,200,000
      Gain on Disposal of Plant Assets 400,000

   b. The cash receipt (¥1,600,000) is reported in the investing section. The gain (¥400,000) is deducted from net income in the operating section.

   5. a. Cash 1,800,000
      Common Stock 100,000
      Paid-in Capital in Excess of Par—Common Stock 1,700,000

   b. The cash receipt (¥1,800,000) is reported in the financing section.

   6. a. Depreciation Expense 2,000,000
      Accumulated Depreciation—Equipment 2,000,000

   b. Depreciation expense (¥2,000,000) is added to net income in the operating section.

2. **(LO 2, 3)** Grand Valley Corporation's comparative balance sheets are as follows:

Prepare statement of cash flows and compute free cash flow.

Grand Valley Corporation
Comparative Balance Sheets
December 31

	2023	2022
Cash	A$ 28,200	A$ 17,700
Accounts receivable	24,200	22,300
Investments	23,000	16,000
Equipment	60,000	70,000
Accumulated depreciation—equipment	(14,000)	(10,000)
Total	A$121,400	A$116,000
Accounts payable	A$ 19,600	A$ 11,100
Bonds payable	10,000	30,000
Common stock	60,000	45,000
Retained earnings	31,800	29,900
Total	A$121,400	A$116,000

Additional information:

1. Net income was A$28,300. Dividends declared and paid were A$26,400. Depreciation expense was A$5,200.
2. Equipment which cost A$10,000 and had accumulated depreciation of A$1,200 was sold for A$4,300.
3. All other changes in noncurrent accounts had a direct effect on cash flows, except the change in accumulated depreciation.

Instructions

a. Prepare a statement of cash flows for 2023 using the indirect method.
b. Compute free cash flow.

Solution

2. a.

Grand Valley Corporation
Statement of Cash Flows
For the Year Ended December 31, 2023

Cash flows from operating activities		
Net income		A$ 28,300
Adjustments to reconcile net income to net cash provided by operating activities:		
Depreciation expense	A$ 5,200	
Loss on disposal of plant assets	4,500*	
Increase in accounts payable	8,500	
Increase in accounts receivable	(1,900)	16,300
Net cash provided by operating activities		44,600
Cash flows from investing activities		
Sale of equipment	4,300	
Purchase of investments	(7,000)	
Net cash used by investing activities		(2,700)
Cash flows from financing activities		
Issuance of common stock	15,000	
Retirement of bonds	(20,000)	
Payment of dividends	(26,400)	
Net cash used by financing activities		(31,400)
Net increase in cash		10,500
Cash at beginning of period		17,700
Cash at end of period		A$ 28,200

*[A$4,300 − (A$10,000 − A$1,200)]

b. Free cash flow = A$44,600 − A$0 − A$26,400 = A$18,200

Practice Problem

Prepare statement of cash flows using indirect and direct methods.

(LO 2, 4) The income statement for the year ended December 31, 2023, for Schneider Manufacturing contains the following condensed information.

Schneider Manufacturing
Income Statement
For the Year Ended December 31, 2023

Sales revenue		€6,583,000
Cost of goods sold	€2,810,000	
Operating expenses (excluding depreciation)	2,086,000	
Depreciation expense	880,000	
Loss on disposal of plant assets	24,000	5,800,000
Income before income taxes		783,000
Income tax expense		353,000
Net income		€ 430,000

The €24,000 loss resulted from selling equipment for €270,000 cash. New equipment was purchased for €750,000 cash.

The following balances are reported on Schneider's comparative balance sheets at December 31.

Schneider Manufacturing
Comparative Balance Sheets (partial)

	2023	2022
Cash	€672,000	€130,000
Accounts receivable	775,000	610,000
Inventory	834,000	867,000
Accounts payable	521,000	501,000

Income tax expense of €353,000 represents the amount paid in 2023. Dividends declared and paid in 2023 totaled €200,000.

Instructions

a. Prepare the statement of cash flows using the indirect method.

*b. Prepare the statement of cash flows using the direct method.

Solution

a.

Schneider Manufacturing
Statement of Cash Flows—Indirect Method
For the Year Ended December 31, 2023

Cash flows from operating activities		
Net income		€ 430,000
Adjustments to reconcile net income to net cash provided by operating activities:		
Depreciation expense	€ 880,000	
Loss on disposal of plant assets	24,000	
Increase in accounts receivable	(165,000)	
Decrease in inventory	33,000	
Increase in accounts payable	20,000	792,000
Net cash provided by operating activities		1,222,000
Cash flows from investing activities		
Sale of equipment	270,000	
Purchase of equipment	(750,000)	
Net cash used by investing activities		(480,000)
Cash flows from financing activities		
Payment of cash dividends	(200,000)	
Net cash used by financing activities		(200,000)
Net increase in cash		542,000
Cash at beginning of period		130,000
Cash at end of period		€ 672,000

*b.

Schneider Manufacturing
Statement of Cash Flows—Direct Method
For the Year Ended December 31, 2023

Cash flows from operating activities		
Cash collections from customers		€6,418,000*
Less: Cash payments:		
To suppliers	€2,757,000**	
For operating expenses	2,086,000	
For income taxes	353,000	5,196,000
Net cash provided by operating activities		1,222,000
Cash flows from investing activities		
Sale of equipment	270,000	
Purchase of equipment	(750,000)	
Net cash used by investing activities		(480,000)
Cash flows from financing activities		
Payment of cash dividends	(200,000)	
Net cash used by financing activities		(200,000)
Net increase in cash		542,000
Cash at beginning of period		130,000
Cash at end of period		€ 672,000

Direct-Method Computations:

*Computation of cash collections from customers:

Sales revenue	€ 6,583,000
Less: Increase in accounts receivable	165,000
Cash collections from customers	€ 6,418,000

**Computation of cash payments to suppliers

Cost of goods sold per income statement	€ 2,810,000
Less: Decrease in inventories	33,000
Less: Increase in accounts payable	20,000
Cash payments to suppliers	€ 2,757,000

Note: All asterisked Questions, Exercises, and Problems relate to material in the appendices to the chapter.

Questions

1. **a.** What is a statement of cash flows?

   b. Nick Johns maintains that the statement of cash flows is an optional financial statement. Is this true? Explain why or why not.

2. What questions about cash are answered by the statement of cash flows?

3. Distinguish among the three types of activities reported in the statement of cash flows.

4. **a.** What are the major sources (inflows) of cash?

   b. What are the major uses (outflows) of cash?

5. Why is it important to disclose certain noncash transactions? How should they be disclosed?

6. Wilma Flintstone and Barny Rublestone were discussing the format of the statement of cash flows of Saltwater Candy Co. At the bottom of Saltwater's statement of cash flows was a separate section entitled "Noncash investing and financing activities." Give three examples of significant noncash transactions that would be reported in this section.

7. Why is it necessary to use comparative balance sheets, a current income statement, and certain transaction data in preparing a statement of cash flows?

8. Contrast the advantages and disadvantages of the direct and indirect methods of preparing the statement of cash flows. Are both methods acceptable? Which method is preferred by the IASB? Which method is more popular?

9. When the total cash inflows exceed the total cash outflows in the statement of cash flows, how and where is this excess identified?

10. Describe the indirect method for determining net cash provided (used) by operating activities.

11. Why is it necessary to convert accrual-basis net income to cash-basis income when preparing a statement of cash flows?

12. The president of Tsz & Chi Company is puzzled. During the last year, the company experienced a net loss of HK$8,000,000, yet its cash increased HK$3,000,000 during the same period of time. Explain to the president how this could occur.

13. Identify five items that are adjustments to convert net income to net cash provided by operating activities under the indirect method.

14. Why and how is depreciation expense reported in a statement of cash flows prepared using the indirect method?

15. Why is the statement of cash flows useful?

16. During 2023, Oliver Company converted A$1,700,000 of its total A$2,000,000 of bonds payable into common stock. Indicate how the transaction would be reported on a statement of cash flows, if at all.

17. In its 2019 statement of cash flows, what amount did **Apple** (USA) report for net cash (a) provided by operating activities, (b) used for investing activities, and (c) used for financing activities? (Apple's financial statements are available online.)

*18. Describe the direct method for determining net cash provided by operating activities.

*19. Give the equations under the direct method for computing (a) cash receipts from customers and (b) cash payments to suppliers.

*20. Ozturk A.S. reported sales of ₺20 million for 2023. Accounts receivable decreased ₺1,500,000, and accounts payable increased ₺3,000,000. Compute cash receipts from customers, assuming that the receivable and payable transactions are related to operations.

*21. In the direct method, why is depreciation expense not reported in the cash flows from operating activities section?

Brief Exercises

BE13.1 (LO 1), C Each of these items must be considered in preparing a statement of cash flows for Brown Ltd. for the year ended December 31, 2023. For each item, state how it should be shown in the statement of cash flows for 2023.

a. Issued bonds for £200,000 cash.

b. Purchased equipment for £180,000 cash.

c. Sold land costing £20,000 for £20,000 cash.

d. Declared and paid a £50,000 cash dividend.

Indicate statement presentation of selected transactions.

BE13.2 (LO 1), C Classify each item as an operating, investing, or financing activity. Assume all items involve cash unless there is information to the contrary.

a. Purchase of equipment.
b. Proceeds from sale of building.
c. Redemption of bonds payable.
d. Cash received from sale of goods.
e. Payment of dividends.
f. Issuance of common stock.

Classify items by activities.

BE13.3 (LO 1), AP The following T-account is a summary of the Cash account of Wiegman Ltd.

Identify financing activity transactions.

Cash (Summary Form)			
Balance, Jan. 1	8,000		
Receipts from customers	364,000	Payments for goods	200,000
Dividends on stock investments	6,000	Payments for operating expenses	140,000
Proceeds from sale of equipment	36,000	Interest paid	10,000
Proceeds from issuance of		Taxes paid	8,000
bonds payable	300,000	Dividends paid	40,000
Balance, Dec. 31	316,000		

What amount of net cash provided (used) by financing activities should be reported in the statement of cash flows?

BE13.4 (LO 2), AP Michel plc reported net income of £2.5 million in 2023. Depreciation for the year was £160,000, accounts receivable decreased £350,000, and accounts payable decreased £280,000. Compute net cash provided by operating activities using the indirect method.

Compute net cash provided by operating activities—indirect method.

BE13.5 (LO 2), AP The net income for Aloha Ltd. for 2023 was NT$2,800,000. For 2023, depreciation on plant assets was NT$700,000, and the company incurred a loss on disposal of plant assets of NT$280,000. Compute net cash provided by operating activities under the indirect method, assuming there were no other changes in the company's accounts.

Compute net cash provided by operating activities—indirect method.

BE13.6 (LO 2), AP The comparative balance sheets for Yang Ltd. show these changes in noncash current asset accounts: accounts receivable decreased HK$800,000, prepaid expenses increased HK$280,000, and inventories increased HK$400,000. Compute net cash provided by operating activities using the indirect method, assuming that net income is HK$1,860,000.

Compute net cash provided by operating activities—indirect method.

Determine cash received from sale of equipment.

BE13.7 (LO 2), AN The T-accounts for Equipment and the related Accumulated Depreciation—Equipment for Castamar SpA at the end of 2023 are shown here.

Equipment					Accum. Depr.—Equipment			
Beg. bal.	80,000	Disposals	22,000		Disposals	5,100	Beg. bal.	44,500
Acquisitions	41,600						Depr. exp.	12,000
End. bal.	99,600						End. bal.	51,400

In addition, Castamar's income statement reported a loss on the disposal of plant assets of €3,500. What amount was reported on the statement of cash flows as "cash flow from sale of equipment"?

Calculate free cash flow.

BE13.8 (LO 3), AP Suppose that during 2023 **Cypress Semiconductor Corporation** (USA) reported net cash provided by operating activities of $89,303,000, cash used in investing of $43,126,000, and cash used in financing of $7,368,000. In addition, cash spent for fixed assets during the period was $25,823,000. No dividends were paid. Calculate free cash flow.

Calculate free cash flow.

BE13.9 (LO 3), AP Aksu A.S. reported net cash provided by operating activities of ₺4,120,000, net cash used by investing activities of ₺2,500,000, and net cash provided by financing activities of ₺700,000. In addition, cash spent for capital assets during the period was ₺2,000,000. No dividends were paid. Calculate free cash flow.

Calculate free cash flow.

BE13.10 (LO 3), AP Suppose **Shaw Communications** (USA) reported net cash used by operating activities of $104,539,000 and sales revenue of $2,867,459,000 during 2023. Cash spent on plant asset additions during the year was $79,330,000. Calculate free cash flow.

Calculate and analyze free cash flow.

BE13.11 (LO 3), AN The management of Chong & Lee Company is trying to decide whether it can increase its dividend. During the current year, it reported net income of S$875,000. It had net cash provided by operating activities of S$734,000, paid cash dividends of S$92,000, and had capital expenditures of S$310,000. Compute the company's free cash flow, and discuss whether an increase in the dividend appears warranted. What other factors should be considered?

Compute receipts from customers—direct method.

*****BE13.12 (LO 4), AP** Suppose **Columbia Sportswear Company** (USA) had accounts receivable of $299,585,000 at January 1, 2023, and $226,548,000 at December 31, 2023. Assume sales revenue was $1,244,023,000 for the year 2023. What is the amount of cash receipts from customers in 2023?

Compute cash payments for income taxes—direct method.

*****BE13.13 (LO 4), AP** Lin Ltd. reported income taxes of NT$3,700,000,000 on its 2023 income statement. Its balance sheet reported income taxes payable of NT$2,770,000,000 at December 31, 2022, and NT$5,280,000,000 at December 31, 2023. What amount of cash payments were made for income taxes during 2023?

Compute cash payments for operating expenses—direct method.

*****BE13.14 (LO 4), AP** Yaddof SE reports operating expenses of €90,000, excluding depreciation expense of €15,000, for 2023. During the year, prepaid expenses decreased €7,200 and accrued expenses payable increased €4,400. Compute the cash payments for operating expenses in 2023.

DO IT! Exercises

Classify transactions by type of cash flow activity.

DO IT! 13.1 (LO 1), C Piekarski Group had the following transactions:

1. Issued €160,000 of bonds payable.
2. Paid utilities expense.
3. Issued 500 shares of preferred stock for €45,000.
4. Sold land and a building for €250,000.
5. Loaned €30,000 to Zarembski Company, receiving Zarembski's one-year, 12% note.

Classify each of these transactions by type of cash flow activity (operating, investing, or financing). (*Hint:* Refer to Illustration 13.1.)

Calculate net cash from operating activities.

DO IT! 13.2a (LO 2), AP Ziba Photography reported net income of S$100,000 for 2023. Included in the income statement were depreciation expense of S$6,300, patent amortization expense of S$4,000, and a gain on disposal of plant assets of S$3,600. Ziba's comparative balance sheets show the following balances:

	12/31/23	12/31/22
Accounts receivable	S$21,000	S$27,000
Accounts payable	9,200	6,000

Calculate net cash provided by operating activities for Ziba Photography.

DO IT! 13.2b (LO 2), AP Scott Industries reported the following information for 2023.

Prepare statement of cash flows—indirect method.

Scott Industries
Comparative Balance Sheets
December 31

	2023	2022	Change Increase/Decrease	
Assets				
Cash	A$ 59,000	A$ 36,000	A$ 23,000	Increase
Accounts receivable	62,000	22,000	40,000	Increase
Inventory	44,000	-0-	44,000	Increase
Prepaid expenses	6,000	4,000	2,000	Increase
Land	55,000	70,000	15,000	Decrease
Buildings	200,000	200,000	-0-	No change
Accumulated depreciation—buildings	(21,000)	(14,000)	7,000	Increase
Equipment	183,000	68,000	115,000	Increase
Accumulated depreciation—equipment	(28,000)	(10,000)	18,000	Increase
Totals	A$560,000	A$376,000		
Liabilities and Stockholders' Equity				
Accounts payable	A$ 43,000	A$ 40,000	A$ 3,000	Increase
Accrued expenses payable	-0-	10,000	10,000	Decrease
Bonds payable	100,000	150,000	50,000	Decrease
Common stock (A$1 par)	230,000	60,000	170,000	Increase
Retained earnings	187,000	116,000	71,000	Increase
Totals	A$560,000	A$376,000		

Scott Industries
Income Statement
For the Year Ended December 31, 2023

Sales revenue		A$941,000
Cost of goods sold	A$475,000	
Operating expenses	231,000	
Interest expense	12,000	
Loss on disposal of plant assets	2,000	720,000
Income before income taxes		221,000
Income tax expense		65,000
Net income		A$156,000

Additional information:
1. Operating expenses include depreciation expense of A$40,000.
2. Land was sold at its book value for cash.
3. Cash dividends of A$85,000 were declared and paid in 2023.
4. Equipment with a cost of A$166,000 was purchased for cash. Equipment with a cost of A$51,000 and a book value of A$36,000 was sold for A$34,000 cash.
5. Bonds of A$50,000 were redeemed at their face value for cash.
6. Common stock (A$1 par) was issued at par for A$170,000 cash.

Use this information to prepare a statement of cash flows using the indirect method.

CHAPTER 13 Statement of Cash Flows

Compute and discuss free cash flow.

DO IT! 13.3 (LO 3), AP Bourne plc issued the following statement of cash flows for 2023.

Bourne plc
Statement of Cash Flows—Indirect Method
For the Year Ended December 31, 2023

Cash flows from operating activities		
Net income		£ 59,000
Adjustments to reconcile net income to net cash provided by operating activities:		
Depreciation expense	£ 9,100	
Decrease in accounts receivable	9,500	
Increase in inventory	(5,000)	
Decrease in accounts payable	(2,200)	
Loss on disposal of plant assets	3,300	14,700
Net cash provided by operating activities		73,700
Cash flows from investing activities		
Sale of investments	3,100	
Purchase of equipment	(24,200)	
Net cash used by investing activities		(21,100)
Cash flows from financing activities		
Issuance of common stock	20,000	
Payment on long-term note payable	(10,000)	
Payment of cash dividends	(13,000)	
Net cash used by financing activities		(3,000)
Net increase in cash		49,600
Cash at beginning of year		13,000
Cash at end of year		£ 62,600

---

a. Compute free cash flow for Bourne plc.

b. Explain why free cash flow often provides better information than "Net cash provided by operating activities."

Exercises

Classify transactions by type of activity.

E13.1 (LO 1), C Zhìmíng Ltd. had these transactions during 2023.

a. Purchased a machine for NT$300,000, giving a long-term note in exchange.
b. Issued NT$500,000 par value common stock for cash.
c. Issued NT$2,000,000 par value common stock upon conversion of bonds having a face value of NT$2,000,000.
d. Declared and paid a cash dividend of NT$130,000.
e. Sold a long-term investment with a cost of NT$150,000 for NT$150,000 cash.
f. Collected NT$160,000 from sale of goods.
g. Paid NT$180,000 to suppliers.

Instructions

Analyze the transactions and indicate whether each transaction is an operating activity, investing activity, financing activity, or noncash investing and financing activity.

Classify transactions by type of activity.

E13.2 (LO 1), C An analysis of comparative balance sheets, the current year's income statement, and the general ledger accounts of Hailey Corp. uncovered the following items. Assume all items involve cash unless there is information to the contrary.

a. Exchange of land for patent.
b. Sale of building at book value.
c. Payment of dividends.
d. Depreciation of plant assets.
e. Conversion of bonds into common stock.
f. Issuance of capital stock.
g. Amortization of patent.
h. Issuance of bonds for land.
i. Purchase of land.
j. Loss on disposal of plant assets.
k. Retirement of bonds.

Instructions

Indicate where each item should be presented in the statement of cash flows (indirect method) using these four major classifications: operating activity (that is, the item would be listed among the adjustments to net income to determine net cash provided by operating activities under the indirect method), investing activity, financing activity, or significant noncash investing and financing activity.

E13.3 (LO 1), AP Hayashi Constructions had the following transactions:

1. Sold land (cost ¥1,200,000) for ¥1,500,000.
2. Issued common stock at par for ¥2,000,000.
3. Recorded depreciation on buildings for ¥1,700,000.
4. Paid salaries of ¥900,000.
5. Issued 1,000 shares of ¥100 par value common stock for equipment worth ¥800,000.
6. Sold equipment (cost ¥1,000,000 accumulated depreciation ¥700,000) for ¥120,000.

Prepare journal entry and determine effect on cash flows.

Instructions

For each transaction above, (a) prepare the journal entry, and (b) indicate how it would affect the statement of cash flows using the indirect method.

E13.4 (LO 2), AP Garcia SA reported net income of R$1,900,000 for 2023. Garcia also reported depreciation expense of R$350,000 and a loss of R$50,000 on the disposal of plant assets. The comparative balance sheets show an increase in accounts receivable of R$150,000 for the year, a R$170,000 increase in accounts payable, and a R$40,000 increase in prepaid expenses.

Prepare the operating activities section—indirect method.

Instructions

Prepare the operating activities section of the statement of cash flows for 2023. Use the indirect method.

E13.5 (LO 2), AP The current sections of Bracewell SE's balance sheets at December 31, 2022 and 2023, are presented here. Bracewell's net income for 2023 was €153,000. Depreciation expense was €27,000.

Prepare the operating activities section—indirect method.

	2023	2022
Current assets		
Cash	€105,000	€ 99,000
Accounts receivable	80,000	89,000
Inventory	168,000	172,000
Prepaid expenses	27,000	22,000
Total current assets	€380,000	€382,000
Current liabilities		
Accrued expenses payable	€ 15,000	€ 5,000
Accounts payable	85,000	92,000
Total current liabilities	€100,000	€ 97,000

Instructions

Prepare the operating activities section of the company's statement of cash flows for the year ended December 31, 2023, using the indirect method.

E13.6 (LO 2), AP The following information is available for Murphy Corporation for the year ended December 31, 2023:

Prepare statement of cash flows—indirect method.

Beginning cash balance	A$ 45,000
Accounts payable decrease	3,700
Depreciation expense	162,000
Accounts receivable increase	8,200
Inventory increase	11,000
Net income	284,100
Cash received for sale of land at book value	35,000
Cash dividends paid	12,000
Income taxes payable increase	4,700
Cash used to purchase building	289,000
Cash used to purchase treasury stock	26,000
Cash received from issuing bonds	200,000

Instructions

Prepare a statement of cash flows using the indirect method.

Prepare partial statement of cash flows—indirect method.

E13.7 (LO 2), AN The following three accounts appear in the general ledger of Tao Ltd. during 2023.

Equipment

Date		Debit	Credit	Balance
Jan. 1	Balance			1,600,000
July 31	Purchase of equipment	700,000		2,300,000
Sept. 2	Purchase of equipment	530,000		2,830,000
Nov. 10	Cost of equipment sold		490,000	2,340,000

Accumulated Depreciation—Equipment

Date		Debit	Credit	Balance
Jan. 1	Balance			710,000
Nov. 10	Accumulated depreciation on equipment sold	160,000		550,000
Dec. 31	Depreciation for year		280,000	830,000

Retained Earnings

Date		Debit	Credit	Balance
Jan. 1	Balance			1,050,000
Aug. 23	Dividends (cash)	140,000		910,000
Dec. 31	Net income		720,000	1,630,000

Instructions

From the postings in the accounts, indicate how the information is reported on a statement of cash flows using the indirect method. The loss on disposal of plant assets was HK$80,000.

Prepare statement of cash flows and compute free cash flow.

E13.8 (LO 2, 3), AP Syal A.S.'s comparative balance sheets are presented below.

Syal A.S.
Comparative Balance Sheets
December 31

	2023	2022
Cash	₺ 143,000	₺ 107,000
Accounts receivable	212,000	234,000
Land	200,000	260,000
Buildings	700,000	700,000
Accumulated depreciation—buildings	(150,000)	(100,000)
Total	₺1,105,000	₺1,201,000
Accounts payable	₺ 123,700	₺ 311,000
Common stock	750,000	690,000
Retained earnings	231,300	200,000
Total	₺1,105,000	₺1,201,000

Additional information:

1. Net income was ₺226,300. Dividends declared and paid were ₺195,000.
2. No noncash investing and financing activities occurred during 2023.
3. The land was sold for cash of ₺49,000.

Instructions

a. Prepare a statement of cash flows for 2023 using the indirect method.
b. Compute free cash flow.

E13.9 (LO 2), AP The following are comparative balance sheets for Cassandra SA.

Prepare statement of cash flows—indirect method.

Cassandra SA
Comparative Balance Sheets
December 31

	2023	2022
Assets		
Cash	€ 68,000	€ 22,000
Accounts receivable	88,000	76,000
Inventory	167,000	189,000
Land	80,000	100,000
Equipment	260,000	200,000
Accumulated depreciation—equipment	(66,000)	(32,000)
Total	€597,000	€555,000
Liabilities and Stockholders' Equity		
Accounts payable	€ 39,000	€ 43,000
Bonds payable	150,000	200,000
Common stock (€1 par)	216,000	174,000
Retained earnings	192,000	138,000
Total	€597,000	€555,000

Additional information:
1. Net income for 2023 was €93,000.
2. Depreciation expense was €34,000.
3. Cash dividends of €39,000 were declared and paid.
4. Bonds payable with a carrying value of €50,000 were redeemed for €50,000 cash.
5. Common stock was issued at par for €42,000 cash.
6. No equipment was sold during 2023.
7. Land was sold for its book value.

Instructions

Prepare a statement of cash flows for 2023 using the indirect method.

E13.10 (LO 2, 3), AP Meyer AG's comparative balance sheets are as follows:

Prepare statement of cash flows—indirect method and compute free cash flow.

Meyer AG
Comparative Balance Sheets
December 31

	2023	2022
Cash	CHF 15,200	CHF 17,700
Accounts receivable	25,200	22,300
Investments	20,000	16,000
Equipment	60,000	70,000
Accumulated depreciation—equipment	(14,000)	(10,000)
Total	CHF106,400	CHF116,000
Accounts payable	CHF 14,600	CHF 11,100
Bonds payable	10,000	30,000
Common stock	50,000	45,000
Retained earnings	31,800	29,900
Total	CHF106,400	CHF116,000

Additional information:

1. Net income was CHF18,300. Dividends declared and paid were CHF16,400.
2. Equipment which cost CHF10,000 and had accumulated depreciation of CHF1,200 was sold for CHF3,300.
3. No noncash investing and financing activities occurred during 2023.
4. Bonds were retired at their carrying value.

Instructions

a. Prepare a statement of cash flows for 2023 using the indirect method.
b. Compute free cash flow.

Compute net cash provided by operating activities—direct method.

*E13.11 (LO 4), AP Fletcher Ltd. completed its first year of operations on December 31, 2023. Its initial income statement showed that Fletcher had sales revenue of £198,000 and operating expenses of £83,000. Accounts receivable and accounts payable at year-end were £60,000 and £23,000, respectively. Assume that accounts payable related to operating expenses. Ignore income taxes.

Instructions

Compute net cash provided by operating activity using the direct method.

Compute cash payments—direct method.

*E13.12 (LO 4), AP Suppose the 2023 income statement for **McDonald's Corporation** (USA) shows cost of goods sold $5,178.0 million and operating expenses (including depreciation expense of $1,216.2 million) $10,725.7 million. The comparative balance sheets for the year show that inventory decreased $5.3 million, prepaid expenses increased $42.2 million, accounts payable (inventory suppliers) increased $15.6 million, and accrued expenses payable increased $199.8 million.

Instructions

Using the direct method, compute (a) cash payments to suppliers and (b) cash payments for operating expenses.

Compute cash flow from operating activities—direct method.

*E13.13 (LO 4), AP The 2023 accounting records of Mega Transport provide the following information.

Payment of interest	A$ 10,000	Payment of salaries and wages	A$ 53,000
Cash sales	48,000	Depreciation expense	16,000
Receipt of dividend revenue	18,000	Proceeds from sale of vehicles	812,000
Payment of income taxes	12,000	Purchase of equipment for cash	22,000
Net income	38,000	Loss on sale of vehicles	3,000
Payment for merchandise	97,000	Payment of dividends	14,000
Payment for land	74,000	Payment of operating expenses	28,000
Collection of accounts receivable	195,000		

Instructions

Prepare the cash flows from operating activities section using the direct method.

Calculate cash flows—direct method.

*E13.14 (LO 4), AN The following information is taken from the 2023 general ledger of Recife Company.

Rent	Rent expense	R$ 300,000
	Prepaid rent, January 1	59,000
	Prepaid rent, December 31	74,000
Salaries	Salaries and wages expense	R$ 540,000
	Salaries and wages payable, January 1	20,000
	Salaries and wages payable, December 31	80,000
Sales	Sales revenue	R$1,600,000
	Accounts receivable, January 1	160,000
	Accounts receivable, December 31	70,000

Instructions

In each case, compute the amount that should be reported in the operating activities section of the statement of cash flows under the direct method.

Problems

P13.1 (LO 1, 2), C You are provided with the following information regarding events that occurred at Campbell Corporation during 2023 or changes in account balances as of December 31, 2023.

Distinguish among operating, investing, and financing activities.

	(1) Statement of Cash Flow Section Affected	(2) If Operating, Did It Increase or Decrease Reported Cash from Operating Activities?
a. Depreciation expense was A$80,000.		
b. Interest Payable account increased A$5,000.		
c. Received A$26,000 from sale of plant assets.		
d. Acquired land by issuing common stock to seller.		
e. Paid A$17,000 cash dividend to preferred stockholders.		
f. Paid A$4,000 cash dividend to common stockholders.		
g. Accounts Receivable account decreased A$10,000.		
h. Inventory increased A$2,000.		
i. Received A$100,000 from issuing bonds payable.		
j. Acquired equipment for A$16,000 cash.		

Instructions

Campbell prepares its statement of cash flows using the indirect method. Complete the first column of the table, indicating whether each item affects the operating activities section (O) (that is, the item would be listed among the adjustments to net income to determine net cash provided by operating activities under the indirect method), investing activities section (I), financing activities section (F), or is a noncash (NC) transaction reported in a separate schedule. For those items classified as operating activities (O), indicate whether the item is added (A) or subtracted (S) from net income to determine net cash provided by operating activities.

P13.2 (LO 2), AN The following account balances relate to the stockholders' equity accounts of Gibson plc at year-end.

Determine cash flow effects of changes in equity accounts.

	2023	2022
Common stock, 10,500 and 10,000 shares, issued and outstanding, respectively, for 2023 and 2022	£160,800	£140,000
Preferred stock, 5,000 shares, issued and outstanding	125,000	125,000
Retained earnings	300,000	270,000

A small stock dividend was declared and issued in 2023. The market price of the shares issued was £8,800. Cash dividends of £20,000 were declared and paid in both 2023 and 2022. The common stock and preferred stock have no par or stated value.

Instructions

a. What was the amount of net income reported by Gibson plc in 2023?

b. Determine the amounts of any cash inflows or outflows related to the common stock and dividend accounts in 2023.

c. Indicate where each of the cash inflows or outflows identified in (b) would be classified on the statement of cash flows.

a. Net income £58,800

Prepare the operating activities section—indirect method.

P13.3 (LO 2), AP The income statement of Hu Na Ltd. is presented here.

Hu Na Ltd.
Income Statement
For the Year Ended November 30, 2023

Sales revenue		HK$76,000,000
Cost of goods sold		
Beginning inventory	HK$19,000,000	
Purchases	44,000,000	
Goods available for sale	63,000,000	
Ending inventory	16,000,000	
Total cost of goods sold		47,000,000
Gross profit		29,000,000
Operating expenses		
Selling expenses	4,500,000	
Administrative expenses	7,000,000	11,500,000
Net income		HK$17,500,000

Additional information:

1. Accounts receivable decreased HK$3,800,000 during the year, and inventory decreased HK$3,000,000.
2. Prepaid expenses increased HK$1,500,000 during the year.
3. Accounts payable to suppliers of inventory decreased HK$3,500,000 during the year.
4. Accrued expenses payable decreased HK$1,000,000 during the year.
5. Administrative expenses include depreciation expense of HK$1,100,000.

Instructions

Net cash provided— oper. act. HK$19,400,000

Prepare the operating activities section of the statement of cash flows for the year ended November 30, 2023, for Hu Na Ltd., using the indirect method.

Prepare the operating activities section—direct method.

Net cash provided— oper. act. HK$19,400,000

*P13.4 (LO 4), AP Data for Hu Na Ltd. are presented in P13.3.

Instructions

Prepare the operating activities section of the statement of cash flows using the direct method.

Prepare the operating activities section—indirect method.

P13.5 (LO 2), AP Moser AG's income statement contained the following condensed information.

Moser AG
Income Statement
For the Year Ended December 31, 2023

Service revenue		CHF970,000
Operating expenses, excluding depreciation	CHF614,000	
Depreciation expense	55,000	
Loss on disposal of plant assets	16,000	685,000
Income before income taxes		285,000
Income tax expense		56,000
Net income		CHF229,000

Moser's balance sheets contained the following comparative data at December 31.

	2023	2022
Accounts receivable	CHF70,000	CHF60,000
Accounts payable	41,000	32,000
Income taxes payable	13,000	7,000

Accounts payable pertain to operating expenses.

Instructions

Prepare the operating activities section of the statement of cash flows using the indirect method.

*P13.6 (LO 4), AP Data for Moser AG are presented in P13.5.

Instructions

Prepare the operating activities section of the statement of cash flows using the direct method.

P13.7 (LO 2, 3), AP Presented here are the financial statements of Drew Company.

Net cash provided CHF305,000

Prepare the operating activities section—direct method.

Net cash provided CHF305,000

Prepare a statement of cash flows—indirect method, and compute free cash flow.

Drew Company
Comparative Balance Sheets
December 31

	2023	2022
Assets		
Cash	A$ 35,000	A$ 20,000
Accounts receivable	20,000	14,000
Inventory	28,000	20,000
Property, plant, and equipment	60,000	78,000
Accumulated depreciation	(32,000)	(24,000)
Total	A$111,000	A$108,000
Liabilities and Stockholders' Equity		
Accounts payable	A$ 19,000	A$ 15,000
Income taxes payable	7,000	8,000
Bonds payable	17,000	33,000
Common stock	18,000	14,000
Retained earnings	50,000	38,000
Total	A$111,000	A$108,000

Drew Company
Income Statement
For the Year Ended December 31, 2023

Sales revenue		A$242,000
Cost of goods sold		175,000
Gross profit		67,000
Selling expenses	A$18,000	
Administrative expenses	6,000	24,000
Income from operations		43,000
Interest expense		3,000
Income before income taxes		40,000
Income tax expense		8,000
Net income		A$ 32,000

Additional data:
1. Depreciation expense was A$17,500.
2. Dividends declared and paid were A$20,000.
3. During the year, equipment was sold for A$8,500 cash. This equipment originally cost A$18,000 and had accumulated depreciation of A$9,500 at the time of sale.
4. Bonds were redeemed at their carrying value.
5. Common stock was issued at par for cash.

Instructions

a. Prepare a statement of cash flows using the indirect method.
b. Compute free cash flow.

*P13.8 (LO 3, 4), AP Data for Drew Company are presented in P13.7. Further analysis reveals the following:
1. Accounts payable pertain to merchandise suppliers.
2. All operating expenses except for depreciation were paid in cash.
3. All depreciation expense is in the selling expense category.
4. All sales and inventory purchases are on account.

a. Net cash provided— oper. act. A$38,500

Prepare a statement of cash flows—direct method, and compute free cash flow.

CHAPTER 13 Statement of Cash Flows

*a. Net cash provided—
oper. act. A$38,500*

Prepare a statement of cash flows—indirect method.

Instructions

a. Prepare a statement of cash flows for Drew Company using the direct method.
b. Compute free cash flow.

P13.9 (LO 2), AP Condensed financial data of Gao Ltd. follow:

Gao Ltd.
Comparative Balance Sheets
December 31

	2023	2022
Assets		
Cash	HK$ 808,000	HK$ 484,000
Accounts receivable	878,000	380,000
Inventory	1,125,000	1,028,500
Prepaid expenses	284,000	260,000
Long-term investments	1,380,000	1,090,000
Plant assets	2,850,000	2,425,000
Accumulated depreciation	(500,000)	(520,000)
Total	HK$6,825,000	HK$5,147,500
Liabilities and Stockholders' Equity		
Accounts payable	HK$1,020,000	HK$ 673,000
Accrued expenses payable	165,000	210,000
Bonds payable	1,100,000	1,460,000
Common stock	2,200,000	1,750,000
Retained earnings	2,340,000	1,054,500
Total	HK$6,825,000	HK$5,147,500

Gao Ltd.
Income Statement Data
For the Year Ended December 31, 2023

Sales revenue		HK$3,884,600
Less:		
Cost of goods sold	HK$1,354,600	
Operating expenses, excluding depreciation	124,100	
Depreciation expense	465,000	
Income tax expense	272,800	
Interest expense	47,300	
Loss on disposal of plant assets	75,000	2,338,800
Net income		HK$1,545,800

Additional information:

1. New plant assets costing HK$1,000,000 were purchased for cash during the year.
2. Old plant assets having an original cost of HK$575,000 and accumulated depreciation of HK$485,000 were sold for HK$15,000 cash.
3. Bonds payable matured and were paid off at face value for cash.
4. A cash dividend of HK$260,300 was declared and paid during the year.
5. Common stock was issued at par for cash.
6. There were no significant noncash transactions.

*Net cash provided—
oper. act. HK$1,769,300*

Instructions

Prepare a statement of cash flows using the indirect method.

Prepare a statement of cash flows—direct method.

*P13.10 (LO 4), AP Data for Gao Ltd. are presented in P13.9. Further analysis reveals that accounts payable pertain to merchandise creditors.

*Net cash provided—
oper. act. HK$1,769,300*

Instructions

Prepare a statement of cash flows for Gao Ltd. using the direct method.

P13.11 (LO 2), AP The comparative balance sheets for Sung Company as of December 31 are as follows:

Prepare a statement of cash flows—indirect method.

Sung Company
Comparative Balance Sheets
December 31

	2023	2022
Assets		
Cash	₩68,000,000	₩45,000,000
Accounts receivable	50,000,000	58,000,000
Inventory	151,450,000	142,000,000
Prepaid expenses	15,280,000	21,000,000
Land	145,000,000	130,000,000
Buildings	200,000,000	200,000,000
Accumulated depreciation—buildings	(60,000,000)	(40,000,000)
Equipment	225,000,000	155,000,000
Accumulated depreciation—equipment	(45,000,000)	(35,000,000)
Total	₩749,730,000	₩676,000,000
Liabilities and Stockholders' Equity		
Accounts payable	₩ 44,730,000	₩ 36,000,000
Bonds payable	300,000,000	300,000,000
Common stock, ₩1,000 par	200,000,000	160,000,000
Retained earnings	205,000,000	180,000,000
Total	₩749,730,000	₩676,000,000

Additional information:

1. Operating expenses include depreciation expense of ₩42,000,000 (₩20,000,000 of depreciation expense for buildings and ₩22,000,000 for equipment).
2. Land was sold for cash at book value.
3. Cash dividends of ₩12,000,000 were declared and paid.
4. Net income for 2023 was ₩37,000,000.
5. Equipment was purchased for ₩92,000,000 cash. In addition, equipment costing ₩22,000,000 with a book value of ₩10,000,000 was sold for ₩8,000,000 cash.
6. 40,000 shares of ₩1,000 par value common stock were issued in exchange for land with a fair value of ₩40,000,000.

Instructions

Prepare a statement of cash flows for the year ended December 31, 2023, using the indirect method.

Net cash provided— oper. act. ₩94,000,000

Expand Your Critical Thinking

Financial Reporting Problem: Apple Inc.

CT13.1 The financial statements of **Apple Inc.** (USA) are available online.

Instructions

Answer the following questions:

a. What was the amount of net cash provided by operating activities for the year ended September 28, 2019? For the year ended September 29, 2018?
b. What was the amount of increase or decrease in cash and cash equivalents for the year ended September 28, 2019?
c. Which method of computing net cash provided by operating activities does Apple use?
d. From your analysis of the September 28, 2019, statement of cash flows, was the change in accounts receivable a decrease or an increase? Was the change in inventories a decrease or an increase? Was the change in accounts payable a decrease or an increase?
e. What was the net cash provided (generated) by investing activities for the year ended September 28, 2019?
f. What was the amount of interest paid in the year ended September 28, 2019? What was the amount of income taxes paid for the same period?

Comparative Analysis Problem: PepsiCo, Inc. vs. The Coca-Cola Company

CT13.2 The financial statements of **PepsiCo** (USA) and **The Coca-Cola Company** (USA) are available online. The complete annual reports of PepsiCo and Coca-Cola, including the notes to the financial statements, are available at each company's respective website.

Instructions

a. Based on the information contained in these financial statements, compute the 2019 fiscal year free cash flow for each company.

b. What conclusions concerning the management of cash can be drawn from these data?

Comparative Analysis Problem: Amazon.com, Inc. vs. Walmart Inc.

CT13.3 The financial statements of **Amazon.com, Inc.** (USA) and **Walmart Inc.** (USA) are available online. The complete annual reports of Amazon and Walmart, including the notes to the financial statements, are available at each company's respective website.

Instructions

a. Based on the information contained in these financial statements, compute the 2019 fiscal year free cash flow for each company.

b. What conclusions concerning the management of cash can be drawn from these data?

Decision-Making Across the Organization

CT13.4 Norman Roads and Mira Sarang are examining the following statement of cash flows for Del Carpio, SLU for the year ended January 31, 2023.

Del Carpio, SLU
Statement of Cash Flows
For the Year Ended January 31, 2023

Sources of cash	
From sales of merchandise	€385,000
From sale of capital stock	405,000
From sale of investment (purchased below)	80,000
From depreciation	55,000
From issuance of note for truck	20,000
From interest on investments	6,000
Total sources of cash	951,000
Uses of cash	
For purchase of fixtures and equipment	€320,000
For merchandise purchased for resale	258,000
For operating expenses (including depreciation)	170,000
For purchase of investment	75,000
For purchase of truck by issuance of note	20,000
For purchase of treasury stock	10,000
For interest on note payable	3,000
Total uses of cash	856,000
Net increase in cash	€ 95,000

Norman claims that Del Carpio's statement of cash flows is an excellent portrayal of a superb first year, with cash increasing €95,000. Mira replies that it was not a superb first year. Rather, she says, the year was an operating failure, the statement is presented incorrectly, and €95,000 is not the actual increase in cash. The cash balance at the beginning of the year was €140,000.

Instructions

With the class divided into groups, answer the following:

a. Using the data provided, prepare a statement of cash flows in proper form using the indirect method. The only noncash items in the income statement are depreciation and the gain from the sale of the investment.

b. With whom do you agree, Norman or Mira? Explain your position.

Real-World Focus

CT13.5 Purpose: Learn about the **U.S. Securities and Exchange Commission (SEC)**.

Instructions

Go to the U.S. SEC website, choose **About**, and then answer the following questions:

a. How many enforcement actions does the SEC take each year against securities law violators? What are typical infractions?

b. After the Depression, Congress passed the Securities Acts of 1933 and 1934 to improve investor confidence in the markets. What two "common sense" notions are these laws based on?

c. Who was the president of the United States at the time of the creation of the SEC? Who was the first SEC chairperson?

CT13.6 You can use the Internet to view **U.S. SEC** filings.

Instructions

Choose a company, go to the **Yahoo! Finance** website, and then answer the following questions:

a. What company did you select?

b. What is its stock symbol? What is its selling price?

c. What recent SEC filings are available for your viewing? (*Hint:* Use the Profile link.)

d. Which filing is the most recent? What is its date?

Communication Activity

CT13.7 Bart Sampson, the owner-president of Computer Services International, is unfamiliar with the statement of cash flows that you, as his accountant, prepared. He asks for further explanation.

Instructions

Write him a brief memo explaining the form and content of the statement of cash flows as shown in Illustration 13.14.

Ethics Case

CT13.8 Babbit Ltd. is a medium-sized wholesaler of automotive parts. It has 10 shareholders who have been paid a total of £1 million in cash dividends for eight consecutive years. The board's policy requires that, for this dividend to be declared, net cash provided by operating activities as reported in Babbit's current year's statement of cash flows must exceed £1 million. President and CEO Milton Williams' job is secure so long as he produces annual operating cash flows to support the usual dividend.

At the end of the current year, controller Jerry Roberts presents president Milton Williams with some disappointing news: The net cash provided by operating activities is calculated by the indirect method to be only £970,000. The president says to Jerry, "We must get that amount above £1 million. Isn't there some way to increase operating cash flow by another £30,000?" Jerry answers, "These figures were prepared by my assistant. I'll go back to my office and see what I can do." The president replies, "I know you won't let me down, Jerry."

Upon close scrutiny of the statement of cash flows, Jerry concludes that he can get the operating cash flows above £1 million by reclassifying a £60,000, two-year note payable listed in the financing activities section as "Proceeds from bank loan—£60,000." He will report the note instead as "Increase in payables—£60,000" and treat it as an adjustment of net income in the operating activities section. He returns to the president, saying, "You can tell the board to declare their usual dividend. Our net cash flow provided by operating activities is £1,030,000." "Good man, Jerry! I knew I could count on you," exults the president.

Instructions

a. Who are the stakeholders in this situation?

b. Was there anything unethical about the president's actions? Was there anything unethical about the controller's actions?

c. Are the board members or anyone else likely to discover the misclassification?

All About You

CT13.9 In this chapter, you learned that companies prepare a statement of cash flows in order to keep track of their sources and uses of cash and to help them plan for their future cash needs. Planning for short- and long-term cash needs is every bit as important for you as it is for a company.

Instructions

Read the online article "Financial Uh-Oh? No Problem" and then complete the following. To access this article, it may be necessary to register at no cost.

a. Describe the three factors that determine how much money you should set aside for short-term needs.

b. How many months of living expenses does the article suggest to set aside?

c. Estimate how much you should set aside based on your current situation. Are you closer to Cliff's scenario or to Prudence's?

CHAPTER 14

Financial Analysis: The Big Picture

CHAPTER PREVIEW

We can learn an important lesson from Li Ka-shing: Study companies carefully if you wish to invest. Do not get caught up in fads but instead find companies that are financially healthy. Using some of the basic decision tools presented in this textbook, you can perform a rudimentary analysis on any company and draw basic conclusions about its financial health. Although it would not be wise for you to bet your life savings on a company's shares relying solely on your current level of knowledge, we strongly encourage you to practice your new skills wherever possible. Only with practice will you improve your ability to interpret financial numbers.

Before unleashing you on the world of high finance, we will present a few more important concepts and techniques, as well as provide you with one more comprehensive review of company financial statements. We use all of the decision tools presented in this textbook to analyze a single company.

CHAPTER 14

Financial Analysis: The Big Picture

FEATURE STORY

Making Money the Old-Fashioned Way

Li Ka-shing likes simple things. He wears a basic electronic wristwatch, basic black dress shoes, and basic business suits. He lives by the philosophy that "If you keep a good reputation, work hard, be nice to people, keep your promises, your business will be much easier." It seems to have worked for him. Business has been good. Li Ka-shing is Hong Kong's richest person, with a net worth of over US$38 billion. That placed him in the top 40 on a recent list of the richest people in the world.

Li was not born rich. His family fled to Hong Kong from mainland China during the upheavals of war in 1940. His father died when Li was in his teens, forcing him to quit school and take a job at a plastics trading company. Within a few years, Li had started his own plastics company. One of his early businesses produced plastic flowers. He produced the parts for the flowers and then paid people to assemble the flowers in their homes. This saved him the cost of additional factory space (space being in short supply in Hong Kong).

Over the years, Li also invested in Hong Kong properties. One long-time business associate recalls that Li was very disciplined when bidding on investments in businesses and properties. He didn't like debt, and he would never bid above a predetermined number. He knew precisely what it would take for his investments to be profitable.

Today, Li's business interests span many industries and virtually all parts of the world. His companies operate in 55 countries with approximately 250,000 employees. He owns ports, retail companies, electricity companies, and energy interests such as oil sands in Canada, shipping companies, and telecom companies. He describes his criteria for doing business in a country as "rule of law, political stability that safeguards investments, ease of doing business and good tax structures."

How can you enjoy similar success? There are no guarantees, but honing your financial analysis skills would be a start. A good way for you to begin your career as a successful investor is to master the fundamentals of financial analysis discussed in this chapter.

Sources: Tom Mitchell and Robin Kwong, "Breaking the Mould," *Financial Times Online* (FT.com) (October 26, 2007); *Forbes.com*. https://www.forbes.com/profile/li-ka-shing/?sh=44ab92a0523f (accessed June 19, 2023).

CHAPTER OUTLINE

Learning Objectives	Review	Practice
LO 1 Apply the concepts of sustainable income.	• Discontinued operations • Comprehensive income • Changes in accounting principle	**DO IT! 1** Unusual Items
LO 2 Apply horizontal analysis and vertical analysis.	• Horizontal analysis • Vertical analysis	**DO IT! 2** Horizontal Analysis
LO 3 Analyze a company's performance using ratio analysis.	• Liquidity ratios • Solvency ratios • Profitability ratios • Financial analysis and data analytics • Comprehensive example	**DO IT! 3** Ratio Analysis

Go to the Review and Practice section at the end of the chapter for a targeted summary and practice applications with solutions.

SUSTAINABLE INCOME

The value of a company like **Google** (USA) is a function of the amount, timing, and uncertainty of its future cash flows. Google's current and past income statements are particularly useful in helping analysts predict these future cash flows. In using this approach, analysts must make sure that Google's past income numbers reflect its **sustainable income**, that is, they do not include unusual (out-of-the-ordinary) revenues, expenses, gains, and losses.

> **LEARNING OBJECTIVE 1**
> Apply the concepts of sustainable income.

- **Sustainable income** is, therefore, the most likely level of income to be obtained by a company in the future.
- Sustainable income differs from actual net income by the amount of unusual revenues, expenses, gains, and losses included in the current year's income. Determining sustainable income requires an understanding of discontinued operations, comprehensive income, and changes in accounting principle.
- Analysts are interested in sustainable income because it helps them derive an estimate of future earnings without the "noise" of unusual items.

Discontinued Operations

Discontinued operations refers to the disposal of a **significant component** of a business, such as the elimination of a major class of customers or an entire activity (see **Decision Tools**). For example, to downsize its operations, **General Dynamics Corp.** (USA) sold its missile business to **Hughes Aircraft Co.** (USA) for $450 million. In its income statement, General Dynamics reported the sale in a separate section entitled "Discontinued operations."

A company reports the disposal of a significant component as follows:

> **DECISION TOOLS**
> The discontinued operations section alerts users to the sale of any major components of a company's business.

- When a company has discontinued operations, the company should report on its income statement both income from continuing operations and income (or loss) from discontinued operations.
- **The income (loss) from discontinued operations consists of two parts: the income (loss) from the operations component and the gain (loss) on disposal of the component.**
- The income from continuing operations as well as the discontinued component are reported net of tax.

To illustrate, assume that during 2023 Garcia Energy SpA has income before income taxes of €800,000. During 2023, Garcia discontinued and sold its unprofitable chemical division. The loss in 2023 from the chemical division's operations (net of €40,000 income tax savings) was €160,000. The loss on disposal of the chemical division (net of €20,000 income tax savings) was €80,000. Assuming a 20% tax rate on income, **Illustration 14.1** shows Garcia's income statement (see **Helpful Hint**).

Note that the statement uses the caption "Income from continuing operations" and adds a new section "Discontinued operations."

> **HELPFUL HINT**
> Observe the dual disclosures: (1) the results of operation of the discontinued division must be separated from the results of continuing operations, and (2) the company must also report the gain or loss on disposal of the division.

- **The new section reports both the operating loss and the loss on disposal net of applicable income taxes.**
- This presentation clearly indicates the separate effects of continuing operations and discontinued operations on net income.

Garcia Energy SpA
Income Statement (partial)
For the Year Ended December 31, 2023

Income before income taxes		€800,000
Income tax expense		160,000
Income from continuing operations		640,000
Discontinued operations		
Loss from operation of chemical division, net of €40,000 income tax savings	€160,000	
Loss from disposal of chemical division, net of €20,000 income tax savings	80,000	(240,000)
Net income		€400,000

ILLUSTRATION 14.1 | Income statement presentation of discontinued operations

---

INVESTOR INSIGHT

iStock.com/Andrey Armiagov

What Does "Non-Recurring" Really Mean?

Many companies incur restructuring charges as they attempt to reduce costs. They often label these items in the income statement as "non-recurring" charges, to suggest that they are isolated events, unlikely to occur in future periods. The question for analysts is: are these costs really one-time, "non-recurring events" or do they reflect problems that the company will be facing for many periods in the future? If they are one-time events, then they can be largely ignored when trying to predict future earnings.

But, some companies report "one-time" restructuring charges over and over again. For example, **Procter & Gamble** (USA) reported a restructuring charge in 12 consecutive quarters, and **Motorola** (USA) had "special" charges in 14 consecutive quarters. On the other hand, other companies have a restructuring charge only once in a 5- or 10-year period. There appears to be no substitute for careful analysis of the numbers that comprise net income.

If a company takes a large restructuring charge, what is the effect on the company's current income statement versus future ones? (Answer is available in the book's product page on www.wiley.com)

Comprehensive Income

Most revenues, expenses, gains, and losses are included in net income.

- However, certain gains and losses that bypass net income are reported as part of a more inclusive earnings measure called comprehensive income.
- **Comprehensive income** is the sum of net income and other comprehensive income items.[1]

Illustration of Comprehensive Income

Accounting standards require that companies adjust most investments in stocks and bonds up or down to their market price at the end of each accounting period. For example, assume that during 2023, its first year of operations, Stassi Corporation purchased bonds for €10,500 as an investment, which it intends to sell sometime in the future. At the end of 2023, Stassi was still holding the investment, but the bonds' market price was now €8,000. In this case, Stassi is required to reduce the recorded value of its investment by €2,500. The €2,500 difference is an "unrealized" loss. A gain or loss is referred to as unrealized when an asset has experienced a change in value but the owner has not sold the asset. The sale of the asset results in "realization" of the gain or loss.

Should Stassi include this €2,500 unrealized loss in net income? It depends on whether Stassi classifies the bonds as a trading security or an available-for-sale security.

---

[1] The IASB defines total comprehensive income as the change in equity during a period resulting from transactions and other events, other than those changes resulting from transactions with owners in their capacity as owners.

- A **trading security** is bought and held primarily for sale in the near term to generate income on short-term price differences.
- Companies report unrealized losses on trading securities in the "Other expenses and losses" section of the income statement.
- The rationale: It is likely that the company will realize the unrealized loss (or an unrealized gain), so the company should report the loss (gain) as part of net income.

If Stassi did not purchase the investment for trading purposes, it is classified as available-for-sale.

- **Available-for-sale securities** are held with the intent of selling them sometime in the future.
- Companies do not include unrealized gains or losses on available-for-sale securities in net income.
- Instead, they report them as part of "Other comprehensive income," which is not included in net income.

Format

Companies report other comprehensive income in a separate statement of comprehensive income. For example, assuming that Stassi Corporation has a net income of €300,000 and a 20% tax rate, the unrealized loss would be reported below net income, net of tax, as shown in **Illustration 14.2**.

Stassi Corporation
Statement of Comprehensive Income
For the Year Ended December 31, 2023

Net income	€300,000
Other comprehensive income	
Unrealized loss on available-for-sale securities, net of €500 income tax savings	2,000
Comprehensive income	€298,000

ILLUSTRATION 14.2 | **Statement of comprehensive income**

Companies report the cumulative amount of other comprehensive income from all years as a separate component of stockholders' equity. To illustrate, assume Stassi has common stock of €3,000,000, retained earnings of €300,000, and accumulated other comprehensive loss of €2,000. (To simplify, we are assuming that this is Stassi's first year of operations. Since it has only operated for one year, the cumulative amount of other comprehensive income is this year's loss of €2,000.) **Illustration 14.3** shows the balance sheet presentation of the accumulated other comprehensive loss.

Stassi Corporation
Balance Sheet (partial)

Stockholders' equity	
Common stock	€3,000,000
Retained earnings	300,000
Total paid-in capital and retained earnings	3,300,000
Accumulated other comprehensive loss	(2,000)
Total stockholders' equity	€3,298,000

ILLUSTRATION 14.3 | **Accumulated other comprehensive loss in stockholders' equity section**

Note that the presentation of the accumulated other comprehensive loss is similar to the presentation of the cost of treasury stock in the stockholders' equity section. (Accumulated unrealized gains would be added in this section of the balance sheet.)

Income Statement and Statement of Comprehensive Income

As discussed, many companies report net income and other comprehensive income in separate statements, such as those shown for Gallop AG in **Illustration 14.4**.

Gallop AG
Income Statement
For the Year Ended December 31, 2023

Net sales		€440,000
Cost of goods sold		260,000
Gross profit		180,000
Operating expenses		118,250
Income from operations		61,750
Other revenues and gains		5,600
Other expenses and losses		9,600
Income before income taxes		57,750
Income tax expense (€57,750 × 20%)		11,550
Income from continuing operations		46,200
Discontinued operations		
Loss from operation of plastics division, net of income tax savings €12,000 (€60,000 × 20%)	€48,000	
Gain on disposal of plastics division, net of €10,000 income taxes (€50,000 × 20%)	40,000	(8,000)
Net income		€38,200

Gallop AG
Statement of Comprehensive Income
For the Year Ended December 31, 2023

Net income	€38,200
Other comprehensive income	
Unrealized gain on available-for-sale securities, net of income taxes (€15,000 × 20%)	12,000
Comprehensive income	€50,200

ILLUSTRATION 14.4 | Income statement and statement of comprehensive income

- The income statement presents the types of items usually found on this statement, such as net sales, cost of goods sold, operating expenses, and income taxes.
- The income statement and statement of comprehensive income show how companies report discontinued operations and other comprehensive income (highlighted in red).

Changes in Accounting Principle

For ease of comparison, users of financial statements expect companies to prepare their statements on a basis **consistent** with the preceding period.

DECISION TOOLS

Informing users of a change in accounting principle helps them determine the effects of this change on current and prior periods.

- A **change in accounting principle** occurs when the principle used in the current year is different from the one used in the preceding year (see **Decision Tools**).
- An example is a change in inventory costing methods (such as FIFO to average-cost).
- Accounting rules permit a change when management can show that the new principle is preferable to the old principle.

Companies report most changes in accounting principle retroactively.[2] That is, they report the results from both the current period and previous periods using the new principle. Thus, the same principle is used in all periods. This treatment improves the ability to compare financial performance across years.

INVESTOR INSIGHT   United Parcel Service (UPS)

More Frequent Ups and Downs

Larry MacDougal/ Canadian Press Images

In the past, U.S. companies used a method to account for their pension plans that smoothed out the gains and losses on their pension portfolios by spreading gains and losses over multiple years. Many felt that this approach was beneficial because it reduced the volatility of reported net income. However, recently some companies have opted to adopt a method that comes closer to recognizing gains and losses in the period in which they occur. Some of the U.S. companies that have adopted this approach are **United Parcel Service (UPS)**, **Honeywell International**, **IBM**, **AT&T**, and **Verizon Communications**. The CFO at UPS said he favored the new approach because "events that occurred in prior years will no longer distort current-year results. It will result in better transparency by eliminating the noise of past plan performance." When UPS switched, it resulted in a charge of $827 million due to the change in accounting principle.

Source: Bob Sechler and Doug Cameron, "UPS Alters Pension-Plan Accounting," *Wall Street Journal* (January 30, 2012).

When predicting future earnings, how should analysts treat the one-time charge that results from a switch to the different approach for accounting for pension plans? (Answer is available in the book's product page on www.wiley.com)

DO IT! 1 ▶ Unusual Items

During 2023, Soule AG had the following amounts, all before calculating tax effects: income before income taxes €400,000, unrealized gain on available-for-sale securities €100,000, loss from operation of discontinued flower division €50,000, and loss on disposal of discontinued flower division €90,000. The income tax rate is 20%. Prepare a partial income statement, beginning with "Income before income taxes," and a statement of comprehensive income.

ACTION PLAN
- Show discontinued operations and other comprehensive income net of tax.

Solution

Soule AG
Income Statement (partial)
For the Year Ended December 31, 2023

Income before income taxes		€400,000
Income tax expense		80,000
Income from continuing operations		320,000
Discontinued operations		
Loss from operation of flower division, net of €10,000 income tax savings	€40,000	
Loss on disposal of flower division, net of €18,000 income tax savings	72,000	(112,000)
Net income		€208,000

---

[2] An exception to the general rule is a change in depreciation methods. The effects of this change are reported prospectively in current and future periods. Discussion of this approach is left for more advanced courses.

Soule AG
Statement of Comprehensive Income
For the Year Ended December 31, 2023

Net income	€208,000
Other comprehensive income	
Unrealized gain on available-for-sale securities, net of €20,000 income taxes	80,000
Comprehensive income	€288,000

Related exercise material: **BE14.1, BE14.2, DO IT! 14.1, E14.1,** and **E14.2.**

HORIZONTAL ANALYSIS AND VERTICAL ANALYSIS

LEARNING OBJECTIVE 2
Apply horizontal analysis and vertical analysis.

In assessing the financial performance of a company, investors are interested in its core or sustainable earnings. In addition, investors are interested in making comparisons from period to period. Throughout this text, we have relied on three types of comparisons to improve the decision-usefulness of financial information:

1. **Intracompany basis.** Comparisons within a company are often useful to detect changes in financial relationships and significant trends. For example, a comparison of **Kellogg's** (USA) current year's cash amount with the prior year's cash amount shows either an increase or a decrease. Likewise, a comparison of Kellogg's year-end cash amount with the amount of its total assets at year-end shows the proportion of total assets in the form of cash.

2. **Intercompany basis.** Comparisons with other companies provide insight into a company's competitive position. For example, investors can compare Kellogg's total sales for the year with the total sales of its competitors in the breakfast cereal area, such as **General Mills** (USA).

3. **Industry averages.** Comparisons with industry averages provide information about a company's relative position within the industry. For example, financial statement readers can compare Kellogg's financial data with the averages for its industry compiled by U.S. financial rating organizations such as **Dun & Bradstreet**, **Moody's**, and **Standard & Poor's**, or with information provided on the Internet by organizations such as **Yahoo!** on its financial site.

We use three basic tools in financial statement analysis to highlight the significance of financial statement data:

1. Horizontal analysis.
2. Vertical analysis.
3. Ratio analysis.

In the remainder of this section, we introduce formal forms of horizontal and vertical analysis. In the next section, we review ratio analysis in some detail.

DECISION TOOLS
Horizontal analysis helps users compare a company's financial position and operating results with those of the previous period.

Horizontal Analysis

Horizontal analysis, also known as trend analysis, is a technique for evaluating a series of financial statement data over a period of time (see **Decision Tools**). Its purpose is to determine the increase or decrease that has taken place, expressed as either an amount or a percentage. For example, here are recent net sales figures (in thousands) of Dubois Céréale SA:

2023	2022	2021	2020	2019
€11,776	€10,907	€10,177	€9,614	€8,812

If we assume that 2019 is the base year, we can measure all percentage increases or decreases relative to this base-period amount with the formula shown in **Illustration 14.5**.

$$\text{Change Since Base Period} = \frac{\text{Current-Year Amount} - \text{Base-Year Amount}}{\text{Base-Year Amount}}$$

ILLUSTRATION 14.5 | Horizontal analysis—computation of changes since base period

Using horizontal analysis, we can determine the following:

- Net sales for Dubois Céréale increased approximately 9.1% [(€9,614 − €8,812) ÷ €8,812] from 2019 to 2020.
- Net sales increased by 33.6% [(€11,776 − €8,812) ÷ €8,812] from 2019 to 2023.

Alternatively, we can express current-year net sales as a percentage of the base period. To do so, we would divide the current-year amount by the base-year amount, as shown in **Illustration 14.6**.

$$\text{Current Results in Relation to Base Period} = \frac{\text{Current-Year Amount}}{\text{Base-Year Amount}}$$

ILLUSTRATION 14.6 | Horizontal analysis—computation of current year in relation to base year

Current-period net sales expressed as a percentage of the base period for each of the five years, using 2019 as the base period, are shown in **Illustration 14.7**.

Dubois Céréale SA
Net Sales (in thousands)
Base Period 2019

2023	2022	2021	2020	2019
€11,776	€10,907	€10,177	€9,614	€8,812
133.6%	123.8%	115.5%	109.1%	100%

ILLUSTRATION 14.7 | Horizontal analysis of net sales

The large increase in net sales during 2020 would raise questions regarding possible reasons for such a significant change. Dubois Céréale's 2020 notes to the financial statements explain that the company completed an acquisition of Quality Foods Company during 2020. This major acquisition would help explain the increase in net sales highlighted by horizontal analysis.

To further illustrate horizontal analysis, we use the financial statements of Dubois Céréale SA. Its two-year condensed balance sheets for 2023 and 2022, showing euro and percentage changes, are presented in **Illustration 14.8** (see **Helpful Hint**).

HELPFUL HINT
When using horizontal analysis, be sure to examine both euro amount changes and percentage changes.

Dubois Céréale SA
Condensed Balance Sheets
December 31 (in thousands)

	2023	2022	Increase (Decrease) During 2023 Amount	Percent
Assets				
Current assets	€ 2,717	€ 2,427	€290	11.9
Property, plant, and equipment (net)	2,990	2,816	174	6.2
Other assets	5,690	5,471	219	4.0
Total assets	€11,397	€10,714	€683	6.4
Liabilities and Stockholders' Equity				
Current liabilities	€ 4,044	€ 4,020	€ 24	0.6
Long-term liabilities	4,827	4,625	202	4.4
Total liabilities	8,871	8,645	226	2.6
Stockholders' equity				
Common stock	493	397	96	24.2
Retained earnings	3,390	2,584	806	31.2
Treasury stock (cost)	(1,357)	(912)	445	48.8
Total stockholders' equity	2,526	2,069	457	22.1
Total liabilities and stockholders' equity	€11,397	€10,714	€683	6.4

ILLUSTRATION 14.8 | Horizontal analysis of balance sheets

The comparative balance sheets show that a number of changes occurred in Dubois Céréale's financial position from 2022 to 2023.

HELPFUL HINT
The increase in the Amount column of €99 results from adding and subtracting the amounts shown. In the Percent column, the 9.9% cannot be determined by adding and subtracting the percentages shown.

- In the assets section, current assets increased €290,000, or 11.9% (€290 ÷ €2,427, in thousands), and property, plant, and equipment (net) increased €174,000, or 6.2%. Other assets increased €219,000, or 4.0%.
- In the liabilities section, current liabilities increased €24,000, or 0.6%, while long-term liabilities increased €202,000, or 4.4%.
- In the stockholders' equity section, we find that retained earnings increased €806,000, or 31.2%.

Illustration 14.9 presents two-year comparative income statements of Dubois Céréale SA for 2023 and 2022, showing euro and percentage changes (see **Helpful Hint**).

Dubois Céréale SA
Condensed Income Statements
For the Years Ended December 31 (in thousands)

	2023	2022	Increase (Decrease) During 2023 Amount	Percent
Net sales	€11,776	€10,907	€869	8.0
Cost of goods sold	6,597	6,082	515	8.5
Gross profit	5,179	4,825	354	7.3
Selling and administrative expenses	3,311	3,059	252	8.2

	2023	2022	Increase (Decrease) During 2023	
			Amount	Percent
Income from operations	1,868	1,766	102	5.8
Interest expense	321	294	27	9.2
Income before income taxes	1,547	1,472	75	5.1
Income tax expense	444	468	(24)	(5.1)
Net income	€ 1,103	€ 1,004	€ 99	9.9

ILLUSTRATION 14.9 | Horizontal analysis of income statements

Horizontal analysis of the income statements shows the following changes:

- Net sales increased €869,000, or 8.0% (€869 ÷ €10,907, in thousands).
- Cost of goods sold increased €515,000, or 8.5% (€515 ÷ €6,082).
- Selling and administrative expenses increased €252,000, or 8.2% (€252 ÷ €3,059).
- Overall, gross profit increased 7.3% and net income increased 9.9%. The increase in net income can be attributed to the increase in net sales and a decrease in income tax expense.

The measurement of changes from period to period in percentages is relatively straightforward and quite useful. However, complications can result in making the computations. If an item has no value in a base year or preceding year and a value in the next year, no percentage change can be computed.

Vertical Analysis

Vertical analysis, also called common-size analysis, is a technique for evaluating financial statement data that expresses each item in a financial statement as a **percentage of a base amount** (see **Decision Tools**). For example, on a balance sheet we might express current assets as 22% of total assets (total assets being the base amount). Or, on an income statement we might express selling expenses as 16% of net sales (net sales being the base amount).

Presented in **Illustration 14.10** are the comparative balance sheets of Dubois Céréale for 2023 and 2022, analyzed vertically. The base for the asset items is **total assets**, and the base for the liability and stockholders' equity items is **total liabilities and stockholders' equity**.

In addition to showing the relative size of each item on the balance sheets, vertical analysis can show the percentage change in the individual asset, liability, and stockholders' equity items.

- Current assets increased €290,000 from 2022 to 2023, and they increased from 22.6% to 23.8% of total assets.

DECISION TOOLS

Vertical analysis helps users compare relationships between financial statement items with those of last year or of competitors.

Dubois Céréale SA
Condensed Balance Sheets
December 31 (in thousands)

	2023		2022	
	Amount	Percent*	Amount	Percent*
Assets				
Current assets	€ 2,717	23.8	€ 2,427	22.6
Property, plant, and equipment (net)	2,990	26.2	2,816	26.3
Other assets	5,690	50.0	5,471	51.1
Total assets	€11,397	100.0	€10,714	100.0

	2023		2022	
	Amount	Percent*	Amount	Percent*
Liabilities and Stockholders' Equity				
Current liabilities	€ 4,044	35.5	€ 4,020	37.5
Long-term liabilities	4,827	42.4	4,625	43.2
Total liabilities	8,871	77.9	8,645	80.7
Stockholders' equity				
Common stock	493	4.3	397	3.7
Retained earnings	3,390	29.7	2,584	24.1
Treasury stock (cost)	(1,357)	(11.9)	(912)	(8.5)
Total stockholders' equity	2,526	22.1	2,069	19.3
Total liabilities and stockholders' equity	€11,397	100.0	€10,714	100.0

*Numbers have been rounded to total 100%.

ILLUSTRATION 14.10 | **Vertical analysis of balance sheets**

- Property, plant, and equipment (net) decreased from 26.3% to 26.2% of total assets.
- Other assets decreased from 51.1% to 50.0% of total assets.
- Total stockholders' equity increased by €457,000 from 19.3% to 22.1% of total liabilities and stockholders' equity.

This switch to a higher percentage of equity financing has two causes.

1. While total liabilities increased by €226,000, the percentage of liabilities declined from 80.7% to 77.9% of total liabilities and stockholders' equity.
2. Retained earnings increased by €806,000, from 24.1% to 29.7% of total liabilities and stockholders' equity.

Thus, the company shifted toward equity financing by relying less on debt and by increasing the amount of retained earnings.

Vertical analysis of the comparative income statements of Dubois Céréale, shown in **Illustration 14.11**, reveals the following:

Dubois Céréale SA
Condensed Income Statements
For the Years Ended December 31 (in thousands)

	2023		2022	
	Amount	Percent*	Amount	Percent*
Net sales	€11,776	100.0	€10,907	100.0
Cost of goods sold	6,597	56.0	6,082	55.8
Gross profit	5,179	44.0	4,825	44.2
Selling and administrative expenses	3,311	28.1	3,059	28.0
Income from operations	1,868	15.9	1,766	16.2
Interest expense	321	2.7	294	2.7
Income before income taxes	1,547	13.2	1,472	13.5
Income tax expense	444	3.8	468	4.3
Net income	€ 1,103	9.4	€ 1,004	9.2

*Numbers have been rounded to total 100%.

ILLUSTRATION 14.11 | **Vertical analysis of income statements**

- Cost of goods sold **as a percentage of net sales** increased from 55.8% to 56.0%, and selling and administrative expenses increased from 28.0% to 28.1%.
- Net income as a percentage of net sales increased from 9.2% to 9.4%. Dubois Céréale's increase in net income as a percentage of sales is due primarily to the decrease in income tax expense as a percentage of sales.

Vertical analysis also enables you to compare companies of different sizes. For example, one of Dubois Céréale's competitors is Park Mills. Park Mills' sales are 1,000 times larger than those of Dubois Céréale. Vertical analysis enables us to meaningfully compare the condensed income statements of Dubois Céréale and Park Mills, as shown in **Illustration 14.12**.

Condensed Income Statements
For the Year Ended December 31, 2023

	Dubois Céréale (in thousands)		Park Mills (in millions)	
	Amount	Percent*	Amount	Percent*
Net sales	€11,776	100.0	€17,910	100.0
Cost of goods sold	6,597	56.0	11,540	64.4
Gross profit	5,179	44.0	6,370	35.6
Selling and administrative expenses	3,311	28.1	3,474	19.4
Income from operations	1,868	15.9	2,896	16.2
Interest expense	321	2.7	196	1.1
Income before income taxes	1,547	13.2	2,700	15.1
Income tax expense	144	3.8	876	4.9
Net income	€ 1,103	9.4	€ 1,824	10.2

*Numbers have been rounded to total 100%.

ILLUSTRATION 14.12 | Intercompany comparison by vertical analysis

Dubois Céréale's results are presented in thousands while those of Park Mills are presented in millions. Vertical analysis eliminates the impact of this size difference for our analysis.

- Dubois Céréale has a higher gross profit percentage of 44.0%, compared to 35.6% for Park Mills.
- But, Dubois Céréale's selling and administrative expenses are 28.1% of net sales, while those of Park Mills are 19.4% of net sales.
- Looking at net income, we see that Dubois Céréale's net income as a percentage of net sales is 9.4%, compared to 10.2% for Park Mills.

ANATOMY OF A FRAUD

Freeman FinTech Corporation Limited (HKG) is a Hong Kong based investment holding company. The company's businesses include (a) trading in securities and futures contracts, (b) lending business, (c) insurance brokerage, and (d) financial planning services.

The Hong Kong Stock Exchange declared on May 4, 2023, that Mr. Wang (former Executive Director) along with three other Directors of Freeman FinTech Corporation was found unsuitable to hold the position of director or any position within the company's senior management or any of its subsidiaries.

The case primarily relates to a money-lending business that was grossly mismanaged by the management of the company. The investigations revealed that Freeman FinTech rapidly expanded its money-lending business between July 2017 and April 2018. The company granted unsecured loans amounting to HK$2.28 billion to borrowers based in the People's Republic of China, and surprisingly 93% of the loans were paid to third-party nominees. Almost all the borrowers defaulted on the loans. As a result, the company incurred a massive loss of HK$1.9 billion.

Mr. Wang and his team need to answer the following:

1. What was the business rationale for granting loans without any scrutiny?
2. Why did the company not follow mandatory processes such as due diligence and evaluation of the creditworthiness of the borrowers?

Lessons Learned

1. The board of Freeman FinTech failed to evaluate the risks and rewards of expanding the money-lending business, which is known for high risk.
2. Companies like Freeman which are in the money-lending business must follow the necessary processes to assess the risk before granting and pricing the loans.

3. A thorough analysis of the risks and ongoing loan portfolio oversight is necessary.

The primary responsibility for the above matters lies with the directors—they must always play an active role in safeguarding the company's interest.

Source: Hong Kong Exchange's disciplinary action against four Directors of Arta TechFin Corporation Limited (stock code 279) (dated May 4, 2023). https://www.mayerbrown.com/en/perspectives-events/publications/2023/05/hkex-censures-directors-for-mismanagement-of-company-business#:~:text=In%20a%20recent%20disciplinary%20action,the%20material%20time%20and%20concluded

---

DO IT! 2 ▶ Horizontal Analysis

Summary financial information for Rosenlap NV is as follows:

	December 31, 2023	December 31, 2022
Current assets	€234,000	€180,000
Plant assets (net)	756,000	420,000
Total assets	€990,000	€600,000

Compute the amount and percentage changes in 2023 using horizontal analysis, assuming 2022 is the base year.

Solution

	Increase in 2023	
	Amount	Percent
Current assets	€ 54,000	30% [(€234,000 − €180,000) ÷ €180,000]
Plant assets (net)	336,000	80% [(€756,000 − €420,000) ÷ €420,000]
Total assets	€390,000	65% [(€990,000 − €600,000) ÷ €600,000]

Related exercise material: **BE14.4, BE14.6, BE14.7, BE14.9, DO IT! 14.2, E14.3, E14.5, and E14.6.**

ACTION PLAN
- Find the percentage change by dividing the amount of the increase by the 2022 amount (base year).

RATIO ANALYSIS

LEARNING OBJECTIVE 3
Analyze a company's performance using ratio analysis.

Ratio analysis expresses the relationship among selected items of financial statement data (see **Decision Tools**).

- A **ratio** expresses the mathematical relationship between one quantity and another.
- The relationship is expressed in terms of either a percentage, a rate, or a simple proportion.

To illustrate, in a recent year, **Nike, Inc.** (USA) had current assets of $13,626 million and current liabilities of $3,926 million. We can find the relationship between these two measures by dividing current assets by current liabilities. The alternative means of expression are as follows:

Percentage: Current assets are 347% of current liabilities.
Rate: Current assets are 3.47 times current liabilities.
Proportion: The relationship of current assets to liabilities is 3.47:1.

DECISION TOOLS

Ratio analysis helps users evaluate mathematical relationships between financial statement items and compare across years, competitors, and industry.

To analyze the primary financial statements, we can use ratios to evaluate liquidity, solvency, and profitability. **Illustration 14.13** describes these classifications.

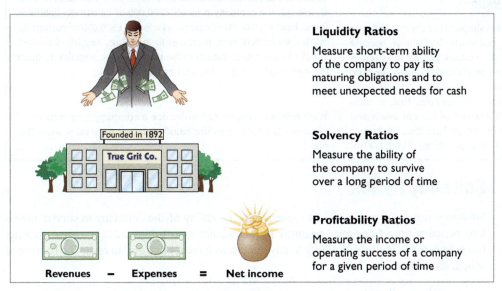

ILLUSTRATION 14.13 | **Financial ratio classifications**

Ratios can provide clues to underlying conditions that may not be apparent from individual financial statement components. However, a single ratio by itself is not very meaningful. Thus, in the discussion of ratios we will use the following types of comparisons:

1. **Intracompany comparisons** for two years for Dubois Céréale.
2. **Industry average comparisons** based on median ratios for the industry.
3. **Intercompany comparisons** based on Park Mills as Dubois Céréale's principal competitor.

Liquidity Ratios

Liquidity ratios (**Illustration 14.14**) measure the short-term ability of the company to pay its maturing obligations and to meet unexpected needs for cash. Short-term creditors such as bankers and suppliers are particularly interested in assessing liquidity.

Liquidity Ratios

1. Current ratio = $\dfrac{\text{Current assets}}{\text{Current liabilities}}$

2. Inventory turnover = $\dfrac{\text{Cost of goods sold}}{\text{Average inventory}}$

3. Days in inventory = $\dfrac{\text{365 days}}{\text{Inventory turnover}}$

4. Accounts receivable turnover = $\dfrac{\text{Net credit sales}}{\text{Average net accounts receivable}}$

5. Average collection period = $\dfrac{\text{365 days}}{\text{Accounts receivable turnover}}$

ILLUSTRATION 14.14 | **Summary of liquidity ratios**

INVESTOR INSIGHT

Nova Stock/SuperStock

How to Manage the Current Ratio

The apparent simplicity of the current ratio can have real-world limitations because adding equal amounts to both the numerator and the denominator causes the ratio to decrease.

Assume, for example, that a company has €2,000,000 of current assets and €1,000,000 of current liabilities. Its current ratio is 2:1. If it purchases €1,000,000 of inventory on account, it will have €3,000,000 of current assets and €2,000,000 of current liabilities. Its current ratio decreases to 1.5:1. If, instead, the company pays off €500,000 of its current liabilities, it will have €1,500,000 of current assets and €500,000 of current liabilities. Its current ratio increases to 3:1. Thus, any trend analysis should be done with care because the ratio is susceptible to quick changes and is easily influenced by management.

How might management influence a company's current ratio? (Answer is available in the book's product page on www.wiley.com)

Solvency Ratios

Solvency ratios (Illustration 14.15) measure the ability of the company to survive over a long period of time. Long-term creditors and stockholders are interested in a company's long-run solvency, particularly its ability to pay interest as it comes due and to repay the balance of debt at its maturity.

Solvency Ratios

6. Debt to assets ratio $= \dfrac{\text{Total liabilities}}{\text{Total assets}}$

7. Times interest earned $= \dfrac{\text{Net income + Interest expense + Income tax expense}}{\text{Interest expense}}$

8. Free cash flow $= \text{Net cash provided by operating activities} - \text{Capital expenditures} - \text{Cash dividends}$

ILLUSTRATION 14.15 | Summary of solvency ratios

Profitability Ratios

Profitability ratios (Illustration 14.16) measure the income or operating success of a company for a given period of time. A company's income, or lack of it, affects its ability to obtain debt and equity financing, its liquidity position, and its ability to grow. As a consequence, creditors and investors alike are interested in evaluating profitability. Profitability is frequently used as the ultimate test of management's operating effectiveness.

Profitability Ratios

9. Return on common stockholders' equity $= \dfrac{\text{Net income} - \text{Preferred dividends}}{\text{Average common stockholders' equity}}$

10. Return on assets $= \dfrac{\text{Net income}}{\text{Average total assets}}$

11. Profit margin $= \dfrac{\text{Net income}}{\text{Net sales}}$

12. Asset turnover $= \dfrac{\text{Net sales}}{\text{Average total assets}}$

13. Gross profit rate $= \dfrac{\text{Gross profit}}{\text{Net sales}}$

14. Earnings per share $= \dfrac{\text{Net income} - \text{Preferred dividends}}{\text{Weighted-average common shares outstanding}}$

15. Price-earnings ratio $= \dfrac{\text{Market price per share}}{\text{Earnings per share}}$

16. Payout ratio $= \dfrac{\text{Cash dividends paid on common stock}}{\text{Net income}}$

ILLUSTRATION 14.16 | Summary of profitability ratios

> ### INVESTOR INSIGHT
>
>
> iStock.com/Ferran Traite Soler
>
> **High Ratings Can Bring Low Returns**
>
> Moody's, Standard & Poor's, and Fitch are three big U.S. firms that perform financial analysis on publicly traded companies and then publish ratings of the companies' creditworthiness. Investors and lenders rely heavily on these ratings in making investment and lending decisions. Some people feel that the collapse of the financial markets in 2008 was worsened by inadequate research reports and ratings provided by the financial rating agencies. Critics contend that the rating agencies were reluctant to give large companies low ratings because they feared that by offending them they would lose out on business opportunities. For example, the rating agencies gave many so-called mortgage-backed securities ratings that suggested that they were low risk. Later, many of these very securities became completely worthless. Steps have been taken to reduce the conflicts of interest that lead to these faulty ratings.
>
> **Sources:** Aaron Lucchetti and Judith Burns, "Moody's CEO Warned Profit Push Posed a Risk to Quality of Ratings," *Wall Street Journal Online* (October 23, 2008); and Alan S. Binder, "A Better Way to Run Rating Agencies," *Wall Street Journal* (April 17, 2014).
>
> **Why are credit rating agencies important to the financial markets?** (Answer is available in the book's product page on www.wiley.com)

Financial Analysis and Data Analytics

In the age of "Big Data," opportunities for investors to apply data analytics to financial data are boundless. Immense quantities and types of data are available to investors. Free financial data about corporations, for example, can be obtained from the U.S. SEC's Edgar database and other sources. Alternatively, database services such as Compustat and WorldScope sell financial and other information regarding a wide range of company and industry characteristics. In addition, each day massive amounts of trading data are collected from financial exchanges.

Professional analysts employ sophisticated computerized valuation models that use financial, nonfinancial, and trading data to identify investment opportunities.

- Since these valuation models frequently rely heavily on accounting data, it is important to have a sound understanding of the financial accounting standards on which the numbers used in the models are based.
- If you desire to someday use data analytics to evaluate companies, the accounting skills and financial analysis tools acquired in this course are a good start.

Comprehensive Example of Ratio Analysis

In this section, we provide a comprehensive review of ratios used for evaluating the financial health and performance of a company. We use the financial information in **Illustrations 14.17** through **14.20** to calculate Dubois Céréale SA's 2023 ratios. You can use these data to review the computations.

Dubois Céréale SA
Balance Sheets
December 31 (in thousands)

	2023	2022
Assets		
Current assets		
Cash	€ 524	€ 411
Accounts receivable (net)	1,026	945
Inventory	924	824
Prepaid expenses and other current assets	243	247
Total current assets	2,717	2,427
Property, plant, and equipment (net)	2,990	2,816
Other assets	5,690	5,471
Total assets	€11,397	€10,714

	2023	2022
Liabilities and Stockholders' Equity		
Current liabilities	€ 4,044	€ 4,020
Long-term liabilities	4,827	4,625
Stockholders' equity—common	2,526	2,069
Total liabilities and stockholders' equity	€11,397	€10,714

ILLUSTRATION 14.17 | Dubois Céréale SA balance sheets

Dubois Céréale SA
Condensed Income Statements
For the Years Ended December 31 (in thousands)

	2023	2022
Net sales	€11,776	€10,907
Cost of goods sold	6,597	6,082
Gross profit	5,179	4,825
Selling and administrative expenses	3,311	3,059
Income from operations	1,868	1,766
Interest expense	321	294
Income before income taxes	1,547	1,472
Income tax expense	444	468
Net income	€ 1,103	€ 1,004

ILLUSTRATION 14.18 | Dubois Céréale SA's income statements

Dubois Céréale SA
Condensed Statements of Cash Flows
For the Years Ended December 31 (in thousands)

	2023	2022
Cash flows from operating activities		
Cash receipts from operating activities	€11,695	€10,841
Cash payments for operating activities	(10,192)	(9,431)
Net cash provided by operating activities	1,503	1,410
Cash flows from investing activities		
Purchases of property, plant, and equipment	(472)	(453)
Other investing activities	(129)	8
Net cash used in investing activities	(601)	(445)
Cash flows from financing activities		
Issuance of common stock	163	218
Issuance of debt	2,179	721
Reductions of debt	(2,011)	(650)
Payment of cash dividends	(475)	(450)
Repurchase of common stock and other items	(645)	(612)
Net cash provided (used) by financing activities	(789)	(773)
Increase (decrease) in cash and cash equivalents	113	192
Cash and cash equivalents at beginning of year	411	219
Cash and cash equivalents at end of year	€ 524	€ 411

ILLUSTRATION 14.19 | Dubois Céréale SA's statements of cash flows

Additional information:		
	2023	2022
Weighted-average common shares outstanding (thousands)	418.7	418.5
Stock price at year-end	€52.92	€50.06

ILLUSTRATION 14.20 | Additional information for Dubois Céréale SA

As indicated in the chapter, we can classify ratios into three types for analysis of the primary financial statements:

1. **Liquidity ratios.** Measures of the short-term ability of the company to pay its maturing obligations and to meet unexpected needs for cash.
2. **Solvency ratios.** Measures of the ability of the company to survive over a long period of time.
3. **Profitability ratios.** Measures of the income or operating success of a company for a given period of time.

As a tool of analysis, ratios can provide clues to underlying conditions that may not be apparent from an inspection of the individual components of a particular ratio. But, a single ratio by itself is not very meaningful. Accordingly, in this discussion we use the following three comparisons:

1. **Intracompany comparisons** covering two years for Dubois Céréale (using comparative financial information from Illustrations 14.17 through 14.20). The ratios for 2022 are given and not calculated because the beginning balances are not provided for this year.
2. **Intercompany comparisons** using Park Mills as one of Dubois Céréale's competitors.
3. **Industry average comparisons** based on **MSN.com** (USA) median ratios for manufacturers of flour and other grain mill products and comparisons with other sources. For some of the ratios that we use, industry comparisons are not available (denoted "na").

Liquidity Ratios

Liquidity ratios measure the short-term ability of the company to pay its maturing obligations and to meet unexpected needs for cash.

- Short-term creditors such as bankers and suppliers are particularly interested in assessing liquidity.
- The measures used to determine the company's short-term debt-paying ability are the current ratio, the accounts receivable turnover, the average collection period, the inventory turnover, and days in inventory. In addition, another measure used to assess liquidity is working capital. **Working capital** is current assets minus current liabilities.

1. **Current ratio.** The **current ratio** expresses the relationship of current assets to current liabilities, computed by dividing current assets by current liabilities. It is widely used for evaluating a company's liquidity and short-term debt-paying ability. The 2023 and 2022 current ratios for Dubois Céréale and comparative data are shown in **Illustration 14.21**.

Ratio	Formula	Dubois Céréale 2023	Dubois Céréale 2022	Park Mills 2023	Industry Average
Current ratio	Current assets / Current liabilities	€2,717 / €4,044 = .67	.60	.67	1.06

ILLUSTRATION 14.21 | Current ratio

What do the measures tell us?
- Dubois Céréale's 2023 current ratio of .67 means that for every euro of current liabilities, it has €0.67 of current assets. (We sometimes state such ratios as .67:1 to reinforce this interpretation.)
- Its current ratio—and therefore its liquidity—increased significantly in 2023.
- It is well below the industry average but the same as that of Park Mills.

2. **Accounts receivable turnover.** Analysts can measure liquidity by how quickly a company converts certain assets to cash. A low value for the current ratio can sometimes be compensated for if some of the company's current assets are highly liquid.

How liquid, for example, are the receivables? The ratio used to assess the liquidity of the receivables is the **accounts receivable turnover**, which measures the number of times, on average, a company collects receivables during the period. The accounts receivable turnover is computed by dividing net credit sales (net sales less cash sales) by average net accounts receivable during the year. The accounts receivable turnover for Dubois Céréale is shown in **Illustration 14.22**.

Ratio	Formula	Dubois Céréale 2023	Dubois Céréale 2022	Park Mills 2023	Industry Average
Accounts receivable turnover	Net credit sales / Average net accounts receivable	€11,776 / ((€1,026 + €945) ÷ 2) = 11.9	12.0	12.2	11.2

ILLUSTRATION 14.22 | Accounts receivable turnover

In computing the rate, we assumed that all Dubois Céréale's sales are credit sales.

- Its accounts receivable turnover declined slightly in 2023.
- The turnover of 11.9 times is higher than the industry average of 11.2 times, and slightly lower than Park Mills' turnover of 12.2 times.
- A higher value suggests better liquidity because the receivables are being collected more quickly.

3. **Average collection period.** A popular variant of the accounts receivable turnover converts it into an **average collection period** in days. This is done by dividing the accounts receivable turnover into 365 days. The average collection period for Dubois Céréale is shown in **Illustration 14.23**.

Ratio	Formula	Dubois Céréale 2023	Dubois Céréale 2022	Park Mills 2023	Industry Average
Average collection period	365 days / Accounts receivable turnover	$\frac{365}{11.9}$ = 30.7	30.4	29.9	32.6

ILLUSTRATION 14.23 | Average collection period

Dubois Céréale's 2023 accounts receivable turnover of 11.9 times is divided into 365 days to obtain approximately 31 days.

- This means that the average collection period for receivables is about 31 days.
- Its average collection period is slightly longer than that of Park Mills and shorter than that of the industry.
- A shorter collection period means receivables are being collected more quickly and thus are more liquid.

Analysts frequently use the average collection period to assess the effectiveness of a company's credit and collection policies. The general rule is that the collection period should not greatly exceed the credit term period (i.e., the time allowed for payment, which is 30 days for many companies).

4. **Inventory turnover.** The **inventory turnover** measures the number of times average inventory was sold during the period. Its purpose is to measure the liquidity of the inventory. A high measure indicates that inventory is being sold and replenished frequently. The inventory turnover is computed by dividing the cost of goods sold by the average inventory during the period. Unless seasonal factors are significant, average inventory can be computed using the beginning and ending inventory balances. Dubois Céréale's inventory turnover is shown in **Illustration 14.24**.

Ratio	Formula	Dubois Céréale 2023	Dubois Céréale 2022	Park Mills 2023	Industry Average
Inventory turnover	$\dfrac{\text{Cost of goods sold}}{\text{Average inventory}}$	$\dfrac{€6{,}597}{(€924 + €824) \div 2} = 7.5$	7.9	7.4	6.7

ILLUSTRATION 14.24 | **Inventory turnover**

Dubois Céréale's inventory turnover decreased slightly in 2023.

- The turnover of 7.5 times is higher than the industry average of 6.7 times and similar to that of Park Mills.
- Generally, the faster the inventory turnover, the less cash is tied up in inventory and the less the chance of inventory becoming obsolete.
- A downside of high inventory turnover is that it sometimes results in lost sales because if a company keeps less inventory on hand, it is more likely to run out of inventory when it is needed.

5. **Days in inventory.** A variant of the inventory turnover is the **days in inventory**, which measures the average number of days inventory is held. The days in inventory for Dubois Céréale is shown in **Illustration 14.25**.

Ratio	Formula	Dubois Céréale 2023	Dubois Céréale 2022	Park Mills 2023	Industry Average
Days in inventory	$\dfrac{365 \text{ days}}{\text{Inventory turnover}}$	$\dfrac{365}{7.5} = 48.7$	46.2	49.3	54.5

ILLUSTRATION 14.25 | **Days in inventory**

Dubois Céréale's 2023 inventory turnover of 7.5 divided into 365 is approximately 49 days.

- An average selling time of 49 days is faster than the industry average and similar to that of Park Mills.
- However, inventory turnovers vary considerably among industries. For example, grocery store chains have a turnover of 10 times and an average selling period of 37 days. In contrast, jewelry stores have an average turnover of 1.3 times and an average selling period of 281 days.
- Within a company, there may even be significant differences in inventory turnover among different types of products. Thus, in a grocery store the turnover of perishable items such as produce, meats, and dairy products is faster than the turnover of soaps and detergents.

To conclude, nearly all of these liquidity measures suggest that Dubois Céréale's liquidity changed little during 2023. Its liquidity appears acceptable when compared to the industry as a whole and when compared to Park Mills.

Solvency Ratios

Solvency ratios measure the ability of the company to survive over a long period of time.

- Long-term creditors and stockholders are interested in a company's long-run solvency, particularly its ability to pay interest as it comes due and to repay the face value of debt at maturity.
- The debt to assets ratio and times interest earned provide information about debt-paying ability.
- In addition, free cash flow provides information about the company's solvency and its ability to pay additional dividends or invest in new projects.

6. **Debt to assets ratio.** The **debt to assets ratio** measures the percentage of total financing provided by creditors. It is computed by dividing total liabilities (both current and long-term debt) by total assets. This ratio indicates the degree of financial leveraging. It also provides some indication of the company's ability to withstand losses without impairing the interests of its creditors. The higher the percentage of debt to assets, the greater the risk that the company may be unable to meet its maturing obligations. Thus, from the creditors' point of view, a low ratio of debt to assets is desirable. Dubois Céréale's debt to assets ratio is shown in **Illustration 14.26**.

Ratio	Formula	Dubois Céréale 2023	Dubois Céréale 2022	Park Mills 2023	Industry Average
Debt to assets ratio	Total liabilities / Total assets	€8,871 / €11,397 = 78%	81%	55%	55%

ILLUSTRATION 14.26 | **Debt to assets ratio**

Dubois Céréale's 2023 ratio means that creditors have provided financing sufficient for 78% of the company's total assets.

- Alternatively, the ratio indicates that the company would have to liquidate 78% of its assets at their book value in order to pay off all of its debts.
- Dubois Céréale's ratio is above the industry average of 55%, as well as that of Park Mills.
- This suggests that it is less solvent than the industry average and Park Mills. Dubois Céréale's solvency improved slightly from that in 2022.

The adequacy of this ratio is often judged in light of the company's earnings. Generally, companies with relatively stable earnings, such as public utilities, have higher debt to assets ratios than cyclical companies with widely fluctuating earnings, such as many high-tech companies.

Another ratio with a similar meaning is the **debt to equity ratio**.

- It shows the relative use of borrowed funds (total liabilities) compared with resources invested by the owners.
- If debt and assets are defined as above (all liabilities and all assets), then when the debt to assets ratio equals 50%, the debt to equity ratio is 1:1.

7. **Times interest earned.** The **times interest earned** (also called interest coverage) indicates the company's ability to meet interest payments as they come due. It is computed by dividing the sum of net income, interest expense, and income tax expense by interest expense. Note that this ratio uses income before interest expense and income taxes because this amount represents what is available to cover interest. Dubois Céréale's times interest earned is shown in **Illustration 14.27**.

Ratio	Formula	Dubois Céréale 2023	Dubois Céréale 2022	Park Mills 2023	Industry Average
Times interest earned	(Net Income + Interest expense + Income tax expense) / Interest expense	(€1,103 + €321 + €444) / €321 = 5.8	6.0	9.9	5.5

ILLUSTRATION 14.27 | **Times interest earned**

For Dubois Céréale, the 2023 interest coverage was 5.8 times, which indicates that income before interest and taxes was 5.8 times the amount needed for interest expense.

- This is less than the rate for Park Mills, but it slightly exceeds the rate for the industry.
- The debt to assets ratio decreased for Dubois Céréale during 2023, and its times interest earned held relatively constant.
- A low debt to assets ratio and high times interest earned suggest better solvency.

8. **Free cash flow.** One indication of a company's solvency, as well as of its ability to pay dividends or expand operations, is the amount of excess cash it generated after investing in capital expenditures and paying dividends. This amount is referred to as **free cash flow**. For example, if you generate €100,000 of net cash provided by operating activities but you spend €30,000 on capital expenditures and pay €10,000 in dividends, you have €60,000 (€100,000 − €30,000 − €10,000) to use either to expand operations, pay additional dividends, or pay down debt. Dubois Céréale's free cash flow is shown in **Illustration 14.28**.

Ratio	Formula	Dubois Céréale 2022	Dubois Céréale 2023	Park Mills 2023	Industry Average
Free cash flow	Net cash provided by operating activities − Capital expenditures − Cash dividends	€1,503 − €472 − €475 = €556	€507 (in thousands)	€895 (in millions)	na

ILLUSTRATION 14.28 | Free cash flow

Dubois Céréale's free cash flow increased slightly from 2022 to 2023.

- During both years, the net cash provided by operating activities was more than enough to allow it to acquire additional productive assets and maintain dividend payments.
- It could have used the remaining cash to reduce debt if necessary.
- Given that Dubois Céréale is much smaller than Park Mills, we would expect Dubois Céréale's free cash flow to be substantially smaller, which it is.

Profitability Ratios

Profitability ratios measure the income or operating success of a company for a given period of time.

- A company's income, or the lack of it, affects its ability to obtain debt and equity financing, its liquidity position, and its ability to grow.
- As a consequence, creditors and investors alike are interested in evaluating profitability.
- Analysts frequently use profitability as the ultimate test of management's operating effectiveness.

The relationships among measures of profitability are very important. Understanding them can help management determine where to focus its efforts to improve profitability. **Illustration 14.29** diagrams these relationships. Our discussion of Dubois Céréale's profitability is structured around this diagram.

9. **Return on common stockholders' equity (ROE).** A widely used measure of profitability from the common stockholders' viewpoint is the **return on common stockholders' equity (ROE)**. This ratio shows how many euros of net income the company earned for each euro invested by the owners. It is computed by dividing net income minus any preferred dividends—that is, income available to common stockholders—by average common stockholders' equity. The return on common stockholders' equity for Dubois Céréale is shown in **Illustration 14.30**.

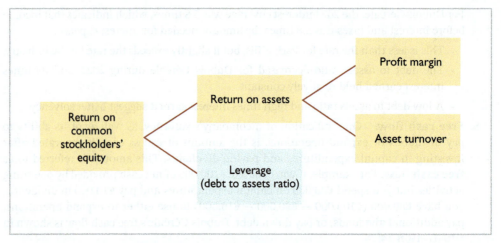

ILLUSTRATION 14.29 | **Relationships among profitability measures**

Ratio	Formula	Dubois Céréale 2023	Dubois Céréale 2022	Park Mills 2023	Industry Average
Return on common stockholders' equity	$\dfrac{\text{Net Income} - \text{Preferred dividends}}{\text{Average common stockholders' equity}}$	$\dfrac{€1{,}103 - €0}{(€2{,}526 + €2{,}069) \div 2} = 48\%$	46%	25%	19%

ILLUSTRATION 14.30 | **Return on common stockholders' equity**

Dubois Céréale's 2023 return on common stockholders' equity is unusually high at 48%. The industry average is 19% and Park Mills' return is 25%. In the subsequent sections, we investigate the causes of this high return.

10. **Return on assets.** The return on common stockholders' equity is affected by two factors: the **return on assets** and the degree of leverage. The return on assets measures the overall profitability of assets in terms of the income earned on each euro invested in assets. It is computed by dividing net income by average total assets. Dubois Céréale's return on assets is shown in **Illustration 14.31**.

Ratio	Formula	Dubois Céréale 2023	Dubois Céréale 2022	Park Mills 2023	Industry Average
Return on assets	$\dfrac{\text{Net income}}{\text{Average total assets}}$	$\dfrac{€1{,}103}{(€11{,}397 + €10{,}714) \div 2} = 10.0\%$	9.4%	6.2%	5.3%

ILLUSTRATION 14.31 | **Return on assets**

Dubois Céréale had a 10.0% return on assets in 2023. This rate is significantly higher than that of Park Mills and the industry average.

Note that its rate of return on common stockholders' equity (48%) is substantially higher than its rate of return on assets (10%). The reason is that it has made effective use of **leverage**.

- **Leveraging** or **trading on the equity** at a gain means that the company has borrowed money at a lower rate of interest than the rate of return it earns on the assets it purchased with the borrowed funds.
- Leverage enables management to use money supplied by nonowners to increase the return to owners.
- A comparison of the rate of return on assets with the rate of interest paid for borrowed money indicates the profitability of trading on the equity.

For example, if you borrow money at 8% and your rate of return on assets is 11%, you are trading on the equity at a gain. Note, however, that trading on the equity is a two-way street. For example, if you borrow money at 11% and earn only 8% on it, you are trading on the equity at a loss.

Dubois Céréale earns more on its borrowed funds than it has to pay in interest. Thus, the return to stockholders exceeds the return on assets because of the positive benefit of leverage. Recall from our earlier discussion that Dubois Céréale's percentage of debt financing, as measured by the ratio of debt to assets (or debt to equity), is higher than Park Mills' and the industry average. It appears that Dubois Céréale's high return on common stockholders' equity is due in part to its use of leverage.

11. **Profit margin.** The return on assets is affected by two factors, the first of which is the profit margin. The **profit margin**, or rate of return on sales, is a measure of the percentage of each euro of sales that results in net income. It is computed by dividing net income by net sales for the period. Dubois Céréale's profit margin is shown in **Illustration 14.32**.

Ratio	Formula	Dubois Céréale 2023	Dubois Céréale 2022	Park Mills 2023	Industry Average
Profit margin	$\dfrac{\text{Net income}}{\text{Net sales}}$	$\dfrac{€1{,}103}{€11{,}776} = 9.4\%$	9.2%	8.2%	6.1%

ILLUSTRATION 14.32 | **Profit margin**

Dubois Céréale experienced a slight increase in its profit margin from 2022 to 2023 of 9.2% to 9.4%.

- Its profit margin was higher, indicating the company earned more profit out of each euro of net sales, than the industry average and that of Park Mills.
- High-volume (high inventory turnover) businesses such as grocery stores and pharmacy chains generally have low profit margins.
- Low-volume businesses such as jewelry stores and airplane manufacturers typically have high profit margins.

12. **Asset turnover.** The other factor that affects the return on assets is the asset turnover. The **asset turnover** measures how efficiently a company uses its assets to generate sales. It is determined by dividing net sales by average total assets for the period. The resulting number shows the euros of net sales produced by each euro invested in assets. **Illustration 14.33** shows the asset turnover for Dubois Céréale.

Ratio	Formula	Dubois Céréale 2023	Dubois Céréale 2022	Park Mills 2023	Industry Average
Asset turnover	$\dfrac{\text{Net sales}}{\text{Average total assets}}$	$\dfrac{€11{,}776}{(€11{,}397 + €10{,}714) \div 2} = 1.07$	1.02	.76	.87

ILLUSTRATION 14.33 | **Asset turnover**

The asset turnover shows that in 2023, Dubois Céréale generated sales of €1.07 for each euro it had invested in assets.

- The ratio rose from 2022 to 2023.
- Its asset turnover is above the industry average and that of Park Mills.
- Asset turnovers vary considerably among industries. The average asset turnover for utility companies is .45, for example, while the grocery store industry has an average asset turnover of 3.49.

In summary, Dubois Céréale's return on assets increased from 9.4% in 2022 to 10.0% in 2023. Underlying this increase was an increased profitability on each euro of net sales (as measured by the profit margin) and a rise in the sales-generating efficiency of its assets (as measured by the asset turnover). The combined effect of the profit margin and asset turnover yields the return on assets for Dubois Céréale shown in **Illustration 14.34**.

Ratios:	Profit Margin	×	Asset Turnover	=	Return on Assets
	$\dfrac{\text{Net Income}}{\text{Net Sales}}$	×	$\dfrac{\text{Net Sales}}{\text{Average Total Assets}}$	=	$\dfrac{\text{Net Income}}{\text{Average Total Assets}}$
Dubois Céréale					
2023	9.4%	×	1.07 times	=	10.1%*
2022	9.2%	×	1.02 times	=	9.4%

*Difference from value in Illustration 14.31 due to rounding.

ILLUSTRATION 14.34 | Composition of return on assets

13. **Gross profit rate.** One factor that strongly influences the profit margin is the gross profit rate. The **gross profit rate** is determined by dividing gross profit (net sales less cost of goods sold) by net sales. This rate indicates a company's ability to maintain an adequate unit selling price above its unit cost of goods sold.

    As an industry becomes more competitive, this ratio typically declines.
    - For example, in the early years of the personal computer industry, gross profit rates were quite high.
    - Today, because of increased competition and a belief that most brands of personal computers are similar in quality, gross profit rates have become thin.
    - Analysts should closely monitor gross profit rates over time.

    Illustration 14.35 shows Dubois Céréale's gross profit rate.

		Dubois Céréale		Park Mills	Industry Average
Ratio	Formula	2023	2022	2023	
Gross profit rate	$\dfrac{\text{Gross profit}}{\text{Net sales}}$	$\dfrac{€5{,}179}{€11{,}776} = 44\%$	44%	34%	30%

ILLUSTRATION 14.35 | Gross profit rate

Dubois Céréale's gross profit rate remained constant from 2022 to 2023, and exceeded that of Park Mills and of the industry average.

14. **Earnings per share (EPS).** Stockholders usually think in terms of the number of shares they own or plan to buy or sell. Expressing net income earned on a per share basis provides a useful perspective for evaluating profitability. **Earnings per share** is a measure of the net income earned on each share of common stock. It is computed by dividing net income by the average number of common shares outstanding during the year.

    The terms "net income per share" and "earnings per share" refer to the amount of net income applicable to each share of **common stock**. Therefore, when we compute earnings per share, if there are preferred dividends declared for the period, we must deduct them from net income to arrive at income available to the common stockholders. Dubois Céréale's earnings per share is shown in **Illustration 14.36**. There were no shares of preferred stock outstanding and no preferred stock dividends.

Ratio	Formula	Dubois Céréale 2023	Dubois Céréale 2022	Park Mills 2023	Industry Average
Earnings per share (EPS)	$\dfrac{\text{Net income} - \text{Preferred dividends}}{\text{Weighted-average common shares outstanding}}$	$\dfrac{€1{,}103 - €0}{418.7} = €2.63$	€2.40	€2.90	na

ILLUSTRATION 14.36 | Earnings per share

Note that no industry average is presented in Illustration 14.36.

- Industry data for earnings per share are not reported, and in fact the Dubois Céréale and Park Mills ratios should not be compared.
- Such comparisons are not meaningful because of the wide variations in the number of shares of outstanding stock among companies.
- Dubois Céréale's earnings per share increased 23 cents per share in 2023. This represents a 9.6% increase from the 2022 EPS of €2.40.

15. **Price-earnings ratio.** The **price-earnings (P-E) ratio** is an oft-quoted statistic that measures the ratio of the market price of each share of common stock to the earnings per share of common stock. The P-E ratio reflects investors' assessments of a company's future earnings. It is computed by dividing the market price per share of the stock by earnings per share. Dubois Céréale's price-earnings ratio is shown in **Illustration 14.37**.

Ratio	Formula	Dubois Céréale 2023	Dubois Céréale 2022	Park Mills 2023	Industry Average
Price-earnings ratio	$\dfrac{\text{Market price per share}}{\text{Earnings per share}}$	$\dfrac{€52.92}{€2.63} = 20.1$	20.9	24.3	35.8

ILLUSTRATION 14.37 | Price-earnings ratio

At the end of 2023 and 2022, the market price of Dubois Céréale's stock was €52.92 and €50.06, respectively.

- In 2023, each share of Dubois Céréale's stock sold for 20.1 times the amount that was earned on each share.
- Dubois Céréale's price-earnings ratio is lower than Park Mills' ratio of 24.3 and lower than the industry average of 35.8 times.
- Its lower P-E ratio suggests that the market is less optimistic about Dubois Céréale than about Park Mills, but it might also signal that Dubois Céréale's stock is underpriced.

16. **Payout ratio.** The **payout ratio** measures the percentage of earnings distributed in the form of cash dividends on common stock (see **Helpful Hint**). It is computed by dividing cash dividends paid on common stock by net income. Companies that have high growth rates are characterized by low payout ratios because they reinvest most of their net income in the business. The payout ratio for Dubois Céréale is shown in **Illustration 14.38**.

HELPFUL HINT
Some formulations of the payout ratio also include preferred stock dividends. Note that our definition is focused on dividends paid on common stock.

Ratio	Formula	Dubois Céréale 2023	Dubois Céréale 2022	Park Mills 2023	Industry Average
Payout ratio	$\dfrac{\text{Cash dividends paid on common stock}}{\text{Net income}}$	$\dfrac{€475}{€1{,}103} = 43\%$	45%	54%	37%

ILLUSTRATION 14.38 | Payout ratio

The 2023 and 2022 payout ratios for Dubois Céréale are lower than that of Park Mills (54%) but higher than the industry average (37%).

- A lower payout ratio means a company has chosen to pay out a lower percentage of its net income as dividends.
- Management has some control over the amount of dividends paid each year, and companies are generally reluctant to reduce a dividend below the amount paid in a previous year.
- The payout ratio will actually increase if a company's net income declines but the company keeps its total dividend payment the same. (Of course, unless the company returns to its previous level of profitability, maintaining this higher dividend payout ratio is probably not possible over the long run.)

Before drawing any conclusions regarding Dubois Céréale's dividend payout ratio, we should calculate this ratio over a longer period of time to evaluate any trends and also try to find out whether management's philosophy regarding dividends has changed recently. The "Selected Financial Data" section of Dubois Céréale's Management Discussion and Analysis shows that over a five-year period, earnings per share rose 45%, while dividends per share grew only 19%.

In terms of the types of financial information available and the ratios used by various industries, what can be practically covered in this text gives you the "Titanic approach." That is, you are only seeing the tip of the iceberg compared to the vast databases and types of ratio analysis that are available electronically. The availability of information is not a problem. The real trick is to be discriminating enough to perform relevant analysis and select pertinent comparative data.

DO IT! 3 ▶ Ratio Analysis

The condensed financial statements of Paul Huber Group, for the years ended June 30, 2023 and 2022, are presented as follows:

ACTION PLAN
- Remember that the current ratio includes all current assets.
- Use average balances for turnover ratios like inventory, accounts receivable, and return on assets.

Paul Huber Group
Balance Sheets
June 30

(in thousands)

	2023	2022
Assets		
Current assets		
Cash and cash equivalents	€ 553.3	€ 611.6
Accounts receivable (net)	776.6	664.9
Inventory	768.3	653.5
Prepaid expenses and other current assets	204.4	269.2
Total current assets	2,302.6	2,199.2
Investments	12.3	12.6
Property, plant, and equipment (net)	694.2	647.0
Other assets	876.7	849.3
Total assets	€3,885.8	€3,708.1
Liabilities and Stockholders' Equity		
Current liabilities	€1,497.7	€1,322.0
Long-term liabilities	679.5	637.1
Stockholders' equity—common	1,708.6	1,749.0
Total liabilities and stockholders' equity	€3,885.8	€3,708.1

Paul Huber Group
Income Statements
For the Years Ended June 30

	(in thousands)	
	2023	2022
Net sales	€6,336.3	€5,790.4
Expenses		
Cost of goods sold	1,617.4	1,476.3
Selling and administrative expenses	4,007.6	3,679.0
Interest expense	13.9	27.1
Total expenses	5,638.9	5,182.4
Income before income taxes	697.4	608.0
Income tax expense	291.3	232.6
Net income	€ 406.1	€ 375.4

Compute the following ratios for 2023 and 2022.

a. Current ratio.
b. Inventory turnover. (Inventory on 6/30/21 was €599.0.)
c. Profit margin.
d. Return on assets. (Assets on 6/30/21 were €3,349.9.)
e. Return on common stockholders' equity. (Stockholders' equity on 6/30/21 was €1,795.9.)
f. Debt to assets ratio.
g. Times interest earned.

Solution

	2023	2022
a. Current ratio:		
€2,302.6 ÷ €1,497.7 =	1.5:1	
€2,199.2 ÷ €1,322.0 =		1.7:1
b. Inventory turnover:		
€1,617.4 ÷ [(€768.3 + €653.5) ÷ 2] =	2.3 times	
€1,476.3 ÷ [(€653.5 + €599.0) ÷ 2] =		2.4 times
c. Profit margin:		
€406.1 ÷ €6,336.3 =	6.4%	
€375.4 ÷ €5,790.4 =		6.5%
d. Return on assets:		
€406.1 ÷ [(€3,885.8 + €3,708.1) ÷ 2] =	10.7%	
€375.4 ÷ [(€3,708.1 + €3,349.9) ÷ 2] =		10.6%
e. Return on common stockholders' equity:		
(€406.1 − €0) ÷ [(€1,708.6 + €1,749.0) ÷ 2] =	23.5%	
(€375.4 − €0) ÷ [(€1,749.0 + €1,795.9) ÷ 2] =		21.2%
f. Debt to assets ratio:		
(€1,497.7 + €679.5) ÷ €3,885.8 =	56.0%	
(€1,322.0 + €637.1) ÷ €3,708.1 =		52.8%
g. Times interest earned:		
(€406.1 + €13.9 + €291.3) ÷ €13.9 =	51.2 times	
(€375.4 + €27.1 + €232.6) ÷ €27.1 =		23.4 times

Related exercise material: **BE14.10, BE14.11, BE14.12, BE14.13, BE14.14, BE14.15, DO IT! 14.3, E14.7, E14.8, E14.9, E14.10, E14.11, E14.12, and E14.13.**

USING THE DECISION TOOLS | Kellogg Company

In analyzing a company, you should always investigate an extended period of time in order to determine whether the condition and performance of the company are changing. The condensed financial statements of **Kellogg Company** (USA) for the current year and previous year are presented here:

Kellogg Company, Inc.
Balance Sheets
(in millions)

	Current Year	Previous Year
Assets		
Current assets		
Cash	$ 281	$ 280
Accounts receivable (net)	1,389	1,231
Inventories	1,217	1,238
Other current assets	149	191
Total current assets	3,036	2,940
Property (net)	3,716	5,166
Other assets	9,598	7,005
Total assets	$16,350	$15,111
Liabilities and Stockholders' Equity		
Current liabilities	$ 4,479	$ 4,474
Long-term liabilities	9,643	8,711
Stockholders' equity—common	2,228	1,926
Total liabilities and stockholders' equity	$16,350	$15,111

Kellogg Company, Inc.
Condensed Income Statements
(in millions)

	Current Year	Previous Year
Net sales	$12,923	$ 13,014
Cost of goods sold	7,901	8,259
Gross profit	5,022	4,755
Selling and administrative expenses	3,076	3,360
Income from operations	1,946	1,395
Interest expense	256	406
Other income (expense), net	(16)	(62)
Income before income taxes	1,674	927
Income tax expense	412	233
Other earnings (loss)	7	0
Net income	$ 1,269	$ 694

Instructions

Compute the following ratios for Kellogg for the current year and discuss your findings (previous-year values are provided for comparison).

1. Liquidity:
   a. Current ratio (previous year: .66:1).
   b. Inventory turnover (previous year: 6.6 times).

2. Solvency:
   a. Debt to assets ratio (previous year: 87%).
   b. Times interest earned (previous year: 3.3 times).

3. Profitability:
   a. Return on assets (previous year: 4.6%).
   b. Profit margin (previous year: 5.3%).
   c. Return on common stockholders' equity (previous year: 33%).

Solution

1. Liquidity

   a. Current ratio:

   Current year: $\dfrac{\$3,036}{\$4,479} = .68:1$ Previous year: .66:1

   b. Inventory turnover:

   Current year: $\dfrac{\$7,901}{(\$1,217 + \$1,238) \div 2} = 6.4$ times   Previous year: 6.6 times

   We see that between the previous year and the current year, the current ratio increased, which suggests an increase in liquidity. The inventory turnover decreased, which suggests a decline in liquidity.

2. Solvency

   a. Debt to assets ratio:

   Current year: $\dfrac{\$4,479 + \$9,643}{\$16,350} = 86\%$ Previous year: 87%

   b. Times interest earned:

   Current year: $\dfrac{\$1,269 + \$256 + \$412}{\$256} = 7.6$ times   Previous year: 3.3 times

   Kellogg's debt to assets ratio decreased in the current year, and its times interest earned increased. Both changes suggest improved solvency.

3. Profitability

   a. Return on assets:

   Current year: $\dfrac{\$1,269}{(\$16,350 + \$15,111) \div 2} = 8.1\%$ Previous year: 4.6%

   b. Profit margin:

   Current year: $\dfrac{\$1,269}{\$12,923} = 9.8\%$ Previous year: 5.3%

   c. Return on common stockholders' equity:

   Current year: $\dfrac{\$1,269}{(\$2,228 + \$1,926) \div 2} = 61\%$ Previous year: 33%

   Kellogg's return on assets, profit margin, and return on stockholders' equity increased. The company experienced a sharp increase in net income, while its total assets, sales, and equity were relatively constant.

REVIEW AND PRACTICE

Learning Objectives Review

LO 1 Apply the concepts of sustainable income.

Sustainable income analysis is useful in evaluating a company's performance. Sustainable income is the most likely level of income to be obtained by the company in the future and omits unusual items. Discontinued operations and other comprehensive income items are presented separately to highlight their unusual nature. Items below income from continuing operations must be presented net of tax.

LO 2 Apply horizontal analysis and vertical analysis.

Horizontal analysis is a technique for evaluating a series of data over a period of time to determine the increase or decrease that has taken place, expressed as either an euro amount or a percentage.

Vertical analysis is a technique that expresses each item in a financial statement as a percentage of a relevant total or a base amount.

LO 3 Analyze a company's performance using ratio analysis.

Financial ratios are provided in Illustration 14.14 (liquidity), Illustration 14.15 (solvency), and Illustration 14.16 (profitability). Analysis is enhanced by intracompany, intercompany, and industry comparisons of these three classes of ratios.

Decision Tools Review

Decision Checkpoints	Info Needed for Decision	Tool to Use for Decision	How to Evaluate Results
Has the company sold any major components of its business?	Discontinued operations section of income statement	Information reported in this section indicates that the company has discontinued a major component of its business.	If a major component has been discontinued, its results during the current period should not be included in estimates of future net income.
Has the company changed any of its accounting principles?	Effect of change in accounting principle on current and prior periods	Management indicates that the new principle is preferable to the old principle. Discussed in notes to financial statements.	Examine current and prior years' reported income, using new-principle basis to assess trends for estimating future income.
How do the company's financial position and operating results compare with those of the previous period?	Income statement and balance sheet	Comparative financial statements should be prepared over at least two years, with the first year reported being the base year. Changes in each line item relative to the base year should be presented both by amount and by percentage. This is called **horizontal analysis**.	Significant changes should be investigated to determine the reason for the change.
How do the relationships between items in this year's financial statements compare with those of last year or those of competitors?	Income statement and balance sheet	Each line item on the income statement should be presented as a percentage of net sales, and each line item on the balance sheet should be presented as a percentage of total assets or total liabilities and stockholders' equity. These percentages should be investigated for differences either across years in the same company or in the same year across different companies. This is called **vertical analysis**.	Any significant differences either across years or between companies should be investigated to determine the cause.
How do mathematical relationships between financial statement items compare to prior years, competitors, and industry?	Financial statements	Various ratios that measure liquidity, solvency, and profitability.	Significant differences from prior-year values, or from competitor or industry values, should be investigated to determine the cause.

Glossary Review

Accounts receivable turnover A measure of the liquidity of receivables; computed as net credit sales divided by average net accounts receivable. (p. 14-20).

Asset turnover A measure of how efficiently a company uses its assets to generate net sales; computed as net sales divided by average total assets. (p. 14-25).

Available-for-sale securities Securities that are held with the intent of selling them sometime in the future. (p. 14-5).

Average collection period The average number of days that receivables are outstanding; calculated as accounts receivable turnover divided into 365 days. (p. 14-20).

Change in accounting principle Use of an accounting principle in the current year that is different from the one used in the preceding year. (p. 14-6).

Comprehensive income The sum of net income and other comprehensive income items. (p. 14-4).

Current ratio A measure used to evaluate a company's liquidity and short-term debt-paying ability; calculated as current assets divided by current liabilities. (p. 14-19).

Days in inventory A measure of the average number of days that inventory is held; computed as inventory turnover divided into 365 days. (p. 14-21).

Debt to assets ratio A measure of the percentage of total financing provided by creditors; computed as total liabilities divided by total assets. (p. 14-22).

Discontinued operations The disposal of a significant component of a business. (p. 14-3).

Earnings per share The net income earned by each share of outstanding common stock; computed as net income less preferred dividends divided by the weighted-average common shares outstanding. (p. 14-26).

Free cash flow A measure of solvency. Cash remaining from operating activities after adjusting for capital expenditures and dividends paid. (p. 14-23).

Gross profit rate Gross profit expressed as a percentage of net sales; computed as gross profit divided by net sales. (p. 14-26).

Horizontal analysis A technique for evaluating a series of financial statement data over a period of time to determine the increase (decrease) that has taken place, expressed as either an euro amount or a percentage. (p. 14-8).

Inventory turnover A measure of the liquidity of inventory. Measures the number of times average inventory was sold during the period; computed as cost of goods sold divided by average inventory. (p. 14-20).

Leveraging Borrowing money at a lower rate of interest than can be earned by using the borrowed money; also referred to as *trading on the equity*. (p. 14-24).

Liquidity ratios Measures of the short-term ability of the company to pay its maturing current obligations and to meet unexpected needs for cash. (p. 14-15).

Payout ratio A measure of the percentage of earnings distributed in the form of cash dividends; calculated as cash dividends paid on common stock divided by net income. (p. 14-27).

Price-earnings (P-E) ratio A comparison of the market price of each share of common stock to the earnings per share; computed as the market price of the stock divided by earnings per share. (p. 14-27).

Profitability ratios Measures of the income or operating success of a company for a given period of time. (p. 14-16).

Profit margin A measure of the net income generated by each euro of net sales; computed as net income divided by net sales. (p. 14-25).

Ratio The mathematical relationship between one quantity and another. The relationship may be expressed either as a percentage, a rate, or a simple proportion. (p. 14-14).

Ratio analysis A technique for evaluating financial statements that expresses the relationship between selected financial statement data. (p. 14-14).

Return on assets A profitability measure that indicates the amount of net income generated by each euro of assets; calculated as net income divided by average total assets. (p. 14-24).

Return on common stockholders' equity (ROE) A measure of the euros of net income earned for each euro invested by the owners; computed as income available to common stockholders divided by average common stockholders' equity. (p. 14-23).

Solvency ratios Measures of the ability of a company to survive over a long period of time, particularly to pay interest as it comes due and to repay the balance of debt at its maturity. (p. 14-16).

Sustainable income The most likely level of income to be obtained by a company in the future. (p. 14-3).

Times interest earned A measure of a company's solvency and ability to meet interest payments as they come due; calculated as the sum of net income, interest expense, and income tax expense divided by interest expense. (p. 14-22).

Trading on the equity See *leveraging*. (p. 14-24).

Trading securities Securities bought and held primarily for sale in the near term to generate income on short-term price differences. (p. 14-5).

Vertical analysis A technique for evaluating financial statement data that expresses each item in a financial statement as a percentage of a base amount. (p. 14-11).

Practice Multiple-Choice Questions

1. **(LO 1)** In reporting discontinued operations, the income statement should show in a special section:
   a. gains on the disposal of the discontinued component.
   b. losses on the disposal of the discontinued component.
   c. neither gains nor losses on the disposal of the discontinued component.
   d. both gains and losses on the disposal of the discontinued component.

2. **(LO 1)** Cool Stools Corporation has income before taxes of €400,000 and a loss on discontinued operations of €100,000. If the income tax rate is 25% on all items, the income statement should report income from continuing operations and discontinued operations, respectively, of
   a. €325,000 and €100,000.
   b. €325,000 and €75,000.
   c. €300,000 and €100,000.
   d. €300,000 and €75,000.

3. **(LO 1)** Which of the following would be considered an "Other comprehensive income" item?
   a. Gain on disposal of discontinued operations.
   b. Unrealized loss on available-for-sale securities.
   c. Loss related to flood.
   d. Net income.

4. **(LO 2)** In horizontal analysis, each item is expressed as a percentage of the:
   a. net income amount.
   b. stockholders' equity amount.
   c. total assets amount.
   d. base-year amount.

5. **(LO 2)** Samuel Apparels plc reported net sales of £300,000, £330,000, and £360,000 in the years 2021, 2022, and 2023, respectively. If 2021 is the base year, what percentage do 2023 net sales represent of the base?
   a. 77%.
   c. 120%.
   b. 108%.
   d. 130%.

6. **(LO 2)** The following schedule is a display of what type of analysis?

	Amount	Percent
Current assets	A$200,000	25%
Property, plant, and equipment	600,000	75%
Total assets	A$800,000	

   a. Horizontal analysis.
   c. Vertical analysis.
   b. Differential analysis.
   d. Ratio analysis.

7. **(LO 2)** In vertical analysis, the base amount for depreciation expense is generally:
   a. net sales.
   b. depreciation expense in a previous year.
   c. gross profit.
   d. fixed assets.

8. **(LO 3)** Which measure is an evaluation of a company's ability to pay current liabilities?
   a. Accounts receivable turnover.
   b. Current ratio.
   c. Both accounts receivable turnover and current ratio.
   d. None of the answer choices is correct.

9. **(LO 3)** Which measure is useful in evaluating the efficiency in managing inventories?
   a. Inventory turnover.
   b. Days in inventory.
   c. Both inventory turnover and days in inventory.
   d. None of the answer choices is correct.

10. **(LO 3)** Which of these is **not** a liquidity ratio?
    a. Current ratio.
    b. Asset turnover.
    c. Inventory turnover.
    d. Accounts receivable turnover.

11. **(LO 3)** Empalagar SpA reported net income €24,000, net sales €400,000, and average assets €600,000 for 2023. What is the 2023 profit margin?
    a. 6%.
    c. 40%.
    b. 12%.
    d. 200%.

Use the following financial statement information as of the end of each year to answer Questions 12–16.

	2023	2022
Inventory	€ 54,000	€ 48,000
Current assets	81,000	106,000
Total assets	382,000	326,000
Current liabilities	27,000	36,000
Total liabilities	102,000	88,000
Common stockholders' equity	240,000	198,000
Net sales	784,000	697,000
Cost of goods sold	306,000	277,000
Net income	134,000	90,000
Income tax expense	22,000	18,000
Interest expense	12,000	12,000
Dividends paid to preferred stockholders	4,000	4,000
Dividends paid to common stockholders	15,000	10,000

12. **(LO 3)** Compute the days in inventory for 2023.
    a. 64.4 days.
    c. 6 days.
    b. 60.8 days.
    d. 24 days.

13. **(LO 3)** Compute the current ratio for 2023.
    a. 1.26:1.
    c. 0.80:1.
    b. 3.0:1.
    d. 3.75:1.

14. **(LO 3)** Compute the profit margin for 2023.
    a. 17.1%.
    c. 37.9%.
    b. 18.1%.
    d. 5.9%.

15. (LO 3) Compute the return on common stockholders' equity for 2023.

 a. 54.2%.
 b. 52.5%.
 c. 61.2%.
 d. 59.4%.

16. (LO 3) Compute the times interest earned for 2023.

 a. 11.2 times.
 b. 65.3 times.
 c. 14.0 times.
 d. 13.0 times.

Solutions

1. d. Gains and losses from the operations of a discontinued component and gains and losses on the disposal of the discontinued component are shown in a separate section immediately after continuing operations in the income statement. Choices (a) and (b) are correct, but (d) is the better answer. Choice (c) is wrong as there is a correct answer.

2. d. Income tax expense = 25% × €400,000 = €100,000; therefore, income from continuing operations = €400,000 − €100,000 = €300,000. The loss on discontinued operations is reported net of tax, €100,000 × 75% = €75,000. The other choices are therefore incorrect.

3. b. Unrealized gains and losses on available-for-sale securities are reported as other comprehensive income. The other choices are incorrect because they are reported on the income statement as follows: (a) a gain on the disposal of discontinued operations is reported as an unusual item, (c) loss related to a flood is reported among other expenses and losses, and (d) net income is a separate line item.

4. d. Horizontal analysis converts each succeeding year's balance to a percentage of the base year amount, not (a) net income amount, (b) stockholders' equity amount, or (c) total assets amount.

5. c. The trend percentage for 2023 is 120% (£360,000 ÷ £300,000), not (a) 77%, (b) 108%, or (d) 130%.

6. c. The data in the schedule are a display of vertical analysis because the individual asset items are expressed as a percentage of total assets. The other choices are therefore incorrect. Horizontal analysis is a technique for evaluating a series of data over a period of time.

7. a. In vertical analysis, net sales is used as the base amount for income statement items, not (b) depreciation expense in a previous year, (c) gross profit, or (d) fixed assets.

8. c. Both the accounts receivable turnover and the current ratio measure a firm's ability to pay current liabilities. Choices (a) and (b) are correct but (c) is the better answer. Choice (d) is incorrect because there is a correct answer.

9. c. Both inventory turnover and days in inventory measure a firm's efficiency in managing inventories. Choices (a) and (b) are correct but (c) is the better answer. Choice (d) is incorrect because there is a correct answer.

10. b. Asset turnover is a measure of profitability. The other choices are incorrect because the (a) current ratio, (c) inventory turnover, and (d) accounts receivable turnover are all measures of a firm's liquidity.

11. a. Profit margin = Net income (€24,000) ÷ Net sales (€400,000) = 6%, not (b) 12%, (c) 40%, or (d) 200%.

12. b. Inventory turnover = Cost of goods sold ÷ Average inventory {€306,000 ÷ [(€54,000 + €48,000) ÷ 2]} = 6 times. Thus, days in inventory = 60.8 (365 ÷ 6), not (a) 64.4, (c) 6, or (d) 24 days.

13. b. Current ratio = Current assets ÷ Current liabilities (€81,000 ÷ €27,000) = 3.0:1, not (a) 1.26:1, (c) 0.80:1, or (d) 3.75:1.

14. a. Profit margin = Net income ÷ Net sales (€134,000 ÷ €784,000) = 17.1%, not (b) 18.1%, (c) 37.9%, or (d) 5.9%.

15. d. Return on common stockholders' equity = Net income (€134,000) − Dividends to preferred stockholders (€4,000) ÷ Average common stockholders' equity [(€240,000 + €198,000) ÷ 2] = 59.4%, not (a) 54.2%, (b) 52.5%, or (c) 61.2%.

16. c. Times interest earned = (Net income + Interest expense + Income tax expense) ÷ Interest expense [(€134,000 + €12,000 + €22,000) ÷ €12,000] = 14.0 times, not (a) 11.2, (b) 65.3, or (d) 13.0 times.

Practice Exercises

Prepare horizontal and vertical analyses.

1. (LO 2) The comparative condensed balance sheets of Roadway Ltd. are as follows:

Roadway Ltd.
Condensed Balance Sheets
December 31

	2023	2022
Assets		
Current assets	HK$ 760,000	HK$ 800,000
Property, plant, and equipment (net)	990,000	900,000
Intangible assets	250,000	400,000
Total assets	HK$2,000,000	HK$2,100,000

Liabilities and Stockholders' Equity		
Current liabilities	HK$ 408,000	HK$ 480,000
Long-term liabilities	1,430,000	1,500,000
Stockholders' equity	162,000	120,000
Total liabilities and stockholders' equity	HK$2,000,000	HK$2,100,000

Instructions

a. Prepare a horizontal analysis of the balance sheet data for Roadway Ltd. using 2022 as a base.

b. Prepare a vertical analysis of the balance sheet data for Roadway Ltd. in columnar form for 2023.

Solution

1. a.

Roadway Ltd.
Condensed Balance Sheets
December 31

	2023	2022	Increase (Decrease)	Percent Change from 2022
Assets				
Current assets	HK$ 760,000	HK$ 800,000	HK$ (40,000)	(5.0%)
Property, plant, and equipment (net)	990,000	900,000	90,000	10.0%
Intangible assets	250,000	400,000	(150,000)	(37.5%)
Total assets	HK$2,000,000	HK$2,100,000	HK$(100,000)	(4.8%)
Liabilities and Stockholders' Equity				
Current liabilities	HK$ 408,000	HK$ 480,000	HK$ (72,000)	(15.0%)
Long-term liabilities	1,430,000	1,500,000	(70,000)	(4.7%)
Stockholders' equity	162,000	120,000	42,000	35.0%
Total liabilities and stockholders' equity	HK$2,000,000	HK$2,100,000	HK$(100,000)	(4.8%)

b.

Roadway Ltd.
Condensed Balance Sheet
December 31, 2023

	Amount	Percent
Assets		
Current assets	HK$ 760,000	38.0%
Property, plant, and equipment (net)	990,000	49.5%
Intangible assets	250,000	12.5%
Total assets	HK$2,000,000	100.0%
Liabilities and Stockholders' Equity		
Current liabilities	HK$ 408,000	20.4%
Long-term liabilities	1,430,000	71.5%
Stockholders' equity	162,000	8.1%
Total liabilities and stockholders' equity	HK$2,000,000	100.0%

2. (LO 3) Taylor Group's comparative balance sheets are presented here:

Compute ratios.

Taylor Group
Balance Sheets
December 31

	2023	2022
Cash	A$ 5,300	A$ 3,700
Accounts receivable (net)	21,200	23,400
Inventory	9,000	7,000
Land	20,000	26,000
Buildings	70,000	70,000
Accumulated depreciation—buildings	(15,000)	(10,000)
Total	A$110,500	A$120,100
Accounts payable	A$ 10,370	A$ 31,100
Common stock	75,000	69,000
Retained earnings	25,130	20,000
Total	A$110,500	A$120,100

Taylor's 2023 income statement included net sales of A$120,000, cost of goods sold of A$70,000, and net income of A$14,000.

Instructions

Compute the following ratios for 2023.

a. Current ratio.
b. Accounts receivable turnover.
c. Inventory turnover.
d. Profit margin.
e. Asset turnover.
f. Return on assets.
g. Return on common stockholders' equity.
h. Debt to assets ratio.

Solution

2. a. (A$5,300 + A$21,200 + A$9,000) ÷ A$10,370 = 3.42:1
   b. A$120,000 ÷ [(A$21,200 + A$23,400) ÷ 2] = 5.38 times
   c. A$70,000 ÷ [(A$9,000 + A$7,000) ÷ 2] = 8.8 times
   d. A$14,000 ÷ A$120,000 = 11.7%
   e. A$120,000 ÷ [(A$110,500 + A$120,100) ÷ 2] = 1.04 times
   f. A$14,000 ÷ [(A$110,500 + A$120,100) ÷ 2] = 12.1%
   g. A$14,000 ÷ [(A$100,130 + A$89,000) ÷ 2] = 14.8%
   h. A$10,370 ÷ A$110,500 = 9.4%

Practice Problem

(LO 1) The events and transactions of Quereus plc for the year ended December 31, 2023, resulted in the following data.

Prepare an income statement and a statement of comprehensive income.

Cost of goods sold	£2,600,000
Net sales	4,400,000
Other expenses and losses	9,600
Other revenues and gains	5,600
Selling and administrative expenses	1,100,000
Income from operations of plastics division	70,000
Gain from disposal of plastics division	500,000
Unrealized loss on available-for-sale securities	60,000

Analysis reveals the following:

1. All items recorded are before the applicable income tax rate of 20%.
2. The plastics division was sold on July 1.
3. All operating data for the plastics division have been segregated.

Instructions

Prepare an income statement and a statement of comprehensive income for the year.

Solution

Quereus plc
Income Statement
For the Year Ended December 31, 2023

Net sales			£4,400,000
Cost of goods sold			2,600,000
Gross profit			1,800,000
Selling and administrative expenses			1,100,000
Income from operations			700,000
Other revenues and gains			5,600
Other expenses and losses			9,600
Income before income taxes			696,000
Income tax expense (£696,000 × 20%)			139,200
Income from continuing operations			556,800
Discontinued operations			
Income from operation of plastics division, net of £14,000			
income taxes (£70,000 × 20%)		£ 56,000	
Gain from disposal of plastics division, net of £100,000			
income taxes (£500,000 × 20%)		400,000	456,000
Net income			£1,012,800

Quereus plc
Statement of Comprehensive Income
For the Year Ended December 31, 2023

Net income	£1,012,800
Unrealized loss on available-for-sale securities, net of £12,000 income tax savings (£60,000 × 20%)	48,000
Comprehensive income	£ 964,800

Questions

1. Explain sustainable income. What relationship does this concept have to the treatment of discontinued operations on the income statement?

2. Ruan Ltd. reported 2022 earnings per share of NT$32.6 and had no discontinued operations. In 2023, earnings per share on income from continuing operations was NT$29.9, and earnings per share on net income was NT$34.9. Do you consider this trend to be favorable? Why or why not?

3. Gibson Shoes Ltd. has been in operation for three years and uses the FIFO method of inventory costing. During the fourth year, Gibson Shoes changes to the average-cost method for all its inventory. How will Gibson Shoes report this change?

4. Explain how the choice of one of the following accounting methods over the other raises or lowers a company's net income during a period of continuing inflation.

   a. Use of FIFO instead of LIFO for inventory costing.

   b. Use of a six-year life for machinery instead of a nine-year life.

   c. Use of straight-line depreciation instead of declining-balance depreciation.

5. Two popular methods of financial statement analysis are horizontal analysis and vertical analysis. Explain the difference between these two methods.

6. **a.** If Erin Company had net income of $300,000 in 2022 and it experienced a 24.5% increase in net income for 2023, what is its net income for 2023?

   b. If 6 cents of every dollar of Erin's revenue results in net income in 2022, what is the dollar amount of 2022 revenue?

7. **a.** Maribel Ortiz believes that the analysis of financial statements is directed at two characteristics of a company: liquidity and profitability. Is Maribel correct? Explain.

   b. Are short-term creditors, long-term creditors, and stockholders interested in primarily the same characteristics of a company? Explain.

8. a. Distinguish among the following bases of comparison: intracompany, intercompany, and industry averages.
   b. Give the principal value of using each of the three bases of comparison.
9. Name the major ratios useful in assessing (a) liquidity and (b) solvency.
10. James Hodzic is puzzled. His company had a profit margin of 10% in 2023. He feels that this is an indication that the company is doing well. Rita Borg, his accountant, says that more information is needed to determine the company's financial well-being. Who is correct? Why?
11. What does each type of ratio measure?
    a. Liquidity ratios.
    b. Solvency ratios.
    c. Profitability ratios.
12. What is the difference between the current ratio and working capital?
13. Nimoy el Mercado, a retail store, has an accounts receivable turnover of 4.5 times. The industry average is 12.5 times. Does Nimoy el Mercado have a collection problem with its receivables?
14. Which ratios should be used to help answer each of these questions?
    a. How efficient is a company in using its assets to produce net sales?
    b. How near to sale is the inventory on hand?
    c. How many euros of net income were earned for each euro invested by the owners?
    d. How able is a company to meet interest charges as they become due?
15. At year-end, the price-earnings ratio of **General Motors** (USA) was 11.3, and the price-earnings ratio of **Microsoft** (USA) was 28.14. Which company did the stock market favor? Explain.
16. What is the equation for computing the payout ratio? Do you expect this ratio to be high or low for a growth company?
17. Holding all other factors constant, indicate whether each of the following changes generally signals good or bad news about a company.
    a. Increase in profit margin.
    b. Decrease in inventory turnover.
    c. Increase in current ratio.
    d. Decrease in earnings per share.
    e. Increase in price-earnings ratio.
    f. Increase in debt to assets ratio.
    g. Decrease in times interest earned.
18. The return on assets for Miller Ltd. is 7.6%. During the same year, Miller's return on common stockholders' equity is 12.8%. What is the explanation for the difference in the two rates?
19. Which two ratios do you think should be of greatest interest in each of the following cases?
    a. A pension fund considering the purchase of 20-year bonds.
    b. A bank contemplating a short-term loan.
    c. A common stockholder.
20. Azra A.S. has net income of ₺2,000,000, average shares of common stock outstanding of 40,000, and preferred dividends of ₺200,000 that were declared and paid during the period. What is Azra's earnings per share of common stock? Elif Deniz, the president of Azra, believes that the computed EPS of the company is high. Comment.

Brief Exercises

BE14.1 (LO 1), AP On June 30, Benito SpA discontinued its operations in Italy. During the year, the operating income was €200,000 before taxes. On September 1, Benito disposed of the Italy facility at a pretax loss of €640,000. The applicable tax rate is 25%. Show the discontinued operations section of Benito's income statement.

Prepare a discontinued operations section of an income statement.

BE14.2 (LO 1), AP An inexperienced accountant for Voldemort plc showed the following in the income statement: net income £337,500 and unrealized gain on available-for-sale securities (before taxes) £70,000. The unrealized gain on available-for-sale securities is subject to a 25% tax rate. Prepare a correct statement of comprehensive income.

Prepare a statement of comprehensive income including unusual items.

BE14.3 (LO 1), C On January 1, 2023, Bryce Inc. changed from the LIFO method of inventory costing to the FIFO method. Explain how this change in accounting principle should be treated in the company's financial statements.

Indicate how a change in accounting principle is reported.

BE14.4 (LO 2), AP Using these data from the comparative balance sheets of Jiang Ltd., perform a horizontal analysis.

Prepare horizontal analysis.

	December 31, 2023	December 31, 2022
Accounts receivable (net)	NT$ 4,600,000	NT$ 4,000,000
Inventory	7,800,000	6,500,000
Total assets	31,640,000	28,000,000

BE14.5 (LO 2), AP Using these data from the comparative balance sheets of Jiang Ltd., perform a vertical analysis.

Prepare vertical analysis.

	December 31, 2023	December 31, 2022
Accounts receivable (net)	NT$ 4,600,000	NT$ 4,000,000
Inventory	7,800,000	6,500,000
Total assets	31,640,000	28,000,000

Calculate percentage of change.

BE14.6 (LO 2), AP Net income was HK$5,000,000 in 2021, HK$4,850,000 in 2022, and HK$5,184,000 in 2023. What is the percentage of change (a) from 2021 to 2022, and (b) from 2022 to 2023? Is the change an increase or a decrease?

Calculate net income.

BE14.7 (LO 2), AP If Tillman SA had net income of R$3,828,000 in 2023 and it experienced a 16% increase in net income over 2022, what was its 2022 net income?

Analyze change in net income.

BE14.8 (LO 2), AP Vertical analysis (common-size) percentages for Dagman Company's net sales, cost of goods sold, and expenses are listed here:

Vertical Analysis	2023	2022	2021
Net sales	100.0%	100.0%	100.0%
Cost of goods sold	60.5	62.9	64.8
Expenses	26.0	26.6	27.5

Did Dagman's net income as a percent of net sales increase, decrease, or remain unchanged over the three-year period? Provide numerical support for your answer.

Analyze change in net income.

BE14.9 (LO 2), AP **Writing** Horizontal analysis (trend analysis) percentages for Phoenix Company's sales revenue, cost of goods sold, and expenses are listed here:

Horizontal Analysis	2023	2022	2021
Net sales	96.2%	104.8%	100.0%
Cost of goods sold	101.0	98.0	100.0
Expenses	105.6	95.4	100.0

Explain whether Phoenix's net income increased, decreased, or remained unchanged over the three-year period.

Calculate current ratio.

BE14.10 (LO 3), AP Suppose these selected condensed data are taken from recent balance sheets of **Bob Evans Farms** (USA) (in thousands).

	2023	2022
Cash	$ 13,606	$ 7,669
Accounts receivable (net)	23,045	19,951
Inventory	31,087	31,345
Other current assets	12,522	11,909
Total current assets	$ 80,260	$ 70,874
Total current liabilities	$245,805	$326,203

Compute the current ratio for each year and comment on your results.

Evaluate collection of accounts receivable.

BE14.11 (LO 3), AN **Writing** The following data are taken from the financial statements of Gladow Ltd.

	2023	2022
Accounts receivable (net), end of year	£ 550,000	£ 540,000
Net sales on account	4,300,000	4,000,000
Terms for all sales are 1/10, n/45		

Compute for each year (a) the accounts receivable turnover and (b) the average collection period. What conclusions about the management of accounts receivable can be drawn from these data? At the end of 2023, accounts receivable (net) was £520,000.

Evaluate management of inventory.

BE14.12 (LO 3), AN **Writing** The following data were taken from the financial records of Feng Company.

	2023	2022
Net sales	HK$64,200,000	HK$62,400,000
Beginning inventory	9,600,000	8,400,000
Purchases	48,400,000	46,610,000
Ending inventory	10,200,000	9,600,000

Compute for each year (a) the inventory turnover and (b) days in inventory. What conclusions concerning the management of the inventory can be drawn from these data?

Calculate profitability ratios.

BE14.13 (LO 3), AN **Staples, Inc.** (USA) is one of the largest suppliers of office products in the United States. Suppose it had net income of $738.7 million and net sales of $24,275.5 million in 2023. Its total assets were $13,073.1 million at the beginning of the year and $13,717.3 million at the end of the year. What is Staples, Inc.'s (a) asset turnover and (b) profit margin? (Round to two decimals.) Provide a brief interpretation of your results.

BE14.14 (LO 3), AN Celyse Company has stockholders' equity of A$400,000 and net income of A$72,000. It has a payout ratio of 18% and a return on assets of 20%. How much did Celyse pay in cash dividends, and what were its average total assets?

Calculate profitability ratios.

BE14.15 (LO 3), AN Selected data taken from a recent year's financial statements of trading card company **Topps Company, Inc.** (USA) are as follows (in millions):

Calculate and analyze free cash flow.

Net sales	$326.7
Current liabilities, beginning of year	41.1
Current liabilities, end of year	62.4
Net cash provided by operating activities	10.4
Total liabilities, beginning of year	65.2
Total liabilities, end of year	73.2
Capital expenditures	3.7
Cash dividends	6.2

Compute the free cash flow. Provide a brief interpretation of your results.

DO IT! Exercises

DO IT! 14.1 (LO 1), AP During 2023, Zacarias SA had the following amounts, all before calculating tax effects: income before income taxes €500,000, loss on operation of discontinued music division €60,000, gain on disposal of discontinued music division €40,000, and unrealized loss on available-for-sale securities €150,000. The income tax rate is 20%. Prepare a partial income statement, beginning with income before income taxes, and a statement of comprehensive income for the year ended December 31, 2023.

Prepare a partial income statement and a statement of comprehensive income.

DO IT! 14.2 (LO 2), AP Summary financial information for Rapture Ltd. is as follows:

Prepare horizontal analysis.

	Dec. 31, 2023	Dec. 31, 2022
Current assets	£ 200,000	£ 220,000
Plant assets	1,040,000	780,000
Total assets	£1,240,000	£1,000,000

Compute the amount and percentage changes in 2023 using horizontal analysis, assuming 2022 is the base year.

DO IT! 14.3 (LO 3), AP The condensed financial statements of Jayden Company for the years 2022 and 2023 are presented as follows (amounts in thousands):

Compute ratios.

Jayden Company
Balance Sheets
December 31

	2023	2022
Current assets		
Cash and cash equivalents	S$ 330	S$ 360
Accounts receivable (net)	470	400
Inventory	460	390
Prepaid expenses	120	160
Total current assets	1,380	1,310
Investments	10	10
Property, plant, and equipment (net)	420	380
Intangibles and other assets	530	510
Total assets	S$2,340	S$2,210
Current liabilities	S$ 900	S$ 790
Long-term liabilities	410	380
Stockholders' equity—common	1,030	1,040
Total liabilities and stockholders' equity	S$2,340	S$2,210

Jayden Company
Income Statements
For the Years Ended December 31

	2023	2022
Net sales	S$3,800	S$3,460
Expenses		
Cost of goods sold	955	890
Selling and administrative expenses	2,400	2,330
Interest expense	25	20
Total expenses	3,380	3,240
Income before income taxes	420	220
Income tax expense	126	66
Net income	S$ 294	S$ 154

Compute the following ratios for 2023 and 2022.

a. Current ratio.

b. Inventory turnover. (Inventory on 12/31/21 was S$340.)

c. Profit margin.

d. Return on assets. (Assets on 12/31/21 were S$1,900.)

e. Return on common stockholders' equity. (Stockholders' equity—common on 12/31/21 was S$900.)

f. Debt to assets ratio.

g. Times interest earned.

Exercises

Prepare a correct partial income statement.

E14.1 (LO 1), AN Writing For its fiscal year ending October 31, 2023, Johnson Group reports the following partial data.

Income before income taxes	A$540,000
Income tax expense (20% × A$420,000)	84,000
Income from continuing operations	456,000
Loss on discontinued operations	120,000
Net income	A$336,000

The loss on discontinued operations comprised of a A$50,000 loss from operations and a A$70,000 loss from disposal. The income tax rate is 20% on all items.

Instructions

a. Prepare a correct partial income statement, beginning with income before income taxes.

b. Explain in memo form why the original income statement data are misleading.

Prepare a partial income statement and a statement of comprehensive income.

E14.2 (LO 1), AP Antier SpA has income from continuing operations of €290,000 for the year ended December 31, 2023. It also has the following items (before considering income taxes):

1. An unrealized loss of €80,000 on available-for-sale securities.

2. A gain of €30,000 on the discontinuance of a division (comprised of a €10,000 loss from operations and a €40,000 gain on disposal).

Assume all items are subject to income taxes at a 20% tax rate.

Instructions

Prepare a partial income statement, beginning with income from continuing operations, and a statement of comprehensive income.

E14.3 (LO 2), AP Here is financial information for Glitter Inc.

Prepare horizontal analysis.

	December 31, 2023	December 31, 2022
Current assets	$106,000	$ 90,000
Plant assets (net)	400,000	350,000
Current liabilities	99,000	65,000
Long-term liabilities	122,000	90,000
Common stock, $1 par	130,000	115,000
Retained earnings	155,000	170,000

Instructions

Prepare a schedule showing a horizontal analysis for 2023, using 2022 as the base year.

E14.4 (LO 2), AP Operating data for Sze Ltd. are presented as follows:

Prepare vertical analysis.

	2023	2022
Net sales	HK$8,000,000	HK$6,000,000
Cost of goods sold	5,200,000	4,080,000
Selling expenses	1,200,000	720,000
Administrative expenses	600,000	480,000
Income tax expense	300,000	240,000
Net income	700,000	480,000

Instructions

Prepare a schedule showing a vertical analysis for 2023 and 2022.

E14.5 (LO 2), AP Hypothetical comparative condensed balance sheets of **Nike, Inc.** (USA) are presented here:

Prepare horizontal and vertical analyses.

Nike, Inc.
Condensed Balance Sheets
May 31
($ in millions)

	2023	2022
Assets		
Current assets	$ 9,734	$ 8,839
Property, plant, and equipment (net)	1,958	1,891
Other assets	1,558	1,713
Total assets	$13,250	$12,443
Liabilities and Stockholders' Equity		
Current liabilities	$ 3,277	$ 3,322
Long-term liabilities	1,280	1,296
Stockholders' equity	8,693	7,825
Total liabilities and stockholders' equity	$13,250	$12,443

Instructions

a. Prepare a horizontal analysis of the balance sheet data for Nike, using 2022 as a base. (Show the amount of increase or decrease as well.)

b. Prepare a vertical analysis of the balance sheet data for Nike for 2023.

E14.6 (LO 2), AP Here are the comparative condensed income statements of Hendi A.S.

Prepare horizontal and vertical analyses.

Hendi A.S.
Condensed Income Statements
For the Years Ended December 31

	2023	2022
Net sales	₺5,980,000	₺5,000,000
Cost of goods sold	4,770,000	4,200,000
Gross profit	1,210,000	800,000
Operating expenses	800,000	440,000
Net income	₺ 410,000	₺ 360,000

Instructions

a. Prepare a horizontal analysis of the income statement data for Hendi, using 2022 as a base. (Show the amounts of increase or decrease.)

b. Prepare a vertical analysis of the income statement data for Hendi for both years.

Compute liquidity ratios.

E14.7 (LO 3), AP Nordstrom, Inc. (USA) operates department stores in numerous states. Selected hypothetical financial statement data (in millions) for 2023 are presented below.

	End of Year	Beginning of Year
Cash and cash equivalents	$ 795	$ 72
Accounts receivable (net)	2,035	1,942
Inventory	898	900
Other current assets	326	303
Total current assets	$4,054	$3,217
Total current liabilities	$2,014	$1,601

For the year, net credit sales were $8,258 million, cost of goods sold was $5,328 million, and net cash provided by operating activities was $1,251 million.

Instructions

Compute the current ratio, accounts receivable turnover, average collection period, inventory turnover, and days in inventory for the current year.

Perform current ratio analysis.

E14.8 (LO 3), AP Bennis SA had the following transactions involving current assets and current liabilities during February 2023.

Feb. 3   Collected accounts receivable of R$150,000.
      7   Purchased equipment for R$230,000 cash.
     11   Paid R$30,000 for a one-year insurance policy.
     14   Paid accounts payable of R$120,000.
     18   Declared cash dividends of R$40,000.

Additional information:
As of February 1, 2023, current assets were R$1,200,000 and current liabilities were R$400,000.

Instructions

Compute the current ratio as of the beginning of the month and after each transaction.

Compute selected ratios.

E14.9 (LO 3), AP Ling Ltd. has these comparative balance sheet data.

Ling Ltd.
Balance Sheets
December 31

	2023	2022
Cash	HK$ 150,000	HK$ 300,000
Accounts receivable (net)	700,000	600,000
Inventory	600,000	500,000
Plant assets (net)	2,000,000	1,800,000
	HK$3,450,000	HK$3,200,000
Accounts payable	HK$ 500,000	HK$ 600,000
Bonds payable (15%)	1,000,000	1,000,000
Common stock, HK$100 par	1,400,000	1,200,000
Retained earnings	550,000	400,000
	HK$3,450,000	HK$3,200,000

Additional information for 2023:

1. Net income was HK$250,000.
2. Sales on account were HK$3,750,000. Sales returns and allowances amounted to HK$250,000.
3. Cost of goods sold was HK$1,980,000.
4. Net cash provided by operating activities was HK$480,000.
5. Capital expenditures were HK$250,000, and cash dividends paid were HK$100,000.
6. The bonds payable are due in 2036.

Instructions

Compute the following ratios at December 31, 2023.

a. Current ratio.
b. Accounts receivable turnover.
c. Average collection period.
d. Inventory turnover.
e. Days in inventory.
f. Free cash flow.

E14.10 (LO 3), AP Selected hypothetical comparative statement data for the giant bookseller **Barnes & Noble** (USA) are presented here. All balance sheet data are as of the end of the fiscal year (in millions).

Compute selected ratios.

	2023	2022
Net sales	$5,121.8	$5,286.7
Cost of goods sold	3,540.6	3,679.8
Net income	75.9	135.8
Accounts receivable (net)	81.0	107.1
Inventory	1,203.5	1,358.2
Total assets	2,993.9	3,249.8
Total common stockholders' equity	921.6	1,074.7

Instructions

Compute the following ratios for 2023.

a. Profit margin.
b. Asset turnover.
c. Return on assets.
d. Return on common stockholders' equity.
e. Gross profit rate.

E14.11 (LO 3), AP Here is the income statement for Rees NV.

Compute selected ratios.

Rees NV
Income Statement
For the Year Ended December 31, 2023

Net sales	€ 400,000
Cost of goods sold	230,000
Gross profit	170,000
Expenses (including €16,000 interest and €24,000 income taxes)	98,000
Net income	€ 72,000

Additional information:

1. Common stock outstanding January 1, 2023, was 32,000 shares, and 40,000 shares were outstanding at December 31, 2023. (Use a simple average for weighted-average.)
2. The market price of Rees stock was €14 on December 31, 2023.
3. Cash dividends of €21,000 were declared and paid.

Instructions

Compute the following measures for 2023.

a. Earnings per share.
b. Price-earnings ratio.
c. Payout ratio.
d. Times interest earned.

E14.12 (LO 3), AN Linchen Ltd. experienced a fire on December 31, 2023, in which its financial records were partially destroyed. It has been able to salvage some of the records and has ascertained the following balances:

Compute amounts from ratios.

	December 31, 2023	December 31, 2022
Cash	NT$ 300,000	NT$ 100,000
Accounts receivable (net)	725,000	1,260,000
Inventory	2,000,000	1,800,000
Accounts payable	500,000	900,000
Notes payable	300,000	600,000
Common stock, NT$1,000 par	4,000,000	4,000,000
Retained earnings	1,135,000	1,010,000

Additional information:

1. The inventory turnover is 3.8 times.
2. The return on common stockholders' equity is 22%. The company had no additional capital accounts.
3. The accounts receivable turnover is 11.2 times.
4. The return on assets is 18%.
5. Total assets at December 31, 2022, were NT$6,050,000.

Instructions

Compute the following for Linchen Ltd.

a. Cost of goods sold for 2023.
b. Net credit sales for 2023.
c. Net income for 2023.
d. Total assets at December 31, 2023.

Compute ratios.

E14.13 (LO 3), AP The condensed financial statements of Keller Company for the years 2022 and 2023 are as follows:

Keller Company
Balance Sheets
December 31 (in thousands)

	2023	2022
Current assets		
Cash and cash equivalents	CHF 330	CHF 360
Accounts receivable (net)	470	400
Inventory	460	390
Prepaid expenses	130	160
Total current assets	1,390	1,310
Investments	10	10
Property, plant, and equipment (net)	410	380
Other assets	530	510
Total assets	CHF2,340	CHF2,210
Current liabilities	CHF 820	CHF 790
Long-term liabilities	480	380
Stockholders' equity—common	1,040	1,040
Total liabilities and stockholders' equity	CHF2,340	CHF2,210

Keller Company
Income Statements
For the Year Ended December 31 (in thousands)

	2023	2022
Net sales	CHF3,800	CHF3,460
Expenses		
Cost of goods sold	970	890
Selling and administrative expenses	2,400	2,330
Interest expense	10	20
Total expenses	3,380	3,240
Income before income taxes	420	220
Income tax expense	168	88
Net income	CHF 252	CHF 132

Compute the following ratios for 2023 and 2022.

a. Current ratio.
b. Inventory turnover. (Inventory on December 31, 2021, was CHF340.)
c. Profit margin.
d. Return on assets. (Assets on December 31, 2021, were CHF1,900.)
e. Return on common stockholders' equity. (Stockholders' equity—common on December 31, 2021, was CHF900.)
f. Debt to assets ratio.
g. Times interest earned.

Problems

P14.1 (LO 2, 3), AN Writing Here are comparative financial statement data for Lionel Company and Barrymore Company, two competitors. All data are as of December 31, 2023, and December 31, 2022.

Prepare vertical analysis and comment on profitability.

	Lionel Company		Barrymore Company	
	2023	2022	2023	2022
Net sales	£1,849,000		£546,000	
Cost of goods sold	1,063,200		289,000	
Operating expenses	240,000		82,000	
Interest expense	6,800		3,600	
Income tax expense	62,000		28,000	
Current assets	325,975	£312,410	83,336	£ 79,467
Plant assets (net)	526,800	500,000	139,728	125,812
Current liabilities	66,325	75,815	35,348	30,281
Long-term liabilities	113,990	90,000	29,620	25,000
Common stock, £10 par	500,000	500,000	120,000	120,000
Retained earnings	172,460	146,595	38,096	29,998

Instructions

a. Prepare a vertical analysis of the 2023 income statement data for Lionel Company and Barrymore Company.

b. Comment on the relative profitability of the companies by computing the 2023 return on assets and the return on common stockholders' equity for both companies.

P14.2 (LO 3), AP The comparative statements of Ernie Bishop Company are presented here:

Compute ratios from balance sheets and income statements.

Ernie Bishop Company
Income Statements
For the Years Ended December 31

	2023	2022
Net sales	€1,890,540	€1,750,500
Cost of goods sold	1,058,540	1,006,000
Gross profit	832,000	744,500
Selling and administrative expenses	500,000	479,000
Income from operations	332,000	265,500
Other expenses and losses		
Interest expense	22,000	20,000
Income before income taxes	310,000	245,500
Income tax expense	92,000	73,000
Net income	€ 218,000	€ 172,500

Ernie Bishop Company
Balance Sheets
December 31

	2023	2022
Assets		
Current assets		
Cash	€ 60,100	€ 64,200
Debt investments (short-term)	74,000	50,000
Accounts receivable (net)	117,800	102,800
Inventory	126,000	115,500
Total current assets	377,900	332,500
Plant assets (net)	649,000	520,300
Total assets	€1,026,900	€852,800

	2023	2022
Liabilities and Stockholders' Equity		
Current liabilities		
Accounts payable	€ 160,000	€145,400
Income taxes payable	43,500	42,000
Total current liabilities	203,500	187,400
Bonds payable	220,000	200,000
Total liabilities	423,500	387,400
Stockholders' equity		
Common stock (€5 par)	290,000	300,000
Retained earnings	313,400	165,400
Total stockholders' equity	603,400	465,400
Total liabilities and stockholders' equity	€1,026,900	€852,800

All sales were on credit. Net cash provided by operating activities for 2023 was €220,000. Capital expenditures were €136,000, and cash dividends paid were €70,000.

Instructions

Compute the following ratios for 2023.

a. Earnings per share.
b. Return on common stockholders' equity.
c. Return on assets.
d. Current ratio.
e. Accounts receivable turnover.
f. Average collection period.
g. Inventory turnover.
h. Days in inventory.
i. Times interest earned.
j. Asset turnover.
k. Debt to assets ratio.
l. Free cash flow.

Perform ratio analysis, and discuss changes in financial position and operating results.

P14.3 (LO 3), AN Writing Condensed balance sheet and income statement data for Clarence Ltd. are presented here:

Clarence Ltd.
Balance Sheets
December 31

	2023	2022	2021
Cash	£ 30,000	£ 20,000	£ 18,000
Accounts receivable (net)	50,000	45,000	48,000
Other current assets	90,000	95,000	64,000
Investments	55,000	70,000	45,000
Property, plant, and equipment (net)	500,000	370,000	358,000
	£725,000	£600,000	£533,000
Current liabilities	£ 85,000	£ 80,000	£ 70,000
Long-term debt	145,000	85,000	50,000
Common stock, £10 par	320,000	310,000	300,000
Retained earnings	175,000	125,000	113,000
	£725,000	£600,000	£533,000

Clarence Ltd.
Income Statements
For the Years Ended December 31

	2023	2022
Sales	£740,000	£600,000
Less: Sales returns and allowances	40,000	30,000
Net sales	700,000	570,000
Cost of goods sold	425,000	350,000
Gross profit	275,000	220,000
Operating expenses (including income taxes)	180,000	150,000
Net income	£ 95,000	£ 70,000

Additional information:

1. The market price of Clarence's common stock was £7.00, £7.50, and £8.50 for 2021, 2022, and 2023, respectively.
2. You must compute dividends declared. All declared dividends were paid in cash in the year of declaration.

Instructions

a. Compute the following ratios for 2022 and 2023.
   1. Profit margin.
   2. Gross profit rate.
   3. Asset turnover.
   4. Earnings per share.
   5. Price-earnings ratio.
   6. Payout ratio.
   7. Debt to assets ratio.

b. Based on the ratios calculated, discuss briefly the improvement or lack thereof in the financial position and operating results from 2022 to 2023 of Clarence Ltd.

P14.4 (LO 3), AN The following financial information is for Nguyen Company.

Compute ratios; comment on overall liquidity and profitability.

Nguyen Company
Balance Sheets
December 31

	2023	2022
Assets		
Cash	A$ 70,000	A$ 65,000
Debt investments (short-term)	55,000	40,000
Accounts receivable (net)	104,000	90,000
Inventory	230,000	165,000
Prepaid expenses	25,000	23,000
Land	130,000	130,000
Building and equipment (net)	260,000	185,000
Total assets	A$874,000	A$698,000
Liabilities and Stockholders' Equity		
Notes payable (current)	A$170,000	A$120,000
Accounts payable	65,000	52,000
Accrued liabilities	40,000	40,000
Bonds payable, due 2026	250,000	170,000
Common stock, A$10 par	200,000	200,000
Retained earnings	149,000	116,000
Total liabilities and stockholders' equity	A$874,000	A$698,000

Nguyen Company
Income Statements
For the Years Ended December 31

	2023	2022
Net sales	A$882,000	A$790,000
Cost of goods sold	640,000	575,000
Gross profit	242,000	215,000
Operating expenses	190,000	167,000
Net income	A$ 52,000	A$ 48,000

Additional information:

1. Inventory at the beginning of 2022 was A$115,000.
2. Accounts receivable (net) at the beginning of 2022 were A$86,000.
3. Total assets at the beginning of 2022 were A$660,000.
4. No common stock transactions occurred during 2022 or 2023.
5. All sales were on credit.

Instructions

a. Compute liquidity and profitability ratios, and indicate the percentage change (to the nearest whole percentage) in liquidity and profitability ratios of Nguyen Company from 2022 to 2023. (*Note:* Not all profitability ratios can be computed, nor can cash-basis ratios be computed.)

b. The following are three **independent** situations and a ratio that may be affected. For each situation, compute the affected ratio (1) as of December 31, 2023, and (2) as of December 31, 2024, and percentage change in each ratio after giving effect to the situation.

Situation	Ratio
1. 18,000 shares of common stock were sold at par on July 1, 2024. Net income for 2024 was A$54,000, and there were no dividends.	Return on common stockholders' equity
2. All of the notes payable were paid in 2024. All other liabilities remained at their December 31, 2023, levels. Total assets on December 31, 2024, were A$900,000.	Debt to assets ratio
3. The market price of common stock was A$9 and A$12 on December 31, 2023 and 2024, respectively. Net income for 2024 was A$54,000. (Use a simple average calculation for EPS.)	Price-earnings ratio

Compute selected ratios, and compare liquidity, profitability, and solvency for two companies.

P14.5 (LO 3), AN Selected hypothetical financial data of **Target** (USA) and **Walmart** (USA) for 2023 are presented here (in millions):

	Target Corporation	Walmart Inc.
Income Statement Data for Year		
Net sales	$65,357	$408,214
Cost of goods sold	45,583	304,657
Selling and administrative expenses	15,101	79,607
Interest expense	707	2,065
Other income (expense)	(94)	(411)
Income tax expense	1,384	7,139
Net income	$ 2,488	$ 14,335
Balance Sheet Data (End of Year)		
Current assets	$18,424	$ 48,331
Noncurrent assets	26,109	122,375
Total assets	$44,533	$170,706
Current liabilities	$11,327	$ 55,561
Long-term debt	17,859	44,089
Total stockholders' equity	15,347	71,056
Total liabilities and stockholders' equity	$44,533	$170,706
Beginning-of-Year Balances		
Total assets	$44,106	$163,429
Total stockholders' equity	13,712	65,682
Current liabilities	10,512	55,390
Total liabilities	30,394	97,747
Other Data		
Average net accounts receivable	$7,525	$ 4,025
Average inventory	6,942	33,836
Net cash provided by operating activities	5,881	26,249
Capital expenditures	1,729	12,184
Cash dividends paid	496	4,217

Instructions

a. For each company, compute the following ratios. Assume all sales were on credit.

1. Current ratio.
2. Accounts receivable turnover.
3. Average collection period.
4. Inventory turnover.

5. Days in inventory.
6. Profit margin.
7. Asset turnover.
8. Return on assets.
9. Return on common stockholders' equity.
10. Debt to assets ratio.
11. Times interest earned.
12. Free cash flow.

b. Compare the liquidity, solvency, and profitability of the two companies.

Expand Your Critical Thinking

Financial Reporting Problem: Apple Inc.

CT14.1 Your parents are considering investing in **Apple Inc.** (USA) common stock. They ask you, as an accounting expert, to make an analysis of the company for them. Financial statements of Apple are available online. The complete annual report, including the notes to its financial statements, is available at the company's website.

Instructions

a. Make a five-year trend analysis, using 2015 as the base year, of (1) net sales and (2) net income. Comment on the significance of the trend results.

b. Compute for 2019 and 2018 the (1) debt to assets ratio and (2) times interest earned. (See Note 3 for interest expense.) How would you evaluate Apple's long-term solvency?

c. Compute for 2019 and 2018 the (1) profit margin, (2) asset turnover, (3) return on assets, and (4) return on common stockholders' equity. How would you evaluate Apple's profitability? Total assets at September 30, 2017, were $375,319 million and total stockholders' equity at September 30, 2017, was $134,047 million.

d. What information outside the annual report may also be useful to your parents in making a decision about Apple?

Comparative Analysis Problem: Columbia Sportswear Company vs. Under Armour, Inc.

CT14.2 The financial statements of **Columbia Sportswear Company** (USA) and **Under Armour, Inc.** (USA) are available online.

Instructions

a. Based on the information in the financial statements, determine each of the following for each company:

1. The percentage increase (i) in net sales and (ii) in net income from 2018 to 2019.
2. The percentage increase (i) in total assets and (ii) in total stockholders' equity from 2018 to 2019.
3. The basic earnings per share for 2019.

b. What conclusions concerning the two companies can be drawn from these data?

Interpreting Financial Statements

CT14.3 **The Coca-Cola Company** (USA) and **PepsiCo, Inc.** (USA) provide refreshments to every corner of the world. Selected data from hypothetical consolidated financial statements for The Coca-Cola Company and for PepsiCo, Inc. are presented here (in millions):

	Coca-Cola	PepsiCo
Total current assets	$17,551	$12,571
Total current liabilities	13,721	8,756
Net sales	30,990	43,232
Cost of goods sold	11,088	20,099
Net income	6,824	5,946
Average (net) accounts receivable for the year	3,424	4,654

	Coca-Cola	PepsiCo
Average inventories for the year	$ 2,271	$ 2,570
Average total assets	44,595	37,921
Average common stockholders' equity	22,636	14,556
Average current liabilities	13,355	8,772
Average total liabilities	21,960	23,466
Total assets	48,671	39,848
Total liabilities	23,872	23,044
Income taxes	2,040	2,100
Interest expense	355	397
Net cash provided by operating activities	8,186	6,796
Capital expenditures	1,993	2,128
Cash dividends	3,800	2,732

Instructions

a. Compute the following liquidity ratios for Coca-Cola and for PepsiCo and comment on the relative liquidity of the two competitors.

1. Current ratio.
2. Accounts receivable turnover.
3. Average collection period.
4. Inventory turnover.
5. Days in inventory.

b. Compute the following solvency ratios for the two companies and comment on the relative solvency of the two competitors.

1. Debt to assets ratio.
2. Times interest earned.
3. Free cash flow.

c. Compute the following profitability ratios for the two companies and comment on the relative profitability of the two competitors.

1. Profit margin.
2. Asset turnover.
3. Return on assets.
4. Return on common stockholders' equity.

Real-World Focus

CT14.4 You can use the Internet to employ comparative data and industry data to evaluate a company's performance and financial position.

Instructions

Identify two competing companies and then go to the **MarketWatch** website. Type the company name in the search box (e.g., **Best Buy** [USA]) and then use the information from the Profile tab to answer the following questions:

a. Evaluate the company's liquidity relative to the industry averages and to the competitor that you chose.

b. Evaluate the company's solvency relative to the industry averages and to the competitor that you chose.

c. Evaluate the company's profitability relative to the industry averages and to the competitor that you chose.

CT14.5 The April 25, 2012, edition of the *Wall Street Journal* contains an article by Spencer Jakab entitled "Amazon's Valuation Is Hard to Justify."

Instructions

Read the article and answer the following questions:

a. Explain what is meant by the statement that "On a split-adjusted basis, today's share price is the equivalent of $1,166."

b. The article says that **Amazon.com** (USA) nearly doubled its capital spending on items such as fulfillment centers (sophisticated warehouses where it finds, packages, and ships goods to customers). Discuss the implications that this spending would have on the company's return on assets in the short term and in the long term.

c. How does Amazon's P-E ratio compare to that of U.S. companies such as **Apple**, **Netflix**, and **Walmart**? What does this suggest about investors' expectations about Amazon's future earnings?

d. What factor does the article cite as a possible hurdle that might reduce Amazon's ability to raise its operating margin back to previous levels?

Decision-Making Across the Organization

CT14.6 You are a loan officer for White Sands Bank of Taos. Paul Jason, president of P. Jason Corporation, has just left your office. He is interested in an eight-year loan to expand the company's operations. The borrowed funds would be used to purchase new equipment. As evidence of the company's debtworthiness, Jason provided you with the following facts:

	2023	2022
Current ratio	3.1	2.1
Asset turnover	2.8	2.2
Net income	Up 32%	Down 8%
Earnings per share	$3.30	$2.50

Jason is a very insistent (some would say pushy) man. When you told him that you would need additional information before making your decision, he acted offended and said, "What more could you possibly want to know?" You responded that, at a minimum, you would need complete, audited financial statements.

Instructions

With the class divided into groups, answer the following:

a. Explain why you would want the financial statements to be audited.

b. Discuss the implications of the ratios provided for the lending decision you are to make. That is, does the information paint a favorable picture? Are these ratios relevant to the decision?

c. List three other ratios that you would want to calculate for this company, and explain why you would use each.

Ethics Case

CT14.7 Robert Turnbull, president of Turnbull Industries, wishes to issue a press release to bolster his company's image and maybe even its stock price, which has been gradually falling. As controller, you have been asked to provide a list of 20 financial ratios and other operating statistics for Turnbull Industries' first-quarter financials and operations.

Two days after you provide the ratios and data requested, Perry Jarvis, the public relations director of Turnbull, asks you to prove the accuracy of the financial and operating data contained in the press release written by the president and edited by Perry. In the press release, the president highlights the sales increase of 25% over last year's first quarter and the positive change in the current ratio from 1.5:1 last year to 3:1 this year. He also emphasizes that production was up 50% over the prior year's first quarter.

You note that the press release contains only positive or improved ratios and none of the negative or deteriorated ratios. For instance, no mention is made that the debt to assets ratio has increased from 35% to 55%, that inventories are up 89%, and that although the current ratio improved, the accounts receivable turnover fell from 12 to 9. Nor is there any mention that the reported profit for the quarter would have been a loss had not the estimated lives of Turnbull's plant and machinery been increased by 30%. Perry emphasizes, "The press wants this release by early this afternoon."

Instructions

a. Who are the stakeholders in this situation?

b. Is there anything unethical in president Turnbull's actions?

c. Should you as controller remain silent? Does Perry have any responsibility?

All About You

CT14.8 In this chapter, you learned how to use many tools for performing a financial analysis of a company. When making personal investments, however, it is most likely that you won't be buying stocks and bonds in individual companies. Instead, when most people want to invest in stock, they buy mutual funds. By investing in a mutual fund, you reduce your risk because the fund diversifies by buying the stock of a variety of different companies, bonds, and other investments, depending on the stated goals of the fund.

Before you invest in a fund, you will need to decide what type of fund you want. For example, do you want a fund that has the potential of high growth (but also high risk), or are you looking for lower risk and a steady stream of income? Do you want a fund that invests only in domestic companies, or do you want one that invests globally? Many resources are available to help you with these types of decisions.

Instructions

Do an Internet search on "Motley Fool Here's How to Determine Your Ideal Asset Allocation Strategy" and then complete the investment allocation questionnaire. Add up your total points to determine the type of investment fund that would be appropriate for you.

APPENDIX A

Time Value of Money

APPENDIX PREVIEW

Would you rather receive €1,000 today or a year from now? You should prefer to receive the €1,000 today because you can invest the €1,000 and then earn interest on it. As a result, you will have more than €1,000 a year from now. What this example illustrates is the concept of the **time value of money**. Everyone prefers to receive money today rather than in the future because of the interest factor.

APPENDIX OUTLINE

Learning Objectives	
LO 1 Compute interest and future values.	• Nature of interest • Future value of a single amount • Future value of an annuity
LO 2 Compute present values.	• Present value variables • Present value of a single amount • Present value of an annuity • Time periods and discounting • Present value of a long-term note or bond
LO 3 Compute the present value in capital budgeting situations.	• Using alternative discount rates
LO 4 Use a financial calculator to solve time value of money problems.	• Present value of a single sum • Present value of an annuity • Future value of a single sum • Future value of an annuity • Internal rate of return • Useful financial calculator applications

INTEREST AND FUTURE VALUES

LEARNING OBJECTIVE 1
Compute interest and future values.

Nature of Interest

Interest is payment for the use of another party's money.

- Interest is the difference between the amount borrowed or invested (called the **principal**) and the amount repaid or collected.
- The amount of interest to be paid or collected is usually stated as a rate over a specific period of time.
- The rate of interest is generally stated as an annual rate.

The amount of interest involved in any financing transaction is based on three elements:

1. **Principal (p):** The original amount borrowed or invested.
2. **Interest rate (i):** An annual percentage of the principal.
3. **Time (n):** The number of periods over which the principal is borrowed or invested.

Simple Interest

Simple interest is computed on the principal amount only.

- Simple interest is the return on the principal for one period (we use an annual interest rate unless stated otherwise).
- Simple interest is usually expressed as shown in **Illustration A.1**.

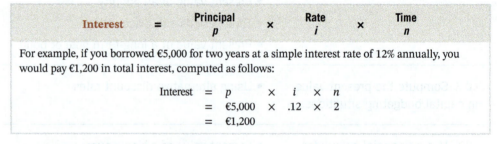

For example, if you borrowed €5,000 for two years at a simple interest rate of 12% annually, you would pay €1,200 in total interest, computed as follows:

$$\begin{aligned}\text{Interest} &= p \times i \times n \\ &= €5,000 \times .12 \times 2 \\ &= €1,200\end{aligned}$$

ILLUSTRATION A.1 | Interest computation

Compound Interest

Compound interest is computed on principal **and** on any interest earned that has not been paid or withdrawn.

- Compound interest is the return on (or growth of) the principal for two or more time periods.
- Compounding computes interest not only on the principal but also on the interest earned to date on that principal, assuming the interest is left on deposit.

To illustrate the difference between simple and compound interest, assume that you deposit €1,000 in Bank Two, where it will earn simple interest of 9% per year, and you deposit another €1,000 in Citizens Bank, where it will earn compound interest of 9% per year compounded annually. Also assume that in both cases you will not withdraw any cash until three years from the date of deposit. **Illustration A.2** shows the computation of interest to be received and the accumulated year-end balances.

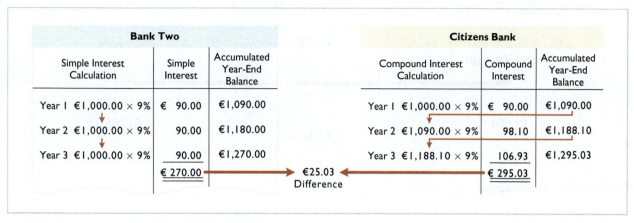

ILLUSTRATION A.2 | **Simple versus compound interest**

Note the following in Illustration A.2:

- Simple interest uses the initial principal of €1,000 to compute the interest in all three years.
- Compound interest uses the accumulated balance (principal plus interest to date) at each year-end to compute interest in the succeeding year—which explains why your compound interest account is larger.

Obviously, if you had a choice between investing your money at simple interest or at compound interest, you would choose compound interest, all other things—especially risk—being equal. In the example, compounding provides €25.03 of additional interest income. For practical purposes, compounding assumes that unpaid interest earned becomes a part of the principal, and the accumulated balance at the end of each year becomes the new principal on which interest is earned during the next year.

Most business situations use compound interest. Simple interest is generally applicable only to short-term situations of one year or less.

Future Value of a Single Amount

The **future value of a single amount** is the value at a future date of a given amount invested, assuming compound interest. For example, in Illustration A.2, €1,295.03 is the future value of the €1,000 investment earning 9% for three years. The €1,295.03 is determined more easily by using the formula shown in **Illustration A.3**.

$$FV = p \times (1 + i)^n$$

ILLUSTRATION A.3 | **Formula for future value**

where:

FV = future value of a single amount
p = principal (or present value; the value today)
i = interest rate for one period
n = number of periods

The €1,295.03 is computed as follows:

$$\begin{aligned} FV &= p \times (1+i)^n \\ &= €1{,}000 \times (1 + .09)^3 \\ &= €1{,}000 \times 1.29503 \\ &= €1{,}295.03 \end{aligned}$$

The 1.29503 is computed by multiplying (1.09 × 1.09 × 1.09). The amounts in this example can be depicted in the time diagram shown in **Illustration A.4**.

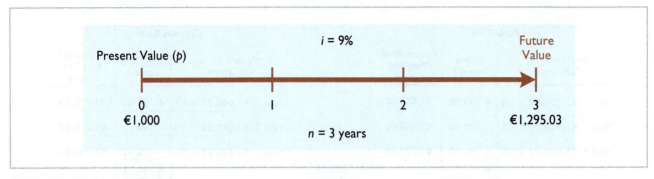

ILLUSTRATION A.4 | **Time diagram**

Another method used to compute the future value of a single amount involves a compound interest table. This table shows the future value of 1 for *n* periods. **Table 1** is such a table.

TABLE 1 | **Future Value of 1**

(n) Periods	4%	5%	6%	7%	8%	9%	10%	11%	12%	15%
0	1.00000	1.00000	1.00000	1.00000	1.00000	1.00000	1.00000	1.00000	1.00000	1.00000
1	1.04000	1.05000	1.06000	1.07000	1.08000	1.09000	1.10000	1.11000	1.12000	1.15000
2	1.08160	1.10250	1.12360	1.14490	1.16640	1.18810	1.21000	1.23210	1.25440	1.32250
3	1.12486	1.15763	1.19102	1.22504	1.25971	1.29503	1.33100	1.36763	1.40493	1.52088
4	1.16986	1.21551	1.26248	1.31080	1.36049	1.41158	1.46410	1.51807	1.57352	1.74901
5	1.21665	1.27628	1.33823	1.40255	1.46933	1.53862	1.61051	1.68506	1.76234	2.01136
6	1.26532	1.34010	1.41852	1.50073	1.58687	1.67710	1.77156	1.87041	1.97382	2.31306
7	1.31593	1.40710	1.50363	1.60578	1.71382	1.82804	1.94872	2.07616	2.21068	2.66002
8	1.36857	1.47746	1.59385	1.71819	1.85093	1.99256	2.14359	2.30454	2.47596	3.05902
9	1.42331	1.55133	1.68948	1.83846	1.99900	2.17189	2.35795	2.55803	2.77308	3.51788
10	1.48024	1.62889	1.79085	1.96715	2.15892	2.36736	2.59374	2.83942	3.10585	4.04556
11	1.53945	1.71034	1.89830	2.10485	2.33164	2.58043	2.85312	3.15176	3.47855	4.65239
12	1.60103	1.79586	2.01220	2.25219	2.51817	2.81267	3.13843	3.49845	3.89598	5.35025
13	1.66507	1.88565	2.13293	2.40985	2.71962	3.06581	3.45227	3.88328	4.36349	6.15279
14	1.73168	1.97993	2.26090	2.57853	2.93719	3.34173	3.79750	4.31044	4.88711	7.07571
15	1.80094	2.07893	2.39656	2.75903	3.17217	3.64248	4.17725	4.78459	5.47357	8.13706
16	1.87298	2.18287	2.54035	2.95216	3.42594	3.97031	4.59497	5.31089	6.13039	9.35762
17	1.94790	2.29202	2.69277	3.15882	3.70002	4.32763	5.05447	5.89509	6.86604	10.76126
18	2.02582	2.40662	2.85434	3.37993	3.99602	4.71712	5.55992	6.54355	7.68997	12.37545
19	2.10685	2.52695	3.02560	3.61653	4.31570	5.14166	6.11591	7.26334	8.61276	14.23177
20	2.19112	2.65330	3.20714	3.86968	4.66096	5.60441	6.72750	8.06231	9.64629	16.36654

- In Table 1, n is the number of compounding periods, the percentages are the periodic interest rates, and the five-digit decimal numbers in the respective columns are the future value of 1 factors.
- To use Table 1, you multiply the principal amount by the future value factor for the specified number of periods and interest rate. For example, the future value factor for two periods at 9% is 1.18810.
- Multiplying this factor by €1,000 equals €1,188.10—which is the accumulated balance at the end of year 2 in the Citizens Bank example in Illustration A.2.
- The €1,295.03 accumulated balance at the end of the third year is calculated from Table 1 by multiplying the future value factor for three periods (1.29503) by the €1,000.

The demonstration problem in **Illustration A.5** shows how to use Table 1.

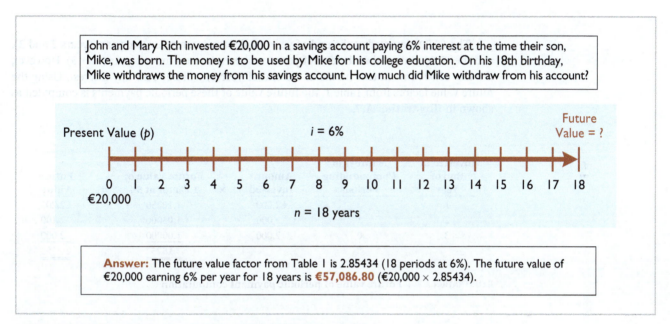

ILLUSTRATION A.5 | Demonstration problem—Using Table 1 for *FV* of 1

Future Value of an Annuity

The preceding discussion involved the accumulation of only a single principal sum. Individuals and businesses frequently encounter situations in which a **series** of equal euro amounts are to be paid or received at evenly spaced time intervals (periodically), such as loans or lease (rental) contracts.

- A series of payments or receipts of equal euro amounts is referred to as an **annuity**.
- The **future value of an annuity** is the sum of all the payments (receipts) plus the accumulated compound interest on them.
- In computing the future value of an annuity, it is necessary to know:
  1. The interest rate.
  2. The number of payments (receipts).
  3. The amount of the periodic payments (receipts).

To illustrate the computation of the future value of an annuity, assume that you invest €2,000 at the end of each year for three years at 5% interest compounded annually. This situation is depicted in the time diagram in **Illustration A.6**.

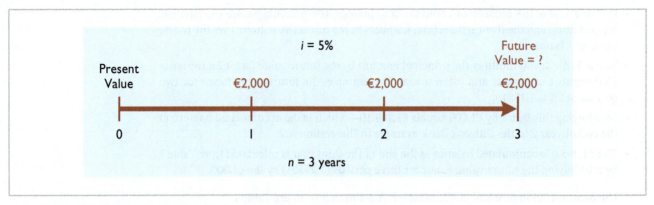

ILLUSTRATION A.6 | Time diagram for a three-year annuity

The €2,000 invested at the end of year 1 will earn interest for two years (years 2 and 3), and the €2,000 invested at the end of year 2 will earn interest for one year (year 3). However, the last €2,000 investment (made at the end of year 3) will not earn any interest. Using the future value factors from Table 1, the future value of these periodic payments is computed as shown in **Illustration A.7**.

Invested at End of Year	Number of Compounding Periods	Amount Invested	×	Future Value of 1 Factor at 5%	=	Future Value
1	2	€2,000		1.10250		€2,205
2	1	2,000		1.05000		2,100
3	0	2,000		1.00000		2,000
				3.15250		€6,305

ILLUSTRATION A.7 | Future value of periodic payment computation

- The first €2,000 investment is multiplied by the future value factor for two periods (1.1025) because two years' interest will accumulate on it (in years 2 and 3).
- The second €2,000 investment will earn only one year's interest (in year 3) and therefore is multiplied by the future value factor for one year (1.0500).
- The final €2,000 investment is made at the end of the third year and will not earn any interest. Thus, $n = 0$ and the future value factor is 1.00000. Consequently, the future value of the last €2,000 invested is only €2,000 since it does not accumulate any interest.

Calculating the future value of each individual cash flow is required when the periodic payments or receipts are not equal in each period. However, when the periodic payments (receipts) are **the same in each period**, the future value can be computed by using a future value of an annuity of 1 table. **Table 2** is such a table.

- Table 2 shows the future value of 1 to be received periodically for a given number of payments. It assumes that each payment is made at the **end** of each period.
- We can see from Table 2 that the future value of an annuity of 1 factor for three payments at 5% is 3.15250.
- The future value factor is the total of the three individual future value factors shown in Illustration A.7. Multiplying this amount by the annual investment of €2,000 produces a future value of €6,305.

The demonstration problem in **Illustration A.8** shows how to use Table 2.

TABLE 2 | Future Value of an Annuity of 1

(n) Payments	4%	5%	6%	7%	8%	9%	10%	11%	12%	15%
1	1.00000	1.00000	1.00000	1.0000	1.00000	1.00000	1.00000	1.00000	1.00000	1.00000
2	2.04000	2.05000	2.06000	2.0700	2.08000	2.09000	2.10000	2.11000	2.12000	2.15000
3	3.12160	3.15250	3.18360	3.2149	3.24640	3.27810	3.31000	3.34210	3.37440	3.47250
4	4.24646	4.31013	4.37462	4.4399	4.50611	4.57313	4.64100	4.70973	4.77933	4.99338
5	5.41632	5.52563	5.63709	5.7507	5.86660	5.98471	6.10510	6.22780	6.35285	6.74238
6	6.63298	6.80191	6.97532	7.1533	7.33592	7.52334	7.71561	7.91286	8.11519	8.75374
7	7.89829	8.14201	8.39384	8.6540	8.92280	9.20044	9.48717	9.78327	10.08901	11.06680
8	9.21423	9.54911	9.89747	10.2598	10.63663	11.02847	11.43589	11.85943	12.29969	13.72682
9	10.58280	11.02656	11.49132	11.9780	12.48756	13.02104	13.57948	14.16397	14.77566	16.78584
10	12.00611	12.57789	13.18079	13.8164	14.48656	15.19293	15.93743	16.72201	17.54874	20.30372
11	13.48635	14.20679	14.97164	15.7836	16.64549	17.56029	18.53117	19.56143	20.65458	24.34928
12	15.02581	15.91713	16.86994	17.8885	18.97713	20.14072	21.38428	22.71319	24.13313	29.00167
13	16.62684	17.71298	18.88214	20.1406	21.49530	22.95339	24.52271	26.21164	28.02911	34.35192
14	18.29191	19.59863	21.01507	22.5505	24.21492	26.01919	27.97498	30.09492	32.39260	40.50471
15	20.02359	21.57856	23.27597	25.1290	27.15211	29.36092	31.77248	34.40536	37.27972	47.58041
16	21.82453	23.65749	25.67253	27.8881	30.32428	33.00340	35.94973	39.18995	42.75328	55.71747
17	23.69751	25.84037	28.21288	30.8402	33.75023	36.97351	40.54470	44.50084	48.88367	65.07509
18	25.64541	28.13238	30.90565	33.9990	37.45024	41.30134	45.59917	50.39593	55.74972	75.83636
19	27.67123	30.53900	33.75999	37.3790	41.44626	46.01846	51.15909	56.93949	63.43968	88.21181
20	29.77808	33.06595	36.78559	40.9955	45.76196	51.16012	57.27500	64.20283	72.05244	102.44358

John and Char Lewis's daughter, Debra, has just started high school. They decide to start a college fund for her and will invest €2,500 in a savings account at the end of each year she is in high school (four payments total). The account will earn 6% interest compounded annually. How much will be in the college fund at the time Debra graduates from high school?

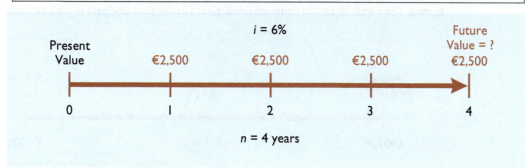

Answer: The future value factor from Table 2 is 4.37462 (four payments at 6%). The future value of €2,500 invested each year for four years at 6% interest is **€10,936.55** (€2,500 × 4.37462).

ILLUSTRATION A.8 | Demonstration problem—Using Table 2 for *FV* of an annuity of 1

PRESENT VALUES

LEARNING OBJECTIVE 2
Compute present values.

Present Value Variables

The **present value** is the value now of a given amount to be paid or received in the future, assuming compound interest.

- The present value, like the future value, is based on three variables:
  1. The euro amount to be received (future amount).
  2. The length of time until the amount is received (number of periods).
  3. The interest rate (the discount rate).
- The process of determining the present value is referred to as **discounting the future amount**.

Present value computations are used in measuring many items. For example, the present value of principal and interest payments is used to determine the market price of a bond. Determining the amount to be reported for notes payable and lease liabilities also involves present value computations. In addition, capital budgeting and other investment proposals are evaluated using present value computations. Finally, all rate of return and internal rate of return computations involve present value techniques.

Present Value of a Single Amount

To illustrate present value, assume that you want to invest a sum of money today that will provide €1,000 at the end of one year. What amount would you need to invest today to have €1,000 one year from now? If you want a 10% rate of return, the investment or present value is €909.09 (€1,000 ÷ 1.10). The formula for calculating present value is shown in **Illustration A.9**.

$$\text{Present Value } (PV) = \text{Future Value } (FV) \div (1 + i)^n$$

ILLUSTRATION A.9 | Formula for present value

The computation of €1,000 discounted at 10% for one year is as follows:

$$\begin{aligned} PV &= FV \div (1 + i)^n \\ &= €1{,}000 \div (1 + .10)^1 \\ &= €1{,}000 \div 1.10 \\ &= €909.09 \end{aligned}$$

The future amount (€1,000), the discount rate (10%), and the number of periods (1) are known. The variables in this situation are depicted in the time diagram in **Illustration A.10**.

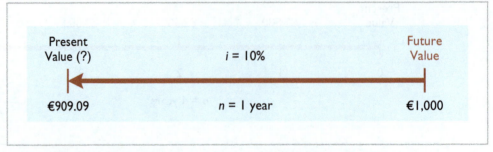

ILLUSTRATION A.10 | Finding present value if discounted for one period

If the single amount of €1,000 is to be received **in two years** and discounted at 10%, the formula $PV = €1{,}000 \div (1 + .10)^2$ is used, where $(1 + .10)^2$ is equal to 1.21 (1.10 × 1.10). Its present value is €826.45 (€1,000 ÷ 1.21), depicted in **Illustration A.11**.

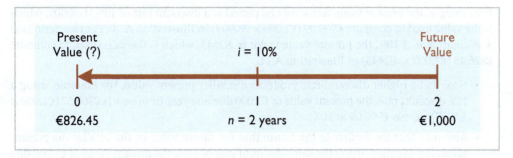

ILLUSTRATION A.11 | **Finding present value if discounted for two periods**

The present value of 1 may also be determined through tables that show the present value of 1 for *n* periods. In **Table 3**, *n* is the number of discounting periods involved.

- The percentages are the periodic interest rates or discount rates, and the five-digit decimal numbers in the respective columns are the present value of 1 factors.
- When using Table 3, the future value is multiplied by the present value factor specified at the intersection of the number of periods and the discount rate.

TABLE 3 | **Present Value of 1**

(n) Periods	4%	5%	6%	7%	8%	9%	10%	11%	12%	15%
1	.96154	.95238	.94340	.93458	.92593	.91743	.90909	.90090	.89286	.86957
2	.92456	.90703	.89000	.87344	.85734	.84168	.82645	.81162	.79719	.75614
3	.88900	.86384	.83962	.81630	.79383	.77218	.75132	.73119	.71178	.65752
4	.85480	.82270	.79209	.76290	.73503	.70843	.68301	.65873	.63552	.57175
5	.82193	.78353	.74726	.71299	.68058	.64993	.62092	.59345	.56743	.49718
6	.79031	.74622	.70496	.66634	.63017	.59627	.56447	.53464	.50663	.43233
7	.75992	.71068	.66506	.62275	.58349	.54703	.51316	.48166	.45235	.37594
8	.73069	.67684	.62741	.58201	.54027	.50187	.46651	.43393	.40388	.32690
9	.70259	.64461	.59190	.54393	.50025	.46043	.42410	.39092	.36061	.28426
10	.67556	.61391	.55839	.50835	.46319	.42241	.38554	.35218	.32197	.24719
11	.64958	.58468	.52679	.47509	.42888	.38753	.35049	.31728	.28748	.21494
12	.62460	.55684	.49697	.44401	.39711	.35554	.31863	.28584	.25668	.18691
13	.60057	.53032	.46884	.41496	.36770	.32618	.28966	.25751	.22917	.16253
14	.57748	.50507	.44230	.38782	.34046	.29925	.26333	.23199	.20462	.14133
15	.55526	.48102	.41727	.36245	.31524	.27454	.23939	.20900	.18270	.12289
16	.53391	.45811	.39365	.33873	.29189	.25187	.21763	.18829	.16312	.10687
17	.51337	.43630	.37136	.31657	.27027	.23107	.19785	.16963	.14564	.09293
18	.49363	.41552	.35034	.29586	.25025	.21199	.17986	.15282	.13004	.08081
19	.47464	.39573	.33051	.27615	.23171	.19449	.16351	.13768	.11611	.07027
20	.45639	.37689	.31180	.25842	.21455	.17843	.14864	.12403	.10367	.06110

For example, the present value factor for one period at a discount rate of 10% is .90909, which is the value used to compute €909.09 (€1,000 × .90909) in Illustration A.10. For two periods at a discount rate of 10%, the present value factor is .82645, which is the value used to compute €826.45 (€1,000 × .82645) in Illustration A.11.

- Note that a higher discount rate produces a smaller present value. For example, using a 15% discount rate, the present value of €1,000 due one year from now is €869.57 (€1,000 × .86957), versus €909.09 at 10%.
- Also note that the farther in the future that the future value is, the smaller the present value. For example, using the same discount rate of 10%, the present value of €1,000 due in **five years** at 10% is €620.92 (€1,000 × .62092). The present value of €1,000 due in **one year** is €909.09, a difference of €288.17.

The following two demonstration problems **(Illustrations A.12 and A.13)** illustrate how to use Table 3.

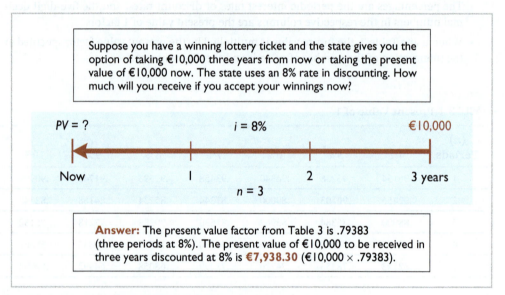

ILLUSTRATION A.12 | **Demonstration problem—Using Table 3 for *PV* of 1**

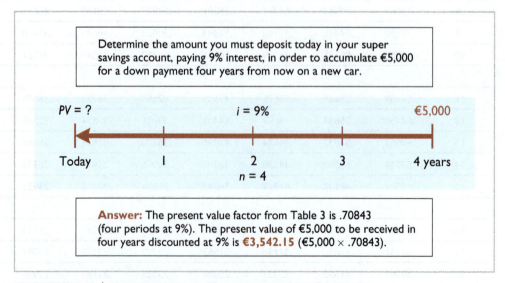

ILLUSTRATION A.13 | **Demonstration problem—Using Table 3 for *PV* of 1**

Present Value of an Annuity

The preceding discussion involved the discounting of only a single future amount. Businesses and individuals frequently engage in transactions in which a series of equal euro amounts are to be received or paid at evenly spaced time intervals (periodically). Examples of a series of periodic receipts or payments are loan agreements, installment sales, mortgage notes, lease (rental) contracts, and pension obligations. As discussed earlier, these periodic receipts or payments are **annuities**.

- The **present value of an annuity** is the value now of a series of future receipts or payments, discounted assuming compound interest.
- In computing the present value of an annuity, it is necessary to know:
  1. The discount rate.
  2. The number of payments (receipts).
  3. The amount of the periodic receipts or payments.

To illustrate the computation of the present value of an annuity, assume that you will receive €1,000 cash annually for three years at a time when the discount rate is 10%. This situation is depicted in the time diagram in **Illustration A.14**. **Illustration A.15** shows the computation of its present value in this situation.

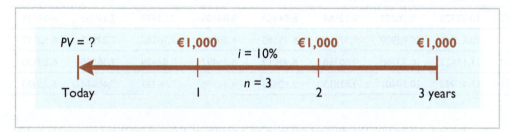

ILLUSTRATION A.14 | Time diagram for a three-year annuity

Future Amount	×	Present Value of 1 Factor at 10%	=	Present Value
€1,000 (1 year away)		.90909		€ 909.09
1,000 (2 years away)		.82645		826.45
1,000 (3 years away)		.75132		751.32
		2.48686		€2,486.86

ILLUSTRATION A.15 | Present value of a series of future amounts computation

This method of calculation is required when the periodic cash flows are not uniform in each period. However, when the future receipts are the same in each period, an annuity table can be used. As illustrated in **Table 4**, an annuity table shows the present value of 1 to be received periodically for a given number of payments. It assumes that each payment is made at the end of each period.

TABLE 4 | Present Value of an Annuity of 1

(n) Payments	4%	5%	6%	7%	8%	9%	10%	11%	12%	15%
1	.96154	.95238	.94340	.93458	.92593	.91743	.90909	.90090	.89286	.86957
2	1.88609	1.85941	1.83339	1.80802	1.78326	1.75911	1.73554	1.71252	1.69005	1.62571
3	2.77509	2.72325	2.67301	2.62432	2.57710	2.53130	2.48685	2.44371	2.40183	2.28323
4	3.62990	3.54595	3.46511	3.38721	3.31213	3.23972	3.16986	3.10245	3.03735	2.85498
5	4.45182	4.32948	4.21236	4.10020	3.99271	3.88965	3.79079	3.69590	3.60478	3.35216

TABLE 4 | (Continued)

(n) Payments	4%	5%	6%	7%	8%	9%	10%	11%	12%	15%
6	5.24214	5.07569	4.91732	4.76654	4.62288	4.48592	4.35526	4.23054	4.11141	3.78448
7	6.00205	5.78637	5.58238	5.38929	5.20637	5.03295	4.86842	4.71220	4.56376	4.16042
8	6.73274	6.46321	6.20979	5.97130	5.74664	5.53482	5.33493	5.14612	4.96764	4.48732
9	7.43533	7.10782	6.80169	6.51523	6.24689	5.99525	5.75902	5.53705	5.32825	4.77158
10	8.11090	7.72173	7.36009	7.02358	6.71008	6.41766	6.14457	5.88923	5.65022	5.01877
11	8.76048	8.30641	7.88687	7.49867	7.13896	6.80519	6.49506	6.20652	5.93770	5.23371
12	9.38507	8.86325	8.38384	7.94269	7.53608	7.16073	6.81369	6.49236	6.19437	5.42062
13	9.98565	9.39357	8.85268	8.35765	7.90378	7.48690	7.10336	6.74987	6.42355	5.58315
14	10.56312	9.89864	9.29498	8.74547	8.24424	7.78615	7.36669	6.98187	6.62817	5.72448
15	11.11839	10.37966	9.71225	9.10791	8.55948	8.06069	7.60608	7.19087	6.81086	5.84737
16	11.65230	10.83777	10.10590	9.44665	8.85137	8.31256	7.82371	7.37916	6.97399	5.95424
17	12.16567	11.27407	10.47726	9.76322	9.12164	8.54363	8.02155	7.54879	7.11963	6.04716
18	12.65930	11.68959	10.82760	10.05909	9.37189	8.75563	8.20141	7.70162	7.24967	6.12797
19	13.13394	12.08532	11.15812	10.33560	9.60360	8.95012	8.36492	7.83929	7.36578	6.19823
20	13.59033	12.46221	11.46992	10.59401	9.81815	9.12855	8.51356	7.96333	7.46944	6.25933

- Table 4 shows that the present value of an annuity of 1 factor for three payments at 10% is 2.48685.[1] This present value factor is the total of the three individual present value factors, as shown in Illustration A.15.
- Applying this amount to the annual cash flow of €1,000 produces a present value of €2,486.85.

The following demonstration problem (**Illustration A.16**) illustrates how to use Table 4.

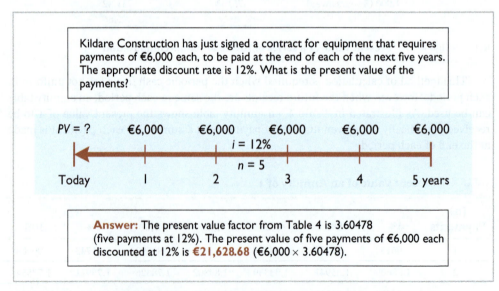

Kildare Construction has just signed a contract for equipment that requires payments of €6,000 each, to be paid at the end of each of the next five years. The appropriate discount rate is 12%. What is the present value of the payments?

Answer: The present value factor from Table 4 is 3.60478 (five payments at 12%). The present value of five payments of €6,000 each discounted at 12% is **€21,628.68** (€6,000 × 3.60478).

ILLUSTRATION A.16 | Demonstration problem—Using Table 4 for *PV* of an annuity of 1

[1]The difference of .00001 between 2.48686 and 2.48685 is due to rounding.

Time Periods and Discounting

In the preceding calculations, the discounting was done on an annual basis using an annual interest rate. Discounting may also be done over shorter periods of time such as monthly, quarterly, or semiannually.

When the time frame is less than one year, it is necessary to convert the annual interest rate to the applicable time frame.

- Assume, for example, that the investor in Illustration A.14 received €500 **semiannually** for three years instead of €1,000 annually.
- In this case, the number of periods becomes six (3 × 2), the discount rate is 5% (10% ÷ 2), the present value factor from Table 4 is 5.07569 (six periods at 5%), and the present value of the future cash flows is €2,537.85 (5.07569 × €500).

This amount is slightly higher than the €2,486.86 computed in Illustration A.15 because interest is computed twice during the same year. That is, during the second half of the year, interest is earned on the first half-year's interest. Each period's €1,000 is received and earns interest six months sooner.

Present Value of a Long-Term Note or Bond

The present value (or market price) of a long-term note or bond is a function of three variables: (1) the payment amounts, (2) the length of time until the amounts are paid, and (3) the discount rate. Our example uses a five-year bond issue.

The first variable (euros to be paid) is made up of two elements:

1. A series of interest payments (an annuity).
2. The principal amount (a single sum).

To compute the present value of the bond, both the interest payments and the principal amount must be discounted—two different computations. The time diagrams for a bond due in five years are shown in **Illustration A.17**.

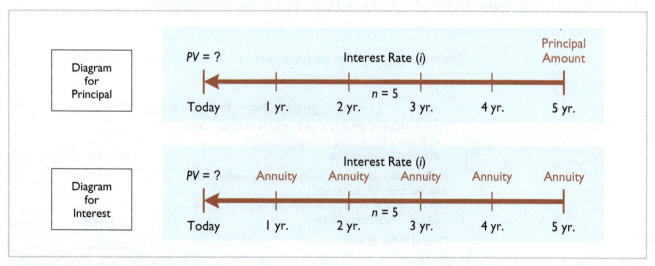

ILLUSTRATION A.17 | **Time diagrams for the present value of a bond**

When the investor's market interest rate is equal to the bond's contractual interest rate, the present value of the bonds will equal the face value of the bonds. To illustrate, assume a bond issue of 5%, 10-year bonds with a face value of €100,000 with interest payable **annually** on January 1.

- If the discount rate is the same as the contractual rate, the bonds will sell at face value.
- In this case, the investor will receive:
  1. €100,000 at maturity.
  2. A series of 10 interest payments of €5,000 each (€100,000 × 5%) over the term of the bonds.
- The length of time is expressed in terms of interest periods—in this case, 10—and the discount rate per interest period, 5%.

The time diagram in **Illustration A.18** depicts the variables involved in this discounting situation.

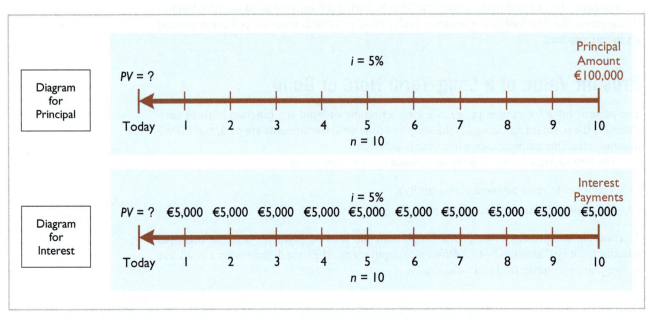

ILLUSTRATION A.18 | Time diagram for present value of a 5%, 10-year bond paying interest annually

Illustration A.19 shows the computation of the present value of these bonds.

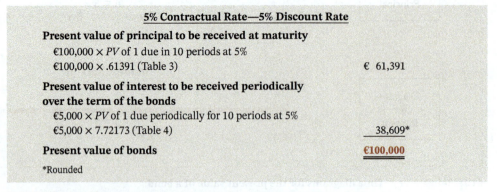

ILLUSTRATION A.19 | Present value of principal and interest—face value

Now assume that the investor's required rate of return (discount rate) is 6%, not 5%. The future amounts are again €100,000 and €5,000, respectively, but now a discount rate of 6% must be used. The present value of the bonds is €92,639, as computed in **Illustration A.20**.

5% Contractual Rate—6% Discount Rate

Present value of principal to be received at maturity
€100,000 × *PV* of 1 due in 10 periods at 6%
€100,000 × .55839 (Table 3) €55,839

Present value of interest to be received periodically over the term of the bonds
€5,000 × *PV* of 1 due periodically for 10 periods at 6%
€5,000 × 7.36009 (Table 4) 36,800

Present value of bonds **€92,639**

ILLUSTRATION A.20 | Present value of principal and interest—discount

Conversely, if the discount rate is 4% and the contractual rate is 5%, the present value of the bonds is €108,111, computed as shown in **Illustration A.21**.

5% Contractual Rate—4% Discount Rate

Present value of principal to be received at maturity
€100,000 × *PV* of 1 due in 10 periods at 4%
€100,000 × .67556 (Table 3) €67,556

Present value of interest to be received periodically over the term of the bonds
€5,000 × *PV* of 1 due periodically for 10 periods at 4%
€5,000 × 8.11090 (Table 4) 40,555*

Present value of bonds **€108,111**

*Rounded

ILLUSTRATION A.21 | Present value of principal and interest—premium

The above discussion relied on present value tables in solving present value problems.

- Calculators, apps, and Excel spreadsheets may also be used to compute present values without the use of these tables.
- Many calculators, especially financial calculators, have present value (*PV*) functions that allow you to calculate present values by merely inputting the proper amount, discount rate, and periods, and then pressing the PV key. (We discuss the use of financial calculators in a later section.)

CAPITAL BUDGETING SITUATIONS

The decision to make long-term capital investments is best evaluated using discounting techniques that recognize the time value of money. To do this, many companies calculate the present value of the cash flows involved in a capital investment.

To illustrate, Dover-Calais Trucking Company, a cross-country freight carrier is considering adding another truck to its fleet because of a purchasing opportunity. **Kent International**, Dover-Calais's primary supplier of overland rigs, is overstocked and offers to sell its biggest rig for €154,000 cash payable upon delivery. Dover-Calais knows that the rig will produce a net cash flow per year of €40,000 for five years (received at the end of each year), at which time it will be sold for an estimated salvage value of €35,000. Dover-Calais's discount rate in evaluating capital expenditures is 10%. Should Dover-Calais commit to the purchase of this rig?

The cash flows that must be discounted to present value by Dover-Calais are as follows:

- Cash payable on delivery (today): €154,000.
- Net cash flow from operating the rig: €40,000 for five years (at the end of each year).
- Cash received from sale of rig at the end of five years: €35,000.

LEARNING OBJECTIVE 3
Compute the present value in capital budgeting situations.

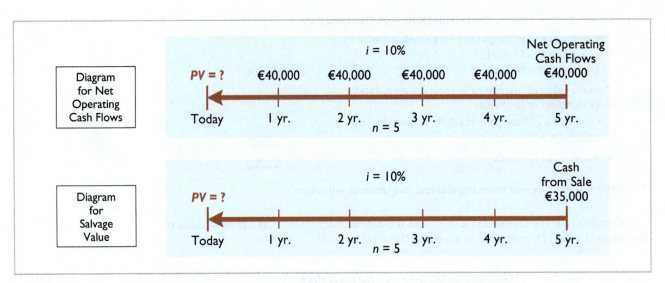

ILLUSTRATION A.22 | Time diagrams for Dover-Calais Trucking Company

The time diagrams for the latter two cash flows are shown in **Illustration A.22**. Notice from the diagrams that:

- Computing the present value of the net operating cash flows (€40,000 at the end of each year) is **discounting an annuity** (Table 4).
- Computing the present value of the €35,000 salvage value is **discounting a single sum** (Table 3).

The computation of these present values is shown in **Illustration A.23**.

Present Values Using a 10% Discount Rate

Present value of net operating cash flows received annually over five years
  €40,000 × PV of 1 received annually for five years at 10%
  €40,000 × 3.79079 (Table 4) €151,631.60

Present value of salvage value (cash) to be received in five years
  €35,000 × PV of 1 received in five years at 10%
  €35,000 × .62092 (Table 3) 21,732.20

Present value of cash **inflows** 173,363.80
Present value of cash **outflows** (purchase price due today at 10%)
  €154,000 × PV of 1 due today
  €154,000 × 1.00000 .... (154,000.00)

Net present value .... € 19,363.80

ILLUSTRATION A.23 | Present value computations at 10%

- The present value of the cash receipts (inflows) of €173,363.80 (€151,631.60 + €21,732.20) exceeds the present value of the cash payments (outflows) of €154,000.00.
- The net present value of €19,363.80 is positive, and **the decision to invest should be accepted.**

Now assume that Dover-Calais uses a discount rate of 15%, not 10%, because it wants a greater return on its investments in capital assets. The cash receipts and cash payments by Dover-Calais are the same. The present values of these receipts and cash payments discounted at 15% are shown in **Illustration A.24**.

Present Values Using a 15% Discount Rate	
Present value of net operating cash flows received annually over five years at 15% €40,000 × 3.35216 (Table 4)	€134,086.40
Present value of salvage value (cash) to be received in five years at 15% €35,000 × .49718 (Table 3)	17,401.30
Present value of cash **inflows**	€151,487.70
Present value of cash **outflows** (purchase price due today at 15%) €154,000 × 1.00000	(154,000.00)
Net present value	€ (2,512.30)

ILLUSTRATION A.24 | **Present value computations at 15%**

- The present value of the cash payments (outflows) of €154,000.00 exceeds the present value of the cash receipts (inflows) of €151,487.70 (€134,086.40 + €17,401.30).
- The net present value of €2,512.30 is negative, and **the investment should be rejected**.

Finally, note that these capital budgeting calculations can also be performed using Excel. A big benefit of using Excel is the ability to quickly experiment with different input variables such as the number of payments, interest rates, or payment amounts. The following shows a sample worksheet:

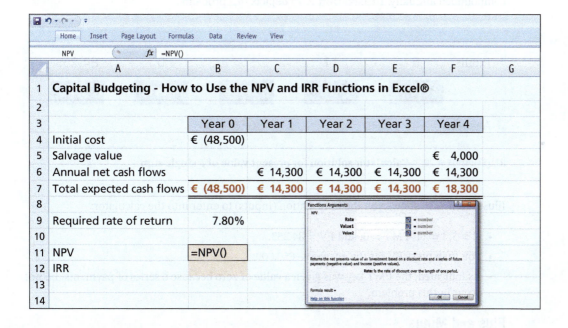

USING FINANCIAL CALCULATORS

The above discussion relied on present value tables in solving present value problems. Calculators may be used to compute present values without the use of these tables. Financial calculators have present value (PV) functions that allow you to calculate present values by merely identifying the proper amount, discount rate, and periods, and then pressing the PV key.

To use financial calculators, you enter the time value of money variables into the calculator. **Illustration A.25** shows the five most common keys used to solve time value of money problems.[2]

LEARNING OBJECTIVE 4
Use a financial calculator to solve time value of money problems.

---

[2]On many calculators, these keys are actual buttons on the face of the calculator; on others, they appear on the display after the user accesses a present value menu.

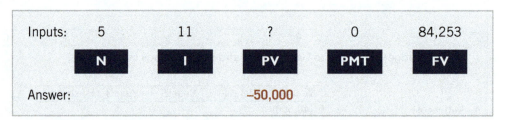

ILLUSTRATION A.25 | **Financial calculator keys**

where:

N = number of periods
I = interest rate per period (some calculators use I/YR or i)
PV = present value (occurs at the beginning of the first period)
PMT = payment (all payments are equal, and none are skipped)
FV = future value (occurs at the end of the last period)

In solving time value of money problems in this appendix, you will generally be given three of four variables and will have to solve for the remaining variable. The fifth key (the key not used) is given a value of zero to ensure that this variable is not used in the computation.

Present Value of a Single Sum

To illustrate how to solve a present value problem using a financial calculator, assume that you want to know the present value of €84,253 to be received in five years, discounted at 11% compounded annually. **Illustration A.26** depicts this problem.

Inputs:	5	11	?	0	84,253
	N	I	PV	PMT	FV
Answer:			−50,000		

ILLUSTRATION A.26 | **Calculator solution for present value of a single sum**

Illustration A.26 shows you the information (inputs) to enter into the calculator:

- N = 5, I = 11, PMT = 0, and FV = 84,253.
- You then press PV for the answer: −€50,000.
- As indicated, the PMT key was given a value of zero because a series of payments did not occur in this problem.

Plus and Minus

The use of plus and minus signs in time value of money problems with a financial calculator can be confusing. Most financial calculators are programmed so that the positive and negative cash flows in any problem offset each other.

- In the present value problem above, we identified the €84,253 future value initial investment as a positive (inflow).
- The answer −€50,000 was shown as a negative amount, reflecting a cash outflow.
- If the 84,253 were entered as a negative, then the final answer would have been reported as a positive 50,000.

Hopefully, the sign convention will not cause confusion. If you understand what is required in a problem, you should be able to interpret a positive or negative amount in determining the solution to the problem.

Compounding Periods

In the problem above, we assumed that compounding occurs once a year.

- Some financial calculators have a default setting, which assumes that compounding occurs 12 times a year.
- You must determine what default period has been programmed into your calculator and change it as necessary to arrive at the proper compounding period.

Rounding

Most financial calculators store and calculate using 12 decimal places. As a result, because compound interest tables generally have factors only up to five decimal places, a slight difference in the final answer can result. In most time value of money problems, the final answer will not include more than two decimal places.

Present Value of an Annuity

To illustrate how to solve a present value of an annuity problem using a financial calculator, assume that you are asked to determine the present value of rental receipts of €6,000 each to be received at the end of each of the next five years, when discounted at 12%, as pictured in **Illustration A.27**.

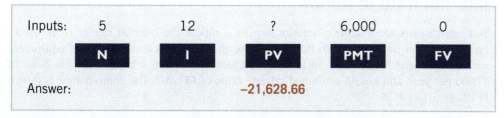

ILLUSTRATION A.27 | Calculator solution for present value of an annuity

In this case, you enter N = 5, I = 12, PMT = 6,000, and FV = 0, and then press PV to arrive at the answer of −€21,628.66.

Future Value of a Single Sum

Now let us look at an investment to illustrate how to solve a future value problem using a financial calculator. Assume that you will invest €20,000 today into a fund and you intend to leave it there for 15 years. The fund earns 7% interest. **Illustration A.28** shows how to compute the future value of the fund at the end of year 15.

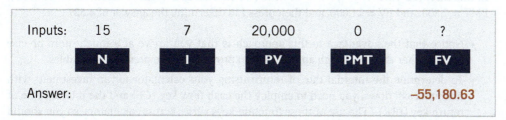

ILLUSTRATION A.28 | Calculator solution for future value of single sum

In this case, you enter N = 15, I = 7, PV = 20,000, and PMT = 0, and then press FV to calculate the future value of −€55,180.63.

Future Value of an Annuity

You can use a financial calculator to solve a future value of an annuity problem for an annuity investment. Assume that you will invest €8,000 into a fund at the end of each of the next eight years. The fund earns 9% interest. **Illustration A.29** shows how to compute the future value of the fund at the end of the eighth year.

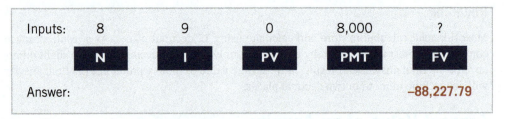

ILLUSTRATION A.29 | Calculator solution for future value of an annuity

In this case, you enter N = 8, I = 9, PV = 0, and PMT = 8,000, and then press FV to determine the future value of −€88,227.79.

Internal Rate of Return

You can also use these same calculator keys to compute the internal rate of return of an investment that has equal cash flows. Suppose that a purchase of a piece of equipment with a seven-year life requires an initial investment of €54,000, has positive cash flows of €7,800 per year, and has an estimated salvage value of €11,000. The computation is shown in **Illustration A.30**.

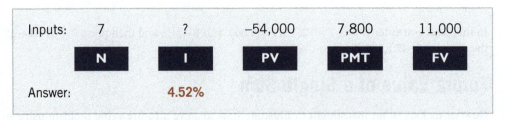

ILLUSTRATION A.30 | Calculator solution for internal rate of return

In this case, you enter N = 7, PV = −54,000 (we entered as a negative since it is an outflow), PMT = 7,800, and FV = 11,000, and then press I to determine the answer of 4.52%.

- Notice that the advantage to this approach is that you arrive at a much more precise result, rather than the rough approximation provided by the present value tables.
- To determine the internal rate of return using your calculator for an investment with unequal cash flows, you need to employ the cash flow key (CF) and the internal rate of return key (IRR). (The use of these function keys varies across calculators, so you should consult the user manual for your calculator or the manufacturer's website for specific information.)

Useful Applications of the Financial Calculator

With a financial calculator, you can solve for any interest rate or for any number of periods in a time value of money problem. Here are some examples of these applications:

Auto Loan

Assume you are financing the purchase of a used car with a three-year loan. The loan has a 9.5% stated annual interest rate, compounded monthly. The price of the car is €6,000, and you want to determine the monthly payments, assuming that the payments start one month after the purchase. This problem is pictured in **Illustration A.31**.

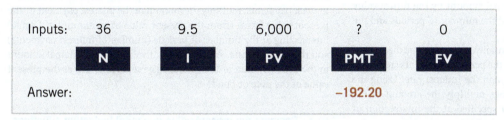

ILLUSTRATION A.31 | Calculator solution for auto loan payments

To solve this problem, you enter N = 36 (12 × 3), I = 9.5, PV = 6,000, and FV = 0, and then press PMT.

- You will find that the monthly payments will be €192.20.
- Note that the payment key is usually programmed for 12 payments per year. Thus, you must change the default (compounding period) if the payments are other than monthly.

Mortgage Loan Amount

Say you are evaluating financing options for a loan on a house (a mortgage). You decide that the maximum mortgage payment you can afford is €700 per month. The annual interest rate is 8.4%. If you get a mortgage that requires you to make monthly payments over a 15-year period, what is the maximum home loan you can afford? **Illustration A.32** depicts this problem. You enter N = 180 (12 × 15 years), I = 8.4, PMT = −700, and FV = 0, and then press PV.

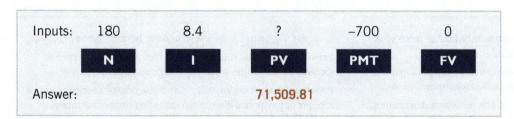

ILLUSTRATION A.32 | Calculator solution for mortgage amount

- With the payments-per-year key set at 12, you find a present value of €71,509.81—the maximum home loan you can afford, given that you want to keep your mortgage payments at €700.
- Note that by changing any of the variables, you can quickly conduct "what-if" analyses for different situations.

REVIEW

Learning Objectives Review

LO 1 Compute interest and future values.

Simple interest is computed on the principal only, while compound interest is computed on the principal and any interest earned that has not been withdrawn.

To solve for future value of a single amount, prepare a time diagram of the problem. Identify the principal amount, the number of compounding periods, and the interest rate. Using the future value of 1 table, multiply the principal amount by the future value factor specified at the intersection of the number of periods and the interest rate.

To solve for future value of an annuity, prepare a time diagram of the problem. Identify the amount of the periodic payments (receipts), the number of payments (receipts), and the interest rate. Using the future value of an annuity of 1 table, multiply the amount of the payments by the future value factor specified at the intersection of the number of periods and the interest rate.

LO 2 Compute present values.

The following three variables are fundamental to solving present value problems: (1) the future amount, (2) the number of periods, and (3) the interest rate (the discount rate).

To solve for present value of a single amount, prepare a time diagram of the problem. Identify the future amount, the number of discounting periods, and the discount (interest) rate. Using the present value of a single amount table, multiply the future amount by the present value factor specified at the intersection of the number of periods and the discount rate.

To solve for present value of an annuity, prepare a time diagram of the problem. Identify the amount of future periodic receipts or payments (annuities), the number of payments (receipts), and the discount (interest) rate. Using the present value of an annuity of 1 table, multiply the amount of the annuity by the present value factor specified at the intersection of the number of payments and the interest rate.

To compute the present value of notes and bonds, determine the present value of the principal amount and the present value of the interest payments. Multiply the principal amount (a single future amount) by the present value factor (from the present value of 1 table) intersecting at the number of periods (number of interest payments) and the discount rate. To determine the present value of the series of interest payments, multiply the amount of the interest payment by the present value factor (from the present value of an annuity of 1 table) intersecting at the number of periods (number of interest payments) and the discount rate. Add the present value of the principal amount to the present value of the interest payments to arrive at the present value of the note or bond.

LO 3 Compute the present value in capital budgeting situations.

Compute the present values of all cash inflows and all cash outflows related to the capital budgeting proposal (an investment-type decision). If the **net** present value is positive, accept the proposal (make the investment). If the **net** present value is negative, reject the proposal (do not make the investment).

LO 4 Use a financial calculator to solve time value of money problems.

Financial calculators can be used to solve the same and additional problems as those solved with time value of money tables. Enter into the financial calculator the amounts for all of the known elements of a time value of money problem (periods, interest rate, payments, future or present value), and the calculator solves for the unknown element. Particularly useful situations involve interest rates and compounding periods not presented in the tables.

Glossary Review

Annuity A series of equal euro amounts to be paid or received at evenly spaced time intervals (periodically). (p. A-5).

Compound interest The interest computed on the principal and any interest earned that has not been paid or withdrawn. (p. A-2).

Discounting the future amount(s) The process of determining present value. (p. A-8).

Future value of an annuity The sum of all the payments (receipts) plus the accumulated compound interest on them. (p. A-5).

Future value of a single amount The value at a future date of a given amount invested, assuming compound interest. (p. A-3).

Interest Payment for the use of another person's money. (p. A-2).

Present value The value now of a given amount to be paid or received in the future, assuming compound interest. (p. A-8).

Present value of an annuity The value now of a series of future receipts or payments, discounted assuming compound interest. (p. A-11).

Principal The amount borrowed or invested. (p. A-2).

Simple interest The interest computed on the principal only. (p. A-2).

Brief Exercises

(Use tables to solve exercises BEA.1 to BEA.23.)

BEA.1 (LO 1), AP Randy Owen invested €6,000 at 5% annual interest, and left the money invested without withdrawing any of the interest for 12 years. At the end of the 12 years, Randy withdrew the accumulated amount of money. (a) What amount did Randy withdraw, assuming the investment earns simple interest? (b) What amount did Randy withdraw, assuming the investment earns interest compounded annually?

Compute the future value of a single amount.

BEA.2 (LO 1), AP For each of the following cases, indicate (a) what interest rate columns and (b) what number of periods you would refer to in looking up the future value factor.

Use future value tables.

1. In Table 1 (future value of 1):

	Annual Rate	Number of Years Invested	Compounded
Case A	5%	3	Annually
Case B	12%	4	Semiannually

2. In Table 2 (future value of an annuity of 1):

	Annual Rate	Number of Years Invested	Compounded
Case A	3%	8	Annually
Case B	8%	6	Semiannually

BEA.3 (LO 1), AP Joyce Ltd. signed a lease for an office building for a period of 12 years. Under the lease agreement, a security deposit of £9,600 is made. The deposit will be returned at the expiration of the lease with interest compounded at 4% per year. What amount will Joyce receive at the time the lease expires?

Compute the future value of a single amount.

BEA.4 (LO 1), AP Bates Company issued $1,000,000, 10-year bonds. It agreed to make annual deposits of $78,000 to a fund (called a sinking fund), which will be used to pay off the principal amount of the bond at the end of 10 years. The deposits are made at the end of each year into an account paying 6% annual interest. What amount will be in the sinking fund at the end of 10 years?

Compute the future value of an annuity.

BEA.5 (LO 1), AP Frank and Maureen Fantazzi invested €8,000 in a savings account paying 5% annual interest when their daughter, Angela, was born. They also deposited €1,000 on each of her birthdays until she was 18 (including her 18th birthday). How much was in the savings account on her 18th birthday (after the last deposit)?

Compute the future value of a single amount and of an annuity.

BEA.6 (LO 1), AP Hugh Curtin borrowed $35,000 on July 1, 2023. This amount plus accrued interest at 8% compounded annually is to be repaid on July 1, 2028. How much will Hugh have to repay on July 1, 2028?

Compute the future value of a single amount.

BEA.7 (LO 2), AP For each of the following cases, indicate (a) what interest rate columns and (b) what number of periods you would refer to in looking up the discount rate.

Use present value tables.

1. In Table 3 (present value of 1):

	Annual Rate	Number of Years Invested	Discounts Per Year
Case A	12%	7	Annually
Case B	8%	11	Semiannually
Case C	10%	8	Semiannually

2. In Table 4 (present value of an annuity of 1):

	Annual Rate	Number of Years Involved	Number of Payments Involved	Frequency of Payments
Case A	10%	20	20	Annually
Case B	10%	7	7	Annually
Case C	6%	5	10	Semiannually

Determine present values.	**BEA.8 (LO 2), AP** **a.** What is the present value of $25,000 due nine periods from now, discounted at 10%? **b.** What is the present value of $25,000 to be received at the end of each of six periods, discounted at 9%?
Compute the present value of a single amount investment.	**BEA.9 (LO 2), AP** Pingtung Ltd. is considering an investment that will return a lump sum of NT$9,000,000 six years from now. What amount should Pingtung pay for this investment to earn an 8% return?
Compute the present value of a single amount investment.	**BEA.10 (LO 2), AP** Lloyd Company earns 6% on an investment that will return $450,000 eight years from now. What is the amount Lloyd should invest now to earn this rate of return?
Compute the present value of an annuity investment.	**BEA.11 (LO 2), AP** Altrix plc is considering investing in an annuity contract that will return £40,000 annually at the end of each year for 15 years. What amount should Altrix plc pay for this investment if it earns an 8% return?
Compute the present value of an annual investment.	**BEA.12 (LO 2), AP** Kaehler Enterprises earns 5% on an investment that pays back $80,000 at the end of each of the next six years. What is the amount Kaehler Enterprises invested to earn the 5% rate of return?
Compute the present value of bonds.	**BEA.13 (LO 2), AP** Blythe Railroad Co. is about to issue €400,000 of 10-year bonds paying an 11% interest rate, with interest payable annually. The discount rate for such securities is 10%. How much can Blythe expect to receive for the sale of these bonds?
Compute the present value of bonds.	**BEA.14 (LO 2), AP** Blythe Railroad Co. is about to issue €400,000 of 10-year bonds paying an 11% interest rate, with interest payable annually. The discount rate is 12% (instead of 10% as in BEA.13). In this case, how much can Blythe expect to receive from the sale of these bonds?
Compute the present value of a note.	**BEA.15 (LO 2), AP** Yilan Ltd. receives a ₺750,000, six-year note bearing interest of 4% (paid annually) from a customer at a time when the discount rate is 6%. What is the present value of the note received by Yilan?
Compute the present value of bonds.	**BEA.16 (LO 2), AP** Gleason Enterprises issued 6%, eight-year, $2,500,000 par value bonds that pay interest annually on April 1. The bonds are dated April 1, 2023, and are issued on that date. The discount rate of interest for such bonds on April 1, 2023, is 8%. What cash proceeds did Gleason receive from issuance of the bonds?
Compute the present value of a note.	**BEA.17 (LO 2), AP** Keller Company issues a 10%, five-year mortgage note on January 1, 2023, to obtain financing for new equipment. Land is used as collateral for the note. The terms provide for semiannual installment payments of CHF48,850. What are the cash proceeds received from the issuance of the note?
Compute the interest rate on a single amount.	**BEA.18 (LO 2), AP** If Colleen Mooney invests £4,765.50 now and she will receive £12,000 at the end of 12 years, what annual rate of interest will Colleen earn on her investment? (*Hint:* Use Table 3.)
Compute the number of periods of a single amount.	**BEA.19 (LO 2), AP** Simon Baker has been offered the opportunity of investing A$36,125 now. The investment will earn 11% per year and at the end of that time will return Simon A$75,000. How many years must Simon wait to receive A$75,000? (*Hint:* Use Table 3.)
Compute the interest rate on an annuity.	**BEA.20 (LO 2), AP** Joanne Quick made an investment of $10,271.38. From this investment, she will receive $1,200 annually for the next 15 years starting one year from now. What rate of interest will Joanne's investment be earning for her? (*Hint:* Use Table 4.)
Compute the number of periods of an annuity.	**BEA.21 (LO 2), AP** Patty Schleis invests €7,793.83 now for a series of €1,300 annual returns beginning one year from now. Patty will earn a return of 9% on the initial investment. How many annual payments of €1,300 will Patty receive? (*Hint:* Use Table 4.)
Compute the present value of a machine for purposes of making a purchase decision.	**BEA.22 (LO 3), AP** Barney Googal owns a garage and is contemplating purchasing a tire retreading machine for $12,820. After estimating costs and revenues, Barney projects a net cash inflow from the retreading machine of $2,700 annually for seven years. Barney hopes to earn a return of 9% on such investments. What is the present value of the retreading operation? Should Barney Googal purchase the retreading machine?
Compute the maximum price to pay for a machine.	**BEA.23 (LO 3), AP** Wei Ltd. is considering purchasing equipment. The equipment will produce the following cash inflows: Year 1, ¥250,000; Year 2, ¥300,000 and Year 3, ¥400,000. Wei requires a minimum rate of return of 11%. What is the maximum price Wei should pay for this equipment?
Determine interest rate.	**BEA.24 (LO 4), AP** Farid Hakimi wishes to invest $18,000 on July 1, 2023, and have it accumulate to $50,000 by July 1, 2033. Use a financial calculator to determine at what exact annual rate of interest Farid must invest the $18,000.
Determine interest rate.	**BEA.25 (LO 4), AP** On July 17, 2022, Keith Urban borrowed A$42,000 from his grandfather to open a clothing store. Starting July 17, 2023, Keith has to make 10 equal annual payments of A$6,500 each to repay the loan. Use a financial calculator to determine what interest rate Keith is paying.

BEA.26 **(LO 4), AP** As the purchaser of a new house, Carrie Underwood has signed a mortgage note to pay the Nashville National Bank and Trust Co. $8,400 every six months for 20 years, at the end of which time she will own the house. At the date the mortgage is signed, the purchase price was $198,000 and Underwood made a down payment of $20,000. The first payment will be made six months after the date the mortgage is signed. Using a financial calculator, compute the exact rate of interest earned on the mortgage by the bank.

Determine interest rate.

BEA.27 **(LO 4), AP** Using a financial calculator, solve for the unknowns in each of the following situations:

Various time value of money situations.

a. On June 1, 2022, Jennifer Lawrence purchases lakefront property from her neighbor, Josh Hutcherson, and agrees to pay the purchase price in seven payments of $16,000 each, the first payment to be payable June 1, 2023. (Assume that interest compounded at an annual rate of 7.35% is implicit in the payments.) What is the purchase price of the property?

b. On January 1, 2022, Gerrard Corporation purchased 200 of the $1,000 face value, 8% coupon, 10-year bonds of Sterling Inc. The bonds mature on January 1, 2032, and pay interest annually beginning January 1, 2023. Gerrard purchased the bonds to yield 10.65%. How much did Gerrard pay for the bonds?

BEA.28 **(LO 4), AP** Using a financial calculator, provide a solution to each of the following situations:

Various time value of money situations.

a. Lynn Anglin owes a debt of $42,000 from the purchase of her new sport utility vehicle. The debt bears annual interest of 7.8% compounded monthly. Lynn wishes to pay the debt and interest in equal monthly payments over eight years, beginning one month hence. What equal monthly payments will pay off the debt and interest?

b. On January 1, 2023, Roger Molony offers to buy Dave Feeney's used snowmobile for $8,000, payable in five equal annual installments, which are to include 7.25% interest on the unpaid balance and a portion of the principal. If the first payment is to be made on December 31, 2023, how much will each payment be?

BEA.29 **(LO 4), AP** Winsdor Corporation is considering two alternative investments in excavating equipment. Investment A requires an initial investment of £184,000, has positive cash flows of £27,500 per year, and has an estimated salvage value of £21,000. Investment B requires an initial investment of £234,000, has positive cash flows of £32,800 per year, and has an estimated salvage value of £19,000. Each piece of equipment is expected to have a 12-year useful life. Use a financial calculator to determine the internal rate of return of each project to decide which is more desirable. (Round to two decimal places, e.g., 9.74%.)

Determine internal rate of return.

Company Index

A
Abercrombie & Fitch (USA), 1-6
Adidas (DEU), 1-20, 7-16
Advanced Micro Devices, 3-4
Airbus (FRA), 2-3
Alaska Airlines (USA), 4-22
Aldi (DEU), 6-1–6-2, 6-18
Allegiant Airlines (USA), 1-17
Allianz Australia Insurance Limited (AUS), 13-13
Amazon.com, Inc. (USA), 5-1–5-2, 5-24–5-25, 6-6, 7-10, 9-9, 13-50, 14-52
American Airlines (USA), 4-22
American Van Lines (USA), 10-7
Anytime Fitness (USA), 6-51
Apple Inc. (USA), 8-4, 13-18, 13-49, 14-51, 14-53
Armani (ITA), 8-3
Armour (USA), 7-12, 14-51
Aryzta (CHE), 1-8
AT&T (USA), 12-9, 14-7
Autodesk (USA), 2-4
AWP Australia (AUS), 13-13

B
Back o' Bourke Cordials Pty Ltd (AUS), 3-1, 3-2, 3-18
Balanced Scorecard Institute (USA), 11-48
Barnes & Noble (USA), 14-45
Best Buy (USA), 14-52
Beverly Hills Fan Company (USA), 7-38
Big Data Pricing (USA), 8-20
BMW (DEU), 1-20
Bob Evans Farms (USA), 14-40
Boeing (USA), 1-16, 7-8
Briggs & Stratton (USA), 10-31
British Airways (GBR), 5-3, 5-10, 6-7, 7-16
British Telecommunications (GBR), 1-4
Buchbinder (DEU), 5-7
Burton Snowboards (USA), 1-9
Button Worldwide (USA), 8-12

C
Caesars Entertainment (USA), 6-9, 6-48
Campbell Soup Company (USA), 12-16, 12-37
Carlsberg A.S., 1-19
Carnival Corporation (USA/GBR), 12-2
CA Technologies (USA), 10-54
Caterpillar (USA), 1-9, 3-8, 4-24
Center Ice Consultants, 3-4
Chanel (GBR), 8-3
Chase (USA), 11-20
Chevron (USA), 8-3
Chipotle (USA), 1-6
Chrysler (USA), 11-17
Cisco Systems (USA), 6-14, 10-16
Clark Equipment Company (USA), 4-13
Clark-Hurt (USA), 4-13
Clarus Technologies (USA), 8-46
Clorox (USA), 7-1
Coal & Allied's (AUS), 12-13
The Coca-Cola Company (USA), 1-8, 1-20, 3-1, 5-47, 10-31, 13-50–13-52
Columbia Sportswear Company (USA), 13-38, 14-51
Compumotor (USA), 4-13
Current Designs (USA), 1-1, 1-2, 1-3, 1-7, 1-8, 1-14, 1-22–1-23, 1-42, 2-40, 3-43, 4-45–4-46, 6-47, 7-36–7-37, 8-42, 9-47, 10-49–10-50, 11-45, 12-34–12-35
Cypress Semiconductor Corporation (USA), 13-38

D
Danske Bank (DNK), 1-5
Dell (USA), 1-4, 4-24, 12-1
Del Monte Foods Company (USA), 6-49
Delta Airlines (USA), 7-39, 11-20
DHL Express (USA), 5-23
Dickey's Barbecue Pit (USA), 9-18
Dick's Sporting Goods (USA), 1-12
DoorDash (USA), 7-1
Dow Chemical, 3-4
DPR Construction (USA), 1-6
Duke Energy (USA), 10-21
Dun & Bradstreet (USA), 14-8
DuPont, 3-4

E
Eastman Kodak (USA), 13-1
E-bay (USA), 11-22
Electronic Arts (USA), 12-21
Eli Lilly (USA), 10-31
Emirates Airlines (ARE), 1-4
Energy Australia (AUS), 10-7
Eni Energy (ITA), 5-4
Environmental Protection Agency (EPA) (USA), 8-46
Erin McKenna's Bakery NYC (USA), 9-1, 9-5, 9-27–9-28
E*Trade (USA), 6-14
Expedia (USA), 13-13
ExxonMobil (USA), 1-18, 2-3, 3-4, 8-3, 12-1

F
Facebook (USA), 1-6
Falfish (GBR), 6-11
Federal Express (USA), 1-4
FedEx Corporation (USA), 5-23, 6-50
Fitch (USA), 14-17
Ford Motor Company (USA), 1-18, 10-21
Fox Broadcasting (USA), 10-10
Freeman FinTech Corporation Limited (HKG), 14-13

G
Gap Inc. (USA), 1-19
General Dynamics Corp. (USA), 14-3
General Electric (GE) (USA), 1-20, 2-20, 3-11, 4-19
General Mills (USA), 3-3, 4-8, 14-21
General Motors Corporation (USA), 1-18, 2-4, 8-4, 14-39
Glassmaster Company (USA), 11-47
Goldman Sachs (USA), 2-19
Goodyear (USA), 7-16
Google (USA), 8-4, 14-3
Great Go Cycles (TWN), 7-11
Gritti Palace (ITA), 5-4
Gulf Craft (ARE), 3-31

H
Harley-Davidson (USA), 4-24
Hewlett-Packard Corporation (HP) (USA), 1-4, 4-26, 7-8, 11-19
Hilton Garden (USA), 5-4
Hilton Hotels (USA), 1-19, 5-4
Holland America Line (USA), 12-1, 12-2, 12-10, 12-22–12-23
Honeywell International (USA), 14-7
H&R Block (USA), 3-3
Hyundai Mobis (KOR), 3-17
Hughes Aircraft Co. (USA), 14-3
Human Rights Watch, 1-21

I
IBM (USA), 11-5, 14-7
Ice Pro, 3-4
IKEA (SWE), 7-11
Inditex SA (ESP), 1-19, 1-43
Intel Corporation (USA), 3-4, 3-17, 8-3, 13-20
iSuppli (USA), 2-12
ISUZU (JPN), 6-7

J
J. Walter Thompson (USA), 3-4
Jiffy Lube (USA), 3-3
Jif Peanut Butter (USA), 3-31
Jostens, Inc. (USA), 11-19

K
Kaiser Permanente, 3-4
Karolinska University Hospital (SWE), 5-3
Kellogg Company (USA), 3-10, 3-12, 3-13, 3-21, 11-12, 14-30, 14-31
Kia (KOR), 8-4
Komag (USA), 6-17

I-1

COMPANY INDEX

Kraft Foods (USA), 11-12
Kroger (USA), 5-10, 5-45

L

Lenovo (HKG), 6-7
Lidl (DEU), 6-1–6-2
Lindt & Sprüngli (CHE), 2-3
Little Caesars (USA), 7-1
Lufthansa (DEU), 7-14

M

Mackinac Center for Public Policy (USA), 9-49
Madison Square Garden (USA), 9-9
Market Watch, 14-52
Marriott Hotels (USA), 8-20
Mars Foods (China) Co. Ltd., 3-31
Mayo Clinic (USA), 2-19, 3-4
McDonald's Corporation (USA), 11-3, 13-44
Merck & Co., Inc. (USA), 8-45
Method Products (USA), 7-1–7-2, 7-8, 7-19
Microsoft (USA), 1-3, 8-2, 13-1, 13-2, 14-39
Motel One (DEU), 10-7
Moody's (USA), 14-8, 14-17
Motorola (USA), 14-4
MSN.com (USA), 14-19
Museum of Contemporary Art (USA), 9-26

N

NBCUniversal (USA), 10-10
Nestle (CHE), 1-19, 5-10, 13-5
Netflix (USA), 14-53
Nike, Inc. (USA), 6-15, 14-14, 14-43
Nissan (JPN), 12-1
Nordstrom, Inc. (USA), 14-44
Novartis (CHE), 1-19

O

Oracle (USA), 1-6
Orica (AUS), 4-17

P

Pandora (USA), 6-17
Parker Hannifin (USA), 4-13
Penske Automotive Group (USA), 11-20

PepsiCo, Inc. (USA), 13-50, 14-51–14-52
Petro-China (CHN), 3-3
Phantom Tac (BGD), 1-21
Pierce Manufacturing (USA), 2-4
Pratt & Whitney (USA), 2-20
PricewaterhouseCoopers (USA), 2-19
Princeton University (USA), 9-26
Procter & Gamble (USA), 1-12, 7-1, 10-16, 11-5, 14-4

Q

Quad Graphics (USA), 2-4
Quaker Oats (USA), 7-1
Qualcomm (USA), 13-20

R

Renault (FRA), 12-1
Rockport (USA), 7-16
Rolling Stones, 5-23

S

Samsung (KOR), 1-4, 1-6, 8-1
San Francisco Giants (USA), 8-20
SAP (DEU), 1-18
Schweppes (CHE), 3-1
Shaw Communications (USA), 13-38
Shell plc (GBR), 7-12
Sherwin Williams (USA), 3-3
Siebel Systems (USA), 10-18
Siemens AG (DEU), 1-19, 10-31
Sina (CHN), 5-18
Singapore Airlines (SGP), 5-3
Small Business Administration, 2-44
Snap Fitness (USA), 6-51
Sony Pictures Entertainment (USA), 8-13
Spotify (SWE), 6-17
Standard & Poor's (USA), 14-8, 14-17
Staples, Inc. (USA), 14-40
Starbucks (USA), 8-4, 11-1, 11-2, 11-17, 11-23–11-24
Sunbeam (USA), 7-5
Synergy (AUS), 5-5

T

Target Corporation (USA), 7-1, 14-50
Tata Steel Europe (GBR), 5-10
Technogym SpA (ITA), 4-1, 4-16, 4-23
Tecumseh Products Company (USA), 12-37

Telstra (AUS), 5-4
the balance, 9-51
Theranos (USA), 1-5
The Roxy Hotel Tribeca (USA), 10-1–10-2, 10-29
3M (USA), 6-9
T-Mobile US (USA), 12-9
Toblerone (CHE), 3-7
Topps Company, Inc. (USA), 14-41
Toyota (JPN), 1-17, 1-18, 8-4
Trek (USA), 8-13

U

Uber (USA), 8-20
Under Armour, Inc. (USA), 14-51
Unilever (GBR), 1-6, 1-19, 7-1, 11-20
United Parcel Service (UPS) (USA), 4-19, 5-23, 14-7
U.S. Navy, 11-5
U.S. Securities and Exchange Commission (SEC), 13-51
United States Steel (USA), 3-3

V

Verizon Communications (USA), 12-9, 14-7
Volkswagen (DEU), 1-4, 5-10

W

Wagner Machine Inc. (USA), 11-16
Walmart Inc. (USA), 1-19, 11-20, 13-50, 14-50, 14-53
Walt Disney Company (USA), 1-21, 2-1–2-2, 2-4, 2-24–2-25, 3-4, 8-5, 8-13
Warner Bros (USA), 3-4, 3-31
Wenonah Canoe (USA), 1-1, 1-42
Whirlpool (USA), 1-9, 11-16
World Bank, 11-5

X

XM Satellite Radio (USA), 9-17

Y

Yahoo! (USA), 14-8
Yahoo! Finance (USA), 13-51
Young & Rubicam, 3-4

Z

Zappos.com (USA), 8-1–8-2, 8-20–8-21

Subject Index

A

ABC. *See* Activity-based costing
ABM (activity-based management), 4-15, 4-17, 4-18, 4-27
Absorption costing, 6-19–6-29
  decision-making concerns, 6-26–6-28
  definition, 6-30
  example, 6-20
  net income effects, 6-22–6-26
  vs. variable costing, 6-20–6-22, 6-28–6-29
Absorption costing income statement, 6-21, 6-23, 6-24, 6-25, 6-27
Absorption-cost pricing, 8-22–8-24, 8-27
Accountability, individual, 2-8
Accounting
  and budgeting, 9-3
  changes in principle, 14-6–14-7, 14-33
  cost, 2-3–2-7, 2-26
  financial, 1-3
  managerial, 1-1–1-45
  across organizations, 9-4, 11-5, 13-5
  responsibility, 10-14–10-24, 10-33
  standard cost, 11-24–11-26, 11-30
Accounts payable, 9-23, 13-12, 13-23
Accounts receivable, 9-23, 13-10, 13-11, 13-22, 13-23
Accounts receivable turnover, 14-19–14-20, 14-33
Accrual accounting
  adjustments for expenses, 13-24
  converting to cash basis from, 13-7, 13-20–13-25
Accumulated depreciation, 9-23
Accumulated other comprehensive loss, 14-5
Activities, 4-5, 4-27
  batch-level, 4-15, 4-16, 4-27
  classification, 4-8
  coordination of, 9-3
  examples, 4-6
  facility-level, 4-15, 4-16, 4-27
  financing, 13-3, 13-4, 13-14–13-15, 13-26
  hierarchy of, 4-16
  identification, 4-8
  investing, 13-3, 13-4, 13-5, 13-14–13-15, 13-26–13-27, 13-30
  noncash, 13-14–13-15
  non–value-added, 4-16, 4-17, 4-27
  operating, 4-16, 13-3, 13-4, 13-5, 13-9–13-13, 13-14–13-15, 13-20–13-26, 13-30
  product-level, 4-15, 4-16, 4-27
  significant noncash, 13-4–13-5
  types of, 4-15, 4-16
  unit-level, 4-15, 4-16, 4-27
  value-added, 4-16, 4-27
Activity-based costing (ABC), 1-18, 4-1–4-48
  allocating overhead to cost pools, 4-8
  assigning nonmanufacturing overhead costs, 4-13–4-15
  assigning overhead costs to products, 4-9–4-10
  benefits, 4-13–4-19
  definition, 1-25, 4-27
  evaluation of, 4-11
  example, 4-21–4-22
  and incremental analysis, 7-5
  key concepts, 4-5
  limitations, 4-13–4-19
  for manufacturers, 4-7–4-13
  reasons for using, 7-5
  for service companies, 4-20–4-24
  steps, 4-6
  vs. traditional costing, 4-22
  when to use, 4-18–4-19
Activity-based management (ABM), 4-15, 4-18, 4-27
Activity-based overhead rates, 4-9
Activity cost pools, 4-5, 4-10, 4-27
Activity flowcharts, 4-16–4-17
Activity index, 5-3, 5-30
  in flexible budgets, 10-9, 10-10
  relevant range, 5-5–5-6
  standard, 11-7
Additional information
  for ratio analysis, 14-18
  for statement of cash flows, 13-8, 13-21
Adjustments
  for changes, 13-11, 13-12
  to cost of goods sold, 2-23
  for depreciation, 13-9
  for expenses, 13-24
Administrative expense budget, 9-16, 9-30
After-tax contribution margin, 8-26
Analysis
  break-even, 5-16–5-20, 6-2–6-3, 6-5, 6-8, 6-9, 6-11
  common-size, 14-11
  cost behavior, 5-3–5-7, 5-30
  cost-volume-profit (CVP), 5-11–5-28, 6-1–6-51
  financial, 14-1–14-54
  horizontal, 14-8, 14-33
  incremental, 6-13, 7-1–7-40
  mixed costs, 5-8–5-11
  ratio, 14-14–14-29, 14-33
  regression, 5-25–5-28, 5-30
  risk, 12-15
  trend, 14-8
  vertical, 14-11–14-13, 14-33
Annual cash flow, 12-11
  equal, 12-7–12-8
  unequal, 12-5, 12-8–12-9
Annual rate of return, 12-19–12-21, 12-24
Annuities, A-22
  discounting, A-8
  future value, A-5–A-7, A-20, A-22
  periodic payments, A-6
  present value, A-11–A-12, A-19, A-22
Assets
  debt to assets ratio, 14-22, 14-33
  equation, 13-27
  noncurrent accounts, 13-14–13-15, 13-25
  operating, 10-26, 10-27
  plant, 13-10, 13-25
  return on, 14-24–14-25, 14-26, 14-33
Asset turnover, 14-25–14-26, 14-33
Authorization process
  corporate capital budgets, 12-3
  not-for-profit organizations, 9-26
Auto loan payments, A-21
Automobile industry, 11-20
Available-for-sale securities, 14-5, 14-33
Average collection period, 14-20, 14-33
Average investment, 12-20
Averages, industry, 14-8, 14-19
Awareness, management, 9-3

B

Balanced scorecard, 1-18, 1-25, 11-20–11-22, 11-30
Balance sheet(s), 1-12, 13-3
  accumulated other comprehensive loss in, 14-5
  budgeted, 9-19–9-24, 9-29
  change in cash, 13-15, 13-27
  comparative, 13-6, 13-8, 13-20, 14-11
  condensed, 14-11, 14-11–14-12
  example, 14-17–14-18
  horizontal analysis of, 14-8–14-11
  stockholders' equity section, 14-5
  vertical analysis of, 14-11–14-12
Banks, regional, 11-20
Batch-level activities, 4-15, 4-16, 4-27
Behavior. *See* Cost behavior analysis; Human behavior
Behavioral principles, 10-17
Benchmarks, 4-18
Bezos, Jeff, 5-1, 5-2, 7-10
Big data, 1-21, 8-20
Big energy, 12-15

I-3

Board of directors, 1-5, 1-25
Bonds: present value of, A-13–A-15
Bonds payable, 13-14, 13-26
Bottlenecks, 1-18
Bottom line, triple, 1-20, 1-25
Bottom-to-top approach, 9-5
Break-even analysis, 5-16–5-20
  basic concepts, 6-2
  cases, 6-5
  contribution margin techniques, 5-17–5-18
  mathematical equation, 5-16–5-17
  weighted-average method, 6-8, 6-9, 6-10
Break-even point, 5-14, 5-16, 5-30
  cost structure and, 6-16
  equations, 5-17, 5-18
  examples, 6-16
  in sales euros, 5-18, 6-4
  in sales units, 5-17–5-18, 6-3, 6-9
Break-even sales, 6-7–6-11
Budget(s)
  cash, 9-19–9-22, 9-29
  definition, 9-3, 9-29
  departmentalized, 9-25
  direct labor, 9-14–9-15, 9-25–9-26, 9-29
  direct materials, 9-11–9-14, 9-30
  financial, 9-7, 9-30
  flexible, 10-7–10-12, 10-32, 11-27
  manufacturing overhead, 9-15, 9-30
  master, 9-7, 9-30
  merchandise purchases, 9-24, 9-25, 9-30
  operating, 9-7, 9-30
  production, 9-10, 9-30
  sales, 9-8–9-9, 9-30
  selling and administrative expense, 9-16, 9-30
  vs. standard costs, 11-4
  static, 10-4, 10-7, 10-8, 10-33
Budgetary control, 10-3–10-4, 10-33
Budgetary optimism, 9-9
Budgetary planning, 9-1–9-51
Budgetary slack, 9-6, 9-29
Budget committee, 9-5, 9-29
Budgeted balance sheet, 9-22–9-24, 9-29
Budgeted classified balance sheet, 9-23
Budgeted income statement, 9-17–9-18, 9-29
Budgeted multiple-step income statement, 9-17
Budgeting
  and accounting, 9-3
  benefits of, 9-3
  bottom-to-top approach, 9-5
  capital, 12-1, 12-3, 12-24, A-15–A-17
  effective, 9-3, 9-4–9-7
  essentials, 9-4–9-7
  and human behavior, 9-5–9-6
  vs. long-range planning, 9-6–9-7
  for nonmanufacturing companies, 9-24–9-26
  for not-for-profit organizations, 9-26
  participative, 9-5–9-6, 9-30
  process, 9-4–9-5
  shortfalls, 9-26
  total budgeted costs, 10-11
  zero-based, 9-49, 10-18
Budget period, 9-4
Budget reports, 10-3
  flexible, 10-7–10-9, 10-12–10-13
  static, 10-4–10-6, 10-8
Budget variance, 10-4
Buildings and equipment, 9-23
  increase, 13-14, 13-25
Burden, 1-8
Business environment, 6-4–6-6, 8-3
Business ethics, 1-19–1-20

C

Calculators, financial, A-17–A-21
Capacity, normal, 11-7, 11-30
Capital
  cost of, 12-9, 12-24
  working, 14-19
Capital budgeting, 12-1
  annual rate of return method, 12-19–12-21, 12-24
  approaches to avoid rejecting projects that should be accepted, 12-12
  big energy, 12-15
  cash flow information for, 12-3–12-4
  cash payback technique, 12-4–12-6, 12-24
  challenges and refinements, 12-12–12-16
  choosing discount rates, 12-9–12-10
  computing present value in, A-15–A-17
  definition, 12-24
  discounted cash flow techniques, 12-6, 12-18–12-19, 12-24
  with equal annual cash flows, 12-7–12-8
  Excel, 12-19
  general process, 12-3
  helpful hint, 12-21
  internal rate of return method, 12-17–12-19, 12-24
  net present value method, 12-6–12-11, 12-24
  post-audit, 12-16, 12-24
  typical cash flows, 12-4
  with unequal annual cash flows, 12-8–12-9
Capital investments: planning for, 12-1–12-38
Cash. See also Net cash
  in budgeted balance sheet, 9-22
  change in, 13-15, 13-27
Cash accounting: converting to, 13-9, 13-19–13-24
Cash budget, 9-19–9-22
Cash disbursements (cash budget), 9-19
Cash flow(s)
  assumptions, 12-10
  capital budgeting, 12-4
  classification, 13-3–13-4
  discounted, 12-6, 12-18–12-19, 12-24
  equal, 12-7–12-8
  even, 12-17
  free, 13-17–13-18, 14-23, 14-33
  from operating activities, 13-4
  statement of cash flows, 13-1–13-52
  unequal, 12-5, 12-8–12-9
Cash flow information, 12-3–12-4
Cash management, 9-21
Cash payback, 12-4–12-6, 12-24
Cash payback period, 12-5
Cash payments, 13-3, 13-21, 13-22–13-23, 13-24
Cash receipts, 13-3, 13-21, 13-22
Cash receipts section (cash budget), 9-19
Cash T-accounts, 13-29
CEO (chief executive officer), 1-6, 1-25
CFO (chief financial officer), 1-6, 1-25
Changes in accounting principle, 14-6–14-7, 14-33
Changes in depreciation methods, 14-7
Charges
  hourly time rate, 8-10
  job, 8-11
  material loading, 8-11, 8-28
  non-recurring, 14-4
  restructuring, 14-4
Chemicals industry, 11-20
Chief executive officer (CEO), 1-6, 1-25
Chief financial officer (CFO), 1-6, 1-25
Classified balance sheet, 9-23
Cloud services, 2-4
Collaboration, 10-16
Collections
  average period, 14-20, 14-33
  from customers, 9-20
Common-size analysis, 14-11
Common stock, 14-26
  on budgeted balance sheet, 9-23
  dividends paid on, 14-27
  increase, 13-14, 13-25
  return on common stockholders' equity (ROE), 14-23–14-24
Comparative balance sheets, 13-6, 13-8, 13-20, 14-10
Comparative rankings, 10-19, 10-20
Comparisons
  with industry averages, 14-8, 14-19
  intercompany, 14-8
  intracompany, 14-8
Competition, 10-16
Compounding periods, A-19
Compound interest, A-2, A-3, A-22
Comprehensive income, 14-4–14-6, 14-33
Compustat, 14-17
Computer systems, 11-20
Condensed balance sheets, 14-11–14-12
Condensed income statements, 14-10–14-11, 14-12, 14-13
Constraints theory, 1-18, 1-25, 6-30

Continuous improvement, 4-17
Contribution margin (CM), 5-12, 5-30
   after-tax, under alternative transfer prices, 8-26
   in break-even analysis, 5-17–5-18
   in cost-based transfer prices, 8-18
   with limited resources, 6-14
   and target net income, 5-21
   total, 6-13
   unit, 5-13–5-14, 5-17–5-18, 5-30, 6-8, 6-12, 8-18, 8-26
Contribution margin (CM) ratio, 5-14–5-15, 5-18
   cost structure and, 6-15
   definition, 5-30
   weighted-average, 6-10
Control accounts, 2-8
Controllability, 10-17
Controllable costs, 10-16, 10-22, 10-32
Controllable fixed costs, 10-25
Controllable margin, 10-22, 10-23, 10-26–10-27, 10-32
Controllable revenues, 10-22
Controllable variance, overhead, 11-26–11-28, 11-30
Controller, 1-6, 1-25
Controlling, 1-4
Conversion costs, 3-11, 3-23
   definition, 3-27
   equivalent units for, 3-22
   total, 3-14
   unit, 3-15
Conversion rate, 6-6
Coordination of activities, 9-3
Corporate social responsibility, 1-20, 1-25, 11-17
Cost(s)
   absorption costing, 6-19–6-29, 6-30
   absorption-cost pricing, 8-22–8-25
   activity-based costing (ABC), 1-18, 1-25, 4-1–4-48
   actual production, 11-9
   assigning to finished goods, 2-16–2-17
   capital, 12-9, 12-24
   controllable, 10-16, 10-22, 10-32
   controlling, 10-23
   conversion, 3-11, 3-22, 3-23
   departmental overhead, 10-4
   direct labor cost, 9-14–9-15
   direct materials purchases, 9-11
   factory labor, 2-6, 2-10–2-12, 3-7
   fixed. *See* Fixed costs
   full-cost pricing, 8-8, 8-22
   inventoriable, 1-9
   job order costing, 2-1–2-44
   joint, 7-12, 7-20
   manufacturing, 1-7–1-8, 1-11, 6-20, 8-22
   manufacturing overhead, 2-6–2-7, 3-7–3-8
   materials, 3-7
   mixed, 5-7, 5-30
   noncontrollable, 10-16, 10-32
   operations costing, 3-17, 3-27
   opportunity, 7-4, 7-9, 7-20, 8-15, 8-28
   overhead, 2-6–2-7, 3-7–3-8, 4-9–4-10, 4-13–4-15
   period, 1-9, 1-25
   physical unit, 3-13, 3-20–3-22. *See also* Unit costs
   pricing considerations, 8-3
   process costing, 3-1–3-45
   product, 1-9, 1-25, 4-11, 7-8
   raw materials, 2-6, 2-8–2-10
   relevant, 7-4, 7-6–7-8, 7-16, 7-20
   standard, 11-1, 11-3–11-8, 11-24–11-26
   sunk, 7-4, 7-20
   target, 8-3–8-5, 8-28
   total budgeted, 10-11
   total conversion, 3-14
   total unit, 9-17
   traditional, 4-3–4-4, 4-20–4-21
   traditional systems, 4-3–4-4
   transfer prices based on, 8-17–8-18
   transfer to cost of goods sold, 3-8
   transfer to finished goods, 3-8
   transfer to next department, 3-8
   underestimating, 2-16
   unit. *See* Unit costs
   variable. *See* Variable cost(s)
Cost accounting, 2-3–2-7
   definition, 2-26
   with variances, 11-26
Cost accounting systems, 2-3–2-7
   definition, 2-26
   types, 2-3
Cost-based transfer prices, 8-17–8-18, 8-28
Cost behavior analysis, 5-3–5-7, 5-30
Cost centers, 10-19–10-21, 10-22, 10-32
Cost control, 4-15–4-17
Cost drivers, 3-8, 4-8–4-9
   definition, 4-5, 4-27
   examples, 4-6, 4-16
   per product, 4-10
Costing systems, 3-17
Cost of goods manufactured, 1-14, 1-25, 2-23
Cost of goods manufactured schedule, 1-13, 1-15
   manufacturing overhead applied, 2-22
Cost of goods sold, 1-13, 2-5, 2-17–2-18, 3-8
Cost-plus pricing, 8-5–8-7, 8-28
Cost pools, 4-8, 4-13–4-15
Cost reconciliation report, 3-24
Cost reconciliation schedule, 3-17, 3-27
   preparation, 3-15, 3-23–3-24
Cost structure, 6-14–6-15, 6-16, 6-30
Cost-volume-profit (CVP) analysis, 5-11–5-15, 5-30
   additional issues, 6-1–6-51
   basic components, 5-11–5-12
   basic concepts, 6-2–6-4
   break-even analysis, 5-16–5-20, 6-2–6-3, 6-4
   cases, 6-4–6-6
   and changes in business environment, 6-4–6-6
   contribution margin techniques, 5-17–5-18, 5-21
   and data analytics, 5-23
   regression analysis, 5-25–5-28
   traditional income statement, 5-13
Cost-volume-profit (CVP) graph, 5-19–5-22, 5-30
Cost-volume-profit (CVP) income statement, 5-12–5-16, 5-30
   comparative statements, 5-15
   examples, 5-14, 6-3, 6-15
Crediting rating agencies, 14-17
Current asset accounts, 13-11
Current assets, noncash, 13-10–13-12
Current Designs case, 5-44–5-45, 6-50–6-51, 7-37–7-38, 8-45, 9-47, 10-47, 11-45, 12-34
Current income statement, 13-7
Current liabilities, 13-10–13-12
Current ratios, 14-16, 14-19, 14-33
Customer collections, 9-20
Customer perspective, 11-20, 11-21, 11-30
Cutoff rate, 12-9
CVP. *See* Cost-volume-profit (CVP)

D

Data analytics, 1-21–1-22, 1-25, 14-17
   CVP analysis and, 5-23
   insights, 1-21, 2-4, 4-19, 8-20, 9-18, 10-13, 10-18, 11-16, 12-21
Database services, 14-17
Data visualizations, 1-21. *See also* Graphic presentation
Days in inventory, 14-21, 14-33
Debt to assets ratio, 14-22, 14-33
Debt to equity ratio, 14-22
Decentralization, 10-15, 10-32
Decision making, 4-18, 7-3
   with absorption costing, 6-26–6-28
   annual rate of return, 12-20
   to eliminate unprofitable segments or products, 7-16–7-18
   incremental analysis approach, 7-3–7-4
   internal rate of return (IRR), 12-18
   make or buy, 7-8–7-10
   management process, 7-3
   net present value (NPV), 12-7
   pricing, 8-1–8-46
   qualitative factors, 7-5
   to repair, retain, or replace equipment, 7-14–7-16
   to sell or process further, 7-11–7-14
Demand, 8-3
Departmentalized budgets, 9-25
Departmental overhead costs report, 10-4

Depreciation
  accumulated, 9-23
  adjustment for, 13-9
  change in methods, 14-7
Depreciation expense, 13-9, 13-23–13-24
Direct fixed costs, 10-22, 10-32
Directing, 1-4
Direct labor, 1-8, 1-25, 10-10, 11-6–11-7
Direct labor budget, 9-14–9-15, 9-25–9-26, 9-29
Direct labor cost, 9-14
Direct labor hours, standard, 11-27
Direct labor price standard, 11-6, 11-30
Direct labor quantity standard, 11-6, 11-30
Direct labor rate standard, 11-6
Direct labor variances, 11-13–11-15
Direct materials, 1-8, 1-25, 11-5–11-6
  costs, 9-11
  payments for, 9-21
  posting, 2-10
  quantity standard, 11-5–11-6
  units to be purchased, 9-11
Direct materials budget, 9-10–9-12, 9-30
Direct materials price standard, 11-5, 11-30
Direct materials quantity standard, 11-5–11-6
Direct materials variances, 11-8–11-13
Discontinued operations, 14-3, 14-4, 14-6, 14-33
Discounted cash flow techniques, 12-6, 12-18–12-19, 12-24
Discounting
  future amounts, A-8, A-22
  time periods, A-13
Discount rates, 12-9–12-10, 12-24
Disposal of plant assets, 13-10, 13-23–13-24
Disposal of significant components, 14-3
Dividends, stock, 14-27
Divisions, 10-15, 10-33
Dunlap, Al "Chainsaw," 7-5

E

Early warning systems, 9-3
Earnings
  price-earnings (P-E) ratio, 14-27, 14-33
  quality of, 14-33
  retained, 9-23, 13-14, 13-25
Earnings per share (EPS), 14-26–14-27, 14-33
Edgar database (SEC), 14-17
Employee safety, 12-13
Energy, big, 12-15
Enterprise resource planning (ERP) systems, 1-18, 1-25
EPS (earnings per share), 14-26–14-27, 14-33
Equal annual cash flows, 12-7–12-8
Equipment, 9-23
  additional considerations, 7-15–7-16
  analysis, 13-14, 13-25
  increase, 13-14, 13-25
  repair, retain, or replace, 7-14–7-16
Equity
  debt to equity ratio, 14-22
  stockholders', 13-14–13-15, 13-26, 14-5, 14-23–14-24, 14-33
  trading on, 14-24–14-25, 14-33
Equivalent units of production, 3-9–3-12
  computation, 3-11, 3-15, 3-22–3-23
  for conversion costs, 3-22, 3-23
  definition, 3-27
  equation, 3-10
  FIFO method, 3-20–3-26
  for materials, 3-22
  weighted-average method, 3-10, 3-25–3-26
  weighted-average method refinements, 3-10–3-12
ERP (enterprise resource planning) systems, 1-18, 1-25
Ethics
  in approving requisition slips, 2-8
  in budgeting, 9-6
  business, 1-19–1-20
  in determining equivalent units, 3-11
  and employee safety, 12-13
  insights, 12-13
  in setting fees, 1-17
  with standards, 11-4
  with statement of cash flows, 13-3
EU Directive 2014/56, 1-20
Euros
  break-even sales in, 6-9–6-11
  margin of safety in, 6-4
  sales, 5-18, 6-4
  target net income in, 6-4
Excel
  capital budgeting calculations, 12-19
  Intercept function, 5-27
  IRR function, 12-19
  NPV function, 12-19
  regression analysis, 5-27
  Scatter function, 5-28
  Slope function, 5-27
Exception: management by, 10-16–10-17, 10-32, 11-19
Exception guidelines, 10-17
Excess capacity, 8-14–8-16
Expenses
  accrued, 13-23
  depreciation, 13-9, 13-23–13-24
  operating, 13-23
  prepaid, 13-11, 13-23
  selling and administrative, 9-16, 9-30, 10-4, 10-6

F

Facility-level activities, 4-15, 4-16, 4-27
Factory labor costs, 2-5
  accumulation, 2-6
  assignment, 2-10–2-12, 3-7
Factory overhead. See Manufacturing overhead
Favorable variances, 11-9
Federal Trade Commission (FTC), 8-45
FIFO (first-in, first-out) method, 3-20–3-26
Financial accounting, 1-3
Financial analysis, 14-1–14-54
  common-size, 14-11
  comparisons with industry averages, 14-8, 14-19
  credit rating, 14-17
  data analytics, 14-17
  horizontal, 14-8–14-11, 14-33
  intercompany comparisons, 14-8
  intracompany comparisons, 14-8
  ratio analysis, 14-14–14-29
  vertical, 14-11–14-13, 14-33
Financial budgets, 9-7, 9-30
Financial calculators, A-17–A-21
Financial measures, 11-22
Financial perspective, 11-20, 11-21, 11-30
Financial ratio classifications, 14-15
Financial statements. *See also specific statements*
  cash budget section, 9-19
  manufacturing costs in, 1-12–1-16
Financing activities, 13-4, 13-30
  direct method, 13-26
  general guidelines for, 13-4
  indirect method, 13-13–13-15
  significant noncash activities, 13-5
  in statement of cash flows, 13-14–13-15
  typical cash inflows and outflows, 13-4
Finished goods
  assigning costs to, 2-17
  transferring costs to, 3-8
Finished goods inventory, 1-12, 2-5, 9-23
First-in, first-out (FIFO) method, 3-21–3-27
Fixed costs, 5-4–5-5, 5-30
  controllable, 10-25
  direct, 10-22, 10-32
  high-low computation, 5-9
  indirect, 10-22, 10-32
  manufacturing, 10-6
  ROI by decrease in, 10-26–10-27
  total, 5-4, 5-6
  unit, 5-4, 8-6, 8-8
Fixed selling and administrative expenses, 10-6
Flexible budget reports, 10-9, 10-12–10-13
Flexible budgets, 10-7–10-9, 10-32
  case study, 10-10–10-12
  development of, 10-9–10-10
  graphic presentation of, 10-12
  with standard direct labor hours, 11-27
Flowcharts, activity, 4-16–4-17
Forecasts, 10-13
  sales, 9-5, 9-30
Fraud, 13-13, 14-13–14-14
Free cash flow, 13-17–13-18, 13-30, 14-23, 14-33

Full-cost pricing, 8-8, 8-22, 8-28
Full disclosure principle, 13-5
Future value
 of annuities, A-5–A-8, A-20, A-22
 calculator keys for, A-18
 calculator solutions, A-20
 of single amounts, A-3–A-5, A-22
 of single sums, A-19

G
Gaming, budgetary, 9-6
Globalization, 8-19, 8-25–8-26
Goods, finished
 assigning costs to, 2-16–2-17
 inventory, 1-12, 2-5, 9-23
 transfer to, 3-8
Goods sold: cost of, 1-13, 2-5
 assignment, 2-17–2-18
 transfer to, 3-8
Graphic presentation
 cost-volume-profit (CVP) graph, 5-19–5-20, 5-22, 5-30
 of flexible budget data, 10-12
 scatter plots, 5-27
Gross profit rate, 14-26, 14-33
Growth. *See* Learning and growth perspective

H
High-low method, 5-8–5-10, 5-28, 5-30
Horizontal analysis, 14-8–14-11, 14-33
Hourly time-charge rate, 8-10
Human behavior, 9-5–9-6
Humanitarian benefits, 12-13
Hurdle rate, 12-9

I
IASB, *see* International Accounting Standards Board
Ideal standards, 11-4, 11-30
IFRS (International Financial Reporting Standards), 13-6, 13-9
IMA (Institute of Management Accountants), 1-20, 1-44, 2-43
IMA Statement of Ethical Professional Practice, 1-20
Improvement, continuous, 4-17
Incentives, 1-19, 11-22
Income. *See also* Net income
 comprehensive, 14-4–14-6, 14-33
 pro forma, 14-33
 residual, 10-31, 10-33
 sustainable, 14-3–14-7, 14-33
Income (margin) measure, 10-26
Income statements, 1-12–1-14, 13-3
 budgetary control report, 10-4
 budgeted, 9-17–9-18, 9-29
 condensed, 14-12, 14-13
 cost-volume-profit (CVP), 5-12–5-16, 5-30, 6-3, 6-15
 current income statement, 13-7
 discontinued operations in, 14-4, 14-6
 examples, 13-8, 13-20, 14-6, 14-18
 horizontal analysis of, 14-11
 non-recurring charges, 14-4
 vs. statement of comprehensive income, 14-6
 variances in, 11-19
 vertical analysis of, 14-12
Income taxes payable, 13-12, 13-24
Incremental analysis, 6-13, 7-1–7-40
 and activity-based costing, 7-5
 additional considerations, 7-7, 7-9, 7-14, 7-15–7-16, 7-18
 basic approach, 7-4–7-5
 decision-making approach, 7-3–7-4
 definition, 7-3, 7-20
 to eliminate unprofitable segments or products, 7-16–7-18
 to make or buy, 7-8–7-10
 multiple-product case, 7-12–7-14
 with opportunity costs, 7-9
 qualitative factors, 7-5
 to repair, retain, or replace equipment, 7-14–7-16
 to sell or process further, 7-11–7-14
 single-product case, 7-11
 of special orders, 7-6–7-8
 types of, 7-6
Indirect fixed costs, 10-22, 10-32
Indirect labor, 1-8, 1-25
Indirect materials, 1-8, 1-25
Industry averages, 14-8, 14-15, 14-19
Institute of Management Accountants (IMA), 1-20, 1-44, 2-43
Insurance, prepaid, 13-10
Intangible benefits, 12-12–12-13
Intercept function (Excel), 5-27
Intercompany comparisons, 14-8, 14-13, 14-15, 14-19
Interest, A-2–A-3, A-22
 cash payments for, 13-24
 compound, A-2, A-3
 simple, A-2, A-3, A-22
 times interest earned, 14-22–14-23
Interest coverage, 14-22–14-23
Interest rates, A-2
 calculator keys for, A-18
 discount, 12-9–12-10, 12-24
Internal process perspective, 11-21, 11-30
Internal rate of return (IRR), 12-17–12-19, 12-24, A-20
International Accounting Standards Board (IASB), 13-7, 13-36, 14-4
International Financial Reporting Standards (IFRS), 13-6, 13-9
Intracompany comparisons, 14-8, 14-15, 14-19
Inventoriable costs, 1-9
Inventory
 analysis of, 13-22
 days in, 14-21, 14-33
 finished goods, 1-12, 2-5, 9-23
 increase in, 13-11
 individual accountability over, 2-8
 just-in-time (JIT), 1-18, 1-25
 raw materials, 1-12, 2-5, 9-23
 work in process. *See* Work in process inventory
Inventory accounts, 1-12
Inventory turnover, 14-20–14-21, 14-33
Investing activities, 13-3
 cash flows, 13-4
 direct method, 13-26
 general guidelines for, 13-4
 indirect method, 13-13–13-15
 significant noncash activities, 13-5
 in statement of cash flows, 13-15
Investment centers, 10-21, 10-24–10-27, 10-32
Investments
 average, 12-20
 big energy, 12-15
 capital, 12-1–12-38
 planning for, 12-1–12-38
 post-audit projects, 12-16
Investors
 insights, 14-4, 14-7, 14-16, 14-17
 restructuring charges, 14-4
iPhones, 2-12
IRR (internal rate of return), 12-17–12-19, 12-24, A-20
IRR function (Excel), 12-19

J
JIT (just-in-time) inventory, 1-18, 1-25
JIT (just-in-time) processing, 4-24–4-26, 4-27
Job charges, 8-11
Job cost sheets, 2-8, 2-9
 completed, 2-16
 definition, 2-26
 direct labor in, 2-12
 direct materials in, 2-10
 manufacturing overhead applied, 2-15
 proof of agreement with work in process inventory, 2-16
Job order costing, 2-1–2-44
 accumulating manufacturing costs, 2-5–2-7
 advantages and disadvantages of, 2-20–2-21
 assigning costs to cost of goods sold, 2-17–2-18
 assigning costs to finished goods, 2-16–2-17
 assigning manufacturing costs, 2-7–2-13
 cost flows, 2-5, 2-18–2-19, 3-4
 document flows, 2-19
 for jobs completed and sold, 2-16–2-21
 with predetermined overhead rates, 2-13–2-16, 2-18–2-19
 for service companies, 2-19–2-20
Job order cost systems, 2-3
 definition, 2-26
 vs. process cost systems, 3-4–3-6

Joint costs, 7-12, 7-20
Joint production process, 7-12
Joint products, 7-12, 7-20
Journal entries, 3-6–3-9, 11-24–11-25, 13-10
Just-in-case philosophy, 4-24
Just-in-time (JIT) inventory, 1-18, 1-25
Just-in-time (JIT) processing, 4-24–4-26, 4-27

L

Labor
   direct, 1-8, 1-25, 11-6–11-7
   direct labor budget, 9-14–9-15, 9-25–9-26, 9-29
   indirect, 1-8, 1-25
   multiskilled work force, 4-25
   standard hours, 11-26, 11-30
Labor costs
   direct labor cost, 9-14
   factory labor costs, 2-6, 2-10–2-12, 3-7
   variable costs per direct labor hour, 10-11
Labor price variance (LPV), 11-14, 11-15, 11-30
Labor quantity variance (LQV), 11-14, 11-15, 11-30
Labor rate, 8-10–8-11
Labor reports, 10-4
Labor variances, 11-13–11-15, 11-30
Land: increase in, 13-14, 13-26
Lean manufacturing, 1-17
Learning and growth perspective, 11-21, 11-30
Ledger accounts
   standard cost accounting, 11-26
   subsidiary, 2-8
Leverage
   equity, 14-24–14-25
   operating, 6-16–6-19, 6-30
Leveraging, 14-33
Liability accounts
   current, 13-10–13-12
   noncurrent, 13-14–13-15, 13-26
Limited resources, 12-14
Line positions, 1-6, 1-25
Liquidity ratios, 14-15, 14-19–14-21, 14-33
Long-range planning, 9-6–9-7, 9-30
Long-term notes, A-13–A-15
Losses
   accumulated other comprehensive loss, 14-5
   on disposal of plant assets, 13-10, 13-25
   unrealized, 14-4
LPV (labor price variance), 11-14, 11-15, 11-30
LQV (labor quantity variance), 11-14, 11-15, 11-30

M

MagicBands, 1-21
Make-or-buy decisions, 7-8–7-10
Management
   awareness of operations, 9-3
   decision-making process, 7-3
   decisions, 4-18
   by exception, 10-16–10-17, 10-32, 11-19
   functions, 1-3–1-5
   insights, 1-6, 1-9, 1-19, 2-12, 2-16, 3-8, 4-11, 4-17, 5-10, 6-6, 6-13, 8-4, 9-12, 10-16, 11-22, 12-9
Managerial accounting, 1-3, 1-25
   basics, 1-3–1-7
   cost concepts, 1-7–1-11
   vs. financial accounting, 1-3–1-4
   trends, 1-16–1-23
Manufacturing, 1-8, 3-3
   lean, 1-17
Manufacturing costs, 1-7–1-11. *See also* Product costs
   accumulating, 2-5–2-7
   activity-based, 4-7–4-13
   assigning, 2-7–2-13, 3-6–3-9
   in financial statements, 1-12–1-16
   fixed, 10-6
   flow of, 2-5
   in job order costing, 2-5–2-13
   per unit, 3-15, 6-20, 8-22
   in process costing, 3-6–3-9
   total, 1-11, 3-15
Manufacturing overhead, 1-8–1-9, 1-25
   accumulating, 2-5–2-7
   applied, 2-15, 2-22–2-24
   assigning, 3-7
   overapplied, 2-22–2-24
   standard, 11-7
   underapplied, 2-22–2-24
Manufacturing overhead budget, 9-15–9-16, 9-30
Manufacturing overhead variances, 11-16–11-17
Margin, profit, 14-25, 14-33
Margin (income) measure, 10-26
Margin of safety, 5-20–5-23, 5-30, 6-4
Margin of safety ratio, 5-22, 6-16
Market-based transfer prices, 8-19, 8-28
Markup, 8-6, 8-28
   in absorption-cost pricing, 8-22
   in cost-plus pricing, 8-7
   in variable-cost pricing, 8-24
Master budget, 9-7, 9-30
Materiality, 10-17
Material loading charge, 8-11, 8-28
Materials
   assigning costs, 3-6
   direct. *See* Direct materials
   equivalent units for, 3-22
   indirect, 1-8, 1-25
   raw. *See* Raw materials
   time-and-material pricing, 8-9–8-13
   total costs, 3-15
   unit costs, 3-15
Materials price variance (MPV), 11-11–11-12, 11-30
Materials price variance (MPV) report, 11-18
Materials quantity variance (MQV), 11-11–11-13, 11-30
Materials requisition slips, 2-8–2-10, 2-26
Materials variances, 11-10–11-13, 11-30
Matrices
   direct labor variances, 11-15
   direct materials variances, 11-12
Merchandise purchases, 9-24
Merchandise purchases budget, 9-24, 9-25, 9-30
Merchandisers, 9-24–9-25
Minimum rate of return, 10-30
Minimum transfer prices, 8-15, 8-16, 8-17
Minus sign, A-18
Mixed costs, 5-7–5-10, 5-25–5-28
Money: time value of, A-1–A-25
Monthly overhead flexible budgets (case study), 10-11
Monthly responsibility reports, 10-23
Mortgage loan amounts, A-21
Motivation, 9-3
MPV (materials price variance), 11-11–11-12, 11-30
MPV (materials price variance) report, 11-18
MQV (materials quantity variance), 11-11–11-13, 11-30
Mutually exclusive projects, 12-14–12-15

N

Negotiated transfer price, 8-14–8-17, 8-28
Net annual cash flow, 12-11
Net cash, 13-5
   conversion to, 13-9, 13-12, 13-20–13-26
   provided/used by operating activities, 13-9, 13-20
Net income, 13-3, 13-5
   absorption vs. variable costing and, 6-22–6-26
   conversion to cash from accrual, 13-9, 13-20–13-26
   conversion to net cash, 13-9, 13-12, 13-20–13-26
   from processing further, 7-11
   reported, 13-3
   target, 5-20–5-22, 5-30, 6-3–6-4
   variable costing and, 6-28–6-29
Net present value (NPV), 12-6–12-11, 12-24
   computation, 12-8, 12-11, 12-14
   evaluation techniques, 12-12
   Excel, 12-19
   with intangible benefits, 12-12–12-13
   vs. internal rate of return, 12-17
   with mutually exclusive projects, 12-14–12-15
   with unequal annual cash flows, 12-8, 12-9
Net sales, 14-9

Noncash activities, 13-4–13-5, 13-14–13-15
Noncash current assets, 13-10–13-12
Noncash expenses, 13-9
Noncash transactions, 13-26
Noncontrollable costs, 10-16, 10-32
Noncurrent asset and liability accounts, 13-14–13-15, 13-26
Nonfinancial measures, 11-22
Nonmanufacturing overhead costs, 4-13–4-14
Non-recurring charges, 14-4
Non–value-added activities, 4-16, 4-17, 4-27
Normal capacity, 11-7, 11-30
Normal standards, 11-4, 11-30
Notes, long-term, A-13–A-15
Not-for-profit organizations, 9-26
NPV. *See* Net present value
NPV function (Excel), 12-19
Number of periods, A-18

O

Open Standards Benchmarking Collaborative, 11-5
Operating activities, 13-3, 13-5, 13-30
   cash flows, 13-4
   direct method, 13-20–13-26
   general guidelines for, 13-4
   indirect method, 13-9–13-13
   net cash provided/used by, 13-9, 13-20
   in statement of cash flows, 13-15, 13-25
   value-added, 4-16
Operating assets, 10-26, 10-27
Operating budgets, 9-7, 9-30
Operating expenses, 13-24
Operating leverage, 6-16, 6-17, 6-30
Operations
   discontinued, 14-3, 14-4, 14-33
   management awareness of, 9-3
Operations costing, 3-17, 3-27
Opportunity costs, 7-4, 7-9, 8-15
   definition, 7-20, 8-28
   incremental analysis with, 7-9
   units sold unequal to units forgone, 8-16–8-17
Optimal pricing, 8-20
Optimism, budgetary, 9-9
Organizational structure, 1-5–1-7
Organization charts, 1-5
Other comprehensive income, 14-6
Outsourcing, 8-19, 8-28
Overapplied overhead, 2-22–2-24, 2-26
Overhead
   actual, 11-16
   allocation to cost pools, 4-8
   assigning to products, 4-9–4-10
   assigning to services, 4-22
   departmental overhead costs report, 10-4
   manufacturing. *See* Manufacturing overhead
   monthly flexible budgets (case study), 10-11
   nonmanufacturing, 4-13–4-14
   overapplied, 2-22–2-24, 2-26
   static budgets, 10-7
   total overhead variance, 11-16, 11-17, 11-30
   underapplied, 2-22–2-24, 2-26
Overhead controllable variance, 11-17, 11-26, 11-27–11-28, 11-30
Overhead flexible budget reports, 10-9, 10-13
Overhead rates
   activity-based, 4-9
   computation, 11-7
   per direct labor hour, 11-7
   predetermined, 2-13–2-16, 2-26
   standard predetermined, 11-7, 11-30
Overhead static budget reports, 10-8
Overhead volume variances, 11-17, 11-26, 11-28, 11-30

P

Partial income statements, 2-23
Participative budgeting, 9-5–9-6, 9-30
Payables
   accounts payable, 9-23, 13-12, 13-23
   bonds payable, 13-14, 13-26
   income taxes payable, 13-12
   salaries and wages, 13-10
Payments
   calculator keys for, A-18
   cash, 13-23–13-24, 13-25
   for income taxes, 13-25
   for interest, 13-25
   for operating expenses, 13-24
   to suppliers, 13-23–13-24
Payout ratio, 14-27–14-28, 14-33
People, planet, and profit
   insights, 1-21, 3-11, 5-5, 6-17, 7-5, 11-17, 12-15
   triple bottom line, 1-20, 1-25
P-E (price-earnings) ratio, 14-27, 14-33
Performance evaluation, 10-16–10-18
Performance measures, 10-22
Performance reports, 10-18
Performance standards, 4-18
Period costs, 1-9, 1-25
Periodic payments, annuity, A-5
Personnel, 9-3
Pharmaceutical industry, 8-45
Physical units, 3-13, 3-20–3-24
   cost flow, 3-13, 3-20–3-22
   definition, 3-27
Planning, 1-4, 9-3, 9-4
   budgetary, 9-1–9-51
   for capital investments, 12-1–12-38
   enterprise resource planning (ERP) systems, 1-18, 1-25
   long-range, 9-6–9-7, 9-30
Plant assets: disposal of, 13-10, 13-25
Plus sign, A-18
Post-audits, 12-16, 12-23
Predetermined overhead rates, 2-13–2-16, 2-26
Preferred stock dividends, 14-27
Prepaid expenses, 13-11, 13-24
Prepaid insurance, 13-10
Present value, A-8–A-15, A-22
   of annuities, A-11–A-12, A-19, A-22
   of bonds, A-13–A-15
   calculator keys for, A-18
   calculator solutions, A-18, A-19
   in capital budgeting situations, A-15–A-17
   discounting, A-13
   of long-term notes, A-13–A-15
   net present value (NPV), 12-6–12-11, 12-24
   of single amounts, A-8–A-10
   of single sums, A-19
   time periods, A-13
Price-earnings (P-E) ratio, 14-27, 14-33
Price standards
   direct labor price standard, 11-6, 11-30
   direct materials price standard, 11-5, 11-30
Price takers, 8-3
Price variances, 11-10
   labor price variance (LPV), 11-14, 11-15, 11-30
   materials price variance (MPV), 11-11–11-12, 11-30
   materials price variance (MPV) report, 11-18
Pricing, 8-1–8-46
   absorption-cost, 8-22–8-24, 8-28
   big data, 8-20
   cost considerations, 8-3
   cost-plus, 8-5–8-7, 8-28
   environmental factors, 8-3
   factors that affect, 8-3
   full-cost, 8-22, 8-28
   objectives, 8-3
   optimal, 8-20
   target costs and, 8-3
   target selling prices, 8-6, 8-28
   time-and-material, 8-10–8-13, 8-28
   transfer prices, 8-13–8-20, 8-28
   variable-cost, 8-8–8-9, 8-22, 8-24–8-25, 8-28
Principal, A-2
Process costing, 3-1–3-45
   assigning manufacturing costs, 3-6–3-9
   cost flows, 3-4, 3-6
   equivalent units, 3-9–3-12
   physical unit cost flow, 3-13–3-14, 3-21–3-22
   for service companies, 3-3–3-4
   transfer to cost of goods sold, 3-8
   transfer to finished goods, 3-8
   transfer to next department, 3-8

Process cost systems, 2-3
　applications, 3-3–3-4
　definition, 2-26, 3-27
　vs. job order cost systems, 3-4–3-6
　overview, 3-3–3-6
Process further, 7-11–7-14
Product costs, 1-9, 1-25. *See also* Manufacturing costs
　data analysis, 7-8
　unit, 4-11
Production
　direct materials units required for, 9-11
　equivalent units of, 3-10
　make-or-buy decisions, 7-8–7-10
　sell-or-process further decisions, 7-11–7-14
Production budget, 9-10, 9-30
Production cost report, 3-12–3-19
　definition, 3-27
　FIFO method, 3-24–3-25
　preparation, 3-16, 3-24–3-25
Production costs
　actual, 11-9
　unit, 3-14–3-15, 3-23, 3-27
Production requirements, 9-10
Product-level activities, 4-15, 4-16, 4-27
Products
　allocation of activity cost pools to, 4-10
　assigning overhead costs to, 4-9–4-10
　cost drivers per, 4-10
　joint, 7-12, 7-20
　unprofitable, 7-16–7-18
Profitability
　cost-volume-profit (CVP) analysis, 5-1–5-48, 6-1–6-51
　gross profit rate, 14-26, 14-33
　operating leverage and, 6-16–6-17
　people, planet, and profit insights, 1-21, 3-11, 5-5, 6-17, 7-5, 11-17, 12-15
　target costs and, 8-4
　unprofitable segments or products, 7-16–7-18
Profitability index, 12-14–12-15, 12-24
Profitability ratios, 14-16–14-17, 14-19, 14-23–14-29, 14-33
Profit centers, 10-21, 10-22–10-23, 10-33
Profit margin, 14-25, 14-33
Pull approach, 4-25
Purchases
　computation, 13-23
　merchandise purchases budget, 9-24, 9-25, 9-30
Push approach, 4-24

Q

Qualitative factors, 7-5, 7-9
Quality of reported net income, 13-3

Quantity variances, 11-10

R

Rate of return
　annual, 12-19–12-21, 12-24
　internal, 12-17–12-19, 12-24, A-20
　minimum, 10-30
　required, 12-9, 12-20, 12-24
Ratio(s), 14-14, 14-33
Ratio analysis, 14-14–14-31, 14-33
Raw materials, 1-8
　accumulating costs of, 2-5
　assigning costs of, 2-8–2-10
　stockpiling, 9-12
Raw materials inventory, 1-12, 2-5, 9-23
Receivables. *See* Accounts receivable
Regional banks, 11-20
Regression analysis, 5-25–5-28, 5-30
Relevant costs and revenues, 7-4, 7-6–7-8, 7-16, 7-20
Relevant range, 5-5–5-6, 5-30
Repair, retain, or replace equipment, 7-14–7-16
Reporting. *See also specific reports*
　responsibility reports, 10-18–10-23, 10-25
　of variances, 11-18–11-19
Required rate of return, 12-9, 12-20, 12-24
Requisition slips. *See* Materials requisition slips
Residual income, 10-30–10-31, 10-33
Responsibility accounting, 10-14–10-24, 10-33
　corporate social responsibility, 1-20, 11-17
　in cost centers, 10-19, 10-21
　in investment centers, 10-21
　in profit centers, 10-21–10-23
Responsibility centers, 10-17, 10-19–10-23
Responsibility reports, 10-18–10-19, 10-33
　example system, 10-19, 10-20
　monthly, 10-23
Restructuring charges, 14-4
Retained earnings
　on budgeted balance sheet, 9-23
　on statement of cash flows, 13-14, 13-27, 13-29
Retained earnings statement, 13-3
Return on assets, 14-24–14-26, 14-33
Return on common stockholders' equity (ROE), 14-23–14-24, 14-33
Return on investment (ROI), 10-24–10-25, 10-33
　in absorption-cost pricing, 8-23
　computation, 10-26, 10-27, 10-30
　in cost-plus pricing, 8-5–8-8
　equation, 10-24
　improving, 10-26–10-27
　measures of inputs, 10-26
　vs. residual income, 10-30–10-31
　in variable-cost pricing, 8-25
Revenues
　controllable, 10-16, 10-22, 10-23
　noncontrollable, 10-16
　relevant, 7-4, 7-20
Risk analysis, 12-15
Risk factors, 7-11
ROE (return on common stockholders' equity), 14-23–14-24, 14-33

ROI. *See* Return on investment
Rounding, A-19

S

SaaS (software-as-a-service), 2-4
Safety
　employee, 12-13
　margin of, 5-20–5-23, 5-30, 6-4, 6-16
Salaries and wages payable, 13-10
Sales
　break-even, 6-5, 6-7–6-11
　horizontal analysis of, 14-9
　net, 14-9
　ROI by increase in, 10-26
　in units, 6-5, 6-7–6-9
Sales budget, 9-8–9-9, 9-30
Sales budget reports, 10-5
Sales forecast, 9-5, 9-30
Sales mix, 6-30
　and break-even sales, 6-7–6-12
　with limited resources, 6-12–6-14
　as percentage of units sold, 6-7
　per unit data, 6-8
Sales report, 10-4
Sales units, 5-17–5-18, 6-3, 6-8
Sarbanes-Oxley Act (SOX), 1-19–1-20, 1-25
Scatter function (Excel), 5-28
Scatter plots, 5-28
Scrap report, 10-4
Securities
　available-for-sale, 14-5, 14-33
　trading, 14-5, 14-33
Securities and Exchange Commission (SEC), 14-17
Segments, 10-15, 10-33
Selling and administrative expense budget, 9-16, 9-30
Selling and administrative expenses, 10-6
Selling expenses report, 10-4
Selling price
　computation, 8-7, 8-8
　target, 8-6, 8-28
Sell-or-process further decisions, 7-11–7-14
Sensitivity ("what if") analyses, 9-23, 12-15, 12-24
Service companies
　activity-based costing, 4-20–4-24
　budgeting, 9-25–9-26
　direct labor budget, 9-25–9-26
　ethics for, 1-17
　insights, 1-17, 2-20, 4-22, 5-18, 5-23, 6-11, 7-10, 8-5, 8-12, 9-9, 9-22, 10-10
　job order costing, 2-19–2-20
　process costing, 3-3–3-4
　traditional costing, 4-20–4-21
　trends, 1-16–1-17
Significant components: disposal of, 14-3
Significant noncash activities, 13-4–13-5
Simple interest, A-2, A-3, A-22
Slope function (Excel), 5-27

Social responsibility, corporate, 1-20, 1-25, 11-17
Software-as-a-service (SaaS), 2-4
Solar power, 6-17
Solvency ratios, 14-15, 14-16, 14-21–14-23, 14-33
Special orders, 7-6–7-8, 8-16
Staff positions, 1-6, 1-25
Standard activity index, 11-7
Standard cost accounting, 11-24
Standard cost accounting system, 11-24–11-26, 11-30
Standard costs, 11-1
   advantages, 11-3
   vs. budgets, 11-4
   case study, 11-5–11-8
   direct labor, 11-6–11-7
   direct materials, 11-5–11-6
   overview, 11-3–11-8
   setting, 11-4–11-8
   total per unit, 11-7–11-8
Standard direct labor hours, 11-27
Standard hours allowed, 11-16, 11-30
Standard predetermined overhead rates, 11-7, 11-30
Standards
   cost, 11-1–11-8
   direct labor price, 11-6, 11-30
   direct labor quantity, 11-6, 11-30
   direct labor rate, 11-6
   direct materials price, 11-5, 11-30
   direct materials quantity, 11-5–11-6
   ideal, 11-4, 11-30
   manufacturing overhead cost, 11-7
   normal, 11-4, 11-30
   Open Standards Benchmarking Collaborative, 11-5
Statement of cash flows, 13-3, 13-30
   analyzing, 13-17–13-20
   vs. balance sheet, 13-15
   direct method, 13-7, 13-20–13-27, 13-30
   example, 13-15, 13-27, 14-18
   example worksheet, 13-27
   format, 13-5–13-6
   free cash flows, 13-17–13-19
   indirect method, 13-6–13-17, 13-30
   operating activities section, 13-26
   preparation, 13-6–13-17
   sources of information, 13-6–13-7
   T-account approach, 13-27–13-29
   usefulness, 13-3
Statement of comprehensive income, 14-5, 14-6
Statement of Ethical Professional Practice (IMA), 1-20
Static budget reports, 10-4–10-6
Static budgets, 10-4, 10-33
Stock, common, 9-23, 13-14, 13-26, 13-29, 14-26
Stock dividends, 14-27
Stockholders' equity
   accounts, 13-14–13-15, 13-26
   balance sheet section, 14-5

   return on common stockholders' equity (ROE), 14-23–14-24, 14-33
Stockpiling, 9-12
Subsidiary ledgers, 2-8
Sunk costs, 7-4, 7-20
Suppliers
   cash payments to, 13-23–13-24
   dependable, 4-25
Sustainable income, 14-3–14-8, 14-33

T
T-accounts, 13-27–13-29
Target costs, 8-3–8-5, 8-28
Target net income, 5-20–5-22, 5-30, 6-3–6-4
Target price, 8-23, 8-24
Target selling price, 8-6, 8-28
Taxes
   after-tax contribution margin, 8-26
   income taxes payable, 13-12, 13-25
Technology, 11-16, 12-9
Telecommunications companies, 1-17
Theory of constraints, 1-18, 1-25, 6-13, 6-30
Time-and-material pricing, 8-9–8-13, 8-28
Time periods
   average collection period, 14-20, 14-33
   budget period, 9-4
   cash payback period, 12-5
   compounding, A-19
   and discounting, A-13
   number of, A-18
Times interest earned, 14-22–14-23, 14-33
Time tickets, 2-10, 2-11, 2-26
Time value of money, A-1–A-25
TLV (total labor variance), 11-13, 11-14, 11-30
TMV (total materials variance), 11-10, 11-11, 11-30
Top-down approach, 9-6
Total amount, standard, 11-4
Total budgeted costs, 10-11
Total contribution margin, 6-13
Total conversion costs, 3-14
Total cost of work in process, 1-14, 1-25
Total direct labor cost, 9-14
Total direct labor variance, 11-14
Total fixed costs, 5-4, 5-6
Total labor variance (TLV), 11-13, 11-14, 11-30
Total manufacturing costs, 1-11, 1-25, 3-15
Total materials costs, 3-14
Total materials variance (TMV), 11-10, 11-11, 11-30
Total overhead variance, 11-16, 11-17, 11-30
Total quality control systems, 4-26
Total quality management (TQM), 1-18, 1-25
Total standard cost per unit, 11-7–11-8
Total unit cost, 9-17

Total units (costs) accounted for, 3-13, 3-27
Total units (costs) to be accounted for, 3-13, 3-27
Total variable costs, 5-4, 5-6
Total variance, 11-9
TQM (total quality management), 1-18, 1-25
Trading on the equity, 14-24–14-25, 14-33
Trading securities, 14-5, 14-33
Traditional costing, 4-20–4-21, 4-22
Traditional costing systems, 4-3–4-4
Transfer prices, 8-13–8-21, 8-28
   alternative, 8-26
   approaches to, 8-14
   cost-based, 8-17–8-18, 8-28
   with excess capacity, 8-15–8-16
   market-based, 8-19, 8-28
   minimum, 8-15, 8-16
   negotiated, 8-14–8-17, 8-28
   with no excess capacity, 8-14–8-15
   objective, 8-13
   outsourcing and, 8-19
Transfers
   to cost of goods sold, 3-8
   between divisions in different countries, 8-19, 8-25–8-26
   to finished goods, 3-8
   to next department, 3-8
Treasurer, 1-6, 1-25
Trend analysis, 14-10. *See also* Horizontal analysis
Triple bottom line, 1-20, 1-25
Turnover
   accounts receivable, 14-19–14-20, 14-33
   asset, 14-25–14-26, 14-33
   inventory, 14-20–14-21, 14-33

U
Underapplied overhead, 2-22–2-24, 2-26
Under budget, 10-9
Underestimating costs, 2-16
Unfavorable variances, 11-9
Unit amount, standard, 11-4
Unit contribution margin, 5-13–5-14, 5-17–5-18, 5-30
   with alternative transfer prices, 8-26
   with cost-based transfer prices, 8-17–8-18
   with limited resources, 6-14
   with negotiated transfer prices, 8-14
   weighted-average, 6-7, 6-8
Unit conversion costs, 3-15
Unit costs
   comparison, 4-10–4-11
   fixed, 5-4, 8-6, 8-8
   total, 9-17
Unit-level activities, 4-15, 4-16, 4-27
Unit manufacturing costs, 8-22
Unit materials costs, 3-15
Unit product costs, 4-11
Unit production costs, 3-14–3-15, 3-23, 3-27

Units
  break-even sales in, 6-5, 6-7–6-9
  required production, 9-10
  target net income in, 6-3–6-4
  total standard cost per, 11-7–11-8
  transferred, 8-16–8-17
Units forgone, 8-16–8-17
Units started and completed, 3-20
Unit variable costs, 5-3, 5-4, 5-8, 8-6, 8-24, 10-8
Unprofitable segments or products, 7-16–7-18
Unrealized loss, 14-4
Unusual items, 14-3

V
Valuation
  future value, A-3–A-8, A-18, A-20, A-22
  net present value (NPV), 12-6–12-11, 12-24
  of operating assets, 10-26
  time value of money, A-1–A-25
Value-added activities, 4-16, 4-27
Value chain, 1-17–1-18, 1-25
Variable cost(s), 5-3–5-4, 6-19–6-28, 8-16
  10% decrease, 10-26–10-27
  budgeted, 10-9
  definition, 5-30, 8-16
  in flexible budgets, 10-10
  importance of identifying, 5-10
  per direct labor hour, 10-11
  total, 5-4
  unit, 5-4, 5-8, 8-6, 8-24, 10-8
Variable costing, 6-19–6-29, 6-30
  vs. absorption costing, 6-19–6-22, 6-27
  advantages, 6-28
  example, 6-21
  net income effects, 6-22–6-26
Variable costing income statement, 6-21, 6-23, 6-24, 6-25, 6-27, 6-28
Variable-cost pricing, 8-8–8-9, 8-22, 8-24–8-25, 8-28
Variable cost ratio, 5-15, 5-30
Variances, 11-8, 11-30
  analyzing, 11-8–11-10
  cost accounts with, 11-26
  direct labor, 11-13–11-15
  direct materials, 11-8–11-13
  favorable, 11-9
  income statement presentation, 11-19
  labor price variance (LPV), 11-14, 11-15, 11-30
  labor quantity variance (LQV), 11-14, 11-15, 11-30
  manufacturing overhead, 11-16–11-18
  materials, 11-10
  materials price variance (MPV), 11-11, 11-12–11-13, 11-18, 11-30
  materials quantity variance (MQV), 11-11, 11-13, 11-30
  overhead controllable, 11-17, 11-26, 11-27–11-28, 11-30
  overhead volume, 11-17, 11-26, 11-28, 11-30
  price, 11-10
  quantity, 11-10
  reporting, 11-18–11-19
  total, 11-9
  total labor variance (TLV), 11-13, 11-14, 11-30
  total materials variance (TMV), 11-10, 11-11, 11-30
  total overhead, 11-16, 11-17, 11-30
  unfavorable, 11-9

Vertical analysis, 14-11–14-13, 14-33
Virtual companies, 8-19
Visualizations, data, 1-21. *See also* Graphic presentation
Volume
  cost-volume-profit (CVP) analysis, 5-11–5-28, 6-1–6-51
  overhead volume variances, 11-17, 11-26, 11-28, 11-30

W
Wages payable, 13-10
Weighted-average contribution margin ratio, 6-10
Weighted-average method, 3-10
  advantages, 3-25–3-26
  break-even analysis, 6-7, 6-8, 6-9
  definition, 3-27
  refinements, 3-10–3-12
Weighted-average unit contribution margin, 6-7, 6-8
"What if" (sensitivity) analyses, 9-22–9-23, 12-15, 12-24
Work force, 4-25. *See also* Labor
Working capital, 14-19
Work in process inventory, 1-12, 2-5, 2-8
  agreement with job cost sheets, 2-15
  beginning, 1-14, 3-20
  definition, 1-12, 1-25
  ending, 1-14, 3-20
WorldScope, 14-17

Y
Year-end balance, 2-23

Z
Zero-based budgeting, 10-18

RAPID REVIEW
Chapter Content

MANAGERIAL ACCOUNTING (Chapter 1)

Characteristics of Managerial Accounting

Primary users	Internal users
Reports	Internal reports issued as needed
Purpose	Special purpose for a particular user
Content	Pertains to subunits, may be detailed, use of relevant data
Verification	No independent audits

Types of Manufacturing Costs

Direct materials	Raw materials directly associated with finished product
Direct labor	Work of employees directly associated with turning raw materials into finished product
Manufacturing overhead	Costs indirectly associated with manufacture of finished product

JOB ORDER AND PROCESS COSTING (Chapters 2 and 3)

Types of Accounting Systems

Job order	Costs are assigned to each unit or each batch of goods
Process cost	Costs are applied to similar products that are mass-produced in a continuous fashion

Job Order and Process Cost Flow

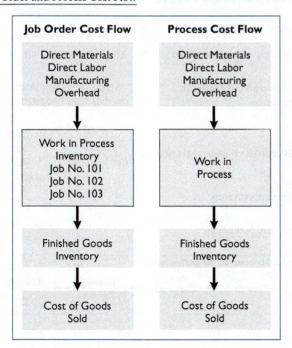

ACTIVITY-BASED COSTING (Chapter 4)

1. **Identify and classify the activities** involved in the manufacture of specific products and **allocate overhead to cost pools**.

2. **Identify the cost driver** that has a strong correlation to the costs accumulated in each cost pool and estimate total annual cost driver usage.

3. **Compute the activity-based overhead rate** for each cost pool.

4. **Assign overhead costs to products** using the overhead rates determined for each cost pool.

COST-VOLUME-PROFIT (Chapters 5 and 6)

Types of Costs

Variable costs	Vary in total directly and proportionately with changes in activity level
Fixed costs	Remain the same in total regardless of change in activity level
Mixed costs	Contain both a fixed and a variable element

CVP Income Statement Format

	Total	Per Unit	Percent of Sales
Sales	€xx	€xx	xxx%
Variable costs	xx	xx	xx
Contribution margin	xx	$xx	xx%
Fixed costs	xx		
Net income	€xx		

$$\text{Unit contribution margin} = \text{Unit selling price} - \text{Unit variable costs}$$

$$\text{Break-even point in units} = \text{Fixed costs} \div \text{Unit contribution margin*}$$

$$\text{Break-even point in euros} = \text{Fixed costs} \div \text{Contribution margin ratio*}$$

$$\text{Required sales in units for target net income} = (\text{Fixed costs} + \text{Target net income}) \div \text{Unit contribution margin}$$

$$\text{Degree of operating leverage} = \text{Contribution margin} \div \text{Net income}$$

*For multiple products, use weighted-average.

RAPID REVIEW
Chapter Content

INCREMENTAL ANALYSIS (Chapter 7)

1. Identify the relevant costs associated with each alternative. **Relevant costs** are those costs and revenues that differ across alternatives. Choose the alternative that maximizes net income.
2. **Opportunity costs** are those potential benefits that are given up when one alternative is chosen instead of another one. Opportunity costs are relevant costs.
3. **Sunk costs** have already been incurred and will not be changed or avoided by any future decision. Sunk costs are not relevant costs.

PRICING (Chapter 8)

External Pricing

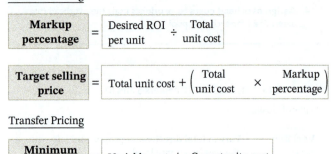

Transfer Pricing

| Minimum transfer price | = | Variable cost + Opportunity cost |

BUDGETS (Chapter 9)

Components of the Master Budget

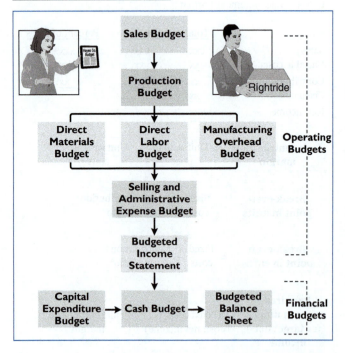

RESPONSIBILITY ACCOUNTING (Chapter 10)

Types of Responsibility Centers

Cost	Profit	Investment
Expenses only	Expenses and Revenues	Expenses and Revenues and ROI

Return on Investment

| Return on investment (ROI) | = | Investment center controllable margin | ÷ | Average investment center operating assets |

STANDARD COSTS (Chapter 11)

Standard Cost Variances

Total materials variance	=	AQ × AP	−	SQ × SP
Total labor variance	=	AH × AR	−	SH × SR
Total overhead variance	=	Actual overhead	−	Overhead applied*

*Based on standard hours allowed.

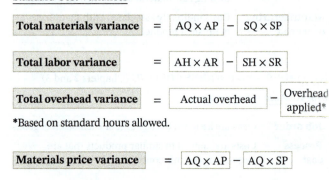

| * Overhead controllable variance | = | Actual overhead | − | Overhead budgeted |

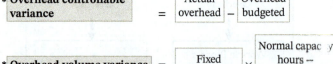

*Appendix coverage.

Balanced Scorecard

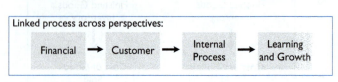

Linked process across perspectives:
Financial → Customer → Internal Process → Learning and Growth

RAPID REVIEW
Chapter Content

CAPITAL BUDGETING (Chapter 12)

Annual Rate of Return

| Annual rate of return | = | Expected annual net income | ÷ | Average investment |

Cash Payback

| Cash payback period | = | Cost of capital investment | ÷ | Annual cash inflow |

Discounted Cash Flow Approaches

Net Present Value	Internal Rate of Return
Compute net present value (an euro amount). If net present value is zero or positive, accept the proposal. If net present value is negative, reject the proposal.	Compute internal rate of return (a percentage). If internal rate of return is equal to or greater than the minimum required rate of return, accept the proposal. If internal rate of return is less than the minimum rate, reject the proposal.

STATEMENT OF CASH FLOWS (Chapter 13)

Cash flows from operating activities (**indirect method**)
    Net income
    Add: Amortization and depreciation   € X
                 Losses on disposals of assets   X
                 Decreases in current assets   X
                 Increases in current liabilities   X
    Deduct: Increases in current assets   (X)
                 Decreases in current liabilities   (X)
                 Gains on disposals of assets   (X)
    Net cash provided (used) by operating activities   € X

Cash flows from operating activities (**direct method**)
    Cash receipts
      (Examples: from sales of goods and services
      to customers, from receipts of interest and dividends) € X
    Cash payments
      (Examples: to suppliers, for operating expenses,
      for interest, for taxes)   (X)
    Net cash provided (used) by operating activities   € X

FINANCIAL STATEMENT ANALYSIS (Chapter 14)

Discontinued operations	Income statement (presented separately after Income from continuing operations).
Changes in accounting principle	In most instances, use the new method in current period and restate previous years' results using new method. For changes in depreciation and amortization methods, use the new method in the current period, but do not restate previous periods.

Income Statement and Comprehensive Income

Sales	€ XX
Cost of goods sold	XX
Gross profit	XX
Operating expenses	XX
Income from operations	XX
Other revenues (expenses) and gains (losses)	XX
Income before income taxes	XX
Income tax expense	XX
Income before discontinued operations	XX
Discontinued operations (net of tax)	XX
Net income	XX
Other comprehensive income items (net of tax)	XX
Comprehensive income	€ XX

RAPID REVIEW
Tools for Analysis

Liquidity

Working capital	Current assets − Current liabilities
Current ratio	$\dfrac{\text{Current assets}}{\text{Current liabilities}}$
Inventory turnover	$\dfrac{\text{Cost of goods sold}}{\text{Average inventory}}$
Days in inventory	$\dfrac{365 \text{ days}}{\text{Inventory turnover}}$
Accounts receivable turnover	$\dfrac{\text{Net credit sales}}{\text{Average net accounts receivable}}$
Average collection period	$\dfrac{365 \text{ days}}{\text{Accounts receivable turnover}}$

Solvency

Debt to assets ratio	$\dfrac{\text{Total liabilities}}{\text{Total assets}}$
Times interest earned	$\dfrac{\text{Net income + Interest expense + Income tax expense}}{\text{Interest expense}}$
Free cash flow	Net cash provided by operating activities − Capital expenditures − Cash dividends

Profitability

Earnings per share	$\dfrac{\text{Net income − Preferred dividends}}{\text{Weighted-average common shares outstanding}}$
Price-earnings ratio	$\dfrac{\text{Market price per share}}{\text{Earnings per share}}$
Gross profit rate	$\dfrac{\text{Gross profit}}{\text{Net sales}}$
Profit margin	$\dfrac{\text{Net income}}{\text{Net sales}}$
Return on assets	$\dfrac{\text{Net income}}{\text{Average total assets}}$
Asset turnover	$\dfrac{\text{Net sales}}{\text{Average total assets}}$
Payout ratio	$\dfrac{\text{Cash dividends paid on common stock}}{\text{Net income}}$
Return on common stockholders' equity	$\dfrac{\text{Net income − Preferred dividends}}{\text{Average common stockholders' equity}}$